Fodor's upCLOSE

CALIFORNIA

the complete guide, thoroughly up-to-date

SAVVY TRAVELING: WHERE TO SPEND, HOW TO SAVE

packed with details that will make your trip

CULTURAL TIPS: ESSENTIAL LOCAL DO'S AND TABOOS

must-see sights, on and off the beaten path

INSIDER SECRETS: WHAT'S HIP AND WHAT TO SKIP

the buzz on restaurants, the lowdown on lodgings

FIND YOUR WAY WITH CLEAR AND EASY-TO-USE MAPS

Previously published as *The Berkeley Guide to California*

FODOR'S TRAVEL PUBLICATIONS, INC.

NEW YORK • TORONTO • LONDON • SYDNEY • AUCKLAND

www.fodors.com/

 Published in the United States by Fodor's Travel Publications, Inc., a subsidiary of Random House, Inc., New York, and simultaneously in Canada by Random House of Canada, Limited, Toronto. Distributed by Random House, Inc., New York.

ISBN 0-679-03438-2

FODOR'S UPCLOSE™ CALIFORNIA

EDITOR: Hannah Borgeson

Editorial Contributors: Jennifer Brewer, Deke Castleman, Kathleen Dodge, Jeanne Fay, Julie Jares, Edie Jarolim, Jonathan Leff, Andrea Lehman, Andy Moore, Daniel Mangin, Amy McConnell, Clark Norton, Marty Olmstead, Cynthia Queen, Sharon Silva, Suzanne Stein, Jennifer Wedel, Sharron Wood, Bobbi Zane

Editorial Production: Linda K. Schmidt

Maps: David Lindroth, Eureka Cartography, *cartographers*; Robert P. Blake, Steven K. Amsterdam, *map editors*

Design: Fabrizio La Rocca, *creative director*; Allison Saltzman, *cover and text design*; Jolie Novak, *photo editor*

Production/Manufacturing: Robert B. Shields

Cover Art: Kaz Chiba/Photonica

SPECIAL SALES

Fodor's upCLOSE™ Guides and all Fodor's Travel Publications are available at special discounts for bulk purchases for sales promotions or premiums. Special editions, including personalized covers, excerpts of existing guides, and corporate imprints, can be created in large quantities for special needs. For more information, contact your local bookseller or write to Special Markets, Fodor's Travel Publications, 201 East 50th Street, New York, NY 10022. Inquiries from Canada should be directed to your local Canadian bookseller or sent to Random House of Canada, Ltd., Marketing Department, 1265 Aerowood Drive, Mississauga, Ontario L4W 1B9. Inquiries from the United Kingdom should be sent to Fodor's Travel Publications, 20 Vauxhall Bridge Road, London SW1V 2SA, England.

PRINTED IN THE UNITED STATES OF AMERICA

10 9 8 7 6 5 4 3 2 1

CONTENTS

2. SAN FRANCISCO 25

3. SAN FRANCISCO BAY AREA 65

4. NORTH COAST 103

5. THE CASCADES 142

6. GOLD COUNTRY 175

7. SIERRA NEVADA AND SAN JOAQUIN VALLEY 205

8. CENTRAL COAST 246

9. LOS ANGELES 280

10. NEAR LOS ANGELES 326

11. SAN DIEGO 354

12. PALM SPRINGS AND THE DESERT 384

13. LAS VEGAS AND THE GRAND CANYON 411

INDEX 435

TRAVELING UPCLOSE

Camp in a national park. Taste wine that's never traveled. Go to a festival. Catch a wave. Climb a mountain. Eat well. And if you want to experience the heart and soul of California, whatever you do, don't spend too much money. The deep and rich experience of California that every true traveler yearns for is one of the things in life that money can't buy. In fact, if you have it, don't use it. Traveling lavishly is the surest way to turn yourself into a sideline traveler. Restaurants with white-glove service are great—sometimes—but they're usually not the best place to find the perfect cassoulet. Doormen at plush hotels have their place, but not when your look-alike room could be anywhere from Düsseldorf to Detroit. Better to stay in a more intimate place that truly gives you the atmosphere you traveled so far to experience. Don't just stand and watch—jump into the spirit of what's around you.

If you want to see California up close and savor the essence of its cities, deserts, mountains, or coast, and its people in all their laid back glory, this book is for you. We'll show you the local culture, the off-beat sights, the bars and cafés where tourists rarely tread, and the B&Bs and other hostelries where you'll meet fellow travelers—places where the locals would send their friends. And because you'll probably want to see the famous places if you haven't already been there, we give you tips on losing the crowds, plus the quirky and obscure facts you want as well as the basics everyone needs.

OUR GANG

Who's "we"? We're artists and poets, slackers and straight arrows, and travel writers and journalists, who in our less hedonistic moments report on local news and spin out an occasional opinion piece. What we share is a certain footloose spirit and a passion for the Golden State, which we celebrate in this guidebook. Shamelessly, we've revealed all of our favorite places and our deepest, darkest travel secrets, all so that you can learn from our past mistakes and experience the best part of California to the fullest. If you can't take your best friend on the road, or if your best friend is hopeless with directions, stick with us.

Jennifer Brewer, a native Californian who updated parts of the San Francisco, Bay Area, and Palm Springs and the Desert chapters, is now a New York–based travel writer. Her work has recently taken her to Eastern Europe, the Middle East, and Asia, but she still thinks the Golden State is one of the most breathtaking and bountiful places on earth.

Deke Castleman covered Reno and Las Vegas for this guide. He learned his budget-traveler skills in the mid-1970s in Alaska, the most expensive state in the country, waiting for a job on the Trans-Alaska Pipeline. He now edits the newsletter *Las Vegas Advisor* in Vegas, the world's greatest bargain-vacation destination.

Kathleen Dodge grew up in the San Francisco Bay Area and still calls it her favorite corner of the world—and home. She's spent the last three years ferreting out the best and most inexpensive places to eat, drink, and be merry while writing and editing for the Berkeley Guides. She worked on parts of the Bay Area chapter.

Jeanne Fay, who updated the Los Angeles chapter, is a writer and researcher at *Buzz* magazine in Los Angeles.

A native Californian, **Julie Jares** grew up believing that Disneyland truly is The Happiest Place on Earth. She covers that attraction and many others in the Near Los Angeles chapter of this book. She learned how to travel on the cheap while living in Florence, Italy, and subsequently returned to Europe to write about budget travel for the *Berkeley Guide to Great Britain and Ireland 1996.*

When **Edie Jarolim** left Manhattan and her job as a senior editor at Fodor's for Tucson, Arizona, she was forced to learn how to budget her travel in order to indulge a sudden, urgent need to buy cowboy boots in every color. She watched her step while updating the Grand Canyon section.

With notepad in hand, car in gear, and feet itching to hit the trails, **Jonathan Leff** left his cozy Berkeley apartment to explore Yosemite and the Sierra Nevada. Since then he's traded in the challenge of the great outdoors to live in Lithuania, where he writes for a weekly newspaper.

Andy Moore, who updated the Sacramento and the Gold Country section and the Basics chapter, was born across the street from Disney Studios near beautiful downtown Burbank. After many years working in the film industry, Andy is now based in San Francisco, where he works on his own independent art films, Film Arts Foundation's *Release Print* magazine, and various book projects. His poetry appears in "Guests' Comments" books in many fine B&Bs throughout the country.

San Francisco–based writer **Clark Norton** is the author of Fodor's *Where Should We Take the Kids? California* and writes for such magazines as *San Francisco Focus* and *California Travel Ideas.* He updated the San Joaquin Valley section of this book.

North Coast and Cascades updater **Marty Olmstead,** who lives in Sonoma, has been visiting the North Coast regularly since 1970 and recently took up fly fishing in the Cascades. Her latest book is *Hidden Tennessee.*

Fancying herself the hostess of San Diego, **Cynthia Queen** likes nothing more than to share her local expertise with eager guests, particularly those looking for the most for their money. The former editor of three San Diego community newspapers, she is a contributor to Fodor's *San Diego* and directs communications for a nonprofit foundation.

San Francisco and Bay Area food updater **Sharon Silva** has been a regular contributor to *San Francisco Focus* magazine for more than a decade and is the coauthor of *Exploring the Best Ethnic Restaurants of the Bay Area* and *The Thrifty Gourmet.*

Suzanne Stein, updater for San Francisco and Bay area Where to Sleep sections, is an expatriate Los Angelina tying up her first decade as a San Franciscan. Backwoods Burmese elephant rides and backpacker's stoop are things of the not-so-distant past and the far-off future—mostly what she budgets now is time.

For the second year in a row, **Jennifer Wedel** traveled the highways and byways of California on half a shoestring. Along the Central Coast, she found the wilds of Big Sur friendliest to the thin-walleted, and the Santa Barbara sun never cost a penny.

Almost everyone **Sharron Wood** meets envies her job as a freelance travel writer. Though she tries to convince people that it's not as glamorous as it seems, she couldn't seem to persuade anyone that writing about San Francisco's nightlife for this book qualified as a job at all.

Bobbi Zane has been searching for travel deals since the 1960s, when she found her first free campsite at Joshua Tree National Monument. More recently she began haunting the thrift and estate-sale shops in the desert for bargains. In addition to updating parts of the Palm Springs and the Desert chapter, she has contributed to a number of Fodor's publications, including the Gold Guides to California and San Diego and *California's Best Bed and Breakfasts.*

A SEND-OFF

Always call ahead. We knock ourselves out to check all the facts, but everything changes all the time, in ways that none of us can ever fully anticipate. Whenever you're making a special trip to a special place, as opposed to merely wandering, always call ahead. Trust us on this.

And then, if something doesn't go quite right, as inevitably happens with even the best-laid plans, stay cool. Missed your train? Stuck in the airport? Use the time to study the people. Strike up a conversation with a stranger. Study the newsstands or flip through the local press. Take a walk. Find the silver lining in the clouds, whatever it is. And do send us a postcard to tell us what went wrong and what went right. You can e-mail us at: editors@fodors.com (specify the name of the book on the subject line) or write the California editor at Fodor's upClose, 201 East 50th Street, New York, NY 10022. We'll put your ideas to good use and let other travelers benefit from your experiences. In the mean time, bon voyage!

INTRODUCTION

The world sees California through the fun-house lens of Hollywood, and it always looks "fabulous, darling." Roses in winter, stretch limos bigger than houses, gym-buffed surfers, and new Beatniks with neatly clipped goatees and a piercing or tattoo—these images of the state abound in movies and on commercials, TV shows, and music videos. Trends in fashion, sports, language, and politics seem to flow magically out of this state and into the other 49; as a wry Jimmy Carter said in 1977, "Whatever starts in California unfortunately has an inclination to spread." But the California of popular conception is based in fantasy rather than fact. Sure, some Californians say "like totally, dude" and resemble a member of the *Melrose Place* cast—Hollywood's clichés have to come from somewhere. But California's population defies stereotypes: This is the most ethnically diverse state in the country, projected to become the first in the nation with a minority of European-Americans soon after the year 2000.

The state's terrain is as varied as its people, from the arid desert of Death Valley, the lowest point in the United States at 282 feet below sea level, to the jagged spine of the Sierra Nevada, with snow-covered peaks reaching higher than 12,000 feet. Almost the entire region north and east of Sacramento, the state capital, is national forest, where towering thousand-year-old redwood trees form cathedral-like glens. Near the Oregon border, Mt. Shasta is either a dormant volcano—one in a Pacific Rim chain that also includes Lava Beds National Monument and Lassen Volcanic National Park—or a mystical world power point, depending on whom you ask. The sun-warmed Central Valley has been pressed into service as the nation's breadbasket; mile after mile of farmlands and orchards line the highways running north from Mexico. To the east, the national parks of the Sierra Nevada hold bubbling hot springs, strange rock formations, and fields of golden poppies. There's no way to absorb the whole state in one trip.

The legend of California's beauty traces back to Spanish explorers who named the land after an earthly paradise described in a popular 16th-century novel. Spain didn't settle California until 1769, when Father Junípero Serra built the first of 21 missions extending from San Diego to Sonoma. But the state remained on the fringes of the New Spain and later Mexico; in 1823 the settler population, mostly *rancheros,* numbered only 3,200. A second legend—gold—would usher in the first "boom" period in California history. The United States claimed the territory from Mexico in 1849, just weeks after carpenter James Marshall discovered the precious nuggets in the foothills of the Sierra Nevada. The news spread fast, and more than 100,000 men descended on the state, tossing social conventions right out the window in favor of boozin', whorin', and grubbin' for gold. The extravagant spending of miners who hit pay dirt helped to make cities out of tin-roof settlements like San Francisco, and the completion of the Transcontinental Railroad in 1869 made it easier for the rest of the country to come out and join in the free-for-all.

The southern half of the state developed more slowly. Using an "if-you-build-it-they-will-come" mentality, a rail line was extended to Los Angeles in 1876. Railroad companies used every available marketing strategy—from pamphlets to free lunches and brass-band concerts—to convince speculators and tourists that the desolate "cow counties" had something to offer. The Rush of the 1880s was on, this time for golden sun and citrus. Forty years later, a second southern boom involved a similar concept, but with interstate highways and a wider range of industrial giants. An advertising campaign that played up Southern California's Spanish past and using images of an exotic Mediterranean-style paradise caused outsiders to confuse Southern California with the whole state; even today, the motion picture industry happily promotes the "sunny California" image—and the world has bought it.

In the minds of millions of Americans, California is still the place where you can discard the baggage of the past and go about the earnest business of re-creating yourself. Just because you come from a family of Southern Baptists (or multimillionaires, or circus performers) doesn't mean you can't move 3,000 miles away and embrace Sufism or take up method acting. Hollywood is an obvious draw, but it's almost matched in income potential by Silicon Valley, an area just south of San Francisco where computer giants such as Apple and Intel were born, and which is now the epicenter of the information superhighway. California's promise has lured a cast of thousands, which explains the decades-old joke defining "Old Settlers" as anyone who's been in the state for more than two years.

The cult of the individual has reached its zenith in California, and the body is its temple. Nowhere else do people devote so much energy to maintaining their physical and emotional selves, whether they're running up and down mountains or ingesting awful-tasting things that are supposed to make them smarter, fitter, or more in tune with their inner child. If these measures fail to add the desired muscle tone or take off the unwanted pounds, there's always a trip to the plastic surgeon.

But California is not a seamlessly perfect state, physically or otherwise. The land has been battered by drought, fires, floods, earthquakes, and even flies, which have caused over $10 million in crop damage annually in the Central Valley since 1993. These disasters come as California crawls out of a recession, aggravated by defense-industry downsizing that eliminated 30,000 jobs annually during its worst years. Economists are now reporting renewed growth, but no one's taking any chances: recently, and for the first time in history, Americans leaving the state outnumbered those coming in. However, immigrants streaming across the southern border from Mexico, and from every other imaginable country, more than make up the difference. Many residents, fighting to keep their piece of a shrinking pie, are looking to antiimmigrant laws despite xenophobic overtones. In 1996, citizens voted to strike down federal affirmative action laws, though critics of the measure claim that voters were duped by language on the ballot that they dubbed "Orwellian newspeak." In the same election, however, a kinder and gentler trend was exemplified by the passage of a "medical marijuana" law allowing very sick people to legally buy some of the state's biggest cash crop if they have a note from their doctor. The Feds are fighting that one too.

Despite a growing sense of instability (both geological and sociopolitical), Californians stay and tourists come to this state precisely because it offers everything imaginable and then some. Yes, California is a land of contrasts, from Disneyland and endless strip malls to untouched scenic wilderness, from great leaps forward in holistic health care to poverty and repression, from Nixon and Reagan to Jerry Brown to Pete Wilson. This is where both humanity and nature show off all their possibilities, whether dreadful or breathtakingly vital and beautiful. So hit the road—soon you'll find yourself with the same rapturous look you see on the faces of many long-term residents. It's a look that comes from the realization that amid all this beauty it's okay to lose yourself a little, and that, yes, you might even rediscover yourself here.

NORTHERN CALIFORNIA

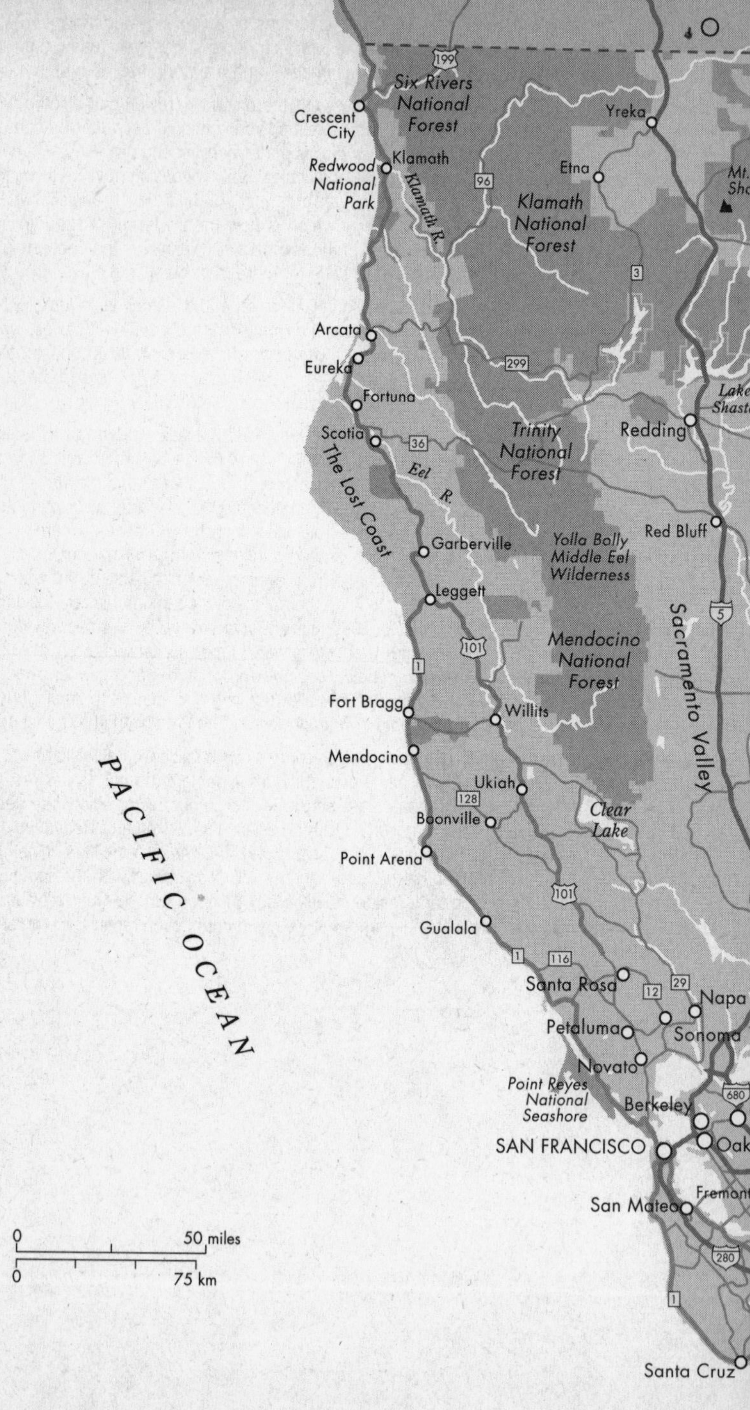

199
Six Rivers National Forest
Crescent City
Yreka
Klamath
Redwood National Park
Klamath R.
96
Etna
Mt. Sha
Klamath National Forest
3
Arcata
Eureka
299
Fortuna
Lake Shasta
Redding
Scotia
36
Trinity National Forest
The Lost Coast
Eel R.
Red Bluff
Garberville
Yolla Bolly Middle Eel Wilderness
Leggett
5
Sacramento Valley
101
Mendocino National Forest
1
Fort Bragg
Willits
Mendocino
PACIFIC OCEAN
Ukiah
128
Boonville
Clear Lake
Point Arena
101
Gualala
1
116
Santa Rosa
12
29
Napa
Petaluma
Sonoma
Novato
Point Reyes National Seashore
680
Berkeley
SAN FRANCISCO
Oakl
Fremont
San Mateo
280
1
Santa Cruz
0 50 miles
0 75 km

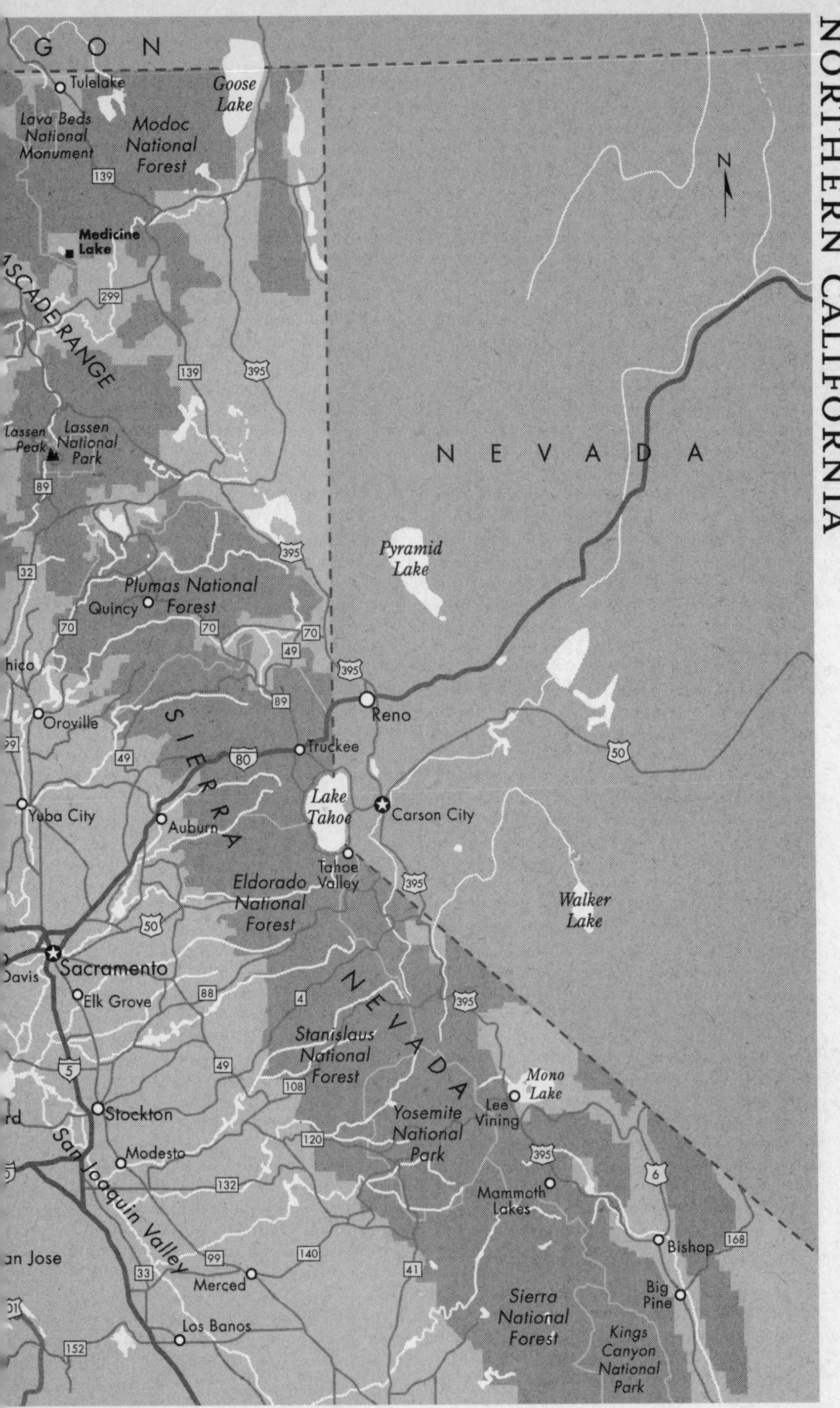
NORTHERN CALIFORNIA
GON
Tulelake
Goose Lake
Lava Beds National Monument
Modoc National Forest
139
Medicine Lake
CASCADE RANGE
299
139
395
N
Lassen Peak
Lassen National Park
89
NEVADA
395
32
Pyramid Lake
Plumas National Forest
Quincy
70
70
70
49
Chico
395
Reno
89
Oroville
SIERRA
Truckee
99
49
80
50
Lake Tahoe
Carson City
Yuba City
Auburn
Tahoe Valley
395
Eldorado National Forest
Walker Lake
50
Sacramento
Davis
Elk Grove
88
NEVADA
4
395
Stanislaus National Forest
5
49
Mono Lake
108
Lee Vining
Stockton
Yosemite National Park
San Joaquin Valley
120
Modesto
395
6
132
Mammoth Lakes
Bishop
168
San Jose
99
140
33
Merced
41
Big Pine
Sierra National Forest
Los Banos
Kings Canyon National Park
152

SOUTHERN CALIFORNIA

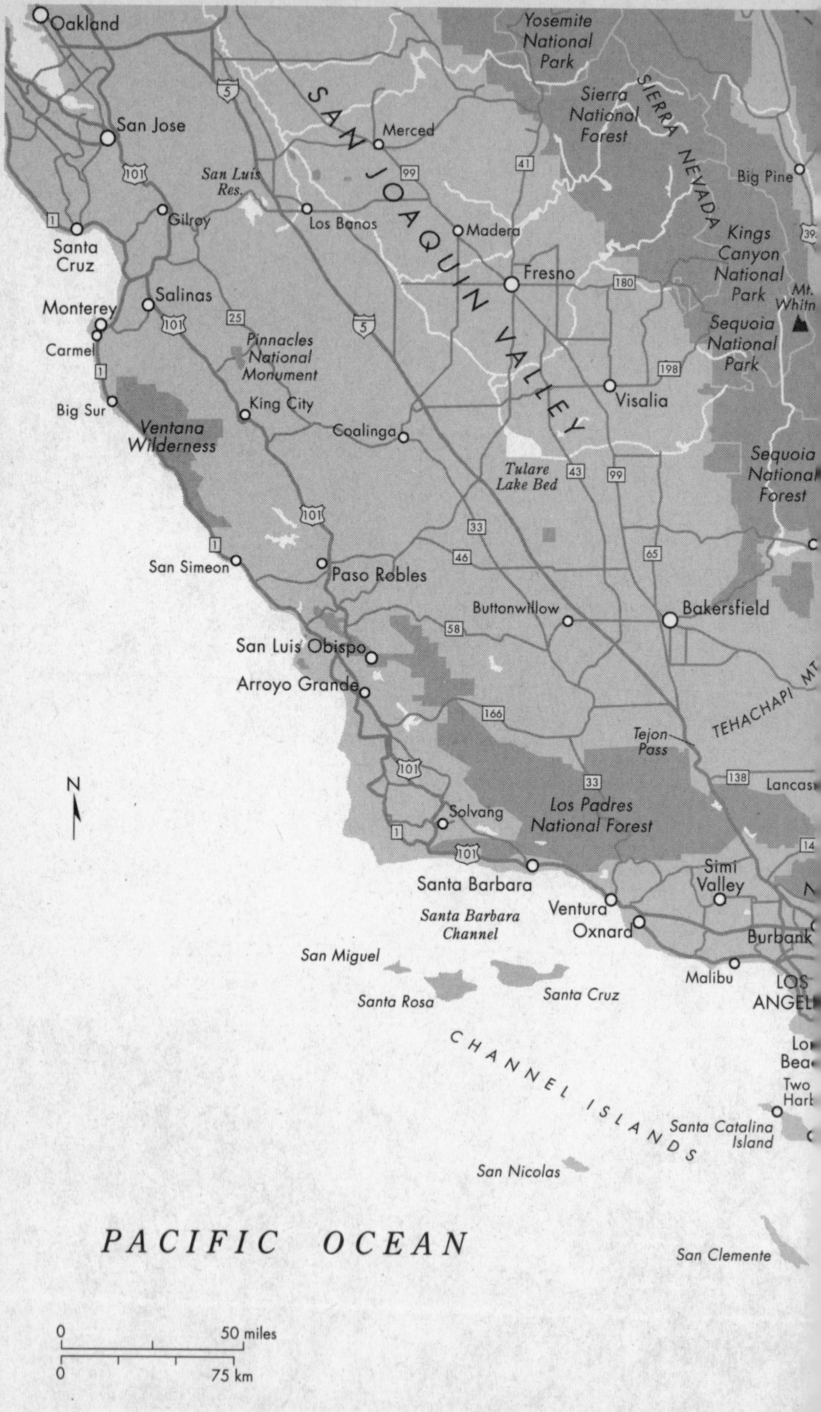

Oakland
Yosemite National Park
San Jose
Merced
Sierra National Forest
SIERRA NEVADA
SAN JOAQUIN VALLEY
San Luis Res.
Big Pine
Gilroy
Los Banos
Madera
Santa Cruz
Kings Canyon National Park
Fresno
Salinas
Monterey
Carmel
Pinnacles National Monument
Sequoia National Park
Visalia
Big Sur
King City
Ventana Wilderness
Coalinga
Sequoia National Forest
Tulare Lake Bed
San Simeon
Paso Robles
Buttonwillow
Bakersfield
San Luis Obispo
Arroyo Grande
TEHACHAPI MT
Tejon Pass
Los Padres National Forest
Solvang
Lancas
Simi Valley
Santa Barbara
Ventura
Oxnard
Burbank
Santa Barbara Channel
San Miguel
Malibu
LOS ANGEL
Santa Rosa
Santa Cruz
CHANNEL ISLANDS
Santa Catalina Island
San Nicolas
PACIFIC OCEAN
San Clemente

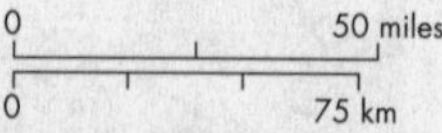

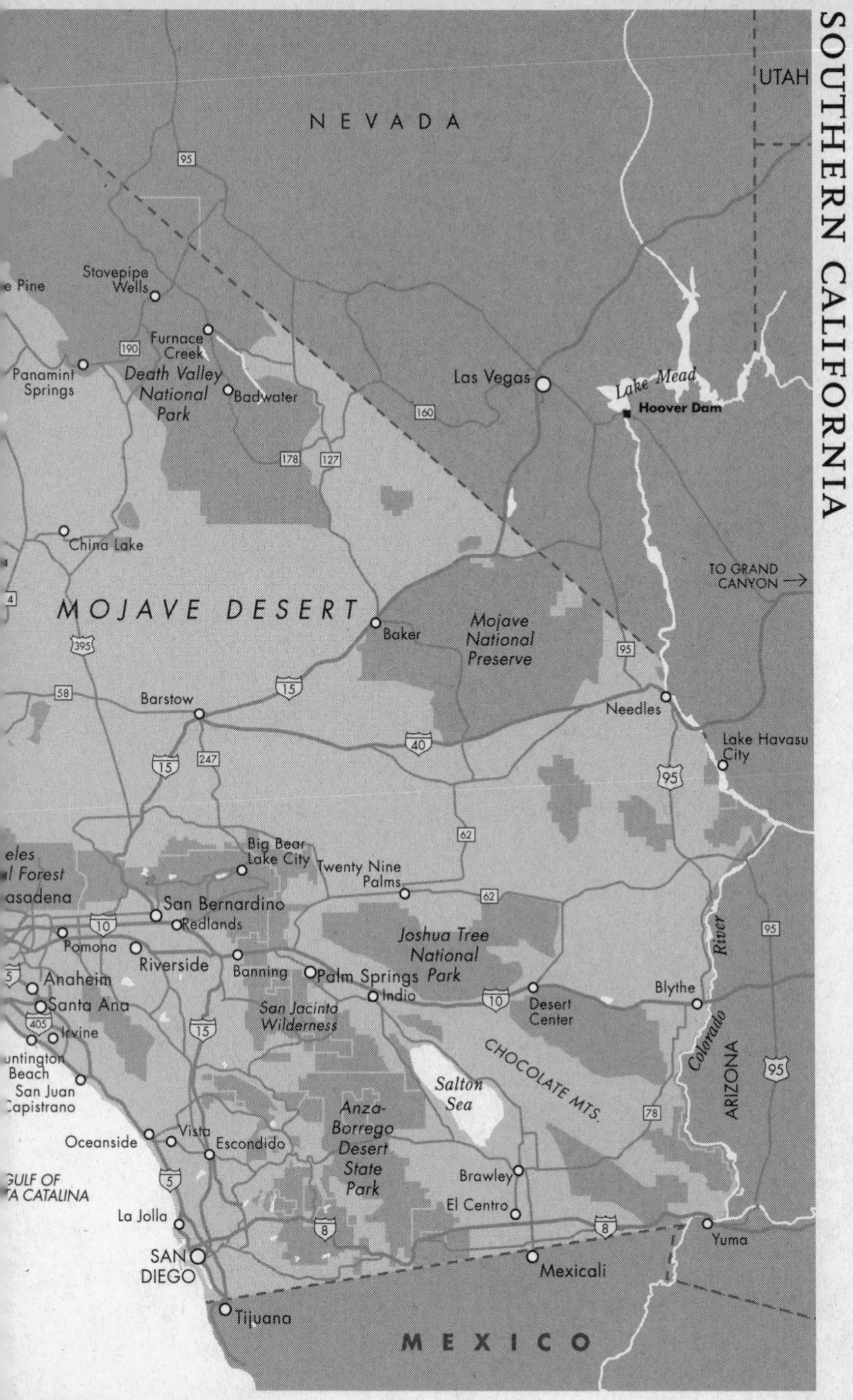
SOUTHERN CALIFORNIA
UTAH
NEVADA
Stovepipe Wells
Furnace Creek
Panamint Springs
Death Valley National Park
Badwater
Las Vegas
Lake Mead
Hoover Dam
China Lake
MOJAVE DESERT
Baker
Mojave National Preserve
TO GRAND CANYON
Barstow
Needles
Lake Havasu City
Big Bear Lake City
Twenty Nine Palms
San Bernardino
Redlands
Pomona
Riverside
Banning
Palm Springs
Indio
Joshua Tree National Park
Anaheim
Santa Ana
Irvine
San Jacinto Wilderness
Desert Center
Blythe
Colorado River
CHOCOLATE MTS.
ARIZONA
San Juan Capistrano
Salton Sea
Anza-Borrego Desert State Park
Oceanside
Vista
Escondido
Brawley
El Centro
La Jolla
SAN DIEGO
Mexicali
Yuma
Tijuana
MEXICO

BASICS

contacts and savvy tips to make your trip hassle-free

If you've ever traveled with anyone before, you know that there are two types of people in the world—the planners and the nonplanners. Travel brings out the worst in both groups. Left to their own devices, the planners will have you goose-stepping from attraction to attraction on a cultural blitzkrieg, while the nonplanners will invariably miss the flight, the bus, and maybe even the point. This chapter offers you a middle ground; we hope it provides enough information to help you plan your trip to California without nailing you down. Stay flexible and remember that the most hair-pulling situations turn into the best travel stories back home.

AIR TRAVEL

Always **bring a photo ID to the airport.** You may be asked to show it before you are allowed to check in.

MAJOR AIRLINE OR LOW-COST CARRIER?

Most people choose a flight based on price. Yet there are other issues to consider. Major airlines offer the greatest number of departures; smaller airlines—including regional, low-cost and no-frill airlines—usually have a more limited number of flights daily. Major airlines have frequent-flyer partners, which allow you to credit mileage earned on one airline to your account with another. Low-cost airlines offer a definite price advantage and fewer restrictions, such as advance-purchase requirements. Safety-wise, low-cost carriers as a group have a good history, but **check the safety record before booking** any low-cost carrier; call the Federal Aviation Administration's Consumer Hotline (*see* Airline Complaints, *below*).

MAJOR AIRLINES • Alaska Airlines (tel. 800/426–0333). **America West** (tel. 800/235–9292). **American** (tel. 800/433–7300). **British Airways** (tel. 800/247–9297). **Continental** (tel. 800/231–0856). **Delta** (tel. 800/241–4141). **Japan Air Lines** (tel. 800/525–3663). **Northwest** (tel. 800/225–2525). **TWA** (tel. 800/892–4141). **United** (tel. 800/241–6522). **US Airways** (tel. 800/428–4322). From the U.K.: **American** (tel. 0345/789–789). **British Airways** (tel. 0345/222–111). **Delta** (tel. 0800/414–767). **United** (tel. 0800/888–555). **Virgin Atlantic** (tel. 01293/747–747). From Down Under: **Qantas** (tel. 008/11–2121) and **Air New Zealand** (tel. 02/13–2476) fly from Sydney and Auckland. **United** (tel. 02/237–8888) flies from Sydney, Auckland, and Melbourne. **Japan Airlines** (tel. 02/9272–1111) flies from Australia and New Zealand with a stopover in Tokyo.

SMALLER AIRLINES • Carnival Air Lines (tel. 800/824–7386). **Midwest Express** (tel. 800/452–2022). **Reno Air** (tel. 800/736–6247). **Southwest** (tel. 800/435–9792).

DON'T STOP UNLESS YOU MUST

When you book, **look for nonstop flights** and **remember that "direct" flights stop at least once.** Try to **avoid connecting flights,** which require a change of plane. Two airlines may jointly operate a connecting flight, so ask if your airline operates every segment—you may find that your preferred carrier flies you only part of the way.

USE AN AGENT

Travel agents, especially those who specialize in finding the lowest fares (*see* Discounts & Deals, *below*), can be especially helpful when booking a plane ticket. When you're quoted a price, **ask your agent if the price is likely to get any lower.** Good agents know the seasonal fluctuations of airfares and can usually anticipate a sale or fare war. However, waiting can be risky: The fare could go *up* as seats become scarce, and you may wait so long that your preferred flight sells out. A wait-and-see strategy works best if your plans are flexible, but if you must arrive and depart on certain dates, don't delay.

GET THE LOWEST FARE

The least-expensive airfares to California are priced for round-trip travel. Major airlines usually require that you **book in advance and buy the ticket within 24 hours,** and you may have to **stay over a Saturday night.** It's smart to **call a number of airlines, and when you are quoted a good price, book it on the spot**—the same fare may not be available on the same flight the next day. Airlines generally allow you to change your return date for a fee $25–$50. If you don't use your ticket you can apply the cost toward the purchase of a new ticket, again for a small charge. However, most low-fare tickets are nonrefundable. To get the lowest airfare, **check different routings.** If your destination or home city has more than one gateway, compare prices to and from different airports. Also price off-peak flights, which may be significantly less expensive, and, look into discounts available through student- and budget-travel organizations (*see* Students, *below*).

Flexibility is the key to getting a serious bargain on airfare. If you can play around with your departure date, destination, amount of luggage carried, and return date, you will probably save money. Ask which days of the week are the cheapest to fly on—weekends are often the most expensive. If you end up biting the bullet and paying more than you'd like for a ticket, keep scanning the ads in newspaper travel sections for last-minute ticket deals or a lower fare offered by desperate airlines. Some airlines will refund the difference in ticket price when they lower fares and you call them on it.

To save money on round-trip flights originating in the United Kingdom, **look into an APEX or Super-PEX ticket.** APEX tickets must be booked in advance and have certain restrictions. Super-PEX tickets can be purchased at the airport on the day of departure—subject to availability.

STANDBY & 3-DAY ADVANCE PURCHASE

Flying standby is almost a thing of the past. The idea is to **purchase an open ticket and wait for the next available seat on the next available flight** to your chosen destination. Yet most airlines have dumped standby policies in favor of three-day-advance-purchase youth fares, which are open only to people under 25 and can only be purchased within three days of departure. Return flights must also be booked no more than three days prior to departure. If you meet the above criteria, expect 10%–50% savings on published APEX fares.

There are also a number of brokers that specialize in discount and last-minute sales, offering savings on unsold seats on commercial carriers and charter flights, as well as tour packages. If you're desperate to get to California by Wednesday, try **Last Minute Travel Club** (tel. 617/267–9800).

CHARTER FLIGHTS

Generally speaking, a charter company either buys a block of tickets on a regularly scheduled commercial flight and sells them at a discount (the prevalent form in the United States) or leases the whole plane and then offers relatively cheap fares to the public (most common in the United Kingdom). Despite a few potential drawbacks—including infrequent flights, restrictive return-date requirements, lickety-split payment demands, frequent bankruptcies—**charter companies often offer the cheapest tickets around,** especially during high season when APEX fares are most expensive. Other charter troubles: Weird departure times, packed planes, and a dearth of one-way tickets. Make sure you find out a company's policy on refunds should a flight be canceled by either yourself or the airline. Summer charter flights fill up fast and should be booked a couple months in advance. You can **minimize risks by checking the company's reputation with the Better Business Bureau and taking out enough trip-cancellation insurance** to cover the operator's potential failure.

Charter companies to try include **DER Tours** (Box 1606, Des Plains, IL 60017, tel. 800/782–2424), **MartinAir** (tel. 800/627–8462), **Tower Air** (tel. 800/34–TOWER), and **Travel CUTS** (*see* Budget Travel Organizations, *above*). The previous list of charter companies is by no means exhaustive; check newspaper travel sections for more extensive listings. Council Travel and STA (*see* Students, *below*) also offer exclusively negotiated discount airfares on scheduled airlines.

AVOID GETTING BUMPED

Airlines routinely overbook planes, knowing that not everyone with a ticket will show up, but sometimes everyone does. When that happens, airlines ask for volunteers to give up their seats. In return these volunteers usually get a certificate for a free flight and are rebooked on the next flight out. If there are not enough volunteers the airline must choose who will be denied boarding. The first to get bumped are passengers who checked in late and those flying on discounted tickets, **so get to the gate and check in as early as possible,** especially during peak periods.

ENJOY THE FLIGHT

For better service, **fly smaller or regional carriers,** which often have higher passenger-satisfaction ratings. Sometimes you'll find leather seats, more legroom, and better food.

For more legroom, **request an emergency-aisle seat**; however, don't sit in the row in front of the emergency aisle or in front of a bulkhead, where seats may not recline.

If you don't like airline food, **ask for special meals when booking.** These can be vegetarian, low-cholesterol, or kosher, for example.

To avoid jet lag try to maintain a normal routine while traveling. At night **get some sleep.** By day **eat light meals, drink water (not alcohol), and move about the cabin** to stretch your legs.

COMPLAIN IF NECESSARY

If your baggage goes astray or your flight goes awry, complain right away. Most carriers require that you file a claim immediately.

AIRLINE COMPLAINTS • U.S. Department of Transportation **Aviation Consumer Protection Division** (C-75, Washington, DC 20590, tel. 202/366–2220). **Federal Aviation Administration (FAA) Consumer Hotline** (tel. 800/322–7873).

AIRPORTS

Major gateways to California are Los Angeles, San Francisco, San Diego, and Oakland International Airports.

Flying time is roughly five hours from New York and four hours from Chicago. Flying between San Francisco and Los Angeles takes one hour.

AIRPORT INFORMATION • **Los Angeles International Airport** (tel. 310/646–5252), commonly called LAX. **San Francisco International Airport** (tel. 650/761–0800). **San Diego International Airport** (tel. 619/231–2100), commonly called Lindbergh Field. **Oakland Airport** (tel. 510/577–4000).

BEACHES

Those who expect California to have the palm-dotted, serene waters of the tropics will be startled to find beaches with a harsh, violent beauty instead. The coast south of Santa Barbara more or less upholds the Hollywood image (prominent lifeguard stands and loads of Beautiful People in skimpy beachwear), but even here the **water is rarely warm** (about 65°F). Along the Central Coast, beaches give way to the majestic cliffs of Big Sur. Summertime is when most people hit the sand, but **don't expect to catch rays on the Central Coast,** which is at its foggiest and dampest then. The Beach Bible is the thorough California ***Coastal Resource Guide*** ($15) published by University of California Press, which details t' coastline beach by beach from Crescent City to San Diego. For a really thorough tan, check out ' Patrick's **California's Nude Beaches** (Bold Type, Inc.; $16).

BICYCLING

Road bikers have long pinpointed **Highway 1,** the coastal road running from Canad the Pacific, as one of America's great rides. But throughout the state, the stunnir wonderful biking. Large cities, resort towns, and national parks rent bikes for about $25 a day and have set aside special routes or trails. While road biking is popular all over the state, mountain bikers particularly should consider trips to the Eastern Sierra, the Angeles and Plumas national forests, the Cascades, Santa Cruz, Big Sur, and Marin County.

Bicycling through California is perhaps the cheapest, most environmentally sound, and—depending on your physical shape—most enjoyable way to see the state. Campgrounds cost less for cyclists and hostels sometimes make room for you even if they're full. Some highways, including stretches of U.S. 101 and Highway 1, accommodate bicyclists, but **the best routes are the less-crowded roads that parallel or branch off the highways. Amtrak** will transport you and your bike ($5 handling fee) on the *Coast Starlight* route. They provide the bike box ($7) but require you to disassemble the bike (bring tools). ***Bicycling the Pacific Coast*** (The Mountaineers; $15), by Tom Kirkendall and Vicky Spring, explores the coastal route from Canada to Mexico.

BIKES IN FLIGHT

Most airlines will accommodate bikes as luggage, provided they are dismantled and put into a box. Call to see if your airline sells bike boxes (about $5; bike bags are at least $100), although you can often pick them up free at bike shops. International travelers can sometimes substitute a bike for a piece of checked luggage for free; otherwise, it will cost about $100. Domestic and Canadian airlines charge a $25–$50 fee.

BUS TRAVEL

Greyhound (tel. 800/231- 2222) offers bus service along U.S. I–5, U.S. 101, and I–80, as well as to a few offshoot towns. The cheapest fares are during low season (Jan.–June and Sept.–Nov.). Their **Ameripass,** valid on all U.S. routes, can be purchased in advance in cities throughout the U.S.; spontaneous types can also buy it up to 45 minutes before the bus leaves from the terminal. The pass allows unlimited travel within a limited time period: seven days ($179), 15 days ($289), 30 days ($399), or 60 days ($599). Foreign visitors can get slightly lower rates.

Green Tortoise is among the least rapid, most memorable ways to traverse California. From Venice Beach to Yreka (and a lot of destinations outside the state), the Tortoise's camper coaches wend their way along a dot-to-dot map of natural (and unnatural) attractions—including Santa Barbara, Berkeley, Yosemite, and Mt. Shasta. Often compared to youth hostels on wheels, the buses feature foam mattresses for sleeping, and communally cooked vegetarian food is included in the price of the trip. Green Tortoise also makes longer treks (e.g., to Mexico, Baja California, Central America, Alaska, the Grand Canyon, and the east coast). Selected fares: San Francisco–L.A., $30; San Francisco–Santa Cruz, $10; Seattle, Washington–L.A., $69, $79 in peak-season. For a free pamphlet, write or call Green Tortoise Adventure Travel, 494 Broadway, San Francisco 94137, tel. 415/821–0803 or 800/867–8647 outside the 415 and 510 area codes. Reservations are recommended for most journeys.

CAMPING

California was made for camping. Most of the state's forests, mountains, deserts, and coastal areas have designated public and private campgrounds whose sites range from primitive (meaning no water and pit toilets) to annoyingly developed (overrun by RVs and arcades). In this book we have three classifications for water at the various camping sites: potable (gulp it down), nonpotable (must be treated or boiled), and no water (dry as a bone). Prices vary accordingly—anywhere from free (for some walk-in campgrounds) to $18 for a public site, more for a private site. For general information about camping, the **Sierra Club** (*see* Hiking, *below*) has a good selection of guidebooks and group tours. For a guide to more than 15,000 campgrounds, splurge on a copy of ***California Camping*** (Foghorn Press, $18), by Tom Stienstra.

CAMPING GEAR

Before packing loads of camping gear, seriously consider how much camping you will actually do versus the hassle of hauling around a tent, sleeping bag, stove, and accouterments. Also consider climate in choosing what to bring. A great place to get equipment, outdoor publications, and useful free pamphlets is **Recreational Equipment, Inc. (REI)** (1700 45th St. E, Sumner, WA 98352, tel. 800/426–4840), with many West Coast locations. Request a free catalog by calling the toll-free number. **The**

North Face (tel. 510/618–3500 or 800/362–4963) has discounted factory outlets in large cities. Call for outlet locations.

Essential camping supplies include a good sleeping bag (preferably stuffed with Qualofil, which provides warmth when sopping wet); a quality backpack (external-frame packs are better suited to rough terrain but are more awkward and less flexible than internal frames); and lightweight, waterproof clothes (layered synthetics are most effective). Tents, which can be expensive, are desirable but not obligatory; a bivouac "bivvy" bag (a water-repellent shell that fits over a sleeping bag) can do the trick, or you can find semi-sheltered areas and risk the rain. Other odds and ends you probably want to have are matches in a waterproof container, a rain poncho, a multiblade knife, something for banging in tent stakes (your shoe will work if it's sturdy enough), a mess kit, water bottle, a water filter or purifying pills, a can/bottle opener, a small cookstove, extra rope, a flashlight or candle lantern, toilet paper, a compass, and extra batteries. Always carry a first-aid kit with lots of adhesive bandages, gauze, aspirin, antibacterial ointment (Neosporin is a good brand), and an emergency procedures guide. Optionals include an elastic bandage, hydrogen peroxide, tweezers, a snake bite kit (if you know how to use it), signal mirror, sunscreen, moleskin with tape for blisters, and a sewing kit. Cellular phones, while expensive to operate, have afforded some modern campers peace of mind (and crucial help) in emergencies.

OFF-ROAD CAMPING

On state park lands, camping is legal only at designated campgrounds, though the *Official Guide to State Parks,* available from the California State Park System (*see below*), lists certain "on-route" spots where you can pull your vehicle off to the side of the road and sleep inside. But there are almost 20 million national forest acres and more than 17 million Bureau of Land Management acres in California—that's two-fifths of the state—that allow free, dispersed camping. With the exception of some national forest campgrounds and towns, these lands are backcountry—no piped-in water, no picnic tables, few paved or maintained roads, maybe an occasional outhouse. Some BLM areas may be the local hot spot for off-road vehicles, but for the most part, national forest and BLM lands are pristine and peaceful. Please be careful to keep it that way. Permits are required for open fires and most camping in wilderness areas (*see below*).

Water from lakes or streams should be purified for drinking or cooking. Purification pills and filters are available at most sporting goods stores, but boiling also works.

For information on BLM lands, write or call the **Bureau of Land Management,** 2800 Cottage Way, Sacramento 95825, tel. 916/979–2800 (for contact information for national and state parks and national forests, *see below*).

PROTECTING THE ENVIRONMENT

Wilderness permits, which outline backpacking rules and help limit the number of people on a trail, are usually required if you plan on any backcountry exploration. They're free and obtainable by mail or at the point of entry to your park (usually no more than a day before you plan to hike). **Consult each park individually for regulations** on trail quotas and mail-in permits. Even if you don't get one, keep in mind some general rules: Always **travel on trails** and, if possible, **camp at previously used sites** to avoid trampling vegetation and causing soil erosion. Also, **don't camp closer than 100 feet to any road, trail, or water source. Hang your food and other smelly items 100 feet away** from camp to deter bears and mountain lions, and always **pack out your garbage**; **bury human waste 8 inches deep, at least 200 feet from water, your camp, and trails.** To wash anything, **use only biodegradable soap,** and never wash directly in a stream or lake—do it at least 100 feet from the water's edge. Very few parks allow you to build fires in the wilderness; if you must, **get a free fire permit** at the nearest ranger station (these are required for any kind of open flame, including cookstoves), and make sure to put the fire out completely.

CAR RENTAL

Rates in Los Angeles begin at $29 a day and $126 a week for an economy car with air conditioning, an automatic transmission, and unlimited mileage. Rates in San Diego begin at $25 a day and $136 a week. Rates in San Francisco begin at $36 a day and $123 a week. This does not include tax on car rentals, which is 8.25%.

CUT COSTS

To get the best deal, **book through a travel agent who is willing to shop around.** When pricing cars, **ask about the location of the rental lot.** Some off-airport locations offer lower rates, and their lots are only minutes from the terminal via complimentary shuttle. You also may want to **price local car-rental companies,** whose rates may be lower still, although their service and maintenance may not be as good as those of a name-brand agency. They sometimes undercut the major agencies on daily or weekly rates, but you may not get unlimited mileage.

Be sure to **look into wholesalers,** companies that do not own fleets but rent in bulk from those that do and often offer better rates than traditional car-rental operations. Prices are best during off-peak periods.

Also **ask your travel agent about a company's customer-service record.** How has it responded to late plane arrivals and vehicle mishaps? Are there often lines at the rental counter, and, if you're traveling during a holiday period, does a confirmed reservation guarantee you a car?

No matter who you rent from, remember to ask about required deposits, cancellation penalties, and drop-off charges if you're planning to pick up the car in one city and leave it in another.

MAJOR AGENCIES • Alamo (tel. 800/327–9633, 0800/272–2000 in the U.K.). **Avis** (tel. 800/331–1212, 800/879–2847 in Canada). **Budget** (tel. 800/527–0700, 0800/181181 in the U.K.). **Dollar** (tel. 800/800–4000; 0990/565656 in the U.K., where it is known as Eurodollar). **Hertz** (tel. 800/654–3131, 800/263–0600 in Canada, 0345/555888 in the U.K.). **National InterRent** (tel. 800/227–7368; 0345/222525 in the U.K., where it is known as Europcar InterRent).

RENTAL WHOLESALERS • Auto Europe (tel. 207/842–2000 or 800/223–5555, fax 800/235–6321). The **Kemwel Group** (tel. 914/835–5555 or 800/678–0678, fax 914/835–5126).

NEED INSURANCE?

When driving a rented car you are generally responsible for any damage to or loss of the vehicle. You also are liable for any property damage or personal injury that you may cause while driving. Before you rent, **see what coverage you already have** under the terms of your personal auto-insurance policy and credit cards.

For about $14 a day, rental companies sell protection, known as a collision- or loss-damage waiver (CDW or LDW) that eliminates your liability for damage to the car; it's always optional and should never be automatically added to your bill. Some states, including California, have capped the price of CDW and LDW.

In most states you don't need CDW if you have personal auto insurance or other liability insurance. However, **make sure you have enough coverage to pay for the car.** If you do not have auto insurance or an umbrella policy that covers damage to third parties, purchasing CDW or LDW is highly recommended.

BEWARE SURCHARGES

Before you pick up a car in one city and leave it in another, **ask about drop-off charges or one-way service fees,** which can be substantial. Note, too, that some rental agencies charge extra if you return the car before the time specified on your contract. To avoid a hefty refueling fee, **fill the tank just before you turn in the car,** but be aware that gas stations near the rental outlet may overcharge.

MEET THE REQUIREMENTS

In the United States you must be 21 to rent a car, and rates may be higher if you're under 25. You'll pay extra for additional drivers (about $2 per day). Residents of the U.K. will need a reservation voucher, a passport, a U.K. driver's license, and a travel policy that covers each driver, in order to pick up a car.

CONSULATES

Canada (In Los Angeles: 300 S. Grand Ave., Suite 1000, 90071, tel. 213/346–2701. Open weekdays 8:30–12:30 and 1:30–4:30). **United Kingdom** (In Los Angeles: 11766 Wilshire Blvd., Suite 850, 90025, tel. 310/477–3322. In San Francisco: 1 Sansome St., Suite 850, 94104, tel. 415/981–3030. Both open weekdays 8:30–5). **Australia** (In Los Angeles: 611 N. Larchmont Blvd., 90004, tel. 213/469–4300. In San Francisco: 1 Bush St., Suite 700, 94104, tel. 415/362–6160. Both open weekdays 8:45–5). **New Zealand** (In Los Angeles: 12400 Wilshire Blvd., Suite 1150, 90025, tel. 310/207–1605. In San Francisco: 1 Maritime Plaza, Suite 700, 94111, tel. 415/399–1455. Both open weekdays 9–5).

CONSUMER PROTECTION

Whenever possible, **pay with a major credit card** so you can cancel payment if there's a problem, provided that you can provide documentation. This is a good idea whether you're buying travel arrangements before your trip or shopping at your destination.

If you're doing business with a particular company for the first time, **contact your local Better Business Bureau and the attorney general's offices** in your state and the company's home state, as well. Have any complaints been filed?

Finally, if you're buying a package, always **consider travel insurance** that includes default coverage (*see* Insurance, *above*).

LOCAL BBBS • Council of Better Business Bureaus (4200 Wilson Blvd., Suite 800, Arlington, VA 22203, tel. 703/276–0100, fax 703/525–8277).

CUSTOMS & DUTIES

ENTERING AUSTRALIA

Australian travelers 18 and over may bring back, duty free: one liter of alcohol; 250 grams of tobacco products (equivalent to 250 cigarettes or cigars); and other articles worth up to AUS$400. If you're under 18, your duty-free allowance is AUS$200. To avoid paying duty on goods you mail back to Australia, mark the package: "Australian goods returned."

ENTERING CANADA

If you've been out of Canada for at least seven days you may bring in C$500 worth of goods duty-free. If you've been away for fewer than seven days but more than 48 hours, the duty-free allowance drops to C$200; if your trip lasts 24–48 hours, the allowance is C$50. You may not pool allowances with family members. Goods claimed under the C$500 exemption may follow you by mail; those claimed under the lesser exemptions must accompany you.

Alcohol and tobacco products may be included in the seven-day and 48-hour exemptions but not in the 24-hour exemption. If you meet the age requirements of the province or territory through which you reenter Canada you may bring in, duty-free, 1.14 liters (40 imperial ounces) of wine or liquor *or* 24 12-ounce cans or bottles of beer or ale. If you are 16 or older you may bring in, duty-free, 200 cigarettes and 50 cigars; these items must accompany you.

You may send an unlimited number of gifts worth up to C$60 each duty-free to Canada. Label the package UNSOLICITED GIFT—VALUE UNDER $60. Alcohol and tobacco are excluded.

INFORMATION • Revenue Canada (2265 St. Laurent Blvd. S, Ottawa, Ontario K1G 4K3, tel. 613/993–0534, 800/461–9999 in Canada).

ENTERING NEW ZEALAND

Although greeted with a "Haere Mai" ("Welcome to New Zealand"), homeward-bound travelers face a number of restrictions. Travelers over age 17 are allowed, duty-free: 200 cigarettes or 250 grams of tobacco or 50 cigars or a combo of all three up to 250 grams; 4.5 liters of wine or beer and one 1,125-ml bottle of spirits; and goods with a combined value up to NZ$700. If you want more details, ask for the pamphlet "Customs Guide for Travellers" from a New Zealand consulate.

ENTERING THE U.K.

From countries outside the EU, including the United States, you may import, duty-free, 200 cigarettes or 50 cigars; 1 liter of spirits or 2 liters of fortified or sparkling wine or liqueurs; 2 liters of still table wine; 60 milliliters of perfume; and 250 milliliters of toilet water; plus £136 worth of other goods, including gifts and souvenirs.

INFORMATION • HM Customs and Excise (Dorset House, Stamford St., London SE1 9NG, tel. 0171/202–4227).

ENTERING THE U.S.

Visitors 21 and older can bring into the United States (1) 200 cigarettes or 100 non-Cuban cigars or 2 kilograms of smoking tobacco, (2) one U.S. liter of alcohol, and (3) duty-free gifts to a value of $400 (this includes the value of your tobacco, cigars and alcohol). Also, you may ship gifts valued up to $100 duty-free. Forbidden are meat and meat products, seeds, plants, and fruits. Avoid illegal drugs like the plague.

DINING

Agriculture is a huge business in California. The Central Valley alone produces a bounty of fresh fruits and vegetables year-round. In addition, organically grown produce and meat products from organically fed animals are becoming more readily available. As befits a place of such ethnic and cultural diversity, California can offer an amazing variety of cuisine within a few city blocks (especially in L.A. and San Francisco). **Mexican restaurants are a good bet** for cheap, fresh, high-quality food throughout the state—in fact, this could easily be considered California's specialty. **Asian restaurants, too, are great for tasty, well balanced meals** including fresh veggies not found in Mexican restaurants. Be wary, however, of Asian restaurants in small towns; their quality varies widely, and some still use MSG though the more enlightened boast its absence. On the pricier side, "California cuisine" is known for its artful presentation; fresh, in-season ingredients; and portions which were once "minimalist" when the trend started but are heartier these days. One of the latest developments on California's culinary front is "fusion" cuisine, blending the best of East and West influences—truly the melting pot in action! Vegetarians will have little trouble finding meatless meals in most areas. For the cheapest food, **try supermarkets,** which charge no sales tax (restaurants do). The budget-minded should also **take advantage of lunch specials and early-evening "happy hours."** Assume that restaurants reviewed in this guide accept credit cards, unless otherwise noted. The price categories refer to the cost of a main course with a nonalcoholic drink.

DISABILITIES & ACCESSIBLITY

ACCESS IN CALIFORNIA

Accessibility may soon have an international symbol if an initiative begun by the Society for the Advancement of Travel for the Handicapped (SATH) catches on. A bold, underlined, capital **H** is the symbol that SATH is publicizing for hotels, restaurants, and tourist attractions to indicate that the property has some accessible facilities. While awareness of the needs of travelers with disabilities increases every year, budget opportunities are harder to find. Always ask if discounts are available, either for you or for a companion. In addition, plan your trip and make reservations far in advance, since companies that provide services for people with disabilities go in and out of business regularly.

INFORMATION • Twin Peaks Press (Box 129, Vancouver, WA 98666, tel. 360/694–2462 or 800/637–2256 for orders only) specializes in books for the disabled, such as *Travel for the Disabled,* which offers helpful hints as well as a comprehensive list of guidebooks and facilities geared to the disabled. Their *Directory of Travel Agencies for the Disabled* lists more than 350 agencies throughout the world. Each is $19.95 plus $3 ($4.50 for both) shipping and handling. Twin Peaks also offers a "Traveling Nurse's Network," which connect disabled travelers with registered nurses to aid and accompany them on their trip. Fees range $30–$125. Whenever possible, reviews in this book will indicate if rooms are wheelchair-accessible. Most hotel chains, such as **Embassy Suites, Radisson,** and the cheaper **Motel 6** can accommodate wheelchair users but rarely offer discounts. **Best Western** sometimes discounts rooms for the disabled, but the offers vary from hotel to hotel. **Red Roof Inns** (tel. 800/843–7663 in U.S. and Canada) have wheelchair-accessible rooms and special alarm systems for deaf and blind guests.

ORGANIZATIONS • Outdoors Forever (Box 4832, East Lansing, MI 48823, tel. 517/337–0018) is a nonprofit organization that works to make the outdoors more accessible to people with physical limitations. Call or write for more information about their magazine, *Outdoors Forever,* or their publications on equipment, techniques, and organizations that plan outings. **Mobility International USA (MIUSA)** (Box 10767, Eugene, OR 97440, tel. 503/343–1284 TDD or 541/343–1284 TDD) is a nonprofit organization that coordinates exchange programs for disabled people around the world. MIUSA also offers information on accommodations and organized study programs for members ($25 annually).

The national park system offers the **Golden Access Passport,** a free, lifetime entry pass that exempts travelers with disabilities and their families or friends from all entry fees and 50% of use fees for camping and parking in federal parks and wildlife refuges. You aren't allowed to register by mail or phone, but you can apply in person with medical proof of disability at all National Park Service and Forest Service offices, Forest Service ranger station offices, national parks that charge fees, Bureau of Land Management Offices, and Fish and Wildlife Service offices. For information, contact the **Outdoor Recreation Information Center** (915 2nd Ave., Suite 442, Seattle, WA 98174, tel. 206/220–7450).

GETTING AROUND

The **American Public Transit Association** (tel. 202/898–4000) in Washington, D.C., has information on transportation options in all U.S. cities for travelers with disabilities. Most major airlines are happy to help travelers with disabilities make flight arrangements, provided they receive notification 48 hours in advance. **Amtrak** (tel. 800/872–7245 or 800/523–6590 TDD) offers a 25% discount on one-way coach fares for travelers with disabilities who show written proof of disability. If notified when reservations are made, Amtrak will provide assistance for travelers at stations. **Greyhound-Trailways** (tel. 800/752–4841 or 800/345–3109 TDD) allows a disabled traveler and a companion to ride for the price of a single fare. No advance notice is required, although you will need to show proof of disability (such as a doctor's letter) to receive the special fare.

Some major car-rental companies are able to supply hand-controlled vehicles with a minimum of 24 hours' advance notice. Given a day's notice, **Avis** (tel. 800/331–1212) will install hand-controlled mechanisms at no extra charge. **Hertz** (tel. 800/654–3131 or 800/654–2280 TDD) asks for 48 hours' advance notice and a $25 cash or credit-card deposit to do the same. **National** (tel. 800/328–4567 or 800/328–6323 TDD) and **Thrifty** (tel. 800/367–2277) have hand-controlled cars at certain locations and ask for at least two days' notice to serve mobility-impaired renters.

TIPS AND HINTS

When discussing accessibility with an operator or reservationist, **ask hard questions.** Are there any stairs, inside *or* out? Are there grab bars next to the toilet *and* in the shower/tub? How wide is the doorway to the room? To the bathroom? When possible, **opt for newer accommodations,** which are more likely to have been designed with access in mind. Older buildings may offer more limited facilities. Be sure to **discuss your needs before booking.**

COMPLAINTS • Disability Rights Section (U.S. Department of Justice, Box 66738, Washington, DC 20035–6738, tel. 202/514–0301 or 800/514–0301, fax 202/307–1198, TTY 202/514–0383 or 800/514–0383) for general complaints. **Aviation Consumer Protection Division** (*see* Air Travel, *above*) for airline-related problems. **Civil Rights Office** (U.S. Department of Transportation, Departmental Office of Civil Rights, S-30, 400 7th St. SW, Room 10215, Washington, DC 20590, tel. 202/366–4648) for problems with surface transportation.

TRAVEL AGENCIES

Some agencies specialize in travel arrangements for individuals with disabilities.

BEST BETS • Access Adventures (206 Chestnut Ridge Rd., Rochester, NY 14624, tel. 716/889–9096), run by a former physical-rehabilitation counselor. **Hinsdale Travel Service** (201 E. Ogden Ave., Suite 100, Hinsdale, IL 60521, tel. 630/325–1335), which offers advice from wheelchair traveler Janice Perkins. **Wheelchair Journeys** (16979 Redmond Way, Redmond, WA 98052, tel. 206/885–2210 or 800/313–4751), for general travel arrangements.

DISCOUNTS & DEALS

While your travel plans are still in the fantasy stage, **start studying the travel sections of major Sunday newspapers**: You'll often find listings for good packages and incredibly cheap flights. Surfing on the Internet can also give you some good ideas. Travel agents are another obvious resource; the computer networks to which they have access show the lowest fares before they're even advertised.

Always **compare all your options before making a choice.** A plane ticket bought with a promotional coupon may not be cheaper than the least expensive fare from a discount ticket agency. (For more on getting a deal on airfares, *see* Air Travel, *above*) When evaluating a package, keep in mind that what you get is just as important as what you save. Just because something is cheap doesn't mean it's a bargain.

CREDIT CARDS & AUTO CLUBS

When you use your credit card to make travel purchases you may get free travel-accident insurance, collision-damage insurance, and medical or legal help, depending on the card and the bank that issued it. So **get a copy of your credit card's travel-benefits policy.** If you are a member of the American Automobile Association (AAA) or an oil-company-sponsored road-assistance plan, always **ask hotel or car-rental reservationists about auto-club discounts.** Some clubs offer additional discounts on admission to attractions. And don't forget that auto-club membership entitles you to free maps and trip-planning services.

DISCOUNTS BY PHONE

Don't be afraid to **check out "1-800" discount reservations services,** which use their buying power to get a better price on hotels, airline tickets, even car rentals. When booking a room, always **call the hotel's local toll-free number** (if one is available) rather than the central reservations number—you'll often get a better price. Always ask about special packages.

CHEAP AIRLINE TICKETS • Tel. **800/FLY–4–LESS.** Tel. **800/FLY–ASAP.**

CHEAP HOTEL ROOMS • **Accommodations Express** (tel. 800/444–7666). **Central Reservation Service (CRS)** (tel. 800/548–3311). **Hotel Reservations Network (HRN)** (tel. 800/964–6835). **Players Express Vacations** (tel. 800/458–6161). **Quickbook** (tel. 800/789–9887). **RMC Travel** (tel. 800/245–5738). **Steigenberger Reservation Service** (tel. 800/223–5652).

SAVE ON COMBOS

Packages and guided tours can both save you money, but don't confuse the two. When you buy a package your travel remains independent, just as though you had planned and booked the trip yourself. Fly/drive packages, which combine airfare and car rental, are often a good deal.

DIVERS' ALERT

Do not fly within 24 hours of scuba diving.

DRIVING

Besides being the most efficient way to navigate this monster state, a car allows you to explore the back roads where mass transportation fears to tread. Renting a car can be economical, but **take your own car if you plan to drive for more than a week or two. I–5** is the fastest route for traveling north–south through the state, but the scenery is mostly flat and uneventful, save for the occasional cow. **Highway 1** is a beautiful but slow drive that hugs the coast north of Santa Barbara all the way up into Oregon. **U.S. 101,** which lies between the two and ends in Leggett when it meets Highway 1, is a compromise in scenery and time. The rolling hills are sometimes pretty but less spectacular than those you'll see on Highway 1; and it takes about 8 hours to travel between Los Angeles and San Francisco, compared to 6 hours on I–5. The north–south route for people who don't like other people is **U.S. 395,** which starts near San Bernardino and climbs north along the eastern slope of the Sierra Nevada, cuts into Nevada and back into northeast California on its way to southeast Oregon. East–west interstate freeways include **I–80** in the north, a fast freeway that can see a lot of messy commute traffic; it heads east from San Francisco through Sacramento and Lake Tahoe on its way across the entire country. In the south, there is I–15, which starts in Los Angeles and travels east through Barstow and the Mojave Desert to Las Vegas; **I–10** shoots east out of Los Angeles into southern Arizona and the great beyond.

DRIVE-AWAY SERVICES

This can be one of the cheapest ways to get around the United States. If you have a current driver's license, are older than 21, and have about $200 for a deposit, you get the keys to a car that someone needs delivered to a specific Point B from a specific Point A. You just worry about gas money and keeping the car clean. Drive-away services usually have time, routing, and mileage limits—these are sometimes very strict. There are services and agents in most major cities; look under "Automobile and Truck Transporting" and "Drive-Away Services" in the Yellow Pages and shop around.

AUTO CLUBS

If you're going to be traveling in the United States and Canada by car, becoming a member of the **Automobile Association of America** (AAA, tel. 800/222–4357) or one of its affiliates is the best investment you can make. Membership generally costs $58 for the first year and $41 annually thereafter, though rates do vary a bit from state to state. Members receive free maps and tour books, personalized itinerary plans, free emergency road service, and discounts at hotels, motels, and some restaurants. If you belong to any type of auto club abroad, AAA may honor your membership; otherwise, consider joining while you're here.

FURTHER READING

A little research before or during your trip can help you make sense or nonsense out of California. Reference works, often pitched to specific kinds of travelers, are legion. Outdoor adventurers should check out

The Pacific Crest Trail (Wilderness Press), a guide to the southern section of the trail (*see* Hiking, *below*). Indoor types might prefer Jack Erickson's *Brewery Adventures in the Wild West* (Red Brick Press).

Besides travel guides, there are countless books on California's culture and politics. Marc Reiser's *Cadillac Desert* explores the significance of water to the history of the state, Mike Davis's excellent *City of Quartz* treats L.A.'s status as a symbol of cultural possibility and political oppression. *The Mayor of Castro Street,* Randy Shilts's biography of late San Francisco Supervisor Harvey Milk (killed together with Mayor George Moscone in 1978), provides insight into the development and politicization of S.F.'s gay community. *The Monkey Wrench Gang,* by Edward Abbey, provides a glimpse into the pristine and untouristed past of places like the Grand Canyon and the greater Southwest. An even better sense of California emerges from the pages of Joan Didion's essays (try *The White Album* or *Slouching Towards Bethlehem*), Tom Wolfe's *The Electric Kool-Aid Acid Test,* Bill Barich's *Big Dreams: Into the Heart of California,* and *West of the West: Imagining California,* an excellent collection of fiction and nonfiction.

Americans and the California Dream by Kevin Starr and *California: An Interpretive History* by Walton Bean are good general California history books, the former concentrating on social and cultural aspects, the latter on politics. William Brewer's *Up and Down California in 1860–1986,* is an unbeatable primary source for pioneer California. In addition, many 20th-century American classics are set in California: John Steinbeck's *Grapes of Wrath* and *Cannery Row* (Monterey), Raymond Chandler's *The Big Sleep* (L.A.), Nathaniel West's *Day of the Locust* (L.A.), and Jack Kerouac's *The Subterraneans* (S.F.) are just a few. More recent titles, like Armistead Maupin's *Tales of the City* series (S.F.) and the surrealistic *Vineland* by Thomas Pynchon (North Coast) make good reading on a long Amtrak ride.

As for film, great images of different parts of the state can be found at revival houses and video stores throughout the country, from the San Francisco of *Play It Again Sam, Vertigo, Dirty Harry, Invasion of the Body Snatchers, Mrs. Doubtfire,* and the revealing documentary *The Times of Harvey Milk;* to the North Coast's *The Birds* and Santa Cruz's *The Lost Boys;* and the Central Valley's *East of Eden* and *American Graffiti,* a vision of youth culture straight out of George Lucas's native Modesto. *Bagdad Café*'s Mojave Desert and *Zabriskie Point*'s Death Valley will make you very thirsty. As for Southern California, leaving aside the more obvious ones (*L.A. Story, The Player, Boyz N the Hood*), a few are essential background: Billy Wilder's *Sunset Boulevard,* the classic film noir portrayal of the darker side of 1940's Hollywood, *Ruthless People* for the lighter side of La La Land, Roman Polanski's *Chinatown,* and two films by Amy Heckerling that say a mouthful about SoCal: *Fast Times at Ridgemont High* (1982) and *Clueless* (1995). You may also want to check out the classic *Rebel Without A Cause* before you visit LA's Griffith Park Observatory, so you can see what the view looked like before the smog set in.

GAY & LESBIAN TRAVEL

Though gay bashing occurs even on the streets of San Francisco, gay men and women enjoy a certain amount of freedom in California. San Francisco and Los Angeles have large gay communities served by many organizations, bookstores, cafés, and other businesses. Many cities have community centers that serve as meeting places and resource clearinghouses; check phone books and individual chapters in this book. Palm Springs and Guerneville, in particular, are popular resort destinations for gay visitors. The **Pacific Center Information Referral Phone Line** (tel. 510/841–6224) is a referral service in the San Francisco Bay Area that provides crisis support and information on social events and emergency housing.

ORGANIZATIONS • The **International Gay Travel Association (IGTA)** (Box 4974, Key West, FL 33041, tel. 800/448–8550) is a nonprofit organization with worldwide listings of travel agencies, gay-friendly hotels, gay bars, and travel services aimed at gay travelers.

PUBLICATIONS • One of the best gay and lesbian travel newsletters is ***Out and About*** (tel. 800/929–2268), with listings of gay-friendly hotels and travel agencies plus health cautions for travelers with HIV. A 10-issue subscription costs $49; single issues are $5. **Ferrari Guides' INN Places** ($16 plus $4.50 shipping) thoroughly covers the United States and is the guide to get for up-to-date listings of gay agencies, hotels, and clubs. Call 602/863–2408 for subscription information. **The Women's Traveller** ($11.95) is a dense guide to bars, hotels, and agencies throughout the United States, Canada, and the Caribbean for lesbians. For either publication, write to Box 422458, San Francisco 94142, or call 415/255–0404 or 800/462–6654. Also look for Fodor's ***Gay Guide to Los Angeles and Southern California*** and ***Gay Guide to San Francisco and the Bay Area.***

GAY- AND LESBIAN-FRIENDLY TRAVEL AGENCIES • **Advance Damron** (1 Greenway Plaza, Suite 800, Houston, TX 77046, tel. 713/682–2002 or 800/695–0880, fax 713/888–1010). **Club Travel** (8739 Santa Monica Blvd., West Hollywood, CA 90069, tel. 310/358–2200 or 800/429–8747, fax 310/

358–2222). **Islanders/Kennedy Travel** (183 W. 10th St., New York, NY 10014, tel. 212/242–3222 or 800/988–1181, fax 212/929–8530). **Now Voyager** (4406 18th St., San Francisco, CA 94114, tel. 415/626–1169 or 800/255–6951, fax 415/626–8626). **Yellowbrick Road** (1500 W. Balmoral Ave., Chicago, IL 60640, tel. 773/561–1800 or 800/642–2488, fax 773/561–4497). **Skylink Women's Travel** (3577 Moorland Ave., Santa Rosa, CA 95407, tel. 707/585–8355 or 800/225–5759, fax 707/584–5637), serving lesbian travelers.

HIKING

California's beautiful scenery and temperate climate make for some of the nation's best hiking. The Sierras, the Cascades, Big Sur, the southern deserts, and the North Coast offer options (the most notable being the Pacific Crest Trail, which zigzags from Mexico to Canada along the length of California) for days or months of hiking. **Wilderness Press** (2440 Bancroft Way, Berkeley 94704, tel. 510/843–8080) publishes excellent guides on hiking in California, including the ***High Sierra Hiking Guide***, complete with topographical maps, for about $12. ***California Hiking*** (Foghorn Press, $19) gives the lowdown on trails.

Sierra Club headquarters (85 2nd St., San Francisco, 94105–3441, tel. 415/977–5653) has information about hiking trips.

INSURANCE

Citizens of the United Kingdom can buy an annual travel-insurance policy valid for most vacations during the year in which it's purchased. If you are pregnant or have a preexisting medical condition, make sure you're covered. According to the Association of British Insurers, a trade association representing 450 insurance companies, it's wise to **buy extra medical coverage when you visit the United States.**

TRAVEL INSURERS • In the U.S., **Access America** (6600 W. Broad St., Richmond, VA 23230, tel. 804/285–3300 or 800/284–8300), **Carefree Travel Insurance** (Box 9366, 100 Garden City Plaza, Garden City, NY 11530, tel. 516/294–0220 or 800/323–3149), **Travel Guard International** (1145 Clark St., Stevens Point, WI 54481, tel. 715/345–0505 or 800/826–1300), **Travel Insured International** (Box 280568, East Hartford, CT 06128–0568, tel. 860/528–7663 or 800/243–3174). In Canada, **Mutual of Omaha** (Travel Division, 500 University Ave., Toronto, Ontario M5G 1V8, tel. 416/598–4083, 800/268–8825 in Canada). In the U.K., **Association of British Insurers** (51 Gresham St., London EC2V 7HQ, tel. 0171/600–3333).

KAYAKING

See White-Water Rafting and Kayaking, *below.*

LODGING

Budget lodging may be ubiquitous or nonexistent, depending on where you are in California. Apart from a quiet beach or the back seat of your Plymouth, the cheapest options are hostels, which charge $10–$15 per person, and campgrounds (sometimes free in national forests, or $4–$35 per site). Hotels and motels usually start at $35 for a double. Bed-and-breakfasts are not the money savers they are in Europe and in fact usually cost more than nice motels.

Throughout the book, the lodging price categories refer to the cost of a double room excluding tax.

HOTELS & MOTELS

About $35–$60 will get you a double room with a private bath in an average hotel. Single travelers usually have to pay the double rate. Budget chains—including Motel 6 and Super 8—permeate the state and can be a reliable and relatively cheap option ($30 and up for a double), although they're usually nondescript. Hotels and motels are cheapest in the off-season and sometimes offer package deals. With the **Entertainment Card,** a promotion run through many credit-card companies, you can get a 50% discount on many moderate to expensive hotels across the country, including about 300 in California. The card costs $49 per year; call 800/548–1116 to enroll. Also look for AAA discounts (*see box* A Driver's Dream, *above*). Assume that hotels reviewed in the book take credit cards unless otherwise noted.

BED-AND-BREAKFASTS

Bed-and-breakfasts are usually out of the budget range, but if you want to splurge for a homey and more personal touch, spend your money here rather than at a large, swanky hotel. B&Bs start as low as $55 in some areas but usually average $80 and up for a double, with occasional discounts on longer stays. The room price includes breakfast, which can range from a Danish and coffee to a five-course feast. Rooms are often without telephones and televisions and sometimes have a shared bath. **Bed and Breakfast International** (Box 282910, San Francisco 94128–2910, tel. 415/696–1690) is a reservation service for more than 500 B&Bs in California and Nevada.

HOSTELS

If you want to scrimp on lodging, **look into hostels.** In some 5,000 locations in more than 70 countries around the world, Hostelling International (HI), the umbrella group for a number of national youth hostel associations, offers single-sex, dorm-style beds and, at many hostels, "couples" rooms and family accommodations.

Hostels affiliated with **American Youth Hostels (AYH),** the American branch of **Hostelling International (HI)** (733 15th St. NW, Suite 840, Washington, D.C. 20005, tel. 202/783–6161 or 800/444–6111), offer a certain welcome predictability, but private hostels are often cheaper and filled with a more eclectic crowd. Membership in any HI national hostel association, open to travelers of all ages, allows you to stay in HI-affiliated hostels at member rates. Members also have priority if the hostel is full; they're eligible for discounts around the world, even on rail and bus travel in some countries. A one-year membership is available to travelers of all ages and runs about $25 for adults (renewal $20) and $10 for those under 18. Family memberships are available for $35, and a lifetime membership will set you back $250.

AYH's facilities vary widely, from lighthouse cabins to small three- or four-bed in-home operations. There are strict rules: Alcohol, drugs, and smoking are forbidden, curfews are enforced, and each visitor is responsible for a simple chore. The maximum stay is three days unless an extension is granted. In high season it's a good idea to book ahead. Some hostels allow you to use your sleeping bag, although officially they require a sleep sack that can be rented for about $1 a night. All hostels have a kitchen, common room, and often useful listings of cheap things to do in the area. Most hostels institute a lockout from 9 AM to 5 PM, during which all guests must leave the premises. AYH publishes a U.S. handbook (free, $3 if you order by mail) that details the location and amenities of each hostel.

ORGANIZATIONS • Hostelling International—American Youth Hostels (HI–AYH; 733 15th St. NW, Suite 840, Washington, DC 20005, tel. 202/783–6161, fax 202/783–6171). **AYH-California** (308 Mason St., San Francisco 94102, tel. 415/788–2525; Los Angeles Council, 1434 2nd St., Santa Monica 90401, tel. 310/393–3413). **Hostelling International—Canada** (HI–C; 400-205 Catherine St., Ottawa, Ontario K2P 1C3, tel. 613/237–7884, fax 613/237–7868). **Youth Hostel Association of England and Wales** (YHA; Trevelyan House, 8 St. Stephen's Hill, St. Albans, Hertfordshire AL1 2DY, tel. 01727/855215 or 01727/845047, fax 01727/844126). **Australian Youth Hostels Association** (YHA; Level 3, 10 Mallett St., Camperdown, New South Wales 2050, tel. 02/565-1699). **Youth Hostels Association of New Zealand** (YHA; Box 436, Christchurch 1, tel. 3/379–9970).

Y's Way International (224 E. 47th St., New York, NY 10017, tel. 212/308–2899) is a network of YMCA and YWCA overnight centers offering low-cost accommodations—anything from dorms to makeshift high-school gymnasiums—at an average overnight rate of $26. Age limits and prices vary, so contact the YMCA in the area you'll be visiting. Some offer special rates for lengthy stays.

UNIVERSITY/STUDENT HOUSING

During summer, universities often rent out dorm rooms by the night or the week; however, it's usually under the pretense that you're there on some sort of school-related business. A good line in such a circumstance is to say you're thinking of attending school there. Generally, **universities are not a real bargain.** Dorms are dreary and costs are high: $30–$40 for a single or double. This book lists, in individual chapters, some universities that offer housing. If you're interested in one not listed, contact the university's housing office.

MONEY

ATMS

Virtually all U.S. banks belong to a network of card-slurping, cash-expectorating ATMs. Before leaving home, **make sure that your credit cards have been programmed for ATM use.**

ATM LOCATIONS • Cirrus (tel. 800/424–7787). **Plus** (tel. 800/843–7587).

COSTS

California is one of the country's most desirable places to live. Unfortunately this means that the state has one of the highest costs of living in the nation. After transportation (car rental, while convenient, is not cheap; long-distance bus travel, while less expensive, is neither cheap nor convenient), food and lodging will probably be the biggest expenses. If you buy food in markets and camp or stay in hostels, expect to spend $20–$30 per person daily; staying in hotels and eating in restaurants is difficult to swing in California without dropping upward of $45 each day. Luckily, cheap nighttime entertainment is easy to come by. Many of the more low-key bars have DJ dancing or even live music with no cover or a small charge of $2 or $3 at the door.

TRAVELER'S CHECKS

They look like play money, have the purchasing power of real money, and—best of all—can be replaced if lost or stolen. To be reimbursed, you *must* produce the purchase agreement and a record of the checks' serial numbers, so it's a good idea to keep those documents separate from your checks.

American Express card members can purchase traveler's checks through many banks (1% commission) or order them by phone (free for gold-card holders, 1% commission for green-card holders). AmEx also issues **Traveler's Cheques for Two,** which can be signed and used by either you or your companion. Lost or stolen checks are often refunded in as little as 24 hours. At their Travel Services offices (about 1,500 around the world) you can buy and cash traveler's checks, write a personal check in exchange for traveler's checks, report lost or stolen checks, exchange foreign currency, and pick up mail. *Tel. 800/221–7282 in the U.S. and Canada.*

The following brands (and occasional others) can be exchanged for cash at banks, select hotels, tourist offices, American Express offices, or currency-exchange offices, usually for a 1%–2% commission. **Citicorp** (tel. 800/645–6556 in the U.S. or 813/623–1709 collect outside the U.S.) traveler's checks are available from Citibank and other banks worldwide. For 45 days from date of check purchase, purchasers have access to the 24-hour International S.O.S. Assistance Hotline and an emergency message center. **MasterCard International** (tel. 800/223–7373 in the U.S. or 609/987–7300 collect from outside the U.S.) traveler's checks are offered through banks, credit unions, and foreign-exchange booths. **Visa** (tel. 800/227–6811 in the U.S. and Canada or 813/623–1709 collect from outside the U.S.) traveler's checks are available in U.S. dollars, British pounds, and various other currencies.

NATIONAL & STATE PARKS

National-park campgrounds are well kept but often crowded. National forests, which are "multiple-use land" areas, have less spectacular but also comparatively uncrowded campgrounds. State parks (usually historically or geologically significant and smaller than national parks) lie somewhere in between in terms of quality of the scenery and campground maintenance. Many campgrounds do not accept reservations, but those in popular spots will take bookings eight weeks in advance. Call **Destinet** 800/436–7275 for national parks, or for state parks call 800/444–7275, for national forests call 800/280–2267 for reservations. Avoid camping or reserve way ahead on Labor Day, Memorial Day, July 4, and any other three-day weekend.

For information on California's eight national parks (Lassen Volcanic, Redwood, Sequoia, Kings Canyon, Yosemite, Death Valley, Joshua Tree, and the Channel Islands) and various national monuments, call the **National Park Service** (Western Region Information Office, Fort Mason, Bldg. 201, San Francisco 94123, tel. 415/556–0560). To find out about national forests, contact the **U.S. Forest Service** (Pacific Southwest Region, 630 Sansome St., San Francisco 94111, tel. 415/705–2874). For information on state parks, such as Big Basin Redwoods near Santa Cruz or Anza Borrego Desert near San Diego, call the **California State Park System** (tel. 916/653–6995). These offices are open 9–5, although you'll probably get a recording during off-hours with some useful information.

National and state parks charge a $4–$7 entrance fee per car, even if you don't plan on camping. This gives you entry to the parks for seven days, and you can come or go as you please. If you're walking or biking in, the fee will be about $2–$3.

You may be able to **save money on park entrance fees** by getting a discount pass, available at park entrances. The Golden Eagle Pass ($25) gets you and your companions free admission to all parks for one year. (Camping and parking are extra). Similar passes for older travelers and travelers with disabilities are also available free by mail.

PASSES BY MAIL • National Park Service (Department of the Interior, Washington, DC 20240).

PACKING FOR CALIFORNIA

Pack as little as possible. Besides the usual suspects—clothes, toiletries, camera, a Walkman, and a good book—bring along a day pack or some type of smaller receptacle for stuff; it'll come in handy not only for day excursions but also for those places where you plan to stay for only one or two days. You can **check heavy, cumbersome bags at the train or bus station** (or leave it at your motel or hostel) and **just carry the essentials** while you are out and about.

Smart—and not terribly fashion-conscious—travelers will bring two outfits and learn to wash clothes by hand regularly. At the very least, **bring comfortable, easy-to-clean clothes.** Californians are, by and large, casual dressers. If you're traveling in summer, pack one pair of pants and a heavy sweatshirt for colder nights (especially in the mountains and along the coast). Pack a raincoat and/or umbrella for the inevitable. If you plan to spend most of your time outdoors, a fleece jacket and **a nylon shell to keep out the wind are indispensable.** Shoes can be your biggest friend or your worst foe: A sturdy pair of walking shoes or hiking boots plus a spare pair of shoes will allow you to switch off and give your barkin' dogs a rest. **Consider taking a pair of heavy-duty sport sandals**—you can bike, hike, or walk in water in them, and they'll protect your feet on communal shower floors.

If you don't have an AmEx gold card, you can still get American Express Traveler's Checks free with an AAA membership. Talk to the cashier at your local AAA office.

Other stuff you might not think to take but will be glad to have: a miniature flashlight, good in dark places; a pocket knife for cutting fruit, spreading cheese, and opening wine bottles; a water bottle; sunglasses; several large zip-type plastic bags, useful for wet swimsuits, leaky bottles, and rancid socks; a travel alarm clock; a needle and a small spool of thread; extra batteries; a good book; and a day pack.

LUGGAGE

In general you are entitled to check two bags on flights within the United States. A third piece may be brought on board, but it must fit easily under the seat in front of you or in the overhead compartment. If your bag is too porky, be prepared for the humiliation of rejection and a last-minute baggage check.

Airline liability for baggage is limited to $1,250 per person on flights within the United States. On international flights it amounts to $9.07 per pound or $20 per kilogram for checked baggage (roughly $640 per 70-pound bag) and $400 per passenger for unchecked baggage. Insurance for losses exceeding these amounts can be bought from the airline at check-in for about $10 per $1,000 of coverage; note that this coverage excludes a rather extensive list of items, which is shown on your airline ticket.

At check-in, **make sure that each bag is correctly tagged** with the destination airport's three-letter code. If your bags arrive damaged or not at all, file a written report with the airline before leaving the airport. If you're traveling with a pack, tie all loose straps to each other or onto the pack itself, so that they don't get caught in luggage conveyer belts.

PASSPORTS & VISAS

AUSTRALIAN CITIZENS

Australian citizens need a valid passport to enter the United States. If you are staying for fewer than 90 days on vacation and have a return or onward ticket, you probably will not need a visa. However, you will need to fill out the Visa Waiver Form, 1-94W, supplied by the airline.

INFORMATION • Passport Office, tel. 008/131–232

CANADIAN CITIZENS

A passport is not required to enter the United States.

NEW ZEALAND CITIZENS

New Zealand citizens need a valid passport to enter the United States. If you are staying for fewer than 90 days on vacation and have a return or onward ticket, you probably will not need a visa. However, you will need to fill out the Visa Waiver Form, 1-94W, supplied by the airline.

U.K. CITIZENS

British citizens need a valid passport to enter the United States. If you are staying for fewer than 90 days on vacation and have a return or onward ticket, you probably will not need a visa. However, you will need to fill out the Visa Waiver Form, 1-94W, supplied by the airline.

INFORMATION • London Passport Office (tel. 0990/21010) for fees and documentation requirements and to request an emergency passport. **U.S. Embassy Visa Information Line** (tel. 01891/200–290) for U.S. visa information; calls cost 49p per minute or 39p per minute cheap rate. **U.S. Embassy Visa Branch** (5 Upper Grosvenor St., London W1A 2JB) for U.S. visa information; send a self-addressed, stamped envelope. Write the **U.S. Consulate General** (Queen's House, Queen St., Belfast BTI 6EO) if you live in Northern Ireland.

ROCK CLIMBING

Lately, more and more folks have been daring to grapple their way up, and rappel down, cliff sides. Favorite spots include Yosemite National Park in the Sierra Nevada, Joshua Tree National Park, Stoney Point in Los Angeles's San Fernando Valley, and Pinnacles National Monument in the Salinas Valley, although climbs of all levels can be found throughout the state. For equipment, advice, and names of climbing schools contact **REI** (*see* Camping, *above*).

SAFETY

Money belts may be dorky and bulky, but it's better to be embarrassed than broke. You'd be wise to carry all cash, traveler's checks, credit cards, and your passport there or in some other inaccessible place: front or inner pocket or a bag that fits underneath your clothes. Waist packs are safe if you keep the pack part in front of your body. Keep your bag attached to you if you plan on napping on the train. And **never leave your belongings unguarded,** even if you're only planning to be gone for a minute.

SKIING & SNOWBOARDING

California offers some of the finest nordic and alpine skiing in the country. Head to Lake Tahoe (*see* Chapter 6), Mammoth Lakes (*see* Chapter 7), Mt. Shasta (*see* Chapter 5), or Big Bear Lake (*see* Chapter 10) for the best trails. Downhill skiing, however, is pricey: Lift tickets cost around $35–$45, and equipment rental is about $20–$25. **Try going midweek,** when resorts and lodges offer lower prices and special deals. Most resorts in California allow snowboards, and you can rent the boots and gear for about the same price as skiing equipment. For details check the ***Skier's Guide to California*** (Gulf Publishing Co.; $16), by Nadine Nardi Davidson.

STUDENTS

The big names in the field are **STA Travel,** with some 100 offices worldwide and a useful website (http://www.sta-travel.com), and the **Council on International Educational Exchange** (CIEE or "Council" for short), a private, nonprofit organization that adminsters work, volunteer, academic, and professional programs worldwide and sells travel arrangements through its own specialist travel agency, Council Travel. **Travel CUTS,** strictly a travel agency, sells discounted airline tickets to Canadian students from offices on or near college campuses. The **Educational Travel Center** (ETC) books low-cost flights to destinations within the continental United States and around the world. And **Student Flights, Inc.,** specializes in student and faculty airfares.

Most of these organizations also issue student identity cards, which entitle their bearers to special fares on local transportation and discounts at museums, theaters, sports events, and other attractions, as well as a handful of other benefits, which are listed in the handbook that most provide to their cardholders. Major cards include the **International Student Identity Card** (ISIC) and **Go 25: International Youth Travel Card** (GO25), available to non-students as well as students age 25 and under; the ISIC, when purchased in the United States, comes with $3,000 in emergency medical coverage and a few related benefits. Both the ISIC and GO25 are issued by Council Travel or STA in the United States, Travel CUTS in Canada, and at student unions and student-travel companies in the United Kingdom. The International Student Exchange Card (ISE), issued by Student Flights, Inc., is available to faculty members as well as students, and the International Teacher Identity Card (ITIC), issued by Travel CUTS, provides similar benefits to teachers in all grade levels, from kindergarten through graduate school. All student ID cards cost between $10 and $20.

STUDENT IDS & SERVICES • Council on International Educational Exchange (CIEE, 205 E. 42nd St., 14th floor, New York, NY 10017, tel. 212/822–2600 or 888/268–6245, fax 212/822–2699), for mail orders only, in the United States. **Council Travel in the United States:** Arizona (Tempe, tel. 602/966–3544). California (Berkeley, tel. 510/848–8604; Davis, tel. 916/752–2285; La Jolla, tel. 619/452–0630; Long Beach, tel. 310/598–3338; Los Angeles, tel. 310/208–3551; Palo Alto, tel. 415/325–3888; San Diego, tel. 619/270–6401; San Francisco, tel. 415/421–3473 or 415/566–6222; Santa Barbara, tel. 805/562–8080). Colorado (Boulder, tel. 303/447–8101; Denver, tel. 303/571–0630). Connecticut (New Haven, tel. 203/562–5335). Florida (Miami, tel. 305/670–9261). Georgia (Atlanta, tel. 404/377–9997). Illinois (Chicago, tel. 312/951–0585; Evanston, tel. 847/475–5070). Indiana (Bloomington, tel. 812/330–1600). Iowa (Ames, tel. 515/296–2326). Kansas (Lawrence, tel. 913/749–3900). Louisiana (New Orleans, tel. 504/866–1767). Maryland (College Park, tel. 301/779–1172). Massachusetts (Amherst, tel. 413/256–1261; Boston, tel. 617/266–1926; Cambridge, tel. 617/497–1497 or 617/225–2555). Michigan (Ann Arbor, tel. 313/998–0200). Minnesota (Minneapolis, tel. 612/379–2323). New York (New York, tel. 212/822–2700, 212/666–4177, or 212/254–2525). North Carolina (Chapel Hill, tel. 919/942–2334). Ohio (Columbus, tel. 614/294–8696). Oregon (Portland, tel. 503/228–1900). Pennsylvania (Philadelphia, tel. 215/382–0343; Pittsburgh, tel. 412/683–1881). Rhode Island (Providence, tel. 401/331–5810). Tennessee (Knoxville, tel. 423/523–9900). Texas (Austin, tel. 512/472–4931; Dallas, tel. 214/363–9941). Utah (Salt Lake City, tel. 801/582–5840). Washington (Seattle, tel. 206/632–2448 or 206/329–4567). Washington, D.C.(tel. 202/337–6464). **Council Travel elsewhere:** France (Paris, 22 rue des Pyramides, 1er, tel. 01-46-55-55-65; Nice, 37 bis rue d'Angleterre, tel. 04–93–82–23–33). **Educational Travel Center:** 438 N. Frances St., Madison, WI 53703, tel. 608/256–5551 or 800/747–5551. **STA in the U.S.:** California (Berkeley, tel. 510/642–3000; Los Angeles, tel. 213/934–8722; San Francisco, tel. 415/391–8407; Santa Monica, tel. 310/394–5126; Westwood, tel. 310/824–1574). Florida (Miami, tel. 305/461–3444; University of Florida, tel. 352/338–0068). Illinois (Chicago, tel. 312/786–9050). Massachusetts (Boston, tel. 617/266–6014; Cambridge, tel. 617/576–4623). New York (Columbia University, tel. 212/865–2700; West Village, tel. 212/627–3111). Pennsylvania (Philadelphia, tel. 215/382–2928). Washington (Seattle, tel. 206/633–5000). Washington, D.C. (tel. 202/887–0912). **STA elsewhere:** Argentina (Buenos Aires, tel. 01/315–1457). Australia (Adelaide, tel. 08/223–2434; Brisbane tel. 73/229–2499; Cairns, tel. 70/31–41-99; Canberra, tel. 06/247–8633; Darwin, tel. 89/41–29–55; Melbourne, tel. 39/349–2411; Perth, tel. 09/227–7569; Sydney, tel. 29/368–1111 or 29/212–1255). Belgium (Brussels, tel. 02/524–0178). Brazil (Rio de Janeiro, tel. 21/259–0023; Sao Paulo, tel. 11/816–1500). Canada (Calgary, tel. 403/282–7687; Edmonton, tel. 403/492–2592; Montreal, tel. 514/284–1368; Toronto, tel. 416/977–5228; Vancouver, tel. 604/681–9136). Chile (Santiago, tel. 02/334–5167). Colombia (Bogota, tel. 01/214–4308). Czech Republic (Prague, tel. 02/26–64–66). Denmark (Holstebro, tel. 97/42–67–33; Copenhagen, tel. 33/55–75–33). Fiji (Fiji, tel. 679/72–27–55). France (Nice, tel. 04/93–13–10–70; Paris, tel. 01/43–43–46–10). Germany (Berlin, tel. 30/285–9826 or 30/311–0950; Cologne, tel. 22/144–2011; Frankfurt, tel. 69/70–30–35 or 69/43–01–91; Hamburg, tel. 40/450–3840; Heidelberg, tel. 62/212–3528). Greece (Athens, tel. 01/322–1267). Holland (Amsterdam, tel. 20/624–0989 or 20/626–2557). Hong Kong (Kowloon, tel. 2730–9407). Hungary (Budapest, tel. 01/111–9898). India (Bombay, tel. 22/218–1431; New Delhi, tel. 11/332–5559). Indonesia (Bali, tel. 361/75–11–40; Jakarta Pusat, tel. 21/230–0336). Israel (Haifa, tel. 04/67–02–22; Jerusalem, tel. 02/25–24–71; Tel Aviv, tel. 03/524–6322). **Student Flights** (5010 E. Shea Blvd., Suite A104, Scottsdale, AZ 85254, tel. 602/951–1177 or 800/255–8000). **Travel Cuts** (187 College St., Toronto, Ontario M5T 1P7, tel. 416/979–2406 or 800/667–2887) in Canada.

SURFING & WINDSURFING

One of California's biggest con jobs has been the image of blond babes and dudes surfing and swimming in warm Pacific waters. The truth is that the water around some of California's most popular surfing towns (Santa Cruz, for example) is cold enough to make you change your mind after sticking one toe in. Heavy surfing abounds in the Bay Area, Santa Cruz, and, of course, Southern California (from Santa Barbara into Baja California), but you can find great spots in the Lost Coast region and even farther up the north coast (bring your wet suit). For tips on starting, try Doug Werner's ***Surfer's Start-Up*** (Pathfinder Publishing; $10). Serious windsurfers will want to make a pilgrimage to the Bay Area, which has some of the finest conditions (and competitions) in the country.

TELEPHONES

For local directory assistance, dial 411. For long-distance help, dial the area code plus 555–1212. Local directory-assistance calls are free from any pay phone. If you don't know the area code or need help with local calls, dial the operator (0); for long-distance or international calls, dial 00. To find out if a particular business has an 800 number, call 800/555–1212.

AREA CODES

Several new area codes have recently been introduced in California, and more changes are planned in the near future. Within this book we have listed the area codes that were scheduled to be in use by early 1998. Following are some recent or coming area-code changes.

NORTHERN & CENTRAL CALIFORNIA • The area south of San Francisco now uses 650 instead of 415. Most of northeastern California except Sacramento and some nearby towns and counties has switched from 916 to 530. In 1997 most of San Gabriel began using 626 instead of 818.

In March 1998, parts of Alameda and Contra Costa counties and small portions of Solano and San Joaquin counties will begin to use 925 instead of 510.

During summer 1998, towns along the Central Coast will switch to 831 from 408.

SOUTHERN CALIFORNIA • In summer 1998, the areas surrounding downtown Los Angeles will begin to use 323 instead of 213. The new code 562 serves the southeastern part of L.A. County and a small piece of Orange County. In mid-1998, L.A. will phase in a new area code for L.A. proper: except for downtown, which will stay 213, the rest of the city previously served by 213 will have the new code 323.

The southern portion of Orange County will begin using 949 rather than 714 in April 1998.

The 209 area code for the Central Valley, Yosemite National Park, and surrounding regions was scheduled to split in late 1998; at press time the new code and exactly which areas would use it had not been determined.

CALLING LONG DISTANCE

AT&T, MCI, and Sprint long-distance services make calling home relatively convenient and let you avoid hotel surcharges. In the United States, you typically you dial an 800 number.

TO OBTAIN ACCESS CODES • AT&T USADirect (tel. 800/874–4000). **MCI** Call USA (tel. 800/444–4444). **Sprint** Express (tel. 800/793–1153).

TOUR OPERATORS

Buying a vacation package can make your trip to California less expensive. The tour operators who put them together may handle several hundred thousand travelers per year and can use their purchasing power to give you a good price. Their high volume may also indicate financial stability. But some small companies provide more personalized service; because they tend to specialize, they may also be more knowledgeable about a given area.

A GOOD DEAL?

The more your package includes, the better you can predict the ultimate cost of your vacation. Make sure you know exactly what is covered, and **beware of hidden costs.** Are taxes, tips, and service charges included? Transfers and baggage handling? Entertainment and excursions? These add up.

If the package you are considering is priced lower than in your wildest dreams, **be skeptical.** Ask about the hotel's location, room size, beds, and whether it has a pool, room service, or programs for children, if you care.

BUYER BEWARE

Each year consumers are stranded or lose their money when tour operators—even large ones with excellent reputations—go out of business. So **check out the operator.** Find out how long the company has been in business, and ask for references that you can check. And **don't book unless the firm has a consumer-protection program.**

Members of the National Tour Association and United States Tour Operators Association are required to set aside funds to cover your payments and travel arrangements in case the company defaults. Nonmembers may carry insurance instead. Look for the details, and for the name of an underwriter with a solid reputation, in the operator's brochure. And when it comes to tour operators, **don't trust escrow accounts.** Although there are laws governing charter-flight operators, no governmental body prevents tour operators from raiding the till. For more information, *see* Consumer Protection, *above.*

TOUR-OPERATOR RECOMMENDATIONS • National Tour Association (NTA, 546 E. Main St., Lexington, KY 40508, tel. 606/226–4444 or 800/755–8687). **United States Tour Operators Association** (USTOA, 342 Madison Ave., Suite 1522, New York, NY 10173, tel. 212/599–6599, fax 212/599–6744).

USING AN AGENT

A good travel agent is an excellent resource. When shopping for one, **collect brochures from several sources** and remember that some agents' suggestions may be skewed by promotional relationships with tour and package firms that reward them for volume sales. If you have a special interest, **find an agent with expertise in that area** (*see* Travel Agents, *below*).

SINGLE TRAVELERS

Remember that prices for vacation packages are usually quoted per person, based on two sharing a room. If traveling solo, you may be required to pay the full double-occupancy rate.

PACKAGES

The companies listed below offer vacation packages in a broad price range.

AIR/HOTEL • American Airlines Fly AAway Vacations (tel. 800/321–2121). **Continental Vacations** (tel. 800/634–5555). **Delta Dream Vacations** (tel. 800/872–7786, fax 954/357–4687). **United Vacations** (tel. 800/328–6877). **US Airways Vacations** (tel. 800/455–0123).

CUSTOM PACKAGES • Amtrak's Great American Vacations (tel. 800/321–8684).

FLY/DRIVE • American Airlines Fly AAway Vacations (*see* Air/Hotel, *above*). **Continental Vacations** (*see* Air/Hotel, *above*). **United Vacations** (*see* Air/Hotel, *above*).

HOTEL ONLY • SuperCities (139 Main St., Cambridge, MA 02142, tel. 800/333–1234).

FROM THE U.K. • British Airways Holidays (Astral Towers, Betts Way, London Rd., Crawley, West Sussex RH10 2XA, tel. 01293/723–121). **Jetsave** (Sussex House, London Rd., East Grinstead, West Sussex RH19 1LD, tel. 01342/312–033). **Key to America** (1–3 Station Rd., Ashford, Middlesex TW15 2UW, tel. 01784/248–777). **Kuoni Travel Ltd.** (Kuoni House, Dorking, Surrey RH5 4AZ, tel. 01306/742–222). **Premier Holidays** (Premier Travel Center, Westbrook, Milton Rd., Cambridge CB4 1YG, tel. 01223/516–688).

THEME TRIPS

ADVENTURE • Access to Adventure (Box 92520 Hwy 96, Somes Bar, CA 95568, tel. 530/469–3322 or 800/552–6284, fax 530/469–3357). **American Wilderness Experience** (2820-A Wilderness Pl., Boulder, CO 80301-5454, tel. 303/444–2622 or 800/444–0099, fax 303/444–3999). **Tahoe Trips & Trails** (Box 6952, Tahoe City, CA 96145, tel. 530/583–4506 or 800/581–4453, fax 530/583–1861). **Trek America** (Box 189, Rockaway, NJ 07866, tel. 201/983–1144 or 800/221–0596, fax 201/983–8551).

ARCHAEOLOGY • Crow Canyon Archaeological Center (23390 Country Rd. K, Cortez, CO 81321, tel. 970/565–8975 or 800/422–8975, fax 970/565–4859).

BALLOONING • Above the West Hot Air Ballooning (Box 2290, Yountville, CA 94599, tel. 707/944–8638 or 800/627–2759). **Bonaventura Balloon Company** (133 Wall Rd., Napa, CA 94558, tel. 707/944–2822 or 800/359–6272, fax 707/944–2220).

BICYCLING • Backroads (801 Cedar St., Berkeley, CA 94710-1800, tel. 510/527–1555 or 800/462–2848, fax 510/527–1444. **Bicycle Adventures** (Box 11219, Olympia, WA 98508, tel. 360/786–0989 or 800/443–6060, fax 360/786–9661). **Cycle America** (Box 485, Cannon Falls, MN 55009, tel. 507/263–2665 or 800/245–3263). **Imagine Tours** (Box 475, Davis, CA 95617, tel. 530/758–8782). **Timberline** (7975 E. Harvard, #J, Denver, CO 80231, tel. 303/759–3804 or 800/417–2453, fax 303/368–1651).

CROSS-COUNTRY SKIING • Backroads (*see* Bicycling, *above*).

ECOTOURISM • Coastwalk (1389 Cooper Rd., Sebastopol 95472, tel. 707/829–6689). **Earthwatch** (680 Mount Auburn, Box 9104, Watertown, MA 02272, tel. 800/776–0188). **Outward Bound** (0110 S. West Bancroft, Portland, OR, tel. 800/547–3312). **Desert Survivors** (Box 20991, Oakland, CA 94620-0991, tel. 510/769–1706).

FISHING • Anglers Travel (3100 Mill St., #206, Reno, NV 89502, tel./fax 702/853–9132). **Fishing International** (Box 2132, Santa Rosa, CA 95405, tel. 707/539–3366 or 800/950–4242, fax 707/539–1320). **Rod and Reel Adventures** (3507 Tully Rd., #B6, Modesto, CA 95356-1052, tel. 209/524–7775 or 800/356–6982, fax 209/524–1220).

FOOD & WINE • *See* Chapter 5.

GOLF • Stine's Golftrips (Box 2314, Winter Haven, FL 33883-2314, tel. 813/324–1300 or 800/428–1940, fax 941/325–0384).

HORSEBACK RIDING • American Wilderness Experience (*see* Adventure, *above*). **Equitour FITS Equestrian** (Box 807, Dubois, WY 82513, tel. 307/455–3363 or 800/545–0019, fax 307/455–2354).

LEARNING • Earthwatch (*see* Ecotourism, *above*) for research expeditions. **National Audubon Society** (700 Broadway, New York, NY 10003, tel. 212/979–3066, fax 212/353–0190). **Oceanic Society Expeditions** (Fort Mason Center, Bldg. E, San Francisco, CA 94123-1394, tel. 415/441–1106 or 800/326–7491, fax 415/474–3395). **Smithsonian Study Tours and Seminars** (1100 Jefferson Dr. SW, Room 3045, MRC 702, Washington, DC 20560, tel. 202/357–4700, fax 202/633–9250).

MUSIC • Dailey-Thorp Travel (330 W. 58th St., #610, New York, NY 10019-1817, tel. 212/307–1555 or 800/998–4677, fax 212/974–1420).

RIVER RAFTING • Access to Adventure (*see* Adventure, *above*). **Action Whitewater Adventures** (Box 1634, Provo UT 84603, tel. 800/453–1482, fax 801/375–4175). **OARS** (Box 67, Angels Camp, CA 95222, tel. 209/736–4677 or 800/346–6277, fax 209/736–2902). **Whitewater Voyages** (5225 San Pablo Dam Rd., El Sobrante, CA 94803, tel. 510/222–5994 or 800/488–7238, fax 510/758–7238).

SAILING • Five Star Charters (85 Liberty Ship Way, Ste. 112, Sausalito, CA 94965, tel. 415/332–7187 or 800/762–6287, fax 415/332–6811).

SPAS • Spa-Finders (91 Fifth Ave., #301, New York, NY 10003-3039, tel. 212/924–6800 or 800/255–7727).

SPORTS • Championship Tennis Tours (7350 E. Stetson Dr., #106, Scottsdale, AZ 85251, tel. 602/990–8760 or 800/468–3664, fax 602/990–8744). **Dan Chavez's Sports Empire** (Box 6169, Lakewood, CA 90714-6169, tel. 310/920–2350 or 800/255–5258). **Spectacular Sport Specials** (5813 Citrus Blvd., New Orleans, LA 70123-5810, tel. 504/734–9511 or 800/451–5772, fax 504/734–7075).

TRAIL RUNNING • Backroads (*see* Bicycling, *above*).

WALKING/HIKING • American Wilderness Experience (*see* Adventure, *above*). **Backroads** (*see* Bicycling, *above*).

WHALE-WATCHING • Pacific Sea Fari Tours (2803 Emerson St., San Diego, CA 92106, tel. 619/226–8224, fax 619/222–0784).

YACHT CHARTERS • Ocean Voyages (1709 Bridgeway, Sausalito, CA 94965, tel. 415/332–4681, fax 415/332–7460).

TRAIN TRAVEL

Amtrak (tel. 800/USA–RAIL) has two main routes in the state. The *Coast Starlight* runs north–south from Los Angeles to Seattle, stopping at cities in between and offering bus connections to outlying towns. Although the name implies that tracks skim the coastline, the *Starlight* does so only south of San Luis Obispo and skips the spectacular scenery of Big Sur. The other route is the *San Joaquin* line, a bus-train combination running north–south between Bakersfield and Emeryville, with stops at cities in the San Joaquin Valley. Round-trip fare on the *San Joaquin* is $69; the trip takes around 6 hours from end to end. Fare on the *Starlight* from S.F. to L.A. runs $72–$142 round-trip, depending upon availability, and takes about 12 hours each way. Reservations are not required, but the *Coast Starlight* tends to fill up, so book ahead. Trains have dining cars on board, but it's cheaper to bring your own food.

DISCOUNT PASSES

The **All-Aboard Pass** is good for people who plan their itinerary in advance. The pass, which is actually a booklet of tickets, allows Amtrak riders special fares for three stops made in 45 days of travel within a region. For travel in or through California, request the All-Aboard Pass for the western United States (about $199, $179 off-season), and choose your own route. Ticket agents need to know your dates of travel and intended destinations for ticketing, so call in advance. Amtrak also provides free but limited shuttle services for pass-holders whose routes don't connect. **USA RailPass** works to the advantage of the foreign budget traveler (it's not available to U.S. or Canadian citizens) because it requires no formal itinerary, works on any of Amtrak's U.S. routes, and allows for spontaneous planning (within a specified time period). Fifteen-day passes start at $200, $340 peak-season; 30-day passes $225, $425 peak-season. Buy them at an international travel agency before entering the United States. In the United States, purchase the pass at any Amtrak station (international passport required for purchase).

TRAVEL AGENCIES

A good travel agent puts your needs first. **Look for an agency that specializes in your destination, has been in business at least five years, and emphasizes customer service.** If you're looking for an agency-organized package, choose an agency that's a member of the National Tour Association or the United States Tour Operator's Association (*see* Payments *and* Tour Operators, *above*).

LOCAL AGENT REFERRALS • American Society of Travel Agents (ASTA, 1101 King St., Suite 200, Alexandria, VA 22314, tel. 703/739–2782, fax 703/684–8319). **Alliance of Canadian Travel Associations** (Suite 201, 1729 Bank St., Ottawa, Ontario K1V 7Z5, tel. 613/521–0474, fax 613/521–0805). **Association of British Travel Agents** (55–57 Newman St., London W1P 4AH, tel. 0171/637–2444, fax 0171/637–0713).

TRAVEL GEAR

Travel catalogs specialize in nifty items that can save space when packing.

MAIL-ORDER CATALOGS • Magellan's (tel. 800/962–4943, fax 805/568–5406). **Orvis Travel** (tel. 800/541–3541, fax 540/343–7053). **TravelSmith** (tel. 800/950–1600, fax 800/950–1656).

U.S. GOVERNMENT

The U.S. government can be an excellent source of inexpensive travel information. When planning your trip, **find out what government materials are available.**

ADVISORIES • U.S. Department of State American Citizens Services Office (Room 4811, Washington, DC 20520); enclose a self-addressed, stamped envelope. Interactive hot line (tel. 202/647–5225, fax 202/647–3000). Computer bulletin board (tel. 202/647–9225).

PAMPHLETS • Consumer Information Center (Consumer Information Catalogue, Pueblo, CO 81009, tel. 719/948–3334) for a free catalog that includes travel titles.

VISITOR INFORMATION

For general information about California, contact the state tourism office; to contact visitors bureaus and chambers of commerce for regional and local information, see individual chapters. Aside from offering the usual glossy tourist brochures, state and local tourist offices can answer general questions about travel and refer you to other organizations for even more information. When writing, ask for brochures on specialized activities, such as boating, horseback riding, or biking—they may not be included in a generic information package.

STATEWIDE INFORMATION • California Division of Tourism (801 K St., Suite 103, Sacramento, CA 95814, tel. 916/322–2881 or 800/862–2543, fax 916/322–3402).

IN THE U.K. • California Tourist Office (ABC California, Box 35, Abingdon, Oxfordshire OX14 4TB, tel. 0891/200–278, fax 0171/242–2838). Calls cost 50p per minute peak rate or 45p per minute cheap rate. Brochures can be obtained by sending to the above address a cheque for £3 made to ABC California.

THE HIGHS AND THE LOWS

Average daily temps (in degrees Fahrenheit and Celsius) stack up as follows:

LOS ANGELES

Jan.	64F	18C	*May*	72F	22C	*Sept.*	81F	27C
	44	7		53	12		60	16
Feb.	64F	18C	*June*	76F	24C	*Oct.*	76F	24C
	46	8		57	14		55	13
Mar.	66F	19C	*July*	81F	27C	*Nov.*	71F	22C
	48	9		60	16		48	9
Apr.	70F	21C	*Aug.*	82F	28C	*Dec.*	66F	19C
	51	11		62	17		46	8

SAN DIEGO

Jan.	62F	17C	*May*	66F	19C	*Sept.*	73F	23C
	46	8		55	13		62	17
Feb.	62F	17C	*June*	69F	21C	*Oct.*	71F	22C
	48	9		59	15		57	14
Mar.	64F	18C	*July*	73F	23C	*Nov.*	69F	21C
	50	10		62	17		51	11
Apr.	66F	19C	*Aug.*	73F	23C	*Dec.*	64F	18C
	53	12		64	18		48	9

SAN FRANCISCO

Jan.	55F	13C	*May*	66F	19C	*Sept.*	73F	23C
	41	5		48	9		51	11
Feb.	59F	15C	*June*	69F	21C	*Oct.*	69F	21C
	42	6		51	11		50	10
Mar.	60F	16C	*July*	69F	21C	*Nov.*	64F	18C
	44	7		51	11		44	7
Apr.	62F	17C	*Aug.*	69F	21C	*Dec.*	57F	14C
	46	8		53	12		42	6

VOLUNTEERING

A variety of volunteer programs are available. **Council** (*see* Students, *above*) is a key player, running its own roster of projects and publishing a directory that lists other sponsor organizations, *Volunteer! The Comprehensive Guide to Voluntary Service in the U.S. and Abroad* ($12.95 plus $1.50 postage). Service Civil International (SCI), International Voluntary Service (IVS), and Volunteers for Peace (VFP) run two- and three-week short workcamps; VFP also publishes the *International Workcamp Directory* ($12).

WHEN TO GO

If *Baywatch* taught you everything you know about California's climate, you're probably going to be disappointed. Summer temperatures in Southern California do hover pleasantly in the 80s, and the inland areas have their share of 100° days; but the northern coasts only rarely see temperatures higher than 70°, and winter temperatures all over the state can dip below 50°. The litmus test to determine seasons: If it's raining, it's probably winter. Summers are very dry and hot in many parts of the state, but the scenic coastal towns are often shrouded with chilly fog in these months (native San Franciscans feel sorry for cable cars full of shivering, goose bumpy tourists wearing shorts—not a pretty sight!). **The optimum times to travel along the coast are mid- to late spring and early to mid-fall**—when fog gives way to sun, tourist hordes abate, and prices plummet.

FORECASTS • Weather Channel Connection (tel. 900/932–8437), 95¢ per minute from a Touch-Tone phone.

FESTIVALS

Californians celebrate anything, anytime, anyplace, so don't be surprised by eccentric, whimsical festivals like the North Coast's February **World Championship Crab Race** (Crescent City, tel. 707/464–3174 or 800/343–8300). Only the major events are highlighted below; look in individual chapters of this book for smaller festivals. Call the California Division of Tourism (tel. 800/862–2543) for a free copy of the Events Calendar and check out *The Festival Hopper's Guide to California and Nevada* (Creative Chaos, $13), by Darrin and Julie Craig, which lists more than 450 affairs.

JANUARY 1 • The **Tournament of Roses Parade** attracts thousands; people sleep overnight on the streets of Pasadena (near Los Angeles) in order to claim a prime slab of concrete from which to view the parade. Their efforts hardly seem heroic compared to those of the glue-gun wielders who affix more than 25 million flowers to the mammoth floats. For more information, contact Pasadena's Tournament of Roses Headquarters (391 S. Orange Grove Blvd., Pasadena 91184, tel. 818/449–4100 or their 24–hr recorded information hot line: 818/449–ROSE).

JANUARY–APRIL • January marks the start of the **whale-watching** season, which takes place all along the coast, as gray whales migrate from Arctic feeding grounds in order to mate and calve off the coast of Baja California. The best spot to watch from land is the Point Reyes National Seashore (tel. 415/663–1092) north of San Francisco. The view from a boat, however, is even better. The California Division of Tourism (*see below*) offers a list of tour operators from Fort Bragg to San Diego.

FEBRUARY • Chinese New Year celebrations in San Francisco's Chinatown are tied to the lunar year and can begin any time from late January to March, culminating with a big parade. In 1998 the Year of the Tiger (4696) marks its official "New Years Day" as January 28th. You can send a SASE to the Chinese Chamber of Commerce (730 Sacramento St., San Francisco 94108, tel. 415/982–3000) anytime after late December for a calendar of events. L.A. celebrates February 14; contact L.A.'s Chinese Chamber of Commerce (977 N. Broadway, room E, Los Angeles 90012, tel. 213/617–0396) for more information.

MARCH • Don't forget Hollywood's prom night, the **Academy Awards** ceremony, held in downtown Los Angeles (usually the last Monday of March). You can't get in without an invite, but you can freely gawk at the movie stars from bleachers set up outside. Contact the Academy (tel. 310/247–3000, information not available until the end of February).

MARCH–JULY • Catch the **Grunion Run** if you're in Southern California. The nighttime fish-breeding orgy allows voyeurs to observe wiggling, ecstatic grunions, the only fish species that comes ashore to mate. Not all Southern California beaches turn on the grunions, so check with state beaches or the Cabrillo Marine Aquarium (tel. 310/548–7562) in San Pedro, which sponsors grunion-peeping programs.

APRIL–JUNE • The **Renaissance Pleasure Faire** (tel. 800/52–FAIRE) is a gathering of fun-loving Elizabethan wanna-be's (some are suspiciously similar in appearance to modern day Deadheads), who re-create 16th century England in San Bernardino county (sometime in late April–mid June) and up north in the Bay Area (sometime in late Aug.–early October). Entrance fees to these events are not for the faint of heart.

MAY • California's huge Latino and Chicano communities celebrate **Cinco de Mayo** (May 5), commemorating Mexico's victory over the French at Puebla in 1862. The most impressive celebrations take place in San Francisco, Los Angeles, San Diego, and San Jose.

The third Sunday in May (May 17 in 1998), San Francisco's **Bay to Breakers** (the largest footrace in the USA) features thousands of serious athletes as well as wacky goofballs who show up in running shorts, G-strings, or crazily inventive individual and team costumes to run from, you guessed it, the bay side of the city to the ocean (about 7.5 mi). Get information from the *San Francisco Examiner* Promotion Department (Box 429200, San Francisco 94142, tel. 415/777–7771).

JUNE • Santa Barbara's **Summer Solstice Celebration** (tel. 805/965–3396) gives new meaning to the word *counterculture*. The festivities, held each year on the Saturday closest to June 21, feature a parade starting at high noon with no motorized vehicles whatsoever. Members of the human train dress every which way (including loose) and act strange.

The **San Francisco Lesbian, Gay, Bisexual, Transgender Pride Celebration** (Pride for short) in San Francisco and the **Los Angeles Gay and Lesbian Pride Parade** in West Hollywood are the largest events during what has been adopted as Gay Pride month in commemoration of the June 1969 Stonewall riots in NYC. Both are rollicking bashes with costumes and floats. San Francisco's fest is held a weekend in the last half of the month: contact the Gay Freedom Day Parade Committee (1390 Market St., Suite 1225, San Francisco 94102, tel. 415/864–3733). Christopher Street West (7985 Santa Monica Blvd., Suite 109–24, West Hollywood 90046–5112, tel. 213/860–0701) plans the LA parade, which is held near the end of June, usually not conflicting with S.F.'s date.

JULY • The **Gilroy Garlic Festival** (Box 2311, Gilroy 95021, tel. 408/842–1625), July 24–26 in 1998, is a huge, aromatic celebration of one of the tastiest plants around. The festival runs all day and offers a rare chance to try, among other taste treats, garlic ice cream.

JULY–AUGUST • During the **International Surf Festival,** amateurs shred on raspy waves along Los Angeles's South Bay beaches, along with the fun runs, swims and lifeguard contests. The festival is usually the first week in August. Contact the L.A. County Department of Beaches and Harbors (tel. 310/305–9546) for information.

SEPTEMBER • Held at the end of the month, the **Valley of the Moon Vintage Festival** is the state's oldest celebration of wine-making. Drink, stomp grapes, and be merry. Contact the Vintage Festival Association (Box 652, Sonoma 95476, tel. 707/996–2109).

OCTOBER • To prepare for Halloween, Half Moon Bay sponsors the **Art and Festival** (tel. 650/726–9652) the third weekend of October, with crafts and the Great Pumpkin Parade.

OCTOBER 31 • The fabulous San Francisco **Halloween** costume party benefits the community groups who put it on: Community United Against Violence, The National Task Force on AIDS, and the Asian AIDS Project. Dress yourself to the nines and join the 100,000 revelers who have done similarly. The event usually runs from 5 PM to 1 AM in the downtown Civic Center, celebrating what has been called the "lesbian, gay, bisexual, and transgender community's high holiday." There's a nominal entry fee. For information call CUAV at 415/777–5500.

NOVEMBER • Pasadena's **Doo Dah Parade** (539 E. Villa #27, Pasadena 91101, tel. 818/449–3689) was conceived as an alternative to the Rose Parade in 1976. Usually held the Sunday before Thanksgiving in the Old Town section of Pasadena, the Doo Dah has grown to alarmingly oddball proportions, a veritable moving art piece of people that includes satirical political humor and community groups.

DECEMBER • Many coastal cities have **Christmas Boat Parades,** with tugboats, yachts, and military ships festively lit to usher in the holiday. Newport Beach's scenic nautical parade runs Dec. 17–23 every year in the harbor. A million people each year come to gawk at the proceedings. Contact the Newport Chamber of Commerce (1470 Jamboree Rd., Newport Beach 92660, tel. 714/729–4400).

WHITE-WATER RAFTING & KAYAKING

Rafting and kayaking have become popular and exciting activities in the spring and summer on the Tuolumne River in Yosemite and on the American River north of Sacramento. Outfitters have also sprung up around the Klamath, Trinity, and Eel rivers, offering half-day to multi-day trips on Class II–Class IV rapids. Check individual chapters for companies and prices, but expect to pay about $40 per half day and $90 for a full-day excursion. The price usually includes lunch and transportation.

SAN FRANCISCO

2

UPDATED BY JENNIFER BREWER, SHARON SILVA, SUZANNE STEIN, AND SHARRON WOOD

San Francisco, love child of the West, is a proud oasis for people and events divergent from the norm. On the tiny tip of a peninsula that separates the Pacific Ocean from San Francisco Bay, this hilly, eminently explorable city continues to go about its business with dignity and aplomb, undaunted by ubiquitous fog, ever-impending earthquakes, Be-Ins, Love-Ins, and one of the world's most severe AIDS epidemics. Whatever's hit the streets, from the drinking and whoring of the gold prospectors to the living and loving of the country's largest lesbian and gay population, has left reminders of its presence in nooks and crannies all over the city.

Without a doubt, San Francisco is a beautiful city, and upon arrival almost every traveler already knows what to see: the Golden Gate Bridge, Alcatraz, cable cars, twisty Lombard Street, and those impossibly steep hills. But don't settle for coffee-table San Francisco. The city's compactness and density beg you to explore on foot, so take advantage of it—just wear sturdy shoes and prepare for lots of climbing. Everywhere you go, you'll find something unexpected: a view continuously changing amid tricks of fog and sunlight, a friendly exchange between an aging hippie and a leather-clad skinhead, or a Victorian home smack in the midst of a warehouse district. And it all happens so quickly—one minute you're marveling at the frenetic pace of Financial District workers, and the next you're strolling through Chinese herb shops and produce markets. Ten minutes after having a cappuccino and biscotti in a noisy North Beach café, you're gazing at the Golden Gate Bridge from the water's edge.

Indeed, the city's greatest strength is its astonishing diversity. When you get on a bus and hear snatches of Mandarin, Thai, Spanish, Vietnamese, and Arabic; when city officials ride in the Gay Freedom Day parade not as a token gesture but because they're gay; when in certain neighborhoods you draw dirty looks because you're wearing a suit and tie—you know you're not in Kansas anymore.

BASICS

A good, all-purpose source of information is the front of the *San Francisco Yellow Pages,* called the **Access Pages.** It contains a list of community organizations, public-transit information, maps, descriptions of famous attractions, and a calendar of events. The best city map—available at most bookstores,

SAN FRANCISCO

Golden Gate Bridge
Fort Point National Historic Site
101
Golden Gate National Recreation Area
PACIFIC OCEAN
The Presidio
1
Lincoln Blvd.
Baker Beach
China Beach
Lands End
W. Pacific Ave
Lincoln Park
Palace of the Legion of Honor
SEACLIFF
Lake St.
Clement St.
Point Lobos
Cliff House
Geary Blvd.
43rd Ave.
34th Ave.
25th Ave.
19th Ave.
Park Presidio Blvd.
8th Ave.
Arguello Blvd.
Geary
Balboa St.
Turk
RICHMOND
Fulton St.
McLaren Lodge
Golden Gate Park
Kennedy Dr.
Middle Dr.
Martin Luther King Jr. Dr.
Stanyan St.
Lincoln Way
Judah St.
Funston Ave.
7th Ave.
Ocean Beach
Great Highway
28th Ave.
Lawton St.
1
Clarendon Ave.
Noriega St.
Ortega St.
19th Ave.
SUNSET
41st Ave.
Sunset Blvd.
Quintara St.
McCoppin Square
14th Ave.
Dewey Blvd.
Taraval St.
Larsen Park
Vicente St.
Portola Dr.
Mt. Davidson
Yerba Buena Ave.
Stern Grove
San Francisco Zoo
Sloat Blvd
Monterey Blvd.
STONESTOWN
Junipero Serra Blvd.
Miramar Ave.
Ocean Ave.
Harding Park
San Francisco State Univ.
Lake Merced Blvd.
Font Blvd.
Holloway Ave.
Garfield St.
Skyline Blvd.
Lake Merced
Plymouth Ave.
N
0
1 mile
0
1 km
Brotherhood Way
Fort Funston
35

SAN FRANCISCO

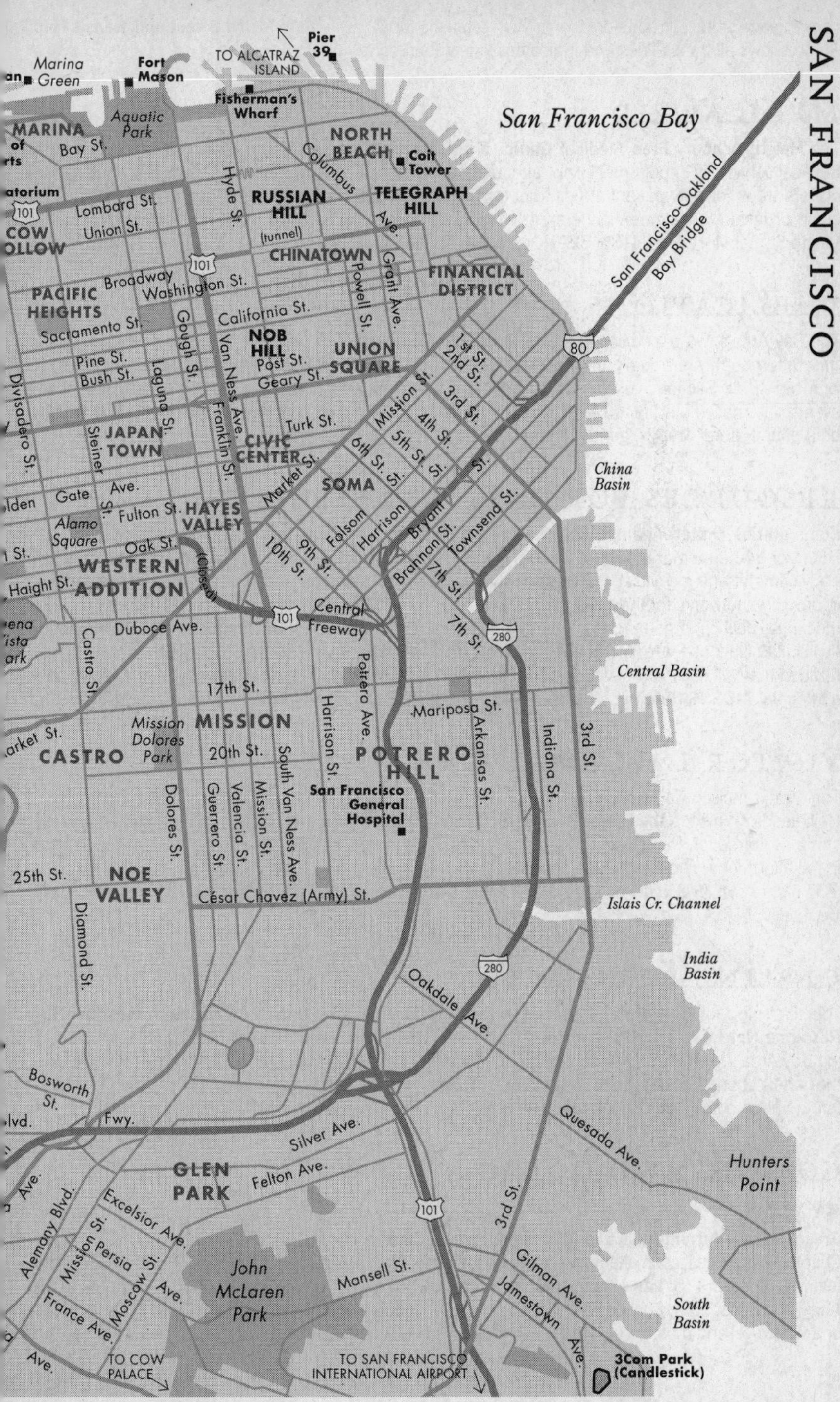

TO ALCATRAZ ISLAND
Pier 39
Marina Green
Fort Mason
Fisherman's Wharf
Aquatic Park
MARINA
Bay St.
San Francisco Bay
NORTH BEACH
Coit Tower
Columbus
RUSSIAN HILL
TELEGRAPH HILL
Hyde St.
Lombard St.
Union St.
COW
OLLOW
101
(tunnel)
Ave.
CHINATOWN
Powell St.
Grant Ave.
FINANCIAL DISTRICT
San Francisco-Oakland Bay Bridge
PACIFIC HEIGHTS
Broadway
Washington St.
California St.
Sacramento St.
Gough St.
NOB HILL
UNION SQUARE
Pine St.
Bush St.
Post St.
Geary St.
1st St.
2nd St.
80
Laguna St.
Van Ness Ave.
Franklin St.
Mission St.
3rd St.
Divisadero St.
Steiner St.
JAPAN TOWN
Turk St.
4th St.
CIVIC CENTER
Market St.
6th St.
5th St.
St.
St.
China Basin
SOMA
Gate Ave.
Fulton St.
HAYES VALLEY
Alamo Square
Folsom
Harrison
Bryant
Brannan St.
Townsend St.
Oak St.
10th St.
9th St.
WESTERN ADDITION
(Closed)
Haight St.
7th St.
101
Central Freeway
Duboce Ave.
280
Castro St.
Potrero Ave.
Central Basin
17th St.
Harrison St.
Mariposa St.
Arkansas St.
Indiana St.
3rd St.
Mission Dolores Park
MISSION
CASTRO
20th St.
POTRERO HILL
Dolores St.
Guerrero St.
Valencia St.
Mission St.
South Van Ness Ave.
San Francisco General Hospital
25th St.
NOE VALLEY
César Chavez (Army) St.
Islais Cr. Channel
Diamond St.
India Basin
280
Oakdale Ave.
Bosworth St.
Fwy.
Silver Ave.
Quesada Ave.
Hunters Point
GLEN PARK
Felton Ave.
Alemany Blvd.
Excelsior Ave.
101
3rd St.
Mission St.
Persia Ave.
Moscow St.
John McLaren Park
Mansell St.
Gilman Ave.
Jamestown Ave.
South Basin
France Ave.
TO COW PALACE
TO SAN FRANCISCO INTERNATIONAL AIRPORT
3Com Park (Candlestick)

convenience stores, liquor stores, and MUNI stations for $2.50—is the **MUNI Street and Transit Map,** which shows all transit lines and indicates all neighborhoods.

MEDICAL AID

The **Haight-Ashbury Free Medical Clinic** (558 Clayton St., at Haight St., tel. 415/487–5632) offers medical service by appointment only; although free, donations are appreciated. There is a waiting list of up to a week for new-patient appointments. To get prescriptions filled after hours, head for one of the chain drugstores: **Walgreen's** offers 24-hour prescription service at two San Francisco locations (498 Castro St., tel. 415/861–3136; 3201 Divisadero St., tel. 415/931–6417).

PUBLICATIONS

The Bay Area's two big dailies, the ***San Francisco Chronicle*** (morning) and the ***San Francisco Examiner*** (afternoon), are equally unremarkable. The combined *Chronicle-Examiner* Sunday paper comes with the "Pink Section," useful for its extensive movie reviews and listings of all sorts of upcoming events. Alternative (and far superior) freebie papers include the weekly ***Bay Guardian*** and ***S.F. Weekly;*** both offer cultural listings, general-interest features, local political commentary, and personal ads.

RESOURCES FOR GAYS AND LESBIANS

Communities United Against Violence (973 Market St., Suite 500, tel. 415/777–5500 or 415/333–HELP for 24-hour emergency hotline) provides crisis counseling and referrals for gays and lesbians who are victims of anti-gay violence. The free weekly ***Bay Area Reporter*** and biweekly ***Bay Times*** serve as information networks for the city's gay, lesbian, and bisexual communities, with listings of clubs, 12-step meetings, political organizations, and gay business classifieds. The **San Francisco AIDS Foundation** (10 United Nations Plaza, Market St., between 7th and 8th St., tel. 415/487–3000) is an umbrella organization that will refer you to whichever of the city's AIDS-related groups best suits you. It also operates a trilingual **AIDS Hotline** (tel. 415/863–2437 or 800/367–2437 in Northern California).

VISITOR INFORMATION

The San Francisco Convention and Visitors Bureau's **Visitor Information Center** is in the lower level of Hallidie Plaza, next to the Powell Street BART station. Before your trip, write or call for a free copy of its "Visitor Information Package." Or stop in for maps, brochures, and MUNI Passports; lines are shortest in the afternoons. The information booth upstairs at the cable car turnaround sells MUNI Passports only. *900 Market St., Hallidie Plaza, San Francisco 94102, tel. 415/391–2000 or 415/391–2001. Open weekdays 9–5:30, Sat. 9–3, Sun. 10–2.*

ON-LINE RESOURCES

Your first stop for Bay Area information on the World Wide Web should be the **San Francisco Bay Resource Net** (www.slip.net/~scmetro/sfbayr.htm), which has links to more than 100 websites covering Bay Area government, transportation, media, entertainment, museums and other points of interest, the arts, sports, restaurants, and more. **Yahoo** has a subsection devoted to San Francisco (sfbay.yahoo.com) that's chock full of links to entertainment, art, housing, travel, you name it.

COMING AND GOING

BY BUS

Green Tortoise Adventure Travel (494 Broadway, San Francisco 94133, tel. 415/821–0803; *see box in* Chapter 1) is a cheap, fun alternative to humdrum bus travel. The journey to Seattle (24 hrs, $49 one-way) features a cookout ($4) and skinny-dipping. Regularly scheduled runs also go from the Bay Area to Los Angeles (12 hrs, $30); Eugene, Oregon (17 hrs, $39); and Portland, Oregon (20 hrs, $39). All fares are for one-way travel and must be paid with cash, traveler's checks, or a money order. Reservations are advised.

Greyhound (tel. 800/231–2222) travels to and from San Francisco all day; major destinations include Seattle (20–26 hrs, $48 one-way), L.A. (7–12 hrs, $32 one-way), and Santa Cruz (2–4 hrs, $15 one-way). In San Francisco, Greyhound operates out of the third floor of the **Transbay Terminal** (1st and Mission Sts., tel. 415/495–1569), where many MUNI lines (*see* Getting Around by Bus, *below*) begin. Plan your arrival for daytime, as this terminal is dicey at night. **Luggage storage** is available for $1.50 per day; you pay for one day up front and for the rest when you pick up your bags.

REGIONAL BUS LINES • AC Transit (tel. 510/817–1717) buses travel between San Francisco and the East Bay 24-hours-a-day, while **SamTrans** (tel. 800/660–4287) serves downtown San Francisco to San Mateo County, south of the city. **Golden Gate Transit** (tel. 415/923–2000) runs north from the city to Marin, Napa, and Sonoma counties. Fares and schedules vary.

BY CAR

From the north, you can reach San Francisco via U.S. 101, which merges with Hwy. 1 (Pacific Coast Highway) and shoots right over the Golden Gate Bridge ($3) and into the city. From the south, you have three routes: north on I–5 to I–580 west, north on U.S. 101, or north on Hwy. 1. From the east, you'll take either I–580 or I–80 west and go over the Bay Bridge ($1). (For car-rental information, *see* Getting Around by Car, *below*.)

BY PLANE

Sure, San Francisco is in California, but you're going to freeze—even in summer—unless you bring some warm clothes.

San Francisco International (tel. 650/876–7809), the biggest Northern California airport, lies about 10 mi south of San Francisco on U.S. 101. All major domestic airlines and many international ones fly into SFO, as it's called; contact individual carriers for specific information. The airport has two **currency exchange** offices, both in the International Terminal. **Baggage storage** (tel. 650/877–0422; open 7 AM–11 PM), in the walkway between the International Terminal and South Terminal, charges according to luggage size: An average bag runs $3.50 per day. There are also lockers inside each terminal near the gates: Small- and medium-size lockers cost $2 for four hours ($4 for 24 hrs); large ones go for $2.50 for four hours ($5 for 24 hrs). There is a three-day maximum on locker use.

AIRPORT TRANSIT • Until BART finally extends its service to the airport (sometime around 2002), you have two basic public transit options: (1) you can take either **SamTrans Buses 7B** (55 min, $2) or **7F** (35 min, $2.50) to San Francisco's Transbay Terminal (1st and Mission Sts.) or (2) **Bus 3X** (20 min, $1) to the Colma BART station, from which you can catch a train to downtown San Francisco (20 min, $1.80). The buses run every half hour: Bus 3X from 6 AM to 11:30 PM; Buses 7B and 7F from about 5 AM to 12:45 AM. Bus 7F restricts you to one small carry-on bag.

Most people, though, feel it's well worth $10 to be delivered door-to-door. Airport shuttle vans will whisk you to the airport anytime, day or night. Fare from San Francisco to SFO usually runs $10–$12; from other Bay Area cities to SFO or Oakland Airport, you'll pay $15–$35. There's often a reduced rate for two or more people, or if you board the shuttle at a major hotel. The **Super Shuttle** chain (tel. 415/558–8500) serves SFO from San Francisco and the Peninsula, as does the reliable **Quake City** (tel. 415/255–4899), an employee-owned business with friendly drivers. **Airport Connection** (tel. 510/841–0150) runs from most Bay Area cities to SFO, Oakland International, and San Jose International airports.

BY TRAIN

Several **Amtrak** (tel. 800/872–7245) lines, including the *Zephyr* from Chicago via Denver, the *Coast Starlight* from San Diego and Seattle, and the *Capitol* from Sacramento and the San Joaquin Valley, stop at five East Bay stations: Richmond (16th St. and MacDonald Ave., adjoining Richmond BART), Berkeley (3rd St. and University Ave.; you can board, but you can't buy tickets here), Emeryville (5885 Landregan St.), Oakland (245 2nd St., at Jack London Square), and San Jose (65 Cahill St.). From the Oakland and Emeryville stations, a connecting Amtrak bus runs to San Francisco's Ferry Building (31 Embarcadero, at the foot of Market St.). Fares vary according to the time of year and other factors: round trip to Seattle (24 hrs one-way) runs $180–$330, to Los Angeles (12 hrs one-way) $78–$155.

REGIONAL TRAIN LINES • CalTrain (tel. 800/660–4287) offers regular service from San Francisco (4th and Townsend Sts.) to downtown San Jose (65 Cahill St.). One-way fare is $4.75 and the trip takes 1½ hours; trains leave hourly between 5 AM and 10 PM. Along the way, the trains stop at a number of Peninsula cities. Bikes are allowed on the trains.

GETTING AROUND

BY BART

Relatively clean and quiet, **Bay Area Rapid Transit (BART)** (tel. 800/817–1717) is a smooth subway system somewhat reminiscent of Disneyland's Monorail. Its primary purpose, however, is not to get you around within the city but to move you from city to city. Its four lines stop at 36 stations serving San Francisco, Daly City/Colma, and the East Bay from Richmond to Fremont and out to North Concord. At press time, BART was scheduled to open a spur line expanding South Bay service to include Castro Valley and Dublin/Pleasanton; call for details. Trains run every 10–20 minutes until midnight, with service starting up again at 4 AM weekdays, 6 AM Saturday, and 8 AM Sunday. Evenings, Sunday, and holidays only the North Concord–Colma and Richmond–Fremont lines operate. All BART stations and trains are wheelchair accessible. The cost of a BART ticket ranges $1–$4 depending on the length of the journey; for example, the 25-minute trip from downtown San Francisco to Berkeley costs $2.35. Riders with disabilities get a good discount: a $16 ticket for $4. Bikes are allowed only during non-commuter hours; call the **BART Office of Passenger Service** (tel. 510/464–7127) for more information.

BY BUS

MUNI (tel. 415/673–6864), San Francisco's bus and streetcar service, runs buses as often as every five minutes in certain well-traveled parts of town (although regular MUNI users will attest to chronically late bus lines). Between 1 AM and 5 AM, the Owl Service offers nine lines that run every 30 minutes. Adult fare is $1 and includes a 90-minute transfer; fare for youths, seniors, and people with disabilities is 35¢. Short-term **Passport** passes allow unlimited access to MUNI (including cable cars) for one day ($6), three days ($10), or seven days ($15). Buy your one-day pass as you board; others can be bought at the Powell-and-Market cable-car turnaround.

BY CABLE CAR

San Francisco's cable cars were the world's first large-scale mechanized street transportation. They run at a pace straight out of the early 1900s—the cables that propel the cars move at 9½ mph. Fare is $2, though many MUNI Passports (*see above*) allow you to ride for free. All three lines run from around 6 AM to a little before 1 AM.

BY CAR

San Francisco is not a car-friendly city. If you ever find a parking space, it might be on the side of a sheer precipice. Remember to curb your wheels, set the emergency brake, and, if you're driving a stick-shift, leave the car in gear.

RENTAL CARS • If you opt for your own wheels, your best bet is to rent at one of the airports; Oakland in particular has good deals. Almost all the rental car agencies also have offices in downtown San Francisco, within five or six blocks of Union Square; look in the *Yellow Pages* for listings.

PARKING • Plenty of parking lots and garages offer hourly and daily rates. Pay close attention to rates as they can get quite steep, especially around prime tourist country like Fisherman's Wharf. In the Union Square area, you can usually find a parking place at the large **Sutter-Stockton Garage** (444 Stockton St., tel. 415/982–7275). It charges a graduated rate: $4 for three hours, $8 for five hours, and $40 for 24 hours. The cheapest lot near Fisherman's Wharf is the **Wharf Garage** (350 Beach St., between Taylor and Mason Sts., tel. 415/921–0226), which charges $7 for day use, open 7:30 AM–11:30PM. Near North Beach and Chinatown, try the lot at the **corner of Sansome and Pacific**; on weekends there's a flat $4 fee that you pay on the honor system. Street parking is hard to come by and tickets are very expensive.

BY FERRY

Ferries are comparable to other forms of transport in terms of speed, and they afford lovely views too. Many ferries depart from the landmark **San Francisco Ferry Building** (on the Embarcadero, at the foot of Market St.). **Golden Gate Ferry** (tel. 415/923–2000) crosses the bay between the SF Ferry Building and Larkspur or Sausalito in Marin County. Ferries depart hourly, 7 AM–8 PM; fare is $2.50–$4.25 and includes free transfer to Golden Gate Transit buses. The **Blue and Gold Fleet** (tel. 415/705–5555 or 415/773–1188) leaves from Pier 41 at Fisherman's Wharf for Sausalito (30 min, $5.50), Tiburon (40 min, $5.50), Alcatraz (*see* Major Sights, *below*) and Angel Island ($10); call for current schedule.

Blue and Gold also operates the **Oakland/Alameda Ferry** (tel. 415/705–5555 or 510/522–3300) which leaves from Oakland's Jack London Square or the Alameda Ferry Dock for the SF Ferry Building (30 min) or **Pier 39** (40 min). Ferries run every one to two hours from 6 AM on weekdays (10 AM on weekends and holidays) until 8:50 PM. Fare is $4; $2.50 youths, seniors, and people with disabilities. Ferry stubs serve as transfers to MUNI and AC Transit buses.

BY TAXI

You can occasionally hail a cab in San Francisco, but most residents phone. All taxis are metered, but you might be able to negotiate a flat rate to the airport at the driver's discretion. The meter rate in San Francisco is $1.70, plus 30¢ each additional ⅙ mi, and 30¢ for every minute of waiting time or traffic delay. Try **Veteran's Cab** (tel. 415/552–1300) or **Yellow Cab** (tel. 415/626–2345). Don't forget to tip the driver; 15% is typical.

WHERE TO SLEEP

For an expensive city, San Francisco has a surprisingly large assortment of reasonably priced accommodations. For a great no-frills deal, stay in one of the city's nine hostels, where a bed will set you back only about $12, or in one of the residential hotels that populate Downtown and North Beach. For a little bit more ($40–$60 a night), many small downtown hotels offer charming "European-style" rooms (i.e., the toilet's down the hall). Only in San Francisco will you find a leather-and-Levi's, gay B&B; an artist's B&B complete with easels and plenty of light; and an inn whose nightly accommodations include "The Summer of Love Room" and "The Japanese Tea Garden Room."

If you don't reserve one to two weeks in advance in summer, you may be exiled to the strip of generic motels along Lombard Street in the Marina District. These motels are about a 20-minute bus ride from Downtown (on Bus 76) but are quite close to Fisherman's Wharf, the Marina Green, and the Golden Gate Bridge. On Lombard, you'll pay $60–$80 for a double—stay here only if you're desperate. The area South of Market (SoMa) has its share of similar "last resort" places on 6th Street but can be unsafe; if you do want to stay in SoMa—near the Museum of Modern Art and much of the city's more hard-core nightlife—try a hostel.

For a map of various lodging options, *see* Exploring, *below.*

HOTELS AND MOTELS

DOWNTOWN

This neighborhood is home to San Francisco's Theater District, a host of shady local bars, and a handful of truly fine restaurants. Its many turn-of-the-century and Victorian buildings lend the area charm, and its central location affords easy access to North Beach, the Financial District, and Chinatown. It also, however, adjoins the seedy Tenderloin. The safest area is west of Mason Street and north of Sutter Street.

UNDER $40 • Nob Hill Pensione. This inn offers basic furnishings in newly remodeled, spacious, sunny rooms, most with shared baths. Doubles start at $40 ($50 with private bath). The hotel's friendly staff and perks (e.g., E-mail, fax, voice-mail service) attract a few live-in residents. *835 Hyde St., near Sutter St., tel. 415/885–2987, fax 415/921–1648. From Powell St. BART/MUNI, walk 5 blocks north to Sutter St., then 10 blocks west or take Bus 2, 3, or 4 to Hyde St. 50 rooms, 8 with bath. Laundry.*

UNDER $55 • Adelaide Inn. The comfortable Adelaide, on a short, dead-end street just minutes from Union Square, is popular with Europeans. Rates include a continental breakfast; some kitchen facilities are also available. Doubles start at $48, depending on room size and availability. All share baths. *5 Isadora Duncan La., near Taylor St., tel. 415/441–2261, fax 415/441–0161. From Montgomery St. BART/MUNI, Bus 38 northwest to Geary and Taylor Sts.; walk ¾ block north on Taylor St. and turn left. 18 rooms.*

Stratford Inn. This tidy little bargain is ideal for those who spend their time out and about. Low-end doubles ($35–$45; hall bath) are dark and spartan, but often large and always clean, and you have free access to an indoor pool and fitness center at the nearby Sheehan Hotel. *242 Powell St., between O'Farrell and Geary Sts., tel. 415/397–7080, fax 415/397–7087. From Powell St. BART/MUNI, walk 2½ blocks north on Powell St. 60 rooms, 30 with bath. Laundry.*

UNDER $65 • Biltmore Hotel. Run by the same folks who run the Amsterdam next door (*see below*), the Biltmore offers clean, sunny rooms at low prices. Rooms, some with great Downtown views, go for $65 (doubles) or $75 (deluxe suites with wet bar, microwave, and refrigerator). *735 Taylor St., tel. 415/775–0630, fax 415/673–0453. 60 rooms, all with bath.*

San Francisco Residence Club. Built in 1910, this family-owned pension offers full breakfast and dinner (Mon.–Sat. only) with a night's stay. Some of the clean, spacious rooms boast spectacular views of Angel Island. Doubles are $60–$95 nightly, $400–$600 weekly. Rates depend on room size and availability of private bath. *851 California St., at Powell St., tel. 415/421–2220, fax 415/421–2335. From Powell St. BART/MUNI, walk 8 blocks north or take cable car to California St. 84 rooms, 6 with bath. Laundry. Reservations advised.*

UNDER $85 • Amsterdam. A comfortable and clean Victorian B&B two blocks from Nob Hill. Doubles start at $89 (deluxe doubles with private Jacuzzi and outdoor patio go for $129). The sunny, cloistered deck garden is a great spot to enjoy the complimentary breakfast. *749 Taylor St., between Sutter and Bush Sts., tel. 415/673–3277 or 800/637–3444. From Montgomery St. BART/MUNI, Bus 2, 3, or 4 west to Sutter St. 34 rooms, all with bath.*

Brady Acres. Come to this small, comfortable hotel if you miss the comforts of home. Each room comes with a microwave, toaster, coffeemaker, and a minifridge filled with chocolates and jam; the bathrooms feature apricot and papaya shampoos; and the beds are laden with colorful quilts. Doubles are $75–$90; after six nights the seventh is free. *649 Jones St., between Post and Geary Sts., tel. 415/929–8033 or 800/627–2396. From Montgomery St. BART/MUNI, Bus 38 west to Geary and Jones Sts. 25 rooms, all with bath. Laundry.*

CIVIC CENTER

The area around the Civic Center ought to be a great place to stay: Davies Symphony Hall, the Opera House, and a host of theaters are all within easy walking distance, and many of the city's public transport lines converge here. Sadly, the Civic Center can be quite dangerous, especially at night, due to an active drug scene in the Tenderloin. After dark, solo travelers—particularly women—should avoid the triangle formed by Market, Polk, and Geary streets.

UNDER $55 • Aida Hotel. Centrally located one block from Civic Center BART, doubles with TV and phone cost $39; rooms with private bath cost $10 more. Show this book to the desk staff and you'll get a $5–$10 discount. The low-grade motel decor wouldn't satisfy a true diva, but the rooms are surprisingly large, and the top floor sunny. Due to the hotel's size, you can probably get a room at the last minute. *1087 Market St., at 7th St., tel. 415/863–4141 or 800/863–2432, fax 415/863–5151. From Civic Center BART/MUNI, walk 1 block northwest on Market St. 174 rooms, 100 with bath.*

UNDER $100 • Albion House. Opened as a saloon in 1906, this B&B is close to Market Street, City Hall, and the Hayes Valley shopping and dining strip; the area is safe at night. Albion House boasts a large, old-fashioned drawing room complete with marble-column fireplace and baby grand piano; complimentary wine and brandy is served here in the evening. The well-appointed rooms start at $95; ask about off-season and senior discounts. *135 Gough St., between Oak and Page Sts., tel. 415/621–0896, or 800/625–2466, fax 415/621–3811. From Civic Center BART/MUNI walk 3 blocks southwest on Market St., right on Gough St. 10 rooms, all with bath. Reservations advised.*

Phoenix Hotel. Bamboo furniture and the piped-in poolside sounds of squawking macaws, croaking frogs, and jungle music make this lively hotel a tropical paradise on the edge of the Tenderloin. The Phoenix—notorious for hosting small- and big-name bands like R.E.M and Pearl Jam—is joined at the hip to the Voodoo Lounge, where you might find yourself tossing one back with a rock star. In high season, you'll pay $90 for a double, but rates go down as much as $20 in winter. *601 Larkin St., at Eddy St., tel. 415/776–1380 or 800/248–9466, fax 415/885–3109. From Powell St. BART/MUNI, Bus 31 west on Eddy St. 44 rooms, all with bath.*

NORTH BEACH

Near Downtown, Chinatown, and Fisherman's Wharf, this is where most tourists congregate—hotel rates are accordingly high. An appealing, low-cost option is the Green Tortoise Guest House (*see* Hostels, *below*). While North Beach is close to many of the city's most popular restaurants, bars, and cafés, another "attraction" to be aware of is the row of tacky strip joints along Broadway.

UNDER $75 • San Remo Hotel. A short walk from Fisherman's Wharf and North Beach, San Remo is an incredible bargain in this pricey area. Doubles with shared bath cost $60–$80; the more you spend, the better your view. The hotel boasts beautiful redwood furnishings and stained-glass windows. *2237 Mason St., between Francisco and Chestnut Sts., tel. 415/776–8688 or 800/352–7366, fax 415/776–2811. From Montgomery St. BART/MUNI Bus 15 north to Chestnut St.; walk 1 block west to Mason St. 64 rooms, 1 with bath. Laundry.*

UNDER $125 • Hotel Bohème. Near the outdoor cafés that sidle up to Columbus Avenue, Bohème offers 15 rooms; plush, striped carpeting; and black-and-white snapshots in the hallway. This was once a hangout for beatnik poets. Doubles are $120; there's also one suite that goes for $125 (for three) or $130 (for four). *444 Columbus Ave., at Vallejo St., tel. 415/433–9111, fax 415/362–6292. From Montgomery St. BART/MUNI, Bus 41 north to Vallejo St. 15 rooms, all with bath.*

THE MARINA

The Marina District is a quiet, safe, residential neighborhood popular with young folks climbing the corporate ladder. It's a long walk from North Beach, Chinatown, and Downtown, but the views of the bay and the Golden Gate Bridge from the nearby waterfront are tremendous. Unfortunately, most of the cheap lodging in this area lies along busy Lombard Street (not on the world's crookedest part), a major thoroughfare leading to the Golden Gate Bridge. The **Travelodge** (1450 Lombard St., at Van Ness Ave., tel. 415/673–0691) isn't too bad—in a last-resort kind of way—with clean doubles for $55; expect $30 rate increases May–November.

UNDER $70 • Marina Motel. This quiet, family-owned motel is an excellent alternative to the general dullness of the Lombard strip. Most rooms ($65–$75) include fully equipped kitchens, garage parking, and views of a courtyard garden and colorful murals by local artists. Off-season, you can rent by the week for $375–$400. *2576 Lombard St., at Divisadero St., tel. 415/921–9406, fax 415/921–0364. From Embarcadero BART/MUNI, Bus 30 northwest to Chestnut and Divisadero Sts., walk 1 block north. 38 rooms, all with bath.*

UNDER $100 • Art Center Bed and Breakfast. The owners like to call this place a country inn with a city built around it. If you want to paint, the proprietors will gladly set up an easel for you, and you can go to the back garden for inspiration. Three studios and a pair of two-room suites ($105 per day) have double beds, TV, and access to a shared kitchen. A three-room apartment with the same amenities runs $145 for two people. *1902 Filbert St., at Laguna St., tel. 415/567–1526 or 800/927–8236. From Embarcadero BART/MUNI, Bus 41 northwest to Laguna St.; walk 1 block north and turn left. 5 rooms, all with bath. Reserve 2 weeks in advance in summer.*

HAIGHT AND WESTERN ADDITION

During its heyday in the 60s and 70s, rock bands (the Grateful Dead), poets (Allen Ginsberg), and runaway hippie children all settled in the Haight. Staying here will give you a sense of the area's history and transformation—contemporary streetwise mottos are more about anarchy and survival than peace and love; expect aggressive panhandling. Much of Haight Street (especially between Laguna and Pierce streets) is dicey at night; the Western Addition, on the other hand, is undergoing something of a revival as artists and musicians discover its (relatively) cheap rents. Nevertheless, caution is advised at night, as it can get hairy in the Western Addition near the subsidized housing west of Webster Street.

UNDER $55 • Metro Hotel. The first thing you'll notice about the Metro is its neon sign, which lights up Divisadero Street, a major thoroughfare in the Western Addition. This is a good middle-range option popular with gay and lesbian travelers, Europeans, and the occasional rock band. High-ceiling rooms (doubles, $50–$94) are large, clean, and comfortable, and the café downstairs serves breakfast and lunch on a sunny outdoor patio behind the hotel. *319 Divisadero St., between Oak and Page Sts., tel. 415/861–5364, fax 415/863–1970. From Market St. downtown, Bus 7 or 71 west to Divisadero and Haight Sts.; walk 1½ blocks north on Divisadero. 24 rooms, all with bath.*

UNDER $70 • Auberge des Artistes. This elegant Edwardian (circa 1901) is nestled on a shady stretch of Fillmore Street, on the outskirts of Alamo Square Park. The neighborhood characters are also a little shady, but the extensive collection of art books, sunny garden, and rich art deco interior make leaving unnecessary. A full gourmet breakfast is served in a dining room graced by a full-scale replica of a Gustav Klimt mural. Luxurious doubles (some with fireplace, one with Jacuzzi tub) range $65–$100. *829 Fillmore St., between Grove and Fulton Sts., tel. 415/776–2530, fax 415/441–8242. From Montgomery St. BART/MUNI, MUNI F, K, L, or M Streetcar to Church St., then Bus 22 Fillmore north to Grove St. 5 rooms, 2 with bath. Reservations advised.*

UNDER $90 • Red Victorian. At the Red Vic, each room is decorated according to a particular theme, for example "The Japanese Tea Garden Room" (double $96); "The Summer of Love Room" (double $86) complete with a tie-dyed canopy and authentic '60s concert posters; and "The Skylight Room" (double $86), painted in deep jewel tones and featuring a skylight ceiling. New double-glass windows insure that even streetside rooms are tranquil, and sweet proprietress Sami Sunchild takes good care of her establishment and her guests. Stays three days or longer garner substantial discounts. *1665 Haight*

St., between Belvedere and Cole Sts., tel. 415/864–1978, fax 415/863–3293. From Market St. downtown, Bus 7 or 71 west to Haight and Cole Sts. 18 rooms, 4 with bath.

CASTRO DISTRICT

As the United States' most prominent gay neighborhood, the Castro naturally offers a wide variety of gay- and lesbian-friendly accommodations and is generally safe at night. Reserve way in advance for the Gay and Lesbian Freedom Day Parade weekend (end of June).

UNDER $55 • Twin Peaks. Firm beds and clean bathrooms compensate for dull decor, and the location is an ideal hub for transport all over the city. Doubles range $35–$41 ($45–$51 with bath); weekly rates are $140–$190 depending on room size. *2160 Market St., between Church and Sanchez Sts., tel. 415/621–9467, fax 415/863–1545. From Montgomery St. BART/MUNI, MUNI F, K, L, or M Streetcar to Church St.; walk 1 block SW on Market St. 60 rooms, 3 with bath.*

UNDER $85 • Inn on Castro. This B&B in a restored Edwardian affords a cheery stay with its hyper-70s pop art decor. The couches around the fireplace are a cozy place to sip complimentary brandy. Prices range from $95 for a double with shared bath to $160 for a suite with private bath and sun deck—all include a full breakfast of fruit, muffins, and pancakes or omelettes. *321 Castro St., near Market St., tel. 415/861–0321. From Montgomery St. BART/MUNI, MUNI F, K, L, or M Streetcar to Castro St.; walk 1 block north. 8 rooms, 7 with bath. Reserve ahead.*

24 Henry. This charming B&B has six doubles (two with bath) and caters to a mostly gay and lesbian clientele. The rooms are colorful and cozy, the showers are big enough for two, and a complimentary breakfast is served in the Victorian-style parlor. Doubles are $75–$90, three-person suites with kitchens $95–$120. *24 Henry St., between 14th and 15th Sts., tel. 415/864–5686 or 800/900–5686, fax 415/864–0406. From Montgomery St. BART/MUNI, MUNI N Judah Streetcar to Noe St.; walk 4 blocks south to Henry St. 5 rooms. Reservations advised.*

MISSION DISTRICT

This lively neighborhood, home to the city's Latin communities, is San Francisco's latest confluence of creativity—artists, musicians, and writers are flocking here. It's not the safest part of the city—stick to Valencia, Dolores, and Guerrero streets and avoid taking a room east of Valencia Street.

UNDER $40 • Curtis Hotel. The owner of this residential hotel works hard to keep the riffraff out—sometimes successfully. The rules prohibit loud noises after 9 PM, alcohol, and parties. If you get too wild, you'll get thrown out. A sweet deal awaits those who can navigate the underworld quality of the halls: Clean singles with shared bath are just $75–$90 per week (no doubles). Talk to the manager about shorter stays. Guests must pay in advance (cash only) and flash a picture ID. *559 Valencia St., near 16th St., tel. 415/621–9337. From Mission/16th St. BART/MUNI, walk 1 block west on 16th St., turn left on Valencia St. 60 rooms, none with bath.*

Dolores Park Inn. One of the best B&Bs in San Francisco, Dolores Park Inn is an 1874 Victorian furnished almost entirely with antiques on a sedate street between the Mission and the Castro, one block south of Mission Dolores Park. Doubles are $99–$165, which includes breakfast and access to the garden and parlor. *3641 17th St., near Dolores St., tel. 415/621–0482. From any downtown BART/MUNI station, MUNI J Streetcar to 16th and Church Sts.; walk 1 block south on Church St. to 17th St. 4 rooms, 1 with bath, all nonsmoking. Two-night minimum.*

HOSTELS

Due perhaps to the dearth of budget lodging in the area, hostels are extremely popular; make reservations before you arrive. In a pinch, you can also try to get one of 12 hostel beds at the YMCA (220 Golden Gate Ave., tel. 415/885–0460). Unless otherwise noted, all the hostels listed below have 24-hour receptions and do not have curfews or lockouts.

AYH Hostel at Union Square. This huge hostel, one block from Union Square, sleeps 230 people in rooms with one to four beds ($16 for members, $19 for nonmembers). Catering mostly to an international student crowd, its amenities include a TV room, smoking room, library, and kitchen (with microwaves, toasters, and fridges). *312 Mason St., between O'Farrell and Geary Sts., tel. 415/788–5604 or 800/909–4776, ext. 02. From Powell St. BART/MUNI, walk 1½ blocks north on Powell St., 1 block west on O'Farrell St., turn right. 230 beds.*

Ft. Mason International Hostel. This AYH hostel, perched high above the waterfront, will dazzle you with its views of the bay and the Golden Gate Bridge. The rules are tedious and complex, however, so listen up: Reservations (by phone or in person) must be made at least 24 hours ahead with a credit card, or by sending the cost of your first night's stay at least two weeks prior to your arrival; include the names and genders of the people in your party and the dates you intend to stay. Get here *really* early if you don't have a reservation—available space often sells out by 8 AM. You're required to perform a chore each day. Beds are $16 a night. No smoking or alcohol allowed. Whew. *Mailing address: Ft. Mason, Bldg. 240, Box A, San Francisco, CA 94123, tel. 415/771–7277 or 800/444–6111, fax 415/771–1468. From Transbay Terminal, Bus 42 to Van Ness Ave. and Bay St.; turn right on Bay St. and follow signs. 160 beds. Check-in varies, lockout 11 AM–1 PM. Kitchen, laundry.*

Grand Central Hostel. This former flophouse, in a central but seedy location, has been transformed into a decent hostel. Dorm space costs $15 per night ($95 per week); doubles are $35. Perks include an exercise room, free coffee, breakfast, social events, free linens, a pool table, a jukebox, table tennis, and TV rooms. All visitors, even Americans traveling within the United States, must show travel documents to stay here. *1412 Market St., at 10th and Fell Sts., tel. 415/703–9988, fax 415/703–9986. From Van Ness Ave. MUNI, walk 1 block NE on Market St. 250 beds.*

Green Tortoise Guest House. From the popular people who have brought you budget bus travel for the past 20 years comes one of the best hostels in San Francisco. Green Tortoise is steps from North Beach on the neon Broadway strip and just blocks from Downtown and Chinatown. European student backpackers fill most of the rooms, which are clean, spacious, and rarely vacant—call ahead. Single bunks cost $15 per night; private doubles $35–$39. *494 Broadway, between Montgomery and Kearny Sts., tel. 415/834–1000, fax 956–4900. From Montgomery St. BART/MUNI, Bus 15 or 9X north. 110 beds. Kitchen, laundry. Cash only.*

Interclub Globe Hostel. Intended for international travelers (but passport-carrying Americans are not turned away), this SoMa hostel has few rules and a warm, relaxed atmosphere—not to mention a pool table and a sun deck that has a grand view of the city. Guests sleep four to a room, and each room has a bathroom; two floors are reserved for nonsmokers. Dorm beds are $15 per night; a few private rooms (doubles, $40) also rent by the week for $224. At the lively adjoining canteen, you can get dinner for less than $5. *10 Hallam Pl., near Folsom St. between 7th and 8th Sts., tel. 415/431–0540, fax 415/431–3286. From Civic Center BART/MUNI, walk 3 blocks south on 8th St., turn left on Folsom St. Laundry.*

Pacific Tradewinds. This friendly, homey place in Chinatown has four rooms; the large, upper floor is partitioned into four-bed private areas. A TV-less common room fosters conversation with your hostel-mates. There's no official lockout and if you want to come in after midnight, the proprietors will give you a key ($20 deposit). Beds are usually $16 per night, but ask about off-season discounts. If you stay seven nights, you pay for only six; in summer, they ask that you pay for the week in advance. *680 Sacramento St., near Kearny St., tel. 415/433–7970, fax 415/291–8801. From Montgomery St. BART/MUNI, walk 1 block west on Post St., then Bus 15 north on Kearny St. 28 beds. Reception open daily 8 AM–midnight.*

San Francisco International Guest House. Tucked away on the outskirts of the Mission District, this clean, 100-year-old hostel is friendly and cozy. With its five-day minimum stay requirement, this hostel is also known for breeding "intimacy." You need international travel documents to stay here; there are no age restrictions but seniors may feel more comfortable elsewhere. There are two full kitchens, a TV room, and a funky, orange-color reading room. Rooms of two to four people go for $13 per person; couples can ask for private rooms. *2976 23rd St., at Harrison St. (next to the laundromat), tel. 415/641-1411. From 24th St. BART/MUNI, walk 1 block north on Mission St. to 23rd St., then 6½ blocks east. 28 beds.*

San Francisco International Student Center. Right in the middle of hip SoMa, the student center has 16 rooms with three to five beds in each, a microwave, and a common room. There are no age restrictions, but the atmosphere is definitely young and funky. Beds cost $13 a night, $84 a week. *1188 Folsom St., near 8th St., tel. 415/255–8800, fax 415/487–1463. From Civic Center BART/MUNI, walk 3 blocks south on 8th St. to Folsom St. Reception open 9 AM–11 PM. 53 beds.*

FOOD

San Francisco has more than 4,000 restaurants, serving everyone from lobster lovers to tofu fanatics. Waves of Asian and Latino immigrants have brought the city a tasty cavalcade of good-deal taquerías, Chinese restaurants, gracious Thai and Vietnamese establishments, reasonably priced sushi houses, and Korean barbecue joints. Just because a restaurant's windows are plastered with reviews doesn't mean it's any good, however; look for recent recommendations from the *Bay Guardian*'s Dan Leone or the *Examiner*'s Jim Wood.

DOWNTOWN/EMBARCADERO

Downtown abounds with both old, classic restaurants that evoke San Francisco's golden years and trendy, new, let's-do-lunch-and-expense-it bistros; both take advantage of the high-rolling Financial District's need to dispose of income. Except for a few options below, it's difficult to find a decent *and* inexpensive sit-down restaurant in this area—but it's usually worth it when you decide to blow a few bucks, especially in the "French Quarter," which offers the almost identical **Café Claude** (7 Claude La., off Bush St. between Grant and Kearny Sts., tel. 415/392–3515) and **Café Bastille** (*see below*). On the other end of the fiscal spectrum, healthy soup-and-salad buffets are not so hard to find.

UNDER $5 • Specialty's. These five tiny take-out stands bake 14 kinds of bread with which they will make any of 40—count 'em—fresh sandwiches (most $3–$5). They also sell coffee and pastries (around $1.50) like zucchini-bran muffins and insanely rich sweets. *312 Kearny St., between Bush and Pine Sts.; 22 Battery St., between Market and Bush Sts.; 150 Spear St., between Mission and Howard Sts.; 1 Post St., at Market St.; 101 New Montgomery St., at Mission. Tel. 415/896–2253 for daily specials, 415/512–9550 for phone orders. Closed dinner, Sat., Sun. Cash only.*

UNDER $10 • 101 Restaurant. Just steps from the Powell Street station toward the Tenderloin, this weary-looking but very reasonable restaurant serves Vietnamese favorites like BBQ beef with rice noodles, lettuce, mint, peanuts, and bean sprouts ($4.50) or chicken in coconut-milk curry with lemongrass ($5.25). The lunch special ($4.75) includes soup, an imperial roll, and your choice of barbecued beef, chicken, or pork. *101 Eddy St., at Mason St., tel. 415/928–4490. Closed Sun.*

UNDER $15 • Café Bastille. Stop by for neat little French appetizers, like onion soup, pâté, or baked goat cheese on eggplant ($4–$6), in a happening, Frenchy atmosphere. For a more substantial meal, try some meat-and-potatoes fare ($7–$12), such as steak with pommes frites. The place is particularly fun and friendly Wednesday through Saturday when there's live jazz. *22 Belden Pl., between Pine and Bush Sts. and Kearny and Montgomery Sts., tel. 415/986–5673. Closed Sun.*

Yank Sing. With a location in the Financial District and one south of Market, and a tasteful, modern setting, Yank Sing is a great place to feast on dim sum. A meal should cost $10–$15, but watch out: Let your appetite run away with you, and next thing you know, your pants are unbuttoned, your head is nodding, stacks of plates are sliding off the table, and the waiter is handing you a bill the size of Beijing. *427 Battery St., at Clay St., tel. 415/362–1640. SoMa location: 49 Stevenson Pl., between 1st and 2nd Sts., tel. 415/541–4949. Closed Sat.*

CIVIC CENTER AREA

This section comprises a few low-lying neighborhoods that aren't exactly what you'd call classy, except, of course, for the area immediately surrounding the Opera House and the Symphony Hall. **Hayes Valley,** to the west of **Civic Center** along Hayes and Grove streets between Franklin and Laguna streets, is a good example of gentrification in progress: You'll find wine bars and chichi restaurants aplenty. Running north of Civic Center on Polk Street, **Polk Gulch** gets some of the sleazy runoff from the nearby Tenderloin, but terrific international and ethnic dives might convince you of the Gulch's seedy charm. Stretching northeast of the Civic Center toward Downtown, very few dining experiences are worth a stroll through the area surrounding Larkin, Market, O'Farrell, and Mason streets (the **Tenderloin**) after dark if you don't know your way around.

UNDER $5 • Aladdin. This casual Mediterranean restaurant in Polk Gulch offers amazing deals on shawerma ($5.49) and falafels ($4.49). This is how it works: They hand you the pita full of meat or falafel, and you fill it up as much as you can at their generous buffet of scrumptious Mediterranean salads, sauces, and grilled veggies. The friendly guys behind the counter are always trying to force-feed you bonus falafel balls. *1300 Polk St., at Bush St., tel. 415/441–2212.*

Swan Oyster Depot. Politicians from nearby City Hall can open their mouths wider than this fish market, which consists of nothing more than one long counter and some of the best seafood in town. The staff welcomes you with open arms and will promptly set you up with a bowl of clam chowder, thick sourdough bread, and an Anchor Steam beer for a fiver. *1517 Polk St., between California and Sacramento Sts., tel. 415/673–1101. Closed Sun. Cash only.*

Tu Lan. Even Julia Child has eaten the famous Vietnamese grub served in this greasy little dive in a seedy section of Downtown. The imperial rolls with rice noodles ($4.50) and lemon beef salad ($4.50) are among the favorite dishes on the menu, which includes quite a few vegetarian choices. Bottles of imported beer are only $2, if you can ever get someone to bring you one. *8 6th St., at Market St., tel. 415/626–0927. Closed Sun.*

UNDER $15 • Nori Sushi. Tucked within a small annex of Market Street in the no man's land between Civic Center and the Castro, this joint consists of an L-shape bar, two booths, and one sushi master, Nori himself. Nori's place is always packed with people who know about his superfresh AND incredibly cheap fish. Most *nigiri* (finger-size pieces of fish on a roll of rice) and six-piece rolls are only $3, so two people can have a sushi fest for less than $25 (not including sake). *1815 Market St., No. 5, between Guerrero and Valencia Sts., tel. 415/621–1114. Closed Mon. Cash only.*

Suppenküche. It's hard to find German food that isn't served in a dark, dingy place full of men with beer bellies. Yet this Hayes Valley restaurant has a lively atmosphere and authentic but dignified German cuisine. Share a bowl of creamy, delicious soup ($3.50), and then brace yourself for a main course, like farmer's sausage with sauerkraut and mashed potatoes ($9.50). The always-busy Saturday and Sunday brunch keeps the kitchen humming. *601 Hayes St., at Laguna St., tel. 415/252–9289. No lunch weekdays.*

UNDER $20 • Zuni Café. Zuni offers a slick atmosphere and extravagant Italian-Mediterranean food for a what-the-hell frame of mind. Lots of people just grab a ringside seat near the perennially packed bar and order appetizers and drinks. Sample from the wide selection of oysters ($1.50 each) or try the Caesar salad ($8)—regulars swear it's the best they've ever had. For a full meal, go for the wonderfully crisp and tender roasted chicken with Tuscan stuffing ($28 for two). But be prepared to get a few sneers from the wait staff if you look any younger than 30. *1658 Market St., between Franklin and Gough Sts., tel. 415/552–2522. Closed Mon.*

CHINATOWN

Finding something to eat in Chinatown is a cinch. Finding something *good* to eat—well, that's a little trickier. Steer clear of the glaringly tourist-oriented places and wander through the heart of Chinatown—**Washington, Clay,** and **Sacramento streets** between Mason and Kearny streets—until you find a restaurant that has the four elements that spell success: small, spare, cheap, and packed with locals. Vegetarians should head to **Lucky Creation** (854 Washington St., tel. 415/989–0818) for fantastic meatless fare. **Stockton Street** is the main market street, where you can load up on chow fun, ginger roots, and live turtles.

UNDER $10 • House of Nanking. A few years back, this legendary Chinatown hole-in-the-wall added a new room to accommodate the hordes seeking Nanking's excellent Shanghai home cooking and righteously low prices. You'll still be crammed into tiny tables with total strangers and the no-nonsense waiters will keep you on your toes, but all that only adds to the experience. Ask for the delicious shrimp cakes in peanut sauce ($4)—they're not on the menu—or try the Nanking chicken ($5), a version of General Tso's chicken. *919 Kearny St., between Jackson and Columbus Sts., tel. 415/421–1429. Cash only.*

Meriwa. This wood-paneled, red-bannered banquet hall is the place for a real Chinatown dim sum experience, chicken feet and all. It may be hard to hear yourself think amidst all the chatting Chinese-American families and gossiping old men sharing rounds of schnapps; but you'll be too busy stuffing yourself with tasty dumplings and sticky rice. A reasonably hungry person can fill up for $6 or less. *728 Pacific Ave., at Stockton St., 2nd Floor, tel. 415/989–8868.*

UNDER $15 • R&G Lounge. No one is going to accuse this restaurant of being too festive, but it's worth the minisplurge for super-fresh Cantonese seafood and other dishes such as clams with spicy black bean sauce ($9.50). When money is no object, order the house special salt-and-pepper crab; its price varies according to how hard the fishermen had to work for the catch. *631B Kearny St., between Sacramento and Clay Sts., tel. 415/982–7877.*

NORTH BEACH/RUSSIAN HILL

The old-time Italian neighborhood of North Beach is about strong espresso, lotsa pasta, fresh tomatoes, and the highest concentration of restaurants (and lowest concentration of parking) in the city. **Columbus Avenue** and **Grant Avenue** north of Columbus are lined with reasonably priced restaurants featuring everything from old-fashioned "American-style" Italian food to trendy neo-Italian cuisine. But watch out for traps—this has been a restaurant district for decades, and many establishments come and go with each tourist season.

UNDER $5 • Golden Boy Pizza. Check out what kind of fat, greasy slices are available in the window of this tiny dive—pesto vegetarian or clam garlic (both $3) are good bets. Wash down your pizza with one of the cheap microbrews on tap ($3). *542 Green St., between Grant and Stockton, tel. 415/982–9738. Cash only.*

UNDER $10 • Il Pollaio. This small Italian kitchen serves up tasty grilled chicken, and lots of it, in a homey atmosphere. It's kind of greasy around the edges, but the Italian old-timers who have been coming here for years don't seem to mind. Fill up on a fantastic half chicken with salad, crusty bread, and wine for less than $10; without wine it's only $6.75. Desserts run from flan and cheesecake to chocolate mousse ($2.25). *555 Columbus Ave., between Union and Green Sts., tel. 415/362–7727. Closed Sun.*

L'Osteria del Forno. Two Italian women have created an affordable menu and a chic-but-casual atmosphere at this tiny restaurant. Antipasti and focaccia sandwiches ($3–$6.50) or thin-crust pizza ($2–$4 by the slice; $10–$13 by the small pie) are deliciously authentic. There are usually only one or two pastas available daily, but they're homemade and stuffed with yummy fillings like spinach or pumpkin ($8). *519 Columbus Ave., at Green St., tel. 415/982–1124. Closed Tues. Cash only.*

UNDER $15 • Caffe Macaroni. This place is tiny and usually packed elbow to elbow (though there's an additional room upstairs). But it's worth the wait for some of the city's most affordable, authentic southern Italian food, served with a Neapolitan flair. Most main plates cost between $12 and $14, and pastas between $8.50 and $9.25; the crowd includes everyone from students to suits from the Transamerica Pyramid looming a few blocks away. Look for specials like squid-ink fettuccine heaped with fresh mussels, clams, calamari, and crab legs. *59 Columbus Ave., at Jackson St., tel. 415/956–9737. Closed Sun. Cash only.*

FISHERMAN'S WHARF AND THE MARINA/COW HOLLOW

Steer clear of the mediocre, high-priced seafood restaurants that compete for tourist bucks all along the wharf. The best dining experience you could have here would involve a loaf of sourdough, some cracked crab, a bottle of wine, a seat on the pier, and a tantalizing dining partner. The only authentically rustic place to sit down and eat is **Eagle Café** (upper level, Pier 39, tel. 415/433–3689), where windows and patio tables look out on the waterfront and Alcatraz. It's a good place to eat a bowl of clam chowder ($4.50) and plan your escape from Fisherman's Wharf. If the crowds are getting to you, soothe your nerves with an Irish coffee at the old-fashioned **Buena Vista Café** (2765 Hyde St., tel. 415/474–5044), which purportedly introduced the drink to America. Although not exactly a budget locale, the **Marina** has recently been flooded with scores of new culinary hotspots. A 10-minute walk west of Fisherman's Wharf brings you to lots of upscale restaurants—from grills to sushi spots to California-cuisine eateries—all along **Chestnut** and **Union streets.**

UNDER $5 • Pluto's. A wall covered with adjectives describing food is part of Pluto's modern decor, but you won't need this to make you hungry after waiting in line with the young Marina folks who come here in droves. The biggest line forms for the salad bar, where you can create a custom-made salad ($3.25–$4.50). The herb-roasted Sonoma turkey ($3.25) with the smashed spuds of the day ($1.45) will make you feel like you're having a top-notch Thanksgiving dinner. Breakfast is served on weekends. *3258 Scott St., at Chestnut St., tel. 415/775–8867.*

UNDER $40 • Greens. Head here for a treat after a long day of museums and cultural enrichment—or any time for that matter—and you'll entirely reevaluate your notion of vegetarian dining. Greens serves state-of-the-art gourmet meals in a beautifully spacious, gallerylike setting with a romantic view of the Golden Gate Bridge. The menu is always fresh and often eclectic: You might see such things as soft polenta with chipotle butter and smoked cheese or a sandwich of charcoal-grilled tofu with horseradish mayonnaise on potato bread. "Cafe Dinners" feature entrées in the $10–$14 range, while the Saturday evening (mandatory) five-course prix-fixe menu costs $38. *Fort Mason, Bldg. A, tel. 415/771–6222. Closed Mon. lunch, Sun. dinner.*

JAPANTOWN

In the **Japan Center** (1737 Post St., between Geary and Fillmore Sts.), the veritable essence of Japantown, a bunch of decent restaurants display their edibles via shiny photos or shellacked, plastic miniatures. If nothing piques your interest, explore the surrounding streets, especially **Buchanan** and **Webster streets** to the north of the center, for older, more divey places that occasionally turn out to be gems. The cheapest option of all is to visit the Japanese market **Maruwa** (open Mon.–Sat. 10–7, Sun. 10–6), on the corner of Post and Webster streets. Along with fruits and vegetables and all manner of Japanese products, the delicatessen offers sushi, rice and noodle dishes, and individual cuts of meat.

UNDER $10 • Isobune. Patrons at this touristy but fun sushi restaurant pack in around a large table and fish their sushi off little boats that bob about in the water in front of them. Kimono-clad chefs deftly mold the sushi and replenish the boats' cargoes as fast as they are emptied. Prices range from $1.20 for two pieces of mackerel or fried bean cake to $3 for two pieces of salmon roe or red clam. It may not be the best sushi you'll ever eat, but it's good enough for the price. *Japan Center, 1737 Post St., tel. 415/563–1030. Oakland location: 5897 College Ave., at Chabot St., tel. 510/601–1424.*

Mifune. A steady stream of Asian and American patrons slurp up cheap, tasty *udon* (thick white noodles), *soba* (thin buckwheat noodles), and *donburi* (rice) dishes in the simple Mifune dining room. The noodles, which are homemade and come with various meats and vegetables—mountain potato, chicken, fish cake, shrimp, seaweed, beef—cost anywhere from $3.50 for a plain broth to $8.50. *Japan Center, 1737 Post St., tel. 415/922–0337.*

THE HAIGHT

The Haight (both Upper and Lower) abounds with good breakfast places full to the brim with today's youth—the ones wearing black and sunglasses, smoking, and sucking on coffee like it's the primal life force. For dinner there are a few trendy hot spots among the pizza joints.

UNDER $5 • Kan Zaman. Patrons pack into this trendy Mediterranean restaurant to listen to hypnotic Middle Eastern music and indulge in hummus ($3.70), baba ghanoush ($3.70), and spinach pies ($3.50). On Friday, Saturday, and Sunday nights the Fat Chance Belly Dancers do their seductive thing. *1793 Haight St., at Shrader St., tel. 415/751–9656. Cash only.*

Taqueria El Balazo. Balazo's appeal is that it *isn't* the Mission—it's new-agey Cal-Mex food instead. Choose from three kinds of veggie burritos (about $4), stuffed with saffron rice, beans, Mexican goat cheese, and/or vegetables sautéed on a vegetarian grill. The burrito vallarta ($5), with sautéed rock prawns, tender nopales cactus, red peppers, and black beans, is so good you'll want to come back tomorrow and eat it again. The kitchen also turns out huge dinner platters (about $5) that are meant to be shared. Eat in the back room and you will sometimes be treated to live flamenco guitar. *1654 Haight St., between Belvedere and Clayton Sts., tel. 415/864–8608. Cash only.*

UNDER $10 • Kate's Kitchen. Get here early, especially on weekend mornings, unless you want to wait forever for a table. The wholesome food, though, is worth the wait. Chummy servers bring you specials like buttermilk-cornmeal pancakes ($4 short, $6 tall) or hush puppies with honey butter ($2.25 for six). The fruit orgy (fresh fruit, yogurt, honey, and granola; $5) is aptly named. *471 Haight St., between Fillmore and Webster Sts., tel. 415/626–3984. No dinner.*

Massawa. If you've never had Ethiopian food, and you (1) like to eat with your hands and (2) relish unusual spices, then you must come here. You get a dinner platter filled with tender lamb or beef ($8–$10), usually with side portions of lentils, greens, or yellow split-pea paste. (Vegetarian dishes run $6–$9). All plates come with *injera,* a flat, spongy bread used instead of silverware to scoop up food. *1538 Haight St., between Ashbury and Clayton Sts., tel. 415/621–4129.*

Squat and Gobble Café. This sprawling café-turned-breakfast-spot serves up home-style breakfasts to Lower Haight types who come armed with the Sunday paper, a pack of Marlboro reds, and nothing to do all day. Try the massive Lower Haight Omelet, with fresh veggies, pesto, and cheese ($5.35), or any number of inventive crêpes. There's also a decent selection of salads and sandwiches. Be aware that coffee refills are not free. *237 Fillmore St., between Haight and Waller Sts., tel. 415/487–0551. Other location: 1428 Haight St., between Ashbury and Masonic Sts., tel. 415/864–8484.*

Ya Halla. Never mind this particularly grimy stretch of the Lower Haight—inside you'll find a peaceful enclave, replete with soothing Middle Eastern music. Chef Nadia attracts loyal customers with extremely fresh, delicious falafel and homestyle main dishes ($5.25–$8). All meals come with a plate of feta and olives, but the *meze* (appetizers; $3.25) are worth getting stuffed for. Both the eggplant musakaa'h (roasted tomato, garlic, pine nuts, and rice pilaf; $6), and the super falafel (hummus, mulabal, and tabouleh in a burrito-style lavash wrap; $4), are incredible. *494 Haight St., near Fillmore St., tel. 415/522–1509.*

A CHEAP TRIP TO THE BORDER

San Francisco and the burrito have a serious love affair going on. For people who lack kitchens and/or money, the hefty concoctions can be a major nutritional staple. Below are some of the best places to get your fix.

Renowned all over the Mission for its homemade tortillas, chips, and salsa, Casa Sanchez (2778 24th St., tel. 415/282–2400) serves up filling combo platters for $4–$5. Stagger in to El Farolito (2777 Mission St., tel. 415/824–7877) for a burrito as late as 2:45 AM (3:45 AM on Fri. and Sat.). If you're in the right state, you might not notice the grimy atmosphere. The always-packed Pancho Villa taquería (3071 16th St., tel. 415/864–8840) is a step above the myriad others. The eclectic, ever-changing artwork is fun to peruse, and mariachi bands often perform on weekends. Taquería Cancun (2288 Mission St., tel. 415/252–9560), a taquería típica, serves one of the best veggie burritos around ($3).

UNDER $15 • Cha Cha Cha. You'll enjoy the skillfully prepared tapas and the pseudo-Catholic icons on the walls, but even though a new room was recently added, you'll still wait all night for a table. Entrées range from $10 to $13, but it's *de rigueur* to stick to tapas ($5–$8) like fried plantains with black beans and sour cream or shrimp sautéed in Cajun spices. Wash down all the spices and other culinary flourishes with plenty of sangria (which can help you pass your possibly two-hour wait). To avoid the crowds, come for a late lunch. *1801 Haight St., at Shrader St., tel. 415/386–7670.*

CASTRO/NOE VALLEY

The Castro teems with cute, slightly pricey restaurants, many with outdoor patios for optimum people-watching. Brunch seems to be the favorite meal, followed closely by after-hours dining: You won't have to travel far for a mimosa or a late-night diner. Just over the hill from the Castro around 24th Street, **Noe Valley** is a placid oasis awash with young liberal professionals, including a sizable lesbian contingent. It's a popular destination on sunny weekend mornings for a lazy brunch and a bit of window-shopping with the dog and/or the stroller. At night Noe gets fairly quiet, as it's mostly residential.

UNDER $5 • Hot 'n Hunky. This little pink restaurant decorated with Marilyn Monroe posters is a Castro institution for thick, juicy burgers. With names like the Macho Man (¾-pounder; $4), I Wanna Hold Your Ham (burger with ham and Swiss; $4), and Ms. Piggy (burger with cheddar and bacon; $3.50), ordering is half the fun. (Veggie garden burgers, at $4, are also dee-lish.) *4039 18th St., near Castro St., tel. 415/621–6365. Cash only.*

UNDER $10 • No-Name (Nippon) Sushi. Everybody calls it No-Name Sushi, even though the proprietors did eventually put up a tiny sign in the window officially dubbing it "Nippon." This small wood-paneled restaurant on Church Street almost always has a line out the door because it serves huge sushi combos at prices that are hard to believe—$6–$10. (For such low prices some freshness is compromised.) No alcohol is served, but most people bring theirs in a bag. *314 Church St., at 15th St., no phone. Closed Sun. Cash only.*

Patio Café. The Castro's premiere brunch spot operates out of an enormous converted greenhouse complete with fake parrots perched among the foliage. Enough Bloody Marys ($3) are consumed here to conk out a small army. Eggs or omelets with home fries go for $4–$7, and sinful cheese blintzes with cherry sauce are $7. Later in the day, you can chow down on sandwiches, burgers, and pastas ($5–$8), or come for a more formal dinner, like a grilled New York steak ($13). *531 Castro St., between 18th and 19th Sts., tel. 415/621–4640.*

UNDER $15 • Thai House on Noe. The rich, spicy curries and elegant dining room make this Duboce Triangle restaurant a popular choice for an intimate dinner. Try the duck on a bed of spinach with hot chili sauce ($9) or the mixed seafood in red curry with vegetables and basil ($10). There's often a wait, so reserve ahead. **Thai House II,** right around the corner on Market Street, has more room. *151 Noe St., at Henry St., tel. 415/863–0374. Thai House II: 2200 Market St., at Sanchez St., tel. 415/864–5006.*

MISSION DISTRICT

Here you can wander from taquería to café to bookstore to taquería again in a salsa-and-cerveza-induced state of bliss. To add to the zillions of Mexican and Central American spots that already crowd the neighborhood, a smattering of trendy restaurants has sprouted up in recent years around the intersection of **16th** and **Valencia streets**—this is the favorite area in town for young hipsters to wine and dine. The Mission's restaurants are accessible from either the 16th St./Mission or the 24th St./Mission BART stations.

UNDER $10 • Ti Couz. An impatient crowd hangs around the bar sipping cider out of *bols,* waiting (no reservations) to get a taste of the succulent, piping-hot crêpes whipped up after the style of Breton crêperies in western France. You'll want one of the light pancakes for dinner *and* dessert. A main course, with savory fillings like ratatouille, smoked salmon, or mushrooms, will run you $3–$6, while a sweet crêpe (i.e., filled with Nutella and banana or fragrant poached pears) will set you back $2–$5. *3108 16th St., at Valencia St., tel. 415/252–7373.*

UNDER $15 • Esperpento. Decorated with colorful Miró-esque touches, Esperpento often has lines snaking out the door on weekends. People might be waiting for delicacies like clams with white beans ($6) and *tortilla de patatas* (potato and onion pancake; $4.75) or huge *paella* dinners ($26 for two). The sangria is tastier and cheaper than at most tapas joints. *3295 22nd St., between Valencia and Mission Sts., tel. 415/282–8867. Cash only.*

Slanted Door. Reserve ahead for this decidedly subdued and elegant, if trendy, upscale Vietnamese restaurant. The vegetarian-friendly menu includes subtle dishes like vegetable curry (shitake mushrooms, yams, and cauliflower; $8), or "spicy squid stir fried" (delicately infused with red pepper, garlic, and other spices; $8.50). Wash it down with a pot of exotic tea ($3–$5) or a microbrew ($3.25). *584 Valencia St., at 17th St., tel. 415/861–8032. Closed Mon.*

SOUTH OF MARKET

If you eat in SoMa, you'll see harried Financial District workers trying to unwind and youthful clubbers fueling up for an evening out on the town. Wander along Folsom Street between 7th and 11th streets, or along 11th and 9th streets between Howard and Harrison streets, and you'll have the SoMa eating scene in the palm of your hand. **Club Za Pizza** (371 11th St., between Folsom and Harrison Sts., tel. 415/552–5599) is a convenient spot for a $3 "zlice" late at night.

UNDER $10 • Hamburger Mary's. The messy hamburgers ($6–$11) and the cluttered decor go together wonderfully. Come by at 1 AM to hang out with SoMa clubbers in various states of inebriation and undress. Vegetarians can feast on the tofu burger ($6) or the Meatless Meaty (a hot sandwich of mushrooms, cream cheese, and olives; $7). Don't pass up the wonderfully spicy home fries. *1582 Folsom St., at 12th St., tel. 415/626–5767.*

Manora's Thai Cuisine. The location on Folsom is trendier than most Thai restaurants in the city, so big crowds pack the bar before being seated—but the fresh, attractive dishes here are worth the wait. Garlic quail is $8, and spicy Japanese eggplant with prawns, chicken, and pork goes for $7.50. If soft-shell crabs are on the menu, don't pass them up. *1600 Folsom St., at 12th St., tel. 415/861–6224. Closed lunch weekends.*

UNDER $20 • Lulu. A nouvelle French/Italian/Californian meal at Lulu's is worth the money. Besides, dishes are served family style, which means that you can try a little of everything and not spend too much. Roasted meat entrées ($11–$16.50) as well as grilled vegetables are the specialties. Pastas ($8.50–$10.50) are fantastically rustic, and thin-crust pizzas ($9–$10.25) taste as amazing as they look. Or, sample oysters ($1.35 each) at the bar or adjacent café—where you can order from the regular menu if the main dining room is full. For a morning fix, unfold your newspaper in the cafe at 7 am and munch on a flaky croissant—or something more substantial—then chase it with a double espresso. *816 Folsom St., at 4th St., tel. 415/495–5775.*

CAFÉS

San Francisco is a city of people who believe in the connection between coffee and the arts. Early acolytes of this philosophy include Beat poets Jack Kerouac and Allen Ginsberg, who held all manner of performances at Caffè Trieste (*see below*) in North Beach. Romantic, European-style North Beach is still a popular place to grab a demitasse on a rainy day, especially if you have someone to hold hands with under the table. Postmodern hipsters will feel more comfortable discussing the revolution in cafés South of Market or in the Haight. The Mission, a hotbed for experimental art in San Francisco, has recently sprouted java dens attracting bohemians new and old. Anywhere in the city, expect to pay $1–$3 for coffee drinks.

Café Flore. Flore is one of the Castro's premier gathering spots for pseudo-artists, political activists, and trendy boys in black turtlenecks. If the outside tables are full, strike a pose until someone makes room—sharing tables is de rigueur. Expect plenty of noise, action, and, in the midst of it all, someone incredibly attractive looking furtively your way. *2298 Market St., at Noe St., tel. 415/621–8579.*

Café Istanbul. The Syrian owner of this unique café serves authentic, delicious Middle Eastern food and drink in an exotic, tapestried setting. The floor is festooned with pillows, and intricately scrolled, gold-color trays function as tabletops. Take off your shoes and settle down with some *dolmas* (stuffed grape leaves), *baklava* (pastry with honey and nuts), or cardamom-spiked Turkish coffee. *525 Valencia St., between 16th and 17th Sts., tel. 415/863–8854.*

Caffè Trieste. This is the legendary home of the Beat generation, where Kerouac and friends oozed cool from every pore. And it hasn't changed—including the '50s jukebox, which spouts opera. Saturday at 2 PM, local Italian performers serenade guests with sentimental Italian tunes, accompanied by a live mini orchestra. *601 Vallejo St., at Grant Ave., tel. 415/392–6739.*

Gathering Café. Jazz aficionados should not miss this spot, which offers nightly live music (weeknights no cover, weekends $2–$3). The small marble tables and black-and-white checkered floor evoke a tiny jazz bar in Paris, not a San Francisco café three blocks from the GIRLS! GIRLS! GIRLS! of Broadway's red-light district. *1326 Grant Ave., between Green and Vallejo Sts., tel. 415/433–4247.*

Horse Shoe. For disaffected youths with tattoos, piercings, and time on their hands, this is the place to be in San Francisco. Regulars come for chess, shouted conversation over cranked-up music, or to peruse the millions of posted flyers. *566 Haight St., between Steiner and Fillmore Sts., tel. 415/626–8852.*

Radio Valencia. This friendly place is all about music, from the vintage instruments on the walls to the carefully chosen tunes playing over the speakers. Owner Don Allen used to work in radio in Wisconsin, and now he (and other staff members) draw up a fresh playlist daily, displayed in a "menu" on each table. Local jazz and indie groups are often featured. Friday through Sunday nights, come in for live jazz, blues, bluegrass, and swing. *1199 Valencia St., at 23rd St., tel. 415/826–1199.*

EXPLORING SAN FRANCISCO

Despite the hills, San Francisco is best explored on foot. For you haven't truly experienced the city until you've climbed up one of Russian Hill's narrow, hidden stairway streets; wandered for a day or two in Golden Gate Park; and bounded from gallery to gallery in SoMa. When you finally tire—as you inevitably will—hop aboard a bus for a higher-speed version of the San Francisco experience: You can get a MUNI "Street and Transit Map" at most liquor and grocery stores for $2.50. The **30 Stockton Bus** travels through some of the city's most interesting neighborhoods, including North Beach, Russian Hill, the Marina, Fisherman's Wharf, the eastern tip of the Presidio, and Chinatown. Pick it up near the Montgomery Street BART station.

MAJOR SIGHTS

The city's "big six" offer something for everyone. Though the carnival air of Fisherman's Wharf is often derided as "too touristy," even the most jaded natives can't help but inhale a reverent breath at the sight of the majestic Golden Gate Bridge. The Alcatraz tour explores such a fascinating place—on such a genuinely stark, scary island—that, for all the hype, it is utterly compelling. And Coit Tower and Golden Gate Park are forever places to get in touch with quintessential San Francisco.

GOLDEN GATE BRIDGE

More than 1 mi long, the bridge-to-end-all-bridges has come to symbolize San Francisco. This masterpiece of design and engineering, which links San Francisco to its wealthy neighbor, Marin County, has withstood wind, fog, the daily load of 100,000 cars, the ignominy of over 1,000 suicides, and the combined weight of more than 200,000 people who showed up all at once to celebrate the suspension bridge's 50th birthday back in 1987. The "Golden" Gate is painted International Orange for visibility in fog—so that seagulls and low-flying planes don't crash into it. To stroll across and back takes about an hour (and the winds can be freezing); Bus 28 will drop you at the toll plaza, where you can begin your walk.

Below the bridge on the San Francisco side is historic **Fort Point** (tel. 415/556–1693). The massive fort was designed to hold 500 soldiers and 126 cannons, though it never fired a single shot. Drop by for free guided tours and "cannon drills" daily 10–5. From U.S. 101 north, exit at Lincoln Boulevard ("last SF exit"), then follow signs.

ALCATRAZ ISLAND

A few years ago, sea lions took over several docks at Pier 39. The owners wanted them removed until they realized the barking mammals were attracting more tourists.

"The Rock" served for 59 years as the nation's most notorious federal penitentiary, holding high-risk prisoners—including Al Capone, Robert "The Birdman" Stroud, and Machine Gun Kelly—in its maw. The prison closed in 1963; six years later, a group of Native Americans occupied the island in an attempt to reclaim it, declaring that an 1868 federal treaty allows Native Americans to use all federal territory not actively being used by the government. After almost two years, the U.S. government forced them off. Today the island is part of the national park system, and tourists visit its grounds in hordes.

The **Red and White Fleet** (tel. 800/229–2784 for information or 415/546–2700 for tickets) ferries you to the island from San Francisco's Pier 41. The price ($10) includes the ferry ride and an audiocassette tour of the prison; tapes are available in several languages, and the average tour takes about 2½ hours including the boat ride. You can skip the cassette tour and pay only $6.75, but the tape, which features former Alcatraz inmates and guards, is one of the best parts of the experience. Ferries leave Pier 41 9:30 AM–2:30 PM year-round (until 4:15 PM June–August). You'll need a Visa, American Express, or MasterCard to reserve tickets by phone and you'll pay a $2 per ticket service charge. If you're buying tickets in person, go to the ferry ticket office (open 8:30–5) at Pier 41. You should reserve or purchase tickets *several* days in advance. Bus 32 will get you to Pier 41 from the Ferry Building downtown.

FISHERMAN'S WHARF

Once the domain of Italian fishermen, the wharf is now San Francisco's prize tourist trap. You won't see many fishermen here unless you arrive in the misty early morning hours (around 5 AM) to watch the fishing boats unload. Otherwise, Jefferson Street, the wharf's main drag, is packed with expensive seafood restaurants, tacky souvenir shops, and "museums" like the **Wax Museum, Ripley's Believe It or Not!,** the **Guinness Museum of World Records, The Haunted Gold Mine,** and the **Medieval Dungeon** (featuring graphic re-creations of torture devices from the Middle Ages). Each can be yours for the low admission price of $6–$10. The only thing that remains fairly authentic (albeit rather pricey) is the array of seafood stands along Jefferson Street. If the weather's nice, buy clam chowder ($3–$4) or a half-pound of shrimp ($7) from one of the sidewalk vendors and a loaf of sourdough bread ($2.50–$3.25) from **Boudin Bakery** (156 Jefferson St., tel. 415/928–1849), and eat on a pier, watching cruise ships and fishing boats glide in and out of the harbor.

Three shopping complexes girdle the wharf: **Pier 39,** the **Cannery,** and **Ghirardelli Square.** Owned by the billionaire Bass brothers of Texas, Pier 39 (tel. 415/981–7437) is a lackluster imitation of a turn-of-the-century New England seaport village. A former Del Monte peach-canning factory, the **Cannery** (2801 Leavenworth St., between Beach and Jefferson Sts., tel. 415/771–3112) is now a gallery of chic boutiques. Chocolate is no longer made on-site at **Ghirardelli Square** (900 North Point St., tel. 415/775–5500), but you can buy it here in bars or atop a huge, tasty ice cream sundae ($6). To reach Fisherman's Wharf, take Bus 32 from the Ferry Building downtown. Or fulfill your other tourist obligation by taking a cable car (*see above*) from Powell Street.

DOWNTOWN SAN FRANCISCO

Sights ●

Ansel Adams Center, **35**

Cable Car Museum, **18**

Capp Street Project, **36**

Cartoon Art Museum, **40**

Center for the Arts, **32**

Chinatown Gate, **30**

Chinese Telephone Exchange, **19**

City Hall, **51**

City Lights Bookstore, **14**

Coit Tower, **15**

"Crookedest Street" (Lombard Street), **8**

Embarcadero Center, **23**

Exploratorium/Palace of Fine Arts, **2**

Fairmont Hotel, **27**

Ferry Building, **24**

Golden Gate Fortune Cookie Factory, **16**

Grace Cathedral, **28**

Haas-Lilienthal House, **7**

Herbst Theatre, **60**

Jackson Square Historical District, **21**

Japan Center, **66**

Justin Herman Plaza, **25**

Kabuki 8 Theatres, **64**

Kabuki Hot Springs, **63**

Louise M. Davies Symphony Hall, **58**

Mark Hopkins Hotel/Top of the Mark, **29**

Mary Ellen Pleasant Memorial, **67**

Painted Ladies, **61**

Peace Plaza, **65**

Portsmouth Square, **20**

San Francisco Main Library, **56**

San Francisco Museum of Modern Art, **33**

Six Sixty Center, **38**

SoMa Flower Market, **39**

South Park, **37**

Tin Hou Temple, **17**

DOWNTOWN SAN FRANCISCO

Transamerica Pyramid, **22**
Transbay Terminal, **31**
UFO, Bigfoot, and Loch Ness Monster Museum, **10**
Union Square, **43**
United Nations Plaza, **53**
War Memorial Opera House, **59**
Washington Square, **11**
Wave Organ, **3**
Yerba Buena Gardens, **34**

Lodging ○
Adelaide Inn, **44**
Aida Hotel, **52**
Amsterdam, **46**
Art Center Bed and Breakfast, **4**
Auberge des Artistes, **62**
AYH Hostel at Union Square, **42**
Biltmore Hotel, **45**
Brady Acres, **49**
Ft. Mason International Hostel, **5**
Grand Central Hostel, **57**
Green Tortoise Guest House, **13**
Hotel Bohème, **12**
Interclub Globe Hostel, **55**
Marina Motel, **1**
Nob Hill Pensione, **48**
Pacific Tradewinds, **26**
Phoenix Hotel, **50**
San Francisco International Student Center, **54**
San Francisco Residence Club, **47**
San Remo Hotel, **9**
Stratford Inn, **41**
Travelodge, **6**

If you lack the stamina or credit rating to shop Fisherman's Wharf, set a course for the **U.S.S. *Pampanito Submarine*** ($5, Pier 45, tel. 415/929–0202) or the **Maritime Museum** (Beach St., at foot of Polk St., tel. 415/556–3002), housed in an art deco building that features all sorts of artifacts from the maritime history of San Francisco. Admission is free, but for $3 you might have more fun walking around on one of the old ships at Hyde Street Pier (between the Cannery and Ghirardelli Square), managed by the Maritime Museum. Docked there are the ***Balclutha***, a 100-year-old square-rigged ship; the ***Eureka***, a newly restored turn-of-the century paddlewheel ferry; and the ***C.A. Thayer***, an equally venerable schooner. Comedian Jonathan Winters was once briefly institutionalized after he climbed the mast of the *Balclutha* and hung from it, shouting "I am the man in the moon!" At the other end of the wharf, **UnderWater World** (Beach St. just east of Pier 39, tel. 415/623–5300) is a 707,000-gallon "diver's-eye view" aquarium, where visitors listen to a taped 30-minute tour as they glide through a 300-ft-long transparent tunnel. Though the two main tanks are full of sharks, rays, anemones, and 10,000 types of fish, many visitors seem more amused by the scuba divers who scrub the tanks each morning. It's entertaining, but the $12.95 admission price is steep for an attraction that you can breeze through in under an hour.

COIT TOWER

Built to memorialize San Francisco's volunteer firefighters, the 210-ft concrete observation tower atop Telegraph Hill is named for the colorful woman who left the funds to build it, Lillie Hitchcock Coit (1843–1929). Heiress Coit was a cross-dresser (she could gain access to the city's more interesting realms in men's clothes) who literally chased fire engines around town. Most people agree the building resembles a fire-hose—supposedly, that's not intentional.

The walls inside the lobby are covered with Depression-era murals in the style of Diego Rivera, painted by local artists on the government dole. **City Guides** (tel. 415/557–4266) offers free descriptive tours of the tower every Saturday at 11 AM, including murals on the second floor, which are normally closed to the public. The elevator ($3) inside the tower will take you to the top for a drop-dead, 360° view of Golden Gate Bridge, the Bay Bridge, and Alcatraz. *Tel. 415/362–0808. From Market and 3rd Sts. downtown, Bus 30 or 45 to Washington Sq.; walk 2 blocks east on Union St., left on Kearny St. Or Bus 39 from Fisherman's Wharf. Tower open daily 10–6:30.*

GOLDEN GATE PARK

Golden Gate Park is San Francisco's pride: 1,000 acres of manicured gardens, museums, playing fields, and bridle paths, not to mention a few Dutch windmills and a paddock full of bison. Wooded areas, wide swaths of open field, formal flower beds, and a zillion other varieties of vegetation are all packed into an area that is 4 mi long and less than a mi wide. And, if you make it all the way to the western end of the park, you'll hit blustery Ocean Beach and the Pacific Ocean. The park's eastern boundary, lying close to Haight Street, has always been a hangout for the countercultural denizens of that neighborhood: Hippie historians should note that Ken Kesey and friends celebrated the first **Human Be-In** here on January 14, 1966. Fittingly, a devotional shrine was erected in tribute to Jerry Garcia's death in 1995. The park has hosted rock concerts ranging from the Grateful Dead and Jefferson Airplane to Pearl Jam and the Beastie Boy's Tibetan Freedom benefit.

Once a lonely stretch of sand dunes, Golden Gate Park is now home to blue gum eucalyptus, Monterey pine, Monterey cypress, and one of the world's foremost horticultural displays. **Strybing Arboretum and Botanical Gardens** (tel. 415/661–1316, $1 donation suggested), near the intersection of 9th Avenue and Lincoln Way, has a dazzling 70 acres of plants, featuring some 5,000 specimens arranged by country of origin, genus, and fragrance. Another star attraction is the **Japanese Tea Garden** (tel. 415/752–4227). The meticulously designed garden features an exquisite 18th-century Buddha and a scanty number of koi in the fish ponds—survivors of raids by local raccoons and hawks. It's open daily 9–6:30 (shorter hrs in winter) and admission is $2.50 (free before 9:30 AM and after 5:30 PM).

Golden Gate Park is bordered by Stanyan Street, the Great Highway, Lincoln Way, and Fulton Street. On Sunday, when flocks of bicyclists, in-line skaters, and skateboarders take over, John F. Kennedy Drive (the park's main thoroughfare) is closed to car traffic between Stanyan Street and 19th Avenue. Several places near the park rent bikes and in-line skates: **Park Cyclery** (1749 Waller St., at Stanyan St., tel. 415/752–8383) rents mountain bikes for $5 an hour or $25 a day. **Skate Pro Sports** (2549 Irving St., between 26th and 27th Aves., tel. 415/752–8776), near a less-traveled part of the park, offers a good deal on blades: $5 per hour or $20 per day, including pads and a helmet. For park information and maps, drop by the **McLaren Lodge** (John F. Kennedy Dr., near Stanyan St., tel. 415/666–7200) weekdays 8–5. From downtown or Civic Center, take Bus 5, 71, or 73 to reach the park.

THE PRESIDIO

The Presidio, a 1,480-acre chunk of prime waterfront land stretching from the western end of the Marina all the way to the Golden Gate Bridge, was originally a fort founded by the Spanish in 1776. The flags of Mexico, the Bear Flag Republic, and the U.S. Army have all flown over the Presidio—one of the oldest military installations in the United States. The land was turned over to the National Park Service in 1994, though it remains to be seen how much will be developed and how much will remain open space: Enjoy the 1,500 acres of rolling hills, forests, and attractive old military buildings while you can. The **Officer's Club** (Moraga Ave.) contains one adobe wall reputed to date from 1776. The free **Presidio Museum** (Funston Ave. at Lincoln Blvd., tel. 415/561–4331; open Wed.–Sun. 10–4) has a collection relating to the Presidio's history.

The easiest way to get to the Presidio is to drive north toward the bay on Van Ness Avenue, turn left on Lombard Street, and then follow the signs. Otherwise, take Bus 38 from Montgomery Street BART/MUNI station to Geary Boulevard and Presidio Avenue, then switch to Bus 43, which travels into the Presidio.

NEIGHBORHOODS

Though the city of San Francisco is a compact 49 square mi, its neighborhoods guard their individuality like medieval fiefdoms. Each district is a distinct entity culturally, socially, and often politically, and they are all fascinating grounds for urban exploration. The best way to experience the city's neighborhoods is on foot: Plan your walk with a map, or just start off in an interesting spot and surrender to the whims of the streets. If you're near the waterfront, try **North Beach** and **Chinatown.** Farther inland, the **Mission, Noe Valley,** and **Castro** districts are all eminently walkable.

Two old-fashioned stairways lead to Coit Tower: "Filbert Street Steps" are narrow wooden walkways through lush private gardens; the concrete "Greenwich Street Stairs" offer stunning views.

DOWNTOWN

For better or worse, Downtown is grand old San Francisco—that of tea dances, cocktail hours, piano bars, fedoras, and big winter overcoats. Looking up at the beautiful architectural details, you might forget what century it is. More recently the downtown area has also become the major concentration of money-making businesses.

UNION SQUARE • Union Square is the physical heart—though not the soul—of the city, especially for tourists who come to shop, browse the galleries, attend the theater, and then sleep in one of the posh hotels. The square, bordered by Powell, Post, Stockton, and Geary streets, was named in honor of pro-Union rallies held prior to the Civil War. Some San Franciscans will tell you the name more appropriately refers to the huge demonstrations held here in the 1930s by labor organizations, which at one point effectively shut down the city for a week. Today Union Square consists of a lackluster park encircled by a ring—make that a solid gold band—of the city's ritziest stores and boutiques, including Neiman-Marcus, Saks, Chanel, Tiffany, Cartier, Hermès, Gump's, Giorgio Armani, Ralph Lauren, and brand-new NikeTown. Combined, Union Square merchants ring up an estimated $1 billion in sales annually. Even so, the park tends toward seediness at night; linger elsewhere.

Maiden Lane, a short alley off the east side of Union Square, was once home to the "cribs" (brothels) of a rowdy, notorious red-light district. Now it's a shopping arcade for the thick-walleted. The building at **140 Maiden Lane** is San Francisco's only Frank Lloyd Wright building, which served as the prototype for the Guggenheim Museum in New York City.

Heading south on Powell Street from Union Square, you'll come to the intersection of Market and Powell streets. Here lie the cable-car turnaround, Powell Street BART station, and **San Francisco Visitor Information Center** (*see* Basics, *above*), the latter found below the street in Hallidie Plaza. Market Street is also home to a string of cheap fast-food joints.

TRANSAMERICA PYRAMID • The Pyramid (600 Montgomery St., between Clay and Washington Sts.) is *the* distinguishing feature of the San Francisco skyline. The interior is less impressive (and closed to the public). Adjacent to the Pyramid is a small, peaceful redwood park (open weekdays 8–6).

BARBARY COAST • In the 1850s, San Francisco was home to the Barbary Coast, one of the most infamous red-light districts ever. It was not uncommon to enter a bar, get drugged, be clubbed, or fall through a trap door, and find yourself a prisoner-sailor heading for the Orient the next morning. The strip of Pacific Street between Sansome Street and Columbus Avenue was the heart of the action: Every

CHINATOWN'S FANCIFUL PAGODAS

Many people blamed a late-1800s job shortage on the Chinese and wanted to completely destroy Chinatown. Thanks to some local politicians, Chinatown was saved and remodeled to attract tourists. American and European architects were put to work, projecting their stereotypes of Asian building styles, to create a Chinese theme park.

building along this street was formerly a saloon, gambling hall, or brothel. Today you can still visit the remains of the Barbary Coast at the **Jackson Square Historical District** just north of the Financial District. To the chagrin of Bible-thumping reformists, many of the buildings survived the 1906 earthquake and fire.

THE EMBARCADERO • The Embarcadero, Spanish for "wharf," looks more like a string of office buildings than anything maritime. One exception is the **Ferry Building** (Embarcadero and Market St.); its 230-ft clocktower was modeled after Venice's Campanile. Ferries depart from here for points around the Bay (*see* Getting Around, *above*). The **Embarcadero Center** (tel. 800/733–6318) is a set of four nearly identical concrete towers with restaurants, 175 chichi shops, a movie theater, and the new **Skydeck** (1 Embarcadero Center, 41st floor, tel. 888/737–5933), an indoor/outdoor observation area ($4) with impressive views. Between the center and the Ferry Building stretches **Justin Herman Plaza,** a favorite of brown-bagging office workers and thrill-seeking young skateboarders. Free concerts happen some weekdays at noon. At one corner Jean Dubuffet's mammoth stainless-steel sculpture *La Chiffonière* poses like a Napoleonic Pillsbury doughboy. At the other lurks Armand Vallaincourt's huge building-block fountain, resembling prehistoric plumbing.

CIVIC CENTER

The Civic Center is the locus of city government and host to many cultural events, including dance, opera, and theater. It's also where a good percentage of San Francisco's homeless have camped out since the 1940s. **City Hall,** built in classic Beaux Arts style, dominates the skyline with its impressive bronze rotunda. Even more impressive is the history City Hall has witnessed: Joe DiMaggio and Marilyn Monroe got married here on January 15, 1954. In 1960, protesters were washed down the central stairway with giant fire hoses while hearings of the House Un-American Activities Committee took place inside. And in 1978 Mayor George Moscone and Supervisor Harvey Milk (the first openly gay elected official in the United States) were murdered here by former city supervisor Dan White. *Between Van Ness Ave. and Grove, McAllister, and Polk Sts.*

Surrounding City Hall are many of the city's cultural mainstays. On Van Ness Avenue the **Louise M. Davies Symphony Hall, Herbst Theatre,** and stately **War Memorial Opera House** are for high culture. Volunteers conduct 75-minute tours ($3) of the three buildings every Monday; call 415/552–8338 for more information. The sparkling new **San Francisco Main Library** (Larkin St. at Grove St., tel. 415/557–4400) is one of the most technologically advanced in the country. It houses a fine collection of books, records, CDs, and San Francisco memorabilia, as well as 300 computer terminals, many with free Web access and CD-ROM capability. Far from a mere place to browse books, it also has a café, a rooftop garden, an incredible children's library, an excellent video library, an African American center, the nation's first Gay and Lesbian Archive Center, an Asian American center, and more, more, more!

If you're walking around the area, head to Hayes Street between Franklin and Webster streets; dubbed **Hayes Valley,** this area is loaded with vintage clothing boutiques, quirky book shops, art galleries, cafés, and restaurants.

Just east of City Hall is the sprawling **Civic Center Plaza,** which has seen its share of protest marches, political rallies (those during the Persian Gulf War drew crowds of over 200,000), and riots. Continue east to the intersection of Market and Seventh streets to find **United Nations Plaza,** commemorating the founding of the United Nations—in San Francisco—in 1945. The plaza is presided over by a dramatic statue of South American revolutionary war hero Simón Bolívar.

POLK GULCH • Once the gay heart of San Francisco, Polk Gulch (Polk Street between Geary and California streets) now takes second place to the even gayer Castro. The Gulch is part yuppie neighborhood, part urban blight: a good place to buy roasted coffee, watch a drug bust, browse a bookstore (there are over a dozen small and special-interest book shops here), and get solicited for prostitution. Once you get past the sleaze, Polk Street provides a pleasant 15-minute walk to Fisherman's Wharf. Bus 19 from Civic Center BART runs along Polk Street on its way to Ghirardelli Square at Fisherman's Wharf.

THE TENDERLOIN • (loosely bordered by Larkin, Market, and Post streets) has traditionally been a dangerous area. In the early days, policemen got higher wages for working these streets, whereby they were able to afford more tender cuts of meat. Hence the name.

CHINATOWN

The real appeal of San Francisco's Chinatown—possibly the most famous immigrant community in the world—is its street life, so arrive hungry and energetic. Despite all the tourists, Chinatown steadfastly remains a residential area, where the largest Chinese community outside Asia has made its home since the 1850s. The original immigrants were refugees from the Opium Wars who came to San Francisco seeking their fortune during the Gold Rush; most ended up working on the railroad.

To reach Chinatown, take Bus 45 from Market and Third streets downtown. You'll know you're in the 16-block neighborhood when the street signs are in Chinese. The best way to enter is through the dragon-crowned **Chinatown Gate** (Grant Ave. at Bush St.), where the sense of being in a different world is suddenly palpable. Or enter through **Portsmouth Square** (Washington and Kearny Sts.), where dozens of old Chinese men gather to gamble and shoot the breeze.

Hop aboard the glass "Tower" elevator at Union Square's posh St. Francis Hotel (335 Powell St.) for an excellent view of the City.

Grant Avenue, the main tourist thoroughfare, also reigns as the oldest street in San Francisco—dating back to 1834. The Chinese characters above Chinatown's Gate read ALL UNDER HEAVEN IS GOOD FOR THE PEOPLE; decide if that's the case as you wander by gimmicky souvenir shops, restaurants, and flocks of wide-eyed visitors clutching $1.50 bamboo back-scratchers. The old **Chinese Telephone Exchange** building, now the Bank of Canton, stands at 743 Washington Street, at Grant Avenue. It's both architecturally and historically interesting: Operators here had to memorize the names of all their customers and speak English and five Chinese dialects. **Stockton Street** is also worth a visit. Its crowded meat and produce stalls resemble the barter and trade section of Hong Kong.

One of Chinatown's most colorful streets is **Waverly Place,** also known as the "street of painted balconies," off California and Clay streets, between Grant and Stockton streets. Chinese temples line Waverly Place—**Tin Hou Temple** (125 Waverly Pl., top floor), is purportedly the city's oldest. Don't miss nearby **Ross Alley,** between Grant and Stockton and Jackson and Washington streets: At the **Golden Gate Fortune Cookie Factory** (56 Ross Alley, tel. 415/781–3956) you can pick up a bagful (40 for $2).

NORTH BEACH

Walk north on Columbus Avenue from the Columbus and Broadway intersection (one of San Francisco's best-known red-light districts) and you'll find yourself in the heart of the legendary Italian district where the Beat movement was born. Nowadays North Beach offers a mouth-watering selection of trattorias, delis, and cafés. Poets and writers, including Jack Kerouac, Lawrence Ferlinghetti, and Allen Ginsberg, came to North Beach around 1953 to write, play music, and generally promote a lifestyle that emphasized Eastern religions, free love, drugs, and crazy new means of artistic expression. Ferlinghetti's **City Lights Bookstore** (261 Columbus Ave., tel. 415/362–8193) continues to publish and sell works by little-known alternative authors.

Those looking to immerse themselves in Beat history can poke around **Vesuvio** (255 Columbus Ave., tel. 415/362–3370), a bar where the boys undoubtedly consumed more than one glass of red, and **Caffè Trieste** (*see* Cafés, *above*). Continue the pilgrimage with a hefty walk over to Russian Hill; you can lay a poem or a stick of incense in front of **29 Russell Street** (between Larkin and Hyde Sts. and Union and Green Sts.), where Kerouac crashed with Neal and Carolyn Cassady for a time in the early '50s. (His relationship with Neal is immortalized in his popular tome *On the Road,* but *The Subterraneans* better evokes Kerouac's North Beach days.)

Washington Square, off Columbus between Filbert and Union streets, is the heart of North Beach. Bordered by bakeries and coffee shops, the square attracts an eclectic crowd of old-time Italian residents, noisome bums, and tourists. Come here early in the morning to see dozens of old Chinese women prac-

SOUND OF THE SEA

The Wave Organ, at the end of the Marina jetty, is a set of pipes that extend underwater beneath the waves of the bay. By placing your ear on the pipe, you will be treated to the soothing musical tones of lapping waves; acoustics are best at high tide. This unusual musical instrument was constructed by artists with help from the Exploratorium.

ticing tai chi in the fog. Nearby, the **UFO, Bigfoot, and Loch Ness Monster Museum** (709 Union St., at Columbus Ave., tel. 415/974–4339) is North Beach's newest—and oddest—attraction ($3). Buses 30 or 45 will get you to North Beach from Market and 3rd streets.

NOB HILL AND RUSSIAN HILL

Long the most elite of San Francisco's districts is Nob Hill (between California, Powell, Broadway, and Leavenworth streets), the locus of San Francisco high society for more than a century. The name comes from the term *nabob,* which refers to a person of great worth or wealth; some residents of the valley below snidely refer to the neighborhood as "Snob Hill." Either way, the hill has great views that even the downtrodden will enjoy, though it's a strenuous walk to the top. North of Nob Hill lies Russian Hill, originally the burial ground for Russian seal hunters and traders, which today houses a combination of old Victorian homes, new high-rises, and more of San Francisco's moneyed class.

A steep walk (or $2 cable-car ride) up Powell Street from Union Square brings you to what once were the hilltop estates of the "Big Four" railroad kings: Leland Stanford, Mark Hopkins, Collis Huntington, and Charles Crocker. Now the city's most luxurious hotels are here, including the **Fairmont Hotel,** at California and Mason streets, and the **Stanford Court Hotel,** at California and Powell streets. Across California Street from the Fairmont is the plush Mark Hopkins Hotel, whose **Top of the Mark** (tel. 415/392–3434) welcomes those in proper attire for high tea, cocktails, and breathtaking views of the city.

CABLE CAR MUSEUM • Between Nob Hill and Russian Hill is this small museum chock-a-block with photographs, scale models, vintage cars, and other memorabilia devoted to the cable car's 125-year history. From the adjacent overlook you can gander at the brawny cables that haul the cars up and down the city's hills, or watch the cables turn from an underground room. *1201 Mason St., at Washington St., tel. 415/474–1887. Admission free. Open daily 10–5 (Apr.–Oct. until 6).*

GRACE CATHEDRAL • A pseudo-Gothic structure that took 53 years to build, the cathedral is essentially a poured-concrete replica of an old European-style cathedral. The gilded bronze doors at the east entrance were taken from casts of Ghiberti's *Gates of Paradise* on the Baptistery in Florence. For a truly sublime experience, come for the singing of **vespers** every Sunday at 3:30 PM or Thursday at 5:15 PM. *1100 California St., at Taylor St., tel. 415/749–6310. From Embarcadero BART/MUNI, Bus 1 west to corner Sacramento and Jones Sts. Admission and guided tours free; donations accepted.*

LOMBARD STREET AND ENVIRONS • The most famous of Russian Hill's manicured streets is undoubtedly Lombard Street, the block-long **crookedest street in the world.** It descends the east side of Russian Hill in no fewer than eight switchbacks, between Hyde and Leavenworth streets. Don't miss the chance to do some strenuous walking around the well-maintained, wealthy neighborhood: If you climb the stairs at the intersection of Taylor and Vallejo streets, you will find a path lined with daisies, roses, and carnations that leads to **San Simone Park,** with its amazing views of Alcatraz and the East Bay.

THE MARINA

The Marina encompasses a gorgeous swath of waterfront between Fort Mason and the Presidio; inland and to the south it's bordered by **Union Street** and all its upscale boutiques and expensive cafés. The Marina is home (or rather, a series of million-dollar, Mediterranean-style homes) for San Francisco's young professionals. But all these folk with stable incomes live on decidedly unstable property; the neighborhood is built on landfill and dangerously susceptible to the whims of Mother Earthquake. You'll probably find yourself wandering the Marina's main drag, **Chestnut Street,** at some point, perhaps for a meal after visiting **Fort Mason** or the **Presidio** (*see* Major Sights, *above*).

FORT MASON • Once an army command post and later a series of warehouses built atop piers on the Marina's eastern border, Fort Mason is now a nexus of artistic, cultural, and environmental organizations; the **African-American** and **Mexican museums** (*see* Museums, *below*), among others, are here. Most days it's fairly quiet, so you can enjoy fantastic views of the bay in peace and solitude. Worth picking up is the Fort Mason monthly newsletter (available free at any of the museums), which details classes, lectures, concerts, and special exhibitions. From Fisherman's Wharf, Fort Mason is a 10-minute walk west: Follow Beach Street past the Municipal Pier, climb the forested hill past the AYH hostel, and as you descend the other side you'll see the neighborhood spread out along the waterfront. *General information: tel. 415/979–3010. Buses 22, 28, 30, 42, 47, and 49.*

PACIFIC HEIGHTS

Pacific Heights is the posh neighborhood of Victorian mansions that rises up from Van Ness and over to the Presidio, between California and Union streets. The district's stately homes were fortunate to survive the great 1906 fire; houses east of Van Ness Avenue were destroyed, and those along the avenue were dynamited to create a firebreak. A good place to start your tour of Victorian Pacific Heights is at the **Haas-Lilienthal House,** the city's only Victorian mansion open to the public. The 1886 Queen Anne–style house, considered modest in its day, is now the pride and joy of **The Foundation for San Francisco's Architectural Heritage** (2007 Franklin St., between Washington and Jackson Sts., tel. 415/441–3000), headquartered here. You must join an hour-long, docent-led tour ($5) to see the house's interior. Tours depart Wednesday noon–3:15 and Sunday 11–4, whenever a small group has gathered. Meet here at 12:30 PM on Sunday for a two-hour walking tour ($5) covering the surrounding blocks of Victorians and Edwardians.

In the next two decades, the National Park Service aims to make the Presidio the country's first self-sustaining national park, equal parts commerce and nature.

JAPANTOWN

Modern Japantown, which spans the area north of Geary Expressway between Fillmore and Laguna streets, unfortunately is dominated by the massive, somewhat depressing shopping complex called Nihonmachi, better known as **Japan Center.** The city's Japanese community was much larger prior to World War II, when California made a practice of "relocating" Japanese-Americans to concentration camps.

Japan Center's **Peace Plaza** and five-story **Pagoda** were designed by architect Yoshiro Taniguchi as a gesture of goodwill from the people of Japan. The plaza is landscaped with traditional Japanese-style gardens and reflecting pools, and in April is the site of the **Cherry Blossom Festival** (*see* Festivals, *below*). To relax after a tough day of sightseeing, try a Japanese steam bath at the **Kabuki Hot Springs** (1750 Geary Expressway, tel. 415/922–6000 for recorded information or 415/922–6002 for appointments), where you can use the communal steam room, sauna, and hot and cold baths for $10, no reservations necessary. A 25-minute shiatsu massage (with unlimited bath use) costs $35, appointment required. The communal area of the baths is reserved for women on Sunday, Wednesday, and Friday; it's men-only the rest of the week. Hours are weekdays 10–10, weekends from 9 AM. Also in the Japan Center, the **Kabuki 8 Theatres** (1881 Post St., tel. 415/931–9800) shows first-run films in a high-tech complex. From the Montgomery Street BART/MUNI station, Buses 2, 3, 4, and 38 will deposit you in Japantown.

HAIGHT-ASHBURY

East of Golden Gate Park sits the Haight-Ashbury District, the name of which still conjures up feelings of peace, love, and happiness. The Haight, nicknamed "Hashbury" by Hunter S. Thompson, began its career as a center for the counterculture in the late 1950s and early '60s, when some Beat writers, several illustrious fathers of the drug culture, and bands like the Grateful Dead and Jefferson Airplane moved in. Attracted by the neighborhood's ensuing liberal atmosphere, several hundred thousand blissed-out teenagers soon converged on the Haight to drop their body weight in acid, play music, and sing days-long renditions of "Uncle John's Band." But like the '60s themselves, Haight-Ashbury's atmosphere of excitement and idealism was pretty much washed up by the mid-1970s. Nowadays, the Haight is a punk-rock haven.

Since the 1970s, the stretch of **Haight Street** between Divisadero and Stanyan streets—often called the Upper Haight—has gone through various stages of seediness and gentrification. With no little irony, its countercultural spirit survives largely in terms of the goods you can buy: rock star T-shirts, bumper stickers, necklaces made with "healing crystals." Neo-hippies still play guitar on the street corner, but the

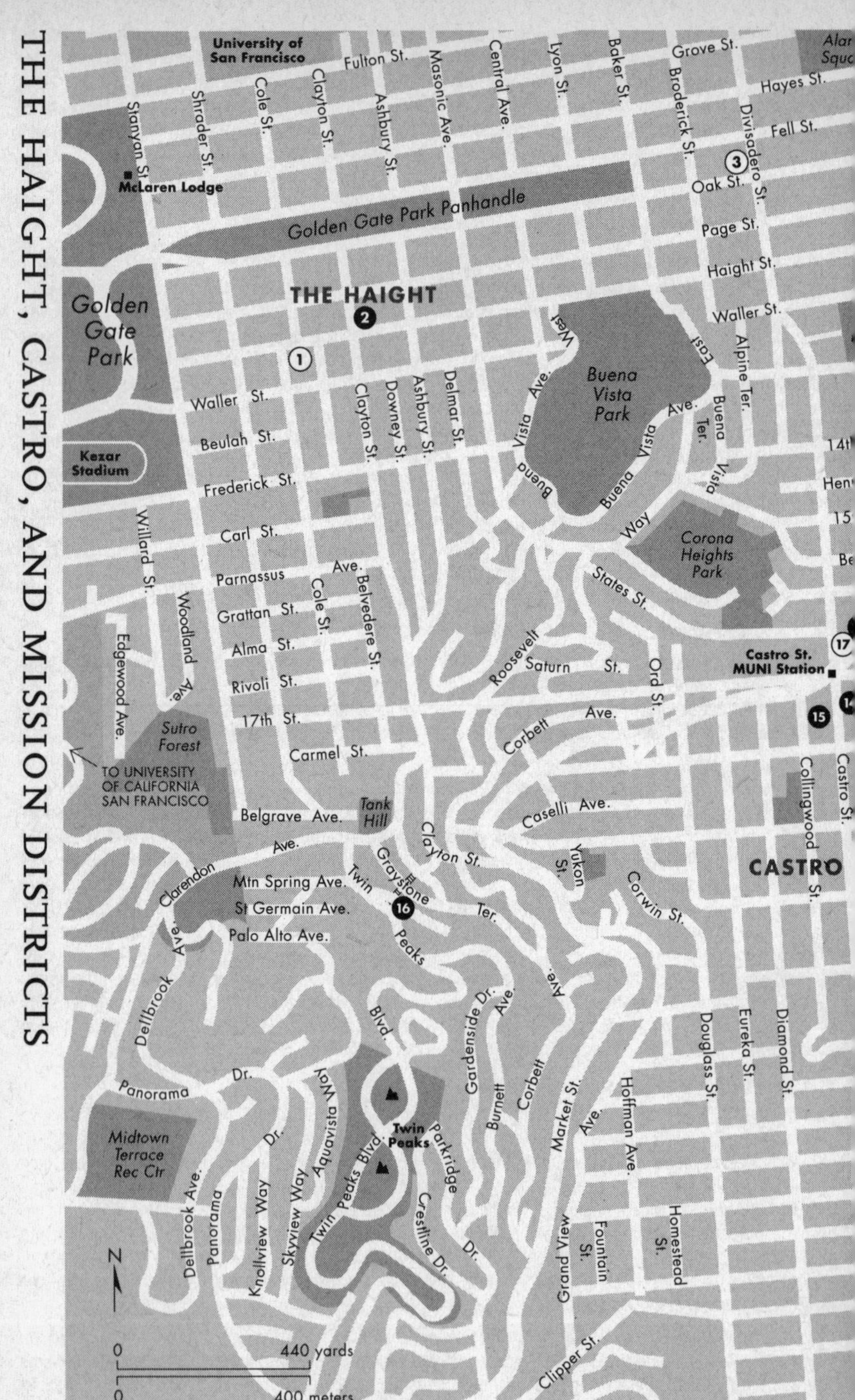
University of San Francisco
Fulton St.
Grove St.
Hayes St.
Fell St.
Oak St.
Page St.
Haight St.
Waller St.
Stanyan St.
Shrader St.
Cole St.
Clayton St.
Ashbury St.
Masonic Ave.
Central Ave.
Lyon St.
Baker St.
Broderick St.
Divisadero St.
McLaren Lodge
Golden Gate Park Panhandle
Golden Gate Park
THE HAIGHT
Buena Vista Park
Buena Vista Ave. West
Buena Vista Ave. East
Alpine Ter.
Buena Vista Ter.
Waller St.
Beulah St.
Frederick St.
Carl St.
Parnassus Ave.
Grattan St.
Alma St.
Rivoli St.
17th St.
Carmel St.
Downey St.
Delmar St.
Belvedere St.
Kezar Stadium
Willard St.
Woodland Ave.
Edgewood Ave.
Sutro Forest
TO UNIVERSITY OF CALIFORNIA SAN FRANCISCO
Corona Heights Park
States St.
Roosevelt Way
Saturn St.
Ord St.
Castro St. MUNI Station
Corbett Ave.
Caselli Ave.
Belgrave Ave.
Tank Hill
Clayton St.
Clarendon Ave.
Mtn Spring Ave.
St Germain Ave.
Palo Alto Ave.
Graystone Ter.
Twin Peaks Blvd.
Yukon St.
Corwin St.
Collingwood St.
Castro St.
CASTRO
Dellbrook Ave.
Panorama Dr.
Midtown Terrace Rec Ctr
Knollview Way
Skyview Way
Aquavista Way
Twin Peaks
Parkridge Dr.
Crestline Dr.
Gardenside Dr.
Burnett Ave.
Corbett Ave.
Market St.
Grand View Ave.
Fountain St.
Hoffman Ave.
Homestead St.
Douglass St.
Eureka St.
Diamond St.
Clipper St.
N
0 440 yards
0 400 meters
1
2
3
15
16
17

Sights ●

Café Flore, **8**

Castro Theatre, **14**

Haight-Ashbury Free Medical Clinic, **2**

Harvey Milk Plaza, **15**

Mission Dolores, **10**

The NAMES Project, **18**

Painted Ladies, **4**

Pemberton Place, **16**

Precita Eyes Mural Arts Center, **20**

Women's Building, **13**

Lodging ○

Albion House, **9**

Auberge des Artistes, **5**

Curtis Hotel, **12**

Dolores Park Inn, **11**

Inn on Castro, **17**

Metro Hotel, **3**

The Red Victorian, **1**

San Francisco International Guest House, **19**

24 Henry, **6**

Twin Peaks, **7**

HOME SWEET HOME

Janis Joplin: 112 Lyon St., between Page and Oak Sts. The Grateful Dead: 710 Ashbury St., at Waller St. The Manson family: 636 Cole St., at Haight St. Jefferson Airplane: 2400 Fulton St., at Willard St. Sid Vicious: 26 Delmar St., at Frederick St. Jimi Hendrix: 142 Central Ave., at Haight St.

revolution is nowhere in sight. What *is* in sight is the gleaming Gap store now standing on the famed corner of Haight-Ashbury.

LOWER HAIGHT AND WESTERN ADDITION • The hip, alternative Haight of the '60s isn't dead, it's just relocated to the Lower Haight—the blocks between **Divisadero** and **Webster streets.** Full of battered Victorian houses, it's a community of angry youth, eccentrics of all ages, mental cases, and—perhaps an amalgam of all three—aspiring artists and writers. At night, the street is loud with the din of '70s funk or '90s hip-hop blaring from the doorway of **Nickie's BBQ** (460 Haight St., tel. 415/621–6508), which overflows with sweaty, dancing youths of all races. For a more laid-back scene, skirt the ornery drunks and drug dealers and head for **Mad Dog in the Fog,** an English-style pub (*see* Bars, *below*). During daylight, the **Horse Shoe** (*see* Cafés, *above*) is a meeting place for neo-psychedelic artists and poetry-writing trust-fund kids. **Naked Eye News and Video** (533 Haight St., tel. 415/864–2985) is best in the city for alternative, avant-garde, and obscure comics, 'zines, and videos.

This colorful haven is itself subverted, however, by the very real poverty of its neighboring district to the north, the Western Addition. Best explored during daylight hours, the Western Addition is worth checking out as a real-life community struggling with a legacy of poverty and discrimination. Today, the main commercial drag is **Fillmore Street** between Oak Street and Geary Expressway: **Marcus Books** (1712 Fillmore St., tel. 415/346–4222) sells an outstanding range of works on African-American literature and history. Nearby, at the corner of **Octavia** and **Bush streets,** a half-dozen eucalyptus trees and a memorial plaque mark the former residence of **Mary Ellen Pleasant** (1816–1904), a heroine of the neighborhood. Rumored to be a madam, a murderer, a witch, or some combination thereof, Pleasant was most renowned for her business savvy, profits from which financed the western leg of the Underground Railroad.

PAINTED LADIES • The most famous row of houses in San Francisco is across from Alamo Square, a block west of Fillmore Street. The six beautifully restored, brightly painted Victorians sit side by side on a steep street with the downtown skyline looming majestically. To snap the obligatory picture, take MUNI Bus 6, 7, 66, or 71 from downtown Market Street to Haight and Steiner streets, and walk north on Steiner to Hayes Street.

CASTRO DISTRICT

You'll know you're in the Castro when you see rainbow flags adorning businesses and homes, and pink-triangle bumper stickers on cars. Since the early 1970s, this neighborhood has been attracting queer men and women from around the world. Before the AIDS epidemic, it was known as a spot for open revelry, with disco music pumping on Castro Street 24 hours a day. Today, the community is less carefree than it was in the first days of open gay pride, but, on weekends it still bustles with people socializing on the streets, in the bars, and at the gyms.

The heart of the district is **Castro Street,** between Market and 19th streets. At the southwest corner of Market and Castro, where the K, L, and M MUNI streetcar lines stop, is **Harvey Milk Plaza,** named in honor of California's first openly gay elected official. On November 27, 1978, Milk and then-Mayor George Moscone were assassinated by Dan White, a disgruntled former supervisor. During his trial, White claimed that the high sugar content of his junk-food diet altered his mental state—the so-called Twinkie defense—and was convicted of voluntary manslaughter by reason of "diminished capacity." The night of the verdict, 40,000 San Franciscans gathered at the plaza and proceeded to City Hall in a candlelight march. The procession is repeated every year on the anniversary of the event.

All the shops, bars, and cafés in the neighborhood cater to the gay community. The **Castro Theatre** (*see* After Dark, *below*) is an impressive art-deco repertory house that hosts the much-loved International Lesbian and Gay Film Festival each summer. The Castro is also a good area to pick up information on gay and, to a lesser extent, lesbian resources—try **A Different Light Bookstore** (489 Castro St., near

18th St., tel. 415/431–0891). Look for special interest listings, abundant free publications, and advertisements for clubs or events in neighborhood shop windows.

The social hub of the neighborhood is east of Harvey Milk Plaza at **Café Flore** (*see* Cafés, *above*), where heads turn and gossip mills churn. Closer to Castro Street, **The Café** (*see* Bars, *below*) is the only bar in the area where women comprise a majority of the clientele, although even The Café has shifted toward a more mixed and male crowd in recent years. At the intersection of Castro and Market streets, **Twin Peaks Tavern** (*see* After Dark, *below*) has the distinction of being the first gay bar in the city with clear glass windows, a celebration of the fact that gay bars no longer risked arbitrary and frequent police raids.

NAMES PROJECT FOUNDATION • For a sobering reminder of the continuing crisis facing the gay community, drop by the NAMES Project Foundation's **Visitor Center and Panelmaking Workshop,** where panels from the now famous *NAMES Quilt*—a tribute to those who have died of AIDS—are displayed. The entire quilt contains more than 30,000 panels. For those who are interested in creating a panel, the foundation provides sewing machines, fabric, and support at its weekly quilting bee (Wed. 7 PM–10 PM). *2362A Market St., at Castro St., tel. 415/863–1966. Visitor center open daily noon–7.*

TWIN PEAKS • When the Spanish came to this area during the 18th century, they named the pair of peaks looming over the bay *Los Pechos de la Choca* (the Breasts of the Indian Maiden). The name's changed, but the Twin Peaks are still truly spectacular: From here, you can see both the bay and the ocean, and everything in between. To reach Twin Peaks, take Bus 37 west from Market and Castro streets. Bring a picnic, and plan on at least 30 minutes to walk up and around.

One of San Francisco's most beautiful staircases, **Pemberton Place** is worth a visit if you're in the Twin Peaks area. Take Bus 33 to Corbett Avenue, and start climbing the stairs off Clayton Street. You will be rewarded with incredible views—and a workout.

MISSION DISTRICT

Unplagued by fog, the sunny Mission district—named after Mission Dolores (*see below*)—was once San Francisco's prime real estate, first for the native Ohlone people and then for Spanish missionaries. Over the years, subsequent Scandinavian, German, Irish, and Italian populations have given way to immigrants from Mexico and Central America. Today the community is low-income and primarily Latino, though it also includes a significant contingent of bohemians, artists, and radicals of all ethnicities. The neighborhood is a colorful and usually friendly place to hang out, but it can also be dangerous. Be particularly careful on Mission Street between 14th and 20th streets, 24th Street near Treat Avenue, and South Van Ness Avenue. Women won't feel comfortable walking alone here at night, and while you can actually find a parking space, you might think twice about leaving your car. Luckily, public transportation is a snap: Two BART stations (one at Mission and 16th streets, the other at Mission and 24th streets) put you right in the heart of things.

Numerous storefront taquerías provide a bounty of cheap, fresh food in the form of huge burritos and succulent tacos (*see box in* Food, *above*). You'll quickly learn the distinction between genuine Mexican fast food and Taco Bell, if you didn't know it already. The area also abounds with specialty bookstores, alternative theater companies, and an increasing variety of bars, some of which offer live music, poetry readings, and dance spaces. A good place to discover the Mission district's offbeat side is Valencia Street (a block west of Mission Street): Check out **Epicenter** (475 Valencia St., 2nd Floor, tel. 415/431–2725) an anarchist's community center with a huge selection of new and used punk albums; **Abandoned Planet** (518 Valencia St., tel. 415/861–4695) and **Dog Eared Books** (1173 Valencia St., tel. 415/282–1901), two among several good used bookstores; **Good Vibrations** (1210 Valencia St., tel. 415/974–8980), a collectively owned, user-friendly vibrator and sex-toy store; and **Botanica Yoruba** (998 Valencia St., at 21st St., tel. 415/826–4967), which sells incense, herbs, and spiritual advice.

Nearby is the **Women's Building** (3543 18th St., tel. 415/431–1180), a meeting place for progressive and radical political groups. The mural *Women's Wisdom Through Time* was completed in 1995 with the help of over 500 artists. You'll see Audre Lorde, Georgia O'Keeffe, Rigoberta Menchú, and many other names woven into the fabric. This is one of approximately 80 murals within an eight-block area in the southeast Mission District. For over 25 years, artists in San Francisco have followed in the tradition of Mexican painter Diego Rivera by painting huge, vibrant works on walls all over the city. The **Precita Eyes Mural Arts Center** (348 Precita Ave., between Folsom and Harrison Sts., tel. 415/285–2287) offers an excellent two-hour tour of many of them, led by one of its muralists-in-residence, along with an introductory slide show. Tours cost $4 and leave from the center every Saturday at 1:30 PM. Otherwise, stop by weekdays 10–5 or Saturday 10–4 to pick up a copy of the handy "Mission Mural Walk" map ($1.50 donation).

CHILLING BY THE OCEAN

Head to the beach in your bikini and flip-flops and you might be in for a shock—the city's beaches rarely greet you with the kind of sun that'll make you crave a swim. **Fort Funston,** *San Francisco's southernmost beach, is great for watching hang gliders and for starting the 7-mi trek to Ocean Beach. From Balboa Park BART, take Bus 88 west.* **China Beach** *is one of the city's safest for swimming, although you must watch out for the rip currents. Take Bus 1 from Clay and Drumm streets (near the Embarcadero Center) to 30th Avenue in the Richmond district. The surfers' beach, the tourists' beach, and the family beach is all-purpose* **Ocean Beach.** *Nearby is the historic Cliff House (tel. 415/386–3330), which houses a popular restaurant. Just west of the Cliff House lie the ruins of the Sutro Baths, a huge complex of fresh and saltwater pools modeled after ancient Roman baths, abandoned in 1966. Take the N Judah streetcar from any downtown underground MUNI station.*

MISSION DOLORES • Though it's made of humble adobe, the oldest building in San Francisco has survived some powerful earthquakes and fires. It was commissioned by Junípero Serra to honor San Francisco de Asis (St. Francis of Assisi) and completed in 1791. The Spanish nicknamed it Dolores after a nearby stream, *Arroyo de Nuestra Señora de los Dolores* (Stream of Our Lady of the Sorrows), and the name stuck long after the river dried up and disappeared. Architecturally, Mission Dolores is the simplest of all the California missions—it's also seen the fewest modifications over the centuries. Look up at the ceiling and you'll see traditional Native American designs handpainted by local Costanoan Indians. The mission bells still ring on holy days and the cemetery next door is the permanent home of a few early *rancheros,* including San Francisco's first mayor, Don Francisco de Haro. Admission ($2) gives you access to the mission, cemetery, and a small display of artifacts; or opt for a worthwhile 45-minute audio tour ($5). *16th and Dolores Sts., tel. 415/621–8203. Open daily 9–4.*

SOUTH OF MARKET

Until recently, SoMa—the area bordered by Mission Street, Townsend Street, the Embarcadero, and 12th Street—was merely a flat, nondescript stretch of abandoned factories. Only in the last decade or so has the region come alive, filling those rows of empty warehouses with art galleries, alternative theaters, dusk-to-dawn nightclubs, and a **flower market** (*see* Cheap Thrills, *below*). The SoMa nightlife scene centers around **Folsom Street,** a heathen's haven of dance clubs (*see* Clubs *in* After Dark, *below*).

The brand-new **Yerba Buena Gardens** and the **San Francisco Museum of Modern Art** (*see below*) are the stars of the SoMa arts scene, both figuratively and literally. Smaller, edgier galleries are relocating to the neighborhood as fast as they can, using light from the big names to draw attention to themselves; there are now dozens of warehouse-cum-gallery spaces within a three-block radius of SFMOMA. One such venture, the **Capp Street Project** (525 2nd St., between Bryant and Brannan Sts., tel. 415/495–7101), sponsors three controversial murals South of Market: "Inner City Home" at 6th and Brannan streets; "One Tree" at 10th and Brannan streets; and "Extinct" at 5th and Folsom streets.

SoMa also attracts bargain hunters with its outlet stores and warehouses; by day, shoppers are out in force hunting leather fashions, beauty products, career clothes, and anything else you can think of. At **Six Sixty Center** (660 3rd St., between Brannan and Townsend Sts., tel. 415/227–0464) you'll find 22 outlet stores under one roof.

YERBA BUENA GARDENS • This 8⅓-acre arts and performance space opened to much fanfare in 1993, after more than 30 years of bureaucratic disputes. On the east side of the garden complex, the

Center for the Arts (701 Mission St., tel. 415/978–2787) houses galleries and a theater, both meant to celebrate the multicultural nature of the Bay Area. Critics point out that the multicultural emphasis may be to the exclusion of mainstream arts. Others smirk at the money spent building the center: a whopping $41 million. Nearby you'll find the **California Historical Society Museum** (678 Mission St., at 3rd St., tel. 415/357–1848; admission $3) and the **Cartoon Art Museum** (814 Mission St., between 4th and 5th Sts., tel. 415/227–8666; admission $4).

MUSEUMS

Although San Francisco has recently trumpeted itself as a city of big, impressive institutions of art—like the newly relocated Museum of Modern Art and the renovated California Palace of the Legion of Honor—the buzz has also been a boon to smaller, edgier spaces. You'll find dozens of galleries and a handful of museums in **SoMa,** particularly around Yerba Buena Gardens (*see above*).

African American Museum. The contemporary art gallery features works by African and African American artists, and an intriguing gift shop sells jewelry and artifacts; there's also a historical archive and research library. Call for information on lectures and performing arts classes. *Fort Mason Center, Bldg. C, tel. 415/441–0640. Admission: $3. Open Tues.–Sun. noon–5.*

A perfect place to relax is South Park (off 2nd and 3rd Sts., between Bryant and Brannan Sts.), an old-fashioned square smack in the middle of warehouse-riddled SoMa.

Ansel Adams Center. If you're even remotely interested in serious photography, come here. The West Coast's largest repository of art photography, the Ansel Adams Center has five rotating exhibits, one of which is devoted to Adams's work (despite the name, there aren't that many works by Adams). Born of the Friends of Photography, a national group founded by Adams, the center serves photographers with publications, awards, an incredible bookstore, and an educational series taught by famous shutterbugs. *250 4th St., between Howard and Folsom Sts., tel. 415/495–7000. Admission: $5. Open Tues.–Sun. 11–5 (until 8 first Thurs. of month).*

Asian Art Museum. Housed in the same building as the M. H. de Young (*see below*), this is the West Coast's largest Asian museum, with more than 12,000 pieces from 40 Asian countries, representing virtually every major artistic period. Highlights include the oldest known Buddha image (AD 338) and superb collections of carved jade and ancient Chinese ceramics. *John F. Kennedy and Tea Garden Drs., Golden Gate Park, tel. 415/379–8801. Admission: $6; free first Wed. of month. Open Wed.–Sun. 9:30–5 (until 8:45 first Wed. of month).*

California Academy of Sciences. This huge natural history complex is subdivided into blockbuster sights that include **Morrison Planetarium,** the **Steinhart Aquarium,** and the **Natural History Museum.** The aquarium's **Fish Roundabout** places you in an underwater world of 14,500 different creatures. The Space and Earth Hall has an "earthquake room" where you can experience the vibrations of an 8.0-magnitude quake. Also worth visiting are the Life through Time Hall, which chronicles evolution from the dinosaurs through early mammals, and the Birds of a Feather exhibit, which explores the languages, physical features, and learning habits of birds. To see the "Sky Show" on the 65-ft dome at the Morrison Planetarium you'll need to pay a separate admission fee ($2.50). **Laserium** shows are $6–$8. *Between John F. Kennedy and Martin Luther King Jr. Drs., Golden Gate Park, tel. 415/750–7145. Admission to Natural History Museum and Steinhart Aquarium: $7. Admission to Morrison Planetarium: $2.50. All exhibits (except Laserium) free first Wed. of month. Open daily 10–5 (until 8:45 first Wed. of the month).*

Exploratorium. This cavernous warehouse contains more than 650 hands-on exhibits, many computer-assisted, about science and technology. It's a fun place for children—and grown-ups—to overcome their fears about science. Advance reservations ($12, includes Exploratorium admission) are required for the enormously popular **Tactile Dome** (tel. 415/560–0362), a series of differently textured, small rooms through which you walk, crawl, and slither in complete darkness. *3601 Lyon St., between Marina Blvd. and Lombard St., tel. 415/563–7337 or 415/561–0360 for recorded information. Admission: $9; free first Wed. of month. Open Tues.–Sun., winter 10–5 (Wed. until 9:30); Memorial Day through Labor Day 10–6.*

Legion of Honor. The California Palace of the Legion of Honor reopened in 1995 after extensive renovations, complete with an underground gallery complex and a full-service restaurant overlooking the

GAY AND LESBIAN SAN FRANCISCO

San Francisco promotes the fact that it is a gay city, and some neighborhood populations are as much as 95% gay; it is feasible here for people to go about their lives dealing almost exclusively with gays and lesbians, both in business and in pleasure. Gays and lesbians are the city's most prominent special-interest group and many hold public offices, ranging from the Board of Supervisors to the Police Commission to the judges on the Municipal Court.

San Francisco's most concentrated gay neighborhood is the Castro district, followed closely by Polk Gulch. Although there isn't a lesbian neighborhood per se, many young lesbians gravitate to the Mission. Bernal Heights seems to attract slightly older women-loving women, while the more upwardly mobile lesbian set heads to Noe Valley. Valencia Street in the Mission is home to the greatest concentration of women-oriented shops.

Pacific Ocean. On display are San Francisco's European fine arts; though the collection isn't stunning, it does include some fine late-19th century pieces. Among them are several Rodin sculptures, including a cast of *The Thinker,* and one of Monet's *Water Lilies. Lincoln Park, Richmond District, tel. 415/750–3600. Admission: $7; free second Wed. of month. Open Tues.–Sun. 9:30–5. From Union Square, take Bus 38 Geary west to 33rd Ave., then transfer to Bus 8 north; park entrance at 34th Ave. and Clement St.*

M. H. de Young Memorial Museum. The de Young is best known for its substantial survey collection of U.S. art, which includes paintings, sculpture, decorative arts, textiles, and furniture dating back to 1670. Artists represented include Sargent, Whistler, Church, and Wood; highlights are George Caleb Bingham's *Boatmen on the Missouri* and Georgia O'Keeffe's *Petunias.* The de Young also houses impressive collections of art from Africa, Oceania, and the Americas. Docent-led tours are offered on the hour. *Golden Gate Park, between John F. Kennedy Dr. and 8th Ave., tel. 415/750–3600. Admission: $6; free first Wed. of month. Open Wed.–Sun. 9:30–5 (until 8:45 first Wed. of the month).*

Mexican Museum. A unique center exploring Mexican and Chicano culture in the United States, this museum—boasting a 9,000-item permanent collection—has had to make do with a relatively small space. Yet it has scored the likes of Diego Rivera and Frida Kahlo exhibits as well as less mainstream shows with themes like Chicano graffiti art. The museum will relocate to more spacious quarters at Yerba Buena Gardens in late 1998 or early 1999. *Fort Mason Center, Bldg. D, tel. 415/441–0404. Admission: $3; free first Wed. of month. Open Wed.–Fri. noon–5 (until 7 first Wed. of month), weekends 11–5.*

San Francisco Museum of Modern Art. SFMOMA's new home, designed by Swiss architect Mario Botta, is dominated by a huge, cylindrical skylight trimmed in black and white stone. The space is twice that of the museum's prior location at the War Memorial Veterans Building, where it opened in 1935 as the West Coast's first museum devoted to 20th-century art. The excellent permanent collection includes works by Jackson Pollock, Jasper Johns, Frida Kahlo, Henri Matisse, and Frank Stella, as well as a healthy representation of contemporary photography. *151 3rd St., tel. 415/357–4000. Admission: $7; free first Tues. of month, half-price Thurs. 6–9. Open Mon. and Tues. 11–6, Thurs. 11–9, Fri.–Sun. 11–6.*

CHEAP THRILLS

The **SoMa Flower Market,** for professional florists, is a heaven-scented place with a dazzling array of blooms for sale, from red roses to zinnias to humble carnations. It's open to the general public on Saturday only, and you'll find incredible bargains if you arrive near dawn. The market opens after midnight and closes by 11 AM. *6th and Brannan Sts.*

The **Midsummer Music Festival** at Stern Grove consists of 10 Sunday afternoons of free symphony, opera, jazz, dance, and pop for an appreciative crowd of picnickers. The amphitheater is in a beautiful eucalyptus grove; concerts start at 2 PM, but you'll want to show up around noon. *Sloat Blvd. at 19th Ave., tel. 415/252–6252. MUNI streetcars K or M.*

Every year the **San Francisco Shakespeare Festival** (tel. 415/666–2221) brings one of the Bard's works to Liberty Tree Meadow (west of the Conservatory) in Golden Gate Park. Free performances are every Saturday and Sunday (1:30 PM) from Labor Day through the first weekend in October.

San Francisco Mime Troupe. This provocative ensemble stages scathing political comedies and musicals—free! They appear in Golden Gate Park and other Bay Area parks between July 4 and Labor Day. Bring a picnic and spend an entertaining sunny afternoon. *Tel. 415/285–1717.*

FESTIVALS

JANUARY

During the one-day **Tet Festival** (late January), the streets around Civic Center come alive with performances by Vietnamese, Cambodian, and Laotian singers and dancers, and numerous booths sell Southeast Asian delicacies. *Tel. 415/391–8050.*

FEBRUARY

Chinese New Year and Golden Dragon Parade. Celebrate the dawn of the Year of the Tiger with North America's oldest Chinese community. Cultural events and festivities take place around January 28, culminating with the fireworks and colorful costumes of the splendid Golden Dragon Parade, in Chinatown. *Tel. 415/982–3000.*

APRIL

Cherry Blossom Festival. Japantown hosts this cultural festival, which extends over two weekends and incorporates such Japanese traditions as the tea ceremony, taiko drum performances, and martial arts and cooking demonstrations. The festivities conclude with a 2½-hour parade. *Tel. 415/563–2313.*

San Francisco International Film Festival. The nation's oldest film festival features two full weeks of films and seminars and many opportunities to mingle with the creative minds behind them. Screenings take place at the Kabuki 8 and the Castro Theatre in San Francisco, the Pacific Film Archive in Berkeley, and at theaters in the South Bay and Marin County. *Tel. 415/929–5000.*

MAY

San Francisco's Mission district explodes with *felicidad* on the weekend nearest May 5th, during the two-day **Cinco de Mayo** fiesta (tel. 415/826–1401) extolling Mexico's independence. Later in the month, on Memorial Day Weekend, the Mission celebrates **Carnaval** (tel. 415/826–1401) with dance, music, arts and crafts, and a parade.

Bay to Breakers. Listed in the *Guinness Book of Records* as the world's largest foot race, this zany 7.5-mi race pits world-class runners against costumed human centipedes and huge safe-sex condom caravans. The half-comical, half-serious event takes place the third Sunday in May (May 17 in 1998) and attracts more than 100,000 people. *Tel. 415/777–7770.*

JUNE

Summer brings out all the neighborhood celebrations, including the **Haight Street Fair** (tel. 415/661–8025), the **Polk Street Fair** (tel. 415/346–9162), the **North Beach Festival** (tel. 415/403–0666), and the **Union Street Spring Festival** (tel. 415/346–9162), all of which feature craft booths, music, and food.

San Francisco Lesbian, Gay, Bisexual, Transgender Pride Celebration. Known as San Francisco Pride for short (tel. 415/864–3733), this is queer San Francisco at its best. June also brings the much-loved and internationally famous **Lesbian and Gay Film Festival** (tel. 415/703–8650).

Making Waves. On June 21st, the longest day of the year, the streets vibrate with the sounds of over 250 bands (everything from local funk to zydeco to jazz to African indigenous music) playing for free on 25 downtown San Francisco stage sites. *Tel. 415/391–0370.*

JULY

Fourth of July Waterfront Festival. San Francisco Bay is illuminated every 4th with fireworks along the waterfront between Aquatic Park and Pier 39. Festivities start in the afternoon with musical performances by Bay Area musicians. *Tel. 415/777–7120.*

SEPTEMBER

San Francisco Blues Festival. Big-name musicians like B. B. King and Robert Cray perform at the country's oldest blues festival, usually the last weekend of the month at Justin Herman Plaza (Market St. at Embarcadero) and Fort Mason's Great Meadow (Marina Blvd. and Laguna St.). Tickets average $20–$30 and advance purchase is recommended. *Tel. 415/979–5588.*

OCTOBER

Halloween. San Francisco's huge, raucous, heavily queer Halloween parade and party recently relocated from the Castro district to Civic Center (between 9th and 10th Sts. north of Market St.). About 300,000 revelers attend each year. Call CUAV (Community United Against Violence; tel. 415/777–5500) for information.

AFTER DARK

San Francisco nightlife leans toward the casual, though there are also plenty of opportunities to put on your best duds and sip a $10 martini, if that's your thing. Look in the *S.F. Weekly* or the *Bay Guardian* for possibilities; you'll find about a hundred different choices. The *Bay Times* is the best source for gay- and lesbian-oriented entertainment listings. Bars and clubs (and liquor stores) are all supposed to close by 2 AM, but several clubs stay open until the wee hours for those who just can't stop dancing.

BARS

The Deluxe. Come on the weekend to this slick, retro bar in Upper Haight, order a martini, and take a look around: You'll get the uncanny feeling that the year is 1945. Patrons enjoy donning their finest '40s duds (hairdos and shoes included) and acting *very* cool. There will usually be a crooner with backup swing band, or at least owner Jay Johnson doing Sinatra his way. *1511 Haight St., between Ashbury and Clayton Sts., tel. 415/552–6949. Cover: $3–$5 weekends.*

500 Club. Here's a little slice of Americana—complete with a huge neon martini sign, two cramped pool tables, and three comfy vinyl booths. The hard-drinking regulars are joined by younger patrons on weekends, when it's difficult to find a place to stand. *500 Guerrero St., at 17th St., tel. 415/861–2500.*

Hi-Ball Lounge. Found near the Wall-to-Wall Sex Parlor, this swank new bar features some of its own red-light district furnishings—leopard-skin drapery and red velvet booths—but none of the sleazy clientele. Before the Hi-Ball days, this spot used to be a hangout for jazz greats such as John Coltrane and Miles Davis, and the bar tries to maintain the legendary atmosphere with nightly live bands, often playing swing. The dance floor, however, is so tiny it starts to resemble a mosh pit when the gents twirl their dates. *473 Broadway St., near Columbus Ave., tel. 415/397–9464. Cover: Thurs. and Sun. $5, Fri. and Sat. $7, free Tues.–Wed.*

Lone Palm. Beyond the huge black door awaits an oasis of class. Dimly lit tables, a '40s atmosphere, and skilled cocktail shakers behind the bar combine to make this an intimate setting to sip martinis with that certain someone. *3394 22nd St., near Guerrero St., tel. 415/648–0109.*

Mad Dog in the Fog. This British-style pub in the heart of Lower Haight is frequented by neighborhood folk who want to watch televised rugby while downing their beer. The Dog offers diversions galore: darts inside, a beer garden outside, and trivia competitions for beer and cash prizes on Monday and Thursday. *530 Haight St., between Fillmore and Steiner Sts., tel. 415/626–7279.*

Place Pigalle. The vibes are hip and European (but definitely not pretentious) at this sleek, low-key, French-owned, Hayes Valley wine bar and gallery space. Stop in for a glass of wine after work and stay for the evening; there's live jazz Thursday through Saturday nights and occasional spoken-word performances during the week. *520 Hayes St., between Octavia and Laguna Sts., tel. 415/552–2671. Cover: up to $5.*

Red Room. Owned by a Manhattan socialite, this lounge-y cocktail bar attached to the Commodore Hotel attracts the trendy, clubbing crowd. Its impressive entrance opens to a curved wall of red bottles stacked to the ceiling and a shockingly red interior. Wear black so you can be seen better, and prepare to match wits against the top 10% of the social food chain. *827 Sutter St., at Jones St., tel. 415/346–7666.*

Vesuvio. A bohemian hangout during the Beat era, Vesuvio has somehow managed to avoid having the life stamped out of it by tourist boots. Have a glass of red and peruse the copy of *Howl!* you just bought next door at City Lights, or listen for words of wisdom from the crowd of wizened regulars. The best seats are upstairs and all the way back, where you can gaze out the large windows down on bustling Columbus Avenue. *255 Columbus Ave., near Broadway, tel. 415/362–3370.*

GAY AND LESBIAN

The Café. Formerly known as Café San Marco, this large, lively bar with mirrored walls and neon lights used to cater mainly to lesbians, although the mix is about 50/50 lesbian/gay male now. If there's no room on the dance floor, you can hang out on the balcony and watch the Castro strut by. *2367 Market St., near Castro St., tel. 415/861–3846.*

The Detour. Minimally decorated with a chain-link fence and pool table, this bar caters to young, good-looking people searching for dates. Saturday night go-go dancers make the scene more extreme. If you can't find it, listen for the music—the black-on-black sign is impossible to see at night. *2348 Market St., between Castro and Noe Sts., tel. 415/861–6053.*

Twin Peaks Tavern. David Lynch has nothing to do with this casual, lounge-like gay bar; in fact, the Peaks has been around for more than 15 years and proudly claims to have been the first gay bar in the city with clear—as in, not tinted—floor-to-ceiling windows. Twin Peaks enjoys its high visibility on the corner of Market and Castro streets; on weekends expect big crowds of both newcomers and an older, established clientele. *401 Castro St., at Market St., tel. 415/864–9470.*

CLUBS

Dance clubs range from the cheap, local, and casual to the expensive, pretentious, and trendy. On the low end, some local bars will just stick a DJ in a corner and clear the tables away—instant disco. For the most eclectic and underground clubs, look in smaller retail and record shops for flyers advertising one-night extravaganzas that take place in changing locations. The *S.F. Weekly* and the *Bay Guardian*, as always, are good resources. Always call ahead; clubs can change as quickly the hair color of their patrons.

STRAIGHT

Bahia Cabana. A multigenerational, international crowd come to samba at this tropical downtown supper club with mural-covered walls. Thursday and Friday are salsa nights; other evenings expect Brazilian and various Latino bands and, on Mondays, techno trance. *1600 Market St., at Franklin, tel. 415/626–3306. Cover: $5–$10.*

DNA Lounge. This dependable choice for after-hours dancing (weekends until 4 AM) has eclectic acts that range from rockabilly nights to tattoo and piercing shows. The crowd isn't afraid to break a sweat on the dance floor, but many come just to kick back in dimly lit corners downstairs. On Friday, dance to the '70s retro-band, Grooveline; DJs usually come on after the live music. On Wednesday, "Afrosheen" features reggae, soul, and R&B. *375 11th St., at Harrison St., tel. 415/626–1409. Cover: $5–$15.*

Nickie's BBQ. Red-vinyl booths and Christmas lights decorate this urban, Lower Haight hole-in-the-wall that's entirely lacking in pretension. Everything from '70s funk, soul, and hip-hop to reggae, Latin, and world beat booms through the speakers nightly. *460 Haight St., between Webster and Fillmore Sts., tel. 415/621–6508. Cover: $3–$5.*

MIXED

The Box. This Thursday-only, artsy-industrial SoMa club plays hard-core hip-hop, funk, soul, and house, and you'll find little attitude here because everybody's out on the dance floor. For an extra treat, go-go platforms mounted on the walls showcase dancers who gyrate at full throttle. The city's most accomplished DJs—including "Mixtress" Page Hodel, S.F.'s most famous queer DJ—and club dance troupes appear here. While the club is lesbian-run, the multicultural crowd includes straights, too. *715 Harrison St., between 3rd and 4th Sts. Cover: $6; $5 for members.*

"TRIPPING" THE LIGHT FANTASTIC

If you find yourself stumbling over two left feet instead of cutting a rug, don't be dismayed. Inexpensive lessons are available at a number of Bay Area locations. At Café du Nord (see *Live Music,* above), *samba, mambo, and cha-cha lessons can be had for the $3 cover Tuesday at 9* PM *while Sunday means free swing lessons at 8* PM*, $3 after 9* PM. *Head to 330 Ritch Street (330 Ritch St., off Townsend St. between 3rd and 4th Sts., tel. 415/522–9558) for free swing lessons (plus $5 cover) on Wednesday at 8:30* PM*, and steamy Latin dance steps Saturday at 8:30* PM *for $5. Ten dollars buys you salsa lessons and dancing every Thursday through Saturday at 8* PM *at Kimballs Carnival* (see *Oakland* in *Chapter 3). Barring the above, a coy glance and a polite inquiry might enlist the company of a willing, and hopefully, capable, partner.*

1015 Folsom. Also called Club 1015, this SoMa spot hosts various clubs on a nightly basis. Three separate "dance scenes"—disco, techno, and house—and theme parties like "Eurotrash" should satisfy any taste in dance music. Saturday, the ever-popular "Release" (tel. 415/337–7457) keeps you up all night with '70s funk and disco, deep house, and hip-hop. Though the club suffers from an ostentatious dress code on weekends, the more casual weeknight after-hours events consistently showcase quality turntable talent, and there's a cozy lounge upstairs conveniently shielded from the blare of the speakers. Call for a complete listing of club nights. *1015 Folsom St., at 6th St., tel. 415/431–1200. Cover: $10 weekends; $5 weeknights.*

The Trocadero. Wednesday only, Trocadero hosts the oldest fetish dance club in California: "Bondage A Go-Go." Other nights, this SoMa club features industrial dancing and live hard-core music. The Trocadero is all-ages when the music is live, and 18-and-over for "Bondage A Go-Go" and DJed events. *520 4th St., between Bryant and Brannan Sts., tel. 415/995–4600. Cover: $4–$7.*

GAY AND LESBIAN

Club Townsend. This vast SoMa disco hosts the high-energy Sunday "Pleasuredome," with local DJs churning out sounds for a largely male crowd followed by a where-do-they-get-the-energy Sunday Tea Dance until 6 AM. "Club Universe" on Saturday is less gender-specific, and the artsy decor changes to create a stunning new illusion each week. *177 Townsend St., between 2nd and 3rd Sts., tel. 415/974–1156. Cover: $10.*

The Stud. This SoMa club is a San Francisco legend and a good watering hole any night of the week. Thursday nights are often set aside for lesbian events; Wednesday, the club draws in a postcollegiate crowd for dancing to '70s and early '80s classics. The Tuesday-night club Trannyshack is especially popular, when cross-dressers enjoy "make-up tips and cheap cocktails." *399 9th St., at Harrison St., tel. 415/252–7883. Cover: $3–$6.*

LIVE MUSIC

While not at the forefront of any musical revolution, San Francisco has an eclectic and energetic music scene. Bars and clubs feature live music on any given night of the week, usually for a modest cover, and sometimes you can see talented bands for free in parks, music stores, bars, and cultural centers. On the other hand, you could pay $15–$25 to see bands on the verge of MTV stardom play at the **Warfield** (982 Market St., between 5th and 6th Sts., tel. 415/775–7722) or the historic **Fillmore** (1805 Geary St., at Fillmore St., tel. 415/346–6000). The gorgeous **Great American Music Hall** (859 O'Farrell St., between Polk and Larkin Sts., tel. 415/885–0750) books an innovative blend of rock and world music, and Boz Scagg's club, **Slim's** (333 11th St., tel. 415/522–0333), specializes in bluesy rock icons and roots music.

BLUES

Blue Lamp. This friendly, downtown bar books a variety of blues, jazz, folk, and rock bands nightly, and attracts an equally diverse mix of patrons. Arrive early to stake your spot near the fireplace. *561 Geary St., between Taylor and Jones Sts., tel. 415/885–1464. Cover: $2 Thurs., $4 Fri.–Sat.*

Grant and Green Blues Club. This dark, smoky bar hosts some raucous blues shows, a welcome change in North Beach, where too many folks sit stiffly in coffeehouses discussing obscure lit-crits over wine. *1731 Grant Ave., at Green St., tel. 415/693–9565. Cover: free–$4.*

Friday and Saturday nights the "Mexican Bus" winds its way through the city depositing dancers at various Latin Clubs. The cost is $30, including cover. Call 415/546–3747.

CLASSICAL

The **San Francisco Symphony,** under Michael Tilson Thomas's baton, plays from September to May. At press time, the musicians were on strike, canceling dozens of performances, but once the strike is resolved this group should return to its home at Davies Symphony Hall. The cheapest balcony seats are $25, though a limited number of $10–$12 center terrace seats (behind the orchestra) go on sale two hours before the show. *Davies Symphony Hall, 201 Van Ness Ave., at Grove St., tel. 415/864–6000.*

San Francisco Opera. In the tradition of expensive wigs, lavish costumes, and lusty sopranos, the San Francisco Opera puts on grand-scale quality performances each season. Tickets prices range from uneconomical ($20–$40), to outrageous (over $100 for the best seats). Student rush tickets for young people and senior citizens often go on sale two hours before curtain and cost $15–$20; call before coming out and they'll tell you your chances of getting a ticket. At press time the War Memorial Opera House (301 Van Ness Ave.) was closed for earthquake retrofitting, but you should be able to see it in all its renovated splendor during the 1997-1998 opera season. *Box office: 199 Grove St., at Van Ness Ave., tel. 415/864–3330.*

JAZZ

Bruno's. Divided into a full-scale restaurant and a lounge-y bar, Bruno's has been wildly popular since its opening a few years ago. Every night of the week, the intimate club showcases local jazz and swing acts—many of them up and coming new stars of the San Francisco scene—though sometimes the patrons here are too busy being fashionable to pay much attention to the band. Relax in the red vinyl booths with a martini, or squeeze up closer (if that's possible) to the band. *2389 Mission St., at 20th St., tel. 415/550–7455. Cover: $3–$5.*

Café du Nord. While hot with urban hipsters, Café du Nord retains a friendly aura. The specialty at this often overcrowded Castro club is jazz you can afford. Saturday night usually features the sultry crooning of local faves LaVay Smith & her Red Hot Skillet Lickers. Wednesday brings the Downhear Experimental Series showcasing some of the finest local talent; other nights feature lounge, salsa, swing, and big band. Because of the club's large size and layout, those more interested in playing pool or socializing can do so in the front of bar, while the music lovers groove uninterrupted in the back. Dinner is served Wednesday through Saturday nights. *2170 Market St., at Sanchez St., tel. 415/861–5016. Cover: $3–$5.*

Elbo Room. This stylish Mission watering hole becomes unmanageably popular as the night progresses. Head upstairs for some of the best local live jazz and hip-hop acts, as well as occasional DJs. Forgot your dancing shoes? Join the locals packed around the pool table—the drinks are cheap ($2–$3). Happy hour is a generous 3–9. *647 Valencia St., near 17th St., tel. 415/552–7788. Upstairs cover: about $5.*

Up and Down Club. This multilevel SoMa supper club has a sleek deco design. Upstairs you'll find a DJ laying down tracks, but little room to dance. Downstairs, jazz, including Latin jazz and acid jazz, heat up the room. *1151 Folsom St., between 7th and 8th Sts., tel. 415/626–2388. Closed Sun. Cover: $5, free Wed.*

ROCK

Bottom of the Hill. Squeeze into this classic dive bar at the bottom of Potrero Hill to acquire a comprehensive sense of the local music scene. You'll be mere feet from promising local talent and touring bands in this eclectic venue, and to make it even better, its sound system was recently improved. On Sunday afternoon, $3 will not only gain you admission to the live music, but also to the all-you-can-eat barbecue (4 PM). *1233 17th St., at Texas St., tel. 415/626–4455. Cover: usually $3–$6.*

Paradise Lounge. The Paradise is like a carnival fun house with something different around every corner: three different musical stages to choose from, Sunday night poetry slams, Tuesday night open mics, pool tables, free-flowing booze, and a constant flow of people. Although the quality of music varies widely (to put it kindly), it's almost always a reliable weekend destination. *1501 Folsom St., at 11th St., tel. 415/861–6906. Cover: about $5.*

MOVIE HOUSES

Castro Theatre. Built in 1922 and the most beautiful place to see a film in San Francisco, the Castro shows a wide selection of rare, foreign, and unusual films that play anywhere from a night to a week or two. However, the specialties are camp, classics of all genres, and new releases of interest to lesbian and gay viewers. And the man who rises out of the floor playing the Wurlitzer organ is guaranteed to make you giggle for the sheer kitschiness of it all. *429 Castro St., between Market and 18th Sts., tel. 415/621–6120. Admission: $6.50.*

Red Vic. Films at this co-op range from artsy to cultish to rare, and you can have your herbal tea in a real mug to accompany your popcorn with yeast. If you arrive early, snag a couch before love birds beat you to it. *1727 Haight St., between Cole and Shrader Sts., tel. 415/668–3994. Admission: $6.*

THEATER

While it doesn't carry the national reputation of New York, Los Angeles, or Chicago, San Francisco has a diverse and affordable theater scene. **ACT** is the city's premier local repertory company, staging about eight plays annually at the Geary Theater (415 Geary St., at Mason St., tel. 415/749–2228), but what San Francisco does best—as usual—is experimental theater with an emphasis on multimedia visual arts and solo performers. Look through the *S.F. Weekly,* the *Bay Guardian,* or the Sunday *Chronicle-Examiner's* "Datebook" for special events.

Magic Theatre (Fort Mason Center, Bldg. D, tel. 415/441–8822) is the city's standby for the mildly experimental, in its showcasing of innovative, modern American works. **Theater Artaud** (450 Florida St., at 17th St., tel. 415/621–7797) regularly programs avant-garde dance, drama, and multimedia work in a cavernous warehouse space. **Theatre Rhinoceros** (2926 16th St., near Mission St., tel. 415/861–5079) is dedicated to all kinds of gay theater.

Beach Blanket Babylon. This treasure trove of San Francisco lore has been selling out most nights for the past three decades. The revue still entertains with talented musicians, polished performers, impeccable timing, extra-large headgear, and a zesty, zany script that changes to incorporate topical references and characters (not to mention an on-going love affair with the British Royal Family). A significant chunk of your $18–$45 ticket goes to local charities. Those under 21 may attend Sunday matinee performances only. *Club Fugazi, 678 Green St., at Powell St., tel. 415/421–4222.*

SAN FRANCISCO BAY AREA

3

UPDATED BY JENNIFER BREWER, KATHLEEN DODGE, SHARON SILVA, AND SUZANNE STEIN

When, or rather if, you tire of San Francisco, there are a host of adventures awaiting you in the greater San Francisco Bay Area: Marin, Sonoma, and Napa counties to the north; Berkeley and Oakland to the east; and Palo Alto, San Jose, and the San Mateo County Coast to the south. These aren't just sleepy second-string cousins to the City by the Bay; each has its own strong flavor, from the hip-hop beat of Oaktown and the hippie parade of Berkeley to the rugged beauty of Marin and the seaside charm of Half Moon Bay. Whether you're looking for a day on the beach or a weekend in the Wine Country, a New Age healing session, or a sizzling blues band, odds are good that you'll find it somewhere in the surrounding Bay Area. Most of the places covered here are within easy reach of San Francisco—by car or on public transportation—and can be covered in day trips or short overnight forays.

BERKELEY

Berkeley and University of California may not be synonymous, but they're so interdependent that it's difficult to tell where one stops and the other begins. You won't find many backpack-toting students in the upscale neighborhoods that buffer the north and east sides of campus, but for the most part Berkeley is a student town, dominated by the massive U.C. campus and its 30,000 undergraduate and graduate enrollees. Because of its offbeat, countercultural reputation, the university attracts every sort of person imaginable—from artists, anarchists, and hypergenius intellectuals to superjocks and fashion slaves, not to mention the stubbornly apathetic and the piously ideological. Recent campus celebrities have included former math professor Theodore Kaczynski (a.k.a. the Unabomber) and former student The Naked Guy (expelled for attending classes in the nude). But anyone who has watched the documentary *Berkeley in the Sixties* might be surprised to find out that the city isn't what it used to be. Berkeley *is* still a breeding ground for alternative social trends both important and inane, for posters and protesters. But with the 1994 election of a more conservative mayor, Shirley Dean, there seems to be a reaction by some Berkeley residents against the city's free-for-all reputation.

Southside, or the area south of campus, is dominated by chaotic **Telegraph Avenue.** A few blocks east, **College Avenue** is lined with boutiques and cafés with a bohemian flair. North Berkeley, a more sedate

THE SAN FRANCISCO BAY AREA

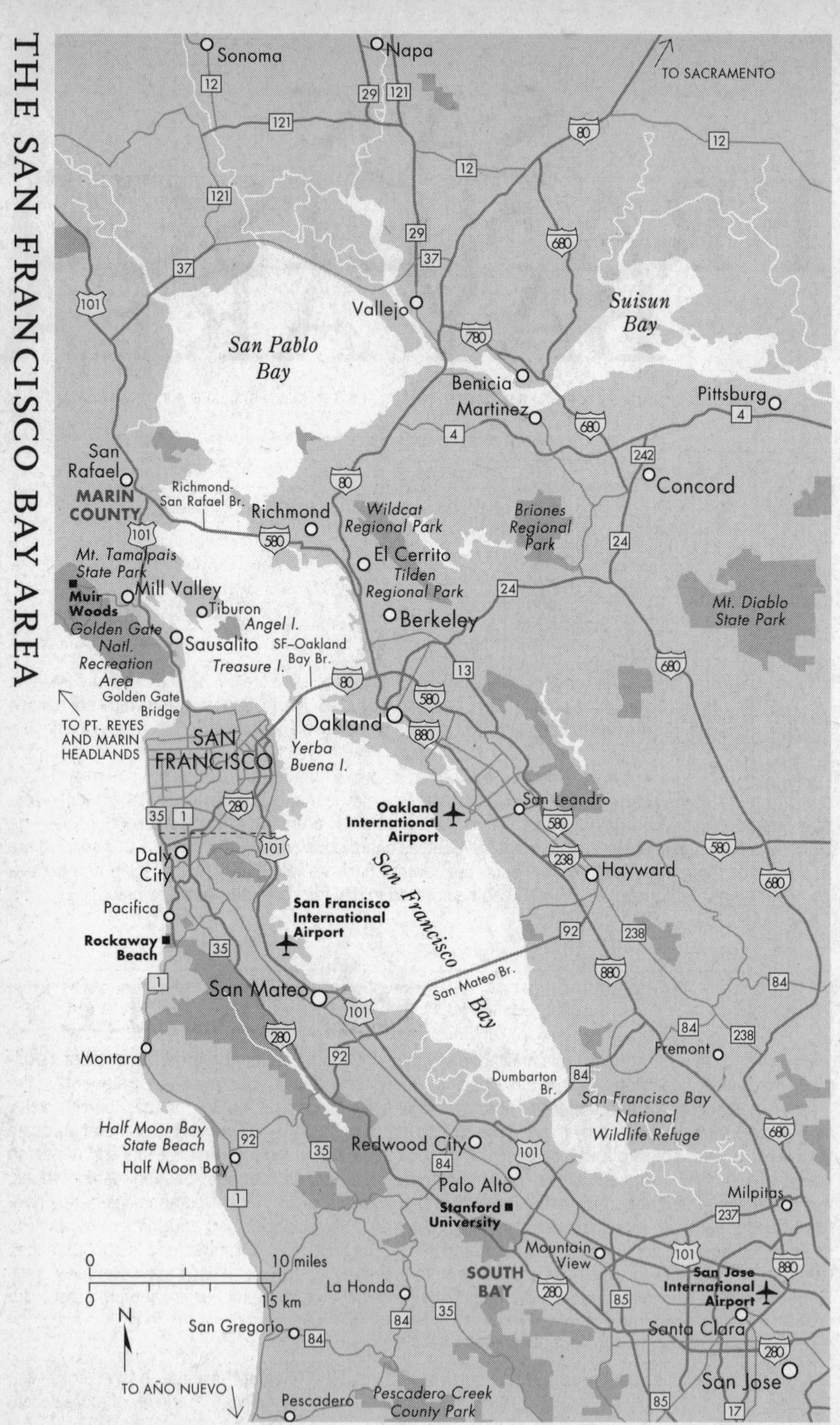

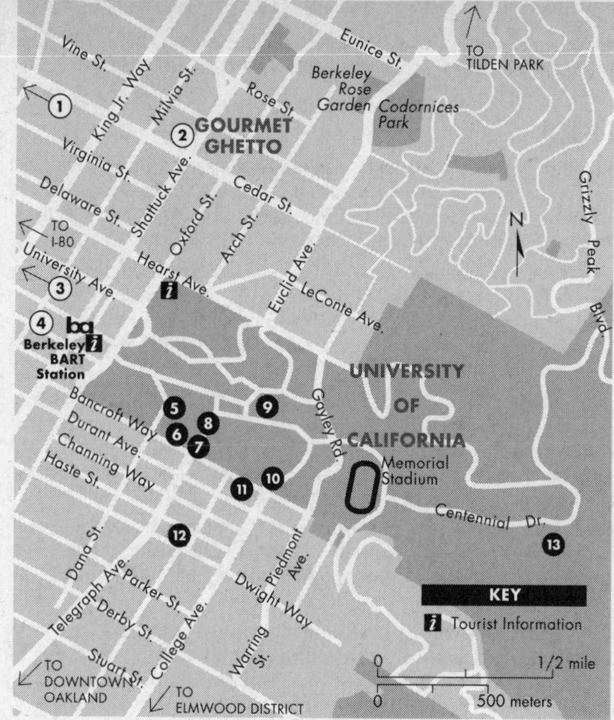

Sights ●
Campanile, **9**
People's Park, **12**
Phoebe Hearst Museum of Anthropology, **10**
Sather Gate, **8**
Sproul Plaza, **7**
Student Union Building, **6**
U.C. Botanical Gardens, **13**
University Art Museum, **11**
Zellerbach Hall, **5**

Lodging ○
Campus Motel, **3**
French Hotel, **2**
Golden Bear Motel, **1**
YMCA, **4**

and residential area, is where you'll find the **Gourmet Ghetto,** home of the famed restaurant **Chez Panisse** (*see below*) and a number of excellent organic food markets. The Berkeley Hills, rising north and east of campus, offer the huge **Tilden Regional Park** and acres of densely forested slopes.

COMING AND GOING

BY BART

Bay Area Rapid Transit (BART) (tel. 800/817–1717) is the easiest way to get to Berkeley. Take it from San Francisco or Oakland to the downtown Berkeley station on Shattuck Avenue. One-way fare from San Francisco is under $3, and the trip takes about 25 minutes. From the station, you can make the 10-minute walk to Telegraph Avenue up Bancroft Way or the five-minute walk to the campus's west entrance on Center Street.

BY BUS

AC Transit (tel. 800/559–4636) offers daily bus service from San Francisco's Transbay Terminal (1st and Mission Sts.): Take Bus F for direct service to Berkeley, or Bus T to Oakland (which connects with Bus 40 to Berkeley). Both transbay bus lines operate until midnight, and fare is $2.20. Within Berkeley, Bus 51 travels from the Marina (*see* Cheap Thrills, *below*) east on University Avenue past the Berkeley BART station, past campus, and south on College Avenue into Oakland.

BY CAR

From San Francisco, cross the Bay Bridge (no toll this direction, $3 other way) and take **I–80** east. Exit east at University Avenue, which ends at the west side of the U.C. campus, near Shattuck Avenue and downtown. For Telegraph Avenue and the main campus entrance, turn right on Shattuck Avenue from University Avenue, and then left on Durant Avenue; Telegraph Avenue is ¼-mi farther. Unless there's heavy traffic, the trip takes 30–40 minutes. Parking is a serious problem, but there's a **parking garage** on Durant just west of Telegraph; look for it on the right side of the street.

BY TRAIN

Amtrak stops in Berkeley (3rd St. and University Ave.)—you can board, but you can't buy tickets—and in nearby Emeryville (5885 Landegran St.), where connecting buses travel into San Francisco.

WHERE TO SLEEP

Lodging in Berkeley is often either shabby or downright expensive—sometimes both. If that isn't enough, it can be hard to come by: In mid-May, when thousands of graduating students don caps and gowns, reservations become *absolutely* essential; most of the nicer hotels sell out four to five months in advance. All Berkeley lodgings add 12% tax to the prices listed below.

Most of the city's motels are on **University Avenue** and most of these are not recommended. Your life isn't necessarily in danger here, but expect a general air of seediness (i.e., velvet curtains, the reek of cheap perfume). It's best to stick to the campus end of University Avenue; the further west you go, the shoddier the surroundings. To reach all of the motels in the vicinity from Berkeley BART, walk two blocks north to University Avenue and head west, or take Bus 51.

Berkeley has no hostels, but the **YMCA** (2185 Milvia St., tel. 510/848–6800, fax 510/848–6835)—open to both men and women—is cheap and within easy reach of Berkeley's sights. Clean, dorm-style singles with shared bath cost $25; there are also a few doubles ($33) and triples ($40). If the price isn't reason enough to stay here, consider that guests have access to a kitchen and a basketball court, weight room, and Olympic-size swimming pool at the fitness center next door.

UNDER $55 • Campus Motel. This place sits right on noisy University Avenue, but it *is* close to campus (6 blocks west) and the rooms are tidy, plain, and cheap, with cable TV and coffee makers. Doubles are $55. *1619 University Ave., between McGee Ave. and California St., tel. 510/841–3844, fax 510/841–8134. 23 rooms, all with bath.*

Golden Bear Motel. One of the nicer budget lodgings in town, the Golden Bear has clean doubles for $49. The surrounding neighborhood isn't that great, so be careful walking around at night. Bus 52 across the street will whisk you to the Berkeley campus. *1620 San Pablo Ave., tel. 510/525–6770, fax 510/525–6999. From North Berkeley BART, walk 3 blocks west to San Pablo Ave. and turn right. 42 rooms, all with bath.*

UNDER $100 • French Hotel. This little hotel in North Berkeley is close to boutique shopping and several gourmet restaurants, including Chez Panisse. Doubles with a minuscule patio cost $85–$95 (there's one room available for $68); those without patio include a complimentary breakfast. A cozy, brick-wall café is downstairs. *1538 Shattuck Ave., between Cedar and Vine Sts., tel. and fax 510/548–9930. From Berkeley BART, walk 6 blocks north on Shattuck Ave. 18 rooms, all with bath.*

UNIVERSITY HOUSING

University Summer Visitor Housing (2601 Warring St., tel. 510/642–4444) offers summer dorm accommodations at 2424 Channing Way for $38–$50 per night. Rooms are nothing to write home about (bed, desk, chair, phone). For an additional $3 per day, you'll get linens, soap, and parking. There are lots of young people around, and the dorms are a very safe place to stay.

FOOD

Berkeleyans take their food very seriously. California cuisine, designer fuel for the yuppie generation, got its start here. It's based on the idea that fresh, home-cultivated ingredients (no matter how costly) are vital to the success of a dish and that portions are to be savored, not shoveled in. This concept has reached its apex at Alice Waters's world-famous restaurant **Chez Panisse** (1517 Shattuck Ave., tel. 510/548–5525), which serves stunning five- to six-course meals for upwards of $65 per person. The area surrounding Chez Panisse, on Shattuck Avenue near Cedar and Vine streets, has become known as the **Gourmet Ghetto** because it contains a number of high-quality restaurants, cafés, and specialty shops. A better bet for budget travelers is **Telegraph Avenue** between Dwight Way and the U.C. campus. Here you'll find a high concentration of supercheap restaurants serving fast food with a Berkeley twist (heaping green salads and gourmet sandwiches are far more common than burgers). West of campus, along **University Avenue,** there's a string of small restaurants, mostly Asian and Indian.

UNDER $5 • Telegraph Avenue near the Berkeley campus is full of places that cater to thin pocketbooks. At Telegraph and Bancroft Way, a cluster of food carts sell everything from burritos and smoothies to Japanese food, falafel sandwiches, and wonderfully stuffed potatoes—try the "Berkeley's Best" spud ($2.75) with pesto and mozzarella. The ever popular **Noah's Bagels** (2344 Telegraph Ave., tel. 510/849–9951) spreads flavored cream cheese shmears around the holes of their chewy New York-style bagels. **Smart Alec's** (2355 Telegraph Ave., tel. 510/704–4000) is a new, vegan fast-food spot, where you can get a veggie burger, air-baked fries, and soda for $3.29. For pizza with an attitude, stop by **Blondie's** (2340 Telegraph Ave., near Durant Ave., tel. 510/548–1129), popular with street freaks and bleary-eyed students in need of a late-night pepperoni fix. The jaded, underpaid employees provide constant entertainment, the stand-up counter is always packed, and your basic, greasy, and filling slice costs $2.

Café Intermezzo. This Berkeley institution with a harried and occasionally rude staff indisputably serves the biggest and best salads around. The Veggie Delight ($4.75) is a family-size mound of greens topped with kidney and garbanzo beans, hard-boiled egg, sprouts, avocado, and croutons. Salads are served with your choice of homemade dressings—try the poppyseed—and include a bookend-size slab of fresh-from-the-oven, honey-wheat bread. Humongous sandwiches go for $4.15. *2442 Telegraph Ave., at Haste St., tel. 510/849–4592.*

Crêpes-a-Go-Go. Slimane Djili, the owner of this small café, used to sell crêpes on the streets of Paris. Now, bless him, he's settled on busy University Avenue, offering sweet and savory crêpes like Nutella and banana ($3.25) or spinach, green onions, and cheeses ($3.55). One is filling, two will leave you staggering out the door. *2125 University Ave., at Shattuck Ave., tel. 510/841–7722. 2 blocks north of Berkeley BART. Cash only.*

UNDER $10 • Blue Nile. This is an excellent Ethiopian eatery, serving everything from thick split-pea stew and pepper-cooked beef to *tej* (honey wine) and freshly blended fruit shakes. The food is served family style, and you use *injera* (spongy bread) instead of silverware to scoop it up. *Kitfo,* minced raw beef laced with spices, is recommended. Lunch goes for about $5 and dinner for $6–$8. *2525 Telegraph Ave., between Dwight Way and Parker St., tel. 510/540–6777. Closed Sun. lunch.*

Cha Am. Although the food is usually more Berkeley than Thai, the airy Cha Am is one of the most popular Thai spots in town. Try the magical *Tom ka gai* (chicken and coconut soup; $7.25) or the mixed seafood plate with chili, garlic, and vegetables ($9). *1543 Shattuck Ave., at Cedar St., tel. 510/848–9664. 7 blocks north of Berkeley BART. Closed Sun. lunch.*

Juan's Place. This traditional Mexican restaurant (stuck on the fringes of Berkeley, surrounded by factories and warehouses) has the feel of an old cantina, complete with piñatas, mirrored beer ads, and cheesy portraits of matadors. Juan's dishes out large portions of standard fare, including tacos, burritos, and tamales. *941 Carleton St., at 9th St., tel. 510/845–6904. 2 blocks west of San Pablo Ave. Closed major holidays.*

Kabana. It's not much to look at, but don't be deterred, or you'll miss out on the deliciously spicy Pakistani food. Choose from vegetarian dishes ($5)—made with eggplant, potatoes, chick peas, or greens—or try a hefty portion of biryani or curry made with lamb ($7) or chicken ($6), both tender as could be from baking in the clay oven. Scoop up flavorful bites with homemade bread. *1106 University Ave., at San Pablo Ave., tel. 845–3355.*

Long Life Vegi House. Just west of campus sits this long-time favorite of locals who appreciate big portions of healthy Chinese food at very reasonable prices. It has daily specials in addition to a long menu of vegetarian dishes, including vegi-chicken, vegi-beef, and vegi-pork options (made with wheat gluten and soy protein), and seafood dishes. Feast on prawns and string beans in black bean sauce ($8.75). Lunch specials, at less than the cost of a bargain matinee, include soup, a spring roll, and entrée over tasty rice. *2129 University Ave., near Shattuck Ave., tel. 510/845–6072.*

UNDER $15 • Pasand Madras Cuisine. If you feel like going for the gusto at this southern Indian restaurant, get a complete *thali* dinner. The ginger-chicken Masala curry ($8.50 à la carte, $11 thali) is a winner, as are the vegetable curries ($6–$9.50)—though even the ones labeled "spicy" are pretty tame. Cross-legged sitar and tabla players whip up a musical frenzy during dinner; a downstairs lounge features live music of various stripes. *2286 Shattuck Ave., at Bancroft Way, tel. 510/549–2559. 2 blocks south of Berkeley BART.*

UNDER $30 • Chez Panisse. Chef Alice Waters started this world-famous restaurant in 1971 with a commitment to serve "produce and meat from local farms and ranches producing ecologically sound agriculture." The four-course dinner menu ($35–$65), served in the downstairs restaurant, changes nightly, but you can be assured of innovative, seasonal combinations such as oven-steamed salmon with curly endive or rabbit confit with noodles. If you would rather not spend your weekly grocery budget on one meal, the upstairs **Chez Panisse Café** serves many of the same dishes for half the price—entrées range from $14–$16. You can make same-day reservations for lunch, but for dinner go early and expect to wait an hour or more for a table. *1517 Shattuck Ave., at Cedar St., tel. 510/548–5049. 7 blocks north of Berkeley BART. Closed Sun.*

CAFES

The People's Republic of Berkeley would collapse without cafés. Students would have nowhere to be seen while "studying"; skate punks would have nowhere to hang while cutting class; artists and poets would have no place to share their angst. Luckily, within a square mile of the U.C. campus, you'll find no fewer than 50 cafés. Smokers should take note: In 1994, Berkeley banned smoking in all indoor *and* outdoor cafés.

Caffè Strada. Strada's sprawling outdoor patio attracts a social mix of students and visiting foreigners (residents of International House, across the street). Relax in the sun with a newspaper, or eavesdrop on your neighbors while sipping latte ($1.60). The free *East Bay Express* and *Daily Cal* are available at a kiosk across the street. *2300 College Ave., at Bancroft Way, tel. 510/843–5282.*

Mediterraneum Caffè. The Med was featured in *The Graduate* and is a longtime hangout for Berkeley's resident thinkers, dreamers, and revolutionaries. It serves sandwiches, pastas, and other such fare at reasonable prices, as well as the usual coffee drinks. *2475 Telegraph Ave., between Haste St. and Dwight Way, tel. 510/549–1128. Kitchen closed for dinner.*

Red Café. Redbrick walls, exposed beam ceilings, and a massive skylight create a warm, welcoming ambiance here. It's a gem of a café/bar, with an older, artsy, postgrad crowd and frequent live jazz. The full kitchen serves vegetarian sandwiches, salads, and pastas ($5–$6), and the café has a fine selection of beers. *1941 University Ave., at Bonita St., tel. 510/843–8607. Closed Sun.*

WORTH SEEING

TELEGRAPH AVENUE

Whether you love it or hate it, the first five blocks of this congested and colorful avenue—which begins at the campus and runs south into Oakland—form the spiritual heart of Berkeley. It's a jumble of cafés, bookstores, used-clothing stores, and cheap restaurants, populated by harried students, long-haired hippies, homeless buskers, metaphysical warriors, and wide-eyed tourists. Every day—rain or shine—street vendors line the avenue's sidewalks, selling everything from handmade jewelry and crafts to crystals, incense, and tie-dye T-shirts. New Age prophets offer tarot and numerology readings to passersby, while baggy-jeaned hip-hop fans skateboard down the sidewalks. Telegraph today is a unique fusion of '60s and '90s counterculture, and the two elements blend nicely.

Shops along Telegraph come and go, but neighborhood landmarks include **Amoeba** (2455 Telegraph Ave., tel. 510/549–1125) and **Rasputin's** (2403 Telegraph Ave., tel. 510/848–9005), both of which feature a huge selection of vinyl, tapes, and CDs. Book lovers should check out **Cody's** (2454 Telegraph Ave., tel. 510/845–7852) and **Moe's** (2476 Telegraph Ave., tel. 510/849–2087). Cody's hosts regular readings and has probably the largest selection of new books, magazines, and 'zines in the area, while Moe's specializes in used and rare books.

UNIVERSITY OF CALIFORNIA CAMPUS

Established in 1868 as the first branch of the statewide University of California system, the "Cal" campus retains some of the beauty and gentility of its early years, as well as vestiges of the revolutionary '60s. For a map, stop by the **Student Union Building** on the west side of Sproul Plaza (*see below*). Free student-led tours of campus leave from the **visitor center** (101 University Hall, 2200 University Ave., at Oxford St., tel. 510/642–5215), on the west side of campus, weekdays at 10 AM. Tours also leave on Saturday at 10 AM from a small visitor center (tel. 510/642–4636), open Saturday only, on the second floor of the Student Union Building.

Sproul Plaza, just north of the Telegraph and Bancroft intersection, is where the Free Speech Movement began in 1964. Look inside imposing **Sproul Hall** for a display of photographs from this first demonstration, in which 3,000 students surrounded a police car containing a U.C. Berkeley student arrested for distributing political flyers. Today Sproul Plaza is a source of endless entertainment for locals and tourists alike, a place where some of Berkeley's most famous loonies congregate: Look out for the Hate Man (the man in a bra, high heels, long skirt, and lipstick), who has professed hatred for everything. **Lower Sproul Plaza,** just west of Sproul Plaza, is the site of occasional free noon concerts as well as weekend jam sessions by a ragtag group of bongo drummers. **Zellerbach Hall,** on Lower Sproul, hosts professional theater and concerts; check the box office for upcoming events.

North of Sproul Plaza, cross over Strawberry Creek to reach **Sather Gate,** the main entrance to campus until expansion in the 1960s. Head uphill (to the right) to find Sather Tower, more commonly known as the **Campanile,** a 307-ft clock tower modeled after the one in Venice's Piazza San Marco. The carillon is played weekdays at 7:50 AM, noon, and 6 PM; Saturday at noon and 6, and on Sunday at 2 for an extended 45 minutes (concerts are suspended during final exams). You can watch the noon performances from the observation deck (open Mon.–Sat. 10–3:30, Sun. 10–1:45), which is reached via an elevator (50¢). Even if you miss the show, the Bay Area views from here are stunning.

Nearby, Kroeber Hall houses the **Phoebe Hearst Museum of Anthropology,** which has rotating exhibits covering everything from ancient America to Neolithic China. Also on display are artifacts used by Ishi, the lone survivor of California's Yahi tribe, who was brought to live on the U.C. campus in 1911, after gold miners had slaughtered the rest of his tribe. *Tel. 510/642–3681. Admission: $2; free Thurs. Open Wed.–Sun. 10–4:30 (Thurs. until 9 during school year).*

UNIVERSITY ART MUSEUM • The UAM houses the largest university-owned art collection in the country. Though the low concrete building may not look like much from the street, the galleries inside are surprisingly airy. Displays could include anything from a 16th-century altar panel to a passel of sugar-candy pastel Bibles made by a Berkeley MFA candidate. One of the museum's most impressive permanent installations is a room full of violently colorful paintings by the abstract expressionist Hans Hofmann. The UAM is also home to the **Pacific Film Archive** (*see* Movie Houses *in* Chapter 6), on the ground floor. Pick up a schedule of upcoming exhibits and movies at the museum entrance. A sculpture garden to the rear of the museum is pleasant during summer. *2626 Bancroft Way, tel. 510/642–0808. Admission: $6; free Thurs. 11–noon and 5–9. Open Wed.–Sun. 11–5 (Thurs. until 9).*

U.C. BOTANICAL GARDEN • Haul yourself up to this horticultural haven to learn more about rare plants, take a tour around the world of flora, or to just stop and smell the roses. Nestled in the hills east of Strawberry Canyon, the garden is a valuable research and education center with a diverse collection of plants—over 10,000 neatly labeled species from around the world. The garden is divided into regional areas with habitats ranging from South African deserts to Himalayan forests. It's especially colorful in spring, when the extensive rhododendron collection is in full bloom. *200 Centennial Dr., tel. 510/642–3343. From Berkeley BART, take Bus 8; or take Hill Service Shuttle (50¢) from Hearst Mining Circle on campus. Admission: $3; free Thurs. Open daily 9–4:45. Tours weekends at 1:30.*

CHEAP THRILLS

Telegraph Avenue is a haven for **street musicians.** Most Fridays a Peruvian band sets up on the corner of Telegraph and Bancroft Way, while other afternoons might bring out folks hammering on dulcimers, drumming on buckets, or strumming on acoustic guitars.

Warm days were meant to be spent at the Berkeley Marina, at the end of University Avenue approximately ½-mi west of I–80. Head for the ¾-mi-long pier jutting out into the bay to enjoy views of the Golden Gate Bridge and Alcatraz Island. Winds along the bay can be quite chilly, which makes nearby **César E. Chávez Park** (formerly North Waterfront Park) a perfect retreat. The hilly, 92-acre park is one of the most popular kite-flying areas in the Bay Area. On the first full weekend of every month, you can catch a free spin around the bay with the **Cal Sailing Club** (tel. 510/287–5905); wear warm, waterproof clothing. To reach the marina from Berkeley BART, take Bus 51M.

North of the Berkeley campus on Euclid Street between Bayview Place and Eunice Street you'll find the terraced **Berkeley Rose Garden,** offering roses, more roses, and a panoramic bay view. To get there from campus, walk north on Euclid Street for 20 minutes; from Berkeley BART, take Bus 65 north.

AFTER DARK

Like everything else in Berkeley, nightlife is eclectic and casual. The bars along Telegraph Avenue can't help but appeal to student tastes and budgets. The campus paper, the *Daily Californian,* regularly lists all student-oriented events, most of which are free or dirt cheap. The free weekly *East Bay Express* contains a complete events calendar for the East Bay, including films, lectures, readings, and musical events. For live music, consult *The List* (found at most independent record stores). For dancing, head

PEOPLE'S PARK

Just east of Telegraph between Haste Street and Dwight Way is People's Park, originally created by students in 1969 on the site of a fenced-off and abandoned asphalt lot. When the university later attempted to replace the park with a dormitory, it touched off protests that ended in the death of one man, the use of tear gas on Sproul Plaza, and the 17-day occupation of Berkeley by the National Guard. Over the years, the park has decayed while activists and university and city officials argue its fate. There isn't that much to do here; you can play basketball or volleyball on the much disputed courts or contemplate why this little plot of land creates such passionate emotions. The homeless and activists remain; elaborately graffitied bathrooms are covered with murals, poetry, antigovernment statements, and witty slogans like "Kill the Narks in People's Park."

across the Bay Bridge to San Francisco; Berkeley's dance club scene is so low-key as to be almost nonexistent—try Blake's (*see below*) in a pinch.

BARS

The Albatross. This no-nonsense watering-hole, the sort of bar where grad students might borrow the bar's Scrabble game and settle in for the evening, attracts both students and working folk. The cheap draft beer (starting at $1.50) tastes even better with the free popcorn, and there's a cozy fireplace and a whole row of dart boards occupying a good-size portion of the bar. *1822 San Pablo Ave., between Hearst Ave. and Delaware St., tel. 510/849–4714. From Berkeley BART, Bus 51 west to San Pablo Ave., walk 1½ blocks north.*

Bison Brewing Company. Homemade stout, cider, ale, and snakebites ($3 a pint) bring in a mix of fraternity brothers and tattooed types. Happy hour (weekdays 4–6, 3–8 during "daylight savings") features $2.25 pints and attracts big crowds during the school year. Live bands, ranging from blues to Irish folk, entertain Thursday through Saturday (occasional $1–$2 cover). Free live jazz often plays on Sunday afternoon. *2598 Telegraph Ave., at Parker St., tel. 510/841–7734. 5 blocks south of U.C. campus.*

Jupiter. This spacious wine-and-beer bar across from Berkeley BART is popular for its outdoor beer garden, 20 microbrews on tap, and free live jazz on weekends. Weekends draw large down-to-earth crowds, but it's almost always mellow enough to allow for conversation. Beers run $2.75–$3.50. *2181 Shattuck Ave., near Center St., tel. 510/843–8277.*

Triple Rock Brewery. At this popular microbrewery, the 1950s reign supreme. The crowd is noisy in a collegiate sort of way, but folks are friendly. The outdoor patio area is the best place to enjoy one of the homebrews ($2.75–$3.25) and excellent munchies (nachos and the like). *1920 Shattuck Ave., at Hearst Ave., tel. 510/843–2739. 3 blocks north of Berkeley BART.*

LIVE MUSIC

Ashkenaz. This world-music emporium has been such a community fixture since the early '70s that everyone was shocked and saddened when owner David Nadel was shot and killed outside the bar in December 1996. At press time Ashkenaz had closed, but Nadel's brother had begun to make plans to reopen the club. *1317 San Pablo Ave., Berkeley, tel. 510/525–5054. From Berkeley BART, Bus 9 west to San Pablo Ave. Cover: $5–$10.*

Blake's. This restaurant and jazz joint opened in the late 1940s, and since then it's become a Berkeley institution. The ground-floor dining room serves decent food, and the upstairs bar (Leona's) provides brews and free popcorn to a sedate, postcollegiate crowd; but the cramped basement downstairs—a no-frills bar with a sawdust-covered floor—hosts some of the best blues and funk acts in the area, plus the occasional alternative rock band. *2367 Telegraph Ave., near Durant Ave., Berkeley, tel. 510/848–0886. 1 block from U.C. campus. Cover: $2–$7.*

924 Gilman Street. This all-ages, alcohol-free cooperative features local hard-core garage and punk bands. Green Day got its start here and has brought the place a fair amount of fame. Most shows cost $5, but you have to buy a $2 membership (valid for one year) to get in the first time. *924 Gilman St., at 8th St., Berkeley, tel. 510/525–9926. From Berkeley BART, Bus 9 north to 8th St.*

Starry Plough. This popular Irish pub near the Berkeley–Oakland border offers an eclectic mix of folk music and not-too-extreme rock bands. Join the older, politically left crowd for a pint or two of Guinness, Bass, or Anchor Steam and a game of darts—or free Irish dance lessons (Mon.). *3101 Shattuck Ave., at Prince St., Berkeley, tel. 510/841–2082. From Ashby Bart, walk three blocks south. Cover: up to $6.*

OUTDOOR ACTIVITIES

Berkeley's **Tilden Regional Park** contains 2,078 acres of eucalyptus trees and rolling hills, filled with hikers, cyclists, picnickers, and poison oak. **Volmer Peak** (1,913 ft) to the south and **Wildcat Peak** (1,250 ft) to the north are two of the highest points in the East Bay. You can hike to Wildcat Peak from **Inspiration Point** along **Nimitz Way,** a 4½-mi road with views of the bay and of the San Pablo and Briones Reservoirs. Stop by the **Environmental Education Center** (tel. 510/525–2233) at the north end of the park for maps and information. Nimitz Way is also popular with bikers. For two-wheel rentals, try **Missing Link Bicycle Co-op** (1988 Shattuck Ave., Berkeley, tel. 510/843–7471), where a mountain bike rents for $25–$35 a day.

From Berkeley BART, AC Bus 67 gets you as far as Spruce and Grizzly Peak on weekdays and directly to **Lake Anza** on weekends. Summers, AC Bus 65 will transport both you and your bike from Berkeley BART to the top of Spruce Street at Grizzly Peak. If you're driving, take University Avenue east from I–80, go left on Oxford Street, right on Rose, and left on Spruce to the top of the hill. Cross Grizzly Peak Boulevard, make an immediate left on Canon Drive, and follow signs.

OAKLAND

Oakland doesn't have the same dazzling effect on visitors as San Francisco, so if you're looking for glitz you might want to save the $2 BART fare for another cable-car ride through Union Square. Voted "All American City" in 1993, predominantly working-class Oakland offers visitors a typical example of a post-1850 American city: a diverse cultural landscape, a struggling downtown, some great architecture, some crime-ridden areas, and high hopes for community renewal. Oakland also has its own special flair as home to the West Coast blues; the Oaktown school of rap (heard in the music of local artists MC Hammer, Digital Underground, Too Short, Tony! Toni! Toné!, Oaktown 3-5-7, and recently deceased rap artist Tupac Shakur); and a vibrant art scene from the many artists who live in the city's plentiful, low-rent warehouse spaces.

Present-day Oakland was founded in the mid-1800s by three unsuccessful gold miners who leveled the area's oak groves and set up a town. Oakland prospered thanks to a thriving port, profitable manufacturing industries, and the arrival of the railroad. These boom days saw a flurry of construction of downtown buildings (many of which are now empty); a bigger, better City Hall (once the tallest building west of Chicago); and the creation of Lake Merritt park. Unfortunately, the growing downtown was shattered by the Depression, the flight of wealthy citizens to the hills, and a poor development plan.

But there's plenty to explore in Oakland. The neighborhoods around **Grand, College,** and **Piedmont** avenues are lined with cafés, reasonably priced and upscale restaurants, bookstores, and boutiques. Wander through **Chinatown** for lively restaurants and markets selling produce, pungent spices, and meats. Check out the downtown revitalization efforts around **Jack London Square** and **City Center** or, if the city is fraying your nerves, head for the parks in the hills to the east.

BASICS

The **Oakland Convention and Visitors Authority** (550 10th St., Suite 214, tel. 510/839–9000), open weekdays 8:30–5, is happy to answer inquiries. Pick up the "Official Visitors Guide," which lists dozens

OAKLAND

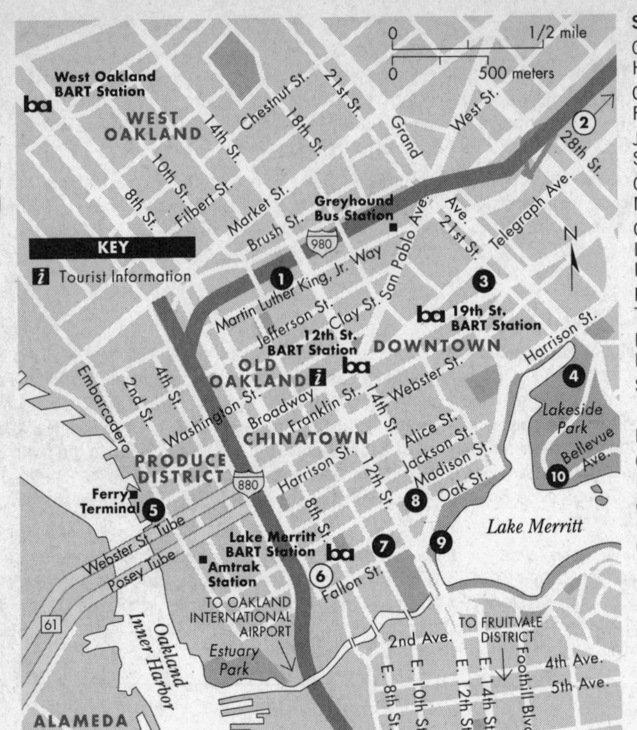

Sights ●

Camron-Stanford House, **9**

Children's Fairyland, **4**

Jack London Square, **5**

Oakland Museum, **7**

Oakland Public Library's Oakland History Room, **8**

Paramount Theatre, **3**

Preservation Park, **1**

Sailboat House, **10**

Lodging ○

Civic Center Lodge, **6**

Claremont Resort, Spa, and Tennis Club, **2**

of museums, historical attractions, and community events. To reach the bureau, take BART to 12th Street Station and walk two blocks south on Broadway. Free walking tours are conducted May–October by **City of Oakland Tours** (tel. 510/238–3234) on Wednesday and Saturday at 10 AM; call for current itineraries.

COMING AND GOING

BY BART

Oakland has eight **BART** stations, but the only ones near downtown are 12th Street, 19th Street, and Lake Merritt. Trains run every 10–20 minutes until midnight, with service starting up again at 4 AM weekdays, 6 AM Saturday, and 8 AM Sunday. The 15-minute ride from San Francisco's Powell Street Station to Lake Merritt Station costs $2.20. For more information, call 800/817–1717.

BY BUS

AC Transit (tel. 510/817–1717) runs from Oakland to points throughout the Bay Area. The adult and youth fare is $1.25; for seniors and persons with disabilities it's 60¢. Transfers (25¢) are good for up to two hours. Lines designated by letters, instead of numbers, go over the Bay Bridge to San Francisco's **Transbay Terminal** (1st and Mission Sts.). Most only run from dawn to dusk; exceptions include the F, T, and N lines, which operate until midnight. Transbay fare is $2.20 for adults ($1.10 youths, seniors, and persons with disabilities). Within Oakland, Bus 40 travels north on Broadway from Jack London Square and into Berkeley, then past the U.C. campus to Berkeley BART. Bus 12 travels from 12th Street BART past Lakeside Park, around Lake Merritt, and east on Grand Avenue.

Greyhound (2103 San Pablo Ave., at 20th St., tel. 510/834–3213 or 800/231–2222 for reservations and ticket information) travels to and from Oakland. Fare to San Francisco is $7 one-way; buses leave once an hour from 12:25 AM to 11:40 PM. One-way fare to Los Angeles is $32.

BY CAR

From San Francisco, take **I-580** to **I-880** south to the Grand Avenue exit for Lake Merritt, or to the Waterfront and Downtown exits for Jack London Square and downtown, respectively. Depending on traffic, the trip takes 30–45 minutes. Once you get to town, Oakland's individual neighborhoods are best explored on foot, even though the city covers a huge geographical area.

BY FERRY

The **Oakland/Alameda Ferry** (tel. 510/522–3300), operated by the **Blue and Gold Fleet,** runs between Oakland's Jack London Square and San Francisco's Pier 39 or the Ferry Building four to five times daily for $4 one-way.

BY PLANE

Oakland International Airport (1 Airport Dr., off Hegenberger Rd., tel. 510/ 577–4000) is a small airport, easily accessed on public transportation from points throughout the Bay Area, and less crowded than San Francisco International. It's often much cheaper to arrive here than at SFO, particularly on **Southwest** (tel. 800/435–9792), which has some 80 flights in and out of Oakland, many of which go to Los Angeles.

The **Air-Bart Shuttle** (tel. 510/562–7700) runs every 15–20 minutes to the Coliseum BART station. Buy tickets ($2) at the BART station or airport terminal before you board. **AC Transit Bus 58** ($1.25) follows the same route, continuing on to downtown Oakland (50 min). A taxi to downtown Berkeley from Oakland International costs about $30–$35.

A much-loved feature of downtown Oakland's skyline is the Tribune Tower, built in 1923. It was the city's first landmark building.

BY TRAIN

Oakland's **Amtrak** station (245 2nd St., tel. 510/238–4320 or 800/872–7245 for reservations) is centrally located near downtown at Jack London Square, less than a mile from 12th Street/Civic Center BART. Both the *Capitol* from Sacramento and the long-distance *Coast Starlight* pass through.

WHERE TO SLEEP

Oakland's budget lodging scene isn't pretty, price-wise or safety-wise. Hotels are either geared toward businesspeople on expense accounts, or they're in grimy, scary neighborhoods. If you're desperate, there are thousands of rooms in faceless chain motels ($50–$75) in downtown Oakland (near Lake Merritt) and around the airport.

Civic Center Lodge. One of the few centrally located and cheap hotels in Oakland, this no-frills place is right next to a highway and a boarded-up gas station but within easy reach of the waterfront, Lake Merritt, and downtown bars and restaurants. Singles cost $38 per night, doubles $48. *50 6th St., tel. 510/444–4139. From Lake Merritt BART, walk 3 blocks down Oak St. to 6th St., turn left. 32 rooms, all with bath.*

Claremont Resort, Spa, and Tennis Club. With its plush rooms (no two are alike), full spa, tennis courts, and pools, you really get what you pay for here—and pay you will. Bay-view doubles go for $239, hillside doubles for $199. Weekend packages sometimes start at $169 per night. The Terrace Bar view of San Francisco, the Bay Bridge, *and* the Golden Gate Bridge, is the most spectacular in the East Bay. *41 Tunnel Road, at Ashby and Domingo Aves., tel. 510/843–3000, fax 510/843–6239. 280 rooms, all with bath.*

CAMPING

Lake Chabot Regional Park. Three campgrounds are perched above Lake Chabot in this park southeast of downtown Oakland. Tent sites in a pleasant wooded area are $14 per night, RV hookups are $20; you also have to pay a $5 reservation charge. The campground has showers and flush toilets and is close to hiking and biking trails. The lake is a popular spot for fishing, so try to reserve ahead in summer. Unfortunately, the nearest bus stop is 1½ miles from the park entrance. *Tel. 510/562–2267. From I-80, I-580 east to Redwood Rd. exit, turn left, follow Redwood Rd. 4½ mi to park gate (it's another 2½–3 mi to campgrounds). 75 sites. Drinking water, fire grates, flush toilets, picnic tables, showers.*

FOOD

From Southern-style shacks to El Salvadoran holes-in-the-wall, Oakland is loaded with cheap and colorful eateries. Because the city's population is so diverse, you can find just about every type of cuisine imaginable. The center for Asian food is **Chinatown,** downtown between Broadway, 7th, 10th, and Alice streets. The **Fruitvale** district, accessed from the Fruitvale BART station, has lots of cheap Mexican and Central American restaurants. It's safest to restrict your visits here to the daylight hours. If you don't feel like having an adventure along with your meal, there are two long avenues in Oakland that offer an array of familiar delis, burger joints, and gringo burrito shops. From downtown Oakland, Bus 59 or 59A will take you north on Broadway to **Piedmont Avenue**; for **College Avenue,** take BART to Rockridge station.

UNDER $5 • Taquería Morelia. Come to this Oakland joint for one of the best *quesadillas* around (fried flour or corn tortilla oozing cheese and sprinkled with chopped tomatoes and cilantro; $2). Locals of all ages flow between the restaurant and adjacent dive bar, Talk of the Town, carrying cold, cheap beer and plastic baskets heaped with tacos and burritos ($2.50–$4 each). *4491 E. 14th St., near High St., tel. 510/535–6030. About 7 blocks southeast of Fruitvale BART.*

UNDER $10 • Asmara Restaurant. Colorful baskets and rugs cheer up this East African restaurant in North Oakland. Sample three of the excellent entrées in the meat ($5.50 lunch, $8 dinner) or vegetarian ($5.50 lunch, $7.50 dinner) combination platter. In keeping with Ethiopian tradition, food is served family style with *injera* bread and a no utensils—use your fingers to scoop up the tasty morsels. *5020 Telegraph Ave., near 51st St., tel. 510/547–5100. No lunch Tue.*

Flint's. Regarded by some as the best barbecue shack in the world, Flint's caters to large appetites during the wee hours. Choose from pork or beef ribs, links, or chicken ($8–$9.75) piled high on a sturdy paper plate, crowned with a couple slices of wheat bread (to soak up the grease) and potato salad. You'll be getting your food to go, as there are no seats here. Keep your wits about you at both locations after dark. *3114 San Pablo Ave., at 31st St., tel. 510/658–9912. 6609 Shattuck Ave., at Alcatraz Ave., tel. 510/653–0593.*

Mama's Royal Café. Although you can get lunch here after 11:30, the restaurant's real raison d'être is breakfast (served until closing). Huge omelets ($6–$9), which come with home-style potatoes, fruit, and a muffin, are available in 31 varieties. Weekend mornings, bring the paper, sign the waitlist, and be prepared to wait outside with everyone else who had the same idea. *4012 Broadway, at 40th St., tel. 510/547–7600. No dinner. Cash only.*

Zachary's Chicago Pizza Inc. Even if you've never been to Chicago, come to Zachary's for a slice (or two) of unforgettable stuffed pizza. People rave about the spinach and mushroom special (medium, $16.40), but whatever toppings you choose will come surrounded by a wall of chewy crust and topped with a layer of oozing mozzarella and stewed tomatoes. Voted #1 East Bay pizzeria for 10 years running, Zachary's typically has a line of adoring fans snaking around the corner. *5801 College Ave., near Rockridge BART, tel. 510/655–6385. 1853 Solano Ave., Berkeley, tel. 510/525–5950.*

UNDER $15 • Le Cheval I. Customers of all sorts come here for delicious Vietnamese food with a French twist. The firepot (small, $10, medium $16, large $20), with prawns, calamari, clams, fish balls, and vegetables, is a standout. Everything is generously proportioned and uniquely spiced. An appetizer not to be missed is the shrimp (or tofu) imperial rolls ($4) served with an addictive peanut sauce. *1007 Clay St., at 10th St., tel. 510/763–8957. No lunch Sun.* **Le Cheval II:** *Kaiser Center, 344 20th St., tel. 510/763–8953. No dinner weekends.*

Spettro. A fine time should be had by all at this funky world-food restaurant near Lake Merritt. The friendly staff creates interesting specials nightly, in addition to main menu treats such as mussels ($8), pastas ($10–$13), and pizzas ($12–$16), with aberrant toppings like peanut butter. On weekend nights, sign your name on the list near the door and join the small crowds waiting happily (thanks to the complimentary house wine or beer) for a table. *3355 Lake Shore Ave., at Mandana Blvd., tel. 465–8320.*

WORTH SEEING

JACK LONDON SQUARE

Although born in San Francisco, Jack London spent his early years in Oakland before shipping out on the adventures that inspired *The Call of the Wild, The Sea Wolf,* and *The Cruise of the Snark.* In an effort to cash in on this legacy, Oakland created Jack London Square on the waterfront west of downtown, at the foot of Broadway. Though several years ago the project resembled a ghost town with more FOR LEASE signs than tenants, the buildings have slowly been filled by boutiques, pricey eateries, a first-run cinema, and popular jazz club **Yoshi's** (510 Embarcadero, tel. 510/652–9200), newly relocated from

Berkeley. These days weekends at the square can be downright bustling. If you're interested in the literary Jack London, visit the Oakland Public Library's **Oakland History Room** (125 14th St., tel. 510/451–8218), which has a collection of his letters, manuscripts, and photographs.

LAKE MERRITT

Lake Merritt, formerly swampland, is now a 155-acre oasis in the middle of urban Oakland. By day the 3½-mi paved path around the lake is filled with sun seekers, joggers, business types on lunch break, and old men feeding the ducks. The 1876 **Camron-Stanford House** (1418 Lakeside Dr., near 14th St., tel. 510/836–1976), near the southwest edge of the lake, is the only remaining Victorian building in this formerly bourgeois neighborhood. Tours ($4; free first Sun. of month) of the meticulously refurbished interior are offered Wednesday 11–4 and Sunday 1–5. **Lakeside Park** (tel. 510/238–3091), on the north shore, has picnic facilities, Japanese and herb gardens, the oldest urban bird sanctuary in the United States (1879), and frequent music events. Nearby, the **Sailboat House** (568 Bellevue Ave., tel. 510/444–3807) rents a variety of rowboats, paddleboats, kayaks, and sailboats for $6–$12 an hour, plus deposit. It's open year-round; call for hours. The **Children's Fairyland** (Grand and Bellevue Aves., tel. 510/238–6876) is a storybook theme park with rides, puppet shows, strange mushroom-, whale-, and shoe-shape buildings, and other miniature delights. Walt Disney reputedly visited Fairyland to gather ideas for his own theme parks. Admission is $3.25 for adults, who are allowed inside only if they bring a child ($2.75).

Each June, Lake Merritt is the site of Oakland's **Festival at the Lake** (tel. 510/286–1061), the East Bay's largest urban fair, and the **Juneteenth Festival** (tel. 510/238–3866). Year-round it's a nice place for a picnic or stroll and easily reached from downtown. Walk a quarter-mile southeast from the 12th Street or 19th Street BART station downtown, or go directly to the Lake Merritt BART station.

OAKLAND MUSEUM

The three permanent-collection halls at the Oakland Museum are devoted to the art, history, and ecology of the Golden State. Extensive mixed-media exhibits document the rise and fall of the Ohlone people (the region's first inhabitants) and tackle the issues of urban violence and Oakland's subsequent deterioration. The changing shows in the art hall feature work by California artists. Be sure to visit the museum's terraced gardens and the nearby Estuary Park, a 22-acre sculpture garden. *1000 Oak St., at 10th St., tel. 510/238–2200. 1 block east of Lake Merritt BART. Admission: $5; free Sun. 4–7. Open Wed.–Sat. 10–5, Sun. noon–7.*

PARAMOUNT THEATRE

A 1931 art deco landmark in downtown Oakland, the Paramount Theatre is a beautifully restored motion picture palace that now houses both the Oakland Symphony and the Oakland Ballet. Classic and silent films are featured intermittently on Friday or Saturday evening, complete with pre-show organ music and old newsreel clips. Live rock or jazz performances are also held at this stately venue. Two-hour tours ($1) are given at 10 AM on the first and third Saturday of the month, no reservations required. *2025 Broadway, near 19th St., tel. 510/465–6400.*

PRESERVATION PARK

As a re-creation of an idyllic 19th-century Oakland neighborhood, Preservation Park has decorative wrought-iron fences and period street lamps and benches. Forty years of architectural history can be seen in the 16 restored houses here (five are in their original location, the others were condemned houses that were moved here), including Queen Anne and Italianate cottages, colonial revival and Craftsman homes. The buildings are private office spaces and aren't open to visitors, but you can stroll the grounds, then visit the **Pardee Home Museum** (672 11th St., at Castro St., tel. 510/444–2187). It's open for guided tours (no reservations required; $5) Saturday at 11, 1, and 2:30. *Martin Luther King Jr. Way at 13th St.*

AFTER DARK

Music, especially blues and jazz, is an integral part of the Oakland scene. For this reason, you may want to venture into that seedy bar or unassuming nightclub down the street—there's no telling what kind of magic may be going on inside. The **White Horse Inn** (6551 Telegraph Ave., at 66th St., tel. 510/652–3820) has DJ dancing Thursday–Saturday under a gleaming disco ball. The scene is low-key, friendly, and primarily gay and lesbian, though other orientations are welcome.

MARCHING TO A DIFFERENT BEAT

Like San Francisco and Berkeley, Oakland has a reputation for being a center of alternative culture and revolutionary politics. In the 1960s, the militant Black Panther Party was founded in Oakland, following a nationwide cry for Black Power. The FBI branded the group "dangerous." In the 1970s, Oakland was headquarters for the Symbionese Liberation Army, who kidnapped Patty Hearst and demanded as part of her ransom that food be distributed to Oakland's poor. In late 1996, the Oakland school board set off national controversy by recognizing Ebonics, or black English, as a distinct language; though board members later backed away from the proposal, many have continued to advocate sweeping changes to the current educational system. Even the city's most famous literary figure, Jack London, was steeped in controversy—an ardent socialist and debauched troublemaker, he wanted California to from the United States.

BARS

The Alley. This bar has been in business since the late 1940s and has the clientele and bar staff to prove it. Live piano music usually begins at 9 PM; drinks are $2.50–$5. *3325 Grand Ave., 3 blocks east of Lake Merritt, tel. 510/444–8505. From 19th St. BART, Bus 12 east to Santa Clara Ave.*

Pacific Coast Brewing Company. In historic downtown Oakland, this brew pub serves four homebrews and has 15 other beers on tap. Its polished appearance attracts a thirstysomething, slightly yuppie crowd, but the beers are top drawer. Drinks are around $3. *906 Washington St., near 10th St., tel. 510/836–2739. From 12th St. BART, 3 blocks SW on Broadway, 1 block west to Washington St.*

Stork Club. Weird tinsel and Christmas-light decor aside, this bar has recently gained a reputation for booking innovative local bands. When they play, the crowd is neatly divided by the bar: the younger, hipper, music-loving crowd is on the left, and the barflies who arrived for the 6 AM opening on the right. Drinks are about $3; live music cover runs $4–$5. *380 12th St., tel. 510/444–6174. 1½ blocks east of Broadway.*

LIVE MUSIC

In the years following World War II, Oakland gave birth to the gritty, hurts-so-bad-I'm-gonna-die music known as the West Coast blues. Even after 50 years, it still flourishes in clubs and bars all over Oakland. Dedicated to the preservation of blues, jazz, and gospel, the **Bay Area Blues Society** (tel. 510/836–2227) sponsors shows and festivals year-round and is a wellspring of information about West Coast blues.

BLUES • Eli's Mile High Club. The reputed birthplace of West Coast blues remains a consistently good bet, continuing to highlight promising local acts plus more renowned performers. It's a small club with a pool table, soul food, and music Thursday–Saturday. The club opens at 8 PM, and the music usually starts around 9:30. *3629 Martin Luther King Jr. Way, Oakland, tel. 510/655–6661. From Berkeley, Bus 15 south on Martin Luther King Jr. Way. Cover: $4–$8.*

Fifth Amendment. High quality blues and jazz acts play to a largely African American crowd of professionals, students, and local old-timers. Dress up a bit for some absolutely searing music. *3255 Lakeshore Ave., Oakland, tel. 510/832–3242. From MacArthur BART, Bus 57 to cnr Lakeshore Ave. and Lake Park Way. No cover.*

JAZZ • Kimball's East. In Emeryville, a small community tucked between Berkeley and Oakland, look for this excellent jazz and supper club, which books well-known jazz musicians Wednesday through Sunday. Downstairs, **Kimball's Carnival** draws big names in Latin jazz and Caribbean music, with an audience of mostly older professionals. *5800 Shellmound St., Emeryville, tel. 510/658–2555. From MacArthur BART, Bus 6 or 57 west on 40th St. to Pacific Park Plaza. Cover: $10–$25.*

Yoshi's. Yoshi's is a renowned club and restaurant, serving up sushi and jazz in sophisticated style. The clientele knows its music, and past acts have included Cecil Taylor, Anthony Braxton, and Ornette Coleman. At press time, Yoshi's was planning to relocate to Jack London Square; check listings or call for its current whereabouts. *6030 Claremont Ave., Oakland, tel. 510/652–9200. Cover: $5–$35.*

OUTDOOR ACTIVITIES

While the hordes head to Muir Woods to see California redwoods, you can slip away to **Redwood Regional Park** in the Oakland Hills. Most of the park's original trees were mowed down at the start of the California gold rush, so only a few virgin redwoods remain, but the second-growth forest is still impressive. From the Skyline Gate entrance, take the 3-mi (one-way) **Stream Trail,** which, after a steep (and often hot and dry) descent to the valley floor, meanders through the redwoods. To return to the Skyline Gate entrance from the valley floor, follow any trail heading up and to the right; you'll soon connect with the West Ridge Trail, which will lead you back to the park entrance. For mountain-bikers, the park offers a moderately difficult, 9-mi bike loop on **East and West Ridge** trails, accessible from the Redwood Gate. Here and at the Skyline Gate entrances you'll find free trail maps. *From I–580, Hwy. 24 east to Hwy. 13 south. Exit north on Joaquin Miller Rd., turn left on Skyline Blvd.; Skyline Gate entrance is about 4 mi further on the right. For Redwood Gate, I–580 east, exit at 35th Ave./MacArthur Blvd. east; park entrance is 3 mi past Skyline Boulevard. Parking: $3 weekends, roadside parking free.*

SOUTH BAY

Heading South on U.S. 101 brings both a change of scenery and pace. As the cosmopolitan frenzy of San Francisco fades away, you sense the quiet blandness of industrial parks, shopping malls, and tract housing. To its credit, the South Bay has its own interesting, amusing, or just plain weird attractions that San Francisco snobs thoroughly underrate (or don't know about). The cities that stretch south from San Francisco to San Jose lie on what locals refer to as the **Peninsula,** a finger of land wedged between the San Francisco Bay on the east and the Pacific Ocean on the west; a number of cities, including Palo Alto, are easy day trips from San Francisco.

The best-kept secret of the South Bay is Hwy. 1 and the secluded **San Mateo County Coast**—more than 75 mi of winding shoreline and gently undulating hills that seem a world away from the overdeveloped inland communities. Along the highway are long, sandy beaches, frequently devoid of any life aside from the local sea lions, surfers, and gulls; small towns just beginning to awaken to their potential as tourist destinations; and redwood groves filled with great hiking trails. The only drag here is the weather: Though hilly inland areas like La Honda and Pescadero are nearly always cool to warm in spring and fall, and hot (but not oppressively so) in summer, the beaches more often than not are windswept and chilly—better suited for a brisk walk than an afternoon of sunbathing. The quickest way to reach the northern end of the San Mateo County Coast from San Francisco is to follow I–280 south to Hwy. 1; it'll only take 10–15 minutes to reach Pacifica from downtown.

BASICS

The **Palo Alto Chamber of Commerce** (325 Forest Ave., tel. 650/324–3121) has maps of the city as well as limited information on sights, restaurants, and lodging. The **San Jose Convention and Visitors Bureau** (McEnery Convention Center, 150 W. San Carlos St., tel. 408/977–0900) is open weekdays 8–5:30, weekends 11–5. Call the bureau's 24-hour **FYI Events Line** (tel. 408/295–2265) for listings on dining, nightlife, arts, and festivals.

The friendly staff at the **Half Moon Bay Chamber of Commerce** (520 Kelly Ave., at Hwy. 1, tel. 650/726–8380), open weekdays 10–4, will give you more information than you ever wanted on Half Moon Bay, as well as a smattering of maps and brochures for the entire coast. The **State Parks District Office** (95 Kelly Ave., Half Moon Bay, tel. 650/726–8820), open weekdays 8–5, is your best source for short descriptions of the coastal parks from Montara to Año Nuevo.

COMING AND GOING

BY BUS

SamTrans (tel. 800/660–4287) runs buses regularly from the Daly City BART station to points throughout San Mateo County and as far as Año Nuevo State Reserve (at the southern end of the county). Bus 1L travels from Daly City BART along the coast to Half Moon Bay about five times daily. Most other buses run weekdays only, though some heavily trafficked routes are covered all week. The fare is $1. No transfers are issued, and bikes are allowed on only at the discretion of the driver.

BY CAR

I–280 (Junípero Serra Freeway) is more scenic than the industry-laden **U.S. 101,** though both connect San Francisco with Palo Alto, Santa Clara, and San Jose. Avoid rush hours, when traffic is bumper-to-bumper, especially on U.S. 101. From Oakland or Berkeley, take I–880 south for San Jose or I–880 south to Hwy. 84 and the Dumbarton Bridge for Palo Alto. I–280 also provides access to the San Mateo County Coast via the east–west **Highway 92** (Half Moon Bay Road), which runs from the interstate to Half Moon Bay. There it connects with **Coastal Highway 1,** the region's only north–south thoroughfare. The only other major road on the San Mateo County Coast is the east–west **Highway 84** (La Honda Road), which connects San Gregorio with La Honda before meeting up with I–280.

BY TRAIN

CalTrain (tel. 800/660–4BUS) offers regular service from San Francisco (4th and Townsend Sts.) to downtown San Jose (65 Cahill St.) with stops at a number of Peninsula cities, including Burlingame, Palo Alto, Mountain View, and Santa Clara. The one-way trip from San Francisco to San Jose is $4.75 and takes 1½ hours; trains leave hourly between 5 AM and 10 PM, more frequently during commuter hours. Bikes are allowed on CalTrain.

PALO ALTO

Palo Alto, about 30 mi south of San Francisco, is mostly known as the location of **Stanford University,** and it's certainly worth the drive just to check out the beautiful 8,200-acre campus. However, contrary to popular Bay Area opinion (in particular that of Berkeley students), the town of Palo Alto itself has some cultural attractions that are worth a look, as well as a cute, if overpriced, downtown area. Off U.S. 101, **University Avenue,** between Middlefield Road and High Street, is Palo Alto's main drag; west of El Camino Real it metamorphoses into **Palm Drive,** Stanford's entrance and main thoroughfare. University Avenue travels through Palo Alto's oldest and wealthiest neighborhood—keep your eyes peeled for mansions. In the downtown area, University Avenue and its side streets are loaded with restaurants, cafés, galleries, boutiques, and bookstores. All are rather upscale for a student shopping district, but the streets are pleasantly punctuated by plazas with benches and plants.

Sometimes called the Ivy League university of the West Coast, **Stanford University** opened its doors to scholars in October 1891. Its cofounder, railroad mogul Leland Stanford, also served as governor and U.S. senator for California. Nicknamed "The Farm" because the land was once a stud farm, Stanford consists of look-alike, mustard-color buildings that combine Romanesque and Spanish mission styles, giving the campus an austere and refined flavor. Some of its more disenchanted students, however, refer to the university as an oversized Taco Bell.

From downtown, enter campus along the aptly named Palm Drive, which will take you to the **quad,** the heart of campus and a popular hangout. You can pick up free maps or take a guided walking tour from the **visitor center** (tel. 650/723–2560) in Memorial Hall. The hour-long tours leave from Memorial Hall at 11 and 3:15 daily. The quad is dominated by the stately, Romanesque **Memorial Church,** best known for its Venetian mosaic. Inquire at the visitor's center about upcoming organ recitals in the church, as it provides inspiring acoustics. Near the entrance to the quad, the grassy **Memorial Court** has a couple of Auguste Rodin statues—dedicated to Stanford men who died for their country—that depict 14th-century French martyrs, *The Burghers of Calais,* "at the moment of painful departure from their families and other citizens." A New Guinean **sculpture garden,** installed in 1995, can be found near the intersection of Lomita Drive and St. Theresa Street. Just to the south of the quad, the 280-ft **Hoover Tower** thrusts mightily into the sky; home to the ultraconservative Hoover Institution for the Study of War, Revolution, and Peace. To get the classic view of campus and parts of Palo Alto, pay $2 to climb to the tower's observation deck, which offers an excellent 360° vista (open daily 10–4:30).

Rodin Sculpture Garden. Since **Stanford's Museum of Art** was seriously damaged in the 1989 Loma Prieta earthquake, this sculpture garden has been the closest you could get to it. The museum is scheduled to reopen in fall 1998, but you should still visit the 20 or so works by French sculptor Auguste Rodin (1840–1917) clustered in a small area to the left of the museum. Most pieces depict nudes in various stages of introspection, ecstasy, or anguish. Check out the particularly intense *Gates of Hell*; the giant iron doors are the scene of lots of wild action. The sculpture garden is open all hours, drawing late-night adventurers out to frolic with the lifelike figures. Descriptive tours are given at 2 PM Wednesday and on weekends; call for details. *Museum Way and Lomita Dr., tel. 650/723–3469. From Palm Dr., turn right on Museum Way, 1 block past Campus Dr.*

Even if you're only vaguely interested in science, make the trek up Sand Hill Road (west from campus toward I–280) to the **Stanford Linear Accelerator.** The 2-mi-long atom smasher is amazing—thousands of house-size machines, dials, diodes, and scientists who get excited when you mention n-orbits and electrons. Reserve space in advance for the twice weekly, free two-hour tour, which includes a slide show and lecture (days and times vary); it's geared toward lay people and is extremely interesting. *2575 Sand Hill Rd., east of I–280 in Menlo Park, tel. 650/926–2204.*

The sprawling campus is best explored by bike, and the biking is even better in the foothills west of the university. For rentals, try **Campus Bike Shop,** which can get you rolling on a mountain bike for $15 or a three-speed for $8 a day. You must leave a deposit equal to the cost of the bike. *551 Salvatierra St., on campus, tel. 650/325–2945.*

The Barbie Hall of Fame (433 Waverly St., at University Ave., tel. 415/326–5841) houses 16,000 of the plastic bombshells. Admission fee: $6.

WHERE TO SLEEP

UNDER $60 • Coronet Motel. Traffic on El Camino Real makes it noisy, but the Coronet wins points for location and value (there's even a tiny pool). It's only a few blocks from Stanford University, and Stanford Shopping Center is a short drive away. Doubles are $55–$60, and the rooms—many with kitchenettes—are comfortable, if not exactly modern. *2455 El Camino Real, between California Ave. and Page Mill Rd., tel. 650/326–1081. From U.S. 101, Embarcadero Rd. exit west, turn left on El Camino Real. 21 rooms, all with bath.*

UNDER $100 • Cowper Inn. The spacious, airy rooms in this Victorian B&B are filled with charming antiques, and all have phones and cable TV. Doubles start at $65 with shared bath, $110 with private bath, and $120 with a kitchenette (breakfast included). Sip sherry and munch on almonds in the parlor, after spending the day exploring the nearby San Mateo Coast. *705 Cowper St., at Forest Ave., tel. 650/327–4475, fax 415/329–1703. From U.S. 101, University Ave. west 2–3 mi, turn left on Cowper St., continue 2 blocks. 14 rooms, 12 with bath. Reservations advised.*

HOSTELS • Hidden Villa Hostel. This is an actual working farm—complete with animals and organic gardens. Set in a 1,500-acre canyon in the Los Altos Hills between Palo Alto and San Jose, the hostel offers easy access to hiking trails and peaceful dirt roads. Large, rustic dorm-style cabins dot the canyon, and each cabin has communal bathroom facilities. HI members pay $10 per night, nonmembers $13. You can also reserve a private room for $23. There's no curfew, but lockout occurs 9:30–4:30. *26870 Moody Rd., Los Altos, tel. 650/949–8648. From San Francisco, I–280 south past Palo Alto to El Monte/Moody Rd. exit, turn right on El Monte Ave., left on Moody Rd. (at stop sign), continue 1.7 mi. Or, from San Francisco, SamTrans Bus 7F from Transbay Terminal (*see Getting In, Out and Around in Chapter 1*) to Palo Alto, then SamTrans Bus 35 to Foothill College; walk 2 mi to hostel. 35 beds. Reception open daily 8–9:30 and 4:30–9:30. Closed June–Aug.*

FOOD

University Avenue is one long food court, with cutesy, yuppified restaurants everywhere you look and prices slightly higher than they should be. For excellent sushi at a decent price, try **Miyake** (140 University Ave., tel. 650/323–9449). **Jing Jing** (443 Emerson St., off University Ave., tel. 650/328–6885) is a Chinese restaurant popular for its spicy dishes (most under $10), and **Mango Café** (435 Hamilton Ave., tel. 650/325–3229) offers Caribbean dishes—with many veggie options—for under $10. At **The Good Earth** (185 University Ave., tel. 650/321–9449), vegetarians and meat eaters alike can count on heart- and health-conscious fare like Chinese chicken salads and garden burgers that actually taste good. Generous portions of salads, sandwiches, and soups (all around $6–$10) are served in a casual, down-to-earth atmosphere.

WALL OF GARBAGE

Californians generate more trash than any other group of people in the world, so what better home for the Garbage Museum? The massive 100-ft "Wall of Garbage" exhibit represents merely one second's worth of what the country is continually throwing out. 1601 Dixon Landing Rd., Milpitas, 5 mi north of San Jose, tel. 408/262-1401. Admission free. Open weekdays 7:30–5.

SAN JOSE

Too sprawling to have cultivated any sort of cohesive identity, Northern California's largest city wallows in misunderstanding. To many, San Jose is another faceless component of **Silicon Valley,** where computer chips whir and scientists diddle day and night with complex equations. In reality, San Jose is part hi-tech wonderland and part minimall suburbia. In effect, a not unlikable metropolis groaning under the strains of growing pains and gentrification. Encircled by mountain ranges and buffered by city parks and gardens, San Jose is home to museums, symphonies, and wineries as well as industrial parks, computer companies, and corporate headquarters.

The new billion-dollar **downtown** is a good place to start exploring. Hop on the **Light Rail** (tel. 408/321–2300) that connects San Jose State University on one end with the Center for Performing Arts on the other (fare is $1.10); its numerous stops should give you a good overview of the city center, which is architecturally interesting in its—generally successful—attempt to meld existing Old West themes with modern styles and materials (note the traditional small-town clock tower built from marble and stainless steel). Cruising the heart of downtown, around the intersection of Market and San Carlos streets, there are a number of pedestrian plazas and a host of museums, including **The Tech Museum of Innovation** (145 W. San Carlos St., across from Convention Center, tel. 408/279–7150), a hands-on technology museum that is great fun for the computer literate and illiterate alike; it's well worth the $6 admission. **Plaza de César Chávez** (S. Market St., in front of Fairmont Hotel) is a pleasant grassy strip that runs for two blocks, complete with benches and a fountain you can play in (the water shoots straight up out of grates in the ground).

Heiress Sarah Winchester was told by a fortuneteller to begin nonstop construction to placate the ghosts of those killed by Winchester guns. She was promised eternal life for doing so—it didn't work, but thus the **Winchester Mystery House** was born: A 160-room Victorian mansion with a floor plan so bizarre, servants needed a map to navigate it. In 1996 San Jose City Council designated the house a city landmark. General building manager Keith Kittle was quoted in the *San Francisco Chronicle* as saying, "I think Sarah Winchester would be proud. We're going to have a seance and talk to her and see." Admission is a steep $13. *525 S. Winchester Blvd., tel. 408/247–2101. From I–280, take Stevens Creek exit to Winchester Blvd.*

The **Rosicrucian Egyptian Museum and Planetarium** houses one of the most impressive collections of Egyptian, Assyrian, and Babylonian artifacts west of the Nile. Truly fascinating are the animal and human mummies, the underground tomb, and the decorative wall reliefs. The planetarium shows also hold their own; call 408/947–3634 for show times and ticket prices. *1342 Naglee Ave., at Park Ave., tel. 408/947–3636. Exit I–880 at Alameda East, turn right on Naglee Ave. Admission: $6. Open daily 9–5, last entry 4:35.*

If you want to be where most of San Jose is during summer, though, head straight for Santa Clara's **Great America** amusement park. Newest is **The Drop Zone,** a 22-story, free-fall drop (world's tallest!). To shave a few bucks off the admission price, call and ask about any current discount schemes. *Great America Pkwy., Santa Clara, tel. 408/988–1776. Take Great America Pkwy. exit off U.S 101, about 10 mi north of San Jose. Admission: $26. Open spring and fall weekends; summer, daily 10–9 (Sat. until 11).*

WHERE TO SLEEP

The **Sanborn Park Hostel,** west of San Jose, is one of the most attractive hostels in California, perfectly situated for avid hikers and bicyclists, and easily reached by public transit. The main cottage, a log cabin that dates from 1908, is surrounded by the dense 300-acre redwood forest of Sanborn Park. Hostelers stay in a large hall and have access to a rec room, volleyball court, grill, laundry facilities, and the standard HI kitchen—all for $9 per night for members or $11 for nonmembers. It's a busy place, but they try to find room for anyone who shows up. You need to bring your own food; the only restaurants and grocery stores are 4 mi away in downtown Saratoga. *15808 Sanborn Rd., Saratoga, tel. 408/741–0166. From San Francisco, I-280 south to Saratoga/Sunnyvale exit, turn right, go 5½ mi to Hwy. 9, turn right (toward Big Basin), go 2½ mi, turn left at SANBORN SKYLINE COUNTY PARK sign, go 1 mi, and turn right. Or, from Sunnyvale CalTrain station, Santa Clara County Transit Bus 54 or 27 to Saratoga post office; call hostel for ride. 39 beds. Reception open daily 5 PM–11 PM, curfew 11 PM, lockout 9–5.*

FOOD

Make a beeline for the incredible Cambodian cuisine at **Chez Sovan** (923 Oakland Rd., 1 block north of Hedding and 13th Sts., tel. 408/287–7619), open weekdays 11–3. The lunch-only menu includes a selection of ginger-cooked meats and vegetables, coconut and leek soups, and other traditional Cambodian specials. Most dishes start at around $5. **Taco Al Pastor** (400 S. Bascom Ave., at San Carlos St., tel. 408/275–1619) has been serving good, cheap Mexican food for more than 15 years. You can fill up on the excellent homemade burritos and tacos for under $5.

After dinner, join the hip, youngish crowd at **Café Matisse** (371 S. First St., at San Carlos St., tel. 408/298–7788), open daily until midnight, where you can sink into an overstuffed chair and nurse a latte.

During Prohibition, the Moss Beach Distillery (Beach Way and Ocean Blvd., tel. 650/728–5595) served as a speakeasy for San Francisco politicians and film stars.

SAN MATEO COUNTY COAST

PACIFICA AND MONTARA

Pacifica and Montara—about 20 minutes south of San Francisco along Hwy. 1—mark the northern end of the spectacular, wind-whipped San Mateo County Coast. Sleepy seaside towns, Pacifica and Montara have somehow escaped the tourist masses and offer an easy escape from urban chaos. The "historic" section of Pacifica, the northernmost outpost of town, is full of bungalow-style homes that once served as weekend retreats for wealthy San Franciscans. Pacifica's small commercial district to the south is an eclectic combination of old mom-and-pop shops and upscale specialty stores, the latter suggesting that the town is growing weary of its backwater authenticity and wants to attract some of San Francisco's yuppie business. Bridging past and present are the old paved promenade and fishing pier, which serve the same purposes today that they have all along. Come here to smell the salt water, feed the pigeons, and watch the local fishermen ply their trade; the pier also affords brilliant views of San Francisco and Marin County.

Pacifica's beaches lie south of town, and they're the attractions that lure most San Franciscans down this way. About 2 mi south of old Pacifica is **Rockaway Beach.** Two large dollops of sand on either end of this gorgeous cove are just large enough for half a dozen sunbathers, and your only other company will be a handful of surfers and fishermen. Immediately south of Rockaway you'll come to the more popular **Pacifica State Beach,** a long, sandy beach favored by surfers and sun worshipers.

Just a few miles farther removed from the city, Montara is pretty much all beach. **Gray Whale Cove State Beach** (tel. 650/728–5336), ½ mi north of town, is an American anomaly: a government-supported, clothing-optional beach. Entrance to the spectacular, secluded cove is $5. In Moss Beach immediately south of the Montara city, the rich tide pools of the **James V. Fitzgerald Marine Reserve** stretch along the coast for 4 mi. Go at low tide to check out abalone, barnacles, and maybe an octopus or two; but remember, this is a reserve: look but don't touch.

WHERE TO SLEEP • Point Montara Lighthouse AYH-Hostel. This functioning lighthouse and its adjoining hostel are perched on a cliff ½ mi south of Montara State Beach; it has incredible views of the coastline and access to a beach and tide pools. Inside, there's a fireplace in the comfortable living room, a communal kitchen, and a dining area; outside, there's a redwood hot tub ($5 a person per hour, two-person minimum). Beds go for $12 per night ($14 for nonmembers), and everyone must perform a small chore. The range of guests is greater than at most hostels; expect to see anyone from locals on a weekend holiday to German travelers on a cross-country trek. Reservations are advised for summer weekends. *Hwy. 1, at 16th St., Montara, tel. 650/728–7177. From Daly City BART, SamTrans Bus 1L or 1C southbound; ask driver to let you off at 14th St. 45 beds. Reception open daily 7:30–9:30 and 4:30–9:30, curfew 11 PM, lockout 9:30–4:30. Laundry.*

Sea View Motor Lodge. Surprisingly modern and spacious for the price, the Sea View offers airy, comfortable doubles, many with an ocean view, for $50 ($70 for a quad with a kitchenette). Hwy. 1 is annoyingly close, but you're within walking distance of the beach and old town. *2160 Francisco Blvd., tel. 650/359–9494. 24 rooms.*

FOOD • Pacifica's and Montara's budget eateries consist almost exclusively of low-end ethnic restaurants. In Pacifica's old town, head straight to Francisco Boulevard just west of Hwy. 1, where you'll find **Pacifica Thai Cuisine** (1966 Francisco Blvd., tel. 650/355–1678) featuring traditional specialties like chicken curry in coconut milk ($7). In Montara, **A Coastal Affair** (Hwy. 1, at 8th St., tel. 650/728–5229), ⅓ mi north of the Point Montara Lighthouse Hostel, is a combination craft gallery and café with excellent espresso drinks ($1.75–$2.75) and freshly made sandwiches (about $4).

OUTDOOR ACTIVITIES • For something a bit more challenging than lying on the beach, **San Pedro Valley County Park** has a number of mellow hiking trails leading through rolling green hills. In winter and spring, try the **Brooks Falls Overlook Trail,** a ½-mi path with views of a three-tier, 275-ft waterfall. To reach the park from Hwy. 1 in Pacifica, turn east on Linda Mar Boulevard; when it dead-ends, turn right onto Oddstad Boulevard; the park entrance and visitor center (tel. 650/355–8289) are 50 yards up on the right.

HALF MOON BAY

In the late 1800's, Half Moon Bay was a sleepy, agricultural hamlet called "Spanish town." That is, until Prohibition paved the way for Canadian bootleggers to seek refuge—and a good time—in Half Moon Bay's decidedly more exciting streets. Today's town rests somewhere in the middle of these two extremes. Famous for growing pumpkins, Christmas trees, and flowers, Half Moon Bay, 28 mi south of San Francisco, is the closest thing to a major town along the San Mateo County Coast. With its seaside/rural/small-town feel, immense surfing waves (*see* Surfing *in* Chapter 8), natural beauty, and wealth of activities, it is no stranger to the tourist. The "revitalized" downtown area centers around **Main Street,** which parallels Hwy. 1; the cozy street is cluttered with craft stores, produce markets, gardens, cafés, and straightforward burger joints. If lolling on the beach is more your speed, follow Kelly Avenue west from Hwy. 1 to the popular **Half Moon Bay State Beach,** actually a series of beaches covering more than 2 mi. To avoid the $5 parking fee, walk from downtown. It will probably get chilly near the water before too long, a perfect excuse to trek 2 mi inland along Hwy. 92 and sample—for free—the local wines at **Obester Winery** (12341 San Mateo Rd., tel. 650/726–9463), open daily 10–5.

Half Moon Bay hosts dozens of annual festivals, any one of which you could plan a visit around. The largest and most popular is the **Art and Pumpkin Festival,** held the weekend after Columbus Day. The high-spirited fall celebration includes live music, local foods, crafts, vendors, a children's parade, and outrageous pie-eating and pumpkin-carving contests. Also popular is the aptly named **Coastal Flower Market,** which takes place on the third Saturday of each month in May through September. Other yearly events include the riotous **Human Race** every May, in which entrants use every wacky scheme they can devise to carry other contestants along the course; the **Brew Ha-Ha** beer and sausage tasting festival each spring; and a daring **California Coast Air Show** that takes place at Half Moon Bay's tiny airport in the fall. For more information, contact the Half Moon Bay Chamber of Commerce.

WHERE TO SLEEP • If you're going to splurge on coastal accommodations, head to the **Old Thyme Inn** (779 Main St., tel. 650/726–1616), a romantic 1899 Queen Anne Victorian complete with a heady, English herb garden. Bordering on cloying, each Laura Ashley–clad room features fresh-cut flowers, a bedside stuffed animal, and charming antiques. A bountiful English breakfast is served in the parlor, where you'll find sherry and candy waiting for you in the evening. Most of the rooms—each named for a separate herb—will run you $90–$125 (or higher for a fireplace and whirlpool bath). On the southern outskirts of town, **Cameron's Inn** (1410 S. Cabrillo Hwy., tel. 650/726–5705) has three clean, simple doubles with shared bath ($60–$70) that are as cheap as you'll find in the area. Big beds and fine-art prints lend some style to the rooms, but that doesn't diminish the noise of big rigs downshifting on the highway.

Half Moon Bay State Beach. Close to downtown, these 55 characterless, first-come, first-served sites ($14) attract teenage partyers and weekend-warrior types, especially during summer. Though you'll fall asleep to the sound of waves and arise to the smell of sea salt, it's hardly the great outdoors. *95 Kelly Ave., west of Hwy. 1, tel. 650/726–8820. Fire pits, flush toilets, food lockers, picnic tables, cold showers.*

FOOD • Half Moon Bay has everything from reasonably priced health-food counters to way-outta-range seafood restaurants. The best of the former is the **Healing Moon Natural Foods Market** (523 Main St., tel. 650/726–7881); if you're not looking for groceries, serve yourself a cup of soup and eat it on the peaceful patio. The Alice in Wonderland-esque decor of **La Di Da** (500 C Purissima St., tel. 650/726–5512) makes it a great place to plan your day with a Cherry Bomb (cherry mocha, $2). The **Half Moon Bay Bakery** (514 Main St., tel. 650/726–4841) serves piping-hot muffins from a 19th-century brick oven. At the **Flying Fish Grill** (99 San Mateo Rd., corner Hwy. 92 and Main St., tel. 650/712–1125), you'll find reasonably priced seafood (a rarity) in a casual environment. Chow down on clam chowder ($3) and a variety of deep-fried and grilled fresh fish ($7–$10).

OUTDOOR ACTIVITIES • Since it occupies a prime spot between the ocean and the hills, Half Moon Bay is a great place to pursue both land and water sports. You'll also find plenty to do at Pacifica and Montara to the north and Año Nuevo State Reserve to the south, all within an hour's drive.

From **Sea Horse Ranch** (tel. 650/726–9903), you can rent a horse and ride, unguided, through 10 mi of verdant trails, ending in a breathtaking stretch of sandy beach that simply invites your horse to break into a canter. One hour will set you back $22, two hours go for $40; tack on $15 if you want an expert guide.

Huck Finn Sportfishing (tel. 650/726–7133 or 800/572–2934 outside northern California) on Pillar Point Harbor offers full-day rock cod or salmon expeditions starting at $40 (tackle and license about $5 extra). Huck Finn will also take you out on whale-watching trips ($20) in season; January through March is the prime time to catch sight of the California gray whale migration.

SAN GREGORIO TO AÑO NUEVO STATE RESERVE

Day-trippers seeking sand, sea, and forest in quiet simplicity are more likely to find it here than in more touristed Half Moon Bay. The desolate stretch of coastline south of Half Moon Bay is nearly deserted year-round. While beaches here are usually cold, and the choice of affordable food and lodging is limited, the very fact that the area is so empty means that with the exception of Año Nuevo State Reserve during the elephant seals' mating season, you don't have to plan ahead to do things here. The rich tide pools at Pescadero State Beach, the cliff-hugging Pigeon Point Lighthouse Hostel, and the sky-high trees lining Hwy. 84 through La Honda all make this chunk of coastline extremely worthwhile for people seeking solitude on short notice.

SAN GREGORIO • Although not much of a destination in itself, San Gregorio is a worthwhile stop if you're traveling the coast between Santa Cruz and Half Moon Bay. The drive to this hitching post of a town, at the junction of Hwys. 1 and 84, is half the fun, even if you don't come via the coast road. Hwy. 84 (also known as La Honda Road) heads west from I–280 and is for the strong of stomach only; a roller-coaster ride on a highway so thick with redwoods it barely sees the light of day. The road spits you out at the isolated **San Gregorio State Beach,** where you can lie back and soak up some rays, or, more likely, throw on a sweater and battle the wind as you watch the fog roll in. Stock up on supplies at the eclectic **San Gregorio General Store** (tel. 650/726–0565; open daily 9–7), 1 mi east of Hwy. 1 on Hwy. 84. It doubles as the town saloon and community center, and weekends bring live bluegrass and Grateful Dead covers as locals, bicyclists, and tourists gather for a little heel stomping and a cold brew.

LA HONDA • After you've had your fill of coastal scenery, head inland to the densely forested community of La Honda, 11 mi east of Hwy. 1. About the size of a postage stamp, La Honda seems almost lost in the shadow of countless giant redwoods on Hwy. 84 (*see* San Gregorio, *above*). As if plucked straight out of rural West Virginia, the town consists of **Pioneer Market** (tel. 650/747–9982), where you can stock up on camping supplies and sandwiches ($3.50); the **Cool Water Café** (tel. 650/742–9600), open daily until 8, offering barbecued chicken sandwiches ($4.50) and espresso drinks (about $2); a post office; and **Apple Jack's Tavern** (La Honda Rd., tel. 650/747–0331), a scruffy bar. Open weekdays noon–2 AM and weekends 10 AM–2 AM, Apple Jack's is today's version of an Old West saloon: The men drink their whiskey straight up, the women are loud and boisterous, and a brawl seems ready to erupt at any minute.

Pescadero Creek County Park (take Hwy. 84 west from La Honda, turn left on Alpine Rd.) has 15 primitive, secluded hike-in tent sites ($7) in dense second-growth forest along the river. Contact the rangers at Portola State Park (tel. 650/948–9098) for details. The most developed sites are in **Portola State Park** (just south of Pescadero Creek County Park; *see below*) and **Memorial County Park** (Pescadero Rd., west of La Honda). Memorial is a thick old-growth forest that offers 135 quiet sites ($12), all with picnic tables, fire pits, and hot showers. Although popular with car campers on summer weekends, the first-come, first-served campground is sparsely visited at other times. The 53 campsites ($14) at Portola State Park have running water, showers, fire pits, and picnic tables. Reserve through Destinet (tel. 800/444–7275).

PESCADERO • More than 100 years ago, all the wooden buildings in the small fishing village of Pescadero were painted white with paint that had washed up on shore when the clipper ship *Carrier Pigeon* crashed into the rocks off Pigeon Point, a few miles south of town. Today, the bank, bakery, general store, and other shops that populate Pescadero retain their whitewashed uniformity, giving this town, in the flatlands a mile inland from the coast on Pescadero Road, a calming, subdued ambience.

After you've rambled around the three blocks that make up Pescadero's commercial district, head straight to **Duarte's Tavern** (202 Stage Rd., at Pescadero Rd., tel. 650/879–0464; open daily 7 AM–9 PM). This combination bar and restaurant has been run by four generations of Duartes since 1894 (and they're in no big hurry to serve you before the next generation takes over). The homey restaurant serves everything from peanut butter and jelly sandwiches ($3) to lamb chops ($14), but it's most famous for its cream of artichoke soup ($4), fresh seafood plates ($6–$20), and homemade pies ($3).

On the coast just west of town, you'll find **Pescadero State Beach,** a long, sandy expanse with some vibrant tide pools, perfect for checking out the Pacific's aquatic community. Immediately north of the beach is the **Pescadero Marsh Reserve** (tel. 650/879–2170), a protected area favored by ornithologists. Free guided walks leave from the parking lot Saturday at 10:30 and Sunday at 1 year-round.

Charming **Butano State Park** (tel. 650/879–0173), 5 mi south of Pescadero on Cloverdale Road, has 20 mi of trails on 2,700 acres. You can reach the park from Hwy. 1 south of Pescadero State Beach; there's a $5 parking fee. The beautiful **Little Butano Creek Trail,** about ½ mi from the entrance, takes you 3 mi along a creek and past old-growth redwoods. Mountain bikes are forbidden on the park's trails, but you can ride on any of the fire roads. Your best bet is to park at the entrance gate near the corner of Cloverdale and Canyon roads, about 1 mi north of the main park entrance, and ride the Butano Fire Road. If you're in pretty good shape you can take it all the way to the Olmo Fire Road, which leads back to the park's main road, and then pedal back to your car.

Pigeon Point Lighthouse Youth Hostel. Perched on a small bluff 5 mi south of Pescadero State Beach are four bungalow-style dorms, along with an outdoor, bluff-side hot tub ($3 a person per half hour). Free tours of the historic lighthouse on the grounds are also available. One night in any of the 54 comfortable beds costs $11 ($14 for nonmembers); another $10 secures a private room for two. Bring your own food to cook up in their kitchen. All guests must do a chore each day of their stay. The maximum stay is three nights. *Pigeon Point Rd. and Hwy. 1, tel. 650/879–0633. From Daly City BART, take SamTrans Bus 1L to Half Moon Bay then SamTrans bus 96C. Reception open daily 7:30–9:30 and 4:30–9:30, curfew 11 PM, lockout 9:30–4:30. Reservations advised.*

Camping. Surprisingly few visitors venture to the 27 campsites ($17) and 18 hike-in sites ($7) in quiet **Butano State Park** (*see above*). The drive-in sites have fire rings, picnic tables, and food lockers but no showers. Reservations (tel. 800/444–7275) can be made up to eight weeks in advance, but are usually not necessary.

AÑO NUEVO STATE RESERVE • Named by explorer Sebastian Viscaino on New Year's Day 1603, the Punta del Año Nuevo is one of few places in the world where you can safely view live elephant seals close up. During mating season (Dec.–Mar.), you'll need to make reservations up to eight weeks in advance through Destinet (tel. 800/444–7275), and you can only visit the reserve on one of its 2½-hour guided walks ($4, plus $4 parking fee). If you're lucky, you may also catch sight of migrating gray whales during the seal mating season.

At other times of the year, you can check out the elephant seals resting on the rocks by obtaining a free visitor's permit when you show up (parking is still $4). The path to the beach from the parking lot is 1½ mi long, and if you come in spring, you'll be treated to the sight of thousands of colorful wildflowers. The reserve, 22 mi north of Santa Cruz, is on Hwy. 1 and can be reached on SamTrans Bus 96C (*see* Coming and Going *in* the South Bay, *above*).

MARIN COUNTY

Marin, just across the Golden Gate Bridge from San Francisco, is one of the richest counties in California, an upscale playground for children old enough to remember Woodstock. Everywhere you turn, you'll see an odd combination of hippie idealism and yuppie wealth: expensive estates buffered by rugged log cabins, Porsches and BMWs parked next to aging VW microbuses.

The reason so many '60s-refugees-turned-'80s-success-stories want to live here—and the reason you'll want to visit despite the price tag—is Marin's incredible natural beauty. The county lays claim to stunning ocean views, thick redwood forests, and rural back roads that wind between sheep ranches and organic-produce farms. You could spend a lifetime describing the pleasures of hiking in **Muir Woods** and the **Point Reyes National Seashore,** and it's hard to act blasé about the views from **Coastal Highway 1,** no matter how many times you've driven the road.

Marin's upscale, tourist-oriented bayside towns, like **Tiburon** and **Sausalito,** are tougher for the budget traveler to love. You'll have to pick your way through an ostentatious show of wealth to find a cheap organic grocery store where you can stock up on supplies for your hike, or an unpretentious restaurant that serves reasonably priced seafood. But these things do exist—and once you find them, you may not want to leave.

BASICS

The **Marin County Convention and Visitors Bureau** distributes information on sights, restaurants, and lodging. *Marin Center, Avenue of the Flags, San Rafael, tel. 415/472–7470. Open weekdays 9–5.* The **West Marin Network** offers information on lodging, restaurants, and activities in the region. *11431 Shoreline Hwy., Suite 15, Point Reyes Station, tel. 415/663–9543. Open Mon.–Sat. 9–5.*

COMING AND GOING

Even the most bucolic corners of Marin County are little more than two hours from San Francisco (except during rush hour, when it can take nearly an hour just to cross the bridge). It's possible to bike across the Golden Gate Bridge from San Francisco, then take a **ferry** (*see below*) back from Sausalito or Tiburon. A final note: If you opt for public transportation in this area, be forewarned of the complexity.

Filmmaker George Lucas lives on Lucas Valley Road in Marin County. Believe it or not, that was the name of the road before Lucas built his Skywalker Ranch on it.

From San Francisco, head north on **U.S. 101** and cross the **Golden Gate Bridge** (no toll this direction, $3 other way). For Sausalito, take the Sausalito exit and go south on Bridgeway to the municipal parking lot near the center of town. Farther north on U.S. 101, you'll see exits for Tiburon (take Tiburon Blvd.) and San Rafael. For Mill Valley, **Highway 1,** and West Marin, follow U.S. 101 north to the Stinson Beach/Hwy. 1 exit. For Mill Valley, turn right on Miller Avenue at the stop light. Or take Hwy. 1 north; as it winds uphill, you'll pass turnoffs for Muir Woods and Mt. Tamalpais. Keep going to get to Stinson Beach (1 hr) and Point Reyes (1½ hrs).

BY BUS

Golden Gate Transit (tel. 415/455–2000 from Marin County or 415/923–2000 from San Francisco) provides service to Marin County. Buses connect San Francisco with the inland cities of Sausalito, Mill Valley, Tiburon, and San Rafael every half-hour during the week. Many buses run weekdays only, dawn to dusk, but some routes (including Buses 20 and 50) run on weekends and as late as 1 AM. There is no direct service from San Francisco to Coastal Hwy. 1; on weekends, you can take Bus 80 (which is the most direct) or Bus 50 from San Francisco to San Rafael, then transfer to Bus 65, which stops in Inverness, Point Reyes, and Olema.

Bus 20 will take you from San Francisco to Marin City, where you can catch Bus 63 to Stinson Beach. Within San Francisco, buses leave from the Transbay Terminal; adult fare costs $1.25–$4.50, depending on the length of your trip. During non-commute hours, a maximum of two bikes per bus are allowed on Bus 40 (El Cerrito del Norte BART–San Rafael) and Bus 80.

BY FERRY

For a change of pace, pack a thermos of coffee and a warm jacket and hop on one of the commuter ferries from San Francisco to Marin County: **Golden Gate Ferry** (tel. 415/923–2000) crosses the bay between the SF Ferry Building (on the Embarcadero, at the foot of Market St.) and Sausalito (30 min, $4.25 one-way) hourly from 7 AM to 8 PM. Tickets include free transfers for Golden Gate Transit buses (*see above*). The **Blue and Gold Fleet** (tel. 415/546–2700 or 800/229–2784) leaves from Pier 41 at Fisherman's Wharf for Sausalito (30 min, $5.50), Tiburon (40 min, $5.50), and Angel Island ($10); call for current schedule.

MARIN HEADLANDS

For a quick taste of what Marin County has to offer nature enthusiasts, cross the Golden Gate Bridge, exit at Alexander Avenue, and drive up Conzelman Road to the Marin Headlands. Consisting of several small but steep bluffs overlooking San Francisco Bay and the Pacific Ocean, the undeveloped, 1,000-acre headlands are a great place to snap a few photos or while away an afternoon. Hundreds of hiking and biking trails meander along the wind-carved hills and cliffs. Rangers sometimes lead mountain-biking tours; for more information on tours and other activities, follow signs from Conzelman Road to the **Marin Headlands Visitors Center** (Field and Bunker Rds., tel. 415/331–1540).

Most weekends—especially in summer—the area is crawling with people, but the farther north you hike, the fewer people you'll see. From the visitor center parking lot, head up the closed-off road (*not* the left stairway) on the **Coastal Trail.** After about 2 mi, turn right onto the **Wolf Ridge Trail,** and head up the grassy hill (alias Wolf Ridge) for 1⅔ mi to the top. When you're ready to stop gazing at Tennessee Valley, continue ¾ mi down the verdant leeward side of the hill until it hooks up with the **Miwok Trail,** which you follow south, back to the visitor center.

WHERE TO SLEEP

Golden Gate AYH-Hostel. Built in 1907, this beautiful, friendly hostel is located in the Marin Headlands in historic Ft. Barry. There's a communal kitchen, laundry room, tennis court, Ping-Pong table, pool table, and a common room with a fireplace. Dorm beds cost $12 per night; in another building private rooms are available for couples and families, starting at $36. Getting to the hostel by public transit is tricky but well worth the effort. From San Francisco, catch Golden Gate Transit Bus 10 or 50 from the Transbay Terminal and ask to be let off at the bottom of the Alexander Avenue off-ramp. From here, it's a stiff 5-mi hike to the hostel. On Sunday only, Bus 76 goes from the Transbay Terminal all the way to the Marin Headlands Visitor Center, 1 block from the hostel. *Ft. Barry, Bldg. 941, tel. 415/331–2777. From U.S. 101, Alexander Ave. exit, cross under freeway, make first right after MARIN HEADLANDS sign, continue 1 mi, turn right on McCullough Rd., left on Bunker Rd., follow signs to visitor center (hostel is just up the hill). 103 beds. Reception open daily 7:30 AM–11:30 PM, lockout 9:30–3:30.*

SAUSALITO

Only a few miles north of San Francisco is Sausalito, which flourished during the 1880s and '90s as a whaling town infamous for its unruly saloons, gambling dens, and bordellos. Even after the town became suburbanized in the 1940s, it continued to attract an offbeat and raffish element, becoming by mid-century a well-known artists' colony. Over the last several decades, however, Sausalito's wharf rats have been replaced by lawyers and investment bankers escaping the San Francisco rat race. Today this is a characterless, wealthy resort town, popular with yachters. If you have unlimited time to explore the Bay Area, Sausalito is worth a gander, but don't go out of your way: Parking is next to impossible, shops and restaurants are shockingly expensive, and camera-toting tourists fill the sidewalks and streets. At the south end of **Bridgeway,** Sausalito's main thoroughfare, is the Sausalito Ferry Terminal. Farther south on Bridgeway is Sausalito's oldest restaurant, built in 1893 and originally known as **Valhalla.** It was used as a backdrop in the classic Orson Welles film *The Lady From Shanghai*; today it's the **Sausalito Chart House Restaurant** (201 Bridgeway, tel. 415/332–0804), part of an upscale seafood-and-steak chain. The views are incredible, and reservations are essential.

WHERE TO SLEEP

Though visitors crowd Sausalito's streets during the day, all but the wealthiest have to find somewhere else to spend the night. The only reasonable alternative is the **Golden Gate AYH-Hostel** (*see* Marin Headlands, *above*), 15 minutes away in the Marin Headlands.

FOOD

Restaurants and cafés line Bridgeway, but they're generally overpriced and touristy. Expect to pay at least $15–$20 for seafood and waterfront vistas. Save your cash and visit **Hamburgers** (737 Bridgeway, tel. 415/332–9471), a lunch-only hole-in-the-wall doing a few variations on the hamburger ($4–$5) and fries ($1.50) theme. If you head one block inland to **Caledonia Street,** you'll find better bargains. Thai food junkies should hit the unpretentious **Arawan** (47 Caledonia St., tel. 415/332–0882), which has attracted a loyal following with dishes such as *pad thai* (noodles) and *gai yang* (barbecued chicken). **Stuffed Croissant** (43 Caledonia St., tel. 415/332–7103) is *the* stop for picnic-packers attempting to avoid Sausalito's overpriced restaurants. The tiny mom-and-pop deli offers sandwiches ($4–$5.50), soups, and decadent desserts. Still, your best bet is to pack a lunch and picnic in the grassy area between Bridgeway and the bay.

AFTER DARK

Tuesday through Sunday evenings a rowdy over-thirty crowd congregates at **No Name Bar** (757 Bridgeway, tel. 415/332-1392) for free live jazz, blues, and Dixieland.

TIBURON AND ANGEL ISLAND

The tiny town of Tiburon lies at the tip of a peninsula jutting into the bay just north of Sausalito. It has a relaxed atmosphere and great views of Angel Island and San Francisco, but it's little more than a waterfront cluster of gift shops and pricey boutiques. Escape uphill to **Old St. Hilary's Landmark and Wildflower Preserve,** which protects both a simple 1889 carpenter's Gothic church (now a historical and botanical museum) and the windswept field of rare black jewel wildflowers that it stands in. *At top of Esperanza St., tel. 415/435–2567. Admission free. Open Apr.–Oct., Wed. and Sun. 1–4.*

The main reason to come to Tiburon, though, is to take the 15-minute ferry ride (*see below*) to **Angel Island,** a 750-acre state park where you can explore sandy beaches and old military installations. The island used to be thickly forested with Australian eucalyptus trees, but in June of 1996 the park set in motion a controversial effort to eradicate all nonnative flora. Park officials assure visitors that the island will soon return to native species, and eucalyptus or no, the surrounding views are stunning. **Ayala Cove,** the area around the ferry landing, is congested with picnickers taking advantage of tables and barbecue grills (BYO charcoal, as wood-gathering is not allowed). The 5-mi perimeter road that rings the island offers access to plenty of scenic and historic sites but is also heavily traveled. To escape the crowds, try the **Sunset Trail,** which begins just southeast of Ayala Cove: It's 2 mi of breathtaking views and ascending switchbacks to reach the 781-ft summit of Mt. Caroline Livermore. Many people bring their bikes to tool around the perimeter road; you can also rent them at the ferry landing for $10 per hour (helmet included). A **visitor center** at Ayala Cove (tel. 415/435–1915 for recorded park information) sells a map/brochure of the island ($2).

For the ultimate deserted-island picnic, tote your fixings about a mile from Ayala Cove to **Camp Reynolds,** which functioned as an army camp from the Civil War to World War II. Plenty of people linger at the Commanding Officer's House along the road, but about a ¼-mi past the old army barracks, at the water's edge, you'll find some isolated picnic tables and an outstanding close-up view of the Golden Gate Bridge. On the other side of the island is an **Immigration Station,** once known as "The Ellis Island of the West," where immigrants (mostly Asian) were detained when trying to enter the United States between 1910 and 1940.

The **Tiburon–Angel Island Ferry** (tel. 415/435–2131) leaves for Angel Island from Tiburon's Main Street Pier (21 Main St.) at 10 AM and 11 AM and 1 PM and 3 PM on spring and summer weekdays, and every hour from 10 to 5 on spring and summer weekends. Boats depart from Angel Island 20 minutes after they dock. Round-trip fares (which include entry fees for the island state park) are $6, plus $1 for bicycles. Cars are not allowed. **WHERE TO SLEEP •** Not surprisingly, chichi Tiburon has no cheap lodging. If you don't want to head to the **Golden Gate Hostel** a few miles south (*see above*), consider a night of camping at **Angel Island State Park.** Nine showerless, hike-in environmental campsites ($10 Sun.–Thur., $11 Fri.–Sat. nights) are scattered around Angel Island. Sites 3 and 4, with views of the Golden Gate Bridge, are the most popular; Sites 1 and 2, surrounded by pine trees and with a view of the East Bay, offer more privacy and shelter from the wind. Reserve a few weeks ahead for a weekend stay; on weekdays, you can almost always get a site on the same day. *Tel. 415/435–1915 for information or 800/444–7275 for reservations. Barbecue grills, drinking water, pit toilets.*

FOOD

One of the least expensive waterfront restaurants, **Sam's Anchor Café** (27 Main St., tel. 415/435–4527) is also the center of Tiburon's nightlife, attracting a lot of locals, who cram onto the deck and sip Famous Ramos gin fizzes ($4.50) and Bloody Marys. Hearty breakfast dishes are $7–$9; if you're feeling adventurous, try the Hangtown Fry omelet ($7.50) with oysters, bacon, scallions, and cheese. Fresh seafood dishes are $8–$16, burgers run $7–$9, sandwiches $5.50 and up.

MILL VALLEY

Mill Valley is a sleepy community of millionaires and mountain bikers, nestled amid California redwoods on the eastern flank of Mt. Tamalpais. It's a mellow town where people have paid enormous sums of money for their solitude—and want to keep it that way. Sneak up on them by taking the East Blithedale exit from U.S. 101.

There aren't any official tourist sights in Mill Valley, but a drive through the forested hills and canyons will explain why this is some of the Bay Area's most coveted real estate. Or take a break from driving and turn off Hwy. 1 onto **Tennessee Valley Road.** From the end of the road you can hike or bike a dirt path leading down to the beach where, in 1853, the steamship *Tennessee* wrecked in dangerous surf—giving the valley its name.

While in Mill Valley stop by the **Depot Bookstore and Café** (87 Throckmorton Ave., at Miller Ave., tel. 415/383–2665), which overlooks the small central plaza. You can enjoy an espresso drink, a salad, or a pita sandwich ($4–$6) and browse through the adjoining bookstore. After sunset, locals mosey over to **Sweetwater** (153 Throckmorton Ave., at Miller Ave., tel. 415/388–2820), where on any given night bluesman Roy Rogers or local resident Huey Lewis might show up to jam. This tiny club is a Bay Area institution, attracting some of the finest blues and R&B talents in the country. Cover ranges from $5 to $20, plus a two-drink minimum.

FOOD

Head to **Joe's Taco Lounge** (382 Miller Ave., at La Goma Ave., tel. 415/383–8164) and hunker down with the locals to enjoy excellent meat and veggie burritos (about $5). The colorful walls lined with hot-sauce bottles and religious memorabilia from Mexico contribute to a festive dining atmosphere at Joe's. If you're anxious to get an early start on the day, funky **Mama's Royal Café** (393 Miller Ave., at La Goma Ave., tel. 415/388–3261) serves unbeatable huevos rancheros ($6.10) and omelets (the cheapest is $4; others are priced according to the fillings). It's full of thrift-store artifacts and psychedelic murals.

SAN RAFAEL

Unassuming San Rafael, set between the foot of Mt. Tamalpais and San Rafael Hill, would attract more day-trippers from foggy San Francisco if people realized it's almost always warmer here than elsewhere in the Bay Area. In fact, that's exactly why the town was founded: In 1817, when Native Americans at San Francisco's Mission Dolores started dying at an alarming rate, missionaries built a hospital here so the sick could receive care in a more hospitable climate. The original buildings of the Mission San Rafael Archangel were torn down in the 1870s, but a replica of the **chapel** (corner 5th and A Sts.), built of stuccoed concrete instead of the original adobe, now sits next to a gift shop selling Catholic kitsch. A block away from the chapel, **4th Street** is the town's main drag, lined with used bookstores, a large contingent of department stores, and some good cafés and clubs, including **New George's** (842 4th St., at Cijos St., tel. 415/457–1515) and **Cafe Kaldi** (835 4th St., at Cijos St., tel. 415/457–6562). Both have won Bay Area polls for "Best Nightlife in Marin." At New George's check out the live jazz, R&B, and acoustic entertainment; airy Cafe Kaldi stays open late and serves up sandwiches ($5) and espresso to the local skater contingent.

Four miles east of San Rafael on North San Pedro Road is **China Camp State Park,** a pristine 1,600-acre wilderness area. Remnants of an old Chinese fishing village are still visible, and the oak knolls and saltwater marshes are great for hiking and camping (30 sites). Park ($3) at China Camp Point for the 5-mi hike along the well-marked **Shoreline Trail.** The steeper **Bay View Trail** is a favorite of park rangers (it's also much less crowded). Pick up a trail map from the **ranger station** (tel. 415/456–0766) about 1 mi from the park entrance on North San Pedro Road.

WHERE TO SLEEP

San Rafael has one of the few hotels in Marin County that you might actually be able to afford. If you're a smoker, however, think again—San Rafael recently passed a no-smoking city ordinance; even lighting up in the privacy of your hotel room is an infraction subject to fine. The **Panama Hotel** (4 Bayview St., tel. 415/457–3993 or 800/899–3993) offers individually decorated rooms (all with TV), a restaurant whose menu will make your mouth water, and a beautiful outdoor area draped with wisteria. Most amazing, the prices are reasonable (at least for this area): Rooms without bath start at $50 ($79–$129 with bath). If you can't get a room in the Panama, **425 Mission** (425 Mission Ave., tel. 415/453–1365) has four great rooms that go for between $85 and $105. The price tag includes a gourmet breakfast and use of the hot tub.

FOOD

Compared with most of Marin County, San Rafael has a down-to-earth restaurant scene with lots of cafés, Mexican joints, and other ethnic eateries lining 4th Street downtown. At the **San Rafael Station Café** (1013 B St., tel. 415/456–0191), locals hang out on weekends reading the paper and ingesting phenomenal amounts of cholesterol. Omelets of every persuasion run $5–$8, and sandwiches are $3.50–$7.50. People all over the Bay Area also rave over **Royal Thai** (610 3rd St., tel. 415/485–1074), which serves up no-frills seafood and curry dishes (under $10) in a restored Victorian house.

MUIR WOODS AND MT. TAMALPAIS

MUIR WOODS NATIONAL MONUMENT

Muir Woods was made a federal preserve in 1908, as a result of John Muir's (1838–1914) campaign to save old-growth forests from destruction. These days, judging from the crowded parking lot and tacky gift shop, it looks like just another overtouristed attraction. However, this 550-acre park contains one of the most impressive groves of redwoods in the world, some more than 250 ft tall and over 800 years old. Neither picnicking nor camping is allowed in the park, but snacks are available at the gift shop, along with every type of redwood souvenir imaginable. The **visitor center** (tel. 415/388–2595) organizes free nature walks through the woods; call for current schedule. The woods lie off U.S. 101, 17 mi northwest of San Francisco; take the Stinson Beach/Hwy. 1 exit and follow signs. The monument is open daily 8 AM–sunset, and parking is free (weekend crowds may force you to park a mile or more from the lot).

To escape the crowds, take one of a dozen rugged trails that meander along the monument's cool, fern-filled ridges: The **Ocean View Trail** ascends for 1⅓ mi before connecting with the **Lost Trail,** which descends through forests of Douglas fir before returning to the redwood groves. Lost Trail hooks up with **Fern Creek Trail,** taking you back to the parking lot. The moderate hike is 3 mi round-trip and passes some of the park's most impressive stands of redwoods. For a more spectacular view and greater workout, head up the **Ben Johnson Trail.** You'll climb up through the forest for 2 mi (the last ½ mi is quite steep) until you reach a hilltop with wonderful views of the Pacific.

MUIR BEACH

If you continue on Hwy. 1 instead of following the turnoff to Muir Woods, you'll come to **Muir Beach,** a quiet strip of sand littered with oddly shaped pieces of driftwood and punctuated by hundreds of tidal pools. The strikingly scenic beach attracts folks looking to relax—not the Budweiser and volleyball crowd you'll find at Stinson Beach, 6 mi farther north.

If you really want to get a feel for Marin's landscape, park your car at Muir Beach and hike the difficult 4-mi **Coastal Trail,** which leads up a steep hill overlooking the ocean and then winds through a series of deserted coves and valleys. Return the same way and you can reward yourself with a pint of Guinness in front of the fire at the **Pelican Inn** (10 Pacific Way, at Hwy. 1, tel. 415/383–6000). The restaurant serves everything from fish 'n' chips ($8) to prime rib ($17) and Yorkshire pudding, along with a healthy sampling of British ales and bitters; open Tuesday–Sunday. The kitchen closes between 3 and 6 in the afternoon.

MT. TAMALPAIS STATE PARK

To see Marin County at its most powerful, go to Mt. Tamalpais. The Coastal Miwok Indians revered Mt. Tam as a spiritual center, and you'll be hard-pressed not to feel it yourself as you wander the forested slopes. With more than 50 mi of trails, Mt. Tam is a weekend pilgrimage for adventurers who hike and bike around the forested canyons and up to the 2,571-ft summit. The **summit** can be reached by car; the gates are open dawn–dusk, and the view of the ocean and Marin's golden hillsides and lakes should not be missed.

A good starting point for your exploration is **Pantoll Ranger Station** (tel. 415/388–2070), where you can pick up one of several topo maps ($1–$6) describing all the trails and roads. Mountain biking is big here, and the map distinguishes the fire trails (where biking is allowed) from the walking trails (where biking nets you a $80–$120 fine). One beautiful and strenuous hike, the 2-mi **Steep Ravine Trail,** takes you down a series of ladders from Pantoll to the Steep Ravine cabins (*see below*). Parking is $5 in the Pantoll parking lot, but you can park for free anywhere along the road. The place is packed on weekends, so you'll have trouble parking if you arrive after noon.

WHERE TO SLEEP • You can camp at one of Pantoll's 15 walk-in sites ($15, $16 weekends) or at its hike-and-bike site ($3 per person), or arrange for a site at the more primitive **Steep Ravine** campground and cabins off the coast highway. Steep Ravine's six walk-in campsites go for $9 per night ($7 off-season), and the cabins (for up to five people), with indoor wood stove and outdoor barbecue, cost $30 per night. If you don't mind a pit toilet, this place is absolutely unbeatable—just you and a few other guests sharing almost the entire dramatic coast as far as the eye can see. Unfortunately, Steep Ravine is not an unknown gem, and the cabins book up well in advance. Reservations for Pantoll and Steep Ravine can be made through Destinet (tel. 800/444–7275).

STINSON BEACH

Six treacherous miles north of Muir Beach on Hwy. 1 lies Stinson Beach, one of Northern California's most popular coastal towns. It's loaded with weather-beaten wooden houses and neighborly general stores, and its 3-mi-long beach has a beach-bum and barbecue appeal that's uncommon north of Santa Cruz. Despite Stinson's isolated location, chilly waters, and lurking sharks, hordes of surfers and sun worshipers descend every spring and summer weekend upon this town of 1,200. The 20-minute (10-mi) drive from Muir Woods to Stinson, past towering cliffs and jagged granite peaks, is incredible. Traffic can be a problem on summer weekends, but there are plenty of scenic overlooks along the way to make the bumper-to-bumper traffic more bearable

The **Livewater Surfshop** (3450 Hwy. 1, tel. 415/868–0333) rents body boards ($8 a day), wet suits ($10 a day), and surfboards ($25 a day) year-round. **Parkside Café** (43 Arenal St., tel. 415/868–1272) has good burgers ($4) and the cheapest prices in town. Turn west at the stop sign on Hwy. 1 and you'll run right into it.

For an encounter with a different sort of wildlife, leave your inhibitions in the car and walk down to **Red Rocks Beach** where, during extremely low tides, caves containing hot springs are revealed—as well as the bare buns of bathers. Even when the caves are concealed by water, the beach is peopled by nudists. To get here, drive ¾ mi south of Stinson Beach and park in the big gravel lot you'll see on the right (it's often full on sunny weekends). A path leads down to the beach.

WHERE TO SLEEP

Stinson Beach is full of nauseatingly quaint bed-and-breakfasts that cost upward of $90 a night. Instead, head to the **Stinson Beach Motel** (3416 Hwy. 1, tel. 415/868–1712), which has inviting doubles with private bath and apartments with kitchens ($60–$80) set around a shady garden. The nearest camping is at Steep Ravine or at Pantoll on Mt. Tamalpais (*see above*).

BOLINAS

Bolinas works hard to avoid notice. Locals are legendary for taking down the sign marking the Bolinas/Olema Road (it's the first left after you curve around the lagoon to your left). If you breeze into town to wander Main Street and do some shopping, you'll feel tolerated at best—locals loathe the idea of tacky Sausalito-style development. **Fourth of July** brings out the town's friendliest faces; past festivities have included outrageous parades and a tug-of-war with Stinson Beach (the loser ended up in the muddy mouth of the estuary between the two towns).

Despite the town's elitism, you'll still find a few bearded radicals hanging out on the street corners, strumming their guitars or fixing their VW microbuses. The **Bolinas People's Store** (14 Wharf Rd., tel. 415/868–1433) is famous for its fresh, high-quality local produce, grown by the same sweaty hippies who once gave the town so much of its character. For a bite to eat, go next door to the **Bolinas Bay Bakery and Café** (20 Wharf Rd., tel. 415/868–0211), which offers fresh baked goods, pasta salads, and pizzas. Many items feature locally grown organic ingredients. The only nightlife in town is **Smiley's Schooner Saloon** (41 Wharf Rd., tel. 415/868–1311), ostensibly the oldest continually operated saloon in California. Huddled around the pool table and jukebox are an odd combination of suit-and-tie professionals and tie-dyed hippies.

POINT REYES NATIONAL SEASHORE

Explore the Point Reyes National Seashore—a 66,500-acre mosaic of marshes, ferocious cliffs, and untrammeled beaches—and you'll feel a lot farther than 40 mi away from San Francisco. With its lush grazing land and rambling farms, Point Reyes could easily pass for the Scottish Highlands or western Ireland, minus the pubs. Even though it's isolated, this hammerhead-shape peninsula, jutting 10 mi into the Pacific, is a manageable 90-minute drive from San Francisco. There are hundreds of hiking trails on the peninsula and, for spending the night, four backpackers' campgrounds and an excellent hostel. Crowds are a problem on summer weekends, but otherwise it's an ideal escape for nature lovers. The peninsula erupts with wildflowers from mid-February through July; and though winter sees a lot of rain, that's when the rivers and ponds teem with life.

Twelve miles north of Bolinas on Hwy. 1, past the block-long town of Olema, look for a sign marking the turnoff for Point Reyes and the **Bear Valley Visitor Information Center** (Bear Valley Rd., tel. 415/663–1092), open weekdays 9–5, weekends 8–5. Here you can see a short orientation film, sign up for ranger-led hikes, explore a small museum of cultural and natural history, or pick up trail maps and camping permits. A short walk away, look for the replica of a typical Coastal Miwok Native American village, built on the ruins of a 400-year-old Miwok farming settlement. Also nearby is the **Bear Valley Trail,** a lightly traveled 4-mi hike that wanders through the woods and down to a secluded beach offering a good overview of the peninsula.

Two miles farther down Bear Valley Road (which turns into Sir Francis Drake Boulevard), you'll pass through the quiet town of **Inverness.** Coming across this town's Czech restaurants and architecture—oddly colored, intricately carved wooden houses—can be disorienting after miles of empty coastline, but the town's Eastern European flavor is genuine. In 1935, after a freighter ran aground in San Francisco Bay, a number of its Czech deckhands jumped ship and settled here. Since then, dozens of Czech families have immigrated to Inverness, bringing their culture, language, and cuisine.

Continue west through Inverness on Sir Francis Drake Boulevard, then take Drakes Beach Road to a massive stretch of white sand called **Drakes Beach**—supposedly, Sir Francis himself landed here on his world tour. A quarter mile north of Drakes Beach, a sign directs you to the **Point Reyes Lighthouse** (tel. 415/669–1534) 6 mi to the west. It's open Thursday–Monday 10–5, except during particularly stormy or windy weather. Admission is free. From the parking lot, a steep trail leads down to the lighthouse, and a dozen or so trails are carved into the surrounding cliffs. The ¾-mi hike to **Chimney Rock** is one of the most scenic; look for the trailhead in the parking lot. From mid-December to April, and especially in January and March, this is a great place to look for the gray whales on their 12,000-mi round-trip migration along the Pacific coast.

COMING AND GOING

From San Francisco, take U.S. 101 north across the Golden Gate Bridge. If speed is more important than scenery, exit at Sir Francis Drake Boulevard and follow it 21 mi to the coast. Eventually, you'll end up 2 mi north of Olema on Hwy. 1. Otherwise, take the Stinson Beach/Hwy. 1 exit and enjoy the curvy, 30-mi scenic drive along the coast. (For bus information, *see* Coming and Going *in* Marin County, *above.*)

WHERE TO SLEEP

Eight miles west of the Point Reyes Visitor Center, the **Point Reyes AYH-Hostel** (Crossroads Rd., tel. 415/663–8811) is popular with foreign travelers, seniors, and weekenders up from San Francisco. The two common rooms have wood-burning stoves and plentiful reading material. Beds cost $12; there is one private room for families with small children. Reservations are advised on weekends and in summer. *Box 247, Point Reyes Station 94956, tel. 415/663–8811. From Hwy. 1, left (west) in Olema on Bear Valley Rd. 1 block beyond stop sign; 1½ mi farther, left at* LIGHTHOUSE/BEACHES/HOSTEL *sign, left after 6 mi on Crossroads Rd. 44 beds. Reception open 7:30–9:30 and 4:30–9:30, curfew 10* PM*, lockout 9:30–4:30. Kitchen.*

CAMPING • Point Reyes National Seashore also has four free campgrounds, open to backpackers only, in isolated wilderness areas. To reserve a campsite up to two months in advance, call 415/663–8054 weekdays between 9 and noon. Trails to the campgrounds leave from the visitor center, which is on the entrance road (turn left off Hwy. 1 just past Olema on Bear Valley Road). All sites have barbecue pits, picnic tables, pit toilets, and food storage lockers; water must be treated before drinking. **Coast Camp** is a 2-mi hike from the youth hostel parking lot (*see above*) or an 8-mi trek from the visitor center, but you'll sleep within a stone's throw (100 yards) of the ocean at any of the 14 sites. People tend to avoid **Glenn Camp** because it's 5 mi from the nearest road, but its 12 sites are in a quiet valley surrounded by trees, perfect for those who want to get away from civilization. The 2 group and 12 individual sites at **Sky Camp** are the most popular; they're a 2½-mi walk from the visitor center and 2 mi from the nearest parking area. For the truly rugged, **Wildcat Camp,** a stiff 6½ mi from the nearest road, has seven sites on a bluff, just a short walk from the beach. Privacy is never a problem.

Six miles east of Point Reyes on Sir Francis Drake Boulevard, **Samuel P. Taylor State Park** (tel. 415/488–9897) has 60 campsites available for $12–$16 per night (hike-in and bike-in sites cost $3 per person) and—blessing of all blessings—hot showers. Reservations can be made through Destinet (tel. 800/444–7275); during summer, even weeknights are booked in advance. Golden Gate Transit Bus 65 stops at the park on weekends and holidays.

FOOD

There aren't too many places to eat in Point Reyes, so stock up in San Francisco or at the **Bovine Bakery** (11315 Hwy. 1, 2 mi north of Olema, tel. 415/663–9420). It has excellent, reasonably priced sandwiches, pastries, and breads—the perfect makings for a picnic. The most popular picnic stop is Inverness's **Perry's Delicatessen** (12301 Sir Francis Drake Blvd., near Vallejo Ave., tel. 415/663–1491). For under $6, you can brown-bag a shrimp or crab sandwich and a pasta salad.

WINE COUNTRY

California's Wine Country lives up to its reputation—it's that beautiful, that elegant, occasionally that snooty, and definitely worth the 50-mi northeast trek from San Francisco. You don't have to be a wine connoisseur to enjoy this region—even philistines appreciate the area's rustic beauty and the opportunity to get a free buzz. Many of the wineries will pour you glass after glass of free samples. Choose carefully though: A number of Napa Valley wineries charge a $2–$5 tasting fee, which can add up if you're making the rounds.

Most vineyards are concentrated in the Napa and Sonoma valleys, but the Wine Country actually stretches north through Healdsburg into Lake and Mendocino counties. Vintners have been making wine here for well over 100 years, but it wasn't until 1976, when a cabernet sauvignon from Stag's Leap won a blind taste test in Paris, that Californians began boasting and people all over the world began buying. Since then, production has skyrocketed: 25 years ago there were only about 25 wineries; now there are almost 300.

Napa Valley has the greatest number, but its wineries are also the most expensive and pretentious. Once upon a time, visitors were greeted with open arms—and flowing bottles—by jolly vintners thankful for even a trickle of business. These days, you'll have to search out Napa's tiniest wineries to get this kind of reception. Better yet, make a beeline for Sonoma Valley. While Sonoma houses a few big, impersonal wineries, it draws fewer tourists and is home to a greater share of rustic family-owned and -operated vineyards. In both valleys, the farther you stray from the main drag, the better off you'll be. Remember that it doesn't always work to just drop in at a winery, especially if you want to take a tour—you may need an appointment.

If you need a break from the wineries, you can luxuriate in the hot springs, bubbling mud baths, and mineral baths of Calistoga; loiter in the lovely Spanish mission and old adobes of Sonoma; or browse through the small museums devoted to former residents Jack London and Robert Louis Stevenson, both of whom wrote about the area. An overnight stay, however, can take a monster-size bite out of your budget. Lodging tends to be more expensive than in San Francisco, and food is pricey as well. You can survive cheaply by eating at roadside produce stands, drinking free wine, and sleeping in a state park. Otherwise, expect to pay through the nose.

BASICS

VISITOR INFORMATION

Before you go (or once you arrive), you may want to call the **Napa Valley Visitors' Bureau** (1310 Napa Town Center, Napa, tel. 707/226–7459), open daily 9–5 (they don't answer the phones on weekends). The friendly local volunteers can help you organize your trip and provide you with more maps than you'll ever need. The **Sonoma Valley Visitors' Bureau** (10 E. Spain St., Sonoma, tel. 707/996–1090), open daily 9–5 (until 7 in the summer), gives advice on what to see and do in the "other" valley. Additionally, most wineries carry *Spotlight's Wine Country Guide*, a free monthly that has maps, coupons, and winery information.

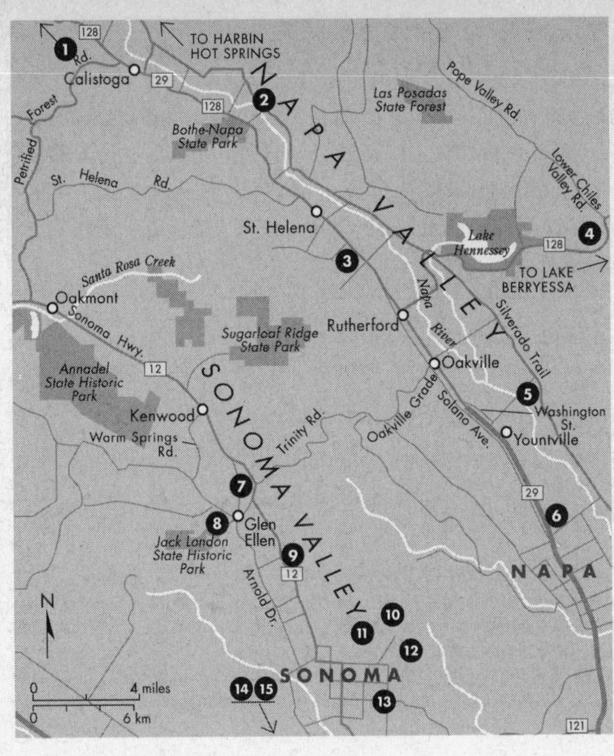

Wineries ●
Bartholomew Park Winery, **10**
Benzinger, **8**
Buena Vista, **12**
Field Stone, **1**
Gundlach-Bundschu, **13**
Hakusan Sake Gardnes, **14**
Nichelini, **4**
Ravenswood, **11**
S. Anderson, **5**
Sutter Home Winery, **3**
Trefethen Vineyards, **6**
Schug, **15**
Valley of the Moon, **9**
Wellington, **7**
Wermuth, **2**

WHEN TO GO

During the autumn harvest season you'll see some real action in the wine cellars. In the spring, wildflowers and mustard bloom amid the endless rows of manicured vines. Try to avoid the Wine Country in summer, when the dry, dusty region becomes even drier and dustier, and the crowds can be suffocating.

COMING AND GOING

If you do go to Napa in summer, stay off gridlocked Hwy. 29 as much as possible and explore the less crowded and more scenic **Silverado Trail,** which runs parallel to Hwy. 29 a mile to the east. In the less crowded Sonoma valley, Hwy. 12 is fine.

BY BUS

Golden Gate Transit (tel. 415/455–2000 or 707/541–2000) provides bus service from San Francisco and Marin County to towns throughout Sonoma County. Bus 90 makes the trek from San Francisco to Sonoma (2 hrs, $4.50) twice daily, but these buses don't run on weekends. Instead, you'll have to take the bus to Petaluma and transfer to Sonoma County Transit (*see* Getting Around, *below*). **Greyhound** has service from San Francisco's Transbay Terminal (*see* Getting In, Out, and Around *in* Chapter 1) once daily to Napa (2½ hrs, $15 one-way) and Middletown (4¼ hrs, $19 one-way), twice daily to Sonoma (3–4 hrs, change in Vallejo or Santa Rosa, $17 one-way). Tickets are cheaper midweek.

BY CAR

Though traffic can be heavy, especially on weekends and during rush hours (7 AM–9 AM and 4 PM–6 PM), the easiest way to reach the Wine Country is by car. From San Francisco, the best option is to take **U.S. 101** north over the Golden Gate Bridge and connect with **Highway 37** east near Ignacio. From here take **Highway 121** north to **Highway 12** north for Sonoma, or follow Hwy. 121 as it curves east toward **Highway 29** for Napa. If you're only visiting the Napa Valley or are coming from the East Bay, it's quicker to take **I–80** north and exit to Hwy. 37 west in Vallejo. Hwy. 37 joins up with Hwy. 29 north

GOURMET TREAT

If you let enough wine go to your head, starve yourself for a week, and reserve two months ahead, you can dine at one of California's best restaurants—Yountville's French Laundry (6640 Washington St., at Creek St., tel. 707/944–2380). The nine-course, prix-fixe ($75) dinner includes California/French delicacies like "braised beef cheek and veal tongue."

to Napa. Even when traffic is heavy it shouldn't take more than two hours; on good days you'll be there in under an hour.

GETTING AROUND

Tempting as the **Napa Valley Wine Train** (1275 McKinstry St., Napa, tel. 707/253–2111) may sound, it's more of a restaurant than a means of transportation—no stopping for a taste of the grape. If you're *still* interested, $24 buys you a ride to St. Helena and back.

BY BIKE

Biking is perhaps the best way to see the Wine Country. Within each region, the wineries tend to be grouped closely together, making them easy to see on two wheels. Bicyclists should stick to the Silverado Trail. Riding on Hwy. 29 means a greater risk of being run over by tipsy drivers, especially on summer weekends. **Napa Valley Bike Tours and Rentals** (4080 Byway E, at Salvador Ave., tel. 707/255–3380 or 800/707–2453), at the northern end of Napa, rents bikes for $6 per hour or $20 per day. They offer biking maps and tour suggestions, so squeeze as much information from them as possible before heading out.

BY BUS

Sonoma County Transit (tel. 707/576–7433) connects all cities in Sonoma County. Buses run daily (some until 10 PM). Fares are less than $2 to most places; buses can get you within walking distance of a few wineries. **Napa Valley Transit** (tel. 707/255–7631) travels between Napa and Yountville ($1).

BY CAR

For the 26-mi grand tour through the Wine Country's major towns and vineyards, take **Highway 29** north from Napa to Calistoga, head west for 12 mi toward Fulton and U.S. 101 on the **Petrified Forest Trail,** drive 4 mi south on **U.S. 101** to Santa Rosa, and then take **Highway 12** south to Sonoma.

SONOMA VALLEY

The town of **Sonoma** may have recently grown into an upscale bedroom community for San Francisco commuters, but behind the trendy restaurants and chic clothing boutiques lies a rich history. It was here that Father Junípero Serra built the last and northernmost of the California missions, **Mission San Francisco Solano** (1st and Spain Sts., tel. 707/938–1519), now a museum housing a collection of 19th-century watercolors by Chris Jorgenson; the $2 admission fee is also good for entry to Lachryma Montis and the army barracks. Just east of the mission lies grassy **Sonoma Plaza,** the epicenter of Sonoma life. Around the plaza, many adobe buildings remain from the days of Spanish and Mexican rule, including old army barracks and the restored **Toscana Hotel** (20 E. Spain St., tel. 707/938–5889). Three blocks west of the plaza lie **Sonoma State Historical Park** and **Lachryma Montis** (3rd St. W, off W. Spain St., tel. 707/938–1519), the ornate home of the last Mexican governor, General Vallejo. Vallejo named the home "mountain tears" after the area's many natural hot and cold springs. Admission to the grounds (open daily 10–5) is $2.

Nearby in **Glen Ellen,** north of Sonoma off Hwy. 12, look for the **Jack London State Historic Park.** Tired of drinking and brawling on the Oakland waterfront, London (1876–1916) came here to build his dream home, Wolf House. The house mysteriously burned down before it was finished, but the impressive stone foundations remain, along with the architects' drawings of what the house would have looked like. A shady ½-mi walk through the oak trees takes you from the Jack London Museum to his grave and the ruins of his home. *Tel. 707/ 938–5216. From Hwy. 12, take Glen Ellen turnoff and follow signs. Parking: $5. Museum open daily 10–5. Park open daily 9:30–7.*

WHERE TO SLEEP

Beds don't come cheap in the Sonoma Valley, so camping or San Francisco day-tripping is advised. Otherwise you'll probably want to make the half-hour drive north on Hwy. 12 to Santa Rosa for an affordable room. Even at Sonoma's least expensive motel, **El Pueblo Inn** (896 W. Napa St., on Hwy. 12, tel. 707/996–3651 or 800/900–8844), a clean and generic double will run you a whopping $80 on weekdays, $94 on weekends ($65 daily in winter). At least the motel has a great swimming pool and is close to the central square and several wineries.

Since prices are comparable, consider staying at one of Sonoma's bed-and-breakfasts. **Hollyhock House** (1541 Denmark St., off 8th St. E, tel. 707/938–1809) attracts adventurous, bohemian types to its old two-story farmhouse on a quiet country road. The two doubles cost $65–$90 on summer weekends ($60 in winter), but you can lower the price of the cheaper room to $60–$65 by staying more than one weekend night or coming on a weekday. In Glen Ellen, the **Jack London Lodge** (13740 Arnold Dr., at London Ranch Rd., tel. 707/938–8510) offers comfortable doubles with antique decor for $75; off-season specials can lower rates to $55–$60. The lodge has a pool, a saloon, and a decent restaurant. Reservations are strongly advised, especially in summer.

CAMPING • Sugarloaf Ridge State Park. Only 8 mi north of Sonoma on Hwy. 12, Sugarloaf has 50 campsites scattered around a large meadow (dry and uninviting in summer). There are 25 mi of trails for hiking, biking, and horseback riding (*see* Outdoor Activities, *below*). If you hike up the trail to your left as you enter the park, you're likely to see deer, especially around sunset when they come out for early evening grazing. Campsites cost $16 ($12 in winter). In summer and on weekends, it's a good idea to reserve ahead through Destinet (tel. 800/444–7275). *2605 Adobe Canyon Rd., Kenwood, tel. 707/833–5712. From Sonoma, Hwy. 12 north, right on Adobe Canyon Rd., which dead-ends at park. Barbecues, drinking water, flush toilets.*

FOOD

Sonoma is *the* place to get your fill of gourmet-pesto this and roasted-goat-cheese that. Fortunately, there are some options for those with expensive tastes but no expense account: Put together a picnic at the **Sonoma Farmer's Market** Friday 9–noon in Depot Park. An additional market is held in the plaza Tuesday evening from 4:30 until dusk. Both markets take place during the summer months. To add to the European flavor of your Wine Country experience, grab breakfast at the **Basque Boulangerie Café** (460 1st St. E, tel. 707/935–7687) where you can dunk the award-winning, made-from-scratch Basque pastries into freshly brewed espresso.

Come dinner time, dive into delicious pasta dishes ($7–$11) on the patio at **Pasta Nostra** (139 E. Napa St., tel. 707/938–4166). Or head down the alley east of the plaza to spirited **Murphy's Irish Pub** (464 1st St. E, tel. 707/935–0660) for homemade lamb stew and vegetables ($6.95), a pint of stout ($3.50), and live Irish tunes (most weekends). For Mexican food, the roadside **Cocina Cha Cha** (897 W. Napa St., tel. 707/996–1735) is open daily and serves crisp tacos with ground beef for only 99¢. Two people can easily split the enormous burrito grande ($7), filled with the works and topped with a spicy homemade sauce.

For an excellent sit-down meal, trek out to the one-street town of Glen Ellen, where you'll find the **Sonoma Mountain Grill** (13690 Arnold Dr., tel. 707/938–2370), open Thursday through Monday 11–9, and Tuesday 11–3. The fresh fish special—with a heaping salad, vegetables, and rice—is the most expensive thing on the menu ($12–$14), but it's well worth it; with an appetizer, it could feed two.

WINERIES

Sonoma Valley is home to some 30 wineries and 6,000 acres of vineyards. It was here that California began its upstart drive to compete with old-world wineries, when Count Agoston Haraszthy, the "father of California wine," brought thousands of European grapevine cuttings to the United States in 1857 and started the **Buena Vista** winery (18000 Old Winery Rd., Sonoma, tel. 800/926–1266). You can easily spend a leisurely day driving along Hwy. 12 through the 17-mi-long valley, stopping to sip a little wine, learn a little history, have a picnic, and nap in the sun. The wineries below are listed in a south to north order.

BEAR FLAG REPUBLIC

For a month in 1846, Sonoma belonged to the little-known Bear Flag Republic—the brainchild of Captain John C. Frémont and a group of Yankee trappers who decided to resolve tensions between the Mexican government and non-Mexican immigrants by imprisoning Mexican General Vallejo and creating their own country. It lasted until the U.S. Navy arrived, but the bear remains on California's flag.

Schug. Walter Schug will pour you free tastes of his European-style wines at this unbelievably friendly, family-run winery. Not many tourists come here, so the family members (who are viticultural experts) have plenty of time to answer questions. They'll give you a tour if you're interested, and you can explore the rooms where wines are aged and bottled. *602 Bonneau Rd., Sonoma, tel. 707/939–9363 or 800/966–9365. From plaza, Hwy. 12 south, then Hwy. 121 west until it hits Hwy. 116 at stop sign; Bonneau Rd. is straight ahead. Open daily 10–5.*

Gundlach-Bundschu. The motto of this 137-year-old, family-owned winery is "We make serious wines, but we don't take our wine too seriously." Indeed, in the main building (surrounded by trellised wisteria), old photographs of the family sit alongside a picture of Bacchus in shades. Then there are the corks, inscribed: "Leave the kids the land and money—drink the wine yourself." Free tasters of up to five different wines get you in the proper mood. If you're visiting in the summer, call ahead for tickets to their outdoor Shakespeare ($17). *2000 Denmark St., Sonoma, tel. 707/938–5277. From plaza, take E. Napa St. east, turn right on E. 8th St., left on Denmark St., and look for sign on left. Open daily 11–4:30.*

Ravenswood. This small, stone winery in the Sonoma foothills has a relaxed, intimate feel, and their merlots and zinfandels are definitely worth writing home about. If you didn't bring a picnic to savor on the terrace, try barbecued chicken or ribs with bread, coleslaw, and potato salad ($6–$7.25), available on summer and early fall weekends only. *18701 Gehricke Rd., Sonoma, tel. 707/938–1960. From plaza, Spain St. east, turn left on 4th St. E, right onto Lovall Valley Rd., left on Gehricke Rd. Open daily 10–4:30.*

Bartholomew Park Winery. Aside from the free tastings, the best thing about Bartholomew is its 400-acre park. Oak-shaded picnic tables, 3 mi of marked hiking trails, and a thick blanket of spring wildflowers will have you questioning whether you came for the vino or the view. All of their grapes are hand-harvested, and you can sample their wares while wandering the adjoined viticulture museum. *1000 Vineyard La., Sonoma, tel. 707/935–9511. From plaza, Napa St. E, turn left on 7th St. E, turn left on Castle Rd, follow to winery entrance. Open daily 10–4:30.*

Valley of the Moon. This intimate winery off the main drag is a breath of fresh air compared to the more crowded vineyards in the upper valley. The staff is friendly and helpful, and in that fine Sonoma Valley tradition, tasting is free. Be sure to sample their port. *777 Madrone Rd., Glen Ellen, tel. 707/996–6941. From Sonoma, Hwy. 12 north 6 mi to Madrone Rd. Open Apr.–Oct., daily 10–5; Nov.–Mar., daily 10–4:30.*

Benziger. You're encouraged to roam the beautiful grounds, enjoy the fragrant rose gardens, picnic in any spot you choose, and indulge in many a free taster. Benziger has torn out some merlot vines to make room for hops and jumped on the microbrewery bandwagon with summer 1997's launch of the **Sonoma Mountain Brewing Company** (2 mi east of the winery), but vino lovers can breathe easy—they plan on continuing their line of wines. *1883 London Ranch Rd., Glen Ellen, tel. 707/935–3000. From Hwy. 12, take Glen Ellen (Arnold Dr.) turnoff and follow signs for Jack London State Park. Open daily 10–5.*

Wellington. Run by a father-son team, this tiny winery just opened its doors in 1994, and it's still obscure enough to escape the hordes. The tasting room is a down-to-earth affair with a small terrace and a view of the Sonoma Mountains. Tastings of their delicious wines are unlimited—be sure to try the Estate Chardonnay, a combination of fruit and clove flavors that tastes like liquid Christmas. *11600 Dunbar Rd., Glen Ellen, tel. 707/939–0708. From Sonoma, Hwy. 12 north 7 mi, exit left at Dunbar Rd. Open daily 11–5.*

NAPA VALLEY

While Sonoma is cheaper and more welcoming, it's Napa Valley, about a 20-minute drive east of Sonoma on Hwy. 121, that lures most visitors to the Wine Country. When the traffic backs up for miles on Hwy. 29, it's clear that Napa Valley has become one of the Bay Area's biggest tourist attractions north of Fisherman's Wharf. The scenery is still beautiful, the wine (in some cases) still free, the town of **Napa** still lined with attractive Victorian houses and California bungalows, but the Napa Valley is losing some of its old-time charm with each trampling tourist.

Wine may take center stage in the Napa Valley, but a fair share of hedonists come here solely for a peaceful soak in hot springs and mud baths, most in or near Calistoga. Though you'd perhaps hesitate to throw yourself in a roadside ditch and roll around in the muck, folks in the Wine Country believe that mud baths and sulfur springs heal all manner of ills. Poverty, however, is not one of them: You'll pay a pretty penny for a day of pampering. On the bright side, you can spend the night at any of several resorts for a decent price, and get free access to mineral pools and Jacuzzis.

WHERE TO SLEEP

Although some of the most expensive lodging in the Wine Country is here in the posh Napa Valley, budget travelers can survive by day-tripping, camping, or checking into one of Napa's lower-end motels. In summer, reserve at least three weeks ahead.

Stock up on groceries in quiet but touristy St. Helena, 16 mi north of Napa on Hwy. 29. You might even bump into resident Francis Ford Coppola.

NAPA • One of Napa's cheapest options is the **Silverado Motel** (500 Silverado Trail, tel. 707/253–0892), where a tacky but cleanish room is $45 weekdays, $65–$75 weekends ($45 daily in winter). The rooms at the **Napa Motel** (314 Soscol Ave., tel. 707/226–1878) are equally homely and equally cheap ($45 weekdays, $55 weekends). The **Napa Valley Budget Inn** (3380 Solano Ave., off Hwy. 29, tel. 707/257–6111) has clean but spartan doubles starting at $60 ($86 on Friday or Saturday). The swimming pool is perfect after a long day at the wineries, many of which are within biking distance. At the **Wine Valley Lodge** (200 S. Coombs St., tel. 707/224–7911), comfy rooms cost $60 on weekdays ($50 if you pick up a flyer at the visitors' bureau), $90 on weekends—unless you want to stay in the room where Elvis slept ($155 for six-person suite). Amenities include a pool and a barbecue in the courtyard.

CALISTOGA • Pleasure-seekers planning to hit both the wineries and the hot springs should consider staying in Calistoga. If you want to stay on the main drag, the **Calistoga Inn** (1250 Lincoln Ave., tel. 707/942–4101) has clean, simple bed-and-breakfast rooms with shared baths and full-size beds for $55 ($68 Fri.–Sat.). For $54 (second night $5 off), you can get a cabin for two at the **Triple S Ranch** (4600 Mt. Home Ranch Rd., tel. 707/942–6730). There's no phone or TV, but the complex does include a swimming pool and a pricey steak house. The ranch is north of Calistoga off Hwy. 128; take Petrified Forest Road west for 2½ mi until you reach Mt. Home Ranch Road. If you can't spend the night without a color TV, try the **Holiday House** (3514 Hwy. 128, tel. 707/942–6174), 3 mi north of Calistoga; watch for the white picket fence. From the outside it looks like you're pulling into a friend's house; the three rooms ($60 one night, $50 if you stay two nights), though, are strictly Motel 6.

CAMPING • Camping is your best budget option in Napa (and the Wine Country in general). Unfortunately, there isn't any public transportation to the campgrounds. Lake Berryessa is 20 mi east from Rutherford on Hwy. 128 and is divided into seven campgrounds, including **Pleasure Cove** (tel. 707/966–2172) and **Spanish Flat** (tel. 707/966–7700), for a total of 225 campsites (about $16) near the water. While you get direct access to swimming, fishing, picnicking, and waterskiing facilities, the area around the lake is barren, dusty, and very hot during summer. Summer weekends, reserve ahead.

Bothe-Napa State Park. This is the Wine Country's most attractive campground, situated in the Napa foothills amid redwoods, madrone, and tan oaks, only 5 mi north of St. Helena and its wineries. The sites are reasonably private, and the park is one of the few with a swimming pool ($3 separate fee), much used on hot summer days. The fee is $15–$16 April–October or $12 off-season, and reservations (tel. 800/444–7275) are suggested in summer, especially on weekends. *3801 St. Helena Hwy. N, Calistoga, tel. 707/942–4575. From St. Helena, north on Hwy. 29. 48 sites. Drinking water, flush toilets, hot showers.*

Calistoga Ranch Club. A mere two minutes north off the Silverado Trail, the Ranch Club scores points for convenience and accessibility. While it's no isolated retreat, it *is* set off the main road with a fair

TASTING WINE LIKE A MASTER

If you want to pass yourself off as a wine aficionado, you'll need to know some rules of tasting. First of all, move from light wines to dark so as not to "clutter your palate." Begin by vigorously swirling an ounce of wine in your glass—put your hand over the glass to hold in the aromas. Raise the glass to your nose and inhale deeply. In young wines, you smell only the grapes (for example, the smell of the pinot noir grape might remind you of black cherries); with aging, the wine becomes more complex, emitting a whole "bouquet" of aromas (in pinot, that can include hints of violets, vanilla, a spicy pepper, or even leather). Next, take a sip—you're encouraged to slurp because air helps you taste the wine. Swish the wine around in your mouth to pick up the more subtle flavors. Before downing the rest of your glass, notice the aftertaste (or "finish"), and then decide what you think.

amount of shade and greenery. Tent sites for four people run $19. The closest thing to a hostel in Napa, you can rent a rustic cabin (sleeps 4) for $49, or . . . an Airstream Trailer (sleeps 5) with kitchen for $89. *580 Lommel Rd., Calistoga, tel. 707/942–6565. From St. Helena, head north on the Silverado Trail. 84 RV sites, 58 tent sites. Drinking water, showers.*

FOOD

If wine tasting is Napa Valley's main attraction, gourmet cuisine runs a close second. The best way to eat well without breaking the bank is to stock up at one of the area's makeshift farmers' markets (*see below*) and picnic on winery grounds at one of the well-placed picnic tables. If you're spending the day in Calistoga, cruise down to **Calistoga Drive-In Taquería** (1207 Foothill Blvd., tel. 707/942–0543) at the west end of Lincoln Avenue. A veggie burrito here runs $3.50, and the tortillas and chips are great.

Fine California cuisine—with fair portions for the price—can be had at the **Calistoga Inn** (1250 Lincoln Ave., tel. 707/942–4101). Try the Moroccan lamb stew with yam, apple, and raisins ($8.50), or cool off in the trellised garden with a home-brewed ale or lagers–only $2 during happy hour (weekdays 4–6). **The Diner** (6476 Washington St., Yountville, tel. 707/944–2626) has been serving huge plates of American or Mexican food for lunch and dinner for more than 20 years. Most meals are in the $7–$10 range, but portions are generous (couples should consider splitting an appetizer and a main course). Pull into **The Red Hen Cantina** (5091 Hwy. 29, tel. 707/255–8125) for excellent fajitas ($25 for two people). You'll be hard pressed to escape the cantina without indulging in one of their margaritas, ranging in size from normal ($5) to *muy grande* ($40).

Napa Valley Farmers' Market. Held on Tuesday in Napa and Friday in St. Helena, this market offers fruits and veggies, cheese, eggs, honey, dressings, cut flowers, baked goods, and countless other edibles. *Napa: West St., between 1st and Pearl Sts., tel. 707/252–2105. Just west of Cinedome Theater, which has free parking. Open May–Oct., Tues. 7:30–noon. St. Helena: Old Railroad Depot, tel. 707/252–2105. East on Adams St. off Hwy. 29, left at stop sign, and 1 block up on right. Open May–Oct., Fri. 7:30 AM–11:30 AM.*

Pometta's Deli. This place is famous for its barbecued chicken platters ($7), but you can also get box lunches ($9.50–$12.50). Especially good is the vegetarian sandwich (about $4) stuffed with avocado, provolone, zucchini, and jalapeños. The restaurant has indoor and outdoor seating. *Hwy. 29, at Oakville Grade in Oakville, tel. 707/944–2365. Open daily.*

WINERIES

With literally hundreds of wineries crammed into the 35-mi-long Napa Valley, it's difficult to decide which to visit. Some, like **Sutter Home Winery** (277 Hwy. 29, St. Helena, tel. 707/963–3104), right on the main drag, are packed with drunken revelers, while others, like **Trefethen Vineyards** (1160 Oak Knoll Ave., Napa, tel. 707/255–7700), draw a sedate crowd able to hold forth about a wine's bouquet and tannins. If you're irked by the idea of paying a $3–$5 tasting fee, you'll have to choose wineries carefully. Seek out the freebies at some of the smaller wineries where the extra attention paid to the product often means better wine.

S. Anderson. Tours are given twice daily, frequently by John Anderson, son of the late Stan (as in "S.") Anderson. He does a wonderful job guiding you through his vineyards and candlelit, stone wine caves, modeled after those in the Champagne region of France. The caves hold over 400,000 bottles of sparkling wine, awaiting their "turn" (champagne bottles are turned by hand in a labor-intensive process that removes the yeast). The tour, with tasting, costs $3—great, bad jokes included—but it's more than worth it. Plan for over an hour—John doesn't need much prompting to extend the visit. *1473 Yountville Crossroad, Yountville, tel. 800/428–2259. From Hwy. 29 in Yountville, take Madison exit and follow signs for Yountville Crossroad. Open daily 10–5; tours at 10:30 and 2:30.*

If you sour on grapes, you can sample warm, cold, and dessert sakes for $1 at Hakusan Sake Gardens (Corner Hwys. 12 and 29, tel. 707/258-6160).

Nichelini. Napa's oldest family-owned winery (since 1890) lies 11 mi east of Rutherford and is worth every minute of the beautiful drive. Outside, under the shade of walnut trees and next to an old Roman grape press (which looks like a giant garlic press), you can sample several wines for free. Winning hands down as the most down-to-earth winery, Nichelini also wins honors for excellent merlots. Summer weekends, picnic to the strains of traditional Italian music on a hill overlooking the countryside. *Hwy. 128, St. Helena, tel. 707/963–0717 or 800/938–2783. Open May–Oct., weekends 10–6; Nov.–Apr., weekends 10–5.*

Wermuth. If you don't come for the notable wines, surely you must come to meet vintner Ralph Wermuth. Referred to fondly by some as "Albert Winestein," Ralph is one part philosopher, one part mad scientist, one part stand-up comedian, and quite a winemaker. For $1 you get tastings of gamay accompanied by chocolate chips to "bring out the flavor" and colombard paired with that gourmet standby, Cheez-Its. Wife and partner Smitty Wermuth designs the winery logos, which depict the old Italian basket presses still used here in the crush. *3942 Silverado Trail, Calistoga, tel. 707/942–5924. From Hwy. 29 north, Hwy. 128 east to Silverado Trail; continue north past Bale La. and look for sign on right. Open Tues.–Sun. 11–5.*

Field Stone. Although technically in Sonoma County, Field Stone is only 15 mi north of Calistoga on Hwy. 128 and is a rare treat. The friendly staff may have to turn down the stereo blasting Bob Dylan when you arrive, but they will quickly set you up with free glasses of their award-winning wines. Don't be fooled by the casual, rural setting; their product is strictly top-notch. Bring some cheese and fruit, and picnic on one of the many wine-barrel tables scattered throughout the beautiful grounds. *10075 Hwy. 128, Healdsburg, tel. 707/433–7266. From Calistoga, 15 mi north on Hwy. 128. Open daily 10–5.*

HOT SPRINGS

The majority of the Napa Valley's mud and mineral baths are in the curious little town of Calistoga, at the northern end of the valley. The town's bubbling mineral spring became a spa in 1859, when entrepreneur Sam Brannan melded the word California with the name of New York's Saratoga Springs resort; Calistoga has been attracting health seekers ever since. Unfortunately, prices at the Calistoga spas are uniformly steep, varying by only a couple of dollars. Be sure to pick up 10%-off coupons at the **Calistoga Chamber of Commerce** (1458 Lincoln Ave., tel. 707/942–6333), open weekdays 9–5, Sat. 10–4, Sun. 10–3.

A cheaper option is open-air bathing at rustic retreats like Harbin Hot Springs or White Sulphur Springs (*see below*). Not only do these resorts offer many of the same amenities as the Calistoga spas, but you get an affordable room for the night to boot. If you opt for one of the indoor spas, call ahead for a reservation. Most accept walk-ins, but nothing is more stressful than being turned away from a longed-for massage.

Golden Haven Hot Springs. A favorite with hetero couples, Golden Haven is the only Calistoga spa to offer private co-ed mud baths. The full treatment (mud bath, mineral Jacuzzi, blanket wrap, and 30-

minute massage) will run you $64 per person. Rooms cost $65 ($49 Sun.–Thurs., Sept.–June), including use of the swimming pool and hot mineral pool. *1713 Lake St., Calistoga, tel. 707/942–6793. From Lincoln Ave. east, left on Stevenson St., right on Lake St. Open daily 9–9.*

Harbin Hot Springs. Forty minutes north of Calistoga, this 1,200-acre, laid-back community is run by the Heart Consciousness Church, a group that advocates holistic health and spiritual renewal. The retreat, popular with gay men, has three natural mineral pools, varying in temperature from tepid to *very* hot, and a cold, spring-fed "plunge" pool, all open 24 hours. To use the pools, you must pay $5 for a one-month membership or $15 for a year (only one member per group required), plus an additional day-use fee ($13 Mon.–Thurs., $18 Fri.–Sun. and holidays). There's also an acclaimed massage school, whose graduates would be happy to show you their stuff ($46 per hour, $60 for 90 minutes). You're welcome to use the vegetarian-only communal kitchen or eat their veggie-only meals ($8–$12). Rustic dorm beds start at $23 ($35 on weekends and holidays), and you have to provide your own sheets or sleeping bag. Private rooms with shared bath are $60 ($90 on weekends). There are campsites along the creek and in nearby meadows, but at $14 per person ($23 Fri.–Sat., $17 Sun.) it's a lot to pay for a night in a tent, especially when the grounds are unkempt and the bathrooms few and far between. Despite the cost, expect a crowd on weekends. *Tel. 707/987–2477 or 800/622–2477 (Northern California only). Hwy. 29 north to Middletown, turn left at junction for Hwy. 175, right on Barnes St.; go 1½ mi to Harbin Springs Rd. and turn left. Rides can be arranged for those taking Greyhound.*

Lincoln Avenue Spa. With pleasant stone-and-wood massage rooms and a central location, this spa is posh for the price. Their Body Mud Treatment ($40) is the ideal alternative for those squeamish about wallowing in mud someone else has already wallowed in: You get your choice of mud (herbal, sea, or mint) slathered over your body, a relaxing nap on the steam table, and a soothing facial mask. *1339 Lincoln Ave., Calistoga, tel. 707/942–5296. Open daily 9–9.*

White Sulphur Springs. If you're planning to stay the night in Napa Valley, this St. Helena resort, established in 1852, is a bargain. For $85, two people gain access to 300 acres of land, plenty of hiking and biking trails, a Jacuzzi, a natural mineral bath, even a stand of redwoods, *and* you get a decent room for the night, either in the rustic, dormitory-style carriage house or in the inn ($105), where each room has a half-bath. It's a day and night of decadence for the price of an hour or two at some of Calistoga's spas. Reserve two weeks ahead of time. Even for day-trippers, a sulphur soak, sauna, Jacuzzi, and hiking trails are a bargain at the $30 day-use fee. *3100 White Sulphur Springs Rd., St. Helena, tel. 707/963–8588. From Hwy. 29 north, turn left on Spring St. in St. Helena and go 3 mi. Note: Do NOT take Sulphur Springs Rd. from Hwy. 29.*

OUTDOOR ACTIVITIES

If you're spending the day in Calistoga, pay a visit to **Robert Louis Stevenson State Park** off Hwy. 29, 9 mi northeast of Calistoga. Here you can hike to the bunkhouse of the Silverado Mine, where the impoverished author honeymooned with his wife, Fanny Osbourne, in the summer of 1880. The stay inspired Stevenson's *The Silverado Squatters.* The park's 3,000 acres on top of Mt. St. Helena are largely undeveloped; picnicking is permitted but overnight camping is not.

Skyline Wilderness Park. Perhaps the best way to experience the beauty of the Napa Valley is to get out and hike, preferably on Skyline's 2½-mi Lake Marie Trail, which runs along a shady creek and past overgrown orchards and ruined stone dairies. Swimming in Lake Marie isn't allowed, but you can try your luck fishing for bluegill and bass. *2201 Imola Ave, tel. 707/252–0481. Open Mon.–Thurs. 9–8, Fri.–Sun. 8–8; shorter hrs in winter.*

NORTH COAST 4

UPDATED BY MARTY OLMSTEAD

Between San Francisco and the Oregon border lie some 400 mi of rugged coastline, presided over by legions of enormous, ancient trees. The inhabitants of small towns dotting the coast are divided between those who live for the trees and those who live by cutting them down. In either case, the North Coast is defined by the giant redwoods, and the trip through Northern California is well worth it if only to pass some time among these ancient beings—which often measure 60 ft around the base and rise to nearly 400 ft. There's a magical quality to the light in a redwood forest. John Steinbeck described it well when he said that a day in the shadow of the towering redwoods consists of a prolonged dawn followed by a prolonged dusk, with little straight daylight in between.

The camping in this part of the state is excellent, especially around Patrick's Point near **Arcata,** in the **Jedediah Smith Redwoods,** north of **Crescent City,** and in the isolated **Lost Coast** and **Northern Coast Ranges.** But it's also worth getting to know the people and lifestyles up here. There's something about the lack of high-rise buildings and the proximity of uncharted wilderness that brings out the friendly side in most folks. You can explore the coast on either Hwy. 1 or U.S. 101, which separate north of San Francisco to become the two main roads through the region. **Highway 1** winds right along the jagged coastline and is one of the most dramatic drives in the United States. North of Westport, it leaves the Pacific and heads east to join U.S. 101. The land for the next 73 mi is so rugged that the state has never extended the highway along the coast. This isolated region, known as the Lost Coast, is accessible only by a series of winding roads that meander through virgin (never logged) redwood forests and open grazing lands overlooking black-sand beaches.

U.S. 101, which parallels Hwy. 1 before joining it at Leggett, is a faster route that takes you through turn-of-the-century farming towns, vineyards, and the impressive **Avenue of the Giants** near Garberville. Farther north on U.S. 101, Arcata is home to Humboldt State University. The town is like a mini-Berkeley, with tofu burritos, repertory film houses, and plenty of live music. This is a great launching point for adventures north into the stunning **Redwood National Forest** or east into the thickly forested wilderness and numerous pristine river valleys of the Northern Coast Ranges.

The **Redwood Empire Association** (2801 Leavenworth St., San Francisco 94133, tel. 415/543–8334), open Tuesday–Saturday 10–6, has a wealth of information on attractions, activities, and regional history. Their 48-page booklet is $3 if you send away for it, but free if you stop by the office, located in the cannery at San Francisco's Fisherman's Wharf.

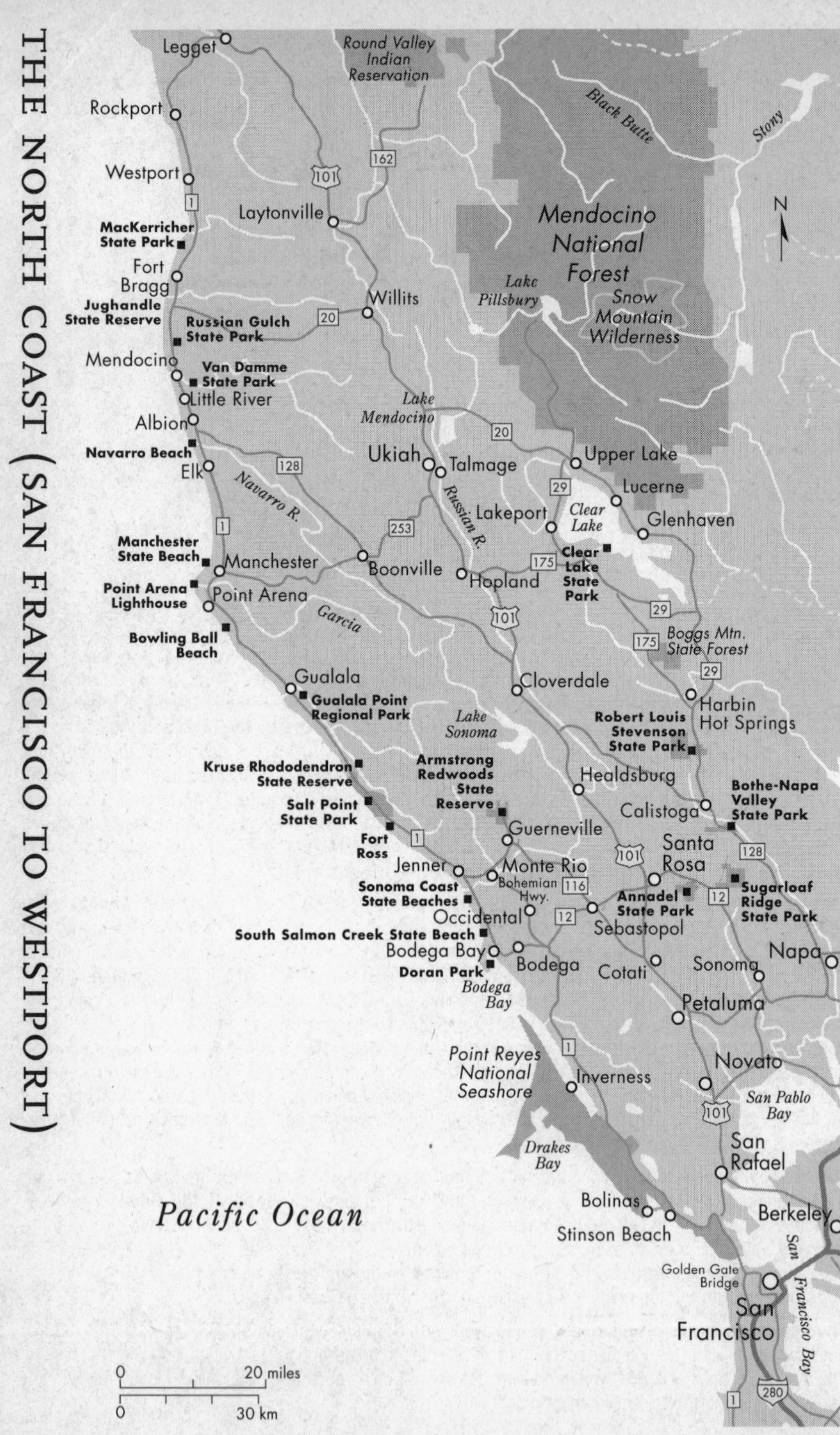
Legget
Round Valley Indian Reservation
Rockport
Black Butte
Stony
162
101
Westport
1
Laytonville
N
Mendocino National Forest
MacKerricher State Park
Fort Bragg
Lake Pillsbury
Snow Mountain Wilderness
Willits
Jughandle State Reserve
20
Russian Gulch State Park
Mendocino
Van Damme State Park
Little River
Lake Mendocino
Albion
20
Navarro Beach
Ukiah
Talmage
Upper Lake
Elk
128
Navarro R.
Russian R.
29
Lucerne
Lakeport
Clear Lake
Glenhaven
1
253
Manchester State Beach
Manchester
Boonville
Hopland
175
Clear Lake State Park
Point Arena Lighthouse
Point Arena
29
Garcia
101
Bowling Ball Beach
175
Boggs Mtn. State Forest
29
Gualala
Cloverdale
Gualala Point Regional Park
Harbin Hot Springs
Lake Sonoma
Robert Louis Stevenson State Park
Kruse Rhododendron State Reserve
Armstrong Redwoods State Reserve
Healdsburg
Bothe-Napa Valley State Park
Salt Point State Park
Calistoga
Fort Ross
1
Guerneville
Santa Rosa
101
128
Jenner
Monte Rio
Bohemian Hwy.
116
Sonoma Coast State Beaches
Annadel State Park
12
Sugarloaf Ridge State Park
Occidental
12
Sebastopol
South Salmon Creek State Beach
Bodega Bay
Bodega
Doran Park
Cotati
Sonoma
Napa
Bodega Bay
Petaluma
1
Point Reyes National Seashore
Inverness
Novato
San Pablo Bay
101
Drakes Bay
San Rafael
Pacific Ocean
Bolinas
Stinson Beach
Berkeley
San Francisco Bay
Golden Gate Bridge
San Francisco
0
20 miles
0
30 km
1
280

THE NORTH COAST (WESTPORT TO OREGON)

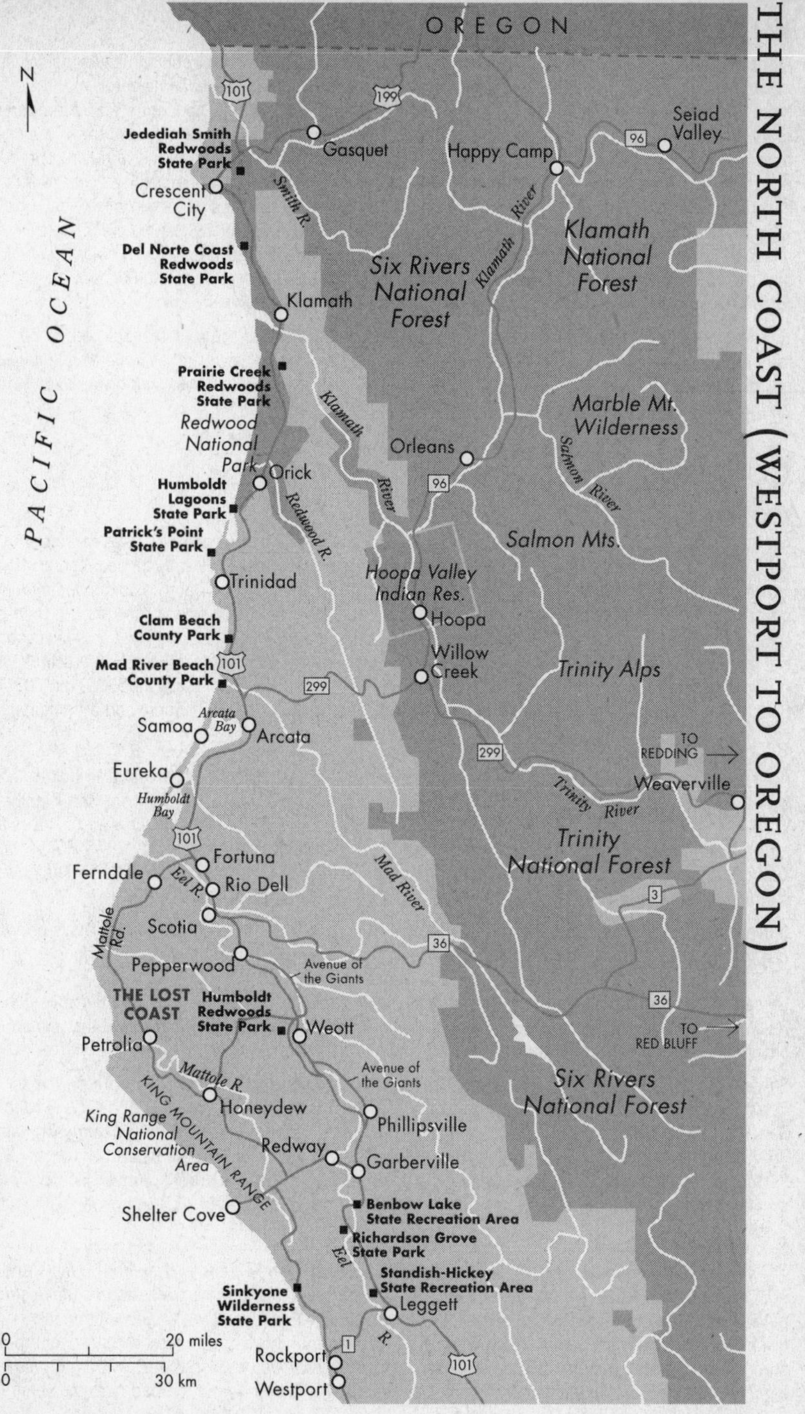
OREGON
PACIFIC OCEAN
N
101
199
Jedediah Smith Redwoods State Park
Gasquet
Happy Camp
96
Seiad Valley
Crescent City
Smith R.
Klamath River
Del Norte Coast Redwoods State Park
Six Rivers National Forest
Klamath National Forest
Klamath
Prairie Creek Redwoods State Park
Klamath River
Marble Mt. Wilderness
Redwood National Park
Orick
Orleans
Salmon River
96
Humboldt Lagoons State Park
Redwood R.
Patrick's Point State Park
Salmon Mts.
Hoopa Valley Indian Res.
Trinidad
Hoopa
Clam Beach County Park
Willow Creek
Mad River Beach County Park
101
299
Trinity Alps
Arcata Bay
Samoa
Arcata
299
TO REDDING
Eureka
Weaverville
Trinity River
Humboldt Bay
101
Trinity National Forest
Fortuna
Ferndale
Eel R.
Rio Dell
Mad River
3
Mattole Rd.
Scotia
36
Pepperwood
Avenue of the Giants
THE LOST COAST
Humboldt Redwoods State Park
36
Weott
TO RED BLUFF
Petrolia
Avenue of the Giants
Mattole R.
Six Rivers National Forest
Honeydew
KING MOUNTAIN RANGE
King Range National Conservation Area
Phillipsville
Redway
Garberville
Shelter Cove
Benbow Lake State Recreation Area
Richardson Grove State Park
Eel R.
Standish-Hickey State Recreation Area
Sinkyone Wilderness State Park
Leggett
0
20 miles
0
30 km
1
101
Rockport
Westport

WHEN TO GO

Along the North Coast, you should abandon your preconceptions about traditional seasons. While the words winter, spring, summer, and fall have some value dividing the year into three-month periods, there are only two true seasons here—rainy and dry. Showers are usually concentrated December–February, though you should come prepared for rain November–April. If you're willing to brave the chance of rain to see the annual whale migrations, January–March can be a prime time to travel. The coast's proximity to the Pacific Ocean keeps temperatures in the cool-to-comfortable range year-round. This can be exhilarating on clear days in spring and fall—or deeply depressing in summer, when you may wish you'd brought ear muffs to the fog-enshrouded beach instead of a swimsuit. One of the best times to see the coast is late spring, when the rolling hills are still a lush green dotted with colorful wildflowers and the summer waves of fog and tourists have yet to begin. Temperature variations are usually more extreme inland: summers are hot and winter lows sometimes fall below freezing.

Warmer and drier weather also means more tourists, though two of the regions explored in this chapter—the Lost Coast and the North Coast Ranges—see little traffic year-round. A general rule to keep in mind, especially in the summer, is that the farther the destination is from major highways like Hwy. 101 and I–5, the fewer folks you'll find.

COMING AND GOING

BY BIKE

Nearly all of U.S. 101 from Ukiah to the Oregon border is bikeable, though you'll have to share the road with RVs, cars, and logging trucks. During summer, a tailwind makes it easy to pedal south through Humboldt County on U.S. 101, and you'll find a parade of other riders in Day-Glo colors out to enjoy the amazing scenery. The rainy season here can last up to eight months, so plan a summer trip unless you don't mind getting very, very wet. Don't even think of riding on the cliff-hugging Hwy. 1 unless you have lots of experience. The best source of information for biking the North Coast is the free "District 1 Bicycle Touring Guide," available from **CalTrans** (Box 3700, 1656 Union St., Eureka 95502, tel. 707/445–6600). The pamphlet contains information on routes, campgrounds, bike shops, and attractions.

BY BUS

Amtrak sticks to inland I–5, so your only choice for public transit is the bus. **Greyhound** (tel. 800/231–2222) runs along U.S. 101 from San Francisco all the way to Seattle. The trip from San Francisco to Eureka, the North Coast's most important transport hub, costs $30 (about 8 hrs one-way). Buses arrive at the **Eureka depot** (1603 4th St., at Q St., tel. 707/442–0370), open weekdays 8–1:30 and 2:30–5:30, Saturday 9–noon. From here, buses depart for Crescent City (2 hrs one-way, $18). The driver will stop at towns along the way if you specify your destination when buying the ticket.

A livelier option is **Green Tortoise** (tel. 415/956–7500 or 800/867–8647; *see* Funky Deals on Wheels *box in* Chapter 1), which offers a six-day Northern California Parks Loop catering to outdoor enthusiasts for $199, plus $51 for food. The loop departs from San Francisco five times each summer and covers Lassen Volcanic National Park and Mt. Shasta (*see* Chapter 5), Crater Lake in southern Oregon, and Redwood National and State Parks (*see below*). Itineraries are flexible, so you may get them to swing by other parks and forests along the way.

Some regional buses hit a few more smaller towns, though they usually only run during the day and don't cover the kind of mileage Greyhound does. **Golden Gate Transit** (tel. 415/923–2000) runs from San Francisco to Santa Rosa several times per day for $4.50 one-way. **Sonoma County Transit** (tel. 707/576–7433 or 800/345–7433) services Santa Rosa to Guerneville eight times per day for $1.95. Farther north, **Redwood Transit System** (tel. 707/443–0826) connects Eureka, Arcata, Scotia, Fortuna, and Garberville at least a dozen times per day; fares are never more than $2.10 one-way.

BY CAR

The best way to explore the North Coast is by car, particularly if you want to stray from Hwy. 1 and U.S. 101. Much of the region is mountainous and remote, and the distances are tremendous. Make sure you have decent tires, and be prepared for rock slides, hairpin turns, road work, and intimidating logging trucks. Be especially careful at night, when tight turns and animals can make driving treacherous. On summer weekends, the tourists are out in force along Hwy. 1—you can spend up to 90 minutes traveling 20 mi on the narrow, difficult roads. On U.S. 101, traffic is usually not too bad north of Santa Rosa.

COASTAL HIGHWAY I

After it crosses the Golden Gate Bridge, Hwy. 1 follows the rugged Northern California coast for close to 200 mi before turning inland and joining U.S. 101 in **Leggett.** The dramatic shoreline here has little in common with popular conceptions of sunny California beaches. Instead you'll find beauty of the stark and chilling variety—the kind that Alfred Hitchcock captured in *The Birds,* filmed in the town of **Bodega.** The twisting highway and foggy weather, especially in July and August, can make your drive positively eerie. (Early spring and late fall are the best times to catch a clear day.) Some of the most beautiful spits of sand lie at the base of jagged cliffs nearly impossible to descend, and the forest extends right to the shore in many places.

The road passes through a number of photogenic towns before reaching **Fort Bragg,** pretty much the only place on the coast that doesn't look like storybook-land. A feasible, if long, day trip is to set out from San Francisco in the early morning, drive up the coast for a late lunch in upscale **Mendocino,** and return to the Bay Area in the evening on U.S. 101. The drive on Hwy. 1 from San Francisco all the way to Leggett takes a minimum of seven hours (longer in foggy weather), but you should take your time. The forested hillsides and rough cliffs along the road provide great hiking, and a night spent camping in any of the coastal state parks could be the most memorable of your trip.

Of course, you can't exactly hide this kind of beauty from the more than 3 million people living in the San Francisco Bay Area. The slow-moving traffic over windswept switchbacks on summer weekends testifies to the area's popularity with everyone from vacationing yuppies to RV trekkers. Nearly all the coastal campgrounds are booked up in advance on summer weekends, and the fragile natural surroundings are endangered by overuse—that's why beach access is often restricted to certain hours. Even greater changes have been wrought by wealthy urbanites from the Bay Area who have developed some of the best-situated property, especially between **Fort Ross** and **Gualala.** Hwy. 1 has been tamed by city dollars, or so it seems in comparison to the pristine Lost Coast farther north. Still, if you're in a position to splurge on a night in a rustic inn or bed-and-breakfast (some charge upwards of $90 per night), this is one of the best places in California to do it.

Driving is by far the easiest way to see Hwy. 1, but the **Mendocino Transit Authority** (tel. 707/884–3723 or 800/696–4682) provides daily bus service from Point Arena to Santa Rosa (3½ hrs one-way, $6.25); weekday routes service Gualala–Ukiah, Gualala–Fort Bragg, and Mendocino–Santa Rosa. Call ahead for schedule information; only one bus per day runs in each direction. The **Fort Bragg and Mendocino Coast Chamber of Commerce** (332 N. Main St., Fort Bragg, tel. 707/961–6300 or 800/726–2780), open Monday–Saturday 9–5, has maps, brochures, and lodging referrals for the Mendocino County coast.

BODEGA BAY

With its rusty schooners, crooked streets, and aging wooden houses, Bodega Bay at first sight looks like an old harbor town. So it is, to a certain extent, but instead of wizened fishermen and old saloons, you're more likely to find real estate agents, overpriced seafood, and developers doing their best to transform this natural harbor into a high-class resort. Developers, however, cannot take credit for the abundant natural beauty. A walk out on the headland leads through tall grasses—and wildflowers in spring and summer—to rocky cliffs; from the top, you can sometimes see migrating gray whales in the spring and fall. Sturdy shoes will enable you to climb down the rocks along the ocean trail to check out the tide pools. If you're in town at the end of April, try to catch the **Bodega Bay Fisherman's Festival** (tel. 707/875–3422), where clergymen stand starboard blessing the fishing fleet, and zany locals turn out for the bathtub race, a Bodega tradition where function takes a back seat to form.

Sportfishing is popular in Bodega Bay, and plenty of charter services vie to sell you a wet line. Several also offer whale-watching trips January–April. For a friendly charter, try the **Boat House** (1445 Hwy. 1, tel. 707/875–3495), which runs daily outings for salmon ($50) and rock cod ($45), plus twice-daily whale-watching trips ($25) on weekends from late December to mid-April. Prefer to surf? Talk to Bob Miller at **North Coast Surf Plus** (1400 Hwy. 1, Pelican Plaza, tel. 707/875–3944; open daily 10–6). He can report on current wave conditions and set you up with a wet suit and surfboard or body board ($13 each per day), or a sailboard ($25 per day). He also offers three-hour lessons ($75 including board and

FRIEND OR ANEMONE?

MacKerricher State Park (see *Near Fort Bragg,* below) *is a great spot for tide pooling, though almost any ranger can direct you to choice pools all along the coast. Tide pools are located in the "intertidal zone," the area that's exposed at low tide; you may want to check a tide table to find the best time of day to go. The rocks around the pools are usually jagged and slippery, so wear tennis shoes, hiking boots, or dive booties. Go ahead and touch most of what you see, but don't detach any creatures from the rocks and keep an eye out for incoming waves. Look for the tiny sea palms—a delicate form of kelp—that inhabit the pools along with starfish and crabs. Don't stick your hands in dark crevices; you might get pinched by a crab or stabbed by a sea urchin quill. Slimy anemones are the most fun to touch. Underwater they resemble translucent rubber flowers; out of the water, they close up and are easily squashed—watch your step.*

wet suit). For those who just want to hang out by the ocean, **South Salmon Creek State Beach** is 5 mi north of town on Hwy. 1 (turn left on Bean St. just south of Salmon Creek Bridge). The beach itself is beautiful, but in light of dangerous rip tides and sneaker waves, the park service strongly discourages swimming. For more information on the area and a small local map, or facts about *The Birds,* stop by the **Bodega Bay Visitor Information Center** (850 Hwy. 1, tel. 707/875–3422), open Sunday–Thursday 10–4, Friday and Saturday 10–5.

WHERE TO SLEEP

The cheapest room in town is at the **Bodega Harbor Inn** (1345 Bodega Ave., east of Hwy. 1 at Boat House, tel. 707/875–3594), which overlooks the harbor. Fourteen simple, cabaña-style rooms stocked with antique furniture start at $48. As with everywhere on the coast, book at least a week ahead in summer, or hope for a cancellation—anything else will run at least $70.

CAMPING • Cold winds whip the coast at night, even in summer, so bring extra blankets and use the driftwood on the beach to build a fire—where it's legal. For more information on campgrounds and day-use beaches in Sonoma County, visit the kiosk at the entrance to Bodega Dunes Campground. If the campgrounds below are full, look for spaces at **Willow Creek** and **Pomo Canyon campgrounds** (*see* Sonoma Coast State Beaches *in* Near Bodega Bay, *below*).

Bodega Dunes Campground. Part of the Sonoma Coast State Beaches (*see* Near Bodega Bay, *below*), Bodega Dunes has 98 sites ($14 weekdays, $16 weekends) in open stretches of sand and grass. Only the first loop of the campground affords much privacy. A 45-minute trail takes you to the beach (also accessible by car). Reserve through Destinet (tel. 800/444–7275). *Hwy. 1, 1½ mi north of Bodega Bay, tel. 707/875–3483. Day use $5. Drinking water, flush toilets, showers.*

Doran Park. This county park on a narrow spit of sand at the southern end of Bodega Bay offers 138 first-come, first-served sites ($14) on barren beaches with little privacy. For tent camping, try to get the Miwok campground, right on the beach. If this is full, try **Shell Campground,** with sites in the dunes and scrub brush. You can fish from the jetty at the end of the park. *Off Hwy. 1 just south of Bodega Bay Lodge, tel. 707/875–3540. Day use $3. Drinking water, flush toilets, showers. No reservations.*

FOOD

If you want good value for your money, skip Lucas Wharf and The Tides, the most touristy spots in town. Locals prefer the restaurants in nearby Occidental (*see* Near Guerneville *in* U.S. 101 to Leggett, *below*). Otherwise, a good bet is **Breakers Café** (1400 Hwy. 1, Pelican Plaza, tel. 707/875–2513). Surfers swear by the breakfast burrito ($5.95) for early morning carbohydrates, but the hummus pita ($5.95) at lunch is equally tasty. The **Sandpiper** (1410 Bay Flat Rd., tel. 707/875–2278) serves a pricey bowl of clam chowder ($4.50), but you can trust it's good. Splurge for the Bodega Bay Melt ($10), an open-face crab and shrimp sandwich with melted cheese.

NEAR BODEGA BAY

SONOMA COAST STATE BEACHES • On the drive along Hwy. 1 to Jenner (*see below*), windswept cliffs lead down to some of California's finest beaches, collectively administered by the California Department of Parks and Recreation (tel. 707/865–2391). Although some rules here may seem rigid (no dogs, gates closed at sunset, no camping, no swimming at a few), they're needed to keep the popular beaches in a more or less natural state. You *can* camp at **Wright's Beach** (6 mi north of Bodega Dunes, tel. 707/875–3483), which has 30 sites ($14 in winter, a couple dollars more in summer) near the ocean, but it's usually overrun with RVs. Sites 0–9, which face the sea, fill up fast, so reserve early through Destinet (tel. 800/444–7275). Day use is $5—but you're certain to find better elsewhere. However, on those rare days when the fog lifts, you'll see great sunsets from camp. If you stop at only one beach, make it the beautiful, albeit popular, **Goat Rock State Beach,** at the northern end of the recreation area. Entrance is free.

About 5 mi north of Goat Rock Beach are two prime environmental (i.e., walk-in, no water) campsites along the mouth of the Russian River ($10 per night). These two campgrounds afford you the best escape. **Willow Creek** has 11 sites set in meadows against a backdrop of alder and willow thickets. **Pomo Canyon** has 22 incredibly green, secluded sites among thickets of berry bushes and stands of redwoods. Both campgrounds are first-come, first-served and relatively unknown, so they may have spots available even on crowded weekends. To reach the campgrounds from Hwy. 1, turn left onto Willow Creek Road just south of the Russian River bridge; after 1 mi, go left at the small tent sign. Pomo Canyon lies 2 mi farther down Willow Creek Road.

JENNER • In the tiny town of Jenner, 10 mi north of Bodega Bay, the Russian River empties into the Pacific, often under the close observation of a colony of harbor seals. At the junction of 116 and Hwy. 1, Jenner is the start of one of the most dramatic stretches of coastline, a series of dizzying switchbacks that takes you up and down steep hills and to the brink of some awe-inspiring cliffs. There's not an affordable hotel within sight, but the wide river makes a fine swimming hole on hot days. After your dip, hit **Sizzling Tandoor** (9960 Hwy. 1, at Willow Creek Rd., 1 mi south of Jenner, tel. 707/865–0625) for the best Indian food this side of New Delhi. The vegetarian entrées are amazing: Try the *saag paneer* dinner ($8.50), a delicate spinach curry over cubes of homemade cheese, served with nan bread and basmati rice. Sit on the deck in nice weather, or get something to take out to the beach.

SALT POINT STATE PARK • The 6,000-acre Salt Point State Park (tel. 707/847–3221) lies 6½ mi north of **Ft. Ross,** a historical park with a sizable reconstructed Russian fort as its centerpiece (*see* Fort Ross—Early Trading Settlement *box, below*). Salt Point itself is an ocean lover's delight, full of white-sand coves, tidal pools, sandstone cliffs, and headlands. The **Reef Campground,** 1½ mi south of Ft. Ross, has 20 sites in a riparian canyon leading down to the beach for $11, $12 on weekends. Half the sites are sheltered and given privacy by second-growth redwoods, but the abalone divers and surfers who love to camp here will take any of the first-come, first-served spots. There are flush toilets and drinking water but no showers. **Woodside,** 8 mi north of Ft. Ross on the east side of Hwy. 1, offers a few secluded sites scattered around a dense forest. If you can carry your stuff ¼ mi, the solitude of the 20 walk-in sites ($13 weekdays, $14 weekends) is worth the extra effort. The 70 drive-in sites are $15 weekdays, $16 weekends, and the 19 hike/bike sites are $3 per person. Both sites have flush toilets and drinking water but no shower. Almost 5 mi north of Ft. Ross, the **Salt Point Lodge** (23255 N. Hwy. 1, tel. 707/847–3234 or 800/956–3437, fax 707/847–3354) makes a great base camp if you didn't bring a tent. Four small, tidy rooms go for $50 (bigger rooms go for up to $137) and include access to a hot tub and a sauna; plus, you're right on the edge of the state park. Reservations are a must in the summer.

Across the highway from Woodside lies **Gerstle Cove,** a smaller campground with matching rates and amenities for 30 sites, and access to the start of the **Salt Point Trail,** which meanders for 3 mi north along the coast to **Stump Beach.** Here intrepid swimmers brave the chill to enjoy the clear blue waters. The beach is also accessible by car from Hwy. 1. A good place to explore tide pools is **Fisk Mill Cove,** 2 mi north of Stump Beach on Hwy. 1, where you'll also find wonderful picnic spots—and toilets. An easy hike leads down the cliffs to the beach from the north parking area. If you park on the highway, you can avoid the $3 day-use fee. However, when you pay a day-use fee at any state park, $3 at Fisk Mill Cove for example, your receipt is valid for all state parks, even if another is more expensive.

FORT ROSS—EARLY TRADING SETTLEMENT

In 1812, 25 Russian fur traders and 80 Native Alaskans landed on the Mendocino coast with the intention of tilling the land to send foodstuffs to trappers up north and bagging a few sea otters while they were at it. They built Fort Ross and equipped it with so many cannons the Spanish thought it was impenetrable. The Russians were notably respectful of the native Pomo people, trading goods for their work in the fields. However, even with help, the Russians didn't turn enough wheat, and the crafty Alaskans decimated the otter population in no time. In 1841, Mother Russia ordered the traders to sell the settlement and return home. Since then sales, earthquakes, and settlements had obliterated most of Fort Ross, but the structures have been painstakingly restored and rebuilt. The state charges a $5 day-use fee for the fort, the grounds, and the small interpretive museum, but the fascinating glimpse into early California history is easily worth the money.

GUALALA, POINT ARENA, AND ELK

At the southern border of Mendocino County, winding Hwy. 1 calms down in time to enter the one-block town of Gualala (wah-LA-la), overlooking the ocean. Once command central for North Coast logging operations, Gualala is now frequented by coastal residents for its well-stocked supermarkets (both on Hwy. 1) and cheap gasoline. At **Gualala Point** (*see* Camping, *below*), you'll find an isolated beach ($2 day-use fee) at the end of an easy walk through scrub.

Eleven miles north of Gualala, keep your eyes peeled for **Schooner Gulch Road** at mile marker 11.41. Park in the turnout (it's across a small, unnamed bridge) and take a five-minute walk down to the water; you'll find one of the most distinctive, and unknown, beaches on the North Coast. If you catch the ocean at low tide, you'll understand precisely why this is known as **Bowling Ball Beach.** Scattered throughout the fine sand, round boulders pepper the coast. To the south, a long slab of sandstone serves as a bowling lane, completing the theme. There's also a rock "tunnel" that leads north to another pristine beach, but keep your eye on the tide to avoid being trapped when the water rises.

Once one of California's smallest cities, state historical district Point Arena is 16 miles north of Gualala and is a good place to take a break from driving. If you're in town between 11 and 3:30 (2:30 in winter), take a $2.50 tour of the 115-ft **Point Arena Lighthouse** (tel. 707/882–2777), the second lighthouse to stand at this location, north of town. (The first, built in 1870, did its job efficiently until it was knocked down by the 1906 earthquake.) The tour requires you to climb the equivalent of a six-story building, but on a sunny day you'll be rewarded by an excellent view of the ocean and the point.

Fourteen miles north of Point Arena, you'll pass through the blink-and-miss-it town of Elk, with its old-fashioned general store and cute, modern Irish pub **Bridget Dolan's** (5910 Hwy. 1, tel. 707/877–1820; closed Tues.–Wed.), which has local microbrews and Guinness on tap. Here, Hwy. 1 begins a series of hair-raising ascents and descents. Just before you reach the Navarro River Bridge near Albion, 26 mi north of Gualala, you'll find the turnoff for **Navarro Beach** (*see* Camping, *below*) at the end of Navarro Bluff Road. The **Navarro River,** south of Albion, is good for relaxed, do-it-yourself kayaking and canoeing. Access to the mouth of the river is easy and free, but you need your own gear.

WHERE TO SLEEP

If you can't camp, try one of the 18 rooms at the inviting **Gualala Hotel** (39301 Hwy. 1, tel. 707/884–3441), where doubles go for $44, ($55 with private bath). Old books and puzzles are scattered around the parlor, which comes complete with a wood-burning heater, while quaint rooms sit above the first-floor saloon—an old Jack London haunt—where loggers once climbed the walls in their spiked boots. For the traditional motel atmosphere and a few more amenities (cable TV, in-room telephone, private bath), your best bet is the **Sea Shell Inn** (135 Main St., Point Arena, tel. 707/882–2000 or 800/982–4298). Prices for the 32 comfortable rooms start at $45; make reservations if you plan to travel during the busy summer weekends.

CAMPING • Gualala Point Regional Park (just south of Gualala, tel. 707/785–2377), the northernmost extension of the Sonoma County Regional Parks, has 19 drive-in and 6 walk-in sites ($14, $3 hike/bike) set in a beautiful redwood forest along the peaceful Gualala River. Running water, flush toilets, and full showers complete this fine and rarely full campground. At **Manchester State Beach** (Hwy. 1, 5 mi north of Point Arena at KOA turnoff, tel. 707/882–2463), you can camp in a grassy park studded with sand dunes and wind-twisted Monterey cypress trees. The nine walk-in sites, ¾ mi off the main camp, are the best. Otherwise, the 42 drive-in sites (both $10 weekdays, $11 weekends) have drinking water and pit toilets but no showers. Make sure to check out the huge driftwood logs on the beach. **Navarro Beach** (no phone) charges $5 to camp on the beach in one of 10 windy, exposed, and extremely small sites. You can legally burn driftwood here to keep warm, and there are pit toilets but no running water. To reach Navarro from Hwy. 1, turn west on Navarro Bluff Road, just south of Navarro River Bridge. None of these campgrounds takes reservations.

FOOD

Bookends. A homey café, bookstore, and gathering spot for residents, this Point Arena culinary haven has a great breakfast including burritos with eggs or tofu ($3 and up) and homemade muffins ($1.25). For lunch, enjoy a huge plate of stir-fried vegetables ($5) or a burrito ($4 and up). *265 Main St., Point Arena, tel. 707/882–2287.*

Gualala Hotel. Huge portions of everything from the steamed vegetable plate ($8.50) to veal scaloppini ($15) all come with salad, soup, and ice cream for dessert. For breakfast, try the hearty homemade corned beef hash, served with two eggs and potatoes ($6). *39301 Hwy. 1, Gualala, tel. 707/884–3441.*

MENDOCINO

Everyone says Mendocino, perched on an oceanside bluff an hour north of Gualala, is the spitting image of a New England town. It's not, although many of the homes were built by settlers from that part of the country in the style of their homeland (Salt Box, for example). The streets are distinctly western—that is, wide—and the houses lack New England shutters. Still, it's prime territory for hordes of tourists eager to poke around weathered wooden homes, small art galleries, and well-packed general stores. If you want a slice of real Mendocino life, visit in winter, spring, or fall, when the tourists aren't around and the town feels like it could have 30 years ago.

You'll notice your dollar doesn't stretch very far in the chichi shops and overpriced bistros of Mendocino, but there's more fine dining here than anywhere else on the coast. Locals in Elk dub their northern neighbor $pendocino.

Most of the action centers around **Main Street,** which parallels the ocean; Lansing Street runs perpendicular to it. Stop by **Mendocino Jams and Preserves** (440 Main St., tel. 707/937–1037) for free samples of excellent jams, chutneys, and mustards, all made in small batches at the store—try the pistachio butter with sour cherry jam. The **Mendocino Ice Cream Company** (45090 Main St., tel. 707/937–5884) sells quarter-pound scoops in waffle cones ($2.50).

If Main Street's too crowded, wander off into **Mendocino Headlands State Park,** the grassy expanse that lies between town and the ocean. December–April, California gray whales pass the coast on their annual migration from the Arctic Ocean and Bering Sea to Baja California. Not only can you spot some of the whales as they pass, but you can learn about them at free nature talks led by docents; times for the talks are posted at the **visitor center** (Ford House Museum, between Kasten and Lansing Sts., tel. 707/937–5397), open daily 11–4. The center is stocked with maps and historical guides, both in print and audio. You can hear more about our large mammalian friends at MacKerricher State Park (*see* Near Fort Bragg, *below*) on weekends at 10 AM in season, or any day during the Mendocino/Fort Bragg **Whale Celebration Weeks** on the first and third weekends in March. For more information, contact the Department of Parks and Recreation, Mendocino District Headquarters (tel. 707/937–5804), 11 mi north of Mendocino.

WHERE TO SLEEP

Mendocino is filled with pricey bed-and-breakfasts; camping is the only real budget option. If you're determined to stay in town, try to get the one $45 room with a toilet and sink but no shower ($75 with full bath) at the **Sea Gull Inn** (44594 Albion St., tel. 707/937–5204). Another B&B option is **McElroy's Inn** (998 Main St., at Evergreen St., tel. 707/937-1734), where one room costs $55 and another goes for $65. Both rooms have private baths. They don't accept credit cards. A great place for families is the Wild West–themed **Blackberry Inn** (44951 Larkin Rd, tel. 707/937–5281 or 800/950–7806), where cheery rooms are tucked behind false fronts purporting to be various frontier town businesses; rates start at $85 and include continental breakfast.

CAMPING • The 30 sites ($15 weekdays, $16 weekends) at secluded **Russian Gulch State Park** (2 mi north of Mendocino on Hwy. 1, tel. 707/937–5804, or Destinet 800/444–7275 for reservations) offer tree-lined privacy and coin-operated hot showers. From the campground you can take the 6-mi Falls Loop Trail past the 36-ft Russian Gulch Falls and around back to camp. The park is closed mid-October–early April. **Van Damme State Park** (*see* Near Mendocino, *below*) is another convenient option for camping close to Mendocino.

FOOD

Pricey gourmet food abounds in Mendocino, though it's possible to put together a meal for under $5. At the **Mendocino Bakery and Café** (10485 Lansing St., tel. 707/937–0836), try the homemade tamales ($2.75) or the spinach lasagna ($4.50). **Mendo Burgers** (tel. 707/937–1111), behind the bakery's patio, has beef, turkey, or veggie burgers ($4). For picnic supplies, stop downtown at **Corners of the Mouth Natural Foods** (45015 Ukiah St., tel. 707/937–5345) for a good selection of organic produce, prepared foods, and baked goods.

Mendocino Café. If you can afford it, splurge on a meal here. The hands-down favorite is the giant Thai burrito, filled with house-smoked meats or tofu, stir-fried veggies, brown rice, and peanut sauce ($8–$10). The burrito costs more at dinner, so come early. If you crave seafood, try the innovative fresh fish specials, served with brown rice and vegetables ($13). *10451 Lansing St., tel. 707/937–2422.*

OUTDOOR ACTIVITIES

The Mendocino area is great for biking, while **Big River,** bordering Mendocino to the south, provides 8 mi of first-rate canoeing. To get outfitted for either sport, stop in at **Catch a Canoe and Bicycles, Too!** (44850 Comptche-Ukiah Rd., tel. 707/937–0273 or 800/320–2453; open daily 9:30–5:30); to get here, drive south of Mendocino on Hwy. 1, cross the Big River Bridge, take the Comptche-Ukiah Road, and look for the store behind Stanford Inn by the Sea. They rent mountain bikes, kayaks (both $10 per hr, $30 per day), and tandem canoes (starting at $16 per hr, $44 per day). If you're planning to go on the river, remember it's tidally influenced—you should call a day in advance to find out about conditions and optimum times. All paddle-craft rentals include life jackets and lessons on basic technique. One option for biking is to start in Mendocino, bike 2 mi south on Hwy. 1 to Van Damme State Park (*see below*), and pedal around the lower portion of the park's **Fern Canyon Trail** (where bikes are allowed). The round trip is 10 mi.

NEAR MENDOCINO

VAN DAMME STATE PARK • Van Damme State Park (tel. 707/937–5804), 2 mi south of Mendocino, has 74 drive-in campsites ($15 weekdays, $16 weekends) and 10 walk-in sites ($10), which often fill up during abalone season (Apr.–June and Aug.–Nov.) and on summer weekends. This park is one of the coast's best spots for abalone diving. (For information on equipment rental, *see* Outdoor Activities *in* Fort Bragg, *below.*) However, the divers usually avoid the 1¾ mi hike through the lush fern canyon to the walk-in sites. Even if you're not here to dive, you'll love the more private upper-loop sites in the dewy coastal forest, and you'll appreciate the coin-operated hot showers. Hikers and bikers share one site for $3 per person. Reserve sites through Destinet (tel. 800/444–7275).

The park's **visitor center** (tel. 707/937–4016) has interesting displays on ocean life and Native American history. The nearby **Pygmy Forest** comprises mile after bizarre mile of wizened trees, some more than a century old, that stand only 3 or 4 ft tall. Highly acidic soil and poor drainage combine to stunt the trees' growth. To reach the forest by car, turn left on Little River Airport Road, ½ mi south of Van Damme State Park, and continue 3½ mi to the clearly marked parking area.

FORT BRAGG

If you're not in the market for quaintness, Fort Bragg is a welcome change. Built in 1857 to oversee the Pomo and Yuki people interned at the Mendocino Indian Reservation, Fort Bragg crashed after the reservation was cited for "gross mismanagement" in 1867. Today, the Georgia Pacific lumber mill occupies the old fort's land. This is just about the only "real" town on this stretch of coast. It's not romantic (the ocean is eclipsed by the steam-belching lumber mill), but appreciate it while you can—the cutesy style (and tourist traffic) of Mendocino, only 10 mi south, has recently begun to creep into Fort Bragg, resulting in a smattering of pricey B&Bs and a restored historic downtown.

Fort Bragg is *the* place to stop for camping and outdoor supplies. Try **PayLess Drug** (490 S. Main St., tel. 707/964–1214) if you're shopping on the cheap, or the **Outdoor Store** (243 Main St., at Redwood St., tel. 707/964–1407) if you want quality equipment. You'll also find reasonable motels, good and inexpensive food, and entertainment in the area bordered by Main, Oak, Franklin, and Pine streets. Don't miss tiny **Noyo Harbor,** just south of downtown Fort Bragg, where you can sit on the docks and watch the fishing boats come in, unloading big plastic crates full of sole, cod, and salmon. For nightlife, everyone travels 4 mi south to the tiny town of Caspar, where the **Caspar Inn** (corner Caspar Rd. and Caspar St., west of Hwy. 1, tel. 707/964–5565) has been booking great jazz, blues, R&B, and rock bands for years. The cover charge on Friday and Saturday is usually $5, more for big names; Sunday and Thursday are open-mic nights, when you get some serious acoustic jam sessions by local talents—or some not-so-serious electrified music—for free. Stop by the **Chamber of Commerce** (332 Main, tel. 707/961–6300 or 800/726–2780) to grab a free map of the town, maps of the coast ($2), and loads of information about Fort Bragg and Mendocino.

WHERE TO SLEEP

Motels are lined up along Main Street like toy ducks in a carnival game, and, like the ducks, few stray from the same boring pattern. Your best bet is Jughandle Farm (*see below*), but if you want a motel, try the **Coast Motel** (18661 Hwy. 1, ¼ mi south of Hwy. 20, tel. 707/964–2852), where rooms start at $36 ($42 in summer). The 28 rooms include the use of a heated pool, cable TV, and—just in case you needed one—a fish-cleaning facility. The nine rooms at the **Ocean Breeze Lodge** (212 S. Main St., at Madrone St., tel. 707/961–1177) have a few more personal touches, including thick, cushy carpets, but they're still rather plain. A double runs $55 weekdays, $58 on weekends late June–early September, $42 otherwise. Reservations are a good idea.

Annie's Jughandle Bed-and-Breakfast Inn. It's a bit costly, but $75 ($85 on weekends) buys you a gourmet breakfast, a tastefully decorated room with private bath, and owners Shannon and Jean's expert advice on what to do in the area. The B&B is 3 mi south of Fort Bragg next to the Jughandle State Reserve. *32980 Gibney La., at Hwy. 1, tel. 707/964–1415. 4 rooms, all with bath.*

Jughandle Farm. This very country Victorian farmhouse (look for the small white sign) on a 40-acre nature reserve, with a huge, spotless kitchen and shared bathrooms, is a fine bargain—basically a hostel without all the rules—where you can sleep on a foam mat or a bed for $18 April–September, $15 October–March. You have the choice of doing a one-hour chore or paying an extra $5. There are also three cabins ($20–$22 per person, plus chore) that usually rent as doubles, or you can camp on the farm for $6 per person. *East side of Hwy. 1, 4 mi south of Jughandle Beach, tel. 707/964–4630. 30 beds. Cash only.*

FOOD

At **Egghead's Restaurant** (326 N. Main St., tel. 707/964–5005), the yellow brick road leads to the "Emerald City" bathroom, and Oz memorabilia cover the walls. Try the omelets ($5–$11) or the "Wicked Witch" ($6.25), a half-pound spicy turkey burger with a side salad. Expect a wait on weekend mornings. For a huge basket of the best fish 'n' chips in town ($6.75), join the fishermen and families at **Cap'n Flints** (32250 N. Harbor Dr., in Noyo Fishing Village, tel. 707/964–9447). The **Headlands Coffeehouse** (120 E. Laurel St., tel. 707/964–1987) acts as a cultural center and local gathering place, featuring live music most nights, and is one of the few places in town open late, every night except Tuesday. If you want to put together your own organic goodies, look for the **Farmer's Market** every Wednesday 3:30–5:30 at Laurel and Franklin streets.

North Coast Brewing Company. To accompany its regionally celebrated beer, this brewpub-restaurant cooks up burgers ($7–$8), sandwiches ($8), and Texas chili ($6.50); for only a little more you can feast on Cajun dirty beans and rice; and for quite a bit more enjoy pastas like linguine frutti di mare (scallops, prawns and clams) for $14. Try the medal-winning Scrimshaw Pilsner, or better yet, ask the staff to rec-

GRASS ROOTS BREWING

Maybe you didn't come to the North Coast for its rolling, golden hills, towering ancient redwoods, or wave-swept beaches—but for the microbrewed beer. While big beer companies substitute cheaper corn and rice for malted barley, use chemical stabilizers, and heat-pasteurize their beers to prolong shelf life, microbreweries offer fresh, unpasteurized brews straight from the source.

*Working your way up the coast, the first stop north of the Bay Area should be the Anderson Valley Brewery (*see *Boonville* in *Near Ukiah,* below*), where you can take your choice of four quality beers on tap. Continue on to Fort Bragg's excellent North Coast Brewing Company. Here, you can shell out $4 for a map that gives directions to every microbrewery in California. Finally, skip up U.S. 101 to the Lost Coast Brewing Company (*see *Food* in *Eureka,* below*) before savoring the Red Nectar Ale produced in Humboldt County (*see *Arcata,* below*).*

ommend a brew to match the spices in your dinner order—they are as meticulous about this issue as the finest French sommelier. Free tours of the brewing area—in a separate building across Main Street—are given Tuesday–Saturday at 1, but beer tasting is *not* included. Some Saturday nights bring live jazz for a two-beer minimum. *444 N. Main St., at Pine St., tel. 707/964–3400. Closed Mon.*

Viraporn's Thai Café. When you're itching for a break from the typical North Coast burgers-and-sandwiches diet, come to this sunny green hut, where excellent vegetarian, vegan, and meat curries go for under $7. The atmosphere is homey and the food authentic. On Sunday and Monday they turn the kitchen around and serve Vietnamese victuals. *Corner Chestnut and Main Sts., across from PayLess Drugs, tel. 707/964–7931. Generally open daily; call ahead.*

Samraat Cuisine of India. Set with white tablecloths and enhanced with tons of green plants, this pleasant room serves good tandoori, kebab, curry, and vegetable specials, mostly under $10. *546 S. Main St., tel. 707/964–0386.*

OUTDOOR ACTIVITIES

For hiking, head 3 mi south to **Jughandle State Reserve.** The highlight here is the Ecological Staircase, a series of five wave-cut terraces created by successive ice ages and seismic activity, each 100 ft higher and 100,000 years older than the one before it. Sportfishing is popular at beaches up and down the coast: Marty at the **North Coast Angler** (1260 N. Main St., at the north end of town, tel. 707/964–8931) is more than willing to give advice and rent you a rod ($5 per day). For deep-sea fishing, the **Noyo Fishing Center** (32450 N. Harbor Dr., tel. 707/964–7609; open daily 6–4 in summer), in Noyo Harbor, provides instruction and equipment. The center can get you in touch with skippers who run five-hour trips for $45. Abalone diving is great along the coast, but you have to be around between April and November (the season is temporarily suspended in July), and only snorkeling gear (no scuba) is allowed. Make sure to follow regulations closely (four abalone per diver, only 7-inch-plus snails are keepers) since rangers are always on the lookout for commercial poachers. **Russian Gulch** (*see* Mendocino, *above*) and Van Damme State Park (*see* Near Mendocino, *above*) are two of the best spots to slip into the ocean in search of abalone. **Sub-Surface Progression** (18600 Hwy. 1, 1 mi south of Fort Bragg, tel. 707/964-3793) rents complete abalone packages for $25 per day, as well as boogie boards and surfboards ($7.50 a day, plus $12.50 for a wetsuit).

NEAR FORT BRAGG

MACKERRICHER STATE PARK • MacKerricher lies 3½ mi north of Fort Bragg on Hwy. 1. The blacktop promenade (an old logging road) fronting the beach is good for biking, though it gets rough at sections that have washed out. Rent a bike from **Fort Bragg Cyclery** (579 S. Franklin St., at Walnut St., tel. 707/964–3509) or from **Ocean Trail Bikes & Rental** (1260 N. Main St., tel. 707/964–1260), a lot closer to MacKerricher. You'll find tide pools near the boardwalk, and January–April you can walk to the end of Laguna Point and watch the whales go by. The easily hiked **Coast Trail** runs parallel to the promenade along the headlands, with plenty of beach access and 9 mi of spectacular ocean views. At **Lake Cleone,** the park's freshwater lake, you can fish for bass or trout or watch flocks of ducks and geese, who migrate in from Mono Lake each summer. Day use of the park is free; get a map showing all the attractions from the **ranger station** (tel. 707/964–9112) at the entrance, open daily 9 AM–10 PM in summer, rarely in winter. The campground here has 140 drive-in sites ($15 weekdays, $16 weekends)—most packed closely among the coastal pines—with drinking water and coin-operated hot showers. The best camping, though, is at the 10 walk-in sites ($15 weekdays, $16 weekends), 50–150 yards from the parking lot but still fairly secluded. Reserve through Destinet (tel. 800/444–7275) in summer for the drive-in campsites; the walk-ins are first-come, first-served. There's also a shared hike/bike site ($3) with room for about 10 people.

U.S. 101 TO LEGGETT

While Hwy. 1 meanders along the coast, U.S. 101 takes the inland route, passing through some 100 mi of gentle, oak-covered hills and dilapidated barns before rejoining Hwy. 1 at Leggett. Once you're north of the Wine Country (*see* Chapter 3), you leave the crowds behind, and the land starts to open up—in short, you're in the country now, and lifestyles reflect that fact. This is where you start to see at least as many hunting and taxidermy shops as vegetarian menus and New Age bookstores.

The towns along U.S. 101—Santa Rosa, Cloverdale, Hopland, Willits, Leggett, Garberville—were stagecoach stops a hundred or more years ago, and they're still destinations for migrating urbanites. People with strong ties to the left and the environmental movement have been relocating here since the '60s. Their presence is widely felt: a funky, unpredictable counterpart to the traditional rural sensibility that dominates the region. To further complicate the mix, a new contingent of yuppies is entering the picture (much to the chagrin of established locals).

On the way to Leggett, U.S. 101 follows the path of the Russian River, which rolls toward the sea from Lake Mendocino. The four-lane highway is a much faster option than Hwy. 1, but drivers who stick to the main road entirely miss the most interesting spots, which usually require a short detour. A drive west on Hwy. 116, for example, will lead you to **Guerneville,** a popular gay vacation spot and a great base for mellow water sports on the lazy Russian River. To the east, via Hwy. 175 or 20, is the resort town of **Clear Lake,** an ideal spot to languish by the water.

GETTING AROUND

As with the rest of California, a car is best for touring. Traffic thins out on U.S. 101 north of Santa Rosa, and gas is reasonably inexpensive. On public transportation, it can be a hassle to travel between transit districts. **Sonoma County Transit** (tel. 800/345–7433) runs buses between Sebastopol, Santa Rosa, Guerneville, and Occidental. Most fares are $1–$3. To the north, the **Mendocino Transit Authority** (tel. 707/462–1422 or 800/696–4682) connects Ukiah with Willits (1 hr, $1.95) six times per day on weekdays. They also service Fort Bragg, Mendocino, and Santa Rosa once a day; $16 covers the whole stretch. (For more information on travel through the region, *see* Coming and Going at the beginning of the chapter.)

SANTA ROSA

When residents of Sonoma County refer to "the city," they no longer mean San Francisco. Once a small farming community, Santa Rosa—an hour's drive north of San Francisco—has become one of California's fastest-growing suburban areas, with shopping malls, mini-marts, and housing tracts sprouting at an alarming rate. Most of old Santa Rosa was destroyed in the 1906 earthquake, but a section called **Railroad Square** (between 3rd, 6th, Wilson, and Davis Sts.) has been preserved. Today the square is the most happening part of town, home to a battalion of cafés, restaurants, and bookstores, as well as **Railroad Park.** The old depot itself has been restored and is the new Santa Rosa Visitors and Convention Bureau **visitor center** (9 Fourth St., tel. 707/577–8674 or 800/404–7673), open Monday 9–5, Tuesday–Friday 8:30–5, weekends 10–2.

Daytime Santa Rosa is pretty slow, peopled almost exclusively by older folks, but the pace picks up with nightfall. Check out **A'Roma Roasters and Coffee House** (95 5th St., at Wilson St., tel. 707/576–7765) for café cuisine and free live jazz, folk, and classical music Friday and Saturday. Night owls can head to the nearby **Funhouse** (120 5th St., at Davis St., tel. 707/545–5483), an urban dance mecca where the grooves start spinning around 10:30 PM and don't slow down until 4 AM.

COMING AND GOING

Greyhound has service to Santa Rosa from San Francisco's Transbay Terminal (1½ hrs, $11 one-way). You can also get here on **Golden Gate Transit** (tel. 415/923–2000 or 707/541–2000) Bus 80, which runs hourly from San Francisco to Santa Rosa (2 hrs, $4.50) until 11 PM daily; you can bring your bike along on this route. Once you're in town, **Santa Rosa City Bus** (tel. 707/524–5306) can get you around town for 85¢.

WHERE TO SLEEP

Santa Rosa has a lot of dumpy motels. Be wary of too-good-to-be-true rates (under $40). A safe, solid, and clean option is **Pelisser Motel** (1875 Mendocino Ave., near Steele La., tel. 707/545–1353), where 20 small, generic doubles go for $35, $40 on weekends. Those looking for something a little more stylish should head to **Hotel La Rose** (308 Wilson St., at 5th St., tel. 707/579–3200) on Railroad Square. Beautifully decorated rooms with antiques and a complimentary continental buffet run $70 weekdays, $90 on weekends. If business is slow, you may get a discount.

CAMPING • Spring Lake Regional Park. Only a few miles from downtown, this park is woodsy but chatty with the sounds of civilization, not nature. Thirty campsites ($14) sit on a bluff overlooking Spring Lake (Site 14 has the best view). You can swim in the lagoon, row, or fish year-round. *Tel. 707/539–8092. From downtown Santa Rosa, Sonoma Ave. east, right on Summerfield Rd., left on Hoen Ave. Hot showers. Campground closed Mon.–Thurs. Labor Day–Memorial Day. Reservations advised.*

FOOD

Santa Rosa has plenty of restaurants that offer good food at affordable prices. The best bet is to catch the extraordinary **Farmers' Market** on 4th Street between Santa Rosa Avenue and E Street. Otherwise, 4th Street, east of the freeway, should have something to fit your fancy. **Mixx** (135 4th St., at Davis St., tel. 707/573–1344) serves such delicacies as grilled Cajun prawns ($9) and crème brûlée ($5.50). **Omelette Express** (112 4th St., tel. 707/525–1690) keeps locals coming back with its 40 varieties of omelets, plus burgers and sandwiches (all in the $6–$7 range).

NEAR SANTA ROSA

COTATI • This progressive farming community 8 mi south of Santa Rosa is popular with students from nearby Sonoma State University. Come in mid-June for the **Cotati Jazz Festival** (tel. 707/523–8378; tickets $12 a day) or in August for the **Cotati Accordion Festival** (tel. 707/664–0444). For great down-home pancakes, homemade biscuits, and other breakfast and lunch staples ($3–$7), try **Mom's Boarding House** (8099 La Plaza St., at Old Redwood Hwy., tel. 707/795–3381). The veggie omelet ($6) is big enough for two. Enormous portions can also be had at **Rafa's** (8230 Old Redwood Hwy., tel. 707/795–7068), a low-key Mexican joint that's packed with locals. The 4-pound Rafa's burrito ($13.50) is not for the faint of heart. Neil Young, Bo Diddley, and Jerry Garcia all played at **The Inn of the Beginning** (8201 Old Redwood Hwy., tel. 707/794–9453) between 1969 and 1982, and these days you can catch national and high-class regional acts. Kick back with a pint of "Death and Taxes," a popular dark beer ($3), or sink your teeth into the Mr. Lucky ($5.50), possibly the only vegetarian sandwich named after a domesticated pig.

GUERNEVILLE AND THE RUSSIAN RIVER

Hwy. 116 passes through the easygoing resort town of Guerneville on its way from U.S. 101 in Santa Rosa to Jenner on the coast. Even when the coast is wrapped in fog (nearly year-round), it'll probably be sunny in Guerneville, and weekend trekkers from San Francisco and points north will be swimming in the Russian River's warm waters. San Francisco's liberal sexual attitudes have found a home in Guerneville as well; **Fife's** (16467 River Rd., tel. 707/869–0656), the first gay-owned resort catering to a like-minded clientele, opened in the mid-'70s and since then the sleepy town has become what some call "the Fire Island of the West." Most disagree, claiming the Russian River creates a mellower atmosphere than the glitzy New York island. Still, the scene around the bar-side pools at Fife's and the **Russian River Resort** (corner 4th and Mill Sts., tel. 707/869–0691) gets pretty cruisey after a few guava coladas. On the last weekends of April and September, Guerneville hosts an event known informally as **Women's Weekend** (tel. 707/869–4522), featuring live music, crafts, and lots of bonding for lesbians and straights alike.

On New Year's Day 1997, the normally benign waters of the Russian River turned into roiling cesspools when heavy rains caused the Russian River to flood—just as it did in 1995 and previous years—submerging just about all of Guerneville. The flooding caused millions of dollars of damage. Luckily, Guerneville—with friendly local cafés and a nearby redwoods reserve—has bounced back and remains a great place to hang out. Though **Johnson's Beach** downtown is packed on summer weekends, you can park for free if you get here early, rent canoes or pedal boats ($5 per hr, $12 per day), and paddle lazily up and down the river. They also rent inner tubes ($3 per day) that carry you down the river with no effort on your part. For an only slightly more high-tech float, take a trip ($30, including free shuttle back) with **Burke's Canoe Trips** (8600 River Rd., 10 mi east of Guerneville, tel. 707/887–1222). Though the 10-mi float (reservations advised) only takes about three hours if you paddle straight through, there's no reason not to bring a swimsuit and lunch, and loll away some time at a remote beach along the way. If you just want to swim accessory-free, try the local's favorite hole under the **Wohler Bridge,** 6 mi east of Guerneville on River Road.

After you've had your fill of water fun, drive 3½ mi east of Guerneville on River Road to **Korbel** (13250 River Rd., tel. 707/887–2294; open daily 9–5) to tour their champagne vineyards and sample a little free bubbly. Despite Guerneville's small size, it sees quite a number of cultural events. One of the biggest is the two-day **Russian River Jazz Festival**—held every year in September at Johnson's Beach—which features some of the world's finest jazz musicians (tickets are about $30 per day). For information and a crude map of town, visit the **Russian River Chamber of Commerce** (16200 1st St., tel. 707/869–9000), open weekdays 9–5, weekends noon–3. Pick up a free copy of the monthly paper *We the People* at **Music Corner** (14045 Armstrong Woods Rd., at River Rd., tel. 707/869–0571) for the scoop on local gay and lesbian issues and events.

WHERE TO SLEEP

In Guerneville, it's almost impossible to find a room during summer without reservations. If you're out of luck, try the first-come, first-served **Armstrong Redwoods State Reserve** (*see* Camping, *below*), spend a night in nearby Occidental (*see* Near Guerneville, *below*), or drive to one of the campgrounds along the coast (*see* Near Bodega Bay, *above*).

Johnson's Beach Resort. Right in town, Johnson's has 10 rundown cabins (with kitchen, bath, and TV) crammed haphazardly near the river for $30–$35 per night ($150–$175 per week). If you yearn for that shantytown feel, stay at their crowded campground on the grassy shore ($7, plus $2 per person). *16241 1st St., off Hwy. 116 just west of Guerneville Bridge, tel. 707/869–2022. Closed Oct.–May.*

Riverlane Resort. It's one block west of Johnson's and far better-maintained. One of the 12 cabins (all with kitchen and access to a pool, hot tub, and private beach on the Russian River) is $45 on weekdays, $55 on weekends and holidays. Most of the rest are $65 on weekdays and $85 on weekends. *16320 1st St., at Church St., tel. 707/869–2323 or 800/201–2324. Reservations a must.*

The Willows. The best bargain in town, The Willows caters to a gay clientele but extends a warm welcome to all, with antique furniture and quiet gardens to lounge in. Doubles with shared bath are $59, including morning pastries, fresh fruit, and coffee; $10 more nets you a private bath. You can also camp by the river for $18 and still get the free breakfast. The kitchen, showers, hot tub, sauna, pedal boats, and canoes for the private beach are available at no charge to all guests. *15905 River Rd., ½ mi east of town, tel. 707/869–2824 or 800/953–2828. 13 rooms, 9 with bath.*

CAMPING • Armstrong Redwoods State Reserve. Just 2½ mi north of Guerneville, you can camp in the reserve's first-come, first-served Bullfrog Pond Campground (no showers) set among the oaks, madrones, and firs. To guarantee yourself a place in one of the 24 drive-in sites ($10) or four hike-in sites ($7), check in early in the morning at the ranger's kiosk. You won't be camping in the redwoods, but you can hike down into the much-visited reserve from camp or explore the backcountry along the moderate 5-mi loop from East Austin Creek Trail to Gilliam Creek Trail and back up East Ridge Trail to Bullfrog Pond. Register with the rangers before entering the backcountry. *Armstrong Woods Rd., 2½ mi from downtown Guerneville, tel. 707/869–2015 or 707/865–2391. Drive-in day use $5, walk-in day use free.*

FOOD

It's easy to eat well on the cheap in Guerneville, but stopping at that would be missing the point—restaurants here are great places to kill time, listen to music, and make friends. There is a Mexican restaurant in town, but those in the know go for the cheaper Mexican fare at the food truck that stops in front of **Safeway** (16405 Main St.) every afternoon and evening; tamales here cost $1.50, extra-large meat burritos $4.50. The better cafés and restaurants are found "downtown"—at the intersection of Main Street and Armstrong Woods Road. Locals lounge for hours at the **Coffee Bazaar** (14045 Armstrong Woods Rd., tel. 707/869–9706) munching custom-built meals of coffee, bagel sandwiches, and salads ($3.50 and up).

Brew Moon Cafe (16248 Main St., tel. 707/869–0201) incorporated the former **Breeze Inn Bar-B-Q** after the latter got flooded out on River Road. Now a combination coffeehouse and barbecue spot, it does offer a few vegetarian options (fettuccine, corn bread, greens), but the Breeze Inn was always famous for its ribs—"slow cooked in our brick oven." A full order (12 ribs and 2 sides) runs $13; half-orders are about $7. The best deals, though, are the pasta dinners—linguine, fettucine, rigatoni—which come with various fixin's and include a salad, all for about $6.

AFTER DARK

At night, Guerneville hops, especially on weekends. You can shake your booty at **Signs,** the club at Fife's (*see* Guerneville, *above*). The space is small and rustic, to say the least, but they have plans for new digs. **Stumptown Brewery** (16135 Main St., next to Chevron station, tel. 707/869–1400) draws a mixed crowd to its cavernous bar notched out of an old movie theater. Five homemade brews, pool tables, and live blues and rock ($2–$10) on weekends flesh out the attractions.

NEAR GUERNEVILLE

OCCIDENTAL • Just 10 mi south of Guerneville on the Bohemian Hwy. lies the quiet town of Occidental, a popular stop for bicyclists touring the valley and travelers looking to escape Guerneville's bustle. A great, if strenuous, bike tour from here is the 25-mi loop on Coleman Valley Road west to Hwy. 1, south to Bodega Hwy., and north up the Bohemian Hwy. back to Occidental. **Mike's Bikes** (16442 Main St., tel. 707/869–1106) rents mountain bikes for $6 per hour or $30 for 24 hours.

Bed down at **Negri's Occidental Lodge** (3610 Bohemian Hwy., tel. 707/874–3623), which has dark rooms with comfy beds, cushy carpeting, and TV ($46, $69 weekends and holidays). The **Union Motel** (corner Main St. and Occidental Rd., tel. 707/874–3635) charges $35 for doubles ($50 on weekends and holidays). Both motels have pools. Locals, tourists, and San Francisco day-trippers flock to Occidental like sharks to bait for the several good restaurants and cafés. The **Bohemian Café** (3688 Bohemian Hwy., tel. 707/874–3931) has tasty Belgian waffles and orange French toast ($4.50) for early risers, but the real treats come later in the day: A medium California-style pizza ($12.50) with funky toppings like apples, walnuts, and Brie is big enough to split. Look for live jazz on Friday and Saturday nights. Across the street, **Howard's Café** (3516 Main St., tel. 707/864-2838) serves up comfort food for breakfast and lunch (blueberry pancakes, veggie melt sandwiches) in a comfortable dining room amid aging black-and-white photographs and out on the deck.

HEALDSBURG

At Healdsburg, 14 mi north of Santa Rosa, the southward-moving Russian River crosses U.S. 101 for the last time before heading to the ocean. In hot weather, this is a good place to stop for a dip. Get off U.S. 101 at the Healdsburg Avenue exit, cross the bridge, park on the street to avoid parking fees, and walk back across the bridge to the beach. You can rent a canoe ($6 per hr, $20 a day) or inner tube ($1.50 per hr, $4 a day) from **Trowbridge Canoe Trips** (20 Healdsburg Ave., tel. 707/433–7247 or 800/640–1386), open summers daily 8–6.

Healdsburg has produced wine since the early 1900s, but only recently has it become a stop on tours of the Wine Country. Wineries are more spread out here and tourists almost nonexistent compared to nearby Napa. Among the established wineries are **Simi** (16275 Healdsburg Ave., 1 mi north of Dry Creek Rd., tel. 707/433–6981), **Clos du Bois** (19410 Geyserville Ave., east on Independence La. from

U.S. 101 and left on Geyserville Ave., tel. 707/857–1651), and **Hop Kiln** (6050 Westside Rd., about 6 mi west of U.S. 101, tel. 707/433–6491), known for its stone hop-drying house and excellent zinfandel. All have free tastings, and Simi offers three tours daily. For a smaller, personal tour through the vineyards (two per day), call the **Michel-Schlumberger Winery** (4155 Wine Creek Rd., tel. 707/433–7427) to make an appointment. For more information about local wineries, including maps, stop by the **Healdsburg Area Chamber of Commerce** (217 Healdsburg Ave., tel. 800/648–9922, 707/433–6935), open weekdays 9:30–5 and weekends 10–2.

The **Cedar Street Deli and Eatery** (304 Center St., on central plaza, tel. 707/433–7224) stocks a good selection of meats, cheeses, beers, and wines, many of which are produced locally. From a stove-top crammed with pots, **El Farolito** (128 Plaza St., ½ block east of central plaza, tel. 707/433–2807) serves up Mexican food so authentic you might have trouble ordering in English. A vegetarian burrito is $3.50, a combination plate (any two items plus rice, beans, and salad) $7.25. From May through December, you can pick up fresh fruit and other produce at the **Farmers Market** (West Plaza Parking Lot at North and Vine streets); there is another market June through October at the same location on Tuesday; both markets run from 9–noon.

UKIAH

The sensible town of Ukiah, 44 mi north of Healdsburg, started life as a rough and rugged lumber village. Its logging roots remain strong, but in recent years it's become an agricultural center, specializing in prunes, apples, and grapes. Ukiah is one of the southernmost outposts of Northern California's "green belt," a band of forest that stretches to Oregon and is home to both loggers and environmentalists.

Though it's no traveler's paradise, Ukiah is a good place to buy supplies or spend a last night in a soft bed before striking out west to the rugged Mendocino coast or east to Clear Lake and Mendocino National Forest. Nearby **Lake Mendocino** (*see* Near Ukiah, *below*) offers camping, hiking, boating, and fishing within 20 minutes' drive of downtown. Surprisingly, the nightlife can be quite eclectic, particularly on weekends. The best bet on a Friday or Saturday night is the live acoustic music at **Coffee Critic** (476 N. State St., tel. 707/462–6333). Another good choice is **The Forks Theater** (on N. State St., 1 block south of Lake Mendocino Dr., tel. 707/468–4336), which shows classic films in a small warehouse decked with padded benches and patio furniture. Movies play weekend nights for $4. For first-run and hard-to-find foreign films, try the recently expanded **Raven Film Center** (115 North St., tel. 707/433–5448.)

WHERE TO SLEEP

Ukiah has a few budget motels along State Street, which runs parallel to U.S. 101 about ½ mi to the west and can be accessed from any of the Ukiah exits. The **Lantern Inn** (650 S. State St., tel. 707/462–6601) makes the most out of its unfortunate cinderblock construction and is easy on the wallet, with doubles for $38 ($33 in winter). Rates climb $5 on holiday weekends.

FOOD

Don't bother with the fast-food chains near U.S. 101; instead, head for reasonably priced restaurants six blocks west on Perkins Street. **Ellie's Mutt Hut and Vegetarian Café** (732 S. State St., near Gobbi St., tel. 707/468–5376) may sound like a strange combination, but who can resist a restaurant that has both chili dogs ($2.95) and vegetarian black-bean chili sandwiches ($5.25) on the menu? To reach the Hut, closed Sunday, exit U.S. 101 at Talmage Road west and go ½ mi north on State Street.

On the south end of town, **Moores' Flour Mill** (1550 S. State St., tel. 707/462–6550; closed Sun.) sells sandwiches ($3 for veggies, up to $3.95 for ones with meat) on fresh-baked bread. You can chow down on the patio next to a giant waterwheel that powers the mill that grinds the flour they use in their bread.

WORTH SEEING

The **Grace Hudson Museum** and adjacent **Sun House** are especially interesting in light of Ukiah's lack of other diversions. The museum features baskets, photographs, and paintings of the indigenous Pomo, as well as rotating exhibitions of local artists. Sun House was home to Grace Hudson and her husband (a doctor who gave up his practice to become a collector-scholar of Native American basketry). Grace painted the scenes of Pomo life that adorn the museum's walls. Half-hour tours of Sun House are given four times daily Wednesday–Sunday. *431 S. Main St., between Gobbi and Clay Sts., tel. 707/467–2836.* 1 block east of State St. Suggested donation: $2. Open Wed.–Sat. 10–4:30, Sun. noon–4:30.

If you're searching for a more profound peace of mind, visit the **Sagely City of 10,000 Buddhas,** a Buddhist community of over 100 people that, surprisingly, resembles a small suburb. (And yes, the temple

HARPIN' BOONT

Boontling, a language native to Boonville, is said to have begun as a children's trick on their parents in the 1880s. It later blossomed into a complete language that locals used to confuse outsiders—and sometimes just to one-up townfolk, a practice called "sharking." These days, only a few remnants exist: If you need to make a local call, deposit 20¢ into the nearest "Buckey Walters." You may be able to eavesdrop on people "harpin' Boont" at the Horn of Zeese on Hwy 128—"zeese" being the word for coffee ever since an early settler named Zeese earned a reputation for his high-octane camp coffee.

walls really are lined with 10,000 tiny Buddha statues.) They stress that only visitors interested in praying or learning more about Buddhism should come: This is not a tourist site but a place of work, study, and worship. The excellent vegetarian restaurant, open Wednesday–Monday 11–6, charges $3.50–$15 for meals—but again, don't come if you're not serious about Buddhism. *2001 Talmage Rd., tel. 707/462–0939. From U.S. 101, take Talmage exit east.*

Skip the overrated **Vichy Springs** and make a beeline for **Orr Hot Springs,** 30 minutes west. Orr has rustic rooms that start at $61 ($73 on weekends) and a community room where you can sleep on a foam futon for $28 ($32 on weekends). The $17 day-use fee ($10 Mon.) buys access to a sauna, a cold pool partially built into the hillside, and a hot pool inside a stained-glass gazebo (cold pool closes on Tues. at noon until Wed. morning). Clothing is required only in the main building, which has a fully equipped kitchen, wood-paneled dining room, and library. Bring your own food and beverages. *13201 Orr Springs Rd., tel. 707/462–6277. From U.S. 101, take North State St. exit, turn north, go ¼ mi to Orr Springs Rd., turn left, and continue 13½ mi.*

NEAR UKIAH

LAKE MENDOCINO • The most accessible camping in the Ukiah area is 20 minutes northeast from town at Lake Mendocino (1160 Lake Mendocino Dr., tel. 707/462–7581), popular with families, jet skiers, and anglers. If you want to spend time on the lake, try the **Lake Mendocino Marina** (north end of lake, tel. 707/485–8644), where you can rent Jet Skis ($55 per hr) or canoes ($15 per hr, $25 a half day). The marina is open 8–8 daily in summer; winter hours vary.

Bu-shay Campground (164 sites) and **Ky-en Campground** (103 sites), at the lake's north end, are fully developed and have showers. The campgrounds line the golden hills around the lake under a light cover of oaks and madrones, but you won't get much protection from families and their dogs. Of the two, Bu-shay is less crowded. You'll pay $14 at both in summer ($16 for a spot next to the lake) and $8 October–mid-April, when only Ky-en is open. **Che-ka-ka Campground** is a cheaper option in the summer with its 23 sites ($8) among scrub trees on a bluff overlooking the southern end of the lake—but no flush toilets or showers. To reach the larger campgrounds and the marina from U.S. 101, take Hwy. 20 east for 3 mi. Ky-en is south of Hwy. 20 off the Lake Mendocino Marina exit; Bu-shay is 1 mi north of Hwy. 20 off the same exit. For Che-ka-ka, take the Lake Mendocino exit and follow Lake Mendocino Drive east to the lake.

HOPLAND BREWERY • It's in the middle of nowhere (13 mi south of Ukiah in the town of Hopland, to be precise), but the Hopland Brewery is one of the best-known brew pubs in California. You can try all four beers in the 4-ounce samplers (75¢ each) for a good overview. There's a good selection of meat and veggie sandwiches (around $6), as well as beer snacks like nachos ($6). Blues bands play on Saturday night ($7–$10 cover). Also look for a slew of annual parties, including Oktoberfest (first Sat. of Oct.), Fourth of July, and their own anniversary (the weekend nearest Aug. 12). *13351 U.S. 101, tel. 707/744–1361.*

BOONVILLE • Boonville is a one-street town halfway between Ukiah and the ocean, in the center of Anderson Valley (Hwy. 253). The first clue that yuppies have arrived is the overpriced golf shirts for sale at the local pub, the **Buckhorn Saloon** (14081 Hwy. 128, tel. 707/895–2337). The microbrewed ales here are truly excellent, especially the Anderson Valley Oatmeal Stout, but the loggers and lefties now look out of place in the sparkling-clean surroundings. The town remains true to its underground politics, though—if you doubt it, pick up a copy of the *Anderson Valley Advertiser,* an independent newspaper. Consider splurging at the gorgeous **Boonville Hotel** (Hwy. 128 at Lambert La., tel. 707/895–2210). The least expensive room, with good art, down quilts, ample space, and access to a flower garden and huge deck, goes for $70 on summer weekends, but they'll knock as much as 20% weekdays and off-season. The hotel's restaurant can get pricey when you're talking tuna and ribeye, but soups, salads, quesadillas and special starters like grilled Japanese eggplant with roasted peppers can be had for less than $7 at lunch (weekends only).

WILLITS • North of Ukiah, U.S. 101 moves into increasingly rugged land. The logging town of Willits, 33 mi north, is fairly unexceptional. You can board the **Skunk Train** (tel. 707/964–6371) here, however, for a trip through the redwoods out to Fort Bragg ($26). Trains depart the station on Commercial Street at 1:20 PM daily, but there's no return jaunt until the following morning at 9:20. You're better off spending the night in Fort Bragg than in Willits, anyway.

There are a few good cafés and cheap eateries, but the best reason to stop in Willits is **Tsunami** (50 S. Main St., tel. 707/459–4750), which offers fresh seafood, chicken, and tofu, prepared in French, Japanese, and Cajun styles ($7–$12 lunch, $10–$16 dinner). They also have wonderful soups (try the zucchini-nutmeg; $3), California-style sushi ($1.10–$1.70), and monstrous salads ($6–$8). Closer to a backpacker's budget, the **Grumpy Peasant Bakery** (3 S. Main St., tel. 707/829–2789) sells veggie sandwiches on fresh bread for $2.25. The **Skunk Train Motel** (500 S. Main St., tel. 707/459–2302) has 17 clean—if a bit rundown—rooms with TVs, and a pool. Their two budget rooms (no phone) run $35 in winter, $40 in summer.

CLEAR LAKE

Once you turn east off U.S. 101 toward Lake County, you begin to breathe the cleanest air in California. As you head toward Clear Lake, California's largest natural lake, you'll see recent retirees shooting the breeze on warm summer evenings, and you can't help thinking that Garrison Keillor would feel right at home. **Lakeport** is the town with the best services and most reasonable prices.

Coming from points north of Ukiah, turn east off U.S. 101 on Hwy. 20; coming from Hopland, take Hwy. 175 east. Along the way you'll probably see trailers loaded with water-ski boats, Jet Skis, and fishing boats (anglers catch crappie, catfish, and largemouth bass year-round). The 580-acre Clear Lake State Park (*see* Camping, *below*) has plenty of quiet inlets that are wonderful for watching grebes, egrets, cormorants, and other waterbirds. The nearby Mendocino National Forest (*see* Near Clear Lake, *below*) offers over a million acres for hiking. The truly sedentary can sit and admire the view of **Mt. Konocti,** a volcano rising 4,200 ft above the southern part of the lake. The moderate **Dorn Nature Trail** (3 mi loop), beginning at the Swim Beach parking lot, has sweeping lake views.

You can rent all the equipment you'd ever need at the dozens of competitively priced shops in Lakeport and around the lake. **On the Waterfront** (60 3rd St., Lakeport, tel. 707/263–6789) rents fishing boats ($40 for 2 hrs) and offers parasailing ($35–$45). If you rent Jet Skis ($35–$60 per hr) on weekdays, you'll get an extra half hour free for every hour you pay.

Clear Lake is also prime biking territory. Drop by the **Lake County Visitor Information Center** (875 Lakeport Blvd., Lakeport, tel. 800/525–3743) weekdays 8:30–5:30 or Saturday 10–4, for maps of 11 different regional biking areas. A good one is the 30-mi **Kelseyville Loop,** which begins at **Library Park** (corner 3rd and Park Sts. in downtown Lakeport). A moderately easy trail with great views, it takes you through orchards and vineyards to the town of Kelseyville and into Clear Lake State Park. Rent a mountain bike ($25 a day) at **The Bicycle Rack** (350 N. Main St., Lakeport, tel. 707/263–1200); they've also got maps for single-tracks and fire roads.

WHERE TO SLEEP

The abundant natural beauty and year-round mild temperatures of Lake County should be appreciated with a tent and a sleeping bag. But, if you're absolutely determined to sleep indoors, you could do worse than the **Rainbow Motel** (2569 Lakeshore Blvd., Lakeport, tel. 707/263–4309), where small rooms with a double bed run only $42 even in the heat of summer; kitchenette units run $50. The hotel is about 1½ mi north of downtown, from Hwy. 101, take Park Way exit, turn right on Lakeshore Boulevard.

CAMPING • Clear Lake State Park. The 147 sites on the western edge of the lake are close together, but you won't feel like you're sleeping in your neighbor's tent. The campground is full almost every sum-

ECO-WARS ON THE NORTH COAST

It may be hard to distinguish a flannel-clad logger from a blue-jeaned activist, but their superficial similarities belie deep differences. The loggers often come from families that have worked in the timber industry for generations. The activists, meanwhile, are passionate about conserving trees; many have migrated from urban areas to spend their lives among forests. The conflict centers on the timber industry's practice of clear-cutting and disregard for shrinking supplies of old-growth forests.

Though the spotted owl, which lives in old-growth forests, is still in danger, recent debate has focused on the marbled murrelet and the Pacific salmon. These species near the top of the food chain serve as indicators for the overall health of forests, and the diagnosis does not look promising. The Clinton Administration attempted to ease tensions with a long-term-use plan for all forests in the Pacific Northwest, but its effects have yet to be felt.

mer weekend, so arrive early to choose between sites in a meadow, near the water, or on a bluff overlooking Soda Bay. Hot springs surface on an island—accessible by boat only—on Soda Bay: Rent a canoe ($30 for 4 hrs) from the **Ferndale Resort** (6190 Soda Bay Rd., 8 mi southeast of Lakeport, tel. 707/279–4866) to explore them. Rates are $15–$21 ($12–$17 off-season); hike/bike sites are $3. *5300 Soda Bay Rd., tel. 707/279–4293 or 800/444–7275 for reservations. From Hwy. 29, take Kelseyville exit and follow signs. Day use: $5.*

FOOD

In good weather, pull up a chair on the outside deck of one of Lakeport's several waterfront hangouts, or—if you're watching the bucks—buy deli sandwiches ($2–$3) from the well-stocked **Bruno's Foods** (355 Lakeport Blvd., tel. 707/263–7337). Eat on the shore at sunny Library Park (*see above*), watching people cast their lines from fishing docks. The best fruits and veggies in town are at **Epidendio Produce** (390 S. Main St., tel. 707/263–6321), which is little more than a fruit stand in a semipermanent building. **Nature's Bounty Herbs and Vegetarian Deli** (301 N. Main St., tel. and fax 707/263–4575) offers a variety of pita sandwiches with potato salad, chick peas, or falafel ($2), as well as large green salads ($3.45) and bowls of yummy soup ($2.70).

Park Place. Perhaps the lake's most popular restaurant, Park Place serves Italian food with an emphasis on fresh, seasonal produce. The pasta ($5–$6.25 lunch, $8–$15 dinner) is made daily. There are plenty of meatless dishes, a great Mediterranean pasta salad ($7), and local beer and wine. Best of all is the lakeside location; sunset is gorgeous on the upstairs open-air deck. *50 3rd St., tel. 707/263–0444. Next to Library Park in downtown Lakeport.*

NEAR CLEAR LAKE

MENDOCINO NATIONAL FOREST • East of U.S. 101 and directly north of Clear Lake on Hwy. 20 lies the southern edge of huge Mendocino National Forest, where the mountains soar to almost 7,000 ft and the lakes, rivers, and unspoiled wilderness are ideal for a quiet retreat. Here you can fish and hike under pines, firs, and scrub oaks that remain green even in the heat of summer. Campgrounds are never more than $10 per night, and you don't have to worry about crowds, reservations, or noise from RVs. The **Snow Mountain Wilderness** area provides the best territory for hiking and backpacking since all vehicles, including bikes, are prohibited.

On Road 18N16, which branches off Road 240B a mile south of Sunset Campground (*see* Where to Sleep, *below*), lies the trailhead for the challenging 8-mi **Lakeshore Loop Trail.** This hike takes you up to a ridgetop and down again to the lake. Another great option is the 7-mi **Waterfall Loop** in the Snow Mountain wilderness. You catch the dramatic falls early on, then continue through one of the largest meadows in Snow Mountain, bursting with wildflowers in the spring and summer. To get to the Summit Springs trailhead, take Elk Mountain Road off Hwy. 20 in Upper Lake, turn right on M-10, and follow signs to Snow Mountain. The ranger station up here is only staffed on holiday weekends; otherwise get maps ($3) and information at the **Upper Lake Ranger District** (10025 Elk Mountain Rd., Upper Lake, tel. 707/275–2361), open weekdays 8–4:30, and the **Mendocino National Forest Headquarters** (1825 N. Humboldt Ave., Willows 95988, tel. 530/934–3316), open weekdays 8–4:30.

As in all national forests, you're allowed to pull to the side of any road and camp for free, though you will need a campfire permit—available gratis from all ranger stations or the Bureau of Land Management in Ukiah—for any open flame. The narrow, rough road leading to the lake keep most RVs away. Navigate the gravel-strewn, 12-mi dirt road (unmaintained during winter) that leads to Lake Pillsbury, and you'll find marshy inlets great for trout fishing and bird-watching, and plenty of free camping: **Oak Flat Campground** is peppered with its namesake trees and has a good view of the lake. The more developed **Sunset Campground** has shady lakeside spots for $8. *From Hwy. 29 north of Lakeport, take Hwy. 20 west 15 mi, go right on Potter Valley Rd. for 6½ mi, right on Eel River Rd. for 5 mi, and right on Mendocino County Rd. 240B for 12 mi. No reservations.*

If you don't want to brave all 12 dusty mi to Lake Pillsbury, pull into small, shady **Trout Creek Campground** (open in summer only) after just 2 mi of dirt on Road 240B, and lie back and listen to the Eel River for the rest of the evening. The 15 thickly wooded sites are distributed on a first-come, first-served basis for $10. There are no showers, but the campground has running water, pit toilets, and a pay phone. Or, on the way to Snow Mountain Wilderness, the **Bear Creek Campground** has wooded sites along a rushing creek. The campground is so remote that you'll probably have the whole place to yourself. From Hwy. 20 in Upper Lake, go north on Elk Mountain Road for 16 mi, turn right on M-10, follow signs to campground. There are no amenities here, but the camping is free.

LEGGETT

Approximately 50 mi north of Willits, U.S. 101 joins Hwy. 1 at Leggett. The town consists of little more than a quarter-mile row of buildings along **Drive-Through Tree Road** (parallel to and just west of U.S. 101), but this is where redwood country begins. From here all the way to Crescent City, you'll be faced with the choice of *which* beautiful grove of ancient or second-growth trees you want to visit. First in line is the **Standish-Hickey State Recreation Area.** It's not the most densely packed redwood grove, but you'll find an excellent (though much-used) swimming hole ¼-mi west of the picnic area; the $5 day-use fee is good for access to any state park for the day. Several hiking trails traverse the park, including the 3½-mi **Big Tree Loop Trail,** which starts at the parking lot and takes you to the biggest tree in the area, the Miles Standish Tree (named for a descendant of the captain of the *Mayflower,* even though the tree is about 800 years older). The 1.7-mi **Grove Trail Loop** begins on the east side of U.S. 101, north of the gas station, and takes you through virgin forest. Campers have a choice of 162 sites ($15, $16 on weekends) in three camp loops or two designated hike/bike areas ($3 a person), many with huge stone fire-pits and all with tables, food lockers, and coin-operated hot showers. In the summer, the rangers open up the 62 sites across the river amid the redwoods. The tent-only sites are the best in the area. *69350 U.S. 101, 2 mi north of Leggett, tel. 707/925–6482 or Destinet, tel. 800/444–7275 for reservations.*

The first weekend in June, thousands of Harley-Davidson owners converge in the town of Piercy, 11 mi north of Leggett, for the **Redwood Run** (tel. 800/438–6786), which is sponsored by the Kiwanis Club. The biker reunion features motorcycle shows, relay games, tattoo and leather accessory booths, steak barbecues, and two nights of live rhythm and blues.

COMING AND GOING

Greyhound (tel. 800/231–2222) stops at the Peg House gas station (2 mi north of Leggett on Hwy. 101) once a day heading north and twice a day heading south.

WHERE TO SLEEP

The **Eel River Redwoods Hostel** is on a sun-warmed stretch of the Eel River in a Mendocino redwood forest. Beds are $12 for members of any hosteling association, $15 for others. Little wooden cabins and separate dorm rooms for "guys" and "girls" make you feel like you're in summer camp. Call ahead to reserve private rooms that sleep two, or dorm rooms that sleep seven. Hostelers (and those who pay a $5 day-use fee) have access to Gene's extensively researched day trips in the area, a hammock, a nine-hole Frisbee-golf course, a well-equipped kitchen, and a sauna and Jacuzzi (open 24 hrs). Most nights you can get a meal at the hostel's pub for $7–$9. Free supplies for pancakes are available every morning. The dorm rooms and the bathrooms are a bit on the grimy side, but the lax enforcement of rules makes up for the unscrubbed walls. Reservations advised in summer. *70400 U.S. 101, 2 mi north of Leggett, tel. 707/925–6425 or 800/500–6464. Follow signs for Bell Glen Resort. 43 beds. Reception open 24 hrs.*

FOOD

If you desperately need picnic supplies, **Garske's Leggett Market** (Drive-Through Tree Rd., tel. 707/925–6279) will cover the necessities, but you'll do better in Willits or Garberville.

U.S. 101 AT THE TOP OF THE STATE

After joining Hwy. 1 at Leggett, U.S. 101 winds through redwood forests, where you can camp among some of the oldest living things on earth. Starting just south of **Garberville,** the highway follows the course of the Eel River, great for fishing. To the west is the stunning, isolated **Lost Coast.** The 80-mi stretch of road between **Arcata** and **Crescent City** winds past windswept shoreline, deserted beaches, rugged forests, and several of the state's finest parks.

The region is not without its touristy side—consider corny, over-hyped sites like the Trees of Mystery in Klamath and Confusion Hill near Richardson Grove State Park (*see* Near Garberville, *below*). But it's easy to avoid all that and enjoy yourself. The massive and spectacular Redwood State and National Parks alone make the drive worthwhile. Here you'll find the world's tallest trees (the highest redwood in Tall Tree Grove was last measured at 367 ft), as well as rare Roosevelt elk and thousands of other animals and plants seldom seen elsewhere. It's a great swath of wilderness and one of the few such places in the state that hasn't been overrun by crowds.

With the proximity to this awe-inspiring amount of nature, it's no surprise that almost everybody in the region is either vocally involved in protecting the environment or turning it to profit. Logging, tourism, and agriculture are some of the major industries in the area. For transportation information, *see* Coming and Going, at the beginning of the chapter, and Eureka and Arcata, *below.*

GARBERVILLE

Two hundred miles north of San Francisco and 65 mi south of Eureka lies Garberville, the first of a stretch of North Coast towns in which the longhair-to-redneck balance tips slightly in favor of the former. At first glance, Garberville and Redway (2 mi north on Redwood Dr.) don't look like much more than the usual string of motels, supermarkets, and diners designed to serve the river of tourists passing through on their way to more redwoods. But these towns serve as metropolitan centers for the back-to-the-landers who inhabit the Lost Coast to the west and for residents of Trinity County (*see* Chapter 5) to the east. For a taste of local life, try a 1½-hour yoga class ($6 minimum donation) at **Standing Wave Yoga Dharma Center** (434 Maple La., 1 block east of Redwood Dr., tel. 707/946–2028); beginner classes start at 4 PM on Thursday.

The first weekend in August, thousands flock to the Eel River, just south of town, for **Reggae on the River**—maybe the best reggae festival in the world outside of Reggae Sunsplash in Jamaica. The 8,000 tickets always go fast, so call the Mateel Community Center reggae hotline (tel. 707/923–4583) in April or early May for ticket outlet locations. In 1997, three-day tickets were $86.50 (no single-day tickets available). The **Redwood Transit System** (133 V St., Eureka, tel. 707/443–0826) runs buses twice a day from Garberville to Scotia (1 hr 20 min, $1.60). From Scotia, buses travel as far north as Trinidad (2 hrs 45 min, $1.60 extra). The **Chamber of Commerce** (733 Redwood Dr., tel. 707/923–2613 or 800/923–2613), open weekdays 10–5, has a wealth of information and good free maps of the Lost Coast and Avenue of the Giants.

WHERE TO SLEEP

You'd do best to stay at the Eel River Redwoods Youth Hostel (*see* Leggett, *above*), since it's only 24 mi south. On the motel circuit, your cheapest option is the **Lone Pine Motel** (921 Redwood Dr., tel. 707/923–3520). During the summer, 17 small, clean rooms go for $35. In the off-season, the price drops $5. The rooms are nothing fancy, but they are right in town and you get access to the pool. Two miles north of town, **Budgetwest Redway Inn** (3223 Redwood Dr., tel. 707/923–2660) has 13 comfortable, slightly outdated rooms with air-conditioning, phones, and HBO for $34–$40 in winter, $40–$50 in summer.

FOOD

It's no surprise that half the restaurants here cater to ethereal health-food enthusiasts and the other half to loggers looking for meat and potatoes. Almost all the food in town can be found on a short stretch of Redwood Drive near the intersection with Sprowel Creek Road. If you think the loggers have the right idea, try **Café Garberville** (770 Redwood Dr., tel. 707/923–3551), where a plate of pork chops and apple sauce with soup, potatoes, and garlic bread costs around $8. A mere two blocks away from Café Garberville, the **Woodrose Café** (911 Redwood Dr., tel. 707/923–3191) is on a different culinary planet. Come for huge omelets ($5–$7), bowls of oatmeal with raisins and banana ($3.50), and sandwiches ($3.50 and up). You'll find several vegetarian options, some organic ingredients, and *no* beef. Stop off at **Chautauqua Natural Foods** (436 Church St., tel. 707/923–2452), one block east of Redwood Drive, for organic produce, vegetarian deli items, herbs, vitamins, and body-care products. You'll find a **Farmers' Market** in the parking lot of Chautauqua Natural Foods on Friday from 11–3.

Mateel Café. This low-key restaurant and coffeehouse in Redway, 2½ mi north of Garberville on Redwood Drive, draws locals and travelers from miles around with its elaborate salads ($6.50), stone-baked pizzas (about $13 for a 12-inch), fresh fish specials ($12–$16), sandwiches ($5–$7), and vegetarian lasagna ($9). You can hang out on the redwood patio sipping a cup of coffee and nibbling on one of the chef's special desserts. Check local papers or the Garberville Chamber of Commerce (*see above*) for discount coupons. *3344 Redwood Dr., next to Redway Liquors, tel. 707/923–2030. Closed Sun. Cash only.*

NEAR GARBERVILLE

RICHARDSON GROVE • Seven miles south of Garberville on U.S. 101, **Richardson Grove State Park** (tel. 707/247–3318) is an easily accessible redwood stop. Unfortunately, this means the place is usually pretty congested in the heat of the summer. Four loop trails and a self-guided nature trail wind around the park. The **Woodland Trail** is a gentle 1½-mi hike through redwoods and tan oaks. The **Toumey Trail** (accessible only in summer) takes you 2 mi through redwoods and up to a panorama viewpoint. Drive-in campers have a choice between 95 oak-forested or 75 redwood-packed sites ($15) with fire rings, picnic tables, food lockers, coin-operated hot showers, and flush toilets nearby. Weekends, families often fill the campground, so reserve through Destinet (tel. 800/444–7275). Hikers and bikers share one site for $3 per person. The day-use hiking fee is $5. If you tell the gatekeeper you're going to the lodge, you can avoid the fee and get a 15 minute pass that you can validate at the giftshop for an additional hour. While there, pick up Metsker's Humboldt County map ($4.50), the best map of the redwoods and the Lost Coast.

BENBOW LAKE • Five miles north of Richardson Grove on U.S. 101, **Benbow Lake State Recreation Area** (tel. 707/923–3238) has 75 campsites with coin-operated hot showers in meadows exposed to the sun. The sites ($15 weekdays, $16 weekends) are private and fill less quickly than Richardson Grove, but most are too close to the highway; reservations are rarely necessary. If you just want to stop for a swim at the seasonal lake (they take the dam out during the winter), the day-use fee is $5. The day-use area west of U.S. 101 rents canoes ($18 for 3 hrs, $43 per day) and inner tubes ($2 per hr). A popular spring activity is to enjoy a 5-mi float on the Eel River from Richardson Grove north to Benbow. Or forget the rentals and the fee and try your Tarzan moves on the rope-swing 200 yards shy of the one-lane bridge that leads to the campground. Look for the wide spot in the road with turnouts on both sides, and ramble through the weeds to the river's edge.

LOST COAST

Because of the rugged terrain, the state of California abandoned hope of extending Hwy. 1 along the Pacific between Rockport and Eureka, and now this whole region goes by the name Lost Coast—in California terms, lack of proximity to a major highway is ample reason for a place to be considered "lost."

But this strange, isolated region earns its name in other ways as well. While California's other coastal areas have been the site of major building and development, the Lost Coast remains in a virtually pristine state. Wherever you go, you get a sense that you've entered another era—redwood trees perch on cliffs 200 ft above rocky shores and black-sand beaches, with nary a condo unit to spoil the view. It's comparable in beauty to Big Sur but not nearly as explored, since most tourists head to places that better accommodate their automobiles.

Only about 2,000 people live in the whole region, and many of them moved here as part of the late '60s hippie migration to Northern California. Hang out at the Hideaway (*see* Food, *below*) in Petrolia on a weekend afternoon to get a feel for the quality of life in these parts. The locals aren't too interested in hordes of people invading their home turf and don't ask people what they do for a living: The question can be a risky one here, as this is one of the world's most celebrated marijuana-growing regions.

WHERE TO SLEEP

Demonstrating the ageless law of supply and demand, lodging proprietors charge relatively exorbitant amounts for the few rooms extant in this region. If you're on a tight budget, think "camping."

HONEYDEW • Mattole River Resort. It's fairly rustic but reasonably priced, with six 1920s redwood cabins that rent by the night or week. The cabins (1 is $45, 2 are $65, the rest are $85–$100) have kitchens and hot showers, and you're across the street from, but within earshot of, the river—good for swimming in summer and fishing (mainly steelhead) in winter. The shady grounds have a few plum and apple trees, as well as grapevines and blackberry bushes, all free for the picking. For $8 a night you can camp in one of six sites, eat the fruit, and take hot showers. They've also got coin-operated washers and dryers. *42354 Mattole Rd., 26 mi west of U.S. 101 and 2¼ mi west of Honeydew, tel. 707/629–3445 or 800/845–4607, fax 707/629–3494. Reservations advised.*

SHELTER COVE • An exception to overpriced motel rooms in Shelter Cove, the **Beachcomber Inn** charges an unbeatable $45 for one of its five clean and spacious rooms. Interiors are personal, with new furniture and kitchenettes, and the inn is only one block away from the cove. The rest of the rooms (all priced for double occupancy) go for $65–$85 ($10 off in winter), in step with the rest of Lost Coast lodgings. Register and make reservations through the Shelter Cove General Store. *7272 Shelter Cove Rd., tel. 707/986–7733 or 800/718–4789. Reservations advised.*

CAMPING • Public land in the Lost Coast is divided between **Kings Range,** north of Shelter Cove and managed by the Bureau of Land Management (BLM), and **Sinkyone Wilderness State Park,** south of Shelter Cove to the spot where Hwy. 1 pulls away from the coast. The chief difference between the two forests is the price of camping. In general, BLM land has fewer regulations and services. The state parks, on the other hand, are usually more pristine with more regulations about where you can camp. The best primitive camping is in the Sinkyone Wilderness State Park, where all campgrounds lie within walking distance of deserted beaches. Stop at the **Needle Rock Visitor Center** (tel. 707/986–7711)—staffed sporadically during daylight hours—to check in and figure out the best camping area. To reach Sinkyone from Garberville (1½ hrs), take Redwood Drive to Redway, then the Briceland Thorne Road west for 25 twisty mi to Four Corners, where you head west on a rough unpaved road for 3 mi to the visitor center (look for signs). All campgrounds in Sinkyone cost $10 ($11 on weekends, $7 in winter), require short walks in, and are first-come, first-served (but you should have no problem finding space, except for holiday weekends).

Of Sinkyone's three campgrounds (17 sites in all, plus trail camps), **Jones Beach** and **Barn Camp,** near the visitor center, are best for beach combing. The three sites at **Bear Harbor,** about 3 mi south of the visitor center, are popular stops on the Lost Coast Trail (*see* Outdoor Activities, *below*). Either way, the settings are truly stupendous—Roosevelt elk cruise the meadows, streams gurgle down canyons, and cool winds sweep across empty beaches. Not many people get out here (you'll see why as you drive the rutted dirt road), but it's well worth the beating to your car.

Another option is **Usal Beach,** 3 mi north of Rockport and 15 mi south of Leggett off Hwy. 1—watch for the hidden driveway at County Road 431 on the west side of Hwy. 1. The beach is also accessible from Garberville via Four Corners; you don't need a 4 x 4, but it will be slow going. Usal's 15 campsites ($10, $11 weekends; $7 in winter) are strung out on the coast road, some among trees, some in an open field, and some next to the beach. There are also 10 campsites ($3 per person) along the **Lost Coast Trail** (*see* Outdoor Activities, *below*) between Bear Harbor and Usal Beach. Pay in advance at the Needle Rock visitor center or Usal Beach.

FOOD

The Lost Coast escapes most tourist itineraries, so it's not surprising that there's almost nothing to speak of in the way of restaurants. Bring your own supplies or plan on eating many meals at the Hideaway.

PETROLIA • The **Petrolia General Store** (40 Sherman St., tel. 707/629–3455) has a range of supplies to help you through: food, sliced deli meat, beer, wine, candy, and ice cream. They don't take credit cards.

Hideaway. You can't help admiring this restaurant-bar on the north side of Petrolia's Mattole Bridge. It features the home cooking of Ed, the owner, who's got an enormous barbecue out back that cooks hindquarters, sides of beef, sometimes even whole hogs. Five bucks gets you a ½-ft-long sandwich of Polish kielbasa on sourdough. On summer weekends there's sometimes an all-you-can-eat barbecue ($6.50–$7.50) with meat, potato salad, macaroni, and coleslaw. You can also buy deli meats and cheeses to take with you. On weekends the Hideaway is quite the local hangout. *Corner Mattole and Conklin Creek Rds., tel. 707/629–3533.*

SHELTER COVE • You won't find anything fancy, but you can put together a solid and affordable meal around Shelter Cove without too much effort. For something hot, try **Mario's Bar & Grill** (533 Machi Rd., tel. 707/986–1199), where the fish 'n' chips ($7) reflect the catch of the day. Fresh snapper goes for $9, and herbivores can munch on a veggie burger ($6). Adventurers with little time for sitting around inside can grab a sack lunch with chicken or ribs for $4.25 at the **Shelter Cove RV Campground and Deli** (492 Machi Rd., tel. 707/986–7474). Or, pick up groceries at the **Shelter Cove General Store** (7272 Shelter Cove Rd., tel. 707/986–7733).

One local disciple of the Hideaway's barbecue dinners claims, "Ed's goal is to make everyone as big as he is"—a prodigious task given Ed's girth.

EXPLORING THE LOST COAST

The only ways to enter the Lost Coast are as follows: from Hwy. 1 in the south, on the barely maintained, dirt County Road 431; from U.S. 101 at Garberville on the Briceland Thorne Road; from Humboldt Redwoods State Park on the Mattole Road, 3 mi north of Weott; or from Ferndale (*see* Near Eureka, *below*) in the north on the Mattole Road. Once in the Lost Coast, almost all roads are marked for the next hamlet along the way; you won't find elaborate signposts on most intersections. You won't need a four-wheel drive to navigate most of the area, but be prepared to drive on stretches of unpaved road no matter which route you take. You can pick up maps of the region at the Chamber of Commerce in Garberville. Topos and more detailed trail maps are at Northern Mountain Supply in Eureka (*see below*).

HONEYDEW • The most accessible of the four routes is the beautiful paved road from Humboldt Redwoods, which heads west toward Honeydew, basically a post office and the **Honeydew Country Store** (44670 Mattole Rd., tel. 707/629–3310). You'll loop around a desolate stretch of coastline before passing east through Ferndale (*see* Near Eureka, *below*) and returning to U.S. 101 just south of Eureka. Budget 3 hours for the 75-mi drive—and bring an extra-heavy sweater, even in summer, if you want to hang out and enjoy the rugged landscape.

OUTDOOR ACTIVITIES

The **Lost Coast Trail** winds past 52 mi of untouched coastline in the King Range and Sinkyone Wilderness. From the northern trailhead at Mattole Campground—at the end of Lighthouse Road just south of Petrolia—it takes three days to a week to hike the 24 mi to **Shelter Cove** in the south. You can camp anywhere your heart desires as long as you get a campfire permit—Cooksie Creek, Spanish Flat, and Shipman Creek are good stopping points. After a few miles on paved roads, the trail begins again in earnest at **Hidden Valley** and stretches south to Usal Beach. Two miles after Hidden Valley, you hit Sinkyone Wilderness State Park. From there on south, you can only camp in designated sites, and you must pay $3 per night. The unkempt trail, best hiked in spring or fall, when the days are warm and the evenings cool, alternates between ridges with ocean views and dark, fern-filled canyons. (Though you can probably find propane bottles at most Lost Coast general stores, camping supplies are sparse and you should stock up before leaving the freeways.) Water appears periodically along the way; don't forget to bring a filter or purification tablets. Check in with the **Bureau of Land Management** in Arcata (1695 Heindon Rd., tel. 707/825–2300) or Ukiah (2550 N. State St., tel. 707/468–4000) weekdays 8–4:30 to get permits and up-to-date trail information (also check tide tables, as a few points may be impassable during high tides). You can request a free map of BLM property in the area. For guidance in the Sinkyone Wilderness, you'll need a "Lost Coast Trail Map"; send a check for $1.50 to 1600 101, #8, Garberville 95542. You can also call 707/986–7711 for information.

The northernmost part of the trail makes a great day hike. Start at the Mattole River Campground and hike 3¼ mi along the coast, past tide pools and sea lions, to the **Punta Gorda Lighthouse,** a forgotten outpost accessible only by foot. Return the way you came or take the four-wheel-drive road for a slight variation.

AVENUE OF THE GIANTS

This 33-mi drive winds through some of the world's largest coast redwoods—and yes, they are giants. The road runs roughly parallel to U.S. 101 between **Phillipsville,** a few miles north of Garberville, and **Pepperwood,** a few miles south of Scotia. Many of the redwood groves are up to 1,500 years old and are named after individuals and organizations that donated money to protect them. With luck, the trees will still be standing long after their names are forgotten.

Most of the Avenue of the Giants is contained within **Humboldt Redwoods State Park,** a truly amazing place to camp, hike, and bike. There's a $5 per vehicle day-use fee for some picnic areas and a couple of campsites, but there's no reason to waste the money; almost the whole park is free. The **visitor center** (2 mi south of Weott on Ave. of the Giants, tel. 707/946–2263) has a staff of friendly volunteers and all the redwood-related items you could want—from books to postcards to ready-to-plant seedlings. It's open daily 9–5 March–October (Thurs.–Sun. 10–4 the rest of the year). Brochures for a self-guided auto tour of the park are available here and at both ends of the avenue (donation requested). For $1 you can also get a map showing hiking and biking trails, campgrounds, and topo lines—well worth it if you plan on exploring, especially since the free map is somewhat inaccurate.

Almost all the tourist traffic keeps to the Avenue of the Giants, but if you head west off the avenue onto Mattole Road (5 mi north of visitor center), you'll pass through equally beautiful old-growth stands where nothing blocks your view. In fact, you could easily keep yourself occupied for weeks without ever visiting such predictable tourist traps as the **Eternal Treehouse**—which offers the remains of a one-time giftshop built inside a redwood as the chief attraction—and the shops that sell redwood carvings and slabs of burl. For an introduction, take the ½-mi, self-guided loop trail through the **Founders Grove,** 4 mi north of the visitor center on Avenue of the Giants, and visit the 362-ft **Dyerville Giant,** which fell in March 1991. No one witnessed the fall, but a neighbor reported hearing "a train wreck" about the time it toppled. The fact that it's now lying down, with its root base jutting up some 35 ft, makes its immensity all the more appreciable.

The **Drury-Chaney Loop** takes you on an easy 1- to 1½-hour hike (almost 3 mi round-trip) through redwood groves where 6-ft-tall lady ferns cover the forest floor. You'll find the trailhead 17 mi north of the visitor center on Avenue of the Giants, just south of Pepperwood at stop 9 on the auto tour. For a longer hike (9 mi round-trip) that's fairly flat the whole way, try the **Big Tree–Bull Creek Flats Loop,** which runs along both banks of Bull Creek through the **Rockefeller Forest,** the largest tract of uncut old-growth redwoods. Start at either Big Tree or Bull Creek Flats parking area (both on Mattole Rd.), choose your bank, and go. Bridges connect the trails on either side of the creek at both parking areas, though the Bull Creek Flats Bridge is only installed in summer.

Several grueling fire roads are open to mountain bikers, but rentals are not available. For a good loop that won't kill you, start at the Grasshopper trail off Mattole Road, 6 mi west of Hwy. 101. Next, cut to Squaw Creek trail, where you'll pedal through giants that those bound to RVs will never see, then take Preacher Gulch down, down, down to Bull Creek Road and loop back. The entire trip is about 15 mi.

CAMPING

If you want to camp on the Avenue of the Giants, skip the overcrowded Burlington Campground (next to the visitor center), and head to the 39 sites at **Albee Creek Campground** (tel. 707/946–2472), 4 mi west of Avenue of the Giants on Mattole Road. You can sleep under the redwoods or out in the open, and solar-powered showers let you wash off. The camp is next to some of the best old-growth forest in the park. All developed sites are $15 ($16 on weekends) in summer, $12 in winter. Reservations for all sites in the park can be made through Destinet (tel. 800/444–7275).

For those trekking through the area under their own power, the **Marin Hike and Bike Campground**—2 mi north of the visitor center on the Avenue of the Giants—is an ideal spot. For $3 per person, you can sleep under the redwoods near the sparkling Eel River; the grounds have picnic tables, flush toilets, and drinking water. To get away from the crowds with minimal effort, see if you can reserve one of the two walk-in sites at **Baxter Campground,** or three walk-in sites at **Hamilton Barn Campground** ($9 each, $7 in winter). The secluded sites, 25 yards to ¼ mi from parking, have fire rings, tables, food-storage boxes, untreated water, and pit toilets. You'll sleep among beautiful second-growth redwoods growing alongside a gurgling stream. Both parking areas are 6 mi west of U.S. 101 on Mattole Road. For all trail and environmental camps, you must register at Burlington Campground, next to the visitor center.

The more adventurous will want to take advantage of the five **Trail Camps** off Mattole Road. This is your chance to strap on a pack and go into the backcountry—the sites are 2½–7 mi in. You must register and pay $3 per person at the visitor center. They'll sell you a serviceable map ($1), identify the trailheads, and let you know if you need to pack water, since the springs sometimes dry up in the summer. Rangers say these camps never fill up, and most of them are located on fire roads, meaning bikers can pedal in.

SCOTIA

A few miles north of the Avenue of the Giants is the one-company town of Scotia. Since its founding in 1869, Scotia has been owned by the Pacific Lumber Company, which runs the churches, the school, and the medical clinic and provides housing for over 270 families. The largest redwood sawmill in the United States sprawls across town, blowing its whistles throughout the day. The effect is eerie, but the town's close-knit residents don't seem to mind. The mill offers a free self-guided tour that's worthwhile for even the staunchest opponent of the timber industry. You see the logs unloaded from trucks, moved through the log pond, stripped of bark with hydro-jets, and whittled into usable lumber—you have to be awed by the sheer magnitude of the operation. Pick up passes for the hour-long tour, offered summer weekdays 8 AM–2 PM, at the **Scotia Museum** (Main St., ½ mi south of Scotia exit, tel. 707/764–2222, ext. 247). Arrive by 1:30 since part of the mill shuts down at 2:30, and get earplugs from the gatehouse at the mill entrance—you'll be sorry if you don't.

Directions for the Pacific Lumber tour are printed on an actual souvenir hunk of redwood—by loggers' reckoning a perfectly renewable resource.

WHERE TO SLEEP

A few blocks north of Scotia in Rio Dell, the **Rio Dell Motel** (53 W. Center St., tel. 707/764–5165) has clean, slightly rickety doubles ($30, sometimes more in summer) with TVs but no phones. In Fortuna, 10 mi north of Scotia on U.S. 101, crash in a pleasant double ($36 in summer) with cable TV and a phone at the salmon-pink **Six Rivers Motel** (531 Fortuna Blvd., between 1st and 2nd Sts., tel. 707/725–1181). Eureka and Arcata (*see below*), with more choices, are only 20–30 minutes north.

FOOD

Diversity is not Scotia's strong suit, and its food is no exception. A good place for camping supplies, Scotia's **Hoby's Market and Deli** (111 Main St., tel. 707/764-5331) is open weekdays 5 AM–9 PM, weekends and holidays 8–8. If you can't push on 10 mi north to Fortuna for a sit-down meal, you can eat amid the sounds of crashing pins at **Ruby's Coffee Shop** (71 Wildwood Ave., Rio Dell, tel. 707/764–3441), located next to Mingo's Bowling Alley. Mill workers start lining up for huge plates of a hearty, farmer's breakfast hash ($4.75) at 4:30 AM. Later in the day, you can get a Cajun cheeseburger for $4.50. Vegetarians can opt for the grilled cheese ($3.75) and are advised to leave their Earth First! T-shirts in the car.

Fortuna's **Hot Brew** is the best café, gallery, and bistro for miles. Try the huge veggie sandwich ($4.50 lunch, $7 dinner) filled with hummus, cream cheese, avocado, slivered almonds, lettuce, tomato, and sprouts. Friday and Saturday bring live jazz and blues by local bands; sometimes there is a cover charge. *904 S. Fortuna Blvd., opposite Safeway, tel. 707/725–2361.*

EUREKA

You'll know you're getting close to Eureka (25 mi north of Scotia) by the stench of its paper mills. Apparently, locals build up some kind of immunity, but short-term visitors may find themselves wincing. The harsh reality is that parts of Eureka are ugly and stinky, with architecture that leans toward strip mall, but it *does* have history—and it is desperately trying to cash in on the tourism trade. In 1807, when whaler James T. Ryan shouted "Eureka!" (Greek for "I've found it!") upon making his way through the narrow entrance to Humboldt Bay, he gave the future state of California its motto. In 1849, miners traveled here to search the Trinity River for gold, but Eureka's distinction came as a whaling and logging town and as a Native American lookout post where soldiers were known to go crazy with boredom.

With the exception of **Old Town** (between 1st, 2nd, C, and M Sts.), a neighborhood of restored Victorians worth a quick exploration on foot, a good deal of today's Eureka is a depressing slough of motels, fast-food joints, gas stations, and city-style dreariness. You probably won't want to stay long. If you're

LIFE ON SKID ROW

Before the days of railroads, North Coast loggers built portable shacks and put them on wooden rails called skids. The whole contraption was then attached to a team of oxen and pulled into the woods. When narrow-gauge railroads made the rigs obsolete, logging companies abandoned the shacks on the outskirts of town and the poor moved in. Townsfolk coined the term skid row.

looking for a place to stop on your drive up U.S. 101, you'll do better to push 10 minutes north to Arcata (*see below*), where the scene is more appealing. However, you might want to hit Eureka for its nightlife. **Hefe's** (432 5th St., tel. 707/443–4333) draws touring blues and alternarock bands and hosts local acts Tuesday–Sunday nights. Call for the line up. The **Eureka Chamber of Commerce** (2112 Broadway, tel. 707/442–3738) is open weekdays 9–7, weekends 10–4 (in winter, weekdays 9–5 only) and can set you up with a free map.

GETTING AROUND

Humboldt Transit System (133 V St., tel. 707/443–0826) runs buses in Eureka for 75¢. For 60¢ more, the bus will take you as far north as Trinidad (1 hr 15 min) or as far south as Garberville. Buses allow bikes, but you'll need to make an appointment at the office to get the $5 lifetime permit. **Greyhound** stops in Eureka twice a day on its way to San Francisco.

WHERE TO SLEEP

Motels are concentrated on Broadway and 4th streets, both of which serve U.S. 101. Most are noisy, grungy places to crash, but for the money they can't be beat. Within walking distance of Old Town, the **Budget Motel** (11400 4th St., at M St., tel. 707/443–7321) offers fairly clean doubles for $34, with queen beds, cable TV, and phones. Right around the corner, the **Royal Inn** (1137 5th St., tel. 707/442–2114) charges $32 for a clean, plain double in the summer.

FOOD

A **farmers' market** convenes 10–1 summer Tuesdays in Old Town, and summer Thursdays (same times) at the Eureka Mall (between Harris and Henderson Sts., east of U.S. 101). More than 60 small farms in Humboldt County participate—this is the place to stock up on fresh fruits and veggies, as well as herbs and honey. If you miss the market but still want some bulk foods, stop by **Eureka Natural Foods** (1626 Broadway, tel. 707/442–6325), open weekdays 8:30–8, Saturday 9–6, Sunday 10–6. The **Humboldt Bay Coffee Company** (211 F St., tel. 707/444–3969) has the finest mocha ($2.40) in town, made from beans roasted right on the premises. It's open Monday–Saturday 7 AM–10 PM, Sunday 9 AM–10 PM. If you've got a sweet tooth, don't miss the panoply of goodies at **Ramone's** (209 E St., tel. 707/445–2923). Among a million other treats, the bread pudding goes for $1.25.

Lost Coast Brewery and Café. They brew their own beer and serve great food, attracting crowds of locals and tourists. The batter on the fish 'n' chips ($6.25) is made with the brewery's own ale, and its hearty sandwiches ($5–$8) come with garlic parmesan fries, salad, or coleslaw. You can sample the beers (at least five are always on tap) for 50¢ per 2-ounce glass. *617 4th St., between H and G Sts., tel. 707/445–4480.*

Cocina Michoacana Restaurant. The antiseptic dining area is cold and boring, but the fiery salsa will shake your senses. Thick red sauce makes all the enchilada plates ($6–$8) a good bet. Two chile rellenos with rice and beans go for $6.95. *427 V St., at 5th St., tel. 707/443–7840.*

Samoa Cookhouse. Some of the best deals in meals can be had at this last surviving cookhouse in the west on the outskirts of town. Samoa's cooks serve three heavy-duty family-style meals every day at long wooden tables. You can call a week in advance to see what's cooking; a typical dinner is chicken fried steak, roast beef, or pork chops (occasionally there's fish at lunchtime) and costs $11, which includes soup, salad, bread, dessert, and tea or coffee. *Cookhouse Rd. (from U.S. 101, cross the Samoa Bridge, turn left on Samoa Rd. then left one block later onto Cookhouse), tel. 707/441–1659.*

WORTH SEEING

For an interesting glimpse of historical Eureka, head to the free **Clarke Memorial Museum** (240 E St., at 3rd St., tel. 707/443–1947), housed in a marble and granite edifice that used to be the Bank of Eureka. It has one of the best Native American displays in California; in addition to the usual arrows and baskets, there's an authentic Yurok dugout boat in the annex. The museum is open Tuesday–Saturday noon–4. While you're in Old Town, walk to the **Romano Gabriel Sculpture Garden** (317 2nd St., at D St.), which houses the crazy folk-art that once filled this local artist and eccentric's front yard. The **Blue Ox Millworks** (1 X St., corner 1st and X Sts., tel. 707/444–3437 or 800/248–4259) offers a self-guided tour ($5) of a working Victorian sawmill and an entirely animal-powered farm. The tour is worth the money if you're dying to see how they splintered the big trees back in the old days. It's open Monday–Saturday 8:30–5 and summer Sundays 11–4.

For a history lesson with style, head to the pier at the foot of C Street in Old Town and board the *Madaket* for the **Humboldt Bay Harbor Cruise** (tel. 707/445–1910). For $9.50 March–November, Eureka native and skipper Leroy Zerlang gives you a 75-minute look at the history of Humboldt Bay, complete with amusing anecdotes. From the ship's decks, you can see harbor seals, Canadian geese, cormorants, lumber mills, and shipwrecks.

OUTDOOR ACTIVITIES

Eureka isn't the most exciting place to enjoy Mother Nature, but you can take a refreshing walk in **Sequoia Park** (W St., take Harris St. east off U.S. 101), a small but dense forest featuring the big trees advertised in its name. **Humboldt Bay** is good for sea kayaking (there are several boat ramps along Waterfront Dr.), and you're not far from beautiful rivers and mountains. The Trinity River, also great for kayaking, is an hour's drive. The 3-mi run from Hayden Flat to Cedar Flat has a Class II–III difficulty. **Northern Mountain Supply** (125 W. 5th St., Eureka, tel. 707/445–1711) has a bevy of trail and topo maps for nearby Lost Coast, Marble Mountain, and Redwood National Park. They also rent sleeping bags ($9–$10 per day), two-person tents ($10–$12 per day), canoes ($30 per day), kayaks ($20–$30 per day), and snowshoes ($10 per day), with significant discounts for multiple-day use. Before you rent or buy, check prices against Humboldt State University's Center Activities (*see* Arcata, *below*).

NEAR EUREKA

FERNDALE • On the north end of the Lost Coast, the fairy-tale town of **Ferndale** is painted pink, blue, and yellow, and instead of the grain stores, open markets, and saloons of yesteryear, it's full of antique shops, touristy boutiques, and candy stores. Because of its Victorian homes and storefronts, the town is a state historic landmark, but the architecture seems incongruous in this otherwise undeveloped area.

For a look at Ferndale's history—which began in 1852 when the first farmers arrived to use the lush pastures for dairy cattle—stop by the **Ferndale Museum** (corner Shaw and 3rd Sts., tel. 707/786–4466). The period rooms and the display on seismology are definitely worth the $1 admission. Ferndale's **Kinetic Sculpture Museum** (corner Main and Shaw Sts., no phone) displays vehicles from past Kinetic Sculpture races, a Memorial Day weekend event requiring participants to travel in human-powered vehicles over a 38-mi course that traverses roads, dunes, bays, and rivers. The ingenious inventions, which are free to inspect, include a human-size hamster wheel and an 8-ft tricycle.

The cheapest room in this sea of pricey B&Bs is at the **Ferndale Laundromat and Motel** (632 Main St., tel. 707/786–9471). The two clean rooms, with microwaves, refrigerators, and TVs, are big enough to sleep five and cost $45. (Beyond two people, it's an extra $5 per person.) Register at the laundromat. If you're looking for something with a bit more class, the **Shaw House** (703 Main St., tel. 707/786–9958) is about as swell as it gets, with ornate architecture, immaculate grounds, robes, slippers, nightshirts, bubble bath, full breakfast, and balconies. A beautiful room filled with antiques goes for $75 year-round. The innkeeper can deliver excellent advice about exploring Ferndale (check out the terraced cemeteries), and bikes are available for guests. For sustenance, the **Ferndale Meat Company** (376 Main St., tel. 707/786–4501; closed Sun.) vends a $3 sandwich that won't leave you hungry. More upscale but still reasonably priced is **Curley's Grill** (460 Main St., tel. 707/786–9696), with tasty grilled sandwiches ($5–$7) for lunch and dinner.

ARCATA

A college, freshwater lagoon, and redwood park are some of the charms of Arcata. Only 8 mi north of Eureka, Arcata avoids the sprawl and the mall, proudly maintaining a close-knit community determined to make the town a great place to live. Most shops, restaurants, and services are within easy walking distance of the town's grassy central plaza (between G, H, 8th, and 9th Sts.), where you can listen to some pretty good buskers. Across U.S. 101, **Humboldt State University (HSU)** (Plaza Ave., off L. K. Wood Blvd. east of U.S. 101, tel. 707/826–4402) deserves its reputation as a hotbed of environmentalism and has many students interested in earning non-traditional degrees.

Seventy-five percent of California's oysters are harvested from Arcata Bay, a fact celebrated in mid-June's **Oyster Festival.** Locals line up to consume the tasty bivalves ($1 each, six for $5) while listening to live folk music. The highlight is the oyster-calling contest (words can't do it justice). Call 707/826–9043 for more information.

BASICS

The **Arcata Chamber of Commerce** (1062 G St., at 11th St., tel. 707/822–3619) has a small, free map of town and copious quantities of regional information. Pick up the free monthly *North Coast Journal,* which highlights local news and happenings. They're open weekdays 10–4, Saturday 9–3. At the **Northcoast Environmental Center** (879 9th St., at I St., tel. 707/822–6918), you can peruse the vast library and find out about everything from hiking trails to volunteer opportunities. Open Monday–Saturday 10–5.

COMING AND GOING

Arcata is the gateway to Redwood National Forest to the north and the mountainous national parks to the east on Hwy. 299 (*see* The Northern Coast Ranges, *below*). If you're without a car, use the **Humboldt Transit System** (133 V St., Eureka, tel. 707/443–0826) from Eureka (20 min, $1.35). The **Arcata and Mad River Transit System** (tel. 707/822–3775) has routes around the city and to the suburbs in the north for 80¢.

WHERE TO SLEEP

Besides the hostel, the only affordable option is the **Fairwinds Motel** (1674 G St., at 17th St., tel. 707/822–4824), six blocks north of the plaza. Generic doubles cost $45–$55 ($8 less in winter); luckily the 27 rooms all face away from the freeway. For $20 more, you can spend a winter weeknight at the **Arcata Hotel** (708 9th St., tel. 707/826–0217 or 800/344–1221), a historic landmark owned by a local Yurok tribe, which has 32 quite decent rooms. Rates include continental breakfast and access to a full-service health club nearby. Also consider camping farther up U.S. 101 (*see* Near Arcata, *below*) or crashing in a cheap motel in Eureka (*see above*).

HOSTELS • Arcata Crew House Hostel. It's an old wooden Victorian with a TV, microwave, barbecue, and five refrigerators. The hostel is only open June 25–August 25. The 18 beds rent for $10 per night (including tax), regardless of whether you're an HI member or not. If you call ahead or get lucky, you may get a private room ($10 per person). Reserve ahead. *1390 I St., at 14th St., tel. 707/822–9995. Reception open daily 5 PM–11 PM, lockout 9 AM–5 PM.*

FOOD

Arcata has a wide range of inexpensive restaurants that cater to the student community. Most are near the plaza or in the area bordered by 16th, 18th, G, and H streets. A breakfast landmark is **TJ's Classic Café** (1057 H St., near 10th St., tel. 707/822–4650), where the weekday-morning special gives you a choice of eggs and potatoes, pancakes, or French toast for $2.50. Some say it's overrated, but hippies love the **Wildflower Café and Bakery** (1604 G St., at 16th St., tel. 707/822–0360), with good tempeh and nature burgers ($4.50) as well as a tempting array of desserts. **Tomo** (708 9th St., in the lobby of the Arcata Hotel, tel. 707/822-1414) has some vegetarian specialties like baby soy beans ($2.50), sashimi, vegetable tempurah ($6.50), and dinners ($11–$14). Closed Tuesday for dinner and weekends for lunch. The **Arcata Co-Op** (corner 8th and I Sts., tel. 707/822–5947) has a great bakery and an excellent selection of produce, cheeses, bulk, and prepared foods. A **farmers' market** convenes on Arcata's central plaza Saturday morning 9 AM–1 PM from May to November.

Hey Juan! Ignore the name and focus instead on the massive, filling burritos ($4.75; small vegetarian versions $1.50) lathered with one of four salsas (beware the "death paste"). Saturday 10:30–2, all veggie burritos are an unbeatable two-for-one. *1642½ G St., near 16th St., tel. 707/822–8433.*

Los Bagels. It's something of a town institution, with outdoor tables, reggae music on the stereo, and a basketball court in back. Expect to see lots of students enjoying the killer bagels (45¢–55¢ each) piled high with toppings (30¢–$2). *1061 I St., near 11th St., tel. 707/822–3150. Closed Tues.*

WORTH SEEING

The **Arcata Community Forest** offers nearly 10 mi of trails through second-growth redwoods. To get here, take 14th Street east over U.S. 101 until it dead-ends in a parking lot within forest boundaries. Much of the forest is open to mountain bikes. **Revolution Bicycles** (1360 G St., at 14th St., tel. 707/822–2562) rents bikes for $25 per day and can point the way to the best tracks. They're open weekdays 8–7, Saturday 9–6, and Sunday 10–5. The Chamber of Commerce (*see* Basics, *above*) has free trail maps, as well as information on the **Arcata Marsh and Wildlife Sanctuary,** a water-treatment experiment headed by HSU professors. The marsh project lets the natural purifying processes of the marshlands erase contaminants from waste-water, allowing the water to be released into the adjoining Humboldt Bay. Foot trails pass throughout the 154-acre facility, allowing prime viewing of the many birds and ducks who call the marsh home. The Audubon Society offers free guided tours of the marsh Saturday morning at 8:30. To reach the marsh, take I Street south to the end.

For $6.50 at the **Finnish Country Sauna and Tubs,** you can have a half hour in a private sauna or outdoor hot tub. At the sauna's Café Mokka Coffeehouse, enjoy the cheapest coffee in town (85¢ for a large), drink hot or cold juice from the juice bar, or browse through stacks of national and international newspapers and magazines. Live acoustic folk music happens here some Friday and Saturday nights. *Corner 5th and J Sts., tel. 707/822–2228. Tubs and coffeehouse open daily noon–11 (Fri. and Sat. until 1 AM).*

AFTER DARK

Arcata is a college town, and its bars and theaters cater to the student population. Laid-back **Humboldt Brewing Company** (856 10th St., at I St., tel. 707/826–2739) draws a local crowd for microbrewed ales ($2.50 a pint) and delicious sandwiches ($6.25), burgers ($6), and salads ($3–$9). Live bands often play on Friday and Saturday nights (about $3 cover). **Jambalaya** (915 H St., just off the plaza, tel. 707/822–4766) also has live entertainment almost every night. Weekly open-mic poetry readings and jazz music appeal to an older, artsy crowd, but on weekends the place books more rockin' bands (about $3 cover).

OUTDOOR ACTIVITIES

Your adventures should begin at Humboldt State's **Center Activities** (2nd floor of University Center, under bookstore, tel. 707/826–3357), open weekdays 10–4 in summer, weekdays 9–8 during the school year. They rent everything from windsurf boards ($18–$28 per day) to canoes and kayaks ($20 per day) to sailboats ($35 per day) to fishing and snow gear, and the knowledgeable staff has up-to-date information on area river conditions. They also rent backpacks ($9 per day), tents ($15 per day), and sleeping bags ($5 per day). There are discounts if you rent for an entire weekend (Fri.–Mon.). **Humboldt Lagoons State Park** (*see below*) is a great place for sailing and windsurfing.

NEAR ARCATA

MAD RIVER BEACH • U.S. 101 hugs the coast north of Arcata, passing by a number of wide, windswept beaches, most of which are great for camping. You can't camp at the first one, Mad River Beach County Park (tel. 707/445–7652), but it's close enough to Arcata (3½ mi) for a brisk morning walk or an afternoon picnic. In mid to late summer, you'll get to tromp through thickets of wildflowers in the dunes, where the Mad River meets the Pacific. Bathrooms are in the boat ramp parking lot. Bring your sweatshirt, as winds range from mild to staggeringly gusty. To get here, take U.S. 101 just north of Arcata to the Guintoli Lane exit, and go west on Janes Road to Upper Bay Road, following the COASTAL ACCESS signs to the end of the narrow country road.

CLAM BEACH • North of Mad River, Clam Beach County Park (tel. 707/445–7652) is—surprise—a good place for clamming during low tides. As the water recedes, look for bubbles coming out of the sand, and then dig (with shovel, pitchfork, or hands). David at **Time Flies** (815 J St., at 8th St., tel. 707/444–8913) can give you the scoop on the critters, including the mandatory license ($9 a day, $15 a year) and tips on how to steam your catch. No clamming is allowed May–October. Camping costs $8 per vehicle; if you arrive on foot or bike it's only $3. There are pit toilets. The campground's 16 sites are right next to U.S. 101, but the beach is wide. Sites closest to the parking lot have easy access to cement picnic tables and barbecue pits, but you'll find more privacy if you park along Clam Beach Drive between the two lots and hike through the waist-high scrub to a secluded patch of sand. To get here take Clam Beach exit off U.S. 101.

PATRICK'S POINT STATE PARK • The campgrounds at Patrick's Point State Park, 20 mi north of Arcata, will make you happy you chose to travel in California. Even in the summer, when the three campgrounds (124 sites in all, coin-operated hot showers) fill to capacity, your site among the trees feels secluded. Sites are $15 ($16 on weekends, $12 in winter). There are plenty of hike/bike sites ($3), and 6 mi of trails traverse the grounds. An especially nice walk from the Agate Beach parking lot follows the **Rim Trail** for 2 mi along ocean bluffs. Periodic offshoots take you out to rocky points ideal for whale and sea lion watching. The yearly ***Brush Dance,*** a healing ritual for children, is performed at the park's reconstructed Yurok village the last weekend in June. *4150 Patrick's Point Dr., tel. 707/677–3570. Follow signs from U.S. 101. Day use: $5. Make camping reservations through Destinet (tel. 800/444–7275).*

TRINIDAD • If your tent pole breaks or you get rained out, take refuge in tiny Trinidad at the **Lighthouse Motel** (3360 Patrick's Point Dr., 1½ mi south of U.S. 101, tel. 707/677–3121). Small but clean rooms go for $42—a bargain in this bed-and-breakfast enclave. The backyard boasts a cliff's-edge view of the ocean and a beautifully maintained garden. No credit cards are accepted. In case you forgot to stock up in Arcata, you can grab a tasty lunch for less than $5 at the campy **El-di-vi Caboose** (702 Patrick's Point Dr., 4 mi south of U.S. 101, tel. 707/677–3389), closed Sunday–Monday.

BIG LAGOON AND HUMBOLDT LAGOONS • A few miles north of Patrick's Point lies **Big Lagoon County Park** (tel. 707/445–7652). The 26 drive-in campsites are set among the trees, but they're not as private as the ones at Patrick's Point. There are no showers, though you will find flush toilets. Do some bird-watching at the lagoon, or just take a peaceful walk at the water's edge. Sites cost $10 per night, and day use is $3. Hikers and bikers share a site for $3 per person. About 8 mi farther north, U.S. 101 runs through **Humboldt Lagoons State Park** (tel. 707/488–2014). The beautiful beaches and lagoons in the park are free for day use, but the 6 walk-in sites, all less than ¼ mi from the parking lot, go for $7. They're first-come, first-served, and you must register at the Patrick's Point campground.

REDWOOD NATIONAL AND STATE PARKS

The mammoth trees that populate the northern coast used to cover almost 2 million acres of California and Oregon, but as of 1993 only 87,000 acres of old growth remained in California—largely due to the trees' value as lumber. Thankfully, 80,000 of the remaining acres of old-growth are within protected parks, most here in Redwood National and State Parks, about an hour north of Eureka on U.S. 101. This is one of the few places on earth where you can enjoy the coast redwoods, some of which are over 350 ft tall, 20 ft in diameter, and more than 2,000 years old.

Redwood National and State Parks, occupying a narrow strip that runs all the way from Orick to Crescent City, encompass much more than redwoods. You're unlikely to have a run-in with one of the park's mountain lions or black bears, but it's easy to get a look at the abundant Roosevelt elk. More patient types can watch for gray whales December–March. The best spots for viewing are the Redwood Information Center (*see below*), where a spotting scope helps you get a closer look, and Klamath Overlook and Gold Bluffs Beach. You may see seals or sea lions almost anywhere along the coast—park rangers can tell you which areas have seen the most activity of late. The park is on one of North America's four major bird-migration routes, and dozens of books and pamphlets sold at the two main ranger stations (*see below*) will help you identify the things flapping above your head.

The park is co-managed by the National Park Service and California State Parks, and within the boundaries of Redwood National Park are the following state parks: **Prairie Creek** (tel. 707/488–2171), **Del Norte Coast** (tel. 707/464–9533), and **Jedediah Smith** (tel. 707/458–3310). The easiest way to approach the parks, though, is as one long continuum—just make forays from the highway wherever desire strikes. But, whatever you do, don't stick only to U.S. 101—the largest trees, best wildlife-viewing opportunities, and most secluded inlets lie a few miles off the highway. If your tour of the redwood parks has to be brief, check out the 45-mi scenic loop that follows U.S. 199 from Crescent City to Howland Hill Road, which will return you to the coast.

BASICS

Pick up maps, get pointers on trails and campgrounds, and get information on ranger-led programs at one of the two main ranger stations: The **Redwood Information Center** (off U.S. 101, 1 mi south of Orick, tel. 707/464–6101, ext. 5265), near the southern park entrance, open daily 8–6 (daily 9–5 off-season); and Crescent City's **Redwood National Park Headquarters** (1111 2nd St., tel. 707/464–6101), open daily 8–5 year-round. The somewhat smaller **Hiouchi Information Center** (off Rte. 199, 10 mi northeast of Crescent City, no phone) is only open May–October.

FEES

Admission to Redwood National Park is free, but you pay $6 per carload in day-use fees for state park facilities, such as picnic grounds or beaches.

WHEN TO GO

July and August bring flocks of hikers and RVers to the park. Temperatures rarely climb above the 60s in this foggy region, though it becomes dramatically warmer as you travel away from the coast. Winter means damp, chilly weather, but it's rarely bitter cold. Expect temperatures between 30°F and 50°F and expect to get wet—average rainfall exceeds 80 inches per year.

WHERE TO SLEEP

You didn't come to redwood country to stay in a hotel. Besides, the few roadside motels in Orick and Klamath are downright depressing. For the money, **Camp Marigold** (16101 U.S. 101, 3½ mi north of Klamath, tel. 707/482–3585 or 800/621–8573) champions the most amenities. The 16 cabins are all equipped with full kitchens, though the carpets are dated and the furnishings tacky. Still, a double goes for $38 at the peak of summer, and it's situated between Del Norte Redwoods and Prairie Creek. Make reservations in the summer and expect cut rates in the winter. Otherwise, continue up the road a few miles to Crescent City (*see below*), where dozens of mostly generic hotels line U.S. 101.

HOSTELS • Redwood Youth Hostel (HI and AYH). Perched above the ocean in Redwood National Park, this turn-of-the-century dairy rancher's mansion is a great base from which to explore the nearby beaches and mountains. (Several good trails begin just steps from the front door.) The hostel is clean and has new furniture, a well-equipped kitchen (with separate stoves for vegetarian and meat cooking), and three showers. Family and couple's rooms are available. The atmosphere is friendly, but the strict rules are somewhat oppressive; expect to do a chore. Reservations (by check or credit card) are suggested in summer. Beds cost $11 a night. If you're not staying the night, a shower is $3. *14480 U.S. 101, 7 mi north of Klamath, tel. 707/482–8265. 30 beds. Reception open daily 7:30 AM–9:30 AM and 4:30 PM–9:30 PM, lockout 9:30–4:30.*

The towering Sequoia Sempervirens, or coast redwoods, were named after Chief Sequoia, a Cherokee from Oklahoma who didn't set foot in California until his dying days.

CAMPING • The cheapest option is to take one of the national park's free campsites (tel. 707/464–6101), distributed on a first-come, first-served basis, but they all require a walk-in. **Flint Ridge** is off the Coastal Drive near Klamath, and the ¼-mi walk there takes you through coastal growth into a quiet redwood forest. The 10 free sites have picnic tables, fire rings, drinking water, and spectacular ocean views. The five free sites at **Nickel Creek** offer tide-pooling opportunities and ocean views. From Crescent City, drive a few miles south on U.S. 101, turn right on Endert's Beach Road, continue to the end, and follow the signs as you hike in ½ mi. Bring your own water and keep your valuables out of sight, as there have been some thefts here. The 10 sites at **DeMartin** are on a grassy prairie a few minutes' walk from the ocean and have drinking water. From U.S. 101, look for signs just north of the Redwood Youth Hostel.

If you want a few more amenities—such as hot showers—try the state parks ($15, $16 on weekends). They attract more people, so reservations are mandatory in summer; call Destinet (tel. 800/444–7275) before setting out. The 25 shoreline sites at **Gold Bluffs Beach Campground** in Prairie Creek Redwoods State Park are exposed, but wind breaks have been put up. There are also three walk-in environmental sites and a hike/bike site here ($3). Traveling north on U.S. 101, turn left on Davison Road a few miles past Orick; the 8-mi drive down the gravel access road discourages trailers and motor homes. The sites at **Elk Prairie Campground** (near Newton B. Drury Pkwy., off U.S. 101) are close together and attract noisy campers, but at least you're among old-growth redwoods. There's also good elk viewing here. **Jedediah Smith Redwoods Campground** has 106 beautiful sites along the Smith River. Its accessibility (right off U.S. 199, which branches off U.S. 101 just north of Crescent City) makes it popular with RVers. Perhaps the best of the lot, **Mill Creek** features private sites among lush ferns and second-growth redwoods. Look for the turnoff 7 mi south of Crescent City. For information on many more camping options, including the numerous environmental sites accessible only with backpacks, ask any park ranger.

FOOD

Within the park, your food options are severely limited. Smart travelers will stock up on groceries on the north edge of the park in Crescent City or 70 mi south of the park in Arcata. Otherwise, make do at one of the three small markets off U.S. 101 in Orick, at the southern edge of the park. Perhaps the best stocked is the **Orick Market** (tel. 707/488–3225) on U.S. 101—if you're heading north, it's on your right just past the post office.

About the only restaurants you'll find in the park are a few greasy spoons and hamburger joints in Orick and Klamath. The best is Orick's **Palm Café** (121130 U.S. 101, tel. 707/488–3381), where local loggers chow chicken-fried steak ($8). A better, but more expensive, option is **Rolf's Park Café** (U.S. 101, at Davison Rd., 2 mi north of Orick, tel. 707/488–3841). The European chef cooks up meaty sandwiches ($6–$8.50) for lunch, hearty German entrées ($10–$16) for dinner, and game dishes—their specialty—morning, noon, and night. Breakfast ($6) here is massive and delicious. In Klamath, stop off at **Kirsten's Klam House Restaurant** (17505 U.S. 101, 4 mi south of Requa, tel. 707/482–7325 or 707/482–5385), usually open daily 8–8, but sometimes closed in the off-season. Here you'll get big portions of deep-fried or sautéed salmon and chips (around $7). A veggie burger is $4.25.

EXPLORING THE REDWOOD PARKS

About 200 mi of trails wind through the park, from old-growth redwood groves that block out almost all light on the forest floor, to driftwood-strewn beaches and estuaries. Pick up a hiking map from one of the ranger offices (*see above*) before you set out—many trails are poorly signposted. The four state park maps, with contours and trailheads, are the best buy at 25¢ apiece.

One of the best forays in the park is the easy ¾-mi jaunt across shallow creeks to **Fern Canyon** in Prairie Creek Redwoods State Park. You have to drive 8 mi on a dirt road to reach the canyon (take the Davison Rd. turnoff west from U.S. 101), but it's worth it. The 40-ft-high canyon walls are covered with five-finger ferns—get a breeze going, and you'll think a million Martians are waving at you.

If you came to Redwood National and State Parks strictly to see redwoods, you'll want to take the **Stout Grove Trail,** where you'll find some of the oldest and largest trees in the park—some 22 ft in diameter. To get here, drive south on U.S. 101 from Crescent City, turn left on Elk Valley Road, and right on Howland Hill Road to the Stout Grove parking area. More ambitious hikers may want to head to the **Redwood Creek Trailhead** (look for signs pointing south after you turn onto Bald Hills Rd. from U.S. 101). From the parking area you can hike about 8 mi (each way) on a trail that's not too steep. If you get a free permit from the Redwood Information Center (*see above*), you can camp anywhere along the trail.

The short **Lady Bird Johnson Grove** offers a decent introduction to the park, but it's always packed. Look for the trailhead 2 mi east of U.S. 101 on Bald Hills Road. A better bet is the **James Irvine Trail,** which follows a lush creek through dense redwoods. If you take the **Clintonia Trail,** at the halfway point you can loop back on **Miner's Ridge** trail for a 5-mi loop. The trailhead is at the Prairie Creek visitor center.

The best place in the park to hang out and watch the wild Roosevelt elk is at Rolf's Park Café (*see* Food, *above*). The field behind the café is so popular with the elk that the park sends rangers out here to explain the habits of the big critters. You're also likely to see the elk along Newton B. Drury Scenic Parkway, accessible from U.S. 101 at the southern end of the park about 6 mi north of Orick, or from U.S. 101 further north, about 4 mi south of Klamath. The rare marbled murrelet, a small seabird that's the latest endangered species to become a pawn in the war to save the old-growth forests, is more elusive but is frequently spotted at Lost Man Creek in summer.

PARK ACTIVITIES

Mountain bikers are prohibited from using most of the trails in the park, but there are several exceptions including the moderately difficult 11½-mi **Holter Ridge Bike Trail.** Your hamstrings will thank you if you start at the scenic overlook off Bald Hills Road (1½ mi north of Orick) and continue down the Old Logging Trail to **The Lost Man Creek Trail. Escape Hatch** (960 3rd St., Crescent City, tel. 707/464–2614 or 800/448–3761) rents bikes for $20 per 24 hours. They're open 10–5 Monday–Saturday.

In past years, rangers have led two low-cost ($6) kayak trips—one at the Klamath River estuary and the other through small rapids on the Smith River at the north edge of the park. At press time, rangers had suspended the tours and were calculating budgets to see if they could reopen. It's worth a call to the Redwood Information Center (*see above*) to see. If not, the folks at **Lunker Fish Trips, Bait and Tackles** (2095 U.S. 199, tel. 707/458–4704, across from Hiouchi Hamlet RV Park) will rent one to you for $10 a day.

CRESCENT CITY

Sixteen miles north of Klamath and 20 mi south of the Oregon border lies Crescent City, the last bastion of good food and well-stocked supermarkets on the Northern California coast. Though Crescent City curves around a gorgeous stretch of ocean and radiates small-town charm, heavy rains and bone-chilling fog dampen the spirit much of the year. Which is too bad—friendly folks around town hope tourism can restore the commerce that left with the mills and is fading among fishermen. Still, the town makes a convenient urban base for trips into Redwood National Park to the south (*see above*) or the Smith River National Recreation Area to the east (*see* The Northern Coast Ranges, *below*).

If you decide to stick around town, there are fine ways to occupy your time at minimal cost. Head over to **Popeye's Landing** (a bait and tackle shop at the bottom of B St. that has no telephone) to try your hand at crabbing, a popular sport here thanks to a prolific Dungeness crab population. You can rent a crab pot (a net strung on a set of flexible rings) and bait at the landing ($5 for 3 hrs weekdays, $8 weekends), and a chair ($2 for 3 hrs). You might find someone at the landing who will cook up your catch for a few bucks and bag it to go (the catch limit is 10 crabs per person). If you'd rather fish for perch, pole rental is $5 for three hours; no fishing license is required.

At low tide April–September, you can walk from the pier across the ocean floor to the oldest lighthouse on the North Coast (1856), **Battery Point Lighthouse** (tel. 707/464–3089), and take a $2 tour Wednesday–Sunday 10–4. A map of the city and copious advice on scenic drives, trails, and nearby forests are available at the **Crescent City/Del Norte County Chamber of Commerce** (1001 Front St., tel. 707/464–3174 or 800/343–8300), open daily Memorial Day–Labor Day (otherwise weekdays) 9–5.

WHERE TO SLEEP

The dozens of hotels lining U.S. 101 near Crescent City charge similar rates: $35–$45 per double in winter, $45–$60 in summer. You can do better, though not by much, if you drive into town. All rooms are not created equal at the **El Patio Motel** (655 H St., at 6th St., tel. 707/464–5114), where most sport wood-paneled walls and dated furniture but some are cleaner. Since you'll drop $34 in summer for a double (two beds), ask to see it first. **The Royal Inn** (102 L St., tel. 707/464–3142) has some rooms with kitchenettes; their basic doubles go for $30 in winter, $45 in summer. Consider making reservations for any of these in the summer; in the winter they'll be begging you to stay with reduced rates.

FOOD

Crescent City's tiny hipster community eats at **Alias Jones** (983 3rd St., tel. 707/465–6987), closed Sunday. Try the pesto omelet or the hot zucchini, mushroom, cheese, and tomato sandwich (both $5.75). They also have great salads, burgers, baked goods, and coffee drinks. At the **Good Harvest Café** (700 Northcrest Dr., at U.S. 101, tel. 707/465–6028), locals rave about breakfast (a large order of french toast is $5.50), but the lunches are just as good (sandwiches are $4.50–$6.75); it's closed for lunch Sunday. While you're in town, restock your backpack at the small health-food market **Harvest Natural Foods** (265 L St., tel. 707/464–1926), closed Sunday.

NORTHERN COAST RANGES

The Northern Coast Ranges are "Bigfoot Country," where the legendary man-ape is sometimes sighted. More frequently sighted are Bigfoot tourist traps, with everything from T-shirts to chain saw–carved sculptures touting the mythical beast. **Bigfoot Days** festivities, the climax of which is the crowning of a Bigfoot king and queen, take place in Happy Camp on Labor Day weekend.

The mountainous regions of the **Six Rivers** and **Klamath** national forests contain some of the state's most spectacular and unpopulated wilderness, with glacial lakes, salmon-filled rivers, and 8,000-ft mountain peaks where the snow doesn't melt until July. The forest's character ranges from the redwood-dominated coastal communities to the inland forests of fir, pine, madrone, and oak—all of which are supported by water from the six major rivers that flow through the region's valleys. You'll find opportunities for fishing, rafting, kayaking, and mountain biking, but best of all is the chance for solitary hiking in wilderness areas untouched by logging. Within Six Rivers National Forest, near the coast, is the **Smith River National Recreation Area,** 315 mi of wild and scenic river. While the beauty of the river and its valley can be awe-inspiring, the chances of your bliss being ruined by crowds are high.

Towns are few and far between, and they're small at that. In the northern part of Klamath National Forest on Hwy. 96, **Happy Camp** makes a convenient launching pad into the Siskiyou or Marble Mountain Wilderness. Since the mill shuttered in 1995 and 75% of townsfolk receive government assistance, the residents of Happy Camp are not, it seems, happy campers. Still, even with its meager resources, the ranger station and grocery store make the tiny town the best stocked in the region. In the south, **Willow Creek** has gas, markets, a few unexceptional eateries, and many rafting companies. The Trinity River flows right through town on its way north through a beautiful valley and offers opportunities for mellow floats or real action on high-intensity white water. Twelve miles north of Willow Creek is the 89,000-acre **Hoopa Valley Indian Reservation,** the first land granted to Native Americans in California after the Gold Rush in 1864. Visitors are welcome to view Hoopa dances, but no cameras or video and tape recorders are allowed. For $10, you can tour the restored village and talk to tribe members. Contact the Hoopa Tribal Museum (Hoopa Valley Shopping Center, tel. 530/625–4110). (For information on adjacent areas, including Weaverville, Lewiston Lake, Trinity National Forest, and the Yolla Bolly–Middle Eel Wilderness, *see* Chapter 5.)

BASICS

VISITOR INFORMATION

You can send away for national forest maps ($3), trail photocopies, and national forest topo maps, and make camping reservations in advance for some campgrounds through all the branches of the national forest office headquarters. Each office has general information about the area it covers, but you'll rarely get rangers with good field experience. For that you should head to a national forest substation in the area you wish to explore.

The **Klamath National Forest Headquarters** (1312 Fairlane Rd., Yreka 96097, tel. 530/842–6131), open weekdays 8–5, is just east of I–5 at the south end of Yreka (*see* Chapter 5). There are substations in Fort Jones (tel. 530/468–5351), Happy Camp (tel. 530/493–2243), Oak Knoll (tel. 530/465–2241), MacDoel (tel. 530/398–4391), and Orleans (tel. 530/627–3291). **Six Rivers National Forest Headquarters** (1330 Bayshore Way, Eureka 95501, tel. 707/442–1721) has maps ($3), books, and staff on hand weekdays 8–4:30. Six Rivers substations are in Gasquet (tel. 707/457–3131), Mad River (tel. 707/574–6233), Orleans (tel. 530/627–3291), and Willow Creek (tel. 530/629–2118). Headquarters for the **Smith River National Recreation Area** are in Gasquet (tel. 707/457–3131).

WHEN TO GO

Prepare for an onslaught of strange weather of almost biblical proportions. Rain (50–70 inches per year), sleet, and hail soak everything, even in summer, and wildfires periodically serve up wilderness barbecue-style. Fall and spring bring more rain, mud slides, the occasional flood, and sometimes even snow. A few areas remain accessible in winter, but the weather is *really* nasty then. Tire chains are a must December–March to get through the mountain passes. While summer temperatures in the valleys average in the 90s, cooler temperatures at higher elevations make long backpacking trips bearable. Snow blocks some high-country trails through July, so be sure to check on trail conditions with the local ranger substations, and carry warm clothing to protect against hypothermia. Late spring through early September is the best time to visit.

COMING AND GOING

The Northern Coast Ranges are bordered by two major north–south highways: **U.S. 101** on the west and **I–5** on the east. The major east–west thoroughfare is **Highway 299,** which you can reach by turning east from U.S. 101, north of Arcata, or west from I–5 at Redding. From Hwy. 299, you can tour both forests, with the option of detouring into the backcountry, by turning north onto Hwy. 3 at Weaverville and looping back south on Hwy. 96, which cruises through Happy Camp and rejoins Hwy. 299 at Willow Creek. The trip will take at least 7½ hours of straight driving, so you'll probably want to take advantage of the excellent camping along the way. Also, **Highway 199,** which begins in Crescent City and cuts the northwest corner of California with a neat, diagonal strip, provides even more access points into Six Rivers. Don't leave the major roads without good tires and a spare—many forest-service roads are gravel-covered and unmaintained.

WHERE TO SLEEP

MOTELS

The quiet little cabins at **Gambi Hill Motel** (40526 Hwy. 299, 1½ mi east of Willow Creek, tel. 530/629–2701) all have kitchenettes and decks. Brimming with character, they're a welcome respite from Motel Generic. Two of the cabins go for $35; four cost $45; a two-bedroom cabin is $80; all come with coffee and the machines to make it. If the less expensive rooms are booked, try **Wyatt's Motel** (39039 Hwy. 299, Willow Creek, tel. 530/629–2142, fax 530/629–4347). The new owners are still renovating, so about half of the 31 rooms are smart and stylish while the others languish in the poor taste of the former owner. Doubles cost $39 year-round. Up Hwy. 96 in Orleans, the **Orleans Hotel** (tel. 530/627–3018 or 530/469–3311) has sheltered travelers since 1870. The 12 small rooms with dated furniture are popular with fishermen, probably because of the low rates—$20 for one person, $5 each additional person. All guests share three bathrooms. Cabins with kitchenettes cost $35, plus $5 for each extra guest. They do not accept credit cards. In Happy Camp, where Indian Creek meets the Klamath River, the **Klamath Inn Motel and RV Park** (110 Nugget Rd., off Hwy. 96, tel. 530/493–2860) has eight doubles with shared bath starting at $33 ($3 more for private bath).

CAMPING

Hundreds of developed and backcountry campsites are scattered throughout the national forests, and you almost never have to worry about crowds hampering your appreciation of nature. Aside from the usual camping gear, be sure to bring the means to secure your supplies from hungry bears. Free camping is available throughout the national forests: Simply throw down a tent or sleeping bag at least ¼ mi away from any developed campground, after picking up the required (free) campfire permit from any ranger station. If you want to camp in the Smith River National Recreation Area, check out **Grassy Flat** (on Hwy. 199, 4 mi east of Gasquet), situated near the Middle Fork of the Smith River. The 19 sites ($8) are spread throughout a hardwood forest and come with fire grills, pit toilets, and drinking water; reservations can be made by calling 800/280–2267.

NEAR WILLOW CREEK • A convenient and popular campground is **Tish Tang**—8 mi north of Willow Creek (3 mi south of Hoopa) on Hwy. 96—with 40 river-accessible and first-come, first-served sites ($6) in a dense forest of live oak, young firs, maples, and madrones. Though it's open year-round, running water is only available late May–October. The noise from Hwy. 96 filters down the canyon, but you're fairly secluded. Keep an eye on your stuff; occasional thefts have been reported here. In the oak, madrone, and fir forest of **Grays Falls** (12 mi east of Willow Creek on Hwy. 299), the 33 sites ($6), open mid-May–early September, are equipped with running water and flush toilets, and the area is so lightly used you'll probably feel like you own the place.

NEAR HAPPY CAMP • The 18 sites ($4) at **O'Neil Creek** (on Hwy. 96, halfway between Happy Camp and I–5) are set under towering firs; some of the sites overlook the Klamath River. Open May–October, the campground has vault toilets and only stream water, so remember to filter or boil before drinking. Nearby **Grider Creek Campground** has 10 free (no drinking water) sites amid old-growth mixed conifer, big leaf maple, and Douglas fir. A trailhead gets you into the Marble Mountain Wilderness along the Pacific Crest Trail, which runs continuously from Mexico to Canada. To get here, turn off on Hwy. 96 at Walker Creek, 1½ mi east of Seiad Valley. Follow signs for 5 mi. The fishing (steelhead and salmon) is fantastic.

One of the better campgrounds around, **Sulphur Springs** offers six secluded walk-in sites along Elk Creek in a mixed forest marked by huge, old-growth firs. Moss-covered rocks crowd the edge of the creek, and campers have easy access to a nearby natural hot spring (about 75°F). Sulphur Springs has only vault toilets and no drinking water and is located 15 mi south of Happy Camp on Elk Creek Road. One mile up the road, **Norcross** has six free sites situated in meadows and second-growth forest with pit toilets and no drinking water. Both Norcross and Sulphur Springs serve as trailheads into the Marble Mountain Wilderness, though you'll have to ford Elk Creek if you start from Norcross. The burned-out chimney between the two campgrounds marks a popular swimming hole on Elk Creek.

FOOD

You'll get a good meal if you're willing to travel to Yreka, Etna, or Weaverville (*see* Chapter 5), but short of that you're looking at mediocrity. In Happy Camp, the **Indian Creek Café** (106 Indian Creek Rd., tel. 530/493–5180), has a 25-page menu that "reads like *Gone With the Wind*," but, while quantity is high, quality suffers, and the cafeteria-style furnishings aren't much to look at. Typical dinners cost $10 and get you a choice of "ten kinds of chicken," pork chops, and the like, with rolls, vegetables, potatoes, and soup or salad. There are fewer options but a friendlier atmosphere at the **Frontier Café** (64118 2nd Ave., Happy Camp, tel. 530/493–2242), open Monday–Saturday 6 AM–8 PM, Sunday 7–2. Try the taco salad or the veggie BLT ($4.25), where fried provolone stands in for the bacon. The only source for supplies is **Larry's Market** (143 Davis Rd., tel. 530/493–2621).

If you're in Willow Creek, you can dry off after a rafting trip at the **Whitewater Café** (39094 Hwy. 299, tel. 530/629–3354). A Gaping Maw, a turkey and cheddar sandwich with hot mustard ($4.95); or the Broken Helmet, egg salad with a pickle ($4.50), might go with your latte ($2.25). You'll pay a bit more for the Old West atmosphere at **Cinnabar Sam's** (19 Willow Way, off Hwy. 299, tel. 530/629–3437). Sandwiches (club, shrimp melt, sour dough melt, veggie) run $4–$10; the pub stays open until 10 in summer, 9 in winter. The bright green–trimmed **Bob's Shopping Center** (Hwy. 299, west of Hwy. 96, tel. 530/629–2457) is the place to stop for trail snacks.

EXPLORING THE NORTHERN COAST RANGES

The "greenbelt" that extends from the Oregon border all the way down to Clear Lake comprises several mountain ranges, national forests, and wilderness areas. Six Rivers National Forest—and the Siskiyou Wilderness—lies to the northwest, Klamath National Forest to the northeast. To the south is Mendocino National Forest (*see* Near Clear Lake, in U.S. 101 to Leggett, *above*), and to the east are Shasta-Trinity National Forest, the Trinity Alps Wilderness, and the Yolla Bolly–Middle Eel Wilderness (*see* Chapter 5). This is all confusing, even on the map, but don't be discouraged.

KLAMATH NATIONAL FOREST

The 250,000-acre **Marble Mountain Wilderness** in Klamath National Forest is one of the most pristine areas in California, and you don't need a wilderness permit to explore it—though you will need a free campfire permit for any open flame (including camp stoves). This is where the wild things are: bears, mountain lions, quail, foxes, deer, elk, red-tail hawks, bald eagles. Black Marble Mountain itself has a 7,442-ft marble-and-limestone peak rising out of the snow. The rugged ridges of the wilderness tower over narrow, winding river valleys and isolated highlands filled with meadows and lakes and a diverse population of trees, including mixed fir, oak, madrone, pine, and mountain hemlock.

SHORT HIKES • A short and easily accessible day hike is the **Dillon Creek Trail,** which follows the picturesque and inviting Dillon Creek for a little more than a mile as it flows through a forested valley toward the Klamath River. The sharp-eyed may catch sight of deer, elk, osprey, fox, or even a bear. You can reach the trail from the **Dillon Creek Campground**; cross the bridge to the north to find the trailhead.

LONGER HIKES • To access the Marble Mountain Wilderness, try the eight free campsites at **Lovers' Camp.** From Hwy. 3 in Fort Jones, take Scott River Road west for 12 mi, turn south toward Indian Scotty Campground, cross the river, and follow signs to Lovers' Camp. From here, the 5-mi **Canyon Creek Trail** leads west into the Marble Valley, a popular backcountry camping spot. One mile into the Canyon Creek Trail, near the Sky High Lakes, the **Red Rock Trail** forks to the south and continues into high mountain meadows, eventually meeting the **Pacific Crest Trail** after 6½ mi. In hunting season (fall and winter), avoid Lovers' Camp and its trails, as the area is popular with drunken marksmen.

SIX RIVERS NATIONAL FOREST

The Six Rivers National Forest stretches like a long finger south from Oregon to the Trinity County line. The forest contains (part of) the 135,000-acre **Siskiyou Wilderness** (the wilderness spills over into Klamath and Siskiyou national forests). Though you won't find the same concentration of lakes and alpine meadows here as in the more popular Marble Mountain Wilderness (*see above*), you will almost always be rewarded for your backcountry efforts with some truly superlative views and solitude. Since the winters here are sometimes very harsh, taking out tall firs like toothpicks, stop in at a ranger station to check on trail conditions.

In the very northwest corner of the forest, east of Gasquet on Hwy. 199, the mountains, streams, and canyons of the **Smith River National Recreation Area** surround the green Smith River, one of the last undammed rivers in California. In summer, you might be able to kayak the scenic Smith for just $6 (*see* Park Activities *in* Redwood National and State Parks, *above*). The river valleys are truly spectacular, though the area's proximity to the coast and its warm summer weather sometimes mean overcrowding.

SHORT HIKES • For an accelerated introduction to the coastal and inland botany of the Smith River National Recreation Area, try the 1-mi round-trip **Myrtle Creek Trail.** This self-guided interpretive trail runs along an old mining ditch near a gurgling stream, passing from a thick redwood forest into a more open pine forest. The trailhead is just off Hwy. 199, 7 mi west of Gasquet; park on the left-hand side just past the South Fork Bridge, cross 199 on foot and walk west 20 yards.

For a short, scenic hike through some of the forest's most impressive—and most secluded—stands of ancient Douglas fir, spend some time along Groves Prairie Creek, on the mile-long **Groves Prairie Trail.** The flat terrain makes for easy hiking, and the 4,200-ft elevation means the air stays pleasantly cool in summer. To reach the trailhead, head east on Hwy. 299 for 11 mi, turn left on Denny Road (Trinity County Road 402), and after 2 mi, turn left onto Forest Service Road 4. After 7 mi turn right on Road

7N04, cross over Groves Prairie Creek (7 mi), and turn right onto Road 7N04P, which leads to the picnic area and trailhead.

Locals rave about the trek to **Mill Creek Lake.** From Hwy. 96 about 1 mi north of Hoopa, take Big Hill Road east 12 mi and follow signs to Mill Creek. It's only about a half-hour hike from the trailhead to the beautiful lake (stocked annually with rainbow trout). You need a wilderness permit for this one, so stop in before you go at the Lower Trinity Ranger District (Hwy. 96, ½ mi north of Willow Creek, tel. 530/629–2118), open Monday–Saturday 8–4:30, with shorter winter hours.

LONGER HIKES • The **South Kelsey Trail** was created in 1851 as an army supply artery from Crescent City to Fort Jones, 200 mi east. Today, it provides over 16 mi of challenging hiking through the Siskiyou Wilderness. After following the south fork of the Smith River, you reach the 5,775-ft Baldy Peak, from which you can view the Pacific Ocean, the rugged Siskiyou Backbone, the Marble Mountains, and Mount Shasta to the east on a clear day. There's plenty of water along the way—boil or filter it before drinking. You can cover the whole trail to Harrington Lake in a great three- to four-day hike. To reach the trailhead from Crescent City, take Hwy. 199 east 7 mi to South Fork Road (County Rd. 427), turn right, and go 14 mi to Forest Service Road 15 (there's no sign, so watch your mileage). Turn right, go 3 mi, turn left onto Forest Service Road 15N39, and follow signs.

For a taste of the Siskiyou Wilderness without trekking through the backcountry for days, the **Buck Lake Trail** takes you by towering old-growth firs on the way to a mountain lake where you can enjoy excellent fishing in almost total solitude. From Gasquet, travel 8 mi north on Hwy. 199, turn right onto Forest Service Road 17N05 (Little Jones Creek Rd.) for 10 mi, then left on Road 6N02 (Big Basin Rd.) for 3½ mi to the Doe Flat Trailhead. Park and take the Doe Flat Trail for 1 mi to the Buck Lake Trail.

FOREST ACTIVITIES

For all their labor, the prospectors who came to California more than 100 years ago to pluck gold nuggets from the Klamath River missed a mother lode. Today's technology allows for more thorough excavations, and each winter run-off washes more wealth down the river. Anyone can get into the action for less than $35 and an afternoon on the banks. You can buy the minimum amount of equipment at the **New 49ers** (27 Davis Rd., Happy Camp, tel. 530/493–2012); a half-hour videotape at the store explains the equipment. Use your new wares anywhere that doesn't have NO TRESPASSING signs tacked to trees.

BIKING

Bicycles are not allowed on trails in the wilderness areas, but most backcountry trails in the three forests are great for mountain biking. Bring your own wheels, because no one in this region rents bikes. In summer, use Hwys. 3 and 96 as departure points for bike trips. The roads are not crowded, and cycling through picturesque mining towns like Callahan, Etna, Seiad Valley, and Somes Bar is a great way to travel. The free, fat biking packet available at the Klamath National Forest ranger station (*see* Visitor Information, *above*) is an excellent resource, listing 17 rides. A moderate, scenic 13-mi ride starts at the far end of Elk Creek Bridge in Happy Camp. You follow asphalt and dirt roads to Sulphur Springs Campground (*see* Camping, *above*), where you can go for a swim. **Shasta Valley Bikes** (215 W. Miner St., Yreka, tel. 530/842–7701), 70 mi east of Happy Camp, can help with mechanical problems.

RAFTING

Most people don't want to make the long trek north to the Klamath River in Happy Camp, but if you do you'll be rewarded with 30 mi of rafting over Class II and III rapids. Local guide **Bryan Joosten** (Box 319, Happy Camp 96039, tel. 530/493–2207) takes private parties on two- to three-day trips for $75 a person per day—he'll negotiate day trips for groups smaller than four if he's not busy. If you want to cut the cost, you can bring your own meals, but his are worth the price. (*See* Redwood National and State Parks, *above,* for the lowdown on cheap ranger-led rafting on the Klamath.)

For a guided white-water adventure on the Trinity River, try the **Bigfoot Rafting Company** (Hwy. 299, behind Cinnabar Sam's in Willow Creek, tel. 530/629–2263 or 800/722–2223). It offers full-day trips for $60 (including lunch) and half-day trips for $39. You can also rent rafts for self-guided Class I and II tours (starting at $36 per day); the staff will recommend good spots. **Tish Tang Gorge** is a 3½-hour Class II run beginning at Big Rock outside of Willow Creek, and ending at the Tish Tang Campground (*see* Camping, *above*). Bigfoot also rents inflatable kayaks ($25 per person) and other river gear and you can arrange for shuttle service to a put-in point (so you can end up at your car) for $6–$15.

5 THE CASCADES

UPDATED BY MARTY OLMSTEAD

Overlooked by international tourists and California residents alike, the north inland expanse of pine forests, alpine mountains, and dormant volcanoes is perhaps the best place in the state to get away from crowds and into the great outdoors. To the east the Sierra Nevadas gradually melt into the Cascade range, to the west the forests and mountain lakes of the Coast Ranges play host to the mythical Bigfoot, and looming over it all is mystical **Mt. Shasta,** whose shadow stretches across the Sacramento Valley. There's never a dull vista—except when you're traveling up I–5, the major highway that runs north–south through the region.

While the oppressively hot mining and shipping towns along I–5—including Red Bluff, Redding, and Yreka—make convenient bases, you'll want to leave the Sacramento Valley as soon as possible and head into the mountains. East of Red Bluff you can enjoy university-sponsored cultural events in **Chico** or opt for solitary hiking or biking in the gentle mountains of the **Plumas National Forest.** West of Red Bluff lies backpacker's paradise: The **Yolla Bolly–Middle Eel Wilderness** beckons with absolute seclusion and pristine mountain streams.

The Cascade Range, formed by volcanic eruptions, begins in Northern California and climbs through Oregon and onward into Washington. It is part of the "Ring of Fire," a virtually contiguous chain of andesitic volcanoes that circle the Pacific Ocean from South America, on through to Alaska, Japan, the Philippines, and New Zealand. Almost as an apology for Redding's dreariness, the area east of it—including **Lassen Volcanic National Park** and **Lava Beds National Monument**—offers an unforgettable taste of the desolate but subtly beautiful volcanic landscape that marks northeastern California. You can explore miles of deserted lava bed caves on your own with just a flashlight in hand. To the west lies the dramatic **Trinity Alps Wilderness**; and in the north, towns like **Dunsmuir** and **McCloud** offer bits of the area's past while keeping a refreshingly rural feel.

Moving from west to east across the region, the weather becomes drier and drier. The Trinity Alps' coastal proximity keeps them wet, while their elevation keeps them snow-capped year-round. The Sacramento Valley is more arid, and in the summer temperatures often soar to over 100°F. The western Cascades are drier than the Trinities but are also dusted with snow year-round. East of the Cascades lies the high desert of Nevada. Keep in mind that some opening hours and rates in the Cascades may change with the seasons and that the timing of the seasons can vary from year to year and region to region.

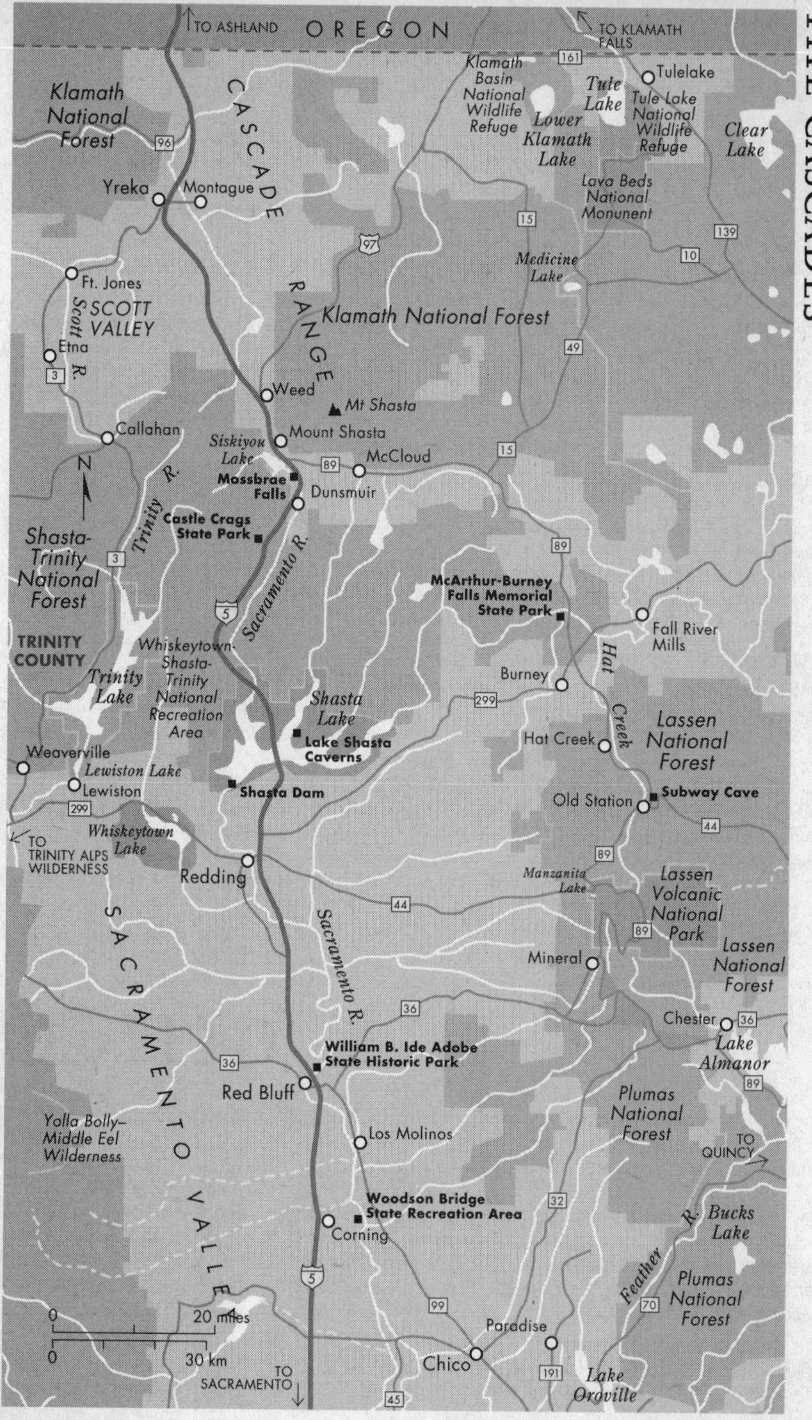

TO ASHLAND
OREGON
TO KLAMATH FALLS
161
Klamath Basin National Wildlife Refuge
Tulelake
Tule Lake
Tule Lake National Wildlife Refuge
Lower Klamath Lake
Clear Lake
Klamath National Forest
96
CASCADE RANGE
Yreka
Montague
Lava Beds National Monument
15
139
97
10
Medicine Lake
Ft. Jones
Scott R.
SCOTT VALLEY
Klamath National Forest
Etna
49
3
Weed
Mt Shasta
Callahan
Siskiyou Lake
Mount Shasta
McCloud
89
15
N
Mossbrae Falls
Dunsmuir
Trinity R.
Castle Crags State Park
Sacramento R.
89
Shasta-Trinity National Forest
3
McArthur-Burney Falls Memorial State Park
5
Fall River Mills
TRINITY COUNTY
Whiskeytown-Shasta-Trinity National Recreation Area
Hat Creek
Trinity Lake
Burney
Shasta Lake
299
Lassen National Forest
Lake Shasta Caverns
Hat Creek
Weaverville
Lewiston Lake
Lewiston
Shasta Dam
Old Station
Subway Cave
299
44
TO TRINITY ALPS WILDERNESS
Whiskeytown Lake
89
Redding
Manzanita Lake
Lassen Volcanic National Park
44
Sacramento R.
SACRAMENTO VALLEY
89
Lassen National Forest
Mineral
36
Chester
36
Lake Almanor
36
William B. Ide Adobe State Historic Park
89
Red Bluff
Plumas National Forest
Yolla Bolly–Middle Eel Wilderness
Los Molinos
TO QUINCY
32
Woodson Bridge State Recreation Area
Feather R.
Bucks Lake
Corning
5
Plumas National Forest
99
70
0
20 miles
Paradise
0
30 km
Chico
191
TO SACRAMENTO
Lake Oroville
45

COMING AND GOING

BY BUS

Greyhound (tel. 530/241–2070 or 800/231–2222) serves Marysville, Chico, Red Bluff, Redding, Weed, and Yreka along I–5, en route from San Francisco to Seattle and points beyond. From San Francisco, the fare is about $38 one-way to Redding or $27 one-way to Chico. You'll pay $33 one-way to Red Bluff; and from here Mt. Lassen Motor Transit (*see* Coming and Going *in* Red Bluff, *below*) can get you near Lassen Volcanic National Park. **Green Tortoise** (*see* Funky Deals on Wheels *box in* Chapter 1) makes a stop in Redding, an access point for Lassen Volcanic National Park, Lake Shasta, and Shasta National Forest.

BY CAR

From the southland or the Bay Area, bomb straight up the monotonous, concrete **I–5,** which runs the length of the state. You may not see noteworthy scenery, but at least you'll get to the mountains quickly. It should take about three hours to reach Chico from San Francisco, 3½ hours to reach Redding, and 4½ hours to arrive at Mount Shasta. The Oregon border is less than an hour north of Shasta. If you're driving, getting around is relatively hassle-free. With the exception of the occasional trundling logging truck, traffic is light, and except for Hwy. 89 in Lassen Volcanic National Park—which is usually shut down November–June due to snow—road closures are rare.

CAR RENTALS • Redding offers the biggest selection of rental agencies, including **Avis** (tel. 530/221–2855 or 800/331–1212) and **Hertz** (tel. 530/221–4620 or 800/654–3131). The agencies are concentrated at the Redding Municipal Airport and near the corner of Cypress and Hilltop avenues. Avis offers lower rates in the winter and a discount for AAA members. Expect to pay about $35 a day on weekends and $250 a week. **California Compacts Rent-a-Car** has an outlet between Mount Shasta and Dunsmuir (tel. 530/926–2519) and at a car wash in Yreka (tel. 530/842–7379). Their rates are slightly lower than the chains—$25 a day and $156 a week, with 70 mi free per day or 700 mi free per week.

BY TRAIN

Amtrak (tel. 800/872–7245) travels between San Francisco and Seattle, stopping in Chico, Redding, Dunsmuir, and Klamath Falls. The best option for those traveling round-trip is to ride the train to Sacramento and then take the Amtrak bus to Chico ($48 round-trip) or Redding ($59 round-trip). If you leave the Bay Area in the morning, you'll be in Redding by afternoon. On the other hand, the six-hour direct train trip straight to Redding will cost $54–$94 round-trip. On top of that, the train leaves at 8:30 PM and you arrive in Redding at 2:45 AM. Your best bet when heading north is to take the same train further north to Dunsmuir (*see* Dunsmuir, *below*) near Mount Shasta. The round-trip costs $72–$122 and takes eight hours (you arrive at 4:35 AM). There's an excellent restaurant across from the train platform and a town with character awaiting you when business hours arrive. None of the Amtrak stations between Sacramento and Klamath Falls, Oregon, are staffed—there is just the train platform and no lockers. Verify departure times and prices before you go.

CHICO

A simple trip on Hwy. 99 north from Sacramento or south from Red Bluff allows you to dodge the monotony of I–5. Better yet, it delivers you to the friendly town of Chico (also accessible from Hwy. 32 east off I–5), home of one of the liveliest branches of the California State University system and gateway to the Plumas National Forest. During the school year, activity in Chico revolves around the Cal State campus, which is north of downtown and attracts a lot of attention for being party-heavy. The agricultural town is slow and sleepy in the hot summers. April is one of the best times to visit; the weather is good and the campus hosts all sorts of cultural events: powwows, luaus, Asian cultural events, and the International Festival. For more information, call 530/898-5701. On Memorial Day weekend the city puts on the **Silver Dollar Festival,** which is like a county fair. The atmosphere here is friendly and diverse, if a bit upscale.

The **Chico Chamber of Commerce** (500 Main St., at 5th St., tel. 530/891–5556 or 800/852–8570), open weekdays 9–5:30 and May–September on Saturday 10–3, houses the visitor center and stocks the "Visitor Guide," a seasonal listing with maps, hot spots, sights, and strolls. The tourist map of Chico costs $1, but there are free brochures with walking tours, bicycle tours, and restaurant guides. The *Chico News and Review,* free every Thursday and available all over town (gas stations, grocery stores, et cetera), has a great weekly calendar. Chico's **Stonewall Alliance** (341 Broadway, Suite 300, at 4th St., tel. 530/893–3338 for recorded information, 530/893–3336 for the office) is the local resource center for all kinds of gay–friendly groups that have events throughout the year.

COMING AND GOING

The **Greyhound** (450 Orange St.., tel. 530/343–8266 or 800/231–2222) station is staffed from 8:30 to 4, but there are no lockers. **Amtrak** (W. 5th and Orange Sts., tel. 800/872–7245) is unstaffed except when trains arrive and depart. The best way to travel around the area, however, is by car. Hwys. 99 and 32, respectively, form the upper and lower boundaries of the university and downtown areas. You can get around the downtown and university areas on foot, but summer heat may have you looking for an oasis. Chico is generally safe, but avoid walking alone at night around campus and Bidwell Park.

Chico is also a great town for bicycling. Just carry lots of water in summer, and walk your bike on campus paths (but not roads) from 7:30 AM to 10 PM—or risk a fine. You can rent bikes at **Campus Bicycles** (*see* Outdoor Activities, *below*). The city buses, run by the **Chico Area Transit System (CATS)/Butte County Transit** (tel. 530/342–0221 or 800/266–6883), have bike racks on the back and can take you from downtown to the outer reaches of Bidwell Park, as well as to some neighboring towns. The fare is 75¢ within the city.

WHERE TO SLEEP

Chico would be a lot friendlier for budget travelers if it had more cheap sleeps. The **Rio Lindo Motel** (2324 Esplanade, tel. 530/342–7555) is one of your better options; brown-tone rooms go for $35 and include the use of a pool. Simple is too fancy a word for the accommodations at the **Safari Garden Motel** (2532 The Esplanade, tel. 530/343—3201 or 800/624—0166), but they are clean and in a good location, plus they have coffee makers and two can sleep in one bed for $45. Downtown is another place to look for budget lodging; try the clean, well-maintained **Thunderbird Lodge** (715 Main St., between 7th and 8th Sts., tel. 530/343–7911), which gives you a $37 double ($34 in winter) near most of what Chico has to offer. There are several cheaper motels nearby, but the sacrifice in quality isn't worth the little money you'll save. Prices go up $10 during graduation weekend in May. Remember to add 10% tax to the room price.

CAMPING

Woodson Bridge State Recreation Area. Right on the Sacramento River, 30 mi north of Chico, this campground has trails (watch out for poison oak) and shady cottonwoods but is best known as a fishing haven—especially for king salmon—from October through April. Conveniences include modern showers, toilets, and fire rings. There are six canoe-in sites. *25340 South Ave., Corning, between I-5 and Hwy. 99, tel. 530/839–2112.*

FOOD

Most of the worthwhile restaurants in town are downtown. **Café Paulo** (642 W. 5th St., at Ivy St., tel. 530/343–0704) stays open until 8 in the summer and offers outdoor seating and culinary delights like the turkey pesto sandwich or spinach salad ($5). For late-night fare, head to **Pizza Face** (128 W. 2nd St., tel. 530/345–3223). **Chada Thai Cuisine** (117B W. 2nd. St., tel. 530/342-7121) is a subterranean restaurant specializing in curries, seafood, and noodles; the best values are vegetarian ($6–$9). No lunch Sunday. Breakfast is a very Chico thing to do. **Oy Vey Café** (146 W. 2nd St., tel. 530/891–6710) serves bagels with veggie cream cheese ($1.75) and the "Jewish Nightmare" omelet ($5), filled with ham or sausage and cheese. There are plenty of major grocery stores around town, but for organic and bulk foods—as well as a deli—stop by **Chico Natural Foods** (818 Main St., at 8th St., tel. 530/891–1713), open 8–9 Monday–Saturday, Sunday 10–6. Better yet, shop at the **Farmers' Market** (tel. 530/893–3276), June–October on Wednesday (10 AM–2 PM, at NVP Mall) or year-round on Saturday (7:30 AM–1 PM, at 2nd and Wall Sts.).

Café Sandino. Organic ingredients make this vegetarian (mostly vegan) restaurant fresh as well as healthy. The spicy tofu tamale ($4.50 lunch, $7.50 dinner), the Del Sol tamale (with artichoke hearts, olives, and sun-dried tomatoes; $5–$7), and the curried vegetable burrito ($5–$6) should satisfy even the carnivores in your group. *817 Main St., between W. 8th and 9th Sts., tel. 530/894-6515. 3 blocks from central plaza. Closed Sun.*

Jasco's California Café. Chico's vigorous competition for your pizza dollar is exemplified in the upscale choices at this high-ceiling, brick-walled corner upstairs in the old Phoenix Building. A small version with spicy chicken is $10.50. For budget meals, try a whopper sandwich like the turkey with avocado ($7), which comes with soup or salad. *300 Broadway, tel. 530/899-8075. Closed Sunday.*

CAFÉS

For a more bohemian scene, try two excellent coffeehouses: the small, hippie-ish **Mana Java** (138 Broadway, between 1st and 2nd Sts., tel. 530/343-1844) has magazines and soy drinks, while stylish **Café Siena** (128 Broadway, between 1st and 2nd Sts., tel. 530/345-7745) has local artists' work on its exposed brick walls. Both serve killer house coffee ($1), and Siena features live bands most weeknights at 8.

WORTH SEEING

Chico's "parents," General John and Annie Bidwell, were pioneers known for their hospitality and generosity. Their legacy is all around—from the land the university occupies to the innumerable trees that shade the town on hot days. Daily tours ($3) are given of the **Bidwell Mansion,** their Victorian-era, Italian villa-style home, which hosted such historical figures as General Sherman and John Muir. *525 Esplanade, at 1st Ave., tel. 530/895-6144. Open weekdays 10-5. Tours on the hour 10-4.*

At Chico's **Sierra Nevada Brewing Company** (1075 E. 20th St., tel. 530/345-2739), free tours (Tues.-Fri. at 2:30, Sat. noon-3) walk you through the mashing, boiling, fermenting, and bottling routine—and include free samples.

An outdoorsy way to enjoy Chico is to head straight for **Bidwell Park,** which runs through the town from Hwy. 99 and E. 8th Street east for about 10 mi and provides plenty of opportunities for urban swimming, biking, and in-line skating. It's swamped with families on summer weekends. Skip the little Nature Center, which has a depressing exhibit of caged owls and snakes. **One Mile** and **Five Mile** are swimming beaches along Big Chico Creek, located (not surprisingly) 1 and 5 mi from downtown. For a real Chico experience, head to **Upper Park** beyond Five Mile, where bathers and tanners go au naturel. Otherwise, grab your mountain bike (and required helmet) and head onto the **Bidwell Park North Rim Trail** in Upper Park or south of town to the nearby **Honey Run,** which leads east from Chico.

AFTER DARK

During summer and fall, the popular Friday night **Concerts in the Downtown City Plaza** feature excellent jazz, rock, bluegrass, and classical musicians. On Tuesday night the plaza features local alternative bands. For Saturday listings call 530/345-6500; for Tuesday shows, 530/899-0491. The **Pageant Theater** (351 E. 6th St., 2 blocks from central plaza, tel. 530/343-0663) shows foreign and domestic films at out-of-this-world prices: tickets are $4.50 ($2.50 on Monday).

BARS

The scene seems divided by factions—fraternities and hippies—but with this many bars, at least there's no lack of choice. Loyalties shift rapidly, but some of the most popular watering holes are funky **Juanita's** (126 W. 2nd St., tel. 530/893-4125), which has live music in the college vein Tuesday-Sunday, and trendy **Lasalle's** (229 Broadway, tel. 530/893-1891), popular with students looking for music from swing to bluegrass and rock 'n' roll. The **Sierra Nevada Brewing Company** (*see above*) also has a bar. **Madison Bear Garden** (316 W. 2nd St., tel. 530/891-1639), a Chico icon, resembles a huge frat house. Every square inch of wall and ceiling is plastered with some sort of bric-a-brac and by day it shows all the effects of all that partying.

The Brick Works. Chico's largest entertainment complex has dancing to top-40 on Friday and Saturday from 9 to 1:45. Friday is Buck Night—$1 cover, $1 beer, $1 well drinks. Live bands are presented frequently, usually starting at about 9:30. *2nd and Wall Sts., tel. 530/895—7700.*

Rascals. Chico's only gay and lesbian bar has a friendly crowd that comes to dance to a live DJ Friday-Sunday 6 PM-2 AM. Beware the "beer bust," Sunday 7 PM-10 PM. *900 Cherry St., at 9th St., tel. 530/893-0900.*

Tres Hombres. More chic than the average Chico night spot, this downtown restaurant/bar has live dance music, with local favorites usually appearing on Thursday. *100 Broadway, tel. 530/342—0425.*

OUTDOOR ACTIVITIES

Bidwell Park (*see* Worth Seeing, *above*) is the center of your outdoor world with its 15 mi of paved biking, jogging, and in-line skating trails. You can rent a bike for $20 a day ($10 per half day on weekdays) at **Campus Bicycles** (501 Main St., at 5th St., tel. 530/345–2081). Pick up the park's free bike-trail map and check out the **Upper Park** and **North Rim** trails, which give you a good few hours' workout in the dry foothills. **Sports Ltd.** (240 Main St., tel. 530/894–1110 or 800/875–4583) charges $15 for the day, $20 if you keep the bike and helmet overnight. After your ride, you can swim in Big Chico Creek (*see* Worth Seeing, *above*). Inner tubing down the Sacramento river is a major Chico activity—rent tubes at, of all places, **Ray's Liquors** (207 Walnut St. at 2nd, tel. 916/343–3249).

Lassen Volcanic National Park (*see below*) is less than 2 hours away, as are the Plumas National Forest (*see* Near Chico, *below*) and Lake Oroville. Year-round, Chico State's **Adventure Outings** (in Chico State's Bell Memorial Union, tel. 530/898–4011), open Tuesday–Friday in summer, plans daylong and overnight hiking, skiing, and rafting trips; nonstudents can sign up if space is available. The Yahi group of the **Sierra Club** (3552 Elk Ave., tel. 530/899–1234) is also very active and plans outings year-round.

NEAR CHICO

Five miles out on Honey Run Road is America's only three-level covered bridge, Honey Run Covered Bridge.

QUINCY

Sixteen mi south of Chico, Hwy. 70 veers northeast off Hwy. 149, passes Lake Oroville, and climbs through the striking Feather River canyon, eventually reaching the town of Quincy (a 2 hr drive). In autumn the trees put on the West Coast's closest approximation of the East's fall foliage. The canyon drive follows the clear, tumbling course of the Feather River, and any pullout provides a great picnic spot.

Quincy (elevation 3,500 ft) is an excellent base for all sorts of activities in the area—not too touristy but with friendly folks who aren't afraid to talk to an out-of-towner. The town amenities and outdoor opportunities are among the best you'll find in Plumas County. The place to find out about all the possibilities to explore—and there are plenty—is the **Plumas County Visitor's Bureau** (Hwy. 70, ¼-mile northwest of Quincy, tel. 530/283–6345 or 800/326–2247), open summer weekdays 8–5, until 7 on Friday; Sat. 10–6; winter weekdays 8–5. The free *Plumas County Visitors Guide* is an amazing source of information on outdoor activities, lodging, and town events. The $2 Plumas County map is worth it for the city maps and detailed topo map. If you have time, check out the **Plumas County Museum**'s (500 Jackson St., behind courthouse, tel. 530/283–6320) Maidu basketry exhibit and other seasonal displays. The museum ($1) is open weekdays 8–5 and May–September, on weekends 10–4. Across the street, the restored 1878 Coburn–Variel Home and gardens will make you wish for Victorian home-building to regain popularity. The **Plumas County Transit System** (522 Lawrence St., tel. 530/283–2538) connects Quincy with Chester to the north. Fares range from 50¢ to $3.

WHERE TO SLEEP • If you've been holding out for a splurge in a Victorian B&B, spend a night at Quincy's **Feather Bed** (542 Jackson St., tel. 530/283–0102). You'll have bikes you can borrow, a full breakfast fresh from the garden, and a library with maps and guidebooks on nearby places to visit. Spacious rooms with private baths start at $75. For something more modest, try the homey, knotty pine cabins and duplexes of the **Pine Hill Motel** (Hwy. 70, just north of downtown, tel. 530/283–1670), with views of the meadow and mountains. All rooms ($42–$52) have private baths, phones, and microwaves, and some have kitchenettes ($5 extra). (For camping, *see* Plumas National Forest, *below.*)

FOOD • Buy groceries at the 24-hour **Safeway** (20 E. Main St., tel. 530/283–1404) or the **Quincy Natural Foods** co-op (30 Harbison St., at Main St., tel. 530/283–3528), great for organic produce and bulk staples. The co-op is open weekdays 10–6:30, Saturday 11–5, Sunday 11–4. The **Morning Thunder Café** (557 Lawrence St., tel. 530/283–1310) serves serious breakfasts daily 7–2. A Frisbee-size blueberry pancake ($2.25) might do it for you; if not, consider a three-egg omelet ($5–$6). For dinner ($10–$16), locals are wild about **Moon's** (497 Lawrence St., tel. 530/283–0765), an Italian restaurant with daily specials and a verdant outdoor patio.

It's worth trekking 10 mi west of Quincy on Bucks Lake Road to the **Ten-Two Bar Café** (8270 Bucks Lake Rd, behind the Meadow Valley Country Store, tel. 530/283–1366). It may look like a roadside diner, but the chef here cooks up some of the most exquisite food in California. Locals make pilgrimages for dishes like Szechuan salmon ($15) and such daily pasta specials as sundried tomato pasta linguine ($14) that they eat outside next to the creek. Reservations are a must on weekends. The café is closed Tuesday and Wednesday in winter.

PLUMAS NATIONAL FOREST

In the huge Plumas National Forest, which surrounds Quincy on all sides, the Sierra Nevada range to the south merges with the Cascade range to the north. Here you're treated to the beauty of Douglas firs, ponderosa pines, massive granite corridors in the Feather River canyon, and a number of dramatic waterfalls—the tallest of which is Feather Falls at 640 ft. The falls are most impressive during spring. Take lots of water and mosquito repellent if you plan to hike the **Feather Falls Trail,** a hilly, 7-mi round-trip hike to the falls (3–4 hrs total); it begins on Trailhead Road, off Lumpkin Road 1 mi west of the town of Feather Falls near the western end of Lake Oroville. Get a map ($3) marking roads, trails, and campsites from the **Plumas National Forest Supervisor's Office** (159 Lawrence St., tel. 530/283–2050, open weekdays 8–5) in Quincy. Just north of Quincy on Hwy. 70 is the **Mt. Hough** (pronounced "Huff") **Ranger District** (39696 Hwy. 70., tel. 530/283–0555, open weekdays 8–4:30); these two offices are your best sources of information on the national forest and its dozens of campgrounds.

A popular and easy trail from **Silver Lake** to Gold Lake starts at the Silver Lake campground, north off Bucks Creek Road, just west of the town of Meadow Valley. Turn north on the dirt road (24N29X) to get to the campground, and once there go past the wooden dock to find the marked trailhead. Gold Lake is about 1½-mi away, and you can take a swim when you arrive. The round-trip is about 2½ hours, with the option of adding on the .9 mi **Granite Gap** trail going to Mud Lake, Rock Lake, and the Pacific Crest Trail.

Mountain-bike routes literally cover Plumas National Forest, but bikes are not allowed on the Pacific Crest Trail or in the Bucks Lake or Caribou wildernesses. One easy trail is the **Summit–Bucks Creek Loop,** which starts at Bucks Creek Road, about 14 mi west of Quincy, just past the Whitehorse Campground. The 3.8-mi ride takes about an hour and gives you great views of meadows and dense forests. For more biking, ask for free maps at the Mt. Hough Ranger Station (*see above*). The best place to rent bikes in the Plumas Forest area is from the legendary **Bodfish Bicycles** (152 Main St., tel. 530/258–2338) in Chester, about an hour north of Quincy near Lake Almanor. Bikes go for $25 a day, $6 an hour with a two-hour minimum. Promoting "quiet mountain sports" that are easy on the terrain, they generate invaluable cycling books—like *Cycling the California Outback* ($11)—renowned for their maps, trail descriptions, history, and advice.

In winter the gentle hills and meadows here are perfect for cross-country skiing. You can rent skis ($10 a day) or snowshoes ($15 a day) from Quincy's **Sierra Mountain Sports** (501 W. Main St., tel. 530/283–2323) or from Bodfish Bicycles (*see above*) for comparable prices.

CAMPING • As with all national forests, primitive camping is free anywhere within Plumas's boundaries. You'll need a free campfire permit, however, which is good all summer. Pick one up at the **Mt. Hough Ranger District** or the **Plumas National Forest Supervisor's Office** (*see above*). Developed campgrounds are generally closed November–March.

Two mi north of Belden on Hwy. 70, about 25 mi west of Quincy, you'll find three campgrounds along **Caribou Road** (look for the Caribou Café and General Store): Gansner Bar, North Fork, and Queen Lily. Sites at all three go for $11 a night, have water and toilets, and are first-come, first-served. There are several turnouts by the river between these campgrounds in which many people camp for free. The secluded, tree-lined campgrounds, open April–October, have access to a trout-fishing creek. There are $3 hot showers and café-diner–type food at the **Caribou Corner Café** (corner Hwy. 70 and Caribou, 2 mi east of Belden, tel. 530/283–0956).

About 10 mi farther east on Hwy. 70, you'll see signs for **Hallstead Campground** on your right. Here, 20 wooded sites with flush toilets go for $9 a night. A quarter mi east from the campground is the **Twain General Store** (130 Twain Store Rd., off Hwy. 70, tel. 530/283–2130), where you can take a hot shower for $2.

The **Whitehorse Campground,** 15 mi west of Quincy on Bucks Lake Road, has 20 huge sites ($11) in a beautiful cedar grove, with pit toilets, fire pits, tables, and running water. Several smaller nearby lakes, such as **Snake Lake,** have free primitive campgrounds (no drinking water)—ask at the Mt. Hough Ranger Station about availability.

RED BLUFF

Like many Northern California towns built on ranching, mining, or logging, Red Bluff retains a mix of Victorian gentility and Old West roughness, with some modern suburban mediocrity thrown in for good measure. Red Bluff got its start in 1850 as a shipping center providing steamer service on the Sacramento River to San Francisco. Today, the city is small, working class, and not used to much tourist traffic, but it's the best place to shop for essentials before heading eastward off the beaten path. The **Red Bluff–Tehama County Chamber of Commerce** (100 Main St., tel. 530/527–6220 or 800/655–6225), open weekdays 8:30–5 (Mon. until 4, Fri. until 4:30), has information on the whole area. If you're heading west off I–5 toward Weaverville, north toward Mt. Shasta, or east to Mt. Lassen, stop here for brochures and maps.

If you can get out onto the Sacramento River, trout, steelhead, salmon, catfish, and bass are here for the casting. Get your permit ($9.20 a day, $16.50 a year), tackle, and gear at **Sports Wild** (327 Walnut St., tel. 530/527–3225). For a taste of local culture, check out April's **Red Bluff Round-Up** (tel. 530/527–5534), the world's third-largest rodeo (seats $6–$18).

Plumas County was so named by 1920s fur trappers who saw Native Americans wearing blankets with feathers woven in them.

COMING AND GOING

Mt. Lassen Motor Transit (22503 Sunbright Ave., 3½ mi south of Antelope Blvd., tel. 530/529–2722 or 800/427–9553) offers sporadic trips from Red Bluff to Reno (4 hrs, $25 one-way). They'll also take you to Mineral, or the southwest entrance to Lassen Volcanic National Park (2 hrs, $6.85 one-way), though from there you're on your own as far as getting around the park. They pick up at the **Greyhound** station (Montgomery Rd., tel. 530/527–0434 or 800/231–2222) at 8 AM sharp Monday–Saturday. For information on Greyhound buses, *see* Coming and Going at the beginning of the chapter. When all is said and done, it's easier to get around in a rental car. **Enterprise Rent-a-Car** (570 Antelope Blvd., at Chester St., tel. 530/529–0177) offers 100 free mi a day, with rates starting at $15 a day.

Downtown Red Bluff lies mainly to the west of I–5. The town centers around the intersection of **Main Street,** which runs north–south (paralleling I–5), and east–west **Antelope Boulevard.** Antelope Boulevard heads east and becomes Hwy. 36, the main road to Mt. Lassen. The Victorian neighborhoods that are the town's claim to fame are to the west of Main Street, within walking distance of the business district.

WHERE TO SLEEP

There's a cluster of nondescript budget motels (all with pools) off Main Street and Antelope Boulevard on either side of I–5. The quiet **Lamplighter Lodge** (210 S. Main St., near Chamber of Commerce, tel. 530/527–1150) has huge, tasteful rooms with queen-size beds, free breakfast, and HBO for $42. **King's Lodge** (38 Antelope Blvd., tel. 530/527–6020 or 800/426–5655) has doubles that overlook the Sacramento River for $37. It fills up the third week in June for the Junior Rodeo at the fairgrounds. The **Sky Terrace Motel** (99 Main St., north of Willow St., tel. 530/527–4145) wins the prize for the cheapest rooms—and the management with the least social graces—with clean and spacious doubles at $30. Add 10% city tax to all prices.

CAMPING

Lake Red Bluff Campground, next to the Tehama-Colusa Fish Facility, has 30 large sites ($10) with access to the Sacramento River and great fishing. The site has some amenities, but be prepared for dusty, exposed sites—and mosquitoes galore—in the hot summer months. *South end of Sale La., off Antelope Blvd., tel. 530/527–2813. Drinking water, fire stands, flush toilets, showers. Closed Dec.–Mar.*

FOOD

The **Snack Box** (257 Main St., at Ash St., tel. 530/529–0227), open daily 7–2, tries a little too hard for the "quaint" look but serves one of the best breakfasts around (which isn't really saying much). Omelets are $5–$6.50, and a stack of buttermilk pancakes is $3.45. Expect a wait on weekends. **Francisco's Mexican Restaurant** (480 Antelope Blvd., tel. 530/527–5311) serves bland Mexican food like the

Memo Special ($6), a quesadilla with lettuce and red or green chile; or the Cuco Special ($5–$6.50), a tostada with spiced meat, shrimp, or vegetarian chili. Szechuan and Mandarin lunch specials at the **Great Wok Restaurant** (490 Antelope Blvd., tel. 530/529–5558) run $3.75–$4.25, and they've got vegetarian selections—a comparative rarity here in beef country. You can buy fresh produce June–October at the **farmers' market,** held Saturday 8–noon in the City Park parking lot.

WORTH SEEING

For a taste of the past, check out Red Bluff's Victorian homes (for a free map of some of the notable ones, ask at the Chamber of Commerce) or do a little antique hunting on Main Street between Antelope and Walnut streets. At the **Kelly-Griggs House Museum** (311 Washington St., at Ash St., tel. 530/527–1129), open Thursday–Sunday 1–4, informative docents lead you on a tour (donation requested) through the renovated rooms of an early 1800's house with antique furnishings and Victorian-garbed mannequins. Be sure to call the museum before showing up—it keeps erratic hours.

Take a dip in the Sacramento River at **William B. Ide Adobe State Historic Park.** In 1846 Ide led a revolt against the Mexican government and for a few weeks was president of the Bear Flag Republic (*see* The Bear Flag Republic *box in* Chapter 3). The U.S. government soon moved in to claim the land as theirs. The shade from the oaks is welcome, and the colors at dusk will make you appreciate Mr. Ide's choice of a homestead. Summer programs re-create life in the 1850s. *21659 Adobe Rd., tel. 530/529–8599. From I-5 north of Red Bluff, take Wilcox Golf Rd. exit and follow signs. Admission free. Open daily 8–5.*

AFTER DARK

Bars are few and far between, and they're all either a little bit honky-tonk or a little bit rock 'n' roll. If you have your heart set on a night out, try the dimly lit **Palomino Room** (723 Main St., tel. 530/527–5470), where the locals are likely to stop talking, turn their heads, and shamelessly stare when a tourist struts in. They offer free live entertainment (country and rock) Friday and Saturday; closed Sunday. The **Brunswick** (343 Walnut St., tel. 530/527–1992), built in 1886, is the oldest bar in Tehama county and a place to shoot pool, reacquaint yourself with classic rock, and rub shoulders with locals. On summer Mondays at 8 PM, catch an old-fashioned band concert at the **Red Bluff City Park,** near the Chamber of Commerce.

NEAR RED BLUFF

YOLLA BOLLY–MIDDLE EEL WILDERNESS

The 155,080-acre Yolla Bolly–Middle Eel Wilderness is perfect for an escape from civilization, especially since there's no public transportation to get you there. About 70 mi from Red Bluff and 230 mi from San Francisco, the wilderness spans the northern sector of Mendocino National Forest, the southern portion of Shasta-Trinity National Forest, and the southeastern part of Six Rivers National Forest. Elevations here range from 2,500 ft to 8,100 ft. "Yo-la" means snow-covered and "Bo-li" high peak in the local Wintu Indian language, apt names when you look up and notice snow-capped **Mount Linn** (elevation 8,092 ft) and its smaller neighbors, **Harvey Peak** (7,361 ft) and **Solomon Peak** (7,581 ft). The wilderness, lush with pine, offers a welcome change from overdeveloped campgrounds, crowded trails, and the din of motorized vehicles. If you're willing to rough it (good drinking water is scarce in summer so carry plenty in), the wilderness will overwhelm you with its stunning mountain peaks, streams, high altitude lakes, fir and pine trees, and incredible wildflowers (at their height in July).

BASICS • Because it's managed by three different forest agencies, the most useful information comes from the agency closest to where you plan to go. Call any of the stations listed here to find the closest place (this list is not comprehensive). For the south side, the nearest station is the **Corning Ranger District** (22000 Corning Rd., ½ mi west of I-5, tel. 530/824–5196. Open weekdays 8–4:30), in the small town of Corning, about 20 mi south of Red Bluff on I-5. For the north you can go to the **Yolla Bolla Ranger District** (Hwy. 36, Platina, 50 mi west of Red Bluff, tel. 530/352–4211), open weekdays 8–4:30, north of the wilderness on Hwy. 36. Get weather and hiking information, a free (and mandatory) campfire permit, and a topo map of the area ($3). Be sure to sign in (and out) at trailhead registries or at the ranger station, leaving a record of when you enter the wilderness and when you plan to leave it.

WHEN TO GO • The lower altitudes of the wilderness are accessible year-round, but everything above 6,000 ft can be snowed-in October–June. The area near the Covelo Ranger District (tel. 707/983–

6118) tends to open earlier than the Corning District's area. Still, July and August are the best months to go: Streams and lakes are at their highest levels, wildflowers are in bloom, and the weather is most consistently cooperative then. You can usually visit May–October, but water becomes scarce late-August–September. At all times, you'll need to bring a water-purifying system and to pack in (and out) everything. The rough logging roads that traverse the wilderness are almost never plowed in winter, so you'll probably be out of luck then. In fact, be ready for lots of unpaved roads whenever and wherever you go—this is a wilderness after all.

CAMPING • Though there are established campgrounds here, you can camp anywhere you'd like on government land if you have a free campfire permit from the ranger station. Check in with the ranger stations to find out where there's piped water, but be prepared to find and treat your own. **Kingsley Glade Campground** (6 sites, open June–Oct.), off Road M2 about 5 mi south of Cold Springs on Road 24N01, is free, and you'll find tables, fire rings, pit toilets, and piped water. A moderate 5-mi hike leads from the adjacent trailhead to **Thomes Creek,** one of the best spots in the area for trout fishing and swimming. The **Ides Cove Campground,** blessed with rings and pit toilets, is the most accessible free campground, less than a mi west of Cold Springs, off Road M2 (take Road M22 for 7 mi). The road is unpaved but well maintained and suitable for most vehicles.

HIKING • Many of the trails are strenuous and at high elevation, so plan ahead to minimize the possibility of unwelcome surprises. Thanks to budget cuts, trails are less well maintained than they have been in the past—it's crucial to have a good map and know how to use it. To access the southeast region of the wilderness, use the **Ides Cove Trailhead,** 56 mi from Corning; a bit further southwest, use the **Green Springs Trailhead,** 65 mi away. For Ides Cove, take Corning/Paskenta Road (County Rd. A9) west to Paskenta, head straight when the road forks on Road M2 to Cold Springs Station, and take another right at the fork on Road M22. For Green Springs, follow the directions above to Paskenta and turn left in Paskenta over the bridge to Road M4 to connect to the M2 (above Government Flat, near Cherry Lake), then head north to the Green Springs Trailhead. Vandalism and fallen signs are a problem here (not to mention narrow, bumpy logging roads)—it's recommended that you check in at an information station to get directions, an official map, and a road log that lists the recommended drives to the trailheads in detail.

The Ides Cove Trailhead offers access to the **Ides Cove Loop National Recreation Trail.** Day hikers should try the moderate 5- to 6-mi loop that passes by **Square Lake,** a popular fishing hole, and then heads north to Burnt Camp and east back to the trailhead, where you can camp for free. More serious hikers will want to do the full loop, which continues past Square Lake to **Long Lake** (with dispersed camping) and meets the **Thomes Trail.** The loop then moves north and east, passing Cedar Basin and Burnt Camp before heading back. The moderately strenuous trip (about 8–9 mi) is a great all-day or overnight hike, but bring plenty of water.

LASSEN VOLCANIC NATIONAL PARK

A link in a volcanic mountain chain that includes Lava Beds National Monument and Oregon's Crater Lake, Lassen Volcanic National Park is one of the finest and most accessible places to explore the glories of mud pots, plug domes, sulfur springs, calderas, and lava pinnacles. Despite its fascinating terrain and crystalline alpine lakes, Lassen is overshadowed by its big-name neighbors Yosemite and Yellowstone and happily remains one of the least crowded national parks. Its empty landscape (shaped by a now dormant volcano) may make you think you've landed on another planet, but you'll wonder why you never made the trip earlier.

Only one 32-mi road (Hwy. 89) runs through Lassen. This leaves most of the park for hiking, the primary activity here. Snow sometimes blocks the road all the way through June, but when the conditions are right, you'll find spectacular hiking, camping, cross-country skiing, and car touring. There are many options: fishing in Manzanita Lake or Hat Creek, snow tubing in Mineral, cross-country skiing on the Emigrant Trail, walking through subway-size subterranean lava tubes, exploring the sulfur geysers at Bumpass Hell, or heading off in the backcountry to Cinder Cone and Butte Lake.

MT. LASSEN BLOWS ITS TOP

On Memorial Day 1914, Mt. Lassen issued the first in a string of eruptions that would continue almost seven years. By March 1915, 150 small, lavaless rumblings had been counted. Then, on May 19, 1915, lava began welling up within the crater. Three days later, the volcano erupted in its largest explosion in recorded history, sending debris 30,000 ft into the air and a 1,000-ft-wide river of lava (still visible from Manzanita Lake) down the east and west sides of the mountain. Northeast of the peak, a section of trees 1 mi wide and 3 mi long was blown completely flat by the explosion. (Still called the Devastated Area, the patch has since been reforested.)

When the eruptions stopped, the lava on top cooled quickly, in essence plugging up the volcano. Lassen is by no means extinct—most days, if you hike up to the peak and down into the crater, you can see steam rising out of vents in the floor.

BASICS

VISITOR INFORMATION

All visitors receive the *Lassen Park Guide* newspaper, which includes detailed information on camping, fishing, hiking, backpacking, and naturalist programs. Highly recommended is the *Road Guide* ($4), which describes each of the 67 spots marked along Hwy. 89 as it goes through the park and includes useful photos and descriptions of the flora, fauna, and volcanic points of interest. **Lassen Park Headquarters** (38050 Hwy. 36 East, tel. 530/595–4444) is just west of Mineral on Hwy. 36 near the park's main entrance. Hours vary, so call ahead. This number has a useful 24-hour system that can give out trail, campground, and road conditions. Come here to get reports on campground availability and hiking conditions. Topo maps, trail guides, and history books are also available here; benefits go to the Park. The $2.50 *Lassen Trails Book* lists 34 trails of varying length and difficulty. The park entrance fee, good for seven days, is $5 per vehicle, $3 if you bike in (bikes are allowed only on the road; not on trails).

The two major entrances to the park are along Hwy. 89 at the southwest and northwest ends of the park (the other entrances are difficult gravel roads). Near the north entrance to the park, the **Loomis Museum and Seismograph Station** (tel. 530/595–4444, ext. 5180), open daily 9–5 mid-June–October, also offers visitor information. The nearby **Manzanita Lake Entrance Station** also has information but is open more sporadically.

Gay-friendly information on the area can be had from the **North Valley Alternative Lifestyle Support Group** (Box 126, Mineral, 96063, tel. 530/529–4105).

WHEN TO GO

Lassen is open year-round, though Hwy. 89, the only road through the park, usually closes from mid-October until Memorial Day or later due to snow pack. You'll find the most access to trails, campgrounds, and the road in August and September. Call or visit the park headquarters for the most current information. Just outside the park, winter brings great sledding, snowshoeing, and cross-country skiing. Hiking, camping, and water recreation predominate in summer. Spring wildflowers and autumn leaves round out the seasons. Even when it's boiling hot outside, you'll want a jacket if you climb to the top of the peak.

GENERAL STORES

Provisions near the park are slim. The best bet if you're coming from the north is the **Mineral Lodge Country Store** (Hwy. 36, Mineral, tel. 530/595–4422), open daily 8 AM–9 PM. It stocks basic groceries and camping supplies at minimart prices. If you're driving up from Plumas County in the south, try the town of Chester, about 35 mi east. The **Manzanita Lake Camper Store** (tel. 530/335–7557), in the north end of the park, stocks groceries, camping supplies, gasoline, propane, soup, and sandwiches. Again, expect to pay more than you're used to for the convenience. You can also shower (50¢ for 4 min) and wash and dry your clothes ($2 per load) here, as well as rent bikes ($11 per day). The showers and laundry are open 24-hours, the store is open daily 9–5 at the beginning and end of the season, 8–8 in the summer. If you're coming from I–5, Red Bluff (*see above*) is the best place to stock up.

COMING AND GOING

Mt. Lassen Motor Transit (*see* Coming and Going *in* Red Bluff, *above*) is the only public transport to the park, and even that only gets you to Mineral, or the southern entrance on Hwy. 36, 1 mi west of Hwy. 89. The cost is $6.50 each way; the bus leaves Red Bluff Monday–Saturday mornings at 8 AM, arriving in Mineral in the late morning. Unfortunately, you won't find any transportation within the park, except your car, bike, or feet; and the Motor Transit does not allow bikes on board. If you're driving from Red Bluff, follow Hwy. 36 east for 48 mi to the park's southern entrance just beyond Mineral. From Redding, follow Hwy. 44 east for 49 mi to the park's northern entrance at Manzanita Lake.

Driving through the park on Hwy. 89 is strictly a summer activity. If anyone tells you it's just a bunch of scenery, drive through anyway; it is, but what scenery. The list of road markers in the *Lassen Park Guide* (*see* Basics, *above*) details the peaks, lakes, and volcanic topography. The 30-plus-mi drive will take you a couple of hours thanks to winding, hilly roads, and a 35 mph speed limit.

WHERE TO SLEEP

Most visitors who don't camp stay just outside the park or in nearby towns like Red Bluff or Redding off I–5, Burney on Hwy. 299, and Chester on Hwy. 36.

Adam's Hat Creek Resort. This well-known fishing resort has been around for decades. In winter there's cross-country skiing 2 mi up the road, and in summer Hat Creek babbles through it. You can stay in the seven-room motel ($45), or in summer rent one of 10 two-person cabins ($50) that will remind you of places you've seen in antique black-and-white photos. The cabins have kitchens. Many of the resort's loyalists reserve a year ahead, but you may get lucky by just showing up. *Hwy. 44/89, Old Station, 11 mi northeast of park's north entrance, tel. 530/335–7121.*

Lassen Mineral Lodge. This 20-room motel has a pool, tennis courts, a restaurant, a bar, a general store, and a ski shop that's open 8–5 when there's snow (cross-country skis rent for $16). There are no phones or TVs in any of the rooms. In summer and on winter holidays, you should reserve a month or two ahead. Doubles start at $70. They also run the adjoining **Volcano Country Camping** (tel. 530/595–3347), which has four tent sites with water, showers, and laundry, each $15 for two people. *Hwy. 36, Mineral, 9 mi from park's south entrance, tel. 530/595–4422.*

Rim Rock Ranch. The Padillas, who own and run the Rim Rock Ranch and General Store, are sweet enough to restore your faith in humanity, and their lodge is in a peaceful meadow with a creek nearby. A double (there are two) runs as little as $33 a night. They have 10 cabins of varying sizes, sleeping 2–12 people and including kitchen, bath, and linens (no maid service). The cabins are closed mid-October–mid-April, except for two newer ones that open the first week in April. A cabin for two costs $40 a night, $50 for three to four people. *13275 Hwy. 89, Old Station, tel. 530/335–7114. To make reservations when the cabins are closed, call 530/663—9016. 14 mi northeast of park's northern entrance. Reservations advised Apr.–mid-Oct.*

CAMPING

Backcountry camping is free with a wilderness permit, obtainable at park headquarters, the southwest information station, the Manzanita Lake entrance station, or the Loomis Museum (*see* Visitor Information, *above*). You can also apply for a permit by mail (Box 100, Mineral, CA 96063–0100). Applications are granted immediately in person, but by mail allow two weeks for processing (they can also hold your permit at the park headquarters). There are seven developed campgrounds in Lassen, all of which operate on a first-come, first-served basis.

INSIDE THE PARK • Manzanita Lake Campground ($12), just inside the park's northern entrance, is the largest (179 sites) and most accessible of Lassen's developed campgrounds. It can be crowded, especially with groups, but has toilets, water, and the Camper Store. It's set in a grove adjacent to Manzanita Lake. You can hike from the nearby trailhead to Chaos Crags Lake (*see* Hiking, *below*) and when you return, get a hot shower (the only such facilities in the park) at the Manzanita Lake Camper Store (*see* General Stores, *above*). When the park gets snowed in, Manzanita Lake is the first campground to get dug out.

Near the southern entrance, **Southwest** ($10) is for tents only, though RVs can park nearby. Most of the 21 sites are on a wooded ridge with great views east to Mt. Canard. Across the road from the Lassen Summer Chalet (*see* Food, *below*), Southwest offers flush toilets, piped water, tables, and fire pits. If it's open, though, a better choice is **Summit Lake** ($12 at 46 northern sites; $10 at 48 southern sites), 12 mi southeast from Manzanita. Not as many people come here, even though the tree-lined sites are quite large and secluded (*see* Hiking, *below*).

NEAR THE PARK • There are over 40 official campgrounds in **Lassen National Forest** (which surrounds the park), with sites $5–12 a night. In the northern area of the forest, 15 mi from the park's northern entrance and near McArthur–Burney Falls, the 46 sites at **Cave Campground** ($11, open year-round) sit just across the road from the Subway Caves and lava tubes (*see* Hat Creek and Burney Falls *in* Near Lassen, *below*). The tree-lined campground isn't very private, but the sunny, large sites are more attractive than those at **Hat Creek Campground,** a few miles south on Hwy. 89. You shouldn't have trouble finding a spot at one of Hat Creek's 75 sites ($9). Naturally, the creek and its great fishing are not far off.

If you want to stay on the park's southern side, check out the 32 sites ($9) at **Gurnsey Creek Campground,** off Hwy. 89, 14 mi west of Chester. Rarely crowded and usually quiet, well-shaded Gurnsey Creek remains cool even in summer. It provides drinking water, toilets, and fire pits. In addition to the official forest campgrounds, you're free to pull off on any road and set up camp (14 days is the maximum stay in one spot). Backcountry exploration is allowed with wilderness permits, but campers should keep an eye on the unpredictable winter weather and heed avalanche warnings.

FOOD

INSIDE THE PARK

Stock up on picnic supplies in nearby towns like Mineral or Chester before you enter the park. The **Lassen Summer Chalet Café** (tel. 530/595–3376), at the park's southern entrance, offers burgers, sandwiches, and breakfasts for less than $5 and an outdoor patio with views of Brokeoff Mountain and Diamond Peak. It's open May–October, daily 9–6, sometimes longer. Unfortunately, you won't find a grocery store here.

NEAR THE PARK

In addition to the restaurants in distant Red Bluff and Redding, the smaller towns closer to the park also offer a few places to eat. Chester, about 35 mi from the south end of the park, has some good choices, including **Mi Casita** (686 Main St., tel. 530/258–1879) and **Ming's Dynasty** (605 Main St., tel. 530/258–2420). The **Mineral Lodge Restaurant and Bar** (tel. 530/595–4422), on Hwy. 36, 9 mi west of the southern park entrance, serves up basic, but expensive, American fare.

About 10 mi south of the park and 25 mi east of Chester on Hwy. 36 are two isolated eateries. The **Black Forest Lodge Restaurant** (off Hwy. 36, in Mill Creek, tel. 530/258–2941) serves large portions of German specialties like sauerbraten ($14) and Wiener schnitzel ($13.50); it is closed Monday. A stone's throw farther east on Hwy. 36 is the **St. Bernard Lodge** (tel. 530/258–3382), offering homemade bread, chili ($5), soup ($3), a full bar, and large portions. For what the owner swears is a low-calorie burger alternative, you can try the half-pound buffalo burger ($7.50); it's closed Tuesday–Wednesday.

EXPLORING MT. LASSEN

NATURALIST PROGRAMS

The park offers free naturalist programs on the stars, volcanic activity, Native American customs, and flora and fauna. The guided tours, hikes, and nature walks really do contribute a lot to your understanding of the park. Programs are usually held late June–late August (January–April for snowshoe programs). Check at park headquarters or one of the ranger stations for current listings (*see* Basics, *above*).

HIKING

A number of popular trails take you past striking volcanic phenomena. Remember that the earth's crust here can be very thin and the mud below can be boiling, so stay on established trails. Very spectacular is the **Lassen Peak Hike,** a 5-mi round-trip (4½ hrs) beginning at 8,500 ft and climbing a strenuous 2,000 ft to the top of the 10,457-ft peak and back. Pick up the trailhead at Road Marker 22. The trail, crowded only by Lassen standards, is totally exposed, so you have to bring sunscreen, a jacket, and plenty of water. Near the top the trail can be snowy, even in July. Near the park's southern entrance, at Road Marker 2, an easier trail heads up **Brokeoff Mountain** past **Forest Lake.** Brokeoff is 1,200 ft shorter than Lassen, and the path to its peak isn't nearly as traveled. What's more, the trail (7½-mi round-trip, 4½ hrs) is shaded until the very top, so you get virtually the same amazing view without the extremes of wind and sun along the way.

Also worthwhile is the 3-mi **Bumpass Hell Trail** (2–3 hrs round-trip), which starts by Road Marker 17 and features the park's largest thermal areas, hot springs, steam vents, and boiling mud pots. Kendall Vanhook Bumpass (pronounced "Bump-us") was a trail guide who in 1865 stepped through the thin crust and burned a leg so badly it had to be removed. One of the easiest trails is the scenic **Manzanita Lake Hike.** Figure on 1½ hours for the 1½-mi walk around the lake. The park also has self-guided ½-mi **Devastated Trail,** beginning at Road Marker 44, with sweeping views of the dramatic terrain created by the massive mudflow resulting from lava-melted snow during the 1915 eruption.

Those wanting extended backcountry hikes to the lakes of Butte, Swan, Horseshoe, or Juniper in the park's eastern sector should head to the **Summit Lake trailhead** south of the Summit Lake Campground (*see above*). The moderately strenuous 8-mi, 6-hour (one-way) trail east to Horseshoe Lake gives you access to the **Pacific Crest Trail,** which runs north–south through the park. Remember to get your free fire permit from the ranger station before heading out.

PARK ACTIVITIES

In addition to biking the 30-mi stretch of Hwy. 89 that runs through the park (you can rent a cycle at Bodfish Bicycles in Chester, *see* Plumas National Forest, *above*), you can try bird-watching, swimming in Manzanita Lake, or fishing (license required, some lakes are closed to fishing, some are catch and release only). The best fishing opportunity is outside the park in Hat Creek, which gets stocked regularly. See Mr. Padilla at the Rim Rock Ranch (*see* Where to Sleep, *above*) for tackle and tips. For information on boat rental and other fishing services, contact the town of Chester's Chamber of Commerce (tel. 530/258–2426 or 800/350–4838).

SKIING

The winter *Lassen Park Guide* lists touring routes for Nordic skiers and snowshoers. Especially popular are the **Manzanita Lake** area, off Hwy. 44 at the north end of the park, and the **Lassen Winter Sports Area** (west of the southwest information center). The moderate 10-mi **Manzanita Creek Trail,** which climbs to the base of Crescent Cliffs, and the easier 6-mi **Emigrant Trail,** which ascends a portion of Table Mountain, are two well-marked treks that depart from Manzanita Lake. Remember that winter weather can be extreme—there's always the danger of avalanche. Snow campers should check in with a ranger to be sure they have the necessary equipment, including extra food in case of an emergency. The Lassen Mineral Lodge (*see* Where to Sleep, *above*) will rent you complete cross-country getup (skis, boots, and poles) for $14 a day. And they can point you to trails (all free) suited to your ability level. Ski rentals can also be had at Bodfish Bicycles (*see above*) or the **Sports Nut** (208 Main St., tel. 530/258–3327) in Chester.

SNOWSHOEING

Naturalist-led snowshoe walks, which emphasize the park's winter ecology and geologic history, are held Saturday at 1:30 PM January 6–April 6. Meet at the snowshoeing sign at the Lassen Chalet at the park's southern entrance. Snowshoes are provided free of charge, although a $1 donation is requested for their upkeep.

SNOW TUBING AND SLEDDING

Next to the Lassen Mineral Lodge in Mineral (*see* Where to Sleep, *above*) is a beautiful slope, popular with sledders and snow tubers. The process for using it is unusual: Since no one can afford to assume responsibility for the land (the liability risk is too great), people have to buy (instead of rent) sleds and inner tubes and then sell them back at the end of the day. The Lassen Mineral Lodge sells sledding disks for $15 (buyback is $10); and the Mineral Gas Mart and Deli (Hwy. 36, tel. 530/595–3222) across the street sells inner tubes for $10 and buys them back (if they still hold air) for $5.

NEAR LASSEN

LASSEN NATIONAL FOREST

The 1.2 million-acre Lassen National Forest, which surrounds the park, has its own schedule of activities and resources. Pick up the *Lassen National Forest Summer* or *Winter Guide* at ranger stations or in Lassen Volcanic National Park. Two ranger stations near the park are the **Almanor Ranger District Office,** in Chester (tel. 530/258–2141), and the **Hat Creek Ranger District Office** (Fall River Mills, off Hwy. 299, 15 mi northeast of Burney, tel. 530/336–5521), both open weekdays 8–4:30. The park also contains three significant wilderness areas. **Caribou Wilderness** to the east is high (6,000 ft) and opens later in the year but is cooler in summer; **Ishi Wilderness** to the south is best visited in spring (in summer it's downright hot); and there is **Thousand Lakes Wilderness** to the north, which is another good summer destination. These California wilderness areas are so little trampled that wilderness permits are not yet required. Thousand Lakes Wilderness is the most accessible of the three and has 22 mi of maintained trails, which wind through volcanic formations, stands of pine and fir, and, of course, plenty of lakes.

Three trailheads mark the main roads through the Thousand Lakes Wilderness. Whichever one you take, stop in first at Hat Creek (*see above*) to pick up a trail map. Turning west off Hwy. 89 at the Ashpan Snowmobile Park (a few miles south of Old Station), you can follow Forest Service Road 16 northwest for 11 mi to the turnoff for Magee Trailhead (go right on Road 32N48 north for 1½ mi to trailhead). From here, the **Magee Peak Trail** runs for 3.7 difficult miles over Magee Peak (8,550 ft) to Magee Lake. This is the highest elevation trail in the wilderness, and it may be closed by snow until mid-July. At the peak, you'll see the Sacramento Valley to the south and the northern Coast Ranges to the west.

HAT CREEK AND BURNEY FALLS

North of the park on Hwy. 89, you'll find world-class stream fishing along Hat Creek, which is stocked regularly by the state. Pick up a fishing permit and equipment in nearby Burney if you don't have them already. You can bring a flashlight (you need *at least* one good one) and explore the third mile long, subway-size corridor of **Subway Cave** (Hwy. 89, north of Old Station). The cave is well marked from Hwy. 89, free, and open all year. This was once a river of molten lava. Though the upper surface cooled and hardened on contact with the outside air, the lava it insulated underneath continued to flow and then finally drained, leaving behind caves made of tubes of volcanic rock. Even on baking summer days, the average temperature inside is 46°F, so bring a jacket. Allegedly the local Atsugewi (Hat Creek) people believed that an "ape man" lived in the cave—Bigfoot's relation? Look out for water puddles below as you walk through and take care not to hit your head above.

McArthur–Burney Falls Memorial State Park (Hwy. 89, 6 mi north of Hwy. 299 junction, tel. 530/335–2777) features one attraction—the 129-ft falls—dwarfed only by the souvenir shops. The falls are quite spectacular (and refreshing on a hot day), but crowds make this a less-than-relaxing picnic spot. This is a park for folks who like their wilderness trails asphalt-paved. People in huge RVs crowd the campground. It's $5 to drive your car in, but if you park outside you can walk in for free and take the 3-mi loop trail to check out the falls. Other short trails take you to the nearby Pioneer Cemetery and Lake Britten. The **McArthur–Burney Falls Campground** has 112 sites with showers for $15–$16. They're full all summer; reserve through Destinet (tel. 800/444–7275).

REDDING

After the straight-as-an-arrow monotony of I–5, many travelers are seduced by the fast-food joints, gas stations, and motels that beckon from the Hilltop Drive/Cypress Avenue exit. Then Redding is seared into their memory by the heat, which shoots past 100°F nearly all summer long. Though it's larger than most towns south on I–5, Redding is not much more than an exhaust-clogged intersection and the transport hub of Northern California; it offers little in the way of unique sights.

The city is useful as a base for trips out into the surrounding wilderness; you can rent bikes, boats, fishing gear, rafts, and just about anything else here. The **Redding Convention and Visitors Bureau** (777 Auditorium Dr., west of I–5 on Hwy. 299, tel. 530/225–4100 or 800/874–7562) has information on Redding and the surrounding area. It's open weekdays 8–5 and weekends 9–5. You can pick up a free map to help you navigate the city streets. The main business area is a maze of one-way streets; you're better off parking and walking around to check out the "sights."

COMING AND GOING

Redding is about 3 hours north of Sacramento on I–5, 4 hours north of San Francisco (I–80 east to I–505 north to I–5), and 2½ hours south of the Oregon border. (For bus and train travel, *see* Coming and Going at the beginning of the chapter.) The **Greyhound** station (1315 Butte St., at Pine St. west of downtown mall, tel. 530/241–2531 or 800/231–2222) offers lockers for $1 a day. The **Amtrak** station (west of downtown mall on southwest corner of California and Yuba Sts., tel. 800/872–7245) is unstaffed.

Within the city, I–5 is like the needle of a compass pointing north toward Mt. Shasta. The Sacramento River winds through the center of town, heading roughly northwest–southeast. Cypress Avenue to the south and Hwy. 299 to the north are the main east–west drags. The municipal bus service, **The Redding Area Bus Authority** (tel. 530/241–2877), serves the city and the nearby towns of Burney (near the Lassen National Forest), Anderson, and Shasta Lake. Fare is 75¢ for anywhere within Redding. Buses run weekdays 6:30–7:30, Saturday 9:30–7:30.

WHERE TO SLEEP

The good news is that you can get a clean double room for around $30 (not including the 10% room tax), but the bad news is there isn't much in the way of character. On Hilltop Drive, which runs parallel to I–5 just to the east, there's a good selection of national chains. The motels on Market and Pine streets, off Hwy. 299 west of I–5, vary greatly in quality and price. Try the friendly **Shasta Lodge** (1245 Pine St., tel. 530/243–6133) for tidy doubles at $39. Across the street, the **Stardust Inn** (1200 Pine St., tel. 530/241–6121) has pretty much the same rooms starting at $28. The free *California Traveler Discount Guide* (available at the Redding Visitors Bureau and at visitor centers all over the state) offers discounts at many fine chain motels throughout the state, including the **Colony Inn** (2731 Bechelli La., off I–5 at Cypress exit, tel. 530/223–1935 or 800/354–5222). Doubles with queen-size beds, bathtubs, and free Showtime go for $34. There's camping 15 minutes west of town at Whiskeytown Lake and 20 minutes north at Shasta Lake (*see* Near Redding, *below*).

FOOD

There are as many major grocery stores as there are car dealerships in Redding. For organic and bulk food, shop at **Orchard Nutrition** (221 Locust St., tel. 530/244–9141). If you're in town on Tuesday or Saturday 7–1, visit the fine **Farmers' Market** (take Hilltop Dr. exit off I–5 past Sears to McFrugals parking lot). Redding's size brings with it an array of mediocre budget dining options. **The Silver Saddle** (401 E. Cypress, at Beverly St., tel. 530/223–6588) is a good place for that cheap, home-style power breakfast with a pancake, egg twins, triplet sausage links, hash browns, and toast ($5). For coffee (try the $2.50 raspberry mocha), make a beeline for the café **Serendipity** (236 Hartnell Ave., at Parkview Ave., tel. 530/223–4497) in the Cobblestone Court strip mall or **Serendipity II** (167 Lake Blvd., tel. 530/244–3780). Both are closed on Sunday.

Buz's Crab Stand. You can't miss the bright orange roof with contrasting blue seascape mural. They continue the nautical motif ahead with fish 'n' chips made with the likes of charbroiled red snapper ($6), calamari ($6), or salmon ($7). There's also a fish market here. *2159 East St., at Cypress Ave., tel. 530/243–2120.*

El Papagayo. They serve what passes for Mexican food in these parts (it's pretty generic), but it's the local choice for burritos and enchiladas. The burrito supreme ($8) is a meat monster—your choice of chicken, beef, or chile verde. Vegetarians can feel good about the beans, prepared with canola oil, or the Vegetarian Burrito ($7). *460 N. Market St., north of river, tel. 530/243–2493.*

WORTH SEEING

Although there's certainly a lot worth seeing *around* Redding, even locals admit that little is actually *in* Redding. If you find yourself with an afternoon to kill, visit the museums in **Caldwell Park,** along the Sacramento River Trail (*see* Outdoor Activities, *below*). The curators of the **Redding Museum of Art and History** (56 Quartz Hill Rd., Caldwell Park, tel. 530/243–8801) consistently assemble high quality shows, both historical and fine art in nature. The museum is open Tuesday–Sunday 10–5; admission is $1.

AFTER DARK

For a listing of movies, theater, special events, and what little nightlife there is in Redding, read the "Spectrum," published every Thursday by the city's newspaper *(The Record Searchlight)*, or *After Five*, a monthly newspaper. Both are available free at the visitor's bureau. Your best bet is to catch up on those movies you meant to see last year at the **UA Cascade Theater** (1731 Market St., south of Hwy. 299, tel. 530/365–4591). Tickets are $1.50 daily and the 1935 art deco building is worth a look, even if just from the outside.

OUTDOOR ACTIVITIES

Rafting or canoeing on the **Sacramento River** is inviting on a hot summer's day, and in winter snow is only an hour's drive away in Lassen Volcanic National Park (Hwy. 44 takes you to the Manzanita Lake entrance). **Park Marina Raft Rentals** (2515 Park Marina Dr., tel. 530/246–8388) will set you up with a two-person raft ($29) for a lazy 12-mi, four-hour float downriver. They even provide shuttle service back to the parking area. No boats are rented after 1:30 PM. **Alpine Outfitters Sports and Bike** (950 Hilltop Dr., tel. 530/221–7333) has skis ($10 a day), in-line skates ($8 a day), bikes ($19 a day), and assorted camping equipment. They'll give you plenty of information on hiking and rafting in the area. You can swim in the Sacramento River, but the water comes from the bottom of the 602-ft Shasta Dam and is cold, so you might want to head to Whiskeytown (*see below*).

NEAR REDDING

WHISKEYTOWN LAKE

Eight mi west of Redding on Hwy. 299 is Whiskeytown Lake, created by the diversion of water from the Trinity River to California's Central Valley. Find your own place to plunge into the lake, or drive to the swimming areas at **Brandy Creek** (JFK Memorial Dr., on south shore) or **Oak Bottom** (Hwy. 299, 4½ mi west of visitor center). You can get fishing permits ($8.40 per day or $25 for the season) and rent canoes ($28 for 4 hrs) or pedal boats ($20 for 4 hrs) at the **Oak Bottom Marina** (tel. 530/359–2269).

Avoid the crowded and dreary campground at Oak Bottom; instead go for one of the free primitive sites back in the hills, all accessible by car. Check in at the **Whiskeytown Visitor Information Center** (Hwy. 299 at Brandy Creek turnoff, tel. 530/246—1225, open daily 10–4) for a free map of the lake and a schedule of ranger-guided activities. Get your free backcountry camping permit a little farther south at the **Whiskeytown Unit's Park Headquarters** (tel. 530/241–6584, ext. 221; open weekdays 8–5, weekends 9–5). The best backcountry option is the camp at **Crystal Creek** at the far western edge of the park but lately many sites have been closed due to lack of funding—check before you go. It has a pit toilet, and crowds are never a problem. Get a hot shower back at the Oak Bottom Campground (75¢ for 5 min), or free, cold, outdoor showers at Brandy Creek.

For an easy and scenic hike following the lakeshore, take the **Davis Gulch Trail** (3 mi each way, about 3 hrs round-trip). You'll find the well-marked trailhead on the road to Brandy Creek, less than 1 mi south of the Whiskeytown Dam. There's also great mountain biking here. Pick up a free copy of "Mountain Bike Riding at Whiskeytown" at the visitor center. The steep and narrow **Boulder Creek Loop** (8½ mi, 6–7 hrs) climbs 1,100 ft for great views; the Boulder Creek Falls are 1 mi from the trailhead. Begin at the Carr Powerhouse, off Hwy. 299 at the northwest end of the lake.

SHASTA LAKE

The sprawling Shasta Lake, 10 mi north of Redding on I–5, is billed as a "full-service" lake (i.e., lots of annoying Jet Skis, motorboats, and all-terrain vehicles). It offers great fishing for rainbow trout, brown trout, and salmon and also supports about 12 pairs of resident bald eagles, the largest nesting population in California. You can rent patio boats, fishing boats, and jet skis at the 11 marinas and resorts around the lake, but expect to pay an arm and a leg. The main office for the Shasta Lake Ranger District (6543 Holiday Dr., tel. 530/275–1587) is in Redding.

The drive to the monstrous **Shasta Dam** at the southern end of the lake (take Central Valley/Shasta Dam exit west from I–5 and go 6 mi) affords great views of the second-largest dam in the country (602 ft by 3,460 ft), exceeded only by the Grand Coulee Dam in Washington. The **visitor center** (southeast of the dam, tel. 530/275–4463), open daily 8:30–5, has an exhibit showing what it took to build the dam. Take the informative and fascinating free tour, offered hourly 9–4; you ride in an elevator from the top of the dam all the way to the bottom.

Follow Gilman Road southeast 2 mi from McCloud Bridge Campground (*see* Camping, *below*) and you'll reach the marked trail to **Samwel Cave** (the road turns sharply to the left and the narrow path leads down and away to the right). The pools inside the cave are considered curative by the local Wintus, and this was an important ceremonial site. It's ½-mi to the cave mouth, where you can gambol for free around a large room (bring a flashlight). If you have the foresight to get a permit at the information center and pay a $10 key deposit, you can get into the locked deeper chambers and recesses, but it involves quite a bit of crawling on your belly, and you *must* have a headlamp or at least a flashlight (bring two just in case). The rock formations in the cave aren't as spectacular as those in Lake Shasta Caverns (*see above*), but here your visit doesn't cost anything. Pick up a free copy of "A Spelunker's Guide to Samwel Cave" at the information center.

BASICS • You'll find many maps and tourist brochures for the area at the well-stocked **Shasta Lake Information Center** (not the same as the visitor center listed above), as well as pamphlets on local sights. If you're headed to Samwel Cave (*see above*), don't forget to ask for the key. *From I–5, take Mountain Gate/Wonderland exit east, tel. 530/275–1589. Open daily 8:30–4.*

CAMPING • For roughing it, any of the 370 mi of shoreline offer free camping, though you'll need a campfire permit from the Shasta Lake Information Center May–October. **Gregory Beach** and **Beehive** are two good spots at the north end of the lake. RVs and boaters flock to the developed sites. Try the **McCloud Bridge Campground** (Gilman Rd., 17 mi east off I–5), with 20 sites ($11), water, and toilets, situated along a narrow finger on the northeast shore of the lake.

Unless you're going into Samwel Cave with rappelling equipment, find out from the ranger where the 75-ft pit is and stay clear.

TRINITY COUNTY

Trinity County's entire population—less than 15,000—is spread out over 3,222 forested, lake-dotted, snow-peaked square miles. In between Eureka and Redding and 278 mi north of San Francisco, Trinity County is a hidden gem with its small artist communities, amazingly lush forests, and small towns preserving their histories of logging and gold mining. Locals, living mostly along Hwy. 299, run the gamut from artists who find the locale inspirational to loggers, miners, and retirees. You won't find a stoplight or parking meter anywhere. Two scenic roads run through the area. The **Trinity Heritage Scenic Byway** begins in Weaverville and heads 111 mi northeast on Hwy. 3—past Trinity Lake, Coffee Creek, and other mining towns. Look for mountains scarred by the gold rush era's hydraulic mining (hillsides were literally washed away by huge water hoses in order to efficiently locate the gold). You can pick up a self-guided auto-tour map, with 20 designated stops, at the **Weaverville ranger office** (*see below*).

The county seat, **Weaverville,** is a gold-rush town with a brick- and wood-fronted Main Street. Here you can procure ingredients for a macrobiotic diet and meet friendly folks willing to talk about their good fortune to be living in such a pristine, comfortable place. Tourism keeps the economy going here; there's no industry to speak of, and the youth often move away from the area in search of jobs. Still, the populace here is pretty engaged with the outside world, many of them having moved from the crazy city to live in the beautiful countryside, and most have a story or two to tell about some old gold mine or fishing hole to explore.

About 15 mi from Weaverville, the blink-and-miss-it town of **Lewiston** still looks much as it did during the gold rush—most of the district is included in the National Registry of Historic Landmarks. The Trinity River (warm, gentle, and shallow here) runs through town, making Lewiston a perfect spot to begin your quest for king salmon.

In fact, if hiking, camping, rafting, or fishing is your thing, you've come to the right place. Like all wilderness areas, the half-million-acre **Trinity Alps Wilderness** does not permit mountain bikes or mechanized vehicles, but for this reason the wilderness plays host to some of the finest backpacking in the state. The **Trinity River,** which flows along Hwy. 299 west from Weaverville, has stretches that are white-knuckle Class VI whitewater and offers prime territory for rafting and kayaking, but you might find its secluded, sandy beaches and warm waters more conducive to lazing around and skinny-dipping than to wave running. This is also one of the best places in the continental United States for fly-fishing—not to mention gold dredging. Kevin Young (tel. 530/623–4227) in Weaverville teaches gold panning techniques and can help you avoid becoming a claim jumper.

BASICS

The **Trinity County Chamber of Commerce** is a great source of information for the whole area. Here you'll find a walking-tour brochure directing you to Weaverville's 116 points of historic interest or pamphlets for car touring in the surrounding area. *317 Main St., Weaverville, tel. 530/623–6101 or 800/421–7259. Open summer, Mon.–Sat. 8:30–4:30, sometimes longer; off-season, weekdays 8:30–4:30.*

COMING AND GOING

The only north–south thoroughfare in Trinity County is Hwy. 3. From the north, Hwy. 3 can be accessed off I–5 from Yreka. To the south, Hwy. 3 meets Hwy. 36 just south of Hayfork in the lower county. Hwy. 36 traverses the county and can be picked up out of Red Bluff from I–5 in the east or just south of Fortuna from Hwy. 101 in the west. A better and more scenic, if winding and slow, east–west route is Hwy. 299, accessed from Redding in the east or Arcata in the west. Greyhound and Amtrak both serve Yreka, Redding, Red Bluff, and Arcata but do not travel through the county.

WEAVERVILLE

Weaverville, 45 mi west of Redding on Hwy. 299, is experiencing the population reductions that come from there being very little industry in the area, but tourist dollars are helping the community stay on its feet. The **Highland Art Center** (503 Main St., tel. 530/623–5111) has rotating exhibits of arts in all media, items for sale by local artists, and some studios on site. You'll see plenty of small galleries, jewelry stores, and artists' studios if you walk around the downtown area.

Weaverville boasts California's oldest active (since 1874) Taoist temple. The **Joss House** (Oregon and Main Sts., tel. 530/623–5284, open July–Aug., daily 10–5, shorter hours in winter) served the Chinese immigrant population from all over the area. The word "Joss" is a corruption of the Portuguese word for God (Deos), a holdover from days when Europeans traveled to China to trade. The nearby museum is free, and you can look at the outside of the temple for free as well; the tour ($2) will clue you in to the significance and symbolism of the objects found inside, including the curved walkways, spirit screens, and why one side of the building isn't painted.

Though it's a tiny town, Weaverville's location at the junction of Hwys. 3 and 299 makes it a hub for travel through the northern Coast Ranges (*see* Chapter 4), especially the spectacular Trinity Alps (*see below*). The **Hays Book Store** (106 Main St., tel. 530/623–2516) has topo maps, hiking guides, and postcards, and **Brady's Sport Shop** (201 Main St., at Court Ham St., tel. 530/623–3121) carries basic camping and fishing gear. Starting July 1 and lasting for four event-packed days, Weaverville has a huge **Fourth of July** celebration.

WHERE TO SLEEP

For a campground near Weaverville, follow Hwy. 3 north out of town, go left on East Weaver Creek Road just past the little airport, and continue for 2 mi. You'll see the **East Weaver Creek Campground** on your left, with 15 sites ($6), water, fire rings, and pit toilets in a pine forest next to the creek. It's beautiful, open year-round, and noticeably cooler than downtown. Your best bet for access to the Trinity Alps Wilderness is **Pigeon Point Campground,** set on the Trinity River off Hwy. 299 about 10 mi west of town. The 10 sites ($5) have tables and firepits, but there's no potable water or showers. Arrive early to get one of the beautiful first-come, first-served riverside spots.

49er Motel. A replica of a gold mine and miner stand in front, making the building easy to pick out. Free local calls are a plus, as is the free Continental breakfast; there's also a lawn and barbecue area. The rooms here are standard and clean. Doubles are $40 in summer, $42 in winter, including use of the pool. *718 Main St., east of downtown, tel. 530/623–49ER, fax 530/623–2049. 13 rooms, all with bath.*

Weaverville Hotel. This 19th-century hotel retains a warm, old-time feeling—some of the rooms even have claw-foot tubs and views of the old Weaverville bandstand. Doubles start at $32. There's a homey sitting room you can relax in that incorporates the walls of an old shed. The charming proprietor, Emilie

Brady, has lots of ideas about what to do in Weaverville. *203 Main St., downtown, tel. 530/623–3121. Check in at Brady's Sport Shop downstairs. 8 rooms, 7 with bath.*

FOOD

Unlike many small towns in Northern California, Weaverville can satisfy your appetite without filling you up on bacon grease. The **Mountain Market Place** (222 Main St., tel. 530/623–2656) is a vegetarian (largely vegan) grocery, juice bar, and deli; closed Sunday. Get a tasty vegetarian burrito ($3) and a large fruit smoothie ($3) and enjoy them on the small back porch. A great place to go for a burger ($4–$6) and microbrew ($2–$3 a pint) is the **1855 Pacific Brewery Restaurant and Bar** (401 S. Main St., tel. 530/623–3000). **La Casita** (254 Main St., tel. 530/623–5797) is a small Mexican place with such fresh, cheap food as quesadillas (including one with roasted chili peppers) and many vegetarian choices.

La Grange Café. West of downtown, you'll get a sizable, tasty dinner at this relaxed Weaverville establishment. The inventive cuisine here is well known and unusual for the area: residents say, "If you want something strange, get it at the La Grange." Locals love Duane's Chicken (sautéed chicken breast with mushroom and wine sauce over California wheat berries; $9.50). Dinners ($8–$17) come with fresh sautéed vegetables, bread, and soup or salad. If gazpacho is the soup du jour, order it. *315 N. Main St., tel. 530/623–5325.*

LEWISTON

As small, historic California towns go, down-to-earth Lewiston, off Hwy. 299 between Redding and Weaverville, is a pretty inviting one. A sleepy town with the feel of an artists' colony, it has a relaxed friendliness that is welcoming. The best time to catch everything open is on weekends: You can picnic along the Trinity River, poke around the antiques in the **Country Peddler** (Turnpike and Deadwood Rds., tel. 530/778–3325 or 530/778–3876), check out the varied multimedia work of local artisan Michele de Oñate (Schoolhouse and Turnpike Rds., tel. 530/778–3323), or take a walking tour along historic **Deadwood Road.** The town boasts a whopping 20 structures listed in the National Register of Historic Places. In late May or early June over 200 vendors set up along Deadwood Road for Lewiston's **Peddler's Faire** (tel. 530/778–3325 or 530/623–6101). The day after Thanksgiving, the town lights up its old steel bridge and puts on a fair.

At **Lewiston Lake,** just south of Trinity Lake (follow Trinity Dam Blvd. to the end and turn right), you can hike, bike, camp, fish, and bird-watch. The 6-mi lakeside trail from Mary Smith Campground (*see* Where to Sleep, *below*) to Ackerman Campground on the northwest shore is perfect for hikers and bikers who want to get a quick lay of the land. Bald eagles and osprey nest in the area, and if you bring a good pair of binoculars, you may see them fighting over a trout or two. You can rent patio boats (covered rafts with seats, $10 per hr, 4 hr minimum) and fishing boats ($7 per hr, 4 hr minimum) at the **Pine Cove Marina** (255 Star Hwy., tel. 530/778–3770). Pick up fly-fishing gear at the **Trinity Fly Shop** (Old Lewiston Rd., tel. 530/623–6757), 1 mi from Hwy. 299 in Lewiston (first Lewiston exit coming east from Weaverville, second heading west from Redding).

WHERE TO SLEEP

There are several places to camp along Lewiston Lake. The sites at the four Forest Service campgrounds (contact the Weaverville Ranger District for information, tel. 530/623–2121) along the western shore of Lewiston Lake all go for less than $10. Close to downtown Lewiston, **Mary Smith Campground,** open May–November, has 18 sites ($8) on the lake's forested, hilly southern banks. You'll find vault toilets and water. A more secluded option, open all year, is the **East Weaver Campground,** north of Weaverville, 2 mi west of Hwy. 3 on E. Weaver Creek Rd. The 15 sites are $6 each, and there's water, toilets, and fire rings. Besides camping, a cheap option is the **Lewiston Valley Motel** (Trinity Dam Blvd., tel. 530/778–3942), which has 12 rooms that are often filled with anglers; reserve early in summer. Doubles go for $39 in summer, $35 in winter.

FOOD

Lewiston Hotel. A restaurant and bar since 1863, this is the town's centerpiece, though it no longer puts up travelers. The walls and ceilings are covered with knickknacks accumulated over the last 120 years, the bar specializes in microbrews ($1.75–$2.50 a bottle), and the humorous menu features embellished Lewiston history. Dishes like Recently Deceased Fish and Vegetarian à la Birkenstock ($7–$16) come with soup, salad, and homemade bread. *Deadwood Rd., tel. 530/778–3823. Restaurant closed for lunch and Mon.–Wed., bar open 3 PM–1 AM.*

GRIN AND BEAR IT

Chances are that all ursine beings will make themselves scarce when they hear your approach. If you do encounter a bear, keep a safe distance, avoid sudden movements, do not tease or play with it, and never get between a mom and her cubs. Make a slow detour, keeping upwind so the bear will smell you and (hopefully) avoid you.

Serendipity. It's cheaper than the Lewiston Hotel and a bit healthier. The menu features sandwiches and pizzas (including veggie, $5) and fresh, tart lemonade ($1). It serves three meals a day and the only espresso in town. The adjacent used bookstore is a good place to pick up some reading for the days you spend fishing. *Deadwood and Turnpike Rds., tel. 530/778–3856, open Wed.–Sun. 8–8.*

TRINITY ALPS WILDERNESS

While the Sierra Nevada and the neighboring Cascade ranges may stand a little larger, the Trinities hold their own in a beauty contest. The area is replete with glaciers, rushing rivers, boisterous waterfalls, granite peaks, alpine lakes, and, in spring, fields of glorious wildflowers. All of this is enhanced by lush fir and ponderosa pine forests. The only thing the area seems to be lacking is mobs of tourists. Only 45 mi west of Redding, just north of Hwy. 299, a winding road that requires slow driving and concentration, the Trinity Alps Wilderness has been discovered by surprisingly few. The Trinity Alps Wilderness hosts the highest concentration of black bears in California—one per square mile—and campers will need to use a little foresight. Pick up the "Bear Country Precautions" handout available at ranger stations for some helpful food storage tips (*see* Some Things to Bear in Mind *box in* Chapter 7). Also look out for wolverines, mountain lions, and . . . Bigfoot.

BASICS

Snowpack reaches 10–20 ft in the higher alps in winter and keeps trails closed through late June. Lower elevation trails generally open in May. In summer, temperatures are in the high 80s in higher elevations and 90s in lower elevations. Even in the heat of summer, sporadic thunderstorms break out and cool things down; bring rain gear. At night, temperatures can dip into the low 40s and 50s, even in August.

Visitors can contact the **Weaverville Ranger District** office on Hwy. 299 for necessary wilderness permits, current trail and weather conditions, trail maps, and other literature. *210 Main St., just north of downtown, tel. 530/623–2121. Open summer, Mon.–Sat. 8–5; off-season, weekdays 8–4:30.*

COMING AND GOING

"Major" cities near the wilderness include **Trinity Center** and **Coffee Creek** to the east and **Big Bar** in the southwest corner, but the only place nearby that even qualifies as a village or town is **Weaverville.** Anywhere else you're not likely to find much more than a minimart, a greasy diner, and a gas station. The last three cities have ranger stations, and the supervisor's office for the wilderness and surrounding Shasta–Trinity National Forest is in Redding (2400 Washington Ave., tel. 530/246–5222).

WHERE TO SLEEP

The only indoor lodging worth mentioning is in Redding, Weaverville, and Lewiston (*see above*). But once in the vicinity of the alps, you'll want to sleep outside anyway. Though there are some developed campgrounds in the surrounding forest (none within the Trinity Alps Wilderness), the entire area becomes a bedroom if you have wilderness and fire permits in hand. Water can be obtained from the abundant streams, creeks, and Trinity River (don't forget to treat it!). (For developed campgrounds, *see* Weaverville and Lewiston, *above.*)

FOOD

If you forgot to stock your food in Redding, Arcata, or Weaverville, you should turn around. In Trinity Center it will cost you over $5 for a gloomy burger and $8–$10 for the chicken or steak at the **Sasquach** (Mary Ave. and Airport Rd., tel. 530/266–3250), open daily in summer. In Coffee Creek, 8 mi north, **The**

Country Store (Derrick Flat Loop Rd., tel. 530/266–3233) has a decent selection of minimart and deli-type food but prices are high. In Big Bar, at the **Outpost Coffee Shop** (off Hwy. 299, tel. 530/623–5434), the menu is only as inspiring as its name, except for the whopping stack of pancakes ($3). Stop by Wednesday–Sunday 8–3 or for the occasional Friday night barbecue special (5–8).

EXPLORING THE TRINITY ALPS

For serious outdoor adventures, the Trinity Alps Wilderness beckons irresistibly with over 60 alpine lakes and soaring cliffs, many visible from miles around. After you check in at the Weaverville Ranger District (*see* Basics, *above*) for up-to-date information, a $4 topo map, and free backcountry and fire permits, you're good to go.

HIKING • Ranger stations have the topo map of the wilderness as well as the "Trail and Lake Information" handout, which are a good start at not getting lost once out on your own. To truly explore the Trinity Alps, hikers should budget at least one week in the backcountry. For day- and weekend-trippers there are many options to choose from. A wonderful all-day hike past alpine streams, falls, and meadows leads to **Canyon Creek Lakes.** From Weaverville, take Hwy. 299 west 7 mi to Canyon Creek Road north (at Junction City), and follow the creek about 15 mi to the trailhead, where there's parking. From there it's a moderate 7-mi hike one-way (3–4 hrs) to the lakes, with a 2,500-ft gain in altitude. If it's too late in the day to start or you just want to camp somewhere secluded, try **Ripstein Campground,** high on a ridge above Canyon Creek, ¼ mi back from the Canyon Creek Lakes trailhead and parking lot toward Junction City. There's no water, but the 10 sites are free and there are pit toilets. Bears are a real presence here, so hang your food when you camp and don't leave yummy-smelling things in your car or tent (*see* Some Things to Bear in Mind *box in* Chapter 7).

Alpen Cellars, Trinity County's only vineyard, is a small, family venture specializing in white Riesling, gewürztraminer, chardonnay, and pinot noir. Call 530/266–9513 for directions.

For a less adventurous hike—an easy day trip if you don't want to camp—take Hwy. 3 about 40 mi northeast of Weaverville to the Eagle Creek Loop, 6 mi north of Coffee Creek, and follow signs to the **Stoddard Lake Trailhead,** 6 mi north. From here it's a moderate 3½-mi hike to Stoddard Lake. Another popular hike begins 30 mi north of Weaverville on Hwy. 3 near Coffee Creek and goes 2 mi to **Big Boulder Lake,** then another mile to **Little Boulder Lake.** To get to the trailhead travel north on Hwy. 3 from Weaverville, turn left at Forest Service Road 37N52 (it's a dirt road near the Powerhouse) before you get to Coffee Creek, and follow the signs to the Boulder Lakes parking lot. The lakes are surrounded by virgin forests and granite cliffs, and there are plenty of quiet places to pitch a tent.

If you have more time, try the 20-mi round-trip **Caribou Lake Trail,** which leads 4,000 ft up through the heart of the alps, carpeted with Douglas fir, ponderosa pine, manzanita, and huckleberry oak. About 8 mi north of Trinity Center on Hwy. 3, look for Coffee Creek Road and proceed west 19 mi to the trailhead at Big Flat Campground.

RAFTING • One of the best ways to see this pristine area is by taking a float down the Trinity River. **Trinity River Rafting** (Hwy. 299, Big Flat, tel. 530/623–3033 or 800/307–4837) offers guided trips (half-day $39, full-day $65) on Class II and III rapids from Pigeon Point, about 10 mi west of Weaverville. The same trips are available by kayak for $10 extra. You can also take self-guided trips on Class I and II rapids for $20 per person, including boat, paddles, life jacket, and shuttle service. A cheaper option is to ask around for inner tubes; a good put-in spot is between Weaverville and Big Bar at Junction City or Helena. Don't go farther west than Pigeon Point, though; the water gets too rough.

MT. SHASTA AND THE UPPER STATE

Perhaps the most famous mountain in the Cascade range is Mt. Shasta, whose dramatic presence played a role in the spiritual life of the local people long before the first European, a Spaniard, described it in 1820. On a clear day, you can see the 14,162-ft dormant volcano from a hundred miles south. Native Americans (notably the Wintus) value Mt. Shasta as the home of the sacred Bohem Puyuik, an

THE NEW AGE OF MT. SHASTA

Many are convinced that Mt. Shasta is the center of a powerful energy vortex. Native American legend pays tribute to Shasta's potency, and some say the mountain's bowels support lost civilizations like the Lemurians, hidden descendants of a 400,000-year-old race from the continent of Mu, which is thought to have sunk into the Pacific Ocean.

important spirit, and many people—particularly those who don't think Waterford when you say crystal—seek a different kind of spiritual power here (*see* The New Age of Mt. Shasta *box, below*). Mt. Shasta dominates the top of California, a region that seems to be more familiar to Oregonians and Washingtonians than to folks from the Golden State. But the tropical Mossbrae Falls in **Dunsmuir** and the sprawling **Scott Valley**—not to mention its excellent Etna Brewery—merit a visit. The Oregon Shakespearean Festival is over the border and through the mountain pass in Ashland. If you really want to launch yourself into the unknown, head northeast to **Tulelake** and the **Lava Beds National Monument**; the spare but richly detailed high-desert landscape may thrill you more than the state's more famous attractions.

Most travelers will want to head to the north state from late spring to early fall, when the snow has largely melted, the roads are clear, the wildflowers are in bloom, and the trout are jumping. The far north is also wonderful in winter, though: Rip up some turf on your cross-country skis, go bird-watching at Klamath Basin, or do some cold-weather spelunking at Lava Beds.

COMING AND GOING

Many of the towns mentioned below (including Dunsmuir, Mount Shasta, Yreka, and Ashland) lie along I–5. **Amtrak** (tel. 800/872–7245) has a station 10 minutes south of Mount Shasta in Dunsmuir (5750 Sacramento Ave., at Pine St.); one-way fare from San Francisco (8 hrs) is $64. **Greyhound** (tel. 800/231–2222) stops seven times a day (four times southbound, three north) in Mount Shasta at 404 North Mt. Shasta Boulevard. One-way fare from San Francisco is $46. **S.T.A.G.E.** (tel. 530/842–8295 or 800/247–8243) provides public transport for the region, traveling through Yreka, Mt. Shasta, Dunsmuir, and McCloud from around 6–6. Fares range 50¢–$4.10.

A car or bike is imperative if you want to venture very far from I–5. The drive from Mount Shasta to Tulelake takes less than two hours. From I–5 at Weed, take Hwy. 97 northeast to Hwy. 161 east, at the Oregon border. After about 15 minutes, you'll hit Hwy. 139, on which you can head south 4 mi to Tulelake and another couple miles to the turnoff for Lava Beds National Monument. Of course, it could take considerably longer than two hours, depending on how often you stop to watch the great blue herons, western grebes, pelicans, cormorants, and (during January and February) hundreds of bald eagles in the Klamath Basin National Wildlife Refuge.

MT. SHASTA

At the foot of the venerable mountain, the city of Mount Shasta embraces both the good-old-boy truckers and the funky New Agers, both of whom have money to drop; Mount Shasta is more than willing to keep what was once a logging and agricultural economy going on tourist dollars, hyping up tales of the few people who actually believe that "Lemurians" live in the mountain in order to generate curiosity about the area. No matter what you've heard about the spiritual aspects, you'll find that Mount Shasta is not much different from many other I–5 towns that are roadstops for desperate travelers.

Mount Shasta's **Fourth of July** celebration draws thousands of people from miles around with a parade, a run, and fireworks that radiate out across Lake Siskiyou. To reach town from I–5, take the central Mount Shasta exit east toward the mountain. This is Lake Street, which crosses Mount Shasta Boulevard; the two roads form the main axes of the town.

BASICS

The helpful staff at the **Mount Shasta Convention and Visitor Bureau** (300 Pine St., at Lake St., tel. 800/926–4865), open Monday–Saturday 9–5 and Sunday 9–3 in summer, Monday–Saturday 10–4, Sunday 10–3 in winter, can give you information as well as a copy of *Siskiyou County Living* and *After Five*, free entertainment monthlies that cover the whole northern part of the state. The **Mt. Shasta Ranger District** (204 W. Alma St., off N. Mount Shasta Blvd., tel. 530/926–4511) is open Monday–Saturday 8–4:30, Sunday 8–11 in summer, weekdays 8–4:30 in winter. They have a list of open campgrounds, roads, and trail conditions, and also sell maps.

WHERE TO SLEEP

The **Evergreen Lodge** (1312 S. Mount Shasta Blvd., tel. 530/926–2143) has 20 drab rooms, a pool, and a hot tub. Doubles are $44, and for $54 (more in summer) you get a fully equipped kitchenette. Another decent option is the **Shasta Lodge Motel** (724 N. Mount Shasta Blvd., north of Lake St., tel. 530/926–2815 or 800/SHASTA1), where your queen bed and bathtub cost $33.

HOSTELS • Alpec Cornerose Cottage Hostel. An independent hostel at the foot of Mt. Shasta, it's also near the local KOA campground, and campers tromp through the unlocked house all day on the way to the shower. Use the lockers if you plan on keeping your towel and soap. For $13 a night, you get a large deck facing the mountain and a shared kitchen with a microwave. Couples can reserve the private room with a queen bed for $30. *204 E. Hinckley St., tel. 530/926–6724. From downtown, walk north 20 min on N. Mount Shasta Blvd., go right at KOA sign on E. Hinckley St. 12 beds. Reception open daily 8–noon and 5–11, curfew 11 PM, no lockout. Laundry ($2).*

Mt. Shasta, the largest stratovolcano in the Cascades, last erupted 200 years ago. Modern monitoring techniques make it unlikely that the next blowup will be a surprise.

CAMPING • Camping costs range from nothing to $8 at the 14 recreation sites in the McCloud and Mt. Shasta ranger districts (you pay more if there's running water at the site). A good choice lies straight up Everitt Memorial Hwy.: **Panther Meadows,** a free, wooded walk-in campground with vault toilets and picnic tables, offers 10 tents-only sites. At 7,400 ft, Panther Meadows is an important meeting ground for all sorts of New Agers. Bring plenty of drinking water; there's none here, though there is a stream with water you can treat. If you can't get into Panther Meadows, drive back down to **McBride Springs,** 6 mi northeast of downtown on Everitt Memorial Hwy. The nine sites ($6), set in a sparse forest, have vault toilets, tables, and drinking water. No reservations are necessary for either campground. Another option is to head to **Lake Siskiyou** (*see* Outdoor Activities, *below*). Otherwise check the camping options at **Castle Crags State Park** (*see below*) or at the McCloud Ranger District, about 12 mi east of Mount Shasta (*see* Basics, *above*).

FOOD

Much of the fare in Mt. Shasta is pretty average and overpriced. One advantage to being in a freeway stop town is that there's usually at least one 24-hour eatery. The **Black Bear Diner** (401 W. Lake St., tel. 530/926–4669) serves breakfasts, lunches, and dinners that are tasty and pretty healthy. Vegetarian pasta is $7.50, chili omelets $6. For a real treat, get the Blackbeary Cobbler ($3). **The Acacia** (1136 S. Mount Shasta Blvd., tel. 530/926–0250) serves three meals a day with an inventive, largely vegetarian menu. The Mediterranean Scramble breakfast ($5.25) is a winner, as is the Creole Pasta with soup ($8.25).

The Pasta Shop (418 N. Mount Shasta Blvd., tel. 530/926–4118), open Monday–Saturday 8–7, makes its own polenta and pasta fresh daily and serves generous portions with marinara sauce ($4.75) or plain to go ($2.75 per lb). **The Avalon Square Heart Rock Café** (401 N. Mount Shasta Blvd., tel. 530/926–4998), closed Sunday in winter, bakes great cinnamon rolls ($1.50), whips up beautiful smoothies ($2.50), and fashions amazing smoked salmon with pesto sandwiches ($6). If you're just looking to stock up on supplies, the **Mountain Song Natural Food Market** (134 Morgan Way, in Mt. Shasta Shopping Center off Lake St., tel. 530/926–3391) has organic produce and other healthy items.

OUTDOOR ACTIVITIES

With hiking, biking, mountaineering, skiing, swimming, and kayaking, Shasta is prime for all those commune-with-nature urges. For equipment, maps, books, and tour guide information, try the **Fifth Season** (300 N. Mount Shasta Blvd., at E. Lake St., tel. 530/926–3606). Crampons and ice axes rent for $13 a day, snowshoes for $8 a day, mountain bikes for $25, cross-country ski packages for $10, and basic downhill getups for $14. The store also rents sleeping bags ($16 for 2–3 days) and tents ($28 for 2–3 days). Call 530/926–5555 for its daily report on mountain conditions.

HIKING • There's hiking galore around Shasta, but the big daddy is the 14,000-ft-plus behemoth itself. While there is no real trail to Shasta's summit, from June to September you can follow the path blazed by climbers on the mountain's south face: the **Avalanche Gulch** route from Bunny Flat (7,000 ft). It's possible to do the 12-mi round-trip from Bunny Flat to the summit and back in a day (8–12 hrs), but the elevation gain is over 7,000 ft (very strenuous), and you'll need crampons and ice axes most of the year. Those who wish to camp can do so at Horse Camp. Above Horse Camp a human waste packout system is in operation—get the bags and information at the ranger station. You can get the required hiking and camping permits (free, with no quotas) from the Mt. Shasta (*see* Basics, *above*) and McCloud ranger stations (*see* Basics, *below*). Day-use permits may be self-issued at both locations; in the off-season all permits can be self-issued from the Mt. Shasta office and in summer from the trailheads as well. You can also stop by the ranger station to ask them to review and advise about your route. Be sure to bring extra clothes and food; Mt. Shasta's unpredictable weather can leave you stranded on the mountain. Check with the ranger station or the Fifth Season (*see above*) for conditions before you go.

You'll get a great view of Mt. Shasta from **Black Butte,** which sits next to the volcano like some smaller, darker alter ego. John Muir once dubbed the 6,325-ft dome "Muir's Peak." It takes about four hours (2½ mi one-way) to hike the trail to the top; bring warm clothes if you want to stop there. To get to the butte, you take Alma Street west from Pine Street, turn left onto Everitt Memorial Hwy. north of town for 2 mi, turn left at the Penney Pines sign, follow the dirt road right 2½ mi, and take the left fork when the road crosses under the powerline. From here it's ½ mi to the trailhead. A topo map from the Fifth Season (*see* Outdoor Activities, *above*) shows all the logging roads leading to the trailhead.

BIKING • You'll find miles of great mountain biking in the Shasta area, much of it on old logging roads. An indispensable resource is the $3.75 *Mount Shasta Mountain Bike Map,* a topo map developed by a local rider and sold at the visitor center (*see above*). The labyrinthine logging roads by McBride Springs (head 1 mi toward the mountain on Everitt Memorial Hwy., turn left on the dirt road past the high school, follow signs to McBride Springs) are great for moderate rides. Stop by Fifth Season (*see above*) for rentals, more maps, and local riding wisdom. The entire forest is open for riding, especially the jeep trails and fire roads; paths are not maintained and can be tricky, though. **Mt. Shasta Ski Park** (*see below*) lets you chairlift to the top in summer ($10) daily 10–4. You can rent bikes and helmets here and zoom down the ski run.

ROCK CLIMBING • For backpackers, climbers, and mountaineers, **Shasta Mountain Guides** (1938 Hill Rd., tel. 530/926–3117) runs a $65 basic mountaineering course to familiarize you with ice axe, crampon, and alpine climbing. They also offer guided expeditions to the summit, which take two to five days and cost $235–$325. They can customize programs for people with special needs and also lead trips to Castle Crags (*see below*). For the beginner, Mt. Shasta Ski Park (*see below*) offers a 24-ft artificial climbing tower with shoes, harness, and assistance for $8 an hour.

RAFTING • White-water enthusiasts should contact **Turtle River Rafting Company** (tel. 800/726–3223), which offers everything from relaxing one-day float trips on Class II-plus rivers ($78) to tough one- to three-day trips on Class V waters ($106–$356, including food). **Living Waters Recreation** (tel. 530/926–5446 or 800/994–7238) runs cheaper all-day excursions on the easy Class I–II section of the Klamath River ($45 half day, $70 per day) or the moderate/challenging Class III–plus runs of the upper Sacramento River ($75 per person). These trips include a light lunch and beverage. They also lead runs on Class IV and V rivers.

WATER SPORTS • **Lake Siskiyou** is a good choice for camping and water activities. For $1 per person per day, you can lounge on the lakeshore or take a dip; pedal boats and canoes rent for $6 an hour and one-person kayaks are $4 an hour. It's a 10 mph lake—no Jet Skis. To get here from I–5, take the central Mount Shasta exit, go west on Hatchery Lane, turn left at the stop sign, bear right onto W. A. Barr Road, and go 3½ mi. For a lesser-known, uncrowded spot, try **Castle Lake** just before you reach the Lake Siskiyou Camp-Resort entrance. Turn south off W. A. Barr Road. About 7 mi into the mountains you'll reach a great spot for an alpine picnic or free lakeside camping (more than 200 ft from the water's edge). Six free sites lie to your left just before you reach the lake.

SNOW SPORTS • Cross-country skiing is very popular near Lake Siskiyou and on Mt. Shasta. The Fifth Season (*see above*) rents equipment ($9 a day). Skiing at **Mt. Shasta Ski Park** (104 Siskiyou Ave., tel. 530/926–8610) is very popular and an integral part of the local economy in the winter. The facilities are constantly being improved. There are currently 24 runs, about evenly divided between beginner, intermediate, and expert. All-day lift tickets are $29 on weekends and $24 weekdays, ski rentals are

$17, and snowboard rentals are $25. Cross-country skiing is also available here. Call 530/926–8686 for snow conditions. To get here, head 10 mi east from town on Hwy. 89 and follow the signs. The park is open daily 9–4 and Wednesday–Saturday 4–10 for night skiing. The season lasts November–April during a typical year.

NEAR MOUNT SHASTA

MCCLOUD • This small town east of Mount Shasta on Hwy. 89 is famous for hosting popular square-dance events at the local Dance Country (tel. 530/964–2578), where people from all over the world come to dress up in elaborate costumes and swing the night away. It's a friendly, relaxed place and does a good job of preserving its history as a logging and railroad town (McCloud used to be owned entirely by McCloud River Lumber Company) without catering too slavishly to the ugly side of the tourist economy and for this reason is much more interesting than the nearby Mount Shasta. With any luck, the upcoming years will see an expansion of services available to travelers, and it will be a worthwhile base from which to explore. The surrounding forests, falls, volcanic areas, and ice caves are a great asset. Information on the area can be requested from the **Chamber of Commerce** (Box 372, McCloud 96057, tel. 530/964–3113 or 800/720–3113). For rest and views that aren't accessible by any road, $9 will get you a ride on the open-air railcars operated by the **McCloud Railway Company** (tel. 530/964–2142 or 800/733–2141). From April through mid-September, trains leave Saturday at 4:30 across from the post office on Main Street. For a fancier—and much more expensive—excursion, the Shasta Sunset Dinner Train runs during the same months on Saturday, and occasionally Friday and Sunday; dinner costs $70, lunch, $49.

Six mi east of McCloud on Hwy. 89, turn south at the FOWLERS CAMPGROUND sign, then turn left (away from the campground) to get to an easy trail of about 2 mi that will take you to **Lower, Upper, and Middle Falls,** three very different and spectacular waterfalls that shoot out of volcanic rock crevasses. Lower Falls, the furthest west of the three, has a deep swimming hole carved out of the rock at its base. Go in the early morning if you want to see deer. During your trek you'll pass through **Fowler Campground,** where the $10-a-night, 39-site campground has water and toilets. The site is well forested, though crowded in summer.

Another great place nearby is the **Jot Dean Cave,** an ice cave that's shallow enough to not need a flashlight but still cool enough that there's ice at the bottom almost year-round. The cave is 9 mi south of Medicine Lake on County Road 49, but it's best to approach it from the other side—the sign pointing it out is only visible if you're traveling north off Hwy. 89 toward it. To find it (and the other volcanic wonders nearby—like lava flows—that you can explore for free), travel 16 mi west of McCloud on Hwy. 89, turn north on County Road 15, and after 22 mi go right at the fork onto County Road 49, keeping your eyes peeled for the sign pointing left to the cave, which is just by the roadside.

For information on the other wonders available in the nearby Medicine Lake Highlands and surrounding forests, go to the **McCloud Ranger District** (Hwy. 89 east of McCloud, tel. 530/964–2184), open weekdays 8–4:30 and summer Saturdays 9–3. They have free handouts with self-guided tours of nearby lava tubes, volcano glass areas, and cinder cones. They can also give information on winter activities like skiing.

McCloud and nearby Dunsmuir (*see below*) are among the cheapest places in the north state to stay at a B&B. For just $55 (shared bath), you can sleep in what was the main office building of the McCloud River Lumber Company at the **McCloud River Inn** (325 Lawndale Ct., tel. 530/964–2130 or 800/261–7831). They also offer snowmobile rental, mountain bike, downhill skiing, and train package deals. Private baths are about $20 more. The **Seraph Inn** (223 Quincy, tel. 530/964–2992) is a two-bedroom vacation flat that houses two for $60, $5 more for each additional person up to a total of six. There isn't much to choose from in the town as far as eats go, but options include a decent barbecue joint, the **North Yard** (Main St., tel. 530/964–2225), and the friendly **Jilly's Summit Club** (127 W. Colombero Dr., tel. 530/964–2227), where there's outdoor seating and a movie or sports event on every night. The dinner special does you right: $4 for a plain cheese personal pizza and large soda. If you feel like splashing out, the dining room at the **McCloud Guest House** (606 W. Colombero Dr., tel. 530/964–3160) goes fancy daily from 5–9 with dinners like the $12 eggplant with marinara sauce.

DUNSMUIR • Nestled in a lush, wooded valley, it's hard to believe that Dunsmuir, south of Mount Shasta, is so close to I–5. Originally named "Pusher," after the special train cars used here to get trains over the summit, the name was changed in 1886 when Scottish-Canadian coal baron Alexander Dunsmuir offered to donate a fountain to the city if it was renamed. He started a town tradition, and today there are 12 public fountains scattered around the small downtown. Call the **Chamber of Commerce**

(4841 Dunsmuir Rd., tel. 530/235–2177 or 800/286–7684), open Tuesday–Saturday 10–4 in summer (shorter hrs in winter), for more information.

There are two nearby waterfalls to the north. Hard to believe, but **Hedge Creek** was slated for demolition when it was decided that I–5 would have to go right where it stands. The diligent work of two local sisters saved it for future generations. The falls are about ¼ mi away from the parking lot and gazebo, which are off Dunsmuir Avenue just north of the North Dunsmuir exit. Further north are the impressively lush and large **Mossbrae Falls.** Getting here is a little complicated but definitely worth the trouble: Follow Dunsmuir Avenue north out of downtown and make a left on Scarlet Way (under the archway to Shasta Retreat). Park at the railroad tracks and walk north along the tracks about 1 mi; trains do run here so watch out. When you see a bridge up ahead, look for paths leading down the hill to your right (about 150 ft shy of the bridge). Standing on the river's edge you'll be facing the falls. Dunsmuir was also a reputed soda springs resort, where people would come to drink the tonic-water-tasting springs for their health. To check out the old soda springs resort, go beyond Mossbrae, cross the railroad bridge, and 150 ft beyond here you'll find a bare spot in the land. Climb its left side to find the original soda spring (the water actually tastes okay—not too minerally). Nearby is the old resort area with old benches. To this day, the water here is touted for its purity; the town even has a mineral water bottling plant.

One of the best times to visit Dunsmuir is the fall, when the broad leaf maples and conifers are at their colorful best. The town is in a transition zone between the two species' habitats, so you will find a mix here you won't see elsewhere. Another good time is in June, for the **Railroad Days** celebration's parade, music, crafts, old railcar rides, and town tours.

Funky and cool accommodations are found at the **Cave Springs** (4727 Dunsmuir Ave., tel. 530/235–2721), which overlooks the Sacramento River and another soda spring. Double motel rooms here are $44, but the best deal is a cozy cabin with kitchen and front porch for $31–$34. They'll even pick you up at the bus or train station if you ask. It's beautifully artsy at the **Nutglade Station** (5827 Sacramento Ave., tel. 530/235–0532), across from the rail station in a building that's been inventively painted and stenciled inside. There are six knotty-pine–walled rooms, all $45 with bath. Everyone from hipsters to Hell's Angels meets to eat at the deservedly popular **Old Rostel Pub and Café** (5743 Sacramento Ave., tel. 530/235–2028). During the winter they have specials like honeynut chicken, ribeye, and steak for $10–$13. Year-round they have great sandwiches like the eggplant hoagie ($6), microbrewed beer, and freshly baked desserts. About a block away, **Cafe Maddalena** (5801 Sacramento Ave., tel. 530/235–2725), open Thursday–Sunday 5:30–9:30, features gourmet Italian food. Fettuccine with mascarpone sauce and proscuitto goes for $9.65, and it's worth every cent. Pizza is about $8–$10.

CASTLE CRAGS STATE PARK • Castle Crags State Park (Box 80, Castella 96017, tel. 530/235–2684) lies right off I–5 south of Dunsmuir and is home to magnificent, soaring granite crags. Hiking on the crags is popular with north staters. Many trailheads branch off the road through the park, which travels up to the Vista Point—look for the signs. Maps and information can be had at the visitor center at the entrance, which keeps irregular hours due to volunteer staffing (someone's usually there on weekends). If you only have a day, don't miss **Castle Dome Trail,** a strenuous 3-mi hike beginning at the Vista Point parking lot that takes you virtually to the top of the crags. Experienced climbers have been known to scamper the last unmarked ¼ mi up the granite dome. Either way, you'll get awesome views of Mt. Shasta and the upper Sacramento River valley. The **Pacific Crest Trail** wanders through the base of the Crags for 10 mi in the park. Day use of the park is $5 (free on bike or foot).

The campground has 64 spacious, forested sites with hot showers ($15–$16). Sites 45–58 are farthest from the freeway. There are also three environmental (walk-in) sites ($7) with pit toilets and no running water, though you can pack in water from the visitor center and parking is close by. Call Destinet (tel. 800/444–7275) for reservations (recommended in summer, not accepted in the winter). For even cheaper and more secluded camping, follow the park road a few miles past the main campground entrance until you enter the national forest. Then just take one of the small logging roads and camp for free anywhere, but don't forget the 14-day limit. If you decide to strike out on your own, you'll need a campfire permit, available at the visitor center.

YREKA

By the time you get to Yreka (pronounced why-REEK-a), about 40 mi north of Mount Shasta on I–5, you'll probably be tired of seeing yet another sign welcoming you to yet another "historic town" begot during the gold rush, even if the streets do feature hitching posts instead of parking meters. Established March 1851 when gold was found nearby, Yreka (originally known as Thompson's Dry Diggings) was the area's central town. Now it's one of those small, friendly, and quiet towns that sees lots of freeway stopover guests. All the town's happenings and nearby outdoor activities are listed at the **Chamber of Commerce** (127 W. Miner St., tel. 530/842–1649 or 800/669–7352). Every Friday in the Miner Street Park you get a chance to hear blues, jazz, country, rock, or a combo of the above for free at 6:30. The city also is worth a look for the interesting **Siskiyou County Museum,** which has well-presented exhibits on pioneer history, gold mining, and fur trapping. A summer-only outdoor wing, which closes at 4:30, offers more tangible historical relics—transplanted original structures from around the county, including a mid-1800s homesteader house, a steam locomotive, a frontier church, and a general store (still using the old cash register to ring up your jawbreakers). *910 S. Main St., tel. 530/842–3836. Take central Yreka exit to Main St. and turn left. Admission is normally $1, but since flood damaged the upstairs exhibits, which won't open again until 1998, none is charged for the time being. Open Tues.–Sat. 9–5.*

If you're curious about old steam engines and have an itch for a slow-moving, 3½-hour round-trip journey (including an hour's stopover for lunch and browsing) with some great views of Mt. Shasta, take a ride on the **Blue Goose Excursion Train.** The train chugs through the hinterlands of Shasta Valley to the little town of Montague, which has stayed small and sleepy despite the hundreds of tourists who disembark there several days a week during summer. *300 E. Miner St., tel. 530/842–4146. From I–5, east at central Yreka exit. Fare: $9. Runs mid-June–early Sept. Departs Wed.–Sun. 10 AM.*

WHERE TO SLEEP

You should be able to find a generic motel for about $30–$35 along Main Street, which runs parallel to I–5. Yreka's motels are all clean and comfortable, with no personality. Add 8% tax. The **Ben Ber Motel** (1210 S. Main St., tel. 530/842–2791) has 36 large rooms surrounding its pool. Doubles go for $38 in summer ($35 in winter). The **Thunderbird Lodge** (626 S. Main St., tel. 530/842–4404 or 800/554–4339) offers a pool and 44 rooms. Doubles are $40–$43, $32 in winter.

FOOD

Ever wanted to eat in bizarre Mexican-grotto surroundings? **Lalo's Restaurant Lounge** (219 W. Miner St., tel. 530/842—2695; closed Sun.) is the place. Many items are rather pricey, but their dinner burritos go for $6 and calamari, steak, and seafood dinners cost about $11. The stained glass Aztec calendar is not to be missed. A healthy choice (espresso excepted) is **Nature's Kitchen** (412 S. Main St., tel. 530/842–1136), open Monday–Saturday for breakfast and lunch, Thursday–Saturday for dinner. Much of the menu here is vegetarian. Try the "dolphin-safe" tuna-salad sandwich for $4 or the chili veggie burger for $5.50 for lunch. They also have a tiny vitamin and supplements shop.

NEAR YREKA

SCOTT VALLEY • Driving through the 28 mi of beautiful farmland that make up the Scott Valley region (take Hwy. 3 southwest from Yreka), you'll see one knockout landscape after another. The town of **Fort Jones** was originally an outpost for white settlers who feared the Rogue River Indians. In 1852, a fort was established in the village of **Etna** (originally named Rough and Ready) to oversee the area, but the native people gave such a fight that Ulysses S. Grant was declared AWOL after failing to quickly take command (he returned later with a good excuse). Check out the **Etna Brewing Company, Inc.** (131 Callahan St., east of Main St., tel. 530/467–5277), which offers free tours and tasting of their beer and root beer, Saturday 1–5.

A couple blocks west along Main Street you'll find **Sengthong's** (434 Main St., tel. 530/467–5668), a highly regarded Thai and Laotian restaurant. The dishes are pricey but a welcome escape from the mediocre food that abounds in the area. Tofu with veggies is $9.50, steamed fish with ginger sauce a dollar more. The dinner-only restaurant is closed Monday and Tuesday and for six weeks in winter, usually reopening at the end of February. Another gem in the area is the **Scott Valley Orchard and Winery** (13611 Meamber Creek Rd., 9 mi west of Fort Jones, tel. 530/468–5297), which sells organic apples, apple-elderberry wine, and hand-pressed apple cider in the fall. To stay the night, try the **Marble View Motel** (12425 Main St., tel. 530/468–2394), just north of Fort Jones on Hwy. 3, where six tidy, spacious doubles go for $35 (no tax, some with fridge), and there's plenty of scenery to fill your window.

ASHLAND • The **Oregon Shakespeare Festival,** held from mid-February through October, has turned Ashland (40 mi north of Yreka) into a staging area for theater of all kinds, from experimental to traditional, though you'll still see a healthy share of the outdoor Elizabethan productions that spawned the festival more than a half-century ago. The flat, pale-green hills make a pretty backdrop for the theatrical whirl. And while you'll find Puck's Doughnuts, the Romeo Inn, and other allusions to the Bard here, Oregonian sensibilities have prevented Ashland's Disneyfication. On the whole, it's an artsy, upscale, college town with a hefty dose of tourists thrown in.

ALL THE WORLD'S A STAGE

The oldest such event in America, Ashland's Oregon Shakespeare Festival has grown to include 11 repertory plays each year (four by Shakespeare), which are performed in three separate theaters, all located in the same courtyard: the beautiful, outdoor Elizabethan Theatre (which has surprisingly good acoustics), the indoor Angus Bowmer Theatre, and the smaller Black Swan stage. Two plays usually go on daily at 2 PM, with two more in the evening. Productions ($19.50–$34, with seasonal discounts, especially for matinees) sell out quickly, but there are always people standing near the Festival box office (15 S. Pioneer St., 1 block south of Main St., tel. 541/482–4331) trying to sell tickets. Standing-room tickets ($10) for the night's play at the Elizabethan Theatre are a good bet. Only 20 standing-room tickets are available for each sold-out performance; get to the box office early (9 AM) to try to get one. Write for a schedule: Box 158, Ashland, 97520.

The **Ashland Chamber of Commerce** (110 E. Main St., at Pioneer St., tel. 541/482–3486), open weekdays 9–5, can give you information as well as a free town map and calendar of events. You'll need that map: the town's main drag, traveling northwest to southeast, changes names—from North Main Street to East Main Street to Siskiyou Boulevard. Public transit in Ashland is courtesy of the Rogue Valley Transportation District (RVTD), tel. 541/779–2877, which runs buses from Medford, Oregon, to Ashland as well as two loops through Ashland. Fare is $1, day passes $4; the fare within Ashland is 25¢.

In addition to full-stage productions, the Festival sponsors all kinds of theater-related events, including **Festival Noons.** There are two ways to go here: cheap or free. Noon happenings in Carpenter Hall are largely lectures and readings by actors, directors, and scholars. Tickets are $4 at the Festival box office (*see box, above*). For free, you can attend the **Talks in the Park,** each an informal hour of questions and answers with directors, costume designers, stage managers, actors, composers, and other theater folk. Talks are most days at noon in Bankside Park, just outside Gate 1 of the Elizabethan Theater. Pick up a schedule of days and speakers at the Chamber of Commerce. Backstage tours of the theater ($9–$10) can be arranged at the Festival box office.

In addition to the festival, there are other ways to entertain yourself in Ashland—many free and near the theater district. **Lithia Park** is a shady spot for picnicking or strolling. The **Pacific Northwest Museum of Natural History** (1500 E. Main St., tel. 541/488–1084), open daily 10–4 (until 5 July–Labor Day; closed Mon. and Tues. in winter), admission $8, farther east on Main Street, sponsors free park walks in the summer. It's the largest natural history museum between San Francisco and Vancouver, with all kinds of hands-on interpretive exhibits on the region.

Ashland is near the Rogue River National Forest, which is divided into Cascade and Siskiyou sections, both with campsites, some free. The Chamber of Commerce has brief information on what's available, but the full story (including mushroom and huckleberry picking, alpine and nordic skiing, mountain biking, and hiking) is at the **Ashland Ranger Station** (645 Washington St., tel. 541/482–3333). Mt. Ashland hosts the reasonably priced, community-owned **Ski Ashland** (1745 Hwy. 66, tel. 541/482–2897), which has downhill and snowboarding trails, and there are some ungroomed cross-country possibilities in the area beyond the complex. Lift tickets are $25 on weekends, $20 during the week; skis, boots, and poles rent for $15 a day, snowboards and boots, $25. **Mountain Supply** (31 N. Main, on the downtown plaza, tel. 541/488–2749) has books on trails in the area; hiking, skiing, and camping gear; and usually bike rentals ($10 for 2 hrs, $25 a day).

Hotel rates climb $10–$20 during summer and holidays. Try the lovely old **Columbia Hotel** (262½ E. Main St., tel. 541/482–3726 or 800/718–2530) downtown if you want bright rooms with antique furniture. A simple double with a country-floral motif and shared bath costs $28 (winter), $49 (summer). Rooms with private bath run $42 (winter)–$85 (summer). The 24 rooms can book up two to three months ahead for summer weekends, so try to call ahead. Besides the hostel (*see below*), the only other way to spend a cheap night here is to camp. **Emigrant Lake County Park** (tel. 541/776–7001) is about 5 mi southeast of Ashland on Hwy. 66, with 42 first-come, first-served sites at $14 a night. You get hot showers, though most spaces lack privacy. Set on an exposed hillside overlooking the lake, the sites can get hot and dusty in summer but are green in spring and fall. The park is closed from mid-October to mid-March.

Ashland Hostel. Ashland's best budget lodging is in a century–old house with a well-kept garden and kitchen. There are 43 dorm beds ($14, $13 for HI members, $11 for Pacific Crest Trail walkers) and three private rooms that fill up quickly in the summer. Send a check to reserve a space (it should arrive seven days ahead of your stay). There's a piano, laundry ($1 wash, 75¢ dry), and lockers ($2). You can pay $2 for a shower if you're just passing through. *150 N. Main St., Ashland 97520, 3 blocks north of the plaza, tel. 541/482–9217. Curfew midnight, 11 PM Oct.—Feb. Lockout 10–5. Reception open 8–10 AM and 5–11 PM.*

For a great selection of organic, bulk, and nutritional foods, shop at the **Ashland Community Food Store Co-Op** (237 N. 1st St., 3 blocks north of E. Main St., tel. 541/482–2237). The **Ashland Bakery & Café** (38 E. Main St., tel. 541/482–2117) makes a chicken sandwich with ortega chilis on sourdough ($7.50) and specials at lunch and dinner daily. **The Beanery** (1602 Ashland St., at Walker St., tel. 541/488–0700) has lunch specials 11–2 and tasty veggie lasagna ($4). Thursday–Saturday they host live music—largely folk—from 8–10. **Geppetto's** (345 E. Main St., tel. 541/482–1138) serves a savory marinated herb, vegetable, and cheddar omelet ($6.25) and has a fine dinner menu as well.

The bald eagle has staged an incredible comeback thanks in part to the Endangered Species Act of 1973, which banned DDT and encouraged recovery programs like the one at Klamath Basin.

Ashland is rather quiet for a college town, but socializing isn't out of the question. The second-story **Black Sheep** (51 N. Main St., tel. 541/482–6414), a homey pub with a roaring fire in the winter, has draft beers and lauded pub "fayre." The **Rogue Brewery** (31B Water St., tel. 541/488–5061) has a nice outside deck.

TULELAKE

Tulelake resembles a small ghost town, but it's just about all there is, civilization-wise, in the northeast corner of California. (By the way, a tule, pronounced "toolie," is a type of bulrush found in marshes.) The town is home to one flashing, red traffic light, lots of farmers, and the University of California's Intermountain Research and Extension Center (where genetic crop experiments are performed). Once you leave I–5 (take Hwy. 97 northeast at Weed to Hwy. 161 east to Hwy. 139 south), the sense of the place will hit you: Tulelake sits in the middle of land that is at once desolate and magnificent. But, sadly, this is a depressed economy with a capital *D*. The town's proximity to Lava Beds National Monument, Klamath Basin National Wildlife Refuge, and Medicine Lake (*see* Near Lava Beds, *below*) makes it a decent place to stock up on groceries and fill your tank, though if you want a forested, backroad drive, you'd do better to approach from McCloud (provided the road isn't blocked by snow).

WHERE TO SLEEP AND EAT

Mike and Wanda's (429 Modoc Ave., tel. 530/667–3226) has sandwiches and burgers ($5) and freshly baked pizza ($7–$15) made with quality (though a bit bland) ingredients. The **Ellis Motel** (tel. 530/667–5242), 1 mi north of town on Hwy. 139 and situated in lovely farmland, charges $35–$40 for doubles, some with kitchens for $4 extra. Some rooms used to be garages and may be a bit chilly; they all fill up fast during duck season (mid-Oct.–mid-Jan.), so reserve ahead.

KLAMATH BASIN

The **Klamath Basin National Wildlife Refuge,** a complex of six waterfront refuges, is partly contained in Northern California and extends well into southern Oregon. Klamath Basin is on the Pacific flyway, the main north–south migration highway for myriad waterfowl, with 75%–80% of all migrating birds stopping here. The birds draw naturalists, bird-watchers, and photographers, as well as hunters. At times during the fall migration (late Aug.–early Nov.) more than a million birds land at Klamath Refuge. The largest concentration of the birds, including the majestic Canadian geese, is in the **Lower Klamath** and **Tule Lake refuges.** Both are easily reached—you skirt the Lower Klamath Refuge (the first waterfowl refuge in the United States) driving east on Hwy. 161, and the Tule Lake Refuge is just southwest of Tulelake—both have auto-tour routes. Park alongside the road, pull out your binoculars, and refer to the free checklist of birds and mammals, including antelope, that's obtainable from the visitor center (*see below*). Newly added near the visitor center is the Discovery Marsh, offering two short hikes of ¼ mi or 1 mi, with observation blinds and lots of interpretive information.

In winter (Nov.–late Mar., peaking in mid-Feb.) as many as 300 bald eagles a night roost in the area. The nearby **Bear Valley National Wildlife Refuge** is set aside specifically for them and boasts a few resident pairs. You're well advised to stop by the **Visitor Center and Refuge Headquarters** (Hill Rd., 5 mi west of Tulelake, tel. 530/667–2231); they can give you up-to-date information on what's open and what animals are around. It's open weekdays 8–4:30, weekends and holidays 10–4. To get here, take East–West Road 5 mi west out of Tulelake, turn left on Hill Road (at the T-junction), and look for the building on your right.

While serious hikers and bikers will have to drive north to the 10-mi trail at the **Klamath Marsh Refuge,** those who want a bird's-eye view of the marshes near the visitor center should head up the **Sheepy Ridge Wildlife Trail** (behind the visitor center), which runs a steep ¼-mi up a volcanic ridge to a cliff face. You'll see raptors, a yellow-bellied marmot or two, and cliff swallows. The Tule Lake Refuge offers a 2-mi marked canoe trail amid a tule marsh that's open July–September. The closest place to rent a boat is north on Hwy. 97 about 15 mi at **Upper Klamath Refuge** off Hwy. 140; you can rent a canoe ($20 half-day; $30 all day) at the Rocky Point Resort (28121 Rocky Point Rd., northwest shore of Upper Klamath Lake, tel. 541/356–2287). For more information, call the **Klamath Ranger District** (1936 California Ave., Klamath Falls, OR, tel. 541/885–3400).

LAVA BEDS NATIONAL MONUMENT

Tucked way up in the northeast corner of the state—west of Hwy. 139 and south of Tulelake—and consequently not on many tourists' itineraries, Lava Beds' spectacular terrain is ripe for exploration. The land is harsh, scarred repeatedly by volcanic activity, but it's what's under the ground that should draw you to this subtly beautiful and often desolate place—350 caves to wander through. You can explore many caves by yourself—borrow lights for free at the visitor center from 8–5:30 (*see below*), wear hard-sole boots, and buy the useful but silly-looking "bump hats" ($3.25)—or bring your bike helmet—to protect your head.

This land was the site of the Modoc Indian War. The U.S. Government, anxious for more land for cattle grazing, forced the Modocs to share a reservation with the Klamath nation. When the Modocs tried to leave, U.S. troops were sent in to force them back. From 1872–1873, Modoc leader Keintpoos, nicknamed Captain Jack by the troops, used the rough terrain and mazelike lava trails, known as the Stronghold, to fend off a well-fortified U.S. Army. On **Captain Jack's Stronghold Historic Trail** at the north end of the park, you can learn about the Modocs' impressive resistance and see how the terrain provided perfect natural fortifications for a Modoc force of fewer than 60 to hold off a U.S. Army 10 times its size. You can borrow the excellent interpretive booklet at the trailhead and take the short ½-mi walk or a longer 1½-mi trail through the stronghold. The Modocs never got their own reservation.

BASICS

The park entry fee is $4 per vehicle, valid for seven days of use. The **visitor center,** at the park's south end on Forest Service Road 10, has maps and plenty of information on which caves are okay to explore on your own. Between mid-June and August, the center organizes daily—and free—two-hour guided walks and a 1- to 1½-hour guided cave tour. There are evening campfire programs too. If you're going to go it alone, it's crucial that you let the visitor center know which caves you're going to explore in case you need your spelunking self saved. Don't forget to bring lights, and pick up a bump hat before you go. The caves are almost always open for exploring, night and day (with some seasonal closures in baby bat season). *Box 867, Tulelake 96134, tel. 530/667–2282. Open daily 8–6 (until 5 in winter).*

WHERE TO SLEEP

The **Lava Beds National Monument Campground,** across from the visitor center at the south end of the park, has 40 sites suitable for tents or trailers. For $10 a night ($6 in winter), the rangers promise: No showers, hookups, dump stations, stores, gas, fast food, or soda machines! Plenty of clean air, crystal-clear, cold drinking water, and beautiful open space. In winter all water at the campground is turned off, but you can fill containers at the visitor center.

If the Lava Beds sites are full (this rarely happens), you can hike into the unspoiled backcountry at Lava Beds and camp for free year-round. Of course, keep in mind the hardships of the terrain and the unpredictability of the weather. Register first at the visitor center, and bring your own water. Rattlesnakes are common. Otherwise, drive 24 mi to Medicine Lake (*see below*) and pitch a tent there. For a shower ($2), make the trek to Tulelake (*see above*) and its **Shady Lanes Trailer Park and Laundromat** (795 Modoc Ave., tel. 530/667–2617).

EXPLORING THE PARK

Perhaps due to its isolation from urban areas, Lava Beds is less trafficked than other comparable parks in the state. The majority of caves open to the public are near the visitor center along **Cave Loop Drive.** Each takes ½–1½ hours to explore—except for **Mushpot Cave,** just outside the visitor center's door; it's lit until 6 PM in summer and 5 PM in winter to allow novices to get acquainted with basic lava-tube formations. **Valentine Cave** is the one the rangers recommend: the lava flows are well-preserved, and you can see the features of the melted rock clearly. Look for tree roots inside, too, as well as a mold called "lava tube slime," which is hydrophobic. It repels water, so the cave is damp and drippy. Two other must-sees in the park are **Fern Cave,** a Modoc spiritual site with pictographs on the wall and a stunning floor of ferns, and **Crystal Cave** (open Dec.–Mar.), full of amazing ice columns, frozen waterfalls, and the like. Both caves can be seen on arranged tours only. They're free, but tours fill up fast, so call the visitor center well ahead of your trip. Don't forget to bring warm clothes for exploring the caves—the temperature drops drastically once you get inside.

Eight miles south of Tulelake on Hwy. 139, keep your eyes open for a monument at the site of a Japanese-American internment camp. During World War II, it was the home of 18,789 refugees.

Otherwise, there's hiking in the lava wonderland outside. Climb **Schonchin Butte,** a ¾-mi path up a volcanic cinder cone that sports fantastic wildflowers in late spring. At the top you get to tour the functioning fire lookout and take in an outstanding view (on a clear day you can see mountains in Oregon, 130 mi away). You'll find the ½-mi dirt road to the trailhead off the park's main road, about 5 mi north of the visitor center (follow signs). Another great hike (1⅓ mi), departing from the main road in the park's southern sector, takes you down into **Skull Cave,** the largest in diameter in the park—the ceiling reaches 84 ft in places. The cave got its name from animal bones and human remains that were discovered when the cave was explored in 1898. Most of the caves average a constant 56°F, winter or summer, but Skull and Merrill caves are just below freezing, so dress warmly.

NEAR LAVA BEDS

MEDICINE LAKE HIGHLANDS • Medicine Lake is a tree-rimmed mountain lake so beautiful you'll find it hard to believe it's this near the desolate Lava Beds. To get there from Lava Beds's southern entrance, travel about 14 mi southwest on the road that heads back to Hwy. 97; at the T-junction, turn left and head south for 24 mi. The road is generally closed by snow from November to mid-May, but there is some sno-park parking available. Four campgrounds with similar facilities surround the lake; the 74 sites are $7 each. There's potable water, fire stands, and pit toilets but no showers. For information prior to coming, contact the **Doublehead Ranger District** (Hwy. 139, in Tulelake, tel. 530/667–2246).

Medicine Lake makes a great fishing and swimming hole. Bring all necessary equipment; you can't rent anything here. The **Medicine Lake Day Use Picnic Area** has a swimming area cordoned off from boats; to get here, follow the myriad signs. One and a half mi from the lake is **Glass Mountain,** where an immense obsidian (glass made from melted rock) flow covers the mountain's peak. The climbing isn't steep, but there is no trail and the volcanic glass can be difficult to negotiate at times—wear good boots and register with a ranger if you plan to do serious trekking. To get to Glass Mountain from the lake, take County Road 97 east to Lyons Loop Road, which goes right by it.

For an awesome view of Little Glass Mountain, green-forested hills and mountains, and Mt. Shasta, go west past the Medicine Campground on a dirt road to the overflow camp. The ranger station is 1 mi past the Medicine Campground—go past it and follow the sign pointing to the Little Mt. Hoffman Lookout, which is 4 mi away. (The same road will take you to Little Glass Mountain, 5 mi away.) The road to the lookout is not accessible by car in the winter—there's snow there even in June—but you can walk it year-round and find few co-explorers. As you climb the road, there's a sheer dropoff to your left, over which you can see the lava flows, now turned to stone and glass. At the top of the climb is an observation tower, picnic tables, and a vista that doesn't easily compare with elsewhere.

6 GOLD COUNTRY

UPDATED BY ANDY MOORE AND DEKE CASTLEMAN

Before high-tech firms, agribusiness, and Hollywood, what made California the Golden State was the precious metal itself. James Marshall's discovery of gold in Coloma in 1848 brought a tidal wave of migrants to California and ushered the territory into the Union. As gold fever seized the nation, California's population of 15,000 swelled to 265,000 within three years. Nearby Sacramento soon became the state capital and today remains a place where old California competes with the state's new definition of itself. The original gold boom has long since subsided (though even today you'll still find a few hopefuls out panning), and the state's population centers have shifted elsewhere. Bustling 19th-century metropolises have been reduced to quaint towns proffering a few antiques shops, or "Wild West" museums that sometimes feel like a piece of Disneyland. If you're interested in what passes for ancient history in California, the towns on Hwy. 49—in particular, **Auburn, Nevada City,** and **Columbia**—have preserved it laboriously.

Many Californians, though, simply pass through Gold Country en route to a night of modern-day mining: gambling under the bright lights of **Reno**'s casinos. But a wealth of treasures awaits the intrepid Gold Country explorer: Besides being a cradle of California history, this region is a haven for those seeking a taste of the great outdoors. Claustrophobes from coastal cities find room to breathe while rafting on the Yuba and American rivers (easily accessible from towns like Coloma and Grass Valley); hiking and biking in the foothills; or skiing in the world-class resorts farther east in **Lake Tahoe.** The Tahoe and Eldorado National Forests cover much of the region, encompassing 19th-century immigration routes and historic gold mines.

SACRAMENTO

Though Sacramento has much to offer, it's a sad fact that even most Californians have never visited the city that's been the state's seat of government since 1854. In California years that's a long time, and the grand Victorians east of downtown and the pioneer graves in the City Cemetery illustrate Sacramento's links to its past. Unlike some of the state's quainter centers of historical self-consciousness, however, Sacramento is a modern city, where a diverse citizenry—African- and Euro-Americans, Latinos, queer

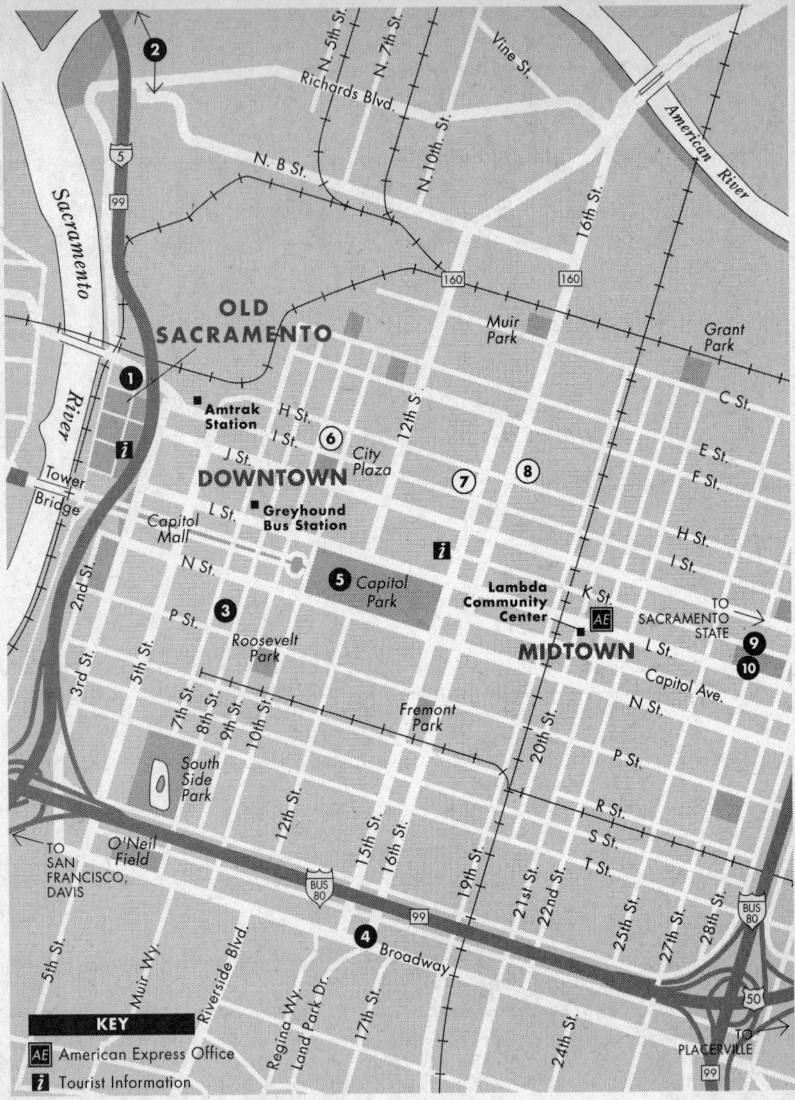

SACRAMENTO

Sights ●

California State Capitol Building, **5**

California State Indian Museum, **9**

California State Railroad Museum, **1**

Discovery Park (Jedediah Smith Memorial Bicycle Trail), **2**

La Raza/Galería Posada, **3**

Sutter's Fort, **10**

Tower District, **4**

Lodging ○

Econo Lodge, **8**

Quality Inn, **7**

Sacramento Hostel, **6**

folk, Asians, young and old—mix it up in cafés, downtown street fairs, and booming, free outdoor concerts. Travelers who join the 1½ million residents for a stay in California's capital will find a large, vibrant city with the friendliness and coffeehouse pace of a smaller town.

BASICS

Sadly, there's little in the way of information at the **Sacramento Convention and Visitors Bureau** (1421 K St., at 15th St., tel. 916/264–7777), open weekdays 8–5. Your best bet for visitor's guides, maps, and useful brochures on restaurants and hotels is the **Old Sacramento Visitor Center** (1101 2nd St., at K St., tel. 916/442–7644), open daily 9–4:30. For current happenings, check the comprehensive listings in the *Sacramento News & Review*, free at newsstands, and the *Sacramento Bee*'s "Ticket" section, a weekend entertainment guide published every Friday. *Alive and Kicking* (tel. 916/448–2582) is a local 'zine that covers the local scene and lists upcoming shows; pick one up at cafés or Tower Records (*see* Cheap Thrills, *below*).

Sacramento's lesbian, bi, gay, and transgender communities are served by the **Lambda Community Center** (919 20th St., between I and J Sts., tel. 916/442–0185); open weekdays 10–7). The community center is also the place to get *Outworld*, River City's hip queer newspaper, and the *Lesbian and Gay Business Alliance Directory*, which lists gay-friendly places of all sorts. *Mom . . . Guess What?* available at the Center and at all Tower Books locations around Sac State (1600 Broadway is the central one) is another decent publication.

COMING AND GOING

BY BUS

Sacramento is a hub for **Greyhound** buses traveling throughout the state. Round-trip fare to San Francisco is $17, and it takes about 2½ hours each way. The station (715 L St., at 7th St., tel. 916/444–7270 or 800/231–2222) is open 24 hours, and lockers are available. **Yolobus** (tel. 916/371–2877) serves Davis for $1; catch it at 10th and N streets or at L Street between 6th and 7th streets. Yolobuses start running around 6:30 AM weekdays (9:40 AM Saturday, 9:10 AM Sunday) and stop around 10:30 PM. Other bus services will run you out to Placerville, Folsom, Auburn, Stockton; call 916/321–2877 for more information, or pick up the $1 timetable from Regional Transit (*see* Getting Around, *below*).

BY CAR

I–80 will take you from San Francisco to Sacramento (1½–2 hrs), but it bypasses the city center to the north, so take the **Capital City Freeway** to get downtown. Merging with the business loop as it cuts east–west through town, **U.S. 50** heads east toward Placerville and Tahoe. For Reno (about 2 hrs), stay on I–80. If you're traveling north to south, **I–5** and **Highway 99** merge as they pass through the city. Outside town, I–5 is a faster thoroughfare (and the direct route to places like L.A., Portland, Seattle, etc.), but Hwy. 99 serves more Central Valley cities. Try to avoid the freeways during commute hours (6–9 and 4–7).

BY TRAIN

Round-trip **Amtrak** fares to San Francisco (2½ hrs each way) are $18; round-trip fares to Los Angeles (14 hrs one-way due to speed restrictions) or Seattle (21 hrs one-way) are $77 and $156, respectively. Reservations are required, and lockers are available. *401 I St. (enter at 5th and I Sts.), tel. 800/872–7245. Open daily 5 AM–midnight.*

GETTING AROUND

Sacramento orients itself around its major highways (*see* Coming and Going by Car, *above*), which collectively form a large "H." Most of what you'll want to do in town falls in the top half of the "H" (the part shown on our map), an area arranged in a grid of numbered and lettered streets. **Old Sacramento,** home to most of the museums and tourist attractions, is at the west end of this area, near I–5 and the Sacramento River. **Downtown** and the capitol are just east of Old Sac (within walking distance), and **Midtown** is still farther east. Bus lines crisscross the city, and a light rail connects downtown with the suburban area east of the city. As with most large urban areas, Sacramento has its share of crime; keep your eyes and ears open while walking around, especially late at night.

BY BUS

Regional Transit (tel. 916/321–2877) covers the whole city and its environs. Service on the most popular downtown routes usually begins by 6 AM and ends around 10 PM; other lines stop running as early as 6 PM. The **Regional Transit Main Office** (1400 29th St., at N St., tel. 916/321–2877) and the **Downtown Service Center** (907 K St.) both sell useful transit time tables ($1) and day passes ($3). Bikes are permitted at no extra charge. Tickets are $1.25, but rides are only 25¢ in the sight-heavy Central Business District 9 AM–3:30 PM, after 6 PM, and all day weekends and holidays. There is also a **free shuttle** that runs from the Convention Center at 12th and K streets west along the K Street Mall to Old Sacramento Monday–Saturday 11–7:30 and Sunday 11–6. Stops are marked by orange and purple FREE SHUTTLE signs.

BY CAR

Downtown is a maze of one-way streets, and parking can be hard to find: Take the bus or walk instead. For short-term stops, consider parking in one of the large garages connected to the shopping mall on L Street between 5th and 4th streets or in the city lot under I–5 at 2nd Street (enter from I Street between 2nd and 3rd streets; about 50¢ an hour). For rentals, try **Enterprise Rent-a-Car** (1401 16th St., at N St., tel. 916/444–7600).

WHERE TO SLEEP

The sheer number of affordable places makes it easy to find a bed, but keep in mind that room tax is 11% throughout Sacramento County. With all the hostel's advantages, you'd be suffering from heat dementia not to stay there. But if you'd prefer a faceless chain motel (or one that looks like one), so be it. The area around the square formed by 16th, G, 11th and J streets has plenty, and the "Sacramento Accommodations" brochure at the visitor's center lists the lot.

Staying near the capitol gives you easy access to Sacramento's main attractions. A stone's throw from the old Governor's Mansion, the **Quality Inn** (818 15th St., at I St., tel. 916/444–3980), formerly the Americana Lodge, has rooms (doubles around $50) in good shape, some with king beds. Best of all, there's a small pool. Two blocks away, the **Econo Lodge** (711 16th St., at H St., tel. 916/443–6631) has clean rooms for about the same price.

HOSTEL

It's been a restaurant, it's been a funeral home, it's been across the street (they moved the building a few years back): The palatial **Sacramento Hostel,** in the heart of downtown, charges $16 ($13 with HI card) for a comfy bed in its renovated 1885 Victorian mansion. Not only is it an easy walk from Amtrak and Greyhound, but the extremely friendly staff here can clue you in on shoestring Sacramento. The clientele runs the gamut from international students to business-suited consultants to families from the suburbs. *900 H St., at 9th St., tel. 916/443–1691 or 800/909-4776 (ext.40). 70 beds, private couple and family rooms available including 1 with private bath, for $5–$10 surcharge. Reception open 7:30–9:30 and 5–10, curfew 11 PM with late entry possible, lockout 9:30 AM–5 PM. Laundry.*

FOOD

Sacramento is a great place for cheap food. Check the *Sacramento Bee* "Ticket" for listings and ratings of dozens of local restaurants. If the weather's nice, pick up lunch at the **Sacramento Natural Foods Co-op** (1900 Alhambra Blvd., at S St., tel. 916/455–2667) and treat yourself to a picnic in Capitol Park (between 10th, 15th, L, and N Sts.). The co-op also has an all-you-can-eat buffet weekdays from 11:30–1:30 and 5–7:30.

In Old Sacramento, **Annabelle's** (200 J St., at 2nd St., tel. 916/448–6239) offers an Italian lunch buffet for $4. For Chinese all-you-can-chow, try **New Lu-Shan** (403 J St., at 4th St., tel. 916/444–2543)—$4.75 lunch, $6.25 dinner. Barbecue lovers should stop by the **Union Restaurant** (117 J St., near 2nd St., tel. 916/448–6466), where $13 gets you salad, veggies, and fries, plus all the ribs you can stomach.

DOWNTOWN

If you wander around the capitol (try J St. between 9th and 13th Sts.), you should have no trouble finding something affordable with either outdoor seating or air-conditioning. Old Sacramento, the tourist center to the west, tends to be pricier and tackier.

Ernesto's Mexican Food. Though the interior is elegant, you don't have to dress up to come enjoy Ernesto's excellent entrées, like the carnitas (lean pork marinated in red wine and herbs; $8.50) or the filling Bonanza Burrito ($4.65). They also feature a vegetarian menu with mouth-watering veggie fajitas ($7.50); eight kinds of Mexican beer and four flavors of margaritas make it just about heaven. *1901 16th St., at S St., tel. 916/441–5850.*

MIDTOWN

Some of the grooviest eateries are scattered around Midtown, especially on 18th and 19th streets between Capitol and I streets.

Greta's Café. This busy deli and bakery is a local institution, with sidewalk seating, mouthwatering desserts, and delicious soups, salads, and sandwiches ($5 or less). Try the buttermilk pancakes ($4.50) for breakfast, then come back for the black-bean chili ($4.75) or the focaccia ($2.75) later in the day. *1831 Capitol Ave., at 19th St., tel. 916/442–7382. No dinner.*

Corner Stone. Arty types chow down on salads and huge sandwiches (around $5) at this busy diner. A two-egg breakfast will run you about $3.25. *2330 J St., at 24th St., tel. 916/441–0948. No dinner Sun.–Wed.*

CAFES

At any time of the day or evening, you can find locals slacking off in several popular coffee spots. You can get beer, wine, sandwiches, and calzones with your coffee at the **Capital Garage Coffee Co.** (1427 L St., at 15th St., tel. 916/444–3633), which really was once a parking garage. **New Helvetia** (1215 19th St., at L St., tel. 916/441–1106), open daily 6:30 AM–11 PM, is an old fire station that's metamorphosed into a dalmatian-theme meeting place for those craving good coffee and focaccia pizza.

WORTH SEEING

If today Sacramento is known as a rather pedestrian political center, in days of old it was famed as a bustling railroad hub. Of course, prior to any of this, diverse Native American tribes inhabited the Central Valley—until pioneer families staked their claim, forcing Native American resettlement and assimilation. Sacramento's museums highlight its patchwork history.

CALIFORNIA STATE CAPITOL BUILDING

Surrounded by the beautiful 40-acre Victorian-style Capitol Park, this 1869 structure was extensively restored in the early 1980s with a lavish 120-ft-high interior rotunda. Sit in the gallery and watch the Assembly flail at the budget when they're in session or head to basement room B-27 for a map, information, and free building tours (given on the hour daily from 9–4). *10th St. and Capitol Mall, near L St., tel. 916/324–0333. Open daily 9–4.*

CALIFORNIA STATE INDIAN MUSEUM

Of interest at this wonderful museum devoted to the arts and crafts of California's earliest inhabitants is a display devoted to Ishi, the last Yahi Indian to emerge from the mountains (in 1911), who provided insight into the existence of this group of Native Americans. Well executed exhibits are worth spending some time viewing, as is the 10-minute video that plays continuously. Call ahead for tours and information on special activities, among them Honored Elders Day in May. *2601 K St., between 26th and 27th Sts., tel. 916/324–0971. Admission: $3. Open daily 10–5.*

CALIFORNIA STATE RAILROAD MUSEUM

This immensely popular museum successfully conveys the awesome amount of work that went into building the first transcontinental railway, completed in 1869 near Ogden, Utah. Exhibits manage to cover the glory of the accomplishment without entirely glossing over the physical toil and loss of life, suffered mainly by Chinese laborers. The best displays, though, have to do with the railroad culture that emerged in the second half of the last century. You can go through a sleeping car that simulates the swaying on the roadbed and the flashing lights of a passing town at night, or glimpse the elegance of the first-class dining car on the *Super Chief,* each of its tables set with a different china pattern. Allow at least a couple hours to experience the museum fully. Though it's expensive, this is probably the most worthwhile stop in Old Sacramento. *125 I St., at 2nd St., tel. 916/323–9280. Admission: $6. Open daily 10–5, last entry at 4:30.*

LA RAZA/GALERÍA POSADA

The experimental art of local and regional artists at La Raza/Galería Posada (704 O St., at 7th St., tel. 916/446–5133) proves that some things still thrive in the River City.

SUTTER'S FORT

Sacramento's earliest settlement was founded by German-born Swiss immigrant John Augustus Sutter in 1839. Visitors walk a self-guided tour, with audio speakers at each stop, which includes a blacksmith's shop, bakery, prison, living quarters, and livestock areas. Costumed docents sometimes reenact fort life, demonstrating crafts, food preparations, and firearm maintenance. *27th and L Sts., tel. 916/445–4422. Admission: $3 ($5 in summer). Open daily 10–5, last tour at 4:15.*

CHEAP THRILLS

Now an international institution, **Tower Records** (2500 16th St., at Broadway, tel. 916/444–3000) began here in 1960. The original store's neon sign is above the **Tower Café** (1518 Broadway, at 16th St., tel. 916/441–0222), a prime coffee spot for people-watching. The adjoining 1940 landmark, **Tower Theater** (16th St. and Broadway, tel. 916/443–1982), shows art films as well as mainstream releases. All three are in what's known as the **Tower District.** During summer months, you can catch the **Starlight Movie Series,** free outdoor showings of old movies on Thursday night at the **1849 Scene** park in Old Sacramento (Front and I Sts.). Call 916/558–3912 for schedules.

After a glitzy spell, the **California State Fair** (tel. 916/263–3000), which runs from mid-August through early September, has thankfully returned to its agricultural roots. The weather is always oppressively hot, but it's worth it to see the animals, who show up to vie for such titles as Supreme Dairy Goat Total Performer. Take I–80 Business Loop to the Cal Expo. The **Sacramento Jazz Jubilee** (tel. 916/372–5277), a 25-year-old international festival featuring blues, zydeco, and traditional jazz, happens every Memorial Day weekend for four days. Concerts are held at five sites throughout the city. Take advantage of discounts by ordering tickets ($10–$75) in advance. On K Street, between the convention center and the mall, the raucous **K Street Fair** takes place every Thursday evening May–October. Merchants tote their wares outside, and live bands play.

AFTER DARK

The **Rubicon Brewing Company** (2004 Capitol Ave., at 20th St., tel. 916/448–7032) is a favored hangout for jocks, ski bums, students, and office types looking to kick back; a pint of Rubicon brew runs $2.75. For those looking for live music or a dance floor, both the *News and Review* (look for it at cafés and newsstands) and the *Sacramento Bee* "Ticket" list dance and music clubs in the area. A good venue for alternative music is **Old Ironsides** (10th St., at S St., tel. 916/443–9751), which has music Thursday–Saturday (the cover's about $5), free movies on Monday, and a comedy talk show on Wednesday for $3. The dance floor at **Faces** (2000 K St., at 20th St., tel. 916/448–7798), Sacramento's largest gay club, attracts a mixed, trendy crowd for its house and country western nights—the cover charge ranges from nothing to $3. **Café Paris** (2326 K St., at 24th St., tel. 916/442–2001) has Spanish poetry readings Monday at 8 PM and $1.75 pints Monday and Wednesday 5–11. Live, mostly indie, music rolls into Paris Thursday–Saturday nights, usually with no cover.

OUTDOOR ACTIVITIES

BIKING

The **Jedediah Smith Memorial Bicycle Trail** starts by the Railway Museum in Old Sacramento and runs along the American River through Discovery Park, ending 32 mi later in Folsom (*see* Near Sacramento, *below*). Along the way, you'll pass by rolling hills, farmland, and wild blackberry bushes. The last 3 mi are steep but doable, and most of the trail is suitable for beginners. Ride smart after dark—if you're worried, latch on to another rider or set off in pairs. You can rent bikes for $15 a day at **City Bicycle Works** (2419 K St., at 25th St., tel. 916/447–2453), open weekdays 10–7, Saturday 10–6, Sunday 11–5. The **Sacramento Singletrack Scorchers** (tel. 916/552–2492) organizes coed and women-only mountain bike rides; call for information and a schedule.

RAFTING

Rafting on the American River during the long, hot summer is a Sacramento tradition. Unless you're a seasoned veteran or are with an experienced guide, stick to the south fork. You can rent equipment from **American River Raft Rentals** (11257 S. Bridge St., Rancho Cordova, tel. 916/635–6400), where four-person rafts go for $30, including life vests and paddles. For another $2.50, you can get a bus ride back when you're done. Dozens of rental outfits will take you on a guided full-day trip for about $75 during the week, $100 on weekends. Check the Yellow Pages under "River Trips," or ask at the tourist centers.

NEAR SACRAMENTO

FOLSOM

East of Sacramento, Folsom has a ho-hum Old Town that could easily be mistaken for any one of a number of historic cities. The town does, however, offer a day-trip's worth of unique delights. The **Folsom Chamber of Commerce** (200 Wool St., tel. 916/985–2698), open weekdays from 9–5, will point you to the nicely assembled, free **History Museum** (823 Sutter St., tel. 916/985–2707) near the old brothel section of town. The museum, open Wednesday–Sunday 11–4, gives details of the African American miners who were the first to mine for gold in the nearby Negro Bar, and the Chinatown here that was third largest in the state after Sacramento and San Francisco. The unusual "gem" of Folsom, though, is the one popularized by Johnny Cash's version of "Folsom Prison Blues." **Folsom Prison** (tel. 916/985–2561), called "the End of the World," has been housing inmates since 1880. Once a house for the insane, the inmates cut the granite stones from a nearby quarry and used them to build the old prison. The **Prison Museum** (north of Folsom on Natoma St.), open daily 8–4, will cost you a donation of your choice to enter and view such grim items as leg irons, photos of pageants the inmates aren't allowed to hold anymore, and knives prisoners made with melted shampoo bottles. For a history of past and present penal systems (this is the eighth largest "housing" unit in the country), no matter how you feel about the American judicial system, this place is a must. Inmate-made items are on sale in the Prison Hobby Shop, open daily 8–5. The **Folsom Commuter Bus** (tel. 916/355–8395) makes the 25 minute trip ($2.50) six times a day from Sacramento, weekdays only. If you're driving, take Hwy. 50 from Sacramento to the Folsom exit.

DAVIS

Despite the University of California at Davis being the state's top school for agricultural studies, Davis's feel is anything but John Deere. The student crowd—an even mix of hippies, gen-x'ers, and greeks—hangs at the cafés and bookstores in the central business district just east of campus, the area between B and G streets, bordered by 1st and 5th streets. Have coffee at grad-student hangout **Delta of Venus** (122 B St., at 2nd St., tel. 916/753–8639) or **Coffee and Classics** (132 E St., at 2nd St., tel. 916/758–7358), a used bookstore and coffeehouse in the Mansion Square complex.

The big event in Davis is **Picnic in the Park,** which takes place—rain or shine—every Wednesday (May–Oct. 4:30–8:30, Nov.–Apr. 2–6) in **Central Park** (4th and C Sts.). There's live music and ethnic food. Larger and more impressive is the Saturday morning **farmers' market,** also in Central Park, where vendors from all over the area converge from 8–noon to sell everything from strawberries to live quail. For quieter distractions, head to the southern edge of campus to Davis's impressive **arboretum** and picnic near the artificially controlled still-water stream. To reach the arboretum from I–80, take the U.C. Davis exit and follow signs from campus.

BASICS • The small **Chamber of Commerce** (228 B St. at 2nd St., tel. 916/756–5160) is open weekdays 9–noon and 1–5 and can give you maps for **Unitrans** (tel. 916/752–2877), the city's public transit. Davis is also accessible by public transit ($1) from Sacramento via **Yolobus** (tel. 916/371–2877).

WHERE TO SLEEP • While lodging is cheaper in Sacramento, Davis has a couple of attractive options. Right off the I–80 Davis exit, the **Davis Inn** (1111 Richards Blvd., tel. 916/756–0910) has sparkling, well-appointed rooms, a movie channel, and a pool. A room with one king bed is $52, with two queen beds $56. Nearer to campus, Pat Loomis's **Davis B&B Inn** (422 A St., at Russell St., tel. 916/753–9611) is a homey bed-and-breakfast. Rooms run $40–$60.

FOOD • In addition to the cafés listed above, Davis has several good restaurants. Just west of campus, the packed **Green Planet Juicery** (301 B St., at 3rd St., tel. 916/753–6000) serves adventurous smoothies ($3–$4) and tasty burritolike concoctions (around $4.50). Located just off the interstate, **Murder Burger** (978 Olive Dr., tel. 916/756–2142) serves up a mean half-pound patty for about $5; it's closed Wednesday.

AFTER DARK • East of the town center, **Sudwerk** microbrewery (2001 2nd St. at Pole Line Rd., tel. 916/758–8700) has year-round and seasonal brews on tap. Come Thursday–Saturday nights for local rock and jazz bands (there's a small cover Thursday). **The Palms Playhouse** (726 Drummond, tel. 916/756–9901), across the railroad tracks and east of Sudwerk, hosts a wide variety of well-known artists playing mostly country and blues. Fans of eclectic blues/country/alternative/garage music should check out the **Davis Saloon** (228 G St., tel. 916/758–3154); cover is usually $1 to $3.

SACRAMENTO RIVER DELTA

The delta is a lazy labyrinth of a thousand or so miles of rivers, streams, and canals connecting Stockton (*see* The San Joaquin Valley *in* Chapter 7) and Sacramento with the San Francisco Bay. The delta's waterways are popular with people in search of a little fishing, swimming, or boating. Yet the year-round population here is eerily sparse, the culture provincial, and the summer weather painfully hot. The delta does make a much more scenic drive than I–80, and as you make the 30- to 40-mi trek on Hwy. 160 between Sacramento and San Francisco, you'll be surprised at how quickly you find yourself in a place that feels several time zones and decades away.

The biggest town in the area is **Rio Vista,** where you'll find visitor information at the Chamber of Commerce (75 Main St., tel. 707/374–2700), shops, banks, and even a supermarket. This is the place to be if you're without a tent come nightfall. The tinier towns of **Locke** and **Isleton** are more historically interesting: Both once hosted thriving Chinese communities that left a curious legacy of Old West and Far East.

Locke—which emerged as a major Chinese community in the early part of this century—is probably the delta's main tourist attraction. What's left of the town is a block-long area on Main Street that includes **Joe Shoong's Chinese School,** where local kids still study Chinese after school; **Al the Wop's** restaurant and bar (tel. 916/776–1800), which has been operating since 1915 and comes complete with dollar bills on the ceiling, steak dinners on the menu, and country music on the jukebox; and the **Dai Loy Museum** (tel. 916/776–1661), an old gambling house that serves as a historical guide to the delta; it's open afternoons Thursday–Sunday and keeps shorter hours in winter. At **Yuen Chong Market** (13924 Main St., tel. 916/776–1818) pick up a great map ($3) listing all the area's marinas, harbors, campgrounds, and recreational areas.

GETTING AROUND • From the Bay Area, take I–80 east to the Hwy. 4 turnoff near Hercules, and go east to Hwy. 160, which follows the Sacramento River through the delta. Heading northeast on Hwy. 160, you'll soon run into Isleton and Locke. From Sacramento, take I–5 south to the turnoff for Hwy. 160. From Stockton, Hwys. 4 and 12 lead west into the delta; Hwy. 12 goes right through Rio Vista, situated about 6 mi northwest of Isleton.

WHERE TO SLEEP • The cheapest option is to camp by the water at **Sandy Beach Regional Park** (take 2nd Street south out of Rio Vista, tel. 707/374–2097), where sites are $12 per vehicle plus $3 for utilities. **Brannan Island State Park** (tel. 916/777–6671), 3 mi south of Rio Vista on Hwy. 160, has sites for $15–$16 per vehicle, $12 from September to mid-May. In summer, reserve through Destinet (tel. 800/444–7275). There are eight tent sites with water and electricity ($17) and RV sites with full hookup ($19) at **Vieira's Resort** (15476 Hwy. 160, tel. 916/777–6661), about 2 mi west of Isleton on Hwy. 160. Vieira's also rents cabins with kitchens ($40 in winter, $45 in summer).

FOOD • During the annual **Crawdad Festival**—held on Father's Day weekend in June—Isleton rises from the dead. Sample a heaping portion fresh from the river at **Ernie's Restaurant and Saloon** (212 2nd St., tel. 916/777–6510), at $6 for an appetizer or $10 for a 2-pound serving. If you have cooking equipment, load up at **Lira's Supermarket** in nearby Rio Vista (609 Hwy. 12, tel. 707/374–5399).

GOLD COUNTRY

Cutting a 350-mi swath down Hwy. 49, from Sierra City in the north to Yosemite in the south, and about 3½ hours east of San Francisco, the Gold Country encompasses wineries, caverns, rushing rivers, and the remnants of old frontier towns. The region's Native Americans—who were some of the last holdouts to white encroachment in the West—lived here for at least 2,000 years before James Marshall picked up a shiny rock from under John Sutter's sawmill. "Boys," he said to the millworkers in his thick New Jersey accent, "I believe I have found a gold mine." So began the 1849 mass migration of "49ers" to the foothills of the Sierra Nevada. Cornish, Peruvian, and Chinese hopefuls joined up with Missourians and Bostonians arriving by covered wagon, all hoping to make their fortune. Even at the height of the rush, though, few actually struck it rich. And by the end of the century, increasingly inaccessible deposits and rising production costs—coupled with environmental opposition and sinking gold value—closed most of the mines. The boomtowns busted, and the Wild West faded into nostalgia.

The main streets of the towns along Hwy. 49 are filled with historical ambiance—commemorative plaques, plank sidewalks, and carriage-ride tours. But the actual drive along Hwy. 49 is almost more spectacular than most of the stops, particularly during early spring, when the flowers are in bloom. Because they sit on major east–west thoroughfares, **Auburn** and **Placerville** are easy access points for quick forays into the region, heavy on motels, fast food, and other conveniences. Tiny towns like **Columbia** and **Murphys** are far better preserved but a little harder to reach and dull (or closed) at night. Towns like **Nevada City** (to the north) and **Sonora** (to the south) strike a balance, feeling different enough from home but giving you some options for eating, sleeping, and meandering.

If you couldn't care less where Mark Twain lived (Angels Camp) or how a mine shaft works, head for the great outdoors. Rollins and Scotts Flat reservoirs, both near Grass Valley, offer excellent boating and fishing. Farther south, **Auburn State Recreation Area** boasts some of the best mountain-biking trails in the region, and the American River is rife with rafting and river sports. For more rugged hiking, camping, fishing, and biking, check out the Tahoe and Eldorado National Forests.

Because delta temperatures hover in the high 90s most of the summer, a dip in the icy-cold river is the first outdoor option you'll want to consider.

BASICS

VISITOR INFORMATION

Tourist offices include the **El Dorado County Chamber of Commerce** (542 Main St., Placerville, tel. 530/621–5885 or 800/457–6279); the **Placer County Visitor Information Center** (13464 Lincoln Way, Suite A, Auburn, tel. 530/887–2111 or 800/427–6463); the **Grass Valley Chamber of Commerce** (248 Mill St., tel. 530/273–4667 or 800/655–4667); the **Nevada City Chamber of Commerce** (132 Main St., tel. 530/265–2692), which has excellent walking tour, hiking and walking, and mountain biking brochures; the **Amador County Chamber of Commerce** (125 Peek St., Jackson, tel. 209/223–0350); the **Calaveras County Visitors Center** (1211 S. Main St., Angels Camp, tel. 800/225–3764); the **Jamestown Visitor Center** (18148 Main St., tel. 209/984–4616); and the **Tuolumne County Visitors' Bureau** (55 W. Stockton St., Sonora, tel. 800/446–1333), which has helpful camping, hiking, and forest information.

For maps and hiking information on the Tahoe National Forest (located north of the Eldorado National Forest) as well as fire permits, head to the **Tahoe National Forest Headquarters** (631 Coyote St. at Hwy. 49, tel. 530/265–4531), right outside Nevada City.

WHEN TO GO

Consider planning your trip around one of the many Gold Country music festivals, including the **Annual Father's Day Weekend Bluegrass Festival,** held on the third weekend of June in Grass Valley. For information on these and other festivals, contact **Foggy Mountain Music** (tel. 530/273–6676) or the **Nevada County Arts Council** (tel. 530/265–3917), both in Grass Valley. To see the pioneers' mode of transport in action, come to Placerville in mid-June for the Main Street **Wagon Train Parade.**

COMING AND GOING

Highway 49 is the north–south backbone of the region, with Placerville (east of Sacramento on **U.S. 50**) roughly in the middle. The route is divided into northern Gold Country (Placerville and north) and southern Gold Country (points south of Placerville). Most of the larger towns on Hwy. 49 are also served by east–west roads that lead back to the coast and out into the Sierra Nevada. **I–80** meets Hwy. 49 at Auburn and continues east to Reno. **Highway 20** goes through Grass Valley and Nevada City, **Highway 4** through Angels Camp and Murphys, **Highway 88** through Jackson, and **Highway 108** through Sonora and Jamestown. Curvy Hwy. 49 can be slow going due to periodic 35-mph speed limits.

Though it's difficult, touring the Gold Country by bus is not out of the question. From Sonora, **Tuolumne County Transit** (tel. 209/532–0404) will get you to Columbia and Jamestown ($2.50) but only weekdays 6 AM–7 PM. For the northern Gold Country, Amtrak runs a bus from San Francisco to Grass Valley three times a day (4½ hrs, $21.50–$33 round-trip) and a train-bus combination to Placerville three times

THE GOLD COUNTRY

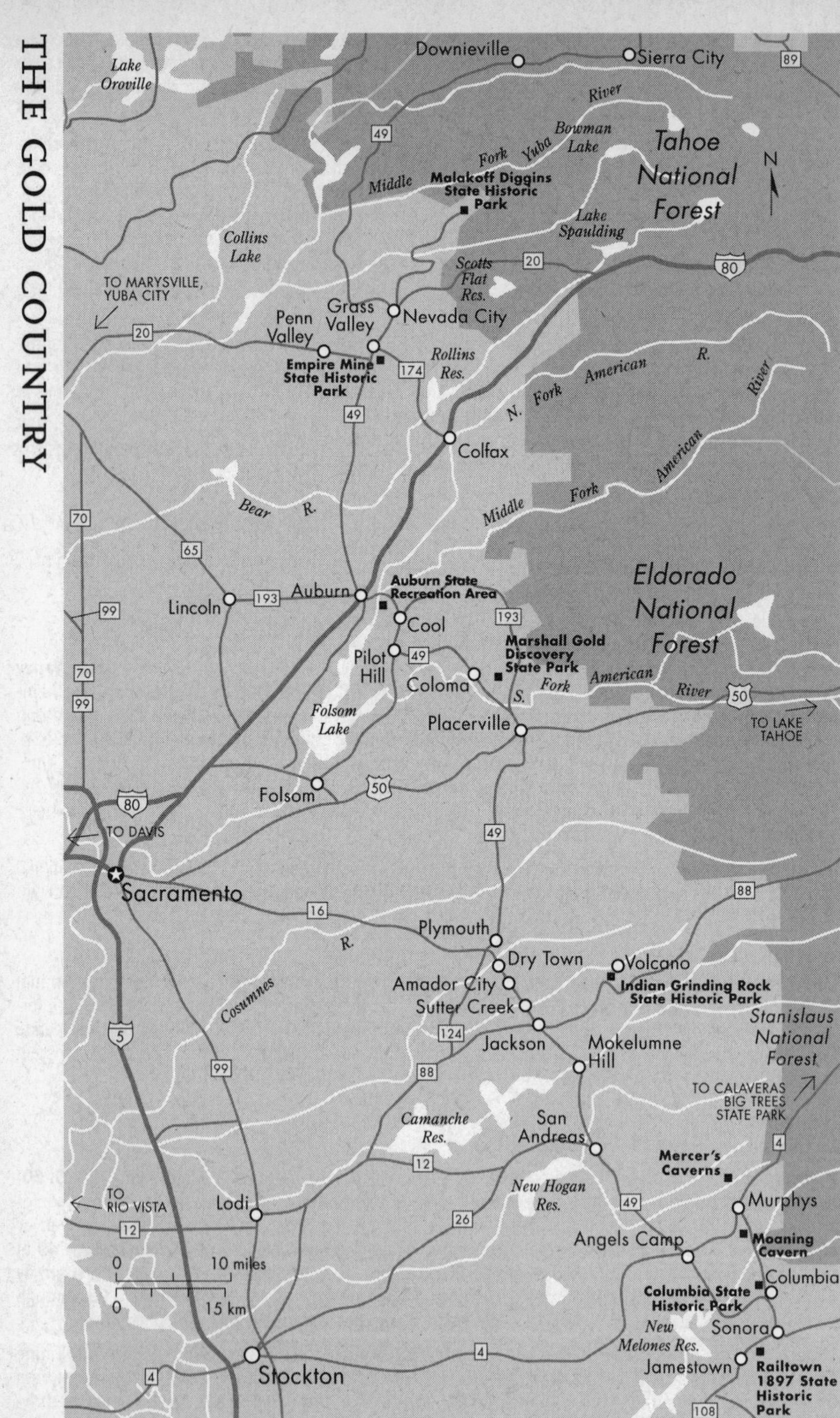

Downieville
Sierra City
89
Lake Oroville
River
Bowman Lake
Tahoe National Forest
49
Fork
Yuba
Middle
Malakoff Diggins State Historic Park
N
Lake Spaulding
Collins Lake
Scotts Flat Res.
20
80
TO MARYSVILLE, YUBA CITY
Grass Valley
Nevada City
Penn Valley
20
Empire Mine State Historic Park
174
Rollins Res.
49
N. Fork
American
R.
River
Colfax
American
Bear
R.
Middle
Fork
70
65
Eldorado National Forest
Auburn State Recreation Area
Lincoln
193
Auburn
99
Cool
193
Pilot Hill
49
Marshall Gold Discovery State Park
70
Coloma
S.
Fork
American
River
99
50
TO LAKE TAHOE
Folsom Lake
Placerville
Folsom
50
80
TO DAVIS
49
Sacramento
88
16
Plymouth
R.
Dry Town
Volcano
Amador City
Indian Grinding Rock State Historic Park
Cosumnes
Sutter Creek
Stanislaus National Forest
5
124
Jackson
Mokelumne Hill
99
88
TO CALAVERAS BIG TREES STATE PARK
Camanche Res.
San Andreas
4
12
Mercer's Caverns
New Hogan Res.
TO RIO VISTA
Lodi
49
Murphys
26
12
Angels Camp
Moaning Cavern
0
10 miles
Columbia
0
15 km
Columbia State Historic Park
New Melones Res.
Sonora
4
Jamestown
Railtown 1897 State Historic Park
Stockton
4
108

daily ($13–$22 round-trip). **Greyhound** (tel. 800/231–2222) also runs frequent buses from San Francisco to Placerville (5 hrs, $57 round-trip). In Placerville, **El Dorado Transit** (tel. 530/642–5383) will bus you to Sacramento for $2.50.

NORTHERN GOLD COUNTRY

PLACERVILLE

Back in the bad old days, Placerville was known as Hangtown in honor of the notorious brand of frontier justice practiced here. Today, it's mostly known as the last major town on U.S. 50 heading east toward Tahoe. If you decide to make this your principle Gold Country stop, you'll likely be disappointed. Main Street boasts only an old bell tower, a few bookstores, and an effigy of a desperado above the **Hangman's Tree** bar on Main Street. But this may be your only chance to sample the town's legendary oyster omelet, the Hangtown Fry—try the **Bell Tower Café** (423 Main St., tel. 530/626–3483). If you're not into spending $6.50 for this odd, possibly stomach-turning concoction that's been trying to win status as the state meal for years, try **A Main Street Cafe** (325 Main St., tel. 530/642–1700) or **Sweetie Pies** (577 Main St., tel. 530/642–0128), cuter-than-thou establishments that serve light lunches (under $10) and heaping portions of fresh baked pies ($2–$3).

Placerville makes a good base for both American River activities and for visiting nearby historic Coloma (8 mi north). Placerville is also the ideal place to nosh homegrown fruit. Pick up a copy of the **El Dorado County farm trails map** or the **Apple Hill growers map** from the chamber of commerce for information on many farms in the area you can visit. Get the fruity booty Saturdays June–October at Placerville's **farmers' market** (Main St, at Cedar Ravine St.).

For a free look back at the area's golden era, take a self-guided tour through the **Gold Bug Mine** (1 mi north of city on Bedford Ave., tel. 530/642–5238), a park with 200 old mines that produced $17 million in gold. At the west end of town at the County Fairground, the **El Dorado County Historical Museum** (104 Placerville Dr., tel. 530/621–5865) is a free museum full of artifacts, both Native American and Gold Rushian. It's open Wednesday–Saturday 10–4, Sunday noon–4, Monday and Tuesday by appointment only (call ahead).

WHERE TO SLEEP • A ½-mi stretch of Broadway offers several places to stay for $35–$45; the cheapest is the **Gold Trail Motor Lodge** (1970 Broadway, tel. 530/622–2906) with doubles from $36, minus a few bucks if you have an AAA card. The highly recommended, family-run **Milton's Cary House** (300 Main St., tel. 530/622–4271) is a Victorian with beautiful etched and stained glass windows, balconies, kitchenettes, and laundry facilities. Spacious doubles are $45. For camping information *see* Eldorado National Forest, *below*.

ELDORADO NATIONAL FOREST

The **Eldorado National Forest** is roughly between Lake Tahoe and Placerville, extending almost as far down as Jackson. The **Eldorado National Forest Information Center** (3070 Camino Heights Dr., tel. 530/644–6048), 5½ mi east of Placerville on Hwy. 50, has information on campsites, cross-country skiing, hiking and biking trails, and work parties. For a cool dip, drive to **Bridalveil Falls,** 17 mi east of Placerville off Hwy. 50, with its swimming holes on the American River. **Lover's Leap** is a popular site for rockclimbing; go to the 42 Mile campsite on Hwy 50, 5 mi west of the eastern end of the Forest, and make a right. From here it's about 1 mi (you can drive) to the unmarked trailhead. Lover's Leap is about 1 more mi up the trail. Even rangers concede that finding the Leap can be confusing—don't be afraid to ask for help at the campsite.

Except for the established sites and places where it's forbidden, camping is free anywhere in the National Forest. Reservations can be made for some sites through Destinet (tel. 800/283–2267), though many are first-come-first-served. At **Sly Park** recreation area (tel. 530/644–2545), 12 mi east of Placerville (from Hwy. 50, exit Sly Park Rd.; follow signs for 5 mi), you can camp in one of 159 campsites for $15 a night. About 18 mi further east on Hwy. 50, the **China Flat** campground has 18 sites on the American River.

COLOMA

Just north of Placerville on Hwy. 49, Coloma offers access to the south fork of the American River, which is filled all summer long with rafts, kayaks, and inner tubes. **Mother Lode River Trips** (6280 Hwy. 49, in Lotus, tel. 530/626–4187 or 800/427–2387) runs four-hour rafting excursions for $59 per person during the week. The site of James Marshall's fateful and fortuitous gold find, Coloma is mostly contained within **Marshall Gold Discovery State Historic Park,** which is home to a historical museum (tel. 530/622–1116), gold-related exhibits along the river, good swimming, and several hikes. The park contains a number of buildings dating back to the Gold Rush, a working replica of John Sutter's mill, and a self-guided trail leading to a monument marking his discovery. The museum here is not as interesting as the outdoor exhibits, which often include a live blacksmith working red-hot metal with a hammer. *Discovery Park: Hwy. 49, tel. 530/622–3470. Day use: $5 per car (main museum and all exhibits included). Park open daily 8–sunset; museum open daily 10–5 (shorter hrs in winter).*

CAMPING • Camp Lotus (5461 Bassi Rd., exit Hwy. 49 at Lotus Rd., tel. 530/622–8672), open March–October, offers secluded camping and modern facilities for $7 per person, with a $21 minimum per site (slightly lower weekdays).

AUBURN

Auburn, at the junction of Hwy. 49 and I–80, is somewhat suburbanized. But being the largest and oldest Gold Country town it also has a fairly well-preserved spirit-of-'49 flavor. Check out the **Placer County Courthouse and Museum** (101 Maple St., tel. 530/889–6500), open Tuesday–Sunday 10–4, an impressive Greco-Roman structure with the new Placer County historical museum inside. The **Bernhard Museum Complex** (291 Auburn-Folsom Rd., near High St., tel. 530/889–4156), a 19th-century Victorian house, re-creates the era's domestic realm. Admission is $1, and it's open Tuesday–Friday 11–3, weekends noon–4. A brochure describing a walking tour of old town is available free at the Placer County Information Center.

WHERE TO SLEEP AND EAT • The **Foothills Motel** (13431 Bowman Rd., tel. 530/885–8444), offering a pool and hot tub, charges $47–$53 for a double room. If Foothills is full, try any of the slew of motels off I–80 at the Foresthill exit. Camp for $7–$11, depending on the time of year, in the Auburn State Recreation Area at **Lake Clementine,** about 2 mi from Auburn off the Auburn-Foresthill Road; reserve through Destinet (tel. 800/444–7275).

When you get hungry, grab some Mexican food at **Trejos Restaurante Mexicano** (1120 High St., tel. 530/889–8401). For all-you-can-eat Mongolian barbecue, head over to **Sum's** (958 Lincoln Way, tel. 530/889–8948).

OUTDOOR ACTIVITIES • The massive **Auburn State Recreation Area** has camping ($7–$9 per site), hiking, swimming, boating, rafting, fishing, and some of the best mountain-biking trails in Northern California (the area's other mountain bike mecca is Downieville). Of Auburn's trails, the 10-mi **Omstead Loop** trail, starting behind the fire station in **Cool** on Hwy. 49, is one of the most beautiful. The **Stagecoach Trail,** running from Russell Road in Auburn to the old Foresthill bridge on the north fork of the American River, is a solid bet for both hiking and biking.

The recreation area's prime location between the north and middle forks of the **American River** makes it ideal for rafting and water sports, but the rough waters call for experienced navigators. If you're a beginner, it's best to stick to the south fork of the river, near Coloma (*see above*). For information and maps, stop in at the **Auburn State Recreation Area Headquarters,** located 2 mi out of Auburn en route east to Cool on Hwy. 49 (tel. 530/885–4527), open 8–4:30 except Wednesday and weekends when it closes at noon.

GRASS VALLEY

On the 23-mi drive from Auburn to Grass Valley along Hwy. 49, you'll shake the familiar vista of fast-food franchises and begin to see the rolling hills that characterize the heart of northern Gold Country. Formerly the center of the so-called Second Gold Rush in 1850, Grass Valley today is a well-groomed little town featuring saloons, antiques stores, and restaurants—all proudly proclaiming to have been in continuous operation since the 1850s. Pick up the *Walking Tour of Historic Grass Valley* brochure at the Chamber of Commerce (248 Mill St., tel. 800/655–4667), which is the site of notorious dancer Lola Montez's former home (her bathtub is still in the front yard, planted with flowers). Montez was supposedly lover to Franz Liszt and Bavarian king Ludwig, who banished her as a witch after she pushed too hard for democracy, according to legend. She ended up in Grass Valley, of all places, in the early 1850's. After you visit the Chamber of Commerce, stroll to the **North Star Mining Museum** (tel. 530/273–4255), at the south end of Mill Street. It's open May–mid-October.

Just east of town is **Empire Mine State Historic Park** (10791 E. Empire St., tel. 530/273–8522), the deepest and richest hardrock mine in the area. When it closed in 1956 it was already 11,000 ft deep and had yielded 362,500 pounds of gold. These days, $3 buys you entrance to the museum and grounds, tours of the mine and the **Bourn Mansion** (where the mine owners lived), and same-day admittance to Malakoff Diggins State Historic Park (*see* Nevada City, *below*). Tours give you a good sense of the often wretched existence led by the miners and the relatively luxurious life led by the mine owners.

WHERE TO SLEEP AND EAT • Grass Valley may be your best bet in the region for an affordable night's sleep. Try the motels on South Auburn Street, including the **Coach 'n' Four** (628 S. Auburn St., tel. 530/273–8009), where doubles start at $46. If you're on a looser budget, the comfortable **Holiday Lodge** (1221 E. Main St., tel. 530/273–4406) has doubles starting at $55. You may also want to try camping at **Greenhorn Campground** (tel. 530/272–6100); it's heavy on the amenities and close to town (take a left off Hwy. 174 towards Colfax on Greenhorn Access Rd.). Sites start at $16. Grass Valley's culinary specialty is pasties, Cornish baked delicacies that can be found at places like **Marshall's Pasties** (203 Mill St., tel. 530/272–2844), where apple, ham and cheese, or sausage versions cost less than $4. For something more elaborate, check out the popular **Tofanelli's** (302 W. Main St., tel. 530/272–1468), where lunch runs around $7, dinner around $10.

NEVADA CITY

During its Gold Rush heyday, Nevada City boasted a population virtually equal to that of San Francisco—over a century later, it's even smaller (and better preserved) than its southern neighbor Grass Valley. Refugees from California's coastal cities have given Nevada City a livelier ambiance than most nearby towns, and you're likely to find a poetry reading, a jazz concert, or a theater production going on as you pass through. Many events take place in the **Miner's Foundry Cultural Center** (325 Spring St., tel. 530/265–5040); pick up a schedule of festivals and performances at the Chamber of Commerce (*see* Visitor Information *in* Basics, *above*).

If you want to soak up Gold Country history, just walk up and down Broad Street. Stick your head into the old **Nevada Theatre** (401 Broad St.), California's oldest theater building in continuous use (Mark Twain, Emma Nevada, and many other "superstars" of bygone days appeared on its stage) and the **National Hotel** (211 Broad St.), the oldest continuously operating hotel west of the Mississippi. The town is also known for its quirky Victorians—the chamber of commerce has information highlighting individual houses.

For a change of pace, drive 11 mi north of Nevada City to the **North Columbia Schoolhouse Cultural Center** (17894 Tyler Foote Rd., tel. 530/265–2826), the hub of activity for a flourishing artists' community that began in the '70s with the likes of Gary Snyder and Allen Ginsberg. These free souls bought up cheap property and started their own mini back-to-the-land movement, building their own homes and organizing craft shows. Most weekends bring live music, art exhibits, and theater presentations to the town's outdoor amphitheater and the cultural center, which also hosts a renowned **Storytelling Festival** the third week in July.

WHERE TO SLEEP AND EAT • Cheap lodging is hard to come by here. The quaint, if a bit shabby, cabins at the '30s-vintage **Motel** (575 E. Broad St., tel. 530/265–2233) are a good deal, starting at $45. The charming old **National Hotel** (tel. 530/265–4551; *see above*) has a few basic rooms for $42, or $68 with private bath. Your best bet is to take advantage of the nearby campgrounds (*see* Outdoor Activities, *below*).

For scrumptious, strictly vegetarian fare, head south of the town center (take Pine St. to Zion St., then go west four blocks) to **Earth Song Café** (135 Argall Way, tel. 530/265–8025), which is open Sunday–Thursday 10–8, Friday and Saturday 10–8:30. You'll be surprised at how well a carrot milkshake ($3) goes with chili over cornbread ($5) or a Gringo enchilada ($7). The attached market is open daily 8 AM–9 PM and sells organic produce, fresh bread, and granola. For deli meals, desserts, strong espresso, and arty culture, try hip **Mekka** (237 Commercial St., tel. 530/478–1517), a gothic warehouse café.

OUTDOOR ACTIVITIES • Biking and hiking are big here, particularly on the dirt roads around town. The **Banner Mountain Trail** is a 10-mi, 800-ft climb starting at the cross of Sacramento Street and the freeway; ride past the Northern Queen Inn to Gracie Road, then follow signs. The **Augustine Agony** trail, an 1,800-ft climb, is for advanced bikers; ride up Cement Hill Road, turn right at Augustine Road, then keep left all the way down to the South Yuba River. **Coyote Adventure Company** (123 Nevada St., tel. 530/265–6909) rents bikes for $30 a day, sells its own maps for 25¢, and also operates a shuttle that will drop you off at the top of popular rides. For more information on rides, call the Bicyclists of Nevada County ride hotline: 530/274–3478. For some light and scenic exercise, drive 7 mi north on Hwy. 49 to the **South Yuba Independence Trail.** After about a 10-minute hike on this relaxing trail, you'll get a good view of the Yuba River—the big payoff comes about ½ mi later when you get to the falls. Follow the wooden ramps down to the bottom, picnic on the rocks, and take a dip if you can stand the cold water.

Just northeast of Nevada City lies **Malakoff Diggins State Historic Park** (tel. 530/265–2740). This 600-ft-deep canyon is a monument to the technological achievement and ecological devastation of hydraulic mining (where miners blasted the gold-bearing rock with high pressure water hoses, eroding away tons of soil). Before outraged Sacramento Valley farmers managed to get a judgment against the mining company in 1884, $3 million in gold was produced here. The park's **museum** is open daily 10–5, weekends only in winter. You can wander along several trails or take a tour—included in the $5 day-use fee—during summer (weekends only in winter). Another attraction here is good camping ($10 per car; reservations: 800/444–7275). The park also has cabins available for $20, but they're primitive—just four walls and a wood stove, so bring your own bedding and $3 for fuel wood. From Nevada City, go north 11 mi on Hwy. 49 to Tyler Foote Road and follow the signs about 15 mi to the park entrance. Slightly closer to Nevada City and ideal for fishing (boat rental $28) and hiking is **Scotts Flat Lake** (18848 Hwy. 20, 5 mi east of Nevada City, tel. 530/265–5302). Campsites with all the amenities go for $18–$22 for four people.

SOUTHERN GOLD COUNTRY

JACKSON

Though it's not as well preserved as some of the smaller Gold Country towns, Jackson makes a good base for quick day trips to smaller towns, such as spruced-up **Sutter Creek** (4 mi north on Hwy. 49); sleepy, unpretentious **Mokelumne Hill** (8 mi south on Hwy. 49); or tiny, engaging **Volcano** (13 mi east of Jackson on Hwy. 88). Nine mi out of Jackson (toward Volcano on Hwy. 88) is the popular **Chaw'se Indian Grinding Rock State Historic Park** (tel. 209/296–7488), a 135-acre park featuring a reconstructed Miwok village and the largest food grinding rock in North America. The park has 23 campsites, complete with brand-new bathrooms and showers, at $15–$16 a night ($12 in the winter). If you're not camping, you can still hike around the park and visit the **Chaw'se Regional Indian Museum** (open weekdays 11–3, weekends 10–4) for $5 per car. Evening ranger programs are free; ask at the museum for more information. In Jackson itself, check out **St. Sava Serbian Orthodox Church** (724 N. Main St.), in the middle of a dramatic, terraced cemetery. It's the mother church of Serbian orthodoxy in the United States. The Amador County Chamber of Commerce (*see* Basics, *above*) has directions to all.

WHERE TO SLEEP AND EAT • Rooms start at $45 at the 135-year-old **National Hotel** (2 Water St., tel. 209/223–0500). If you stay at the **Jackson Holiday Lodge** (850 Hwy. 49, tel. 209/223–0486) you get a pool but much less history; doubles start at $46. For steak and egg cuisine, locals flock to **Mel and Faye's Drive-In** (tel. 209/223–0853) on the southbound side of Hwy. 49 near the center of town. Two mi up Hwy. 49 in Martell is the gaily festooned **Antonio's** (12496 Depot Rd., tel. 209/223–4664), packed Tuesday–Saturday with folks sucking down the area's finest margaritas. Try the light enchilada dinner, with rice, beans, and salad for $7.

ANGELS CAMP

Mark Twain lived in a cabin on the nearby Jackass Hill and set his popular short story "The Celebrated Jumping Frog of Calaveras County" in Angels Camp, where Hwy. 49 joins the east–west Hwy. 4. Homage is paid to the Missouri-born satirist in the form of the annual **Calaveras County Fair and International Jumping Frog Jubilee.** Held the third weekend in May at the fairgrounds (2 mi south of town on Hwy. 49), the festival includes carnival rides, a rodeo, and music to put you in the mood for the big frog jumping contest (don't worry if you left your frog at home—you can buy a contestant at the Jubilee). Admission is $7–$9 a day. For more information on the town's history, the **Angel's Camp Museum** (753 S. Main St., tel. 209/736–2963), admission $1, has 3 acres of it both inside and out.

WHERE TO SLEEP AND EAT • The **Gold Country Inn Motel** (720 S. Main St., tel. 800/851–4944) has large, clean doubles for $49–$69. **Glory Hole** (tel. 209/536–9094), at New Melones Lake (*see* Outdoor Activities, *below*), has 144 sites not far from the water for $10. Angels Camp has few restaurants, and even fewer of them stay open for dinner. **Mike's Pizza** (294 S. Main St., tel. 209/736–9246) will deliver free to your motel and has burgers and sandwiches (most under $5) in addition to pizza. **Dave's Diner** (451 S. Main St., in Alta Village Shopping Center, tel. 209/736–8080) features a '50's motif and is open for breakfast and lunch only Sunday–Thursday 6–2, plus dinner Friday and Saturday until 8.

OUTDOOR ACTIVITIES • **The Mountain Pedaler** (352 S. Main St., tel. 209/736–0771) rents bikes for $20 a day and will advise you on good local rides. For boating, fishing, waterskiing, and swimming, go south a couple miles on Hwy. 49 to the Beacon station and follow signs for **New Melones Lake.** Bass, crappie, catfish, and trout can be pulled from the reservoir.

MURPHYS

A short drive east of Angels Camp on Hwy. 4 is the meticulously restored town of Murphys, a little upscale for lodging and other practicalities but a nice place to spend a day. If the summer heat is killing you, take a dip in **Murphys Creek,** a block from tree-lined Main Street. Across the way at the **Nugget Restaurant** (75 Big Trees Rd., tel. 209/728–2608), you can grab a cheeseburger ($5) and wash it down at the adjacent bar. Murphy's has had a wine industry since the Gold Rush: Get information on local tastings by calling the **Wine Association** at 800/225–3764. The **Murphy's Creek Brewing Company** (Murphy's Grade and Lower French Gulch Rd., tel. 209/736–2739) microbrewery also has tastings on weekends from 11–5.

The **Old Timers Museum** (470 Main St., tel. 209/728–1160) is a unique conglomeration of curios and photos donated by the town's residents. The museum is open weekends 11–4, and donations are requested. One of Murphys's biggest attractions is **Mercer Caverns** (tel. 209/728–2101), about 1 mi north of Main Street on the old Sheep Ranch Road. Discovered in 1885 by a gold prospector, the caverns consist of 10 chambers with awesome crystalline stalactites and stalagmites. They're open daily 9–5 from Memorial Day–September, weekends and holidays 11–2:30 during the off-season. Admission is $5 and includes a 45-minute tour.

Fifteen miles out of Murphys (head east on Hwy. 4) is **Calaveras Big Trees State Park.** The Miwok and Washo Indians had been living around these giant sequoia groves for years before an enterprising promoter—feeling the pinch of waning mining fortunes in Murphys—began touring the country with a 116-ft strip of bark from one of the trees: A tourist attraction was born. This state park is home to some of the largest (and rarest) living things on the planet—150 magnificent giant sequoia redwood trees. Some are almost 3,000 years old, 90 ft around at the base, and upwards of 250 ft tall. The North Grove offers easy hikes, while the South Grove is the place to go if you want a feel for the wilderness. Guides for the park's trails, which crisscross 6,000 acres of land, are available at the visitor center; day use is $5. **Camping** is available in the north grove and at Oak Hollow ($14); (reservations 800/444–7275). Both campsites and trails are liable to be closed from late November until late April due to snow. Call the park (tel. 209/795–2334) for updates.

COLUMBIA

In 1854, the "Gem of Southern Mines" came within two legislative votes of beating out Sacramento for state capital. Twenty years and $87 million worth of gold later, Columbia's population had nearly vanished, leaving the town (2 mi north of Sonora on Parrotts Ferry Road) to eventually become a state historic park. One of the best preserved Gold Rush towns, this could well be *the* place to visit or to avoid, depending on your attitude toward Gold Country nostalgia. In addition to stagecoach rides and elegant hotels, Columbia offers a restored schoolhouse that's worth a quick visit. The **City Hotel** (Main St., tel. 209/532–1479) has a nationally known restaurant that serves an incredible four-course dinner for $31.50, but it's worth it. The adjoining What Cheer Saloon is right out of a western movie. If you can't afford the fancy dinner, at least have a drink in the saloon.

For one of the most beautiful drives in the area, take **Parrotts Ferry Road** (County Rd. E18) from Columbia north toward Hwy. 4. About 2 mi north of town, a turnoff leads down to a spot where you can take a warm-water dip (look for the DAY USE ONLY sign). Another 1½ mi north, the no-longer-so-secret watering hole can be found at the end of the **Natural Bridges Trail.** Look for the sign for the trail, park your car, hike down ¼-mi, and swim under the amazing caverns. Locals are less than thrilled to have their hangout written up in guidebooks, so be considerate and don't leave any trash behind. Camp at **Marble Quarry RV Park** (11551 Yankee Hill Rd., tel. 209/532–9539), where sites 10 minutes from downtown are $18–$25.

The famous **Moaning Cavern,** whose main chamber is large enough to store the Statue of Liberty, is on Parrotts Ferry Road between Columbia and Murphys. So named for the sounds that emanate from it (less so now than in the past), the main source of moaning nowadays is from budget travelers who've come all the way up the road to find that it costs $75 for the three-hour rappel-spelunking tour of the prehistoric cave (reservations required). For $6.75 take the traditional, no-thrills, 45-minute tour of the main chamber via a 235-step spiral staircase. This archaeological site contains the oldest human remains yet found in America (before the stairs were added, some unlucky person fell into the cavern an average of once every 130 years starting back 13,000 years ago!). *Parrotts Ferry Rd., tel. 209/736–2708. Open summer, weekdays 9–6, weekends and holidays 10–5; winter, weekdays 10–5, weekends 9–5.*

SONORA AND JAMESTOWN

At the junction of Hwys. 49 and 108, Sonora is larger and more crowded than most towns in the region. As you walk down Washington Street, the main drag, you'll recognize the trademark elements—Western-style storefronts, second-story porches, and old hotels—that have made this a popular movie location. It's also a pleasant stopover en route to Stanislaus National Forest or Yosemite (*see* Chapter 7). Pick up a map at the Tuolumne (say it: To-ALL-o-mee) County Visitors' Bureau (*see* Visitor Information *in* Basics, *above*) and wander around.

A couple miles southwest on Hwy. 49 is small, gift shop–ambianced **Jamestown** (or Jimtown, as it's sometimes called), Hollywood's favorite "Wild West" movie set. The town is named after a certain gentleman scoundrel, George F. James, who promised high wages to miners to work the area, then ran off with the gold. A subsequent attempt to change the town's name was unsuccessful. **Railtown 1897 State Historic Park** (end of 5th Ave., tel. 209/984–3953) preserves the remnants of the region's glorious rail culture. "The most photographed railroad in the world," this railroad has appeared in more than 200 movies and television productions. The other tourist attraction in Jamestown is the prospecting tour; recent rains have replenished the streams, so you may strike it even richer. **Gold Prospecting Expeditions** (18170 Main St., tel. 209/984–4653) guarantees that anyone who goes on a trip of at least two hours ($30 for one person, $60 for families of up to five) and follows its instructions will find some gold. Shorter trips are available at a lower cost.

WHERE TO SLEEP • A bunch of motels lie on Hwy. 108 between Jamestown and Sonora, but your best lodging bets are in Sonora itself. Call ahead during the school year to reserve a bed in the **Sonora hostel** (11800 Columbia College Dr., tel. 209/533–2339)—the "hostel" actually comprises dorms on the Columbia College campus, though you don't have to be a student to stay there. To reach the hostel from Sonora, take Hwy 49 north, turn right at Parrotts Ferry Road, right at Sawmill Flat Road, enter the campus grounds and make a hard right at the fire station. From there follow the signs to STUDENT HOUSING. Beds are $15 per night. The **Gunn House** (286 S. Washington St., tel. 209/532–3421), the first two-story structure built in town, retains an antique charm with old furniture and wrought-iron beds. Doubles start at $45 with continental breakfast and use of the pool. The restored 1922 **Royal Hotel** (18239 Main St., tel. 209/984–5271) in Jamestown has doubles starting at $45 (breakfast included). Otherwise, camp at **Moccasin Point** (tel. 209/852–2396) on Don Pedro Lake for $14 (no dogs allowed), or at **Pine Mountain Lake** (tel. 209/962–8625) for $12 ($18 with water and electricity). Both are east of Chinese Camp off Hwy. 120.

FOOD • In Sonora, **Alfredo's** (123 S. Washington St., tel. 209/532–8332) has the best Mexican food in the county; most dinner dishes (except for seafood) are in the $7–$10 range. The nearby **Bagel Bin** (83 N. Washington St., tel. 209/533–1904) has fresh, doughy bagels for 65¢. For a great breakfast, come to **Wilma's Café** (275 S. Washington St., tel. 209/532–9957). In Jamestown, another find is **Michaelangelo's** (18228 Main St., tel. 209/984–4830), serving gourmet pasta and pizza dishes for $7–$11.

AFTER DARK • There are several bars on South Washington Street in Sonora, including the **Flying Pig Saloon** (273 S. Washington St., tel. 209/532–8305), which has roots music, largely blues, every night, with a cover of $2–$3 on Friday and Saturday. Head to the **Brass Rail** (131 S. Washington St., tel. 209/533–1700) for mo' blues, old-time rock, and a nominal cover. The **Arts Center/Stage 3 Theater Co.** (208 S. Green St., tel. 209/536–1778) puts on a variety of events emphasizing contemporary plays by new playwrights. There's also a funky café next door called Cups, which includes a bookstore and gallery.

LAKE TAHOE

Straddling the border of California and Nevada on the northern flank of the Sierra Nevada range, Lake Tahoe is one of the West Coast's most popular outdoor playgrounds. During spring and summer, when temperatures hover in the 70s, the lake (about a 3½-hour drive east of San Francisco on I–80) offers boating, fishing, waterskiing, and jet skiing; and the mountains surrounding Tahoe Basin satiate the desires of even the most demanding rock climbers, hikers, bikers, equestrians, and anglers. During the winter season (usually December–April, sometimes extending into May), attention shifts to downhill and cross-country skiing and snowboarding. Tahoe has earned a worldwide reputation for its "extreme" con-

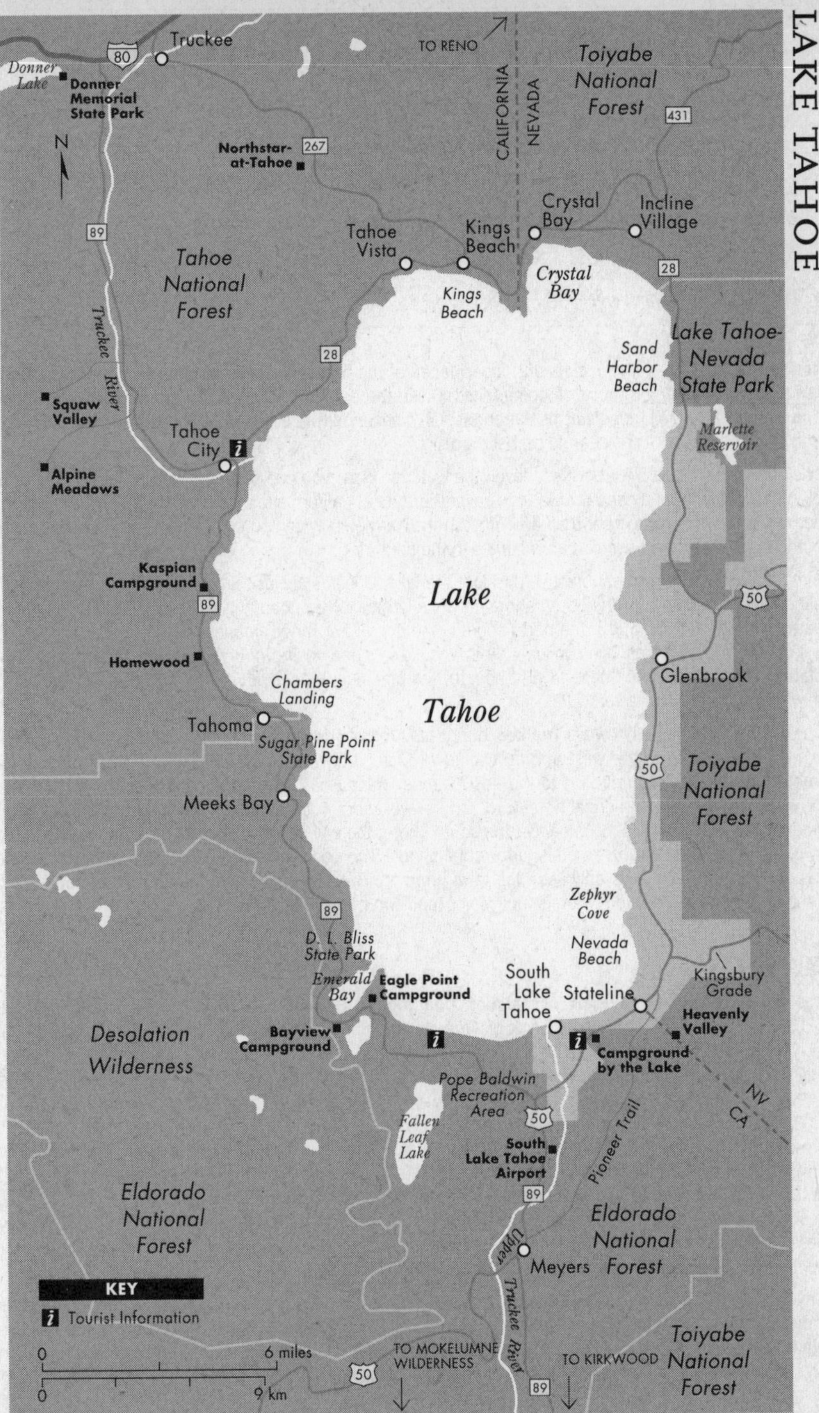

Truckee
80
TO RENO
Donner Lake
Donner Memorial State Park
Toiyabe National Forest
CALIFORNIA
NEVADA
431
N
Northstar-at-Tahoe
267
Crystal Bay
Incline Village
89
Tahoe Vista
Kings Beach
Tahoe National Forest
28
Crystal Bay
Kings Beach
Truckee River
28
Sand Harbor Beach
Lake Tahoe-Nevada State Park
Squaw Valley
Marlette Reservoir
Tahoe City
Alpine Meadows
Kaspian Campground
89
Lake
50
Homewood
Glenbrook
Chambers Landing
Tahoe
Tahoma
Sugar Pine Point State Park
50
Toiyabe National Forest
Meeks Bay
89
Zephyr Cove
D. L. Bliss State Park
Nevada Beach
South Lake Tahoe
Kingsbury Grade
Emerald Bay
Eagle Point Campground
Stateline
Heavenly Valley
Desolation Wilderness
Bayview Campground
Campground by the Lake
NV
CA
Pope Baldwin Recreation Area
50
Fallen Leaf Lake
Pioneer Trail
South Lake Tahoe Airport
Eldorado National Forest
89
Eldorado National Forest
Upper Truckee River
Meyers
KEY
Tourist Information
Toiyabe National Forest
0
6 miles
0
9 km
50
TO MOKELUMNE WILDERNESS
TO KIRKWOOD
89

KEEP TAHOE BLUE

With so many visitors and local interests, it takes work to keep Lake Tahoe magnificent. The League to Save Lake Tahoe (around since 1957; tel. 530/541–5388 or 530/546–5410) is responsible for halting north shore casino development, buying up land for public use, ensuring that environmental regulations are being followed, and all those "Keep Tahoe Blue" bumper stickers. It also hosts free hiking, biking, and skiing tours.

ditions, thanks to the sheer cliffs and steep faces of the Sierra Nevada, while the Donner Summit is famed for its challenging rock climbing faces. Given the array of pleasures, it's no wonder Lake Tahoe draws up to 100,000 tourists at peak periods. On weekends, the traffic on I–80 between the Bay Area and Lake Tahoe has to be seen to be believed.

The lake itself is 6,225 ft above sea level, the water so clear you can see 75 ft below the surface, and, plunging 1,625 ft, it has enough water to cover the state of California to a depth of 14 inches. Those who come to the lake only to spend all their time in the hermetically sealed casinos are missing out on one of the most varied and scenic natural areas in the country.

Although it's a somewhat subjective division, the lake's locales are usually designated as belonging to either the north shore or the south shore. Thanks largely to the popularity of 15 or so ski areas (compared with two in the south), the north shore is the domain of Tahoe's athletic set. The south shore, on the other hand, is largely overrun with family vacationers and casino-bound gamblers. Places like **Desolation Wilderness** have "been loved to death," as one local ranger put it, and have quotas regulating how many people can enter.

The north shore's largest town is **Truckee,** about a 30-minute drive (12 mi) north of the lake, with a modern downtown area to the west and an Old Town (complete with board sidewalks, wood-frame storefronts, and an ancient railroad) to the east. Donner Pass Road connects the two sides of town and serves as the main commercial boulevard. On the west shore of the lake, **Tahoe City** has a small-town warmth largely lacking in Truckee. On the south shore, the city center of **South Lake Tahoe** is packed to the gills with restaurants, motels, and rental shops. The pace never flags in summer and in winter, popular ski areas like Heavenly keep the town jumping. Butting up against the east side of South Lake Tahoe is **Stateline,** Nevada, with its four major (and two minor) hotel-casinos.

BASICS

The **North Lake Tahoe Resort Association Chamber of Commerce** (245 Hwy. 89, Tahoe City, tel. 530/581–6900) lies north of the Bank of America across from the Tahoe City "Y" (the intersection of Hwys. 89 and 28 that is impossible to miss). This site provides free guides and maps, lots of community and historical facts, information on kids' activities, resources for travelers with disabilities, and details on camping. The **North Lake Tahoe Resort Association Visitors and Convention Bureau** in Tahoe City (950 North Lake Blvd., near the Safeway, tel. 530/583–3494 or 800/824–6348) has deals on activity and accommodation packages year-round. The **Lake Tahoe Forest Service Visitor Center** (Hwy. 89, between Emerald Bay and South Lake Tahoe, tel. 530/573–2674) has beach access and nature trails. The staff will tell you all you want to know about the lake's natural and human history. This is also the place to pick up campfire and wilderness permits for the Desolation and Mokelumne wilderness areas. Permits are free, but only a limited number are available. Depending on funding, the visitor center may be closed on certain days of the week—call ahead.

Gay-friendly information on recreational activities, support groups, businesses, and accommodation is found through the **Tahoe Gay Hotline** (tel. 530/541–4297). **Disabled Sports USA of Northern California** (6060 Sunrise Vista Dr., Suite 3030, Citrus Heights, CA 95610, tel. 530/722–6447) has information on skiing, waterskiing, rafting, and other outdoor activities.

COMING AND GOING

BY BUS

Greyhound (tel. 800/231–2222) runs seven buses a day between San Francisco and Truckee (5–10 hrs, $34 one-way) and five between Truckee and Reno (1 hr, $9 one-way). If you're headed to the south shore, Greyhound makes the trip between Sacramento and **Harrah's Hotel and Casino** in Stateline, NV (3 hrs, $19 one-way), twice a day, with a $5 cash bonus on arrival. Both Amtrak and Greyhound use the **Transit Depot** (Donner Pass Rd., in Old Town Truckee, tel. 530/587–3822), a safe place to wait for connections or pick up information at the tourist office. There are a few coin-operated lockers here.

BY CAR

Both routes to Lake Tahoe take 3½–4 hours from the Bay Area when road and traffic conditions are at their best. To reach the north shore, follow I–80 east all the way to Truckee. For the south shore, take U.S. 50 east from Sacramento, which leads directly to South Lake Tahoe. You won't be allowed into the mountains without chains if it snows; bring your own, or you'll have to pay inflated prices for a set near the CalTrans checkpoint. Even if you bring your own, consider paying (about $10) to let someone else put them on for you. You will see swarms of jumpsuit-clad people with numbers on their backs at every checkpoint waiting to perform this service.

For recorded information on road conditions, call CalTrans at 800/427–7623. If snow doesn't slow you down, traffic might, especially on Friday and Sunday afternoons and during summer and holiday weekends. If you must drive to Tahoe on Friday, wait until 7 PM or 8 PM. Traffic is usually worst on I–80, so consider taking U.S. 50, even if you're headed for the north shore.

Besides being deep and blue, Lake Tahoe is mighty cold (40°F–70°F throughout the year). You can swim in it, but most visitors just dip their feet.

BY PLANE

At press time, no commercial airline was flying into **South Lake Tahoe Airport** (off Hwy. 89, about 2 mi south of the "Y" in South Lake Tahoe, tel. 530/542–6180). Your best bet is to get a flight to the **Reno Tahoe International Airport** (2001 E. Plumb La., tel. 702/328–6499), then catch a **Tahoe Casino Express** bus (702/785–2424 or 800/446–6128) to South Lake Tahoe. It offers daily transportation from Reno starting at 6:15 AM, then hourly from 8:15 AM to 3:15 PM, and every two hours starting at 5:30 PM until 12:30 AM.

BY TRAIN

Amtrak (tel. 800/872–7245) runs three train/bus routes a day between Emeryville and Truckee (transfer in Sacramento, 5 hrs, $69 round-trip). If you're coming from San Francisco, take the free bus from the CalTrain Station at 4th and Townsend streets to the Emeryville Amtrak Station (5885 Landregan St., at Powell St., tel. 510/450–1081). Amtrak also has four trains a week traveling the hour-long route between Truckee and Reno ($13 one-way). All trains arrive at the Truckee Transit Depot (*see* By Bus, *above*). Another train/bus combination serves South Lake Tahoe from Emeryville (transfer in Sacramento, 5 hrs, $38 round-trip).

GETTING AROUND

Three intersecting highways form a loop around the lake: **Highway 89** (a.k.a. Emerald Bay Road) skirts the western shore of the lake between Tahoe City and South Lake Tahoe; **U.S. 50** (a.k.a. Lake Tahoe Boulevard) intersects Hwy. 89 in South Lake Tahoe and follows the lake's eastern shore; and **Highway 28** (a.k.a. North Lake Boulevard or Lake Shore Boulevard) runs along the north part of the shore back into Tahoe City. The intersections of Hwys. 28 and 89 in Tahoe City and Hwy. 89 and U.S. 50 in South Lake Tahoe are commonly referred to as the **Tahoe City "Y"** and the **South Lake Tahoe "Y,"** respectively.

Tahoe Area Regional Transit (TART) (tel. 530/581–6365 or 800/736–6365) buses, most equipped with ski and bike racks, serve the north and west shores of Lake Tahoe, traveling from Tahoma (Meeks Bay in summer) on the southwest shore to Incline Village in the north and up Hwy. 89 to Truckee. The fare is $1.25, and buses run from 6:30 AM to 6:30 PM year-round. Between **BUS PLUS** (tel. 530/542–

6077) and the **South Tahoe Area Ground Express (STAGE)** (tel. 530/573–2080), service runs 24 hours from the South Lake Tahoe "Y" to Stateline, Nevada; the fare is $1.25 for STAGE. BUS PLUS ($3–$5) is for people who are too far from bus stops; if you call the number (*see above*) they will pick you up and drop you at the nearest STAGE stop. Schedules and maps are available from the tourist information centers. Pending continued funding, the **Lake Lapper** (tel. 530/542–5900) is a great deal—$5 for an all-day pass on coaches that circle the lake, stopping at points of interest, connecting with STAGE and TART, and running 8 AM to 1:45 AM in summer and 6 AM to 4:30 PM in winter.

WHERE TO SLEEP

You face a mind-boggling number of options in choosing a place to stay in Tahoe. Hostels, motels, condos, cabins, and campgrounds abound. If you're just passing through for a night or two in summer, a motel or campground is the cheapest and most convenient alternative. But if you're coming for a week in winter to ski with a group of friends, consider a condo or cabin on the north shore: It's more affordable than you might think (*see below*).

The quickest way to find a cheap (and perhaps fleabaggy) place to crash is to head to U.S. 50 between South Lake Tahoe and Stateline—cruise the strip and keep your eyes open for the neon. For a safer, quieter stay, opt for the area west of the South Tahoe "Y," and travel up to either the north shore or Stateline from there. If you like to be in the middle of the action, look for cheap deals at the casinos on the Nevada side of both the south and north shores. No matter where you stay, reserve as far ahead as possible. On holidays and summer weekends everything is completely packed, despite the fact that most places raise their prices indiscriminately at these times.

SOUTH SHORE

El Nido Motel. If you're seeking comfort at a reasonable price, the El Nido should end your search. Its excellent amenities include a hot tub and small, modern rooms with TV, VCR, and telephone. Flawlessly clean doubles start at $40 on weekdays, $50 on summer weekends; in the winter prices are about $10 lower. Call for details on discount lift ticket deals. *2215 Lake Tahoe Blvd. (U.S. 50), tel. and fax 530/541–2711. About ½ mi northeast of South Lake Tahoe "Y." 21 rooms, all with bath.*

Emerald Motel. The well-maintained building is 35 years old, making for a homey setting with exceptionally friendly proprietors. Pope Beach and the woods are less than 2 mi away. Standard doubles start at $45 on weekdays and $50 on weekends, with rates $10 lower in winter; groups get the best deal—two beds, sleeping four, for $45 on summer weekdays. Rates are negotiable for stays of four nights or more. *515 Emerald Bay Rd. (Hwy. 89), tel. 530/544–5515, fax 530/544–2510. 1 mi north of South Lake Tahoe "Y." 9 rooms, all with bath.*

Ridgewood Inn. Set on a 2-acre lot (complete with Jacuzzi), these clean, well-kept rooms, some with kitchenettes, are a swell deal. Doubles in summer are $45, and a self-contained suite that sleeps five goes for $110. Some rooms even have tubs for a private post-hike soak. *1341 Emerald Bay Rd., tel. 530/541–8589 or 800/800–4640, fax 530/541–8712. 1 mi south of "Y." 12 rooms, all with bath.*

NORTH SHORE

It's hard to find a budget motel on the north shore, especially in Truckee. For better prices and better location, check out the smaller communities around the lakeshore, like Tahoe Vista or Kings Beach. One of the cheapest hotels on the North Shore is in Kings Beach: **The Big 7** (8171 North Lake Blvd., tel. 530/546–2541 or 800/354–6970), with weekday doubles at $35–$45, $45–$65 weekends.

North Shore Lodge. Across from Kings Beach, $60 gets you a double with a kitchen and the smell of stale smoke. The cabins are the best deal: one sleeps six ($115), another eight ($125). Negotiate in winter, they've been known to take what they can get—sometimes as low as $25. In summer, you have use of a heated pool. *8755 North Lake Blvd. (Hwy. 28) at Chipmunk St., tel. 530/546–4833, fax 530/546–0265. In Kings Beach, 1 mi west of California–Nevada border. 11 rooms, all with bath.*

River Ranch Lodge. For a great splurge, head to the classy River Ranch Lodge, beside the Truckee River between Truckee and Tahoe City. The rustic rooms (all nonsmoking) come complete with tasteful wallpaper and antique furniture, and half have small decks overlooking the river. Doubles start at $40 on spring and fall weekdays ($50 on weekends), $55 on winter and summer weekdays ($80 on weekends). Several of the noisier rooms above the bar go for $10 less, and there's a cheaper double facing the parking lot. *Hwy. 89 and Alpine Meadows Rd., tel. 530/583–4264 or 800/535–9900. 21 rooms, all with bath. Continental breakfast.*

Tamarack Lodge Motel. This is the best budget lodging on the North Shore. The air smells great (it's the pines), the beach is a short walk away, and friendly managers lay on the charm. Knotty pine paneling and bike trail access bring people back here year after year. The TART bus stops across the street. Doubles start at $36 weekdays, kitchenettes are $10 more, and rates go up by $10 in high season. Stay over four nonholiday days, and it's 15% off the total. *2311 North Lake Blvd. (Hwy. 28), 1 mi north of Tahoe City, tel. 530/583–3350 or 888/824–6323, fax 530/583–3531. 21 rooms, all with bath.*

HOSTELS

Clair Tappaan Lodge. Managed by the Sierra Club, this coed hostel is about 45 minutes away from Tahoe City. There are cross-country trails on site and snowshoes and nordic skis for rent in winter. In the summer staff members lead bird-watching, wildflower, and hiking workshops. Summer rates are $39 for nonmembers ($35 members) and include three meals per day. Rates in winter are about $4 higher. *19940 Donner Pass Rd., Norden, tel. 530/426–3632, fax 530/426–0742. From Tahoe City, take Hwy. 89 E, exit at Soda Springs/Norden. 140 beds. No curfew.*

Doug's Mellow Mountain Retreat. Billed as "The Perfect Place to Chill Out," this laid-back private hostel rents bikes for $5 per day, offers laundry services for $3, and has a Rastafarian theme. Doug will let you sit in front of the fireplace and watch movies (he has over 200), use his kitchen, and have barbecues on the deck. He'll even pick you up from the Greyhound station at Harrah's if you call ahead. Beds in coed rooms go for $13. Reserve ahead; if you're a party of three, ask for the studio ($35) with its own kitchen, TV, and bath. *3787 Forest St., just west of CA–NV border, tel. 530/544–8065. From South Lake Tahoe, U.S. 50 east, right on Wildwood Rd., left on Forest St. 15 beds in 3 rooms. No curfew, no lockout. Reception hours flexible.*

Squaw Valley Hostel. This privately run hostel, within walking distance of the Squaw Valley ski area, opens only during winter, usually from mid-November to mid-April. During the week a dorm bed runs $22, $27 weekends. On weekends, when the hostel hosts groups, it's next to impossible to get a room unless you call well in advance. *1900 Squaw Valley Rd., tel. and fax 530/581–3246. From Truckee, Hwy. 89 south, right on Squaw Valley Rd. 100 beds in 9 rooms.*

WEEKEND AND WEEKLY RENTALS

The more people in your group and the longer the stay, the more affordable rentals become. Contact the **Lake Tahoe Visitors' Authority** (1156 Ski Run Blvd., South Lake Tahoe, tel. 530/544–5050 or 800/288–2463) or the **North Lake Tahoe Resort Association Visitors' and Convention Bureau** (tel. 530/583–3494 or 800/824–6348) to find out about weekend or weekly rentals. You should be able to find a basic two- to four-person condo for about $100 a night or $500 a week in the off-season, with prices rising roughly 10% in summer. **R. RENT** (tel. 530/546–2549) specializes in north-shore budget rentals. If you have the time, you can save a few bucks by arranging a rental directly through a property owner. To find out what's available, check the classified ads in the *Tahoe Daily Tribune* for south-shore listings, or the *Tahoe World,* a north-shore paper that comes out each Thursday.

CAMPING

You can hardly drive 5 mi in Lake Tahoe without bumping into a public or private campground, and almost all of them lie in beautiful pine forests. For obvious reasons, all campgrounds close in winter until about Memorial Day. Temperatures can fluctuate widely in the region (from 60°F to less than zero in a day), and many of the areas have snow until May. It's a good idea to call the Forest Service (*see* Basics, *above*) for advice and weather conditions before setting out. Free camping in the Tahoe area is restricted but still available at some lesser-known primitive campgrounds scattered around the lake. The Forest Service has maps, tips, and directions to free spots as well as a complete listing of campgrounds.

SOUTH SHORE • Two inviting campgrounds are just south of Emerald Bay on Hwy. 89. **Bayview** (tel. 530/544–5994, reservations 800/280–2267), on the inland side of Hwy. 89, has 10 primitive sites amid the pines, with picnic tables and fire pits but no drinking water. A stopping-off point for journeys into Desolation Wilderness, it imposes a two-night limit on stays; but for those two nights, you'll sleep for free. If all the sites in Bayview are full, head just up the road to beautiful **Eagle Point** (Hwy. 89, 1 mi south of Emerald Bay, tel. 530/525–7277 or 800/444–7275 for reservations). Here you'll find 100 well-spaced sites ($14)—all with fire pits, barbecues, drinking water, picnic tables, food lockers, and access to bathrooms and showers—on a hillside covered with brush and pines. Some sites offer incredible views of Emerald Bay.

NORTH SHORE • On the north shore, dispersed camping is available near Homewood ski resort in **Blackwood Canyon.** From Hwy. 89 south of Tahoe City, look for a sign to BLACKWOOD CANYON on the right. After 2½ mi, veer to the right on an unmarked dirt road, and camp anywhere you please.

William Kent Campground (off Hwy. 89, tel. 530/544–5994 or 800/444–7275 for reservations) is a 95-site National Forest campground set well off the highway, 2 mi south of Tahoe City. William Kent lies in a moderately dense pine forest and is within walking distance of the lake. Sites are $12. Just down the road to the south, is the **Kaspian Campground** (tel. 530/544–5994).

FOOD

On the south shore, eateries are concentrated along U.S. 50 between South Lake Tahoe and Stateline, Nevada. In Stateline itself, you can get your fill of bargain eats at casino snack shops and all-you-can-eat buffets. On the north shore, there's a heap of restaurants in downtown Truckee (especially on Donner Pass Road) and on Hwy. 28 in Tahoe City. For fresh organic produce and bulk foods, head to **Grass Roots** (2040 Dunlap Dr., at South Lake Tahoe "Y," tel. 530/541–7788) on the south shore.

SOUTH SHORE

Ernie's Coffee Shop. An unpretentious greasy spoon serving breakfast and lunch only, Ernie's has a host of regulars who keep their personalized coffee mugs hanging on the wall. Breakfast is served all day in retro green vinyl booths. Meals range from the standard two-egg-and-toast breakfast ($4) to more adventurous creations like the tostada omelet ($6.50). *1146 Emerald Bay Rd. (Hwy. 89) at C St., South Lake Tahoe, tel. 530/541–2161. ¼ mi south of South Lake Tahoe "Y." No dinner.*

Hunan Garden. The friendly, sometimes wisecracking staff makes this a good place to refuel at the end of the day. Special vegetarian dishes, no MSG, and a willingness to alter any order are also pluses. They have a lunch buffet (11:30–2:30) for $5.50 and another, for $7.95, at dinner (5–9). *900 Emerald Bay Rd. (Hwy. 89), just northwest of South Lake Tahoe "Y", tel. 530/544–5868 or 530/544–7268.*

Sprouts. At South Lake Tahoe's vegetarian paradise, you can feast on great sandwiches ($4–$6), rice and vegetable plates ($4.25–$4.75), tempeh burgers ($4.50), incredible fruit smoothies ($2.50–$3), and beer. The produce is largely organic. The restaurant itself is small and cheery, with a few wooden tables and a small outdoor patio. *3123 Harrison Ave., at U.S. 50, South Lake Tahoe, tel. 530/541–6969. Intersection of U.S. 50 and Alameda Ave.*

Taquería Jalisco. With a rockin' jukebox and great food, this spot attracts Tahoe's sizable Latino population. Hidden behind Rojo's eatery, Taquería Jalisco sells burritos, nachos, and tacos (some vegetarian) for under $2.50. *3097 Harrison Ave. at San Francisco Ave., South Lake Tahoe, tel. 530/541–6516. No breakfast.*

NORTH SHORE

Bridgetender Tavern and Grill. Housed in an old wooden cabin with high-beam ceilings and tree trunks poking through the roof, the Bridgetender is a worthy burgers-and-beer spot. Huge beef patties ($4) and tasty veggie burgers ($6) are both served with hefty french fries. Sit on a patio overlooking the Truckee River, or drink beer and shoot pool inside. *30 Emerald Bay Rd. (Hwy. 89), Tahoe City, tel. 530/583–3342. Next to bridge at Tahoe City "Y." No breakfast.*

China Garden. One of Truckee's best restaurants serves up veggie dishes ($6–$6.50), seafood ($7–$9), and other Mandarin standards (no MSG) in a family-style dining room. Lunch specials (soup, egg roll, fried rice, and your choice of entrée) run just $4.25–$5.25; dinner specials for two or more start at $8.50; Mongolian BBQ buffet goes for $6.95–$8.95. *11361 Deerfield Dr., tel. 530/587–7625. In Crossroads Center, off Hwy. 89 just south of I–80. No breakfast, no lunch Sun.*

Truckee River Coffee Company. For coffee and dessert in Truckee, head to this homey café furnished with couches, a few tables, and a piano. You can get a calzone for $3, but the real reason to come is for a final course. Try the old-fashioned hot chocolate ($1.75) or the Coffee Nut ($4), made of hazelnut espresso, hazelnut syrup, and vanilla yogurt. *11373 Deerfield Dr., Truckee, tel. 530/587–2583. In Crossroads Center just south of I–80/Hwy. 89 junction.*

AFTER DARK

Events on the south shore are covered in *Lake Tahoe Action,* a free weekly entertainment magazine put out by the *Tahoe Daily Tribune,* *. The *Tahoe–Truckee Review* covers the north shore, and both are available at most motels.

SOUTH SHORE

The south shore is surprisingly quiet by night. On the Nevada side of the border in Stateline, you'll find a number of casinos and the usual array of shows and headliners. Just north of the stateline, **Faces** (270 Kingsbury Grade, just west of Hwy. 50, tel. 702/588–2333) is the gay club, offering a relaxed and friendly atmosphere with dancing three nights a week until 4 AM (no cover). **The Brewery at Lake Tahoe** (3542 U.S. 50, tel. 530/544–2739), 1½ mi west of the California–Nevada border, is a microbrewery and restaurant popular with the après-ski crowd. There's usually something to perspire for at the **Embassy Suites** (4130 Lake Tahoe Blvd., tel. 702/544–5400); the Atrium Bar hosts lounge bands nightly and Turtle's Sports Bar sports the disco DJ.

NORTH SHORE

Tahoe City is without a doubt the center of the lake's nightlife. Loud, crowded, and filled with hard-drinking youth, **Humpty's** (877 North Lake Blvd., 1 mi northeast of Tahoe City "Y," tel. 530/583–4867) features the best live indie music in the area most nights (cover $3–$20). When Humpty's is sold out, the overflow crowd heads to **Rosie's Cafe** (571 North Lake Blvd., Tahoe City, tel. 530/583–8504), a large restaurant and bar housed in an old cabin full of Tahoe City memorabilia. Across the street at the **Blue Water Brewery** (850 North Lake Blvd., behind Safeway in Tahoe City, tel. 530/581–2583) you can down microbrews, munch on veggie chili ($7) or fish-and-chips in beer batter ($7.50), and shoot pool.

Alpine Meadows is home to the Tahoe Handicapped Ski School (tel. 530/581–4161), and it is one of the few resorts that does not allow snowboarders.

Catering to a mellower clientele, the **Naughty Dawg** (255 North Lake Blvd., ¼ mi northeast of Tahoe City "Y," tel. 530/581–3294) has a good selection of high-quality beers, as well as surprisingly good salads, burgers, and pizza ($3–$7). With a large deck next to the Truckee River and a stylish indoor bar, the **River Ranch Lodge** (*see* Hotels and Motels, *above*) is an excellent place for a quiet drink. During the summer this place hosts an outdoor concert series with eclectic bookings ranging from jazz to hard rock (cover $5–$25).

SKIING

Whether you prefer downhill or cross-country, you've come to the right place: With more than 24 ski resorts, Lake Tahoe offers ample opportunity for beginners and experts alike on downhill and cross-country slopes. In addition to the millions of discount rental and lift ticket flyers you'll find all over the area, the tourist centers can give you the *Skier's Planning Guide*, the *Winter Travel Planner*, and the *Winter Visitor's Guide*. All have information on the various lift operators and advice about skiing in the area. Call the **North Lake Tahoe Resort Association Chamber of Commerce** (*see* Basics, *above*) for information on skiing specials—they change throughout the season.

EQUIPMENT RENTAL

As a rule of thumb, the closer you get to the ski resorts, the higher the cost of renting equipment. On the other hand, if you choose to rent from the shops run by the resorts, it'll be easier to get an adjustment, repair, or replacement midday. The best deal anywhere is the south shore's **Don Cheepo's** (3349 U.S. 50, about ¾ mi west of Heavenly, tel. 530/544–0356), which offers full downhill and cross-country rental packages (skis, boots, and poles) for $9. Snowboards rent for $20, including boots—a very competitive price.

Of north-shore rental outfits, **Porter's** has low rates (full ski packages $11–$15, snowboards $15–$22) and three locations, including one in Tahoe City (501 North Lake Blvd., just east of Tahoe City "Y," tel. 530/583–2314) and one in Truckee (in Crossroads Center on Hwy. 89, south of I–80, tel. 530/587–1500).

DOWNHILL

The "Big Five" ski resorts (*see below*) all charge in the neighborhood of $41–$45 a day, but if you're careful, you can avoid paying these prices. Buying multiple-day or weekday tickets will save you $3–$7 per day; also scour local papers, motels, gas stations, and supermarkets (try Safeway) for discounts and deals. Beginners and intermediate skiers can save money and still get their money's worth at one of the smaller, less expensive resorts, some of which even offer midweek discounts. If you're coming from the Bay Area, you can save 30–45 minutes driving time by skiing at any of the Donner Pass ski resorts—

Soda Springs, Sugar Bowl, Donner Ranch, Boreal, or Tahoe Donner. Of these five, **Sugar Bowl** (tel. 530/426–3847 for snow report), off the Soda Springs/Norden exit of I–80, is the largest and most beautiful. It's especially attractive for experienced skiers, with 50% of its runs designated advanced, including some of the best tree skiing in Tahoe. A few miles farther down the road, **Donner Ranch** (Soda Springs/Norden exit off I–80, tel. 530/426–3635 for snow report) is Tahoe's cheapest ski resort, with lift tickets starting at just $10 on weekdays and $22 on weekends. If you have more than a day for skiing, consider the underrated, 1,260-acre **Ski Homewood** (Hwy. 89, between Tahoe City and South Lake Tahoe, tel. 530/525–2900 for snow report). Homewood offers outstanding views of the lake and a wide variety of terrain. Lift tickets go for $35 full day and $26 half day. Wednesday is two-for-one day.

BIG FIVE • Squaw Valley (on Hwy. 89, 8 mi south of Truckee, tel. 530/583–6955 for snow report) is a vast resort with over 8,000 acres of open bowls, 2,850 vertical ft, and more than 25 chairlifts. Squaw Valley is unofficially known as the home of "extreme" skiing, but it's truly an all-around ski area—70% of the mountain is suited to beginning and novice skiers. **Alpine Meadows** (off Hwy. 89, 6 mi northwest of Tahoe City, tel. 530/581–8374 for snow report) has a high base elevation of 7,000 ft (allowing for a longer season) and 12 lifts serving over 100 runs. Alpine has built its reputation on the abundant snow and sunshine that grace its two mountains—most locals agree that Alpine Meadows is the best place for spring skiing. **Northstar-at-Tahoe** (Hwy. 267, 7 mi south of Truckee, tel. 530/562–1330 for snow report) certainly tries to be all things to all people, with a split of 25% beginner runs, 50% intermediate runs, and 25% advanced runs. It's definitely worth coming here for a day, if only for the incredible views of the basin from the top of the 8,610-ft **Mt. Pluto. Heavenly** (west entrance off Lake Tahoe Boulevard, in South Lake Tahoe, tel. 530/541–7544 for snow report) is officially the largest ski area in the United States. That means you'll find over 4,300 acres of skiable terrain, an incredible 3,500-ft vertical drop, and 25 lifts scattered over no fewer than nine peaks. **Kirkwood** (Hwy. 88 east, off Hwy. 89 south from South Lake Tahoe, tel. 209/258–3000 for snow report) boasts the driest snow, which experienced skiers know means the best powder—all told, 85% of Kirkwood's runs are designated intermediate or advanced.

CROSS-COUNTRY SKIING

You'll have no problem finding a trail to suit your abilities at Tahoe's 13 cross-country ski areas, the most famous of which is the north shore's **Royal Gorge** (Soda Springs/Norden exit south from I–80, tel. 530/426–3871 or 800/500–3871), the largest cross-country ski resort in the United States. You can choose from 200 mi of trails running along a ridge above the north fork of the American River; fees are $18 midweek.

Strictly for skiers with at least some experience, **Eagle Mountain** (tel. 530/389–2254), dubbed "one of the area's best-kept secrets" by locals, offers incredible vistas along 45 mi of trails (fee $12). About an hour west of Truckee, Eagle is Tahoe's closest nordic resort. Exit I–80 at Yuba Gap and follow signs. Two other cross-country resorts on the north shore, **Northstar-at-Tahoe** (tel. 530/562–1330; fee $14), and **Squaw Creek** (tel. 530/583–6300; fee $10) are right next to downhill ski areas (*see above*), making them great choices for groups with divided loyalties. Of the two, Northstar, with 40 mi of trails, is more exciting.

On the south shore, only **Kirkwood** (tel. 209/258–7248; *see above*) offers both alpine and nordic ski trails, with over 50 mi of cross-country for skiers of all levels ($12). The best deal on the south shore is **Hope Valley** (Hwy. 88 east, off Hwy. 89, tel. 530/694–2266), located in a beautiful valley of the Toiyabe (say it: Toy-AH-bee) National Forest, on the grounds of Sorenson's Resort. It offers 60 mi of trails for all levels—free! (Donation requested.) The North Lake Tahoe Resort Association Visitors & Convention Bureau (*see* Basics, *above*) can also hook you up with packages, such as a $33 three-day ticket that can be used at any of seven resorts.

SUMMER ACTIVITIES

Lake Tahoe offers opportunities for just about every fair-weather sport imaginable. An abbreviated list would include hiking, biking, fishing, sailing, waterskiing, jet skiing, rock climbing, hot-air ballooning, parasailing, horseback riding, and river rafting. Of course many of the more exotic adventures are pricey, but Tahoe is a great place to splurge. Your best printed matter on the possibilities is *Tahoe–Truckee Outdoors,* which gives trail maps, tips, and the latest news on biking, boating, hiking, and rafting, among other sports, as does *Tahoe Mountain News.* Tourist offices or the Forest Service (*see* Basics, *above*) have detailed information about all these sports. Barring droughts, whitewater rafting on the American River is a possibility—the Forest Service can point you in the right direction. **Don Cheepo's** (*see* Equipment Rental *in* Skiing, *above*) rents everything from water skis to backpacks and other camping supplies. A good source of information and equipment for all sorts of outdoor sports in Tahoe City is **Alpenglow Sports** (415 North Lake Blvd., tel. 530/583–6917). **Gravity Works Rock Gym** in Truckee (10095 West River St., tel. 530/582–4510) is a good rock climbing resource.

HIKING

Almost every acre in the Lake Tahoe Basin is protected by some national, state, or local agency. **Tahoe National Forest** lies to the northwest, **Eldorado National Forest** to the southwest, and **Toiyabe National Forest** to the east. What this means for visitors is a whole lot of hiking trails, from easy scenic walks to strenuous climbs over mountain passes. The Lake Tahoe Forest Service Visitor Center (*see* Basics, *above*) has a complete list of day hikes.

One of the more popular short walks is **Vikingsholm Trail,** a mi-long (one-way) paved path leading from the parking lot on the north side of Emerald Bay to the shoreline and the 38-room Vikingsholm Castle, a Scandinavian-style castle built in 1929. From the castle you can walk farther to **Eagle Falls,** the only waterfall that empties into the lake. For something a little more woodsy, try the **Mt. Tallac Trail,** ½ mi north of the Lake Tahoe Forest Service Visitor Center (follow the marked asphalt road opposite Baldwin Beach to the trailhead parking lot). A moderate hike takes you 2 mi through a beautiful pine forest to Cathedral Lake. For a serious day-long trek (with no potable water along the way), continue on the trail another 3 mi as it climbs past a series of boulder fields to the peak of Mt. Tallac, the highest point in the basin at 9,735 ft. At the top you'll find excellent views of the lake and Desolation Wilderness. The trip up and back should take seven–eight hours.

Going to the chapel? You won't be alone—the wedding industry is second only to casinos in bringing business to the Tahoe area.

If you're looking to do extensive backcountry camping, you're going to have a hard time choosing where to go. Off the southwest corner of the lake, the 63,473-acre **Desolation Wilderness,** filled with granite peaks, glacial valleys, subalpine forests, and more than 80 lakes, is one of the most beautiful and popular backcountry destinations in the area. South of the lake, **Mokelumne Wilderness,** straddling the border of Eldorado and Stanislaus national forests, has terrain similar to Desolation without the crowds. Before you enter any wilderness area, either for a day or for an extended visit, it's crucial to pick up a wilderness permit from the Lake Tahoe Forest Service Visitor Center (*see* Basics, *above*)—if you don't, you may be kicked off the trails.

BIKING

Lake Tahoe has everything from mellow lakeshore trails to steep fire roads and tricky single-tracks. The Forest Service has detailed trail information, and the Tahoe North Visitors' and Convention Bureau (*see* Basics, *above*) puts out an excellent brochure called "North Lake Tahoe Mountain Biking" that lists bike tours, trails, bike parks, and bike shops for rentals. Several paved, gently sloped paths skirt the lakeshore: Try the 3.4-mi **Pope Baldwin Bike Path** in South Lake Tahoe, at the Pope Baldwin Recreational Center, or the **West Shore Bike Path,** which extends about 10 mi south from Tahoe City to Sugar Pine Point State Park near the town of Tahoma. Also worthwhile are the path along the **Truckee River** between Alpine Meadows and Tahoe City and the **U.S. Forest Service Bike Trail,** an 8½-mi paved path (through pine forest and rare aspen grove) that starts at Emerald Bay Road just west of the South Lake Tahoe "Y" and ends at the lake.

Experienced riders should dare the famous **Flume Trail,** a 24-mi ride past several lakes and along a ridge with sweeping views of Lake Tahoe. The trail begins at the parking lot of Lake Tahoe–Nevada State Park, just north of Spooner Junction on the lake's eastern shore (take Hwy. 28 east from Tahoe City). A map is crucial. The "**High Sierra Biking Map**" ($6) and its accompanying book ($9) offer a detailed description of the Flume Trail (including a way to cut the ride in half for people with two cars), along with several dozen other excellent rides in the area. If you like the idea of riding downhill all day, **Northstar-at-Tahoe, Donner Ranch, Kirkwood, Squaw Valley,** and **Sugar Bowl** (*see* Skiing, *above*) all open a number of ski runs for mountain biking June–September. All-day tickets run $10–$21 (bike rental $30–$45).

BIKE RENTALS • Dozens of shops around Tahoe rent mountain bikes, generally for $4–$6 an hour or $15–$22 a day. On the south shore there's **Don Cheepo's** (*see* Equipment Rental *in* Skiing, *above*), near the east end of the Pope Baldwin Bike Path. On the north shore try **Porter's** (501 North Lake Blvd., tel. 530/583–2314), on Hwy. 28, east of the Tahoe City "Y."

BEACHES

Dozens of beaches are scattered around the chilly lake's shore, some charging $2–$5 for parking. Two of the best include **Chamber's Landing** south of Tahoe City, a favorite of young north-shore locals, and **Baldwin Beach,** a gorgeous and usually uncrowded sand beach between South Lake Tahoe and Emerald Bay. **Nevada Beach,** a more populated spot just across the Nevada border in Stateline, has great mountain views. **Sand Harbor,** a crescent-shape beach off Hwy. 28 south of Incline Village, is ideal for sunsets.

WATER SPORTS

Despite Lake Tahoe's often frigid waters, there's no lack of rental outfits specializing in sailing, waterskiing, jet skiing, windsurfing, kayaking, canoeing, and parasailing. Prices fluctuate a bit, but, in general, sailboats go for $30–$35 an hour, $85–$95 a day; Jet Skis run $50–$90 an hour; Windsurfers rent for $10–$15 an hour, $30–$40 a half day; and canoes go for $10–$15 an hour, $30–$40 a half day. Parasailing rides, which usually last about 15 minutes, range from $35 to $50.

On the south shore, the **Ski Run Boat Company** (tel. 530/544–0200), with motorboats, canoes, kayaks, and other toys, is one of several shops operating out of **Ski Run Marina,** off U.S. 50 about ½ mi west of the California–Nevada border. On the north shore, you'll find rental outfits in the **Sunnyside Marina,** about 2 mi south of Tahoe City on Hwy. 89.

FISHING

Like nearly everything in Tahoe, fishing options are abundant. The most convenient spot is (can you guess?) **Lake Tahoe,** stocked occasionally with rainbow trout by the folks at the Fish and Wildlife Service (to find the section of the lake most recently stocked, call 530/355–7040 or 530/351–0832). Also popular is the stretch of the **Truckee River** between Truckee and Tahoe City—just pick a spot and cast your line. Wherever you fish, licenses ($9 a day, $24 a year) are required by law and available from most sporting-goods shops. For sport fishing on the lake, contact **Tahoe Sportfishing** (tel. 530/541–5448 or 800/696–7797) in the Ski Run Marina or **Don's Sport Fishing** (tel. 530/541–5566) in South Lake Tahoe. Half-day trips generally start at $60–$70, full-day trips at $75–$85.

RENO

As you cross the state border and approach Nevada's second-largest city, the billboards and neon lights leave little doubt in your mind as to the town's main attraction. The city's history as a center of legalized vice is longer than that of Las Vegas, though Reno made a conscious decision not to become Las Vegas, and it shows. Reno is smaller, prettier, lower-keyed, and friendlier than Sin City in the south. But dirt-cheap hotels and low table minimums are, if anything, a bit scarcer here, particularly on the weekends, when hotel prices can jump by $60. The reason to choose Reno is not for friendlier baccarat dealers but for its location. Set just over the Sierra, near Lake Tahoe, Donner Lake, and Pyramid Lake, Reno has much cooler weather than Las Vegas; and if you do manage to catch some sleep here, you'll wake up to a gorgeous view of snowcapped mountains outside your hotel window.

The locals are friendlier the farther away you get from the glittery spectacle of North Virginia Street, and the natural sites near the area are worth a day trip—as are some of the city's museums. Reno is also the international bowling capital, and the National Bowling Stadium complex has to be seen to be believed.

The **Reno Visitor Center** (300 N. Center St., tel. 800/367–7366), in the lobby of the National Bowling Stadium (look for the building with the huge silver ball on top), has gregarious staffers who can answer just about every question, as well as provide hotel, casino, and sightseeing information. It's open daily 8–5. You can also get information at the commercial **Tourist Center** (354 N. Virginia St., tel. 702/333–6739), which is open daily 9–5; besides gaming coupons and hotel information, they will give you free dice (for good luck) and then try and rope you into watching a video on land in southern Nevada. Even if you're not interested in buying real estate, go for the video—you get various gifts (like discounted show tickets) just for sitting through it. Finally, you can also get most information you may need at the registration desks of the big hotel-casinos.

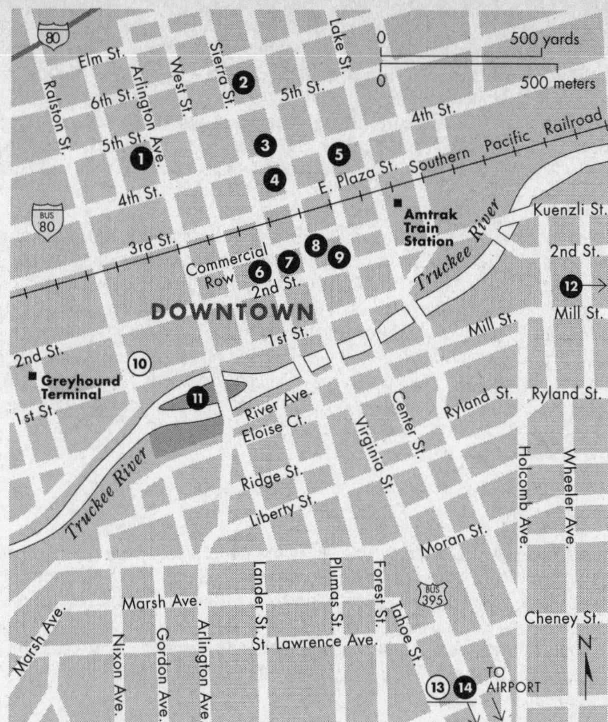

Sights ●
National Bowling Stadium, **5**
Wingfield Park, **11**

Lodging ○
Romance Inn, **13**
Truckee River Lodge, **10**

Hotel-Casinos ●
Circus Circus, **2**
Eldorado Hotel, **3**
Flamingo Hilton, **6**
Harrah's, **9**
Nevada Club, **8**
Nugget, **7**
Peppermill, **14**
Reno Hilton, **12**
Silver Legacy, **4**
Sundowner, **1**

COMING AND GOING

BY BUS

The best **Greyhound** deal in Reno is the casino fare. The bus deposits you right into the Eldorado, where you'll get $10 cash, $3 food credit, 50¢ keno play, and two-for-one cocktails, or John Ascuaga's Nugget ($10 cash, $3 food credit). The catch is that there's a maximum four-day stay. Buses arrive regularly from San Francisco ($27 round-trip) and Sacramento ($22 round-trip). You can also buy more flexible-stay tickets to the 24-hour **Greyhound Terminal** (155 Stevenson St., tel. 702/322–2970 or 800/231–2222 for reservations), but expect prices to be about $25 higher for round-trips. Smaller companies also run gambling tour buses that can be the least expensive way to get to Reno from the Bay Area. **Lucky Tours** (1111 Mission St., San Francisco, tel. 415/864–1133) offers daily round-trips for $30, most of which is returned to you as cash, food credits, and coupons. The catch: You leave San Francisco at 10 AM and depart Reno at 2:15 AM. **Mike Lee Tours** (tel. 415/442–1828), which leaves from S.F.'s Transbay Terminal (*see* Coming and Going *in* Chapter 2) and drops you at the Silver Legacy or John Ascuaga's Nugget ($30 round-trip), gives similar cash perks for casinos and allows you to return anytime within seven days. They also have departures from several East Bay cities. Check ads in the Sunday "Datebook" section of the *San Francisco Chronicle* or in other Sunday papers.

BY CAR

Reno lies on **I–80,** about three hours from Sacramento and just under four hours from the Bay Area. You can't possibly miss the city, whose sudden appearance in the distance a few miles after you cross the Nevada border can be quite spectacular, particularly at sunrise. Most of the major casinos are easily spotted from a few miles away. For downtown, take the Virginia Street exit, which is also the business loop of **U.S. 395,** the road serving Reno from points north and south. Be sure to carry chains during winter, as the highway can be treacherous in the higher altitudes between Auburn and Truckee.

BY PLANE

Upstart carrier **Reno Air** (tel. 800/736–6247) offers affordable round-trips to the **Reno Tahoe International Airport** (2001 E. Plumb La., tel. 702/328–6499). With a 14-day advance purchase, a round-trip ticket from Los Angeles costs about $99. **United Airlines** (tel. 800/241–6522) has flights from San Francisco five times a day ($89 round-trip with 14-day advance purchase, $121 with 7-day advance purchase). **Southwest** (tel. 800/435–9792) has good deals from the Bay Area; you'll pay $59 one-way from Oakland or San Jose if you reserve 21 days in advance. The Reno airport is southeast of town on U.S. 395.

BY TRAIN

Amtrak (135 E. Commercial Row, at Lake St. downtown, tel. 800/872–7245) runs from San Francisco all the way across the country along I–80, passing through Reno. On the four days a week that the *California Zephyr* runs through, the train goes direct from the TransBay Terminal; otherwise, you take a bus from the Transbay Terminal to the Emeryville station and catch the train to Reno from there. Round-trip fares San Francisco–Reno are $102.50; you'll pay $96 from Sacramento. The trip is slow (in the neighborhood of six hours from San Francisco), and though traveling by train the whole way has atmosphere, it costs three times the price of the bus, and you need to reserve well in advance. If all you plan to do in Reno is gamble, consider taking the train to Stateline, NV (in the Lake Tahoe area), instead: The fares for the train-bus are 30% less than those to Reno. Amtrak passengers can store luggage for free in the station daily 8 AM–4:30 PM (the desk is closed for lunch 11:30 AM–1 PM).

GETTING AROUND

Once you're in its confines, the self-designated "biggest little city in the world" is quite easily navigated on foot, and there's not much reason to touch your car once it's in a validated parking lot or valeted at one of the bigger casinos. Most of the casino action is concentrated downtown between the Truckee River and I–80, though a few large casinos (the Peppermill, John Ascuaga's Nugget, and the Reno Hilton, formerly Bally's) lie a couple of miles away. The University of Nevada is north on Virginia Street. **RTC/Citifare** (tel. 702/348–7433, a 24-hour line) is the city's public transit (fare is $1). Bus 1, which runs north–south on Virginia Street, operates 24 hours.

Reno is a city where the bottom line for many is relieving you of your cash. There is a desperate seediness that pervades much of the downtown area, and you should use common sense, wherever you are. In particular, avoid walking alone around 4th and Lake streets, and 9th and Sutro streets.

WHERE TO SLEEP

Reno is packed with hotels and motels in every nook and cranny, but many of the best deals, financially at least, are in the most obvious and imposing places—the downtown hotel-casinos. Even if you're just passing through Reno for the night, you should try to get a room at a place like the **Sundowner** (450 N. Arlington Ave., tel. 800/648–5490)—which is often the least expensive bet with off-season rooms for $26 and summer rates starting at $36. **Circus Circus** (500 N. Sierra St., between 5th and 6th Sts., tel. 800/648–5010), with its midway carnival and circus, so thoroughly epitomizes the Reno experience that it behooves every traveler to spend the night here at least once. Rooms start as low as $22 for a double off-season ($42–$52 during summer). The price of lodging (even outside the casinos) varies considerably from weekday to weekend and from season to season (summer being highest). Reservations are definitely recommended, and remember to figure in the 9% room tax.

If you shoot your point enough times at the crap table, consider an evening at the ritzy **Eldorado Hotel** (345 N. Virginia St., tel. 800/648–4597). Some of its 800-plus rooms can run as low as $50 for a double midweek. Honeymooners and romantic types should check out the various couple-oriented hotels, such as the **Romance Inn** (2905 S. Virginia St., tel. 702/826–1515 or 800/662–8812), where rooms are $75–$150 on summer weekdays, depending on how elaborate the room theme is. You'll find a Jacuzzi and a complimentary bottle of wine (tell them you're on your honeymoon, and they'll send champagne) in some rooms.

Truckee River Lodge. An incredible find amidst gambling-oriented lodging, the emphasis is on physical (and financial) health here. Well-located near downtown, the Greyhound depot, and the Truckee river, you'll find a fitness center, bike rental, information on outdoor activities, and the excellent **Pneumatic Diner** (*see below*). Huge nonsmoking doubles (couch, tub, full fridge, microwave, TV) go for $40–$65, depending on the season. *501 W. First St., tel. 702/786–8888 or 800/635–8950, fax 702/348–4769. 227 rooms, all with bath.*

FOOD

Unlimited quantity is the name of the game when it comes to downtown dining. One-pound steaks and prime rib, ham-and-egg specials, and the much-heralded all-you-can-eat buffets are as central to the ambience of Reno as the slot machines. At the buffets, you can be completely sated for as little as $3–$4. If you find a feeding frenzy unappetizing, Reno has plenty of other options. You can put together a cheap and tasty meal at the vegetarian friendly **Dandelion Deli** (1170 S. Wells Ave., tel. 702/322–6100).

CASINO BUFFETS

One caveat is in order: These buffets are designed to lure you into the casinos. After you've dropped 30 bucks at the crap table while waiting for a table, your meal may seem like less of a bargain, especially when nutritional value comes into the equation. This said, the cheapest buffet is at **Circus Circus** (*see* Where to Sleep, *above*)—where the top-price meal is $5—but you may want to pay $2–$3 extra at a place like the **Eldorado Hotel** (*see* Where to Sleep, *above*) for better quality control. The best spread in town is out at the **Atlantis** (3800 S. Virginia St., tel. 702/825–4700), with its extensive salad bar and Mongolian barbecue. Buffet prices start at $4.99 breakfast and rise to $9.99 for dinner on Friday and Saturday.

Every June 15, Deux Gros Nez (two big noses) sponsors the Tour De Nez, a bike race and community party known to cyclists the country over.

RESTAURANTS

Blue Heron. An island of vegetarianism in a sea of beef buffets, this busy restaurant has sandwiches and an assortment of Mexican and healthy entrées ($5–$7). It uses organic products when possible (90% of the time). Smoothies, salads, and fresh desserts are all up to par, and you can buy a fresh loaf of bread for the road. *1091 S. Virginia St., at Vassar St., tel. 702/786–4110.*

Deux Gros Nez. Hidden at the back of the Cheese Board and Wine Cellar building, climb the west fire escape into this bicycle-racing–theme café (check out the hanging retro biking jerseys). Try the feta and bell pepper focaccia ($6.25), muesli ($2.75), quiches, and their signature frappés—a mixture of ice cream and whatever you want added in like fruit, pie, or cookies. The excellent coffee is organic. *249 California Ave., tel. 702/786–9400.*

Pneumatic Diner. Sporting a menu with attitude, this hopping café-style eatery serves up coffee and espresso like the "Godzilla," frozen espresso mixed with milk and sugar. The produce is organic, and the pies (give the tart rhubarb a try—$3) are this side of heaven. Eat a salad ($2–$4.25). Go wild. *501 W. First St., at Ralston, tel. 702/786–8888 ext. 106.*

DESSERT AND COFFEEHOUSES

Java Jungle (246 W. 1st St., tel. 702/324–5282) is a trendy, smokeless hangout—popular among college students and business types—that serves a superior cup of coffee. A couple blocks south and east of Java Jungle, **Café Royale** (236 California Ave. at Hill St., tel. 702/322–3939) has outdoor seating, a full bar, sandwiches ($5), and pours some of the strongest coffee around.

WORTH SEEING

CASINOS

No matter what your prejudices, a visit to the casinos is obligatory once you decide to stop in town. Reno's newest addition is the **Silver Legacy** (407 N. Virginia St., tel. 800/687–8733), which features 1,720 rooms, five theme restaurants, the world's largest dome roof, 2,300 slot machines, and a shopping mall. Among the other downtown options, **Harrah's** (219 N. Center St., tel. 800/427–7247) is probably the fanciest. If you're willing to drive a couple of miles south on Virginia Street, the **Peppermill** (2107 S. Virginia St., tel. 702/826–2121) has a certain exploitative appeal. To really make your gambling dollar last, try the small **Nevada Club** (224 N. Virginia St., tel. 702/329–1721), where the bet minimums are extremely low (including 25¢ roulette). For that reason, it's a good place to learn the ropes of an unfamiliar game.

In many respects, the nicest place to gamble is the **Flamingo Hilton** (255 N. Sierra St., tel. 702/322-1111), where you might find yourself next to a Roy Orbison impersonator (*see* After Dark, *below*) at the roulette wheel. But the most compelling reason to play here is the superior blackjack rules. Because you're allowed to double down on any two cards (*see* Blackjack Tips *box in* Chapter 13) and to double after a split, your odds are better here than in other Reno casinos.

CHEAP THRILLS

The Sierra Arts Foundation publishes the bi-monthly **Encore**; for detailed theater, gallery, music, and museum information, this is invaluable, and many of the shows are free or very cheap. If you can't find a copy at the tourist center, call 702/329–1324 to get one. Reno's **National Bowling Stadium** (300 N. Center at Fourth St., tel. 702/334–2600) is a monument to a sport that's been experiencing a renaissance lately, though most of the people who come here (technically known as keglers) have been at it for years. One floor up from ground level is an 80-lane bowling alley designed to absorb sound. The bowling is strictly league, but you can bring a lunch (or buy one at the attached concession) and sit in one of 1,200 seats watching a sport that's graceful at its best. The fifth floor has a huge movie theater (tel. 702/334–2634) showing 70mm films on a screen four stories high. Admission is $5.

Just a few blocks west of Virginia Street along the Truckee River, you'll run into **Wingfield Park,** a nice spot for a picnic and the site of free summer concerts. Even better, head east on I–80 and take the Pyramid exit up to **Pyramid Lake.** The drive only takes about 45 minutes, but when you see the desolate desert hills that surround the lake, including sand dunes and the otherworldly Tufa formations made of calcium carbonate deposits, you may think you've traveled to the moon. The area is sacred land to the Paiutes, who now manage the site, and for $5 you can camp anywhere you like.

FESTIVAL

Reno's annual **Hot August Nights** (tel. 702/356–1956) celebrates classic cars and popular symbols of 1950s culture. Visitors drive their pre-1970 cars in a 2,500-vehicle parade, participate in a huge automobile auction, and crowd into the 24-hour Hamburger Haven soda fountain. The town gets decked out in poodle skirts, greased hair, and rolled-up T-shirts, and there's even a prom. Hotel rates go through the roof and rooms become seriously scarce. In 1998, this all takes place August 5–9.

AFTER DARK

Top-name entertainers (well, they were once at the top) make well-advertised appearances in Reno showrooms. If you're looking for some real casino kitsch at bargain prices, check out the celebrity impersonators at the **Flamingo Hilton** (tel. 702/785–7080 for show reservations).

The hard-drinking crowd hangs out at the **Blue Lamp** (241 N. Sierra, tel. 702/786–6004), behind the Pioneer Inn. Reno has the largest gay community in the area, with several gay bars, including **Bad Dolly's** (535 E. 4th St. at Valley Rd., tel. 702/348–1983), a predominantly lesbian country-western and house club featuring two-step and line dancing (call for lesson times). The **1099 Club** (1099 S. Virginia St., tel. 702/329–1099) provides a largely male social environment. Every June, people come from miles around for the annual coronation of the drag emperor and empress at the convention center. Ask at the bars for details. **Visions** (340 Kietzke La., tel. 702/786–5455) draws clubbers from as far away as Tahoe, for the music, the in-house leather shop, and the $1 beer pitchers Sunday and Wednesday.

7 SIERRA NEVADA AND SAN JOAQUIN VALLEY

UPDATED BY JONATHAN LEFF AND CLARK NORTON

To one of the first explorers it was "a specimen of chaos, which has defied the finishing hand of time." To naturalist John Muir it was "the Range of Light, the most divinely beautiful of all the mountain chains." And for millions of visitors today, the Sierra Nevada—the largest continuous mountain range in the United States—is one of the most spectacular natural settings in the world. Trade in the strip malls of the lowlands for mile-high panoramas and lush alpine scenery; motel swimming pools for crystal-clear mountain lakes; and faceless high-rises for towering peaks and granite cliffs. Only four hours east of San Francisco and three to eight hours north of Los Angeles lie **Yosemite National Park**; **Inyo National Forest**; **Sequoia** and **Kings Canyon national parks**; and **Sierra, Stanislaus,** and **Sequoia national forests**—an unparalleled collection of natural wonders 400 mi long and 80 mi wide.

Roughly translated from Spanish, Sierra Nevada means "snowy mountain range." And indeed, the Sierra's tallest peaks—many topping 14,000 ft—are capped by snow year-round. The weather is subject to drastic fluctuations: Even in summer, clear blue skies can suddenly give way to awesome thunderstorms or hazardous blizzards. In higher altitudes, temperatures can drop below freezing year-round or climb to 100°F in summer; in lower altitudes, summer temperatures are likely to soar as high as 110°F. The sudden changes in terrain and climate wreaked havoc on early settlers attempting to cross the mighty mountains in their quest for rich farmland or gold, but the same factors provide an exciting, intense environment for well-prepared hikers, campers, and backpackers.

On the whole, the Eastern Sierra is far less crowded than the western slope, except at Mammoth Lakes during ski season and on the Whitney Portal Trail in summer. In spring and fall, tourists don't create the hassles they do in summer. If you seek well-developed facilities, the national parks are for you. But if you want to bring your dog on a hike or ride your mountain bike up a peak, head to the national forests or wilderness areas, which have far fewer facilities and regulations. If you don't have a car, you'll have to do some creative travel planning.

Droves of vacationers escape to the Sierra Nevada, but most Californians would agree that the San Joaquin Valley, directly to the west, is a place to escape *from.* Unfortunately, if you plan on getting from one end of the state to the other, chances are good you'll find yourself in Stockton, Merced, Fresno, or another of the valley's sprawling cities. The good news is you'll be able to use your air conditioner—this place is as flat as a pancake. As long as you can stand oppressive heat and omnipresent country music, your stopover doesn't have to be a miserable one; most towns have a rowdy nightlife, and some even boast a few cafés.

THE SIERRA NEVADA AND SAN JOAQUIN VALLEY

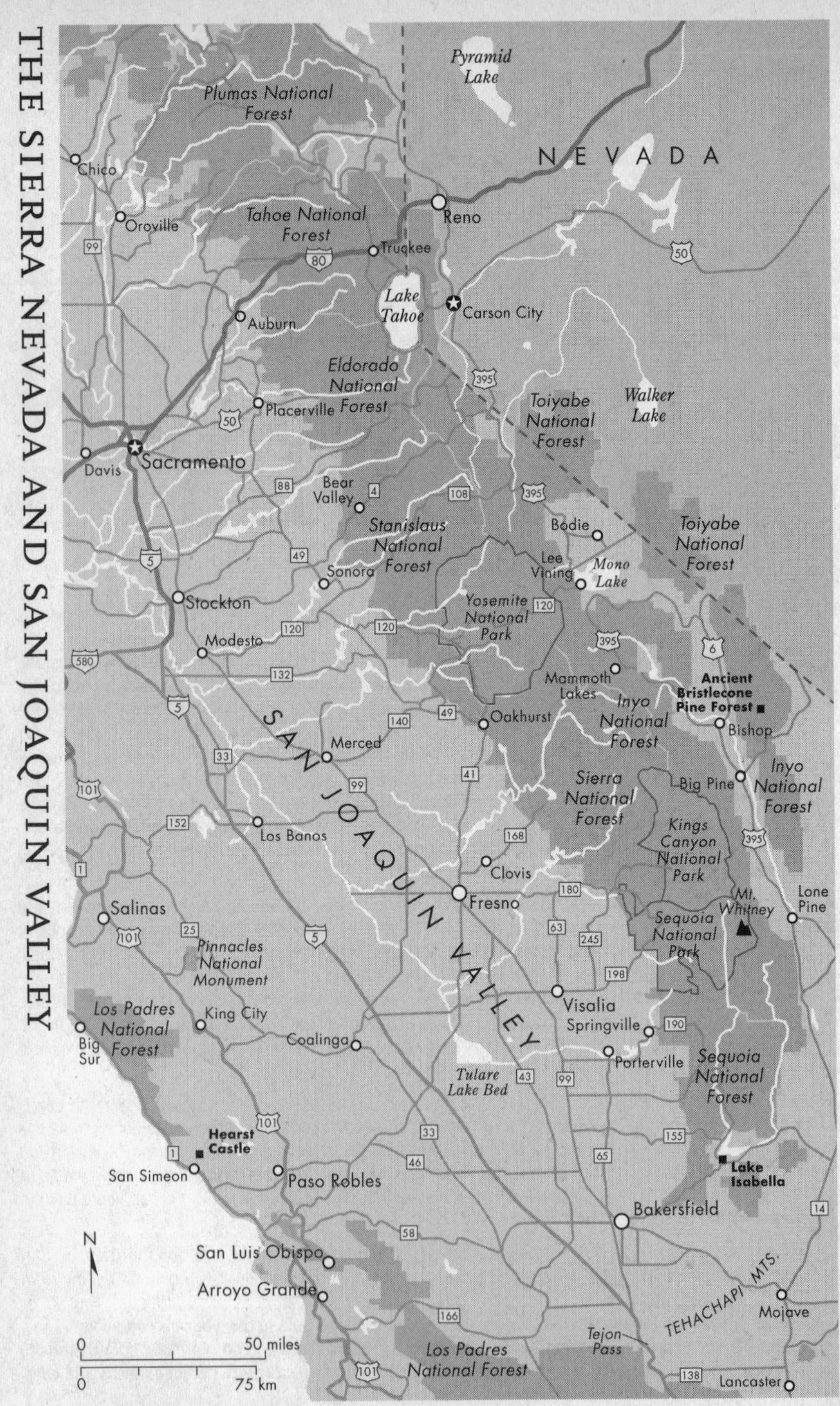

YOSEMITE NATIONAL PARK

For centuries Yosemite Valley was inhabited by the Ahwahneechee, while the Miwok and Paiute people lived in settlements in the surrounding mountains. Unfortunately, the Mariposa Battalion, the first group of whites to enter the valley (in 1851)—who came originally to remove, or destroy, the natives then inhabiting the area—saw Yosemite as prime hunting and fur-trapping ground. By the late 19th century whites conquered the Ahwahneechee and established a lucrative lumber business and trading outpost. We have naturalists John Muir and Galen Clark—named Yosemite's first guardian—to thank that today Yosemite Valley is more than a timber company parking lot. The Yosemite Grant, enacted in 1864, created the world's first state park, and thanks largely to Muir it was declared a national park in 1890.

Ever since, tourists have been flocking to, awestruck by, and—all too often—abusive of Yosemite National Park. A hundred years ago this abuse came in the form of a carved-up giant sequoia (a hole big enough to drive a car through) and atrocities against native peoples; today the damage is from too much attention. Between 1986 and 1996, the number of visitors to the park increased from 3 to over 4 million—most came in the summer, and most went straight to the 7-mi stretch called **Yosemite Valley.** They came to gawk at **Half Dome** and **El Capitan**—two breathtaking but treacherous granite formations—as well as **Yosemite, Nevada,** and **Vernal falls.** The heavy attention given these few sites earned the park the nickname Disneyland of National Parks. Officials have long known that this traffic was damaging the park (not to mention visitors' appreciation of it), but much-needed changes were moving at a slow pace until 1996, when nature took matters into her own hands.

Although Yosemite is much accustomed to the "est" syndrome—it's got the tallest waterfall in North America (Yosemite Falls), the largest single exposed granite rock on earth (El Capitan), and some of the biggest living things in the world (the giant sequoias)—a few new records have been added to the book more recently: The Ackerson-Complex fires burned 59,000 acres north of Tioga Road in August, making them the biggest in park history; a government shut-down closed the park for a record 21 days; and a rock slide behind the Happy Isles Nature Center was 500 ft wide, weighed 80,000 tons, and freefell 1,800 ft at 160 mph. What could top that in 1997? Well, warm, tropical drops of rain started falling early in the morning on January 1 and didn't stop for three days. One of the biggest floods in recorded park history was most destructive along the Merced River, the central waterway in Yosemite Valley, which carved new channels for itself, in the process destroying two campgrounds, washing out big chunks of Hwy. 140, and wreaking havoc with drinking water, sewage systems, and power lines.

The cleansing effect of the flood was naturally beneficial, but this nature-imposed closure of the valley also gave officials time to restructure the way the park worked—proposing to reduce the number of visitors by instituting a day-use reservations system. The major upside of all this is that there will be fewer overall visitors to the valley; what this means for the undisturbed, forested backcountry, with its massive granite formations and plunging waterfalls, is yet to be seen. But already the nonvalley areas of Yosemite—**Tuolumne Meadows** (pronouned too-*all*-o-mee), along Tioga Road; the giant sequoias of **Mariposa Grove,** off Hwy. 41 in the southwest corner of the park; **Glacier Point,** near Badger Pass; and the **Hetch Hetchy Reservoir** (north of Big Oak Flat)—all fairly easy to reach from the highway, are more heavily visited.

Whatever the case, these natural "disasters" haven't dulled the natural, glorious sheen of this land formed by glacial sculpturing and prehistoric activity at the earth's mantle. Slightly smaller than the state of Rhode Island, Yosemite is still packed with waterfalls, sheer granite cliffs, lush forests, and generous expanses of alpine meadows, and you can still find a quiet spot to call your own.

BASICS

VISITOR INFORMATION

For current events in Yosemite, check out the *Yosemite Guide,* available at all entrance stations. The visitor centers stock maps and brochures and distribute free wilderness permits (required for overnight camping in the backcountry). The **Yosemite Valley Visitor Center** (shuttle stops 6 and 9) is 11 mi east of the Hwy. 140 entrance and open daily 8–7 (mid-June–early Sept.), 9–5 (off-season). The **Tuolumne Meadows Visitor Center,** open daily 8–7:30 (summer only), is toward the east end of the park on Tioga

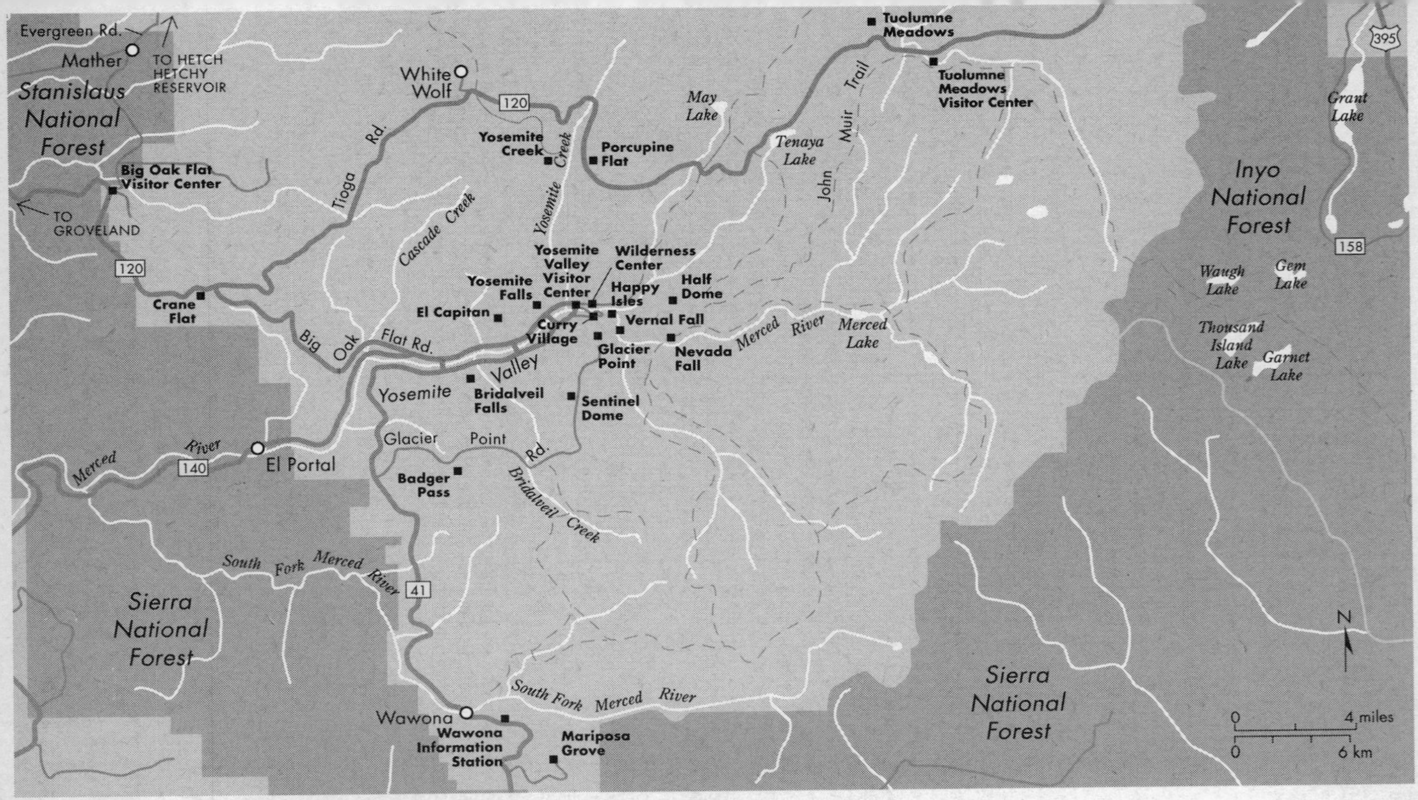

YOSEMITE NATIONAL PARK

Road. Though the **Wawona Information Station,** at the south end of Yosemite on Hwy. 41, doesn't have much of a tourist desk, it does offer wilderness permits weekdays 8:30–5, summer only. The **Big Oak Flat Visitor Center,** at the Hwy. 120 west entrance, is open daily 9–5 from Memorial Day to Labor Day. The **Public Information Office** (Box 577, Yosemite National Park 95389, tel. 209/372–0265) is the place to begin your search for information on Yosemite from afar, though getting through on the phone can be a task. Send a self-addressed, stamped envelope for free brochures and maps, or call weekdays between 9 and 5. For automated information, call the Yosemite National Park information line (tel. 209/372–0200). If you crave some human attention, call the park's new 95¢-per-minute ($1.95 for the first minute) line (tel. 900/454–6739), where you can chat about weather, campgrounds, or anything else; all proceeds benefit the Yosemite Association.

DAY-USE PERMITS

Beginning in May 1997, Yosemite started limiting the number of travelers—or, more specifically, cars—allowed into the park. Visitors in a private vehicle who don't have overnight reservations within the park are required to reserve a day-use permit to gain entrance. At press time, the park service hadn't decided whether this would affect the valley or the whole park. Call 209/372–0265 to get the latest word.

WILDERNESS PERMITS

In 1972 Yosemite had to institute a permit system to limit the number of backpackers on the trails each day. Half the park's permits are reserved, while half are distributed on a first-come, first-served basis one day in advance. To make a reservation (available up to 24 weeks in advance), you'll need to pay a reservation fee of $3 per person and send your dates of arrival and departure, specific trailheads of entry and exit, your main destination in the park, the number in your party, and alternative dates in case your first choices aren't available to **Wilderness Reservations** (Wilderness Center, Box 545, Yosemite 95389). You may also call 209/372–0740 to reserve by phone.

For free first-come, first-served permits, head to the new **Wilderness Center** (closed in winter), located two buildings east of the Yosemite Valley Visitor Center (*see above*). When the Wilderness Center is closed, you should go to the Wilderness Permit station nearest to your planned destination. Permits go quickly (some in just minutes)—particularly for popular areas such as the valley and Tuolumne Meadows—so arrive early the day before your hike with a detailed itinerary, including trails and estimated overnight stops.

FEES

The park fee for one week is $20 per car or $10 per hiker, bicyclist, or bus passenger. You can purchase an annual pass for unlimited access to the park.

WHEN TO GO

If possible, visit during spring or early fall, when crowds are less oppressive. Spring (late April–late May) is especially spectacular—the wildflowers are in bloom and the waterfalls are at their peak of sound and fury as snowpack melts in the high country. Of the more than 4 million people who visit each year, 70% arrive during summer (June–August), when temperatures reach a high of 90°F and a low of 40°F. In winter (November–March), temperatures drop to a chilly 45°F by day and a downright frigid 15°F by night—Tioga Pass and Glacier Point Road usually close by November due to inclement weather.

WHAT TO PACK

Rain gear is essential year-round. Water-repellent "shell" pants and a warm jacket with polar-fleece lining are a smart idea, and don't forget wool or wick-dry socks. If you plan to camp in winter you'll need a subzero sleeping bag and a waterproof (or at least water-resistant), four-season tent. Hiking boots are a must for exploring the backcountry, as are snowshoes or crampons if you want to blaze your own trail.

GENERAL STORES

If you're coming into the park from Hwy. 120, stop first at Oakdale's friendly, well-stocked **Newdeal Market** (888 Hwy. 120, tel. 209/847–5919), open daily 7 AM–10 PM. If you're headed in on Hwy. 41, you'll want to avail yourself of the **Vons, Longs Drugs,** and/or **Raley's** in Oakhurst. Otherwise you're stuck with the grocery and camping stores in pricey Yosemite Village (at shuttle stops 3, 5, and 10). The **Village Sport Shop** (tel. 209/372–1286), open from spring to fall, has fishing and camping gear. Both the **Village Store** (tel. 209/372–1253), open daily 8 AM–10 PM (8–8 in winter), and the **Wawona Store** (Hwy. 41, near south end of park, tel. 209/375–6574), open daily 8–8 (9–6 in winter), stock groceries and basic camping supplies.

SOMETHING TO BEAR IN MIND

Yosemite black bears have developed an appetite for your sunscreen, soap, toothpaste, hairspray, and other scented articles. This diet requires a high level of curiosity: Your tent, ice chest, backpack, and car are all fair game. Store all food and related supplies in the metal storage boxes provided at campsites, or rent or buy bear-proof containers for backcountry trips.

Badger Pass Sport Shop (tel. 209/372–8430), open Thanksgiving through Easter (weather permitting), has ski clothing and equipment, as well as limited picnic supplies. It's near Wawona and the Badger Pass ski slopes, off Hwy. 41 about 5 mi south of Yosemite Valley. In Curry Village, at the far eastern end of Yosemite Valley (shuttle stop 14), you'll find a host of stores, including the **Curry Village Mountain Shop** (tel. 209/372–8396), where you can purchase overpriced rock-climbing supplies and topographic maps, and the **Yosemite Mountaineering School** (tel. 209/372–8344), where you can rent camping equipment at reasonable prices.

MEDICAL AID

The **Yosemite Medical Clinic** in Yosemite Village offers full medical service and 24-hour emergency care. *Between visitor center and Ahwahnee Hotel, tel. 209/372–4637. Open daily 8–5.*

COMING AND GOING

BY BUS AND TRAIN

There is no direct bus service to Yosemite from San Francisco; all lines stop in either Fresno or Merced, where you have to change coaches. A cheap option from either Merced or Fresno is **VIA Adventures** (tel. 209/384–1315 or 800/369–7275), which runs three buses a day (2½ hrs, $20 one-way) from Merced's Greyhound station on 16th and N streets, and two buses a day (3 hrs, $20 one-way) from Fresno's airport and several downtown hotels (call to let them know you're coming). **Amtrak** (tel. 800/872–7245) in conjunction with VIA Adventures can take you from San Francisco to the park and back for $78. The train stops in Emeryville and in Merced, where you board the bus to Yosemite. All buses stop at Yosemite Lodge, Curry Village, and Yosemite Village. From San Francisco, **Green Tortoise** (tel. 415/956–7500 or 800/867–8647) runs a three-day Yosemite and Eastern Sierras tour out of San Francisco that goes through much of the park and surrounding forest. The tour costs $109, plus $31 for food (for more information on Green Tortoise travel *see* Bus Travel *in* Chapter 1); it also has two-day winter trips for $75 including food. **Incredible Adventures** (tel. 415/759–7071 or 800/777–8464) leads three-day trips to Yosemite from San Francisco for $169 (everything included) that feature camping, swimming, high-county hiking, and fireside cookouts.

BY CAR

You can reach Yosemite on three routes: **Highway 41** from the south, **Highway 140** from Merced in the west, and **Highway 120** from San Francisco and from the east when Tioga Road is open. From San Francisco, take I–580 east to I–205 and connect to Hwy. 120 (4 hrs one-way). Hwys. 41 and 140 terminate in Yosemite Valley, and Hwy. 120 becomes Tioga Road inside the park; Big Oak Flat Road connects the latter with the Valley. The eastern portion of Hwy. 120 (from Crane Flat headed east to the Tioga Pass and into Inyo National Forest and Lee Vining) closes in winter until May or June, as does Glacier Point Road. Be forewarned that summertime traffic is frequently bumper to bumper.

From late fall to early spring you should carry snow chains. The highways can get treacherous, and the California Highway Patrol often closes the roads to all traffic without snow gear. If you get stuck, you'll have to buy an expensive set of chains ($60) from a gas station. For road and weather conditions, call 209/372–0200, 916/445–1534, or 800/427–7623.

All this said, plans for a carless Yosemite (or at least a carless Yosemite Valley) are in motion. If this happens, the gateway towns of Groveland, Mariposa, Oakhurst, and others will become places where park visitors leave their cars and hop on shuttle buses into Yosemite. Although this will probably not be the case while you're reading this book, look for big news by the turn of the century.

GETTING AROUND

Curvy **Tioga Road** (Hwy. 120) runs the entire 60-mi, east–west length of the park, climbing 4,000 ft in elevation. If you're on a bicycle (*see* Biking, *below*), you may want to limit yourself to the valley, since both Hwy. 41 and Tioga Road are often narrow and have steep elevation gains.

BY PARK SHUTTLE

Free shuttle buses operate throughout the year, though service hours vary according to season. The **Yosemite Valley Shuttle** operates year-round (schedule varies) between Curry Village, Yosemite Village, the Yosemite Lodge, and campgrounds and points of interest in between (*see* Where to Sleep, *below*). Starting in mid-April, the shuttle operates 7 AM–10 PM for most stops (excluding Happy Isles, the Mirror Lake Trail, and North Pines campground, when service stops at 7:30 PM; campers in North Pines can easily walk from Shuttle Stop 19 at Lower Pines). In winter, hours are reduced, and some stops receive no service at all. Check the *Yosemite Guide* for a current schedule. During ski season a free shuttle leaves Yosemite Lodge for the **Badger Pass** ski area in the morning and returns in the afternoon. Another shuttle ($10 one-way, $19.50 round-trip) runs three times daily from mid-May to early October (weather permitting) between Yosemite Lodge and **Glacier Point** (*see* Scenic Drives and Views, *below*). Tickets can be purchased at a **Yosemite Transportation** desk in all hotels. From July until Labor Day, an early-morning backpackers' shuttle ($20 round-trip) runs once daily between Yosemite Lodge and Tuolumne Meadows with stops in between. It returns each day to Yosemite Valley. Call a visitor center for schedules.

WHERE TO SLEEP

Close to the ground—that's the way to experience Yosemite, and camping and backpacking are the best ways to do it. The privilege of four thin walls and a bed doesn't come cheap anyway. Beds and campsites go like hotcakes, and reservations are required at most.

One of the best kept secrets of Yosemite accommodations is the **Yosemite Lakes Hostel** (31191 Hardin Flat, 17 mi east of Groveland, tel. 209/962–0121), found 5 mi west of the park on Hwy. 120. Here are all sorts of sleeping options: hostel rooms that sleep two ($19), cabins that sleep four ($28), fully equipped yurts (circular dome tents) that sleep up to four ($89), and wooded tent sites ($16). Washing machines, a TV, and microwaves are all found on the premises. And—best of all—they often have space for walk-ins. They're open mid-May to September.

HOTELS AND CABINS

Hotel reservations can be made up to 366 days in advance, and believe it or not, most places actually fill up that far ahead. All lodging reservations are handled through **Yosemite Concessions Services Corp.** (5410 E. Home Ave., Fresno 93727, tel. 209/252–4848). Because Yosemite is so mobbed, consider yourself lucky if you can find a single vacancy. Otherwise try the hostel (*see above*) or check out the nearby towns of El Portal, Fish Camp, and Oakhurst (*see* Sierra National Forest *in* Near Yosemite, *below*), all of which have reasonably priced lodging.

For getting out of moonlight, most people prefer the **Yosemite Lodge** (Yosemite Valley), which has rooms for two starting $87 (with private bathroom); although all shared-bath rooms ($70) were wiped out in the flood, they should be rebuilt by 1998. For the same shared-bath price you can get a nicer, antique-filled room at the charmingly Victorian **Wawona Hotel**; the fact that you'll be about an hour from the Valley madhouse can either be a boon or a curse. Accommodations in **Curry Village** include canvas tent cabins (starting at $41) and simple wood cabins ($56, $73 with private bath). The fee for extra people in the tent cabins is $5.50, in the wood cabins $6–$8. The valley shantytown called **Housekeeping Camp** is for people who want to camp but don't want to lug the equipment; here over 250 identical concrete-and-canvas "tent" units huddle close together. They're not particularly comfy, but each structure houses up to four people—in bunk cots—for only $44 per night (extra cots are $4 more). The camp is open from April to late October. A grocery store, laundry, bathroom, and showers are nearby.

CAMPING

Yosemite Valley's developed campgrounds share a number of characteristics: They're all large, flat, near a major road, and shaded by pine trees—and extremely crowded. Most have picnic tables, fire pits, flush toilets, piped water, and food-storage lockers, but none has direct access to showers (for that, you'll have to head to Housekeeping Camp or Curry Village). Reservations are a must. Campground reservations are available up to five months in advance through a very complicated reservations system. On the 15th of every month, you can make reservations for all dates between four and five months from that day (example: on Feb. 15, you can get campground reservations for every day between June 15 and July 14). Call **Destinet** (tel. 800/436–7275) to get more information, and get your dialing finger in good shape, because these sites go early (Destinet opens at 7 AM PST). If you're stuck, show up at one of the campground kiosks (at Curry Village, Big Oak Flat, and at Tuolumne Meadows) and put your name on the waiting list in case there's a cancellation (don't forget that without reservations you'll still need to get a day-use permit in advance). The campground kiosks usually call off names around 3 PM for cancellations and no-shows.

If you can't get a reservation at any of the major campgrounds, there are a few first-come, first-served sites you can try. In particular, check out the valley's only walk-in campground, **Sunnyside,** located near Yosemite Lodge in Yosemite Valley. In the '70s, Sunnyside was called Camp 4 and was known to host a particular kind of Bay Area crowd in between Dead shows. Today it's the favorite Yosemite campground of a new kind of subculture: hard-core rock climbers. Sunnyside has 35 sites ($3 per person) with running water and toilets; note that the campground manager will pack each site with the six-person maximum, so you could be sharing close quarters with strangers. For walk-ins outside the valley, try **Tuolumne Meadows** (*see above*), where 25 sites are reserved for backpackers with Wilderness Permits; **Backpackers' Camp,** located behind North Pines campground in Yosemite Valley, is a one-day-max ground used only by hikers the day before they head out and the day after they return. Tuolumne also reserves half its sites for same-day reservations. Other first-come, first-served sites have, in the past, included **White Wolf** (Tioga Pass Rd., about 10 mi east of Crane Flat) with 87 sites ($10), **Porcupine Flat** with 52 sites ($6), and **Yosemite Creek** with 75 sites ($6). The latter two are both off Tioga Road east of White Wolf. Keep in mind that all the Tioga Road campgrounds close in winter, usually mid-September or early October to early June. For information on backcountry camping, *see* Longer Hikes, *below.*

INSIDE YOSEMITE VALLEY • The 1997 floods knocked out a whopping 300-plus campsites—and two entire campgrounds (Upper and Lower River)—in the Valley. Although campsites will be rebuilt, when and where is uncertain. Regardless, **Upper Pines** is the biggest campground, with 238 tent and RV sites ($15) available April–November. It's conveniently located at shuttle stop 15, near trailheads to Mirror Lake and Vernal Fall. Misanthropes be warned: This place gets extremely crowded and the RVs pack together like sardines. Across the street at Shuttle Stop 19, **Lower Pines** is open year-round, with 80 tent and RV sites ($15) sandwiched between the Merced River and Storeman Meadow. Expect the same pack of RVs and families you see at Upper Pines. **North Pines Campground,** with 85 sites ($15) available April–October, is conveniently located at shuttle stop 18. Open to both tent campers and RV-owners, this campground sports spectacular views of Yosemite Falls and has many sites along the sandy (sometimes soggy) shores of the Merced River. It is also a great starting point for the short hike to Mirror Lake.

OUTSIDE YOSEMITE VALLEY • Look for **Tuolumne Meadows,** an enormous riverside campground perfect for exploring the eastern side of the park. Its 314 sites ($12) lie along Tioga Road (Hwy. 120) and are usually open mid-June–September, depending on the weather. This campground, in some of the park's most beautiful country, attracts its share of day hikers, but it's still one of the last to fill up. **Hodgdon Meadow,** just past Hwy. 120 at the Big Oak Flat entrance on the west side of the park, allows you to escape the chaos of the valley and still remain within striking distance (30–40 min). It draws nature-loving car campers year-round, except when snow closes the road (sometimes until late spring).

FOOD

If you plan on camping, bring as much food as possible. Prices in Yosemite's stores (*see* General Stores, *above*) are predictably high. A dull variety of American eateries, from fast-food cafeterias to expensive sit-down restaurants, is the only other choice.

The **Yosemite Village** complex, 11 mi east of the Hwy. 140 entrance, has the largest selection of food in the park. The **Pasta Place** (shuttle stop 5, tel. 209/372–8381, closed in winter) is a cafeteria-style restaurant with basic pasta-with-sauce plates (from $4.60) to choose from. You might want to stuff yourself with the dinner special ($9–$10): a full pasta plate, Caesar salad, bread, and a large drink. Also in Yosemite Village, **Degnan's Deli** (tel. 209/372–8454), the Valley's healthiest spot, has made-to-order sandwiches ($4–$5) and salads ($2–$4).

In **Curry Village** (tel. 209/372–8333), on the west side of the Valley near Happy Isles, there's a cafeteria, a burger stand, and a small pizzeria adjoining a bar.

EXPLORING YOSEMITE

It can take anywhere from a few days to the rest of your life to familiarize yourself with Yosemite. To get a good overview in summer, drive along **Tioga Road** (Hwy. 120), stopping to take a walk or a hike wherever you're inclined. Scores of trails meander through the park, from relaxing strolls to highly demanding backcountry excursions. Many trailheads are easily reached by shuttle bus (*see* Getting Around, *above*). In the winter, be sure to check trail conditions with the rangers before heading out. Not all trails and roads are open year-round; trails in Tuolomne Meadows and Glacier Point may be inaccessible. Those venturing off the beaten path will need serious snow gear in the winter months.

ORIENTATION AND TOURS

The **Yosemite Valley Visitor Center** (*see* Basics, *above*) offers a worthwhile slide program on the park's geography and history. The free 20-minute show runs throughout the day; check the *Yosemite Guide* for times. Ranger programs (nature walks and storytelling) in the valley last 30 to 90 minutes and are great ways to learn more about the park; programs in Toulumne and elsewhere can last longer.

All kinds of guided bus tours originate in the valley, from two-hour excursions ($16) along the valley floor (every half hr daily 9–4) to a day-long grand tour ($42) of Mariposa Grove and Glacier Point (late spring to late fall). For reservations, contact the **Yosemite Lodge Tour Desk** (tel. 209/372–1240) or go to one of the tour booths at Curry Village, the Ahwahnee Hotel, or the Village Store in Yosemite Village.

SHORT HIKES

Yosemite Falls, also known simply as "The Falls," is the highest waterfall in North America and the fifth highest in the world. It's divided into the upper falls (1,430 ft), the middle cascades (675 ft), and the lower falls (320 ft). From the parking lot, a ¼-mi trail leads to the base. To reach the top, head to Sunnyside Campground and take the strenuous 3½-mi (one-way) **Yosemite Falls Trail,** which rises over 2,700 ft. The views from the top are breathtaking. If you're not up to the full trek (6–8 hrs round-trip), stop at **Columbia Rock,** just over 1 mi along the trail. You'll still get a good workout and dizzying vistas of Half Dome and the valley. Get off at shuttle stop 7 and follow the signs.

The easy and popular 3-mi trail around **Mirror Lake/Meadow** (Shuttle Stop 17), at the east end of the valley, is the gentlest in the park. From the Happy Isles Trailhead (Shuttle Stop 16), the difficult 6-mi round-trip trail to **Vernal Fall** (317 ft) and **Nevada Fall** (594 ft) takes five–six hours roundtrip, but the view from the top is phenomenal. The first half of the trail (aptly named **Mist Trail**) is a great place to soak yourself on a hot day. A fantastic overnight hike continues past Nevada Fall to Half Dome (*see* Longer Hikes, *below*). If you arrive in Yosemite along Hwy. 41, your first view of the valley will be of **Bridalveil Falls,** a ragged 620-ft cascade that's often blown as much as 20 ft from side to side by the wind. The Ahwahneechee called it *Pohono* (Puffing Wind). An easy ¼-mi trail leading to its base starts from the parking lot. For fabulous views of some of Yosemite's finest, follow the **Pohono Trail.** The trek starts at Hwy. 41 at the Wawona Tunnel and terminates at Glacier Point. If you start on the west side of the tunnel it's 1 mi to Inspiration Point where, looking eastward up the valley floor, you can bask in the shadow of El Capitan and Bridalveil Falls.

Numerous day hikes begin at **Tuolumne Meadows,** including an easy ½-mi trail to **Soda Springs**—a potable, naturally carbonated spring. A lovely but arduous (3 hrs, 5 mi round-trip) hike to emerald **Elizabeth Lake** wanders through mountain hemlock and lodgepole pine and across boisterous Unicorn Creek. These trails are less crowded than those originating in the valley.

LONGER HIKES

There are hundreds of possible day hikes in Yosemite, but to beat the crowds you'll need to backpack away from the stench of civilization. All trails are limited to a certain number of backpackers to prevent overuse, and free wilderness permits are required for overnight stays (*see* Wilderness Permits *in* Basics, *above*). With a permit, you can wander along the 800 mi of trails (ranging from 5 to 20 mi long) crisscrossing Yosemite's wilderness. These often involve strenuous climbs along jagged paths no more than a foot wide, and some trails take upward of a week to complete. Fire rings are interspersed along the

PACIFIC CREST TRAIL

From the California–Mexico border all the way to the Great White North of Canada, the Pacific Crest Trail winds through 24 national forests, 7 national parks, and 33 wilderness areas for 2,638 mi of pure hiking satisfaction. You can hook up with it out of Tuolumne Meadows. For more information contact: The PCT Association, 5325 Elkhorn Boulevard, Suite 256, Sacramento 95842, tel. 800/817–2243.

way, but you'll need to bring your own tent and provisions, including a water filter or iodine tablets to treat water. You can rent special 3-pound bear-proof canisters for $3 at Yosemite Valley Sports Shop, Curry Village Mountain Shop, Crane Flat Grocery, Wawona Store, and Tuolomne Meadows Sports Shop (*see* Something to Bear in Mind *box, above*). Order maps and a pamphlet of hiking suggestions from the **Yosemite Association Bookstore** (Box 230, El Portal 95318, tel. 209/379–2648). At any of Yosemite's bookstores, you can buy topographic USGS maps ($4), but experienced backpackers swear by Trails Illustrated's waterproof topo map ($8.95).

If you're in top physical condition, take the hike out of Yosemite Valley, following either the John Muir or Mist Trail to **Half Dome.** Follow the trail to Nevada Fall (*see* Short Hikes, *above*), and continue past Little Yosemite Valley Campground to the Half Dome turnoff; then be prepared to climb and climb an additional 2,700 ft until you've risen a total of 4,800 ft. This trip (10–12 hrs, 17 mi round-trip) is not for those with vertigo or weak wills. You can make the trek an overnighter by camping at **Little Yosemite Valley Campground.** You can leave your pack at the campground or just before the final cables section and climb the last 4 mi without extra weight.

Hetch Hetchy, one of California's largest reservoirs, has irked conservationists since it was built early in the century. Environmentalists like John Muir fought actively against the damming of the Tuolumne River, which, they argued, would irreparably harm the region's wildlife. But politicians in San Francisco wanted mountain-fresh drinking water. Guess who won? Today, despite the massive Hetch Hetchy dam and the fires in 1996, the area still retains much of its beauty, and it contains the wonderfully isolated, moderately difficult **Rancheria Falls Trail** (13 mi round-trip), which leads to the eponymous lonely falls. You can do this trail in a day. To reach the Rancheria Falls Trailhead, exit the west side of the park on Tioga Road (Hwy. 120), turn right on Evergreen Road after 1 mi, and continue for 8 mi (you'll see signs).

The area north of Tuolumne River is wild and untrammeled. The numerous trailheads near **Tuolumne Meadows** are great for backpackers who want to spend at least a few days in the wilderness. Serious hikers should consider the **Tuolumne Grand Canyon Trail** (accessed from either Tuolumne Meadows or White Wolf). It's a rough 29-mi hike to White Wolf if you begin at Tuolumne Meadows. The first 4 mi follow the river along the forest and then drop down along a series of waterfalls and cascades, where the trail gets steeper as it descends through the Muir Gorge into Pate Valley and then up to White Wolf. This strenuous hike requires at least three full days. Another popular trip out of Tuolumne Meadows from the John Muir Trailhead is an excellent two- to three-day hike (about 30 mi round-trip) that leads to **Vogelsang Lake.** Hike up Lyell Canyon on the **John Muir Trail** to the **Rafferty Creek Trail,** which becomes steep and difficult. This is a popular trip, so get your permits early.

SCENIC DRIVES AND VIEWS

During summer you can drive up to **Glacier Point** for a spectacular view of the valley and surrounding mountains. The 16-mi road starts at Chinquapin junction on Hwy. 41. Better yet, take a shuttle (*see* Getting Around, *above*) to the top and take Four Mile Trail back down into the valley (3–4 hrs), coming out on South Side Drive. **Tuolumne Meadows,** the largest subalpine meadow in the High Sierra and the site of several backcountry trailheads, is on Tioga Road, 25 mi west of Lee Vining and U.S. 395. This is a gorgeous part of Yosemite, with delicate meadows surrounded by huge granite formations, and it's usually much less crowded than the Valley. Tioga Road is closed during winter.

PARK ACTIVITIES

For those who want to take it easy, the National Park Service rents binoculars ($3) for **bird-watching.** Free 1½-hour **photography walks,** which lead you to prime spots for shooting Yosemite, leave several times a week around 8:30 AM from the Yosemite Lodge or the Ahwahnee Hotel; reservations are recommended. **Horseback rides** originate at the stables in Toulumne (in the summer). A four-hour trip is $45. In summer, you can take a leisurely 3-mi float (they call it "rafting") down the Merced in June and July for $13. Sign up at the **rafting** area in Curry Village, open daily 10–4. For more information on all these activities, consult the *Yosemite Guide* or check with the visitor center (tel. 209/372–0299).

BIKING

Bikes are not permitted on any hiking trails, but Yosemite Valley has 8 mi of paved bike paths. Try the spectacular trail to Happy Isles and (halfway to) Mirror Lake, off the road to Curry Village; the easy 3-mi loop takes well under an hour unless you stop for a ½-mi walk to Mirror Lake. Rent bikes ($5 per hour, $20 a day) from **Curry Village** (tel. 209/372–8319) or **Yosemite Lodge** (tel. 209/372–8367). Serious cyclists should consider the 15-mi round-trip from Tuolumne Meadows to Olmstead Point along Tioga Road. The grades are difficult and the roads narrow, but the views are spine chilling.

If you're coming in on Route 41 at the southern end of the park, be sure to stop at the majestic Mariposa Grove, Yosemite's largest stand of giant sequoias.

ROCK CLIMBING

Yosemite is a mecca for world-class rock climbers. Basic and intermediate lessons ($150 for one person, $90 each for two) are available mid-April to mid-October with the **Yosemite Mountaineering School** (tel. 209/372–8444). They organize trips from Yosemite Valley and Tuolumne Meadows. You can't rent climbing equipment in the park without enrolling in a class.

SKIING

Yosemite's ski season usually lasts from early December to March. Call 209/372–0200 for weather conditions.

DOWNHILL • Yosemite has a small ski area, **Badger Pass** (tel. 209/372–8430 or 209/372–1000 for snow report), that won't pose much of a challenge to accomplished skiers. It's a good place to learn, however, and there are enough relatively uncrowded trails to keep intermediate skiers entertained. It's open daily 9–4:30 in winter. Lift tickets cost $22–$28, depending on the number of lifts open, which in turn depends on snowfall. They have five lifts with three advanced runs and six intermediate runs. Ski rentals are $18 a day, snowboards $30 a day. Look for Badger Pass 6 mi east of Hwy. 41 on Glacier Point Road.

CROSS-COUNTRY • Yosemite has 90 mi of marked cross-country trails through the Badger Pass ski area to Glacier Point. A free shuttle from the Valley runs to Badger Pass, departing twice in the morning and returning in the afternoon. **Glacier Point Road** is a good place to start: Beginners will enjoy the groomed track, and advanced skiers will get a workout if they take the whole 21-mi round-trip along the rim of the valley. The **Yosemite Cross-Country Ski School** (tel. 209/372–8444) offers two-hour lessons ($19) and four-hour lessons ($40, including rentals). A guided overnight trip—including meals and lodging—is $110 per person. Badger Pass (*see above*) has rentals ($12 half day, $15 full day). The **Tuolumne Grove of Giant Sequoias Trail** (3 mi round-trip), which starts at Crane Flat a few miles east of the Big Oak Flat entrance station, has a steep drop, but you get to ski among the largest living things on earth.

SNOWSHOEING

National Park Service Naturalists conduct regular two-hour snowshoe walks from Badger Pass and sometimes at Crane Flat. These easy walks ramble around the ski areas and the Tuolumne Grove of Giant Sequoias; snowshoes are available for $2. The Yosemite Mountaineering School (tel. 209/372–8444 in winter) rents snowshoes at Badger Pass for $11.50 per day.

NEAR YOSEMITE

STANISLAUS NATIONAL FOREST

Encompassing a sizable chunk of the Sierra Nevada—more than a million acres in all—just northwest of Yosemite, Stanislaus National Forest has it all: steep peaks, deep valleys, tranquil meadows, scores of mountain streams and lakes, and free camping almost anywhere within forest boundaries. And, wonder of wonders, the backcountry, particularly the **Mokelumne** and **Carson-Iceberg wildernesses,** has hiking trails that are significantly less crowded than Yosemite's; to cap it all, the required permits can be obtained on the day of the hike. Still not convinced? Stanislaus is an excellent choice for mountain biking and fishing (*see* Forest Activities, *below*), with forested dirt roads and stocked lakes that Yosemite can only dream of; unfortunately, Stanislaus is also big with hunters. While there are plenty of places in Stanislaus to commune with Mother Nature tête-à-tête, those looking to do so should give wide berth to the resort communities of **Pinecrest** and **Lake Alpine** between June and September.

During winter, Stanislaus has cross-country and downhill skiing and snowmobiling, but plan to stay in a hotel or by the side of the road; only one campground is open between May and October. Before you venture into the park, pick up a copy of the free *Summit Passage,* available at the Summit Ranger Station in Pinecrest (*see below*), for detailed descriptions of activities and programs in Stanislaus.

VISITOR INFORMATION • All ranger stations offer camping and lodging suggestions, hiking and road maps ($4–$8.50), and free wilderness and campfire permits. The **supervisor's office** is in Sonora (19777 Greenley Rd., tel. 209/532–3671). Otherwise, contact the businesslike **Summit Ranger Station** (Hwy. 108, in Pinecrest, tel. 209/965–3434); the well-prepared **Groveland Ranger Station** (Hwy. 120, in Groveland, tel. 209/962–7825); or the friendly **Mi-Wok Ranger Station** (Hwy. 108, in Mi-Wuk Village, tel. 209/586–3234); visit the **Calaveras Ranger Station** (Hwy. 4, in Hathaway Pines, tel. 209/795–1381) only as a last resort. All are open daily 8–4:30 in the summer and weekdays 8–4:30 in the winter; Summit is also open Saturday 8–4:30 in the winter.

GENERAL STORES • In the forest, the **Pinecrest Market** (401 Pinecrest Lake Rd., Pinecrest, tel. 209/965–3661) is well stocked and has lower prices than others in the area. The market is open summer, daily 7 AM–11 PM; winter, daily 9–6. Farther up the road, there are also general stores at Strawberry, Dardanelle's Resort, and Kennedy Meadows, though the last two are closed in winter. Hours vary, but 8–8 is a good bet in the summer; in the winter it's closer to 9–5. For back-home prices, however, it's best to stock up on the way in. Sonora (*see* Chapter 6), about 10 mi west of Stanislaus on Hwy. 108, has a few stores that sell camping gear; **Sierra Nevada Adventure Co.** (173 S. Washington St., tel. 209/532–5621), open Monday–Saturday 10–7 and Sunday 10–5, specializes in hiking, climbing, skiing, and kayaking gear. They also rent snowshoes and kayaks. For general supplies, head south on Washington Street, Sonora's main thoroughfare, and turn left on Mono Way, where you'll find two shopping centers, a **Save Mart** and a **Payless** drugstore.

COMING AND GOING • Three highways traverse Stanislaus in a roughly east–west direction: **Highway 4** to the north, **Highway 108** in the middle, and **Highway 120**—which connects Stanislaus with San Francisco and Yosemite—to the south. Before heading to the high country, check road conditions at the ranger station in Sonora or Calaveras, or call 800/427–7623 for recorded information—the mountain passes are sometimes closed until late June because of ice and snow. Driving time from San Francisco to Stanislaus (via Hwy. 120) is 3½ hours; from both Stockton (via Hwy. 4) and Modesto (via Hwy. 108) it's two hours. **Tuolumne County Transit** (tel. 209/532–0404) runs buses ($1.50) weekdays only from Sonora into Stanislaus National Forest, passing through the towns of Twain Harte, Mi-Wuk Village, and Sierra Village.

WHERE TO SLEEP • If none of the following options strike your fancy, cruise through the Sonora (*see* Chapter 6). Within the forest, a number of "resorts" with cabins or cottages allow you to get that rustic feeling without actually camping. None of the resorts is dirt cheap, but most have a few reasonably priced rooms. Open year-round, **Pinecrest Lake Resort** (off Hwy. 108 in Pinecrest, tel. 209/965–3411) has motel rooms that sleep four for $80. **Kennedy Meadows** (Hwy. 108, 28 mi from the Summit Ranger Station, tel. 209/532–9632) has 19 comfortable cabins (most with kitchens) for $50–$120, sleeping 2–12 people; they're usually open late April–mid-October.

Just outside the forest's western border, the **Mi-Wuk Motor Lodge** (Hwy. 108, Mi-Wuk Village, tel. 209/586–3031) offers doubles with TVs and VCRs, brass beds, and pine furniture for $55–$110 (pricier rooms have Jacuzzis and fireplaces). A spa, a heated pool, barbecue equipment, and movie rentals ($2) sweeten the deal. Just inside the forest to the north is the comfortable **Wehe's Meadowmont Lodge** (Hwy. 4, Arnold, tel. 209/795–1394) offering simple doubles for $60. For an extra $10 you can get a kitchen or a space for your buddy.

CAMPING • To temporarily free yourself from the bonds of civilization, simply find an appealing spot at least 100 ft off any paved road and pitch your tent. If you plan to have a fire of any kind—including a camp stove—you'll need to pick up a free fire permit from one of the ranger stations first (*see* Visitor Information, *above*). Stanislaus also has dozens of developed campgrounds, ranging in cost from free to $15. Campgrounds in the **Stanislaus Forest** are divided by the four ranger districts—**Mi-Wok** (tel. 209/586–3234), **Summit** (tel. 209/965–3434), **Calaveras** (tel. 209/795–1381), and **Groveland** (tel. 209/962–7825)—and most are open May–October. Be forewarned that there are a few campgrounds with the same name located in entirely different parts of the forest. All developed sites except those at popular **Pinecrest** (on Hwy. 108, behind the Summit Ranger Station) are first-come, first-served. Should you want to vie for one of Pinecrest's 200 sites ($13), open year-round, call the **U.S. Forest Service Reservation Center** (tel. 800/280–2267) up to 240 days in advance. But you'd do better—in terms of your pocketbook and your search for quiet beauty—to go elsewhere. For ideas, ask at a ranger station for the free brochure "Camping in Stanislaus Forest."

In the Mi-Wok District, **Fraser Flat Campground** (3 mi north of Hwy. 108 at Spring Gap turnoff, between Mi-Wuk Village and Pinecrest) is terrific for fishing or just hanging out near the south fork of the Stanislaus River. The 32 sites go for $9. In the Summit District, **Mill Creek Campground** (on Hwy. 108, 14 mi east of the Summit Ranger Station) is located in a pine-studded meadow. Seventeen trailer and tent sites go for $4, and as promised it's next to a creek. **Boulder Flat Campground** (on Hwy. 108, 20 mi east of the Summit Ranger Station) has 20 sunny campsites ($9) hidden among large boulders with nearby fishing. At **Sand Flat Campground** (note that there are several Sand Flats—this one is 20 mi east of the Summit Ranger Station and left on Clark's Fork Rd. for 6 mi), you can escape the RV masses by opting for one of the walk-in sites. Skeeters aside, the nine free sites at **Mosquito Lakes** campground in the Calveras District (6 mi east of Lake Alpine on Hwy. 4) are well worth a visit (open June—October). For easy wilderness access, motor on to the 35 sites ($5) at **Highland Lakes Campground** (7 mi south of Hwy. 4 on Highland Rd., which is 1½ mi west of Ebbetts Pass). This is a great area to begin hikes into the Carson-Iceberg Wilderness (*see below*).

FOOD • Expect to encounter standard burger and steak joints in the forest's small smattering of restaurants. On Hwy. 108, the **Pie in the Sky Pizzeria** (Hwy. 108, Sierra Village, tel. 209/586–4251) caters to truckers in summer and skiers in winter. A small pizza, really enough for two, and a beer will run you just over $12. One of the only exceptions to the greasy-spoon norm is **The Strawberry Inn** (Hwy. 108, Strawberry, tel. 209/965–3662). A California-style omelet (artichoke hearts, mushrooms, and mozzarella; $5.95) makes an excellent breakfast—and their luncheon salads ($4–6) can really fill your roughage quota—but skip dinner, when the food doesn't quite merit the prices. Along Hwy. 4, be sure to stop at the friendly **Snowshoe Brewing Co.** (Hwy. 4, Arnold, tel. 209/795–2272), where you can knock back a pint of handcrafted ale for $2.75 and get a burrito ($4.50) or New York steak ($11) to go with it.

EXPLORING STANISLAUS • To get a sense of Stanislaus's often dramatic terrain, take a drive on Hwy. 4 or Hwy. 108, both of which traverse the 77-mi-wide forest west to east. Along the way you'll find dozens of turnouts with excellent views and trailheads for day hikes. On Hwy. 108, stop at **Donnell Vista** for spectacular views of Dardanelle's Cone—dark rocky crags atop the mountains that are the remnants of ancient lava flows some 9 million years ago. If you're a geology nut, take the short hike to the **Columns of the Giants** (Hwy. 108, 1½ mi east of the town of Dardanelle). These giant solidified lava columns were formed from volcanic eruptions over 150,000 years ago. For stellar views of the area, follow Hwy. 108 to Sonora Pass and hike in either direction up the steep **Pacific Crest Trail.** On Hwy. 4, stop at **Calaveras Big Trees State Park,** 10 mi into the forest, which has some 150 giant sequoias. You can enjoy them in relative solitude on the 5-mi, three-hour walk around the **South Grove Loop**; the hordes take the easier 1-mi **North Grove Loop.**

If you have a few days for exploring, try one of Stanislaus's three well-preserved wilderness areas. Before setting out, plan a specific route and obtain a wilderness permit and topo maps ($4) from any ranger station. Be sure to pick up the forest service flyer entitled "Emigrant Wilderness Trailhead Locations." On the eastern fringes of Stanislaus, the 112,000-acre **Emigrant Wilderness** is the most popular, though solitude can still be found among its lakes, meadows, rushing streams, and granite-walled domes and canyons. The **Gianelli Cabin Trail** is a steep ½-mi ascent to the spectacular views at **Burst Rock.** For some serious backpacking, continue along **Burst Rock Trail,** which will take you deep into the great beyond. A sign just before the Dodge Ridge Ski Resort, off of Hwy. 108, will point you down 9 mi of gravel road to the trailhead.

To the north, the **Mokelumne Wilderness** straddles the border between the Stanislaus and Eldorado national forests; this rough, rugged terrain, most noted for the Mokelumne River Canyon, is hard to hike, but trails originate along Hwy. 4 at **Lake Alpine, Woodchuck Basin,** and **Sandy Meadow.** The 160,000-acre **Carson-Iceberg Wilderness,** with its steep ridges, narrow valleys, and lava-formed mountain peaks, is more easily accessible and therefore more popular. Committed hikers enjoy the 8-mi (one-way) **Clark Fork Meadow Trail,** beginning at St. Mary's trailhead on Hwy. 108 at the eastern edge of the forest, and ending at Clark's Fork Road. From Clark Fork, hikers should check out the moderate 14-mi (round-trip) **Arnot Trail** to the Highland Lakes. Maps, information, and the required wilderness permits for this hike are available at the Summit Ranger Station (*see* Visitor Information, *above*).

FOREST ACTIVITIES • All of Stanislaus's dirt roads are fair game for mountain bikers, but most people stick to the Calaveras Ranger District, off Hwy. 4. The folks at **Bear Valley Mountain Bikes** (Hwy. 4 at the Texaco in Bear Valley, tel. 209/753–2834) rent bikes ($20 half day, $30 full day); you can also purchase a bike trail guide ($4) here. A good introduction to the area's bike trails is the 3-mi **Lake Alpine Loop.** If you need more peddling room, head south on Slick Rock Road, on the west side of Lake Alpine.

Stanislaus is one of the Sierra's most popular fishing destinations, with hundreds of streams and lakes stocked with trout. Among the mainstays are the South Fork of the **Stanislaus River, Pinecrest Lake,** and **Donnell Reservoir,** all on Hwy. 108; and **Mosquito Lake** and the **Mokelumne River,** both off Hwy. 4. Bring your own gear, as rental equipment is nonexistent. In winter, **Dodge Ridge Ski Resort** (off Hwy. 108, near Pinecrest, tel. 209/965–3474) attracts intermediate skiers to its seven lifts and 29 runs. Lift tickets are $34 and rentals $20. Snowboarders take up almost half of the mountain, and the new terrain parks provide challenges. Rent boards and boots at Dodge Ridge ($32), or grab them for less ($28) at Pure Boardom (Hwy. 108, Sierra Village, tel. 209/586–6697) on the way up. On Hwy. 4, **Bear Valley Ski Area** (near Lake Alpine, tel. 209/753–2301) offers nine chair lifts and over 60 runs but still not much for expert skiers. Lift tickets cost $33, skis $20, and snowboards $32. Just 3 mi south of the downhillers is **Bear Valley Cross-Country** (off Hwy. 4, 3 mi before Lake Alpine, tel. 209/753–2834), with over 40 mi of groomed trails; daily fees are $15 and skis cost $14 (snowshoes $12).

SIERRA NATIONAL FOREST

The proximity of Sierra National Forest to the city of Fresno seems a miracle of sorts. After an hour's drive, the landscape transforms from a vast expanse of car dealerships and tract houses into lakes and coniferous forests, a blessing to valley residents and visitors alike. Unfortunately, this stroke of geological good fortune has resulted in heavy use and extensive development around the bigger lakes and reservoirs, specifically **Bass, Shaver,** and **Huntington lakes,** which are renowned for their party atmosphere. Still, Sierra National Forest, which lies between Yosemite and Sequoia/Kings Canyon national parks, is great for a day or weekend trip. Even backpackers craving isolation can find a niche here. In contrast to the development in the western part of the forest, almost the entire eastern half is protected wilderness: the **Ansel Adams Wilderness,** the **Dinkey Lakes Wilderness,** the **John Muir Wilderness,** and the **Kaiser Wilderness.**

The western areas, including **Pine Flat Reservoir** and **Kerckhoff** and **Redinger lakes,** lie at lower elevations and have camping and hiking opportunities year-round. Temperatures climb into the 90s during summer, so try to hit the forest in spring or fall, when screaming teens and the blistering sun are less of a problem. The higher elevations (above 7,000 ft) are generally closed November–April due to snow, but by mid-May the camping season is usually in full swing, and lower temperatures make it worth the extra climb. The best time to visit the high country is July–early September, when the snow melts and the wildflowers bloom.

VISITOR INFORMATION • For information on camping, hiking, and other activities, as well as backcountry fire and wilderness permits, stop by one of the ranger stations in the park's western corridor: **Oakhurst/Mariposa Ranger Station** (43060 Hwy. 41, 6 mi north of Oakhurst, tel. 209/683–4665); **Minarets Ranger Station** (in North Fork, tel. 209/877–2218); **Pineridge Ranger Station** (29688 Aubery Rd., in Prather, tel. 209/855–5360); and **Trimmer/Kings River Ranger Station** (34849 Maxon Rd., near Pine Flat Reservoir, tel. 209/855–8321). All are open weekdays 8–4:30; on weekends, try Pineridge. You'll also find a number of smaller ranger stations near major trailheads. If you're coming to Sierra from the west, stop for information at the **Sierra National Forest Supervisor's Office** (1600 Tollhouse Rd./Hwy. 168, in Clovis, tel. 209/297–0706), 15 minutes east of Fresno; it's also open weekdays 8–4:30. For regional road and weather information, call 800/427–7623.

GENERAL STORES • Shaver Lake and Bass Lake, two overdeveloped resort areas, have grocery stores, restaurants, gas stations, and overpriced lodging. You'll save money, though, by shopping before charging into the forest; in Clovis, check out the competitive prices at **Peacock Market** (1427 Tollhouse Rd., at Sunnyside Ave., tel. 209/299–6627). If you're approaching through Oakhurst on Hwy. 41, you'll pass a **Vons** and a **Longs Drugs.**

COMING AND GOING • Aside from the **VIA bus** (tel. 800/396–7275), which runs twice daily from Fresno to Yosemite and will drop you in Oakhurst or Fish Camp (*see* Coming and Going *in* Yosemite

National Park, *above*), there's no public transportation into the forest. Also, Sierra National Forest is accessible only from the west. **Highway 168** (Tollhouse Rd.), the primary route from Fresno and nearby Clovis, runs northeast–southwest to Shaver and Huntington lakes. South of Hwy. 168, east–west **Highway 180** links Fresno with Pine Flat Reservoir via Trimmer Springs Road, then continues into Kings Canyon National Park. **Highway 41** runs north from Fresno into the northern end of the forest; Oakhurst, the last major town on this road, is less than 10 mi west of Bass Lake.

WHERE TO SLEEP • If you lack camping equipment or if weather forces a retreat, **Camp Fresno** (53849 Dinkey Creek Rd., tel. 209/841–2535 in summer or 209/298–5632 in winter), 13 mi east of Shaver Lake in Dinkey Creek, rents rustic cabins with electricity and running water at an amazingly reasonable price June–October: one-bedroom cabins that sleep up to four go for $24–$29 a night, $132–$147 a week. They're not particularly clean or comfortable, but at these prices no one seems to mind. For non-Fresno residents, reservations can only be made after May 1 and a maximum of 10 days in advance. The **Mono Hot Springs Resort** (Kaiser Pass Rd., near Mono Hot Springs, tel. 209/325–1710), open mid-May through October, offers similar accommodations and boasts (human-made) hot springs ($4 to soak). Two-person cabins at Mono start at $28. To stay within striking distance of both the forest and Yosemite, take one of the six rustic rooms at **Snowline Lodge** (42150 Hwy. 41, just north of Oakhurst, tel. 209/683–5854) for just $45–$55. If you've got to be *in* the forest, bang on the four doors of the **South Fork Motel** (57714 Mammoth Pool Rd., just north of North Fork, tel. 209/877–2237), where a run-down room costs just $38. It's best to call ahead for both hotels.

CAMPING • Sierra National Forest offers a variety of camping choices, from dispersed wilderness camping to crowded and loud developed campgrounds. The most popular developed areas are the banks of **Shaver, Huntington,** and **Bass lakes,** all of which generally require advance reservations year-round (**U.S. Forest Service Reservation Center,** tel. 800/280–2267). If you have no specific reason to be near the water, head for one of the smaller, less crowded high-country campgrounds. It's well worth the extra 15-minute drive to escape the din of RV generators and speedboats. For more information on specific campgrounds, call the administrating ranger station.

The **Mariposa Ranger District** is ideal as a base for excursions—by foot or car—into Yosemite. Dispersed camping (*see* Camping *in* Chapter 1) is allowed everywhere except around Bass Lake, making Mariposa a good backup in case Yosemite is booked solid. Call the ranger station (*see* Visitor Information, *above*) for information and fire permits. A series of primitive campgrounds (no running water) lines Road 632/Sky Ranch Road, which extends east from Hwy. 41 about 5 mi north of Oakhurst. All of these secluded, first-come, first-served spots provide tables, vault toilets, and barbecue pits. The nicest of the seven campgrounds are **Kelty Meadow, Nelder Grove,** and **Little Sandy**; Kelty is $10 a night, the latter two are free.

In the **Minarets Ranger District,** head straight for **Clover Meadow** (Minaret Rd., at Beashore Rd.) and nearby **Granite Creek** (above Clover Meadow, north of Minaret Rd.)—two wonderfully secluded campgrounds on the edge of the Ansel Adams Wilderness. Clover Meadow has seven free tent sites with drinking water, fire pits, tables, and toilets. Granite Creek has 20 free sites with the same amenities but no potable water, and it offers swimming. Plan to stay a few days; the drive is long. To get here from the town of North Fork (7 mi south of Bass Lake), follow the Sierra Vista Scenic Byway north on Minaret Road for about 1½ hours. Both first-come, first-served campgrounds are open June–October.

Secluded campgrounds and dispersed camping opportunities abound in the **Pine Ridge Ranger District.** For true seclusion, try the 44 lovely sites ($12) at **Jackass Meadow Campground** on Florence Lake. Tables, stoves, and toilets—but no drinking water—are at your disposal. **Vermilion Campground,** on Edison Lake, has 31 sites ($12) with drinking water and nearby swimming. Both grounds are off Kaiser Pass Road, a continuation of Hwy. 168, and should be reserved ahead of time (tel. 800/280–2267) for July and August weekends.

In the southernmost part of the forest (Pine Flat Reservoir and east along the Kings River), the **Kings River Ranger District** (tel. 209/855–8321) gets frightfully hot in the summer; dispersed camping here would be best in the spring or fall. If you follow Trimmer Springs Road along the Kings River to its end, you'll come across small **Kirch Flat** campground. These free, no-frills sites lack facilities, but they're terrific escapes from the reservoir crowds; just be sure to pack in plenty of water. Northeast of Pine Flat Reservoir, temperatures drop as you make your way toward the Dinkey Lakes Wilderness off Hwy. 168. Camping, dispersed or developed, is especially good near the two high-country reservoirs, **Wishon** and **Courtright.**

FOOD • Stock up on picnic supplies (*see* General Stores, *above*); otherwise you'll find mostly roadside cafés with variations on the burgers, fries, and black coffee theme. One exception is Shaver Lake's **Sierra House Restaurant** (Hwy. 168, tel. 209/841–3576), open weekdays 11–9 and weekends 11–10—excellent pastas ($9) and monster-size burgers ($6). Another is **La Cabaña** (32754 Road 222, in North Fork, tel. 209/877–3311), closed Monday and Tuesday, which serves homemade Mexican eats ($3–$4) through a parking-lot window. In Oakhurst, the inexplicably Greek **Pete's Place** (40093 Hwy. 41, at Hwy. 41 and Hwy. 49, tel. 209/683–0772) looks like a fast-food outlet because that's exactly what it is; the difference, however, is in the big and delicious falafels ($3.29), breakfast burritos ($3.79), and ¼-pound burgers ($3.79).

EXPLORING SIERRA NATIONAL FOREST • For weekend boaters, waterskiers, and anglers from the Central Valley, the forest's main attractions are its lakes (*see* Forest Activities, *below*). If water sports don't interest you, the terrific forest activities should.

The high-altitude **Mariposa Ranger District,** which borders Yosemite, contains **Nelder Grove,** home to over 100 giant sequoias. Here you'll find several short hiking trails, including the 1-mi **Shadow of the Giants Trail,** a self-guided hike with signs describing the ecology of giant sequoia trees. To reach Nelder Grove, take Hwy. 41 north from Oakhurst for 5 mi, turn east on Road 632/Sky Ranch Road, and follow the signs. For a full-day hike, locals recommend heading to **Goat Mountain.** The trailhead is at the Forks Campground and this 8-mi (round-trip) hike culminates at Spring Cove Campground; both grounds are on the south side of Bass Lake.

In the northeast, the **Minarets Ranger District** contains a popular 100-mi drive known as the **Sierra Vista Scenic Byway.** From the town of North Fork, the byway makes an inspiring loop up Minaret Road, eventually taking you to Cold Springs Summit at 7,308 ft. The road is only open from June or July to September, and only 75 mi are paved. You can make the drive in four hours, but there are plenty of places to camp and hike along the way. About a third of the way into the drive, stop at the Mile High Overlook—the views of the Ansel Adams, John Muir, and Kaiser wilderness areas will knock your socks off. Farther on, the **Fernandez Trailhead** leads to a series of lakes, including the highly recommended **Madera Lakes,** 4 mi away. To reach the trailhead, take the byway to Clover Meadow Campground and follow signs.

In North Fork, you can learn about Mono Indian culture at the **Mono Indian Museum** (Rd. 255/Rd. 228, in North Fork, tel. 209/877–2115), stocked with artifacts, cultural displays, and lots of stuffed critters. Admission is $2 and the museum is open Monday–Saturday 9–4.

The **Pineridge Ranger District** cuts a wide swath through the middle of the forest, extending from Shaver Lake and Redinger Lake in the west to the John Muir and Dinkey Lake wilderness areas in the east. After a slow, one-lane, one-hour drive from Huntington Lake on Kaiser Pass Road, you'll come to **Mono Hot Springs,** where short trails lead relaxation-seeking backpackers and friendly locals to the hot mineral baths. The **Mono Hot Springs Resort** (*see* Where to Sleep, *above*) offers a synthetic version of the springs, but the natural version is much more satisfying. On the way to Mono, ask at the Ranger Station (near Edison Lake, off Hwy. 168, tel. 209/877–3138) about smaller springs, like **Little Eden** (1 mi past ranger station on left side of road just before small bridge). The folks here also issue wilderness permits and offer hiking suggestions for the many trails into the **John Muir Wilderness** from Edison and Florence lakes, a few miles east of Mono Hot Springs. With daunting granite formations, windswept pastures, small lakes, and incredible views, you can't go wrong on any trail, but a good day-hike is the 4-mi (one-way) trek from the Florence Lake Trailhead, on the north end of the lake, to **Crater Lake.**

Encompassing the southern portion of the forest from Shaver Lake in the west to the Dinkey Lakes Wilderness in the east, the terrain of the **Kings River Ranger District** varies widely: Chaparral and woodland vegetation surround **Pine Flat Reservoir** and **Kings River,** two popular water recreation spots; farther north, the elevation increases and the vegetation changes to ponderosa, black oak, and sugar pine, providing shadier and cooler summer camping. **Courtright** and **Wishon reservoirs** lie in the eastern portion of the district; many trails that head east into the high alpine terrain of the John Muir and Dinkey Lakes wildernesses begin here. The **Dinkey Lakes Trailhead,** off Dinkey Lakes Road from Shaver Lake, offers hikers a choice of scenic trails.

FOREST ACTIVITIES • Mountain bikes are allowed on dirt roads but prohibited on hiking trails. You'll find some good, uncluttered roads off the **Sierra Vista Scenic Byway** (*see* Exploring, *above*); one trail gaining in popularity is the four-hour huff-n-puff from the south end of Bass Lake to Graham Mountain. In Shaver Lake, **Four-Season** (41781 Tollhouse Rd., tel. 209/841–2224) rents bicycles for $5 an hour or $20 a day. **D&F Pack Station** (on Hwy. 168, ½ mi north of Lakeshore Village on Huntington

Lake, tel. 209/893–3220 or 800/434–7433) offers guided horseback rides June–October from Huntington Lake: Two-hour rides ($30) lead to nearby meadows; half-day rides ($50) go to Potter Pass and mountain lakes; and day-long trips ($75) follow the Kaiser Loop Trail (20 mi). D&F also has a stable at Shaver Lake (tel. 209/841–8500), which has different routes but comparable prices.

From kayaking to jet skiing, water sports are a popular summertime activity all around Sierra National Forest, especially at Bass, Shaver, and Huntington lakes. At Bass Lake, the **Pines Marina** (tel. 209/642–3565) rents Jet Skis ($50 an hour) and pedal boats ($15 an hour). The **Sierra Marina** (tel. 209/841–3324) at Shaver Lake rents fishing boats ($50 a day) and 10-person pontoons ($110 a day) April–September. **Rancheria Marina** (tel. 209/893–3234) at Huntington Lake rents fishing boats and pedal boats at comparable rates, as well as kayaks and canoes ($20 for two hours). To run the Class III and IV rapids of Kings River, take a guided tour with **Kings River Expeditions** (tel. 209/233–4881) or **Zephyr River Expeditions** (tel. 209/532–6249), both based at Kirch Flat (*see* Camping, *above*). River raft trips don't come cheap; one-day runs $100–$135, while two-day trips start at $195.

Sierra Summit (tel. 209/233–2500), near Huntington Lake, is a downhill ski resort with five lifts. Advanced skiers may find the slopes disappointing, but beginners and intermediates should thoroughly enjoy themselves. Lift tickets are $32 on weekends. At the bottom of the mountain, the **Sierra Summit Inn** (tel. 209/233–1200) offers basic accommodations from $50 per night. **Goat Meadow,** near the town of Fish Camp, has free cross-country trails into the southernmost part of Yosemite National Park. Get detailed maps ($5) and trail suggestions at the **Oakhurst Ranger Station** (*see* Visitor Information, *above*). **Tamarack Meadow,** on Hwy. 168 between Huntington and Shaver lakes, offers miles of marked trails and a plowed parking area. It's managed by the **Pineridge Ranger Station** (tel. 209/855–5360), which sells detailed maps ($5) of the area.

John Muir summed up Mono Basin as "Frost and fire working together in the making of beauty." It could also be accurately described as a science-fiction netherworld run amok.

EASTERN SIERRA AND INYO NATIONAL FOREST

Whether you approach from Yosemite or Los Angeles, you're bound to be startled by the dramatic and austere beauty of the eastern slope of the Sierra Nevada. Inyo National Forest, which extends from Mono Lake in the north to Mt. Whitney in the south, is one of California's most diverse and unique national forests—the striking terrain ranges from piñon trees and sage in the lower elevations through mixed coniferous forests at mid-mountain to the lakes and meadows that abound above the timberline. The Eastern Sierra is also pitted with volcanic craters and explorable caves, especially around **Mono Lake,** one of the strangest bodies of water in the world.

Most visitors are drawn by the resort town of **Mammoth Lakes.** In summer, crowds flock here for biking, backpacking, and fishing; in winter, skiers congregate at Mammoth Mountain. The resort is usually overrun from December to April, though in recent years late snows and earthquakes have kept many visitors away. May is a great time to visit, as the skiers have emptied out and the summer visitors haven't yet arrived. South of Mammoth on U.S. 395, the unavoidable town of **Bishop** provides a departure point for exploring the stark White Mountains or rock climbing in the Owens River Gorge. The only other towns of note are three-block-long **Lee Vining** with its few shoddy motels and greasy diners (worth mentioning only because it's near Mono Lake), and **Lone Pine,** 61 mi south of Bishop, which offers little more than a great 24-hour coffee shop, a bar, and a base for folks heading out to nearby **Mt. Whitney**—the highest peak in the lower 48 states.

The hiking and camping season usually begins around May 15, when Hwy. 120 opens (weather permitting). Some may feel that the warm weather and volcanic terrain make for less attractive hiking than on the western side of the Sierra, but the relative absence of crowds here, even in summer, as well as the presence of some of the country's finest hot springs, more than make up for the dust. Once snow starts falling, the roads become treacherous and the price of accommodations rises. If you can withstand these conditions, however, you'll be treated to some excellent skiing.

BASICS

COMING AND GOING

U.S. 395 cuts north–south through the Eastern Sierra and Inyo National Forest, connecting the region's major towns: Lee Vining, Mammoth Lakes, Bishop, Big Pine, and Lone Pine.

BY CAR • To reach U.S. 395 from Los Angeles, take **Highway 14** north through Mojave; it eventually turns into U.S. 395 north. From San Francisco, the trip is a bit more difficult. In summer (June/July–Sept./Oct.), it's easiest to access U.S. 395 at Lee Vining via **Highway 120** (Tioga Pass Rd.) through Yosemite (you still pay for park admission). When snow closes Hwy. 120 (and Hwy. 18 and Hwy. 4), the only choice is to take **I–80** east to Sacramento, then **U.S. 50** east past Lake Tahoe, where it meets U.S. 395. Before heading to the Eastern Sierra, check with **CalTrans** (tel. 800/427–7623) for road conditions.

Rental cars—including four-wheel-drive Jeeps—are available at **U-Save Auto Rental** (550 Old Mammoth Rd., Mammoth Lakes, tel. 760/934–4999 or 800/272–8728); economy cars cost $36 a day, Jeeps are $50 a day.

BY BUS • Greyhound (tel. 800/231–2222) buses run once a day north from Los Angeles, stopping in Lone Pine, Bishop, Mammoth, and Lee Vining. The round-trip to Bishop costs $84 (8 hrs each way). Spend as little time at the Bishop station as possible; unfriendly sorts hang about.

CAMPING

In the vast Inyo National Forest, camping outside developed campgrounds, 100 ft from the nearest road or trail, is permitted above the 1941 watermark in the Mono Lake area and east and west of U.S. 395. Dispersed camping is not allowed in many areas; ask rangers for specifics, but a general rule of thumb is that where there is developed camping, dispersed camping is forbidden. Inquire about the "no fire" areas in Inyo; in any case, you'll need a fire permit, available at any ranger station (*see below*), if you plan to use a stove or build a campfire.

WILDERNESS PERMITS • Increased popularity is not always a good thing, and there are now quota restrictions placed on overnight visits to Inyo National Forest. To make a reservation (available up to six months in advance), you'll need to pay a reservation fee of $3 per person, and send your dates of arrival and departure, specific trailheads of entry and exit, your main destination in the forest, and the number in your party to **Wilderness Reservation Service** (mailing address: Box 430, Big Pine 93513). You may also call toll-free 888/374–3773 or 760/938–1136 to reserve by phone, or fax 760/938–1137. Luckily, this area is still not the tourist-clogged wilderness that Yosemite can be, and some room for spontaneity still exists: Any unreserved permits are available on a first-come, first-served basis at the ranger station closest to your planned destination. Anyone entering the **Mt. Whitney Zone** (the area immediately surrounding Mt. Whitney), day hikers included, is required to have a special Mt. Whitney endorsement; this, too, is available through Wilderness Reservations. Mt. Whitney backpacking permits cost $4, while day-hike permits cost $2. Pacific Crest Trail through-hikers must request a Mt. Whitney Zone stamp from the agency where they receive their wilderness permits.

MONO LAKE

At the end of the thrilling 2,700-ft drop from Tioga Pass sits one of the eeriest bodies of water in the state. Follow U.S. 395 south to where it connects with Hwy. 120 east, about 5 mi south of Lee Vining, and take 120 east and make a left turn to reach **Panum Crater,** the area's most accessible volcano. Take either the **Plug Trail** or the **Rim Trail,** both short and non-strenuous; the latter gives you great views of the lake and the volcanic cones south of Mono, but the former takes you into the belly of the blaster. Next get back on Hwy. 120 and follow it to the **South Tufa Grove** turnoff. On the short self-guided trail you wander among the spiny Tufa columns formed when calcium in Mono's freshwater springs encounters carbonates in its salty and alkaline lake water. Normally the columns would remain underwater and out of sight, but since 1941 the level of Mono Lake has dropped 40 ft due to the L.A. water district's siphoning of four of the five streams that once fed the lakes. The resulting damage to the lake's ecosystem has made it a favorite cause of California environmentalists. Much effort, and some progress, has been made to replenish the lake, which is three times saltier than the ocean, and a new national mandate to raise the water level by 10 ft has hopes riding high—though it will be several decades before Mono can once again sustain a hearty animal population beyond the trillions of brine shrimp and alkaline flies. In the meantime, the **Mono Lake Committee** (tel. 760/647–6595) offers hour-long guided canoe trips ($15 per person) on the south shore, weekends mid-June–early September. Tours begin at 8, 9:30, and 11; they fill up quickly, so reserve ahead.

Half a mile south of South Tufa Grove, **Navy Beach** provides the most buoyant swimming this side of the Dead Sea. The reason is simple: Although five streams flow into the lake, none flow out; the minerals brought in by the fresh water have nowhere to go, making the water very dense. It gets crowded on weekends and holidays, but in the summer heat you may not care who's floating next to you. If you're unhappy with the film left on your body after a dip, drive about 5 mi south on U.S. 395 and rinse off in June Lake. Even better than floating your body on the soft waves of Mono is floating a kayak, which allows you to get right up next to the tufa; look for vendors renting their boats for $20–$40 per day in the Navy Beach parking lot. If none are around, call **Sierra Country Canoes and Kayaks** (tel. 760/924–8652). Go early in the day, before the afternoon winds turn your pleasure paddle into an endurance test.

If land-based activities are more your suit, ask at the Mono Basin Visitor Center (*see below*) for a current list of ranger-guided activities, including free sunset tours of creek restoration projects, as well as a 1½-hour discussion of the area's geology, plant life, and history. In winter, when Hwy. 120 closes, South Tufa Grove, Navy Beach, and Panum Crater are accessible only on cross-country skis.

VISITOR INFORMATION

The **Mono Basin Visitor Center and Ranger Station** (U.S. 395, ¼ mi north of Lee Vining, tel. 760/647–3044), open daily 9–5 in summer and Thursday–Monday 9–4 in winter, is helpful with information on Mono Lake happenings, has all sorts of literature, and shows a good short film about the area.

FEES

Mono Lake has recently turned to charging fees to support itself. The $2 per person fee is payable at the visitor center or South Tufa Grove and is good for a week.

WHERE TO SLEEP AND EAT

In Lee Vining, it's slim pickings. The **Blue Skies Motel** (U.S. 395, at 2nd St., tel. 760/647–6440) is backpacker-friendly and offers standard rooms ($55) but is only open in the summer. The rustic exterior of **Murphy's Motel** (U.S. 395, north end of town, tel. 760/647–6316) belies the standard AAA rooms, which cost $38 in winter, double that in summer. Stock up on basic groceries at marginally decent prices at **Lee Vining Market** (next to the laundromat on U.S. 395, tel. 760/647–6301); open daily 8 AM–9 PM in summer and 8–6:30 in winter. **Nicely's Restaurant** (U.S. 395, tel. 760/647–6477) has sandwiches ($3.50–$5) and burgers ($4.50).

CAMPING • In warm spring and summer months, you're better off camping. **Lundy Lake Campground,** open May–October, is a good spot to fish, hike, or begin a backpacking trip. Trailers are permitted, though, and most folks staying at Lundy have them. The 60 primitive (pit toilets, no potable water) sites scattered among the trees near Lundy Lake go for $5 a night. To get here from Lee Vining, take U.S. 395 north to the LUNDY CANYON sign and go west 3 mi. Another camping option is secluded, spectacular **Sawmill Walk-In,** just east of Tuolumne Meadows. Set in a meadow surrounded by rocky peaks, it has 12 free walk-in sites. Be sure to bring warm clothing: It gets pretty darn cold at 9,800 ft, even in summer. Sites include tables and pit toilets, but there's no drinking water (just a stream). To get here from Lee Vining, take Hwy. 120 about 10 mi back up Tioga Pass and turn right following the signs to Saddlebag Lake; Sawmill is on your left after about 15 minutes. If you want to stay closer to the hustle and bustle of Lee Vining, check into the **Lower Lee Vining Campground** (Hwy. 120, 2 mi west of Lee Vining); it has 60 sites ($5) and is near a meadow with a fabulous view of the mountains. There are picnic tables and Porta-Pottis, and drinking water can be found just off Hwy. 120, 1½ mi back toward town.

OUTDOOR ACTIVITIES

North of Mono Lake on U.S. 395, **Lundy Canyon** has spectacular hiking trails that wind along alpine lakes, canyons, and jagged mountain ridges. If you follow the mile-long dirt road at the end of Lundy Canyon Road past Lundy Lake, you can pick up the **Lundy Canyon Trail** into the **Hoover Wilderness.** After 5 mi, you'll pass a pair of waterfalls and a number of beaver ponds, and farther on you'll cross Lundy Pass and reach Saddlebag Lake. The trip is 8–10 strenuous mi (4–6 hrs) one-way. For an

SUMMER MUSIC

During the annual Jazz Jubilee (tel. 760/934–2478) in July, Mammoth is graced by some of the biggest names in jazz, blues, and Dixieland. Tickets cost $25 a day or $50 for three days. Those with more "classical" interests should check out the Sierra Summer Festival Concert Series (tel. 760/934–2409) in late July/early August. Some concerts are free, others cost $6–$15.

overnight trip, you can camp at Saddlebag Lake. Otherwise, call **Dial-a-Ride** (tel. 760/872–1901 or 800/922–1930) to pick you up at Saddlebag and take you back to Lundy.

NEAR MONO LAKE

BODIE • Desolate and unforgiving ghost-town country lies off U.S. 395 about an hour north of Mono Lake. As you round the first switchback of Bodie Pass (where U.S. 395 makes a 180° turn), look to the right for a small dirt road. Follow it for ½ mi, park your car, and walk to deserted **Rattlesnake Gulch,** a mining town that went bust in the 1890s. This is do-it-yourself exploration: No brochures, no tours—just a chunk of history, a great view of Mono Lake, and, yes, plenty of snakes. A few miles farther north on U.S. 395, you'll meet Hwy. 270 (sometimes closed in winter). Follow it east for 13 mi (3 of them on difficult dirt roads) to reach **Bodie Ghost Town and State Park** (tel. 760/647–6445). It costs $5 per car to enter (and another $1 for an informative booklet). This is one of the best-preserved ghost towns in the state, complete with a small Chinatown and an abandoned mine shaft. Named after W. S. Body, who discovered gold here in 1859, and most probably renamed by an illiterate sign painter, evidence of Bodie's wild past survives at the excellent, free history museum, where you can see the red light of town harlot Rosa May. It's open daily 10–5 from Memorial Day–September. Park hours are 9–7 Memorial Day–Labor Day, 9–4 in winter.

MAMMOTH LAKES

The Mammoth Lakes Basin is a series of glacial lakes with fishing, boating, and trail access to the John Muir Wilderness. Basically, if you can do it outdoors, you can do it at Mammoth, as the basin offers decent skiing, extraordinary mountain biking, rock climbing, canoeing, and kayaking, plus horseback or llama tours, dogsled tours, and even bobsledding. For an overview of the area and a gorgeous day hike, try the moderately difficult 4.4-mi (one-way) **Duck Pass Trail,** accessible from Coldwater Campground (*see* Where to Sleep, *below*).

West of the town of Mammoth Lakes, at the end of Minaret Road (an extension of Hwy. 203), is **Devils Postpile National Monument,** a unique set of uniform rock columns formed by cooling lava less than 100,000 years ago—the blink of an eye in geologic time. From the parking lot, the monument is an easy ½ mi; after another 2 mi you'll come to the 101-ft **Rainbow Falls.** Nearby **Red's Meadow** affords access to the protected Ansel Adams Wilderness, a long stretch of mountainous terrain running along the western border of Inyo National Forest from Mono Lake to Mammoth. Check with ranger stations for wilderness permits and recommendations for extended backcountry treks.

VISITOR INFORMATION

The **Mammoth Ranger Station** (Hwy. 203, Main St., 3 mi west of U.S. 395, tel. 760/924–5500), open daily 8–5, offers great guidance for outdoor activities. In the same building, the **Mammoth Lakes Visitors Bureau** (tel. 760/934–2712 or 800/367–6572), open daily 8–5, has maps and suggestions for activities and lodging in town.

GETTING AROUND

Mammoth Lakes has a **shuttle bus** (tel. 760/934–2571) between the Mammoth ski area and Devils Postpile ($7 round-trip) that stops at all campgrounds and trailheads along the way. It runs daily June 15–September 15, every 15 minutes 7:30–5:30. During shuttle hours Minaret Road from the Devils Postpile entrance is closed to auto traffic, so the shuttle is the only way to travel between these points, other than walking or biking. Look for the SHUTTLE BUS signs in the Mammoth Mountain parking lot or along the highway. **Dial-a-Ride** (tel. 760/872–1901 or 800/922–1930) lets hikers reserve a one-way shuttle from the end of any trail back to the beginning—ideal if you don't want to trek round-trip. During winter, the free **Mammoth Area Shuttle** (tel. 760/934–0687) runs every 15 minutes 7–5:30 between Mammoth Village and the mountain. Pick up a free shuttle map at the visitor center on Main Street (*see above*).

WHERE TO SLEEP

In Mammoth Lakes, the **ULLR Lodge** (5920 Minaret Rd., tel. 760/934–2454) rents three-person rooms with private baths ($46–$57) and two dorm rooms with shared bath ($16–$18); rates are highest during ski season (Nov.–Apr.). It has a communal kitchen, a common area with a fireplace, and a sauna popular with skiers. This place is packed with young budget travelers. Those looking for quieter accommodations in downtown Mammoth, near the shuttle to skiing and mountain-bike trails, should go to **Zwart House** (76 Lupin St., south of Main St., tel. 760/934–2217), which has reasonable rooms (doubles $40 in summer, $50 in winter). Reservations and a deposit are required; the units, which come with a kitchen, private bath, and cable TV, sleep two to eight people. They'll charge you an extra $10 for each additional person.

North Village Inn (103 Lake Mary Rd., tel. 760/934–2525 or 800/257–3781), at the northern edge of Mammoth, on the shuttle route and within stumbling distance of the Mammoth Brewing Co. (*see below*), offers cozy rooms (some with microwave, minifridge, and TV) for $55–$85. Near Mammoth in stunningly beautiful June Lake, **Fern Creek Lodge** (Hwy. 158, 4 mi west of southern June Lake Loop exit off U.S. 395, tel. 760/648–7722 or 800/621–9146) offers quaint wood cabins starting at $48. Each unit has a kitchen, bath, and TV, and there's a general store at the lodge.

CAMPING • Coldwater Campground. This popular campground is strewn with boulders, shaded by pine, and close to several chilly lakes and streams favored by anglers. The 78 sites ($11) offer access to several excellent trails, including Duck Pass (*see above*). *Tel. 760/924–5500. From U.S. 395, 8 mi west on Hwy. 203, then continue west on Lake Mary Rd. Barbecue pits, drinking water, flush toilets. Open mid-June–late Sept.*

Sherwin Creek. The most secluded campground in the Mammoth Village area offers 87 rustic sites ($10) shaded by pine trees and an occasional aspen grove. The best are the 15 walk-in, tents-only creekside spots; they're usually empty, except on weekends and holidays. Half of the sites in the campground are available for reservation; call the National Recreation Reservation System at 800/280–2267. *Tel. 760/924–5500. From U.S. 395, 3 mi south of Mammoth, take gravel Sherwin Creek Rd. east 3½ mi. Drinking water, fire pits, flush toilets, picnic tables. Open mid-May–mid-Sept.*

FOOD

The Good Life Café (126 Old Mammoth Rd., at Tavern Rd., tel. 760/934–1734), open daily 6:30–3, serves filling breakfasts (full stack of whole-wheat pancakes with fruit, $5). The *chorizo con huevos* (Mexican sausage with eggs; $7) at **Roberto's Café** (271 Old Mammoth Rd., tel. 760/934–3667) is another excellent breakfast option; or stop by later in the day for burritos ($4–$7) or enchiladas ($2.25–$3). Roberto's is open Monday–Thursday 11–9 (Fri.–Sun. until 10). At **Matsu To Go** (Main Frontage Rd., at Joaquin St., tel. 760/934–8277), open weekdays 11:30–9 and weekends 4:30–9:30, a take-out pint of shrimp fried rice is only $3, and chicken teriyaki runs $4.50 per pound.

Angels (Main St., at Sierra Blvd., tel. 760/934–7427) does good, hearty home-cooking. Open weekdays 11–10, weekends 4–10, Angels will barbecue just about anything—but the beer-batter Icelandic cod fish 'n' chips plate ($6.95) might be enough, at least to start. Down the street, the **Looney Bean Coffee Roasting Company** (3280 Main St., near Napa Auto Parts, tel. 760/934–1345), open daily 6–6 (Fri.–Sat. until 10), has the best coffee on U.S. 395, plays upbeat tunes, and is full of conversation you'd actually want to overhear. After hours, head up to the **Mammoth Brewing Co.** at Whiskey Creek (24 Lake Mary Rd., tel. 760/934–2337), open daily from 5 PM until they feel like closing. Start with the Double Nut Brown ($3.75), and stick around for live bands. They have great food, too.

OUTDOOR ACTIVITIES

For equipment rentals and tips on mountain biking, skiing, snowboarding, fishing, or rock climbing, head to **Kittredge Sports** (Main St., at Forest Trail, tel. 760/934–7566).

MOUNTAIN BIKING • During summer (late June–Sept.), the Mammoth Ski Area converts its peak into the outrageously fun **Mammoth Mountain Bike Park** (tel. 760/934–0606 or 888/228–4947), open daily 9–6. For $23 a day, you can take the gondola up and zoom down 70 mi of single-track trails. Rentals go for $35 a day, but you can save a few bucks by renting in town at Kittredge Sports (*see above*),

HAVE SOME BUBBLY

What do you get when you cross volcanic magma with water? Hot springs! You'll find dozens along U.S. 395, many kept secret by locals. One well-known spring is the free Hot Creek Geologic Site. From Mammoth go 9 mi south on U.S. 395. Take the Owens River Road exit to the Hot Creek Fish Hatchery, go south on the road behind the Mammoth airport, then turn left on the dirt road and drive a few miles to the parking area. A more secluded spring is Wild Willy's, 3 mi south of Mammoth on U.S. 395 (left on Benton Crossing Road and right at third cattle crossing; spring is down the slope to your left after about 1 mi). For a complete list of lesser-known sites, check out George Williams's Hot Springs of the Eastern Sierra *($11), available at the Booky Joint (Minaret Village Shopping Center, in Mammoth, tel. 760/934–3240).*

where bikes rent for $9 an hour or $30 a day. **Knoll's Trail,** a moderate 10-mi loop through pine forests with excellent views, comes highly recommended. The trailhead lies ¼ mi past Shady Rest Campground, just west of the ranger station. If you're driving around Mammoth, be sure to check out the extraordinary 17-mi June Lake Loop, off U.S. 395 about 10 mi north of Mammoth. You'll pass a number of high-altitude lakes, including June Lake, in some of the Sierra's most spectacular mountain scenery.

FISHING • Thousands of fishing enthusiasts after the almighty trout head for the Eastern Sierra each year. Though favorite spots differ, mainstays include **Mammoth Lakes,** off Hwy. 203; **June Lakes,** off Hwy. 158 between Mono Lake and Mammoth; and the streams of **Rock Creek Canyon,** off Rock Creek Canyon Road between Mammoth and Bishop. Most sporting goods stores in the area have the required permits ($9 a day), and Kittredge Sports (*see above*) rents gear.

SKIING • Mammoth Mountain (tel. 760/934–2571) and **June Mountain** (tel. 760/648–7733) are two of the most popular and crowded ski resorts in California, particularly if there's a good snow pack. Mammoth has far and away the best skiing south of Tahoe. Plan to spend $45 for a lift ticket and at least that much on lodging; budget-hounds should hit the more low-key June Mountain on Wednesday, when lift tickets are just $10. Both mountains allow snowboarders. At **Wave Rave** (3203 Main St., Mammoth Lakes, tel. 760/934–2471), a snowboard and boots rent for $18 a day. Cross-country skiers should contact Mammoth's ranger station (*see* Visitor Information, *above*) for maps of popular routes.

BISHOP

It's hard to miss the looming, barren **White Mountains,** south of Mammoth Lakes on the east side of U.S. 395. Even harder to miss—and, indeed, many have tried—is the town of **Bishop.** Sandwiched between the Eastern Sierra and the White Mountains in the Owens Valley, this boondocks cowtown is the commercial hub of the Eastern Sierra, and since passing through is inevitable, take advantage of its facilities. The **White Mountain Ranger Station** (798 N. Main St., U.S. 395, north end of Bishop, tel. 760/873–2500), open daily 8–4:30 (weekdays only in winter) in summer, has maps and other information on the White Mountains and the John Muir Wilderness (*see* Sierra National Forest, *above*).

WHERE TO SLEEP

The **El Rancho Motel** (274 Lagoon St., tel. 760/872–9251), one block south of the makeshift Greyhound station, has spacious rooms starting at $36 in winter, $40 in summer; add $8 for a kitchen. The management is friendly and knowledgeable about the area. In Bishop Creek Canyon—a stone's throw from Lake Sabrina and trailheads for the John Muir Wilderness—sits **Sabrina Campground** (Hwy. 168, 17 mi south of Bishop, tel. 760/873–2500), one of Inyo National Forest's most unblemished camping spots. The 18 spacious sites ($11) are shaded by aspens and lie on the banks of a tranquil stream; all have tables, fire pits, vault toilets, and drinking water. The campground is open mid-May to second week in September.

FOOD

Pricey **Holmes Health Haven** (192 W. Line St., 1 block west of Main St., tel. 760/872–5571) is the only place south of Mammoth that sells organic goods and dried food in bulk. Otherwise, the cheapest option for groceries is one of the two **Vons** stores (U.S. 395 on north side of town and U.S. 395 at Eastline St.) open 24 hours.

For a hot meal, head to the **Bishop Grill** (281 N. Main St., tel. 760/873–3911), open daily 6 AM–7:30 PM, a meat-and-potatoes diner where the waitress calls you "hon" while refilling your coffee for the 10th time. A burger and fries or a turkey sandwich goes for $3.25. Next door, **Amigos** (285 N. Main St., tel. 760/872–2189), open daily 11–9, serves excellent Mexican food. Dinner combos run $5–$10, but a filling plate of beans and rice with homemade chips and salsa is only $2.50. For coffee and espresso drinks, stop by the huge **Schat's Bakery** (763 N. Main St., tel. 760/873–7156); they also serve sandwiches ($4.75–$6.75).

OUTDOOR ACTIVITIES

If it doesn't have much else, Bishop does have one of the best outdoors stores in the Eastern Sierra. While its specialty is mountaineering and backpacking supplies, **Wilson's Eastside Sports** (224 N. Main St., tel. 760/873–7520) can give you loads of tips on other outdoor activities in the area.

On Methuselah trail, try to guess which tree is the 4,800-year-old "Methuselah," the oldest living tree on the planet. Forest officials keep its identity secret.

HIKING • The desolate White Mountains don't retain much water, so be sure to bring your own if you're thinking of hiking here. A good rule of thumb is 5 gallons for the car and 1 gallon per person daily. This is the high desert—you'll need it. One area that explodes with life is the **Ancient Bristlecone Pine Forest,** a thick forest of gnarled, twisted bristlecone pines, among the oldest living things on Earth, having survived over 40 centuries. To reach **Schulman Grove** take Hwy. 168 12 mi east from Big Pine (15 mi south of Bishop on U.S. 395) and follow signs for 10 mi north—about 45 minutes driving time—on White Mountain Road to the brand new pine-wood visitor center. There are two self-guided trails at Schulman Grove: Discovery Walk (1 mi) and Methuselah Trail (4¼ mi). Twelve miles farther up the mountain via a rough dirt road is **Patriarch Grove.** Here wind and weather have molded trees into eerie abstract sculptures. A self-guided trail leads past the Patriarch Tree, the largest Bristlecone Pine in the world. From Patriarch Grove, you can drive as far as the locked Barcoff Gate (provided you have a four-wheel drive vehicle), and from there it's a strenuous 7½-mi trail to the summit of **White Mountain,** the highest peak in the range at 14,246 ft.

Ten miles west of Big Pine is **Big Pine Canyon** and the **Palisade Glacier,** the largest in the Sierra. To get a good view, follow **Big Pine Canyon Trail** 6 mi from the Big Pine Trailhead **Third Lake,** whose waters appear turquoise because of mineral-rich glacial runoff. You'll have to climb another 2,000 ft (a moderately strenuous 3 mi) to reach the glacier itself. Though you can complete the hike in a day, consider camping at the lake if you have time. The glacial terrain gets dicey; inexperienced hikers should not attempt the last mile and experts should bring crampons and icepicks.

About 30 mi north of Bishop and 15 mi northwest of U.S. 395, **Rock Creek Canyon** provides access to a series of remarkable glacial lakes, canyons, and granite formations. For a good day hike, try the trails from Mosquito Flat to either **Morgan Pass** or the more difficult **Mono Pass,** both about 4 mi each way (6–8 hrs round-trip). For extended trips, the ranger station (*see above*) can give advice and permits.

ROCK CLIMBING • The Owens River Gorge, a steep, well-protected area with world-famous sport climbing, is among the best places in the Eastern Sierra for scaling some rock; best of all, you don't necessarily have to be experienced to handle the holds. The time to climb is spring or fall. For the indispensable guide *Owens River Gorge Climbs* ($10), stop by **Wilson's Eastside Sports** (*see above*). Directions to the gorge are tricky; buy the guide or ask at Wilson's.

MT. WHITNEY

The biggest attraction in Inyo is 14,496-ft Mt. Whitney—the highest peak in the contiguous United States. Every year thousands of hikers make the strenuous 11-mi trek to the summit from the **Whitney Portal Trailhead** (13 mi west of Lone Pine on Whitney Portal Rd.); rangers recommend three days for the trip. Reservations and wilderness permits are required—even for day hikers (*see* Wilderness Permits *in* Basics, *above*). You can also approach the mountain from trails originating in Sequoia National Park or Sequoia National Forest, both of which rarely fill their allowable quotas for accessing the Whitney trails. These hikes will take a good 7–10 days. If you don't want to climb all the way to the top, you can follow the **Whitney Portal National Recreation Trail** (4 mi) from the lower trailhead at Lone Pine Campground, and you won't need a permit. You'll get a moderate workout and spectacular views of Mt. Whitney, the Alabama Hills, and the Owens Valley. The ranger station (640 S. Main St., Lone Pine, tel. 760/876–6200), open weekdays 8–4:30, will give suggestions for surrounding areas. For maps and such, head to the Interagency Visitor Center (corner U.S. 395 and Hwy. 136, just south of Lone Pine, tel. 760/876–6222), open daily 8–4:45.

The one-stoplight tourist town of **Lone Pine** sits in the mountain's shadow, providing little more than food and lodging for the intrepid mountaineers who mob the area. Mt. Whitney looms above the town, surrounded by nearer peaks like 12,994-ft **Lone Pine** and **Mt. Williamson,** a mere 121 ft shorter than Whitney. Twelve miles north of Lone Pine on U.S. 395 stands **Manzanar National Historic Site,** a solemn reminder of America's abominable treatment of Japanese Americans during World War II. Today little remains of Manzanar, which once held over 10,000 Japanese Americans during the chaotic fear and frenzy of this period. The **Eastern California Museum** (155 N. Grant St., 6 mi north of the site in Independence, 619/878–0258), open Wednesday–Monday 10–4, has more information and historical exhibits covering all of the Eastern Sierra.

WHERE TO SLEEP

Lone Pine's cheapest lodging is at the **Dow Hotel** (310 S. Main St., tel. 760/876–5521), where a room with shared bath is $25 ($35 with private bath). Recently renovated, the Dow offers cable TV, Jacuzzi, and a great pool.

CAMPING • In warmer months, serenity can be yours at one of the 44 sites ($12) of **Whitney Portal Campground** (elev. 8,000 ft)—12 mi west of Lone Pine on Whitney Portal Road—with the desolate Alabama Hills to the north and snow-capped Mount Whitney towering above to the west. On colder nights, try the lower elevation of **Lone Pine Campground,** only 7 mi west of Lone Pine, with 43 sites ($8). Both Whitney Portal and Lone Pine have potable water, fire rings, and toilets; both are also reservable through the **U.S. Forest Service Reservation System** (tel. 800/280–2267). For free camping, head for **Tuttle Creek Campground,** which has pit toilets but no drinking water. To reach the campground, follow directions to Horseshoe Meadow Trailhead (*see* Outdoor Activities, *below*); the campground is only 3½ mi down the road.

FOOD

If it's after hours, swing by **PJ's Bake 'n' Broil** (446 S. Main St., Lone Pine, tel. 760/876–5796), the quintessential 24-hour coffee shop—no frills and filled with regulars. Go for the homemade soups ($2); the biscuits and gravy ($3); the Alabama Hills Salad with turkey, ham, cheese, and green pepper (half order, $4); and, of course, the bottomless cup of coffee (65¢). The air-conditioning is a definite plus on 100°F summer days. For good eats, locals recommend **Totem Café** (131 S. Main St., tel. 760/876–5204). The vegetarian omelet ($5.50) with broccoli, zucchini, tomatoes, peppers, and onion is a platefull. For dinner try the shrimp scampi on linguini ($9.95), with soup or salad and garlic toast. Open daily 7 AM–9 PM. For a good time after hours, swing into **Jake's Saloon** (119 N. Main St., tel. 760/876–5765) where you can knock back a cold one; if you're lucky, you might see the bartender and a couple locals reenact the notorious 1870s gunfights of the Alabama Hills Gang.

OUTDOOR ACTIVITIES

Not up for hiking Mt. Whitney? Check out **Taboose Creek,** a popular day-hiking area 10 mi north of Independence off U.S. 395. Better yet, locals highly recommend the trails from **Horseshoe Meadows** through the mixed conifer forests of the Golden Trout Wilderness. A popular trip from the Horseshoe Meadows Trailhead follows the **Cottonwood Pass Trail** to Cottonwood Pass (4½ mi), Big Whitney Meadow (another 4–5 mi), and finally Rocky Basin Lakes (a strenuous 5 mi more), a spectacular backcountry camping and fishing spot. To reach the main trailhead, take Whitney Portal Road 3½ mi west of Lone Pine to Horseshoe Meadows Road and drive south 20 mi.

Mountain bikers will get a good workout on a scenic 17½-mi loop that affords terrific views of Mt. Whitney. From Lone Pine, take Whitney Portal Road about 3 mi west to unpaved **Movie Flat Road,** which will meet **Hogback Road,** also unpaved, and take you back to Whitney Portal.

SEQUOIA AND KINGS CANYON NATIONAL PARKS

After entering Sequoia and Kings Canyon National Parks, expect to find yourself craning your neck to get a view of the giant sequoias for which the southern park is named. While Mt. Whitney, the highest peak in the lower 48 states, is officially within Sequoia National Park, to climb it or even catch a glimpse of its peak, you'll have to head east to Inyo National Forest. The parks are almost completely covered with virgin forest, making them exquisite for either day hikes or serious wilderness camping. Best of all, Sequoia and Kings Canyon retain a rustic feel even in their most developed areas, a pleasant contrast to their congested neighbor Yosemite. You'll find it easy to visit both parks in one trip, as they share the same highways and administrative facilities.

BASICS

VISITOR INFORMATION

All visitors are given a free copy of the quarterly *Sequoia Bark,* which contains some general articles about park conditions as well as camping and lodging information. A somewhat complicated phone system will answer most of your questions, including road and weather conditions and campground accessibility; call 209/565–3341. The **Foothills Visitor Center** (Hwy. 198, Sequoia, 1 mi from southern entrance) is open daily 8–5 in summer and 8:30–4:30 in winter. The **Lodgepole Visitor Center and Ranger Station** (Generals Hwy., Sequoia, tel. 209/565–3782) is open daily 8–6 in summer. The **Cedar Grove Ranger Station** (end of Hwy. 180, Kings Canyon, tel. 209/565–3793) is open daily 9–5 in summer. The **Grant Grove Visitor Center and Ranger Station** (Hwy. 180, Kings Canyon, tel. 209/335–2856) is open daily 9–5 in winter and 8–6 in summer. For general road conditions call CalTrans (tel. 800/427–7623).

FEES AND PERMITS

The entrance fee is $10 per car or $5 per person if you enter by bus, motorcycle, bicycle, or on foot. This entitles you to a week in both parks. Visitor centers and ranger stations (*see above*) distribute free **wilderness permits,** required for overnight camping in the backcountry. Permits are issued only for the trails within a particular center's district and can only be reserved after March 1 and at least three weeks in advance; after October 1, they're only available on the spot. For an application, write to Wilderness Permit Reservations, Sequoia and Kings Canyon National Parks, Three Rivers 93271. One-third of all the permits are handed out on a first-come, first-served basis; sign up at the visitor center at 1 PM the day before you intend to hike. A lot of people try this strategy, so arrive early. The good news is that Sequoia and Kings Canyon fill their quotas much less frequently than Yosemite. Call **Backcountry Information** (tel. 209/565–3708) for weather and trail conditions and permit availability.

GENERAL STORES

Fresno and Visalia are the best places to stock up on supplies, but if you miss your chance, **Dixon's Village Market** (40869 Sierra Dr., Hwy. 198, tel. 209/561–4441) in the small town of Three Rivers has the essentials Monday–Saturday 8–7 and Sunday 9–5 (shorter hrs in winter). Inside the park, your best bet is the **Grant Grove Market** (Hwy. 180, across from the visitor center), open daily 9–6 in winter and 8 AM–9 PM in summer. In the summer both the **Lodgepole Market** (Generals Hwy., across from the visitor center) and the **Giant Forest Market** (Generals Hwy., in Giant Forest Village) are open daily 8 AM–9 PM; for more information call Sequoia/Kings Canyon Park Services (tel. 209/335–2314). Prices are high, but in a jam you can buy what you need; all markets within the park carry sandwiches and bag lunches.

WHEN TO GO

Summer in the high country (above 7,000 ft) means mild days, occasional afternoon thundershowers, and nights that can dip below freezing. In the foothills (1,500–5,000 ft), summers are hot and dry. Crowds are a problem during high season, especially in late August. Fall is the best time to visit: The weather is still warm, yet crisp, and there are fewer visitors. During winter, most of the park is blanketed with snow, and though the roads to Cedar Grove (Hwy. 180) and Mineral King (east of Hwy. 198) close, much of the park remains open. That said, it is not uncommon for the Generals Highway to be closed

SEQUOIA AND KINGS CANYON NATIONAL PARKS

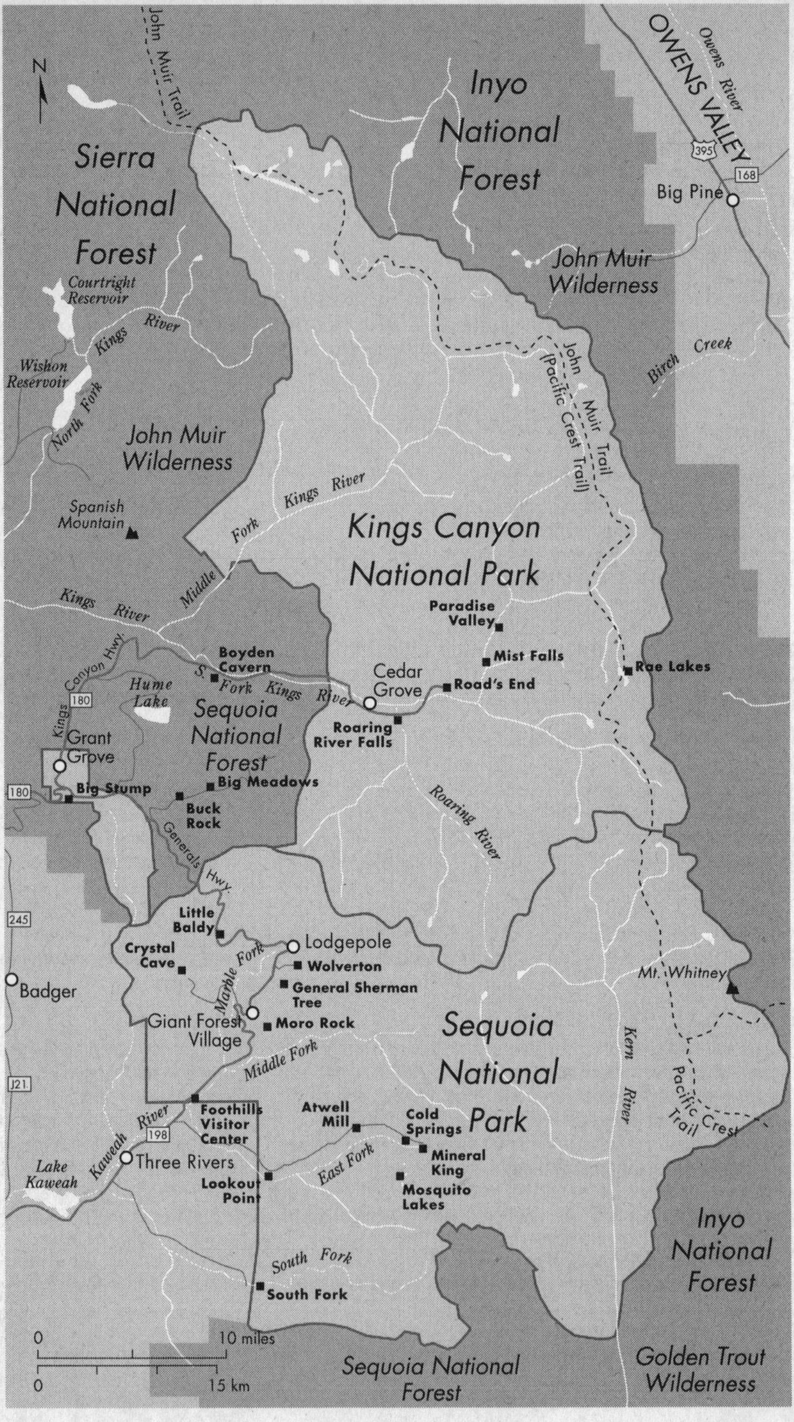

N
Sierra National Forest
Inyo National Forest
OWENS VALLEY
Owens River
395
168
Big Pine
John Muir Trail
John Muir Wilderness
Courtright Reservoir
Kings River
Wishon Reservoir
North Fork
John Muir Wilderness
Birch Creek
John Muir Trail (Pacific Crest Trail)
Spanish Mountain
Middle Fork Kings River
Kings Canyon National Park
Kings River
Paradise Valley
Mist Falls
Rae Lakes
Boyden Cavern
Cedar Grove
Road's End
Kings Canyon Hwy.
180
Hume Lake
S. Fork Kings River
Sequoia National Forest
Roaring River Falls
Grant Grove
Big Stump
Big Meadows
Buck Rock
Roaring River
Generals Hwy.
245
Little Baldy
Crystal Cave
Marble Fork
Lodgepole
Wolverton
General Sherman Tree
Badger
Giant Forest Village
Moro Rock
Mt. Whitney
Sequoia National Park
Middle Fork
J21
Foothills Visitor Center
Atwell Mill
Cold Springs
Mineral King
Kern River
Pacific Crest Trail
Kaweah River
198
Three Rivers
Lake Kaweah
Lookout Point
East Fork
Mosquito Lakes
Inyo National Forest
South Fork
South Fork
0 10 miles
0 15 km
Sequoia National Forest
Golden Trout Wilderness

during and after snowstorms—often for up to two weeks! Either way, be prepared for freezing temperatures and snowbound campsites, and don't forget snow chains. The permanent wintertime fate of the Lodgepole area—which was closed winter 1996–97—had not been decided at press time; ask at the entrance station whether the Lodgepole ranger station and market are open.

COMING AND GOING

BY CAR

Both parks are only one–two hours by car from Fresno and Visalia. **Highway 198** runs roughly east–west between Visalia and Sequoia National Park, entering at the park headquarters at Ash Mountain. The road continues north through Giant Forest to meet **Highway 180** at the Grant Grove area after about two hours; the switchback-filled stretch where the two roads merge is known as **Generals Highway.** Ongoing construction means you should expect additional delays of between 20 minutes and one hour. Hwy. 180 enters Sequoia at the northern Big Stump entrance and provides easy access to Kings Canyon National Park via Grant Grove. It runs primarily east–west from Fresno. In the Central Valley, both roads meet the north–south **Highway 99.** The trip from San Francisco or Los Angeles takes five hours.

From the Eastern Sierra, no pass leads directly to Kings Canyon or Sequoia. You'll have to come via Yosemite's **Tioga Pass** (Hwy. 120) or skirt the south end of the range below Sequoia National Forest at Bakersfield. If you opt for the northern route, take **Highway 120** west at Lee Vining, then **Highway 41** south from Yosemite Valley to Hwy. 180 east at Fresno. If you *must* take the southern route, pick up **U.S. 395** south to **Highway 14** south to Mojave, where you'll pick up **Highway 58** north to Bakersfield. Hwy. 99 will then take you north to Visalia, where you connect to Hwy. 198 east—this route *is* faster than taking Sherman Pass Road across the forest.

SHUTTLES • In the past, summertime **shuttles** ($1 a person per trip or $4 for an all day pass) have run half-hourly between Lodgepole and Giant Forest Village and even down Moro Rock Road. Check with the Lodgepole visitor center for the current schedule—and about whether the service is still running.

WHERE TO SLEEP

Since 1996, all concessions in the parks are managed by **Sequoia/Kings Canyon Park Services** (Box 909, Kings Canyon National Park 93633). At press time, many changes were being made, the biggest of which being the slated demolition of many buildings in Giant Forest Village; if this comes through, look for a new development north of Lodgepole called Wuksachi, which will probably have the usual ranger station/market/lodge setup. In summer most hotels and cabins book 6–10 weeks in advance, so be sure to call and reserve early (tel. 209/335–2314, fax 209/335–5502). Most rooms managed by the concessionaire are overpriced at $80–$100 a night. Of the bunch, the spruced-up **Snowline Lodge** (44138 E. Kings Canyon Rd., 8 mi west of the Big Stump entrance on Hwy. 180) has the least expensive digs: eight small but pleasantly furnished rooms cost $70 and a cabin that accommodates four to six people goes for $95 ($8 extra for each person over two). The cheapest accommodations within the park are Grant Grove's **Rustic Cabins**—24 cabins open year-round with shared (new) washhouses and wood-burning stoves in addition to electric heaters ($55; $8 for each additional person up to six); other summer-only tent cabins are even cheaper ($45), but the lack of electricity may not be worth the marginal savings. Higher-end cabins with in-house toilets are available for $75. If you're smart enough to come in the spring, your special bonus could be the **Montecito-Sequoia Lodge** (*see* Park Activities, *below*), which offers a bed-and-breakfast deal in their rustic cabins between mid-April and mid-May ($49).

The **Sierra Lodge** (43175 Sierra Dr., Hwy. 198 in Three Rivers, tel. 209/561–3681), 6 mi west of Foothills entrance, has accommodations at a comparable price ranging from small, bizarrely asymmetrical rooms (example: one half of an antelope rack) with low, low showerheads to huge, tasteful rooms with private bath, some with a patio or fireplace; prices vary accordingly: $42–$70 in winter, $58–$75 in summer (extra person $3). The **Lazy J Ranch** (39625 Sierra Dr., Hwy. 198, in Three Rivers, tel. 209/561–4449 or 800/341–8000) has slightly cheaper summer prices ($42–$62), with large, cinderblock rooms. The two-room, four-person suite ($80) is quite the bargain for groups.

CAMPING

From mid-May to Labor Day, the large, crowded **Lodgepole** and **Dorst** campgrounds in Sequoia accepts reservations through Destinet (tel. 800/365–2267) up to five months in advance. Lodgepole lays claim to 250 sites ($14), a mixture of tents and small RVs, that flank the Kaweah River and provide easy

SHOCK TREATMENT

Brown bears breaking into parked cars have become such a headache for the park service that they decided to start doing a little breaking of their own—of habits, that is. In one campground, they rigged up a car with food and an easily visible cooler. The catch? The car is electrified. Any bear trying to get an easy snack here is in for quite a shock.

access to the Tokopah Falls Trail (*see* Exploring, *below*). Dorst's 218 sites ($14) are another 8 mi down Generals Highway. You'll find a few too many noisy families at both campgrounds, but for short stays they're not bad. All other campgrounds in Sequoia and Kings Canyon are available on a first-come, first-served basis. Lodgepole, Grant Grove, and Cedar Grove have pay showers. Brown bears have been a recurrent problem, and each campsite is now equipped with a bearproof box—use it.

South Fork Campground, in the southwest corner of Sequoia National Park, is the smallest in the area (13 sites, $6) and definitely one of the nicest. The sites lie in a grove of oak and pine trees, and all have tables and fire pits. There's no potable water, so bring a good supply. Arrive early at this first-come, first-served campground on summer weekends and holidays. *South Fork Dr., 13 mi from Hwy. 198. Open year-round.*

Head north on Hwy. 198 and east on Mineral King Road just before the Foothills entrance to Sequoia and you'll come across two campgrounds pleasantly shaded by pines and a few sequoias: **Atwell Mill** (20 mi east of Hwy. 198) and **Cold Springs** (25 mi east of Hwy. 198), both usually open April–November. The extremely curvy road discourages RVs and trailers, making this area quieter than the central campgrounds. The sites (61 total), with pit toilets, tables, barbecue pits, and water (after late May only), go for $6 a night.

In Cedar Grove, along Hwy. 180 deep in the heart of Kings Canyon, **Sentinel Campground** and **Sheep Creek Campground** (both open May–Oct.) offer a total of nearly 200 spacious, well-shaded sites ($12). Neither takes reservations, but if you arrive early you may be able to snag one of the prime spots along the Kings River. This is terrific hiking territory: Road's End (where Hwy. 180 dead-ends 5 mi east of the campgrounds) is the starting point for hikes to Mist Falls, Paradise Valley, and the Pacific Crest and John Muir trails (*see* Exploring, *below*). Both campgrounds feature potable water, flush toilets, fire pits, and picnic tables—and despite all the people, they still feel isolated.

Just outside park boundaries, there are two excellent free campgrounds in the Sequoia National Forest's Hume Ranger District. Take the road marked BIG MEADOWS off Generals Highway east of Grant Grove. After 4 mi, you'll come to **Buck Rock Campground,** which has five sites with tables, fire pits, and toilets. Two miles farther lies **Big Meadows Campground,** with 25 sites, tables, stoves, and vault toilets. Pack plenty of water; there's none at the sites. Crowds stay away (probably because visitor centers don't steer them here), and the area has fantastic hiking to the Jennie Lakes Wilderness (*see* Near Sequoia and Kings Canyon, *below*), as well as the best cross-country skiing in the region.

FOOD

Prices at the markets in Grant Grove, Giant Forest, Lodgepole, and Cedar Grove are steep, so stock up before entering (*see* Basics, *above*). Prepared food ranges from greasy and cheap to not-quite-so-greasy and expensive. The new concessionaire, however, has promised better quality. Most lodging centers have both buffet-style dining and a sit-down restaurant, the former with food under $8 and the latter with food under $15. If you must eat indoors, try the **Grant Grove Restaurant** (Hwy. 180, in Grant Grove), open daily 7 AM–9 PM (shorter hrs in winter). The prices are steep ($6–$12), but it's all you can eat and may be just the ticket after a day of dehydrated milk and gorp. They also offer box lunches with a sandwich, fruit, and dessert—give them at least eight hours notice.

Cedar Grove, Lodgepole, and Giant Forest Village also have decent eateries. At the **Cedar Grove Cafe** (Hwy. 180, in Cedar Grove Village), open daily 7 AM–9 PM May–October, a three-egg omelet with toast and hash browns fetches $5 and a bowl of chili is $3. On Generals Hwy. in Giant Forest Village, the **Fireside Pizza Pub** dishes out tasty, cheese-drenched (and -filled) pizza and calzones ($6.95 and up) 11–9 daily; unfortunately, this cozy spot, which also serves beer and wine in front of its large stone fireplace, is only open in the summer.

Lodgepole Deli. The best find in the park serves good food at decent prices. Hearty egg-and-sausage breakfasts go for $5, sandwiches are $5–$6, and a new pizza oven turns out sinful pies starting at $6.95. After you get your sandwich, step to the side for a cone at the **Lodgepole Ice Cream Shop.** *Generals Hwy., Lodgepole. Open mid-May–mid-Sept., daily 7 AM–8 PM.*

Clingan's Junction Restaurant. The best find *near* the park, this pleasantly cluttered roadside restaurant has nothing to do with the mythically ugly *Star Trek* villains but does serve outstanding (if predictable) food at unbelievable prices: two plate-filling flapjacks for $2.50, a hefty ¼-pound burger for $3.25. They'll keep you going all day. *35591 Hwy. 180, 12 mi west of Grant Grove, tel. 209/338–2559. Open daily 7 AM–9 PM in summer, 8–8 in winter.*

EXPLORING SEQUOIA AND KINGS CANYON

Altitude in the two parks ranges from less than 1,300 ft to more than 14,000 ft, combining low-elevation chaparral and semidesert environments with cool, forested high country. Much of the territory here isn't accessible by road, so your best bet is to get out of the car and hike through the backcountry. There are hundreds of easy one- to three-hour treks in the area, especially around Mineral King, Giant Forest, Grant Grove, and Cedar Grove. Hwys. 180 and 198 are both incredibly scenic though sometimes difficult to navigate (*see* Scenic Drives and Views, *below*).

ORIENTATION AND TOURS

Foothills, Lodgepole, and Mineral King in Sequoia National Park, and Cedar Grove and Grant Grove in Kings Canyon offer free daily activities in summer that focus on ecology, wildlife, and geology. Ask at the visitor centers for times. On winter weekends, programs are offered at Grant Grove; if conditions permit, rangers also lead snowshoe walks ($1) on weekends and holidays. Reservations are recommended; call the Grant Grove Visitor Center (*see* Visitor Information, *above*).

If you approach Sequoia from the Foothills entrance (Hwy. 198), don't miss **Hospital Rock,** 5 mi north of the visitor center. It has an outdoor display devoted to the Native American population of the Sierra Nevada and a series of pictographs possibly painted by the Monache people, who lived here until 1870. Before tackling the rest of the park, take the easy, self-guided ½-mi paved **Trail for All People,** also called Round Meadow (¼ mi north of Giant Forest Village on Generals Hwy.), which circles a peaceful meadow and features special written exhibits about the ecology of the sequoia groves.

SHORT HIKES

The two parks are oriented around a number of "communities"—developed areas that usually contain a ranger station, grocery store, campground, cafeteria, and trailheads for hikes that range from ¼ mi to 8 mi or more: **Grant Grove** is on the west side of Kings Canyon, where Hwy. 180 meets the Generals Highway; farther east on Hwy. 180 is **Cedar Grove.** On the west side of Sequoia, on the Generals Highway, is **Giant Forest,** which contains **Lodgepole** and **Giant Forest Village**; **Mineral King** is in the southern part of Sequoia.

CEDAR GROVE • Cedar Grove is about an hour's drive (32 mi) east of the popular Grant Grove on Hwy. 180. On this road, built by convict labor in the 1930s, you can see how stunning the canyon is, particularly the glacier-carved valley. On your way into the area, you'll pass by **Boyden Cavern** (tel. 209/736–2708), a large cave filled with stalagmites and stalactites. To see it, you have to take a sometimes crowded 45-minute tour (on the hour, $7)—tours are given June–September, daily 10–5; May and October, daily 11–4. The road to the cavern was closed in 1997 but should open again by the time you read this; call ahead just to be sure.

About 10 mi farther east on Hwy. 180, just past Cedar Grove Village, a ¼-mi path leads to thunderous **Roaring River Falls,** one of the canyon's largest waterfalls. From here you can stroll along the flat 1½-mi trail (or drive on a paved road) to idyllic **Zumwalt Meadow,** which locals claim is the most beautiful in the Sierra; explore the meadow on an easy 2-mi loop trail. At the end of Hwy. 180, near the aptly named Road's End, you'll find **Muir Rock,** a famous spot of cogitation for the renowned naturalist. From the Road's End parking lot, you can walk along the south fork of the Kings River for an easy 9-mi round-trip to refreshing **Mist Falls,** or continue 3 mi farther to **Paradise Valley,** a quiet section of river just begging for a picnic. The moderately strenuous round-trip takes four–five hours. Beware: Mosquitoes reign here.

GRANT GROVE • Grant Grove lies at the northwestern boundary of the parks; you'll pass through it if you come east on Hwy. 180 from Fresno. This is one of the most developed sections of Kings Canyon, but the short trail around the grove will give you an idea of what it feels like to stand among the monumental giant sequoias, which grow to the size of a city skyscraper (up to 310 ft), weigh up to 2.7 million pounds, and sometimes live as long as 3,200 years. A gentle ½-mi trail passes the **General Grant Tree**—the third-largest sequoia in the world and the nation's official Christmas Tree. After the tree, you'll pass the 19th-century **Gamlin Cabin,** once inhabited by the Gamlin brothers, a pair of cattle ranchers and loggers. Also in Grant Grove is the easy mile-long **Big Stump Trail** loop, where you can see firsthand the devastation caused by logging in the late 19th century. To escape the crowds, check out the **North Grove Trail,** a 1½-mi loop (1½ hrs) that starts from the parking lot of the General Grant Tree Trail. About 15 minutes northeast of Grant Grove, off Hwy. 180 in Sequoia National Forest, **Hume Lake** is a nice place for a picnic or a swim.

LODGEPOLE • Behind the visitor center at Lodgepole, a short nature trail leads down to **Marble Fork** on the Kaweah River, where you'll find a pebbly makeshift beach. The river is normally ice-cold, but you're free—though not encouraged—to swim. A quarter mile north of Lodgepole campground, the 2-mi one-way **Tokopah Falls Trail** (2 hrs) leads up through the hills to the 2,000-ft cascade.

Two miles south of Lodgepole, just off Generals Highway, is the **General Sherman Tree,** the largest living tree. It's 275 ft tall and 103 ft around at the base, and the first branch is nearly 130 ft up. Every year, it grows enough additional wood to create another tree 60 ft tall. The easy, paved **Congress Trail** (2 mi, 1–2 hrs round-trip) leads from here past some of the park's other well-known giants. Two miles south of the tree lies **Giant Forest Village,** an overdeveloped resort with two restaurants, a deluxe motel, and convenience stores. The only reason to bother with this place is to access its trailheads. Soon you won't have to bother with it at all: Almost all the buildings are slated to be demolished by 2000 in order to let the big trees—whose root systems are being damaged by constant repairs and rebuilding—lead their lives unmolested. For giant sequoias and a panorama of the Great Western Divide—a dramatic, second crest of the Sierra—head from Giant Forest Village to **Moro Rock** via the **Soldiers Trail Loop** (4⅔ mi), a moderate hike of three–four hours. Eleven miles north of Giant Forest Village on Generals Hwy., you'll come across Little Baldy Saddle. From here, the **Little Baldy Trail** climbs 700 ft in 1.7 mi and ends with a stunning view of the surrounding countryside.

Crystal Cave, 9 mi southwest of Giant Forest Village, is plagued by summer crowds, but the 50-minute tour ($4) will appeal to spelunkers. It's only 48°F inside, so bring a jacket. The cave lies at the end of a rough 7-mi spur road off Generals Hwy.; follow signs from Giant Forest. *Tel. 209/565–3134. Open mid-June–Labor Day, daily 10–3 with tours on the half hour; May and Sept., Fri.–Mon. 10–3 with tours on the hour. 2-hr advance ticket purchase (at Foothills or Lodgepole visitor center) required; no tickets sold at cave.*

MINERAL KING • The southernmost attraction in Sequoia is Mineral King, a secluded, relatively uncongested valley accessible only in summer. Numerous trails lead from here to peaks, meadows, and high lakes, as well as to campgrounds and a ranger station. The 3⅔-mi (one-way) **Mosquito Lakes Trail** winds its way up a series of switchbacks to granite-bound Mosquito Lakes, a secluded area surrounded by a forest of red firs. The **Eagle Lake Trail** (7 mi round-trip), with breathtaking vistas of the southern Sierra, makes a terrific day hike or overnighter. With a permit, you can camp at Eagle Lake (10,000 ft). Both hikes start at the Eagle-Mosquito parking lot; head west to Mosquito Lakes when the trail forks or continue straight for Eagle Lake. To reach Mineral King, take the winding and steep 25-mi Mineral King Road from Hwy. 198 just north of Three Rivers; the trip takes about an hour and a half.

BACKCOUNTRY TRIPS

Both parks make excellent bases from which to explore the wondrous Sierra Nevada backcountry; for permit information, *see* Basics, *above.* In Kings Canyon, most backpackers depart from Road's End, where you can do the 45-mi **Rae Lakes Loop**—a strenuous five- to seven-day trip past alpine lakes—that eventually hooks up with the **John Muir** and **Pacific Crest trails.** In Sequoia, trails leave from Lodgepole, Giant Forest, Buckeye Flat, and Mineral King heading toward Atwell Mill to the west, Franklin Pass to the south, and Sawtooth to the east. Before you choose one, check in with a visitor center or ranger station (*see* Basics, *above*) for maps, trail suggestions, and wilderness permits, and pick up a copy of the newsletter *Backcountry Basics.*

SCENIC DRIVES AND VIEWS

From the northern entrance, the winding **Highway 180** descends into Kings Canyon toward Cedar Grove, providing views of daunting cliffs as well as vistas of the entire canyon. Between Foothills and Giant Forest, **Generals Highway** (Hwy. 198 outside the park) climbs more than 5,000 ft with 23 switchbacks, giving you a firsthand look at the stunning differences between the dry, chaparral-covered foothills and the high sequoia groves. On a clear day, you get excellent views of the valley and surrounding peaks.

PARK ACTIVITIES

BIKING

Biking on unpaved trails in national parks is illegal, but in Sequoia National Forest between Grant Grove and Cedar Grove you'll find a moderate—and legal—16½-mi round-trip trail that travels through sequoia groves and provides great views of the **Monarch Divide.** To get to the trailhead from Hwy. 180 going east, turn right on Hume Lake Road, just past Princess Campground; follow signs to Hume Lake Christian Camp, turn off on the side road leading to public beaches, and park on Forest Service Road 13505.

HORSEBACK RIDING

Guided rides are available in Sequoia at the **Wolverton Pack Station** (between Lodgepole and Giant Forest Village, tel. 209/565–3445) or the **Mineral King Pack Station** (on Mineral King Rd., tel. 209/565–3404), and in Kings Canyon at the **Cedar Grove Pack Station** or the **Grant Grove Stables** (tel. 209/565–3464 for both). Most stables open in mid-June and close at the end of September, except for the Cedar Grove Station, which opens mid-May and runs until early October. Expect to pay around $15–$20 an hour, $70 a day, and $150–$175 (including food) for overnighters.

FISHING

Still going for that elusive trout? You can cast off along several forks of the **Kaweah** and **Kings rivers.** Day licenses ($9.45) and tackle are available at the Lodgepole, Grant Grove, and Cedar Grove markets (*see* Basics, *above*). You can angle for certain fish year-round, but trout season runs from late April through November 15. After your fifth catch (ha!), you have to throw them back.

CROSS-COUNTRY SKIING

The **Sequoia Ski Touring Center** (Wolverton, tel. 209/565–3435) offers cross-country rentals and lessons. Similar services are provided by the **Grant Grove Ski Touring Center** (Grant Grove, tel. 209/335–2314). The facilities are usually open November–April, but be sure to call for conditions. There's no winter lodging near the Sequoia Ski Touring Center, but they do operate a snack shack. Off Generals Hwy., **Big Meadows Nordic Ski Trail** offers 1-mi beginner loops as well as more adventurous treks into Big Meadows. **Grant Grove** and **Giant Forest** also have miles of marked, sometimes groomed routes.

You'll find 52 mi of cross-country trails at **Montecito-Sequoia** (off Hwy. 198, 8 mi south of Hwy. 180, tel. 800/227–9900). It costs $12 a day to use the trails; with ski rentals the cost is $25. The **Montecito-Sequoia Lodge and Resort** (tel. 209/565–3388 or 800/843–8677) offers a midweek winter package: For $72 per person per night, with a two-night minimum, you get a comfortable rustic cabin, three buffet meals, access to a spa, ice-skating on the lake, free ski lessons, and a trail pass.

NEAR SEQUOIA AND KINGS CANYON

SEQUOIA NATIONAL FOREST

Though Sequoia National Park usually takes credit for the grandeur of *sequoiadendron giganteum,* it is actually the neighboring national forest that holds most of these giants within its boundaries. Sequoia National Forest is stunning, replete with coniferous trees, massive granite formations, alpine lakes, and trout-filled streams. Beyond this, its main advantage is its proximity to the San Joaquin Valley. Of course, this also means crowds are a serious problem between May and September. Luckily, most of the RV and ATV enthusiasts seem to cluster around Lake Isabella and the Kern River. As long as you avoid these areas, the weekenders shouldn't get in your way.

Most of the action takes place in the forest's western and southern portions; backcountry hiking, though, is best in the eastern sector. The **Tule River Ranger District,** in the northwest, extends south to Dome Rock and east to the Kern River. The southern **Greenhorn Ranger District** (which comprises the Lower

Kern River and Lake Isabella) and the **Hot Springs Ranger District** (which includes the western forest) are accessible by paved roads and are quite popular in summer. For greater solitude, head east to the **Cannell Meadow Ranger District,** from which you can access the **South Sierra** and **Golden Trout wilderness areas,** as well as **Sherman Pass Road,** the southernmost pass across the towering Sierra Nevada.

VISITOR INFORMATION • Wilderness permits, fire permits, maps, hiking suggestions, and a list of park activities are available from all ranger stations. All stations are open weekdays 8–4:30; on weekends try Cannell Meadow or Greenhorn. Stations include the **Cannell Meadow Ranger Station** (10 mi north of the town of Lake Isabella, in Kernville, tel. 760/376–3781); the **Greenhorn Ranger Station** (4875 Ponderosa Dr., off Hwy. 155 in Lake Isabella, tel. 760/379–5646); the **Hot Springs Ranger Station** (Hwy. J22, a.k.a. Hot Springs Dr., in California Hot Springs, tel. 805/548–6503); the **Hume Lake Ranger Station** (36273 Hwy. 180, 30 mi east of Fresno in Dunlap, tel. 209/338–2251); and the **Tule River Ranger Station** (32588 Hwy. 190, Springville, tel. 209/539–2607).

GENERAL STORES • Before heading into the backcountry, stock up on supplies in Porterville (18 mi outside the park on Hwy. 190), Fresno, or Bakersfield. A great place to stop is the cheap **Save-Mart Supermarket** (900 W. Henderson Ave., Porterville, tel. 209/781–1447), open 6 AM–midnight; it also has a pharmacy (tel. 209/781–1590). Within the forest, **Ponderosa, Pine Flat, Kernville,** and **Kennedy Meadows** have small, pricey stores with limited selections.

COMING AND GOING • Public transportation into the forest does not exist. If you have wheels, reach Sequoia from Porterville (less than 20 mi west) and other points west (including Hwy. 99) via **Highway 190,** known as the **Western Divide Highway** within Sequoia's boundaries. For the southern Cannell Meadow area, take **Sierra Way (Mountain Road 99)** north from Kernville to **Sherman Pass Road,** where many wilderness trailheads originate. The Hot Springs area is accessible from the San Joaquin Valley by **Highway J22 (Hot Springs Drive or Mountain Road 56)** and from the south via Kernville and Sierra Way. Whichever way you go, fill the tank outside the forest; inside, gas prices are criminally high.

WHERE TO SLEEP • Looking for a hotel? If so, make a beeline for Fresno, Bakersfield, or Visalia. It's hard to believe, but affordable hotels and motels are on Sequoia's endangered species list. In nearby Porterville, try one of the budget chains off Hwy. 65 or head to the **Sundance Inn** (676 N. Main St., tel. 209/784–7920), which has nicely remodeled doubles ($30) and a pool.

CAMPING • Dispersed camping (*see* Camping *in* Chapter 1) is allowed throughout the forest with a fire permit (obtainable at a ranger station) and is especially popular in the secluded **Sherman Pass** area of the Cannell Meadow Ranger District. You can phone the **U.S. Forest Service Reservation Center** (tel. 800/280–2267) for reservations ($8.25 per site) at developed campgrounds, but you're unlikely to need them except on holidays and during July and August weekends.

The Tule River Ranger District (along Hwy. 190 from Porterville) offers four quiet campgrounds. One of the nicest is **Quaking Aspen,** roughly 13 mi past the Hwy. 190 entrance to the forest. The 32 sites ($12), with fire pits, toilets, tables, and drinking water, are usually open mid-May–mid-November. The campground makes a great base for exploring Golden Trout Wilderness, and its high altitude (7,200 ft) means cool weather year-round. At **Coy Flat Campground,** the 19 sites ($10) give you access to toilets, potable water, and Bear Creek Trail (*see* Exploring, *below*). The campground is 20 mi east of Springville; take the Camp Nelson exit off of Hwy. 190 and follow the signs on Coy Flat Road.

In the Hot Springs Ranger District, the most convenient campground is **Leavis Flat** ($10), on Hot Springs Road (Hwy. J22) a quarter mile before California Hot Springs Resort (*see* Exploring, *below*). The low elevation and proximity to the road make this a popular place, so solitude-seekers should head instead to **Redwood Meadow,** on the Western Divide Highway a few miles north of its junction with Sherman Pass Road. Just across the street from the Trail of a Hundred Giants (*see* Exploring, *below*), this small campground offers the opportunity to sleep under giant sequoias. The 15 sites ($12) have tables, fire pits, and drinking water. Popular **Lower Peppermint Campground,** 10 mi north of Johnsondale on Lloyd Meadow Road, lies near some of the best views of Dome Rock. The 17 first-come, first-served sites ($10) have tables, fire pits, pit toilets, and piped water. These campgrounds are only open May–October.

EXPLORING SEQUOIA NATIONAL FOREST • The **Tule River Ranger District** offers superb day hiking and popular access points to the Golden Trout Wilderness, including Lewis Camp, Jerkey, and Summit trailheads. If you want to study the lay of the land from above, as opposed to within, drive to **Dome Rock** (take marked dirt road 2 mi south of Ponderosa Lodge on Western Divide Hwy.). The short trail to the top (7,221 ft) is a breeze—and you'll be treated to spectacular views of Slate Mountain to the west, Needles Rock to the northeast, and the Kern Basin to the south. For a bit more exercise, take the moderate 2½-mi (one-way) trail to **Needles Rock.** Give yourself a good four hours for the whole trek—

you'll want to explore the fire lookout tower (as long as it's not being used) and check out views of Mt. Whitney and the Kern Basin. Bring plenty of water. To reach the trailhead, take Needles Road (½ mi south of Quaking Aspen Campground) east 3 mi.

For more hikes, flip through *Upper Tule Hiking Trails* ($2.50), available at the Tule River Ranger Station. One of the best hikes is the Bear Creek Trail, a steep and strenuous 6-mi trek through several sequoia groves to the summit of Slate Mountain. The trailhead, accessible from mid-April through October, is ¼ mi before Coy Flat Campground (*see* Camping, *above*). For some of the best high-altitude hiking in the area, follow signs from Hwy. 190 to the **Lewis Camp Trailhead**: From here you'll get spectacular views of glacier-carved valleys and you can hike into the pristine Golden Trout Wilderness. A good day-trip is the 7-mi loop (4–5 hrs) through Grey Meadow and over the bridge to the other side of Bear Creek; you'll depart on the **Lewis Camp Trail** and circle back on the **Old Jordan Trail.**

The **Hot Springs Ranger District** features two groups of giant sequoias: the **Trail of a Hundred Giants** on Western Divide Highway just north of Sherman Pass Road; and the **Deer Creek Grove,** 3 mi south of the ranger station (follow signs). Both have short trails you can easily walk in an hour. Despite the name, the ranger district contains only one public hot springs: **California Hot Springs Resort** (42177 Hot Springs Dr., in California Hot Springs, tel. 805/548–6582) lets you soak in hot mineral tubs for only $7 a day. Bring a bathing suit; clothing is not optional here.

Climbers, get out your gear. The towering granite spires of Needles Rock (8,245 ft) provide exhilarating, world-class high-country climbs.

The **Cannell Meadow Ranger District** provides trail access to the Dome Land, South Sierra, and Golden Trout wildernesses. The rugged **Dome Land Wilderness,** the southernmost in the Sierra, is covered by piñon and Jeffrey pines. Trailheads are at Big Meadow (Cherry Hill Rd., off Sherman Pass Rd., 38 mi from Kernville) and Taylor Meadow (southeast of Big Meadow). The **South Sierra Wilderness,** north of Dome Land, is notable for its meadows, granite formations, and diverse topography, ranging from gentle hills to steep peaks. To get to its trailheads, take Sherman Pass Road to the Jackass Road turnoff past Black Rock Station and follow signs. The **Golden Trout Wilderness** lies just south of Sequoia National Park. Its pine forests, streams, and meadows can be reached from the trail-head at the Black Rock Station on Sherman Pass Road.

The **Hume Lake Ranger District** in the north (*see* Sequoia and Kings Canyon National Parks, *above*) offers easy access to the **Jennie Lakes Wilderness,** one of the most pristine retreats south of Yosemite. Trails begin on Big Meadows Road, off Generals Hwy. From Big Meadows Station, you can hike 5 moderate-to-strenuous mi (an all-day outing) to **Jennie Lake,** passing the ominous **Bop Out Pass** along the way. To see the Jennie Lakes Wilderness by car, drive along Hwy. 180 east into Kings River Canyon.

FOREST ACTIVITIES • Besides enjoying the rigors of high-country hiking, those itching for action can undertake mountain biking or rafting expeditions; the more sedentary can lazily pursue a day of fishing, swimming, or easy biking.

Bicycles are allowed on almost all forest roads, including fire trails and unimproved dirt roads. The heaviest concentration of trails is in the Hot Springs Ranger District. For an easy pedal, check out **Horse Meadows Road** between Redwood and Holey Meadows campgrounds, off the south end of the Western Divide Highway. Serious cyclists can tackle the 6½-mi climb to **Mule Peak,** which offers stunning views. From Horse Meadows, the dirt path follows Horse Meadows Creek north, and the high altitude will make the 1,400-ft ascent feel like 3,000 unless you're already acclimated. For bike rentals ($15 half day, $28 full day), head to Kernville's **Mountain and River Adventures** (11113 Kernville Rd., tel. 760/376–6553).

Fishing—particularly for trout—is popular along the Tule River, in the high lakes and streams of the Golden Trout and Jennie Lakes wildernesses, and at Hume Lake. You can fish year-round on the North Fork Tule River and all its forks and tributaries above the confluence with Pine Creek (about 50 yards upstream from the Blue Ridge Road, about 12¼ mi north of Springville). You may use only artificial lures with barbless hooks. Pick up a license ($9.45 a day) at any sporting goods store. Springville (on Hwy. 190), the self-proclaimed "Gateway to the Golden Trout Wilderness," is good for supplies; try **Gifford's Market** (35637 Hwy. 190, tel. 209/539–2637).

Several companies run raft trips along the Kern River, which boasts Class III and IV rapids. Trips range from 1½-hour outings ($15) to multiple-day adventures ($195–$275). Contact **Chuck Richard's Whitewater** (11200 Kernville Rd., tel. 760/379–4444), which seems to beat the competition by a couple dollars across the board.

GRAPES OF WRATH

The San Joaquin Valley is one of the most productive agricultural regions in the world, but those who work in the fields pay a price for its success. According to the United Farm Workers of America (UFW), 300 million pounds of pesticides are used each year in California, resulting in the poisoning of nearly 300,000 farm workers yearly. The Food and Drug Administration is supposed to regulate hazardous products, yet a third of the pesticides used on grapes are known to cause cancer. In one farm community, the cancer rates were 1,200% higher than the national average. In 1962, César Chávez founded the UFW in hopes the union could address such problems. His efforts resulted in a grape boycott, which began in 1965 and continues today. Conscientious consumers can ask at stands off the highway for union-friendly fruit or check for the union label at markets.

Most streams are too shallow or too cold for swimming, but **Coffee Camp,** along Hwy. 190 just inside forest boundaries, is a blessed exception, offering pools carved into huge granite formations. There are also several swimming holes along the Wishon Fork. The day-use fee is $5 per vehicle. Be careful when swimming in these areas; the spring melt-off can make the water treacherous.

SAN JOAQUIN VALLEY

In a state whose image is symbolized by beaches and movie stars, California's San Joaquin Valley is something of a forgotten land. To many outsiders, the hot, flat, 225-mi stretch of tract homes and minimalls separating San Francisco and Los Angeles from the Sierra Nevada is just a pit stop, stocked with enough cheap fuel and food to get them to their real destinations. Still, this is one of the fastest-growing regions in the state, and no area is so central to California's economic health. The valley has long supplied agricultural products to the rest of the country, thanks to the irrigation and the labor of migrant workers. Now its cities are growing spectacularly, becoming bedroom communities for commuters to Los Angeles and San Francisco.

Odds are you won't fall in love with this area. But with a healthy sense of the absurd, you can enjoy the time you spend zipping along **I-5** and **Highway 99,** the region's principal thoroughfares. Don't despair if you find yourself in Stockton, Merced, Fresno, or Bakersfield. Head out to the minor-league baseball park, hit a country-western bar, find a comfy room in a chain motel with king beds and a pool, and have an all-American adventure.

STOCKTON

Both farm capital and bedroom community, Stockton is really two towns in one: one of gun shows and El Caminos, the other of malls and 80-mi commutes. If you're passing through this inland port—which brought you author Maxine Hong Kingston and rock star Chris Isaak—you'll have no trouble finding a budget motel with a pool or a cheap, authentic Mexican meal. Wandering around the seedy downtown area, where Market and Main streets meet Wilson Way, you'll get a feel for the town as it was before the gangs took up residence and the industry took off for greener pastures.

While some people use Stockton as a base for exploring the waterways of the Sacramento River Delta (*see* Chapter 6), you don't have to rent a houseboat or go waterskiing to find something to do here. Head to **Louis Park** and spend an afternoon at the kitschy wonderland of Pixie Woods (*see* Cheap Thrills, *below*). At **Victory Park** you'll find the free **Haggin Museum** (1201 N. Pershing Ave., tel. 209/462–4116), open Tuesday–Sunday 1:30–5, which showcases an unusual juxtaposition of antique farm equipment and 19th-century French paintings. If you're in town on the fourth weekend of April, check out the annual **Asparagus Festival** (tel. 209/943–1987), a three-day blowout at Oak Grove Regional Park that celebrates the spring harvest with music, games, and plenty of fresh green spears enlivening soup, pasta, salads, and stir fries.

VISITOR INFORMATION

The **Stockton/San Joaquin Convention and Visitors Bureau** has information on the entire region, including a great street map ($2) and loads of brochures on lodging, dining, and recreation. *46 W. Fremont St., at Center St., tel. 209/943–1987 or 800/350–1987. Open weekdays 8–5.*

COMING AND GOING

I–5 runs north–south along the western fringes of Stockton. **Highway 99** runs north–south along the eastern edge of the city and leads south to Modesto, Merced, Fresno, and Bakersfield. **Highways 4, 26,** and **88** all run east toward the Gold Country (*see* Chapter 6). **Amtrak** (735 S. San Joaquin St., tel. 209/946–0517) runs trains from Stockton to the Bay Area (2 hrs each way, $18 round-trip) and down to Bakersfield, with bus service to Los Angeles (6½ hrs each way, $71 round-trip). The depot is open daily 8–7:30, but don't linger, and keep a tight grip on your wallet or purse. **Greyhound** buses to the Bay Area ($17 round-trip) take as long as trains and are less comfortable. Lockers at the downtown station (121 S. Center St., tel. 209/466–3568), open daily 6 AM–midnight, are available for $1 per 24 hours.

GETTING AROUND

A mediocre bus system ($1.10, transfers 5¢) covers most of the city from 6 AM to 7:30 PM. Bus 1 will get you from downtown to the Amtrak Depot. Pick up maps and schedules at the visitor center (*see above*). For more information, call the **San Joaquin Regional Transit District** (tel. 209/943–1111).

Stockton is a freeway town. If you're driving, use Hwy. 99 and I-5—which run north–south on the east and west sides of the city, respectively—to connect to almost anywhere. Travelers, especially solo women, should avoid Wilson Way, off Hwy. 99, and Charter Way, off I–5. These streets are known for prostitution, drug-dealing, and gang activity. From Hwy. 99 the downtown area is accessible off the Fremont Street exit; just follow the road west to Fremont and Center streets.

WHERE TO SLEEP

Budget motels abound near I–5 and Hwy. 99. The Waterloo Road exit off Hwy. 99 has some excellent options, which are more modern than the dives on Wilson Way off Hwy. 99. Near the Greyhound station and downtown, the **City Center Days Inn** (33 N. Center St., tel. 209/948–6151) has comfortable rooms at $45 for a queen bed.

FOOD

Large Asian- and Mexican-American populations have helped Stockton spice up its standard selection of fast-food chains with cheap, hearty eateries. Still, sometimes it seems the prime local cuisine is donuts. Try **Town Donuts** (347 East Weber St., tel. 209/460–0866), where they custom-fill 'em. You load up on fresh produce at Stockton's large **farmers' market** (tel. 209/943–1830) held 7 AM–11:30 AM every Saturday beneath the crosstown freeway that connects I–5 and Hwy. 99. For a quick, tasty sandwich or burger (about $3.50), go to **Manny's California Fresh** (1612 Pacific Ave., at Harding St., tel. 209/463–6415). Near the Greyhound station downtown, popular **Arroyo's Café** (324 S. Center St., at Lafayette St., tel. 209/462–1661) serves great burritos and soft tacos for under $3. On Saturday night you can listen to live Latin music here, but bring a friend: The neighborhood can be questionable after dark.

UNDER $10 • Cancun. Besides being a fine Mexican restaurant, Cancun is beautifully decorated with murals of pre-Columbian scenes. The combo plate (rice, beans, and two additional items) runs about $5. *248 N. El Dorado St., at Miner St., tel. 209/465–6810.*

On Lock Sam. Check out the exotic touch of Stockton's old-time Chinatown at this landmark restaurant (now ensconced in a modern, pagoda-style building): some booths have curtains that can be drawn for complete privacy. The Cantonese food would be ho-hum in San Francisco but is among the Valley's best. Try the eight-piece foil-wrapped chicken ($7.75) or the *mu-shu* pork ($6.95). *333 S. Sutter St., between Sonora and Lafayette Sts., tel. 209/466–4561.*

BUY ME SOME PEANUTS AND CRACKER JACKS

Though it's only Class A (the highest being AAA), the century-old California League features high-quality baseball played by future stars. (About 25% of major leaguers have done time in "the Cali.") The 10 teams are concentrated in sweltering towns along Hwy. 99 and points south, including Stockton (Ports), Modesto (A's), Visalia (Oaks), and Bakersfield (Blaze).

CHEAP THRILLS

Pixie Woods. Wandering around this unusual park, dotted with cement replicas of your favorite fairy-tale characters, is the perfect excursion for the young at heart. It's set in Louis Park near the San Joaquin River. *Tel. 209/937–8220. Pershing exit off I–5, left on Monte Diablo Ave. Admission: $1.50. Open June–Aug., Wed.–Fri. 11–5, weekends 11–6; Mar.–May and Sept.–Oct., weekends noon–5; closed Nov.–Feb.*

Stockton Ports. A perennial powerhouse of minor-league baseball, the Ports trace their lineage back to a Stockton team called the Mudville Nine, believed to have inspired Ernest L. Thayer's poem "Casey at the Bat." Stockton's pride plays at Billy Hebert Field in Oak Park from early April to September. *Alpine and Sutter Sts., tel. 209/944–5943. Admission: $5 (reserved seats, $7).*

AFTER DARK

Though Stockton's nightlife caters mostly to a conservative sports-bar crowd, other options exist. If anything exciting is happening in town, you'll probably find out about it at the **Blackwater Café** (912 N Yosemite St., at Acacia St., tel. 209/943–6938), a casual coffee spot where the young and hip pass evenings sipping stimulants, and the serious play chess all night long. If you're thirsty for a pint of Guinness, pop in at the **Bull 'n' Bear** (2301 Pacific Ave., at Tuxedo Ave., tel. 209/937–0228), a British-style pub. Grab a pint ($3.50) and some fish 'n' chips ($6.25) and challenge someone to a darts match; the games get serious here. The **Valley Brewing Company** (157 Adams St., off Pacific Ave., tel. 209/948–2537), the city's first microbrewery, serves up yam fries ($3.50) and a beer lovers' stout float ($3.25).

NEAR STOCKTON

MODESTO • Less than an hour south of Stockton on Hwy. 99, Modesto lies deep in the heart of fruit and fertilizer country—you'll smell it before you see it. Travelers use the town as a gateway to Yosemite and the Sierra Nevada (via Hwy. 132) and usually escape without confronting much of the sizable city. In previous years, the main lure for visitors was Graffiti Night, a massive celebration of 1950s car culture in the town that inspired native son George Lucas's movie *American Graffiti*. Recent outbursts of gang violence, however, led the city to outlaw it, though you can still cruise 10th Street between G and K streets to recapture the *Graffiti* days—as long as the police don't view you as a chronic offender. For more nostalgia, catch the minor-league **Modesto A's** (general admission $3.50) at John Thurman Field (Tuolumne exit from Hwy. 99, left on Neece Dr., tel. 209/572–4487). The **Modesto Stanislaus Firehouse Pub & Grille** (924 15th St., tel. 209/575–3473) has warm-weather outdoor tables and good pub food (chili, garlic fries, buffalo wings, about $4–$6) to go with its selection of 117 beers. For a surprisingly good time and a look at Modesto's definition of hip, drop by the **J Street Café** (1030 J St., at 11th St., tel. 209/577–8007) for espresso, cake and ice cream ($1–$3), and Tuesday-night poetry readings. For upscale dining on a budget, hop up to the bar at **Tressetti's World Caffe** (927 11th St., tel. 209/572–2990) for tasty Cajun, Mexican, Mediterranean, and Italian food. The artichoke ragout (artichokes, bell peppers, onions, and tomatoes tossed with fettucini; $6) is a winner.

There's not a whole lot to do after dark in Modesto—even many locals will tell you the best thing to do is leave town—but if you're here for the night, try **Gilligan's Beach House** (1640 Princeton Ave., at Carver St., tel. 209/549–0595), a dance club set in a two-story warehouse.

FRESNO

Forget all the jokes about Fresno being the gateway to Bakersfield: This is the best spot in the San Joaquin Valley. Smack between Stockton in the north and Bakersfield in the south, Fresno provides a happening nightlife (by regional standards) and a hip, alternative neighborhood. If you have any time at all, check out the **Tower District** (E. Olive Ave., west of N. Van Ness Ave.), playground of the city's bohemian, gay, punk, and hippie populations, whose slim numbers force them into an unusually friendly coexistence. The architectural center of the district is the **Tower Theater** (815 E. Olive Ave., tel. 209/485–9050), which books comedy and musical acts. Down the block at **Java Café** (*see* Food, *below*), you can pick up free copies of some local alternative papers and get the scoop on the various cultural scenes. Other hot spots include **Valentino's Alternative Apparel** (814 E. Olive Ave., tel. 209/233–6900), with the best of Los Angeles's Melrose or San Francisco's Haight at half the price. To get to the Tower, take Olive Avenue east from Hwy. 99, or take McKinley Avenue west from Hwy. 41, then go left on South Wishon Avenue.

Downtown, the demography and architecture give the area a Latino feel, while the construction of large office buildings around M and Fresno streets would seem to portend some redevelopment that hasn't yet taken hold. There's not much foot traffic here; most commercial action takes place along **North Blackstone Avenue,** which runs parallel to Hwy. 41. Shopping centers and multiplex theaters dominate this strip, but nearly lost amid the sprawl is a café or two.

During summer, temperatures hover in the FM-radio range, but you can find shade in **Roeding Park** (between Olive and Belmont Aves., near Olive Ave. exit off Hwy. 99, tel. 209/498–4239), open daily 9 AM–10 PM. The **Chaffee Zoological Gardens** (tel. 209/498–2671), open March–October, daily 9–5 and November–February, daily 10–4, is California's third largest zoo, a leading endangered species breeding center, and home to more than 500 species of mammals, birds, and reptiles. Park entrance is free for pedestrians and $1 for cars (charged from Feb.–Oct.); zoo admission is another $4.50.

Fresno's most unusual—and compelling—attraction is the **Forestiere Underground Gardens** (5021 W. Shaw Ave., tel. 209/271–0734), open Memorial Day–Labor Day, Wednesday–Sunday 10–4; Easter–Memorial Day and Labor Day–Thanksgiving (weather permitting), weekends noon–3. Sicilian immigrant Baldasare Forestiere spent 40 years carving out this 10-acre subterranean realm of rooms, tunnels, grottoes, alcoves, and arched passageways. Skylights allow a variety of exotic, full-grown fruit trees to flourish as far as 22 ft below ground. Explore it all for $6 a head.

VISITOR INFORMATION

The **Fresno Convention and Visitors Bureau** distributes a useful free booklet that includes important phone numbers, public transportation routes, and some inexpensive dining and lodging options. *808 M St., between Kern and Inyo Sts., tel. 209/233–0836 or 800/788–0836. Open weekdays 8–5.*

COMING AND GOING

Highway 99, the valley's lifeline, angles down Fresno's western edge. **Highway 41,** which extends 90 mi north to Yosemite National Park, provides a quick way to get around the sprawling city. If you're coming from Los Angeles, pick up Hwy. 41 from Hwy. 99 just south of the city. **Highway 180** runs east to Kings Canyon and Sequoia National Parks, while **Highway 168** goes northeast to the Shaver Lake area of the Sierra National Forest.

Greyhound (1033 Broadway Blvd., tel. 209/268–1829) runs four buses daily to San Francisco (5 hrs, $21 one-way) and 14 daily to Los Angeles (5½ hrs, $19 one-way). The station is open 24 hours. Both Greyhound and Amtrak are located in a less savory part of town, so it's not a bad idea to time your arrival for daylight. Trains run from Fresno's **Amtrak** station (2650 Tulare St., Bldg. B, just south of city hall, tel. 209/486–7651) to San Francisco via a bus connection in Emeryville (4½ hrs, $25 one-way) and to Bakersfield, with bus connections to Los Angeles (4½ hrs, $23.50 one-way). The station is open 6 AM–9:30 PM (closed 7:30–8:30 PM). Passengers can stow luggage behind the ticket counter for free for up to 72 hours. Another cheap and fast connection to Southern California is **Transportes Inter California** (1333 Broadway Blvd., at Tuolomne, tel. 209/233–7488), which has three buses daily to Los Angeles (4 hrs, $22 one-way). Call for information on other Southland destinations.

GETTING AROUND

Major north–south routes through town include Blackstone Avenue and Hwy. 41. Downtown is the only area accessible by foot from the train and bus stations. **Fresno Area Express** (tel. 209/498–1122) buses run all over town for 75¢ (with one free transfer). Most lines run every 30 minutes (hourly on Sunday);

service stops around 7 PM. Important routes include Bus 30 (downtown to N. Blackstone Ave.), Bus 28 (downtown to the Tower District), and Bus 33 (crosstown on Olive Ave. from the Tower District to Hwy. 99, where you can disembark for cheap motels). Like all big cities, Fresno has its seedier areas. Two of them—the Downtown (C St. exit off Hwy. 99) and the Motel Drive exit off Hwy. 99—are known for derelicts, drug dealing, gang activity, and prostitution. A safer and cooler destination is the Tower District (Olive Ave. exit off Hwy. 99), where bars and cafés are plentiful.

WHERE TO SLEEP

Your best bet is the Olive Avenue exit off Hwy. 99, as long as you don't mind sleeping to the clang of the Southern Pacific. Some hotels on Olive Avenue cater to an hourly business; generic chain motels are usually a safe way to avoid this kind of activity. You'll find **Motel 6** (1240 N. Crystal Ave., tel. 209/237–0855) right next to Roeding Park, a little more than 1 mi down Olive Avenue from the Tower District; it offers HBO and a pool for $32. The **Thrift Lodge** (777 N. Parkway Dr., tel. 209/237–2175) lacks a pool, but doubles start at $30. There's also a Motel Drive exit off Hwy. 99, with cheap lodgings right along the tracks, but these motels are dingier than the ones at Olive Avenue. Offerings are sparse downtown, but if you're stuck try the **Super 8** (2127 Inyo St., tel. 209/268–0621), within three blocks of the bus station. One double bed runs about $40.

FOOD

Thanks to its Mexican-American, Southeast Asian, and Armenian communities, Fresno has a number of ethnic restaurants worth seeking out. **Belmont Avenue,** east of Broadway, has popular Thai and Cambodian places, while Armenian restaurants are scattered mostly in the north end of the city. **Armenian Cuisine** (742 W. Bullard Ave., at Palm Ave., tel. 209/435–4892) offers hearty meat-and-pilaf dinners ($9.75–$12) and sandwiches (about $6). Though it sounds like a produce fair, the **Farmers' Market** (Blackstone Ave., at Shaw Ave., tel. 209/221–0182), open Wednesday from 3 PM–7 PM and Saturday morning, is actually a collection of reasonably priced (around $5) ethnic eateries. In the Tower District, **Piemonte's** (616 Olive Ave., tel. 209/237–2038), closed Sunday and Monday, is great for take-out sandwiches ($2.85–$3.99).

UNDER $5 • Rafael's Sabroso Foods. Part Mexican deli, part restaurant, and part tortilla factory, Rafael's serves some of the best and cheapest eats in all of Fresno. Enchiladas with rice and beans are $5, and for $4.25 you get the Sabroso burrito with shredded beef or chicken. *94 E. Belmont Ave., near Palm Ave., tel. 209/264–1684. No dinner Sun.*

UNDER $10 • Grandmarie's Chicken Pies. It's always refreshing to see ol'-timer cowboys and young gay men eating together in peace. Delectable chicken pies with gravy, mashed potatoes, and salad are $6.50. It may be worth the price just to see this unofficial museum of America's diner heritage. *861 E Olive Ave, in the Tower, tel. 209/237–5042. Closed Sun. No dinner Sat.*

Tamiko's Soul Food Kitchen. Tamiko serves up African-American Southern-Mississippi–style cooking a its best. Try the Southern catfish fillet dinner ($7.75) for three tasty pieces of fish, two side entrées (suc as black-eyed peas, homemade potato salad, collard greens) and a roll. Don't skip dessert—homemad sweet potato pie is $2.25. *433 E. Clinton Ave., at Cedar Ave., tel. 209/252–5087. Closed Sun.*

CAFÉS • In the heart of the Tower District, **Java Café** (805 E. Olive Ave., tel. 209/237–5282) is the city's hippest hangout, but there's less attitude than you might expect. You can sip your espresso ($1.75) o indulge in vegetarian dishes (starting at $3.50) on the outdoor patio until 11 on weeknights and midnigh on weekends. **Café Intermezzo** (747 E. Olive Ave., tel. 209/497–1456) has a ceiling painted like the sk and theater and movie posters on the wall. Ingest amazing desserts ($3), fine pizzas ($7.50–$10), an something from the generous wine and beer lists until 11 PM during the week and midnight on weekends **Krakatoa Coffee & Trading Co.** (5138 N. Palm Ave., at Shaw Ave., Fig Garden Village, tel. 209/221–7961) has gourmet sandwiches ($4.25) along with heavenly gelato to help you beat the heat.

AFTER DARK

Fresno has loads of nightlife options. Cheap drinks, dancing, and even live music are easy to find in th Tower District and downtown, though you won't get a bus ride home until morning. **Butterfield Brewin Company** (777 E. Olive Ave., tel. 209/264–5521) in the Tower serves five of their own microbrews fc $2.75 a pint and hosts jazz and blues on weekends. Fresno's premier gay bar, the **Express** (708 N Blackstone Ave., at Bremer Ave., tel. 209/233–1791) is packed with dancers throughout the wee Expect a $1–$5 cover and try to park your car in the lot, as the bar is in a rough part of town. Fresn has only one lesbian bar: the **Palace Saloon,** on the far east side of town (4030 E. Belmont Ave., Cedar Ave., tel. 209/264–8283), with a DJ on Friday and Saturday.

Pick up a free mag at **Java Café** (*see* Food, *above*) to find out what's happening at the clubs. For blues, try **Zapp's Park** (1105 N. Blackstone Ave., near Olive Ave., tel. 209/266–0334), a crowded little bar with live music every night and a $1–$3 cover most nights. Pay a varying cover or ticket charge and join the young and the pierced at **Club Fred** (1426 N. Van Ness Ave, in the Tower, tel. 209/233–3733), a good place to scope out reggae, blues, and other bands. **The Eclipse** (50 E. Herndon Ave., at Blackstone Ave., tel. 209/436–8703), on the other side of town, is a nightclub with a two-level dance floor and pool tables. It attracts a yuppie crowd that likes to shake it up until 1:45 AM on weekends. Expect a $3–$5 cover after 9 PM and look for drink specials such as two domestic pints for $2 on Thursday evening.

On summer Tuesday evenings at 6, head to the Tower District's **street fair.** Or on any evening June–August, head over to the west-facing wall of the **Tower Theater** at sundown (bring a chair) for free movies. You can catch free bluegrass, jazz, or big band concerts Monday evening during the summer at **Woodward Park** north of town (Audubon Dr. and Friant Rd., Friant exit off Hwy. 41). Ask about the concert schedule at the visitor center.

NEAR FRESNO

MERCED • About 70 mi south of Stockton and 50 mi north of Fresno on Hwy. 99, Merced is the valley's preferred gateway to Yosemite, so thousands of travelers pass through here every year. Most pick up Hwy. 140 and speed right out of town, but Merced—hardly a hotbed of tourist delights—does have plenty of cheap motels. Motels cluster along Hwy. 99; the Motel Drive off-ramp is your best bet for good rates. The **Days Inn** (1199 Motel. Dr., tel. 209/722–2726) is loaded with amenities for the price ($48 for a double) and has a small outdoor pool. The small **Merced Gateway Home Hostel** (tel. 209/725–0407), not far from town, has only eight beds, four for each sex ($15, $12 with AYH card), so reservations are essential. They welcome travelers of all ages and will give you directions when you call. One of the most striking sights in the area (and free to boot) is the Victorian Italianate-style **Merced County Courthouse Museum** (21st and N Sts., tel. 209/723–2401), open Wednesday–Sunday 1 PM–4 PM, which displays everything from old gas pumps to a Taoist shrine (a vestige of the Chinese community that built the Southern Pacific Railroad). If it's not too crowded, and it seldom is, a docent will take you on a free tour.

VISALIA • A few miles east of Hwy. 99 on Hwy. 198 (43 mi south of Fresno), Visalia makes a good pit stop on the way to Sequoia National Park, 55 mi east on Hwy. 198. You can stock up on groceries on West Mineral King Avenue at the west end of town or on Noble Avenue at the east end. The **Marco Polo Hotel and Restaurant** (4545 W. Mineral King Ave., on Hwy. 198 at Linwood Ave., tel. 209/732–4591) has small, newly carpeted rooms starting at $38, with balconies, HBO, and a pool. The Indian restaurant on the premises serves dinner only.

Though you can no longer order from your car, the 58-year-old **Mearle's Drive-In** (604 S. Mooney Blvd., tel. 209/734–4447) still serves up sandwiches ($3–$6), diner food ($8 and under), and plenty of ice cream. For an authentic Mexican meal, head to **Colima** (111 E. Main St., tel. 209/733–7078), where great combo plates are less than $7. You might not expect to find a place like **Java Jungle** (208 W. Main St., tel. 209/732–5282) in a town with such rural roots, but would-be urbanites have carved a niche even in Visalia. On Saturday night from 11 PM to 2 AM you can bowl all you want for $9.95 (as DJs spin rock music and award door prizes) at spacious **Visalia Lanes** (1740 W. Caldwell Ave., tel. 209/625–2100). To make your all-American visit complete, catch the local minor-league team, the Visalia Oaks, at **Recreation Park** (440 N. Giddings Ave., near downtown north of Hwy. 198, tel. 209/625–0480). Tickets go for $4.

Restaurant-nightclub **El Presidente** (539 N. Santa Fe, tel. 209/733–0535) serves up hearty Mexican/American fare and offers free munchies during happy hour at the bar Tuesday–Friday 5 PM–7 PM. After dark they have a variety of DJ and live music including country, hip hop, new wave, and, on Sunday, great live Latin music. Music begins around 9 PM and El Presidente keeps it lively until 2 AM.

BAKERSFIELD

In the past, travelers headed to the Sierra Nevada from Southern California rarely stepped out of their cars as they passed through this much-maligned city—and if they did it was for a fill up or a Big Mac and fries. Bakersfield never ranks high in the list of "Best Places to Live." Yet despite the heat and a landscape etched with oil derricks and shopping centers, Bakersfield's population continues to swell with folks happy to commute two hours to Los Angeles everyday in return for mortgage payments that more nearly resemble car insurance premiums in West Hollywood. This conservative town offers plenty of cheap motels, truck-stop diners, and a half-dozen good Basque restaurants: Kern County is home to one of the largest Basque communities outside the Pyrenées. If country music, drive-ins, and girlie bars still leave you cold, you can always use Bakersfield as a base for day trips to nearby Lake Isabella, the largest freshwater lake.

Bakersfield does have two attractions that may lead you to postpone that jaunt to Lake Isabella, especially if the temperatures are tolerable enough for outdoor sightseeing. The **Kern County Museum/Lori Brock Children's Discovery Center** (3801 Chester Ave., tel. 805/861–2132), open weekdays 8–5, Saturday 10–5, Sunday noon–5, forms one of the valley's top museum complexes. The indoor–outdoor Kern County Museum is highlighted by an open-air, walk-through historic village with more than 50 restored or re-created buildings from the 1860s to 1940s. The adjacent Children's Discovery Center wows the kiddies with hands-on displays and activities. Joint admission is $5. On the outskirts of town, the *California Living Museum* (14000 Alfred Harrell Hwy., take Hwy. 178 east, then 3½ mi northwest on Alfred Harrell Hwy; tel. 805/872–2256), is a combination zoo, botanical garden, and natural history museum, displaying species native to the state. (If you like rattlesnakes, this is the place.) It's open Wednesday–Sunday 9–4 and costs $3.50.

VISITOR INFORMATION

The helpful staff at the **Kern County Board of Trade** offers guides for food, lodging, and regional transit. *2101 Oak St., at 21st St., tel. 805/861—2367 or 800/500–5376. Open weekdays 8–5.*

COMING AND GOING

Highway 99 runs north–south through town, connecting Bakersfield to Los Angeles (112 mi south) and Fresno (110 mi north). If you're coming from San Francisco, pick up **Highway 58** off I–5 at Buttonwillow, and follow it 23 mi east into town. East of the city, Hwy. 58 runs over the Tehachapi Pass into Barstow (130 mi), where you can pick up I–15 and I–40. **Highway 178** goes northeast up the Kern River Canyon toward Lake Isabella and Sequoia National Forest.

Greyhound (800/231–2222) runs six buses daily to San Francisco (8–9 hrs each way, $54 round-trip) and 18 buses daily to Los Angeles (2½–4 hrs each way, $24 round-trip). The station (1820 18th St., at F St. downtown, tel. 805/327–5617) is open 24 hours and has lockers for $1. **Amtrak** (800/872–7245) has trains to the San Francisco Bay Area (6½ hrs each way, $68 round-trip). There's no rail service to Los Angeles; Amtrak runs frequent buses (2½–3 hrs each way, $34 round-trip). The train station downtown (15th and F Sts., tel. 805/395–3175) is open daily 4:15 AM—8:45 PM and 9:45 PM–12:15 AM. Storing luggage in the baggage room costs $1 per piece per day.

GETTING AROUND

Downtown, roughly the area between F and M streets and 15th and 24th streets, encompasses the train station, the bus station, and any remnants of character the town once possessed. The **Golden Empire Transit District** (21st St. and Chester Ave., tel. 805/327–7686) sells transit maps (50¢) and schedules for city GET buses (75¢, transfers free), which run Monday–Saturday 6:30 AM–7:15 PM.

WHERE TO SLEEP

Budget accommodations are Bakersfield's main draw. The Olive Drive exit off Hwy. 99 (just north of town), and Union and South Union avenues on the east side, are good bets, but the prime location is the intersection of Hwy. 58 (Rosedale Hwy.) and Hwy. 99. Here your options include the affordable **E-Z 8 Motel** (2604 Pierce Rd., Pierce Rd. exit off Hwy. 99, tel. 805/322–1901), with comfortable rooms (doubles $32) and a pool where you can splash around with the truckers. Within walking distance of the bus and train stations, the **Downtowner Inn** (1301 Chester Ave., at 13th St., tel. 805/327–7122) is your best bet. Doubles go for $38 and up, and you get free breakfast, HBO, and pool.

FOOD

Bakersfield specializes in an unlikely pairing of greasy truck-stop fare and hearty Basque food. A half dozen Basque restaurants serve up lavish multicourse meals that include good homemade bread, soup, beans, and spicy meats; you won't leave hungry. Several of the restaurants still serve family-style in one large sitting for all patrons. If you're partial to diner food, try **Zingo's** (3201 Pierce Rd., tel. 805/321–0627), a 24-hour-a-day eatery that has pancakes and eggs ($4) for breakfast and a tasty roast beef dinner ($6). **Dewar's** (1120 Eye St., near California St., tel. 805/322–0933), an old-fashioned soda fountain and candy shop, has been a town institution since 1909.

UNDER $10 • Garden Spot. This place offers an all-you-can-eat salad bar ($5.50, $6.45 with soup) that puts Sizzler to shame. The veggies are fresh and the homemade soups good and filling. *3320 Truxtun Ave., at Oak St., tel. 805/323–3236. Closed Sun.*

UNDER $15 • Bootleggers Brewing Co. At the town's only restaurant microbrewery, you can enjoy Drunken Chicken Fajitas ($8.95) and wash them down with a pint of Voluptuous Blonde Ale ($2.75). *4301 Chester Ave., tel. 805/323–2739.*

Chalet Basque. Work up a serious appetite before embarking on the adventure disguised as a meal at this unpretentious Basque restaurant. You get soup, beans, hors d'oeuvres, vegetables, and potatoes, *plus* a main course (such as roast leg of lamb or ox-tail stew). These trencherman-size meals start at $9 for lunch and $12 for dinner. *200 Oak St., tel. 805/327–2915. Closed Sun.–Mon.*

AFTER DARK

A monument to a more glamorous time, the **Hotel Padre** (1813 H St., tel. 805/322–1419) towers above downtown like a lighthouse, often with some of its neon lights burnt out (you may recognize it as HOT PADRE or even HOT PAD). It has a popular piano bar, drawing young folks and barflies for serious drinking and Sinatra sing-alongs. A block away, down the alley between 18th and 19th streets, **Guthrie's Alley Cat** (1525 Wall St., tel. 805/324–6328) is probably the hippest bar in town. You'll pay $1.75 for a mug of beer and $2.25 for well drinks. **Suds Tavern** (1514 Wall St., tel. 805/322–2265) is a 21-and-over rock and blues club with a $3 weekend cover.

8 CENTRAL COAST

UPDATED BY JENNIFER WEDEL

Half the romance of the 360-mi stretch of coastline that runs between San Francisco and Los Angeles is that it's the end of the road in the contiguous United States. The other half is that it looks like the end of the earth. As the treacherous road rockets to cliffs, cuts back sharply toward immense redwood canyons and then falls to the coast, it takes your breath away along with your stomach.

But beauty has a price. Native Californians and millions of out-of-state and international travelers coming to witness this splendor have worn a well-beaten tourist trail, but anything remotely off their dog-eared itineraries remains nearly empty and unstudied. In **Monterey,** for example, thousands pack commercialized Cannery Row, while the buildings from which the Mexican government ruled California until 1846 echo in silence. Silent, too, are the arches of the 21 missions (most within this region) that Spanish priests built at the end of the 1700s with "borrowed" native labor. In **Big Sur,** busloads of photo-snappers are dumped in front of McWay Falls, while only a few head toward stunning Pico Blanco where the nomadic Esselen Indians lingered. Life does, in fact, exist beyond the visitor's information desk, and you'll find great variation among towns that share the same coast. In the south, affluent **Santa Barbara** caters to conservative retirees and BMW-driving yuppies. To the north, **Santa Cruz** surfers compete for the best wave while environmentalists duke it out with logging companies over open space. Linking the two cities are a handful of smaller towns: student-filled **San Luis Obispo,** hardworking **Salinas,** the old-time beach town of **Avila,** and tiny **San Simeon,** best-known for **Hearst Castle.**

The best way to explore the coast is with a car, some camping equipment, a sturdy pair of shoes, and a map. Head straight for **Highway 1,** a.k.a. the Pacific Coast Highway or PCH (this stretch of highway's drawbacks include its shortage of affordable hotels and spotty public transportation). The best time to explore the coast is not during summer, when the seaboard is frequently blanketed with fog, but in late spring or fall, when the mist gives way to clear skies and temperatures linger in the 70s. Winter days tend toward the cool and clear, whereas early spring often means weeks of blinding rain. If you're just looking for a speedy trip between San Francisco and Los Angeles, you can scurry down the Salinas Valley on **U.S. 101** in seven hours, or take the even quicker **I–5** through the San Joaquin Valley for a quick (6 hrs) but tedious trip—but you'll be missing one of the most spectacular chunks of California.

THE CENTRAL COAST

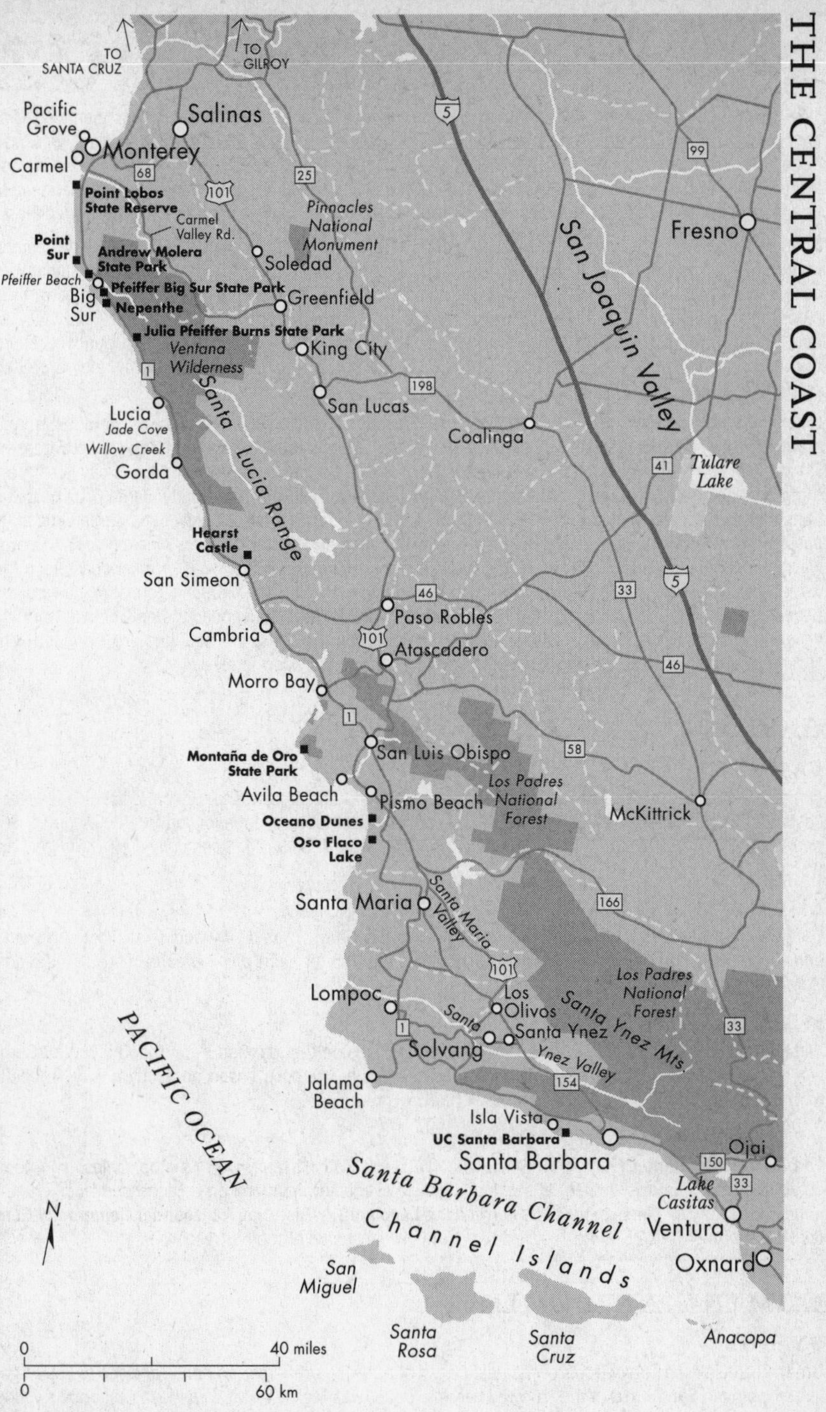
TO SANTA CRUZ
TO GILROY
Pacific Grove
Monterey
Salinas
Carmel
68
Point Lobos State Reserve
101
25
Pinnacles National Monument
Carmel Valley Rd.
5
99
San Joaquin Valley
Fresno
Point Sur
Andrew Molera State Park
Soledad
Pfeiffer Beach
Big Sur
Pfeiffer Big Sur State Park
Nepenthe
Greenfield
Julia Pfeiffer Burns State Park
Ventana Wilderness
King City
1
Santa Lucia Range
198
San Lucas
Lucia
Jade Cove
Willow Creek
Gorda
Coalinga
41
Tulare Lake
Hearst Castle
San Simeon
46
Paso Robles
33
Cambria
Atascadero
Morro Bay
Montaña de Oro State Park
San Luis Obispo
58
Avila Beach
Pismo Beach
Los Padres National Forest
McKittrick
Oceano Dunes
Oso Flaco Lake
Santa Maria
Santa Maria Valley
166
Lompoc
Los Olivos
Santa Ynez
Santa Ynez Valley
Santa Ynez Mts.
Solvang
Jalama Beach
154
Isla Vista
UC Santa Barbara
Santa Barbara
PACIFIC OCEAN
Santa Barbara Channel
Channel Islands
150
Ojai
Lake Casitas
Ventura
Oxnard
San Miguel
Santa Rosa
Santa Cruz
Anacopa
N
0
40 miles
0
60 km

SANTA CRUZ

Originally founded during the late 18th century as a mission town, Santa Cruz has several identities. Old-time residents, many of Italian descent, still look askance at the liberal students and hippies who have been migrating to the town ever since the University of California opened its "alternative, no-stress" branch here in the 1960s. Back then, Santa Cruz was a city-size incarnation of the hippie, and while that's no longer the case, the fact that people still call Santa Cruz a hippie town has somehow made it so.

Though Santa Cruz's reputation as a happy beach town stretches far and wide, it has its fissure points, including the Loma Prieta fault, which runs through the mountains east of town. Bicycle riders spar with car drivers about bike lanes; small-business owners roll their eyes at the mangy folks clogging their cafés and panhandling on their sidewalks. Anti-immigration hysteria is taking its toll here, too, as migrant farm workers, mostly Mexicans and Mexican-Americans, move to Santa Cruz County in record numbers to work on nearby farmlands. Though they fit snugly into the local economy, they are often made to feel unwelcome by the largely homogeneous (i.e., white) community.

Downtown has risen fully from the rubble of the 7.1-magnitude Loma Prieta earthquake of 1989, and many say the squeaky-clean new buildings and chain stores symbolize a sea change toward conservatism. But even if the walking mall is blander than before, Santa Cruz's sloppy individuality is still very much in place.Though subject to the conflicts of any sizable California community, Santa Cruz holds on to its idyllic beach-town atmosphere better than many. The carnival-like **Boardwalk** is Santa Cruz at its flashiest, drawing legions of crazed teenagers from Salinas and San Jose every weekend. The Boardwalk's most popular attraction is the 1924 **Giant Dipper,** one of the oldest wooden roller coasters in the world. The ride affords you a brief panorama of Monterey Bay before plunging you down toward the beach. If your stomach's not up to such antics, try the Ferris wheel or just head to Santa Cruz's stunning coast. The rocks off the craggy shore are favored perches for seals, the beaches are thronged with surfers and their retinue, and the surrounding hills fade into redwood forests.

BASICS

LAUNDRY

Not your average laundromat, **Ultramat** serves coffee and assorted noshes. Each load in the washer costs $1.25, and dryers are 25¢ for 10 minutes; or have your laundry done for you for 90¢ a pound (10-pound minimum). *501 Laurel St., at Washington St., tel. 408/426–9274. Open daily 7 AM–midnight; last wash at 10:30.*

LUGGAGE STORAGE

Lockers are available at the **Greyhound** station, open weekdays 7 AM–11 AM and 1 PM–7 PM and weekends 7 AM–11 AM and 2 PM–7 PM for $1 for the first day, $5 for each day thereafter (*see* Coming and Going, *below*).

MEDICAL AID

Westside Health Center (1119 Pacific Ave., Suite 200, inside the Planned Parenthood office, at Cathgart St., tel. 408/425–5028) offers general medical care at low cost, based on ability to pay. Appointments are required; open weekdays 8:30–4 (Mon.–Thurs. til 7).

VISITOR INFORMATION

The **information center** (701 Front St., tel. 408/425–1234) isn't really worth a stop, unless you need one of their $1.50 maps; limited dining, lodging, and events information can be accessed by phone 24 hours a day. Gay and lesbian travelers can call the **Lesbian/Gay/Bisexual/Transgender Community Center Hotline** (tel. 408/425–5422) for listings of upcoming events and other resources.

COMING AND GOING

BY BUS

Green Tortoise (*see* Funky Deals on Wheels *box in* Chapter 1) lumbers from San Francisco to Los Angeles, stopping in Santa Cruz at the Safeway parking lot (2018 Mission St., at Younglove St.), once a week.

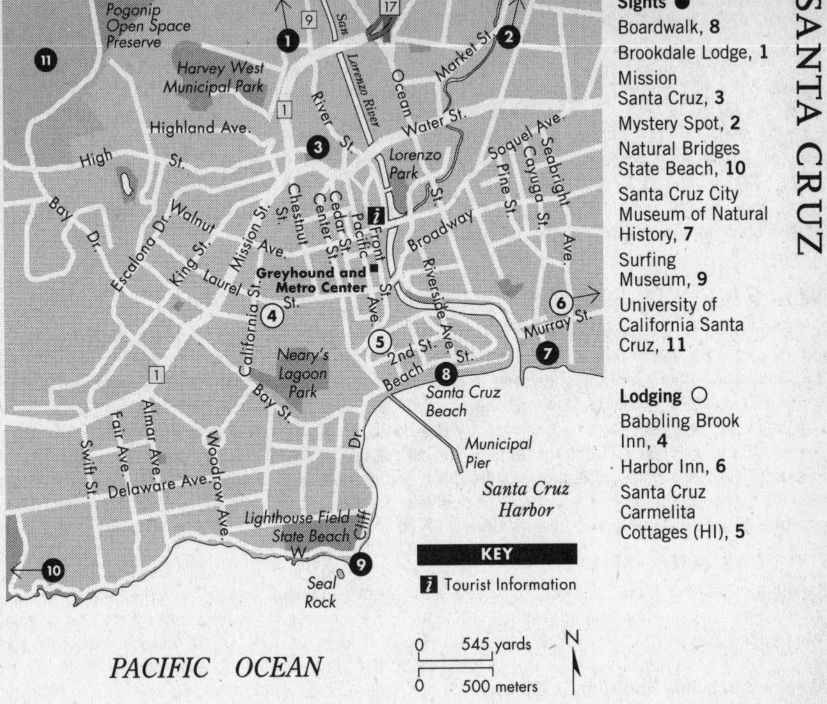

Buses from San Francisco (3 hrs, $10) arrive in Santa Cruz Friday at 11 PM. From L.A., buses arrive Monday morning (9–12 hrs, $30). Reserve one week ahead in the summer. *Tel. 415/956–7500 in California or 800/867–8647.*

Greyhound (425 Front St., at Laurel St., tel. 408/423–1800) has direct service between Santa Cruz and San Francisco twice daily (½ hr, $14 one-way, $15 weekends) and three times daily from Los Angeles (10 hrs, $51 one-way). Amtrak buses (tel. 800/872–7245) roll between San Jose CalTrain depot and the Santa Cruz Metro Center roughly every hour between 4 PM and 10 PM for $5 each way ($8 for two tickets).

BY CAR

The most scenic route from either San Francisco, 1½ hours north, or Monterey, an hour south, is along **Highway 1.** San Jose is about 45 minutes away on curvy **Highway 17,** which meets up with I–280, I–880, and U.S. 101, and is the faster drive to San Francisco and the East Bay. Avoid Hwy. 17 weekend mornings (when the entire Silicon Valley seems to head for the beaches) and at night, when the sharp curves of the road are difficult to navigate.

GETTING AROUND

Santa Cruz is insanity on a map and even more confusing in practice. On the edge of Monterey Bay and bisected by the San Lorenzo River, the town is full of crooked and puzzling streets. From both directions, Hwy. 1 becomes **Mission Street** when it enters Santa Cruz. **Bay Street** and **High Street** both funnel into UCSC, which is located on a hill 2 mi northeast of downtown, while the Boardwalk is on **Beach Street** just west of the river. The Boardwalk and downtown (which centers around **Pacific Avenue** and **Front Street**) are within comfortable walking distance (20 min) of each other.

BY BIKE

For many, biking is the best way to get around Santa Cruz. Many streets have wide bike lanes, and the weather is moderate, especially in spring and summer. It's best to bring your own bike if you can, since renting can be expensive. **Pacific Avenue Cycles** (709 Pacific Ave. at Laurel St., tel. 408/423–1314), at the end of the Pacific Garden Mall, charges $23 per day.

BY BUS

Bus service is efficient and fairly easy to use. The Santa Cruz Metropolitan District Transit (SCMDT), also known as Metro, operates from the **Metro Center** (920 Pacific Ave., at Laurel St.) adjoining the Greyhound station. Any bus in town will eventually take you to the Metro Center, where you can pick up a copy of "Headways," a free pamphlet that lists all bus routes. Bus fare is $1, but you can purchase a special all-day pass for $3 on any bus or at the Metro Center. Exact change, in coins or one-dollar bills, is required; change machines are available at the Metro Center. *Tel. 408/425–8600. Phones and information booth in Metro Center lobby staffed weekdays 8–5.*

WHERE TO SLEEP

In the summer, especially on weekends, finding a budget room in Santa Cruz is next to impossible. During the rest of the year, hotels slash prices to rope in boarders. Year-round, the best deal is at the hostel if you can get a bed. Camping is popular in summer, evidenced by the saturated campgrounds. If the campgrounds listed below are full, call the headquarters after 5 PM, when Manresa and Sunset State beaches open overflow sites. Failing that, try Big Basin Redwoods State Park (*see* Near Santa Cruz, *below*), 45 minutes away. The dorms at U.C. Santa Cruz (tel. 408/459–2611) accept guests on "official business" (in other words, college visits) from the end of June to the beginning of September, but the rooms are spartan, uncentral, and pricey. A double is $30 per person, $37 with full board. A few faculty apartments are available for rent year-round at $70 nightly—call ahead to check availability.

HOTELS AND MOTELS

Facing the Boardwalk on 2nd and 3rd streets and Riverside Avenue are some motels that lie in what some consider a sketchy area known as "The Flats." These places rarely fill up, but you'll find comparably priced places clustered on Mission and Ocean streets that are much more comfortable and equally convenient if you have a car. For a decadent treat, stay at one of several good B&Bs. At the downtown **Babbling Brook Inn** (1025 Laurel St., tel. 408/427–2437, fax 408/427–2457), rooms with country-French decor are surrounded by manicured gardens and a beautiful brook. Twelve rooms come complete with private bath and a fireplace or Jacuzzi. Double rooms, which include a full breakfast, range $85–$165 per night.

UNDER $50 • Harbor Inn. In a residential area 10 minutes southeast of town, this inviting inn has doubles (starting at $45 in summer, $35 in the off-season) with a hodgepodge of old furniture and wooden beds. The antidote to characterless chain motels, the Harbor often fills in summer, so call ahead for reservations. Most rooms have kitchenettes, and groups of four can get a suite ($65–$85, depending on the season). *645 7th Ave., tel. 408/479–9731. From downtown, cross river on Laurel St., right on San Lorenzo Blvd., left on Murray St., left on 7th Ave. Or Bus 67 or 6 to 7th Ave. 19 rooms, 14 with bath.*

HOSTEL • Santa Cruz Carmelita Cottages (HI). The cottages—two blocks from the Boardwalk on Beach Hill—are actually a cluster of houses made hosteler-friendly, which, thanks to an 11 PM curfew and a no-alcohol rule, are quiet ($13 members, $16 nonmembers). Private and family rooms (three to five people) cost $30–$40, depending on the number of beds. Cyclists can use the on-site repair and tune-up shop. You're almost sure to snag a spot as they leave most beds unreserved: Eager beavers show up around 3 PM for the 5 PM first-come first-served check-in; arrive in a car and you get last dib but free parking. If you show up during lockout, use the complimentary outside lockers for your luggage and return at check-in time for the key. Write two weeks ahead (Box 1241, Santa Cruz 95061) or call for reservations. *321 Main St. at 2nd St., tel. 408/423–8304. From Metro Center, Bus 7 to Main St. 25 beds. Reception open daily 8 AM–10 AM and 5 PM–10 PM, curfew 11 PM, lockout 10 AM–5 PM.*

CAMPING • Henry Cowell Redwoods State Park. Five mi north of Santa Cruz, this 113-site campground is buffered by a redwood forest and rests under madrone and mixed pine trees near several trailheads. In summer, RVs and screaming teens tend to overrun the place, but otherwise it's great. Bike campers share one large, shady site for $3 each. Both tent and RV sites are $17 weekdays, $18 weekends. *101 N. Big Trees Park Rd., Felton, tel. 408/335–4598 or 408/438–2396, reservations tel. 800/444–7275. From Hwy. 1, Hwy. 9 north; from Metro Center, Bus 35. Drinking water, flush toilets, showers. Closed Dec.–Feb.*

New Brighton State Beach. High above the ocean on a large cliff, this popular tent-only campground in Capitola, 5 mi southeast of Santa Cruz, offers an incredible view of the coast from some of its 112 sites, but few of them offer any privacy. A steep path leads downhill to the soft beach below. Reservations (tel. 800/444–7275) are a must between May and October, when the place is invariably filled. Sites go for $16 weekdays, $19 weekends. Follow signs from Hwy. 1. Otherwise, Bus 71 will take you to the corner of Soquel and Park avenues, leaving you with a long walk. *1500 Park Ave., tel. 408/464–6330.*

Sunset State Beach and **Manresa State Beach.** Offering slightly more space and privacy than New Brighton, these two campgrounds, both about 10 minutes south of Santa Cruz, are short walks from wide, sandy beaches. Sunset has 90 campsites, all with fire rings, picnic tables, and hot showers. Spaces, reserved through Destinet (tel. 800/444–7275), are $17 weekdays, $18 weekends. On the way to Sunset, you'll pass Manresa, which has 64 walk-in sites 100 yards from the parking lot, with the same facilities, prices, and reservation system as Sunset. Sites are on a plateau above the beach or set back in a sparse sprinkling of trees. Both campgrounds open overflow sites when they're all booked up; Manresa overflow accommodates RVs only, and Sunset puts tent campers in the picnic area. *San Andreas Rd.; Sunset: tel. 408/763–7063, Manresa: tel. 408/761–1795. Hwy. 1 south to San Andreas Rd./Larkin Valley exit, right at bottom of ramp, right onto San Andreas Rd.*

FOOD

Healthy cuisine and yummy yuppie vittles are the heir apparent of Santa Cruz's hippie legacy. For fresh produce, much of it organically grown, head to the **farmers' market** held every Wednesday 2–6 on the corner of Pacific Avenue and Walnut Street; then trot over to Lorenzo Park (River St., between Water St. and Soquel Ave.) for a picnic. Also, look for the markets along Mission Street.

UNDER $5 • For a tasty slice of late-night pizza ($1.75)—or at lunchtime, when they have specials—head to **Uppercrust Pizza** (2415 Mission St., tel. 408/423–9010), on the west side of town near the Hwy. 1 turnoff for Natural Bridges State Beach. For heaping portions of Mexican food, hit **Taquería Vallarta** (608 Soquel Ave., 1 block east of Ocean St., tel. 408/457–8226). Enormous burritos ($3.25 vegetarian, $3.70 with meat) are served up daily 10 AM–midnight.

The Bagelry. This Santa Cruz institution specializes in hybrid bagel spreads like the Pink Flamingo (cream cheese with lox and dill, $2.65) and the Luna spread (pesto, ricotta, and almonds, $2.50). The "three-seed slug"—a wide bagel without the hole (55¢) is as cheap as it gets. *320A Cedar St., at Laurel St., tel. 408/429–8049.*

Zachary's. The basic breakfast—two eggs, tasty home fries, and your choice of homemade breads—sells for a reasonable $5 here. On the more elaborate side, the huge stack of pancakes ($4.50) and the family-size omelets ($5.50 and up) are definitely worth the price. Usually crowded with students and locals alike, Zachary's has outstanding food that justifies the wait (except maybe on weekends, when it can take up to an hour to get a table). *819 Pacific Ave., between Laurel and Maple Sts., tel. 408/427–0646. Closed Mon.*

UNDER $10 • Dolphin Restaurant. Wade your way through tacky tourist traps to the end of Santa Cruz's municipal pier for crispy, fresh-caught fish and chips ($4.75) or a burger ($5.50). You could sit inside, but it's more expensive and the picnic tables adjacent to the Dolphin's serving window provide ample space. *End of pier, tel. 408/426–5830. Winter hrs vary.*

Saturn Café. The interior of the Saturn is something like a pizza parlor in a parallel universe, with theme tables (*Charlie's Angels,* Richard Nixon, and Madonna, to name a few) and flying-saucerlike lamps. The mostly veggie menu offers stellar tomato-garlic pesto sauce over the pasta of the day and a small salad for $6.25, and soul-warming chili for $3.50. The Chocolate Madness ($4.50) frightens even the sweetest tooth with a mess of chocolate cookies, ice cream, mousse, and chocolate chips smothered in hot fudge. *1230 Mission St., near Laurel St., tel. 408/429–8505. No credit cards.*

CAFÉS

In a town with more than 15,000 college students, the need for nighttime diversions for the under-21 set has fueled a serious café scene. In addition to being popular hangouts for college students, cafés are also frequented by locals looking for lively debate or a place to read a good book.

Caffè Pergolesi. In a big, rambling Victorian house blessed with a huge outdoor deck, the Perg has all the trappings of a good café: good coffee that won't put a hole in your stomach ($1.25), espresso drinks that will ($1–$3), and several teas. Try *chai,* the milky Indian spice tea ($2) for a new caffeine vice. The limited menu offers veggie lasagna ($5) and quiche ($4.10), as well as bagels ($2) and pastries ($1.50–$2). The crowd ranges from UCSC Earth muffins to Euro travelers. *418A Cedar St., at Elm St., tel. 408/426–1775.*

Herland Book-Café. Although men are allowed, this bookstore/café was conceived as a safe haven for women. The books, grouped in categories like "Women of the Wild West" or "Women Respond to the Men's Movement," are all (surprise) female-authored. The café serves coffee, tea, espresso drinks, and snacks. *902 Center St. at Locust St., tel. 408/429–6636.*

Jahva House. The Jahva House is in a large, airy, comfortable warehouse softened by big Oriental rugs and leafy ficus trees. The long coffee bar serves up a multitude of coffees and teas, including organically grown varieties of both. Try a Mexican mocha (coffee, chocolate, and cinnamon; $2.60) or a slice of excellent pie ($3). *120 Union St., near Cedar St., tel. 408/459–9876.*

WORTH SEEING

Most of Santa Cruz's sights are downtown, within a walkable area. To explore the jagged coast, though, you'll definitely need a car or an excellent mountain bike. Downtown, the **Pacific Garden Mall** is the center of the action, strewn with specialty stores, antiques shops, restaurants, and cafés and is an easy destination for an afternoon of window-shopping. **Logos** (1117 Pacific Ave. near Lincoln St., tel. 408/427–5100) is Santa Cruz's premier used-book and music store. Good for a leisurely afternoon walk, the **Mission Santa Cruz** (126 High St.), built in 1791, destroyed by an earthquake in 1857, and rebuilt as a half-size replica in 1931, has grounds overrun with colorful gardens and fountains.

SANTA CRUZ BEACH BOARDWALK

Thick with the smell of suntan oil and hairspray, the Boardwalk provides the stickiest, lewdest, most commercialized sun-and-sand carnival west of Coney Island. Rows and rows of pinball machines help you lose your quarters. The Boardwalk is free, so pony up $2–$3 for only the rides you want and skip the overpriced unlimited ride passes. *400 Beach St., tel. 408/423–5590 or 408/426-7433 for recorded information. From Front St. follow the signs to the ocean. Rides open weekends year-round, daily in summer.*

U.C. SANTA CRUZ

UCSC boasts one of the most beautiful campuses in California. Like the environs, the bookstore at the center of campus is woody and natural, resembling a ski lodge more than a student union. The **admissions office** (tel. 408/459–4008) at the campus entrance is open weekdays 8–5 and has maps and tour schedules. Investigate the **limestone quarry** near the campus bookstore—it's a nice spot for a picnic—and take a self-guided or docent-led tour of the 29-acre organic growing system at the **Farm and Garden Project** (tel. 408/459–4140), located near the base of campus. If you park along Meder Avenue at the far west end of campus and catch the free shuttle at Bay and High streets, you can avoid the on-campus parking fee. Otherwise take Bus 1 from the Metro Center to the west entrance of campus.

SANTA CRUZ CITY MUSEUM OF NATURAL HISTORY

The museum is small but full of information about the Ohlone Indians—who originally populated the area—and the seals and sea lions that still do. A slippery touch pool allows you to finger weird sea slugs and anemones. In January, it sponsors the **Fungus Fair,** celebrating the mushrooms that blanket the forest floor. *1305 East Cliff Dr., tel. 408/429–3773. From downtown, walk or drive east on Laurel St., cross river, turn right on San Lorenzo St. (which becomes East Cliff Dr.). Or take Bus 67 from Metro Center. Admission: $2 donation requested. Open Tues.–Sun. 10–5.*

SANTA CRUZ SURFING MUSEUM

At Lighthouse Point on West Cliff Drive, there's a tiny exhibit on surfing from its Hawaiian origins to the present. The museum is dedicated to the memory of an 18-year-old surfer who drowned in 1965. Also on display is a board bitten by a great white shark in 1987, testimony to the real danger posed by sharks along the coast from Santa Cruz to Pigeon Point. Plop down outside the lighthouse and watch the surfers on Steamer's Lane, one of the best surf spots in California. A little farther out you'll see Seal Rock, the summertime home of thousands of barking, shiny seals. *Mark Abbott Memorial Lighthouse, West Cliff Dr., tel. 408/429–3429. Bus 3A to Lighthouse Field. Admission free. Open Mon., Wed.–Fri. noon–4, weekends noon–5.*

NATURAL BRIDGES STATE BEACH

Two miles west of town, the secluded and spectacular Natural Bridges State Beach is the perfect place to escape the overwhelming sensory stimulation of Santa Cruz. As its name implies, the beach features a mudstone bridgelike formation, a nesting spot for pelicans, as well as excellent tidal pools, picnic tables, barbecue pits, and plenty of soft, warm sand to stretch out on. Also on the grounds of the park is a **monarch butterfly colony,** where you can witness the amazing sight of thousands of brightly colored butterflies clustering in the trees (mid-October to February). Call ahead for the latest (and to make a reservation for guided walks). Park on Delaware Avenue just east of the park entrance to avoid the $6 parking fee. *West Cliff Dr., tel. 408/423–4609. From boardwalk, follow West Cliff Dr. until you see signs. Or Bus 3B from Metro Center. Open daily 8* AM*–sunset.*

BROOKDALE LODGE

An oasis of drink during Prohibition, the bizarre Brookdale Lodge's Mermaid bar had a window that looked underwater into a swimming pool full of prostitutes. Men chose a date, met her in the secret passage behind the fireplace, and used a tunnel to get to the bordello across the street. Manager Terry offers free tours once a day. *9 mi from Santa Cruz on Hwy. 9, tel. 408/338–6433.*

MYSTERY SPOT

This quirky little place lies in the redwoods 3 mi north of Santa Cruz and, in the minds of true believers, is at the center of a mysterious force that makes people taller and compels balls to roll uphill—basically, the Spot is a life-size physics experiment. A tacky tourist trap, to be sure, but its gift shop is filled with one-of-a-kind souvenirs and kitschy knickknacks. Your $4 admission also buys you a Mystery Spot bumper sticker (that's why you see them everywhere). *465 Mystery Spot Rd., tel. 408/423–8897. From downtown, go south on Water St., left on Market St., go 2½ mi, then follow signs. Open summer, daily 9–8:30; winter, daily 9–5.*

CHEAP THRILLS AND FESTIVALS

The oceanside town of **Capitola,** along the coast about 5 mi southeast of Santa Cruz, is popular with locals for its wide, quiet, sandy beach and rickety wooden pier—a welcome change from the sometimes frenetic pace of Santa Cruz. After you're done soaking up the sun, head straight to **Mr. Toot's** (221 Esplanade, tel. 408/475–3679), a café full of old wood tables, comfortable couches, and a deck overlooking the beach. Catch Bus 59 from Santa Cruz's Metro Center, or take Hwy. 1 south to the Capitola/Park Avenue exit and head toward the Pacific. For a groovy Santa Cruz experience, go at sunset to **It's Beach,** immediately west of the lighthouse. Almost every summer evening, locals gather here to drum and dance as night falls. You can hang back or jump right in to the middle of the fun. Also check out the numerous street performers on **Pacific Avenue** and the area surrounding the Boardwalk.

The **Cabrillo Music Festival,** usually held during the first week of August, has food, symphonic music, and other live entertainment. Call the Santa Cruz Civic Auditorium Box Office (tel. 408/429–3444) for more information. Tickets cost $6–$25 depending on the performance and seating. From mid-July to August, UCSC hosts **Shakespeare Santa Cruz** (tel. 408/459–2121): six weeks of the Bard's works set against a backdrop of beautiful redwoods. Tickets ($15–$21) should be reserved a few days in advance.

AFTER DARK

Drinking—either in cafés or bars—is the main nighttime activity in Santa Cruz. Only a few bars feature live music, listing upcoming shows in the weekly newspaper *Good Times.* Unless there's a big name playing, skip **The Catalyst** (1011 Pacific Ave., tel. 408/423–1336)—it has few redeeming qualities. The **Kuumbwa Jazz Center** (320 Cedar St. at Laurel St., tel. 408/427–2227) hosts jazz and blues shows throughout the year. Call for tickets ($2–$14) and scheduling information. And if you like to shoot stick you're in luck—in Santa Cruz pool tables are ubiquitous.

If you've got a car, why not celebrate a dying American tradition at the **Skyview Drive-In Theater** (2260 Soquel Ave. at Thurber La., tel. 408/475–3405), where you can watch a double feature on the big screen for $5 a head. Each screen (there are two) plays a different first-run film and then a not-quite-on-video flick year-round starting around 7:30 in winter and 9 in the summer. Call ahead.

The Blue Lagoon. This is Santa Cruz's premier (read: only) gay and bisexual nighttime hangout. There's a $2 cover on weekends and Tuesday, but it's worth it for some of the best DJ dance music in town; straight- and bi-friendly. *923 Pacific Ave., across from Metro Center, tel. 408/423–7117.*

Boulder Creek Brewing Company. Even though it's 25 minutes north of Santa Cruz, Boulder Creek combines great beer and the best live music in the area. Try their Ghost Rail Pale Ale ($3) and Redwood

Ale ($3); for heartier appetites there's the Mudslide Stout ($2.75), billed "thick as a mudslide, twice as tasty." When live bands play there's usually a cover ($3 and up). Flamenco dancers, Middle Eastern musicians, and blues artists have all performed here. *13040 Hwy. 9, tel. 408/338–7882.*

Seabright Brewery. Despite the pastel-color stucco building and bland interior, the Seabright is incredibly popular with locals, especially on Tuesday's "Neighborhood Night" when homeowners mingle with renting students on the concrete patio. Fridays bring live rock and blues from 6 PM to 10 PM. Six or seven varieties of award-winning pints go for $3 a pint; skip the food. *519 Seabright Ave. at Murray St., 7 blocks east of the river, tel. 408/426–2739.*

The Red Room. This snazzy dive bar is a true UCSC institution, especially among the über-hip. Occasionally you can catch rockabilly and alternarock in the rear Crown room. Don't look for a sign out front; there isn't one. Some nights you pay a minimal cover. *1003 Cedar St. at Locust St., tel. 408/426–2994.*

OUTDOOR ACTIVITIES

HIKING AND MOUNTAIN BIKING

The redwood-filled hills surrounding Santa Cruz provide some of Northern California's best hiking and mountain-biking. Two or three times a week, the local chapter of the Sierra Club sponsors group outings—hikes, camping, and canoe trips. Stop by their office (903 Pacific Ave., tel. 408/426–4453) for a listing of upcoming wilderness forays. To go on your own, head directly to **Big Basin Redwoods State Park** (*see* Near Santa Cruz, *below*). Closer to town, **Henry Cowell Redwoods State Park** (*see* Camping, *above*) has 20 mi of tamer trails, many of which meander through virgin redwood forests. Bikes are allowed on designated fire and service roads but not on hiking trails. For a beautiful, albeit crowded, stroll among some of the park's tallest trees, take the **Redwood Grove Trail**; you'll find the trailhead off Hwy. 9. For more of a workout, head 2 mi uphill to the observation deck for a beautiful view of the valley (walk up Pipeline Rd. from the nature center and turn left on Ridge Fire Rd.). To get here from Downtown, follow Hwy. 9 toward Felton.

Hiking and biking locals adore the **Forest of Nisene Marks** (southwest of Santa Cruz; exit Hwy. 1 at Seacliff, take Soquel Ave. ½ mi east to Aptos Creek Rd., tel. 408/763–7063), partly because most tourists ignore it. Amid the creeks, redwoods, and steep trails, you can view the ruins of a Chinese labor camp or walk 2 mi to the epicenter of the 1989 Loma Prieta earthquake; the trail is clearly marked from the end of the park's driveable road. There are also a few trails that mountain bikers are allowed to navigate—ask at the main gate. Bike rentals are available back in town (*see* Getting Around, *above*).

SURFING

Santa Cruz is the surf capital of Northern California. **Steamer's Lane,** between the Boardwalk and the lighthouse, always has a decent break and plays host to several competitions in the summer; consult the free quarterly *Ocean Life* for dates. The city's **parks and recreation department** (tel. 408/429–3663) offers the best surf lesson deals: Four hours of lessons in two days go for $68; surfboards are included, and wetsuits can be rented for $10 per class. If you're already waveworthy but left your board at home, the Cowell's Beach Shop (corner Beach and Front Sts., across from the wharf, tel. 408/427–2355) rents surfboards ($15) and wet suits ($10) by the day.

NEAR SANTA CRUZ

BIG BASIN REDWOODS STATE PARK

The first forest deemed a California State Park, Big Basin (23 mi northeast of Santa Cruz off Hwy. 9) overwhelms you with acres of gigantic old-growth redwoods that have been here about 1,500 years longer than you have, lofty Douglas firs, rushing streams, and flowing waterfalls. All sorts of wildlife call Big Basin home, including black-tailed deer and an occasional fox, bobcat, coyote, or mountain lion. Worthy of at least a day's visit ($5 per car), this is one park where you must get away from the main roads to fully appreciate nature's splendor.

Just past the main entrance you'll come to the **park headquarters** (tel. 408/338–8860), where you can buy a map ($1) and get advice from rangers on which trails best suit your desires and energy level. If you just have an hour or so, your best chance for drama is to head for the gorgeous **Silver Falls** and **Golden Falls** about three quarters of a mi along the Skyline-to-the-Sea trail. For a less crowded hike, try the **Howard King Trail** from the parking lot to Mt. McAbee. Along the way you'll traverse several different ecosystems, from the redwoods to the chaparral, and be rewarded with an ocean view at the peak. You can return on Hammond Road for a round-trip of 5 mi in about two–three hours.

The truly fit should tackle the scenic 12½-mi **Skyline-to-Sea Trail,** which travels over hill and dale all the way to the coast. This is the park's most popular trek, and those who've done it rave about how satisfying it is to reach the water after gazing at it earlier in the trail. Leave a second car at the trail's endpoint at Waddell Beach, and either pay scrupulous attention to a map or accept the possibility of getting semi-lost, since several trailheads converge a few miles into the hike. Mountain biking is only allowed on fire roads in the park, and unfortunately there are few good loops: Your best bet is to follow North Escape Road a short distance from park headquarters to **Gazos Creek Road,** a 12-mi fire trail that stretches to the coast, and then return on Johansen Road via Middleridge Road.

COMING AND GOING • To reach Big Basin from Santa Cruz, follow Hwy. 9 north for 12 mi, then follow the signs for another 9 mi from Boulder Creek. If you're coming from the north on I–280, take Hwy. 85 south from Cupertino to Hwy. 9 south, then pick up Hwy. 236 into the park. Bus 35 will take you 2½ mi short of the campgrounds. Hike the rest of the way.

CENTRAL COAST DRIVE

Poised 280 ft above the crashing surf, the Point Sur Lighthouse, with its stark beauty and isolation, somehow encapsulates the 131-mi drive between Monterey and San Luis Obispo. The lighthouse reigns over the stretch of Hwy. 1, carved into the mountains by convict labor in 1937, that links the odd bedfellows of northern and southern coastal California. The road twists its way past stately redwoods, endless ocean views, and rolling mountains. Historically, this area has been difficult to explore. Low-bottom boats called Tender Ships were custom-built to navigate the rocky shores, and even the intrepid Spanish explorers avoided this territory, commuting inland to bypass the most difficult terrain. Before them, only the nomadic Esselen people, a kin group of natives, populated the land. Only 60 years after the Mexican government vacated its capital on the Monterey Peninsula, San Francisco's bohemians retreated to Carmel after the 1906 earthquake, then later joined Henry Miller and beat poet Gary Snyder for solitude at Big Sur.

Today much of this territory is still difficult to explore and somewhat isolated: Few roads run east–west between Hwys. 1 and 101, leaving a gigantic chunk of land that can only be accessed by miles of hiking trails. Outdoor types with a tent and some time could easily spend a week here, but the lack of budget motels and the poor public transportation can be a real hardship for others. If you just want to enjoy some scenery, you can easily do it in a long day trip from either Los Angeles or San Francisco, though two days are preferable and still shamefully short. If you decide to traverse the whole strip, start in **Monterey,** a heavily touristed but historically fascinating coastal town 48 mi south of Santa Cruz. Heading south, you'll pass by the beautiful and wealthy **Carmel** before entering the rugged heart of **Big Sur.** After an intoxicating four or five hours you'll hit San Simeon—home of the ridiculously ornate **Hearst Castle**—and, finally, **San Luis Obispo,** a surprisingly lively college town. Outside San Luis Obispo, Hwy. 1 meets U.S. 101 and continues south to Santa Barbara and Los Angeles. If you can, make the trip during the week or in late fall or early spring, when hotels and motels chop $5–$10 off their prices.

COMING AND GOING

BY BUS

Traveling up and down the entire Central Coast on public transportation is impossible, but with some ingenuity and a lot of patience you can travel among a few towns. In the north, **Monterey-Salinas Transit** (tel. 408/899–2555) runs Bus 22 (which can carry bicycles) summers only into the heart of Big Sur (*see* Coming and Going *in* Monterey, *below*); in the south, **Central Coast Area Transit** (tel. 805/541–2228) runs along the coast between San Simeon and San Luis Obispo ($2); there's direct service Saturday, no service Sunday, and on weekdays you'll have to transfer. The San Simeon stop is 4 mi from Hearst Castle but right in the center of a budget lodging area.

BY CAR

The best way to experience the 131-mi stretch of coastline is to drive it. It's nearly impossible to get lost—the only road is Hwy. 1. To reach Highway 1 from the north, take I–280 (from San Francisco) or U.S. 101 to Hwy. 68 (from San Jose or the Peninsula). If you're coming from Southern California, U.S. 101 meets the highway in San Luis Obispo. In the off-season, the coastal drive takes less than six hours, but summer traffic on Hwy. 1 will add a good two hours to your driving time.

If you don't have a car, think seriously about renting one. Many agencies will let you pick up a car on one end and drop it off at the other for a "small" fee. San Francisco and Los Angeles tend to be the cheapest endpoints. At press time, Hertz (tel. 800/654–3131) had one-way rentals from those cities for about $220 and one-ways from Monterey to San Luis Obispo at about $50 daily with free unlimited mileage; weekly round-trip rates from San Luis Obispo are $170 and include 1,050 mi; round-trips from Monterey are $210 weekly with free unlimited mileage. In Pacific Grove, near Monterey, try **Rent-a-Wreck** (95 Central Ave. at David Ave., tel. 408/373–3356); cars go for about $140 a week with 1,000 free mi but must be returned to the Pacific Grove location.

BY TRAIN

Amtrak (tel. 800/872–7245) runs the *Coast Starlight* line between Oakland and Santa Barbara (9 hrs, $40–$73 one-way, $80–$146 round-trip), stopping along the way in San Jose, Salinas, Paso Robles, and San Luis Obispo. Though parts of the ride give a feel for the Central Coast's beauty, you'll be missing a whole lot of scenic turnoffs.

MONTEREY

Monterey—with the possible exception of nearby Carmel—is California's tackiest and most unabashedly commercial seaside resort. John Steinbeck (1902–1968) immortalized the busy fishing port in *Cannery Row* and *Sweet Thursday,* describing it as "a poem, a stink, a grating noise, a quality of light, a tone, a habit, a nostalgia, a dream." By the 1950s, however, the sardines were gone, along with much that was poetic. Visitors will still find the fascinating Monterey Bay Aquarium a worthwhile stop; unfortunately, much of the rest of the town has a Disneyland-by-the-sea feel—pricey gift shops sell plastic sardines and lackluster restaurants feature "Steinbeck Specials." Still, Monterey's wealth has funded extensive public-space improvements—there's always a bench surrounded by a blooming garden just around the corner. And, off Cannery Row and Fisherman's Wharf, historical conservation has preserved much of Monterey's past—it was the capital when Spain and Mexico ruled California from 1775 to 1846.

VISITOR INFORMATION

The Monterey Peninsula Chamber of Commerce (380 Alvarado St. at Franklin St., tel. 408/649–1770) offers free maps, 24-hour recorded information, and information about the world-famous **Monterey Jazz Festival** (tel. 408/373–3366) held in late September and the late June **Monterey Blues Festival** (tel. 408/394–2652).

COMING AND GOING

Greyhound buses have regular service to Monterey from San Francisco (4 hrs, $18 one-way) and from Los Angeles (12 hrs, $49 one-way) via Salinas. The Monterey **Greyhound station** (42 Del Monte Ave., tel. 408/373–4735), in a gas station on the eastern end of town, is open daily 8 AM–10 PM.

Green Tortoise (tel. 415/956–7500 or 800/867–8647) buses don't go directly to Monterey, but their Monday morning northbound to San Francisco ($10) stops at the **Salinas Transit Center** (Salinas St. at Gabilan Dr., tel. 408/424–7695) at 5:15 AM. The ride takes four hours. The southbound bus to Los Angeles takes 8–11 hours, stops at the Salinas Transit Center at 11:45 PM Friday night, and costs $30 (*see* Funky Deals on Wheels *box in* Chapter 1).

Monterey-Salinas Transit (tel. 408/899–2555) has regular connections to Carmel, Santa Cruz, and Salinas, and a summertime-only connection to Big Sur from Monterey ($1.50–$6). All buses depart from the downtown **Monterey Transit Plaza** (corner Tyler and Pearl Sts.). For Big Sur, take Bus 22; it will get you as far as the Nepenthe restaurant on Hwy. 1.

GETTING AROUND

From Hwy. 1, the Pacific Grove/Del Monte Avenue exit will take you straight into downtown. The main drag is north–south **Alvarado Street,** with Fisherman's Wharf at the north end and Cannery Row (and the aquarium) 1½ mi farther northwest.

Once in town, your best bet for getting around is on foot or by bus. Because of summer tourism, both parking and crowds are a serious problem for drivers. The most reasonable parking garage downtown (between Alvarado, Franklin, Washington, and Del Monte Sts.) charges $1 an hour; the meters near Cannery Row charge 25¢ per 30 minutes. A bike/pedestrian path (*see* Outdoor Activities, *below*) parallels the shore from the historic downtown area to Fisherman's Wharf and Cannery Row. During summer and on holiday weekends catch the **Wave** (tel. 408/899–2555)—$1, transfers free—a shuttle bus with frequent service and stops throughout the downtown/Cannery Row area. Otherwise Bus 1 travels from the Transit Plaza to Fisherman's Wharf, Cannery Row, and the aquarium for $1.50. Buses 4 and 5 travel between the Monterey Transit Center and Carmel for $1.50.

WHERE TO SLEEP

Monterey is almost devoid of cheap lodging—but if you're persistent (or if you have a tent) you may be able to scare up something reasonable. A slew of motels along North Fremont Street are close to downtown and the routes of Buses 9 and 10. Across from Del Monte Beach and one block east of the Greyhound station, **Del Monte Beach Inn** (1110 Del Monte Ave., tel. 408/649–4410, fax 408/375–3818) is a small bed-and-breakfast offering 18 rooms ($50–$60) decorated by a Martha Stewart disciple. Check in before 9 PM.

Lone Oak Motel. At this flawlessly clean (albeit dull) motel the price of a double—$42 weekdays, $80 weekends—includes unlimited access to a Jacuzzi and sauna room, providing a great way to unwind after a hard day's traveling. Call ahead, as prices fluctuate. *2221 N. Fremont St., tel. 408/372–4924. 46 rooms, all with bath.*

Paramount Motel. Eight mi north of Monterey in the town of Marina, the Paramount looks shabby on the outside, but the proprietor is friendly and the rooms ($33 for a double) are secure, clean, and comfortable. No reservations are accepted so arrive early. *3298 Del Monte Blvd. at Beach St., tel. 408/384–8674. Hwy. 1 north from Monterey to Del Monte Ave.; or Bus 7 to Beach Rd. 6 rooms, all with bath.*

CAMPING • Laguna Seca. Most of the 160 campsites here have RV hookups, but a few undeveloped spaces are reserved for tent campers. Considering its location on the grounds of an auto-racing track—the site of various concerts and festivals in summer—the area is surprisingly scenic. Unfortunately, the sites themselves are pretty ugly and cost $16. It's advised to call ahead in summer to find out whether special events or racing are closing the campground for the dates you're interested in. *Hwy. 68, tel. 408/755–4899 or 408/422–6138. 9 mi east of Monterey off Hwy. 68 (follow signs); or Bus 23 from Transit Plaza and walk 1 mi up a steep hill.*

Veteran's Memorial Park Campground. Just five minutes from downtown, this first-come, first-served campground lies on a grassy knoll in a quiet valley. Although it's not exactly the great outdoors, it's well-maintained and better overall than Laguna Seca. Some of its 40 tightly packed sites ($15) are shadier and more secluded than others. Hikers and cyclists share one large site for $3 per person. Showers are available, but bring your own food. *Via del Rey, tel. 408/646–3865. From downtown, take Jefferson west; or Bus 3 from Transit Plaza.*

FOOD

On Tuesday afternoon Alvarado Street downtown is closed off for a **farmers' market**; at all other times you can find a plethora of seafood and health-food restaurants here, but most are overpriced. The **Lighthouse Bagel Bakery** (201 Lighthouse Blvd. at Reeside Ave., tel. 408/649–1714) has the best deal in town for breakfast or lunch: Tasty bagels are 40¢–50¢, and you can add such toppings as cream cheese (60¢), Jack or Swiss cheese (35¢), avocado (70¢), and sandwich meat ($1.50). **Tillie Gort's Café** (111 Central Ave., Pacific Grove, tel. 408/373–0335) serves delicious sandwiches, Mexican, and Mediterranean food, with an emphasis on vegetarian dishes. A mushroom garden burger will set you back $6.25, and the turkey sandwich goes for $5.75.

Fishwife. One of the Peninsula's best pasta and seafood restaurants, this casual place serves fish dishes that start at $9 and all its pastas are less than $9. *1996 ½ Sunset Dr., Pacific Grove, tel. 408/375–7107. Near Asilomar State Beach. Closed Tues.*

Papá Chano's. This taquería offers tasty, large portions of Mexican basics. Tacos run $2–$3, and a gigantic burrito ($3.50–$4.50) is a meal in itself. *462 Alvarado St. at Del Monte Blvd., tel. 408/646–9587.*

Toastie's Café. When you walk in you may feel like you're trapped in a lacy, pink dollhouse, but the fluffy yogurt-and-buckwheat pancakes ($4.25) and waffles smothered in blueberries ($4.25) should win you over. *702 Lighthouse Ave., Pacific Grove, tel. 408/373–7543. West of downtown Monterey. Open for breakfast and lunch only Mon., Sun.*

POOR MAN'S 17-MILE DRIVE

Probably the most notorious road on the Central Coast, 17-Mile Drive charges cars $6.50 to drive by manicured golf courses and multimillion-dollar mansions. The preferred alternative is "The Poor Man's 17-Mile Drive," really only 6 mi but equally dramatic (and gratis). From Monterey, head west on Ocean View Drive and follow the road as it bends southward past spectacular Asilomar State Beach.

WORTH SEEING

Monterey's main attraction is the justifiably world-famous **Monterey Bay Aquarium** (886 Cannery Row, tel. 408/648–4800), open daily 10–6 (9:30–6 late May–Aug.), where you'll find sharks and sea otters in convincingly natural habitats and a three-story kelp-forest aquarium. The new outer-bay exhibit, featuring the world's largest viewing tank, is engineered to make visitors feel like they've taken a dive—odd jellyfish drift by and mackerel schools circle endlessly. Admission is $14.75. Avoid hour-plus waits during the summer by purchasing your tickets in advance (tel. 408/648–4937 or 800/756–3737 in California). From Hwy. 1 south, follow signs from the Pacific Grove/Del Monte Avenue exit.

Cannery Row lies along the waterfront south of the aquarium, ending at **Fisherman's Wharf.** Both places have seen better days. The Laida Café—an "institution of commercialized love" in Steinbeck's time—is now a bright-yellow ice cream parlor called **Kalisa's** (851 Cannery Row, no phone). At **Bargetto Winery** (700 Cannery Row, tel. 408/373–4053), open daily 10:30–6, you can sip the wares for free. Upstairs, **A Taste of Monterey** (700 Cannery Row, tel. 408/646–5446), open daily 1–6, charges $2 for tasting—but think of it as a fee for the superlative bay views.

"The Path of History Walking Tour," a brochure from the Chamber of Commerce (*see above*) or a $2 guided tour organized by **Monterey State Historic Park** (20 Custom House Plaza, tel. 408/649–7118) highlights the town's history. Monterey's old buildings are fascinating and well-preserved, but most tourists ignore them for the artificial flash of Cannery Row. Don't miss Colton Hall, where the state constitution was written, the Cooper Molera Adobe, or the Custom House. Most buildings on the tour are free, but some charge $2 for a look inside. A $5 pass (good for two days) buys you admission to all of the buildings.

When you've had enough quill pens and adobe walls, head for the water. Don't waste time at windy **Monterey State Beach**—it's nothing compared to **Asilomar State Beach** (tel. 408/372–4076), which features tide pools and enormous waves crashing on the rocky shore; look for it 2 mi west of Monterey in the quiet town of **Pacific Grove** (Bus 1 will get you within walking distance). Here, between October and March, you can glimpse thousands of monarch butterflies who make their winter homes in **Washington Park** (corner Pine Ave. and Alder St.). Pacific Grove is also home to the 1855 **Point Piños Light Station** (Ocean View Blvd. at Point Piños, tel. 408/648–3116), the oldest continuously operating lighthouse on the West Coast, is open Thursday–Sunday 1–4.

AFTER DARK

The nightlife around Cannery Row caters to tourists in search of gimmicky clubs and drink specials. It's where you'll hear low-rent bands playing shoddy covers of "Brown-Eyed Girl." Less than intrigued? Try the **Three Spirits Gallery** (361 Orange Ave., tel. 408/393–2787; from Del Monte Blvd. north, turn west on Contra Costa St., first left is Orange Ave., or Bus 20), a tiny art space found in the middle of a warehouse district in Sand City, 5 mi northeast of downtown Monterey. On some nights (make sure to call first) the gallery hosts solid go-go, surf, or indie rock bands for a $3–$5 cover. For more laid-back atmosphere—something along the lines of a café decked out like a medieval castle—**Morgan's Coffee & Tea** (498 Washington St. at Pearl St., tel. 408/373–5601) serves excellent coffee and sometimes features local folk and jazz performers. The publike **Sly McFlys** (700 Cannery Row, tel 408/649–8050) is a popular watering hole.

Business is slower since the Ft. Ord military base shut down a few years ago, but gay men still get down on the dance floor at **After Dark** (214 Lighthouse Ave. at Reeside Ave., tel. 408/373–7828). Deep house on Thursday night attracts straights who want to boogie as well.

CHEAP THRILLS

Next to the Custom House at the foot of Fisherman's Wharf, aging Italian men spend entire afternoons at the **boccie ball court**; anyone can play with free equipment from the Custom House (tel. 408/649–7118), open daily 10–4. If you're challenged and lose, cheer yourself up with a few 85¢ go-arounds on the 1904 carousel housed inside the **Edgewater Packing Company** (640 Wave St., tel. 408/649–1899).

OUTDOOR ACTIVITIES

BIKING AND MOPEDS • Moped Adventures (1250 Del Monte Ave., at Sloat St., tel. 408/373–2696) rents beach cruisers ($15 a day) and mopeds ($20 for the first hour, then $10 an hour; $50 a day). Call ahead to reserve and verify hours; a driver's license and deposit are required. For $20 a day you can rent a mountain bike from **Bay Bikes** (640 Wave St., 1 block inland from Cannery Row, tel. 408/646–9090) and make tracks for the paved path (4 mi) that stretches from the wharf past Cannery Row and Lover's Point or pedal down 17-Mile Drive (*see box, below*) for free, then on into Carmel or back to Monterey. Bicyclists don't have to stop at the pay booth and can catch quite a few spectacular ocean views between the hoity-toity homes. Bay Bikes will allow you to leave the bike in Carmel (near the south end of the drive) for an extra $8.

There are no sidewalks, no street lighting, and no residential mail delivery in Carmel-by-the-Sea. Locals pick up their mail at the post office, where they hang out and exchange gossip.

FISHING AND WHALE-WATCHING • For salmon- and tuna-related fun, contact **Chris's Fishing Trips** (tel. 408/375–5951) on Fisherman's Wharf for half-day sportfishing trips ($28–$32 plus $15 for a license and equipment). Chris's also offers two-hour whale-watching trips ($15) between December and March, when Monterey Bay is filled with migrating gray whales.

KAYAKING • Kayaking is superb right out from Cannery Row in downtown Monterey: a raft of otters spends most of the year straight out from the **Adventures by the Sea** shop (tel. 408/372–1807), and 300 yards up or down the coast you'll run into either sea lions or harbor seals. The shop can outfit you with a kayak, oars, wet suit, and a half-hour lesson for $25. Open summers 9–6, hours vary in winter.

SNORKELING AND SCUBA DIVING • Monterey Bay attracts divers from around the world with its vast kelp beds and magnificent underwater terrain. The bluffs and underwater caves off Ocean View Drive (between the aquarium and Asilomar Beach) are some of the best scuba and snorkeling spots in the area. Better yet are the pristine waters of Whaler's Cove in Point Lobos (*see below*). **Aquarius Dive Shop** (32 Cannery Row, tel. 408/375–6605) offers moderately priced equipment rentals for certified divers (about $70 the first day, $35 each additional day). More feasible for most people is snorkeling. Aquarius has gear for less than $34—not bad considering you'll need a wet suit, boots, gloves, and a hood to brave Monterey Bay's freezing waters. Snorkeling lessons and a tour will set you back $50 more.

CARMEL

Perched on a rocky bluff 8 mi south of Monterey, this quiet, affluent beachfront town doubles as an artists' colony. While Carmel *does* possess a gorgeous coast, don't believe the hype; Carmel is a strange place—an aloof bastion of conservatism known for its provincial attitudes and some of the most restrictive laws in the nation (high heels, for instance, are illegal). Downtown establishments do not have street addresses; and don't expect to find after-hours food or midnight revelry. No live entertainment is allowed in local drinking holes or restaurants. Instead, Carmel hosts its live shows and movies at the bring-your-own-blanket **Outdoor Forest Theater** (corner Mountain View Ave. and Santa Rita St., tel. 408/626–1681), located between Hwy. 1 and downtown.

Carmel fancies itself a small and private community, yet it's mercilessly invaded each day by tourists hopping from gift shop to art gallery to "quaint" café, and it managed to elect a huge celebrity—Clint Eastwood—as mayor. Above Clint's Hog's Breath Inn restaurant sits the **visitor center** (San Carlos St., between 5th and 6th Sts., tel. 408/624–2522), open weekdays 9–5, weekends 11–3.

WHERE TO SLEEP

Carmel is *not* amenable to those on a budget. Even the beat-up motels price their rooms as if they were lush suites in an upscale B&B. Your best bet is to camp—Andrew Molera State Park (*see* Camping *in* Big Sur, *below*) is only 21 mi south of Carmel. Otherwise, Monterey (*see above*) has a few reasonably priced motels.

The Homestead. Right in town, this place fits into the overdone country inn category—going too far out of its way to be quaint and cozy. However, it *is* awfully comfortable. Doubles start at $55 in winter, $65 in summer; three-person cottages with kitchens are $95. *Lincoln St. and 8th Ave., tel. 408/624–4119. Exit Hwy. 1 at Ocean Ave., then left on Lincoln St. 8 rooms, 4 cottages, all with bath. Reservations advised.*

CAMPING • Saddle Mountain. This well-groomed, commercial campground is the only one near Carmel. Twenty-five tent sites ($22 per night) lie on a terraced hillside. If you don't have camping gear, you can rent a cabin or teepee for $32. Hobnob at the clubhouse or poolside if you don't feel like going into Carmel. *Tel. 408/624–1617. Take Carmel Valley Rd. off Hwy. 1, turn right at Schulte Rd. Showers available. Reservations advised.*

FOOD

Unique and expensive are the norms here: Taverns, tearooms, al frescos, and broilers. If you'd rather picnic, hit the **Mediterranean Market** (Ocean Ave. and Mission St., tel. 408/624–2022), where you can create your own sandwich (around $5), snack on tasty salads, or buy meats and imported cheeses by the pound and eat in the little park across the street. Four doors down, **Wishart's Bakery** (tel. 408/624–3870) has bagels (60¢) and homemade soup ($2.95).

Friar Tuck's. This friendly, quasi-English place is down to earth compared to the rest of Carmel. Burgers, salads, and sandwiches run $4–$6. For breakfast try one of the outstanding omelets ($7.25). *5th Ave. and Dolores St., tel. 408/624–4274.*

WORTH SEEING

Your first stop in Carmel will be the downtown area, easily accessed from Hwy. 1 via Ocean Avenue. Here you'll find a parade of pricey and often snobby gift shops, boutiques, restaurants, and art galleries. At any gallery or at the **Carmel Art Association** (Dolores St., between 5th and 6th Aves., tel. 408/624–6176) you can pick up a map that locates over 35 local galleries, many clustered on Dolores Street.

Carmel's **public beach,** at the end of Ocean Avenue, is the place for a game of volleyball or a nap in the sand protected from the blistering sun and howling winds by cypress trees. For a more spectacular and less populated beach, head about 1 mi south along Scenic Road (off Ocean Ave. just above public beach) until you come around the hairpin curve to **Carmel River State Beach,** known to locals as Oliver's Cove. When you see the view from here, you'll realize how poet Robinson Jeffers, a naturalist obsessed with classical mythology, remained inspired for so many years—his home, known as the **Tor House** (26304 Oceanview Ave., 2 blocks from Scenic Rd., tel. 408/624–1813), is a stone's throw away. Jeffers, one of Carmel's most famous personalities, built Tor House and the adjacent Hawk Tower from rocks he carried up from the beach, creating one of California's most unique "natural" dwellings. Guided tours ($7 and worth it) are available by appointment Friday and Saturday 10–3. Otherwise, Scenic Road affords an excellent view of the house.

The **Carmel Mission** (Rio Rd. and Lasuen Dr., tel. 408/624–3600), founded in 1770 by the busy Padre Juníperro Serra (who initiated California's missions for Spain and is buried here), includes a stone church, museum, and gardens. Winter hours are Monday–Saturday 9:30–4:30 and Sunday 10:30–4:30; in summer it's open daily until 7:30, and it's always worth the $2 donation. To get to the mission take Rio Road west from Hwy. 1.

OUTDOOR ACTIVITIES

The main attraction in Carmel for bicyclists is 17-Mile Drive (*see* Outdoor Activities *in* Monterey, *above*); you can also pedal south on flat coastal roads for a few miles to Point Lobos, where there are a few further miles of paved roads. **Bay Bikes II** (tel. 408/625–2453) will deliver a mountain bike to your doorstep from Monterey for $22 a day.

The inspiration for Robert Louis Stevenson's *Treasure Island,* **Point Lobos State Reserve** (Hwy. 1, 3 mi south of Carmel, tel. 408/624–4909) is a stunningly beautiful day-use park where sea lions, harbor seals, and otters frolic; it's also a good spot to watch gray whales on their southward migration from December to May. The hikes are not strenuous, but tide pooling and vistas prompt lengthy diversions from the trails. The **Cypress Grove Trail** loops past a rare species of cypress; the **Sea Lion Point Trail** leads to a magnificent series of sea coves; and the **South Shore Trail** takes you to Weston Beach, site of the reserve's best tidal pools. Less crowded are the trails without ocean views, where you'll find paths lined with brilliant orange sticky, money flowers, alligator lizards, and western skinks. Park for free across the street from the main entrance on Hwy. 1; otherwise you'll pay $6 per vehicle. The park is open daily 9–4:30 in winter and until 6:30 in summer.

The reserve allows up to 45 people on any given day to dive in **Whaler's Cove** among the otters, seals, and sea lions. Snorkelers and divers (with proof of certification) must have a partner and pay a $6 fee; reserve for either activity through Destinet (tel. 800/444–7275). To rent equipment, contact the Aquarius Dive Shop in Monterey (*see* Outdoor Activities *in* Monterey, *above*).

BIG SUR

Of all the scribes who've attempted to capture Big Sur on paper, locals call Henry Miller their patron saint. Miller, who made a shack in Big Sur his home for many years, wrote of the land as "a region where extremes meet, a region where one is always conscious of weather, of space, of grandeur, of eloquent silence." Spanish settlers in the 1770s had called this forbidding wilderness *el pais grande del sur* (the big country to the south), which got shortened to Big Sur in the early 1900s. Everyone defines Big Sur differently, but all agree that the region's precipitous cliffs, rocky beaches, and redwood forests make it one of the most dramatic stretches of coastline in the world. The harsh geography, helped along by a core of adamantly protective locals, has precluded development; as a result the area is sparsely populated. The closest thing to a town is the group of stores surrounding the **River Inn,** 22 mi south of Carmel. Locals head over to the inn on Saturday night to hear live jazz or drum music; about 1 mi further south, **Fernwood** (408/667–2422) hosts occasional live rock and roll on summer Saturday nights.

After the 1993 opening of the enviro-chic Post Ranch Inn (Hwy. 1, tel. 408/667–2200), competing hoteliers discovered they too could charge close to $500 a night.

Much of Big Sur lies within the 167,000-acre **Ventana Wilderness** in Los Padres National Forest, with its deep, wide valleys, waterfalls, hot springs, natural pools, perennial streams, and undisturbed wildlife (deer and a few bears). **Big Sur Station** (Hwy. 1, just south of Pfeiffer Big Sur State Park, tel. 408/667–2315), open daily 8–6, is loaded with information on camping and exploring the surrounding wilderness. If you want to pay for printed word on *el sur,* rangers will recommend *Hiking the Big Sur Country* ($16). Although primarily a tourist rag, *El Sur Grande* offers a history lesson, a detailed map, and hiking tips in each issue. One tip hikers won't find, however, is a suggestion to park at one of Hwy. 1's turnouts and avoid paying $6 on state lots.

WHERE TO SLEEP

If you want to sleep indoors, you'll have to pay handsomely for the privilege. If you don't have camping gear, your best option is to rent a tent cabin at a private campground for $30–$40. One of the nicest is **Big Sur Campground and Cabins** (tel. 408/667–2322), 3 mi south of Andrew Molera State Park (*see below*), where cabins sleeping two start at $45.

Deetjen's Big Sur Inn. The secluded inn and cabins behind redwoods off Hwy. 1 are romantic-rustic to the core—no phones, no TVs, thin walls, and old bathrooms. Each room has its own name and is uniquely decorated with homey, personal stuff and a down comforter (you'll need it). Both the atmosphere and the people who run the place are top-notch, and short walking trails lie behind the inn. Doubles start at $85. The expensive on-site restaurant is outta this world. *Hwy. 1, tel. 408/667–2377. 3 mi south of Big Sur Station, ½ mi south of Nepenthe. 20 rooms, 15 with bath. Reservations required.*

Riverside Campgrounds and Cabins. Twenty-five mi south of Carmel, Riverside provides the cheapest indoor accommodations in all of Big Sur. Five excellent rooms graced with gorgeous redwood interiors start at $50. The two larger double cabins will set you back $80. *Hwy. 1., tel. 408/667–2414. Reservations advised in summer.*

CAMPING • With more than 1,000 campsites up and down the coast, Big Sur is an ideal place to pitch a tent. You can camp for free in **Los Padres National Forest** as long as you hike 100 ft from a paved road and don't light a fire (*see* Camping *in* Chapter 1). Good access roads can be found all along Hwy. 1: If you've got four-wheel drive, try Willow Creek Road just north of Gorda, otherwise head up Nacimiento Road about 4 mi south of Lucia (*see* Camping, *below*). The Forest Service runs 11 designated campgrounds ($5) in the Nacimiento area, all with fire pits and drinking water. For maps, fire per-

SYKES HOT SPRINGS

If you have two days and backpacking gear, make the 10-mi trek to Sykes Hot Springs, one of the Central Coast's most enticing natural wonders. After a long hike up steep ridges and along a river valley crowded with redwoods, you can soak in the thermal spring and sleep under the stars. The largest of the spring's rock-dam tubs holds four people. The trail begins at the Big Sur Station parking lot.

mits, and information, contact Big Sur Station (*see above*) or the **U.S. Forest Service District Headquarters** (406 S. Mildred St., King City 93930, tel. 408/385–5434).

One of the few access points to the interior of Big Sur, Nacimiento Road, 4 mi south of Lucia, twists and turns to reach eight $5 sites at **Nacimiento Campground** (11 mi from Hwy. 1) and 23 $10 sites at **Ponderosa Campground** (13½ mi from Hwy. 1). Both peaceful campgrounds, devoid of massive RVs year-round, lie on the bank of a babbling brook, but neither has showers and only Ponderosa has flush toilets; make sure to bring your own water or a purifier. A more hard-core option is to turn off Nacimiento Road after 7 mi onto the precarious **Central Coast Ridge Road** (commonly called Cone Peak Road) at an elevation of 2,800 ft. The dirt road is bumpy and slow going but definitely traversable for 6 mi. Along it you find a few sites forged by other adventurous souls, trailheads leading deep into the Ventana Wilderness, total silence, and one of the best views of the ocean from any spot in Big Sur.

Andrew Molera State Park. Andrew Molera has more than 4,000 largely undeveloped acres with beach access and camping. Campers pay $3 per person. Don't try to get by without putting your money in the self-payment box—a ranger *will* come around at 8 AM to collect the cash and hand out $25 tickets to the weasels. The campsites are set against trees in a flat 10-acre meadow, ½ mi from the parking area. Beware of staying here on summer weekends, when Cub Scouts and preteens can make life hell. The 50 tents-only sites are first-come, first-served, but they never turn anyone away, which means the park can become a beehive when overflow campers from other campgrounds stack up on weekends. Call Big Sur Station (*see above*) for more information. *West of Hwy. 1, 10 mi south of Palo Colorado Rd.*

Bottcher's Gap. If you want to soak up a view of a tremendous valley among the majestic madrones and oaks of the Ventana Wilderness, trek to the 11 first-come, first-served campsites ($12) at Bottcher's Gap. There's no phone and no showers, but you'll have running water, and if you come on a weeknight, you'll have peace and solitude. For the best information on the trails and the campground, call Big Sur Station (*see above*). *5 mi south of Garrapata State Beach, go east 8 mi on Palo Colorado Rd.*

Pfeiffer Big Sur State Park. Although there are more than 200 RV and tent sites ($16) here, the redwood groves and gurgling stream still make this sprawling campground one of the best of Big Sur's developed campgrounds. There's a general store, a laundromat, and hot showers for your convenience. It's crowded in summer, and sites should be reserved (tel. 800/444–7275). *Hwy. 1, 26 mi south of Carmel, tel. 408/667–2315. Fire pits, flush toilets, picnic tables.*

Julia Pfeiffer Burns State Park. Save the short McWay Falls Trail, the huge redwoods and shady oaks of this park receive much less attention than Pfeiffer Big Sur. The jewel here for hikers and tent campers is the chance of getting a space at one of two secluded environmental sites ($17 weekdays, $18 on weekends), set in a cypress forest on bluffs overhanging the ocean. Even without potable water or flush toilets, these spots book early. For information on both environmental and developed camping, call or stop by Big Sur Station (*see above*). *Hwy. 1, 38 mi south of Carmel, reservations tel. 800/444–7275.*

FOOD

Wise travelers will stock up at the supermarket in Carmel or San Luis Obispo. If you forget to pack the cooler, the **Center Deli** (Hwy. 1, 30 mi south of Rio Rd. next to Big Sur post office, tel. 408/667–2225) has groceries, a host of pasta salads, and the cheapest sandwiches around ($3–$5), as well as fruit smoothies ($3) in summer. The **Big Sur Pub** (Hwy. 1, next to Deetjen's River Inn, tel. 408/667–2355) has a filling veggie burrito ($5.25) and sandwiches for less than $5.

Café Kevah. Part of the Nepenthe restaurant complex, this café has daily brunch and lunch menus with interesting dishes like apple-bread pudding ($6.75) and spicy chicken brochettes ($6.75), as well as the priciest espresso drinks this side of Paris ($3.25 and up). The food is overpriced, but what you're really paying for is the fantastic view from the deck. The upstairs Nepenthe dining room is outrageously expensive. *Hwy. 1, tel. 408/667–2344. 29 mi south of Carmel.*

EXPLORING BIG SUR

Eleven mi south of Carmel, Palo Colorado Road winds its way east from Hwy. 1 through the Ventana Wilderness for 8 serpentine mi until it ends at **Bottcher's Gap.** From the parking lot, **Skinner's Ridge Trail** climbs 4 mi (roughly three hours) to Devil's Peak, which affords incredible views of Ventana's dramatic wooded peaks and valleys. South off Skinner's Ridge Trail, the eight-hour round-trip hike to **Pico Blanco**—a rugged, marble mountain peak that the Esselen Indians, Big Sur's earliest human inhabitants, thought of as the top of the world and the site of human creation—offers stunning views but winds through private property. The hike's not legal, but people do it anyway, trekking along the Boy Scout Service Road past the Boy Scout Camp and all the way up **Little Sur Trail.**

Back on Hwy. 1, south of Palo Colorado Road, look for the **Bixby Creek Bridge,** a 550-ft concrete span built in 1932. Just before the bridge, the circular **Old Coast Road** curves inland for 10 mi and meets back up with Hwy. 1 opposite the entrance to Andrew Molera State Park. This is California at its rugged best—craggy cliffs, majestic redwoods, and views of the Little Sur River running its way toward the ocean. If you're the four-wheeling type, you'll like the road's gravel- and mud-plagued inclines; a regular car should be fine if the weather's been dry.

Between 1 AM and 3:30 AM, you can relax (naked) in Esalen's natural hot springs, perched on a cliff overlooking the Pacific for just $10. Call the institute to make reservations.

Double back ½ mi north from Andrew Molera to check out the **Point Sur Light Station** (tel. 408/625–4419), which was built in 1889 on a strange and gargantuan rock outcropping to prevent shipwrecks along this rocky and often foggy stretch of coast. Tours of the lighthouse are available on weekends and Wednesday May–October ($5). Call first for times and make sure to show up a half hour early so the docents can let you through the gate. Once the site of a Monterey Jack cheese factory and a dairy farm, **Andrew Molera State Park** offers more than 10 mi of hiking and mountain-biking trails. The strenuous hike up the **Ridge Trail** takes you through 4 mi of stunning coastal scenery to the top of a ridge. Collapse on the bench, take a deep breath, and savor the spectacular view of the Pacific before you head down the **Panorama Trail** to the **Bluffs Trail,** which is especially striking in spring when the wildflowers bloom.

About 5 mi south of Andrew Molera State Park, **Pfeiffer Big Sur State Park** (east side of Hwy. 1, tel. 408/667–2315) is one of the most popular camping and hiking spots on the coast, especially during summer. Don't waste your time at **Pfeiffer Falls**—the hike is crowded and the falls are less than spectacular. Instead, just south of Pfeiffer on the same side of the highway, Big Sur Station (*see above*) is the starting point for the **Pine Ridge Trail,** a local favorite that leads into the Ventana Wilderness and **Sykes Hot Springs** (*see box, below*).

Sycamore Canyon Road, 1 mi south of Big Sur Station, is unmarked save for a stop sign. If you can find it, brave the road for 2 mi and you'll land at **Pfeiffer Beach,** a turbulent, windswept cove with huge rock formations and an angry ocean that's definitely not suitable for swimming. About 2½ mi farther south lies **Nepenthe** (tel. 408/667–2345; *see* Food, *above*), an expensive restaurant with an extraordinary view (also the last stop of the summers-only Bus 22 from Monterey).

Head south from Nepenthe to the **Henry Miller Library** (Hwy. 1, ¼ mi south of Nepenthe, tel. 408/667–2574). More like a bookstore with a precise collection of literature, the tiny one-room library displays the bohemian author's artifacts (sorry, no steamy letters to Ms. Nin) and has rotating exhibits on artists and writers associated with Miller or Big Sur. The library is open daily 11–5 in summer, hours vary in the winter.

More spectacular than Pfeiffer Big Sur State Park, **Julia Pfeiffer Burns State Park** (12 mi south of Big Sur Station, tel. 408/667–2315) has excellent and often less crowded hiking trails. But most people pay the $6 entrance fee to see **MyWay Falls**—the most breathtaking sight in all of Big Sur before parking lots, postcards, and crowds demystified some of its natural wonder. From the parking lot, a short ½-mi path leads to a bluff with an incredible view of the creek at the head of the falls. Better, and far less crowded, the 6-mi **Ewoldsen Trail** loop is a fantastic rugged hike that offers one of the best vegetation samplings of the Big Sur coast.

Three mi south of Julia Pfeiffer, a sign on the right side of the road reads: ESALEN INSTITUTE–RESERVATIONS ONLY. At the end of the road you'll find the world-famous **Esalen Institute** (tel. 408/667–3000), which specializes in the "exploration of human value and potentials." Locals tend to scoff, but the institute was one of the first places to introduce Gestalt therapy in the late '60s. Today's classes, for instance "Awakened Mind II: Advanced Brainwave Training," will be lucky to achieve similar acceptance. These days the grounds and natural hot springs are closed to the public during the day. Stop by anyway, and the guard will hand you a catalog of the outrageously expensive workshops. Class titles and descriptions will keep you chuckling for miles down the road.

The southern stretch of Big Sur—between the tiny towns of Lucia and San Simeon—is less populated and has a gentler geography than the sometimes violently beautiful north. There's not much to see besides the continually unfolding coastline, but you will come across some choice beaches every now and then. Ten mi south of Lucia, **Jade Cove** is a secluded, rocky beach with sweeping views both up and down the coast. Just north of Gorda, quiet **Willow Creek** is gorgeous, rocky, and a local favorite.

OUTDOOR ACTIVITIES

The main activity in Big Sur is hiking (*see* Exploring Big Sur, *above*), but lots of people also bicycle along Hwy. 1. Cyclists should be experienced and familiar with the narrowness of the highway and the lack of road shoulder. One benefit of pedaling the coast is that most of the state parks offer cheap campsites (usually $3) to those on two rather than four wheels.

Andrew Molera State Park is the only Big Sur park with single-track trails for mountain biking. Mountain bikers in tip-top shape can take on the steep, strenuous **Ridge Trail,** which is more than 2 mi long and has an elevation gain of 1,200 ft. For a more relaxing ride, try the **River** and **Cottonwood trails** (2 mi), both of which wind through the park's meadows. Most trails start at the parking area or ½ mi away at the beach. Elsewhere in Big Sur, you'll have to stick to the fire and service roads, or risk a fine. One possibility is to head up **Nacimiento–Ferguson Road,** 4 mi south of Lucia off Hwy. 1 (*see* Camping, *above*). Bikes are not allowed to the left into the Ventana Wilderness, but off the right side of the road you'll see a few trails, most of which are quite steep in sections.

HEARST CASTLE

Possibly the most colossal monument to an individual ego that the United States has ever produced, Hearst Castle crowns a hilltop above the tiny town of San Simeon, 44 mi south of Lucia. Though designed by Julia Morgan, the mammoth compound was the brainchild (and bankrolled) by publishing magnate William Randolph Hearst, best known as the inheritor of the *San Francisco Examiner,* an architect of yellow journalism, and the model for Orson Welles's *Citizen Kane*. You can glimpse the castle from the highway, but for a closer inspection of the eclectic and disgustingly opulent "Enchanted Hill," take one of four guided tours ($14, $25 spring and fall evenings) that leave from the visitor center (*see below*) off Hwy. 1.

The tours last 1¾ hours, including bus transportation up the private 5-mi road that leads to the site (sit on the right-hand side of the bus for the best views). Although they're pricey, the tours of the ornately decorated rooms, gold-plated indoor pool, flower beds, and sculpture-lined gardens are worth the money, if only to marvel at the horrifically poor taste of the nouveau riche. First-time visitors usually opt for Tour 1, a general overview of the main house and the gardens, but Tour 2 groups are smaller and venture into the personal chambers. All tours cover the lush gardens and the oft-photographed indoor and outdoor pools. Reservations are advised but not entirely necessary; call 800/444–4445.

If you want a sneak preview of your tour or cannot afford the castle's steep admission, check out the free exhibit at the huge **visitor center** (west side of Hwy. 1, tel. 805/927–2020) at the bottom of the hill. It documents the history of the Hearst family and the building of the castle, which was begun in 1919 and was left unfinished after 28 years. The center is generally open daily 8–5:30, but hours may vary, so call ahead.

WHERE TO SLEEP

Loads of motels are clustered about 2 mi south of Hearst Castle in a strip known as San Simeon Acres, but they're all overpriced. For a better deal, head 6 mi down Hwy. 1 into tiny Cambria, where you'll find the **Cambria Palms Motel** (2662 Main St., tel. 805/927–4485) at the south end of the main drag. It's got simple rooms (no phones) with thick walls and cozy beds; the friendly Brits who run the place charge $55 for doubles in summer, $35 off-season. To camp near the beach, head to the unspectacular **San Simeon State Park Campgrounds** (Hwy. 1, tel. 805/927–2035), which include San Simeon Creek Campground, with 134 modern sites (i.e., with showers) for $17 weekdays and $18 on weekends, and Washburn Campground, with 70 primitive sites for $10 weekdays and $11 on weekends. San Simeon Creek has some shady trees, while Washburn is on a flat hilltop with no shade and lots of scrub brush; it's a wasteland in the summer but tolerable the rest of the year. It's wise to reserve through Destinet (tel. 800/444–7275), especially for summer weekends.

FOOD

There's not much to choose from in Cambria and San Simeon. **Creekside Gardens Café** (2114 Main St. in Redwood Shopping Center, Cambria, tel. 805/927–8646) is a great place for breakfast, with omelets ($5.50) and applesauce pancakes ($3.50). Tuesday–Saturday nights, the same space becomes **Creekside De Noche,** a Mexican restaurant with combination platters for $5.50. At **Robin's** (4095 Burton Dr. off Main St. in Cambria, tel. 805/927–5007), closed Sunday, you get home cooking with an ethnic edge. Try the hot-and-spicy tempeh or the fresh pasta primavera with vegetables; both are under $8.

SAN LUIS OBISPO

The inland burg of San Luis Obispo sits 34 mi south of San Simeon and 110 mi north of Santa Barbara and is surrounded by rocky hills and volcanic peaks, called *morros.* Half the town is made up of students who attend California Polytechnic State University (Cal Poly) and nearby Cuesta College, so the population drops dramatically in summer. There's not all that much to do here—Californians sometimes refer to it by its acronym "SLO." But if you need a place to stop for the night on the drive from San Francisco to Los Angeles, San Luis Obispo is a convenient halfway point, and you can find enough diversions to keep you happily occupied for an evening. Stop in at the **visitor center** (1039 Chorro St. at Higuera St., tel. 805/781–2777 or 800/676–1772) for a free map and information on goings-on. Gay travelers should call the **Gay and Lesbian Alliance** hot line (tel. 805/541–4252) for upcoming events and local resources.

Throwing a little shindig? You can rent the grounds of Hearst Castle (but not the building) to the tune of $3,000 an hour.

For starters, check out the tacky pink-and-white **Madonna Inn** (100 Madonna Rd., tel. 805/543–3000), southwest of downtown and visible from U.S. 101. At this popular hotel, no two of the flamboyant rooms are alike. The management won't let you visit the Cave Room (complete with waterfall) or the Old Mill (featuring a working waterwheel) unless you have a reservation, but postcards in the lobby detail each of the $87–$240 rooms. When you've had your fill of kitsch, head into San Luis Obispo's long and narrow downtown area, which is packed with record stores, restaurants, cafés, and movie theaters. The main drag, **Higuera Street,** runs roughly east–west, with Palm Street and Marsh Street paralleling it. Intersecting these long commercial avenues, Broad Street to the west and Toro Street to the east form a rectangle within which lie all the downtown sights.

In the center of town, the Mission San Luis Obispo (751 Palm at Chorro, tel. 805/543–6850) was built in 1772 by Chumash Indians. The on-site museum devotes more space than most missions to Indian artifacts and history and asks for a $1 donation to check out the unique L-shape sanctuary and exhibits. The surrounding plaza and gardens are favored by locals for picnicking. Nearby is the first Chinese mercantile establishment in the United States, the **Ah Louis Store.** Built by its namesake in 1884, it served as a post office, bank, and supply shop for the Chinese coolies who dug tunnels for the Southern Pacific Railroad. Today the store mostly peddles carved Buddhas and incense burners. On Thursday evening 6–9, year-round, an excellent **farmers' market** on Higuera Street features fresh produce, hot food, and live music.

COMING AND GOING

San Luis Obispo lies at the junction of Hwy. 1 and U.S. 101, both of which run north–south. Just north of where the highways split, Hwy. 1 becomes North Santa Rosa Street for several blocks. If you're making the trip between San Francisco and Los Angeles, San Luis Obispo is the natural halfway point; it's roughly four hours from each city on U.S. 101.

BY BUS • From the San Luis Obispo **Greyhound station** (150 South St., at Parker St., tel. 805/543–2121 or 800/231–2222), buses run north along U.S. 101 to San Francisco (6 hrs, $42 one-way) five times a day, and south to Los Angeles (5½ hrs, $32 one-way) six times a day. The station, where you'll find overnight lockers for $1, is open daily 7:15 AM–9:30 PM. **Green Tortoise** (tel. 800/867–8647) stops in San Luis Obispo at the Denny's restaurant on Los Osos Valley Road; buses to San Francisco ($15) pass through San Luis Obispo at 2:15 AM Monday, and buses to Los Angeles ($15) pass through at 2:45 AM Saturday. Call a week ahead to make reservations. *See* Funky Deals on Wheels *box in* Chapter 1.

SLO Transit (tel. 805/541–2877) runs bus service within the city limits (75¢) until 7 PM on weekdays; two bus routes operate on weekends until 6 PM. Bus 5 connects the Greyhound station to downtown, though you can easily walk the quarter mile.

BY TRAIN • Amtrak's *Coast Starlight* trains stop at the **San Luis Obispo depot** (1011 Railroad Ave., at Santa Rosa St., tel. 800/872–7245) once a day in each direction. Going south, you can reach Santa Barbara (2½ hrs, $24 one-way) or Los Angeles (6 hrs, $32 one-way); northbound trains go to Emeryville, where you board a bus to San Francisco (6–6½ hrs, $42 and up for train and bus). The train is slower and more expensive than Greyhound and only travels along the coast between San Luis Obispo and Santa Barbara, yet seats fill up quickly—reserve well in advance. The station's open daily 6:15 AM–9 PM. SLO Transit Bus 5 (*see above*) connects the station to downtown.

WHERE TO SLEEP

If you're in town during graduation week (mid-June) or Mardi Gras (mid-February) you'll be hard pressed to find a double for less than $80. At all other times of the year rooms are plentiful and usually less than $50. Motels are sprinkled around the city, with many concentrated on **Monterey Street** east of Santa Rosa Street. No buses go far enough down Monterey to reach the motels, but you can easily walk from Mission Plaza, ½-mi away.

Budget Motel. Within walking distance of the Greyhound station, the Budget Motel has spotless, if somewhat saccharine, doubles starting at $45. Four-person suites go for $78. *345 Marsh St., at Archer St., tel. 805/543–6443. From Hwy. 1, exit east on Madonna Rd., turn left on Higuera St. to Marsh St. 51 rooms, all with bath.*

HOSTEL • San Luis Obispo Coast Hostel (HI). At this environmentally minded, homey hostel ($13 HI members; $16 nonmembers) in the foothills near the Cal Poly campus, you'll share the yard with friendly chickens and organic gardens. The proprietor organizes free hikes with the Sierra Club on weekends, will rent you a bike for $5 a day, provides tennis rackets for the nearby courts, and will cook you a homemade meal (price varies). *1292 Foothill Blvd., tel. 805/544–4678. From N. Santa Rosa St. (Hwy. 1) turn east on Foothill Blvd., follow ½ mi. 20 beds, 2 private rooms ($30–$32). Reception open daily 5 PM–10 PM, curfew 11 PM (flexible), lockout 9:30–5. Laundry.*

CAMPING • There are a number of campgrounds in the semi-arid hills around San Luis Obispo. If you prefer to camp on the beach, head 25 minutes west to Montaña de Oro State Park (*see* Near San Luis Obispo, *below*) or 15 minutes south to Pismo Beach. **Cerro Alto Campground** (tel. 805/461–5437) is contracted out by the Forest Service; to get here from town, take Hwy. 1 to Morro Bay, then Hwy. 41 toward Atascadero (watch for signs). The 21 first-come, first-served primitive sites ($10) fill up with overflow from the beach campgrounds. The sites lie in a wooded valley bisected by a narrow stream and are a great base for exploring the nearby mountains. Thirteen mi north of San Luis Obispo and sandwiched between a golf course and a natural reserve, **Morro Bay State Park Campground** (State Park Rd., tel. 805/772–7434) contains 135 developed sites ($17 weekdays, $18 weekends) complete with showers and flush toilets. Under the canopy of eucalyptus, the sprawling grid attracts loads of RVs. From Hwy. 1 turn east on South Bay Boulevard, fork right onto State Park Road; reservations are a must in the summer.

FOOD

David Muzzio's Market (870 Monterey St., between Chorro and Morro Sts., tel. 805/543–0800), closed Sunday, has imported groceries and a deli counter with specialty sandwiches ($4–$6). If you're looking for tacos ($2) or veggie burritos ($3), head to **Tio Alberto's** (1131 Broad St., tel. 805/546–9646; or 295 Santa Rosa St., tel. 805/542–9321), the best Mexican taquería in town. **Big Sky** (1121 Broad St., between Higuera and Marsh, tel. 805/545–5401) serves stellar rosemary potatoes with inventive breakfasts ($4–$6); dinner entrées start at $7.

Natural Flavors. Perhaps one of the best Vegan eateries in California, this cafeteria-style health mecca serves sandwiches ($5.50), pastas ($5), and delicious burritos ($4.50). The massive salad bar with organic greens ($2.75 for a small bowl) shouldn't be missed. Eat on the patio or on a bench along the creek. *570 Higuera St., near Napoma, tel. 805/781–9040. Closed Sun.*

AFTER DARK

San Luis Obispo hops when school's in session (Sept.–May), and nightlife is largely student-oriented; to check out what's going on, pick up a copy of the free weekly *New Times.* The action is centered in the downtown commercial district. Popular with the more grown-up variety of students, the **S.L.O. Brewing Company** (1119 Garden St. at Higuera St., upstairs, tel. 805/543–1843), is a large, airy brick-and-wood microbrewery with live music most Thursday–Saturday nights (cover up to $5). **Mother's Tavern** (725 Higuera St., tel. 805/541–8733) has frequent swing and big band nights (cover varies), but steer clear of the fraternity crowds Thursday–Saturday. **Breezes** (11560 Los Osos Valley Rd., near Madonna Rd., tel. 805/544–8010), in the Laguna Village Shopping Center, is a raucous gay- and straight-friendly bar and dance club with a $2–$4 cover. DJs spin tunes except Thursday, which is audience participation (i.e., karaoke) night. Breezes (open Thurs.–Sat.) is shopping for a new location, so call ahead.

For something mellower, check out the popular **Linnaea's Café** (1110 Garden St., tel. 805/541–5888), where you can enjoy your java in the great outdoors on a large patio in the back. On weekends and some other days the café hosts poetry readings, and live blues, folk, or alternarock music. **Palm Theatre** (817 Palm St., tel. 805/541–5161) shows three art-house or foreign films daily 4–9 for $5.50; weekend matinees begin around 1 PM.

NEAR SAN LUIS OBISPO

MONTANA DE ORO STATE PARK • This is one of the most beautiful parks on the coast. Twelve mi northwest of San Luis Obispo at the end of Los Osos Valley Road, its 8,000 acres of mostly undeveloped land turn golden (*oro* means gold) every spring and summer when the poppies and mustard bloom. You can get a free map at **park headquarters** (tel. 805/528–0513), open daily noon–4 during summer but weekends only in winter; follow signs to the Old Spooner Ranch House from the entrance gate. Head down to **Spooner's Cove,** once popular with Prohibition-era bootleggers, for a gorgeous vista of crashing waves and a whiff of sea spray. For a more distant view of spume and foam, the **Valencia Peak Trail** climbs 1,347 ft to the summit of the park's namesake in 2 mi, crossing marine terraces thick with coastal sage. The trailhead is just south of park headquarters. Mountain bikers are offered several good loops. **Islay Creek Road** winds past the Old Spooner Ranch barn and back to park headquarters via the grueling **Ridge Trail** for a round trip of 11 mi.

Not to be missed at the Madonna Inn is the urinal in the men's room—a large waterfall that's activated by lasers (women should knock and look in).

Montaña de Oro has 50 primitive sites (no showers, chemical toilets) for $10 ($11 in summer) and four secluded walk-in sites; bring your own water and prepare for ocean views and total solitude. Reservations (tel. 800/444–7275) are taken year-round for the walk-in sites and from Memorial Day to Labor Day for the others. Central Coast Transit (tel. 805/541–2228) does not go to park headquarters, but Bus 7 can drop you at Pine Street and Los Osos Valley Road, about 3 mi from Spooners Cove. Weekdays, the bus runs five times a day (8 AM–5 PM); Saturday, three times 9 AM–5 PM (from San Luis Obispo's City Hall). The trip costs $1.50.

AVILA BEACH AND PISMO BEACH

If you follow U.S. 101 south for 12 mi from San Luis Obispo (turn off at San Luis Bay Dr. and follow it to Avila Beach Rd.), you'll hit **Avila Beach.** Just before you cross into town, look for the **Diablo Canyon nuclear power plant** exhibit at the **PG&E Community Center** (6588 Ontario Rd., tel. 805/546–5280); open weekdays 9–noon and 1–5, it details the history of the power plant, which opened in 1986 and supplies 5% of the state's energy. Diablo is one of the country's most controversial nuclear plants, on account of safety questions raised by its location on top of a major fault line. Drop by and listen to what a siren will sound like in the event of a meltdown (the answer is: scary). The three-hour, Monday–Saturday tours are free (though not free from propaganda), but you must call ahead to reserve a space.

Avila Beach has a wonderfully rickety wooden pier and harbor boardwalk. If the public beach there is too crowded, head up Cave Landing Road (off Avila Beach Road, opposite the golf course on the way back to U.S. 101) to the popular **Pirate's Cove** (officially known as Mallagh Landing), one of the few nude beaches in the area. Both ends of the cave—gay to the north and straight in the southern areas—boast warm waters with towering cliffs as backdrop. Nudists claim the cove is one of the most idyllic settings on the California coast, but women may feel more comfortable—and avoid hecklers—with a partner. Farther down Avila Beach Road, you'll pass **Avila Hot Springs** (250 Avila Beach Dr., tel. 805/595–2359), a crass, developed resort that charges $9 an hour for the use of its private hot mineral baths and $7.50 a day to use the regular and hot pools and public mineral pool.

Pismo Beach, a few miles south of Avila off U.S. 101, is the ultimate "has-been" town. In the 1930s it was one of *the* beachside getaways for Hollywood's elite, including part-time residents Clark Gable and Spencer Tracy. Today the stars and starlets are gone, and the town's once impressive clam population has been nearly obliterated by fishing and pollution. But visitors can still enjoy the wide beaches and undulating sand dunes. In fact, Pismo has become one of the cheapest seaside towns in central California.

Pismo's north end, which lies between wide, sandy Pismo State Beach and an old wooden fishing pier near Price Street, serves as a downtown area. The southern end of town is dominated by the sand dunes, some of which have been designated the only state vehicular recreation area on a California beach, meaning you can drive a car or other motorized vehicle on the sand. If you've got a four-wheel drive, deflate your tires for traction and go nuts. If you don't have one and you're seriously addicted to adrenaline, you can rent an ATV (starting at $45 for 2 hrs) from **B.J.'s ATV Rentals** (197 Grand Ave., at Hwy. 1, tel. 805/481–5411). There are plenty of more benign ways to enjoy Pismo (*see* Outdoor Activities, *below*), not the least of which is simply lying on the usually uncrowded beaches and soaking up the sun.

COMING AND GOING

Monday through Saturday, **Central Coast Area Transit** (tel. 805/541–2228) runs three buses a day between San Luis Obispo's county courthouse and Pismo Beach; the trip takes 25 minutes and costs $1. Bikes are allowed on these buses.

WHERE TO SLEEP

Avila Beach has only one motel. Newly renovated and eyeing the wallets of wealthier vacationers, the **Inn at Avila Beach** (256 Front St., tel. 805/595–2300) has large posh doubles that cost $45–$190 depending on the season, view, and the presence or absence of hot tubs. Some rooms have kitchenettes. In Pismo you can stay at the **El Pismo Inn** (230 Pomeroy Ave., tel. 805/773–4529), the now stylishly cluttered spot where Carole Lombard and Tyrone Power used to romp. Rooms range $25 (off-season) to $55 (summer), making it one of the better deals on the coast, which is not a secret—reserve ahead, especially on summer holiday weekends. Try to get a room with large bay windows.

CAMPING • There are no public campgrounds in Avila. **Avila Hot Springs** (*see above*) offers tent camping for $16.50 a night (campers also get a 40% discount on pool fees), but the sites are packed with RVs and closer to the highway than to the beach. Campers would do better—though not by much—heading to Pismo Beach. Pismo's campgrounds have great beach access, but they're the unfortunate targets of family reunions and ATV sand warriors. **Pismo State Beach** (tel. 805/489–2685) has two campgrounds: **North Beach State Campground** (off Hwy. 1) has 103 tightly packed sites in a grassy area near the beach. Try to get one near the sand dunes. **Oceano Campgrounds** (555 Pier Ave., off Hwy. 1) offers access to a lagoon, but the 40 tent sites are too close to the 42 RV sites for solitude. Both campgrounds have showers, charge $14 off-season and $17–$18 in summer (RV sites are $24). **Pismo Dunes** (on Pier Ave.) offers beach camping on soft sand in the same area where motors roar. Rangers claim no one's been run over yet. There are no sites here—simply drive or walk out onto the beach and pitch a tent for $6. To reserve any of these sites, call Destinet (tel. 800/444–7275).

FOOD

In Avila your best bet is **Avila Grocery and Mercantile** (354 Front St., tel. 805/595–2098), where you'll find all the makings for a cheap picnic on the beach. In Pismo, locals line up at **Pismo Beach Fish and Chips** (505 Cypress St., at Stimson Ave., tel. 805/773–2853), closed Monday, for fish 'n' chips ($5.95) made from a family recipe refined over three generations. **Jalpeños Taco Hut** (246 Pomeroy Ave., tel. 805/773–3806), also closed Monday, serves up a huge veggie burrito for $5. Start your day right with a cheap bagel and coffee ($1.50) at the charming **Black Pearl** (230 Pomeroy Ave., tel. 805/773–6631); the café also delivers a mean ice coffee and is one of the few places in town to catch decent live music Saturday after dark.

OUTDOOR ACTIVITIES

To go for a bike ride around town or along the boardwalk, come to **Pismo Bike Rentals** (519 Cypress St., 3 blocks south of pier, tel. 805/773–0355): beach cruisers rent for $15 per half day, $25 per full day; mountain bikes go for $21 per half day, $35 per full day (25% off during summer months); three-wheeled low riders that roll easily over the sand rent for $5 an hour. On the right day, the surfing, body surfing, and body boarding next to the Pismo pier is excellent. Pismo Bike Rentals also has surfboards for half-day rental ($12) and wet suits ($6).

The **Pismo Dunes Preserve,** an area popular in the 1930s with bohemian squatters, was once thought to be the center of a powerful and benign energy. The last of the "dunites" settlement died in the early 1970s, but you can still experience the power of the dunes by taking a trek among its wildflowers and vegetation. No set trails exist, and hikers should be careful not to step on any plant life. Look for the preserve on Hwy. 1, just south of town at the end of Pier Avenue. Sixteen mi south of Pismo Beach, freshwater **Oso Flaco Lake** is the crown jewel of the Pismo Dunes. Secluded and removed from the roar of the dirt bike savages, hikers can romp through a grove peppered with chirping songbirds, cross the lake on an extended bridge, and tackle one dune before reaching a magnificent (and usually empty) beach. The walk is 1¼ mi long; day use costs $2. *Tel. 805/473–7220. From Pismo Beach follow Hwy. 1 south for 13½ mi, turn west on Oso Flaco Lake Rd.*

SANTA BARBARA

You cross an invisible line as you enter Santa Barbara, and a small but noticeable change in attitude tells you this is no longer Northern California. Considered the northernmost coastal outpost of "SoCal" (Southern California), Santa Barbara is too wealthy and aloof to fit comfortably with the more genial towns of San Luis Obispo and Santa Cruz, yet it's too picturesque and relaxed to be seen as an extension of Los Angeles, only 92 mi south. An exceedingly wealthy and conservative community—Ronald Reagan has his ranch here—the scenery is Riviera-esque in its beauty, and the locals all look as if they do nothing but sit on the beach. A scruffier and less daunting contingent lurks in town, too, ranging from mellow U.C. Santa Barbara students to the vagabond homeless. But the city works hard to retain its sanitized Mediterranean image. Everything here is architecturally designed around a Spanish-Moorish theme, with red-tile roofs, wrought-iron gates, and red adobe. Despite the fact that Santa Barbara takes itself much too seriously, it's still one of Southern California's most engaging coastal towns, buffered by golden beaches, a historic mission, a few museums, and tons of thriving outdoor cafés and restaurants. Despite $2 million worth of damages (since repaired) from floods and mud slides in the mid-1990s, surfers, shoppers, and students alike seem to have only sunshine on their minds.

The first motel (1925) in America rests, unoccupied, at the Grand Avenue entrance to Hwy. 101. Though the Hotel Inn's entrepreneur visualized a chain, he never made it out of town.

BASICS

The busy **visitor center** (1 Santa Barbara St. at Cabrillo Blvd., tel. 805/965–3021) stocks brochures, maps, and information on local accommodations. It also has guides to the "Red Tile" walking tour, which highlights Santa Barbara's architecture. The **Gay and Lesbian Resource Center** (126 E. Haley St., Suite A-17, tel. 805/963–3636) provides information on local gay and lesbian events weekdays and recorded information at all times, and counseling for anyone who just wants to talk.

COMING AND GOING

BY BUS

Green Tortoise (tel. 800/867–8647) runs a bus from Los Angeles ($10) on Sunday night that stops in Santa Barbara before heading on to San Luis Obispo ($15) and San Francisco ($30). The bus stops at the Banana Bungalow International Hostel (*see* Where to Sleep, *below*). **Greyhound** (34 W. Carrillo St., next to Transit Center, tel. 805/965–7551) has frequent service from Santa Barbara to San Francisco (7½ hrs, $36.50 one-way) and Los Angeles (2½–3 hrs, $12 one-way). The station is open weekdays 5:30 AM–8 PM, weekends until midnight. Lockers ($1 per 24 hrs) are available for passengers.

BY CAR

U.S. 101, which connects Santa Barbara to Los Angeles (92 mi south) and San Luis Obispo (100 mi north), is the main highway through the city. Other arteries include **Highway 154** (San Marcos Pass Rd.), which leads north out of Santa Barbara to Lake Cachuma and Santa Ynez (*see* Cheap Thrills, *below*) and eventually rejoins U.S. 101 north of Buellton.

BY PLANE

The small **Santa Barbara Airport** (500 James Fowler Rd., Goleta, tel. 805/683–4011), 8 mi north of downtown Santa Barbara, is served by several major airlines' shuttle services, including America West and United. Generally, one-way tickets to San Francisco hover around $150 and those to Los Angeles

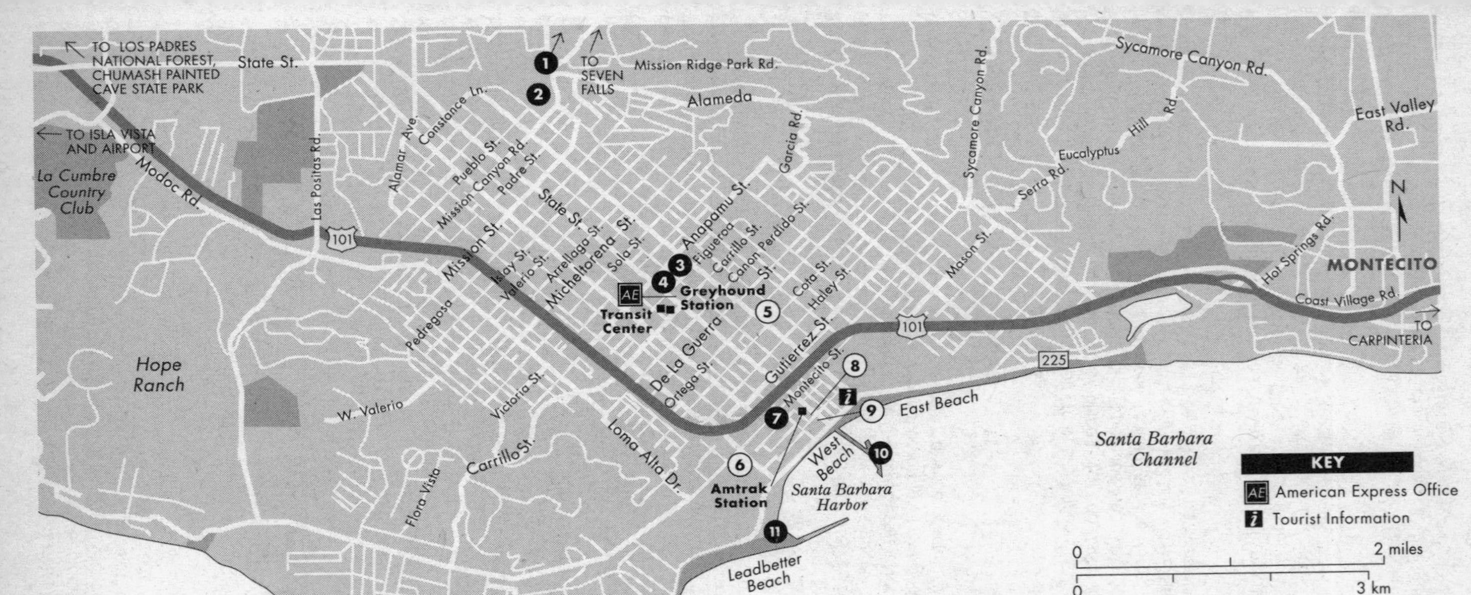

Sights ●
Botanical Gardens, **1**
County Courthouse, **3**
Mission Santa Barbara, **2**
Moreton Bay Fig Tree, **7**
Museum of Art, **4**
Santa Barbara Yacht Harbor, **11**
Stearn's Wharf and Sea Center, **10**

Lodging ○
Banana Bungalow International Hostel, **5**
Californian Hotel, **9**
Inn by the Harbor, **6**
Hotel State Street, **8**

SANTA BARBARA

are about $54. Transit to and from downtown is via **Santa Barbara Metropolitan Transit District** buses (tel. 805/683–3702). Line 11 serves the airport and can be picked up at the Transit Center (*see below*) and along upper State Street (40 min, $1). The bus runs 6 AM–11:15 PM on the half hour. **SuperRide** (tel. 805/683–9636) is Santa Barbara Airport's door-to-door shuttle. Fare is $15 from the airport to downtown Santa Barbara, and credit cards are accepted.

BY TRAIN

Amtrak trains stop once daily at the Santa Barbara depot (209 State St., tel. 805/963–1040 or 800/872–7245 for reservations) on the way to San Francisco (9–10 hrs, $71) or to Los Angeles (3 hrs, $21). The station is open daily 7 AM–8 PM, but the ticket window opens and closes according to train schedules. Luggage storage costs $1.50 per bag for 24 hours.

GETTING AROUND

The first thing to remember is that the Pacific Ocean is south, not west, and the mountains surrounding Santa Barbara run east–west, not north–south. Most restaurants, shops, and nightspots are densely concentrated on **State Street,** so the easiest way to orient yourself downtown is by this street, which starts at Stearn's Wharf and runs north toward the town of Goleta, where it becomes Hollister Avenue. The beach and Stearn's Wharf are less than a mile from downtown; walking is the best and easiest way to get around.

About 3,000 giant blue whales (each approximately 100 ft long, 150 tons, and with a tongue heavier than an elephant) currently live off the coast of Santa Barbara.

BY BUS

All local bus routes pass through the **Transit Center** (1020 Chapala St., tel. 805/683–3702), which has information on routes and is open weekdays 6 AM–7 PM, Saturday 8–6, and Sunday 9–6. Buses run 6 AM–11:15 PM; fare is $1. Bus 5 travels to the Amtrak depot, while Buses 6 and 11 take you from the Amtrak depot to upper State Street's budget hotels. A convenient 25¢ shuttle travels daily along State Street between Stearn's Wharf and Sola Street downtown. Shuttles run daily 10–6 and until 8 PM on summer weekends; stops are marked SANTA BARBARA SHUTTLE.

For $4 you can get an all-day pass on the **Santa Barbara Trolley** (tel. 805/965–0353), which will whisk you up from Stearn's Wharf along State Street, through the city's main historical districts, out to the mission, and back to the beach. Tours run every 90 minutes from 10–4, and you can hop on and off at any stop.

WHERE TO SLEEP

Santa Barbara's Mediterranean climate draws a beach crowd year-round, and the city's hotels and motels are overpriced, especially during summer, when prices jump by $3–$30 (ouch!). If all the cheap lodgings are booked, you can usually find something affordable in **Carpinteria,** about 12 mi east. Try **Casa Del Sol Motel** (5585 Carpinteria Ave., tel. 805/684–4307), which charges about $40 for a single or double; or the **Reef Motel** (4160 Via Real, north of U.S. 101, tel. 805/684–4176), which has doubles for $40 ($46 for four people). To get to Carpinteria, take Santa Claus Lane exit from U.S. 101 or Bus 20 from Transit Center.

In Santa Barbara, upper State Street is where you'll find the cheap—and truly indistinguishable—motels. Prices fluctuate wildly depending on the season, but midweek you can almost always find singles in the $50–$70 range. On summer weekends, these same motels balloon to $125. If you want to be closer to the action downtown and on the beach, try to find something reasonable on lower State Street. If you're traveling in a pack of four, try the **Inn by the Harbor** (433 W. Montecito St., between U.S. 101 and Cabrillo Blvd., tel. 805/963–7851 or 800/626–1986), which has large, elegant, nonsmoking rooms just two blocks from the beach, complete with kitchens, beautiful furniture, and plenty of floor space. A couple pays $89 for a room with two queen beds (add $10 on weekends), but extra guests pay only $5, and everyone gets to frolic in the pool and spa. If you ask nicely, the manager may forego the extra-head charge.

UNDER $70 • Hotel State Street. This place is cursed with roaring noise from nearby train tracks, but for a spotless room, safe environment, and fantastic location, it's hard to beat. The friendly management charges $65 for double rooms with shared bath (knock off about $10 in winter). Continental breakfast is included. *121 State St., tel. 805/966–6586, fax 805/962–8459.*

UNDER $80 • Californian Hotel. This tall, ancient hotel is one block from the beach and a half block from the train tracks. When Amtrak thunders through at 2 AM you may go deaf, but the convenient locale makes up for the noise and the musty smell. Doubles start at $75 and soar to $125 (add $10 in summer). *35 State St. at Mason St., tel. 805/966–7153.*

DIRT CHEAP • Banana Bungalow International Hostel. Formerly a homeless shelter, this newly converted hostel is close to the beach but not particularly comfortable or hygienic. Beds cost $14–$18, depending on where you sleep. *210 E. Ortega St. at Santa Barbara St., tel. 805/963–0154 or 800/346–7835, fax 805/963–0184. 40 beds. Reception open 8 AM–midnight.*

CAMPING • Carpinteria State Beach. Twelve mi south of Santa Barbara, Carpinteria offers 262 tent and RV spaces on a dirt and grass area beside the beach. Sites ($14–$17) are close together, so privacy is a serious problem, as is the noise from both the highway and train tracks. Showers are available and a grocery store/restaurant is nearby. Crowds are a hassle during summer, so reserve through Destinet (tel. 800/444–7275). *U.S. 101, Carpinteria, tel. 805/684–2811. Bus 20 from Transit Center.*

El Capitan State Beach. Despite the shady palm trees and the pleasant beach nearby, the sardinelike conditions and 140 scraggly grass sites ($14–$18) are nearly enough to ruin El Capitan's appeal. Nonetheless, its location about 15 minutes north of Santa Barbara makes it more convenient than the campgrounds in the hills (*see below*). Showers and a grocery store (the latter open summer only) are on the premises. It's crowded most of the year and reservations (tel. 800/444–7275) are highly recommended. **Refugio State Beach,** 2½ mi north, has 82 sites indistinguishable from El Capitan. *El Capitan: U.S. 101 between Gaviota and Santa Barbara. Tel. for both: 805/968–3294.*

FOOD

The Mexican food stands on **Milpas Street** are popular with UCSB students; tacos and burritos go for less than $5. **El Escondido** (316 N. Milpas St., tel. 805/965–2690) is perhaps the best of the lot. On State Street authentic Mexican food can be found at **Don Pepe's** (617 State St., tel. 805/962–8072). Two can easily share a plate ($3–$7) that includes an entrée, refried beans, rice, and salad. Two weekly **farmers' markets** are good for stocking up on locally grown produce, flowers, and fish. The first is held on the 500 block of State Street Tuesday 3–7, the second at Cota and Santa Barbara streets Saturday 8–noon. For cheap eats, also try Isla Vista (*see* Near Santa Barbara, *below*).

UNDER $5 • Natural Café. On sunny afternoons (almost every day) the granola contingent overflows onto the street in front of yet another healthy place to grab a bite. Try a big, fresh salad ($4.75–$5.75) or a tofu hot dog ($4.50) with a shot of wheatgrass juice ($1). *508 State St. at Haley St., tel. 805/962–9494.*

UNDER $10 • Esau's Coffee Shop. Esau's serves up huge orders of the standards—eggs, hash browns, and pancakes—to a mixed crowd of surfers and old-timers for $4–$6. *403 State St., tel. 805/965–4416. Open for breakfast only.*

UNDER $20 • Palace Café. Businesspeople in suits and students in Birkenstocks coexist here peacefully, drawn by the best Cajun and Creole cuisine in Santa Barbara—perhaps in all of California. Try the Cajun popcorn shrimp ($9) or any of the fish dishes ($13–$25). Vegetarians will love the Mardi Gras Vegetarian Pasta Primavera ($9 half, $14 full). If you're daring, the Cajun martini is sure to sizzle your sinuses and put a spark in your step. For more moderate prices, look for the café's spin-off, **Palace Express,** in the food court of the Paseo Nuevo Mall (State St. at Chapala St., tel. 805/899–9111). *8 E. Cota St. off State St., tel. 805/966–3133. Open evenings only.*

CAFES

If you're tired of staring at tanned bodies and neon clothing, you might enjoy the more wan-faced crowd in Santa Barbara's cafés, most of which are concentrated downtown. There's live music Friday and Saturday nights, open-mic poetry Wednesday, scorching-hot tango on Sunday, and organic and decaf espresso drinks every evening at **Café Neruda** (22 W. Mission St. off State St., tel. 805/569–5977). The 24-hour **Hot Spots** (36 State St., ½ block from Stearn's Wharf, tel. 805/564–1637) plays host to students during the day, alterna-teens in the early evening, and boisterous travelers late at night—all sipping $1.90 cappuccinos. The **Santa Barbara Roasting Co.** (321 Motor Way at Gutierrez St., tel. 805/962–0320) is a real locals' spot. Voted the best coffeehouse in town five times in a row, this mellow place is hard to beat.

WORTH SEEING

Any tour of Santa Barbara should begin with a stroll down palm-lined **State Street,** packed to the hilt with boutiques, import shops, bookstores, restaurants, and cafés. The visitor center (*see* Basics, *above*) has a self-guided tour map covering historical sites downtown.

Santa Barbara's **Botanical Gardens** (1212 Mission Canyon Rd., tel. 805/682–4726) offers hundreds of trails and floral specimens for horticultural buffs willing to pay the $3 admission fee. Besides admiring the Joshua trees and redwoods, you can visit Mission Dam, constructed by the Chumash Indians in 1806. The mammoth **Moreton Bay Fig Tree** (Montecito and Chapala Sts.), transplanted from Australia in the late 1800s, is one of Santa Barbara's most striking sights. Check it out during the day, as its largely exposed root system makes it a popular homeless hangout at night.

Stearn's Wharf (Cabrillo and State Sts.), the oldest operating wharf on the West Coast, has one of the least touristed piers in California. Next to it are the aquariums and petting pools of the **Sea Center** (211 Stearn's Wharf, tel. 805/962–0885), a small hands-on museum that charges only $2 and is open daily at least noon–5. To the west of Stearn's Wharf lies the **Santa Barbara Yacht Harbor.** Walk to the end of its artificial breakwater for an outstanding view of the coast and shoreline. When you've had enough of the sights, head to **East Beach,** a wide, sweeping beach that rarely gets overcrowded—you can't miss it if you're at Stearn's Wharf.

MISSION SANTA BARBARA

One of the city's best attractions, Mission Santa Barbara is considered the crown jewel of California's missions. Built in 1786 with the "help" of the local Chumash people, this Spanish Renaissance structure has come to define the Santa Barbara architectural style with its red tile roof, orange adobe facade, and wrought-iron gates and fixtures. If you visit during Memorial Day weekend you can catch the *I Madonnari,* a three-day festival where internationally famous street artists, local artists, and children create elaborate chalk drawings in front of the mission. Visitors should keep in mind that this is a working mission, and tours are short for this reason. *Laguna St. at Los Olivos St., tel. 805/682–4713. Bus 22 from the Transit Center. Admission: $3. Open daily 9–5.*

COUNTY COURTHOUSE

The 114-ft tower provides a 360° view of the city, and the courthouse itself is full of ornate murals and elaborate Spanish tile work. You can wander around by yourself or take a free guided tour (call ahead for schedule). *Anapamu and Anacapa Sts., tel. 805/962–6464. Open weekdays 8–5, weekends 9–5.*

MUSEUM OF ART

A modest collection of French impressionists and German expressionists—Monet to Kandinsky—are on display here, as well as classical Greek and Roman sculptures. *1130 State St., tel. 805/963–4364. Admission: $4; free Thurs. and first Sun. of month. Open Tues.–Sat. 11–5 (Thurs. until 9), Sun. noon–5.*

CHEAP THRILLS

Sunday between 10 AM and 4 PM, dozens of artisans display their wares on the boardwalk running along **East Beach.** Then at sunset on Sunday, a mellow drumming circle comes together at **Palm Park** (east of Stearn's Wharf, near Red Lion's Resort). You can occasionally catch a free concert at **De la Guerra Plaza** between State and Anacapa streets. Also, on summer Sundays at 3 PM, free concerts take place at **Alameda Park** (corner Anacapa and Micheltorena Sts.).

The old pioneer towns of Santa Ynez and Los Olivos are 50 mi northwest of town on Hwy 154. Any local gas station or market can provide you with a free map of the region's eight wineries, which are best known for their chardonnays. North of Los Olivos off U.S. 101, **Firestone Vineyard** (5017 Zaca Station Rd., 2 mi west of U.S. 101, tel. 805/688–3940), one of California's largest, offers free tours, wine tasting, and a grassy picnic area. It's open daily 10–5. If you're feeling a bit wacky, hop in your car to get to **Santa Claus Lane** (U.S. 101, ½ mi west of Carpinteria), one of the strangest "theme malls" in the country—sun, surf, sand, and Christmas year-round—a symbol of California's determination to have it all.

FESTIVALS

On the Saturday closest to June 21, the **Summer Solstice Celebration** (tel. 805/965–3396) kicks off, giving Santa Barbara's fringe element a chance to let loose. Unlike their Northern California counterparts who take to the mountains indulging in all the fresh air and meditation a person can handle, these lunatics parade the streets in wildly provocative costumes celebrating the longest day of the year. No cars or promotional posters are permitted—just processions of people dressed in bizarre costumes, some dancing or performing short plays. At the end of the parade there's food and live music in one of the local parks.

Every summer, usually in July, thousands of people head to the beach for the **Sandcastle and Sculpting Contest** (tel. 805/965–0509), where artists from around the world make outlandish sand creations. Dates change each summer, so call for details. The **Old Spanish Days Fiesta** (tel. 805/962–8101) is a big event in early August—five days of celebrating Santa Barbara's Spanish and Mexican heritage. Highlights include a carnival, free music, parades, vociferous street vendors, and lots of beer. On the last day of the Fiesta, locals grab their old beach cruisers and take over the streets en masse. If you want to partake in this annual tradition, meet at Stearn's Wharf at 11 AM. In unofficial honor of the god of guacamole, the **California Avocado Festival** (tel. 805/684–0038) is held every October in Carpinteria. For two fun-filled days, exotic avocado concoctions are featured along with art exhibits and entertainment. Call for precise dates.

AFTER DARK

Santa Barbara has a lively nightlife. The action centers around lower State Street, where most bars feature live music—rock, reggae, folk, or funk—every weekend and often weekdays as well. For an events calendar, pick up a copy of *The Independent,* the county's free weekly, at any café or bookstore.

Live bands (cover free–$12) play Tuesday–Sunday at **Toe's Tavern** (416 State St. at Haley St., tel. 805/965–4655)—your basic sand and surf extravaganza. At Caribbean-inspired **Calypso Bar and Grill** (514 State St., between Cota and Haley Sts., tel. 805/966–1388) there's live jazz and blues two nights a week, dance music weekend nights, and other types of tunes every other day. No cover Sunday–Wednesday; about $2 other nights. A historic landmark, **Joe's Café** (536 State St., tel. 805/966–4638) is revered for its deadly stiff drinks and down-home charm. Joe's attracts all sorts, from locals to tourists to UCSB students. **Mel's** (6 W. De la Guerra St., in the Paseo Nuevo Mall, tel. 805/963–2211) is filled with some of Santa Barbara's grittiest barflies. Wild man Hunter S. Thompson used to hang out in Mel's back booth.

Fathom (423 State St., between Gutierrez and Haley Sts., tel. 805/730–0022 or 805/882–2082 for recorded club information) is the hottest dance spot around, gay, lesbian, whatever. Don't miss their famous drag shows. Sunday evening brings the gut-busting Barbecue and Beer Bust—all you can eat and drink for $5.

OUTDOOR ACTIVITIES

HIKING

There are hundreds of great walks in and around Santa Barbara. Close to downtown, one of the best trails takes you up a creek bed to a series of swimming holes and a seven-tier waterfall aptly known as **Seven Falls.** Although the falls dry up following less rainy winters, the pools remain year-round. To reach this choice spot, drive east on Mission Street, turn right on Foothill Road, veer left onto Mission Canyon Road and left at the next fork onto Tunnel Road; from the end of the road, follow the paved path to the bridge and either climb up the rocks for about 20 minutes or keep going on the path to the end. The walk takes 45 minutes to an hour.

BIKING/IN-LINE SKATING

Whether you like to pedal along the coast or in the hills, you're in for a treat in Santa Barbara. Aside from the boardwalk and the hiking trail listed above, which are both open to bikers, there's the short (about 2½ mi) bluffside dirt trail in Isla Vista (*see* Near Santa Barbara, *below*) and all sorts of fire roads off Hwy. 154 (San Marcos Pass Rd.). **Beach Rentals** (22 State St., tel. 805/966–6733) is the best place to rent cruisers ($6 an hour, $24 a day) or mountain bikes ($7 an hour, $26 a day). It also rents in-line skates ($5 an hour, $15 per day). Bladers take off along the boardwalk and also skate from the end of Modoc Road in Goleta along the path to UCSB.

OCEAN ACTIVITIES

SURFING

The most popular break near Santa Barbara—if not on the whole Central Coast—is **Rincon,** 3 mi south of Carpinteria on Hwy. 1. Outside Rincon, you'll find better surfing in Isla Vista (*see below*) than in Santa Barbara, at spots like **Sands Beach** near the end of the UCSB campus. **Beach House** (10 State St., tel. 805/963–1281) rents boards ($21 a half-day) and will provide wet suits.

BEACHES

Bask in the sunshine, stomp around barefoot, build a sandcastle, heck, take a dip—this is why you came here. **Leadbetter Beach,** between Shoreline and Loma Alto drives, has a secluded cove, making it an ideal spot to picnic, surf, or windsurf. **Isla Vista Beach** (Del Playa Dr. at Camino Corto) offers low-tide walks to UCSB and excellent bird-watching. For swimming, **East Beach** (on Cabrillo Blvd.) is popular and has lifeguards on duty as well as volleyball courts, picnic tables, and boogie board rentals. The less-crowded **Goleta Beach** boasts similar amenities to East beach.

WHALE-WATCHING

For the past 20 years, humpback and blue whales have been coming to the coast of California during the summer months. If you'd like to catch a glimpse of these majestic creatures as they feed off the coast of Santa Rosa and San Miguel Islands (*see* Channel Islands, *below*), hop on board with **Captain Don's Whale Watching and Coastal Cruises** (tel. 805/969–5217 for reservations). Tours (2½ hrs) cost $24 for adults and leave twice daily at 9 and noon from Stearn's Wharf, June–September. A 40-minute narrated boat ride around Santa Barbara Harbor, including a visit with local sea lions, is only $10 noon–6 weekdays and 11–6 weekends, June–September.

For a sense of how difficult student life is at U.C. Santa Barbara, check out the main library—it's got ocean views and a third-floor sun deck.

NEAR SANTA BARBARA

ISLA VISTA

Built in the 1950s on the site of a military complex used in World War II, the University of California at Santa Barbara (UCSB) is perched on a bluff overlooking the Pacific Ocean, 12 mi west of downtown Santa Barbara, dominating the town of Isla Vista. It's one of the country's few institutions of higher learning with its own surfing beach, known as Campus Point. The campus sits right on the ocean, and its enticing lawns, lagoon, and sandstone buildings are pleasant, if not exactly inspiring.

Much more interesting than the UCSB campus is the town of Isla Vista (known to locals as I.V.), packed to the gills with thousands of raucous students. In the center of town, **Anisq'oyo Park** (near El Colegio Rd.) is the site of often excellent free concerts on spring and fall weekends and a good place for a picnic otherwise. On weekend nights during the school year, the town lives up to its unfortunate reputation as a mindless party town: around **Del Playa Street,** at all hours, bleary-eyed students stumble from one kegger to the next.

To reach UCSB from Santa Barbara, take U.S. 101 north to Los Carneros Road, head south (toward the ocean) 1 mi, then turn left on El Colegio Road and right on Embarcadero del Mar, a U-shape street that serves as I.V.'s main drag. Otherwise, take Bus 24 (25 min) from the Transit Center in Santa Barbara.

FOOD • I.V. has some great cheap eats. At any time of the day or night at **Freebird's** (879 Embarcadero del Norte, tel. 805/968–0123), you can gorge yourself on fat breakfast burritos with beans, potatoes, salsa, and eggs for 95¢–$1.50. For lunch or dinner try the famous Monster Chicken burrito ($4.50), or—if you have two or three people—the Super Monster ($7.50). Also popular is the pizza at **Woodstock's** (928 Embarcadero del Norte, tel. 805/968–6969). The I.V. crowd takes its java on the sun-drenched patio of **Espresso Roma** (6521 Pardall St., tel. 805/968–5101).

AFTER DARK • If you're looking for a game of pool or a bite to eat, head over to **I.V. Beer Co.** (935 Embarcadero del Norte, tel. 805/961–4488), with live music provided by mostly local talent once a week (occasional $2 cover after 9 PM).

LOS PADRES NATIONAL FOREST

Inland from Santa Barbara lies over 211 mi of trails with opportunities for day hiking, horseback riding, mountain biking, fishing, rock climbing, backpacking, and camping within the Ojai Ranger District of the Los Padres National Forest. The terrain varies wildly from the densely covered chaparral foothills to the high bluffs of Nordhoff Ridge to the distinctive sandstone formations that comprise Piedra Blanca. The **Ojai Ranger District** (1190 E. Ojai Ave., tel. 805/646–4348), open weekdays 8–4:30, has topo maps, books, handouts, postcards, permits, and a wealth of information on the local area. Pick up a free trail map here before setting out; it outlines hikes of varying degrees for the entire area. If you're looking for an easy day hike, try the **Potrero John Trail.** This easy 1.6-mi (one-way) trail follows a stream channel into the Sespé Wilderness. The trail begins on Hwy. 33 just north of the Beaver campground. For a longer hike, try the **Matilija Canyon Trail.** This trek (8 mi one-way) is appropriate for a day trip or as an overnighter. To find the trailhead, drive 27.1 mi down Hwy. 33 and turn left on the rough dirt road up to Cherry Canyon. The trail starts at the southern section of the parking area at the ridge top. Be sure to bring plenty of water. All water from streams must be treated.

Also in the Los Padres National Forest is the sagebrush- and oak-covered hills of the **Santa Ynez Recreation Area,** rife with 21 mi of excellent trails. At the end of Paradise Road, the **Red Rock Trail** winds along and across the Santa Ynez River for 3½ mi—past rocky enclaves and some exceptional swimming holes—to the Gibraltar Dam. For a steeper climb, follow the **Santa Cruz Trail** for 6½ mi through oak and pine trees to the Happy Hollow campground on Little Pine Mountain, a beautiful spot to spend the night (pack your own water). To reach Los Padres, take U.S. 101 north to Hwy. 154 (San Marcos Pass Rd.) and turn right on Paradise Road. For more trail recommendations, call the Santa Barbara Ranger District office (tel. 805/967–3481).

CAMPING • There are five designated campgrounds on Paradise Road in the forest outside of Santa Barbara, as well as unlimited acres of free camping, a perk available at all national forests. If you're looking for privacy and want to head out on your own, take U.S. 101 north to Hwy. 154 (San Marcos Pass Rd.), turn right on East Camino Cielo Road, follow it to the Santa Ynez Recreation Area, and pick a spot—it's bare as a bone but free. Check with the ranger station before you head out—you will need a visitor's permit if you intend to camp outside a designated campsite. Fire permits are also required in nondesignated campsites during fire season and in high risk areas. Permits are free and can be obtained through the **Forest Supervisor's Office** (6144 Calle Real, Goleta, tel. 805/683–6711) or any of the five ranger district offices. Bring plenty of water; no potable water is available outside designated sites and any stream water must be treated.

For the next step up, continue on Hwy. 154 to Paradise Road, hang a right, and follow the signs to the designated campgrounds ($8). These all have picnic tables and fire pits on the site and flush toilets and potable water. The 15 sites at **Paradise** are ugly and crammed too close for comfort, but they're the most popular. Most secluded are the 25 spacious sites at **Upper Oso.** Whatever your pleasure, you'll be surrounded by the Santa Ynez Mountains and more scrub brush than you ever imagined. Arrive early at the designated sites; they fill up fast. *Tel. 800/280–3267 for reservations.*

CHUMASH PAINTED CAVE STATE PARK • In the Los Padres National Forest, 12 mi northwest of Santa Barbara, this state park houses the faded remains of centuries-old Chumash cave paintings. A locked metal screen keeps you from actually entering the cave, and the lack of light makes viewing the paintings a bit difficult, but you can still make out the colorful animal figures and decorative designs from outside. While anthropology buffs may get excited over this, few others will. *Take U.S. 101 north to Hwy. 154 (San Marcos Pass Rd.), turn right on Painted Cave Rd. However, this road is often subject to closures; when this happens, continue north on Hwy. 154 to San Marcos Summit. At the summit, take East Camino Cielo Rd. to Painted Cave Rd. Admission free.*

OJAI

Hidden away in a shallow, oak-lined valley about 40 mi southeast of Santa Barbara, Ojai (say it: "Oh, hi!") is a quintessentially Californian community: hot, scenic, laid-back, and populated by an eclectic mix of beautiful people. Here, affluent made-it-in-L.A.-and-moved-to-the-country types drive $60,000 Range Rovers from their ranch-style homes to the town's posh mineral baths, while New Agers ramble around town in road-worn VW Beetles on their way to the **Krotona Institute** (off Hwy. 33, south end of town, tel. 805/646–2653)—the largest theophilosophical library on the West Coast—or the **Krishnamurti Library** (1130 McAndrew Rd., tel. 805/646–4948), closed Mondays, part of a complex dedicated to the teachings of the eponymous Indian spiritual leader.

Even those who have trouble finding their third eye will enjoy **Bart's Books** (302 W. Matilija St. at Canada St., tel. 805/646–3755), a sprawling outdoor bookstall filled with thousands of used paperbacks. You can soak up some culture at the studios of local artists willing to expose their work to the uninitiated public; check the listings of open studios at the **Ojai Visitor Center** (150 W. Ojai Ave. at Blanch St., tel. 805/646–8126). If you find your stomach growling after dizzying discussions of chiaroscuro or color harmonies, head to the **Ojai Café Emporium** (108 S. Montgomery St., tel. 805/646–2723), which serves vegetable lasagna ($6) in its large outdoor patio. One of the best things about Ojai is the drive into town. From U.S. 101 south of Santa Barbara, follow Hwy. 150 for 20 mi past vast orchards, wooded hills, wide valleys, and Lake Casitas; then turn north on Hwy. 33 (Maricopa Hwy.) and go 2 mi.

Ojai Farm Hostel. On an organic fruit farm 10 minutes from Ojai, this charming hostel offers 12 beds ($12) in two sex-separated, air-conditioned dorms. The friendly management graciously shares the various fruits from the trees with visitors. There are six bicycles available for use at no charge to guests, and they can give you directions for hikes to some of Ojai's more elusive hot springs. A foreign passport is required to stay in this strictly nonsmoking hostel, and cooking in the kitchen is limited to the preparation of vegetarian meals. Call the hostel from downtown, and they'll either pick you up or guide you back. Reservations are advised. *Box 723, Ojai, CA 93024, tel. 805/646–0311. Free pick-up from Ventura Greyhound and sometimes Amtrak. Reception open 7 AM – 10 PM.*

The Albinger Archaeological Museum was a muffler shop until Chumash arrowheads were discovered in the backyard.

VENTURA AND THE CHANNEL ISLANDS

Halfway between Santa Barbara and Los Angeles is the unassuming town of **Ventura,** a beachside community being slowly engulfed by tract homes and mini-malls. At least Main Street and the historic downtown area—with a mission, museums, and plentiful thrift shops—retain some charm. For maps and information, stop by the **visitors' bureau** (89C S. California St. off Main St., tel. 805/648–2075 or 800/333–2989). The **San Buenaventura Mission** (enter through gift shop at 225 Main St., tel. 805/643–4318) and tiny adjacent **museum** ($1) are located near the most interesting sight downtown, the **Albinger Archaeological Museum** (113 E. Main St., tel. 805/648–5823), open Wednesday–Sunday 10–4 (winters until 2). The museum features artifacts from over 200 years of the area's history. Ventura's raison d'être, though, is its endless miles of wide sandy beaches; at the end of California Street you'll find **Main Beach,** complete with a pier, surfers, and sun worshipers. For food and drink, **Bombay Bar & Grill** (143 S. California St., between Thompson and Santa Clara Sts., tel. 805/643–4404) has a full bar with happy-hour specials weekdays 5–8 and serves burgers and veggie fare in the $4–$7 range.

Island Packers (1867 Spinnaker Dr., tel. 805/642–1393 or 805/642–7688 for recorded information) runs eco-conscious excursions from the Ventura harbor to the **Channel Islands,** one of California's least accessible and most pristine wildlife preserves. Most trips include guided walks with knowledgeable naturalists. Day trips start at $37, while overnight trips for those who want to camp on the islands start at $48. The island chain is situated where the warm waters of the tropics meet the cold waters of the Arctic, creating an exceptional breeding ground for a myriad of plants and animals. Visitors who make their way out here will find 25 types of sharks, 27 species of whales and porpoises, five kinds of sea lions and seals, and one of the largest populations of brown pelicans in the world. The Channel Islands also contain ruins of Paleolithic villages, considered by some to be the oldest settlements of this type in North America. Primitive camping is allowed—and free—on any of the five islands except Santa Cruz, but you need a permit from park headquarters. For maps and information contact the visitor center at **Channel Islands National Park Headquarters** (1901 Spinnaker Dr., Ventura Harbor, tel. 805/658–5730), open daily 8–5:30 from Memorial Day to Labor Day and daily 8:30–4:30 off-season.

Anacopa is the closest island at only 14 mi from Ventura. Most visitors head to East Anacopa Island, where there is a small visitor center. Picnicking, diving at Cathedral Cove, and camping are all permitted on the eastern island. Visitors during the months of January through March should keep an eye out for gray whales. On Middle Anacopa Island, divers can check out the wreckage of the steamer *Winfield Scott,* which sank in 1853. West Anacopa Island is home to a research-natural area dedicated to protecting the endangered brown pelican. **Santa Cruz,** at 24 mi long the largest of the islands, once housed the Chumash Indians for over 6,000 years. Home to steep cliffs, enormous sea caves, and sandy shores, Santa Cruz is unfortunately one of the most complicated islands to reach; you need a permit to land unless you are on an authorized boat trip. **Santa Rosa** is the best island for serious hikers and birdwatchers, but obtain a backcountry permit before venturing beyond the beach.

U.S. 101

If you choose to make your trip from San Francisco to Los Angeles on U.S. 101, you'll find yourself in a long agricultural valley flanked by rolling hills, some of which you drive through on the southernmost portion of the journey. Along the way you'll pass a series of small towns and minor attractions, none—save Pinnacles National Monument—true destinations in themselves but some worthy of a quick stop.

All of the small towns along the way have heaps of cheap motels; get off at any highway exit marked LODGING and you should find a decent double for less than $40. One of the best overnight stops is San Luis Obispo (*see* The Central Coast Drive, *above*), about halfway into the drive. There are also a few places to camp, most in the vicinity of Pinnacles National Monument. Bring picnic supplies: Along the road you'll see some fast-food chains but little else in the way of nourishment.

If you pass by at the right time of year, you can gorge yourself at one of the region's agricultural festivals. Best known is the **Garlic Festival** (tel. 408/842–1625) held each July in Gilroy, 35 mi south of San Jose and 27 mi north of Salinas. One of the largest crop-oriented events in the country, the festival draws garlic lovers from all over California. Taste the garlic-based foods and drinks (including free garlic ice cream) or try bathing with garlic soaps and shampoos. Greenfield, a tiny town between Salinas and Soledad, hosts a **Broccoli Festival** (tel. 408/674–3222) each Labor Day. To the south, Templeton (between Paso Robles and Atascadero) is the site of a small **Apple Festival** (Cider Creek Farms, tel. 805/238–5634) every October. Finally—and perhaps juiciest of all—the **Strawberry Festival** (tel. 805/489–1488) is held on Memorial Day weekend in Arroyo Grande, a small farming town between San Luis Obispo and Santa Maria.

COMING AND GOING

As usual, the easiest way to make the seven- to eight-hour trip between San Francisco and Los Angeles on U.S. 101 is by car; if you don't have one, consider renting (*see* Coming and Going *in* Chapter 1). **Greyhound** runs daily buses from San Francisco to Salinas (2½–4 hrs, $15 one-way) and to Paso Robles (5 hrs, $20 one-way). From Los Angeles the trip to Salinas takes about six hours ($34 one-way), six–eight hours to Paso Robles ($32 one-way).

SALINAS

Driving U.S. 101 south from San Francisco or San Jose, the first major town you hit is Salinas, famed for its bountiful fields of lettuce and cabbage. However, what really put Salinas on the map was not its greenery but the success of native son John Steinbeck, the Pulitzer Prize–winning author of *Grapes of Wrath* and countless other novels and short stories, many of which use central California as a backdrop. The three small Steinbeck sights in town are all moderately interesting. The **Steinbeck Room** (350 Lincoln Ave., tel. 408/758–7311)—part of a public library, closed Sunday—contains photos, an original manuscript, and some of the author's personal items. The **Steinbeck House** (132 Central Ave., tel. 408/424–2735), where the man himself was born, has been turned into a restaurant that serves lunch (at 11:45 and 1:15) for $7.50, dessert for $3; open Tuesday–Saturday, the price also includes a tour. Call to make sure they're not hosting a group on the day you want to visit. True fans should also check out the **Steinbeck Center Foundation** (371 Main St., tel. 408/753–6411), where several displays map out his life and work. The foundation also puts on a **Steinbeck Festival** the first weekend of August; popular among California's literati, the $5 registration gets you into as many lectures and movies about Steinbeck as you can stomach.

Experience the culinary expertise of the local Mexican American community at **Rosita's Armory Café** (231 Salinas St., tel. 408/424–7039), where $5–$7 will buy you a tasty plate of rice, beans, salad, and an entrée. To sample some of the famed local produce, head to a roadside stand on the outskirts of town along Hwy. 146 (a few can also be found along U.S. 101); not only are prices lower, but the stuff's grown 50 yards from the stand—deliciously fresh.

PINNACLES NATIONAL MONUMENT

Pinnacles National Monument is a rocky outpost in the middle of the San Joaquin Valley, full of wickedly jagged spires (some over 600 ft high). Foot trails (of varying difficulties) and dark caves wind through the remnants of an ancient volcano. Although most trails are not long (1–5 mi), they are steep and exposed—

not pleasant in the hot summer sun. If you do visit in summer, be sure to hike only in the early morning or late afternoon. But the best time to come to Pinnacles is definitely in spring, when the weather is moderate and the valley surrounding the monument blooms with colorful wildflowers. The west entrance to Pinnacles is accessed from U.S. 101, via Soledad and King City (follow signs); the east entrance via Hwy. 25 from Hollister.

You can't drive from the west side of Pinnacles to the east—only hiking trails connect the two entrances. There's an entrance fee of $4. There is a **visitor center** (tel. 408/389–4485) on the east side and a helpful **ranger station** on the west, and both sides have campgrounds (*see below*). There are no concessions in the park, so pack a cooler and lots of water. Those in the know claim that the west side has better hiking through the lava formations, while the east side is the place for cave exploration. The 5-mi **High Peaks Loop,** which takes you through the remnants of an extinct volcano to the Pinnacles formations, can be accessed from the east on **Condor Gulch Trail** and from the west on **Juniper Canyon Trail.** The round-trip takes three–four hours. Both trailheads are near the parking lots.

Experienced rock climbers will have a great time scrambling up any one of the oddly named climbing areas. The closest climbs are on **Tourist Trap** from the eastern Bear Gulch side (a 10-min walk up Moses Spring Trail) and from the west on **Passion Play** and **Game Show.** Don't attempt the **Balconies,** a massive shelf perched 200 ft off the valley floor, unless you know what you're doing. For bouldering head to **Discovery Wall** on the Bear Gulch side. Those who have only climbed on granite should give themselves some time to get used to climbing on softer volcanic rock. Before you do anything, be sure to stop by the ranger station to pick up topo maps. Some formations may be closed January–July to protect the nesting area of falcons and hawks. While these closures are voluntary, if you ignore them and end up disturbing nesting birds or other wildlife, you will likely be fined.

James Dean died in a car crash in 1955 at the junction of Hwys. 41 and 46 east of Paso Robles. A nearby memorial reads, "Death in youth is life that glows eternal."

WHERE TO SLEEP

Two campgrounds serve Pinnacles, a private one at the east entrance and a public one just inside the west entrance on Hwy. 146. Sites at both places are first-come, first-served, but the privately run campground to the east has more sites, more facilities, and—most importantly—more shade. The public one, **Pinnacles National Monument Chaparral Campground** (tel. 408/389–4485), charges $10 per night for each of 18 desolate sites set in scrub with about enough tree cover for a field mouse. There are no showers. This place is closed for camping on weekends from Presidents' Day to Memorial Day, when the campsites are reserved for use as picnic areas.

Shady trees, a small creek, a pool, and showers make **Pinnacles Campground, Inc.** (408/389–4462) the better choice for campers. The 78 tent sites go for $6 per person, with a $24-per-site maximum. A small market on the premises is good for stocking up on bare necessities. Off Hwy. 146, drive five minutes from east entrance.

PASO ROBLES

Midway between Los Angeles and San Francisco, an hour north of San Luis Obispo, Paso Robles is one of California's fastest growing winery towns, with over 20 wineries in a 2-mi radius. One of the oldest and most attractive is **York Mountain** (7 mi west on Hwy. 46, from U.S. 101, 1½ mi north on York Mountain Rd., tel. 805/238–3925), with a dark, musty cellar and a wonderfully atmospheric tasting room ($1 per person). The region is primarily known for its red wines, especially zinfandel.

Between November and March, bald and golden eagles come to **Lake San Antonio,** west of U.S. 101 between King City and Paso Robles, to escape the winters of northern California. You can picnic on the shore (day-use fee $6) and watch the rare creatures wing their way into the great unknown, or you can take a boat tour with the county parks department (tel. 805/472–2311 for information and reservations) for close-up views of the massive birds. Overdeveloped camping with plenty of shade is available on the south shore of the lake, and shadeless, more secluded sites sit right on the shore on the north side; all sites are $16), with drinking water, toilets, and showers. To reach the lake from the north, take the Jolon Rd. exit (north of King City) west for 40 mi and follow signs; from the south take the Nacimiento and San Antonio Lakes exit (in Paso Robles) west for 30 mi.

9

LOS ANGELES

UPDATED BY JEANNE FAY

Los Angeles: land of 24-hour celebrity coverage, drive-through sushi bars, *Baywatch* fantasies, and macabre Charles Manson and Nicole Brown Simpson realities. The 44 Spanish, native, and black settlers who founded El Pueblo de la Reina de Los Angeles on September 4, 1781, were cajoled into moving from northern Mexico by the Spanish crown's promise of free land, cash, and cows. More than 200 years later, their peaceful farming community has exploded into an unbounded megalopolis of more than 15 million people speaking some 120 tongues. This is the second-largest city in the United States, and it's still spreading into new suburbs like a low-budget Hollywood *Blob.* If you ask for a map of Los Angeles, you'll probably get something that includes most of Southern California. Within these vague boundaries exists a mixture of people of diverse origins, wealth, and outlooks. Just consider the city's main districts: Hollywood, Watts, Beverly Hills, South Central, Bel Air, Malibu.

The last few years have not been kind to Los Angeles. After enduring massive wildfires attributed to arsonists, heavy rains followed by mud slides, and renewed racial friction as police officers acquitted of beating black motorist Rodney King faced retrial, the last thing Angelenos needed was the 6.7-magnitude earthquake of January 17, 1994, which caused more than $10 billion in damage—Angelenos are still paying off debts incurred from rebuilding costs, and many still break into a cold sweat at the slightest temblor. Los Angeles's arid climate, inadequate drainage systems, and spider's web of earthquake faults make it fertile breeding ground for natural disasters. Malibu alone has endured an apocalyptic cycle of fires, mud slides, and floods in the 1990s, yet locals remain fiercely loyal to this paradisiacal enclave.

But Los Angeles's faults, geological and otherwise, should not deter you from visiting. For every tale of smog and traffic, there's a story of wide beaches, mild climate, superb museums, outrageously varied and bizarre nightlife, and, hey, surfboards for rent. Move beyond the tourist strips of Hollywood Boulevard, Universal Studios, and the Santa Monica Pier and you'll be rewarded; master the grid of freeways and avenues and you'll find an adventure. True Angelenos are used to traveling long distances in search of the coolest nightspot (heading to Malibu for dinner, Venice for drinks, West Hollywood for dancing, and Santa Monica for a snack), and visitors must be prepared to follow suit. It'll sneak up on you, to be sure, but one morning you just might wake up and realize that you're addicted.

BASICS

Due to the increasing number of phone lines, faxes, cellular phones, and people in L.A., there is an ever-growing need for new area codes. The new code 562 serves Long Beach, and in mid-1998 L.A. will introduce another area code for the city proper—downtown will remain 213, but the rest of the city will change to 323.

AMERICAN EXPRESS

American Express has seven offices in Los Angeles County, where cardmembers may cash personal or traveler's checks and replace lost or stolen cards. *Downtown: 901 W. 7th St., at S. Figueroa St., tel. 213/627–4800. Open weekdays 8–6. Midtown: 8493 W. 3rd St., at La Cienega, tel. 310/659–1682; open weekdays 9–6, Sat. 10–5.*

GAY AND LESBIAN RESOURCES

Los Angeles has a large and out bisexual, lesbian, and gay population, particularly in Hollywood and West Hollywood. The **Gay and Lesbian Community Services Center** (1625 N. Schrader Blvd., 4 blocks west of Vine St., tel. 213/993–7400, fax 213/993–7699), in Hollywood, offers information on community events, civil rights advocacy, a 24-bed youth shelter, and support groups for youths and adults every Monday through Saturday 9 AM–10 PM and Sunday 10–6. Anyone can stop by for free HIV testing or to visit the center's STD clinic. Report hate crimes to the **Anti-Violence Project** (tel. 213/993–7670).

Gay people can find news, essays, political cartoons, roommate listings, and the lowdown on what's up in the city's numerous gay-oriented weeklies and microzines, available in bookstores and cafés, particularly in West Hollywood. Among the most widely distributed are *Edge, Frontiers, Planet Homo,* and *Spunk.* Women should also check out the *Lesbian News, Female FYI* and *L.A. Girl Guide.* The *Gay and Lesbian Times* covers events and issues in Los Angeles and San Diego.

MEDICAL AID

The **Los Angeles Free Clinic** (8405 Beverly Blvd., between Fairfax Avenue and La Cienega Boulevard., tel. 213/653–1990) provides free general medical services. Call weekdays 9 AM–11 AM for a same-day appointment. The **rape hotline** in the Los Angeles area is 310/392–8381. The **suicide prevention hotline** is 213/381–5111.

PUBLICATIONS

The *Los Angeles Times* (25¢, Sunday $1.50), widely considered the West Coast's best newspaper, is especially valuable on Sunday: The "Calendar" section contains a trove of entertainment information. For slightly hipper, up-to-the-minute entertainment listings, pick up a copy of *L.A. Weekly* or *New Times,* both free weeklies available at cafés, supermarkets, and bookstores; new issues hit the stands on Thursday. *L.A. Weekly* is the more comprehensive.

VISITOR INFORMATION

The **Los Angeles Convention and Visitors Bureau** maintains two convenient offices, both with multilingual staff members. Get free brochures, low-priced city maps, and an abbreviated but invaluable list of city bus routes at the downtown branch (stuffed in the Omni Hotel) or the **Hollywood Visitor Information Center** (in a much nicer mansion on Janes House Square). *Downtown: 685 S. Figueroa St., between Wilshire Blvd. and 7th St., tel. 213/689–8822. Open weekdays 8–5, Sat. 8:30–5. Hollywood: 6541 Hollywood Blvd., near Hudson Ave., tel. 213/236–2331; open Mon.–Sat. 9–5.*

If you're concentrating on the coast, you may want to drop by the **Santa Monica Visitors Center,** north of the pier in Palisades Park. The staff has route information for the "Big Blue Bus" (*see* Getting Around, *below*) and special events. *1400 Ocean Ave., between Broadway and Santa Monica Blvd., tel. 310/393–7593. Open summer, daily 10–5; winter, daily 10–4.*

LOS ANGELES

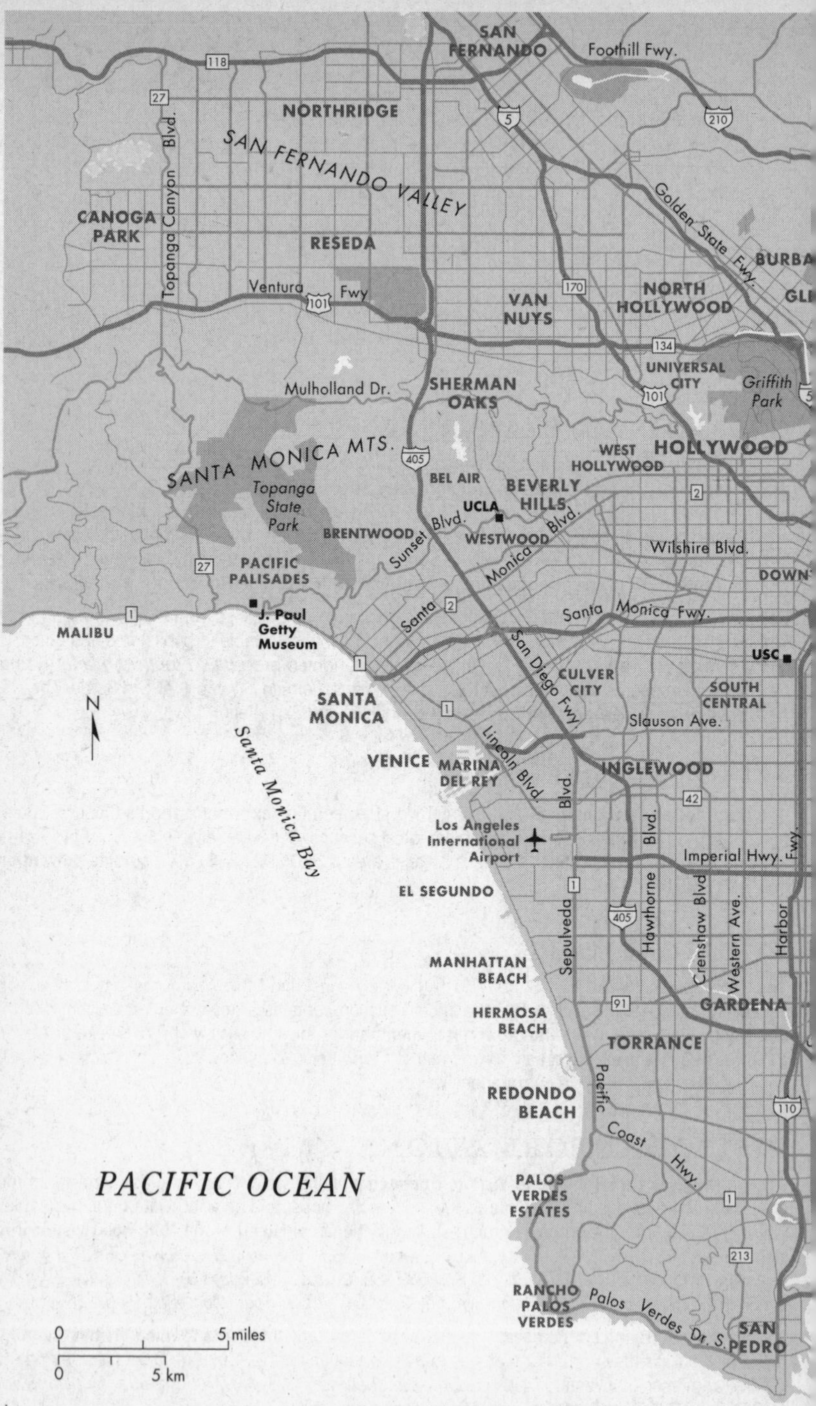

SAN FERNANDO
Foothill Fwy.
118
27
5
210
NORTHRIDGE
SAN FERNANDO VALLEY
Topanga Canyon Blvd.
CANOGA PARK
RESEDA
Golden State Fwy.
BURBA
GLE
Ventura Fwy.
101
170
VAN NUYS
NORTH HOLLYWOOD
134
UNIVERSAL CITY
Griffith Park
Mulholland Dr.
SHERMAN OAKS
101
SANTA MONICA MTS.
405
WEST HOLLYWOOD
HOLLYWOOD
Topanga State Park
BEL AIR
BEVERLY HILLS
2
UCLA
Sunset Blvd.
BRENTWOOD
WESTWOOD
Monica Blvd.
Wilshire Blvd.
PACIFIC PALISADES
27
DOWNT
Santa
2
Santa Monica Fwy.
1
MALIBU
J. Paul Getty Museum
San Diego Fwy.
USC
1
CULVER CITY
SOUTH CENTRAL
SANTA MONICA
1
Slauson Ave.
N
Santa Monica Bay
VENICE
MARINA DEL REY
Lincoln Blvd.
INGLEWOOD
42
Los Angeles International Airport
Blvd.
Imperial Hwy.
Fwy.
1
EL SEGUNDO
405
Sepulveda
Hawthorne Blvd.
Crenshaw Blvd
Western Ave.
Harbor
MANHATTAN BEACH
91
HERMOSA BEACH
GARDENA
TORRANCE
Pacific Coast Hwy.
REDONDO BEACH
110
PACIFIC OCEAN
PALOS VERDES ESTATES
1
213
RANCHO PALOS VERDES
Palos Verdes Dr. S.
SAN PEDRO
0 5 miles
0 5 km

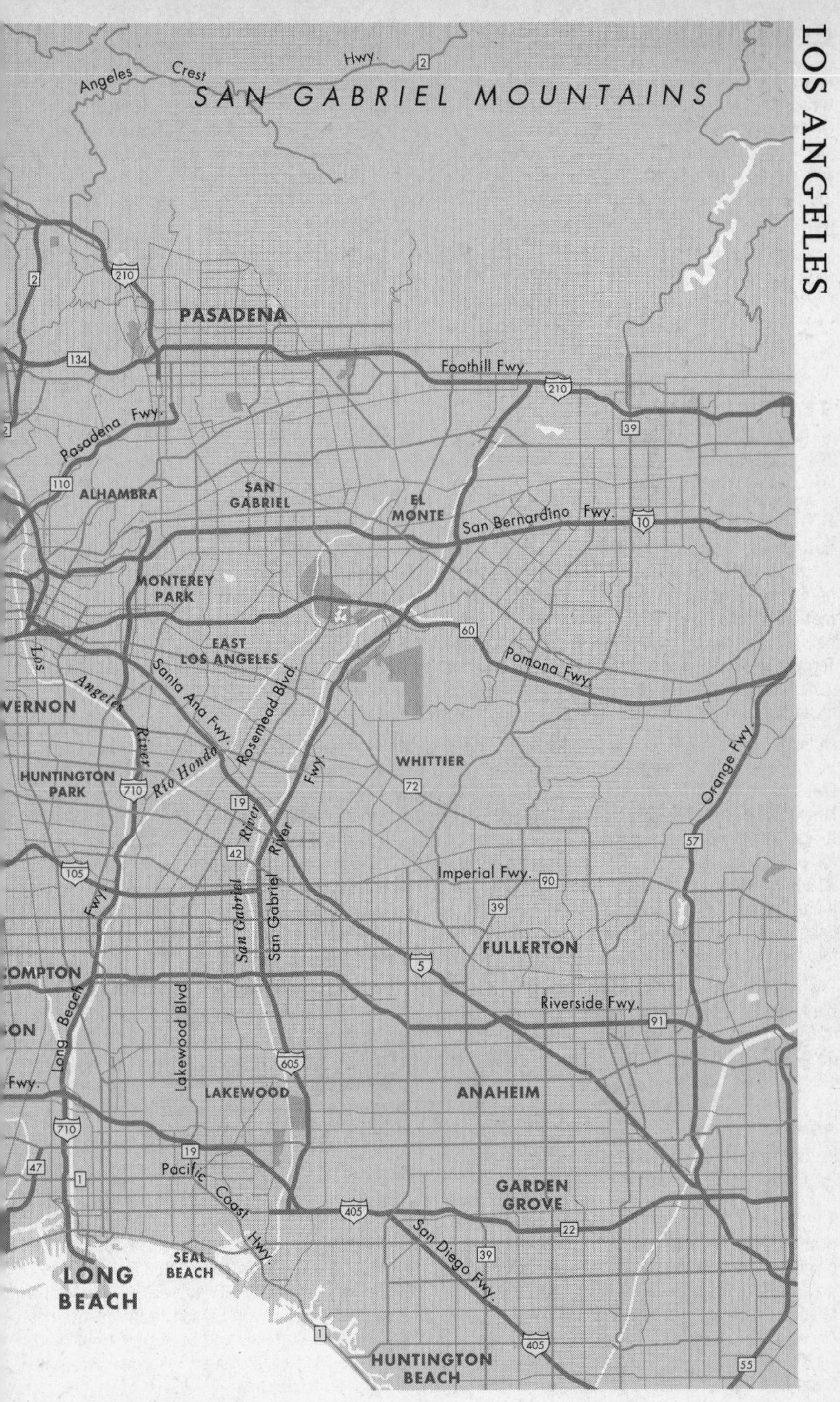

SAN GABRIEL MOUNTAINS
Angeles Crest Hwy.
2
210
2
PASADENA
134
Foothill Fwy.
210
39
Pasadena Fwy.
110
ALHAMBRA
SAN GABRIEL
EL MONTE
San Bernardino Fwy.
10
MONTEREY PARK
60
EAST LOS ANGELES
Pomona Fwy.
Los Angeles River
VERNON
Santa Ana Fwy.
Rosemead Blvd.
Rio Hondo
HUNTINGTON PARK
710
WHITTIER
72
Fwy.
19
San Gabriel River
42
Orange Fwy.
57
105
Fwy.
Imperial Fwy.
90
39
FULLERTON
5
OMPTON
Long Beach Fwy.
Lakewood Blvd
Riverside Fwy.
91
ON
Fwy.
605
LAKEWOOD
ANAHEIM
710
47
19
1
Pacific Coast Hwy.
GARDEN GROVE
405
22
San Diego Fwy.
39
LONG BEACH
SEAL BEACH
1
405
HUNTINGTON BEACH
55

COMING AND GOING

BY BUS

Incontestably the cheapest—and potentially the most entertaining—way of getting to Los Angeles is by **Greyhound** (tel. 800/231–2222), which offers service to Los Angeles's downtown station from many U.S. and Canadian cities, including San Francisco (8–12 hrs, $61 round-trip) and San Diego (3 hrs, $21 round-trip). Neither the downtown station (1716 E. 7th St., at Alameda St., tel. 213/629–8400) nor the Hollywood station (1409 N. Vine St., between Sunset Blvd. and De Longpre Ave., tel. 213/466–6384) is in the best of neighborhoods, so try to arrive during daylight hours.

For perennially rootless road warriors, **Green Tortoise Adventure Travel** (tel. 800/227–4766) runs bus tours to San Francisco, Alaska, Baja California, the Grand Canyon, and the California desert (*see* Funky Deals on Wheels *box in* Chapter 1). From Los Angeles, round-trip fare to San Francisco (12 hrs nonstop) is $60; for Seattle (2 days) you'll pay $138. Green Tortoise stops in Hollywood, downtown Los Angeles, Santa Monica, LAX, Long Beach, and Huntington Beach once weekly; call for schedule and pickup locations.

BY CAR

Just about every freeway in California seems to lead to Los Angeles eventually. From the north, take I–5, U.S. 101, or coastal Highway 1. From San Diego in the south, take I–5 to I–405. From the east, I–10 leads into town (*see* Getting Around by Car, *below*).

BY PLANE

Los Angeles International Airport (LAX), 17 mi southwest of downtown Los Angeles off I–405, is a snarl of traffic and tourists. It's the third-largest airport in the country, and every airline you can think of flies here. International terminals (2, 5, and the Bradley Terminal) have **currency exchange** offices and **information booths** open daily 7 AM–11 PM. In addition to dispensing tourist pamphlets, the staff here can help you find accommodations. **Luggage storage** is available in Terminals 1, 3, 4, and 7 and the Bradley Terminal; prices range from $2 to $10 per bag per day, depending on size. Baggage storage facilities are generally open daily 6 AM–10 PM. All terminals have lockers, which cost $1 for the first 24 hours and $2 for each additional 24-hour period. The main information line for LAX is 310/646–5252.

Outside the baggage claim area in each of LAX's terminals is a Quick-Aid computer that provides ground transportation information. Public bus routes from the airport include No. 3, Big Blue Bus, to Santa Monica and Brentwood; No. 439 southbound to beach cities down to Palos Verdes; and No. 232 to Long Beach. Another possibility is to take the G shuttle to the Green Line metro station at Aviation and I–105. More costly transport options include shuttle buses, such as **Super Shuttle** (tel. 213/775–6600; for pickup call 5–6735 from any courtesy phone in baggage claim) or **Airport Flyer Express** (tel. 818/376–1234, for pickup go to the blue Van Stop outside baggage claim). Both will take you anywhere in the greater L.A. area, 24 hours a day, for $10–$30 per person, depending on pickup or drop-off location. Taxis, though convenient, are expensive unless you're traveling with a crowd and can divide the fare. A ride to Santa Monica will set you back about $20, to Hollywood about $30.

The smaller **Burbank-Glendale-Pasadena Airport** (2627 N. Hollywood Way, at Thornton Ave. in Burbank, tel. 818/840–8847), close to Hollywood and only 1 mi south of I–5, is served by Alaska (tel. 800/426–0333), America West (tel. 800/247–5692), American (tel. 800/433–7300), Sky West (tel. 800/453–9417), Southwest (tel. 800/435–9792), and United (tel. 800/241–6522). These airlines often offer the best fares on journeys up and down the West Coast (to San Francisco, say, or Seattle) because landing at small airports like Burbank costs less than touching down at major hubs like LAX. To reach downtown from the Burbank Airport take Bus 94; to reach Hollywood take Bus 212.

leads into town (*see* Getting Around by Car, *below*).

BY TRAIN

The slow but romantic way to reach Los Angeles is by train, arriving at the beautifully restored **Union Station** (800 N. Alameda St., at Cesar Chavez St., tel. 213/683–6729), in a somewhat disreputable neighborhood downtown. **Amtrak** (tel. 800/872–7245) sends several trains daily to San Francisco (12 hrs, $75), San Diego (3 hrs, $25), Chicago (2 days, $242), New York City (3 days, $266); round-trip fares are often only slightly higher. Several public transport lines link Union Station to the rest of Los Angeles: MTA Bus 434 heads to Santa Monica and Malibu; Bus 60 takes you to Sunset Boulevard, where you can catch Buses 1–4 to Hollywood; the Metro Red Line light-rail serves downtown; and **Metrolink** (tel. 213/808–5465) offers commuter service to far-flung suburbs.

GETTING AROUND

BY BUS

The orange-and-white buses of the **Metropolitan Transit Authority (MTA)** (1 Gateway Plaza, tel. 213/626–4455), emblazoned with "Travel Smart . . . Take Metro," provide thorough but plodding transportation through Los Angeles for a flat $1.35 (2-hr transfers 25¢). Carry exact fare ($1 bills are okay), because drivers cannot make change. Generally, MTA buses numbered 1–99 serve downtown Los Angeles, Buses 100–199 run east–west, and Buses 200–299 run north–south. Bus stops are obvious and well marked by orange and white signs (which list the bus numbers and final destination) and buses arrive every 10–30 minutes, depending on routes and days. Late-night service is skimpy, so stop by a visitor center (*see* Visitor Information, *above*) for a schedule. Call 1/800–COMMUTE for route information during daytime hours.

As its name suggests, **DASH** (Downtown Area Short Hop) buses serve the downtown area, including Chinatown, Little Tokyo, Olvera Street, and Union Station, during the daytime only. The 25¢ fare includes one free transfer. During rush hours (5 AM–8 AM and 3 PM–6 PM), express buses run from downtown to more distant destinations like Hermosa Beach (Bus 438, $1.10) and Westwood (Bus 534, $1.50). *Tel. 213, 310, or 818/808–2273.*

Even if you're not planning to take the Red Line subway, duck into the Civic Center Station (1st and Hill Sts.) to check out the mannequins suspended from the ceiling.

Though some MTA buses loop through the city of Santa Monica, more thorough service is provided by Santa Monica's **Big Blue Bus** (tel. 310/451–5444), which also takes passengers from the beach to LAX, Westwood, and downtown Los Angeles. Fare is 50¢ ($1.25 to downtown) with one free transfer. Transfers to MTA bus lines are available for 25¢. Additionally, a city-operated shuttle called **The Tide** (tel. 310/451–5444) connects several downtown Santa Monica attractions, including Main Street, the Promenade, the pier, and some motels. The shuttle operates daily from noon–10 PM, with departures every 15 minutes; fare is free.

BY CAR

Traffic in Los Angeles is less apocalyptic than it's often portrayed in movies and on TV, though not by much. And while the popularity of drive-by shootings has waned, carjacking incidents are on the rise. The ***Thomas Guide to L.A. County*** *($15.95) is almost heavy enough to fulfill any self-defense needs, but its primary purpose is to help you figure out where you are and how to get where you're going. Worshipped throughout the Southland, this comprehensive book of maps and indexes is available in area bookstores and gas stations, and should be the first thing a visiting driver buys.*

I–5 (the Golden State Freeway) runs through downtown, continuing north to Sacramento and south to San Diego. **I–10** (the Santa Monica Freeway) runs east from Santa Monica, continuing through to Palm Springs and points beyond. **I–405** (the San Diego Freeway) runs parallel to but west of I–5; take this to reach LAX and points south. **Highway 1,** also known as the **Pacific Coast Highway (PCH),** meanders along the coastline, passing through Los Angeles's beach communities on its way north to San Francisco and south toward San Diego.

RENTAL CARS • Independent agencies are usually cheaper than the bigger corporations. When making a reservation at a smaller company, be sure to get a confirmation number, or at least the name of the person you speak with. Almost all companies offer insurance (usually about $10 per day), but check first with your own car-insurance company and your credit-card company—chances are that the rental will already be covered. You may save cash if you're a member of AAA, or if you rent by the week rather than by the day. Some hostels (*see* Where to Sleep, *below*) offer rental discounts. Most companies without an office at LAX will send a shuttle to the airport to pick you up.

At LAX, **Bob Leech's** (4490 W. Century Blvd., tel. 310/673–2727 or 800/635–1240 for reservations and free airport pickup) rents cars for $25 a day or $129 a week. For an extra $50, you can drive the car up the coast and drop it off at their San Francisco office. You're allowed 150 free mi per day; it's 20¢ for each additional mile. **Lucky** (8620 Airport Blvd., LAX, tel. 310/641–2323 or 800/400–4736 for reservations and free airport pickup) charges $23 a day or $139 a week. **Fox** (10210 La Cienega Blvd., LAX, tel. 310/641–3838) rents economy cars for $30 a day or $150 a week. For free pickup call from the courtesy phone in baggage claim.

Avon (8459 Sunset Blvd., near La Cienega Blvd. in West Hollywood, tel. 310/277–4455) charges $25 a day or $150 a week for low-end cars. Avon does not provide shuttle service to and from area airports.

DRIVER'S ED: THE ACCELERATED COURSE

You and your car will feel right at home if you follow these few simple steps: Call Interstate 5 "The Five" and U.S. 101 "The One-oh-One," and have your auto "detailed," not "washed." Rent a cellular phone, so you can conduct animated conversations while weaving recklessly. Never concede space on the freeway to merging traffic.

Penny and **Rent-a-Wreck** (14308 Ventura Blvd., at Beverly Glen in Sherman Oaks, tel. 818/786–1733) are jointly owned, and both rent nice, normal cars for $21–$27 a day or for $139 and up a week. They do not operate a shuttle service but can arrange to pick up travelers at Burbank Airport free of charge.

BY SUBWAY

In 1990 the first line of Los Angeles's limited metro system opened, and now three lines link Los Angeles with MacArthur Park/West Lake, Norwalk, El Segundo, and Long Beach. Plans include extending the system to North Hollywood, Pasadena, and East Los Angeles, and optimists say that by 2001 the Metro will run 300 mi throughout the greater Los Angeles area. We'll believe it when we see it. Red Line trains, which run every 10 minutes 5 AM–7 PM, make eight stops in the downtown area, continuing on to Union Station, where they connect with Amtrak and Metrolink. The Blue Line makes the one-hour journey from downtown Los Angeles to downtown Long Beach daily 5 AM–10:40 PM. The Green Line runs from Norwalk to El Segundo. There are plans to link the Green Line directly to LAX, but right now there's only a connecting shuttle. The Red and Blue lines converge at the 7th Street Metro Center (corner Flower and 7th Sts.). The Blue Line meets the Green Line at the Imperial Highway/Wilmington stations. Metro maps are available at the Visitor Information Centers. *Tel. 213/626–4455 or 800/266–6883. Fare: $1.35 one-way.*

BY TAXI

Usually, you can't hail a taxi on the street; you must phone for one. **L.A. Taxi** (tel. 213/627–7000) and **United Independent Taxi** (tel. 213/653–5050) charge an initial $1.90, plus $1.60 per mi. Most taxi companies operate 24 hours daily.

WHERE TO SLEEP

Hotels and motels range from grossly opulent to flea-infested. Some of the most pleasant, safe, and convenient motels lie in the Wilshire District, along Beverly Boulevard and Fairfax Avenue. Hostels are an even better choice for those who want to save money and meet other travelers. Hollywood, Venice, and Santa Monica offer several hostels in key locations, some with private rooms similar in price and quality to those at standard inns. Figure out what you want to do and see in Los Angeles before choosing a hotel or hostel so that you don't spend half the day fighting traffic. If you're an AAA member or a student, ask about discounts; you could shave as much as 10% off your bill just by presenting ID. Many hotels recommend reservations during the busy summer months, as well as on weekends and holidays throughout the year. Keep in mind that a 12%–14% room tax will be added to listed prices. Unless otherwise noted, all the rooms listed below have private bath, and all come with free parking.

HOTELS AND MOTELS

DOWNTOWN

City planners and private investors have recently poured large amounts of money into the downtown area, giving Los Angeles a long-needed center of business activity. They've moved businesspeople in and struggled to move the homeless out. As a result, the neighborhood now offers plenty of impressive hotels for executives on expense accounts, as well as a surviving host of dives unsafe for the budget traveler. Though staying downtown puts all the freeways at your fingertips, you're better off staying in the Wilshire District (*see below*). For a map of downtown lodging, *see* Exploring L.A., *below.*

UNDER $40 • Orchid Hotel. Amidst a sea of pricey Sheraton types, the Orchid is a welcome respite. Clean, comfortable doubles are a refreshing $35 ($184 a week); triples (with three single beds) are $47 ($228 a week). The clientele includes an odd mix of backpackers and pensioners; the 24-hour reception desk keeps the place safe and orderly 'round the clock. *819 S. Flower St., between 8th and 9th Sts., tel. 213/624–5855 or 800/874–5855. From LAX, Bus 439 to 8th and Flower Sts. 62 rooms. Laundry.*

UNDER $60 • Hotel Stillwell. Framed East Indian prints line the halls of this freshly painted high-rise near the heart of downtown, and the rooms have tastefully matched curtains and linens. The management can be effusively friendly. You'll even find some families staying here, a testimony to the building's excellent security. Doubles are $49. *838 S. Grand Ave., between 8th and 9th Sts., tel. 213/627–1151 or 800/553–4774. From LAX, Bus 439 to 8th and Figueroa Sts. 250 rooms. Laundry.*

HOLLYWOOD

This is a place of sin and excess. Even in Hollywood's nicer motels crime can be a problem, and at night, muggings on the streets are common. But if you're fearless, stupid, or handy with Mace, you can see it all here: leather-clad Iron Maiden fans; glossy, giggling transvestites; between-gig glam rockers; and the assorted hopefuls seeking success in the City of Broken Dreams. For a map of Hollywood lodging, *see* Exploring L.A., *below.*

Even if you don't have $100 burning a hole in your pocket, a subtle cruise through the Roosevelt's lobby and pool area will give you a taste of legendary, but long-gone, Hollywood.

UNDER $55 • Hollywood Towne House Motel. The decor here is low-budget Gothic, with dark wood paneling, gilt mirrors, and antiquated rotary phones. Otherwise, this two-story motel, just blocks away from Sunset Boulevard's clubs, is clean and cheap: Doubles are $45 ($220 a week). *6055 Sunset Blvd., between N. Gower St. and N. Bronson Ave., tel. 213/462–3221. Just west of U.S. 101. 32 rooms.*

Liberty Hotel. Quiet, charming, and unlike anything you'd expect to see in Hollywood, this low-rise hotel is the place to stay if you have high standards of personal hygiene. Though it's on a tree-lined side street, it's only a block north of the everlasting carnival sideshow surrounding Mann's Chinese Theater (*see* Exploring L.A., *below*). Doubles start at $45. *1770 Orchid Ave., between Franklin Ave. and Hollywood Blvd., tel. 213/962–1788. 20 rooms.*

UNDER $120 • Hollywood Roosevelt Hotel. Built in 1927, this swank hotel is an unofficial historic landmark. It reputedly hosted Marilyn Monroe, provided a trysting spot for Clark Gable and Carole Lombard, and was a hangout for Ernest Hemingway and F. Scott Fitzgerald. The first Academy Awards were held here in 1929. The Spanish-Moorish architecture, lush palm trees, and David Hockney–painted pool provide a luxurious retreat from the grime of Hollywood. Doubles start at $119, but call ahead to get special seasonal deals. *7000 Hollywood Blvd., between La Brea Ave. and Orange Dr., tel. 213/466–7000 or 800/252–7466. 320 rooms. Restaurant.*

WILSHIRE DISTRICT

A string of ridiculously priced hotels lines Sunset Boulevard between Crescent Heights and La Cienega boulevards, most notably the **Chateau Marmont,** long a favorite of the rich and famous, and the **Mondrian Hotel,** recently remodeled by a hip New York designer and painted plain white, making its name meaningless. Admire and move on; you'll find much cheaper lodging a few blocks south, around the intersection of Beverly Boulevard and Fairfax Avenue. Prices are a bit higher than in Hollywood or downtown Los Angeles, but you're paying for comfort, security, and prime locale. Peruse the Melrose café scene, visit museums and the La Brea Tar Pits, or drive 20 minutes to downtown or Santa Monica Beach. To locate lodging, *see* the West L.A. map *in* Exploring L.A., *below.*

UNDER $50 • Bevonshire Lodge Motel. This is a small and unremarkable motel with a Chihuahua-size pool and fatigued furnishings. It does win bonus points for location: CBS is a block away. Doubles, all with refrigerators, are $48; an extra $7 will get you a room with a kitchenette. *7575 Beverly Blvd., between Fairfax Ave. and Gardner St., tel. 213/936–6154. 25 rooms.*

UNDER $65 • Beverly Laurel Motor Hotel. Tastefully furnished, spacious rooms make it a pleasure to stay at this well-situated three-story motel. All rooms have refrigerators; doubles are $60, $70 with kitchenette. Extras include a downstairs coffee shop (open Sat.–Thurs. 6:30 AM–2 AM, Fri. and Sat. 6:30 AM–4 AM) and a pleasant tiled pool. *8018 Beverly Blvd., 2 blocks west of Fairfax Ave., tel. 213/651–2441, fax 213/651–5225. 52 rooms.*

UNDER $85 • Farmer's Daughter Motel. This three-story motel, across from the Farmer's Market (*see* Exploring L.A., *below*), hasn't seen any real farmers—or their daughters—for decades. Large, immaculate doubles, complete with refrigerators, start at $65 in summer, $58 in winter. There's also a pool and sundeck. *115 S. Fairfax Ave., between Beverly Blvd. and 3rd St., tel. 213/937–3930 or 800/334–1658, fax 213/932–1608. 64 rooms.*

WESTWOOD AND BEVERLY HILLS

Budget travelers are not likely to find lodging in Beverly Hills' illustrious 90210 zip code. You'll have better luck and more fun in Westwood, home to thousands of UCLA students. To locate lodging, *see* the West L.A. map *in* Exploring L.A., *below.*

UNDER $65 • Westwood Inn. Don't be turned off by the shabby exterior. The rooms—equipped with phone, TV, and sofa—are spacious and comfortable. The motel is close to UCLA, with easy access to cheap eateries. Doubles go for $62 a night (10% weekly discount). It's popular with young backpackers, so you'll need to make reservations two to three weeks in advance during summer. *10820 Wilshire Blvd., between Westwood and Selby Blvds., tel. 310/474–3118. From LAX, Bus 560. 21 rooms.*

UNDER $100 • Beverly Terrace Hotel. On the border of West Hollywood and Beverly Hills, this motel is centrally located, newly refurbished, clean, and welcoming. The clientele consists mainly of families and couples. Doubles start at $95. *469 N. Doheny Dr., at Santa Monica Blvd., tel. 310/274–8141. 39 rooms. Restaurant.*

SANTA MONICA, VENICE, AND MALIBU

Malibu, remote and relatively inaccessible, has long been a favorite of the wealthy and famous. However, it's retained a laid-back air, and budget travelers looking for a few days of solitude (and surfing) will want to stay here. Santa Monica is ideal for beach lovers also looking to explore Los Angeles's interior; the city has a range of motels and hotels, a huge number of young people, and easy freeway access. Also consider one of the excellent hostels in nearby Venice, a beach town that's a nonstop riotous carnival of skating Rastafarians, posing bodybuilders, and sidewalk shiatsu massage therapists. For a map of lodging, *see* the Santa Monica and Venice map *in* Exploring L.A., *below.*

UNDER $50 • Palm Motel. Palm trees, flower pots, and painted flags cheer up this bungalow-style motel. The rooms are airy and relatively clean, and doubles are only $40 ($256 a week). The clientele ranges from gregarious elderly residents to young hip-hop types. *2020 14th St., at Pico Blvd., Santa Monica, tel. 310/452–3861. 26 rooms.*

UNDER $65 • Pacific Sands Motel. Directly across from the Santa Monica Pier, this motel is peeling in some places and patched in others, but overall it's clean and comfortable. There's a pool, too, if you can find it. During summer, the Pacific Sands is usually packed with a college-age crowd, so reserve at least a week in advance. Doubles run $56 in winter, $62 the rest of the year; lower weekly rates are available. *1515 Ocean Ave., between Broadway and Colorado Ave., Santa Monica, tel. 310/395–6133. From LAX, Big Blue Bus 3 to 4th St. and Broadway. 40 rooms, 52 during summer.*

UNDER $85 • Bayside Hotel. You can't beat the location of this attractively landscaped motel, just across the street from the beach. Comfortable doubles without phones go for $64–$74 depending on season; some have kitchens, and all come with plenty of free coffee. On Friday and Saturday nights you'll pay $5 more. *2001 Ocean Ave., south of Pico Blvd., Santa Monica, tel. 310/396–6000. From LAX, Big Blue Bus 3, get off at 4th St. and Pico Blvd. 45 rooms.*

Jolly Roger Hotel. Despite its colorful name, this three-story hotel is a bit on the bland side, with a decor that sticks too close to a beige-and-brown theme. But the price (doubles $72) and location (a five-minute drive from Venice Beach) are bonuses. *2904 Washington Blvd., between Lincoln and Abbot Kinney Blvds., Marina del Rey, tel. 310/822–2904 or 800/822–2904. From LAX, Big Blue Bus 3. 82 rooms. Courtyard café, Jacuzzi, pool.*

UNDER $100 • Hotel Carmel. One of Santa Monica's original grand hotels, the Carmel has been carefully tended over the decades, as you'll see from the elegant lobby and well-appointed rooms. It's hoity toity, but it's in the heart of downtown Santa Monica, two blocks from the beach and around the corner from the Third Street Promenade (*see* Exploring L.A., *below*). Double rooms start at $83; rates higher in summer. *201 Broadway, at 2nd St., Santa Monica, tel. 310/451–2469 or 800/445–8695. From LAX, Big Blue Bus 3, get off at 4th St. and Broadway. 102 rooms.*

Malibu Surfer Motel. Ideally located 1 mi south of Surfrider State Beach, this charming blue-and-white stucco motel has bright, clean rooms with refrigerators, king-size beds, and balconies. There's a small pool and sundeck, and a hilltop patio and picnic area. Doubles range $62–$95 in winter, $95–$110 in summer; the highest prices are for weekend stays. *22541 Pacific Coast Hwy., between Carbon Canyon and Malibu Canyon Rds., Malibu, tel. 310/456–6169. 17 rooms.*

SOUTH BAY

The South Bay includes Manhattan Beach, Hermosa Beach, and Redondo Beach, all linked to the rest of Los Angeles by the Pacific Coast Highway (also known as PCH, Hwy. 1, or sometimes Sepulveda or Lincoln boulevard). Budget lodgings here line the highway, and room rates get progressively higher as you near the water. But presumably, you're here for the beaches, so it might be worth it. Manhattan and Redondo beaches are more commercialized than their quirky small-town neighbor Hermosa.

UNDER $50 • East-West Inn. A great bargain considering it's only a five-minute walk from the beach, the East-West lets doubles for $45 a night or $224 for the week. Clean, newly furnished rooms, fresh paint, and scattered tubs of small palm trees give the hotel a little personality. *435 S. Pacific Coast Hwy., at Ruby St., Redondo Beach, tel. 310/540–5998. South of Torrance Blvd. 40 rooms.*

UNDER $70 • Sea Sprite Motel. It lacks character, but the Sea Sprite is nirvana for beach-seeking travelers: If it were any closer to the ocean, you'd need a life raft. All rooms have a microwave and refrigerator, and rates vary from $55 for economy one-bed rooms to $118 for ocean-view doubles; reserve at least a week in advance during summer. *1016 The Strand, at 10th St., Hermosa Beach, tel. 310/376–6933, fax 310/376–4107. 70 rooms. Laundry.*

Seahorse Motel. Don't let the *Miami Vice* pink-and-aqua pastel exterior dissuade you: The rooms are large, clean, pleasantly furnished, and equipped with HBO. It's a five-minute drive to the ocean and the Manhattan Beach Pier, and there's a pool on the premises. Double rooms are $48–$68, depending on season, or $314 a week. *233 N. Sepulveda Blvd., between 2nd St. and Manhattan Beach Blvd., Manhattan Beach, tel. 310/376–7951 or 800/233–8057, fax 310/379–3328. 33 rooms. Closed Nov.–Jan.*

UNDER $80 • Grandview Motor Hotel. This tiny, modern three-story hotel sits steps from the beach; spacious rooms come complete with refrigerator and private balcony, and friendly managers give the place a comfortable feel. Doubles start at $76; weekly rates are available in winter. *55 14th St., off Hermosa Ave., Hermosa Beach, tel. 310/374–8981. 17 rooms.*

NEAR THE AIRPORT

There's no reason to linger here, unless you're fond of the sound of DC-10s. Keep in mind that many beachside and Hollywood hostels offer free airport shuttle service.

UNDER $65 • Hacienda Hotel. If you're determined to stay near LAX, head straight for this labyrinthine hotel. The modern rooms are almost antiseptically clean, and the fern- and fountain-bedecked ground floor might be mistaken for a Mediterranean palazzo. The bar is open daily 11 AM–1:30 AM. Extras include movie channels, free champagne and hors d'oeuvres during happy hour (weekdays 4:30–6:30), free 24-hour airport shuttle service, and free country-and-western dance lessons on Friday and Saturday nights. Doubles start at $54. *525 N. Sepulveda Blvd., at Mariposa Ave., El Segundo, tel. 310/615–0015 or 800/421–5900. 630 rooms. 24-hr coffee shop, laundry.*

HOSTELS

Hostels in Los Angeles usually offer a variety of sleeping options, from double rooms with private baths to warehouse-like dorms sleeping 20 or more. Many independent hostels hold their cheapest dormitory options for international and out-of-state travelers, particularly during summer. Los Angeles's hostels usually require passports, even of U.S. citizens, so they can discourage locals from using their hostel as a permanent home. Despite these restrictions, hostels are an excellent lodging alternative: Most offer free airport pickup, and some even have arrangements with rental car companies for discount car rentals.

HOLLYWOOD • Banana Bungalow Hotel and Hostel. Near U.S. 101 and the Hollywood Bowl (*see* Exploring L.A., *below*), this well-run hotel/hostel offers so much that you may forget to venture down to frothy Hollywood Boulevard for fun. Dorms sleeping four to six people are $18 per person; doubles are

$45. There's always a crowd floating between the pool, weight room, basketball courts, sundeck, and arcade. Other extras include free airport pickup; free breakfast; free movie nights; free shuttles to the beach, studios, and amusement parks; and a reasonably priced café/restaurant. A passport (foreign or domestic) and proof of international travel is required for dormitory space. *2775 Cahuenga Blvd. W, 1 mi north of Franklin Ave., tel. 213/851–1129 or 800/446–7835. 250 beds. Reception open 24 hrs. Kitchen, laundry. Reservations advised in summer.*

Hollywood International Guest House and Hostel. Two blocks east of Mann's Chinese Theater, this clean, relatively new hostel is right in the thick of Hollywood insanity—and it's still quiet. Dorms sleep two to four people ($13 per person), and doubles are $30. Free movie nights, the occasional barbecue, a lounge area with a pool table, an exercise machine, and a common-use kitchen are perks. *6820 Hollywood Blvd., at Highland Ave., tel. 213/463–0797 or 800/750–6561. 42 rooms. Reception open 24 hrs. Kitchen, laundry.*

Hollywood Wilshire YMCA International Youth Hostel. If you want to get in shape while you're visiting Hollywood, you might enjoy free access to two swimming pools and a fitness room at this hostel. Of course, you'll have to put up with two pages of rules, which prohibit opposite sexes from entering each other's dorms, and anyone from eating or smoking in the building. Beds are $16 a night. *1553 N. Schrader Ave., at Selma Ave., tel. 213/962–4685. 42 beds. Lockout 10 AM–4 PM. Laundry.*

Orange Drive Manor. This 1918 boarding house is the perfect spot to relax after a hard day of touring Hollywood Boulevard. The rooms are big and clean and have charming antique furnishings. Dorms with four beds are $17 per person, and doubles are $34. *1764 N. Orange Dr., between Hollywood Blvd. and Franklin Ave., tel. 213/850–0350, fax 213/850–7474. 35 rooms, some with bath. Reception open 9 AM–11 PM. Kitchen. Reservations advised in summer. Cash only.*

SANTA MONICA AND VENICE • Airport Hostel. Recognizable from the road as the two-story structure with a perpetual string of drying laundry suspended from the balcony, the Airport Hostel offers a cheap place to sleep, free airport pickup, discount rentals on cars and bikes, and a reasonable standard of hygiene. There's one 30-bed dorm and several smaller ones that run $12–$14 a night or $84 a week; a handful of double rooms go for $32. The common room features a pool table and TV. The management gives preference to foreign and out-of-state visitors, particularly in summer; a passport is required. *2221 Lincoln Blvd., near Venice Blvd., Venice, tel. 310/305–0250. 70 beds. Reception open 24 hrs. Kitchen, laundry. Cash only.*

Cadillac Hotel. The Cadillac is a stylishly renovated art deco hostel/hotel less than a block from Venice Beach. Thirty of the rooms are standard hotel-type, and five additional hostel rooms house four dorm-style beds each. Dorms are $20 per person; double rooms go for $59–$79. The hostel offers airport pickup for $5, and guests have access to a sauna, sundeck, gym, pool table, and laundry facilities; discount car rentals and studio tours are also available. *8 Dudley Ave., at Ocean Front Walk, Venice, tel. 310/399–8876. 85 beds. Reception open 24 hrs.*

Jim's at the Beach. A stone's throw from the water, Jim's has a laid-back, homey atmosphere. Beds in six-person dorm rooms go for $17, $120 weekly, and $450 monthly. Breakfast and dinner are included. A domestic or international passport is required to stay here. *17 Brooks Ave., at Pacific Ave., Venice, tel. 310/399–4018. From LAX, take Dani's shuttle (hostel will pay). 40 beds. Reception open 9 AM–midnight. Kitchen, laundry.*

Santa Monica American Youth Hostel. Perhaps the best hostel in Los Angeles, this place is almost a self-sufficient community; its amenities include laundry machines, a spacious courtyard, kitchen facilities, and a travel store. The proprietors have preserved the brick-and-wood charm of the historic building, a former town hall. (It's quite a contrast to the neighboring Pussycat Adult Movie Theater, the only blemish in an otherwise respectable neighborhood.) The hostel, one block from the 3rd Street Promenade (*see* Exploring L.A., *below*), is open year-round to both AYH members and nonmembers on a first-come, first-served basis. Dorm rooms are $21–$24, and doubles are $27 a person. Add $3 if you are not an HI member. All dorms are single-sex. *1436 2nd St., south of Santa Monica Blvd., Santa Monica, tel. 310/393–9913. Call for free airport pickup. 200 beds. Reception open 24 hrs. Kitchen, laundry. Reservations strongly advised in summer.*

Share Tel Apartments. Across the street from Jim's at the Beach (*see above*), this social hostel hosts free dinner-and-keg nights for guests. Dorm beds cost $17 or $112 a week, and free airport pickup is provided. A foreign passport is required. *20 Brooks Ave., at Pacific Ave., Venice, tel. 310/392–0325. 150 beds. Reception open 8 AM–11 PM. Kitchen, laundry.*

Venice Beach Cotel. Well-scrubbed and literally steps from the beach, the high-rise Cotel offers both dorm- and hotel-style accommodations. Studio tours, an inexpensive weekly shuttle to San Diego, and discount car rentals are all available. Dorms sleep three to four people; beds in rooms with a shared bath down the hall cost $13 ($15 with adjoining private bath and ocean view). Double rooms with ocean views are $32–$44. The management suggests that hostelers arrive soon after checkout time (11 AM) to get a bed; a passport is required. *25 Windward Ave., 1 block west of Pacific Ave., Venice, tel. 310/399–7649. From LAX, take Coast Shuttle. 70 beds. Reception open 24 hrs.*

Venice Beach Hostel. It's a carnival out on Ocean Front Walk, and it's a jungle in here. All the hallways are painted to represent different places—the jungle, the Grand Canyon, Venice Beach at the foot of Mount Fuji. Private rooms go for $39, and dorms with 4–10 beds per room go for $17 per person ($112 a week). Think rustic. *1515 Pacific Ave., at Windward Ave., tel. 310/452–3052, fax 310/821–3469. 100 beds. Reception open 24 hrs. Kitchen, laundry, lockers.*

CAMPING

While it would indeed be a shock to find camping within L.A. city limits, a few oceanside state parks offer you a place to pitch your tent within striking distance of the city. Most are in or around Malibu and all offer fully developed sites; for reservations, contact Destinet (tel. 800/444–7275). At **Leo Carillo State Beach** (tel. 818/880–0350), 25 mi west of Santa Monica on PCH, you'll find 127 sycamore-shaded campsites ($17 Sun.–Thurs.; $18 Fri.–Sat.), as well as rugged cliffs, tide pools, hidden coves, and miles of hiking trails. **Malibu Creek State Park** (1925 Las Virgenes Rd., 4 mi south of U.S. 101 in Calabasas, tel. 818/880–0367) has 60 sites ($15 Sun.–Thurs.; $16 Fri.–Sat.) in a pleasant clearing amidst the Santa Monica Mountains.

Back in 1948, California's first drive-thru hamburger stand was born, and ever since In-N-Out Burger has been king of fast-food restaurants.

FOOD

Los Angeles has a diverse, lively, and even affordable dining scene. The city's burgeoning selection of ethnic eateries reflects its large immigrant population: Thai, Peruvian, Mongolian, Japanese, Filipino, Cuban, Indian, Korean, Italian, and Mexican restaurants, among others, rub shoulders here. Many cafés offer sandwiches and light, reasonably priced fare; scan *L.A. Weekly* or one of the other free papers (*see* Basics, *above*) for news of the newest and best. Keep an eye out for lunch specials, particularly in the downtown area. Especially thrifty eaters should look for farmers' markets (*see* Hollywood and West Hollywood *and* Westwood and Beverly Hills, *below*).

DOWNTOWN

Downtown Los Angeles has plenty to see on the cheap, but the central museum area suffers from a dearth of inexpensive eateries. Most Westside restaurants are geared toward executives and theatergoers with credit cards, but within the **Grand Central Market** (317 S. Broadway, between 3rd and 4th Sts., tel. 213/624–2378) and along the surrounding Broadway strip, you'll find many cheap options. **Geraldine's Fresh Food and Juice Bar** (317 S. Broadway, between 3rd and 4th Sts., tel. 213/629–2787) provides the area's health food, offering a wide array of freshly squeezed juice combos including pomegranate, alfalfa, prune, and garlic. Chinatown's vast selection of Chinese and Vietnamese restaurants is a safe bet for decent budget food.

UNDER $5 • Clifton's Brookdale Cafeteria. Clifton's dorm-style food and curious interior (a waterfall and a wallpaper redwood forest) give it cult status among young locals. The typical diner fare (fried chicken or roast beef with choice of vegetables) at this 1930s relic generally runs less than $5. *648 S. Broadway, at 7th St., tel. 213/627–1673.*

Philippe the Original. Catercorner from Union Station, Philippe's (established 1908) is another beloved downtown institution, with faded photographs, communal tables, and sawdust on the floor. It's also the reputed birthplace of the French-dip sandwich (less than $4). You'll find all sorts lunching here, from bankers to beggars (and plenty of tourists). A cuppa joe is still just a dime. *1001 N. Alameda St., at Ord St., tel. 213/628–3781. Cash only.*

UNDER $10 • Jeepney Grill. A minimall filled with upscale Korean restaurants is probably not the first place you'd think of looking for Filipino food. Nonetheless, here it is—and with a gaudily painted Jeep from Manila parked right in the center of the small dining area. Traditional pork and beef barbecue dishes, many marinated in a surprisingly tasty concoction of banana sauce, honey, and spices, are $4.75 and up. *3470 W. 6th St., at Alexandria, tel. 213/739–2971.*

Original Pantry Café. This classic American greasy spoon isn't the place to drag a vegetarian: They've been carving up about 7,200 cows a year since 1924. Pot roast ($6), stewed chicken ($6), and creamed tuna ($5) are menu staples. With red-vinyl stools, stainless-steel countertops, and employees with names like Vera, Flo, Mel, and Alice, the whole joint could qualify as a living museum. Next door, the **Pantry Bake Shoppe** is a less greasy alternative, serving decent, moderately priced sandwiches, soups, and salads. *875–877 S. Figueroa St., at 9th St., tel. 213/972–9279 (Original Café) or 213/627–6879 (Bake Shoppe).*

Shabu Shabu House. There's only one dish on the menu here, traditional Japanese *shabu shabu.* You cook the parchment-thin slices of beef yourself, in a broth of vegetables and noodles. Though it's at the center of touristy Japanese Village, this is an authentic cultural experience. Lunchtime portions start at $5.75, dinner at $10. Wash it all down with Japanese beer ($2.50–$4.50) or sake ($3.75). *127 Japanese Village Plaza Mall, between San Pedro and Center Sts., Little Tokyo, tel. 213/680–3890. Closed Mon.*

UNDER $15 • El Cholo. Tasty Mexican food (since 1927) and attentive service make this festive restaurant well worth the drive. Try the cheese-filled enchilada *suiza* ($8.75) or the carne asada ($11). To make your wait for a table fly by, grab a margarita ($6) at the bar. *1121 S. Western Ave., between Pico and Olympic Blvds., tel. 213/734–2773. 2 mi west of downtown.*

Monkee's Seafood Restaurant. In the heart of Chinatown, Monkee's serves reasonably priced Cantonese poultry, pork, beef, and vegetable dishes ($6–$10). But this place is famed for its seafood—from exotics like sea cucumber and abalone ($12 and up) to more familiar dishes like oyster and crab ($7.25 and up). Residents from all over the city come here. *679 N. Spring St., between Ord St. and Cesar Chavez, tel. 213/628–6717. Closed Sun.*

Woo Lae Oak. At this classic Korean barbecue, you grill your dinner at the table, choosing from chicken, squid, beef, pork, and other meats ($12.50 and up). Noodle dishes start at $9 and require no cooking skills. Cavernous ceilings and a fountain add a touch of grandeur. *623 S. Western Ave., between Wilshire Blvd. and 6th St., tel. 213/384–2244.*

HOLLYWOOD AND WEST HOLLYWOOD

Red-jacketed valets signal a dangerously high concentration of pricey restaurants on just about every boulevard in Hollywood and West Hollywood. Fortunately, budget travelers can choose from an equally ample selection of quirky, inexpensive eateries—or succumb to one of the many cheap, greasy burger joints and taco stands along Santa Monica Boulevard. F. Scott Fitzgerald was once a regular customer at **The Musso and Frank Grill** (6667 Hollywood Blvd., at Cherokee Ave., tel. 213/467–7788), but don't let that tempt you into eating at "the oldest restaurant in Hollywood." Instead, make like Gatsby: Pass up the overpriced food (corned-beef sandwich $10, steak $20) and head straight for the cocktails. On Sunday from 8:30 AM to 1 PM, pick up organic produce at the **Hollywood Farmers' Market** (Ivar Ave., between Hollywood Blvd. and Selma Ave., tel. 213/463–3171).

UNDER $5 • For low-priced, high-viscosity chili concoctions, head to **Carney's** (8351 Sunset Blvd., at Sweetzer Ave. in West Hollywood, tel. 213/654–8300), which dispenses burgers and dogs (both less than $4) from a train caboose 11 AM–midnight (until 2 AM Friday and Saturday).

UNDER $10 • Flowering Tree. Focusing on organic, no-artificial-anything dishes—from wheat-free waffles to sugarless chocolate mousse pie—this tiny, friendly, Formica-counter joint features an inventive and surprisingly affordable menu. Turkey and tempeh burgers are $6 and turkey-chili burritos are $7. *8253 Santa Monica Blvd., between La Cienega and N. Crescent Heights Blvds., West Hollywood, tel. 213/654–4332.*

Prizzi's Piazza. Pick up something at the corner liquor store before going to Prizzi's, a charming restaurant serving giant portions of pasta (most plates under $10). They're justifiably famous for their garlic bread sticks. Sidewalk tables provide excellent people-watching opportunities, with the Scientology Center across the street and the Bourgeois Pig (*see* Cafés, *below*) nearby. *5923 Franklin Ave., between Bronson and Tamarind Aves., Hollywood, tel. 213/467–0168. Open daily 5:30 PM–11 PM (Fri.–Sat. until 1 AM).*

Swingers Diner. This '50s-style diner enjoyed a stint as a late-night hangout for cast members of *Beverly Hills 90210.* With the stars gone, what remains is better-than-average diner fare (most dishes cost about $7) and smart drinks (about $6) with names like Thermite Bomb and Female Love. *8020 Beverly Blvd., at Laurel Ave., Hollywood, tel. 213/653–5858.*

Thai California Kitchen. Items on the menu are labeled VERY MILD, SPICY, HOT, and NO, NO; only the very daring should sample the chili sauce at each table, labeled LEAVE ME ALONE. The food is tasty and unique—try the drunkard's pasta ($5), a sweet-basil Thai dish with a slight mint flavor that allegedly counteracts inebriation. The atmosphere is weirdly disco, with a strobe light and MTV. *414 N. La Cienega Blvd., between Beverly Blvd. and Melrose Ave., West Hollywood, tel. 310/652–6808.*

Toi on Sunset. Toi offers Thai food as it's never been seen in Thailand. The creative menu caters to a vegetarian diet; the vegetable curries ($7) come highly recommended. The decor is definitely avant-grunge; pierced and Puma-shod patrons complete the scene. Most dishes can be prepared meat-free for vegetarians. *7505½ Sunset Blvd., at Gardner St., Hollywood, tel. 213/874–8062.*

MELROSE AND THE WILSHIRE DISTRICT

Between Santa Monica Boulevard and the Santa Monica Freeway (I–10), you'll find excellent dining options. Around trendy Melrose Avenue (between Fairfax and La Brea Aves.), chic restaurants and sidewalk burgers-'n'-dogs stands predominate.

UNDER $5 • For the absolute best chili creations in town, come to **Pink's Famous Chili Dogs** (709 N. La Brea Ave., at Melrose Ave., tel. 213/931–4223). They've been stuffing buns daily 9:30 AM–2 AM (Fri.–Sat. until 3 AM) since 1939. At **Eat a Pita** (465 N. Fairfax Ave., at Rosewood Ave., tel. 213/651–0188), pick up a falafel sandwich ($2.75), a Greek salad ($2.95), or baklava ($1.50) 11 AM–10 PM.

*Philippe the Original's (*see Food, above*), a wonderful ancient lunch counter across from Union Station, is filled with faded photos of people long since dead and buildings long since demolished.*

UNDER $10 • California Chicken Café. This casual restaurant is a favorite with the office lunch crowd and stray café types. Chicken—pita chicken sandwiches ($5.75–$6.75), chicken salad ($4.50–$7), and rotisserie chicken ($4 a half, $14 for a whole with side dishes)—dominates the menu, but vegetarians can choose from a few salads. *6805 Melrose Ave., between La Brea and Highland Aves., tel. 213/935–5877. Cash only. Closed Sun.*

El Coyote Café. The only way to explain the enormous popularity of El Coyote—site of the last meal of Manson victims Sharon Tate and Co.—is the abundance of cheap liquor ($2.50–$3.50) and tasty margaritas. The food is almost awful, the decor a tacky Tinseltown approximation of Mexican. Nonetheless, it continually draws a crowd, including a fair number of celebrities. Combination plates (select from enchiladas, tacos, tamales, etc.) are $5. On weekend evenings, the bar fills with clubgoers fueling up on frosted margaritas. *7312 Beverly Blvd., just west of Poinsettia Dr., tel. 213/939–2255.*

Flora Kitchen. This corner café is a popular place to pick up the makings for a gourmet picnic at Hollywood Bowl (*see* Hollywood *in* Exploring L.A., *below*). It's also an ideal spot for a sit-down lunch at tables surrounded by the buckets of fresh-picked flowers from the adjacent florist. The quasi–California-cuisine menu includes sandwiches ($6–$10), salads ($5–$8), and sinful desserts ($4). *460 S. La Brea Ave., at 6th St., tel. 213/931–9900.*

Mario's Peruvian Seafood. In an unassuming strip mall near Paramount Studios (*see* Studios *in* Exploring L.A., *below*), Mario's serves excellent, generous portions of sautéed or fried red snapper, shrimp, and squid ($7–$11), with side orders of Peruvian-style rice and vegetables. *5786 Melrose Ave., at Vine St., tel. 213/466–4181.*

UNDER $15 • Authentic Café. The eclectic menu at this popular Southwestern-style eatery combines Latin American, Asian, and Middle Eastern cuisines to create some inspired dishes. Try the zesty, wood-grilled Yucatán marinated chicken breast with citrus and Mexican spices ($10) or the fresh corn tamales ($5.50). Be prepared to wait a half-hour or longer for a table in the company of a young and clean-cut but casual crowd. *7605 Beverly Blvd., at N. Curson Ave., tel. 213/939–4626.*

Caffé Luna. Luna keeps late hours for a good reason: There's always a crowd (including the occasional hoping-not-to-be-noticed celebrity). The menu includes a wide selection of pastas (buckwheat fettuccine, $8.75) and pizzas that feed two ($10). The best tables are on an outdoor patio meant to look like an Italian village square, and all come equipped with crayons for between-course scribbling. *7463 Melrose Ave., at Gardner St., tel. 213/655–8647.*

Louis XIV. You could easily spend your entire dinner hour staring at the beautifully prepared dishes (appetizers $4–$9, entrées $8.50 and up). The darkly lit, narrow interior is impressively furnished with

SO YOU WANT TO SELL YOUR SCREENPLAY?

Or be discovered as an actor? A musician? You won't be able to afford the food at these places, but you can down drinks at the bar, provided you keep that dog-eared copy of Entertainment Weekly's *annual "100 Most Powerful People in Hollywood" hidden. A gross number of celebrities and behind-the-scenes power brokers frequent Morton's (8764 Melrose Ave., West Hollywood, tel. 310/276–5205) and Spago (176 N. Cañon Dr. at Wiltshire, Beverly Hills, tel. 310/385–0880). For a more low-key encounter, try Dalt's Grill (3500 W. Olive Blvd., in Union Bank Building, tel. 818/953–7752) in Burbank. You'll find affordable Mexican food, peons from the nearby studios, and DJs from KROQ (106.7 FM), a popular alternative radio station that broadcasts from upstairs. If you just want to gawk at a celebrity (not be one), Patrick's Roadhouse in Santa Monica (106 Entrada Dr., at PCH, tel. 310/459–4544) offers mediocre grill food and great sightings of folks like Zsa Zsa Gabor, Sean Penn, and Arnold Schwarzenegger.*

majestic carved chairs, gilt mirrors, and chandeliers. The waiters and much of the clientele are imported from France. The cuisine is continental, and a cool bar scene develops in late evening. *606 N. La Brea Ave., at Melrose Ave., tel. 213/934–5102.*

WESTWOOD AND BEVERLY HILLS

The majority of affordable restaurants in West Los Angeles cluster around Westwood Village and the UCLA campus. Farther south and east are a sprinkling of eclectic eateries worth the extra drive. Stop by the large **farmers' market** held every Thursday 2–7 on Weyburn Avenue (between Glendon Avenue and Westwood Boulevard near UCLA).

UNDER $5 • Walk southeast from the UCLA campus along Broxton Avenue, and you'll pass the majority of Westwood's cheapest eats. **Tommy's** (970 Gayley Ave.) is a 24-hour grease shack notorious for its chili burgers (around $2). **Stan's Donuts** (10948 Weyburn Ave., at Broxton Ave., tel. 310/208–1943) is a late-night favorite.

UNDER $10 • Apple Pan. The menu hasn't changed one iota since the Pan opened in 1947—why bother, since it's widely considered the city's best burger joint? It serves fries ($1.75) and homemade apple pie ($2.25) in addition to the much-loved burgers ($4). *10801 W. Pico Blvd., at Westwood Blvd., West L.A., tel. 310/475–3585. Cash only. Closed Mon.*

Mongols BBQ. This cafeteria-style joint is always mobbed by students who know a good deal when they eat one. For $5.50 you get your choice of meat, vegetables, or noodles, all grilled Mongolian-style with a variety of spicy oils and served with rice, soup, and a sesame bun. *1064 Gayley Ave., between Weyburn and Kinross Aves., Westwood, tel. 310/824–3377. Cash only.*

Versailles. As you drive by, the perennial long line and delicious smells should tip you off to this local favorite, where cordial Cuban waiters serve up a taste of Old Havana. The house special, roasted garlic chicken ($6.50), comes with generous portions of rice, black beans, and fried plantains. Robust *café cubana* (espresso) is only 75¢. *1415 S. La Cienega Blvd., south of Pico Blvd., tel. 310/289–0392. Culver City location: 10319 Venice Blvd., tel. 310/558-3168.*

UNDER $15 • Crazy Fish. The sushi chefs at Crazy Fish mold giant rolls ($2–$12) as big as footballs, filled with unusual combinations of fish, chicken teriyaki, asparagus, or Cajun spices. The names of dishes are equally strange: Crazy Rock 'n' Roll, Baked Hawaiian Volcano, or Oy Vey Salmon Sashimi. There's usually a wait for a seat in the small, brightly lit restaurant, which is extremely popular with Los Angeles's sushi-mad populace. *9105 W. Olympic Blvd., at Doheny Dr., Beverly Hills, tel. 310/550–8547.*

Dive! Okay, okay, so Dive! is overpriced and designed with the tourist in mind—it's still fun. Built to resemble a giant yellow submarine, it has porthole windows offering diners views à la *20,000 Leagues Under the Sea* and a giant TV screen that broadcasts aquarium shots. The menu features submarine sandwiches (about $10); investor Steven Spielberg's favorite is the spicy Nuclear Sicilian. *10250 Santa Monica Blvd., Century City Shopping Mall, tel. 310/788-3483.*

SANTA MONICA AND VENICE

Aside from stands selling cheap and greasy food on the Venice boardwalk and the Santa Monica Pier, the dining scene in Venice and Santa Monica is quite tasteful. The restaurants that line **Main Street** in both neighborhoods range from elegantly expensive to funky and affordable; stroll south from Pico Boulevard if you've been stricken with diner's indecision.

UNDER $5 • Cheap eats in Venice are mostly of the undistinguished, deep-fried, boardwalk variety, with a few exceptions. Meat-eaters should head to **Jody Maroni's Sausage Kingdom** (2011 Ocean Front Walk, in Venice, tel. 310/306–1995)—the self-proclaimed "home of the haute dog"—for all-natural and original variations on the frankfurter, such as the Toulouse Garlic ($4). In Santa Monica, both carnivores and herbivores will enjoy the tasty, thin-crust pizza ($1.50–$2 a slice) at **Pizzarito** (1439 Third Street Promenade, in Santa Monica, tel. 310/458–2838).

UNDER $10 • **Rose Café.** More than a restaurant, the Rose is part of the daily routine for many Venice natives. You'll see bodybuilders and unemployed scriptwriters taking coffee at 10 AM; actors showing up for a bite around noon; and artists hunkering in for a meal after dark (a gallery displays local work). From croissants ($1.50) to chicken tacos ($7), the kitchen and bakery crank out a wide range of fresh, reasonably priced food in an open, social atmosphere. *220 Rose Ave., at Main St., tel. 310/399–0711.*

Van Go's Ear. A visit to the Ear can provide unexpected entertainment: Mornings, bodybuilders fuel up before hitting Muscle Beach (*see* Exploring L.A., *below*), and café types filter in after midnight. Omelets, sandwiches, and salads range in price from $4.25 to $9. Desserts are baked in-house daily, and plenty of vegetarian dishes are available. *796 Main St., between Rose and Brooks Aves., Venice, tel. 310/314–0022. Cash only.*

Wildflour Boston Pizza. Come here if you crave traditional pizza in a city where guacamole often replaces pepperoni as the topping of choice. It's a great choice for a 15" pie (cheese, $10.25) or a slice ($1.50). Inexpensive sandwiches and pastas ($4–$8) round out the menu. *2807 Main St., near Ocean Park Blvd., Santa Monica, tel. 310/392–3300.*

UNDER $15 • **Nawab of India.** One of the best, most affordable Indian restaurants in Los Angeles is a short drive inland from Santa Monica Beach. Nawab offers tasty tandoori dishes ($8–$15), vegetarian plates ($7), and delicious curries ($10–$12); particularly good is the tandoori chicken *makhanwala* ($12)—cooked in tomato sauce and cream. Though it's nothing fancy, the dining room is pleasantly serene. *1621 Wilshire Blvd., between 16th and 17th Sts., Santa Monica, tel. 310/829–1106.*

California Pizza Kitchen. The main event is pizza ($6–$10) with unusual toppings like Peking duck, Thai chicken, guacamole, or smoked salmon. Downtown L.A.: 330 S. Hope St., between 3rd and 4th Sts., tel. 213/626–2616. West Hollywood: 121 N. La Cienega Blvd., in Beverly Center, tel. 310/854–6555. Redondo Beach: 1815 Hawthorne Blvd., at Artesia Blvd., tel. 310/370–9931.

Chin Chin. Los Angeles's hip come here for Chinese food, California-style. The Chinese chicken salad ($6.50) is a favorite. West Hollywood: 8618 Sunset Blvd., between La Cienega Blvd. and Doheny Dr., tel. 310/652–1818. Marina del Rey (near Venice): 13455 Maxella Ave., at Lincoln Blvd., tel. 310/823–9999.

Gaucho Grill. This sparse but stylish nouveau Argentinean restaurant features moderately priced, grilled chicken and beef dishes (around $9), as well as sandwiches and salads. West Hollywood: 7980 Sunset Blvd., at Laurel Ave., tel. 213/656–4152. Santa Monica: 1253 Third Street Promenade, tel. 310/394–4966.

Jerry's Famous Deli. This 24-hour deli, popular after-hours with the clubbing crowd, serves massive sandwiches (around $8). West Hollywood: 8701 Beverly Blvd., at San Vicente Blvd., tel. 310/289–1811. Westwood: 10925 Weyburn Ave., between Broxton Ave. and Westwood Blvd., tel. 310/208–3354.

Louise's Trattoria. Sizable Italian dishes, served al fresco with a California twist for under $10. West Hollywood: 7505 Melrose Ave., at Gardner St., tel. 213/651–3880. Santa Monica: 1008 Montana Ave.,

NOT YOUR AVERAGE CHAINS

Reconsider any prejudices against chain restaurants when visiting Los Angeles. A number of locally owned chains keep residents coming back for great, reliable eats.

between 10th and 11th Sts., tel. 310/394–8888. Redondo Beach: 1430 Pacific Coast Hwy., at Ave. G, tel. 310/316–5236.

Tommy's. A 24-hour grease shack notorious for its chili burgers ($2). Downtown L.A.: 2575 Beverly Blvd., at Rampart Blvd., tel. 213/389–9060. Santa Monica: 1900 Lincoln Blvd., at Pico Blvd., tel. 310/392–4820. Burbank: 1310 N. San Fernando Rd., at Burbank Blvd., tel. 818/843–9150.

SOUTH BAY

Manhattan, Hermosa, and Redondo Beaches have excellent food, but you'll never find it if you stay on the Pacific Coast Highway. As you move closer to the shore, generic spots give way to locally owned kitchens offering fresh seafood and inexpensive California cuisine, particularly in health-conscious Hermosa Beach. In Manhattan Beach, the **Manhattan Beach Brewing Company** (*see* After Dark, *below*) serves up excellent entrées, such as wood-fired pizzas, burgers, and sandwiches ($5–$7.50), with its own homebrew.

UNDER $5 • In Manhattan Beach, filling and cheap burritos ($3.50) can be found four blocks in from the beach at the diminutive counter of **El Tarasco** (316 Rosecrans Ave., at Highland Ave., tel. 310/545–4241). Also in Manhattan Beach, **Sloopy's** (3416 N. Highland Ave., at 35th St., tel. 310/545–1373) has a garden patio, open fireplace, and tasty milk shakes, sandwiches, and salads ($3–$6). In Hermosa Beach, **Rosa's** (322 Pacific Coast Hwy., at 3rd St., tel. 310/374–9094) has served tasty, traditional Mexican dishes at reasonable prices for 25 years. Try the pork tacos *adobadas* (barbecued pork tacos; $2) or the bean-and-cheese burrito ($2).

UNDER $10 • Fat Face Fenner's Falloon. More than just a local pub (though it serves that purpose quite nicely), "FFFF" has raised burger making to an art form. The half-pound Falloon Burger ($5) can be topped with 19 items, including pineapple and artichoke hearts. Weekends 8 AM–1 PM, chow down on brunch staples like eggs and home fries ($2–$4). *837 Hermosa Ave., at 9th St., Hermosa Beach, tel. 310/376–0996.*

Good Stuff. Home-cooked food, California-style (vegetarian burgers, massive burritos, omelets), tastes even better when served right on the beach. On weekend mornings the line for brunch can be formidable, but locals never seem to mind—it's just one more opportunity to tan. Lunch and dinner run $5–$10; breakfast is $2–$6. *1286 The Strand, at Pier Ave., Hermosa Beach, tel. 310/374–2334. Manhattan Beach location: 1300 Highland Ave., tel. 310/545–4775.*

Martha's 22nd Street Grill. Breakfast on the heavenly patio here is a tradition among laid-back locals. There's frequently a wait to get in, but don't despair: The healthy soups ($2–$5) and hearty sandwiches ($5–$8) are also available to go from **Martha's Corner** next door. *25 22nd St., at Hermosa Ave., Hermosa Beach, tel. 310/376–7786.*

Ocean View Café. A cross between a coffeehouse and a restaurant, the Ocean View serves up excellent salads and sandwiches ($4–$7), light breakfasts ($4–$5), and wonderful espresso drinks. Try the soup du jour with a baguette ($2) and freshly squeezed orange juice. Both the view of the Pacific from the outdoor patio and the staff's mellow attitude are big bonuses. *229 13th St., off Highland Ave., Manhattan Beach, tel. 310/545–6770. Cash only.*

Ragin' Cajun Café. Mobbed by visitors and locals alike, this tiny restaurant dishes up authentic Cajun food—crawfish, red beans and rice, gumbo, and jambalaya—cooked by a Lafayette native. Coffee and *beignets* (N'awlins-style donuts) are served Sunday morning 8–11:30. *422 Pier Ave., between Pacific Coast Hwy. and Hermosa Ave., Hermosa Beach, tel. 310/376–7878. Closed Mon.*

The Spot. You don't need to be a vegetarian to enjoy this very popular health-food restaurant. Everything—from fresh-baked bread to soups, lasagna, and Mexican food—is made in-house without refined sugar or animal products, using purified water. *110 2nd St., at Hermosa Ave., Hermosa Beach, tel. 310/376–2355. Redondo Beach location: Green's at the Beach, 247 Avenida del Norte, at Via El Prado, tel. 310/316–9451.*

UNDER $15 • Takeout Taxi. This service delivers the best of South Bay eateries to your door; just call and request that beloved dish from your favorite restaurant, and some polite chap will bring it to you in under an hour. Choose from a wide selection including Chinese, Mexican, Italian, Indian, Thai, and Californian cuisine. A $5 charge is added to all deliveries. *Tel. 310/301–7074. Open daily 10:30–2 and 5–9:30.*

CAFÉS

Los Angeles now bristles with quirkily decorated coffee bars offering a variety of entertainment to patrons quaffing espresso drinks strong enough to take lacquer off a wall. But as you might expect, the café has been woven nicely into the fabric of the city's nightlife, a hip addition to clubbing. Many cafés stay open after bars and clubs close up, offering live music and poetry readings as well as backgammon boards, magazines, used paperbacks, and free local weeklies. *Caffeine,* the café scene's own (free) magazine, prints poetry, art, fiction, and the praise of coffeehouses. Pick it up at any café. Prices for coffee drinks are fairly uniform; unless specified below, you'll pay $1–$3, depending on size, strength, and the number of frills (whipped cream, sprinkles, etc.).

HOLLYWOOD AND WEST HOLLYWOOD

All-Star Theatre Café and Speakeasy. Located in the Hollywood Knickerbocker Hotel, the self-proclaimed "ultimate 1920s coffeehouse" has comfortably overstuffed club chairs and oversized drinks. Come for the art deco decor and the speakeasy atmosphere, but stay for a glimpse of the oft-seen ghost of Valentino. *1714 N. Ivar Ave., ½ block north of Hollywood Blvd., Hollywood, tel. 213/962–8898.*

Bourgeois Pig. With red lights illuminating the erotic-political paintings on the black walls and thrift store–clad patrons at the pool table, this is an achingly hip caffeine outlet. Despite the lack of alcohol, it's got a barlike social quality, and its denizens are engaging in their own studied way. *5931 Franklin Ave., at Beachwood Dr., Hollywood, tel. 213/962–6366.*

Living Room Café. Furnished with gold-painted mirrors and velvet thrift-shop chairs, the Living Room is the nighttime headquarters of Los Angeles's poseur youth. Besides espresso, they have an extensive and appetizing menu of pizzas, pastas, and sandwiches (all about $8) and various breakfast items ($4–$7). *112 S. La Brea Ave., at 1st St., tel. 213/933–2933.*

The Onyx. This art gallery-cum-café is where Los Angeles's small population of the unaffected gather to play card games with friends, write dissertations on laptop computers, or improvise on the piano. Poetry readings, live music, and comedy happen sporadically. The café serves veggie quiche ($3) and a few daily specials, as well as desserts. *1802 N. Vermont Ave., between Franklin Ave. and Hollywood Blvd., Los Feliz, no phone.*

MELROSE AND WILSHIRE DISTRICT

Highland Grounds. Don't let the graffiti-covered exterior frighten you: This café is mellow and friendly, with excellent breakfasts (omelets and pancakes $4–$7), and lunch and dinner items available after 11 AM. Come nightfall, it transforms into a demi-club, with art openings, open-mic poetry, and live music. There's an occasional small cover charge for some entertainment. *742 N. Highland Ave., ½ block north of Melrose Ave., tel. 213/466–1507.*

Insomnia Café. This velvet-couch-and-chandelier haunt is open 'til the wee hours. There's a small selection of pizzas and sandwiches ($2–$6), and the Thai iced tea ($2.50–$3.50) is heavenly. It's a friendly, social café. *7286 Beverly Blvd., at Poinsettia Pl., tel. 213/931–4943. Other location: 8164 Melrose Ave., between Crescent Heights and La Cienega Blvds., tel. 213/655–3960.*

Stir Crazy. You'll be so cozy within this café's faux log walls and low ceilings, you'll want to camp out for a few hours, maybe play a board game, or snuggle up on a couch to read a magazine. You won't even have to lift a finger as your cup o' joe is refilled for free. *6917 Melrose Ave., east of La Brea., tel. 213/934–4656.*

SANTA MONICA AND VENICE

Anastasia's Asylum. Check out the shrine in the blood-red bathroom and pray for deliverance from the smog of the city. Among the perks here are the almost completely vegetarian menu, the free live music/open-mic every night, and the 10% off all coffee drinks before 6 PM. *1028 Wilshire Blvd., at 11th St., Santa Monica, tel. 310/394–7113.*

Café Collage. Come here to get away from the Venice Beach circus. Modernist interpretations of Renaissance paintings hang on the terra-cotta walls, and wrought-iron furnishings add to the funky atmosphere. There's the regular café cuisine as well as original espresso drinks like the Palermo (chocolate, espresso, orange peel, and nutmeg; $3.25). *1518 Pacific Ave., at Windward Ave., Venice, tel. 310/399–0632.*

Lulu's Alibi. Small and cheerful, Lulu's is a popular meeting place for those catching a show at the nearby Nuart Theater (*see* After Dark, *below*). Stop by on weekdays 5–7 for happy hour, when prices are slashed by half on caffeinated drinks. Brazilian appetizers and entrées ($2–$9) dominate the food menu. *1640 Sawtelle Blvd., at Santa Monica Blvd., West L.A., tel. 310/479–6007.*

Newsroom Espresso Café. Only at Newsroom can you catch CNN updates while sipping Bolt Coke ($2.25), a mix of espresso and cola. In other words, this is a habitat for tightly wired media junkies. Normal, well-adjusted types will enjoy the large magazine rack and tasty range of entrées, including tandoori chicken and pesto pizza (each about $6). *530 Wilshire Blvd., at 6th St., Santa Monica, tel. 310/319–9100.*

Novel Café. This is where the literati of Venice and Santa Monica congregate. Elegant, aging couches and floor-to-ceiling shelves of used hardbacks give the café/bookstore a clubby feel. Nosh on inexpensive soups, salads, and sandwiches while attempting to plow through Joyce or Faulkner. *212 Pier Ave., at Main St. , Santa Monica, tel. 310/396–8566.*

Wednesday's House. Its proximity to the artsy Main Street strip makes this the perfect place for a post-gallery java. The outlandish collection of overstuffed furniture and the display of velvet Elvis paintings could only be the work of a gifted postmodernist decorator. On some evenings, musical friends of the owner drop by to jam. *2409 Main St., at Hollister St., Santa Monica, tel. 310/452–4486.*

SOUTH BAY

Hungry Mind. Feed your head and tummy in this cozy living room–cum-café. Young mothers, bronzed joggers, and recent college grads vie for spots on the sofas and sidewalk patio. Reading from their newsstand goes well with specialty coffee drinks. *916 Manhattan Ave., Manhattan, tel. 310/318–9029.*

Java Man. Housed in a Victorian home two blocks from the beach, this café also functions as a gallery, displaying works by local artists. Strong cups of joe ($1.20) can be refilled twice for only 25¢ before 6 PM daily. Salads and sandwiches are about $6. *157 Pier Ave., at Manhattan Ave., Hermosa Beach, tel. 310/379–7209.*

Sacred Grounds. This intimate space houses a performance stage and is the locus of San Pedro's thriving art scene. Live music or spoken-word entertainment begins nightly around 8 PM. *399 W. Sixth St., San Pedro, tel. 310/514–0800. Cover $2–$5.*

EXPLORING LOS ANGELES

Los Angeles has long been characterized as "19 suburbs in search of a metropolis." One of the reasons this tag has stuck is because sights are incredibly spread out, and public transit is slow and tedious. Unless you rent a car (*see* Getting Around, *above*) to drive between communities, you'll feel like a prisoner of the MTA bus system. There's plenty to see within certain neighborhoods, though, so if you have the time, don't try to tackle more than one neighborhood a day—unless sweating it out on the freeway is your idea of the L.A. experience.

DOWNTOWN LOS ANGELES

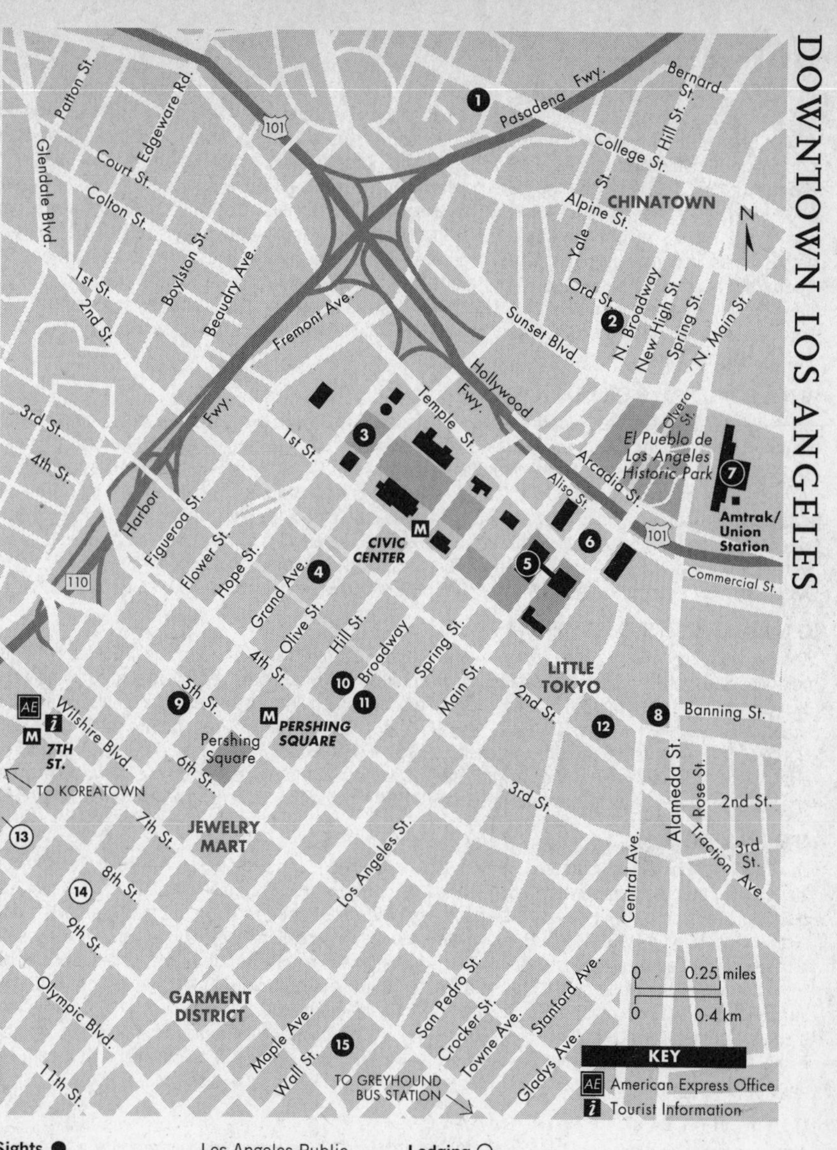

Sights ●

Bradbury Building, **11**

Children's Museum, **6**

City Hall, **5**

Dodger Stadium, **1**

Flower Mart, **15**

Grand Central Market, **10**

Japanese Village Plaza, **12**

Los Angeles Public Library, **9**

Museum of Contemporary Art, **4**

Music Center, **3**

Temporary Contemporary, **8**

Teo Chow Association, **2**

Union Station, **7**

Lodging ○

Hotel Stillwell, **14**

Orchid Hotel, **13**

DOWNTOWN

To most, it's shocking to learn that somewhere amid Los Angeles's strip malls and tract houses there lurks a real downtown. But yes, the city's got it all: skyscrapers and sidewalk shoeshine stands, one-way streets bracketed by brass-and-marble shopping complexes, and a very visible homeless and transient population. Downtown proper is right in the middle of the freeway jumble where the Hollywood, the Pasadena, the Santa Ana, and the Harbor freeways overlap. Stand at the corner of Hill and 6th streets and look northeast for a view of futuristic buildings that house museums, office buildings, and expensive hotels. The stretch of Broadway between 3rd Street and Olympic Boulevard is an alternate universe where Times Square meets Tijuana, with bustling shops and lively crowds. Further east toward San Pedro, the buildings thin out and the terrain turns to vacant lots, wholesalers, and single-room-occupancy hotels. Inexpensive parking lots ($2–$3.50 daily) can be found in the blocks around 9th Street, between Main and San Pedro streets on the fringes of downtown, and the area is serviced by DASH lines A, B, C, D, and E.

BRADBURY BUILDING

Constructed in 1893, the Bradbury Building was designed by an obscure draftsman named George Wyman as a textile factory for mining millionaire Lewis Bradbury. Wyman created a masterpiece of light and form, later made famous by the films *Blade Runner* and *Citizen Kane*. The building was majestically restored to its original condition in 1991, and law offices replaced the sweatshops long ago. While the outside is unassuming, the interior is literally breathtaking. Elaborate wrought-iron staircases and elevator cases ascend to a massive skylight five stories above. The effect is so peaceful, you'd never know you were 2 ft from the crazed Broadway strip. *304 S. Broadway, between 3rd and 4th Sts., tel. 213/626–1893. Across from Grand Central Market; DASH Route D. Building open Mon.–Sat. 9–5.*

CHILDREN'S MUSEUM

At this colorful downtown museum, kids—and adults who think like kids—can construct forts and tunnels with giant Velcro cushions, create music in a professionally equipped recording studio, animate their own drawings, or learn more about recycling. Interactive entertainment and exhibits on history and multiculturalism abound. *310 N. Main St., L.A. Mall, tel. 213/687–8800. Just south of U.S. 101; DASH Route B or D. Admission: $5. Open weekends 9:15–1 year-round; in winter, weekdays 9:15–1:30 with advance group reservations (although groups of fewer than 10 should call 213/687–8801 to see if there's space); in summer, open to everyone weekdays 11:30–5 (and groups with reservations, 9:15–11:15).*

CHINATOWN

Los Angeles's Chinatown, bordered by Yale, Bernard, Spring, and Ord streets, is actually in its second incarnation; much of the original neighborhood was razed in 1933 to make way for Union Station (*see below*). Today's small Chinese enclave is a five-minute walk from downtown, north of U.S. 101—or an even shorter hop on DASH Route B. Along North Broadway you'll encounter Buddhist temples fragrant with burning incense, acupuncturists, vendors hawking live poultry and fish, and pungent shops purveying rare teas and dried herbs. Step into the **Teo Chow Association** (649 N. Broadway, at Ord St.), a temple and community organization, to make an offering of incense or fruit to one of the Chinese idols. If you seek a meal, visit Monkee's or one of the many other cheap restaurants in the neighborhood (*see* Food, *above*). During February, Chinese New Year (*see* Festivals, *below*) culminates with a parade of dancing dragons and fireworks.

CITY HALL

Although the 1928 Los Angeles City Hall is now dwarfed by surrounding skyscrapers, as an icon it stands larger than life. Its gracious form contrasts markedly with the dreary architecture of most civic buildings. TV addicts have seen the building in many guises—it served a stint as the *Daily Planet* office in the *Superman* TV series and stood in for the Vatican in the TV movie *The Thorn Birds*. Though the observation area (27th–29th floors) is closed indefinitely for seismic renovation, you can still get a good look at the interior—and a peek inside the mayor's office (3rd floor)—by taking a free guided tour. The area around this building tends to be iffy, especially after dark. *200 N. Spring St., between Temple and W. 1st Sts., tel. 213/485–4423. DASH Route A, B, or D. Free tours weekdays 10 AM and 11 AM; reservations are the only sure ticket, but you can drop by and try your luck.*

FLOWER MART

Each day before dawn, florists make a pilgrimage to this block-long series of fragrant shops and stalls crowded into several large buildings on Wall Street (between 7th and 8th Sts.). From 8 AM (6 AM on Tues day, Thursday, and Saturday) early risers jostle with wholesalers and florists to pick out enormous bouquets of every imaginable flower at wholesale prices. Most stalls close down by about 11 AM, with slightly longer hours on Wednesday and Friday. If precious gems are your preferred indulgence (and you have credit to spare) check out the **Jewelry District,** mainly on Spring St. between 5th and 7th streets. In addition to marked-down Cartier baubles and Rolex watches, this urban gold mine has wafer-thin gold leaf pendants ($5) and a brilliant selection of loose gemstones.

GARMENT DISTRICT

A slew of cut-rate clothing stores is wedged into the blocks between Santee Street, Maple Avenue, 12th Street, and Pico Boulevard—though looking for stylish bargains can be frustrating. The four-floor **Cooper Building** (860 S. Los Angeles St., at 9th St., tel. 213/622–1139), open Monday–Saturday 9:30–5:30 and Sunday 11–5, is filled with ugly, overpriced department store leftovers, including garb by Calvin Klein and DKNY, but the prices don't promote impulse buying. It's at the smaller shops, like **Fashion Mart** (930 S. Santee St., #219, tel. 213/689–8700) and **Comedy Club** (930 S. Santee St., #7, tel. 213/891–9311), that you'll find cheap and decent stuff. Most stores close on Sunday.

GRAND CENTRAL MARKET

Wander through this maze of produce and fishmongers' stalls, butcher shops, bakeries, and ethnic fast-food stands, and you'll rub elbows with Mexican housewives, chefs from ritzy Santa Monica restaurants, and just about every other kind of Angeleno imaginable. *317 S. Broadway, between 3rd and 4th Sts., tel. 213/624–2378. DASH Route D. Open Mon.–Sat. 9–6, Sun. 10–5:30.*

KOREATOWN

The Korean section of Los Angeles covers a large area, and it's not exactly clear where it begins and ends. Just west of downtown, the boundaries are loosely defined by Wilshire Boulevard to the north and Pico Boulevard to the south, but the only real clue that you've arrived is that the signs above the strip malls are in Korean. Mostly residential and commercial, Koreatown does not cater much to tourists. In fact, the **Korean Cultural Center** (5505 Wilshire Blvd., at Dunsmuir, tel. 213/936–7141), which has an art gallery and a library, is located outside the neighborhood. Nevertheless, it's a reasonable starting point: Gallery exhibits range from ancient calligraphy to postmodern sculpture, and if you can find a human being working there, you may get tips on further exploration. Korean restaurants tend to be fancy and expensive. Woo Lae Oak (*see* Downtown Food, *above*) is moderately priced, but for truly cheap eats, poke around the many shopping centers for more accessible Korean barbecue.

LITTLE TOKYO

More like a mall than a neighborhood, Little Tokyo (bordered by Temple, Los Angeles, 3rd, and Alameda streets and served by DASH Route A) nonetheless offers many bits of interest amid lots of touristy schlock. Within the **Japanese Village Plaza** (on 1st and 2nd streets between San Pedro and Central avenues, tel. 213/620–8861) you can ignore the overpriced gift shops and focus on the bookstores, pharmacies, and grocery stores, along with many restaurants of all price ranges, depending on whether you prefer sushi, teriyaki, or shabu-shabu (*see* Food, *above*). The **Japanese-American National Museum** (369 E. 1st St., at Central Ave., tel. 213/624–0414) has small but very well-presented temporary exhibits on subjects like internment and Japanese-American veterans. Admission is $4, and the museum is open Tuesday–Sunday 10–5 (on Thursday until 8; admission is free the third Thursday of every month). The adjoining row of buildings, known as the **Little Tokyo Historic District,** lets you envision the Japanese-American community before their forced relocation during World War II. Across the street and down a small alley, the **Koyosan Buddhist Temple** (342 E. 1st St., at Central Ave., tel. 213/624–1267) occupies a beautiful building and offers an English-language service open to the public every Sunday at 10.

LOS ANGELES PUBLIC LIBRARY

Recently reopened after a seven-year hiatus forced by a devastating fire, the library houses exquisite murals depicting the founding of Los Angeles, as well as the third-largest library collection in the United States. *630 W. 5th St., tel. 213/228–7000.*

MUSEUM OF CONTEMPORARY ART

The stark interior of MOCA is a startling contrast to the urban clutter of the outside world. The elegant red sandstone building—designed by Japanese architect Arata Isozaki—displays works from the museum's permanent collection, including paintings by abstract expressionists Mark Rothko and Jackson Pollock, along with special installations of contemporary pieces. A separate annex, the **Temporary Contemporary** (152 N. Central Ave.), had been scheduled for abandonment when MOCA was com-

THE FIRE THIS TIME

Issues of race, ethnicity, and economics have lent the city of Los Angeles a segregated geography—residents of various communities often only cross paths on the freeway. This separatist lifestyle exploded in April 1992, when devastating riots followed the acquittal of four white officers charged in the videotaped beating of black motorist Rodney King.

Several years later, the Rodney King riots have taken their place in the history books next to the riots that shook Watts in 1965. But South Central has grown disillusioned with government "solutions." Instead, grassroots organizations are initiating their own revitalization programs. GED preparation courses, employment training, small business loans, job placement programs, and alliances with other economically depressed ethnic communities have recently been implemented in an attempt to strengthen the economy from the ground up.

pleted in 1986, but its popularity forced museum officials to reconsider. A free shuttle runs between the two buildings. *250 S. Grand Ave., at 3rd St., tel. 213/626–6222. DASH Route B. Admission: $6; free Thurs. after 5 PM. Open Tues.–Sun. 11–5 (Thurs. until 8).*

MUSIC CENTER

One of three performance spaces at the Music Center is the **Dorothy Chandler Pavilion** (named for the *L.A. Times* publisher's widow, who helped finance it), which trades off with the Shrine Auditorium as host to the annual Academy Awards. Jacques Lipchitz's hydrated sculpture in the courtyard outside is refreshing just to look at. Look across Hope Street from the Music Center to see an even more extravagant display of water: The Department of Water and Power is ringed by an actual moat, which at night spouts a pinkly lit fountain. For information on concert, ballet, and opera tickets at the center, *see* After Dark, *below.* *Grand Ave., at 1st St., tel. 213/972–7211. DASH Route B. Free tours available; call for schedule.*

OLVERA STREET

On cobblestone, pedestrian-only **Olvera Street,** you'll find carts groaning with hand-tooled leather goods and open-air restaurants serving delicious *churros* (Mexican donuts), *carne asada* (grilled meat on a tortilla with beans), and frosty margaritas. The street is part of **El Pueblo de Los Angeles Historic Park,** a collection of low wooden buildings that made up the original city, circa 1800. At around noon daily, the historic plaza becomes a stage for folkloric and Aztec dancers. The park also plays host to numerous special festivals (*see* Festivals, *below*), including the springtime Blessing of the Animals, *Cinco de Mayo* (5th of May), and *Día de los Muertos* (Day of the Dead) in November. Built in 1818, the **Avila Adobe** on the east side of Olvera Street is the oldest house in Los Angeles. The carefully restored rooms are open to the public daily 10–5, free of charge. The park is bordered by Alameda, Arcadia, Spring, and Macy streets; it's one block east of Union Station, where most MTA buses stop. *Visitor center: Sepulveda House, 622 N. Main St., tel. 213/628–1274. DASH Route B or D. Open Mon.–Sat. 10–3. Free park tours hourly Tues.–Sat. 10–1 on the hour.*

UNION STATION

Union Station and the Union Pacific Railroad helped transform Los Angeles from an underpopulated farming community into a bustling metropolis in the era before the superhighway. An eclectic mix of Spanish colonial, Southwestern, and art deco styles, the station is also the best example of 1940s architecture in Los Angeles—a rare combination of marble floors, wrought-iron gas lamps, wood paneling, and engraved ceilings. It's now an Amtrak depot, linked with regional and local mass-transit lines. *800 N. Alameda St., tel. 213/683–6729. Just north of I–101. DASH Route B or D.*

SOUTH CENTRAL L.A.

Southwest of downtown LA lies the historically African American communities collectively known as South Central, bordered by **Crenshaw Boulevard** to the west, **Manchester Avenue** to the south, **Central Avenue** to the east, and **Slauson Avenue** to the north. Recently emigrated Latinos and Pacific Islanders continue to settle here in droves. Most people's preconceptions about the neighborhood involve images of gang warfare and riots. To be sure, gangs do operate here, though their main targets are usually other gangs. Generally, the predominantly African American middle-class neighborhoods north of Slauson Avenue, where most of South Central's tourist attractions lie, are less troubled by urban violence than the areas to the south. If you visit during the day, you'll be relatively safe, but it's hard not to be disconcerted by the rampant evidence of poverty, from boarded-up delis to exhausted and sagging apartment complexes. Juxtaposed against the poverty of most of this area are the exclusive, private **University of Southern** and **Exposition Park,** home to several museums and sporting stadiums.

EXPOSITION PARK

Created in 1880, Exposition Park is beginning to show signs of age and exhaustion (it hosted Olympic festivities in 1932 and 1984), but it's worth a visit nonetheless. Take a stroll in the centrally located 14-acre **Sunken Rose Garden** before tackling one of the park's fascinating museums. The free **California Science Center** (700 State Dr., tel. 213/744–7400), open daily 10–5, houses everything from an authentic space capsule and fighter planes to hands-on computers and robots. At the museum's **IMAX Theatre** (tel. 213/744–2014), a larger-than-life movie experience is $6 ($4.75 students). The **Natural History Museum** (900 Exposition Blvd., tel. 213/744–3466), open Tuesday–Sunday 10–5, contains gems and minerals, fossils, and the obligatory stuffed mammals in lifelike poses. Admission is $6 ($3.50 students) and is free the first Tuesday of the month. The free **California Afro-American Museum** (600 State Dr., tel. 213/744–7432) explores the history, art, and culture of African American people in the United States. Stop by Tuesday–Sunday 10–5. The Olympic torch burns atop the **Coliseum,** which, like the adjacent **Sports Arena,** is home to some pro and collegiate sports teams (*see* Outdoor Activities, *below*).

LEIMERT PARK

You might easily overlook this tiny triangle of shops and greenery in a middle-class community about 1 mi north of Slauson Avenue. But Leimert Park (cnr Crenshaw Blvd. and Vernon Ave.) is an oasis of prosperous African American culture amid the blight of South Central's boarded-up storefronts. The shops on 43rd Place and Degnan Boulevard feature African clothing, art, jewelry, and food. Stop by **5th Street Dick's Coffee Company** (3347½ W. 43rd Pl., tel. 213/296–3970) for a powerful cup of Ethiopian coffee ($3) and some of the best jazz in Los Angeles, as well as poetry, drama, and rap. The customers and the men playing dominoes tend to go out of their way to be friendly. During the week after Christmas, Leimert Park is the site of the annual **Kwanzaa Festival** (*see* Festivals, *below*). To reach the park, take Crenshaw Boulevard south from I–10 or Vernon Avenue west from the Harbor Freeway (I–110).

UNIVERSITY OF SOUTHERN CALIFORNIA

Founded in 1880, USC (dubbed the "University of Spoiled Children" by rivals) is the West Coast's oldest major private college. Tree-shaded Spanish-style and contemporary brick buildings provide the backdrop for this enclave of wealth and privilege—a gated and fenced village some 30,000 students strong—in a sea of relative poverty. The film school has graduated the likes of George Lucas, Ron Howard, and John Singleton; and the football team, the Trojans, once starred O. J. Simpson. A stroll across campus can be rewarding for movie buffs: *The Graduate, The Hunchback of Notre Dame,* and parts of *Forrest Gump* were all shot here. Worthwhile stops include the beautiful main lobby and reading rooms of **Doheny Memorial Library,** the oddly shaped **Shrine Auditorium,** and tiny **Widney Hall,** constructed in the early 1880s. Maps are available at all eight entrance gates. *Campus information: tel. 213/740–2311. From I–110, exit at Exposition Blvd. Enter campus at Gate 1 on Exposition Blvd., or turn right on Figueroa St. and enter at Gate 2. Free 1-hour walking tours weekdays 10–3; for reservations call Alumni House, tel. 213/740–2300.*

WATTS TOWERS ARTS CENTER

A masterpiece of Los Angeles folk art, the Watts Towers were constructed by Italian immigrant Simon Rodia entirely of discarded objects (for example, scrap iron, abandoned bedsteads, and shards of bottles and seashells) he collected between 1921 and 1954. The tallest of the three main structures stands an impressive 99½ ft tall. Art historians compare the steel and wire towers (embedded with colorful glass shards) to Gaudí's Barcelona cathedral but to the average traveler, the Watts Towers are simply a strik-

PURSUING THE HOLLYWOOD GRAIL

Though years have passed since the last failed starlet did a swan dive from one of its 50-ft-tall O's, questions about the famous HOLLYWOOD *sign are routinely intercepted by Griffith Park rangers with a curt "It's off-limits." One look at the expressway-size trails blazing up the hillside from the ends of Deronda and Innsdale drives, though, and you know people are hiking up there.*

ing and imaginative work looming over South Central Los Angeles with peculiar majesty. Despite several private and city-led efforts to raze them, the structures now stand in a state historic park. There aren't any tours while the towers are being restored, but you can come anytime and peek through the fence. This is not a place you want to linger after dark. *1727 E. 107th St., at Graham Ave., tel. 213/847–4646. Take I–110 to I–105 east; exit north at S. Central Ave., turn right onto 108th St., left onto Graham Ave.*

HOLLYWOOD

Modern Tinseltown came from inauspicious beginnings: The city's first movie was filmed in a German immigrant's barn at the corner of Sunset Boulevard and Gower Street in 1914. At the time, the area was called Hollywoodland, and most residents made a living farming fruit. Forty years later, Hollywood had shed the cumbersome last four letters of its name and emerged as the Movie Capital of the World. In the decades since, its star has dimmed slightly; studio after studio has slipped over the hills to cheaper real estate in Burbank. People around the globe still dream of a glamorous Hollywood, and wanna-bes still flock to Tinseltown hoping to trade their pasts for more promising futures. But in reality, the only stars you'll see here are those embedded in the sidewalk along Hollywood Boulevard.

The eternal pimp-vs.-cop struggle of Hollywood Boulevard seems finally to have been won by the latter, and streets once dominated by boarded-up buildings are slowly being infiltrated by the *très chic* and their attendant string of hip cafés and taverns. The newly arrived naïf should still exercise caution, but don't be afraid to check out the experimental theaters on Santa Monica Boulevard (*see* After Dark, *below*) or explore the emerging, laid-back social scene on Franklin and North Vermont avenues in East Hollywood (*see below*).

To make a sweep through the obligatory tourist sights, take MTA Bus 1 along Hollywood Boulevard. The bronze stars embedded in the pavement of Hollywood Boulevard will be your first clue that you've broached the much-ballyhooed **Hollywood Walk of Fame**—if the tour buses and snap-happy retirees didn't already give it away. You can easily do the walk in an afternoon. The **Hollywood Wax Museum** (6767 Hollywood Blvd., tel. 213/642–8860), **Guinness World of Records Museum** (6764 Hollywood Blvd., tel. 213/463–6433), and **Ripley's Believe It or Not!** (6780 Hollywood Blvd., tel. 213/466–6335) offer lots of Marilyn Monroe and other trivialities, each for $9 admission. Save your money for a movie.

If you have a map and some patience, you may stumble across a sliver of park northeast of the **Upper Hollywood Reservoir,** which offers a fantastic view of the legendary HOLLYWOOD sign. You'll also see some of Los Angeles's architectural jewels, including homes designed by Frank Lloyd Wright, R. M. Schindler, and Richard Neutra.

HOLLYWOOD BOWL

The Hollywood Bowl, a striking white bandshell nestled in the Hollywood foothills, is the summer home of the **Los Angeles Philharmonic** and the **Hollywood Bowl Orchestra.** On clear summer nights, thousands of picnic-toting Angelenos head here for performances of classical, jazz, and contemporary music. Thirteen picnic areas surround the Bowl, and they get crowded; arrive an hour or two before the performance to claim a spot. You can pick up any supplies you forgot at the Bowl's concession stands: hot dogs, beer, pesto chicken, wine, whatever—though you'll pay for the convenience. Seat prices vary by type of performance and proximity, usually ranging from about $1 (the stage looks awfully small from here) to about $25. You can catch a rehearsal for free Tuesday–Friday 9:30–noon. Call ahead to make

HOLLYWOOD

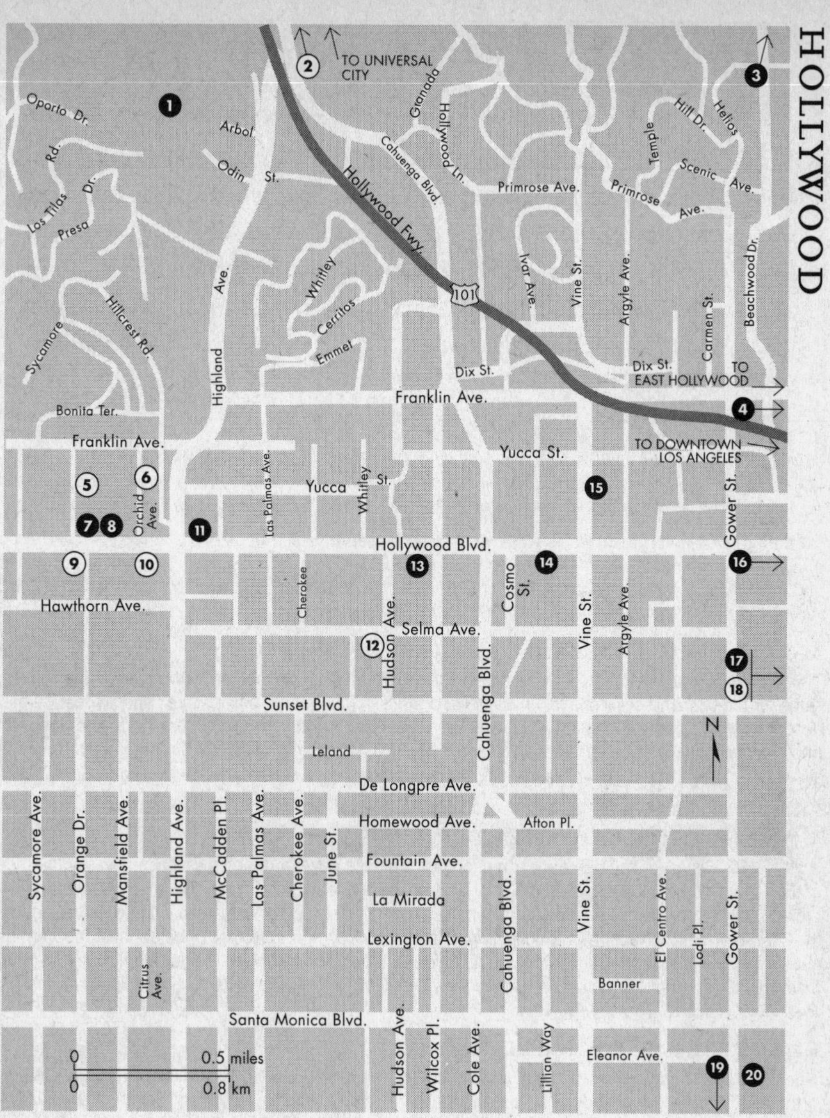

Sights ●

Capitol Records Tower, **15**

Eco-Home, **4**

Fox Televison Studios, **17**

Frederick's of Hollywood, **13**

Hollyhock House, **16**

Hollywood Bowl, **1**

Hollywood Memorial Park Cemetery, **20**

HOLLYWOOD Sign, **3**

Hollywood Walk of Fame, **14**

Hollywood Wax Museum, **11**

Mann's Chinese Theater, **8**

Motion Picture Coordination Office, **7**

Paramount Studios, **19**

Lodging ○

Banana Bungalow Hotel and Hostel, **2**

Hollywood International Guest House and Hostel, **10**

Hollywood Roosevelt Hotel, **9**

Hollywood Towne House Motel, **18**

Hollywood Wilshire YMCA International Hostel, **12**

Liberty Hotel, **6**

Orange Drive Manor, **5**

WALK OF FAME DO-IT-YOURSELF TOUR

Alfred Hitchcock: 7013 Hollywood Blvd. W. C. Fields: 7004 Hollywood Blvd. Michael Jackson: 6927 Hollywood Blvd. Olivia Newton-John: 6925 Hollywood Blvd. Greta Garbo: 6901 Hollywood Blvd. Groucho Marx: 6821 Hollywood Blvd. Elvis Presley: 6777 Hollywood Blvd. Marilyn Monroe: 6776 Hollywood Blvd. Charlie Chaplin: 6751 Hollywood Blvd. Sylvester Stallone: 6712 Hollywood Blvd. Lucille Ball: 6436 Hollywood Blvd. Bette Davis: 6225 Hollywood Blvd. Clark Gable: 1608 Vine St. John Lennon: 1750 Vine St.

sure a rehearsal is scheduled. *2301 N. Highland Ave., ¾ mi north of Hollywood Blvd., tel. 213/850–2000 for performance and Bowlexpress information. Bowlexpress Park & Ride service ($2.50 round-trip) from 15 locations in L.A. County; or MTA Bus 212 or 420. Performances June–Sept., Tues.–Sun.*

On the grounds of the Bowl is the **Hollywood Bowl Museum,** which houses a permanent collection of photos and documents charting the history of the structure, as well as exhibits about guest composers and special performances. Come here only if you're going to the Bowl already. *Tel. 213/850–2058. Admission free. Open Tues.–Sat. 10–4:30 (until 8:30 concert nights).*

MOTION PICTURE COORDINATION OFFICE

This is an invaluable resource if you're determined to see at least one celebrity (though you may have to settle for the cast and crew of a low-budget HBO thriller). Pick up the office's free "shoot sheet," which describes what's being filmed around town each day: It lists the kind of shoot (film, TV, music video, still photography), who's involved, and when and where it's happening. Once you find the set you may be allowed a closer inspection—perhaps even an autograph—if you remain polite and calm. *7083 Hollywood Blvd., 5th floor, tel. 213/957–1000. Open weekdays 8–6.*

MANN'S CHINESE THEATER

Built in 1927 as an outlandish approximation of a Chinese pagoda, Mann's Chinese is easily the most garish structure on Hollywood Boulevard. During the glorious '30s, opening nights drew enormous crowds anxious to glimpse arriving stars in person. Today—though movies are still shown in the opulent theater—the main attraction is a collection of some 160 cement imprints of celebrities' feet, hands, guns, cigars, and so forth outside the lobby. If you watch a movie here, make certain it's playing in the main theater and not the bland secondary theaters. *6925 Hollywood Blvd., between Highland and La Brea Aves., tel. 213/464–8111.*

FREDERICK'S OF HOLLYWOOD

The legendary purveyors of licentious lingerie also have a well-endowed **Bra Museum** (admission free) in the back of the store. Besides its "History of the Bra" display, there's a riveting "Celebrity Lingerie Hall of Fame," with undergarb once worn by Mae West, panties from Zsa Zsa Gabor, a Madonna bustier—even one of Milton Berle's bras. Though the museum was looted during the 1992 riots, most stolen bras were later returned—one remorseful man turned in his booty to a bemused priest. *6608 Hollywood Blvd., at Wilcox Ave., tel. 213/466–8506. Open Mon.–Thurs. and Sat. 10–6, Fri. 10–9, Sun. noon–5.*

CAPITOL RECORDS TOWER

When Capitol Records needed new offices in 1956, singer Nat King Cole and songwriter Johnny Mercer suggested that the company build a cylindrical tower resembling a stack of records. And voilà, it was done. If you peek through the window you can see the lobby, where numerous awards for gold and platinum albums line the walls. The crowning bit of kitsch: The red beacon atop the tower spells out Hollywood nonstop in Morse code. *1750 North Vine St., at Hollywood Blvd.*

HOLLYWOOD MEMORIAL PARK CEMETERY

Fame *is* immortal. Just ask the Memorial Park gardeners, who have seen countless tourists drive up in rented convertibles, stand on the gravesites of their favorite stars, and take snapshots of the tombstones with disposable cameras. The remains of Mel Blanc; Douglas Fairbanks, Sr.; Marion Davies; and other celebrities are here, denied anonymity even in death by a tour-of-the-dead-stars map available free in the cemetery office. *6000 Santa Monica Blvd., between Gower St. and Van Ness Ave., tel. 213/469–1181. Open daily 8–5.*

HOLLYHOCK HOUSE

Hollyhock House stands in the middle of **Barnsdall Art Park,** a small art community founded by oil heiress Aline Barnsdall. It is the first—and probably the most unusual—of the many L.A. projects designed by architect Frank Lloyd Wright. Built in the 1920s, the house is filled with quirky touches, like a water-filled moat surrounding the living-room fireplace and inward-sloping walls on the second floor. Mayan designs and hollyhock flowers are motifs used throughout the house. A few doorways measure only 5′7″—the "perfect" height for a door, according to short-of-stature Wright. The Art Park is also home to the **Los Angeles Municipal Art Gallery** (tel. 213/485–4581), known for its excellent contemporary art exhibits. *4800 Hollywood Blvd., at Vermont Ave., tel. 213/662–7272. Tours ($2) on the hour, Wed.–Sun. noon–3.*

If you approach anyone holding a clipboard at Mann's Chinese Theater, you'll likely walk away with free movie preview tickets.

ECO-HOME

Los Angeles, land of smog and excess, is hardly the place you'd expect to find Eco-Home, an ecologically sound household that features all sorts of low-cost, earth-friendly features, from solar energy panels to xeriscapes (low-water, low-maintenance landscaping). In order to see the house, you have to go on a two-hour tour, during which you'll get tips on how your house can be an eco-home. *4344 Russell Ave., near Vermont Ave., Los Feliz, tel. 213/662–5207. Admission: $7. Tours Oct.–June, Sun. 2–4:30; July–Sept., Sun. 4–6:30. Reservations required.*

EAST HOLLYWOOD

If you're tired of Melrose attitude and Hollywood grime, head east to East Hollywood. Here, around the intersection of Franklin and North Vermont avenues, you'll find a newish café and club scene that has so far avoided the pretense that accompanies almost every emerging L.A. trend. On Franklin, have a coffee at the **Bourgeois Pig** (*see* Cafés, *above*) or dine at **Prizzi's Piazza** (*see* Food, *above*). On Vermont, wax critical about the art on the walls at **The Onyx** (*see* Cafés, *above*) while you wait for a spontaneous performance to develop out of thin air (and it will). After a hard day's window-shopping and people-watching, stop by the **Dresden Room** (*see* After Dark, *below*) for liquid refueling to the accompaniment of Sinatra tunes.

GRIFFITH PARK

Griffith Park's 4,213 acres in the Santa Monica Mountains, northeast of Hollywood, are part of a dwindling number of "nature zones" within L.A. county limits. Though portions have been developed for human pursuits, the bulk has been left in a relatively pristine state. Hiking, cycling, and horseback riding are all options (*see* Outdoor Activities, *below*); for safety, solo travelers should remain on maintained, populated trails, and leave before dark. *Visitor center and ranger headquarters: 4730 Crystal Springs Dr., at Griffith Park Dr., tel. 213/665–5188. West of I–5, between Hwy. 134 and Los Feliz Blvd. From I–5, exit at Los Feliz Blvd., Griffith Park, or Zoo Dr., and follow signs. From Hwy. 134, exit at Forest Lawn Dr. Park open daily 5:30 AM–10 PM.*

AUTRY MUSEUM OF WESTERN HERITAGE

If ever there were a politically correct cowboy museum, this is it. Funded by Gene Autry's estate, the huge, sophisticated collection of artifacts (and props from TV Westerns) presents a fond look at the Old West without perpetuating myths and stereotypes about the era. It's just across the parking lot from the zoo (*see below*). *4700 Western Heritage Way, tel. 213/667–2000. Enter at Griffith Park Dr. and follow signs. Or MTA Bus 96, 97, or 412. Admission: $7.50, $5 students. Open Tues.–Sun. 10–5.*

GRIFFITH OBSERVATORY

The copper-dome observatory houses a science museum, a planetarium, a laserium, and a 12-inch telescope. Film crews love this place, as viewers of *Rebel Without a Cause* and *The Terminator* can attest. If you're wondering how much you'd weigh on Mars, head to the **Hall of Science** (free), with interactive computers and exhibits designed for both kids and adults. In the main hall, you can buy tickets for the hour-long **Planetarium** presentation ($4) or for **Laserium** ($7), a laser-art show set to the tunes of bands like Led Zeppelin, U2, and Pink Floyd. (Beware the hordes of red-eyed youths who flock here on Friday and Saturday nights.) On clear evenings from 7 to 9:45, peer through the telescope (free) at Jupiter or the Orion nebula. *2800 E. Observatory Rd., tel. 213/664–1191. Enter Griffith Park from Los Feliz Blvd. and follow signs. Call for Laserium and Planetarium show times. Observatory open summer, daily 12:30 PM–10 PM; winter, Tues.–Fri. 2 PM–10 PM, weekends 12:30 PM–10 PM.*

L.A. ZOO

If you need a break from the urban jungle, head to the zoo. Considerable effort (and a lot of corporate money) has been spent to give the 1,200 animals here some semblance of a natural habitat, making L.A.'s zoo comparatively humane. The newest exhibits are **Tiger Falls,** where a pair of Bengals frolic in waterfalls, and **Adventure Island,** which houses bats, mountain lions, and other natives of the American Southwest. The vast zoo is well worth an afternoon's exploration, so wear comfortable shoes. *5333 W. Zoo Dr., tel. 213/666–4650. Enter Griffith Park at Los Feliz Blvd. or Zoo Dr. and follow signs. Admission: $8.25 (look for discount coupons at city visitor centers). Open daily 10–5; ticket sales stop at 4.*

WEST HOLLYWOOD

West Hollywood is home to some of Los Angeles's best bars, cafés, clubs, and galleries, most of which line **Santa Monica Boulevard** between Doheny Drive and La Cienega Boulevard. This is a commercial and social center for the gay, lesbian, and bisexual community. But on Saturday night, the sidewalks are thronged with club-hopping couples both gay and straight. Begin your visit with a look at the landmark **Pacific Design Center** (south of Santa Monica Blvd. on San Vicente Blvd.), closed to the public but fun to admire from outside; locals refer to the colorful glass-and-steel structure as "the Blue Whale." Santa Monica Boulevard is served by MTA Bus 4.

At **A Different Light Bookstore** (8853 Santa Monica Blvd., near San Vicente Blvd., tel. 310/854–6601), you'll find an excellent selection of gay and lesbian literature. The tiny shop **Don't Panic** (802 N. San Vicente Blvd., at Santa Monica Blvd., tel. 310/287–3250) sells T-shirts with pro-queer messages for about $18 each. **Little Frida's,** one of the few spots along the strip for the ladies, has good strong coffee, friendly service, and pleasant ambience. At the **Troubadour** (*see* After Dark, *below*), some of the biggest names in rock have played as relative unknowns.

SUNSET STRIP

Wild-child **Sunset Strip** (Sunset Blvd., between Doheny Dr. and Crescent Heights Blvd.) was Los Angeles's locus of hippie youth, anti-war protests, and rock and roll during the 1960s and '70s; though you'll still find an industrial-strength concentration of nightclubs, things are much tamer than they used to be (partly due to the subduing effect of the AIDS epidemic). Closed is the Dionysian den Gazzarri's, where the Doors, Van Halen, and Guns 'N Roses all climbed from obscurity. There's still the self-consciously cool **Roxy** and groupie-jammed **Whiskey A Go Go,** as well as the trendy new **House of Blues,** owned by actor Dan Ackroyd (for more on nightclubs, *see* After Dark, *below*). These days, though, you're more likely to encounter yuppies on their way to catch headline acts at the **Comedy Store** (8433 Sunset Blvd., tel. 213/656–6225) than beer-swilling glam rockers in leather.

MELROSE AND THE WILSHIRE DISTRICT

The area bordered by Melrose Avenue to the north, Wilshire Boulevard to the south, and I–405 and I–110 to the west and east, respectively, is Los Angeles's "midsection," the stuff most tourists skip over in their haste to get from Hollywood and Beverly Hills to coastal towns like Malibu and Santa Monica. Don't make the same mistake: This is archetypal Los Angeles, where you can glimpse stars in their sneakers, be served lunch by an aspiring actor, and check out a large contingent of tattooed plastic-surgery recipients. It's also home to a growing number of excellent museums on Wilshire Boulevard. MTA Bus 10 serves Melrose Avenue, Bus 14 runs down Beverly Boulevard, and Buses 20–22, 320, and 322 travel Wilshire Boulevard.

MELROSE AVENUE

The epicenter of L.A. trendy, Melrose is lined with cafés, restaurants, avant-garde art galleries, and a jumble of stores purveying '60s and '70s furniture, clothing, and kitsch. Even if you lack the capital to

WEST LOS ANGELES

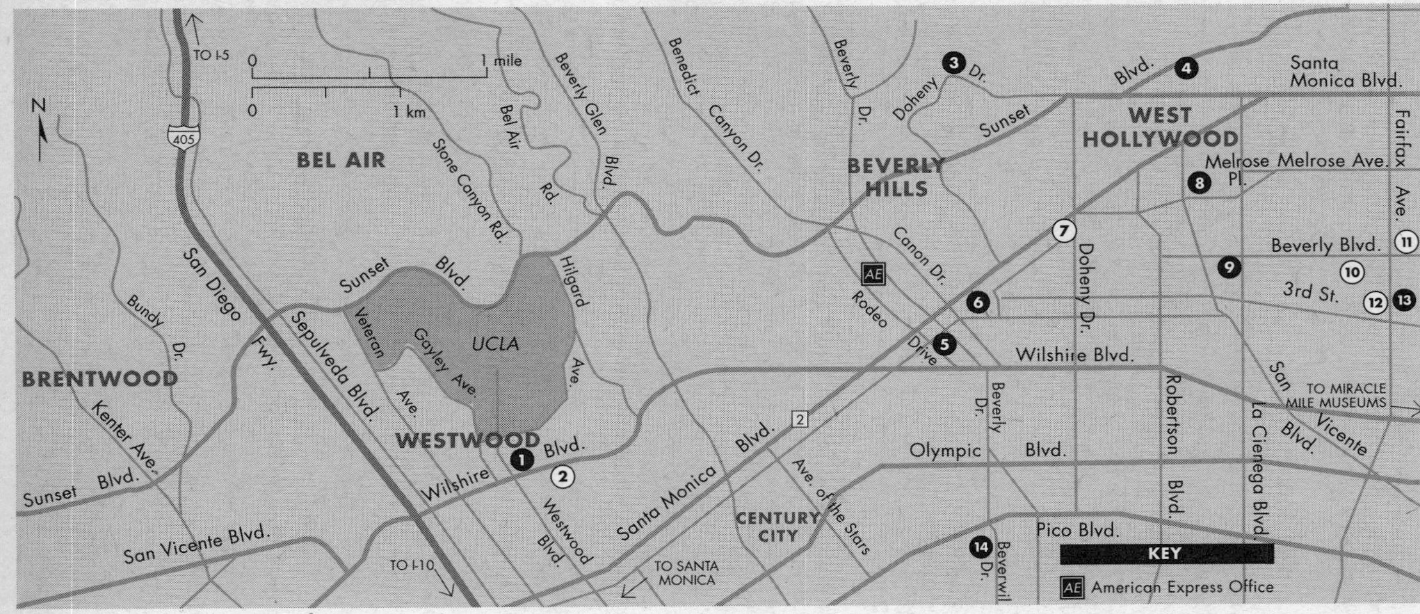

Sights ●
Armand Hammer Museum of Art, **1**
Beverly Center, **9**
Beverly Hills Civic Center, **6**
Farmers' Market, **13**
Greystone Mansion, **3**
Museum of Television and Radio, **5**
Museum of Tolerance, **14**
Pacific Design Center, **8**
Sunset Strip, **4**

Lodging ○
Beverly Laurel Motor Hotel, **10**
Beverly Terrace Hotel, **7**
Bevonshire Lodge Motel, **11**
Farmer's Daughter Motel, **12**
Westwood Inn, **2**

CELEBRITY ADDRESSES

Aaron Spelling's château (the house that "Charlie's Angels," "Dynasty," and "Melrose Place" built): On the 500 block of North Mapleton Drive in Bel Air. With 123 rooms, it's only nine short of the White House.

Madonna's old estate: On Canyon Lake Highway, near the Hollywood Reservoir. When the Material Girl moved into this former casino, she painted the entire thing in horizontal red and yellow stripes.

Ronald Reagan's house: On the 600 block of St. Cloud Road, in Bel Air. Wife Nancy created minor postal havoc by insisting on a number change—the original address was 666.

O.J.'s former residence at 375 North Rockingham Avenue in Brentwood. Site of the bloody glove, the bloody sock, and who knows what bloody else.

purchase a studded leather bodysuit, it's fun to gawk at the duds and the youthful celebs attempting to shop incognito. Let the 6900–8200 blocks of Melrose (between Highland Ave. and Crescent Heights Blvd.) be your starting point; you can park on surrounding residential streets, but pay attention to posted restrictions.

Pick up a glossy fashion magazine—or the local paper, whichever you prefer—at **Melrose News** (647 N. Martel Ave., at Melrose Ave., tel. 213/655–2866). The **Cosmopolitan Book Shop** (7017 Melrose Ave., tel. 213/938–7119) has a good selection of used, 50¢ paperbacks perfect for a café read. At **Off the Wall Antiques** (7325 Melrose Ave., tel. 213/930–1185), marvel at the latest pop trophy for sale; previous offerings have included Elvis Presley's Corvette convertible and several life-size fiberglass cows ($2,400 per heifer).

Before heading south down La Brea Avenue to admire the ultra-chic furniture stores or to shop for used clothing, grab a chili dog at **Pink's** (*see* Food, *above*); then stop by **Fréwil** (605 N. La Brea Ave., tel. 213/934–8474), one of many havens of interior design along this street. Parallel to and south of Melrose is **Beverly Boulevard,** where you'll find lots of shops selling custom-made garb that looks street but costs steep. Admire and move on to **Insomnia** (*see* Cafés, *above*) for your third or fourth cappuccino of the afternoon.

FAIRFAX AVENUE

While the Jews who founded the Hollywood motion picture industry kept their ethnicity under wraps, the Orthodox Jews of the Fairfax district have no problem showing their colors. Kosher delis, religious shops, and Jewish community organizations line Fairfax Avenue between Beverly and Melrose. **Canter's** deli (419 N. Fairfax, tel. 213/651–2030), a longtime Fairfax institution, hosts a substantial and diverse crowd, serving its famous matzo ball soup ($3) 24 hours a day. After midnight, the restaurant's bar, **The Kibitz Room,** tends to fill up with club-hoppers in leopard prints and black vinyl. Although there aren't many formal sights in the neighborhood (except for the historical mural of Jewish Los Angeles on the side of Canter's) walk down the Fairfax strip and check out the shops. **Damiano Mr. Pizza** (412 N. Fairfax, tel. 213/658–7611) offers authentic N.Y. pizza, if kosher is not your scene. Farther down at 3rd Street, the **Farmer's Market** has decent produce, cute eateries, and chintzy souvenir shops.

MIRACLE MILE MUSEUMS

You can spend at least a couple of days exploring the Wilshire District's museums. If you drive out here, however, be warned: Parking lots along Miracle Mile—the strip of Wilshire Boulevard between Fairfax and Curson avenues—can be expensive. Luckily, most lots will give discounts to those with validated museum tickets—check before you park. To reach the Miracle Mile museums from I–10 eastbound, exit north on Fairfax Avenue; from I–10 westbound, exit north on La Brea Avenue.

CAROL AND BARRY KAYE MUSEUM OF MINIATURES • Across the street from the LACMA you can find the teeny-weeny version of everything under the sun: tiny towns, tiny furniture, tiny famous people, tiny houses—you get the picture. Most interesting is the life-size violin in which a tiny violin workshop has been painstakingly re-created, complete with a half-dozen miniature instruments. Pop into the gift shop and check out the not-so-tiny prices; a miniature person retails for about $3,000. *5900 Wilshire Blvd., tel. 213/937–6464. Admission $7.50. Open Tues.–Sat. 10–5, Sun. 11–5.*

CRAFT AND FOLK ART MUSEUM • The permanent collection is a small but beautiful display of Guatemalan *hüipiles* (woven shawls). Temporary exhibits can focus on a wide range of geographic areas. Recent shows have included classic American pottery (from turn-of-the-century moonshining jugs to 1950s dinnerware) and the arts and crafts of Morocco. *5800 Wilshire Blvd., at Curson Ave., tel. 213/937–5544. Admission $4. Open Tues.–Sun. 11–5 (Fri. until 8).*

LA BREA TAR PITS • About 10,000–40,000 years before freeways and tract houses, Los Angeles was a lush basin filled with strange mammals and exotic plants. Fossil remains of these early inhabitants were excavated from La Brea's subterranean tar pits when oil was discovered in the 1890s, and recovery of Ice Age remains continues today. Look for fossilized animal bones in the sticky pools by the observation area; the adjacent small museum displays recreations of more spectacular finds, including California saber-toothed cats, an American mastodon, and a 9,000-year-old woman. *5801 Wilshire Blvd., at Curson Ave., tel. 213/857–6311. Admission to museum: $6; free first Tues. of month. Open Tues.–Sun. 10–5.*

LOS ANGELES COUNTY MUSEUM OF ART • With the help of corporate money, LACMA has put Los Angeles on the art-world map. If you've got the stamina, you could easily pass an entire day exploring its four vast galleries. The **Pavilion for Japanese Art** is a soothing world of subdued light and gently flowing water; the collection features scrolls of paper and silk from the 13th to 16th centuries. The **Ahmanson Building** showcases a variety of ancient treasures. Permanent exhibits include ornamental gold and silver; Mayan statuary dating from AD 800; amazing collections of Egyptian, Greek, and Roman statuary; and Neolithic and dynastic Chinese artifacts. The **Hammer Building** houses special exhibits that change seasonally. The **Anderson Building** features rotating displays and permanent collections of 20th-century art, including a Donald Judd minimalist sculpture and Andy Warhol's infamous *Brillo Boxes.* At the **Leo S. Bing Center,** take tea at the café, catch films and lectures at the theater (Wed. 1 PM), or visit a basement gallery of impressive local artwork. *5905 Wilshire Blvd., at Ogden Dr., tel. 213/857–6000. Admission: $6; free second Wed. of month. Open Tues.–Thurs. 10–5, Fri. 10–9, weekends 11–6; call for hrs of individual galleries.*

PETERSEN AUTOMOTIVE MUSEUM • You could call this new museum inevitable, given the city's fondness for auto travel. It displays over 130 cars and motorcycles—including Joan Crawford's '33 Cadillac and a vehicle custom-built for Elvis's *Easy Come, Easy Go.* Some may actually weep when they see the museum's 1957 Ferrari 250 Testa Rossa, especially upon learning that test drives are not allowed. *6060 Wilshire Blvd., at Fairfax Ave., tel. 213/930–2277. Admission: $7. Open Tues.–Sun. 10–6.*

WESTWOOD AND BEVERLY HILLS

Beverly Hills has glitzy shops and showy houses with a nationally known zip code, and Westwood is full of UCLA students ditching classes. If you have a car, also consider a spin through exclusive **Bel Air.** Look for local kids hawking **Star Maps** ($3–$7), which allegedly—and for the most part inaccurately—identify movie stars' addresses. MTA Bus 8 travels Westwood Boulevard; Rodeo Drive is walkable, especially if you're only window-shopping and don't have to lug all those heavy purchases around.

BEVERLY HILLS

Everything you've ever heard about the enormous wealth of Beverly Hills is true, so pack a lunch and make it a low-cost day trip of window-shopping and people-watching. **Rodeo Drive** is the fabulous shopping avenue of the rich and famous; all the major names are here, including Gucci, Armani, and Chanel. Notice that very few people actually *shop* in these by-appointment-only boutiques satirized in *Pretty Woman* and *LA Story.* The **Counterspy Shop** (9557 Wilshire Blvd., near Rodeo Dr., tel. 310/274–7700) carries lie-detector telephones, bulletproof vests, and discreet personal microphones for aspiring 007s. The opulent **Beverly Hills Civic Center** (444 N. Rexford Dr., at Santa Monica Blvd.) has an improbable pseudo-Spanish colonial tower and tile-mosaic dome. Still more shopping can be found at the **Beverly Center** (Beverly Blvd., at La Cienega Blvd., tel. 310/854–0070), an eight-story temple of fashion that's also home to the ubiquitous Hard Rock Cafe (*see* After Dark, *below*). Restore your inner tranquillity with a stroll through the perfectly manicured gardens of beautiful **Greystone Mansion** (905 Loma Vista Dr., at Doheny Rd. north of Sunset Blvd., tel. 310/550–4796). Though the $100 million house is closed to the public, the grounds are open daily 10–6 in summer and 10–5 in winter, and admission is free.

MUSEUM OF TELEVISION & RADIO • This museum houses 60,000 radio and tv programs covering a 70-year time span. Visitors have full access to this vast collection of 20th-century pop culture. The museum also has archives of news programs, documentaries, children's programming, sports, and advertising, and regularly puts on special screening series. *465 N. Beverly Dr., near Santa Monica Blvd., tel. 310/786-1000. $6. Open Wed.–Sun. noon–5 (Thurs. until 9).*

MUSEUM OF TOLERANCE • Housed inside a mammoth glass-and-steel building, this unforgettable conceptual museum asks tough questions about racism and prejudice. High-tech displays unflinchingly explore historical acts of oppression and genocide against groups as diverse as 18th-century Native Americans and World War II European Jews. Most exhibits encourage visitor participation and are designed to provoke—look for an authentic re-creation of a Holocaust gas chamber or the list of some 250 hate groups currently active in the United States. There's also an examination of the issues underlying Los Angeles's 1992 riots. It's a roller-coaster ride of revelation, revulsion, and self-doubt, occasionally heavy-handed but ultimately extraordinary. *9786 W. Pico Blvd., at Roxbury Dr., tel. 310/553–8403. Admission: $8 (advance ticket purchase recommended Fri., Sun., and holidays). Open Mon.–Thurs. 10–4, Fri. 10–1, Sun. 10:30–5.*

WESTWOOD/UCLA

The streets of Westwood Village teem with well-scrubbed kids from the University of California at Los Angeles (UCLA). Most of the action takes place on **Broxton Avenue,** lined with student-oriented shops and eateries, as well as 10—count 'em, 10—movie theaters. Before visiting campus, stop by **Diddy Riese** (926 Broxton Ave., at Le Conte Ave., tel. 310/208–0448) for a cookie (25¢). On campus, worthwhile stops include **Ackerman Student Union,** which has a well-stocked bookstore; the **Tree House** (main level), a popular place to pick up a snack; and **Melnitz Hall** (tel. 310/206–3456), which often has free showings from the Department of Film and Television's extensive collection of old movie reels. At the campus's free **Fowler Museum of Cultural History** (tel. 310/825–4361), open Wednesday–Sunday noon–5 and until 8 on Thursday, you'll find fascinating exhibits of non-Western art. Stroll among works by Rodin and Matisse at the **Franklin D. Murphy Sculpture Garden.** Reserve ahead for a guided walking tour of the garden, weekdays only, at the Art Council (tel. 310/825–3264). *UCLA switchboard: tel. 310/825–4321. Visitor center: tel. 310/206–0616. Exit I–405 and follow signs to Westwood Blvd. Pass Westwood Village, cross Le Conte Ave. to UCLA parking lots. Free maps at kiosk, just past main entrance.*

ARMAND HAMMER MUSEUM OF ART • The permanent collection at this richly endowed museum, located just south of campus, includes oils by van Gogh, Cassatt, Rubens, Monet, and Rembrandt, as well as original manuscripts penned by Leonardo Da Vinci and an extensive collection of works by 19th-century French lithographer and sculptor Honoré Daumier. *10899 Wilshire Blvd., at Westwood Blvd., tel. 310/443–7000. Admission: $4.50; free Thurs. after 6 PM. Open Tues.–Sat. 11–7 (Thurs. until 9), Sun. 11–5. Free tours daily at 1 PM.*

GETTY CENTER • Scheduled to open in late 1997, the Getty Center is the new home of much of the art collection of the late oil billionaire J. Paul Getty, as well as a center for art scholarship, education, and conservation. Getty began collecting art in the 1930s, concentrating on three areas: Greek and Roman antiquities, Baroque and Renaissance paintings, and 18th-century decorative arts. Until 1997 the collection was kept in the J. Paul Getty Museum in Malibu, which is now being renovated to house only the antiquities.

The Richard Meier–designed museum is organized as a series of pavilions around an outdoor courtyard, containing permanent collections as well as loaned exhibitions. Furniture, carpets, tapestries, clocks, chandeliers, and small decorative items made for the French, German, and Italian nobility are in the decorative arts collection. All major schools of Western art from the late 13th to the late 19th centuries are represented in the painting collection, which emphasizes Renaissance and Baroque art and includes works by Rembrandt, Rubens, de la Tour, Van Dyck, Gainsborough, and Boucher. Recent acquisitions include Old Master drawings, medieval and Renaissance illuminated manuscripts, works by Picasso, van Gogh's *Irises,* and select Impressionist paintings, including some by Claude Monet.

From the parking structure, take the tram uphill to the museum, restaurants, bookstore, and gardens. The restaurant has a beautiful view of the ocean; artist Robert Irwin designed the central garden. The

105-acre grounds also include a conservation institute with scientific labs and training facilities and a research institute with library and archives. *1200 Getty Center Dr., tel. 310/440–7300. Admission: free ($5 parking charge; reservations necessary). Open Tues. and Wed. 11–7, Thurs. and Fri. 11–9, weekends 10–6.*

SANTA MONICA AND VENICE

If you like the beach—and even if you don't—Santa Monica and Venice are full of diversions. At all hours, Beautiful People whiz by on the **Promenade/Ocean Front Walk,** a paved pathway for bicyclists, skaters, and pedestrians that links the two coastal communities. You have to wonder what these people do for a living. In each of these beach towns, Main Street is lined with shops, restaurants, art galleries, and museums aplenty.

SANTA MONICA

Santa Monica is an ironic mixture of beach town and urban blight. On Main Street, crowds of cappuccino drinkers read *The New York Times* and bask in the glow of their own success; on strips of beach near the pier, a vaguely menacing throng makes the potential for mugging almost as good as that for getting a tan. The **Santa Monica Pier** (tel. 310/458–8900) is one of the main tourist destinations, though some may find the popularity of its arcade games and greasy fast-food stands unfathomable. Here you can ride a restored 1922 carousel (open June–Sept., Tues.–Sun.; Sept.–May, weekends only) for 50¢, or stare at the water over a fishing pole ($3/hr) rented from **SM Pier Bait and Tackle** (tel. 310/576–2014). In the Pacific Park amusement area at the foot of the pier, a **roller coaster** with a 30-ft drop and an 11-story Ferris wheel that affords a great view of Santa Monica Bay are fresh additions. Exercise caution when hanging around the pier after dark. You can also stroll the adjacent shady **Palisades Park,** or rent Rollerblades (*see* Outdoor Activities, *below*) and cruise the waterfront promenade. Watch for people with clipboards—they may be studio flunkies distributing free movie tickets.

Look for the Frank Gehry–designed offices of the TBWA Chiat/Day advertising agency (340 Main St., Venice). The building's facade is shaped like giant three-story binoculars.

Beyond the beach, Santa Monica is a mecca of small museums and shops. The **18th Street Arts Complex** (1639 18th St., at Olympic Blvd., tel. 310/453–3711) includes artists' residences, galleries, and a performance space that often features gay and lesbian events. Do your art criticism down the street at **Wednesday's House** (*see* Cafés, *above*), among the velvet Elvis paintings. A few more blocks northwest, look for **Bergamot Station** (2525 Michigan Ave., between Pico and Olympic, tel. 310/829–5854), an art gallery complex housed in a restored railroad depot, where you'll find a high concentration of intriguing works by young, up-and-coming artists, and the newly relocated **Santa Monica Museum of Art,** hosting unusual exhibits of contemporary paintings.

If you're interested in Golden State history, step into the **California Heritage Museum** (2612 Main St., at Ocean Park Blvd., tel. 310/392–8537), housed in an 1894 American Colonial revival home. Rotating displays of California history are on the second floor; the first floor has rooms furnished in turn-of-the-century styles. Admission is $3. If fighter planes get your blood pumping, pay $7 to see the **Museum of Flying** (2772 Donald Douglas Loop N, at Santa Monica Airport, tel. 310/392–8822). You can check out Spitfires, Sopwith Camels, jet fighters, and the 1986 *Voyager,* the first plane to make a nonstop, unrefueled around-the-world flight. For $2 a shot, you can fly in a simulation ride; the stomach-turning Tornado is not to be missed.

Two inland areas lend themselves to people-watching. The **Third Street Promenade** is a Disneyfied version of hip, worth a quick walk-through. This pedestrians-only bazaar between Wilshire Boulevard and Broadway features topiary dinosaurs that look like giant Chia pets and Generation X chains like Z Gallerie and Urban Outfitters. Browse the shelves in the **Midnight Special Bookstore** (1318 3rd St., tel. 310/393–2923), which has Friday evening poetry readings (*see* Cheap Thrills, *below*). **Benita's Frites** (1437 3rd St., tel. 310/458–2889) serves up tasty Belgian-style fries with dipping sauces like peanut curry satay. The scene grows increasingly sophisticated as you move north toward **Montana Avenue** between Ocean Avenue and Lincoln Boulevard. Shops here sell artsy jewelry, one-of-a-kind furniture, and whimsical (if pricey) clothing. Every other storefront is a coffee shop, so take a break here and watch celebs stroll by with their kids.

SANTA MONICA AND VENICE

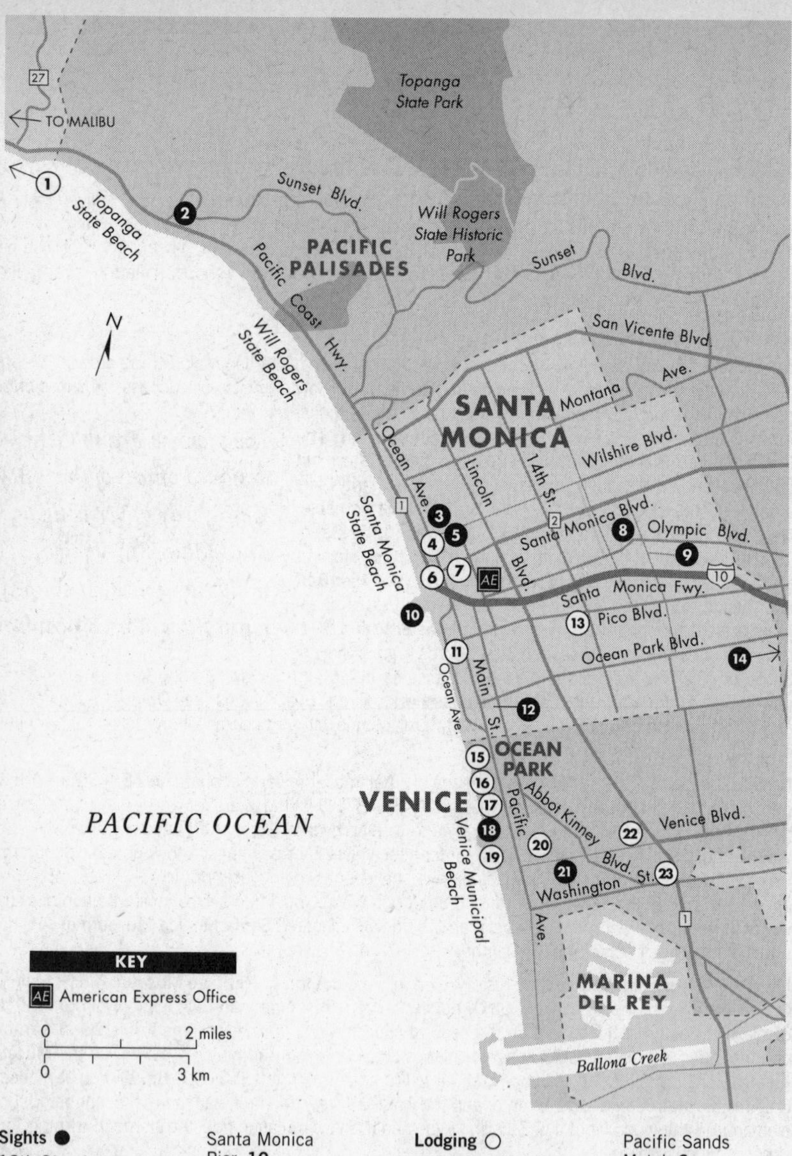

Sights ●

18th Street Arts Complex, **8**

Bergamot Station, **9**

California Heritage Museum, **12**

Muscle Beach, **18**

Museum of Flying, **14**

Palisades Park, **3**

Santa Monica Pier, **10**

Self-Realization Fellowship Lake Shrine, **2**

Third Street Promenade, **5**

Venice Boardwalk, **18**

Venice Canals, **21**

Lodging ○

Airport Hostel, **22**

Bayside Hotel, **11**

Cadillac Hotel, **15**

Hotel Carmel, **4**

Jim's at the Beach, **16**

Jolly Roger Hotel, **23**

Malibu Surfer Motel, **1**

Pacific Sands Motel, **6**

Palm Motel, **13**

Santa Monica American Youth Hostel, **7**

Share Tel Apartments, **17**

Venice Beach Cotel, **19**

Venice Beach Hostel, **20**

VENICE

The undisputed magnet for L.A. eccentrics is Venice Beach. Even its birth involved bizarre circumstances: At the turn of the century, cigarette manufacturer Abbot Kinney bought up land south of Santa Monica and built a replica of Italy's Venice, complete with a small-scale copy of St. Mark's Cathedral and 16 mi of saltwater canals. Alas, canal-making in California was an engineering problem, and anti-gondola snobbery ran rampant in the new automobile age. Most of Kinney's underappreciated constructions were torn down when the city of Los Angeles annexed Venice in 1925. A few residence-lined canals remain, south of Venice Boulevard and east of Ocean Avenue. Only recently dredged of stinky algae, they're now a pleasant place for a stroll. The **Venice Boardwalk** is perennially thronged with bikini-clad rollerbladers, T-shirt hawkers, street musicians and artisans, and New Age prophets; several characters, such as the chain-saw juggler and the rollerblading Rastafarian guitarist, could qualify as boardwalk ambassadors. At **Muscle Beach** (1800 Ocean Front Walk), perfectly pumped bodybuilders from Gold's Gym flex and lift weights in the open air. If you yearn to become a part of the Venice scene, rent a bike or a pair of 'blades (*see* Outdoor Activities, *below*). Otherwise, grab a beer (about $3) at the **Sidewalk Café** (1401 Ocean Front Walk, at Horizon Ave., tel. 310/399–5547), sit back, and enjoy the show. Try to avoid the area between Lincoln and Abbot Kinney boulevards after dark: It's a notorious arena for gang warfare.

MALIBU

The city of Malibu extends along 27 mi of coastal cliffs and canyons. Besides sprawling estates and expensive restaurants, it includes one of the least developed stretches of beach in Los Angeles; nearby are acres of rugged state parklands. Though beach crowds can be annoying in summer, most of the area remains as undeveloped as it was 40 years ago, when Malibu and neighboring **Pacific Palisades** first became popular with reclusive celebrities. Local mailboxes still read like a *Who's Who* of the film world: Robert Redford, Shirley MacLaine, Dustin Hoffman, and Jack Lemmon live here, to name a few. You won't be able to see the stars' homes without a boat or a helicopter, though.

Who needs to look at aging celebrities anyway with these views of the Pacific? If the water looks tempting, check out **Malibu Surfrider State Beach** (tel. 818/880–0350), just east of Malibu Canyon Road on PCH. Here, locals carry on the tradition of longboard surfing, sometimes with antique wooden boards (for surfboard rentals, *see* Outdoor Activities, *below*). Or continue several miles farther west to **Zuma Beach County Park** (tel. 310/457–9891), a favorite escape for L.A. natives. Nudists gravitate to **Point Dume,** just north of Malibu.

Those more interested in classic nudes will be dismayed to learn that the **J. Paul Getty Museum** is closed for renovations. Although the post-Greek and -Roman works are on display in the Getty's new Brentwood space (*see* Westwood and Beverly Hills, *above*), the gorgeous Getty villa and the remainder of its amazingly well-endowed collection will be under wraps until the year 2001.

MALIBU CREEK STATE PARK

If this park triggers TV or film flashbacks, it's probably because it served as a stand-in for Korean scenery in the hit series *M*A*S*H* and as alien landscape in *Planet of the Apes.* Film crews still make the trek out here for on-location shoots. Covering 6,000 acres of the Santa Monica Mountains, the park has over 20 mi of hiking and mountain-biking trails and a cliff face popular with rock climbers. You'll want to pick up a trail map ($1) at the park entrance station. Worth exploring is the easy 1-mi trail from the park entrance to the picnic area at **Century Lake,** where camping is available (*see* Where to Sleep, *above*). *1925 Las Virgenes Rd., Calabasas, tel. 818/880–0367. 4 mi south of U.S. 101. Admission: $5 per vehicle (includes all area state parks and beaches for one day). Park open daily 8–sunset.*

SELF-REALIZATION FELLOWSHIP LAKE SHRINE

A tiny pocket of paradise only occasionally punctured by the buzz of traffic from Sunset Boulevard, this 10-acre park is maintained by the Eastern-influenced Self-Realization Fellowship. Their doctrine promotes the universality of all religions—which may explain why the chapel is housed in a Dutch-style windmill, while across the small lake a lotus-top arch flanks a stone sarcophagus containing a portion of Mahatma Gandhi's ashes. Along the gravel walkways, secluded benches encourage meditation. *17190 Sunset Blvd., Pacific Palisades, tel. 310/454–4114. ½ mi north of Pacific Coast Hwy. Admission free. Open Tues.–Sat. 9–4:30, Sun. noon–4:30.*

TAKE A WALK ON THE MILD SIDE

Universal CityWalk (tel. 818/622–4455) is Universal Studios' privately administered two-block "city"—a response to the fears about Los Angeles's carjackings, drugs, and gang warfare— conveniently cleansing the "streets" of any undesirable urban elements. Your $6 parking fee (redeemable at any of the 18 cinema screens on the premises) is the only admission price for this weird world.

WILL ROGERS STATE HISTORIC PARK

Cowboy, philanthropist, philosopher, actor, journalist, lasso artist, and naturalist Will Rogers lived at this sprawling ranch in the Santa Monica Mountains in the 1920s and '30s. In 1944, Rogers's house became a museum of the Old West, with displays of Navajo rugs, Native American arrowheads, antique saddles, cowboy boots, and a stuffed Texas longhorn bull. One wing is preserved with furnishings from Rogers's time here. Visitors can picnic on the polo grounds (for information on polo matches, *see* Outdoor Activities, *below*), or follow trails that lead from the lodge into the surrounding hills. The 1-mi hike up to **Inspiration Point** ends with a stunning view of the ocean. *14235 Sunset Blvd., between Amalfi Dr. and Brooktree Rd., Pacific Palisades, tel. 310/454–8212. Admission: $5 per vehicle. Park open daily 8–sunset. House tours daily 10:30–4:30.*

SOUTH BAY

The three beaches that make up the South Bay—Manhattan, Hermosa, and Redondo—embody many visitors' preconceptions about Southern California. The local attitude is laid-back (bordering on torpid near the water), and the pace of life is slow and undemanding. Rent and thrills are at their lowest in Redondo—proceed to the touristy pier at your own risk. If you stick to the Pacific Coast Highway (PCH), you'll see nothing but car dealerships and minimalls, but as you approach the water the distinctive features of each town emerge. Stop at any convenience store on PCH for a free copy of *Beach Reporter* or *Easy Reader*; both weeklies cover entertainment and list rentals in the South Bay.

MANHATTAN BEACH

Manhattan Beach Boulevard leads into the heart of Manhattan Beach, intersecting PCH about 3 mi south of the airport and ending at the pier. More upscale than Hermosa and less commercial than Redondo, Manhattan Beach has lots of condos, relatively few unemployed surfers, and plenty of attitude. At its northern boundary begins the **Strand,** part of a 22-mi, two-lane beachfront "highway" open to bicyclists, skaters, and pedestrians. This is *the* place to gawk and be gawked at along the South Bay coast. The gloriously clean sands host a seemingly endless string of volleyball nets. Stroll down the end of the municipal pier to the free **Roundhouse Aquarium,** where you can check out spiny lobsters, menacing crabs, and slinky sea slugs in an almost-natural environment.

HERMOSA BEACH

If you're looking for the archetypal Southern California seaside town, head for Hermosa Beach, just south of Manhattan. Though multimillion-dollar houses line the water, there's an antiestablishment feel; even the Mercedes Benzes sport Grateful Dead stickers. To reach Hermosa's low-key jumble of shops and restaurants from PCH, look for Pier Avenue, 2 mi south of Manhattan Beach (it leads to the municipal pier). You'll look out of place unless you're sporting equipment here: At **Jeffers Beach Rentals** (39 14th St., just off the Strand, tel. 310/372–9492), you'll find in-line skates ($6/hr), body boards ($4–$5/hr), and volleyballs ($2/hr). Lower rates are available for full-day rentals. At **Hermosa Cyclery** (20 13th St., just off the Strand, tel. 310/376–2720) bike rentals are $6–$12 an hour or $19–$36 a day.

If you tire of watching the take-no-prisoners volleyball being played by the pier, take a jaunt to **Hamilton Gregg Brewworks** (58 11th St., between the Strand and Hermosa Ave., tel. 310/376–0406), where customers brew their own beer in giant steel kettles ($100 gets you 48 bottles). If you're just passing through, you won't be able to brew; the beer requires two weeks of aging. It's fun to watch, however, and the display of witty personalized labels rivals many art galleries in creativity. Farther inland, the **Either/Or Bookstore** (124 Pier Ave., just east of Hermosa Ave., tel. 310/374–2060) offers a heady selection of obscure and enlightened fiction, nonfiction, and periodicals; you are encouraged to plop down and browse until 11 PM nightly.

STUDIOS

Most of the movie and television studios, apart from Fox and Paramount, aren't actually in Los Angeles; they're in the San Fernando Valley (*see* Chapter 10). But because the studios are an integral part of the L.A. tourist experience, all are listed below. In choosing a studio to tour, weigh admission prices against your interests. If it's rides and spectacle you're after, head for the Universal Studios extravaganza. If you want a more straightforward glimpse of life behind the camera, try the cheaper and subtler NBC or Paramount tours. If you prefer an intimate group of 12 or fewer people accompanying you, pay extra for Warner's "personalized" tour.

FOX TELEVISION

Those hoping to be discovered as the next Pamela Lee will be disappointed to learn that Fox TV does *not* offer back-lot tours. The consolation prize: You can pick up free tickets to various situation comedies taped here at the Fox Television Center box office weekdays 9–3. Tickets are available beginning each Wednesday for the following week on a first-come, first-served basis. Be warned, however, that the most popular shows have a two-year waiting list. You can write requesting hot items well in advance by sending a self-addressed stamped envelope to Fox Television, 100 Universal City Plaza, Building 153, Universal City, CA 91608, or you can play it casual and drop in on a sleeper. *5746 Sunset Blvd., 1 block west of U.S. 101, Hollywood,; call Audiences Unlimited to order tickets by phone: 818/506–0043.*

NBC STUDIOS

NBC's excellent tour takes you to working studios and sets; you might get a peek at *The Tonight Show* or an outdoor set for *Days of Our Lives.* The 1¼-hour guided walking tour of the network's facilities in Burbank also stops by the special effects, makeup, and wardrobe departments. Free tickets for *The Tonight Show* (and other programs on occasion) are available weekdays on a first-come, first-served basis; you may also request tickets by mail (with an SASE) at least two weeks in advance. *3000 W. Alameda Ave., Burbank 91523, tel. 818/840–3537. Admission: $7. Ticket office open weekdays 8–5. Tours weekdays 9–3 on the hour, 10–2 some summer Sat. Tours are on a first-come, first-served basis.*

PARAMOUNT STUDIOS

Paramount, one of the last great movie studios remaining in Hollywood proper, offers a two-hour guided walking tour through its back lots. You'll hear plenty of history and see whatever's happening around the lots on that particular day. From August through April you can also join the live studio audience for one of several television shows. In the dog-eat-dog world of the entertainment business, however, you never know what's on the chopping block and what's sizzling, so call ahead to investigate your options. Tickets, distributed on a first-come, first-served basis, are free at Paramount's box office weekdays 8:30–4. *5555 Melrose Ave., Hollywood, tel. 213/956–1777. 2 blocks east of Vine St.; park in the lot on Bronson Ave. Admission: $15. Tours hourly weekdays 9–2.*

UNIVERSAL STUDIOS HOLLYWOOD

Many of Universal's past and present film props are displayed on the 420-acre grounds, but the emphasis is on thrilling the pants off visitors with high-tech extravaganzas and stunt shows involving explosions, mechanical monsters, and simulated gunfire. Hefty admission prices reflect that the studio has become a theme park, and thrill-seekers will have many opportunities to lose their lunch. Scream through time on *Back to the Future*: The Ride, or narrowly miss death at the jaws of a T. Rex in the new *Jurassic Park: The Ride.* Quiver as you experience the re-created carnage of San Francisco's subway in a major earthquake! Sweat as you're cast into the movie *Backdraft* without singeing a hair on your head! Though there's no opportunity to see an authentic working studio, Universal is still jammed every summer; go early in the day, if at all. Look for discount coupons at motels and visitor centers. *100 Universal City Plaza, Universal City, tel. 818/508–9600. Admission: $34. Summer: box office open daily 7:30 AM–6 PM; park closes at 10. Winter: box office open daily 8:30–4; park closes at 7. Park hrs vary, so call ahead.*

WARNER BROTHERS STUDIOS

At Warner Brothers, there is no formal tour schedule; guides try to take you "behind the scenes" to wherever the action is on that particular day. You might drop by the old *Dukes of Hazzard* set before checking progress on the newest blockbuster mega-movie. Then stroll by set-construction facilities, sound stages, and the new costume warehouse. Walking tours last about two hours. *4000 Warner Blvd., at Olive Ave., Burbank, tel. 818/972–8687. Admission: $29. Tours weekdays 9–3; call for schedule. Reservations advised.*

CHEAP THRILLS

At the **West Hollywood Playhouse** (666 N. Robertson Ave., south of Santa Monica Blvd. in West Hollywood, tel. 818/762–7547), Mice, the self-billed "Improv Comedy All-Stars," perform Saturday at around 9 PM for free. Jerome Cleary hosts free comedy improv workshops every Thursday at 7:30 inside **The Actor's Lab** (1514 N. Gardner Ave., at Sunset Blvd. in West Hollywood, tel. 213/878-2688). Check the *L.A. Weekly* (*see* Basics, *above*) for the latest acts.

In summer, (free) music fills the air around Los Angeles. Besides practice sessions at the Hollywood Bowl (*see* Exploring L.A., *above*), you'll find free summer concerts at the **UCLA Summer Chamber Music Festival,** in the university's Schoenberg Auditorium (tel. 310/825–4401). Musicians from the L.A. Philharmonic, L.A. Chamber Orchestra, and UCLA's Music Department perform on Monday and Thursday afternoons. **Jazz at the Wadsworth** (tel. 310/794–8961), a series of free concerts that takes place the first Sunday of each month at UCLA's Veterans Wadsworth Theatre, has featured such artists as Tito Puente, Branford Marsalis, and Maceo Parker. The Santa Monica Pier's **Twilight Dance Concerts** (tel. 310/458–8900) feature a different sound each week, from big band to reggae; bands play Thursday evening 7:30–9:30. At downtown's **California Plaza** (350 S. Grand, at Olive St., tel. 213/626–1901), you can catch local and international musicians Wednesday, Friday, and Sunday afternoons or Friday and Saturday evenings. Past performers have included the Japanese group Shoukichi Kina, and El Vez ("the Mexican Elvis") and his Memphis Mariachis.

Open-mic poetry readings draw the new beatniks of Los Angeles's café society. They're usually free-wheeling (and free) affairs—audience members stand up and read their own work while Wordsworth spins in his grave. On Santa Monica's Third Street Promenade, the **Midnight Special Bookstore** (1318 3rd St., tel. 310/393–2923) has open readings on Friday starting at 8 PM. And in Hollywood, the folks at **Highland Grounds** (*see* Cafés, *above*) open their café to musicians and poets at 7:30 PM Wednesday. Participation is never required, but if you've composed a modern *Iliad,* arrive half an hour early to sign up for a reading time.

At **Melrose Weekend Market,** at the corner of Melrose and Fairfax avenues on Sunday from 9 to 5, you'll find both junk and salvageable curios among the antiques, jewelry, and vintage clothing. Live jazz and fresh baked goods are groovy extras.

FESTIVALS

The Los Angeles **Cultural Affairs Department** (tel. 213/485–2433) publishes a large "Festivals of Los Angeles" booklet, available at visitor centers (*see* Basics, *above*). It should be especially appealing to lovers of jazz and film, for which monthly festivals abound.

JANUARY

During the first week of the month, look for the **Tournament of Roses Parade** and the **Rose Bowl** in Pasadena (*see* Chapter 10). In Little Tokyo, the **Oshogatsu Festival** (tel. 213/625–0414) ushers in the Japanese New Year.

FEBRUARY

The Golden Dragon Parade—which falls on a different day in February each year—marks the height of the month-long **Chinese New Year** festivities (tel. 213/617–0396) in Chinatown.

MARCH

The **Los Angeles Marathon** (tel. 310/444–5544), held the first Sunday of the month, attracts international competitors and hordes of spectators. At the **St. Patrick's Day Parade** in Century City, expect green beer—and people who like to drink it. The **Academy Awards** are usually held the last week of the month—you can lurk outside the Dorothy Chandler Pavilion (135 N. Grand Ave., at 1st St.) or the Shrine Auditorium admiring arriving celebrities.

MAY

The entire city comes alive for the celebration of **Cinco de Mayo** (tel. 213/625–5045), the anniversary of Mexico's independence from France. A 36-block section of downtown hosts Latino music, carnival rides, and traditional food and drink. At the end of the month, UCLA holds a free, two-day **Jazz and Reggae Festival** (tel. 310/825–9412). During the last weekend of May, **Chalk It Up** (tel. 213/850–4072), the world's largest chalk mural festival, happens in West Hollywood on San Vicente Boulevard—great for eating, drinking, and gawking.

JUNE

The **Lesbian and Gay Pride Festival and Parade** (tel. 213/860–0701), in West Hollywood, commemorates the 1969 Stonewall riots in New York City and honors queer people past and present. In 1998, Pride events will be held on the last weekend of the month; check out the day-long festival on Saturday in West Hollywood Park.

JULY

Watch the **Fourth of July Fireworks** from coastal communities such as Marina del Rey; most take place around sunset. The **Lotus Festival** (tel. 213/485–1310), held in Echo Park north of downtown, celebrates Pacific Rim cultures with crafts, music, and dragon boat races. **Shakespeare Festival/LA** (tel. 213/489–1121) runs July and August in West Los Angeles, and it's free with a donation of canned food.

SEPTEMBER

Los Angeles's Birthday (tel. 213/680–2821) is celebrated with festivities on Olvera Street in El Pueblo de Los Angeles Historic Park. A civic ceremony and festivities will honor the 44 black, mestizo, and Spanish founders. At the end of the month, South Central's one-day, free **Watts Towers Jazz Festival** (tel. 213/485–1795) attracts top performers from all over the world. For more than 20 years, the annual **Koreatown Festival** (tel. 213/730–1495), celebrated at the end of the month, has included a lavish parade, traditional dancing, and martial-arts demonstrations.

OCTOBER

The three-day **Santa Monica Oktoberfair** (tel. 310/393–9287, ext. 326), which takes place at the beginning of the month, is an epic street fair, with German oompah bands, carnival rides—and maybe just a little beer.

NOVEMBER

Día de los Muertos (tel. 213/628–1274 or 213/625–5045), or Day of the Dead, is celebrated at the beginning of the month on Olvera Street with activities both silly and somber, from dancing humans dressed as skeletons to a candlelight procession at dusk.

DECEMBER

Skip the traditional **Hollywood Christmas Parade** (tel. 213/469–8311) in favor of the annual African American **Kwanzaa Festival and Parade** (tel. 213/789–5654), held shortly after Christmas in Leimert Park.

AFTER DARK

Most bars, clubs, and bistros in this go-go-go city have a shelf life shorter than the vinyl skirts at Melrose boutiques. Sometimes, appearance in print equals instant social death. Hollywood, the locus of L.A. nightlife, is without question the place to start your search. Look for flyers in record stores or check the **KROQ Concert and Events Line** (tel. 818/566–7625 or 818/843–5050). The station (106.7 FM) often sponsors free shows by cool bands and has frequent ticket giveaways. Though bars close at 2 AM, many cafés are open until all hours, hosting live music, open-mic poetry readings, and screenings of cult and classic films (*see* Cafés, *above*). Tickets to many concerts and mainstream theater performances can be obtained directly through a venue's box office or by calling **Ticketmaster** (tel. 213/480–3232), which adds a service charge. The nights that dance clubs are open change frequently; call ahead to check the current status.

BARS

Barney's Beanery. Half bar, half restaurant, the Beanery serves up over 300 different beers, including a few of their own brews. The crowd clustered at the long bar and near the pool tables is hip but not haughty. *8447 Santa Monica Blvd., between La Cienega and Crescent Heights Blvds., West Hollywood, tel. 213/654–2287.*

Cat & Fiddle Pub and Restaurant. You'll find a mixed crowd of yuppies and hipsters drinking pricey beers and espressos on the large, breezy outdoor patio. There's live jazz on the patio Sunday evening, blues on Monday, and an open-mic Tuesday (no cover). *6530 Sunset Blvd., between Vine St. and Highland Ave., Hollywood, tel. 213/468–3800.*

Dresden Room. Dark and smoky, and the senior citizens who live for the happy-hour buffet and teenage lounge lizards who filter in after dark like it that way. Crooners Marty & Elayne hold forth on the piano Monday–Saturday among furnishings unchanged since the '60s. *1760 N. Vermont Ave., near Hollywood Blvd., East Hollywood, tel. 213/665–4294.*

Formosa. This is a Chinese restaurant and bar partially housed in a converted railroad car, with a photographic shrine to Hollywood's movie legends. The fun crowd is fittingly eclectic. *7156 Santa Monica Blvd., at Formosa Ave., West Hollywood, tel. 213/850–9050.*

Good Luck Club. Chinese lanterns, comfy sofas, funky music, and a crowd that's willing to line up outside are sure signs this is a hot hangout. It stocks powerful Chinese rose and melon whiskeys ($4.50) meant for sipping. *1514 Hillhurst Ave., at Hollywood Blvd., East Hollywood, tel. 213/666–3524.*

Hollywood Athletic Club. Legend has it that a drunken John Wayne once pelted passing cars with the club's billiard balls. You, too, can pay $4–$14 (plus valet parking) for an hour of pool at this swank stomping ground for the see-and-be-seen crowd. Check out live blues on Monday night. *6525 Sunset Blvd., just east of Highland Ave., Hollywood, tel. 213/962–6600.*

Lava Lounge. Occupying a two-tier strip mall in a dicey neighborhood, this is the latest dimly lit den of Los Angeles's chic society. Look for the faux lava-rock fountain and a variety of weird lounge acts (was that a xylophonist?). *1533 N. La Brea Ave., between Sunset and Hollywood Blvds., Hollywood, tel. 213/876–6612. Cover $1–$3.*

Manhattan Beach Brewing Company. As the beach (two blocks away) empties in late afternoon, this place fills. The homebrewed ales, bitters, and stouts go for $3.50 a pint, beers in shot-glass "tasters" are $1. *124 Manhattan Beach Blvd., at Ocean Dr., Manhattan Beach, tel. 310/798–2744.*

Micky's. Bartenders at this packed and popular gay bar are more than occasionally bare-chested, and video screens dominate the walls. *8857 Santa Monica Blvd., between La Cienega and San Vicente Blvds., West Hollywood, tel. 310/657–1176.*

San Francisco Saloon. Magnanimously dedicated to Los Angeles's main rival, the saloon has S.F. beer (Anchor Steam on tap) and S.F. baseball (Giants games on a big-screen TV); it's popular with a laid-back younger crowd. *11501 W. Pico Blvd., at Exposition Blvd., West L.A., tel. 310/478–0152.*

Ye Olde King's Head. Guinness is on tap at this fish 'n' chips refuge for Irish and British ex-pats and other Anglophiles; on Saturday night the crowds are as thick as the accents. *116 Santa Monica Blvd., between Ocean Ave. and 2nd St., Santa Monica, tel. 310/451–1402.*

CLUBS

Arena. A favorite among the hip gay men of Hollywood, this 22,000-square-ft former ice-making factory literally thumps with house music Tuesday and Thursday–Sunday under dramatic lights. Techno, industrial, and disco are on the decks on Friday; live Latin music takes center stage Saturday, with a drag show around 11:30 PM; Sundays, families show up for more live Latin rhythms. *6655 Santa Monica Blvd., between Highland Ave. and Vine St., Hollywood, tel. 213/462–0714. Cover: $6–$10. Usually 18 and up.*

Dragonfly. Dragonfly offers different music nightly, always at the cutting edge of Los Angeles's club scene. *6510 Santa Monica Blvd., between Highland Ave. and Vine St., Hollywood, tel. 213/466–6111. Cover: 99¢–$10.*

Kingston 12. Reggae reigns on the Kingston's two dance floors and is enjoyed by locals and visitors alike. Friday and Saturday nights feature live bands; on Thursday and Sunday, a DJ spins. *814 Broadway, at Lincoln Ave., Santa Monica, tel. 310/451–4423. Open Thurs.–Sun. Cover: $5.*

LunaPark. Dark, elegant, and elaborate, Luna has two stages, three bars, and a restaurant. Patrons are befittingly sleek. Nightly entertainment ranges from deejayed world music to live bands and alternative comedy acts. *655 N. Robertson Blvd., between Melrose Ave. and Santa Monica Blvd., West Hollywood, tel. 310/652–0611. Cover: $5–$12.*

Mayan. This Friday and Saturday night venue is utterly dedicated to the dithyrambic powers of disco, retro, hip-hop, and salsa. Dress your best or the powers that be may not let you over the threshold of this renovated former art-deco movie house. The downtown club has secured parking; take advantage, and be careful walking around here at night, as it can be a sketchy neighborhood. *1038 S. Hill St., near 11th St. downtown, tel. 213/746–4287. Cover: $12.*

The Palms. Los Angeles's oldest exclusively women's nightclub offers different DJs nightly, pool tables, and cheap drink nights (50¢ Wed., $1 Thurs.). Music runs the gamut from live blues, rock, and jazz (Tues.) to house and dance mixes (Wed.–Mon.). *8572 Santa Monica Blvd., at N. La Cienega Blvd., West Hollywood, tel. 310/652–6188. Cover: $3–$5; no cover Mon. and Thurs.*

The Probe. There's a different club every night of the week, each with its own groupies. Tuesday, Club Flex (tel. 818/980–4793) plays reggae and hip-hop; Stigmata (tel. 213/462–7442) gives techno and industrial fans a place to party on Friday; on Saturday, Probe (tel. 310/281–6292) is a gay men's night with Euro-pop tunes; and the extremely popular Club '70s (tel. 213/957–4855) revives disco on Sunday. The crowd is a mix of gay and straight folk. For some clubs, you must buy a $2 membership, good for one year. *836 N. Highland Ave., between Santa Monica Blvd. and Melrose Ave., Hollywood. Cover $5 and up.*

The term "go-go girl" was supposedly coined at the Whiskey in the 1960s to refer to drugged-out dancers who enjoyed gyrating naked onstage.

Rudolpho's. Salsa is king at this Mexican restaurant in Silver Lake. Orchestras and DJs take turns laying down the grooves nightly for a young, downwardly mobile crowd. Dance lessons ($6–$8) take place on Monday and Wednesday around 8 PM. The Venue also hosts Dragstrip 66, the legendary "dress up, drag down" club, on the second Saturday of every month (tel. 213/969-2596); and Salsa con Clase, a strictly gay affair, on the first and last Saturdays of the month. *2500 Riverside Dr., Silver Lake, tel. 213/662–4021. Cover $8–$10.*

LIVE MUSIC

Los Angeles has long been one of the best cities in the country to catch promising rock acts, or to check out jazz, blues, and classical tunes.

CLASSICAL

The downtown Music Center's Dorothy Chandler Pavilion (135 N. Grand Ave., at 1st St.) offers rush tickets an hour before show time. The renowned **L.A. Opera** (tel. 213/972–8001) and the **Philharmonic** (tel. 213/850–2000) both play there. The **Hollywood Bowl** (2301 N. Highland Ave., tel. 213/850–2000) also offers rush tickets for weekday performances of classical, jazz, and contemporary music, available the day of (or one day prior to) the performance. UCLA hosts a free **Summer Chamber Music Festival** with weekly performances (*see* Cheap Thrills, *above*).

JAZZ AND BLUES

Blues Cafe. Nothin' but the blues plays six nights a week at 9 PM on the waterfront in Long Beach. The café has plenty of full-size pool tables, afternoon jam sessions, and deli fare. *210 The Promenade, Long Beach, tel. 562/983–7111. Cover: $2–$10.*

The Derby. This swank, retro club is housed in an impressive, domed room and comes complete with private booths, an oval-shape bar, and plush furnishings. There's live jazz, blues, rockabilly, and swing, and free swing lessons. *4500 Los Feliz Blvd., at Hillhurst Ave. south of Griffith Park, Los Feliz, tel. 213/663–8979. Cover: $5*

Harvelle's. Smoke and thick crowds are de rigueur for a great blues house, and Harvelle's proves no exception. Nightly sessions start at 8:30 PM and last until 2 AM. *1432 4th St., at Santa Monica Blvd., Santa Monica, tel. 310/395–1676. Cover $3–$7; no cover Mon.*

House of Blues. Actor Dan Ackroyd's $9 million plaything offers a glitzy interpretation of the South that makes it hard to concentrate on the quality blues, funk, and rock acts. *8430 Sunset Blvd., east of La*

Cienega Blvd., West Hollywood, tel. 213/650–1451 (information) or 213/650–0476 (box office). Cover: $10 and up. Some shows all ages.

Jack's Sugar Shack. Is it a blues bar or a beach bungalow? The Sugar Shack has an all-out faux-tropical decor with bamboo trellises, plastic birds, and beach landscapes painted on the walls. There are also 16 beers on tap (in addition to live music nightly). *1707 N. Vine St., at Hollywood Blvd., Hollywood, tel. 213/466–7005. Cover: $5.*

ROCK

Al's Bar. Every so often an unknown grunge, jazz, or neo-punk band shows up in this large brick warehouse downtown and blows people away. A popular hangout of the pierced and tattooed set, the bar hosts live music on Thursday, Friday, and Saturday nights, and an occasional Sunday barbecue. *305 S. Hewitt St., between Alameda St. and Santa Fe Ave. downtown, tel. 213/625–9703. Cover: $5, free Tues. and Wed.*

Anti-Club. This was once a vanguard of Los Angeles's music scene: Henry Rollins, the Red Hot Chili Peppers, and Dwight Yoakam all played here early in their careers. Now you're more likely to find subthrash bands playing to crowds of hyperactive skatebrats. *4658 Melrose Ave., between Western and Normandie Aves., Hollywood, tel. 213/661–3913 or 213/667–9762. Cover varies. All ages.*

Canter's Kibitz Room. Adjoining the landmark kosher deli Canter's (*see* Fairfax *in* Exploring, *above*), the Kibitz Room often has jazz and blues in addition to rock acts. *419 N. Fairfax Ave., between Melrose Ave. and Beverly Blvd., Fairfax, tel. 213/651–2030. No cover.*

Troubadour. With a reputation for hosting some of the biggest names in rock when they were still relatively unknown, the multilevel Troubadour is an excellent place to catch budding and established alternative bands. *9081 Santa Monica Blvd., between Doheny Dr. and San Vicente Blvd., West Hollywood, tel. 310/276–6168. Cover: $6–$12. All ages.*

Whiskey A Go Go. In past years, the club was *the* venue of the L.A. punk scene. The Whiskey was home to The Minutemen, Black Flag, and of course, X. Some of the city's best alternative rock bands still play here, hoping to impress scouts. *8901 Sunset Blvd., near San Vicente Blvd., West Hollywood, tel. 310/652–4202. Cover: $3–$15. All ages.*

MOVIE HOUSES

The city that makes 'em is also the city that screens 'em—movie houses are a big part of life in Los Angeles. Call 777–3456 in the 213, 310, and 818 area codes for recorded information on movie times and locations. Offbeat flicks and revived classics can be found at UCLA's **Melnitz Theater** (call 310/206–3456 for information) and the L.A. County Museum of Art's **Bing Theater** (for more on either, *see* Exploring L.A., *above*). **Sunset 5** (8000 Sunset Blvd., at Crescent Heights Blvd. in West Hollywood, tel. 213/848–3500) is just another big movie complex—until midnight on weekends, when they screen five of the weirdest low-budget flicks they can find (like *Surf Nazis Must Die*).

L.A. Connection, a comedy troupe that imposes hysterical improvisational plots and dialogue on cheap horror flicks, appears sporadically at **Nuart Theater.** *11272 Santa Monica Blvd., at Sawtelle Blvd. in West L.A., tel. 310/478–6379. Cost: $7.50.*

THEATER

The strip of Santa Monica Boulevard between Cole and Seward streets in Hollywood promotes itself as "Theater Row." Here, a loose federation of micro-theaters hosts an eclectic and usually obscure range of one-act and experimental plays with cheap ticket prices. **Actors' Gang** (6209 Santa Monica Blvd., one block east of Vine St., tel. 213/465–0566) was founded by actor Tim Robbins and is well known for both its original productions and its innovative adaptations of established plays; tickets cost $5–$15. In Santa Monica, **Highways** (1651 18th St., tel. 310/453–1755) presents performance art, dance, theater, comedy, and any combination thereof; it's always avant-garde, wild, weird, and affordable ($10–$15). If you feel like splurging on a big Broadway-style production, check out downtown's **Ahmanson Theatre** (135 N. Grand Ave., between 1st and 2nd Sts., tel. 213/365–3500).

Mark Taper Forum. This theater in the downtown Music Center frequently offers public rush tickets for shows nightly (except Saturday). You'll want to get in line with cash at least an hour early for these $10 tickets (usually $30 and up). Shows at the Forum often go on to New York City's Broadway. *135 N. Grand Ave., at 1st St., tel. 213/972–0700.*

Groundling Theater. This is where Pee Wee Herman and many *Saturday Night Live* cast members got their start. The Groundling puts on several different shows a week, from scripted sketches to improvisational and audience-interaction pieces. *7307 Melrose Ave., near La Brea Ave., tel. 213/934–9700. Tickets: $10–$17.50.*

Theatre/Theater. The troupe here can always be counted on to come up with something witty and weird. Recent efforts include *The Dysfunctional Show,* which lampooned daytime talk shows. Audience participation is integral. *1713 Cahuenga Blvd., near Hollywood Blvd., Hollywood, tel. 213/871–0210. Tickets: around $10.*

OUTDOOR ACTIVITIES

There are plenty of outdoor options in Los Angeles. Of course, smog can pose a serious threat to your health, but the air is clearer in the surrounding hills and along the coast. If you plan to hit the sand, Los Angeles has over 20 public beaches from which to choose. Start on the Pacific Coast Highway (PCH) in Malibu and drive south along the ocean—you're sure to find your niche by the time you reach Venice. Especially attractive is **Leo Carillo State Beach** (tel. 818/880–0350), 25 mi west of Santa Monica off PCH, with rugged cliffs, tidal pools, hidden coves, and miles of hiking trails, as well as a developed campground (*see* Where to Sleep, *above*).

PARTICIPANT SPORTS

In the 9,000-acre **Topanga State Park** (tel. 310/455–2465), explore the Musch Trail, a 4-mi round-trip to a pleasant waterfall. Park admission is $5; you can reach the entrance on Topanga Canyon Boulevard from either PCH in Malibu or U.S. 101 in the San Fernando Valley. There are also miles of trails in **Will Rogers** (tel. 310/454–8212) and **Malibu Creek** (tel. 818/880–0367) **state parks,** near Malibu (*see* Exploring L.A., *above*).

BIKING

Some 5 mi of gravel trails provide excellent mountain biking at **Sullivan Canyon** in the Santa Monica Mountains; from different points along the trails you'll find great views of the Pacific. To get here, take Sunset Boulevard to Mandeville Canyon Road (about 3 mi west of I–405 in Brentwood), turn north, and then go west on Westridge Road to the end. **Griffith Park** (*see* Exploring L.A., *above*) restricts bicyclists to paved paths. Try two unmaintained paved roads that are closed to vehicular traffic: the 5-mi **Mt. Hollywood Road,** which branches off Griffith Park Drive near the Travel Town Museum, and the 5-mi **Vista del Valle Road,** which you pick up from Commonwealth Avenue near the Roosevelt Golf Course. Both offer good views and solitude. Mountain bikers will also find miles of trails at **Malibu Creek State Park** in Malibu (*see* Exploring L.A., *above*).

If a cruise on the coast sounds more appealing, head to the strand of concrete that stretches 22 mi along the ocean; it's parallel to PCH and connects the South Bay beaches to Pacific Palisades. Bike rentals cost $5–$8 per hour ($14–$30/day) at **Rental on the Beach** (3100 Ocean Front Walk, at Washington Blvd. in Venice, tel. 310/821–9047) and **Spokes and Stuff** (1715 Ocean Front Walk, at Loews Hotel in Santa Monica, tel. 310/395–4748). Near Griffith Park's southeast entrance, **Woody's Bicycle World** (3157 Los Feliz Blvd., just east of I–5, tel. 213/661–6665) rents mountain bikes by the day ($15) or the week ($65). For more information on biking in Southern California, contact the **L.A. County Transportation Commission** (818 W. 7th St., Suite 1100, tel. 213/244–6539), which distributes an invaluable full-color L.A. County bike map free of charge.

HIKING

In the Santa Monica Mountains, **Franklin Canyon** has beautiful hiking trails. To reach them, take Beverly Drive north to the stoplight in Coldwater Canyon Park. Continue on Beverly Drive (you'll have to turn left), then turn right onto Franklin Canyon Drive. During full moons, rangers lead two-hour night hikes through Franklin Canyon with views of the city lights far below. In **Griffith Park,** you can ascend to the summit of Mt. Hollywood, a trip with amazing views; the trail (3 mi round-trip) begins at the parking lot of the Griffith Observatory (*see* Exploring L.A., *above*). At the **Hollywood Reservoir** (Lake Hollywood Dr.)—in the Santa Monica foothills west of Griffith Park—a 3½-mi path loops the shore, blissfully secluded among stands of pine and eucalyptus. It's a popular circuit for racewalkers and runners. From U.S. 101, take Cahuenga Boulevard north, go right on Barham Boulevard, and make a right on Lake Hollywood Drive.

HORSEBACK RIDING

The **Los Angeles Equestrian Center** rents horses for a maximum of two hours at a mere $15 per hour. No riding test or reservations are required. *480 Riverside Dr., tel. 818/840–8401. From Hwy. 134, exit at W. Alameda Ave., turn right on Main St., and follow signs. Open daily 8–5.*

IN-LINE SKATING

Sea Mist Rentals in Santa Monica rents roller skates and in-line skates, offering two ways to see and be seen on the 22-mi beachside bike path that winds south from Pacific Palisades. Beware: On summer weekends the route is completely clogged with knock-kneed Rollerblade neophytes. Skates are $4 for the first hour ($3 each additional hr, $10 per day); blades are $5 for the first hour ($4 each additional hr, $14 per day). Photo ID is required as a deposit. *1619 Ocean Front Walk, across from Santa Monica Pier, tel. 310/395–7076. Open daily 9–8.*

SURFING AND BODY SURFING

Popular L.A. surf spots include Topanga, Zuma, and Leo Carillo beaches—but locals don't take kindly to being invaded by fumbling beginners. Novices should head to **Malibu Surfrider State Beach** for gentler breaks and kinder companions. The nearly clairvoyant recording of the **Surfline/Wavetrak** (tel. 714/976–7873) is worth the $1.50-per-minute price; wave predictions are accurate to within a foot, up to two weeks in advance. If your interest in surfing is of the "sit on the beach and watch" variety, keep an eye out for the professional surfing competitions that surface during summer in Manhattan Beach and Malibu. For information on dates and locations, call the Associated Surfing Professionals (714/851–2774) or U.S. Surfing (714/366–4584). *See* Go Ahead—Make My Wave *box in* Chapter 10.

Across from the pier in Malibu, **Malibu Ocean Sports** (22935 Pacific Coast Hwy., tel. 310/456–6302) rents longboards and regular "sticks" for $25 a day, with a credit card or $400 cash deposit. Wet-suit and boogie-board rentals are $8 and $12 a day, respectively, and windsurfing boards go for $30 a day. In Venice, **Rental on the Beach** (*see* Biking, *above*) rents boogie boards for $3 an hour or $10 a day.

WHALE-WATCHING

Redondo Sport Fishing, on the pier at the Redondo Beach Marina, sends out two boats a day during whale-watching season (Jan.–Mar.). Trips last about three hours and cost $7–$10 per person ($12 on weekends). *233 N. Harbor Dr., Redondo Beach, tel. 310/372–2111 or 213/772–2064. Reservations advised.*

SPECTATOR SPORTS

BASEBALL

Bundle up—preferably in the team colors blue and white—if you're headed to a night game. All the overpriced beer in the world can't keep you warm if the fog rolls into Dodger Stadium, beloved home of the beloved **Los Angeles Dodgers.** The stadium is just northwest of downtown, off Highway 110 north of U.S. 101. Call 213/224–1400 for game information, or 213/224–1448 for tickets (there's a $1 per ticket handling fee for phone orders). Seats start at $6.

BASKETBALL

Los Angeles Lakers seats ($21 and up) are easily obtained for most home games. Home court is the Great Western Forum in Inglewood, near Los Angeles International Airport. To reach the stadium, take I-405 to Manchester Avenue (Hwy. 42) east, then turn right on Prairie Avenue. The season runs October–April. Call 310/419–3100 for a schedule and tickets. For general information call 310/419–3865.

The **Clippers** are Los Angeles's "other" basketball team. The city hasn't yet decided whether to love or hate them, and this won't change until they win a championship (or at least don't finish second to last). The Clippers play at the L.A. Sports Arena (3939 S. Figueroa St.) in Exposition Park, and tickets start at $10. To reach the park from downtown, take I–110 to Exposition Boulevard and turn left on Figueroa Street. For tickets and game information, call 213/748–8000.

BEACH VOLLEYBALL

Professional volleyball competitions take place February–September on the sand in Manhattan Beach, Hermosa Beach, and Malibu. Tournament dates and sites change year to year; call the **Women's Pro Volleyball Association** (tel. 310/726–0700) or the **Association of Volleyball Professionals** (tel. 310/577–0772).

FOOTBALL

Now that the Rams have transplanted their franchise to St. Louis and the Raiders are back in Oakland, Angelenos rely on college pigskin. Luckily, one of the most heated college rivalries in the country—between the **USC Trojans** and the **UCLA Bruins**—provides ample entertainment. The competition alternates between the Rose Bowl and the L.A. Coliseum and culminates on the Saturday before Thanksgiving, when the two teams clash and the winner walks away with a year's worth of bragging rights. Tickets to see either team play cost about $20–$25. To reach the UCLA ticket office call 310/206–6831; the USC ticket office can be reached at 213/740–GOSC.

Before you don your hiking boots, check the newspaper for air-quality predictions. In the L.A. hills, pollution can reach unhealthy concentrations 80 or more days per year.

ICE HOCKEY

Blood, gore, and random acts of violence: a **Los Angeles Kings** tradition. Tickets for Kings' games, held November–April at the Forum (for directions, *see* Basketball, *above*), start at $11. For tickets and game information, call 310/419–3100.

Professional ice hockey team the **Mighty Ducks** (named after the 1992 movie starring Emilio Estevez and owned by the savvy Walt Disney Corporation) play at the Pond in Anaheim, a $100 million stadium 28 mi south of downtown Los Angeles. For information on tickets (starting at $14) and games, call 714/704–2701.

POLO

Long ago, Will Rogers built a polo field so his friends could enjoy an afternoon chukker and barbecue. The polo field is still in use at **Will Rogers State Historic Park** (1501 Will Rogers State Park Rd., tel. 310/454–8212), where you can park ($5) and picnic on the sidelines. Games are played in the spring and summer, Saturday 2–5 and Sunday 10–1; rain cancels. The polo field is in the hills of Pacific Palisades, just off the 14000 block of Sunset Boulevard.

NEAR LOS ANGELES

UPDATED BY JULIE JARES

Most people who live in or even near L.A. County will tell you that they're from Los Angeles, when in fact they're from one of the myriad cities that surround it. Residents of the **San Fernando Valley,** for instance, vote in L.A. elections and are subject to most of L.A.'s ordinances, but they're separated from the city by the Santa Monica Mountains. Here they've carved out a distinct cultural niche, with its own vernacular and an identity based in the land of shopping malls and ironed hair.

Of course, Los Angeles sprawls in many directions. In the South Bay, the clifftop estate community of **Palos Verdes** remains impervious to the encroachment of its less affluent neighbors to the east—**San Pedro** and the ever-expanding industrial town of **Long Beach.** Far enough from downtown L.A. to merit their own identities, these towns are still close enough to the city to serve as bedroom communities. They're also the most convenient departure point for **Santa Catalina Island,** 22 mi offshore and a world apart, with a profusion of marine activities and a rugged, undeveloped interior.

Oil rigs and port facilities line the shore near Long Beach and southern Los Angeles, but as you head farther south along the **Orange County** coast the scenery gives way to pristine stretches of beach and dramatic hillsides. Though parts of the coast are notorious for their conservative politics, the area is also immensely popular with surfers and artists. Galleries fill the streets of progressive Laguna Beach, a delightful place to spend some time on your way south toward San Diego or Mexico. **Pacific Coast Highway (PCH)** is often congested with traffic during summer, so if you're in a hurry to reach San Diego you'll want to take I–5. But the coast road is the best way to discover Southern California's golden beaches firsthand, from healing ocean vistas to the tacky bric-a-brac of the tourist trail.

Disneyland, on nearly every tourist's itinerary, is not in Los Angeles but in Orange County, encircled by the inland city of **Anaheim.** As if the Magic Kingdom weren't enough, Orange County also gives us the **Knott's Berry Farm** theme park in the city of Buena Park. It's true that inland Orange County is unwieldy suburbia that lacks any central focus—but it isn't nearly as bad as Angelenos make it out to be. So blaze your own trail through the tangle of freeways; most sights are within easy reach of L.A.

PASADENA

Pasadena, derided as traditional, residential, and out-of-touch, has long been an uncomfortable cousin to Los Angeles. (Poignantly, the town's comeback is to point with pride at being named the "most livable city in the United States"—in 1939.) But Pasadena does not deserve such harsh criticism, and after L.A.'s fires and riots, quite a few Pasadena-snubbing Angelenos have eaten their words. This is, after all, home to some of L.A. County's best museums and historic buildings.

In fact, Pasadena is slowly becoming cool. City planners have aided this transformation by gentrifying **Old Pasadena,** an eight-block section of town bordered by Pasadena Avenue, Arroyo Parkway, and Green and Union streets. This is the place to check out historic bungalows on tree-shaded streets and restored two-story buildings that made up the city's business district at the turn of the century. The heart of Old Pasadena lies at the intersection of Colorado Boulevard and Fair Oaks Avenue; here you'll find a jumble of restaurants, bars, and shops—and guilty-looking L.A. natives enjoying the scene. Because Old Pasadena knows it's charming, expect to pay for parking at meters (until 8 PM) or at city-owned lots.

On New Year's Day, Pasadena is the site of the **Tournament of Roses Parade** and the **Rose Bowl** football game. If you're in town on Thanksgiving, check out the **Doo Dah Parade,** a takeoff on the Tournament of Roses in which business executives march with their briefcases. For lodging and dining tips, plus schedules of current area events, pick up *Pasadena Weekly* or *In Pasadena* magazine; both are available free of charge at most bookstores, cafés, restaurants, and supermarkets. The **Pasadena Chamber of Commerce** offers free maps and a glossy community guide for an outrageous $10. *117 E. Colorado Blvd., at Arroyo Pkwy., tel. 626/795–3355. Open weekdays 9–5.*

COMING AND GOING

From downtown Los Angeles, take Hwy. 110 north. From Orange County, take I–5 north to I–605 north to I–210 west. From the San Fernando Valley, take U.S. 101 east to Hwy. 134 east. **Metro Transit Authority (MTA)** (tel. 213/626–4455 or 800/266–6883) provides frequent bus service from downtown L.A. to Old Pasadena daily 6 AM–midnight. Catch Pasadena-bound Bus 483 at Olive and 7th streets in L.A.; fare is $1.85 for the 45-minute ride. The Pasadena **Greyhound** station (645 E. Walnut St., at N. El Molino Ave., tel. 626/792–5116) has a ticket office open weekdays 7–4:50 and Saturday 7–2.

Like most of the L.A. area, Pasadena is much too spread out to cover on foot. MTA provides bus service around town; the fare is $1.35, transfers 25¢ (disabled patrons pay 45¢ per ride and 10¢ for transfers). For local routes, pick up a schedule at the public library or the nearest Thrifty drugstore.

Pasadena's free ARTS buses are a city project that takes the concept of public art and makes it mobile. Each of 10 theme buses—including the Community Fabric bus and the Peace bus—travels daily along Colorado Boulevard, Green Street, and South Lake Avenue.

WHERE TO SLEEP

Most of Pasadena's budget motels lie along **East Colorado Boulevard,** just east of the city's happening area. Accommodations get more expensive as you head toward Fair Oaks Avenue and the heart of Old Pasadena. Rates are comparable to much of L.A., except during the week surrounding the January 1 Rose Bowl—when prices soar and vacancy signs disappear.

Despite being a wide, palm-lined avenue, Colorado Boulevard is quite ugly in places. You can always head for the safety of **Travelodge** (2131 E. Colorado Blvd., west of Sierra Madre Blvd., tel. 626/796–3121), with doubles for $50 per night. However, an even better bet lies so far east it borders the neighboring town of Arcadia: The **Regal Inn Motel** (3800 E. Colorado Blvd., at Rosemead Blvd., tel. 626/449–4743) is extremely clean, with doubles for $35 ($182 per week) and kitchenettes for $5 extra per night. Closer to the action is the **Saga Motor Hotel** (1633 E. Colorado Blvd., tel. 626/795–0431 or 800/793–7242), which has 70 spacious rooms (doubles $59–$69) and a heated pool.

TIMES CHANGE, EVEN AT DISNEY

In a nod to the politically correct '90s, the new-and-improved Pirates of the Caribbean showcases lascivious pirates chasing food instead of women. By 1998, Disneyland's Tomorrowland will be whisked out of the '70s and thrust into imagination and beyond, thanks to a much-needed facelift. Look forward to high-speed rocket cars and an interactive pavilion of technology.

FOOD

Having increased its number of restaurants from three to around 100 since 1991, Old Pasadena has surely reached a zenith in its gustatory renaissance. People not only flock from L.A. to dine here—they actually wait in line to do so. In particular, walk-in customers at the reasonably priced Italian kitchen and bakery **Mi Piace** (25 E. Colorado Blvd., near Fair Oaks Ave., tel. 626/795–3131) face waits of up to an hour almost every night. Plan ahead and make reservations. Across from Mi Piace is the more authentic and less crowded **Sorriso** (46 E. Colorado Blvd., tel. 626/793–2233), where you'll pay $10–$13 for pasta dishes like risotto with mushrooms. If you're in the mood to splurge, head for the shaded patio, cool interiors, and stocked bar of the **Clearwater Café** (168 W. Colorado Blvd., at Pasadena Ave., tel. 626/356–0959). Seafood entrées start at $12. Peruse the blocks surrounding **Fair Oaks Avenue** and **Colorado Boulevard.** Another crop of restaurants lies just south of Colorado, along **Lake Avenue.**

Burger Continental. Part bar, part restaurant, and part belly-dancing venue, Burger Continental is popular with almost everyone in Pasadena. Besides cheap pitchers of beer, you'll find an excellent selection of Middle Eastern dishes; justifiably famous is the delicious chicken Corinthian ($9), baked in phyllo dough with spinach and feta cheese. Most nights, a quartet of Greek musicians delights diners on the outdoor patio. *535 S. Lake Ave., at California Ave., 5 blocks south of Colorado Blvd., tel. 626/792–6634.*

Ernie Jr.'s Taco House. Fast, cheap, and tasty. It doesn't look like much from the outside, but Ernie's makes some of the best tacos and carne asada burritos in town ($3–$6). *126 W. Colorado Blvd., between Pasadena Blvd. and De Lacey Ave., tel. 626/792–9957.*

WORTH SEEING

If you tire of museums, check out the kitsch for sale at Pasadena's two well-known flea markets. **Pasadena City College** (1570 E. Colorado Blvd., at Hill St., tel. 626/585–7906) holds one the first Sunday of each month from 8 AM to 3 PM. The mother of all swap meets, though, takes place at the **Rose Bowl** (1001 Rosebowl Dr., tel. 626/577–3100 or 213/560–7469) the second Sunday of each month. Admission is $5.

GAMBLE HOUSE

This house was built for David and Mary Gamble (of Procter and Gamble fame) in 1908 by Pasadena's illustrious architects Charles and Henry Greene. Known for their love of open space and elaborately carved wood, the Greene brothers built the 8,400-square-ft mansion as a winter cottage, at a time when Pasadena was nothing more than a wild prairie of sagebrush. Next door, the **Unitarian church** at 2 Westmoreland Place is another Greene and Greene house, and nearby lies **Arroyo Terrace,** a curved street full of bungalows designed by the famous duo. Only the Gamble House gives tours, though. *4 Westmoreland Pl., tel. 626/793–3334. From Hwy. 134, take Orange Grove Blvd. exit north, first left after Walnut St., first right onto Westmoreland Pl. Admission: $5. Tours several times an hr, Thurs.–Sun. noon–3.*

HUNTINGTON LIBRARY

Built in 1919 on the grounds of Henry E. Huntington's 207-acre estate, the Huntington Library contains a gallery specializing in British and French art of the 18th and 19th centuries (including Gainsborough's *Blue Boy*); a library of rare books and manuscripts (featuring a Gutenberg Bible and the Ellesmere manuscript of Chaucer's *Canterbury Tales*); and 15 botanical gardens (including a Zen garden of raked gravel and an herb garden). The Patio Restaurant on the grounds has sandwiches and salads for about $6; in the Rose Garden Tea Room, you can nibble on nine kinds of finger sandwiches. *1151 Oxford Rd., San Marino, tel. 626/405–2100 or 626/405–2274 for directions. Admission: $7.50. Library, art collections, and gardens open Tues.–Sun. 10:30–4:30; shorter hrs in winter; garden tours available but hrs vary.*

NORTON SIMON MUSEUM

The Norton Simon Museum contains one of the best collections of art on the West Coast, with more classic pieces than you'll find at L.A.'s Museum of Contemporary Art or the Los Angeles County Museum of Art. Rooms full of works by Rembrandt, Picasso, Van Gogh, Degas, Manet, and Monet are set among manicured parks, fountains, and sculpture gardens. Although the rather eccentric Norton Simon is no longer around to arrange the displays himself, the museum still has a personal, intimate charm. *411 W. Colorado Blvd., at Orange Grove Blvd., near I–210 and Hwy. 134, tel. 626/449–6840. Admission: $4. Open Thurs.–Sun. noon–6.*

PACIFIC ASIA MUSEUM

One of the few museums in California that specializes in Asian and Pacific Basin art, it's housed in a building constructed in the Chinese Imperial Palace style, complete with a center courtyard garden and a pond filled with koi fish the size of schnauzers. Exhibits include Japanese and Chinese woodworks, illuminated manuscripts, and pottery. *46 N. Los Robles Ave., ½ block north of Colorado Blvd., tel. 626/449–2742. Admission: $4. Open Wed.–Sun. 10–5; tours Sun. 2 PM.*

If Pasadena's heat becomes oppressive, cool off at the ice skating rink in Pasadena Center (300 E. Green St., tel. 818/793–2122). Lessons are available.

AFTER DARK

Old Pasadena is where several alternate universes collide. Weekend nights, the streets clog with everything from the white stretch limos of the nouveau riche to the Kustom Klass low riders of visiting gangstas. Slick sorts queue up at **Q's Billiard Club** (99 E. Colorado Blvd., one block west of Arroyo Pkwy., tel. 626/405–9777), where it costs up to $16 an hour just to play pool—*if* they find your attire suitable (no plain tees, tank tops, or torn items allowed). Otherwise, head across the street to **Freddie's 35er Bar** (12 E. Colorado Blvd., tel. 626/356–9315), which has billiards and beer for less. **The Colorado** (2640 E. Colorado Blvd., at Altadena Dr., tel. 626/449–3485) has a dimly lit, well-worn ambience that's a far cry from the clean-cut veneer of Old Pasadena. In the afternoons you'll find old-timers who know each other by name, but at night a younger crowd prevails in this bar. South of Colorado Boulevard is **Crown City Brewery** (300 S. Raymond Ave., at Del Mar Blvd., tel. 626/577–5548), which pours over 170 kinds of beer ($2–$6). If you're more interested in live theater than microbreweries, contact the well-known **Pasadena Playhouse** (39 S. El Molino, tel. 626/356–7529), which performs both revivals and new works.

NEAR PASADENA

BIG BEAR LAKE

L.A. County's suburbs would probably continue to multiply were it not for the abrupt mountain ranges demarcating the **Angeles** and **San Bernardino national forests** (the two are divided by the ribbon of I–15). Though you may not believe it as you stand in smog-filled Los Angeles, an entirely different world awaits two–three hours northeast and 5,000–10,000 ft above sea level. Within this vast acreage lies Big Bear Lake, a source of year-round diversion for generations of grateful L.A. residents. On the south shore, **Big Bear Lake City** is home base for most vacationers.

VISITOR INFORMATION • The **Big Bear Chamber of Commerce and Visitor Center** (633 Bartlett Rd., tel. 909/866–7000) has an excellent visitor's guide, many brochures, and limited information on campgrounds and hiking. The **Big Bear Ranger Station** (North Shore Dr., 3 mi east of Fawnskin, tel. 909/866–3437) has maps and detailed information on campgrounds and trails. The station also dispenses permits required for camping at undeveloped sites.

COMING AND GOING • From L.A., take I–10 east to Redlands and pick up Hwy. 30 north; it becomes Hwy. 330 and then turns into Hwy. 18 at Running Springs. Here, turn right onto Hwy. 18 east, which takes you to Big Bear Lake City. The lake's north shore can be reached via Hwy. 38 (North Shore

Dr.), which meets Hwy. 18 at the dam. To reach Big Bear Lake from Pasadena, take I–210 east to I–10 east and follow the directions above. In winter be sure to carry chains.

WHERE TO SLEEP • The city of Big Bear Lake is chock-full of expensive matchbox cottages tucked between pines, with names like Snuggler's Cove and Cuddly Inn. A few budget options exist: **Motel 6** (42899 Big Bear Blvd., at Division Rd., tel. 909/585–6666) offers some of the cheapest lodging in the area, with doubles for $46 weekdays and $56 weekends. The nearby **Hillcrest Lodge** (40241 Big Bear Blvd., tel. 909/866–7330 or 800/843–4449) is an appealing mountain cabin with 12 unique, clean, and comfortable rooms for $35–$45 in summer ($39–$59 in winter) and a soothing spa to relax in.

Camping at one of Big Bear's six campgrounds is your best option during summer months. **Pineknot** (south on Summit Blvd., near Snow Summit ski area, tel. 800/280–2267 for reservations) has 48 pine-studded spots ($15) available from mid-May through the end of September. Two miles east of the north-shore community of Fawnskin, **Serrano** (North Shore La., off Hwy. 38, tel. 800/280–2267 for reservations) has 132 sites ($15) open May–November and more amenities than Pineknot (including showers and electrical hookups). The sparse foliage here means that privacy will be minimal. For information on Big Bear's other campgrounds, contact the ranger station or Chamber of Commerce (*see* Visitor Information, *above*).

FOOD • Local restaurants must rely on the appetite-inducing fresh mountain air to increase the appeal of their fare—less-than-fabulous cuisine abounds. **Mongolian Palace** (40797 Lakeview Dr., west of Pine Knot Blvd., tel. 909/866–6678) lets carnivores and vegetarians alike fill up on all-you-can-eat Mongolian barbecue for lunch ($6) and dinner ($8). **Thelma's Twin Pines Restaurant** (337 Big Bear Blvd., near Hwy. 38, tel. 909/585–7005) offers a hearty breakfast special ($2.75) that includes two slices of thick french toast, two eggs, and bacon or sausage weekdays 6 AM–3 PM and weekends 6 AM–8 AM. The area's most convenient and well-stocked market is **Vons** (Interlaken Shopping Center, Hwy. 18 near Stanfield Rd., tel. 909/866–8459).

OUTDOOR ACTIVITIES • Look for the monthly newspaper *Big Bear Today* at motels and restaurants; it's a handy resource for Big Bear's many outdoor activities.

A compass and a good map are essential for any hike; **Franko's Map of Big Bear** ($3), hand drawn by local Frank Nielsen and complete with anecdotes on the back, is one of the best. It's available at the ranger station (if they haven't run out of copies). The **Cougar Crest Trail** is a 2-mi, moderately difficult trail that begins a half-mile west of the ranger station on Hwy. 38. The trailhead is at the north end of the parking area, just off the Highway. It traverses a mixed conifer forest of juniper, Jeffrey pine, and piñon, and provides beautiful views of the lake. The easy, .3-mi **Champion Lodgepole Trail,** an interpretive trail, begins at the end of Forest Service Road 2N11, meanders through subalpine forest, and finishes at the **Lodgepole Pine Trail.** From Mill Creek Road take Forest Service Road 2N10 for 4½ mi, turn right on 2N11; it's 1 mi to the trailhead located on the right.

Mountain biking is popular during summer; purchase a map of bike trails ($4) at the Big Bear Ranger Station (*see* Visitor Information, *above*) or at a local sporting goods store. For $7, a ride up the **Snow Summit** ski lift (Summit Blvd., south of Big Bear Blvd., tel. 909/866–5766) puts you and your bike on top of 40 mi of roads and trails. A full-day pass gives you unlimited runs for $18; bike rentals are an additional $6.50 an hour ($22 a day). Spectacular scenery is accessible to bikers on trails of varying difficulty, including the moderate 2-mi **Cougar Crest Trail** (*see* Hiking, *above*). Contact **Team Big Bear** (tel. 909/866–4565) for more information.

During summer, you can fish for trout, bass, and silver salmon from any secluded spot along the shore or struggle for casting space at **Dana Point** in the tiny north-shore community of Fawnskin, where some swear the fish bite better. **Jack's Tackle Shop** (39730 Big Bear Blvd., at Iris St., tel. 909/866–6525) rents gear ($10 a day, $35 deposit), sells bait (about $4), and dispenses the required permit ($9.45 a day, $26.50 per season). You can rent a fishing boat or a pontoon at any of the lake's marinas, including **Pleasure Point Boat Landing** at Metcalf Bay (603 Landlock Landing Rd., at Cienega Rd., tel. 909/866–2455), where rates start at $14 an hour. The **Get Wet Water Sports Center** (38573 North Shore Dr., tel. 909/878–4386) rents Jet Skis and Waverunners (about $55–$65 an hour) and offers waterskiing packages ($88 an hour) that include optional instruction.

During winter, Big Bear fills up with those eager to shred the slopes of **Bear Mountain Ski Resort** (43101 Goldmine Dr., east of Big Bear Lake City, tel. 909/585–2519), **Snow Summit** (Summit Blvd., south of Big Bear Blvd., tel. 909/866–5766), and **Snow Valley** (Hwy. 18, 5 mi east of Running Springs, tel. 909/867–2751). Though they'll never be mistaken for the Swiss Alps, all three resorts offer downhill runs ranging in difficulty from novice to expert. Bear Mountain has the highest elevation, as well as several ungroomed, experts-only canyons (snow conditions permitting). Lift tickets sometimes sell out on weekends, so consider purchasing in advance by telephone; the smallest resort, Snow Valley, is least likely to have crowds. Snowboarders may want to head straight for Snow Summit; locals claim it has the best hills for catching air. They'll rent you a snowboard for $28 (plus $300 deposit). Lift tickets at all three places will set you back about $40, with equipment an extra $25. It's wise to call for snow conditions: Get the Bear Mountain ski report (tel. 909/585–2519) or county weather and road conditions (tel. 909/866–7669). Cross-country skiers should pick up the cross-country skiing brochure at any of the ranger stations. It outlines some favorite local spots and includes a handy map. Most of the spots are off Forest Service Roads and require a 4-WD to get to. On Big Bear Boulevard, rental shops sprout as soon as the first snowflake falls.

SAN FERNANDO VALLEY

Ever since the early-'80s movie *Valley Girl,* the San Fernando Valley has basked in the spotlight of dubious international fame. Locals may not be proud that phrases like "gag me with a spoon" and "like, fer sure" were first coined here, but most residents don't mind that people from around the world have heard of the Valley and its infamous shopping mall, the **Galleria** (cnr Ventura and Sepulveda blvds., Sherman Oaks). By now, of course, even original Valleyspeak queen Moon Unit Zappa (daughter of Frank) wouldn't, like, be caught *dead* talking that way.

It takes a certain suspension of aesthetics to embrace the Valley, an area carved from orchards and ranchlands during an unchecked postwar housing boom. The 1994 earthquake left scars on Sherman Oaks, Van Nuys, and Northridge, but these bedroom communities have kept busy rebuilding their frantic boulevards, strip centers, and tract houses. The eastern Valley's proximity to the rest of L.A.—including the movie studios—makes it bearable, but don't linger. Just north of the Valley is where you'll find most of the nonstudio attractions, including **Six Flags Magic Mountain** (*see* Worth Seeing, *below*), with its gut-wrenchingly swift roller coasters.

COMING AND GOING

BY BUS

MTA (tel. 213/626–4455 or 800/266–6883) runs to almost every part of the Valley, but avoid the bus unless you have hours to kill (no joke). Fare is $1.35 ($2.35 to downtown L.A.). For long-distance travel, **Greyhound** has three stations in the Valley: North Hollywood (11239 Magnolia Blvd.), Glendale (400 W. Cerritos Ave.), and San Fernando (1441 Truman St.). Call the general information number (tel. 800/231–2222) for tickets and timetables.

BY CAR

The Valley's main streets are **Ventura Boulevard,** which runs east–west, and **Van Nuys Boulevard,** which runs north–south. Traffic is worst 7–10 AM and 3–7 PM, but even at nonpeak hours the highways look much like parking lots. The main freeways are the north–south **I–5** and **I–405,** which follows the coast to San Diego. **U.S. 101** runs east–west through the southern edge of the Valley, eventually leading north to San Francisco. To get to the Valley from West L.A., take I–405 north or follow **Coldwater Canyon Boulevard, Laurel Canyon Boulevard,** or **Beverly Glen Boulevard.** These three streets can be accessed from Sunset Boulevard, and all eventually lead to Ventura Boulevard.

BY METRO

Metrolink (tel. 800/371–5465) offers service to greater L.A. weekdays from stations throughout the Valley. The trip from Burbank (201 N. Front St., at Olive St.) takes 20 minutes and costs $3.50; from Van Nuys (7720 Van Nuys Blvd.) it's 30 minutes for $4.50; and from Northridge (8775 Wilbur Ave.) it takes 40 minutes and costs $5.50.

BY PLANE

The **Burbank Airport** (2627 N. Hollywood Way, at Thornton Ave., tel. 818/840–8847) offers service within and outside California. All international flights are handled by LAX (*see* Coming and Going *in*

Chapter 9). Rental cars are available at the airport. **Easy Rent-a-Car** (tel. 818/848–4885) is one of the cheapest agencies, with cars starting at $33 per day.

BY TRAIN

Amtrak (tel. 800/872–7245) has two stations that serve the Valley. In Glendale (400 W. Cerritos Ave., at San Fernando Rd., no phone) you can catch trains departing for all points along the Pacific coast; prices and travel times are similar to those from Los Angeles's Union Station (*see* Coming and Going *in* Chapter 9). From Burbank (3750 Empire Ave., near airport at Hollywood Way, no phone) trains run only to Santa Barbara (2½ hrs, $12) and San Diego (3½ hrs, $17).

WHERE TO SLEEP

With few exceptions, lodging in the Valley falls into one of three categories: expensive, sleazy, or uncomfortably near earthquake damage. Avoid all three by staying in a similarly priced place in L.A. proper (you also won't spend half your day schlepping up and down U.S. 101). If you must stay in the Valley, your budget options lie along Sepulveda Boulevard, north of Ventura Boulevard. But keep in mind, if it's under $35 it's probably dodgy.

777 Motor Inn. The combination of baroque headboards, tropical bedspreads, and garish carpets may make you dizzy, but the rooms are clean and in good repair. Doubles go for $38; they charge an additional $5 for a third or fourth person. Continental breakfast is included. The motel is next door to that Valley-child mecca, the Galleria. *4781 Sepulveda Blvd., Sherman Oaks, tel. 818/788–3200. 1 block north of Ventura Blvd. 37 rooms, all with bath.*

Starlite Cottage. This English country-style inn seems like a fish out of water on Sepulveda Boulevard with its manicured shrubs, gentle pastel colors, and neatly painted trim. Rooms are clean, fresh, and furnished with care. Basic doubles go for $45; $10 extra puts you in a theme room (French cottage, safari, Ralph Lauren Polo). All room rates rise $5 on Friday and Saturday nights. *5450 Sepulveda Blvd., between Magnolia Ave. and Burbank Blvd., tel. 818/997–9754. North of Ventura Blvd. in Sherman Oaks. 11 rooms, all with shared bath, all nonsmoking. No check-in Sun.*

FOOD

The Valley is blighted by countless indistinguishable chain eateries. Stray west beyond Sherman Oaks and the food becomes expensive as well as generic. In the eastern part of the Valley, however, it's possible to eat cheaply. In Van Nuys, head to **Dr. Hogly Wogly's Tyler Texas BBQ** (8136 Sepulveda Blvd., south of Roscoe Blvd., tel. 818/782–2480) for L.A.'s undisputed best barbecue sandwiches ($6) on home-baked bread. If you can ignore the plastic booths, mirrored walls, and framed pictures of food in the window, **ZanKou Chicken** (5658 Sepulveda Blvd., at Burbank Blvd., tel. 818/781–0615) is a splendid place for falafel sandwiches ($2.75) or spicy roast chicken and pita ($3.75 for a half chicken).

Vegetarians should make a beeline for Canoga Park's **India Sweets and Spices** (22009–11 Sherman Way, cnr Topanga Canyon Rd., tel. 818/887–0869). It doesn't look like much from the outside, but this corner café/store serves up fantastic Indian food for next to nothing. Two can eat here for $7. Food is served cafeteria-style; everything is vegetarian and all of it absolutely mouth-watering. If you want to splurge, try one of the nicer eateries along Ventura Boulevard's budding "restaurant row." It's easy to spot the black and yellow awning of **La Frite Cafe** (15013 Ventura Blvd., at Lemona Ave., tel. 818/990–1791), which offers a scrumptious array of French and Italian dishes ($9 and up). You may have to wait for a shaded table on the front patio. The marvelous food at **The Great Greek** (13362 Ventura Blvd., nr Woodman Ave., tel. 818/905–5250) is almost beside the point; it's the singing and dancing waiters that draw the crowds. Try the Macedonia shrimp pasta ($16) or a few appetizers ($4–$9) while you inspect the Greek newspapers that line the walls.

WORTH SEEING

Several of the major studios, including **Universal** and **Warner Brothers,** lie at the eastern end of the Valley. For more information, *see* Exploring the Studios *in* Chapter 9.

SIX FLAGS MAGIC MOUNTAIN

On these 260 acres in Valencia, north of the Valley off I–5, sit more than 100 roller coasters, rides, shows, and attractions. Magic Mountain's coasters are fast and wicked; the newest is **Superman, the**

Escape, a 40-story free-fall billed as the tallest, fastest thrill ride. Eight other "monster coasters," with names like **Viper, Colossus,** and **Psyclone,** should reduce you to a quivering, jelly-kneed lump. When you've had enough of roller coasters, head to the **Hurricane Harbor** ($18) and cool off on more than 20 acres of water slides and rides. Look for coupons worth $2–$12 off the admission price in Six Flags brochures, available at L.A.-area tourist offices and some motels. *Magic Mountain Pkwy., off I–5 in Valencia, tel. 805/255–4100 or 818/367–5965 from L.A. From L.A., I–405 north to I–5 north to Valencia. Admission: $34, parking $6. For information on group discounts (10 or more) call 805/255–4500. Open year-round (Nov.–Mar., weekends and holidays only); hrs vary, so call ahead.*

MISSION SAN FERNANDO REY DE ESPANA

At the northern edge of the Valley, far from tourist haunts, lies this carefully restored 1797 mission. It's small, but its 35-bell carillon casts an enchanting spell over the surrounding gardens. The church's interior is decorated with Native American design and artifacts of Spanish craftsmanship depicting the mission's 18th-century culture. *15151 San Fernando Mission Blvd., Mission Hills, tel. 818/361–0186. From I–405, Mission Blvd. exit east. From I–5, Mission Blvd. exit west. Admission: $4. Open daily 9–4:30.*

LOS ANGELES PET MEMORIAL PARK

For those left unsatisfied by a dead-celebrity fix at the Hollywood Memorial Park Cemetery (*see* Exploring Hollywood *in* Chapter 9), there is, thankfully, a celebrity pet cemetery. If you stroll the hill bordering the riding academy, you'll see the final resting place of the African lion Tawny (1918–40), and celeb companions like Mae West's monkey and Hopalong Cassidy's horse. The staff is friendly but they can't do much more than point you in the general direction of a celebrity gravesite. Dead pets deserve privacy, too. *5068 N. Old Scandia La., Calabasas, tel. 818/591–7037. From U.S. 101, Parkway Calabasas exit to Ventura Blvd., left onto Old Scandia La. and follow signs. Admission free. Open daily 8:30–4:30.*

AFTER DARK

Get in the car and drive to Los Angeles. The Valley is the land of restless teens with shiny cars, shiny clothes, and midnight curfews. If you insist on staying after dark, head for the Valley outpost of L.A.'s too-hip: **The Nerve Lounge** (13718 Venture Blvd., Sherman Oaks, tel. 818/990–0051), where you can drink over-priced cappuccino or throw down a quarter to surf the Net. **Studio City Bar & Grill** (11002 Ventura Blvd., Studio City, tel. 818/763–7912) is a blues bar that has live bands three nights a week; you can shoot pool, play darts, and knock back a couple of cold ones at this laid-back spot. There's a two-drink minimum but no cover when bands play. At the other end of town, discover **Coffee Junction** (19221 Ventura Blvd., Tarzana, tel. 818/342–3405), a coffee house that boasts a wide variety of live music on Friday and Saturday nights (8 PM–11 PM). The daring can audition on Sundays.

DISNEYLAND AND INLAND

Far and away the most popular attraction that inland Orange County has to offer is **Disneyland,** though you will find a couple of noteworthy destinations nearby. Disney's new "Indiana Jones Adventure" with its individually programmed cars and 160,000 ride variations is almost guaranteed to hold your attention. Besides **Knott's Berry Farm,** with its notable ghost town complete with authentic relocated buildings, there's Dr. Schuller's testament to Christianity, the **Crystal Cathedral,** one of the world's largest churches. Fans of the late Richard Nixon will enjoy the **Richard M. Nixon Library and Birthplace,** which presents a detailed history of the highs and lows of America's 37th president (he was buried on the grounds on April 27, 1994). Disney and Knott's lie in Anaheim and Buena Park, respectively, while the other sights are in surrounding suburbs easily reached by car. Accommodations are cheaper here than along the shore, but what you save in dollars you certainly lose in beauty—for the most part, this is a ghastly panorama of tedious suburbs, tightly buckled to the ailing defense industry.

ORANGE COUNTY

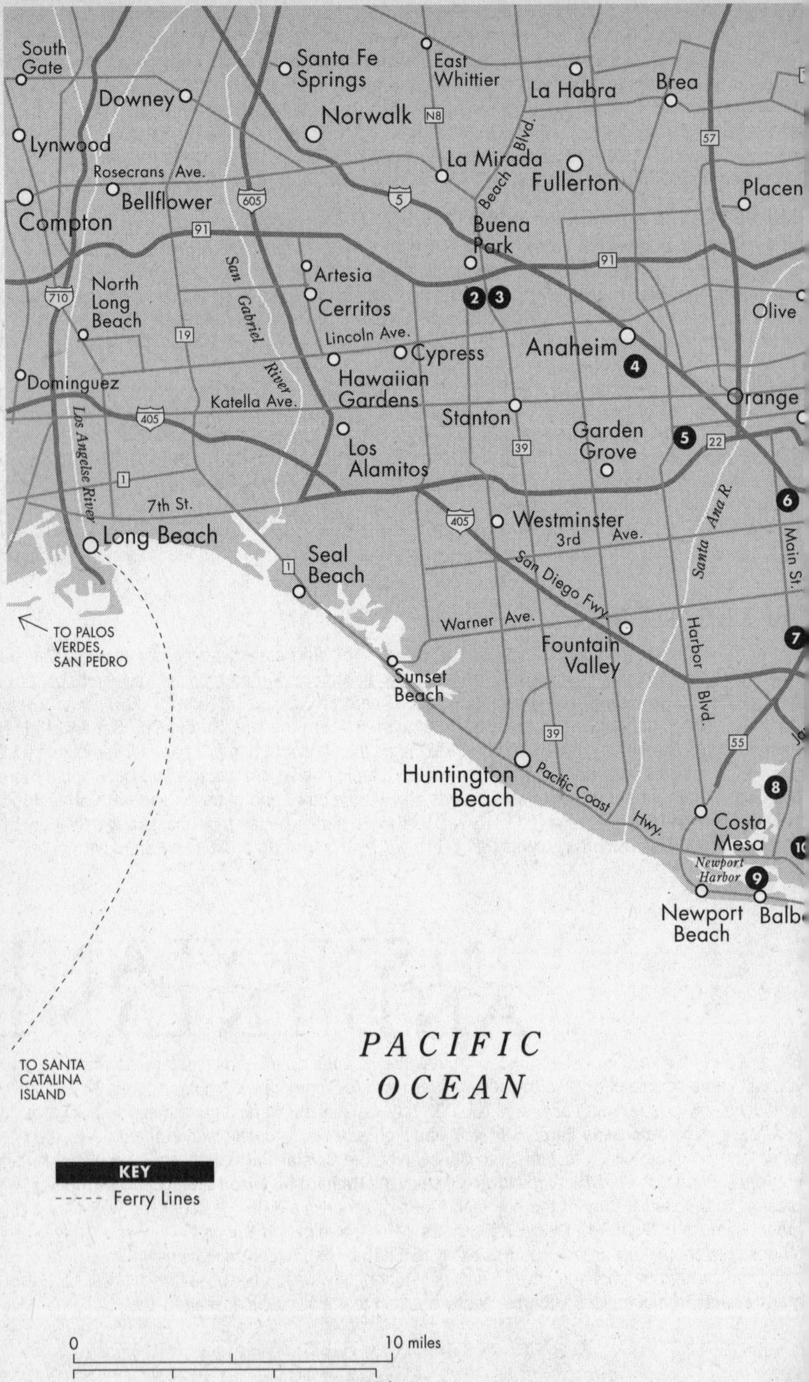

South Gate
Downey
Santa Fe Springs
Norwalk
East Whittier
N8
La Habra
Brea
57
Lynwood
Rosecrans Ave.
La Mirada
Beach Blvd.
Fullerton
Placen
Compton
Bellflower
605
5
91
Buena Park
North Long Beach
710
Artesia
Cerritos
San Gabriel River
19
Lincoln Ave.
Cypress
Anaheim
Olive
Dominguez
Hawaiian Gardens
Katella Ave.
405
Stanton
Orange
Los Angelse River
Los Alamitos
39
Garden Grove
22
1
7th St.
Long Beach
Seal Beach
Westminster
3rd Ave.
San Diego Fwy.
Santa Ana R.
Main St.
TO PALOS VERDES, SAN PEDRO
Warner Ave.
Fountain Valley
Harbor Blvd.
Sunset Beach
39
55
Huntington Beach
Pacific Coast Hwy.
Costa Mesa
Newport Harbor
Newport Beach
Balb
2 3 4 5 6 7 8 9 10

TO SANTA CATALINA ISLAND

PACIFIC OCEAN

KEY

- - - - - Ferry Lines

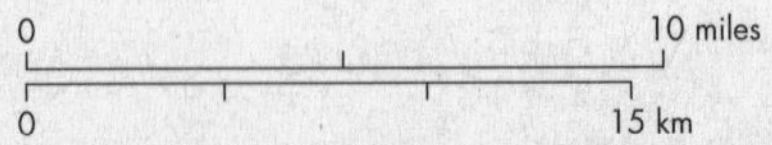

Balboa Island, **9**
Bowers Museum, **6**
Crystal Cathedral, **5**
Disneyland, **4**
Knotts Berry Farm, **2**
Laguna Beach Museum of Art, **12**
Mission San Juan Capistrano, **13**
Movieland Wax Museum, **3**
Orange County Museum of Art, **10**
Orange County Performing Arts Center, **7**
Richard M. Nixon Library and Birthplace, **1**
Sherman Library and Gardens, **11**
Upper Newport Bay Ecological Reserve, **8**

COMING AND GOING

BY BUS

Greyhound (tel. 800/231–2222) has a station in Anaheim (100 W. Winston Rd., at Anaheim Blvd., tel. 714/999–1256), across I-5 from Disneyland. The bus runs daily every hour from L.A. (1 hr, $8 one-way) 5:15 AM–6:15 PM. From Los Angeles, **MTA** (tel. 213/626–4455) offers limited service to Orange County; Bus 460 leaves downtown L.A. for Anaheim, Disneyland, and Knott's Berry Farm ($3.35 one-way). Within Orange County, call the **Orange County Transportation Authority (OCTA)** (tel. 714/636–7433, ext. 10) for routes, schedules, and bus information. It's open weekdays 6 AM–8 PM, weekends 8–5.

BY CAR

The easiest way to reach Anaheim is via **I-5** (a.k.a. **Golden State Fwy.** or **Santa Ana Fwy.**). There are hundreds of signs once you get near Disneyland and Knott's Berry Farm. Traffic can be a serious problem during rush hour (7–10 AM and 3–7 PM); otherwise, it shouldn't take you more than an hour by car from downtown L.A. or about 2½ hours from San Diego.

BY TRAIN

All **Amtrak** trains (tel. 800/872–7245) between Los Angeles and San Diego stop at **Anaheim Station** (2150 E. Katella Ave., tel. 714/385–1448), which lies at the east end of the Anaheim Station parking lot, a short drive east from Disneyland. From the Anaheim station, Bus 50 (Katella) heads to Disneyland every half hour. It takes only nine minutes to shuttle you to the Magic Kingdom. The first bus leaves weekdays at 5:25 AM and the last departs at 10:30 PM. On weekends, the last bus is at 9:20 PM. Fare is $1. The station, open 5:15 AM–11 PM, offers luggage storage. Amtrak also serves **Fullerton Station** (120 E. Santa Fe Ave., at Harbor Blvd., tel. 714/992–0530), 6 mi from Knott's Berry Farm and the city of Buena Park. From the Fullerton Station, Bus 43 (southbound) connects to Disneyland. The bus runs about every 8 minutes on weekdays from 4:50 AM to 11:09 PM. The last bus Saturday is 10 PM and Sunday 9:30 PM. On weekends, service is every 20–30 minutes. From the Fullerton Station to Knott's Berry Farm, take Bus 47 to Anaheim and transfer to Bus 42 heading west. Bus 47 runs about every 30 minutes. Fare is $1.

WHERE TO SLEEP

You'll find ample lodging around Disneyland (Katella Ave. and Harbor Blvd. in Anaheim) and Knott's Berry Farm (south of Hwy. 91 on Beach Blvd. in Buena Park). However, most accommodations are rundown, and they're priced maddeningly like nicer hotels ($35–$100 a night). Even worse, you must reserve a room at least a week in advance, especially during summer, when hordes of tourists invade the area. Your best bet is the area's lone hostel (*see below*), but if you do opt for a hotel, remember that an AAA card can often get you a discount.

NEAR DISNEYLAND

Anaheim Motel. This average-looking motel is just far enough from the chaos of Disney (about a 5-minute drive) to make a stay pleasant. And it has a pool and Jacuzzi to soothe your aching legs after a long day of walking around the theme parks. Doubles go for around $40. *426 W. Ball Rd., at Harbor Blvd., Anaheim, tel. 714/774–3882. 33 rooms, all with bath. Reservations advised.*

Desert Palm Suites. A few hundred yards from Disneyland, this very comfy hotel offers spacious, clean rooms with refrigerators, microwaves, and Continental breakfast. Rooms run about $69; they often fill with corporate types from the Convention Center down the block, so reservations are advised year-round. *631 W. Katella Ave., at Harbor Blvd., Anaheim, tel. 714/535–1133 or 800/635–5423, fax 714/491–7409. 105 rooms, all with bath. Free shuttle to Disneyland.*

Magic Carpet and Magic Lamp Motel. Tidy rooms, two pools, and cheap prices make these co-owned, neighboring motels a bargain. The bedspreads are colorful and the bathrooms immaculate—so you can forgive the orange carpet. Rooms are $34 per person, plus $4–$6 for each additional person. They no longer have a magic carpet to take you to Disneyland, but the 10-minute walk is painless. *Magic Lamp: 1030 W. Katella Ave., tel. 714/772–7242; Magic Carpet: 1016 W. Katella Ave., tel. 714/772–9450. Both: tel. 800/422–1556. 81 rooms, all with bath.*

NEAR KNOTT'S BERRY FARM

Colony Inn. This spankin' clean blue-and-white inn feels fresher than most budget places. Doubles start at $50 in summer; for $58 you can get a minisuite that sleeps up to six. The pool-sauna complex and a location across from Knott's Berry Farm attract colonies of families. *7800 Crescent Ave., at Beach Blvd. (Hwy. 39), Buena Park, tel. 714/527–2201 or 800/982–6566, fax 714/826–3826. 130 rooms, all with bath. Laundry.*

Covered Wagon Motel. Although this motel looks like a charmless hole-in-the-wall from the outside, the rooms ($30 and up) are comfortable, the "grounds" include a pool, and you can't beat the location—directly across from Knott's. *7830 Crescent Ave., at Beach Blvd. (Hwy. 39), Buena Park, tel. 714/995–0033. 20 rooms, all with bath. Reservations advised.*

HOSTEL

Fullerton-Hacienda AYH-Hostel. For price and location, the Fullerton-Hacienda is your best value. One mile from Amtrak's Fullerton Station (*see* Coming and Going, *above*), it's served by numerous public buses and is only a short car ride from both Disneyland and Knott's Berry Farm. Lockout is 10:30 AM–5 PM, but there's no curfew. The rate for members is $10.45, for nonmembers $13.45. To reach Disneyland from here, take OCTA Bus 41 south to Chapman and transfer to OCTA Bus 43 south. *1700 N. Harbor Blvd., tel. 714/738–3721. 3 mi north of Hwy. 91 on Harbor Blvd., in Brea Dam Park. From Fullerton Station, Bus 41 west (sign says La Habra) to Brea Dam Park. 20 beds. Laundry, linen ($1), lockers, on-site parking. Reservations strongly advised.*

FOOD

In one year, Disneyland uses more than 20,000 gallons of paint while guests buy 4 million hamburgers, 1.2 million gallons of soft drinks, and 2.8 million churros.

Most restaurants and food stands within the theme parks are overrated and overpriced—as in $3 ice-cream cones and $15 plates of leathery chicken and cold potatoes. The one exception is **Mrs. Knott's Chicken Dinner Restaurant** (8039 Beach Blvd., on Hwy. 39, tel. 714/220–5225), in the Berry Farm parking lot, where the fresh-baked berry pies and fried chicken dinners ($10) still taste homemade and smell heavenly. If you'd rather pack your lunch, the **K&C Market** (8465 Western Ave., at Crescent Ave., tel. 714/828–9141) near Knott's has basic items; near Disney, the behemoth **Food 4 Less** (1616 W. Katella Ave., at Euclid St., tel. 714/539–7497) is open 24 hours and carries whatever you desire in numbing quantities.

PoFolks. If you're in the mood for a hearty homestyle meal in a slightly hokey setting (a sticker in the window boasts, "I'm Po but I'm Proud"), this is your place. Country-fried steak, barbecued ribs, and Southern-style catfish are all under $10. Finish your meal with a scrumptious Mississippi mud pie ($3). *7701 Beach Blvd. (Hwy. 39), between Hwy. 91 and La Palma Ave., Buena Park, tel. 714/521–8955.*

Restaurant Ararad. Don't be dismayed by the unassuming exterior —you can't go wrong with the delicious Armenian and Middle Eastern dishes here. Pick out a few appetizers ($2–$4) to share, or go for the generous kabob combo dinner ($8.75). Vegetarians should try the creamy smooth metabbal appetizer, a tantalizing mix of blended eggplant, sesame, and garlic. Superb slathered on pita bread ($2.25). Call ahead on weekend evenings to make sure the restaurant isn't closed for a private party. *1827A W. Katella Ave., between Euclid and Brookhurst Sts. in Anaheim, tel. 714/778–5667. No lunch; closed Mon. and Wed.*

WORTH SEEING

DISNEYLAND

Ever since it opened in 1955, adults and children have been making pilgrimages to this childhood mecca of the West. If you haven't been here for a few years, you'll be surprised at how little it's changed: **Sleeping Beauty's Castle** still stands; the **Haunted Mansion** is still looking for its "1,000th ghost"; and the **Mad Tea Party** is still spinning over-gorged youngsters wildly about. Recent additions include **Mickey's Toontown,** home to a host of well-known cartoon characters, and the incredible laser-light and fireworks symphony **Fantasmic**—staged several times nightly from **Tom Sawyer's Island.** Also of note is the new **Indiana Jones Adventure,** a rough ride through the Temple of the Forbidden Eye. It's turbulent, fast-moving, and guaranteed to make those prone to motion-sickness lose their lunch. In other words: thumbs up. Disneyland is currently undergoing a slight facelift; nips and tucks consist of an attempt at a futuristic **Tomorrowland,** a new theatrical show to grace Main Street, and a speedier **Space Mountain** with a new techno sound.

Long lines—sometimes two hours or longer—are a real problem at all Disneyland attractions; your best bet is to visit the main rides early in the morning, late at night, or during popular shows. The park also has a number of bandstands and music venues—some free, some not. Stop by City Hall (near entrance) for concert information and prices. Disney's best restaurant is the Southern-style **Blue Bayou,** in the **Pirates of the Caribbean** complex. Reservations are advised, and they must be made in person. A full dinner runs about $15. *1313 Harbor Blvd., Anaheim, tel. 714/781–4565. Admission: $34. Hrs vary, so call ahead.*

KNOTT'S BERRY FARM

What began as a temporary diversion for customers waiting for one of Mrs. Knott's famed chicken dinners (*see* Food, *above*) has now expanded into six different theme areas spread over 300 acres—the oldest theme park in America. In contrast to Disneyland, Knott's has an undeniable down-home charm and more hair-raising rides. The park's **Ghost Town,** modeled after an 1890's Old West mining town, includes the Old Trails Hotel, a famous landmark relocated from Prescott, Arizona. You can also pan for gold or ride a train through a 19th-century gold mine complete with explosions and cave-ins. Check out **Bigfoot Rapids,** a whitewater ride guaranteed to leave you soaking wet, and the park's $10 million **Mystery Lodge,** full of weird special effects (including a time-traveling Native American storyteller). The strong-stomached will enjoy **Boomerang,** which flips you upside down six times in less than a minute; **Montezooma's Revenge,** which catapults you through a fearsome, seven-story loop and back again; and their largest, fastest roller coaster, **Jaguar,** which whips past a Mayan temple. One of the latest attractions is **Hammerhead,** 360° of head-spinning fun.

In mid-October, Knott's Berry Farm becomes **Knott's Scary Farm** with disorienting special effects, 1,000-plus monsters, and lots of fog and chainsaws. Come December, it transforms into **Knott's Merry Farm,** a Victorian Christmas village with 100-plus costumed characters and live performances of *Gift of the Magi* and Dickens's *A Christmas Carol.* Like Disneyland, Knott's is also prone to ridiculously long lines. *8039 Beach Blvd., (Hwy. 39), ½ mi south of Hwy. 91, Buena Park, tel. 714/220–5200. Admission $29.95, $14.95 after 4 PM. Hrs vary so call ahead.*

MOVIELAND WAX MUSEUM

Just a stone's throw from Knott's Berry Farm lies an extensive collection of immortalized celebrities. Covering the spectrum of Hollywood history from silent stars to action heroes, the museum showcases the likenesses of Michael Jackson, Little Richard, Bruce and Brandon Lee, Marilyn Monroe, and James Dean, among others. Figures are displayed in a maze of realistic sets from films such as *Star Trek, The Wizard of Oz,* and *Home Alone. 7711 Beach Blvd., tel. 714/522–1155. Admission $12.95. Open daily 9–7.*

BOWERS MUSEUM

The Bowers Museum has numerous ethnographic displays from the Americas, the Pacific Rim, and Africa. Exhibitions include Native American arts and crafts, traditional African costumes and clothing, and a first-rate display of international photography. Everything from African icons of power to pre-Columbian deities to a selection of impressionist paintings. Visit the museum's Topaz Cafe (tel. 714/835–2002) for Southwestern cuisine with unique spices; lunch runs about $6–$10. *2002 N. Main St., Santa Ana, tel. 714/567–3600. Exit I–5 at Main St., go ½ mi south. Admission: $6. Open Tues.–Sun. 10–4 (Thurs. until 9 PM).*

CRYSTAL CATHEDRAL

Designed by postmodern architect Phillip Johnson, the Crystal Cathedral is a 10,661-pane glass superstructure that looms over surrounding Garden Grove in peculiar majesty. Home to Dr. Robert Schuller and his *Hour of Power* ministry, and housing a pipe organ with 16,271 pipes, it looks like something out of a bad science-fiction movie. And though the glass ceiling may afford an excellent view of the Garden Grove skyline (smog, tract housing, and minimalls), it's about as inviting as a jail cell. You're free to inspect the cathedral at your leisure, but keep in mind this is a working church—conservative dress is recommended. *12141 Lewis St., Garden Grove, tel. 714/971–4013. Admission free. Tours available; donation suggested.*

RICHARD M. NIXON LIBRARY AND BIRTHPLACE

Built on the grounds of Nixon's childhood home, this 9-acre tribute to the life and times of the late 37th president was opened by Presidents Bush, Reagan, Ford, and Nixon on July 19, 1990. There are several things that are easy to mock: the 30-minute film *Never Give Up*; the "World Leaders" exhibit (littered with life-size bronze statues of Nixon's picks for the 20th century's greatest leaders); and carefully chosen snippets from the infamous Watergate tapes. But there's something both sad and stirring about the shiny marble headstone at the base of the Rose Garden. *18001 Yorba Linda Blvd., Yorba Linda, tel. 714/993–3393. Follow signs from Hwy. 91. Admission: $6. Open Mon.–Sat. 10–5, Sun. 11–5. Free parking.*

AFTER DARK

Inland Orange County isn't known for its exciting nightlife. Except for a few dance clubs and Top 40 hangouts, you'll find your options sorely limited. You may want to see what's playing at the **Orange County Performing Arts Center** (600 Town Center Dr., Costa Mesa, tel. 714/556–2787); it frequently hosts the American Ballet Theatre, the L.A. Philharmonic, and the New York Opera. Performances cost a small fortune ($30–$70), and student and senior discounts are available one hour before some shows. In Irvine, the **Improv** (4255 Campus Dr., tel. 714/854–5455) offers live stand-up comedy nightly; the best acts appear on Friday and Saturday. Since Irvine is home to a University of California campus, it's easy to find concerts and other activities around here. For the latest, pick up the *O.C. Weekly* at record stores and cafés.

The Olde Ship is a traditional British pub and a laid-back local watering hole. If you're at all hungry, order the not-so-cheap-but-awfully-good Tiddler; one large piece of fish with chips, $5.95. If you're short on cash, try the traditional Irish meal: Guinness. Be sure to check out the loo, where British tabloids line the walls. *709 N. Harbor Blvd., Fullerton, tel. 741/871–7447.*

SANTA CATALINA ISLAND

This small island resort 22 mi off the coast of San Pedro is perfect for a weekend respite from L.A. and Orange County. Catalina was home to Native Americans for over 7,000 years, before the yacht club set hit its sandy shores. In 1542, these natives received the first European explorer, Don Juan Rodriguez Cabrillo and probably weren't happy about it. However, it was Don Sebastian Viscaino of Spain who named the island, 60 years later, after St. Catherine of Alexandria. The island has also housed Native Americans, Russians, and Aleutians who snubbed Spain's ownership claims and hunted sea otter to their hearts' desire. Yankee smugglers camped out here during the Mexican era and in later years American cattlemen squatted on the island. The development of Avalon, Catalina's main hub, was carried out by the Wrigley family of Chicago (the gum magnates), who acquired majority ownership in the Santa Catalina Island Company in 1919. The Wrigleys made the mountainous island into a tourist resort and a spring training ground for their baseball team, the Chicago Cubs. The Cubs don't train here anymore, but the island has become a venue for world-class sailing regattas, as well as competitive and recreational sportfishing. During summer, the small marina overflows with luxury yachts, sailboats, and cruise ships from around the world. Catalina, however, is not an exclusive playground: Snorkeling, scuba diving, and backpacking are popular pursuits with reasonable price tags. In 1975, the Santa Catalina Island Conservancy bought the title to 86% of Catalina so as to preserve and protect the land and its many varied inhabitants; ensuring that it would remain beautiful for years to come.

The island has two hubs: **Avalon,** the larger and more populated, sees the heaviest traffic and is where you'll find all the food, bars, shopping, and nightlife. The more rustic **Two Harbors** (23 mi northwest of Avalon by road, 13 by boat) has limited food and facilities but is quieter, equally (if not more) scenic, and offers seaside and beach camping at secluded Parson's Landing as well as access to the island's five wilderness campgrounds (*see* Where to Sleep, *below*). The extra time and effort required to reach this remote but attractive village means that it's less likely to be overrun by day-trippers. The **Catalina Island Chamber of Commerce** (tel. 310/510–1520), on Avalon's green Pleasure Pier, has maps, brochures, a visitor's guide, and information on hotel availability. The **visitor center** at the end of the pier in Two Harbors (tel. 310/510–0303) can advise you on the town's activities and amenities. For information on camping, hiking, and biking permits, *see* Where to Sleep *and* Outdoor Activities, *below.*

Avalon's most famous sight is the **Casino Building,** an art-deco masterpiece built in 1929. Marking the end of **Crescent Avenue Walkway** on the north side of the bay, this enormous circular landmark once

WHERE THE BUFFALO ROAM

Writer Zane Grey spent a lot of time on the island, and his biggest contribution—buffalo—is still evident today. For the movie version of Grey's book "The Vanishing America," buffalo had to be ferried across from the mainland. A small herd remains, grazing Santa Catalina's interior. Pigs, goats, and deer were also shipped over, but they lost out on the starring roles.

hosted top-notch big bands of the '30s and '40s. It now houses a renovated movie theater, a historical museum (tel. 310/510–2414, admission $1.50), and a tiny, free art gallery showcasing local talent. Ballroom dancing and evening concerts are still held here occasionally; check the Chamber of Commerce for schedules (*see above*). At the foot of the building is the **Underwater Dive Park,** a marine preserve with two shipwrecks, kelp forests, and school after school of fish. It's a terrific site for scuba diving, with some shallow areas suitable for snorkeling (for equipment rentals, *see* Outdoor Activities, *below*). In the hills above the Casino Building, look for the **Zane Grey Pueblo,** now a luxury hotel. A short walk up the road from the Pueblo is the **Chimes Tower,** commissioned by Ida Wrigley. The pleasant ringing of its bells every quarter hour can be heard throughout the streets of Avalon. About 1½ mi southwest of Avalon, at the end of Avalon Canyon Road, the **Wrigley Memorial and Botanical Gardens** (tel. 310/510–2288, admission $1) feature a tribute to William Wrigley, Jr., and a collection of the island's indigenous plant life.

COMING AND GOING

The ideal way to experience Santa Catalina is to sail over on your own and drop anchor in a secluded cove. For the rest of us, ferries depart regularly from Long Beach, San Pedro, and Newport to Avalon. Newport's **Catalina Flyer** (400 Main St., Balboa, tel. 714/673–5245) is fast (75 min) but expensive ($33 round-trip). Excessive baggage is not allowed, and reservations are required. **Catalina Cruises** (320 Golden Shore Blvd., Long Beach, tel. 800/228–2546) offers the cheapest round-trip fare to Avalon at $23. The trip takes two hours, and you depart from Catalina Landing in downtown Long Beach. Service to Two Harbors is the same price, but requires an additional 1¼ hours of travel time. Several ferries depart daily during summer; call ahead for schedule. For a few extra bucks, **Catalina Express** (tel. 310/519–1212) speeds over to Avalon in one hour from Berth 95 in San Pedro (follow signs from I–110) or from the Queen Mary in Long Beach (off Queen's Way Dr.). Round-trip tickets cost $36. They also have direct ferries to Two Harbors from San Pedro only; call ahead for the (erratic) schedule. All three ferry lines charge $6–$7 extra round-trip for bicycles and surfboards. Boats have both indoor and outdoor seating and snack bars. Reserving two weeks ahead is a must, especially during summer. Since the waters around Santa Catalina can get rough, you may want to bring along some seasickness pills.

GETTING AROUND

Only residents are allowed to have cars on Catalina, and an electronic key is required to drive through the gates of Avalon to outlying areas. The **Catalina Safari Bus** (tel. 310/510–2800) offers regular transportation between Avalon, Two Harbors, and several campgrounds for $36 round-trip. Buses depart from Island Plaza in Avalon and from the bus station just outside town in Two Harbors. In summer only, **Catalina Express** (tel. 310/519–1212) has an express boat that shuttles between Avalon and Two Harbors for $25 round-trip. The town of Avalon is small enough to explore on foot, making the notion of renting a **golf cart** ($30 per hour plus $30 deposit) seem ridiculous; nonetheless, they're quite popular—distracted pedestrians beware. **Bicycles** are another option, though you'll need a $50 permit to ride outside the town limits of Avalon and Two Harbors (*see* Outdoor Activities, *below*).

WHERE TO SLEEP

If you want to stay overnight without camping, prepare to lay down a lot of cash. In Avalon, your cheapest option is the **Hermosa Hotel and Catalina Cottages** (131 Metropole St., between Crescent Ave. and Beacon St., tel. 310/510–1010 or 800/666–3383), where you can get tidy, sparse rooms with shared bath for $35–$50 in summer, or private cottages with kitchen and bath for $80–$95. On most weekends March–October there's a two-night minimum stay. At **Hotel Atwater** (125 Sumner Ave., ½ block inland from Crescent Ave., tel. 800/851–0217), decent doubles in an institutional building go for $57 weekdays and $91 weekends during summer. The cheerful, yellow **Catalina Lodge** (235 Sumner Ave., at Beacon St., tel. 800/974–1070) has only 15 rooms ($58 weekdays, $68 weekends, $96 daily in summer), but it's clean and cozy and a jovial proprietor keeps things lively.

CAMPING

Avalon's only campground is **Hermit Gulch** (tel. 310/510–8368), 1 mi southwest of town at the end of Avalon Canyon Road. With room for 240 people in 68 sites, this could hardly be classified as "getting away from it all"; the campground is usually filled with families and large groups. However, it's an easy walk into town (summer tram service available, $1 one-way), and at $8.50 per person it's cheaper than any Avalon inn. It also rents tepees ($20–$25 per night). Reservations are recommended in summer and required in July and August.

If you can, experience the island's rugged outback and secluded coves. Inland **Black Jack Campground,** midway between Avalon and Two Harbors, offers stunning mountain vistas, while **Little Harbor Campground,** 7 mi south of Two Harbors on the opposite coast, overlooks a serene beach. Both can be reached by shuttle (*see* Getting Around, *above*) or hiking, and both have showers and chemical toilets. The **Two Harbors Campground,** ¼ mi outside the eponymous community, has tent cabins and tepees ($48–$72) as well as tent sites ($8.50–$9.50 per person). If you really want to get away from it all, bring everything you'll need to survive—this includes food and water—and hike on out to **Parson's Landing.** Parson's is found 7 mi west of Two Harbors on the island's northwest shore. Summers, there is a scheduled shoreboat shuttle service from Two Harbors to Emerald Bay; from Emerald Bay, it's a 1-mi hike to Parson's. Off-season you have to hoof it. There are six sites, and each can hold up to eight people. All sites are located on the beach and include picnic table, fire ring, and barbecue. Supposedly 2½ gallons of water and a bundle of firewood are provided each day, but to be on the safe side, especially off-season, bring your own. Unfortunately, Parson's is no bargain at $16.50 for the first person and $6.50 for each additional person. Reservations for all these year-round campgrounds must be made through **Catalina Camping Reservations** (Box 5044, Two Harbors 90704, tel. 310/510–7265). If you plan to hike to your campground, you must also pick up a free hiking permit in Avalon or Two Harbors (*see* Outdoor Activities, *below*).

FOOD

Santa Catalina's eateries are secure in the knowledge that they play to a captive audience; the food ranges from decent to awful and will sit best with those who enjoy a good dose of grease. The **Catalina Cantina** (311 Crescent Ave., tel. 310/510–0100) serves Mexican cuisine at moderate prices; try an enormous "big and wet" burrito for $8 and wash it down with a beer or a fresh-fruit margarita from the bar. Live bands play here on weekends. At the **Blue Parrot** (205½ Crescent Ave., tel. 310/510–2465), on the second level in the Metropole Marketplace, you can get Creole cuisine for $10–$14. Tropical drinks from the bar, views from all tables, and whimsical decor almost make the prices worthwhile. After hours, don your favorite aloha shirt and slip into **Luau Larry's** (509 Crescent Ave., tel. 310/510–1919) for a fantastic variety of tropical drinks. If you're on a tight budget, you'll find bread, cheese, fruit, and bottled water at the **Vons** supermarket on Metropole Avenue, a half block inland from Crescent Avenue.

OUTDOOR ACTIVITIES

Santa Catalina's varied terrain makes it an enticing place to hike, bike, and get your feet wet; however, efforts to preserve the island have led to costly permits and limited trail access. **Wet Spot Rentals** (tel 310/510–2229), next to the ferry landing, rents kayaks and paddleboats for $10–$17 an hour or $30–$50 a day (kayaks only).

BIKING AND HIKING

Mountain biking on the island can be a blast, but you'll need to buy a $50 permit if you want to ride outside Avalon or Two Harbors. In Avalon, permits are available at the **Catalina Island Conservancy** (125 Claressa St., at 3rd St., tel. 310/510–2595). Permits are valid from May 1 until April 30 of each year, and applicants must have a mountain bike and helmet. You can rent both at **Brown's Bikes** (107 Pebbly Beach Rd., near ferry landing, tel. 310/510–0986) for about $20 a day. They also rent tandems and six-speed bikes ($6–$12 per hr) for in-town cruising.

The required hiking permit is free and available at the conservancy or at Hermit Gulch Campground (*see* Where to Sleep, *above*). In Two Harbors, both permits are available at the **visitor center** (tel. 310/510–7265) at the end of the pier. It's possible to hike or bike between Avalon and Two Harbors, starting at the Hogsback gate above Avalon, though the 28-mi journey has an elevation gain of 3,000 ft and is not for the weak. For a pleasant 4-mi hike out of Avalon, take Avalon Canyon Road to Wrigley Gardens and follow the trail to Lone Pine. At the top you'll have an amazing view of the Palisades cliffs and, beyond them, the sea.

FISHING

Year-round, the sportfishing is tremendous in the waters off Catalina, with an abundance of yellowtail, calico bass, and barracuda. The once large shark population, however, is rapidly diminishing. You can rent fishing equipment ($5 plus for 4 hrs) at **Joe's Rent-a-Boat** (tel. 310/510–0455) on Avalon's Pleasure Pier. Joe also rents single ($10 per hr) and double ($17 per hr) kayaks. **Earl and Rose's Seafood,** at the pier's end, sells bait ($1–$2). For a small fee, they'll also fillet and freeze whatever you catch. No permit is necessary to fish off Pleasure Pier or from the end of the cement ferry landing. While barracuda, bonito, and mackerel bite at either location, some say the larger fish are found at the ferry landing.

SNORKELING AND SCUBA DIVING

If you prefer your fish live, rent scuba (certification required) or snorkeling gear in Avalon at **Catalina Diver's Supply** (end of Pleasure Pier, tel. 310/510–0330) for $50 and $23 respectively in summer all day. Noncertified divers can scuba with the aid of an instructor for $85. The shop offers guided and package tours, but you can easily enjoy the Underwater Dive Park (*see* Catalina Island, *above*) on your own for free. Snorkelers should head to the shallow waters of **Lover's Cove Marine Preserve,** a short walk east past the ferry landing; this is also a good spot to swim, since it's free of the boat traffic that jams Avalon Bay.

NEAR SANTA CATALINA ISLAND

PALOS VERDES

The Palos Verdes peninsula rises dramatically from the sea: a green-and-gold mass of rolling hills and steep cliffs peppered with elegant estates. Once a vast, treeless ranch owned by José Dolores Sepulveda—whose name graces one of the longest boulevards in Los Angeles—the peninsula was purchased for $1 million in 1913 by a wealthy businessman and turned into an exclusive residential community. Its pocket-size beaches, though difficult to reach, are worth a visit. You can get to Palos Verdes from L.A. by taking I-110 south to Hwy. 91 west (Artesia Blvd.). Take Artesia to Highway 1 (Pacific Coast Hwy.) and head south to **Palos Verdes Drive.** Tiny beaches pocket the steep bluffs west of **Palos Verdes Estates**; one of the most attractive is **Bluff Cove,** accessible to the nimble via a winding trail from Paseo del Mar (at Flat Rock Point). Turn left on Hawthorne Boulevard to get to the center of town, or keep going on Palos Verdes Drive South to the main inorganic attraction: the **Wayfayer's Chapel** (5755 Palos Verdes Dr. S, tel. 310/377–1650), designed by the son of famed architect Frank Lloyd Wright. This thrilling natural sanctuary, built almost entirely of glass and surrounded by redwoods, is open daily 9–5.

SAN PEDRO

Quite a contrast to its ritzy neighbor Palos Verdes, this working-class neighborhood at the southern edge of the peninsula is home to **Los Angeles Harbor,** one of the major departure points for ferries to Santa Catalina (*see* Coming and Going *in* Catalina Island, *above*). Besides the **Cabrillo Marine Aquarium** (3720 Stephen White Dr., tel. 310/548–7562), the official main attraction here is **Ports O'Call Village** (Harbor Blvd. terminus, tel. 310/831–0287), a 15-acre cluster of pierside shops gussied up to look like New England. Visit on a Thursday to peruse the expansive Farmer's Market. The city's real personality (cautiously avant-garde) can be found in the blocks surrounding the intersection of **Gaffey** and **6th**

streets; inexpensive cafés and restaurants abound (*see* Food, *below*), and sidewalk plaques honor various athletes. Scuba divers and snorkelers may want to explore the **Underwater Dive Trail** just east of Royal Palm State Beach (Western Ave., at S. Paseo del Mar), which winds through kelp beds and sulfurous hot springs. **Pacific Wilderness and Ocean Sports** (1719 S. Pacific Ave., tel. 310/833–2422) rents scuba gear for about $50 a day and offers certification classes. Stop by the **San Pedro Chamber of Commerce** (390 W. 7th St., 4 blocks east of Gaffey St., tel. 310/832–7272), open weekdays 9–5, to pick up a visitor's guide, trolley schedule, or detailed city map. To reach San Pedro from downtown L.A., take I–110 south.

GETTING AROUND • The **Electric Trolley** runs Thursday through Monday 10–6, stopping at the Catalina Air and Sea Terminal, Ports O'Call Village, downtown San Pedro, the Los Angeles Maritime Museum, and other points of interest. Fare is 25¢; routes and schedules are available at the Chamber of Commerce (*see above*).

WHERE TO SLEEP • San Pedro International AYH-Hostel. Set in Angel's Gate Park, with a panoramic view of the Pacific and the Korean Friendship Bell, this 60-bed hostel is one of the best deals in the area. It's near downtown San Pedro, easily accessible by bus and only a 10-minute walk from the beach. Private rooms go for $29, semiprivate rooms (two beds) for $16 a person, and dorm beds for $11.50. There's a kitchen, a TV room with movies, a reading room, a volleyball court, a barbecue, and laundry facilities. Backpackers and foreign travelers pack the place during summer, so make reservations. All guests must have a sleep sheet, which you can rent for $2. *3601 S. Gaffey St., Bldg. 613, tel. 310/831–8109, fax 310/831–4635. From LAX, free shuttle to the Metro (Green Line). Take Metro to 110 Harbor Fwy., transfer to Bus 446 ($1.60) to Korean Bell and Hostel. From L.A. Greyhound, Bus 446 south from 6th and Grand Sts., get off at Angel's Gate Park. By car, I–110 south to San Pedro, follow to end, then left on Gaffey St. 60 beds. Lockout 11–4. Checkout 11 AM. No curfew. Key ($10 deposit).*

FOOD • For once, you don't have to avoid the "nice" restaurants if you're on a tight budget. Even the most highbrow places offer meals for around $10–$15. Top-rate Greek food and live Greek dancing have made **Papadakis Taverna** (301 W. 6th St., at Center St., tel. 310/548–1186) one of the most popular restaurants in San Pedro; catch one of two nightly informal performances (usually at 6 and 9) while you dine. Popular with locals and backpackers alike, the **Lighthouse Deli/Café** (508 W. 39th St., tel. 310/548–3354) offers big, messy sandwiches like the vegetarian submarine with curry sauce ($5.95) or the huge, multigrain waffle ($2.95). From the youth hostel, it's a 10-minute walk: Head back to Gaffey Street, walk down the hill, and take a left on 39th. **Sacred Grounds** (399 W. 6th St., tel. 310/514–0800) is the place to sample alternative tunes and fresh-brewed java.

LONG BEACH

Long Beach, just across the Vincent Thomas Bridge from San Pedro, seems like a contradiction in terms—a seaside resort amid towering oil refineries and massive natural-gas processing plants. Yet somehow (probably thanks to gross infusions of wealth), parts of the city have shaken that industrial image—maybe it's the 5½ mi of sandy white beaches. There's plenty to explore in Long Beach, from the landmark deco buildings of downtown to a nascent artists' community to the cluster of funky cafés, shops, and restaurants that constitute the twentysomething haunt of Belmont Shore. The city is also one of Southern California's most socially diverse and well worth a visit before catching the ferry to Catalina.

VISITOR INFORMATION • As is fitting in a city eager for tourist dollars, the **Long Beach Area Convention and Visitors Bureau** delights in distributing a comprehensive area map and guide, as well as the extremely helpful handout "101 Things to Do in the Long Beach Area." The staff is also knowledgeable about San Pedro and Palos Verdes. *1 World Trade Center, Suite 300, tel. 562/436–3645 or 800/452–7829. Between Magnolia Ave. and Ocean Blvd. Open weekdays 8:30–5.*

COMING AND GOING • To get to Long Beach from L.A., take I–710 south. From the south, take I–405 to I–710 or I–110. **Greyhound** (tel. 800/231–2222) has a station in downtown Long Beach (464 W. 3rd St., at Magnolia Ave., tel. 562/432–1842) with service to L.A. (1 hr, $8), San Diego (3 hrs, $11), and San Francisco (10 hrs, $32). The Metro's **Blue Line** runs between L.A. and downtown Long Beach every 10–20 minutes, stopping at the Long Beach Transit Mall (*see* Getting Around, *below*) and 1st Street; the ride costs $1.35 each way. For more information, call 800/266–6883. Both **Catalina Express** (tel. 310/519–1212 or 800/618–5533) and **Catalina Cruises** (tel. 800/228–2546) offer regular service to Santa Catalina Island (*see above*).

Long Beach Airport (4100 E. Donald Douglas Dr., tel. 562/570–2600) is served by American West (tel. 800/235–9292) and several charter services. Prices for in-state and national flights are the same as at LAX or slightly higher (all international travel is handled by LAX). Unfortunately, there's no public transportation to the airport; private shuttles will bring you to your hotel or downtown for about $15, and **Yellow Cab** (tel. 562/421–7180) can do the same for $18–$20.

GETTING AROUND • Public buses (90¢) are operated by **Long Beach Transit** (tel. 562/591–2301). Obtain schedules and catch most bus lines at the **Transit Mall** (1st St., between Long Beach Blvd. and Pacific Ave.). The **Runabout Shuttle** (no tel.) offers frequent free service from Downtown (Ocean or Pine Blvd.) to the ferry terminal and the Queen Mary. Shuttles run 7–6 weekdays and 10–5 weekends. For 90¢ it connects with Belmont Shore.

Ocean Boulevard is the main thoroughfare along the coast of Long Beach and heading north over the bridge to San Pedro and south into Belmont Shores and Seal Beach. Downtown is comprised of five districts: **Pine Avenue,** with many bars and cafés; quaint **Shoreline Village** with an old seaport feel; **East Village**'s arts community; the financial district of **West Side**; and the residential **North End.** These areas are bordered by Shoreline Drive on the far northwest corner, 10th Street on the easternmost side, Golden Avenue to the west, and Lime Street to the south.

WHERE TO SLEEP • Long Beach has a large selection of motels, though many cater to the convention center's big spenders. The **Rodeway Inn** (50 Atlantic Ave., ½ block from Ocean Blvd., tel. 562/435–8369, fax 562/432–3799) has immaculate, attractive rooms with refrigerators for $42–$48 a night. A meager Continental breakfast is included. Farther from the center of town, the beachside **Surf Motel** (2010 E. Ocean Blvd., at Cherry Ave., tel. 562/437–0771) has a pool and small, clean rooms starting at $45 ($55 with ocean view). Rates rise in summer. If these are full, look on Atlantic Avenue, which houses the majority of the city's budget accommodations.

FOOD • In the area known as Belmont Shore, 2nd Street is lined with restaurants catering to the young but not necessarily rich. Locals jam into the **Shore House Café** (5271 E. 2nd St., at La Verne Ave., tel. 562/433–2266), open 24 hours, which has a lengthy list of sandwiches for $5–$7. The salmon alla checca or the chicken marsala dinners will set you back about $10. At **Midnite Espresso** (4925 E. 2nd St., tel. 562/439–3978), pick up the namesake coffee drink (a mocha-cinnamon/whipped cream wake-up call) for about $3, and then cut the caffeine with a starchy snack (under $4).

A young, artsy crowd fills the cluster of restaurants near the intersection of Pine Avenue and Broadway Street downtown. **M Bar and Grill** (213A Pine Ave., at Broadway St., tel. 562/435–2525), which doubles as a gallery, features an eclectic calendar of live music as well as delicious, skillfully prepared food. The menu includes a sautéed red-snapper sandwich ($8) and toasted feta and goat cheese salad ($7.50). People flock to **Alegria** (115 Pine Ave., at Broadway St., tel. 562/436–3388) for the potent sangria ($16.50 per liter), the occasional live flamenco dancers, and the novel menu of hot and cold *tapas* (appetizers; $4–$8).

AFTER DARK • If you want to shake it up, **Jillians** (110 Pine Ave. at 1st St., tel. 562/628–8866) boasts a velvet draped lounge, a wooden bar snaking its way through the main floor, and two dance floors. A dance party is held every Thursday through Saturday around 9 PM ($7 cover, 21 and over), and while fetish gear isn't mandatory, it's certainly not discouraged. **Blue Café** (210 Promenade N, at Broadway, tel. 562/983–7111) features live blues every night of the week except Monday. Play a few rounds of pool on one of the many tables upstairs, or down a cold one and hide out in the dark interior. Cover $2–$10.

WORTH SEEING • If you're interested in architecture, head to the small residential community of **Belmont Shore,** at the east end of Ocean Boulevard (Bus 12 stops here). Developed in the 1940s, it has some of the town's oldest beach homes and bungalows. The unofficial inland boardwalk is **2nd Street** (between Livingston Dr. and Bay Shore Ave.), a hot spot lined with bars, cafés, and nightclubs where twentysomethings gratefully shed job angst. Across from Belmont Shore in Alamitos Bay is the upscale island community of **Naples** (Little Italy), home to Long Beach's wealthiest families. Like Venice, this community was designed around an extensive canal system—you can even take gondola rides in authentic Venetian gondolas. Second Street crosses Naples's main island on its way to Pacific Coast Hwy. (Hwy. 1).

To get a feel for the city's funkier side, explore **Broadway,** the downtown drag between Pacific and Cherry avenues. The art-deco feel is authentic; if you have any doubts check out the terra-cotta detailing and vibrant colors of the **Bradley Building** (201 Pine St.). Other landmarks include **Villa Riviera** (800 E. Ocean Blvd.), a 16-story high-rise built in 1929 with a mix of Gothic, Tudor, French, and Italianate architectural styles; and the **Breakers Hotel** (200 E. Ocean Blvd.), a Spanish Revival–style resort built in 1926. Covering the entire exterior of the Long Beach Arena (300 E. Ocean Blvd.) is **Planet Ocean,** whose life-size depictions of whales and other frolicsome sea creatures qualify it as the world's largest mural. A shuttle ride away (*see* Getting Around, *above*) lies the historic **Queen Mary** (tel.

562/435–3511), an ocean liner that ferried U.S. troops to Europe during World War II and returned with the bodies of fallen soldiers. It's permanently docked at the harbor and boardable for $10 (though rumor has it this boat is in such horrible disrepair that it's in danger of sinking into the harbor).

ORANGE COUNTY COAST

The 50-mi stretch of coast between Seal Beach and San Clemente is fondly known as the "American Riviera," the most scenic and lively seaside region on California's coast. **Seal Beach,** only 10 mi south of Long Beach, is a quirky, uncommercial small town—the perfect place to begin your coastal odyssey. The adjacent **Sunset Beach** offers no-frills sand and surf and budget motels. A little farther south you'll come across **Huntington Beach,** a trendy enclave filled with bleached-blond surfers and their suntanned groupies. The average age here seems to be 18–25. Sprawling **Newport Beach,** one of Southern California's most exclusive seaside playgrounds, is just 40 mi south of downtown Los Angeles; its size makes it the unofficial coastal capital, particularly for boat trips of all types. At rugged **Laguna Beach,** the coast earns its Riviera nickname—it's beginning to resemble Prince Rainier's cliffside Monaco. Laguna has also been a colorful coastal stop since the '60s, when Timothy Leary and his hippie cronies hung out in the town's fast-food joints. The final two stops are **San Juan Capistrano** and **San Clemente,** both worth a short visit—the former for its historic mission and the latter for its narrow, crowd-free beaches. Wherever you go, pay attention to the brown COASTAL ACCESS signs; they may lead you to a completely untouristed stretch of sand.

The famous three-hour tour of the SS Minnow (the wrecked ship of "Gilligan's Island" fame) set sail from Long Beach's Alamitos Bay in 1964.

Nothing comes cheap on this part of California's coast, including lodging. There is a youth hostel in San Clemente, and you'll find excellent campgrounds near San Juan Capistrano, but otherwise be prepared to spend upward of $40 for lodging along the coast. You'll also pay anywhere from $2 to $10 for daytime parking at most beaches.

COMING AND GOING

BY BUS

The **Santa Ana Greyhound Station** (1000 E. Santa Ana Blvd., at Santiago Blvd., tel. 714/542–2215 or 800/231–2222) lies in the Transit Center just off the Santa Ana Freeway, 10 mi north of Newport Beach and the coast. Connections from this station include San Diego (2 hrs, $11 one-way), Riverside (2 hrs, $9 one-way), Los Angeles (1½ hrs, $9 one-way), Santa Barbara (4 hrs, $10 one-way), San Luis Obispo (8 hrs, $38 one-way), and San Francisco (10 hrs, $32 one-way). The ticket office is open 6 AM–8 PM daily, and buses leave hourly throughout the day. To reach the coast from here you need to take OCTA Bus 85 to Main Street and Santa Ana Boulevard and then Bus 53 south to Newport Beach; a taxi will run you about $25.

In **San Clemente,** Greyhound picks up and drops off passengers in front of Dad's Liquor and Deli (2421 S. El Camino Real). Buses head north from here to Santa Ana (45 min, $9 one-way), L.A. (2½ hrs, $13 one-way) and beyond, and south to Oceanside (40 min, $7 one-way) and San Diego (1½ hrs, $11 one-way). You pay for the trip at the next station along your route.

Call the **OCTA** for routes, schedules, and public bus information for all of Orange County. *Tel. 714/636–7433, ext. 10. Open weekdays 6 AM–8 PM, weekends 8–5.*

BY CAR

The scenic stretch of Hwy. 1 called Pacific Coast Hwy. traverses the coast from L.A. to San Juan Capistrano, where it merges with I–5. To save some time and still see some of Orange County's most rugged beachfront, you can take I–405 south from L.A., cross to the coast on Hwy. 55 (to Newport Beach) or Hwy. 133 (to Laguna), and continue south.

SURF'S UP

If you're just starting out, try mellow Redondo and Huntington beaches, both of which are wide enough to offer plenty of waves for beginners as well as experts. If you're confident in your ability, hit the landmarks: Malibu, Ventura County Line, San Clemente, and Carlsbad, all of which have a point break. A word of caution, though—these are largely "locals only" surf spots.

BY TRAIN

Between Los Angeles and San Diego, the main stop for Amtrak trains is the **San Juan Capistrano Depot.** You can head to L.A. (1½ hrs, $9 one-way) and to San Diego (1½ hrs, $9.50 one-way). Public buses run between this depot, Laguna, and San Clemente hourly 9–7. *26701 Verdugo St., west of Camino Capistrano, tel. 714/240–2972. Office open weekdays 7–2:30, weekends 7–6:30.*

Otherwise, you can get off the train at the **San Clemente Auxiliary Amtrak Station,** at 1850 Avenida Estacion at El Camino Real. There's no staff here, and outgoing passengers can't purchase tickets at the station; you must either already have a ticket or be prepared to pay for one in cash when you step on board. Call **Amtrak** (tel. 800/872–7245) for more information. To reach Laguna Beach from the San Clemente station, take OCTA Bus 91 south to the last stop, then hop on Bus 1 heading north; to reach Disneyland, take Bus 85 north to Laguna Hills Transportation, then switch to Bus 51 north.

SEAL BEACH

If you blink, you could easily miss this mellow seaside community 10 mi south of Long Beach. Even though it offers no real tourist attractions, Seal Beach has a wonderfully quirky, 1950s beach-town feel. **Main Street** has managed to ward off most of the evils of tourism (only one or two shops sell Seal Beach T-shirts). In the simply named **Book Store** (213 Main St., tel. 562/598–1818), you can browse among haphazard stacks of used books; behind one of them you may even uncover the proprietor. The **municipal pier,** Seal Beach's pride and joy despite recurrent electrical fires, sits in the center of a wide, sandy half shell of beach, bordered by enormous houses. Though the view of oil rigs is less than inspiring, it's fun to stroll along the pier or pause to fish for rock cod. The sportfishing shop at the pier's end rents rods ($10) and sells bait ($3). The beach itself is fantastic for swimming, with its mellow waves and sandy shore. Surfers will probably want to head elsewhere.

For information on local events, contact the **Seal Beach Chamber of Commerce** (201B 8th St., tel. 562/799–0179) between 10 AM and 4 PM weekdays. The town's accommodations are few and cater to the very wealthy. You're better off in nearby Sunset or Huntington beaches (*see below*), where rooms go for about half the price.

Start with an Irish pub, fill it with surfers and lifeguards, then add a dash of country music and seaside charm, and you've got **Hennessy's Tavern** (140 Main St., tel. 562/598–4419), part of a small chain of beachside pubs and one of Seal Beach's more popular hangouts. It has sandwiches ($5–$8) and salads (about $7), but most people prefer beer and make small talk at the bar. Line up at **Nick's** (223 Main St., tel. 562/598–5072) for beach fuel, including the tasty breakfast burrito ($3) and the vegetarian sandwich ($3.50). Otherwise, head to **Ruby's** (tel. 562/431–7829), at the end of Seal Beach's pier. This '50s-style diner (part of an Orange County chain) has hefty burgers (beef, turkey, veggie, or chicken) starting at $4.

NEAR SEAL BEACH

SUNSET BEACH • Barely 2 mi long, this no-frills town is bordered by **Seal Beach Boulevard** (to the north) and **Warner Boulevard** (to the south). It's got the same sand and lifeguard towers you'll find in Huntington Beach in a more residential, less crowded setting. While the surf is not as good as that at Huntington, it's a fabulous place to swim. The shores are lined with a trim collection of two-story cottages, and you'll find free parking along North and South Pacific avenues, parallel to PCH. You can't camp on the beach, but you can stay a mere half block from it at the reasonably clean, slightly seedy **Islander Motel** (16545 Pacific Coast Hwy., at 21st St., tel. 562/592–1993) for as little as $30 a night ($45 with kitchenette). To register, head next door to the Econo Lodge (16555 Pacific Coast Highway). The better-kept but misleadingly named **Oceanview Motel** (16196 Pacific Coast Hwy., tel. 562/592–2700) has rooms with no views starting at $35. Though you may be tempted to pay $30 more for a private Jacuzzi, the secret is that it's just a bathtub with jets. You're better off indulging yourself at the **Harbor House Café** (16341 Pacific Coast Hwy., at Anderson St., tel. 562/592–5404), which serves the best omelets in Orange County ($6–$9) 24 hours a day.

HUNTINGTON BEACH

Huntington Beach is Surf City U.S.A. Twelve miles south of Seal Beach on PCH, this was once a quiet town, but robust development has left the city bustling with glittery, spanking-new shops and restaurants along **Main Street.** You'll also find heaps of pseudo-Spanish terra-cotta condo complexes. Appropriately, beaches here are huge and filled with conveniences (including tons of stands hawking slush puppies, soft tacos, firewood, boogie boards, and beach umbrellas). Pay $5–$6 for the privilege of parking near the action, or park for free on Beach Boulevard and walk. Huntington is also home to the **International Surfing Museum** (411 Olive Ave., 1 block west of Main St., tel. 714/960–3483), in case you didn't get enough of the real thing down at the shore. Huntington Beach is a haven for recently graduated working stiffs clinging to their youth. At any moment of the day, a steady stream of them can be found jaywalking across PCH with surfboards, in-line skates, and overexcited Labradors. At night the same throng packs into Main Street bars. Fourth of July festivities are notorious here: General chaos prevails as drunken revelers whoop it up.

You can get sun and a little exercise playing pickup sand volleyball on the courts next to the pier. Be warned, though, that locals take their volleyball pretty seriously. **Robert August** (301 5th St., at Olive St., tel. 714/960–2266) rents surfboards for $25 per day. You can set up lessons with a pro surfer for $35 per 90 minutes; the price includes your board and wet suit.

From mid-September until mid-November (but especially weekends in October), locals exhaustively celebrate **Oktoberfest** with German food, music, and, of course, beer. Lots of it. Call the Old World German Restaurant (tel. 714/895–8020) for more details.

VISITOR INFORMATION

Huntington Beach Conference and Visitors Bureau. The staff will assail you with glossy material on restaurants, lodging, and activities. *101 Main St., Suite 2A, tel. 714/969–3492 or 800/729–6232. At Pacific Coast Hwy. Open weekdays 9 AM–5 PM.*

WHERE TO SLEEP

If you're willing to forgo beachside digs, reasonably priced motels abound along **Beach Boulevard (Hwy. 39),** about a mi inland. The visitor's bureau (*see above*) can refer you to several.

Huntington Shores Motel. Ping-pong, horseshoes, HBO, and a pool are among the amenities you'll find at this motel, located across the highway from the beach. Doubles cost $60 in winter, $80 in summer. Make reservations at least 10 days in advance in summer—it books up fast. *21002 Pacific Coast Highway, between Huntington St. and 1st St., tel. 714/536–8861 or 800/554–6799, fax 714/536–0060. 50 rooms, all with bath.*

Huntington Surf Inn. With a second-story sundeck and the ocean just across PCH, this is the place to be, especially if you're seeking contact with real-life surfers. Doubles are $80 (with a $5 charge per extra person). Other than a few stray surfing stickers, rooms are well-kept, and the management aims to keep them that way. "Unregistered guests" (read: parties) are forbidden after 10 PM. *720 Pacific Coast Hwy., north of 8th St. pier, tel. 714/536–2444. 9 rooms, all with bath. Laundry. Reservations advised 2 weeks in advance during summer.*

FOOD

The Huntington Beach Brewing Company (201 Main St., at Walnut Ave., tel. 714/960–5343) has live jazz and blues and views of the beach, not to mention "armadillo eggs" (stuffed jalapeños, $6.35) and other fillers for less than $10. The pub overflows with overtanned yuppies on weekend nights, and brews ale with a name (Huntington Beach Blonde) that cries out for bad jokes. If you need to power up before catching some waves, head to the **Beach Café Deli** (328 11th St., at Orange St., tel. 714/960–7008), where barefoot surfers chow down breakfast burritos ($2.50). Still hungry? Two eggs with homefries and toast is only $2.30.

CHEAP THRILLS

After you wipe out on a massive swell, be sure to pay your respects along **Huntington Beach's Surfing Walk of Fame.** Every year surfers who have made significant contributions to the culture of surfing receive a golden stone on the walk of fame. To see the stars, begin at the corner of PCH and Main Street. On Fridays from 2 PM to 7 PM, buy produce, flowers, or arts and crafts at the **Farmers Market,** on Main Street between Walnut and Orange Streets. Nature lovers—especially bird watchers—will want to check out the **Bolsa Chica Ecological Reserve.** A 1½-mi loop trail traverses the Bolsa Bay, highlighting the archaeology, ecology, and biology of the reserve. Explore on your own, or take free guided tours; offered 9 AM–10:30 AM on the first Saturday of the month from September to April. Call 714/897–7003 for more information. The reserve is located at Huntington Harbor, off PCH.

NEWPORT BEACH

Newport Beach, 5 mi south of Huntington Beach on PCH, is an aloof bastion of high society, yacht clubs, and multimillion-dollar beachfront homes. But, during the summer, Newport's beaches are swamped with visitors, transforming the city's quiet boardwalk into a crowded and colorful promenade. It's the largest of Orange County's beachfront communities, with tons of organized scuba-diving, sport-fishing, and whale-watching possibilities. There's also a daily ferry to Catalina Island (*see above*).

You can explore the happening parts of the city on foot, starting on the beach near the **Newport Pier.** If you want to blend in with the locals, rent a bicycle or a pair of in-line skates from any of the shops along the waterfront. Otherwise, head for the **FunZone,** a small amusement park in Balboa Pavilion with an old-fashioned Ferris wheel ($2) and penny arcades. From here it's only a 5-minute walk to the town's liveliest nightspot—the stretch of beach and bars between **Balboa Boulevard** and **Ocean Front Avenue.** Lunatics may want to check out **The Wedge** (end of Balboa Blvd., 20 min from pier), one of the most famous—and dangerous—body-surfing breakwaters in the world. Be warned: The Wedge is for experienced swimmers only, and surfboards are not allowed. Waves range anywhere from 8 to 25 ft, and the water is extremely shallow. Any day of the week you can watch local body surfers getting knocked silly by the infamous swells. The minipalazzos of the city's wealthy are shoehorned onto **Lido Island** in the center of Newport Harbor. Farther inland lies **Fashion Island** (which is neither fashionable nor an island), the location of the fine Orange County Museum of Art (*see below*).

VISITOR INFORMATION

Newport Beach Visitors and Conference Bureau offers the usual: tourist brochures, maps, and sound advice. *3300A W. Coast Hwy., at Newport Blvd., tel. 714/722–1611 or 800/942–6278. Open weekdays 8–5.*

WHERE TO SLEEP

You'll find a string of reasonably priced (although some are unreasonably shabby) motels ($25–$40) along Newport Boulevard in **Costa Mesa.** You won't have an ocean view (more likely a view of Hwy. 55), but Costa Mesa is only a 10-minute drive from the beach. The **Sandpiper Motel** (1967 Newport Blvd., near 19th St., tel. 714/645–9137), where doubles start at $45, is probably the best of the bunch. The only two affordable hotels in Newport proper are the **Newport Channel Inn** (6030 W. Coast Hwy., between Brookhurst and Superior Aves., tel. 714/642–3030), with rooms starting at $44 in winter and $75 in summer; and the **Newport Classic Inn** (2300 W. Coast Hwy., at Tustin Ave., tel. 800/633–3199), with rates from $69 on weekdays and from $76 on weekends. Both are well-maintained, clean, and seconds from the beach. They're also popular with summer crowds, so reservations are advised.

CAMPING • Newport Dunes. This privately owned facility is primarily an RV trailer park, but a limited number of tent sites go for a brutal $25–$30 a night, depending on the season. Don't expect the great outdoors, either: The gravel sites don't have a tree or verdant hillside in sight. However, Newport Dunes is only minutes away from Balboa Island and the peninsula, Newport Beach's hot spot. You'll find a few restaurants and stores near the campground, and the beach is a 10-minute walk away. *1131 Back Bay Dr., off Jamboree Rd., tel. 714/729–3863 or 800/288–0770. 406 sites (79 tent sites). Barbecues, drinking water, fire grates, flush toilets, picnic tables, showers. Reservations advised.*

FOOD

Newport's cheap eats lie between **Balboa Boulevard** and **Ocean Front Avenue,** 1 block from the beach and pier. Along with ice-cream parlors and yogurt shops, there's a decent selection of breakfast and burger joints, as well as a healthy sampling of bars.

The Crab Cooker. This no-frills place serves tasty seafood on paper plates and offers the best clam chowder ($3.25 large, $1.40 small) for miles around. Dinner entrées range from skewered scallops with bacon ($10.75) to cracked crab ($13). You can sit down in the restaurant or get your food to go from the adjoining market. *2200 Newport Blvd., tel. 714/673–0100.*

Taquería Tia Rosa. This tiny hole-in-the-wall serves up some of the best Mexican food in town. A hefty carne asada burrito fetches $3.49; a veggie burrito with beans, rice, cilantro, onions, salsa, cheese, and guacamole is $2.89. They don't serve chips, but you won't miss 'em. *2307 Balboa Blvd., tel. 714/675–6574. No credit cards.*

WORTH SEEING

Newport's main attraction is **Balboa Island,** connected to the mainland by Jamboree Road. You can catch a ferry that shuttles between island and peninsula constantly, docking on the peninsula at the end of Palm Street (follow BALBOA FERRY signs from PCH). The fun five-minute ride is a bargain at $1 per car, 50¢ per bike, or 35¢ per passenger. **Marine Avenue** is Balboa Island's main drag, with more than 70 shops and restaurants. It's touristy, but it still has a seaside charm that most of California's overdeveloped beach towns lost years ago. Back on the peninsula, the Victorian **Balboa Pavilion** (400 Main St., off Balboa Blvd.) is the architectural jewel of the city. Built in 1906 as a bathhouse, the pavilion became a haven for big-band sounds in the 1940s. Today, it's the place to go for deep-sea fishing ($23 a half day) and whale-watching (*see* Outdoor Activities, *below*).

One of Newport's edible attractions is the Balboa Bar—a frozen, chocolate-dipped creation that was invented here (so locals claim) in the 1940s.

The **Orange County Museum of Art,** near Newport Center, recently spent 1.8 million dollars renovating what was once an unremarkable brown building. The museum collects and displays art from the turn of the century to the present, including the works of post–World War II California artists. *850 San Clemente Dr., tel. 714/759–1122. From Pacific Coast Hwy., Jamboree Rd. north and follow signs. Admission: $5. Open Tues.–Sun. 11–5.*

The **Upper Newport Bay Ecological Reserve** (end of Back Bay Dr., tel. 714/640–6746) offers year-round viewing of a protected natural-wetland habitat—home to more than 30 species of indigenous and migratory birds. You'll get a good sense here of what the California coast looked like 100 years ago: lush flora and chatty fauna accompanied by the peaceful rumble of the sea. The road that follows the shore is popular among bicyclists, joggers, and in-line skaters. To get to the preserve from PCH, turn inland onto Jamboree Road, veer left on Back Bay Drive, and follow it to the end.

AFTER DARK

Newport Beach has long had a reputation as *the* oceanside playground of Orange County's young and available. Though many have defected lately for the crush of new bars in Huntington Beach, Newport will always be King. Most of the late-night action takes place on the Balboa peninsula, particularly in the strip of restaurants and bars near **Newport Pier** and in **Lido Village.** Solo women and those who don't enjoy exchanging sexual *bons mots* might prefer to explore the area's cafés, which are a bit more low-key.

BARS • Across the street from the Newport Pier, **Blackies by the Sea, Inc.** (2118 W. Ocean Front, tel. 714/675–1074), the apotheosis of all things Californian, dispenses cheap beer with an attitude; the sign on the door reads SORRY—WE'RE OPEN. On the other side of the peninsula and a world apart, **The Cannery** (3010 Lafayette Ave., at Newport Blvd., tel. 714/675–5777) draws crowds into its maw for happy hour (weekdays 4–6) and karaoke (Wed.). Weekends bring bands playing rock classics, as well as a $5 cover. Old-timers and young people frequent **Snug Harbor** (517 30th St., tel. 714/673–3170) for the cozy atmosphere and stiff drinks.

CAFÉS • Jazz lovers should make a beeline for **Studio Café** (100 Main St., at Balboa Blvd., tel. 714/675–7760), which presents top-rate jazz and blues musicians nightly. The café has a full-service bar and dining room; try the savory shrimp scampi ($15.50) or the barbecued ribs ($11.50). The **Alta Coffee Warehouse and Roasting Co.** (506 31st St., off Newport Blvd., tel. 714/675–0233) has jazz, folk, and blues singers weekly (no cover). The food is simple, the coffee strong.

OUTDOOR ACTIVITIES

Newport Beach seems to revolve around sporting activities, most of which take advantage of the town's prime coastal location. **Balboa Bikes 'n' Beach Stuff** (601 E. Balboa Blvd., Balboa, tel. 714/723–1516) rents bikes and skates for about $6 an hour. If these guys don't have what you're looking for, just keep walking down the street; there's no shortage of rental places.

FISHING • Fishing is allowed from either of Newport's two piers without a permit. You can buy your bait ($2) at **Glen's Tackle** (1145 Baker St., Costa Mesa, tel. 714/957–1408). Both **Davey's Locker** (400 Main St., tel. 714/673–1434) and **Newport Landing** (309 Palm St., Suite F, tel. 714/675–0550) organize fishing trips year-round for rock cod, mackerel, bonito, barracuda, or whatever else is biting (about $23 per half-day). Both are located in the Balboa Pavilion (*see* Worth Seeing, *above*).

SNORKELING AND SCUBA DIVING • In Newport Beach, the **Aquatic Center** (4537 W. Coast Hwy., at Balboa Blvd., tel. 714/650–5440) rents scuba gear ($60 a day) and snorkeling equipment ($10 a day). Photo ID and a deposit are required, and scuba divers must bring certification papers. Call their 24-hour hotline (tel. 714/650–5783) for diving conditions. But the best dive spots along this stretch of coastline are not in Newport; they're farther south in Corona del Mar and Laguna Beach.

WHALE-WATCHING • If you're in the area between December and March, check out the gray-whale migration, during which herds of grays head from Alaska to Mexico and back along the California coast. Whale-watching boats ($14 per person) are run by Davey's Locker (*see above*) at the Balboa Pavilion.

NEAR NEWPORT BEACH

CORONA DEL MAR • Only 3 mi south of Newport, this small coastal community has an exceptional beach and some of the county's toniest stores and ritziest restaurants. You can search for starfish and anemones in the tide pools around the breakwater, or walk clear out into the bay on a rough-and-tumble rock jetty and watch local anglers reel in barracuda and perch. Corona del Mar is off-limits to boats *and* it has two colorful reefs, making it an ideal place for snorkeling and diving. Unfortunately, no one rents gear, so bring your own or stop first in Newport Beach's Aquatic Center (*see* Outdoor Activities, *above*). The **Sherman Library and Gardens** (2647 E. Coast Hwy., at MacArthur Blvd., tel. 714/673–1880 or 714/673–2261), a botanical garden and library specializing in Southwestern flora, offers a fun diversion from sun and sand. Colorful seasonal flowers adorn the grounds, and you can have pastries and coffee in the tea garden. Corona del Mar's golden beaches are ideal for a late-afternoon walk, but past sunset there isn't much to do. Unless you're prepared to pay $50 for a suit-and-tie meal in one of the town's swank restaurants, you're better off stopping here for an hour or two on your way somewhere else.

LAGUNA BEACH

Laguna Beach, 17 mi south of Corona del Mar, is home to one of Southern California's largest gay communities and is one of the state's largest artist colonies. This is an "alternative" city tailor-made for artists, hippies, and counterculture dropouts, a place where even Jaguar drivers are likely to have a SAVE THE HARBOR SEALS bumper sticker. Laguna has somehow managed to maintain a balance between luxury tourism and communal values. The county's largest housing project for AIDS patients, for example, is only blocks from the town's $200-a-night hotels.

In Laguna's 100 art galleries, you'll find everything from traditional seascapes to 6-ft Day-Glo marlin sculptures made by Todd the Fish Man. The **Laguna Beach Museum of Art** (307 Cliff Dr., at Pacific Coast Hwy., tel. 714/494–6531), one block north of Main Beach, has some spectacular temporary exhibits of offbeat and ultramodern local artists. Admission is $5. Laguna has plenty of outdoor diversions, too: At **Main Beach,** you can join a game of pickup basketball or volleyball, or watch the ubiquitous guitar-strumming beachniks. Some of the best scuba diving in the county is here; join an organized expedition originating in Newport (*see* Outdoor Activities *in* Newport Beach, *above*), or rent equipment at one of the many local dive shops, including **Laguna Sea Sports** (925 N. Coast Hwy., at Wave St., tel. 714/494–6965). A complete rental will cost you $36–$45 a day. In particular, **Moss Point** (off Pacific Coast Hwy. at Moss St., south of Main Beach) is an excellent and rarely crowded dive spot. Only a few short miles north of Laguna Beach, **Crystal Cove State Park** (8471 N. Pacific Coast Hwy., tel. 714/494–3539) has a 1,000-acre **underwater park** for scuba divers and snorkelers. The inland portion of the park, almost destroyed in an October 1993 fire, has become popular again with hikers and mountain bikers. Rangers offer free guided tours most weekends.

To find out where Laguna Beach's true action is, check out the posted flyers at the de facto counterculture headquarters that is **Underdog Records** (812 S. Coast Hwy., at St. Ann's Dr., tel. 714/494–9490). The infamous **Boom Boom Room** (1401 S. Coast Hwy., tel. 714/494–7588), located within the Coast Inn, is a hot spot for gay and lesbian travelers. This nightclub/bar has a laid-back, welcoming atmosphere—you can step right off the beach and onto the dance floor.

VISITOR INFORMATION

Laguna Beach Visitor Information Center. Call for recorded information on lodging, restaurants, and activities, or stop by for maps and brochures. *252 Broadway, tel. 800/877–1115. Open weekdays 9–6.*

WHERE TO SLEEP

Laguna is the most popular stopover south of Newport, but it's priced way out of the budget traveler's reach. The **Crescent Bay Inn** (1435 N. Coast Hwy., at Crescent Bay Dr., tel. 714/494–2508) isn't the classiest place in town, but the rooms ($45–$60 weekdays, $55–$90 weekends) are clean and comfortable, and some even have kitchens and partial views of the ocean. On the other side of town, the **Trade Winds Motor Lodge** (2020 S. Coast Hwy., at Diamond St., tel. 714/494–5450) charges $40–$110, depending on the season and the night. A large sundeck and proximity to a beautiful pocket-size beach compensate for the annoying roar of cars on PCH, audible from every room.

FOOD

Laguna's hotels and galleries may be prohibitively expensive, but finding a cheap, well-prepared meal is easy. In the center of town are more than 30 restaurants, ranging from greasy spoon to china-and-crystal. **Royal Thai Cuisine** (1750 S. Coast Hwy., tel. 714/494–8424) has delicious, authentic dishes for less than $10, and the inexpensive **Wahoo's Fish Tacos** (1133 S. Coast Hwy., tel. 714/497–0033), a popular local hangout, serves the best—repeat, the *best*—fish tacos on the coast. Another local favorite is stylish **Café Zinc** (350 Ocean Ave., tel. 714/494–6302), which does brisk business at lunch (pizzettas, $6) and brunch (huevos rancheros, $6.25). The outdoor tables are wonderful for lingering. For a Thai chicken pizza ($9.25) or a hand-crafted ale, come to the **Laguna Beach Brewing Company** (422 S. Coast Hwy., tel. 714/494–2739).

FESTIVALS

Laguna's many festivals give it a worldwide reputation in the arts community. The **Pageant of the Masters** (tel. 714/494–1145; for tickets call 800/487–3378), held in July and August, is by far the town's most impressive event. Each evening at a park on Laguna Canyon Road actors re-create some of the world's most famous paintings in stunning detail. Participants must hold a perfectly still pose while on stage; though you may not realize it at first, every figure in these life-size paintings is alive—from the man in the bathtub in Jacques-Louis David's *Death of Marat* to the picnickers in Georges Seurat's *Sunday on La Grande Jatte.* Tickets for the pageant start at $15. The **Sawdust Festival** (tel. 714/494–3030), also held in July/August on Laguna Canyon Road, is a raucous "Auld Tyme Faire" featuring handmade arts and crafts, strolling minstrels, mimes, and hearty tankards of ye olde ale and wine. Tickets are $5. Parking for both events is limited, and it's recommended that you park in one of the marked lots along Laguna Canyon Road. A $1 shuttle runs between the lots and the festival grounds. Advance ticket purchases are advised for both events. Call the visitor center (*see* Visitor Information, *above*) for exact locations.

SAN JUAN CAPISTRANO

Just 6 mi south of Laguna, San Juan Capistrano is a serene inland town—a welcome respite from the frenzied commercialism so common in other coastal towns. Aside from visiting surfers who sometimes meet on the shores of **Capistrano Beach** at dawn, most people see San Juan only from the freeway. Don't make that mistake: The town's clean beaches and historic **Mission District** deserve a day's visit. The **Mission San Juan Capistrano** (Camino Capistrano and Ortega Hwy., tel. 714/248–2049; admission $5), founded in 1776 by Father Junípero Serra, was once the major Roman Catholic outpost between Los Angeles and San Diego. Although an 1812 earthquake left the great stone church in ruins, many of the mission's adobe outbuildings have been restored. One of them, the **Serra Chapel,** is believed to be the oldest building in California in continuous use. In the week surrounding St. Joseph's Day (Mar. 19), the mission hosts the ***Fiesta de las Golindrinas*** (Festival of the Swallows), celebrating the springtime return of the swallows from Argentina. The tradition dates to the days of the mission padres, and includes a parade, a rodeo, traditional music, and the strangely out-of-place "hairiest beard" contest. One block north of the mission is the striking **San Juan Capistrano Library** (31495 El Camino Real, tel. 714/493–1752), built in 1983 by postmodern architect Michael Graves. It has a peaceful and shady courtyard with private spots for reading. The library is open to the public Monday–Wednesday 10–9, Thursday 10–6, and Saturday 10–5.

WHERE TO SLEEP

Mission Inn. It's close enough to the mission (architecturally and geographically) to be mistaken for part of it, and it's only two blocks from the train station. Rooms are clean, the service is friendly, and guests have use of a pool, Jacuzzi, and a VCR (videos are $2). You're encouraged to pick fruit from the orange trees on the premises. Double rooms start at $50 during the week, $59 on weekends. *26891 Ortega Hwy., tel. 714/493–1151, fax 714/496–5102. 31 rooms, all with bath.*

CAMPING • Doheny State Beach. Overlooking the ocean, the campground sits on Dana Point, nestled among sand dunes and trees. Facilities include fishing areas, swimming, a general store, and food service. An inland site fetches $17–$18, a beachfront site $22–$23. This campground is popular with backpackers and families, so reserve through Destinet (tel. 800/444–7225). *25300 Harbor Dr., Dana Point, tel. 714/496–6172. Near intersection of I-5 and Pacific Coast Hwy. at entrance to Dana Point Harbor. 122 sites (82 RV or tent spaces, 33 beachfront sites, 5 hike/bike sites). Firewood ($5). Drinking water, fire grates, flush toilets, picnic area, showers.*

Ronald W. Caspers Wilderness Park. Other than not allowing people under 18 to hike, except in ranger-led groups, because of the presence of mountain lions (really, the likelihood of seeing a mountain lion is no greater than at other parks), this is a great place for car campers and RVs. Tents are allowed, but the ground is uneven and strewn with rocks. Hordes of retired folks flock here, so excessive noise isn't tolerated. All campers must obtain a free wilderness-use permit, available on the premises. Camping costs around $12 per night per site. Numerous hiking trails and scenic walks surround the campground, but the beach is a disappointing 10 mi away. *33401 Ortega Hwy., tel. 714/728–0235 or 714/728–3420. Off Hwy. 74 (Ortega Hwy.) 7½ mi east of I-5. 88 developed sites.*

FOOD

Those who are camping or pinching pennies should head to the **Marbella Plaza Farmers Market** (31109 Rancho Viejo Rd., north of Ortega Hwy., tel. 714/248–0838), which has the usual staples, plus artfully arranged produce, a full deli and bakery (sandwiches $5), and several indoor tables. Near the mission lies a string of unremarkable taco shops, but the delicious Mexican entrées at sprawling **El Adobe** (31891 Camino Capistrano, south of Ortega Hwy., tel. 714/493–1163) are worth the extra $5–$10; portions of the romantic, dark, honeycombed interior were once the town's *juzgados* (jails). The crowd at **Sarducci's Café and Grill** (31751 Camino Capistrano, across from Amtrak station, tel. 714/493–9593) may look like tourists in their aloha shirts and Bermuda shorts, but they're natives. This place has outdoor seating and serves light, original pasta dishes like the Thai chicken in peanut sauce. Pasta dishes and sandwiches ($6–$8) are reasonable, but the jalapeño lobster and other entrées will cost you $13–$17.

SAN CLEMENTE

San Clemente, the southernmost city in Orange County, is only 15 mi south of Laguna Beach on I-5, but in lifestyle and spirit it's a world apart. San Clemente looks like the California that Hollywood portrays: Blondes in bikinis, surf dudes streaking nude across the pier, and surfboards resting against the lifeguard stand as the sun sets. Well . . . except for the reactors of the San Onofre Nuclear Power Plant looming in the distance. The town is probably best remembered as the site of **Casa Pacifica,** Nixon's "Western White House." The massive 25-acre estate is visible from San Clemente State Beach; just look up to the cliffs for a large Spanish-style mansion (one of several) perennially surrounded by flowers. Because of its proximity to **Camp Pendleton,** one of the largest military bases in the state, San Clemente is a popular weekend beach retreat for military personnel. The town's main street is **Avenida del Mar,** which winds through picturesque hills of stucco-and-tile houses, eventually reaching the **Municipal Pier. South El Camino Real** is main street for the motel business, so if Motel San Clemente is booked, don't despair.

WHERE TO SLEEP

Motel San Clemente. This spotless and incredibly comfy motel lies inland from the coast, but many rooms still have ocean views. Rooms cost $40 during the week, $45 on weekends. There's a $5 charge per extra person. *1819 S. El Camino Real, near exit off I-5, tel. 714/492–1960.*

HOSTEL • San Clemente Beach AYH-Hostel. You're likely to be greeted by a make-shift barbecue and gregarious international hostelers at this imminently friendly, laid-back young spot. The hostel provides affordable, spotless, and safe lodging only 2½ blocks from a tranquil beach. There's even an Amtrak stop on the beach nearby, the San Clemente Auxiliary (*see* Coming and Going *in* Orange County Coast, *above*), where you can catch a bus to Disneyland or Laguna Beach. Members pay $10 a night, nonmembers $14. *233 Av. Granada, tel. 714/492–2848. From Amtrak stop, walk 3 blocks uphill on Av. Granada; it's on right-hand side. 40 beds. Curfew 11 PM, lockout 11 AM–4:30 PM. Reception open 9–11 AM and 4:30–11 PM, checkout 11 AM. Kitchen, laundry. Closed Nov.–Apr.*

CAMPING • San Clemente State Beach. Developed sites at this campground, atop bluffs overlooking the beach, are open to both tent and RV campers, and additional undeveloped sites are available. During peak season (Mar.–Nov.) fees are $17, $23 with hookups; on the weekends you'll pay an extra buck. Facilities include picnic areas, hiking trails, and fishing. Bring your own food, since there are no stores (although the county beach immediately to the north has a snack shack). Reservations (tel. 800/444–7275) are recommended during summer. *3030 Av. del Presidente, tel. 714/492–3156. From I–5 south, Av. Calafia exit and follow signs. 157 developed sites, 72 with hookups. Barbecues, drinking water, fire grates, picnic area, showers.*

FOOD

Come to **Fisherman's Restaurant** (San Clemente Pier, tel. 714/498–6390) for the stunning view but not the pricey mediocre food (dinners run around $15). Across the street, the **Tropicana Grill** (610 Av. Victoria, tel. 714/498–8767) has standard restaurant fare (burgers, Caesar salads, pasta) for less than $10; you'll also hear live jazz and local rock bands most weekend evenings. Also in the vicinity is **Cassano's Pizza** (626 Av. Victoria, tel. 714/361–0522), where a tempting slice of pepperoni is only $1.50. Vegetarian dishes—including the delectable tofu burger with avocado ($4) and delicious fruit-and-yogurt drinks ($2.75)—can be found at the inviting counter of **Captain Culver's Counter Culture** (149 Av. del Mar, at Ola Vista, tel. 714/498–8098).

II SAN DIEGO

UPDATED BY CYNTHIA QUEEN

Cool ocean breezes and more than 300 days of sunshine a year give San Diego—the genesis of Southern California's stereotype of sun, surf, and sand—a sublime Mediterranean climate. Laid-back San Diegans spend a great deal of their time outside; even at night, you'll find a lot of people kicking back on the beach rather than in nightclubs.

Regarded as California's birthplace, the San Diego area has been controlled by Native Americans, Spaniards, and Mexicans, the last surrendering California to the United States in 1848 after a brief war. During the negotiations, it was a toss-up on which side of the border San Diego would fall, and the influence of different cultures is still very visible in the architecture, the cuisine, the sizable Latino population—and street names. Untold numbers of Mexicans and Central Americans still cross the border at Tijuana—legally or illegally—every day in search of higher wages (*see* Border Trouble *box, below*), contributing in part to a population explosion that makes San Diego one of the fastest-growing cities in the country.

Long a sleepy Navy town, with an economy based on the military and defense industries, San Diego has grown into a biotechnology hub and science center. Its Mexican-influenced architecture and the hilly terrain conspire to give the sprawling city an enduring charm. To the north is the wealthy enclave of La Jolla, home of U.C. San Diego; at the other end you have downtown and Balboa Park with its museums and world-famous zoo; in between are miles of sand and neighborhoods like Ocean Beach and Hillcrest. With a rejuvenating economy and abundant aesthetic appeal, this city of 1.2 million has also lured Hollywood, its picturesque skyline now featured in several TV series (including *Renegade* and *Silk Stalkings*) and TV movies. Spend a day here and you'll feel the allure, but you'll need more time—San Diego proper is just the nucleus of gigantic San Diego County (pop. 2.7 million), which includes 17 other incorporated cities, stretching from Orange County to the Mexican border.The surrounding hills and mountains afford plentiful opportunities for camping, hiking, and apple-pie eating.

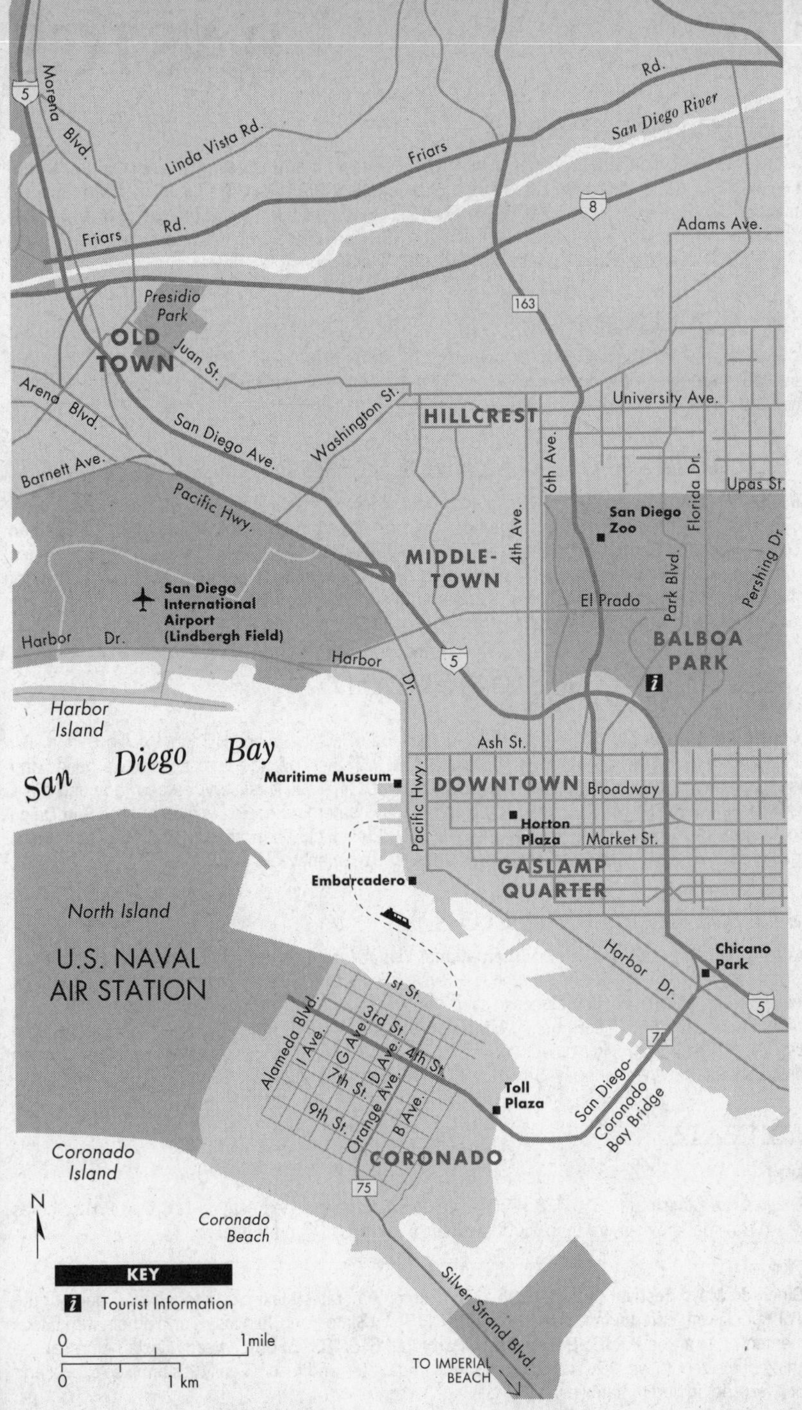

Morena Blvd.
Linda Vista Rd.
Friars Rd.
Friars
Rd.
San Diego River
Adams Ave.
Presidio Park
OLD TOWN
Juan St.
Arena Blvd.
San Diego Ave.
Washington St.
HILLCREST
University Ave.
Barnett Ave.
Pacific Hwy.
6th Ave.
4th Ave.
Florida Dr.
Upas St.
San Diego Zoo
MIDDLE-TOWN
Park Blvd.
Pershing Dr.
El Prado
San Diego International Airport (Lindbergh Field)
Harbor Dr.
Harbor Dr.
BALBOA PARK
Harbor Island
Ash St.
San Diego Bay
Maritime Museum
Pacific Hwy.
DOWNTOWN
Broadway
Horton Plaza
Market St.
GASLAMP QUARTER
Embarcadero
North Island
U.S. NAVAL AIR STATION
Harbor Dr.
Chicano Park
1st St.
Alameda Blvd.
I Ave.
G Ave.
3rd St.
4th St.
7th St.
D Ave.
Orange Ave.
9th St.
B Ave.
Toll Plaza
San Diego-Coronado Bay Bridge
CORONADO
Coronado Island
Coronado Beach
N
KEY
Tourist Information
0
1 mile
0
1 km
Silver Strand Blvd.
TO IMPERIAL BEACH

BASICS

AMERICAN EXPRESS

AmEx has three offices in San Diego, all of which accept client mail and cash personal checks: **Downtown** (258 E. Broadway, at 3rd Ave., San Diego, 92101, tel. 619/234–4455); **La Jolla** (1020 Prospect St., at Girard Ave., La Jolla, 92037, tel. 619/459–4161); and just north of downtown in **Mission Valley** (7610 Hazard Center Dr. near intersection of Hwy. 163 and Friar's Rd., Mission Valley, 92108, tel. 619/297–8101), the only one open Saturday (10–3). All are open at least weekdays 9:30–5.

PUBLICATIONS

For a window onto San Diegan life, pick up a copy of the fat, free weekly ***Reader***, issued on Thursday and available throughout the city (look for it in 7-Eleven stores). It has extensive restaurant and entertainment listings and well-written articles on local issues.

RESOURCES FOR GAYS AND LESBIANS

Though San Diego is undeniably a conservative town, the gay and lesbian community has a visible presence, especially in the Hillcrest neighborhood. For information on gay resources, contact the **Lesbian and Gay Community Center** (3916 Normal St., at University Ave., tel. 619/692–4297), which is open weekdays 9 AM–10 PM, Saturday 9–4. Look for free weeklies ***Update***, a community bulletin board for social events, and ***Gay & Lesbian Times***, Southern California's most widely distributed lesbian and gay publication, in cafés and bookstores downtown and in Hillcrest.

RESOURCES FOR WOMEN AND PEOPLE OF COLOR

The **Center for Community Solutions** (4508 Mission Bay Dr., at Bunker Hill St., Pacific Beach, tel. 619/272–5777) operates a 24-hour live hotline (tel. 619/272–1767) to address women's needs and provide referrals; the center itself, open weekdays 8–4:30, provides legal services and rape and crisis counseling. San Diego doesn't have a specific community center for people of color, but the **San Diego Urban League** (4261 Market St., near I–805, tel. 619/263–3115) can answer questions or provide referrals to help for legal, medical, social, or violence issues; open weekdays 8–5.

VISITOR INFORMATION

The multilingual staff at the downtown **International Visitor Information Center** (11 Horton Plaza, First Ave. and F St., tel. 619/236–1212), on the first level of Horton Plaza, offers free maps and information on local activities, attractions, and places to stay. The office is open year-round Monday–Saturday 8:30–5, as well as Sunday 11–5 in summer. The **Mission Bay Visitor Information Center** (2688 East Mission Bay Dr., tel. 619/276–8200) is a clearinghouse for informational pamphlets about Mission Bay and San Diego as a whole. It's open Monday–Saturday 9–5, Sunday 9:30–4:30.

FESTIVALS

APRIL

San Diego Crew Classic (tel. 619/488–0700) is a collegiate rowing competition at Crown Point Shores in Mission Bay that draws more than 2,000 athletes from the U.S. and Canada.

MAY

The **Cinco de Mayo Festival** (tel. 619/296–3161) commemorates Mexico's victory over France at the battle of Puebla with entertainment and booths in Old Town State Park. Join locals and others with tatoos and pierced parts at the **Pacific Beach Block Party** (tel. 619/483–6666), a yearly fiesta held near the beginning of the month with live music, prizes, arts and crafts, and food. (Really, it's a mixed crowd and fun for everyone, including families.)

JUNE–SEPTEMBER

San Diego county's **Del Mar Fair** (tel. 619/755–1161 or 619/793–5555 for a 24-hr events hotline), held just north of San Diego at the Del Mar Fairgrounds, is a popular June pastime featuring the usual midway, carnival, livestock shows, and nightly entertainment. Even better at the fairgrounds racetrack are the **Del Mar Races,** featuring champion Thoroughbreds and people-watching entertainment, daily except Tuesday in the late summer. The **Old Globe Festival** (tel. 619/239–2255) features contemporary plays, Shakespearean works, and other classics at the Simon Edison Centre for Performing Arts in Balboa Park throughout the summer. Tickets cost $22–$39. At the can't-miss **Ocean Beach Street Fair and Chili Cook-Off** (tel. 619/224–4906), usually held the weekend before the 4th of July, there's lots of fun stuff to buy, from hemp clothing to jewelry from Central America. Arrive early Saturday to procure your tickets for chili samples!

JULY

The **Over-the-Line Tournament** (tel. 619/688–0817) on Fiesta Island in Mission Bay is basically an excuse for thousands of people to get drunk and sunburned, while competing in a sport that's a cross between softball and stickball. Essential elements of OTL include particularly creative team names and the politically incorrect Miss Emersom contest.

AUGUST

Hillcrest's Cityfest Street Faire (tel. 619/299–3330) happens on a couple of barricaded blocks of 5th Avenue near University Avenue. The Navy's Blue Angels flying team headlines the **Miramar Air Show** (tel. 619/537–6289), five hours of stunts and flying formations straight out of *Top Gun.* Admission and parking are free. At **Sand Castle Days** (tel. 619/424–6663), America's largest sand castle–building event, you can enter your own replica of the Sphinx or the USS *Enterprise.*

DECEMBER

The first Friday and Saturday of the month, **Christmas on El Prado** (tel. 619/239–0512) features a candlelight procession, carolers, and free admission to all museums.

COMING AND GOING

BY BUS

The **Greyhound** station is not a place you'd want to linger, but it's in the heart of the downtown lodging area, just five blocks east of the train station. A small number of lockers are available for rent for about $6 per day; otherwise, passengers can check baggage at the parcel desk for $8 daily. The station is open 24 hours. More than 15 buses leave for L.A. daily (2½ hrs, $12 one-way). *120 W. Broadway, at 1st Ave., tel. 619/239–3266 or 800/231–2222 for reservations.*

BY CAR

I–5 passes through the heart of Downtown and has its southern terminus in San Ysidro at the U.S.–Mexico border. Farther inland, **I–15** acts as the unofficial eastern border of the city and heads northeast through San Bernardino to Las Vegas. **I–8,** the main east–west freeway, starts at Ocean Beach and travels past Old Town State Historic Park and through Mission Valley toward the desert.

BY PLANE

One of the very few truly downtown airports in the United States, **San Diego International Airport** (tel. 619/231–2100), commonly called Lindbergh Field, lies about 2 mi northwest of downtown on Harbor Drive. Be sure to enjoy the view—cars parked on top of Laurel Travel Building, fancy downtown restaurant Mr. A's, the Coronado Bridge—during the landing. The airport is served by all major airlines. Although the airport does not have lockers, it's open 24 hours and has restaurants, snack bars, and ATMs, as well as three **Traveler's Aid** information desks (one in East Terminal, two in West Terminal, tel. 619/231–7361) that stay open until 11 PM. Traffic jams, flight delays, and detours should be subsiding with completion of the airport's West Terminal renovations, which is not likely until spring '98 or later.

AIRPORT TRANSIT • San Diego Transit Bus 2 or **2A** (aka the "30th and Adams bus") goes from the airport to downtown in about 10 minutes. The fare is $1.50, and buses leave every 10–30 minutes from 5 AM to 1 AM. The bus drops you off at 3rd Avenue and Broadway downtown, putting you near Horton Plaza, Seaport Village, and the Amtrak and Greyhound terminals. **Public Shuttle** (tel. 619/990–8770) can whisk you downtown from the airport shuttleport in about 15 minutes for $4 per person, 24 hours a day. Taxis to downtown cost about $5, plus tip, via **San Diego Cab** (tel. 619/226–8299 or 800/368–2947).

BY TRAIN

Daily, nine **Amtrak** trains make the three-hour trek between San Diego and Los Angeles ($33 round-trip excursion fare). The historical **Santa Fe Depot,** easily accessible by bus and trolley, is open 5:30 AM–midnight, and luggage storage is available for passengers ($1.50 per bag per day). A tourist booth offers information on transportation and area attractions. *1050 Kettner Blvd., at Broadway, tel. 619/239–9989 or 800/872–7245 for recorded information on reservations and train schedules. Ticket office open daily 5:30 AM–9 PM.*

GETTING AROUND

It may take a few wrong turns before you feel comfortable navigating the sprawl, hills, and valleys of San Diego. As is almost always the case in California, a car is the most convenient way to travel. However, the relative safety of the streets and the widespread availability—if not the efficiency—of public transit makes other options feasible. Two major interstates bisect San Diego and meet near Sea World: **I–8** runs east–west, while **I–5** meanders north–south, running just east of the Gaslamp Quarter and Downtown. Outside the more densely populated areas of the city, you won't be able to find your way around the wide, anonymous boulevards, freeway ramps, and miles of condo developments without a map.

BY BIKE

San Diego is fairly well set up for bicycle travel, and it's especially convenient within San Diego's individual communities or along the stretch of coast from Ocean Beach to Pacific Beach. For a free county bike map that marks bike paths, designated lanes, and shared right-of-ways (but not hill grade or very many street names), call or stop by the **California Department of Transportation Bicycle Information Line** (4040 Taylor St., near Old Town State Historic Park, tel. 619/231–2453) or the downtown **International Visitor Information Center** (*see* Basics, *above*).

Rental shops are concentrated downtown and in Pacific and Mission beaches. For beach cruisers and information on recreational riding, *see* Outdoor Activities, *below.* Most rentals include a helmet, a lock, and a map. Many shops will discount rates for rentals of two or more bikes, and some shops take reservations so they can be sure to provide you with the bike you want. On the beach, **Hamel's** (704 Ventura Pl., the giant castlelike structure on the Mission Beach Boardwalk, tel. 619/488–5050) will set you up with two wheels for $10 daily or $50 weekly. Downtown**, Gaslamp Bike Rentals** (523 Island Ave., between 5th and 6th Aves., tel. 619/595–0211) also rents $10 daily or $50 weekly.

BY BUS

The $5 Day Tripper Transit Pass gives one day's unlimited use of city buses, the San Diego Trolley, and the San Diego–Coronado Ferry. **San Diego Transit** lines extend from the San Ysidro border north past La Jolla into the other towns of San Diego County. You can call the harried folks at the **San Diego Regional Transit Information Line** (tel. 619/233–3004) 5:30 AM–8:30 PM weekdays (until 5 PM weekends) to find out which buses you need to catch, or pick up a bus map at the International Visitor Information Center (*see* Basics, *above*). The regular fare is $1.50, $1.75 for express buses, and $2 for certain longer routes. If you have to switch buses, be sure you get a transfer when you first board. At **The Transit Store** (103 E. Broadway, at 1st Ave., tel. 619/234–1060) you can buy several types of bus passes and pick up free maps and bus schedules; the store is open weekdays 8:30–5:30, weekends noon–4.

The **Handicap Pass** ($12.25 per month) allows passengers with disabilities unlimited rides on trolleys and most buses. Buses with a wheelchair lift serve each route at least hourly. In addition, **MTS Access** (tel. 619/266–9000) provides taxi service throughout San Diego for passengers with disabilities. **LIFT** (tel. 619/726–1111 or 619/436–5632 in Del Mar) provides the same service throughout the North County.

BY CAR

For rentals, it's best to use a local company—they're usually less expensive and more flexible. Rental car insurance can cost up to $15 extra per day, but if you have a major credit card and auto insurance, you're probably already covered. However, if you're planning to venture into Mexico, you should buy one-day (or longer) insurance, widely available near the border. Some rental companies will not allow their cars to be driven into Mexico.

At **Bargain Auto Rental** (3860 Rosecrans St., near I-5, tel. 619/299–0009), you pay $17 a day or $95 a week for budget or compact cars. They'll accept a cash deposit with proof of insurance. Bargain has no pick-up or drop-off service. Also try **Rent a Wreck** (1904 Hotel Circle N in Mission Valley, tel. 619/ 223–3300).

BY TROLLEY

The two lines of the bright red **San Diego Trolley** (tel. 619/233–3004) are generally faster and more comfortable than the bus. The **East Line** begins at the Convention Center in the Gaslamp Quarter, circles counterclockwise through downtown, and extends into the East County to El Cajon. The **North/South Line** leads from Old Town through downtown to the U.S.–Mexico border, where Tijuana is but a hole in the fence away. The finishing touches are being completed on the North/South Line's extension east into Mission Valley and Jack Murphy Stadium—oops, now QUALCOMM Stadium. Trolleys run weekdays every 10–15 minutes from 4:30 AM to 9 PM and every 30 minutes until midnight (after which you should check a schedule). Weekend service is more limited, but the trolley to the border runs all night Saturday. Fares range from $1 to $1.75 each way, depending on the distance traveled. Purchase tickets from the vending machines at each station before boarding. For information about trolley passes for passengers with disabilities, *see* Getting Around by Bus, *above*.

Dial up the new, automated Information Express line (tel. 619/ 685-4900) for schedule and fare information for buses, trolley, and Amtrak's Coaster.

WHERE TO SLEEP

San Diego has plenty of budget hotels, many convenient to public transport. Staying anywhere near the water will cost you more—especially during the peak summer season—unless you stay in a beach hostel. However, if you live to surf or sunbathe, it may be worth it. The cheapest places are generally downtown, but the area can be sketchy after dark; be careful, particularly when traveling alone. Reservations are advised everywhere in the summer months, especially July and August. San Diego has a 10½% tax on hotel rooms, and many hotels require a key deposit when you pay with cash.

There are no public campgrounds that allow tent camping within city limits, but the surrounding towns and parks (*see* Near San Diego, *below*) offer a variety of terrain—including beach, woodlands, and desert—where you can pitch your tent.

DOWNTOWN

Although staying downtown puts you out of immediate reach of the ocean, the area is the city's transportation hub, and you're always within walking distance of a beach-bound bus. Choose downtown for quick access to Gaslamp Quarter nightlife, the world-famous San Diego Zoo in Balboa Park and the neighboring museums, and Hillcrest's shopping and gay and lesbian scene. If you're yearning to experience opulence of the 1890s, stay at one of two historic downtown hotels: the **U.S. Grant** (326 Broadway, between 3rd and 4th Aves., tel. 619/232–3121 or 800/237–5029) or the **Horton Grand** (311 Island Ave. between 2nd and 3rd Aves., tel. 619/544–1886 or 800/542–1886). However, if you're going to spend $90–$150 a night, for better service and opulence to spare, go to the **Westgate,** (1055 2nd Ave. across from Horton Plaza, tel. 619/238–1818, 800/221–3802, or 800/522–1564 in CA). For a map of downtown hotels, *see* Exploring San Diego, *below.*

UNDER $20 • Astor Hotel. The location is ideal—right next to Horton Plaza in the heart of downtown—and the price is unbeatable if you're going to stay awhile (doubles $100 a week; no nightly rates). It's mostly a residential hotel, with refrigerators and TVs in all the rooms. *421 E St., at 4th Ave., tel. 619/232–4642. 29 rooms, all with bath. Deposit ($50), kitchen, laundry, luggage storage. No credit cards.*

UNDER $30 • Golden West Hotel. One of the cheapest downtown flophouses, Golden West is surprisingly clean and well kept. Doubles with private bath (translation: a bathtub in the closet) go for $27

WHERE TO "CAMP" IN SAN DIEGO

Hotel Churchill (827 C St., tel. 619/234–5186) lies about five blocks east of Horton Plaza and looks like it was designed by Walt Disney's less-gifted brother. Admire the medieval castle decor in the lobby before heading to the "Chrome-a-Rama" room, the "Jungle Safari" room, or one of 22 other atrociously over-themed lairs (starting at $42). Run-of-the-mill singles with shared bath start around $27.

a night and $130 weekly. *720 4th Ave., at G St., tel. 619/233–7594. 234 rooms, most with shared bath. Key deposit ($2), laundry, luggage storage. No reservations. No credit cards.*

UNDER $40 • Pickwick Hotel. At first glance, this place looks a bit shabby, but you'll find yourself in a clean room for only $35. Unless you're partial to peeling paint, try to get one of the remodeled rooms on the sixth or seventh floor. *132 W. Broadway, tel. 619/234–9200 or 800/826–0009, fax 619/544–9879. 248 rooms, all with bath. Key deposit ($10), laundry.*

UNDER $50 • La Pensione. This downtown budget hotel has daily (doubles $65), weekly (doubles $275), and monthly rates, and it's pleasant enough that you might imagine an extended stay. Rooms are modern, clean, and well designed, with good working areas and kitchenettes. The hotel is convenient to the restaurants of the city's version of Little Italy, now a hip design district. *1700 India St., at Date St., tel. 619/236–8000 or 800/232–4683. 81 rooms, all with private bath. Laundry.*

MISSION BAY AND THE BEACHES

You'll pay more to be near the water, but that might be why you came to San Diego. Sea World is close by, Mission Bay Park is good for biking, and you're near the nightlife in Pacific and Ocean Beaches, both of which are safe neighborhoods after nightfall. In general, you'll be more likely to find a cheap bed in Mission or Ocean Beach rather than in Pacific Beach.

If you're the plan-ahead type, you and five of your closest pals can rent a house or apartment in Mission Beach for as little as $1,000 a week (less than $200 per person); of course, oceanfront rentals cost more (try $1,800 a week on for size). Inquiries are best made in December and January, and a good place to start is **Cairncraft and Mission Bay Vacations** (2990 Mission Blvd., tel. 619/539–7220 or 800/882–8626). If your personality is more Type B, explore the "courts" (Nantasket Ct., Dover Ct., etc.) that branch off from Mission Boulevard north and south of Belmont Park, particularly on the Bay side, and keep your eyes peeled for FOR RENT signs.

UNDER $40 • Ocean Beach Motel. A lot of surfers make the OB Motel their summer home and for good reason: The beach and municipal pier are right across the street. The good-size rooms are clean and, like the rest of OB, a little behind the times interior-design–wise. The best deals here are the small studios in the back of the secured building that rent for $90-$160 weekly; these go like hotcakes—reserve early. If any are available, the management will rent them for $48 nightly. Otherwise, doubles with balconies—some with ocean view—go for $60. Kitchens are $8 extra, and if you stay five nights the next two are free. Rates drop about $10 in winter. *5080 Newport Ave., at Abbott St., tel. 619/223–7191. From I–8 west, Sunset Cliffs Blvd., right on Newport Ave. to end. Or Bus 35 from downtown to Cable St. and Newport Ave., walk 2 blocks northwest to Abbott St. 60 rooms, all with bath. Laundry, phone deposit ($10), parking, cable TV.*

UNDER $55 • Ocean Villa Motel. A block from Ocean Beach and a short drive from Mission Bay, this place is nothing fancy; but it does offer peace, quiet, and a pool. Doubles start at $48 in summer, and rooms with full kitchen are $53 per night. Winter rates are $10 cheaper. *5142 W. Point Loma Blvd., at Voltaire St., tel. 619/224–3481 or 800/759–0012, fax 619/224–9612. From I–5, Sea World Dr. west to Mission Bay Dr. south, to Sunset Cliffs Blvd., right on W. Point Loma Blvd. Or Bus 35 from downtown to Cable and Voltaire Sts., walk 3 blocks northwest on Voltaire St. 53 rooms, all with bath. Laundry.*

UNDER $65 • Pacific View Motel. About the only thing this place—and its circa 1975 decor—has going for it is that it's the cheapest motel on the water in Pacific Beach. This means $57–$65 nightly ($37–$45 in winter). All rooms have kitchenettes, none has private phone. *610 Emerald St., at the water, tel. 619/483–6117. From I-5, exit Grand/Garnet, west on Garnet Ave., right on Bayard St., left on Emerald St. Or Bus 30 from downtown to Grand Ave. and Mission Blvd., walk 4 blocks north to Emerald St. 26 rooms, all with bath.*

LA JOLLA

Stay in La Jolla if you want easy access to scuba, snorkeling, surfing, boutique shopping, fun places to eat, and beautiful people. Most accommodations near La Jolla Cove are prohibitively expensive for budget travelers, but La Jolla Cove Suites has some affordable rooms and there are a few reasonably priced beach motels along La Jolla Boulevard south of Windansea Beach.

UNDER $65 • Sands of La Jolla. This nondescript roadside motel halfway between Windansea Beach and Tourmaline Surfing Park has some of La Jolla's lowest rates. In winter, a room goes for as low as $40, though regular rates are normally $44–$64. The small but clean rooms have coffeemakers, refrigerators, and complimentary Continental breakfasts; weekly rates, kitchenettes, and ocean views are available. *5417 La Jolla Blvd., near Colima St., tel. 619/459–3336, fax 619/454–0922. From I-5, Grand/Garnet exit, west on Garnet Ave., right on Mission Blvd., left on La Jolla Blvd. Or Bus 34/34A from downtown. 39 rooms, all with bath. Pool.*

HOSTELS

In keeping with San Diego's easygoing attitude, none of the following hostels has a curfew or lockout; all have kitchens and TV rooms.

AYH-Hostel Gaslamp Quarter. Newly relocated from Broadway to the trendy Gaslamp Quarter, this hostel offers beds for $14–$16, bike rentals, trips to Tijuana, movie nights, and more. You'll need a photo I.D. *521 Market St., at 5th St., tel. 619/525–1531, fax 619/338–0129. 98 beds. Reception open late. Kitchen, laundry.*

Grand Pacific Hostel. Depending on the time of year, $12–$16 will get you a bed in a dorm, $35 a private room with microwave and fridge. Housed in a recently renovated Victorian in the Gaslamp Quarter, this spacious hostel welcomes international travelers and accepts Americans with travel documents. They'll pick up two or more people from the airport, train depot, or bus station. Organized fun includes weekly keg parties, trips to Tijuana, free breakfast, and Sunday beach barbecues. Ask the staff about weekly rates in the winter months. *437 J St., at 5th Ave., tel. 619/232–3100 or 800/438–8622. 60 beds. Laundry.*

Ocean Beach International Backpacker Hostel. This is definitely the cheapest and best bet for seaside lodging, as it's only 1½ blocks from the beach. Formerly a historic hotel, Hell's Angels hangout, and rehabilitation center, this friendly hostel has been miraculously cleaned up, with a prime front porch spot on the main drag, Newport Avenue. Every Wednesday a farmer's market transforms the block in front of OBIBH into an afternoon carnival. The management prefers hostelers with proof of international travel. A dorm costs $13, a double room is $15 per person. Perks include free boogieboard and surfboard rental for guests, $10 per day bike rentals, and weekly pasta and barbecue nights. *4961 Newport Ave., between Bacon and Cable Sts., tel. 619/223–7873 or 800/339–7263. From I-5, Sea World Dr. west to Sunset Cliffs Blvd., right on Newport Ave. Or Bus 35 to Newport Ave. 85 beds. Reception open 7 AM–11 PM. Laundry.*

Point Loma–Elliot AYH-Hostel. Spacious, with a large kitchen, common area, and outdoor patio, this hostel offers lots of peace and quiet. It's in the boonies, but it's great if you don't mind walking or biking—a challenging full-day ride leads to Sunset Cliffs and Ocean Beach. Beds are $12 for members, $15 for nonmembers. (Be sure to eat at the Venetian Italian restaurant around the corner, 3663 Voltaire St., 619/223–8197, your first night, as you'll likely love it and want to return.) *3790 Udall St., tel. 619/223–4778. From the end of I-8, Sunset Cliffs Blvd. SW, left on Voltaire St., right on Worden St. Or Bus 35 to Worden St. and Voltaire St. 60 beds. Office open 8 AM–10 PM. Laundry.*

FOOD

San Diego has a wide enough variety of excellent, inventive restaurants to keep anyone's mouth watering. Budget travelers are especially lucky here, since the cheapest and most satisfying places are also some of the best—the city's innumerable, quality taco shops. Some of the better chain taquerías are **Rubio's,** which locals worship for the fish tacos and healthy preparation; **Bahia**; and **Roberto's,** open 24 hours. **Fins** is a new addition and worth a try.

Restaurant coupons for meal deals can be found in the *Reader,* the otherwise useless *Visitor* (check hotel lobbies), and in community newspapers. Only eat in places that receive an A rating from the city's Environmental Health Services; the grade will appear on a small white sign with a large blue letter. For fresh produce and baked goods, head for the daily **Farmers' Bazaar** at the corner of 7th Avenue and K Street downtown.

DOWNTOWN

Downtown's main eating center is the Gaslamp Quarter, especially on 4th and 5th avenues, where you'll find primarily here-today-gone-tomorrow–type places: trendy bistros and tourist-savvy bar-and-grills. Inexpensive restaurants do exist, though—there's no need to do anything rash, like eating at the overpriced Horton Plaza food stalls. A number of cheap Chinese restaurants are clustered on 4th Avenue above Broadway, and all of them can fill your stomach for less than a fiver. **Eastern Chinese Restaurant** (1065 4th Ave., tel. 619/233-6090), open daily, has a $4 all-you-can-eat buffet or $2.75 combo plate special.

For pasta, make a beeline for **Little Italy** (around India and Date streets). Here, you'll dine authentically at **Filippi's Pizza Grotto** (1747 India St., between Date and Elm Sts., tel. 619/232–5095 or 619/232–1346). Pizzas ($8–$11) are big enough for two or three people, and the pasta dishes ($5–$10) and Italian sausage sandwiches ($3.50) get rave reviews from locals who know their Italian.

UNDER $5 • El Indio. Another in San Diego's infinite series of well-under-$5 taquerías, El Indio apparently coined the term "taquito" to refer to flautas (rolled tacos) in 1940 and sells them for 60¢ a pop. Try the fish-taco plate ($3.75)—it comes with beans, rice, and chips. There's also an extensive vegetarian menu. *409 F St., at 4th Ave., tel. 619/239–8151. Other locations: 3695 India St., between Old Town and Hillcrest, tel. 619/299–0333; 4120 Mission Blvd., Pacific Beach, tel. 619/272–8226.*

Lee's Café. Looking for a downtown diner where you don't have to take your life or your pocketbook in your hands just to get a decent meal? Head to Lee's, and sink your teeth into cheap, passable, and filling Chinese or American fare. Two eggs, hashbrowns, toast, and coffee or tea goes for $1.39, as does a short stack of hot cakes. Spaghetti with meatballs, with soup, bread, and coffee or tea is $2.33, and vegetarian chop suey is $2.20. *738 5th Ave., between F and G Sts., tel. 619/239–1621.*

UNDER $15 • Fio's Cucina Italiana. If you're sick of eating fish tacos on the sidewalk, dust off a respectable outfit and hightail it to Fio's. The pizza à la Genovese (spicy shrimp with pesto, mozzarella, and goat cheese; $11) feeds one easily, two with dainty appetites ($3 split charge). Also try the rich, filling *cappellini al basilico con pollo* (pasta with chicken, basil, and sun-dried tomatoes; $11). *801 5th Ave., at F St., tel. 619/234–3467.*

MILLION DOLLAR VIEW AND A BUDGET DINNER • Fish Market. Located on San Diego's beautiful downtown harbor, the dining area faces Coronado Island to the West. Go early for lunch or a sunset dinner and sit on the outside deck, at the bar waiting area, or at the oyster bar instead of in either of the main restaurant areas. Order a pint of microbrew ($3.75), sourdough bread, and clam chowder ($3.35), or pasta rustica ($4.50) and smoked fish; enjoy the scene; and feel like you're living extravagantly. *750 North Harbor Dr., next to Seaport Village, tel. 619/232-3474.*

HILLCREST

Hillcrest, just northwest of Balboa Park, is a common mealtime destination for suburban kids, gourmet foodies from San Diego's wealthier districts, and AWOL downtown businesspeople desperate for decent and reasonably priced food. The stretch of University Avenue between 4th Avenue and Park Boulevard is lined with a mix of cheap and pricey eateries.

UNDER $5 • For utterly dependable, cheap Mexican food 24 hours a day, locals head to **La Posta #8** (3980 Washington St., at 3rd Ave., tel. 619/295–8982). The tasty, filling bean burrito is just $1.39. For breakfast or lunch, grab a bagel at popular **Big City Bagel** (1010 University Ave., at 10th Ave., tel. 619/574–7878). The sandwich meal deal (any bagel sandwich—including egg salad or chicken salad, a side order, and a soft drink; $4.95) is a favorite.

UNDER $10 • Kung Food. Stop in here for one of the most diverse and unique menus in the city, with tasty, all-vegetarian food. You can't go wrong with the garden burger ($5.50) and a papaya smoothie with protein powder ($3.70). You're welcome to peruse the New Age crystals and scented oils in the adjoining gift shop while you wait for your food. *2949 5th Ave. at Quince St., near main Balboa Park entrance, tel. 619/298–7302.*

Pasta Nostra. The overflowing patio makes the popularity of this place—quality fast food, Italian-style—readily apparent. Fresh, authentic pasta dishes—including eggplant parmigiano, vegetarian lasagna, and cheese ravioli al pesto—come complete with homemade soup or salad for $5. A half bottle of house wine sells for $3.50. *1040 University Ave., at 10th Ave. in the Uptown District Shopping Center, tel. 619/574–2800.*

Taste of Thai. At the local favorite for Thai food, choose the basis of your meal (chicken, roast duck, shrimp, vegetarian, etc.), then choose among 14 ways to have it prepared—including hot basil (green peppers, chili, garlic, onions, and shredded carrots), red curry, and choochi curry (sweet and mild curry, coconut milk, peas, and carrots). Lunch is around $5, dinner $6–$9. The patio on University Avenue is people-watching heaven. *527 University Ave., at 6th Ave., tel. 619/291–7525. No lunch Sun.*

Long a Baja staple, the fish taco has made it to San Diego. It's basically chunks of grilled or fried fish folded with cabbage and salsa into a soft flour tortilla.

OLD TOWN

Restaurant prices are inflated for tourists and the atmosphere is generico México, but Old Town nevertheless offers culinary quality. The Bazaar del Mundo in Old Town State Historic Park has three restaurants with reasonable prices that attract long lines of tired, sunburned folk every weekend: **Rancho El Nopal** (tel. 619/295–0584), which may be the most cost-effective of the three (daily $6 special, and a weekday happy hour when beef and fish tacos and chile relleno are $1.75); **Lino's Italian Restaurant** (tel. 619/299–7124); and **Casa de Pico** (tel. 619/296–3267).

UNDER $5 • Carne Estrada's. There used to be a Taco Bell here, and Carne Estrada's still looks like a fast-food joint, but the taste and quality are a couple cuts above. Owned and operated by the same guys that run the overcrowded **Old Town Mexican Café** (2489 San Diego Ave., two blocks east of Old Town Plaza, tel. 619/297–4330), this place offers excellent food—the carne asada in particular—for less money, in less time. *2502 San Diego Ave., 2 blocks east of Old Town Plaza at Harney St., tel. 619/296–1112. No credit cards.*

UNDER $15 • Casa de Bandini. In a mansion that was once the center of Old Town's social life (rumor has it that the first tango in San Diego was danced here), this restaurant is decorated with colorful murals and tapestried chairs. The fajita dinner plate is $9; cheese enchilada plates go for around $7. There's sometimes a wait, but it's worth it—just enjoy chips and a margarita (the *medium* margarita is the best deal) on the patio. If the waiting list is really, really long or if you're in a big hurry, order from the appetizer menu on the waiting patio. *2754 Calhoun St., tel. 619/297–8211. In Old Town State Historic Park.*

BEACHES

You'll be pleasantly surprised if the word "beach" makes you think of greasy snack-shack fare. Pacific and Ocean beaches, in particular, have several casual restaurants that serve excellent, inexpensive food. Try the areas along Garnet Avenue, Mission Boulevard, and Newport Avenue or Voltaire Street.

UNDER $5 • Glutton's. Right across from the beach just south of the Pier in Ocean Beach is this little deli owned by two local guys. The toasted sandwiches and french fries ($5.25) are outstanding and they have good beer on tap. *5083 Santa Monica Ave., tel. 619/223–4059.*

Ortega's. OB'S best-kept secret, this southern-style Mexican café is operated by the Ortega family, who have been feeding Obecians for more than a decade. Best bets for the AM are the breakfast quesadilla, huevos rancheros, omelettes, chili quiles, and the granola. For later in the day: homemade tamales, chili rellenos with fresh roasted chilis, shrimp taco plate, and the carne asada tacos. It's all good. *4888 Newport Ave. between Cable and Sunset Cliffs, tel. 619/222–4205.*

Ichiban PB. Very popular with beach locals and UCSD students, Ichiban serves complete Japanese meals for unbelievably low prices. Try one of the specials ($4.50) or the Ichiban stamina noodles ($5). Sodas are free ad infinitum with a $4 purchase. Arrive early—the place is often busy, and you'll have to wait 20 minutes or more if you get here after 5:30. It's a longish walk from the water (10–15 minutes), but it's by far the best dinner deal near the beach. *1441 Garnet Ave., Pacific Beach, tel. 619/270–5755. No credit cards. Sundays, dinner only.*

Kono's Café. Step up to the counter and order anything you like without taking more than a $5 bill out of your swimsuit. Kono's serves not-so-standard American beach fare, with a Cal-Mex twist. The Egg Scramble (eggs, optional bacon, onion, green pepper, and cheese, served with English muffin and Kono's potatoes; $3.50) is a breakfast hit. For lunch, try the quesadillas ($1.75) or the $4 chili burger. Ask your friendly counterperson to direct you to the outside patio overlooking the beach. *704 Garnet Ave., directly across from Crystal Pier on the Boardwalk, Pacific Beach, tel. 619/483–1669. Open daily 7–3 (until 4 on weekends).*

UNDER $10 • The Venetian. Since 1965, this Italian restaurant has been a favorite among locals and they, of course, know best. For pizzas (the best in town; about $10), always order a large, though everything on the menu is excellent. Brothers Joey and Frank Giacalone now have a full bar on the enclosed patio. *3663 Voltaire, near the corner of Chatsworth in Point Loma, just east on Voltaire from Ocean Beach (parking lot in back), tel. 619/223–8197.*

UNDER $15 • Yakitori II. This sushi bar, located in a nondescript shopping center right next to the San Diego Sports Arena, is the best in town. The entire restaurant comprises two sushi bars, a bar/lounge, and a Japanese restaurant, also superb. For sides, try the lettuce and ginger salad, and, oddly enough, the onion rings—tempura terrific. Wherever you sit, you can order from other parts of the restaurant. There's often a wait for the sushi bars. *3740 Sports Arena Blvd., tel. 223–2641.*

CORONADO ISLAND

UNDER $5 • Nite & Day Café. As the name suggests, it's a 24-hour greasy spoon—a cheap, friendly place where you can brood unmolested—except perhaps by the sometimes surly waitstaff—over coffee and scrambled eggs at 4 AM while mournful '30s music plays on the jukebox. The Belgian waffle with blueberries ($3) is a good breakfast bet. *847 Orange Ave., at 8th St., tel. 619/435–9776.*

UNDER $10 • Mexican Village. This famous Mexican restaurant has long been a favorite with the military and the old Hollywood crowd—Ronald Reagan, Red Skelton, Vincent Price, and Liberace, among others. The Village admirably maintains its commitment to reasonable prices: Most items are under $10, and a veggie burrito costs $6.25. *120 Orange Ave., tel. 619/435–1822.*

LA JOLLA

The cheapest ocean-view dining in La Jolla is at the **Living Room** (1010 Prospect St., near Herschel Ave., tel. 619/459–1187). A sandwich on fresh-baked bread costs about $5.

UNDER $5 • Bahia Mexican Restaurant 2. (There are three total.) Located in the southern Bird Rock section of La Jolla, this delicious taco shop has an endless menu ranging from 99¢ fish tacos to $6 lobster enchiladas. *5504 La Jolla Blvd., at Midway, tel. 454–8940.*

Come On In. This hip little café-bakery has wonderful chili ($3.75) and chicken salad sandwiches ($4.75). *1030 Torrey Pines Rd., on corner of Herschel, tel. 551–1063. Open daily till 3, closed Monday.*

Don Carlos Taco Shop. First in the area to include black beans on its menu, Don Carlos serves up great vegetarian burritos ($2.50) and other tasty dishes, including the *Don Carlos especial*—five rolled tacos with guacamole, rice, and beans ($3). Don Carlos's specialty is the 69¢ potato taco, which tastes much better than it sounds. *737 Pearl St., near Faye Ave., tel. 619/456–0462.*

UNDER $10 • Ocean Kitchen. The emphasis at this low-key restaurant is on quality Chinese food, not the decor (which combines elements of a diner, a seaside shanty, and China). Ocean Kitchen uses no MSG, brown rice is an option with every dish, and you can dine inside or on the small outdoor patio with a view of La Jolla Boulevard in all its glory. The snow peas and water chestnuts ($7) and the chicken with black bean sauce ($7) both come highly recommended. If you come at lunch ($4–$6) you'll save a couple of bucks. *5525 La Jolla Blvd., tel. 619/459–3993 or 619/459–9909.*

UNDER $15 • George's at the Cove. Many San Diegans might not believe it, but one of the premier restaurants in all of San Diego, George's, can be had without breaking the bank. The trick is to go for lunch or an early dinner and sit on the upstairs balcony, with a view of the coast all the way up to Dana Point. The food is terrific, just like in the fancy dining room—try the rock shrimp pasta ($10.50) or the chicken quesadilla ($9.25). *1250 Prospect St., above La Jolla Cove, tel. 619/454–4244.*

CAFÉS

Within the past few years the number of cafés in San Diego has skyrocketed—though many seem to be just a brief flash in the pan. Besides serving espresso and café cuisine, coffeehouses serve as nightspots—gallery spaces for struggling artists and venues for local bands, poetry readings, and open-mic nights. *The Espresso,* a think tabloid available in most coffeehouses, lists café happenings alongside the usual angst-ridden commentary on the wretched state of the world.

DOWNTOWN

Café Bassam. This café is spacious and elegantly decorated, but you won't be able to see the furnishings if you show up on a weekend after 2 AM, when cosmopolitan clubbers of all ages—anybody not ready to call it a night—pack the place. Bassam usually stays open until 4, and some nights they don't even bother to close. On Monday evening you might be treated to piano music, and on weekends one of the waiters and two other tenors sing Italian opera. *401 Market St., at 4th Ave., tel. 619/557–0173.*

Gas Haus. You'll have to vie with young, pierced, urban guerrilla–type regulars for a shot at the pool tables, but at least you'll wait in comfort—there are enough soft old armchairs to make you think you're in your own living room. Coffee drinks ($1.50–$3) and breakfast cereals ($2.50) are the nourishment of choice. *640 F St., at 7th Ave., tel. 619/232–5866. Open late every evening, closed during the day Sunday.*

HILLCREST

David's Place. Billing itself as "a positive place for positive people and their friends," this spacious café is one-of-a-kind in San Diego: David's donates all its proceeds to local AIDS charities. The crowd is intergenerational and primarily gay and male, although some women and straight folks round out the clientele. An excellent departure point for Hillcrest's social and political gay scenes, David's serves up coffee, desserts, and reasonably priced café fare. *3766 5th Ave., between University and Robinson Aves., tel. 619/294–8908.*

BEACHES

Java Joe's. Though it's hard to imagine sitting inside a café when the waves and sand of Ocean Beach are but a block away, this high-ceilinged, musty café sees a steady stream of daytime beach traffic—teen runaway lookalikes, surfers, and local beach bums all hit Joe's at least daily for a caffeine fix. Wednesday through Sunday, Joe's picks up in the evenings with the help of local bands (usually free, occasional $3–$5 cover Friday and Saturday nights). *4994 Newport Ave., Ocean Beach, tel. 619/523–0356.*

Mission Coffeehouse. The Mission is a large, sunny space with overstuffed furniture and the best espresso drinks on the beach. It's also a popular breakfast and lunch spot with surfers and local business folks—try the blackberry pancakes with real maple syrup ($5) or the veggie burrito grande ($4). Bread and pastries are baked on the premises. *3795 Mission Blvd., at San Jose Pl., Mission Beach, tel. 619/488–9060.*

LA JOLLA

Bernini's. Half country kitchen, half modern art museum, Bernini's serves breakfast, as well as pasta ($5), salads ($5), and sandwiches ($4–$5). Browse through the well-stocked newsstand as you sip your coffee. It's located in downtown La Jolla, and the crowd metamorphosizes as the day progresses—from businesspeople to escapees from the local high school to UCSD students too young or too mellow for the bar scene. *7550 Fay Ave., near Pearl St., tel. 619/454–5013.*

EXPLORING SAN DIEGO

Within each of San Diego's very different neighborhoods, walking is the most sensible way to get around, but you'll probably need to hop on a bus or trolley to get from one community to another. If you only have a couple of days, spend one of them in central San Diego, checking out downtown and Balboa Park and the Zoo, and then eat dinner in Old Town or Hillcrest. The rest of San Diego's attractions are strung out along the coast, and they emphasize fun in the sun. Loll on the beach, but leave time for Mission Bay and picturesque La Jolla a little farther north.

DOWNTOWN

Modern downtown began in 1867 when Alonso Horton visited what is now Old Town, decided San Diego was in the wrong place, and bought up 1,440 acres of land near San Diego Bay for 26¢ an acre to begin building the city as we now know it. Today, despite revitalization efforts, downtown San Diego hardly has the bustling feeling you'd expect from the center of a growing city. The centerpiece of the "redevelopment program"—code words for getting rid of remnants of San Diego's '70s drug culture—is the inescapable, confection-color, 11½-acre **Horton Plaza** (between Broadway and G St. and 1st and 4th Aves., tel. 619/239–8180), a shopping mall masquerading as a tourist attraction. A more recent—and decent—downtown addition is the **Museum of Contemporary Art** (corner Broadway and Kettner Blvd., tel. 619/454–3541), the sister gallery to the one in La Jolla (*see below*). It costs $4 to view the special exhibitions and selections from the permanent collection; admission is free the first Tuesday of the month. The museum is open Tuesday–Saturday 10–5, Sunday noon–5, Friday until 8.

The **Embarcadero** is the parklike section of the waterfront that follows Harbor Drive along the curve of San Diego Bay. The strip's main attractions are its views of the bay and its docked boats, ranging from huge cruise ships to old sailing vessels. The **San Diego Maritime Museum** (1306 N. Harbor Dr., at Ash St., tel. 619/234–9153) displays three restored ships, including the *Berkeley,* an 1898 riverboat that ferried passengers between Oakland and San Francisco after the 1906 earthquake. It's open every day 9–8 (until 9 in summer), and admission is $5.

Seaport Village (849 W. Harbor Dr., at Kettner Blvd., tel. 619/235–4014) is a touristy, open-air shopping mall, where more than 65 specialty shops vie to sell out-of-towners fudge, cookies, nautical kitsch, and expensive souvenirs. Check out the **Boardwalk Flying Horses Carousel** ($1), whose handcrafted horses were brought from Coney Island. Make a trip down here after dark, when the views of downtown and the Coronado Bridge are excellent. Once you're here, also drop by **Upstart Crow** (tel. 619/232–4855), a cozy bookstore/café with fancy coffee drinks. **The Fish Market** (*see above*) is just up the sidewalk.

CHICANO PARK

When the largely Mexican and Mexican-American community of Logan Heights was vivisected by the construction of the Coronado Bridge in 1969, residents organized, chained themselves to bulldozers, and started planting cactus and flowers in the upturned dirt. Already cut in half by the completion of I–5 a few years earlier, the community was in danger of extermination. After serious negotiations, the city acquired the land underneath the bridge and a community park was born. Numerous oversized and inspiring murals form the heart of the park, which is found under the bridge at the corner of Logan Avenue and Crosby Street. Park supporters are concerned that scheduled retrofitting of the bridge and freeway may endanger the murals; already, community activists are rallying in support of the bright, hopeful, angry art. The best day of the year to visit Chicano Park is on its festive yearly anniversary (tel. 619/691–1044), celebrated at the end of April; otherwise, the neighborhood is safest during the day, and solo women may be more comfortable in the park with a friend. Chicano Park can be accessed via the Barrio Logan stop on the North/South Line trolley.

GASLAMP QUARTER

Named for the elegant gas lamps (now electric) that line the streets, the Gaslamp Quarter was a flourishing business center during the 19th century and features some of the city's finest Victorian architecture. When the business center moved west at the turn of the century, the Gaslamp Quarter became the city's seedy underbelly and red-light district for more than 60 years. After concerted

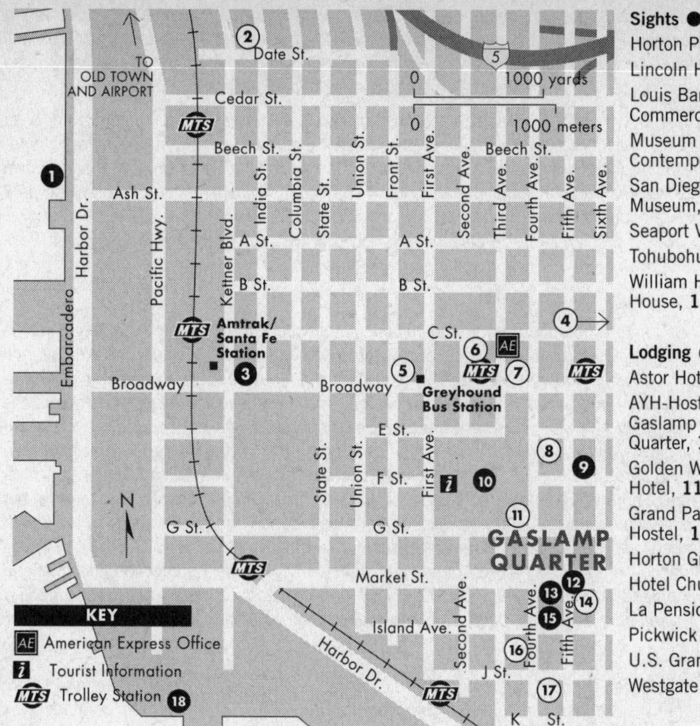

DOWNTOWN SAN DIEGO

clean-up efforts, the whorehouses and gambling parlors have been replaced by trendy restaurants and clubs, art galleries, and boutiques. If you're interested in history, contact the **Gaslamp Quarter Historical Foundation** (tel. 619/233–4692) about its Saturday morning neighborhood tours that leave from the **William Heath Davis House** (410 Island Ave., at 4th Ave.), the oldest building in the quarter. Check out the Mini Photo Museum at **Gaslamp Antiques** (413 Market St. between 4th and 5th Aves., tel. 619/237–1492).

The Gaslamp Quarter can entertain any architecture or history buff with its mix of late 19th century and early 20th century art deco structures. Buildings worth a detour include the baroque revival **Louis Bank of Commerce** (5th Ave., between E and F Sts.), built in 1888; the 1913 **Lincoln Hotel** (5th Ave., between Market and Island Sts.), with its combination of Chinese and art deco elements; and the 1886 **Horton Grand Hotel** (311 Island Ave., between 3rd and 4th Aves.), which is actually two hotels renovated and reopened as one.

Tohubohu (548 5th Ave., tel. 619/338–8153), with its disturbing **Museum of Death** ($4), exhibits body bags, a photo exhibit of infamous and anonymous killings, and various coffins and shrines. The "curator" plans to open a Funny Farm USA, where he will display a two-headed turtle, seven-legged pig, and other live oddities. Admission will be $3, although for now, "the amazing two-headed devil turtle" can be seen for just a buck. The best places to wade into the cultural morass of the Gaslamp, though, are its bars and cafés, especially after dark (*see* After Dark, *below*). Stop in at **Johnny M's** (801 4th Ave., tel. 619/233–1131), which features a beautiful stained-glass dome ceiling and a mahogany bar.

BALBOA PARK

Straddling two mesas that overlook downtown, Balboa Park offers visitors a gorgeous respite from urban San Diego. Its 1,400 acres hold a world-famous zoo and a complex of museums and gardens, including the **Japanese Friendship Garden,** a **Sculpture Garden,** lush **Palm Canyon,** and a **Rose Garden.** Most museums are grouped around **El Prado,** the park's central pedestrian mall, and are housed in big

Spanish–Moorish buildings that were constructed for the Panama-California International Exposition of 1915. The **visitor center** (Plaza de Panama, tel. 619/239–0512) offers general park information as well as the "Passport to Balboa Park," which allows weeklong entry to nine museums for $18. Every Tuesday, select museums will let you in for free; call the visitor center to find out which ones.

Blundering along downtown's thoroughfares, it's almost impossible *not* to slam into Balboa Park or at least a sign pointing the way. From the west side of downtown, take any east–west street to Park Boulevard, and drive north into the park. From Old Town, take I–8 east to Hwy. 163 south into the park. From I–5, take any of the well-marked exit signs. Or take Bus 7/7A from downtown, which traverses the park along Park Boulevard. Inside the park, numerous signs along El Prado point the way to the attractions. The **Balboa Park Tram** runs regularly during the day from the Inspiration Point parking lot off Park Boulevard to all museums.

SAN DIEGO ZOO

World famous for its large and exotic animal and botanical collection, the Zoological Society is at the forefront of endangered species research. You'll also want to see its second campus, the Wild Animal Park (*see* Escondido *in* North County Coast, *below*), so buy the discount double package. Arrive close to opening, get a hot drink and a *churro* (a Mexican pastry), and then head for the exhibits before the crowds; use the map they give you at the entrance to plot a course. Best-kept secrets are the hummingbird aviary (sit quietly and observe), Fern Canyon, and riding the Skyfari at night (great view anytime) during extended summer hours. One of only two zoos in America to exhibit Chinese giant pandas, the zoo has two they're hoping will mate. You'll get your exercise hiking around the 100–acre park, but there are lots of spots to rest and eat, and all proceeds from food stands and gift shops go to the zoo. If you have special needs, a few motorized, four-wheel scooters are available for rent ($25). For $4, you can see most of the zoo from an open-air double-decker bus. On Zoo Founder's Day, the first weekend in October, everyone is admitted free. *Tel. 619/234–3153 for recorded information or 619/231–1515. Admission: $15. Open Labor Day–Apr., daily 9–4; May–Labor Day, daily 9–9.*

MUSEUMS

Centro Cultural de la Raza. This cultural and activism center in a former water cistern is set apart from the more complacent neighboring museums by its colorful murals. The Centro exhibits contemporary Chicano, Mexican, and Native American art, and also hosts performing arts and literary and film events. *2125 Park Blvd., near Pepper Grove, tel. 619/235–6135. Admission free. Open Wed.–Sun. noon–5.*

Museum of Photographic Arts. Excellent rotating exhibits, ranging from artistic to journalistic, greatly augment a small permanent collection. The museum store sells a plethora of photography books. *Casa de Balboa, tel. 619/239–5262. Admission: $3.50. Open daily 10–5.*

Natural History Museum. In the halls of Ocean, Shore, and Desert Ecology, you'll find lots of stuffed animals (the kind that used to be alive, that is); the Hall of Mineralogy has a variety of pretty rocks; and the Insect Zoo has live insects. There are many hands-on and interactive exhibits. *Tel. 619/232–3821. Admission: $6, half-price Thurs. 4:30–6:30 PM. Open daily 9:30–4:30 (Thurs. until 6:30).*

Reuben H. Fleet Space Theater and Science Center. The Omnimax theater here can simulate trips on a wild roller-coaster through the desert, on the space shuttle, along the ocean floor, or inside the human body. The science center, a futuristic playhouse filled with interactive exhibits, is most entertaining for children. *Park Blvd., tel. 619/238–1233. Admission to science center only $2.50; to space theater $6 ($1 more for science center). Open Mon.–Tues. 9:30–9, Wed.–Thurs. 9:30–10, Fri.–Sat. 9:30–11, Sun. 9:30–10; longer summer hrs.*

San Diego Museum of Art. The museum features a notable permanent collection of Spanish baroque and Italian renaissance works, including the only authenticated Giorgione in America, as well as Dutch, American, and Asian art. The temporary exhibits—ranging from big-name modern art to an exhibit of Fabergé eggs—are very popular and cost a few dollars more. Come play with the new IMAGE system, which allows you to research many of the museum's works on computer; for a couple bucks you can print out a color copy of your favorite. *Tel. 619/232–7931. Admission: $7 Tues.–Thurs., $8 Fri.–Sun. Open Tues.–Sun. 10–4:30.*

Timken Museum of Art. This small collection includes some impressive samples of European Old Master paintings, as well as 18th- and 19th-century American paintings. *Tel. 619/239–5548. Admission free. Open Tues.–Sun. 10–4:30.*

HILLCREST

Just northwest of Balboa Park lies Hillcrest, an oasis of cafés, bookstores, record shops, and restaurants—and the most visible center of San Diego's gay and lesbian community. Hillcrest's heart is the area around the intersection of University and 5th avenues, although interesting shops stretch all the way down to Park Boulevard. Stray businesspeople looking for lunch in Hillcrest mix with interns in hospital scrubs from the nearby UCSD Medical Center, and lost-looking sailors pass by fashionable young gays.

Blue Door Bookstore (3823 5th Ave., tel. 619/298–8610) stocks a number of books with a queer emphasis, as well as general-interest titles. Catch a flick at the **Guild Theater** (3827 5th Ave., at University Ave., tel. 295–2000); it shows old and new artsy movies, with a focus on camp. You'll find a number of vintage—don't call them "thrift"—stores along Park Avenue, south of University. Hillcrest merchants sporting TUESDAY NITE OUT signs in their windows offer discounts in the evening from 6 to 8. Hillcrest is best accessed from the Washington Street exit off I–5. Bus 3 from downtown travels north on 5th Avenue and then east on University Avenue.

OLD TOWN

Horton Plaza's architecture combines the open-air, breezy feeling of a Mediterranean plaza with large, primary-color shapes and big objects that don't make any apparent sense.

Old Town, a few miles north of downtown near the I–5/I–8 interchange, is simply a collection of remnants of the original San Diego, the first European settlement in California. The former pueblo is now preserved as a state historic park, containing several original and reconstructed buildings. Old Town is a tourist spot and is predictably ringed with numerous "Apache Trading Post Shoppe"–type stores. Avoid the schlocky **Bazaar del Mundo.** Park rangers lead free, informative tours of Old Town starting at 2 PM daily from the **Robinson-Rose House/ State Park Visitor Center,** on the Wallace Street side of the plaza. An information-packed booklet for a self-guided tour is also sold here for $2, and free maps are available from almost any shop in the park. Buses 4 and 5 and the North line trolley serve Old Town from downtown.

The settlement began as a suburb of California's first mission, **San Diego de Alcalá** (10818 San Diego Mission Rd., tel. 619/281–8449), founded by Padre Junípero Serra in 1769. It's been relocated east of town near the San Diego River. The cool adobe structures are pleasant enough, although the Padre Luis Jayme Museum's exhibits are limited. Masses are held daily, and private weddings book the chapel on Saturdays—during these times no admission is charged; otherwise, it's $2. The mission is open daily 9–5; take Bus 43 from downtown, or take I–8 east, take Mission Gorge Road north, then go left on Twain Avenue for a half mile.

CASA DE ESTUDILLO

Despite the earthquakes that have rattled Southern California, many of Old Town's first adobe buildings, erected in the early and mid-1800s by Spanish military officers from the nearby Presidio, are still standing. The largest remaining adobe is Casa de Estudillo, built in the early 1800s by Captain José M. Estudillo. You can view the mansion's 13 luxurious rooms and then rest in the courtyard with its modest garden and fountain. *Across Mason St. from the plaza, tel. 619/220–5426. Open Apr.–Oct., daily 10–5; Nov.–Mar., daily 10–4.*

PRESIDIO PARK

In 1769 a Spanish presidio (fort) was built next to the original site of Padre Serra's mission, in what is now Presidio Park. The park is a short, vigorous hike (or a brief car ride) up a hill from the core of Old Town. Its 40-odd manicured acres, covered with grass and trees, offer an uninspiring view of Old Town, the freeways, and the golf course below. Constructed in 1929, the **Junípero Serra Museum** is one of San Diego's most well-known landmarks, visible from both I–5 and I–8. Although small, the museum does an excellent job of outlining San Diego's Spanish and Mexican history, with displays of furniture, clothing, tools, and household items (native artifacts, however, are relegated to a small room off the main museum). The excavation of the Presidio is going on right next to the museum. *2727 Presidio Dr., tel. 619/297–3258. Admission: $3. Closed Mon.*

WHALEY HOUSE

The oldest brick structure in Southern California houses a surprisingly interesting collection of early California photographs, period furnishings, and other antique trinkets. Built by Thomas Whaley in 1856, the building is one of the only two houses in California listed by the U.S. Department of Commerce as haunted. Join the crowds to find out why. *2482 San Diego Ave., at Harney St., tel. 619/298–2482. Admission: $4. Open daily 10–5, closes around 4 in the winter.*

MISSION BAY

Locals and visitors looking for aquatic fun head to this 4,600-acre park of islands, coves, inlets, points, and open water in droves. Terrestrial types can jog, play basketball, picnic, or toss a Frisbee along 27 mi of bayfront beach or on one of two main islands, Vacation Isle and Fiesta Island. The winds striking the Tecolote Shores area near East Mission Bay Drive produce especially good kite-flying conditions. Although the staff won't win any congeniality awards, **Mission Bay Park Headquarters** (2581 Quivira Ct., on Hospitality Pt., Mission Bay, tel. 619/221–8899) are the folks to see about water-use permits or other rules and regulations. Mission Bay is pretty much clogged on summer weekends; go early to find parking (or midweek) if possible.

SEA WORLD

Easily the most famous attraction in Mission Bay, Sea World displays fish and captive marine mammals, including sea otters, dolphins, seals, and the trademark killer whales. The newest attraction, Shamu Backstage, gives you an opportunity to get *very* up close and personal with one of the three orcas. If you're not thrilled by contrived shows, check out the park's diverse aquarium displays. The California stereotype comes to life with "Baywatch at Sea World," a water ski and aerial stunts show. For $2, you can be hydraulically shoved 320 ft into the air on Southwest Airlines' **Skytower,** which offers an excellent view of greater San Diego. A tip: The free beer samples at the Anheuser-Busch Hospitality Garden are limited to two, but there are three different shifts of bartenders daily. Look for coupons at visitor centers, hotels, McDonald's, and the like, to save on admission. *Sea World Dr., 1 mi west of I–5, tel. 619/226–3901 for recorded information. Bus 9 from downtown. Admission: $31. Open June–Aug., Mon.–Thurs. 9 AM–10 PM, Fri. and Sat. 9 AM–11 PM; Sept.–May, daily 10 AM–5 PM. Parking ($5).*

BEACHES

The stretch of sand on which you choose to stretch your towel says as much about who you are as your accent or the clothes you wear. San Diego's coast stretches from Pacific Beach, where a "no shirt, no shoes, no problem" attitude prevails, all the way to the tip of Point Loma, where the Naval Reservation and National Cemetery set the tone. The lifeguards everywhere can point you toward designated swimming or surfing areas and explain strategies for escaping potentially deadly rip currents and undertows.

PACIFIC BEACH

Known locally as PB, Pacific Beach is one of San Diego's most popular hangout and pick-up spots. You'll find ample quantities of sunburned flesh and kids on rented body boards and a smattering of longboard surfers. Adolescents whiz along the concrete strip that runs parallel to the beach on bicycles, skateboards, in-line skates, and LSD. Longhaired, bare-chested young men sit on the porches of rented beach bungalows, and hippie girls sell handmade necklaces and offer to wrap your hair in yarn. You can rent all manner of beach-bumming equipment, including in-line skates ($5 an hour, $20 a day) and body boards ($4 an hour, $8 a day), at **PB Sun & Sea** (4539 Ocean Blvd., at Felspar St., tel. 619/483–6613). Bus 34 or Express Bus 30 will get you here from downtown.

The only strip of ocean in San Diego devoted exclusively to surfing, **Tourmaline Surfing Park,** at the north end of PB, teems with boards, although the waves can be scant. Surf veterans sit like tribal elders on the park's benches, bragging about the gigantic waves they rode decades ago. Take Tourmaline Street off Mission Boulevard to reach the beach. The most local of locals regularly mob **Lahaina Beach House** (near Pacific Beach Dr., on Ocean Front Walk, tel. 619/270–3888), a beach social center first, and a burger-and-beer joint second. **Garnet Avenue** (pronounced gar-NET) is the undisputed main drag of PB's business district, with trendy new and used clothing stores, campy novelty shops, and the inevitable surfwear boutiques. PB also has a happening nightlife, from mellow bars to cheesy discos.

MISSION BEACH

Mission Beach is PB with attitude or else Ocean Beach (*see below*) plus tourists. You get teenage skateboard punks in stocking caps in addition to the more common varieties of beachgoer. Bikers, joggers, and sun-bleached teenagers all flow along the concrete strip of **Ocean Front Walk,** running the length of the 3-mi beach all the way to Pacific Beach. **Hamel's** (tel. 619/488–5050), right on the Boardwalk at Ventura Place, can rent you blades or a bike for $5 an hour, a body board for $10 a day, or a surfboard for $10 a day. Bus 35 from downtown goes to Mission Beach.

BELMONT PARK

Near the ocean at the end of West Mission Bay Drive, Belmont Park is family fun by day and here-today-gone-tomorrow bars at night. The park's three main attractions are: The great-view-from-the-top **Giant Dipper** rollercoaster ($2.50), the reconstructed **Liberty Carousel,** and **The Plunge** pool—all relics of a 1925 amusement park. On Family Night (Friday at press time but call to check: tel. 619/491–2988), the roller coaster costs a flat buck and all other rides are only 50¢. The Plunge (tel. 619/488–3110) was once a saltwater showplace that hosted the likes of Esther "Vaseline" Williams and Johnny Weismuller. It's now a public pool, and admission is $2.50.

OCEAN BEACH

Sometimes called OB, this community is among San Diego's liveliest and friendliest. Long-time locals often compare OB to the Venice or Malibu of 20 years ago, and it is true that the '80s and '90s appear to have washed over this relatively isolated and untouristed piece of San Diego without doing much damage. On the smallish, clean beach, local families picnic, adolescent boys with tattoos watch the surf, and illicit "business" transactions seem to occur with regularity near the pier—all under the cover of the dull roar of commercial jets taking off from nearby Lindbergh Field. Unlike Mission and Pacific beaches, OB is not the place for the neophyte surfer. Instead, walk out onto the **Municipal Pier** to watch better-than-average regulars carve up the wave sets. Near the end of the pier, **Ted's Tackle** (tel. 619/226–3474) will rent you a pole and bait for $9/day ($25 deposit), and you can try your luck with local populations of shark and stingray, or—more edible—sea bass and halibut. If you make a good catch, talk to Ted about convincing the cook at the adjacent coffeeshop to cook it up for you.

Don't miss **Newport Avenue,** Ocean Beach's main drag, where you'll find a plethora of bars and restaurants, a few clothing boutiques, and, of course, surf shops. For picnic supplies OB-style, well-stocked **People's Natural Foods Market** (4765 Voltaire St., near Sunset Cliffs Blvd., tel. 619/224–1387) can do you right with fresh organic produce, prepared salads and sandwiches, or all-natural sunscreen. Also, the **Olive Tree Market** (corner Sunset Cliffs Blvd. and Naragansett Ave., tel. 619/223-2230) has a great deli and friendly service. Bus 35 serves Ocean Beach from downtown.

CABRILLO NATIONAL MONUMENT

Perched at the end of the Point Loma peninsula, the 144-acre park's rugged cliffs and shoreline offer truly spectacular views of the harbor and coastline, and the park is a prime viewing spot for the migration of the California gray whale (mid-December to mid-March). The visitor center offers films and lectures about the monument, the sea-level tide pools, and the gray whale migration. The **Old Point Loma Lighthouse** began operating in 1855, the light from its lens visible for 25 mi on a clear day—but ships' navigators were usually unable to see it in the fog. The lighthouse stopped operating in 1891, but visitors can still tour it. *Tel. 619/557–5450. From Old Town Transit Center, Bus 26 into the park. Admission: $4 per vehicle, $2 on foot or bike, free on public transit. Open July 4–Labor Day, daily 9–6:15; Labor Day–July 3, daily 9–5:15.*

CORONADO ISLAND

Across the water from the downtown Embarcadero lies Coronado Island, a combination of wealthy suburb and naval air base. Coronado—actually the tip of the peninsula that creates San Diego Bay—attracts a lot of retirees and stiff military types (the North Island U.S. Naval Air Station takes up the northern tip of the island). The easiest way to reach Coronado is on the **Bay Ferry** (tel. 619/234–4111). The 15-minute ride from the San Diego Excursion Dock of the Broadway Pier (1050 N. Harbor Dr., at the foot of Broadway) to the ferry landing in Coronado costs $2 each way, and an additional 50¢ for bicycles. Ferries leave San Diego every hour 9 AM–9 PM, except on Friday and Saturday, when they run until 10 PM. The ferry docks at the touristy **Ferry Landing Marketplace** (1201 1st St., at B Ave., tel. 619/435–8895); from there a trackless trolley (50¢) runs down Orange Avenue, the island's main strip, to the

Hotel del Coronado (*see below*) and the beaches. If you have a car, you can cross the San Diego–Coronado Bay Bridge, but rush-hour traffic may cause delays. The toll into Coronado is $1, but cars with two or more passengers cross for free—just make sure you're in the carpool lane. The **Coronado Visitor Information Center** (1047 B Ave., at Orange St. in the La Avenida complex, tel. 619/437–8788 or 800/622–8300) offers brochures on shopping, dining, and lodging.

HOTEL DEL CORONADO

Referred to as the "Hotel Del" by locals, this place is the ultimate in Victorian architecture. Its tall circular turrets, hand-carved wooden pillars, and sheer size represent the pinnacle of San Diego affluence and clout. Opened in 1888, the Hotel Del has hosted a veritable *Who's Who* of the world, including the Prince of Wales and several U.S. presidents (including the Clintons); and it was the backdrop for Marilyn Monroe's *Some Like It Hot.* Rumor has it that one of the rooms is haunted: explore at night for maximum effect. If you want to stay here, you're going to have to dig deep: Standard nonview rooms go for $179, and the best room in the house costs $350. *1500 Orange Ave., tel. 619/435–6611. From Coronado Bridge, left on Orange Ave. and drive 6 blocks. Or Bus 901 from downtown. Open to public 5 AM–10 PM.*

SILVER STRAND BEACH

Follow Hwy. 75 east from Coronado (or take Bus 901 from downtown) and you'll hit the slim, 2-mi-long **Silver Strand Beach State Park,** which connects the mainland at Imperial Beach to the south with Coronado. Named for the silver shells found at the water's edge, the beach offers calm bay on one side and pounding surf on the other. The park is open 8 AM–9 PM and charges a $4 parking fee, though parking is available for free outside the park entrance. South of Silver Strand on Hwy. 75, also on Bus 901's route, lies **Imperial Beach,** home to the famous and elaborate sand castles constructed at the annual **Sand Castle Days Festival** (*see* Festivals, *above*). In other parts of the year, the big surf here would probably draw bigger crowds were it not for the fairly regular sewage leaks and drug busts.

LA JOLLA

La Jolla—in Spanish, "the jewel"—lives up to its name in both beauty and expense, with dramatic ocean coves, spectacular views, and ritzy homes. Boutiques and restaurants generally cater to the affluent local gentry, but there are fun bargains to be had—so take a look. The largely unspoiled scenery is still free, and La Jolla is the best place in San Diego to see underwater marine life. In addition, UCSD, the Museum of Contemporary Art, and the world-famous Scripps Institution of Oceanography, with a new aquarium-museum, are all clustered here within a few minutes' driving time of one another. **Prospect Street** and **Girard Avenue** are the two main drags, with plenty of pricey restaurants and boutiques. The short stretch of Pearl Street around Fay Avenue and La Jolla Boulevard as it heads south are La Jolla's only strips—good places to find cheaper eats, gas stations, convenience stores, food, drug stores, and divier bars. To reach them, take Bus 30 or 34 from downtown; exploring hilly La Jolla on foot will give you a serious workout. But within "the village" of La Jolla, walking is easy. If you're driving north on I–5, exit at Ardath Road; from I–5 southbound take the La Jolla Village Drive exit to Torrey Pines Road. You'll go left where the sign says DOWNTOWN LA JOLLA.

U.C. SAN DIEGO

UCSD students are remarkably studious, considering that their classes have to compete with the sun and the sea. The campus is reputed to be drab, but a hike through its eucalyptus groves may surprise you with some unique features. Pick up a map at the information booth in the **Price Center** (tel. 619/534–3362) or at the booths at the north and south entrances. The campus features lots of harsh, parking garage–like structures, but more architecturally interesting is the **Geisel Library** (tel. 619/534–3336), which may remind you of a spaceship—although it was designed to look like a tree. The library is named in honor of Dr. Seuss, who lived in La Jolla for much of his life, and houses the complete collection of his original artwork, as well as fan mail, magazine stories, and cartoons. A small selection is always on display to the left of the main entrance, and any particular piece can be viewed in the Special Collections room, which is open weekdays 9–5 (Wed. until 9) and Saturday 10–1. The library lies diagonally across from the even wackier Structural Systems Laboratory, lit by night with neon that flashes the names of the Seven Sins and the Virtues. The "decoration" is part of the Stuart Collection, an attempt to spice up the campus with public artwork commissioned from well-known contemporary artists like Jenny Holzer and William Wegman. Two more pieces, in the thinning stand of eucalyptus trees nearby, are the **Singing Tree** (singing everything from country and western to opera) and the **Talking Tree** (which chants or whispers poetry).

WINDANSEA BEACH

Considering the beauty of San Diego's beaches, the quality of the local breaks, and the general disdain some surfer's have for novices, it's little wonder that a "locals-only" wave territorialism developed in San Diego. In particular, Windansea Beach gained a reputation in the early 1960s—made famous by Tom Wolfe's story "The Pumphouse Gang"—for harshly punishing violations of the unwritten rules of surfing etiquette. Interloping beginners who made mistakes—dropping in on someone else's wave, or cutting in front of someone more experienced—were summarily dealt with through verbal abuse, an "accidental" flip of the board, or a mysteriously slashed tire in the parking lot. Although threats of litigation have somewhat softened Windansea's traditional hard line, it's still not the best place for a beginner to learn. If you're still interested, take Nautilus Street west from La Jolla Boulevard to Neptune Place to check it out. If you're not brave enough for the waves, this is still a great spot for sunning and beautiful-people watching.

BLACK'S BEACH

If you're feeling constricted by your swim trunks, head to **Black's Beach,** where only about half of the mostly male sunbathers wear clothes. The area in which nudity is "tolerated" by the state parks department is the area south of Mussel Rock and north of Regent Street—you will probably be cited if you take your nudity north of Mussel Rock. The beach is beautiful and popular with surfers but doesn't attract a crowd. To get to Black's Beach by car, take I–5 north to La Jolla Village Drive west, turn left on La Jolla Shores Drive, and right almost immediately on La Jolla Farms Road. Follow the road down the hill; you'll pass one gate on your left; park near the second gate and follow the well-worn trail down the cliff for less than a quarter-mile. Bus 34 will take you as far as the intersection of La Jolla Shores Drive and La Jolla Farms Road, but then you're in for a steep, mile-long walk.

MOUNT SOLEDAD

East of downtown La Jolla, Mount Soledad reigns as the highest point in the area. Though Soledad's peak has long been topped by a cross, in 1991 the more secular of San Diego's populace began an effort to remove it, since it then stood on public land. The city transferred ownership of the few square feet beneath the cross to a nonprofit historical society to get around the problem. Conflict aside, Mount Soledad is still worth its salt as a scenic view: From I–5 north, take Ardath Road exit and make a left at the third light.

SCRIPPS PARK

Strolling along the walkway that borders Coast Boulevard and Scripps Park, you'll understand why people pay so much to live in La Jolla. The park, a sea-cooled patch of manicured grass, makes a great site for a seaside picnic, attracting everyone from wet-suited scuba divers to the tassel-loafered lunch crowd. The ocean is stunningly clear, and La Jolla Cove's largest beach—usually just called **The Cove**—hosts sunbathers, snorkelers, and divers attracted by the good underwater visibility and swirling schools of fish (*see* Outdoor Activities, *below*). Would-be swimmers take note: The wave action here is sometimes strong and often unpredictable, and the rocky reef nearby can make ocean play very hazardous. Keep your eyes peeled for sea lions and harbor seals sunning themselves on the rocks, as you continue south toward the tide pools—with anemones, crabs, sea urchins, and small fish—that dot the coast farther south. A safer place for swimming is the Children's Pool (aka Seal Rock) located just south of the Cove. Here you may also be treated to the company of a group of about 20 seals, who have taken up residence on the Children's Pool's small beach for the last couple of years.

MUSEUM OF CONTEMPORARY ART SAN DIEGO

MCA displays a small permanent collection of modern American works—including Warhol soup cans and Lichtenstein lithographs—dating from the 1950s to the present. The collection is housed in a newly renovated, neoclassical building with exterior neon accents. Through the glass walls of some exhibit rooms, the sparkling ocean serves as a nice backdrop. *700 Prospect St., at Silverado St., tel. 619/454–3541. Admission: $4. Open Tues.–Sat. 10–5 (Wed. until 8), Sun. noon–5.*

STEPHEN BIRCH AQUARIUM-MUSEUM

The aquarium-museum emphasizes the educational, in an attempt to promote Scripps Institution's work and oceanography in general. One of the more popular exhibits in the small museum is the floor-to-ceiling kelp-forest aquarium: The living spectacle of leopard sharks, giant sea bass, and other species cruising serenely around a tangle of swaying kelp is trance-inducing. Skip the "Deep Diver" simulation—it certainly can't compete with Disneyland. For a spectacular view of La Jolla Cove, Scripps Pier, and the Pacific, walk out to the observation deck by the artificial tide pool, itself an excellent example of the teeming life that inhabits these miniature marine ecosystems. Try to arrive after 2 PM, when school groups have dispersed. Bus 34 will drop you at the intersection of La Jolla Village Drive and Torrey Pines Road, but you still have a steep half-mile walk. *Tel. 619/534–3474. From La Jolla Village Dr., take North Torrey Pines Rd. and follow signs. Admission: $6.50; parking $3 (20 minutes free). Open daily 9–5.*

TORREY PINES STATE RESERVE AND BEACH

Home to one of the world's two groves of Torrey pines—hardy, scraggly pines that would probably survive even if they were planted *in* the ocean—the hilly, 2,000-acre reserve lies just north of La Jolla. With only about 8 mi total of trails, the reserve is imminently explorable and worth every minute spent in the cool shadows of its pine groves or along its breathtakingly steep, sandstone cliffs. You can hike and bike (road biking only) in the reserve: To get a decent workout as well as a gander at all that Torrey Pines has to offer, follow the **Razor Point Trail** as it takes you away from the visitor center past a tall red-rock butte and along the edge of a deep canyon. Follow the trail northward to link up with the **Beach Trail,** which will take you out to Flat Rock, with its tidepools and access to Black's Beach (*see above*). To return to the visitor center, follow **North Fork Trail** up a few steep switchbacks past Fern Canyon, then follow the paved road south back to the parking lot. Alternately, from Flat Rock, walk north along the beach to the park entrance. Total trail distance is about 4 mi. *Tel. 619/755–2063. From I-5 north, exit Genessee Ave. west, go right on North Torrey Pines Road about 1 mi. Or North County Transit District Bus 301 from University Towne Centre in La Jolla. Parking: $4; free parking available outside park entrance. Open daily 9 AM–sunset.*

CHEAP THRILLS

Cheap thrills are most abundant near San Diego's beaches; the whole coastal strip is one big people-watching opportunity on most days. In summer months, if you position yourself at the north end of Ocean Beach, anywhere in Mission Bay, or at the south end of Mission Beach, you can catch Sea World's nightly fireworks extravaganza. **Kobey's Swap Meet** (tel. 619/226–0650) is a big flea market in the parking lot of the San Diego Sports Arena that takes place Thursday–Sunday 7–3. Admission is a mere 50¢ Thursday and Friday, $1 on weekends.

In Balboa Park (*see above*), the road that branches off south from El Prado at the parking lot by the Museum of Art leads to the **Spreckels Organ Pavilion** (tel. 619/226–0819). Proclaimed the "world's largest outdoor musical instrument," the 4,445-pipe organ is played for the public free of charge every Sunday afternoon 2–3. Monday-evening concerts are also held during summer. The concerts are a fun way to relax, if you can drown out the sounds of aircraft landing downtown. You can catch more free tunes on summer Sundays at Scripps Park in La Jolla—probably the only time you'll get somethin' for nothin' in this part of town. The 2–4 PM concerts usually feature mellow jazz or big band sounds.

AFTER DARK

San Diego has tried hard in recent years to establish a nightlife fit for a true city and has succeeded here and there. The Gaslamp Quarter jumps on weekends, with DJs and live music on every block, but since the clientele tends to sport tight black dresses and European suits, budget travelers might feel out of place. For a jeans-and-beer crowd, head to Garnet Avenue in Pacific Beach or, for even less pretense, to Newport Avenue in Ocean Beach. Where San Diego comes into its own after dark, though, is at its coffeehouses—many showcase local musicians (*see* Cafés, *above*) and are more popular than bars. For events listings, consult the *Reader* (*see* Basics, *above*). *Revolt in Style,* a small underground publication with local listings, is available at most cafés and some trendy boutiques, as are flyers for roving dance clubs.

BARS

The Alibi. The doorwoman wears a pink polyester pantsuit and reads *Soap Opera Digest,* Patsy Cline's on the jukebox, and a casual combination of young, hip kids and old-time regulars sip 23-ounce Buds ($1.75) side by side. This is the ultimate cheap dive, red lights and all. *1403 University Ave., at Richmond St. in Hillcrest, tel. 619/295–0881.*

José's. In a town where the nightlife scene often resembles a meat market, José's is somewhat of an exception. You can still pick up or be picked up in this casual bar, though you may have a hard time finding a suitable partner in the dim lighting. Free chips and salsa go nicely with the margaritas ($2.75), especially during low-key happy hour (weekdays 3:30–7:30), when they're a buck off. *1037 Prospect St., between Herschel and Girard Aves., tel. 619/454–7655.*

Pacific Shores. This fabulously decorated OB institution is usually filled with locals of several generations enjoying the great drinks at great prices. *4927 Newport Ave., near Cable St. in Ocean Beach, tel. 619/223–7549.*

Society Billiard Café. At this very '80s pool hall, the lighting is indirect, and lots of things are lacquered black. A large selection of beers and a decent menu complement the 15 pool tables, which stay busy all day. An hour of pool costs $3–$5 during the day and up to $10 an hour at night, depending on the day of the week and the number of people shooting stick. *1051 Garnet Ave., Pacific Beach, tel. 619/272–7665.*

Sunshine Company. This large OB bar boasts an outdoor upstairs patio and ample pool tables. *5028 Newport Ave., near the Ocean Beach Pier, tel. 619/222–0722.*

LIVE MUSIC

San Diego has been dubbed "the next Seattle" by several national music publications. Whether this is a blessing or a curse is hard to tell, but now's the chance to check out a large number of excellent local bands—including the B-Side Players and the Greyboy All-Stars just entering the limelight.

CLASSICAL

The closing of the San Diego Symphony in 1996 was a tremendous blow to the city's fine arts program. **La Jolla Chamber Music Society** (tel. 619/459–3724) offers classical music throughout the year. For half-price tickets contact **Art Tix** (*see below*).

JAZZ AND BLUES

While there are few exclusively jazz joints in San Diego, somewhere usually has it going on—check the *Reader.* The local favorite is **Croce's Restaurant and Jazz Bar** (802 5th Ave., tel. 619/233–4355), which has a $5 cover, plus a $5 minimum on drinks or food. Next door, **Croce's Top Hat Bar and Grille** offers nightly R&B.

Blues offerings are similarly limited. In Ocean Beach, **Winston's** (1921 Bacon St., Ocean Beach, tel. 619/222–6822) features live blues for $1 on Sunday, giving over other nights to reggae, Dead covers, and anything else that will promote its nightly drink specials.

Blind Melons. San Diego would be lost in a blues-less world were it not for Blind Melons—the name honors legendary blues singer Blind Melon Chittlin—where you can get live blues, reggae, rock, or zydeco every day (and sometimes twice a day) for a $5–$25 cover. *710 Garnet Ave., between Mission Blvd. and the beach in Pacific Beach, tel. 619/483–7844.*

LATIN

Venues with a Latin theme are a dime a dozen in San Diego. **Café Sevilla** (555 4th Ave., at Market St., tel. 619/233–5979) attracts a fun international crowd for its nightly music, which ranges from samba to flamenco to Spanish rock-and-roll. The music is accompanied by appropriate food and drink (i.e., tapas and margaritas) and dance lessons some evenings (cover $4–$6). For Latin jazz, try **Café Bravo** (4th Ave. and E St., tel. 619/234–8888).

ROCK

The Casbah. A key venue in San Diego's alternative music scene, the Casbah headlines cream-of-the-crop local bands nightly, with smaller nationally acclaimed acts every now and again. A tight-knit group of regulars frequents the small club (which is underneath an apartment complex), but everyone is friendly. *2501 Kettner Blvd., at Laurel St. downtown, tel. 619/232–4355. Cover: up to $10.*

Tiki House. Local bands like to play at Tiki, and the low-key crowd likes to hear them. This narrow, dark bar serves up beer, wine, and live blues and rock Wednesday through Sunday, though it's a nice place for a drink and a game of Foozball or pool any time of day. *1152 Garnet Ave., Pacific Beach, tel. 619/273–9734. Cover: $3–$5 Thurs.–Sun.*

CLUBS

Green Circle Bar. Green Circle's impressive DJ keeps this place hopping all week long with ambient/groove and "trip-hop." In addition to house music, live jazz is featured twice weekly and a dance party goes on every Sunday. The mostly straight crowd here is more casual than other downtown spots—they're also young, fashionable, and sexy. *827 F St., at 9th St. downtown, tel. 619/232–8080. Cover: up to $5. Closed Mon.*

Olé Madrid. A Spanish-inspired tapas bar, this downtown joint attracts mellow, mid-20s downtowners with live and DJ music in the basement. You'll hear everything from '70s disco and deep house to reggae to salsa, depending on the night. *751 5th Ave., between F and G Sts., tel. 619/557–0146. Cover: $7–$10.*

GAY AND LESBIAN NIGHTLIFE

San Diego is no Los Angeles, and it is certainly no San Francisco—but for lesbian and gay clubs and bars, check either *Update* or *Gay & Lesbian Times,* both free and available in shops and cafés in Hillcrest.

Between **Rich's** (1051 University Ave., tel. 619/497–4588) and the **Brass Rail** (3797 5th Ave., at Robinson Ave., tel. 619/298–2233), the dancing week is covered, though only just. Rich's is definitely the more happening spot, especially on Thursday, when Club Hedonism ($4 cover) will rock your world with three DJs, visual effects, and a sea of dancers; Rich's is also open Friday–Sunday, with go-go boys and erotic dancers (cover $3–$5). At the smaller Brass Rail, Thursday's Noche Latina—San Diego's only gay Latino dancing night—packs the place from wall to wall and from ceiling to floor ($3 cover); Monday and Tuesday are drag-show nights ($4 cover), and other nights are given over to go-go dancers and drink specials.

The Flame. This multiroom, multibar, women-only club (except on Tuesday, which is "boys' night") features regular events like trash disco, salsa, Monday-night football, country-western, and soul. *3780 Park Blvd., near Cypress Ave. in Hillcrest, tel. 619/295–4163. Cover: up to $3.*

THEATER

A good way to take advantage of San Diego's great theater offerings without paying an arm and a leg is through **Times Art Tix** (Horton Plaza, 3rd St. and Broadway, tel. 619/497–5000), where you can get half-price tickets (cash only) for same-day shows at all area theaters. The box office is open Tuesday–Saturday 10–7; the best time to go is weekday mornings, since shows during the week don't usually sell out. Tony award-nominated director of *Rent,* Michael Greif, is currently artistic director at the **La Jolla Playhouse** (2910 La Jolla Village Dr., tel. 619/550–1010), which has sent several productions to Broadway. Other theater hotspots include the **San Diego Repertory Theatre** (79 Horton Plaza, tel. 619/235–8025), and the **Old Globe** (Balboa Park, tel. 619/239–2255), famous for its Shakespearean productions and top-flight actors.

OUTDOOR ACTIVITIES

With an ideal climate year-round, San Diego offers lots of ways to get your body out into the sun. Most beaches have at least one shop or waterfront shack that rents in-line skates, bikes, and body boards. Many coastal communities with piers also have bait shops that rent fishing gear. For more information, *see* Beaches *in* Exploring San Diego, *above.*

BIKING

For tips on commuter biking, *see* Getting Around, *above.* Recreational cycling is huge in San Diego. The **California Department of Transportation** (tel. 619/688–6699) puts out a free map of all county bike paths. Probably the most popular route is **Old Hwy. 101,** the 18-mi coastal road that runs from La Jolla north to Oceanside. Although the road is narrow and windy, experienced riders like to follow **Lomas Santa Fe Drive** in Solana Beach (*see* Near San Diego, *below*) east into beautiful Rancho Santa Fe. For more leisurely rides, Imperial Beach, Mission Bay, San Diego Harbor, and the Mission Beach Boardwalk are all flat and scenic. You can rent bikes all over town for $20 a day or less. Try **Hamel's** in Mission Beach (704 Ventura Pl. on the Boardwalk, tel. 619/488–5050), where a beach cruiser will cost only $10 per day.

BOATING

Mission Bay's smooth water and consistent winds provide easy sailing, especially for beginners. However, if you want better views (of downtown and big Navy ships), head to San Diego Bay. **Seaforth Boat Rentals** (1641 Quivira Rd., Mission Bay, tel. 619/223–1681; or 1715 Strand Way, Coronado, tel. 619/437–1514) rents sailboats from $30 an hour, as well as motorboats ($65 an hour) and canoes and kayaks ($10 an hour). **Mission Bay SportCenter** (1010 Santa Clara Pl., Mission Bay, tel. 619/488–1004) has a wide selection of aquatic gear, including sailboats and sailboards from $16 an hour.

SNORKELING AND SCUBA DIVING

The ecological reserve at La Jolla Cove provides some of the best snorkeling in Southern California. Look out for the bright-orange garibaldi, known for its friendliness. Off Torrey Pines State Beach, snorkelers should look for garibaldi, as well as rays, sea bass, and the formerly endangered spiny lobster. **La Jolla Surf Systems** (3132 Avenida de la Playa, tel. 619/456–2777) will rent you a full snorkeling rig (mask, flippers, snorkel) for $4 a half-day, and it's within spitting distance of the beach. If you're certified for scuba diving, **San Diego Diver's Supply** (4004 Sports Arena Blvd., near I–8, tel. 619/224–3439; 5701 La Jolla Blvd., La Jolla, tel. 619/459–2691) can fix you up with all the equipment you need, including fins, snorkel, tank, and mask, for $40 a day. You can scuba off the beach at La Jolla Cove, but you'll need a boat to access the best diving; San Diego Diver's Supply can take you out (locally for $55; to the Coronados for $60), or contact **Seaforth Boat Rentals** (*see* Boating, *below*) about charters.

SPORTFISHING

San Diego is world renowned for high-quality sportfishing. Several fleets and individual boats run fishing operations in both U.S. and Mexican waters. **Seaforth Sportfishing** (1717 Quivira Rd., tel. 619/224–3383) has a good variety of trips: A shark-boat ticket runs $30, a twilight boat goes for $18, and a full day trip to Mexico's Coronado Islands is $45. Rod and reel rental costs an extra $6–$10, and a one-day California fishing license is $6.

SURFING

Contrary to popular mythology, you need a wet suit if you're going to surf in San Diego any time other than the summer months. If you are an experienced surfer, you should head for the pier at Ocean Beach, Tourmaline Surfing Park in Pacific Beach, Windansea or Black's Beach near La Jolla, or Swami's (Sea Cliff Roadside Park) in Encinitas. Boards rent for about $4–$8 an hour or $17–$30 a day, and you need a major credit card to rent one. You can rent foam boards at **Star Surfing Company** (tel. 619/273–7827) in Pacific Beach, real or foam boards at **La Jolla Surf Systems** (*see* Snorkeling and Scuba Diving, *below*) in La Jolla, and real boards at **101 Sports** (tel. 619/942–2088) in Encinitas. Beginners should definitely stick to beach breaks; ask at these surf shops about lessons, which run about $10 an hour in a small group or $20–$40 an hour for private time with one of the big guys.

WHALE-WATCHING

The best terrestrial vantage point for watching California gray whales on their annual southern migration (late Dec.–Mar.) is the Cabrillo National Monument at the tip of Point Loma (*see* Beaches *in* Exploring San Diego, *above*). If you want to get closer, **Helgren's Sportfishing** (315 Harbor Drive S, Oceanside, tel. 619/722–2133) offers narrated tours of the San Diego migratory route mid-December 17–late March for $4 a person. Helgren's also offers a variety of sportfishing tours throughout the year.

BORDER TROUBLE

Nowhere in California are anti-immigrant sentiments more rampant than in San Diego, whose border with Tijuana is the busiest in the United States. Since October 1994, "Operation Gatekeeper" has attempted to curb illegal crossings using agents and surveillance equipment; in the same year, California voters passed Proposition 187, seeking to deny public services to undocumented workers and to require teachers and healthcare workers to report them to the Immigration and Naturalization Service. Although a U.S. District Court judge declared most of the law unconstitutional in 1995, parts of Prop. 187 will probably be argued before the Supreme Court. Within this antagonistic climate, there have been several cases of racially motivated murders of Mexican immigrants in recent years; more than 15 immigrants annually die at or near the border as a direct result of violence. But without the cheap labor they provide, it is difficult to imagine how California's economy would function efficiently.

NEAR SAN DIEGO

TIJUANA

San Diego likes to bill itself as "a two-nation vacation destination," and nearly every visitor heads for what is reputed to be the most heavily crossed border in the world. If you're looking for an authentic Mexican vacation, you'll have to go a lot farther than "TJ," as the city largely attracts those with a single objective: to party. Popular wisdom holds that Tijuana is more a mix of Mexican and gringo cultures than a "real" Mexican city. In certain respects this is accurate, and those shy of crowds of tourists and made-for-export *artesanía* (crafts) may want to avoid the main tourist drag of **Avenida Revolución**; instead, head one block west to **Avenida Constitución,** where microphone-wielding salesmen and strolling families could be part of any Mexican city.

Tijuana is also home to the second-largest bullring in the world, the beachside **Plaza de Toros Monumental.** Fights take place May–September on Sunday at 4 PM; tickets start at $7 for seats in the sun, $11.50 for shade. Buy tickets at the *caseta,* or ticket office (Revolución, between Calles 3 and 4, tel. 66/85–22–10), open weekends 10 AM–7 PM, or at the ring (Hwy. 1D, by the ocean). To reach the Plaza take a Mexi-Coach bus (½ hr, $2) at 3:30 PM from Revolución (between Calle 6 and 7). Get there early to guarantee yourself a ticket.

BASICS

Anyone can visit a Mexican border town for up to 72 hours without a border card: U.S. and Canadian citizens should present a driver's license or birth certificate at the border; citizens of Hong Kong, South Africa, Brazil, and Taiwan need a visa; citizens of other countries need a passport. When making adventure to Tijuana, don't worry about a Spanish phrase book—your English will get you by just fine.

CHANGING MONEY • All prices below are listed in U.S. dollar values due to the instability of the Mexican economy. While dollars are accepted and often encouraged, you'll generally get a better value if you change dollars into pesos: when you get to Tijuana, simply look around for a place with competitive rates. To buy or change traveler's checks, try the **American Express office** (Sánchez Taboada, at Clemente Orozco, tel. 66/34–36–60), open weekdays 9–5 and Saturday 9–1; you do not have to be a cardmember. ATMs accepting Visa and MasterCard can be found at most banks. Try **Bancomer** (on Constitución, at Calle 5a) or **Bital** (on Revolución and Calle 2a.

VISITOR INFORMATION • The most centrally located tourist office is run by **CANACO** (Revolución, at Calle 1a, tel. 66/88–16–85), the Tijuana Chamber of Commerce. It has friendly, English-speaking staff, decent maps, and a public phone and restroom; open daily 9–7.

COMING AND GOING

If your plans only include Tijuana proper, public transportation into and around the city is your best bet. The tourist areas are compact and walkable, and buses are affordable and straightforward. The **San Diego Trolley** (*see* Getting Around *in* San Diego, *above*) runs from downtown San Diego to the border at San Ysidro, and this is definitely the best way to get to the border. Many trolley stations along the line provide free parking, which can save you $6 in parking expenses at San Ysidro. Be sure to park in a guarded and lighted lot. The easiest way to get to downtown from the border is via taxi ($7); the easiest way to get from downtown back to the border is on a **Mexi-Coach** bus ($1), which leaves from Revolución (between Calle 6 and 7) every half hour between 9 AM and 9 PM.

Greyhound/Trailways (tel. 66/21–29–48) travels to Tijuana from San Diego (50 min, $5 one-way), stopping at one of two bus stations: **Central Viejo** (Madero, at Calle 1a 1 block east of Revolución, tel. 66/88–07–52) is more conveniently located than **Central Camionera.**

If you do cross by car, the less central **Otay Mesa** border crossing (10 minutes east of San Diego) has shorter lines but is only open 6 AM–10 PM. On weekends and holidays, the wait to enter the United States by car at the main **San Ysidro–Tijuana** crossing can be two hours. While only required for trips further south, it is recommended that you purchase one-day (or more) Mexican car insurance at the border (less than $10 a day), since U.S. insurance is not valid.

WHERE TO SLEEP AND EAT

At clean, quiet **Hotel Catalina** (Calle 5a, at Madero, tel. 66/85–97–48) you can get a or a double ($16) in the heart of the tourist area. Reservations are advised on weekends. Tijuana is a great place to sample the diversity of Mexican cuisine, because people move here from all over Mexico. The fabulous **La Vuelta** (Revolución, at Calle 11, tel. 66/85–73–09) doubles as an all-hours nightclub featuring live mariachi music at 8 PM Monday–Saturday and 6:30 PM on Sunday. If you've reached taco overload, head to the 24-hour **Restaurant Los Norteños** (Constitución 530, near Calle 2, tel. 66/85–68–55), where breakfast costs less than $2 and meat or veggie sandwiches go for $2–$3. The outdoor tables here provide a clear line of sight to the nonstop action on Plaza Revolución.

AFTER DARK

Finding something to do at night is not a problem here. Revolución (between Calle 1 and 7) is jam-packed with blaring no-cover discos. Typically, a margarita costs $3–$4, a beer about $2.50. If you get tired of dancing with the underdressed and underage, try to keep up with the locals at the restaurant/nightclub **La Vuelta** (*see* Where to Sleep and Eat, *above*). The most popular gay disco in town is **Mike's Disco** (Revolución 1220, near Calle 6, tel. 66/85–35–34); the main draw here is the midnight and 3 AM shows, where men dress up like famous Mexican actresses and sing torch songs.

NORTH COUNTY COAST

North County's seaside towns each have a distinct history and character, and all are manageable day-trips from San Diego. **Solana Beach** is a small, very beach-oriented town with a mellow demeanor and scads of sand. **Encinitas** is justly famous for its fabulous fields of flowers and gardens, which extend inland from excellent surfing waters, and **Oceanside** shows off its restored mission. If you want to stay the night, Oceanside is your best bet. Other North County coastal towns include ritzy **Del Mar** and the spa town of **Carlsbad.**

COMING AND GOING

The coastal portion of North County is best accessed via **I–5,** but **Highway S21** (Old Hwy. 101) will give you a better feel for the individuality of each town. **Amtrak** (tel. 619/239–9021 or 800/872–7245) stops regularly in Solana Beach and Oceanside en route to L.A. and San Diego. Amtrak's *Coaster* (tel. 800/262–7837) runs north to Oceanside and south to San Diego's Old Town Transit Center Monday–Saturday, with late-night service Friday until about midnight. **Greyhound-Trailways** (tel. 800/231–2222) stops in Oceanside on the L.A.–San Diego route. Bus 800 of the **San Diego County Transit Express**

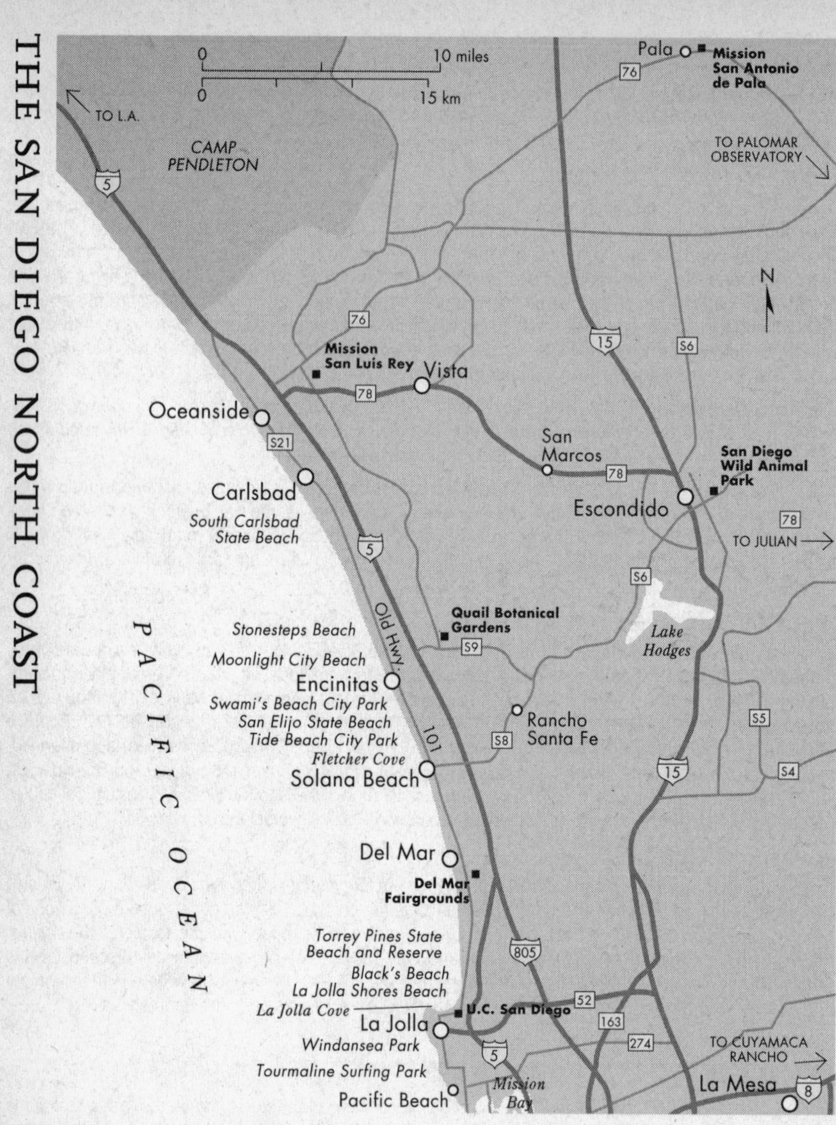

takes I–5 as far north as Oceanside from downtown San Diego. Bus 30 meanders along the coast from downtown San Diego up to La Jolla, whereupon you must transfer to **North County Transit District** (tel. 619/722–6283) Bus 301, which also ends up in Oceanside via Old Hwy. 101. The **NCTD** also operates a whole network of bus routes within the North County coastal area.

SOLANA BEACH

Dwarfed in size and population by its North County neighbors, Solana Beach is a classic beach town, though in sprucing itself up for tourists it's losing a lot of charm. **Fletcher Cove,** at the western terminus of Lomas Santa Fe Drive (past where it becomes Plaza Street), provides the powdery sand. Slightly less crowded is **Tide Park Beach,** to the north on Pacific Avenue at Solana Vista. Once you descend the steep stairs, you'll find a nearly level beach that is perfect for sunbathing and skim boarding.

Drop in for a box of fresh, locally grown fruit at **Solana Beach Produce** (343 S. Hwy. 101, next to Bank of America, tel. 619/259–3866). For more substantial food, try **Pizza Port** (135 N. Highway 101, tel. 619/481–7332), also known as the Solana Beach Brewery, which has great food and beer. There's also **Jocks Sports Cafe and Museum** (145 S. Hwy. 101, south of Loma Santa Fe Drive, tel. 619/792–7521), a casual pizza-and-pasta joint. Check out its horse-racing museum, emphasizing the nearby Del Mar Racetrack. Ask anyone in North County where to go for Mexican food, and they're sure to tell you **Fidel's** (607 Valley Ave., at Genevieve St., tel. 619/755–5292). Gorge yourself on a combination plate, including rice, beans, and tortillas ($8), in an old Spanish-style villa.

ENCINITAS

Encinitas is worth a stop for its numerous natural attractions. Foremost among them is **Quail Botanical Gardens** (230 Quail Gardens Dr., off Encinitas Blvd., tel. 619/436–3036), a conservation preserve for threatened or rare plants that houses the largest bamboo collection in the United States. Take Encinitas Boulevard east from I–5 and follow signs; the park is open 9–5 daily and admission is $3. If you want to get around Encinitas without damaging its natural appeal, rent a bike at Coast Cyclery (553 1st St., tel. 619/753–5867) for $6 an hour, $23 a day.

Encinitas also has a number of notable beaches. **Stonesteps,** so-called despite the newer wooden ones, is rocky and pebbly; but you get an excellent view of the water from halfway down the stairs, which are located along the 1600 block of Neptune Avenue near Portal Street. Slightly south of Stonesteps is **Moonlight Beach** (4th and B Sts.), with a lot of white, fluffy sand for the family picnic-and-barbecue set. Farther south lies the beach known as **Swami's** (1st St., just past K St.), in dubious deference to the adjacent Encinitas branch of the Self Realization Fellowship. The "beach" at Swami's is much like Stonesteps—only the few and the brave surf, swim, or sunbathe here.

Stop by **Juanita's Taco Shop** (290 S. Hwy. 101, tel. 619/753–9625) for some good food in a snack-shack setting. The carnitas ($5 with rice and beans) are locally famous, and a bean and cheese burrito will set you back only $1.50. In general, most of what's worthwhile in Encinitas is on (or near) 1st Street, which turns into Old Hwy. 101 as it crosses the town's other main drag, Encinitas Boulevard. The north end of town—in what used to be Leucadia—is both more low-rent and low-key. For staying the night, **San Elijo State Beach** (look for signs off Old Hwy. 101, Cardiff, tel. 619/753–5091 for information or 800/444–PARK for reservations) has 171 sites ($14–$21); the 226 sites at nearby **South Carlsbad State Park** (Carlsbad Blvd., at Poinsettia Ln., tel. 619/438–3143) are indistinguishable. If you want to sleep indoors, the **Pacific Surf Inn** (1076 N. Hwy. 101, tel. 619/436–8763 or 800/795–1466, fax 619/436–6751) can put you up in a roomy, newly renovated double with a kitchen for $50 a night or about $275 a week; the friendly manager has been known to bargain. For more information on local events or lodging, contact the **Encinitas Chamber of Commerce** (138 Encinitas Blvd., tel. 619/753–6041).

OCEANSIDE

Oceanside would probably not exist were it not for Camp Pendleton, the enormous U.S. Marine base just to the north, but it does have other charms. Among them is the 1798 **Mission San Luis Rey** (4050 Mission Ave., on Hwy. 76, tel. 619/757–3651), the largest of California's Spanish missions. For $3, you can walk through the chapel, a good-sized museum, and reconstructions of the mission's past, getting a sense of the asceticism of the friars and their patronizing attitude toward the native residents. For more information on Oceanside and a free map, contact the **Visitor Information Center** (940 N. Coast Hwy., tel. 619/721–1101). Oceanside's two main drags are Hill Street, running north–south, and Mission Avenue, running east–west.

Oceanside's second most visited attraction is the **California Surf Museum** (273 N. Coast Hwy., at Pier View Way, tel. 619/721–6876, open Thurs.–Sun. 10–4). For no charge you can peruse the museum's lovingly put together exhibits of antique boards, photos, and other surfing artifacts. For fishing, venture westward to the pleasant **Oceanside Municipal Pier** (end of Pier View Way). You can rent a pole for $2 an hour (with $25 deposit and ID) at the **Bait Shop** on the pier, but there are no public benches (chair rentals are $10 a day, plus $100 deposit and ID). Surfers frequent the water near the pier; you can take a shot at the waves or bike along the beach. **Action Beach** (310 W. Mission Ave., tel. 619/722–7101) will rent you a surfboard for $5 an hour or $20 a day; volleyball sets run $10 a day.

If all this activity is wearing you down, stop in at the **Hill Street Coffee House** (524 S. Coast Hwy., tel. 619/966–0985), *the* caffeine depot in Oceanside. For serious travel fuel, the always-hopping **Johnny Manana's** (308 Mission Ave., 1 block from beach, tel. 619/721–9999) will serve you a healthy Mexican breakfast, lunch, or dinner for $2–$6. Oceanside has some of the cheapest lodging in the San Diego area; avoid the hotels on North Coast Highway above Mission Avenue, though, where shootings are not uncommon. The **Dolphin Hotel** (133 S. Coast Hwy., tel. 619/722–7200) bills itself as "Oceanside's Grand Hotel," and the narrow rooms with vintage furnishings do suggest at least a faded grandeur. Rooms start at $27 a night, plus TVs and refrigerators; and it's only four blocks from the beach.

INLAND NORTH COUNTY

When you venture east of the coast, the tourist trappings of fun-in-the-sun California fall away. At first, the hills are covered with oak and pine and interspersed with wineries, missions, and freshwater lakes. As you go farther east, the land breaks down into arid desert and scrub. Linked only by winding, hilly country highways, the small and scattered towns of the inland north are infrequently served by the **Northeast Rural Bus System** (tel. 619/765–0145). Fare is $2.50, and the system doesn't include the town of Palomar Mountain; but it does serve Escondido, Julian, Cuyamaca, and Borrego Springs. Buses are small, so you should make reservations. The **Escondido Transit Center** (700 W. Valley Pkwy., at Quince St., Escondido) serves as the hub for buses of the **North County Transit District** (tel. 619/743–6283) and **Greyhound** (tel. 619/745–6522), both of which offer service from San Diego.

ESCONDIDO

This quiet, suburban lake community is 18 mi east of the Pacific and 30 mi north of San Diego at the intersection of Hwy. 78, which heads east from Oceanside, and I–15, which connects San Diego to Riverside and points north. Escondido is a major transport hub for trips inland to Palomar Mountain and Julian (*see below*). Other than that, it has little to offer except the nearby Wild Animal Park (*see below*). Most motels are on Washington Avenue; to get there from the transit center, walk north on Quince Avenue. Try the **California Motel** (420 W. Washington Ave., at Centre City Pkwy., tel. 619/745–6566) for a borderline clean single with private bath ($25); more motels are a few blocks north on Centre City Parkway. The nearest camping is about 15 mi north in the dusty, dry Cleveland National Forest; call the **Palomar Ranger District** (tel. 619/788–0250) for information. For dining and sightseeing tips, contact the **North County Convention and Visitors Bureau** (720 N. Broadway, between Washington and Mission Aves., tel. 619/745–4741).

SAN DIEGO WILD ANIMAL PARK • Opened in 1972 as an extension of the San Diego Zoo in Balboa Park, this 2,200-acre park allows the animals to roam freely in natural-looking habitats with other species normally found in their environments. Humans view the area via a 50-minute, 5-mi monorail trip. The park is also fun to explore on foot: With plenty of steep hills, the 1¾-mi **Kilimanjaro Hiking Trail** can prove exhausting. A totally different feel than Sea World or the San Diego Zoo, the Wild Animal Park is more for the animals than for humans. At Lorikeet Landing you can feed these rainbow birds while they rest on your arm. *Tel. 619/234–6541 or 619/480–0100. Follow signs from I–15 north. Or NCTD Bus 307 from downtown Escondido. Admission: $19, parking $3. Open Sept.–May, daily 9–4; June–Aug., daily 9–6 (Thurs.–Sun. until 8).*

MISSION SAN ANTONIO DE PALA • The only mission still serving Native Americans, the small, somber chapel and museum are worth a stop, and the grounds—dotted with ancient, gnarled pepper trees—are a pleasant place for a stroll or a picnic. The focus on the native history rather than on the conquerors, the old campo (cemetery), and wooden-beam chapel ceiling are just some of the reasons this mission, established in 1816, stands out from the others. *23013 Hwy. 79, 6 mi east of I–15, tel. 619/742–1600. Admission free to chapel and grounds, $2 to museum. Chapel open daily 24 hrs; museum open Tues.–Sun. 10–4.*

PALOMAR OBSERVATORY

About 30 mi northeast of Escondido along windy, wooded Hwy. S6 is the Hale Telescope at the Palomar Observatory. With its 200-inch diameter mirror, the telescope is one of the largest in the world, with a range of approximately one billion light-years. Images taken by the telescope are shown at the observatory museum, as is a video history of the telescope. *North end of Hwy. S6, tel. 619/742–2119. Admission free. Open daily 9–4.*

At the town of Palomar Mountain, if you turn off onto S7 instead of continuing on S6 to the observatory, you'll come to **Palomar Mountain State Park** (tel. 619/742–3462). Camping among pine and cedar forests is allowed in the park at **Doane Valley,** which has 31 sites. The campground has restrooms and showers, and the $14 small sites each have table, stove, and fire ring. You should reserve in summer through Destinet (tel. 800/444–7275). The **Palomar Mountain General Store** (tel. 619/742–3496), at the intersection of Hwys. S6 and S7 in Palomar Mountain, sells everything from candy to astronomy-related items but is light on basic camping supplies. **Mother's Kitchen** (tel. 619/742–4233) next door has inexpensive salads and burgers as well as erratic hours (Mon., Thurs., Fri. 11–5, Sat. 10–6, Sun. 10–5; closed Tues., Wed., closes an hour earlier in winter).

CUYAMACA RANCHO STATE PARK

A little more than an hour's drive east of San Diego and just west of Anza-Borrego Desert State Park (*see* Chapter 12), Cuyamaca Rancho is a richly forested and mountainous area that you would never expect to find tucked into the surrounding desert. More than half the park's 25,000 acres are classified as wilderness, which prohibits all vehicles in order to preserve the park's natural beauty. The hiking can be quite challenging, and mountain lions are a real presence, but the serenity and sylvan surroundings make the effort worthwhile. **Cuyamaca Peak Trail** is a reasonably difficult trek that climbs at a 20% grade for 3½ mi on a paved fire road with little shade to the 6,500-ft summit, where your reward awaits—you can gaze at both the desert and the ocean on clear days. The trailhead is 2½ mi north of park headquarters; park at one of the paved pull-outs and look for signs. The moderate **Azalea Glen Loop** follows one of the park's few year-round streams through tall stands of coniferous forest, returning through an open meadow that affords fine views of Stonewall Peak (4 mi total). The trailhead is located at Paso Picacho campground. The short **Paso Self-Guided Nature Trail** at the Paso Picacho campground is an easy introduction to the area's native plants.

With all its cheap campgrounds, Cuyamaca Rancho is a great place to stay. Reservations through Destinet (tel. 800/444–7275) are advised, especially if you plan on visiting during one of Julian's many festivals. The 85 sites at **Paso Picacho,** a secluded, tree-covered campground, are $12–$14 as are those at the park's other drive-in campground, **Green Valley. Arroyo Seco** (about 1½ mi west of Green Valley) and **Granite Springs** (about 4½ mi east of Green Valley) are primitive sites—essentially clearings with no facilities. The only way to get there is on your own two feet, but you pay only $3 a night.

As bagels are to Brooklyn, so are apple pies to Julian. Get yours (or pastries and breads) at the renowned Dudley's Bakery (Hwys. 78 and 79, Julian, tel. 800/225-3348).

The easiest way to get to the park from San Diego is to take I–8 east to Hwy. 79 north. If you're using the Northeast Rural Bus System (*see* Coming and Going, *above*), you want Bus 878 from Escondido. The **park headquarters** (tel. 619/765–0755) on Hwy. 79 provides information on trails, camping, and other sights in and near the park.

12 PALM SPRINGS AND THE DESERT

UPDATED BY JENNIFER BREWER AND BOBBI ZANE

Exploring the California desert is like enduring a pentathlon: The conditions may be harsh, but the rewards are great. From a distance, the desert seems arid, sun-scorched, brown, and lumpy, the geographic equivalent of a plate of refried beans. But with preparation and the right temperament, visitors can grow to appreciate the stark beauty of this seemingly barren world, which extends along California's eastern border from Mexico to just south of Fresno.

In geologic time, the California desert is a recent development. Only a few thousand years ago lakes and rivers covered the area, creating lush valleys populated by an assortment of now-extinct giant mammals. While sweating through 100°F heat to the top of a 100-ft sand dune in Death Valley, consider that this was once the floor of an ancient lake. When the climate was milder, people lived here, too: On the canyon walls of almost every desert, prehistoric *pictographs* (stone paintings), *petroglyphs* (stone etchings), and *geoglyphs* (large-scale arrangements of rocks, like Stonehenge) provide clues to early civilizations.

There's still life in the desert, despite its cruel summer temperatures. You'll find ranch families who fled to the desert a century ago when Los Angeles boomed; retirees from crowded coastal cities; and even a few diehard prospectors searching the desolate buttes and washes for wealth. And though annual rainfall rarely exceeds a few inches, certain animals and insects have adapted to the terrain: Look for colorful beetles, giant tarantulas, kangaroo rats, rattlesnakes, roadrunners, and jackrabbits. At higher elevations, you may find bighorn sheep. During spring, the valleys are covered with a riotous carpet of blooms that attracts swarms of amateur photographers. Since the show changes from week to week and location to location, you may want to check the Theodore Payne Society's **wildflower hotline** (tel. 818/768–3533) before planning a trip. Wildflower viewing is particularly popular at **Anza-Borrego Desert State Park** and **Joshua Tree National Park.** The twisting, tufted plants that give Joshua Tree its name offer a dramatic vista year-round; the park is also a mecca for rock climbers from around the world.

When night rolls around, you'll most likely camp (free in many locations) or flop down in a forgettable motel in **Barstow,** the de facto desert capital. Avoid the desert in summer unless you're truly masochistic. If you do show up in July or August, at least reward yourself by staying in a motel with a swimming pool in the sunny resort town of **Palm Springs,** a surreal oasis where the green leaves your wallet just as quickly as it sprouts on the golf course; where gay and lesbians can take their lovers by the hand and frolic in exclusive resorts; and where the oppressive heat and sand of the desert is kept at bay just long enough to allow frazzled souls to relax.

BASICS

COMING AND GOING

The vast desert is poorly served by public transportation; the only way to see it is by car. Plan carefully—carry about 5 gallons of water at all times (enough for you *and* your car radiator), and keep the gas tank full and the engine in good working order. (Note that the few gas stations throughout the area charge about 30¢ more per gallon than you'll pay along the interstate.) In the summer, you can easily drive dozens of miles without seeing a soul, so be sure to bring along a good roadside repair kit, and keep an eye on the temperature gauge. Also check your oil and tire pressure and bring antifreeze to soothe an overheated engine. If the temperature gauge in your car does get close to the red line, roll down the windows and turn on the heater full blast. This actually cools the water that will then pass through the engine and radiator. Sounds like fun? It gets better: Should your car overheat anyway, pull to the side of the road but leave your engine and the heater on. Get out of the car, find or make some shade, and allow the engine to cool. If you have a breakdown, stay with the car until someone comes by—AAA towing and auto repair are available at Furnace Creek in Death Valley.

DESERT SURVIVAL

To survive the desert's dry heat, you need a constant supply of water. Drink 1–3 gallons per day, depending on the season and your level of activity. Don't wait until you're thirsty before taking a gulp—by then, you may already be dehydrated. Avoid caffeine and alcohol, which only make you more dehydrated. Desert hikers should consume plenty of high-sugar, carbohydrate-rich foods (dried banana chips are excellent). Skip high-protein or fatty foods, which require a lot of water to digest.

It may seem like torture, but when driving up the steep grades in the park, turn off your air conditioner to avoid overheating the engine.

If you're going to spend time outdoors (especially during summer), you must also protect your skin. Thick-sole shoes are a must, as ground temperatures can reach a blistering 200°F. Wear a hat, sunglasses, and a high-SPF sunscreen, and remain fully clothed at all times—a sweat-soaked T-shirt, though uncomfortable, may be the only thing slowing the evaporation of your bodily fluids. In the evenings, especially during winter, temperatures can drop to near freezing, so bring extra layers for warmth.

Whether you're hiking or camping, always let someone know where you're headed; usually, you'll need to register at the park's ranger station before setting off on your trip. A compass is absolutely essential for desert navigation—learn how to use it before you arrive. And in the event that you do get lost, carry a small signal mirror. Even if its reflection doesn't draw help, it will probably scare off the buzzards.

You also have to prepare for flash floods, which are a possibility in the water-thirsty land. Don't linger in low-lying washes (any area where a river is or has been) and canyons; a storm can blow in without warning and dump thousands of gallons of water onto the desert floor in less than a minute. Rainfall channeled into a wash carries stones and other debris and sweeps away everything in its path. To protect yourself from whiteouts (sand blizzards), carry a bandanna. Whiteouts rarely last longer than 15 minutes; if you're driving, pull over immediately. If you're outside, crouch down and cover your face while you wait it out. Other desert dangers include abandoned mines with unstable structures and hidden shafts; admire these from a safe distance. In addition to mining, a good deal of military training has taken place here over the past four decades. If you see something metallic glittering in the sun, don't think "souvenir." Think "unexploded shell," give it a wide berth, and report your find to a ranger or the local police department.

DANGEROUS FLORA AND FAUNA • There are a few unfriendly desert inhabitants to watch out for. The deadly female **black widow spider,** ½-inch in size, is easily identified by her shiny black abdomen and red underbelly. The males are smaller, brown, have white lines on their sides, and are far less venomous. **Tarantulas** are a common sight, especially in fall. These fat, furry spiders, measuring up to 7 inches, are unfairly labeled as killers: Tarantulas will only bite if threatened or antagonized and their bite, while painful, is not dangerous. Of all the desert's inhabitants, you're most likely to encounter **rattlesnakes,** the only poisonous snakes in California. While not all rattlers rattle (some hiss instead), they all have diamond-shape heads and rattles on their tails. Use caution in the early morning, especially in spring, when rattlers come out to sun themselves. Another common desert creature is the **scorpion.** These nocturnal relatives of the spider can be black or cream-color and range 2–4 inches in length. A scorpion's stinger is at the tip of its tail, which it curves over its back. Fortunately, Californian scorpions are only mildly poisonous. Still, they occasionally sneak into tents and hotel rooms and have even been

MIXED BLESSING?

In 1994 the U.S. Congress passed the California Desert Protection Act, upgrading Joshua Tree and Death Valley to the status of national parks and the Mojave to that of national preserve. These desert areas will get more protection—but also more visitors. Environmentalists hope this won't prove to be a contradiction in terms.

known to crawl into sleeping bags or between sheets in search of a cool, dry hiding place. The key is to shake out your belongings (hiking boots, bedding, clothing) before using them.

While common sense will tell you not to touch a plant covered with 6-inch spikes, every year dozens of people find out the hard way by backing into the bristly **yucca plant,** also known as the Spanish Bayonet. The **jumping cholla cactus** is another prickly dance partner whose spines are extremely painful and difficult to remove. If you accidentally brush against a cholla, use a comb, stick, or fork to flick the branch away. (If you use your fingers you'll be speared by its spines.) Remaining stickers can be plucked away with tweezers or needle-nose pliers.

DEATH VALLEY NATIONAL PARK

It's a wasteland with searing summer temperatures and the possibility of being fatal to the ill-prepared (*see above*), yet Death Valley still draws a crowd, intrigued by its fierce reputation as one of the least hospitable places on earth. Each year, more than a million adventurous or macabre-minded travelers come away moved by the valley's stark beauty and the legends of its crumbling ghost towns. Most are astonished to learn that these blistered badlands support over 600 species of plants and a wide variety of mammals, reptiles, birds, and insects—some of which are so highly adapted that they can survive without free-standing water.

It all began nearly 3 million years ago when plates under the earth's crust separated, creating a sunken valley almost 100 mi long and up to 25 mi wide. This open-face geological taco consists of craggy mountains, sand dunes, inhospitable salt flats, natural oases, and volcanic craters. Human history here began around 9000 BC, when Native American tribes inhabited Grapevine Canyon. At the time, the valley floor was covered with water and big game roamed freely. Today, the rivers and lakes have all but vanished, and less than 5 inches of rain fall every year. Birds dropped dead in mid-flight on July 10, 1913, when the temperature in Furnace Creek reached 134°F, the hottest weather ever recorded outside the Sahara.

Death Valley's modern era began in 1849, when about 40 emigrant families stumbled onto it en route to gold country in the Sierra Nevada mountain range. They found a way out only after one died and the rest had burned their wagons to roast the meat of their gaunt oxen; hence the name. Though myths, rumors, and occasional successes brought waves of prospectors searching for gold and silver, the real find was the rich boron deposits that are still mined at the edge of the valley. In 1933, Death Valley was declared a national monument; in 1994, with the addition of 1.3 million acres and a change in name, it became the largest national park—at over 3 million acres—outside Alaska.

The best way to enjoy Death Valley in the summer is to stay in the shade during the day and trek along the dunes and trails in early morning or late afternoon. A winter trip requires less planning, since temperatures are comfortable during the day (though sometimes very cold at night). Civilization (restaurants, lodging, gas stations, and potable water) exists in three places: **Furnace Creek Ranch, Stovepipe**

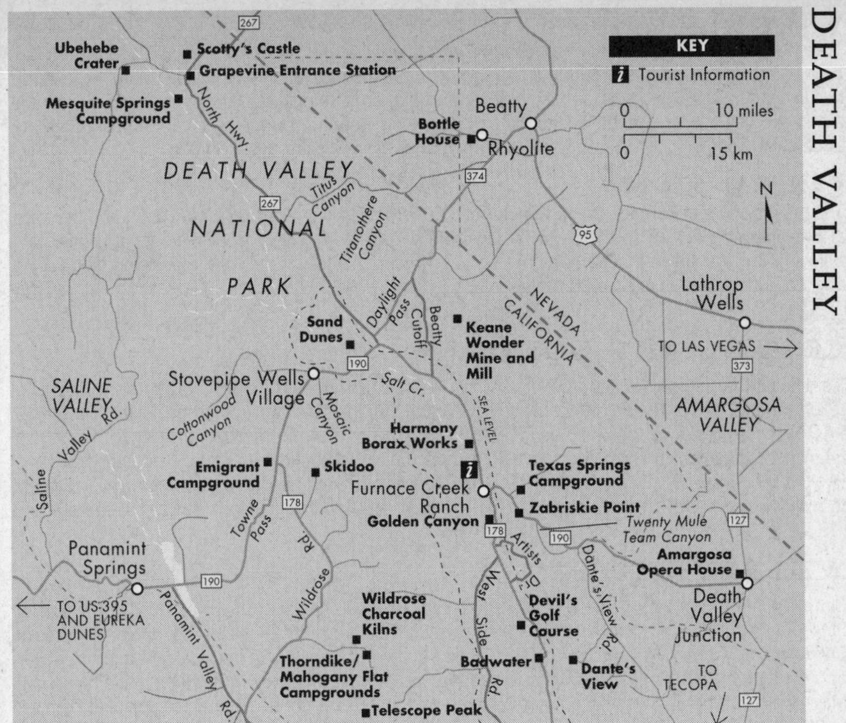

Wells Village, and **Panamint Springs,** though food and gas are also available at **Scotty's Castle.** Prices at all these places run as high as the temperatures.

BASICS

VISITOR INFORMATION

The **Furnace Creek Visitor Center** (1½ mi north of junction of Badwater Rd./Hwy. 178 and Hwy. 190) near the center of the park, is the best starting point for visitors. For a quick overview of the park, check out the small adjacent museum and 18-minute orientation film. Rangers lead evening programs and daytime walks on a regular basis in high season, November to March, and on a more limited basis in off-season. Pick up a free guide, road map ($3.95), topo maps, or lists of bike routes, campsites, and trails. During the summer, request the free pamphlet "Hot Weather Hints: How to Survive Your Summer Trip Through Death Valley." (For a crash course on dealing with the desert, *see* Desert Survival, *above.*) *Tel. 760/786–2331. Open daily 8–5.*

FEES

Entrance permits, valid for seven days, are $5 per vehicle, $3 for hikers and cyclists. Fees are collected at the Furnace Creek Visitor Center, the Grapevine Ranger Station, and Stove Pipe Wells Ranger Station.

PUBLICATIONS

The **Death Valley Natural History Association** (Box 188, Death Valley 92328, tel. 760/786–3285) has maps and guides that you can order in advance or pick up at the visitor center (*see above*). The most complete guidebook on Death Valley and its recent addition to the U.S. Park System is *The Explorer's Guide to Death Valley National Park,* by T. Scott Bryan and Betty Tucker-Bryan. The best general guide for getting around the desert is *Adventuring in the California Desert,* by Lynne Foster. Hikers will want *Trails Illustrated* ($9), a topo map covering the entire Death Valley.

WHEN TO GO

The choice times to visit are in fall and spring, when temperatures hover in the mid-70s. The park can be busy in winter, particularly during Thanksgiving and Christmas, and in the spring (March–mid-April) due to academic spring breaks and the blooming wildflowers. During these times, daytime temperatures are in the low 60s and nighttime temps can dip below freezing. During summer, temperatures are unbearably hot (up to 120°F), and some campgrounds close altogether.

GENERAL STORES

The general store at **Furnace Creek Ranch** (tel. 760/786–2345), open daily 7 AM–10 PM, and the store at **Stovepipe Wells** (tel. 760/786–2387), open daily 7 AM–9 PM, sell groceries, camping goods, cold drinks, and ice at inflated prices. You'll need to buy your charcoal or firewood here if you didn't bring any; collecting wood in the park is not permitted.

COMING AND GOING

It's difficult to see Death Valley without your own wheels, as no mass transportation runs through. To reach **Furnace Creek Ranch,** the center of civilization and the starting point for most excursions, take I–10 east from Los Angeles to I–15 north. At Baker, 60 mi northeast of Barstow, take Hwy. 127 north for 84 mi to Death Valley Junction, then drive 30 mi north on Hwy. 190. From Northern California, take Hwy. 99 south to Hwy. 178 near Bakersfield, then travel east on 178 to U.S. 395 north, where you'll connect to Hwy. 190 east. (If you're new to driving in the Desert, *see* Coming and Going *in* Basics, *above.*)

WHERE TO SLEEP

Camping is the best alternative for price and location—if you can stand the heat. Lodging prices at Stovepipe Wells and Furnace Creek generally range from expensive to ridiculous. The luxurious **Furnace Creek Inn,** a historic, 70-year-old rambling stone structure set amid lush landscaped gardens, is well out of budget travelers' means in winter, when doubles average $245. However, during summer (mid-May to mid-October) prices on those same rooms drop to $150. Both the inn and the adjacent Furnace Creek Ranch (*see below*) are operated by the concessionaire Fred Harvey, Inc.; call 760/786–2345 for reservations.

On the western edge of the park, independently owned Panamint Springs offers more reasonable prices, but it's a lengthy drive away from the park's main sights. The visitor center (*see above*) has a partial list of area motels. Beatty, Nevada (Junction of Hwys. 374 and 95), has motels and RV parks, making it a decent base for trips to Titus Canyon.

HOTELS

Furnace Creek Ranch. What was originally crew headquarters for a borax company is now a family-oriented motel with views of an 18-hole golf course. Though it exudes a certain rustic charm, facilities inside are thoroughly modern. Double-occupancy cabins are $85, double rooms are $105–$125 (depending on their proximity to the motel's pool). *Tel. 760/786–2345, fax 760/786–2514. On Hwy. 190, 1½ mi north of junction with Hwy. 178. 224 rooms, all with bath. Restaurant, coffee shop, bar.*

Panamint Springs Resort. Don't be alarmed by the fancy moniker: This is really a simple roadside motel, just inside the park's western boundary. You'll pay $49–$56 for a clean, comfortable, room. The restaurant/bar on the premises is well worth the money. *Tel. 702/482–7680, fax 702/482–7682. On Hwy. 190, 48 mi east of Lone Pine and 35 mi west of Stovepipe Wells. 14 rooms, all with bath. Restaurant, bar.*

Stovepipe Wells Village. Comfort and convenience are key at this sprawling, Old West–style establishment. Extremely clean, attractive rooms, each with two beds and a shower (but without TV, phone, or drinkable water) are $53; rooms with water you can drink, a bathtub, and a refrigerator are $76. Take an afternoon dip in the adjacent swimming pool, or unwind at the Badwater Saloon. *Tel. 760/786–2387, fax 760/786–2389. 24 mi NW of Furnace Creek Visitor Center on Hwy. 190. 83 rooms, all with bath. Restaurant, bar. Reserve 2 weeks ahead.*

HOSTEL

Desertaire Hostel. This small hostel in the town of Tecopa, a one-hour drive south of Death Valley, offers visitors free access to hiking and mountain-biking trails, hot springs, a date farm, a volleyball court, and a watchtower from which you can observe the starry nighttime sky. Dorm-style beds are $15, or $12 for HI members. There are two private rooms ($35 and $45) for up to four persons each. Though the hostel accepts walk-ins, the manager requests that people write in advance (with a deposit) or at least call 24 hours before arrival. *2000 Old Spanish Trail Hwy., at Hwy. 127, tel. 760/852–4580. Mailing address: Box 306, Tecopa 92389. 12 beds. Reception open 5 PM–9 PM, curfew 11 PM. Cash only.*

CAMPING

All of the designated campgrounds except Furnace Creek operate on a first-come, first-served basis. Many campgrounds on the valley floor are closed April–October, and some at higher elevations are closed in winter. During hot weather, head for higher elevations, where campgrounds are cooler, more isolated, and sometimes even shaded by trees. Showers, a pool, and a laundromat are all available for a fee at Furnace Creek Ranch.

Emigrant. On Hwy. 190, 9 mi west of Stovepipe Wells Village, this small, free campground may be just a patch of flat gravel, but it's much cooler than Stovepipe, thanks to its 2,100-ft elevation. Fires are not allowed. *10 sites. Drinking water, flush toilets, picnic tables. Closed Nov.–Mar.*

Furnace Creek. This uninspiring campground 196 ft below sea level owes its popularity to its location: The entrance is ½ mi north of Furnace Creek Ranch. To get a spot ($16), shaded with a handful of spindly cottonwood trees, arrive by 8 AM. From October to April, make campsite reservations up to five months in advance through Destinet (tel. 800/365–2267). *136 tent and RV sites. Drinking water, fire grills, flush toilets.*

Mesquite Springs. In contrast to the barren campsites nearby, this shaded campground ($10; elevation 1,800 ft) is surrounded by shrubbery. But there's a catch—its location, near the park's northern boundary, is far from most of the park's attractions. *Off Hwy. 267 near Scotty's Castle, 52 mi north of Furnace Creek. 30 sites. Drinking water, fire rings, flush toilets, picnic tables.*

Stovepipe Wells. This is nothing more than an open, treeless patch of ground parceled into campsites ($10; elevation sea level)—although a few of the tent sites have shrubs that provide much-needed shade. But it *is* near Stovepipe Wells Village, which consists of a motel, a restaurant, a general store, and, best of all, a swimming pool. Campers may use the pool and showers for $2. *24 mi NW of Furnace Creek on Hwy. 190. 200 sites. Drinking water, flush and pit toilets. Closed May–Sept.*

Texas Springs. Located 1½ mi south of Furnace Creek off Hwy. 190, Texas Springs (elevation sea level) is a designated "quiet" campground: Since RVs may not use their generators, many rely on solar paneling. The parking lot looks like a scene from Mad Max, but there is a tents-only section of about 40 sites ($10). *92 sites. Drinking water, fire rings, flush and pit toilets, picnic tables. Closed May–Sept.*

Thorndike and **Mahogany Flat.** These adjacent free campgrounds are for serious solitude-seekers only or for hikers planning a trip to the top of 11,000-ft Telescope Peak (*see* Longer Hikes, *below*). At 7,500 and 8,200 ft respectively, these sites are much higher than other campgrounds in the park. They are accessible only via several miles of rough, unpaved road that isn't passable by RVs or by cars without four-wheel drive. Neither campground has potable water. *From Emigrant Campground, follow signs 25 mi south of Hwy. 190 on Wildrose Rd. Thorndike (elev. 7500 ft): 8 sites. Mahogany Flat (elev. 8200 ft): 10 sites. Both have fire rings, pit toilets, picnic tables. Both closed Dec.–Feb.*

BACKCOUNTRY CAMPING • Backcountry camping is permitted anywhere in the park, as long as you're at least 2 mi from maintained roads, 200 yards from any water source, and 5 mi from developed areas, including campgrounds. Fires are not permitted. You may follow trails or strike out cross-country; in either case you'll want to pick up maps and check conditions at the Furnace Creek Visitor Center first. While you're there, fill out a voluntary backcountry registration form so someone knows your whereabouts; you may also register at ranger stations at Stovepipe Wells Village or the Furnace Creek Visitor Center. Water found in the valley is an undrinkable concoction of salts and minerals, so plan on packing in at least a gallon per person per day. (For hot-weather hiking tips, consult rangers and *see* Desert Survival *in* Basics, *above*.) **Hanaūpah, Johnson,** and **Warm Springs canyons**—all off the unpaved West Side Road—are excellent destinations if you're looking for a day or more of desert solitude. West Side Road branches southwest from Hwy. 178/Badwater Road about 10 mi south of Furnace Creek Ranch and is accessible to high-clearance vehicles like Jeeps and pickups. Conditions may require four-wheel drive—ask at the ranger station.

SANDBLASTS

Created when ancient lakes dried up and their sandy bottoms were teased into stiff peaks by the wind, Death Valley's awe-inspiring sand dunes tower up to eight stories high. Wandering among the windswept slopes may be a mesmerizing experience, but don't lose sight of your car. Should an abrupt gust of wind cover your tracks with sand, you may suddenly become lost.

FOOD

Unfortunately, unless you've discovered a way to digest creosote bushes, you'll need to spend a lot for a meal. You'll find food in only four locations in Death Valley or at two grocery stores in the park (*see* General Stores, *above*). **Furnace Creek Ranch** has a handful of sit-down or buffet-style restaurants: At one end of the spectrum, the **Inn Dining Room** serves delectable $30 entrées to the jacket-and-tie crowd. At the other end, the mellow **49er Coffee Shop** offers burgers, sandwiches, omelets, and such, for $6 and up. The **Toll Road Restaurant** in Stovepipe Wells Village serves everything from cheese sandwiches ($3) to filet mignon ($19) and has a well-stocked salad bar. At the remote northern boundary, a snack bar at **Scotty's Castle** (*see* Exploring Death Valley, *below*) serves spicy fries and good grilled sandwiches for under $5, though it doesn't sell hamburgers May–October due to the heat.

The best deal on quality food is at the family-run **Panamint Springs Resort** (*see* Where to Sleep, *above*), where you can get a bowl of spicy vegetable soup for $3.50 or a burger for about $6. If you think you'll beat these prices by providing for yourself, think again: The two grocery stores in the park are no cheaper. If you're truly interested in saving your dollars you'd be wisest to fill a cooler with goodies before you leave home.

EXPLORING DEATH VALLEY

Travelers who prepare accordingly will be intrigued by the park's unique sights, including 200 square mi of crusty salt beds, a string of 11,000-ft peaks, and whipped mounds of weirdly hued soil. The intense heat often makes lengthy hikes impossible; fortunately, the park is packed with shorter trails that can be explored during early morning or late afternoon and evening, when desert sands assume luminous purple, orange, and gold hues. Most points of interest are accessible from the paved main roads.

HIKING

The Furnace Creek Visitor Center (*see* Visitor Information, *above*) has a comprehensive list of day hikes, as well as trail guides and topo maps for sale. Most trails lie near Furnace Creek or farther north. Remember to carry plenty of water.

SHORT HIKES • In addition to established trails, you may want to explore the valley's **sand dunes.** They aren't particularly tough to climb, though you'll find the experience most pleasant when the sands are cool (in early morning or evening). A parking and picnic area is accessible from Hwys. 190 and 267, near their intersection with Mid-Canyon Road. To reach the tallest dunes, look for a roadside marker on Hwy. 190 about 4 mi east of Stovepipe Wells Village; park and hike 1 mi north.

Golden Canyon. If you only have time for one hike, make it to Zabriskie Point. The views at sunset are absolutely stunning. From the trailhead on Badwater Road, 3 mi south of Furnace Creek, take this relatively easy trail (2 mi round-trip), which climbs through colorful layers of rock bearing the ripple marks of an ancient lake. After ½ mi, you have two options for magnificent views of the valley: A short trek to the sheer cliffs of **Red Cathedral,** or a steep and strenuous 2-mi ascent to **Zabriskie Point** (*see* Scenic Drives and Views, *below*) one of Death Valley's most famous viewpoints.

Keane Wonder Mine and Mill. This steep 2-mi round-trip trail follows a defunct aerial tramway to the abandoned remains of one of Death Valley's most successful mines. A one-eyed butcher and his prospector partner discovered gold here in 1904; by 1911 they'd hauled out almost $1 million worth. Though you shouldn't enter the mine, you can safely enjoy spectacular views of the valley floor below.

To reach the trail from Furnace Creek, drive 10 mi north on Hwy. 190, then go east on Beatty Cutoff Road. Turn south onto a marked but unpaved access road and continue 3 mi to the parking area.

Mosaic Canyon. Take this easy uphill trail (2 mi one-way) to see the unique geologic mosaic for which the canyon is named. Portions of the narrow canyon walls have been polished to marblelike smoothness by draining water; in other places, the workings of time have "glued" rock fragments together. Follow signs to the trailhead 3 mi west of Stovepipe Wells Village off Hwy. 190. Use caution: The unpaved access road can be rough. The actual canyon head is a steep 9 mi from the parking area, but you only need to venture a few miles to witness the remarkable landscape.

Ubehebe Crater. Around 3,000 years ago, molten lava oozed into contact with groundwater under the valley floor, creating explosions of steam and gas that spewed debris over 6 square mi. From the wreckage was born this crater, nearly ½ mi wide and 600 ft deep. Though the 3-mi trail to the bottom may be a lark, bear in mind that it will take you twice as long to climb back up. The trail is at the northern edge of the park, 5 mi west of the Grapevine Entrance Station; follow signs from Hwy. 267.

LONGER HIKES • If it's not too hot (i.e., below 95°F), you have a choice of several day hikes. Let your water supply and internal thermometer—not your ego—help you decide when to turn back (*see* Desert Survival *in* Basics, *above*). Experienced hikers in excellent physical condition may want to purchase topographic maps (*Trails Illustrated* is best) at the visitor center and plan a cross-country trek through isolated **Johnson, Warm Springs,** and **Hanaupah canyons** (*see* Backcountry Camping, *above*).

Telescope Peak. If you have abundant energy and six to nine hours, the strenuous 7-mi hike to the summit of 11,049-ft Telescope Peak affords panoramic views of Death Valley and the High Sierra. In winter, the last ice-covered mile to the summit requires special preparation and equipment. The trailhead is comfortably above the valley floor, about 25 mi south of Hwy. 190 on Emigrant Canyon Road; follow signs from Mahogany Flat Campground or, if you lack four-wheel drive, from the Wildrose Charcoal Kilns (*see* Historic Buildings, *below*); the kilns are an additional 2 mi from the summit.

Titanothere Canyon. This moderately strenuous hike is named for one of the largest mammals ever to roam North America. A cousin of the rhinoceros, the now-extinct Titanothere inhabited the area more than 30 million years ago, and you can follow in its gigantic hoofprints. The day-long hike through the canyon has an elevation change of 4,700 ft. The hike starts 11 mi down the Titus Canyon Road, and though the trailhead is marked you'll want to carry a topo map. As you descend the wash (12 mi to Scotty's Castle Road), you'll encounter underground springs, fascinating geologic formations, and spectacular views of Death Valley. It helps if you have a second car so you can walk all the way down the canyon. If not, hike 4½ mi to Lost Man Spring and return the same way.

SCENIC DRIVES AND VIEWS

The valley's attractions are spread out over hundreds of miles, so you won't be able to see everything in less than at least three days. A great drive begins at **Badwater,** 18 mi south of the visitor center on Hwy. 178. This brackish pool is the remnant of an ancient lake. At 279.8 ft below sea level, it's also the second-lowest point in the United States. (The lowest point is ½ mi away and 2 ft farther down.) Drive 4 mi north of Badwater on Hwy. 178/Badwater Road to **Devil's Golf Course,** a craggy expanse of crystallized salt beds. Another 4 mi farther north, turn onto **Artist's Drive,** which loops through colorful rock and mineral deposits. The most vibrant ones are at **Artist's Palette,** an overlook about halfway along the drive. The scenic detour rejoins Hwy. 178 about 5 mi south of the visitor center.

Zabriskie Point, 4 mi south of Furnace Creek Ranch on Hwy. 190, provides a striking panorama of weathered, cinnamon-color hills from a height of 710 ft. One mi farther south, a 3-mi unpaved drive loops through **Twenty-Mule Team Canyon** before returning to Hwy. 190. The canyon is named for the teams once used to haul wagons laden with boron (20 tons at a time) out of the desert. Tunnels made by prospectors are still visible from the road. Continue 4 mi south to a marked 13-mi paved road leading through the Black Mountains to **Dante's View** scenic lookout, 5,000 ft above the valley floor. From here, the bleak landscape includes the Devil's Golf Course (*see above*), the green oasis of Furnace Creek, and the incongruous, snow-capped Telescope Peak (*see* Longer Hikes, *above*). On a clear day, look for Mt. Whitney's imposing profile on the western horizon.

The **Saline Valley,** 130 mi west of Stovepipe Wells Village on Hwy. 190, is chock-full of eerie mine ruins, shaggy wild burros, and waterfalls. But the real reason people come to this site is for the clothing-optional hot springs. Over the years, **Lower Warm Spring** and **Palm Spring** have been modified so that their waters flow into stone and cement soaking tubs; team labor has also provided crude showers, toilets, and a primitive campground. During spring it's crowded but always congenial—as long as you

BEST LITTLE OPERA HOUSE IN DEATH VALLEY

The desert snags wandering souls the way barbed-wire fences collect tumbleweeds. Case in point: New York artist and dancer Marta Becket's car broke down near the all-but-dead burg of Death Valley Junction years ago. Once the gaskets were fixed, Becket's travel fuse had blown out; she stayed. The town lacks necessities like a gas station and restaurant, but darned if it doesn't have some of the highest culture west of Manhattan, in the form of the one-woman ballet at Becket's Amargosa Opera House. Marta's repertoire of 47 different characters is world famous (well, almost), as are her murals on the walls and ceilings of the theater. She often plays to sell-out crowds, so call ahead for reservations (tel. 760/852-4441). Admission is $8; shows happen Saturday and Monday at 8:15 PM in November and February–April, Saturday only in October, December, January, and May.

respect the fragile environment. *From Hwy. 190, pass Panamint Springs, right on unpaved Saline Valley Rd. for 4 mi, right when road forks, left at Painted Rock, left again after 4 mi.*

HISTORIC BUILDINGS

Harmony Borax Works. The abandoned adobes and weathered buildings here are not the remains of a typical ghost town: This is the former site of a plant that processed raw boron into borax through the early 20th century. You may have seen the Harmony Borax Work's wagons immortalized in ads for the old radio and TV show *Death Valley Days,* hosted by none other than Ronald Reagan. Borax is used in ceramics, welding, paint, gas, fertilizer, the Space Shuttle heat shields, and as an insecticide. *Off Hwy. 190, 2 mi north of Furnace Creek Ranch.*

Scotty's Castle. This sprawling Spanish-style compound seems as incongruous in the desert as an igloo would be in Tahiti. The castle was built with no expenses spared between 1922 and 1933 as a vacation retreat for Chicago millionaire Albert Johnson and his wife, Bessie; the Johnsons entertained Hollywood types here, including Will Rogers and Betty Grable. The name sprang from Johnson's unusual friendship with local eccentric Walter Scott (a.k.a. Death Valley Scotty), who was allowed to live on the property and brag that it was his own. The castle's lavish interiors are worth seeing, but the crowds, especially on holidays, can be maddening. If you don't feel like parting with $8 for a guided tour, or waiting one or two hours for the privilege of doing so, take a walk on your own around the grounds instead. *Tel. 760/786–2392. 3 mi north of Grapevine Entrance Station on Hwy. 267. Tours on the hour (sometimes more often) daily 9–5; grounds open until 6.*

Wildrose Charcoal Kilns. The kilns, which look like a row of monstrous beehives, are 10 huge ovens (each about 25 ft high and almost 10 yards across) used by miners to turn wood into the coal needed to process silver. To get here, drive east on Wildrose Canyon Road from the Wildrose Campground. After 4 mi the pavement ends; you can either hike the final 1½ mi or bump along slowly in your car.

PARK ACTIVITIES

BIKING

Bicycles are permitted on anything cars and trucks may drive upon but are banned from hiking trails and open terrain. Be sure to bring lots of extra water, food, tools, a first-aid kit, and maps, as a backcountry breakdown could equal a huge ordeal. And bring your own mountain bike, too—there's no place to rent within 100 mi.

For a moderate workout over mostly level ground, try the 12-mi round-trip to the once-booming ghost town of **Skidoo.** Little is left of the town (you may see a few tin cans), though the stamp mill that once crushed gold-impregnated rock is still fairly intact. Use caution; one day it might collapse on some hapless tourist. Pick up the unpaved road to Skidoo about 12 mi south of Hwy. 190 on Wildrose Road. Ambitious cyclists may want to explore **Cottonwood Canyon.** The fairly level road, sandy in spots, extends westward for 20 mi from the Stovepipe Wells campground. You'll see Native American petroglyphs 15 mi in; otherwise, enjoy the occasional shade of cottonwood trees.

HORSEBACK RIDING

In fall, winter, and spring, **Furnace Creek Ranch** (tel. 760/786–2345) offers guided horseback rides, starting at $20 per person for one hour. During the full moon, they have one-hour moonlight rides ($30 per person). Carriage rides go for $10 per person. Make reservations for all activities.

NEAR DEATH VALLEY

EUREKA SAND DUNES NATIONAL NATURAL LANDMARK

The Eureka Dunes are technically within Death Valley boundaries but are considered a separate preserve. Spectacular, unspoiled, and uncrowded, these are the tallest sand dunes in California—some of them reach heights of nearly 700 ft. Fifty plant species thrive here, including three that grow nowhere else in the world. At dawn, look for the tracks of sidewinder snakes and tiny mammals on the windswept dunes. Because getting here can be a trek, you'll probably want to camp a night or two, though the only nod to human needs is a single pit toilet off the roadside as you approach the dunes. The dunes lie approximately 43 mi from Scotty's Castle and 50 mi from Big Pine on a graded dirt road (sometimes accessible only by four-wheel drive). To reach them from Big Pine (*see* Eastern Sierra and Inyo National Forest *in* Chapter 7) on U.S. 395, go 2⅓ mi east on Hwy. 168, south on Death Valley Road, and past the Saline Valley turnoff to South Eureka Valley Road (40 mi from U.S. 395). The dunes are 10 mi away.

RHYOLITE

In 1904, two miners stumbled across a "crackerjack" of a hill, bursting with gold nuggets. The ensuing scramble to lay claims and collect ore spawned Nevada's desert city of Rhyolite (named for the type of rock in which the gold was embedded). In its heyday, this was a classic boomtown. But in 1916, a combination of financial misfortune and waning mine profits put the lights out in Rhyolite for good. Though the town has been empty since, the train depot and the **Bottle House,** built of 50,000 beer and liquor bottles, are still intact, and a portion of the jail remains. Caretakers lead tours of the town October–April whenever people arrive; during the summer months, tours are less frequent. To get here, drive 37 mi northeast of the Furnace Creek Visitor Center on Hwy. 374, and follow signs north on the short paved road.

MOJAVE DESERT

If you've only flipped to this page because you're zooming through the desert en route to somewhere else, perhaps east to Las Vegas or west to Los Angeles, consider that some people visit the Mojave Desert by choice. There's an entire subculture of desert groupies who make annual pilgrimages to see a particular flower that blossoms for one week in the year; who have been panning for gold for years; or who caravan in ATV's (all-terrain vehicles), searching for off-road thrills. While you may not become a regular, take some time to contemplate the beauty of arid, stark plains, quiet canyons, and the desert's maddening vastness. In particular, the 600-ft-high **Kelso Dunes,** 95 mi east of Barstow in the **Mojave National Preserve,** are just begging to be climbed at sunrise. With its many crags and rocky mountains, creosote bushes, and gnarled Joshua trees, the Mojave's magic has crystallized in many a solitude-lover's heart. Arrive in the Mojave as the sun sweeps across hunched-over cacti and then slides behind mud-color mountains composed of old volcanic basalt, and you, too, may feel compelled to someday return.

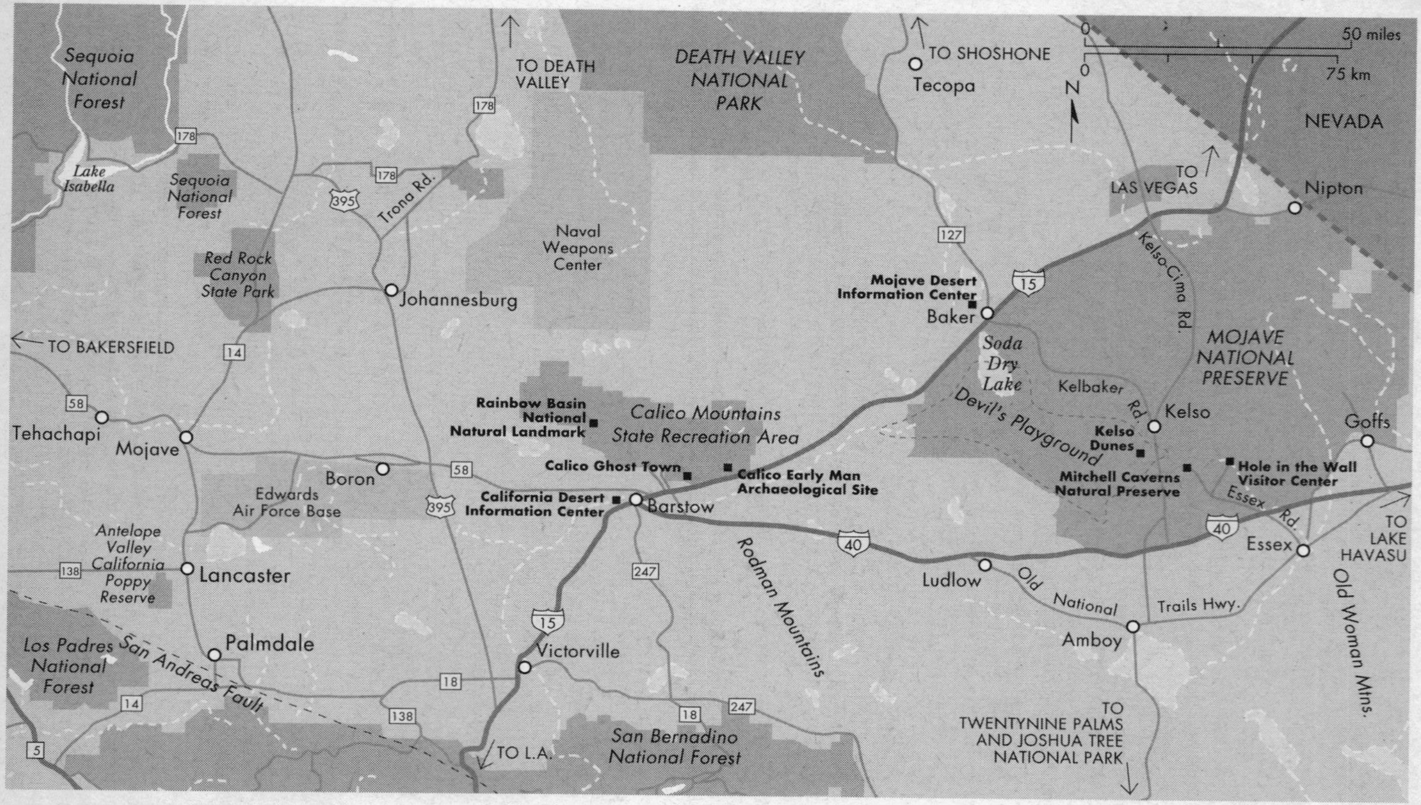

MOJAVE DESERT

BARSTOW

On holidays and weekends, some 4,000 people pass through this high-desert town, halfway between Los Angeles and Las Vegas at the intersection of I–15 and I–40, but few do more than stretch their legs and slap on some sunscreen. There's not much here besides the Santa Fe Railroad and Fort Irwin, a Marine training base. The **California Desert Information Center** (831 Barstow Rd., between Virginia Way and Mountain View St., tel. 760/255–8760), open daily 9–5, has indoor exhibits about desert life and brochures on nearby attractions.

If you're stuck in Barstow overnight, at least you won't have to pay a lot for the privilege. Try the **Barstow Inn Motel** (1261 E. Main St., tel. 760/256–7581), where doubles start at $30, or the **Desert Inn** (1100 E. Main St., tel. 760/256–2146), which has cheap but uninspiring doubles for $38. Perhaps the most interesting place to eat here is, well, **McDonald's** (1611 E. Main St., tel. 760/256–8023). This one is built like an old rail car and has a candy shop, a bakery and deli, a liquor store, and a gift shop. If you're looking for something with a little less grease, **Di Napoli's Firehouse** (1358 E. Main St., Barstow, tel. 760/256–1094) is an Italian restaurant sporting a firefighter motif. Small pizzas cost $5–$7, pasta dinners $7.

NEAR BARSTOW

CALICO GHOST TOWN • The town of Calico was abandoned for 44 years before suffering a worse fate—in 1951, it was taken over by Walter Knott, owner of the Knott's Berry Farm theme park in Los Angeles. The ghost town is contrived, but the museum exhibits, silver mine, and gold-panning school provide an enjoyable afternoon's break from desert driving. *Tel. 760/254–2122. Exit I–15 12 mi NE of Barstow at Calico Ghost Town Rd. and follow signs. Admission: $6. Open daily 9–5.*

CALICO EARLY MAN ARCHAEOLOGICAL SITE • Depending on who you ask, the Calico site is the most significant archaeological find in the United States—or an experiment in how far the human imagination can be stretched. The Friends of the Calico Early Man Site, who run ongoing excavations, claim that over 200,000 years ago this was a workshop, quarry, and campsite located on an idyllic lake. Indeed, noted archaeologist Dr. Louis Leakey, who began excavations here in 1964, contends that it is the oldest known archaeological site in the New World. On the other side of the ring is Dr. Haynes, of the University of Arizona, who claims that Calico flints are geo-facts (made by nature) and not Pleistocene-era tools. For obvious reasons, employees at the site volunteer little information about the controversy. The site is accessible only by 45-minute guided tour; show up Wednesday 1:30 or 3:30, or Thursday–Sunday 9:30–4 to judge for yourself. Public and private camping is available near the site. For more information contact the California Desert Information Center (*see* Barstow, *above*). *15 mi east of Barstow. From I–15, exit Minneola Rd. and follow dirt road north 2¼ mi. Suggested donation $1. Limited drinking water available.*

RAINBOW BASIN NATIONAL NATURAL LANDMARK • Twelve to sixteen million years ago, Rainbow Basin was the bottom of a large lake, its shores grazed by a circus of creatures, including three-toed horses, camels, dog-bears, and mastodons. When these animals died, their skeletons stuck in the mud; the resulting fossils have been perfectly preserved in the cliff walls. Also fascinating are the red-, orange-, and green-hued striations on the walls of the basin. The 6-mi round-trip scenic drive on a dirt road is perfect for an afternoon's visit. The more ambitious can meander in one of the many washes (where water once or still flows), the most interesting of which is **Owl Canyon Wash,** just off the scenic drive. If one day is simply not enough, you can stay in one of the 31 sites ($4) in the **Owl Canyon Campground** (tel. 760/256–3591). Drinking water is limited, and there are pit toilets. *8 mi north of Barstow. Hwy. 58 west to Fort Irwin Rd., go north 5½ mi to Fossil Bed Rd. (a graded dirt road), and head west 3 mi.*

MOJAVE NATIONAL PRESERVE

Mojave's rock spires, sand dunes, and bare mesas, combined with the nearly total absence of human life, either inspire or torment visitors. Stretching more than 50 mi east and about 40 mi south from the flyspeck town of Baker to the Arizona and Nevada borders, the 1½-million-acre national preserve can be accessed from several points along I–15 to the north and I–40 to the south. As always, avoid visiting during the sweltering summer months and make sure to fill up the gas tank and several water jugs before leaving civilization. Information on the preserve is available daily 9–5 at the **Mojave Desert Information Center** (72157 Baker Blvd., at I–15, tel. 760/733–4040) located in Baker, 60 mi east of Barstow. The

NEED A DRINK?

Hikers, off-roaders, and other desert enthusiasts gather at the Nellie E. Saloon (open weekends only, closed June–Aug.), 35 mi south of Lake Havasu City in the Buckskin Mountains. Look for the dirt turnoff to Cienega Springs Road off the east side of Hwy. 95. The bar has no electricity or plumbing, and its entire water supply is stored in a 500-gallon fire truck.

Hole in the Wall Visitor Center (Black Canyon Rd., 19 mi north of I–40, tel. 760/928–2572) is open sporadically in spring and fall; follow the Essex Road to Black Rock Canyon Road.

Those wishing to be immersed in the solitude of the Mojave should camp at the **Hole in the Wall Campground,** near the Hole in the Wall Visitor Center on Black Canyon Road. The 36 unshaded, open-desert sites ($10), located near volcanic-rock towers and canyons, have water, pit toilets, picnic tables, and grills. The first-come, first-served campground is open year-round, but temperatures are most pleasant between February and May. If you come in summer, prepare yourself for the incessant caterwauling of 5 million insects. You may also want to stay away during hunting season (Oct. and Nov.), when you could be mistaken for a bighorn sheep—wear bright colors. From the nearby picnic area, the strenuous ¼-mi **Rings Trail** descends into Banshee Canyon via iron rings (hence the name).

Visiting the extraordinary **Kelso Dunes** at the preserve's western boundary involves a worthwhile detour. More than 600 ft high, these are some of the tallest sand dunes in the United States. From I–15 at Baker, drive 43 mi south on Kelbaker Road, pass the almost nonexistent town of Kelso, and follow signs 3 mi west on the dirt road to the parking area. From there, you walk ½ mi to the pristine dunes, but be sure to bring a compass so you can find your car again. There are no facilities at the dunes or in the town, which consists of six shacks, some trailers, and a handful of people. Also off Kelbaker Road (look for the parking area and small sign on the right 9 mi south of I–15) is the **Teutonia Peak Trail,** leading 2 mi through a Joshua tree forest to a 5,755-ft peak that overlooks more than 30 young volcanic cones and the 75-square-mi Cima Dome.

Another worthwhile diversion is **Mitchell Caverns Natural Preserve,** 116 mi from Barstow in a patch of mountainous desert designated as the Providence Mountains State Recreation Area. Driving up the steep inclines to your destination, you'll have a spectacular view of the desert valleys that stretch all the way to Kingman, Arizona. The underground caves are riddled with astonishing rock and mineral formations, and you can expect cool 65°F temperatures in the caverns year-round—a great break from the desert heat. The 4,200-ft elevation also makes the six campsites ($12), which come complete with running water, flush toilets, and fire rings (bring wood), more bearable in the summer heat. *Tel. 760/928–2586. From Barstow, I–40 100 mi east to Essex Rd., follow signs NW 16 mi. Guided tours ($6) Sept.–May, weekdays 1:30, weekends and holidays 10, 1:30, and 3; June–Aug., weekends 1:30.*

LAKE HAVASU

Formed when the Colorado River was blocked by Parker Dam in 1938, Arizona's Lake Havasu, off I–10 160 mi south of Las Vegas and 330 mi east of Los Angeles, provides water for thirsty Los Angelenos. Its claim to fame is not as a reservoir, however, but an authentic **London Bridge,** which stands incongruously at the center of Lake Havasu City. In 1968 Robert P. McCulloch, the city's founder, negotiated with the British government to purchase the slightly used, 150-year-old bridge, which had been slowly sinking into the Thames River. At $2.46 million it was, according to the *Guinness Book of Records,* the most expensive antique ever sold. For almost 30 years, the bridge has drawn more than 1 million visitors annually from all over the globe, ranking it second only to the Grand Canyon among Arizona's tourist attractions. Naturally, overzealous city officials market "New England" to its fullest extent. The result: **English Village,** a tourist trap with inflated prices, warranting only a single walk-through.

In the last decade or so, Lake Havasu has become immensely popular with a new breed of lake lover: party-minded college students. Late March through early May, the area is clogged from shore to shore with zillions of bobbing houseboats, crewed by boisterous, overtanned coeds on spring break. At **Havasu Springs Resort** (Hwy. 2, tel. 520/667–3361), 20 mi south of Lake Havasu City off Hwy. 95, houseboat rental rates are $1,855–$2,500 per week March–September, and $1,175–$1,700 per week October–February. Houseboats sleep a maximum of eight persons.

VISITOR INFORMATION

The **Lake Havasu Visitor Center,** run by the city's chamber of commerce, offers camping, motel, and dining guides, city maps, and a barrage of brochures on water sports; some brochures include discount coupons. Hikers should ask for "Desert Walk Routes," which outlines several hikes and their degree of difficulty. The city charges $3 for parking in English Village, so park at the big hotel up the hill and walk down the staircase. *420 English Village, Lake Havasu City, tel. 520/855–5655. North of London Bridge. Open summer, daily 9–4; winter, daily 9–5.*

For maps on Arizona's Bureau of Land Management Wilderness stop in the **Lake Havasu Field Office** (2610 Sweetwater Ave., at Rte. 95, tel. 520/505–1200), open weekdays 7:45–4:30.

WHERE TO SLEEP

Moderate evening temperatures nearly year-round make camping more inviting than a cheap motel. The real Havasu experience, though, is renting a houseboat (*see above*). If your ship (or houseboat) has failed to come in, the **Windsor Inn** (451 London Bridge Rd., ¾ mi north of London Bridge, tel. 520/855–4135 or 800/245–4135) has clean doubles for $35–$42 weekdays, $45–$49 weekends. Guests have use of a pool and spa, and the inn is within walking distance of Windsor State Beach.

The official California state reptile title is held by the slow-moving, camouflaged desert tortoise, common in the Mojave National Preserve.

CAMPING • The **Windsor Beach Unit of Lake Havasu State Park** (2 mi north of London Bridge, tel. 520/855–2784) has 75 first-come, first-served lakeside campsites ($12). Though the boat launches to the north and south are dominated by beer-guzzling powerboaters, the grounds themselves draw a more mellow crowd (and a number of desert rodents, like rabbits and bats). Amenities include flush toilets, hot showers, and a fantastic swimming beach.

FOOD

Restaurants abound in the **English Village,** but the Brits were never noted for culinary genius, and being transported to Arizona hasn't helped matters. However, you can get a pint of fine English ale at **London Arms Pub and Restaurant** (422 English Village, tel. 520/855–8782), and chances are good that you'll see the local bobby at the bar. **Scotty's Broasted Chicken and Ribs** (410 El Camino Way, near S. Palo Verde Blvd., tel. 520/680–4441) may look like your average rubber-chicken pit stop from Hwy. 95, but the food is excellent and cheap. A two-piece chicken dinner, cooked using an oil-free "broasting" process and served with potatoes, roll, and slaw, will set you back just $3.85. **Taco Hacienda** (2200 Mesquite Ave., at Acoma Blvd. S, tel. 520/855–8932) is a classy establishment with mouth-watering *chimichangas* and other delicious authentic Mexican entrées ($5.50–$10).

OUTDOOR ACTIVITIES

Most people come to Lake Havasu to frolic in the water, and the lake buzzes year-round with Jet Skis, speedboats, waterskiers, and fishing boats. But unless you've brought your own equipment, all this aquatic fun can be costly. **Arizona Jet Ski Rentals** (655 Kiowa Ave., tel. 520/453–5558) rents tandem Jet Skis ($35 an hour) and 15-ft motorboats ($50 an hour) and will deliver equipment to the dock. Ascetics and the thin-walleted may eschew the pricey floating stuff in favor of a dip in the lake at **Rotary Community Park** (west end of Smoke Tree Ave., off Hwy. 95), open daily until 10:30 PM. The beach has a $5 day-use fee and is furnished with volleyball courts and picnic tables. Hikers are better off heading to **Buckshine State Park.** To get there, head north about 5 mi from Cienega Springs Road. At the park there are marked trails that begin on both sides of Hwy. 95. For detailed maps stop in at the BLM's Lake Havasu Field Office (*see* Visitor Information, *above*).

WHAT'S IN A NAME

Joshua trees are not really trees, but a type of large yucca plant. The name came about when early 20th-century Mormon settlers saw in their reaching branches the beckoning arms of the prophet Joshua. The "trees," which can be up to 40 ft tall, hold beautiful creamy white blossoms at the end of their arms in the spring.

JOSHUA TREE NATIONAL PARK

Many visitors approach Joshua Tree with the vague feeling that it must be cool: After all, Irish rockers U2 named an album for it in 1987. But to visit this desert preserve, which encompasses about 794,000 acres, including many forests of spiky, twisted Joshua trees and boulders piled high like giant bowling pins, is to encounter a sublime, unexpected, and almost surreal beauty. Joshua Tree National Park actually comprises two separate deserts, joined together raggedly at the center of the park. To the west lies the higher-elevation **Mojave Desert,** covered with Joshuas and other thick (for the desert) vegetation; to the east lies the drier **Colorado Desert,** bristling with spindly clumps of ironwood, ocotillo, and creosote. Throughout the park, granite monoliths rise from the landscape like the products of a strangely fertilized garden. The majority of campgrounds and trails lie within the Mojave sector, though both types of desert support an incredible variety of life, despite extreme temperatures and sparse precipitation. Don't skip the less-colorful Colorado portion—two of the park's cool, green palm oases lie to the east, near the south entrance station.

For humans, the deserts have always been inhospitable; early explorers expressed their disgust by giving mountainside washes unappealing names like Fried Liver, no doubt cursing the rumors of a hidden mother lode. More recently, though, angst-ridden Angelenos have rediscovered the value of a weekend's desert escape, as have Winnebago warriors determined to see all of America; springtime wildflower enthusiasts; and an international crowd of thrill-hungry rock climbers. The greatest present-day difficulty may be the struggle for a campsite during the peak season (late fall through spring), but if you're willing to hike a mile or so away from the road to pitch your tent, you can have any patch of ground your heart desires.

Summer can bring temperatures well over 100°F, but it's considerably less crowded than spring, when desert blooms draw capacity crowds. Winter and fall are the best times for solitude and reasonable weather (daytime highs in the 60s, lows of around 35°F at night). Water sources are very limited within the park, so bring plenty (*see* Desert Survival *in* Basics, *above*). You can fill your canteen at the Oasis Visitor Center, Indian Cove ranger station, and Cottonwood Springs and Black Rock Canyon campgrounds. There are five palm fan oases in the park; named for their huge fan palm trees, these are lush places where water occurs naturally near the ground surface. But don't look to the oases for drinking water or swimming—what little there is, is for the desert's full-time inhabitants.

BASICS

VISITOR INFORMATION

At the **Oasis Visitor Center,** you can pick up the free park newspaper, *The Joshua Tree Guide,* and free maps, purchase detailed rock-climbing and hiking guides, and check backcountry camping regulations. Rangers lead nature walks and short hikes on weekends from mid-October to mid-December and mid-February to May. *74485 National Park Dr., Twentynine Palms 92277, tel. 760/367–7511. Just south of Hwy. 62 at northern park boundary. Open daily 8–5 (until 4:30 in winter).*

Smaller visitor centers are in the northwest part of the park at **Black Rock Canyon** (4½ mi south of Hwy. 62, on Joshua La.), open most days October–May, and at **Cottonwood Springs** (South Entrance Rd., 7 mi north of I–10, no phone), open daily 8–3. Both are subject to occasional closures due to staff shortages.

FEES

Park entrance fees, good for seven days, are $10 per car, or $3 for walk-ins and cyclists.

GENERAL STORES

The town of **Twentynine Palms** is full of small convenience stores, but you'll find a larger selection of supplies in **Yucca Valley,** 23 mi west of the Oasis Visitor Center along Twentynine Palms Highway. Try the **Vons** supermarket (57950 Twentynine Palms Hwy., Yucca Valley, tel. 760/365–8998), open daily 6 AM–11 PM.

MEDICAL AID

In an emergency, call (collect) the 24-hour San Bernardino Ranger Dispatch Center (tel. 909/383–5651). A single pay phone is located at the Oasis Visitor Center in Twentynine Palms. Otherwise, you can find pay phones in Joshua Tree, at the Indian Cove Market, and at Chiriaco Summit (12 mi southeast of Cottonwood).

COMING AND GOING

The park is 140 mi east of Los Angeles. Take I–10 east to the Twentynine Palms Highway (Hwy. 62), which leads to the two northern entrances: The West Entrance Station, in the town of Joshua Tree; and the Oasis Visitor Center, in Twentynine Palms. The park is an hour from Palm Springs; take I–10 to the southern entrance at Cottonwood Springs, 25 mi east of Indio. The park's main paved road—Park Boulevard—loops westward through the park from the Oasis Visitor Center to the town of Joshua Tree. A second paved road branches off from Park Boulevard and heads south to the Cottonwood Visitor Center.

A car is really necessary for exploring the park. However, you can get to Twentynine Palms from the Palm Springs Airport or Greyhound station via **Morongo Basin Transit** (tel. 760/367–7433), which provides service to Twentynine Palms from Palm Springs (1½ hrs, $9 one-way) weekdays; buses leave Palm Springs in the afternoon and return the next morning. Reserve 24 hours in advance.

WHERE TO SLEEP

The streets of Twentynine Palms are lined with a slew of mostly forgettable motels that primarily accommodate marines on R-and-R from the nearby military base. The **Sunset Motel** (73842 Twentynine Palms Hwy., 2 blocks east of Adobe Rd., tel. 760/367–3484) has nine spacious rooms starting from $40 ($10 extra for kitchenette). The 84 rooms and suites at **Best Western Gardens Motel** (71487 Twentyine Palms Hwy., tel. 760/367–9141) start at $65; some have kitchens and three have whirlpool tubs. Both motels have swimming pools. If you like kitsch, the best lodging this side of Graceland is at the **Oasis of Eden Inn** (56377 Twentynine Palms Hwy., Yucca Valley, tel. 760/365–6321). You can curl up in a room decorated like a cave, safari, or the roaring '20s (among other options) for $79–$149. Theme rooms are equipped with Jacuzzis. Regular rooms start at $55.

CAMPING

Many of the 500 campsites in the park are free. Campgrounds have pit toilets, picnic tables, and fire pits, though you must bring your own wood and water. Only Cottonwood and Black Rock Canyon have flush toilets and water. Campgrounds are limited to six people and two cars. Make reservations for Black Rock, Indian Cove, and all group sites by calling **Destinet** (tel. 800/365–2267). All others are first-come, first-served, so arrive well before noon during winter and spring, particularly on weekends and holidays. Note that rangers close some campgrounds during summer heat waves; stick to those at higher, cooler elevations and you'll have no trouble finding a space. A popular scheme at full campgrounds is to ask fellow campers if you can park your car at their site (each site has two parking spaces). Promise to camp at a discreet distance (or offer to share your s'mores), and they'll probably agree.

Backcountry camping is a wonderful way to experience Joshua Tree's grandeur. You may pitch your tent anywhere that's at least 1 mi from the road, 500 ft from any trail, and ¼ mi from all water sources. Avoid making camp in the valley washes; while they may look invitingly flat, remember that they got this way because flash floods swept rocks, vegetation, and the odd camper out of the way. Check with rangers for further regulations and weather conditions. You must also register at one of 12 backcountry boards, located at trailheads throughout the park. Fires are not permitted in the backcountry. Pack out all trash.

Black Rock Canyon. Scattered piñon pines provide some shade and the high elevation gives relief from the heat. This campground (elevation 4,000 ft) is close to several trails, including the High View Nature Trail (*see* Short Hikes *in* Exploring Joshua Tree, *below*), and fills quickly during winter and spring. To be sure of getting a spot, reserve ahead. The fee is $10 per night. *Joshua La., 4½ mi south of Hwy. 62. 100 sites. Drinking water, flush toilets.*

Cottonwood Springs. The lowest-elevation campground in the park (3,000 ft) has unshaded sites ($8) in the open desert with views of Eagle and Hexie mountains. A moderate, 7½-mi round-trip hike leads from the camp to Lost Palms Oasis, the largest of the park's oases. *South entrance, 7 mi north of I–10. 62 sites. Drinking water, flush toilets.*

Hidden Valley. Legend has it that this was once a hideout of cattle rustlers; nowadays, this tiny, enclosed valley (elevation 4,200 ft) is a favorite of rock climbers and those who like to watch them. Joshua trees and towering rock formations provide a spot of shade, and sites are free. The Barker Dam Trail (*see* Exploring Joshua Tree, *below*) begins nearby. *From Oasis Visitor Center, go 20 mi south on Park Blvd., follow signs to the 1½-mi winding road into Hidden Valley. 39 sites.*

Jumbo Rocks. This secluded, free campground (elevation 4,400 ft) is ideally located among the enormous granite boulders and Joshua trees of Queen Valley, at the center of the park. A short nature trail leads to the aptly named Skull Rock. *12 mi south of Oasis Visitor Center on Park Blvd. 125 sites.*

FOOD

The coolest place in the desert—in attitude as well as temperature—is **Jeremy's Cappuccino Bar and Beer Haus** (61597 Twentynine Palms Hwy., near Park Blvd., Joshua Tree, tel. 760/366–9799), open daily 8–midnight. Vegetarian and other sandwiches on pita bread go for about $4.50; for breakfast, try the bagel with hummus ($2.50). If you're feeling dry, Jeremy's has 75 beers, four on tap. Musicians such as Brent Lewis, Clive Wright, and others (some with gold and platinum albums) drop by to play rock, blues, ska, reggae, or classical music.

For breakfast or burgers, stop by **Andrea's Charbroiled Burgers** (73780 Twentynine Palms Hwy., near Adobe Rd., Twentynine Palms, tel. 760/367–2008), which serves three-egg omelets, burgers, and other delights for less than $4. The **Finicky Coyote** (73511 Twentynine Palms Hwy., Twentynine Palms, tel. 760/367–2429) makes fantastic pita sandwiches ($4). Chase one with an iced cappuccino with whipped cream ($2.25) and, whatever you do, stay away from the fudge (it's addictive).

EXPLORING JOSHUA TREE

Hikers, rock climbers, and a hardy band of mountain bikers are big fans of the park. If you only have a few hours or are loath to leave your car, traverse Park Boulevard (about 34 mi total) for a scenic overview. Informative exhibits explain the sights at frequent roadside pullouts.

HIKING

Five palm oases lie within the park. To reach the man-made one at **Cottonwood Springs,** drive to the parking lot 1 mi east of the Cottonwood Visitor Center. More secluded is the **Lost Palms** oasis, the park's largest group of fan palms. A moderate to strenuous 7½-mi round-trip hike to this lovely spot begins from Cottonwood Springs Campground.

SHORT HIKES • The **Oasis of Mara** trail, at the Oasis Visitor Center, and the **Cap Rock** trail, which begins southeast of Hidden Valley Campground at Keys View Road, are both easy ½-mi loops. The 1.1-mi **Barker Dam Trail Loop** leads to a turn-of-the-century reservoir at the Wonderland of Rocks (*see* Scenic Drives and Views, *below*). Migrating birds liven the scene in the spring and fall, but the reservoir's not much to look at during summer—unless you're interested in mud. The return portion passes Native American petroglyphs recently painted over by film crews for the making of Disney's *Chico the Misunderstood Coyote* and *Burro of the West.* Those petroglyphs are now lost forever . . . thanks to Mickey Mouse. To reach the trailhead, follow the dirt road from Hidden Valley Campground approximately 1 mi.

The painless, ¼-mi **Cholla Cactus Garden** nature trail is ideal for a leisurely desert stroll. Be sure to wear thick-soled shoes: The barbed spines of the *bigelow cholla* almost reach out and grab you. (It's not uncommon for misguided nature lovers to run into the visitor center wildly waving cholla-covered arms and legs.) The trailhead is 20 mi north of the Cottonwood Springs Visitor Center, off the main park road.

You get excellent views at the midpoint of the **High View Nature Trail,** near Summit Peak (4,500 ft). It starts at the South Park parking area, just northwest of Black Rock Canyon Campground; the trail is moderately steep, but at 1⅓ mi, it's not too taxing.

LONGER HIKES • The ruins of one of the park's most successful gold mines can be seen at the end of the **Lost Horse Mine Trail.** The site was abandoned in 1936, 11 years after the owner was found—dead, mummified, and clutching a single strip of bacon. The 4-mi round-trip is only moderately strenuous, so you won't suffer the same fate as the former owner. If you continue an additional ¼ mi beyond the mine, you'll reach the summit of **Lost Horse Mountain** (5,278 ft). The hike begins at the parking area about a mile east of Keys View Road.

The strenuous but rewarding hike up **Ryan Mountain** is a 3-mi (round-trip), three-hour haul with a total elevation gain of about 1,000 ft. Once you're at the summit, you can sit back and enjoy 360° views of Lost Horse, Queen, and Pleasant valleys. Start the trail at the Ryan Mountain parking area or slightly farther east at Sheep Pass Campground. The 3-mi hike to **Mastodon Peak,** which begins at Cottonwood Springs Campground, is easier than the one up Ryan Mountain and provides similar stunning views. In the distance, look for the Salton Sea, a vast, salty inland lake with a maximum depth of 12 ft.

SCENIC DRIVES AND VIEWS

Keys View. As long as smog doesn't choke the sky, you can see clear to Signal Mountain, Mexico, from here. Below, you'll notice topographic proof of the writhings of the San Andreas Fault. To reach the viewpoint from Quail Spring Road, go south on Keys View Road to the parking lot.

Wonderland of Rocks. Weird stone massifs abound inside the park, but the most impressive collection of giant granite boulders lies to the north, covering roughly 20 square mi between the Indian Cove and Hidden Valley campgrounds. It's a mazelike jumble of caves and boulder piles, with a resident population of bighorn sheep. Off-trail exploring without a compass and topo map is foolhardy; instead, take a walk along the Barker Dam Trail (*see* Hiking, *above*).

Prior to becoming a protected preserve, the Joshua Tree area was mined for gold and ore. Don't attempt to rappel down into abandoned structures, as one unfortunate climber did.

PARK ACTIVITIES

During cooler months, mountain biking is popular, but you'll need to bring your own bike; rentals are not available in the park. Bikes are restricted to paved or unpaved roads and may not be taken on trails or ridden cross-country through the desert. Check the free *Joshua Tree Guide* for bike routes. The 13-mi dirt road in **Covington Flats** passes some of the park's largest Joshua trees. For magnificent views, continue about 4 mi beyond the Lower Covington Flats picnic area along a steep path to get to **Eureka Peak.** To reach Lower Covington Flats from Hwy. 62 in Yucca Valley, follow Yucca Trail Road to La Contenta Road. The self-guided **Geology Tour Road** passes through a variety of remarkable desert terrain on a sandy, occasionally bumpy track (four-wheel drive recommended). The trailhead for the 18-mi round-trip is at a road marker on the south side of Park Boulevard, 2 mi west of Jumbo Rocks Campground.

Joshua Tree is one of the world's most popular rock-climbing destinations, with hundreds of evocatively named climbs (Up Chuck, Bloody Knuckles, Heart of Darkness) and the highest density of established routes anywhere—more than 3,500. The **Saddle Rocks** formation at Ryan Mountain (*see* Hiking, *above*) has some of the longest climbs, and **Astro Dome** in the Wonderland of Rocks (*see* Scenic Drives and Views, *above*) contains some of the most extreme terrain. These and other established routes are serious endeavors, suitable only for climbers with proper equipment and training. Beginning climbers should find a gently sloping giant boulder on which to engage in a bit of innocuous "scrambling" or take a class: **Joshua Tree Rock Climbing School** (Box 29, Joshua Tree 92252, tel. 760/366–4745 or 800/890–4745) in Joshua Tree offers one- and two-day weekend instruction programs for beginner to intermediate climbers for $75 to $145 including equipment. There are no classes in July and August.

NEAR JOSHUA TREE NATIONAL PARK

PIONEERTOWN

If you're in the vicinity of Yucca Valley and in the mood for an offbeat detour, head for Pioneertown. It's an authentic Hollywood-built western town, created in 1946 by Roy Rogers and Gene Autry for the

HOORAY FOR HOLLYWOOD

To compete with newer down-valley megaresorts and gated golf enclaves owned by wealthy retirees, Palm Springs has reinvented itself using its glamorous Hollywood past. Palm Canyon Drive, once exclusively for wealthy sophisticates, now lures a nighttime crowd that strolls the Star Walk, sips drinks at outdoor cafés, and checks out the old photos in the Show Biz Museum.

famous *Gunfight at the OK Corral* and later used as a backdrop for dozens of other cowboy films. Bikers, musicians, Desert Storm vets, and anyone with a friendly face and a sense of humor are welcome, though the town is most popular with recording artists looking to jam, relax, or work on some tunes. Eric Burdon from The Animals has been known to pop in for breakfast and contemporary artists like Sheryl Crow and Cracker have stopped by to record at the town's garage-style studios.

Pappy and Harriet's Pioneertown Palace (tel. 760/365–5956) is the center of all the action; while there's no real address, it's one of only two buildings in town. Pappy passed away in 1993, but Harriet's still welcoming all with a warm smile and a hot meal. Wednesday and Thursday the Palace is open for dinner ($7–$17) only, with country dance lessons Wednesday at 7 PM. Lunch ($3–$7) and dinner is served on Friday, and on weekends the Palace serves three hearty, homecooked meals a day (reservations recommended for dinner). Friday and Saturday evenings, grab a beer and listen to live music country, blues, and rock until 1 AM. Sunday evening (6–10:30) is reserved for jam sessions—a mixture of local talent and visiting artists, such as Vic Chesnutt or Victoria Williams. The town's other building is the **Pioneertown Hotel** (tel. 760/365–4879), which has basic country-style doubles for $35 weekdays or $43 weekends. To get here from Yucca Valley, follow Hwy. 62 to Pioneer Road. If you're coming from the direction of Twentynine Palms, the turnoff is on your right just after the abandoned liquor store. Follow the road as it winds uphill into Pioneertown.

PALM SPRINGS

Between a string of burlap-color mountains and the barren desert, this incongruous resort community has for decades held a reputation as a playground for the rich and famous. It first became a haven for Hollywood stars when Ginger Rogers, Humphrey Bogart, and Clark Gable joined the Palm Springs Racquet Club in the 1930s. Today, the celebrity contingent is still present, cowering behind the high hedges that screen their huge houses from stargazing bus tours. However, most of Palm Springs' recent growth has come from a potpourri of less-tinseled visitors: The fastest-growing group of Palm Springs vacationers is gays and lesbians from all over the country, who enjoy being pampered at expensive, exclusively gay or lesbian resorts. Palm Springs's vocal gay community grabbed headlines during the 1995 mayoral race, when local transvestite Miss Kitty Cole gleefully campaigned on a platform that called for the return of "mobsters and movie stars" to the city. She finished fourth in a field of nine. One of Palm Springs's previous celebrity mayors was pop singer Sonny Bono.

Palm Springs and the seven neighboring cities of the Coachella Valley, collectively called "The Springs," have the climate—and unfortunately, the high prices—of a true resort. Even in the dead of winter, when snow crowns the top of nearby San Jacinto Peak, temperatures are regularly in the 70s and rarely dip below freezing at night. Notwithstanding the fact that this is the desert, developers have built more than 90 verdant golf courses here. Six times that many tennis courts and 30,000 swimming pools fill whatever land is left—and golf, tennis, and poolside lounging are the primary pursuits of visitors. There are other options, however, from hiking the palm oases of Indian Canyons to ascending a Swiss-style tram for a view of the desert from the 10,000-ft peaks of the San Jacinto Wilderness. During the summer,

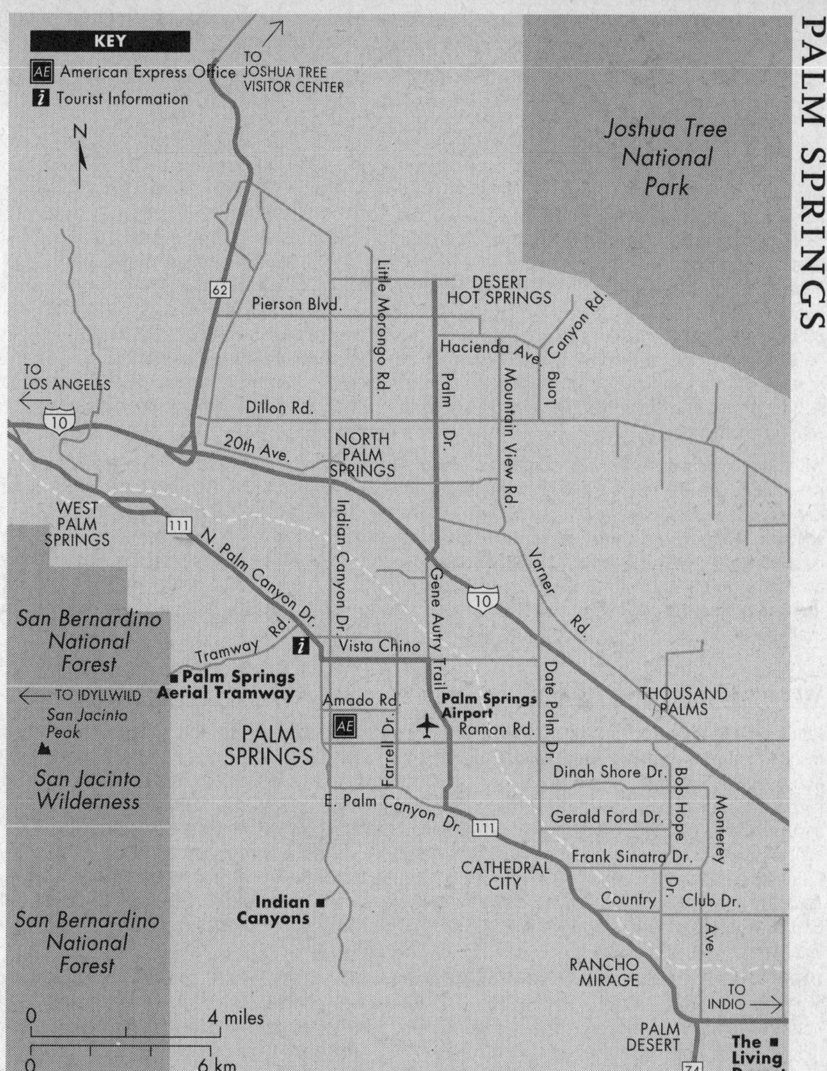

motel prices fall as temperatures rise, so if you can take the heat (90°F to 100°F), you'll be able to negotiate outrageous bargains.

VISITOR INFORMATION

The **Palm Springs Visitor Information Center** (2781 N. Palm Canyon Dr., tel. 760/778–8418 or 800/347–7746; open daily 9–5) makes gratis lodging reservations (often securing cut-rate prices) and distributes a free city map, a visitors' guide, brochures, and copies of the biweekly *Bottom Line,* which lists gay hotels, bars, restaurants, and nightclubs in Palm Springs and surrounding communities. The **Palm Springs Desert Resorts Convention and Visitors Bureau** (tel. 800/967–3767) makes hotel reservations (tel. 760/770–9000), operates a visitor center at the Palm Springs Regional Airport (3400 E.

Tahquiz Canyon Way), and maintains a 24-hour Events Hotline (tel. 760/770–1992). Check out the "Weekend" section of the Friday *Desert Sun* for nightlife listings and restaurant bargains.

COMING AND GOING

Palm Springs lies 110 mi southeast of Los Angeles, a drive of approximately two hours; take I–10 east to Hwy. 111 south. From San Diego, it's a 2½-hour drive (about 140 mi) northeast; from I–15 north, take Hwy. 215 north to Hwy. 60 east, which connects with I–10 east. You can also reach Palm Springs by plane, bus, or train. **Palm Springs Regional Airport** (tel. 760/323–8161), 2 mi east of downtown, is served by Alaska Airlines, American/American Eagle, Northwest, America West Express, Reno Air, Sky West, United/United Express, U.S. Airways Express, and several charter services. **Greyhound** (311 N. Indian Canyon Dr., tel. 760/325–2053, or 800/231–2222 for ticket information) has direct service between Palm Springs and Los Angeles (3½ hrs, $14 one-way). **Amtrak** (45050 Jackson St., Indio, tel. 800/872–7245) runs three trains weekly from Los Angeles to downtown Indio, 20 mi east of Palm Springs (2½ hrs each way, $50–$66 round-trip). From Indio, **Sunbus** (*see below*) provides public transportation to Palm Springs; if you're planning an Amtrak/Sunbus connection, keep in mind, however, that Amtrak arrives in Indio at 1:05 AM, but the last Sunbus leaves at 9:15 PM. Unless urban camping suits you, try another option.

Within the city limits, Hwy. 111 is known as **Palm Canyon Drive**; the section of the highway between Amado and Ramon roads constitutes the town center and is open to southbound traffic only (Indian Canyon Dr., 1 block east, handles downtown's northbound flow). South of Ramon Road, Palm Canyon splits; continue on East Palm Canyon Drive (Hwy. 111) to reach other desert resort communities, including Cathedral City and Rancho Mirage. **Sunbus** (tel. 760/343–3451) serves the entire Palm Springs area from Desert Hot Springs to Coachella, including Indio, for only 75¢ (transfers are 25¢). The natural-gas powered buses run 5 AM–11 PM (not all lines run until 11). Schedules and route guides are available at the visitor center (*see above*) and most other tourist locations.

WHERE TO SLEEP

Admire the luxury resorts from afar, then check into one of the area's reasonably priced inns, hotels, or resorts (many of which are really motels). Indeed, these days you'll find a good selection of chain motels and budget lodgings strung out along Hwy. 111 from Palm Springs to Indio; there are five Motel 6 complexes, including one in Rancho Mirage that's visible from the haughty Ritz-Carlton's nature trail. Rest assured that almost any establishment comes with a heated pool. Room rates are steepest in high season, October–May, and on summer holiday weekends; reservations are a must during these times. Camping isn't an option unless you hike 3 mi from the top of the Aerial Tramway (*see* Worth Seeing, *below*) or drive half an hour to **Lake Cahuilla Riverside County Park** (58075 Jefferson, La Quinta, tel. 619/564–4712), where you can camp for $12 to $16 per night. All rooms listed below come with private bath.

DIRT CHEAP • Ambassador Health Spa Motel. Rooms (and most guests) appear to be ancient and a bit frayed around the edges, but, at $39–$45 for a roomy double, consider this motel about 10 mi north of Palm Springs a budget resort. Water is piped into the Jacuzzi and pool from hot springs below the AstroTurf. Après-soak, slip into the sauna. *12921 Tamar Dr., Desert Hot Springs, tel. 760/329–1909, fax 760/251–1021. From I–10, take Palm Dr. north to Hacienda Ave. east, then left onto Tamar Dr. 18 rooms, all with bath and kitchen.*

UNDER $60 • Hampton Inn. This chain motel at the north end of Palm Springs occupies nicely landscaped grounds against a backdrop of Mt. San Jacinto. Winter rates start around $60 per night including continental breakfast. Appointments are nothing special, but the inn has a swimming pool, outdoor spa, and barbecues to save you money on dinner. *200 N. Palm Canyon Dr., Palm Springs, tel. 760/320–0555, 800/732–7755, fax 760/320–2261. 96 rooms.*

Mira Loma Hotel. This cozy, affordable oasis has immaculate and luxurious rooms, some with private patios. Guest quarters encircle a small pool (in which Marilyn Monroe purportedly swam), and the congenial management provides plenty of thick towels for sunbathing. Travelers looking to escape families with youngsters will enjoy the serenity this refuge affords. Rates start around $45 in summer and $65 the rest of the year. In summer, they serve a complimentary continental breakfast, and there's free poolside ice-tea and lemonade year-round. *1420 N. Indian Canyon Dr., tel. 760/320–1178, fax 760/320–5308. 15 rooms, some with kitchenette.*

Vagabond Inn. Rooms are smallish but clean and comfortable at this centrally located motel; they go for around $40 in summer, $65 in winter. For that you can hang out by the swimming pool, sauna, and outdoor spa. There's a coffee shop adjacent too. *1699 S. Palm Canyon Dr., Palm Springs, tel. 760/325–7211 or 800/522–1555, fax 760/322–9269. 120 rooms.*

UNDER $100 • Ingleside Inn. You can star gaze at the Ingleside and keep your budget somewhat intact. The guest register here lists top Hollywood names, ranging from Greta Garbo to Elizabeth Taylor to John Travolta. Many of the 30 rooms have antiques, fireplaces, whirlpool tubs and steam showers, stocked refrigerators, and private patios. Although prices at the Ingleside run up to $295 for the digs favored by celebrities, a few less expensive rooms start at just $95 in season, continental breakfast included. *200 W. Ramon Rd., 92264, tel. 760/325–0046 or 800/772–6655, fax 760/325–0710.*

FOOD

Once considered a culinary wasteland where restaurants served terrible food at sky-high prices, the Springs now supports a wide range of eateries, from inexpensive to luxurious. Early bird specials are common, as are menus that feature low-fat, heart-healthy items. You'll find plenty of vegetarian choices on most menus. Check the "Weekend" section of the Desert Sun for specials.

UNDER $5 • The resort set may chow down overpriced pasta at swanky bistros, but you needn't join them. A good bet for breakfast is **Bit of Country** (418 S. Indian Canyon Dr., Palm Springs, tel. 760/325-5154), which serves down-home breakfast and lunch, with $3 specials before 8:30. Casual coffeehouse **Le Peep** has two locations. Each serves huge platters of breakfast and lunch starting at about $3. Deep-skillet entrées—sausage, eggs Benedict, omelets, and frittatas—anchor the huge breakfast menu. *73-725 El Paseo, Palm Desert, tel. 760/773–1004; 2665 E. Palm Canyon Dr., Palm Springs, 760/416–1444.*

UNDER $10 • Daily Grill. The smell of cookies baking might make you more hungry than you thought you were. Good thing, because portions—such as a dinner-plate-size chicken pot pie—are huge at this bustling deli–coffee shop. Best buys (starting at $6) are the blue-plate specials, which include soup or salad and turkey meatloaf, a beef-dip sandwich, or turkey steak plus unlimited lemonade. *73-061 El Paseo, Palm Desert, tel. 760/779–9911.*

La Donne Cucina Italiana. This is a real find for lovers of Italian food. Families like this busy restaurant-deli and its large portions of homemade pasta, risotto, chicken, and other dishes. Good food and good value make reservations essential. *72-624 El Paseo, Palm Desert, tel. 760/773–9441. Closed Sun.*

Las Casuelas Terraza. Cool, adobe-walled Las Casuelas is a Palm Springs institution, always filled with convivial locals. Its hearty Mexican dishes are served up with an emphasis on health; most are low salt, low fat. Entrées average $6–$10. *222 S. Palm Canyon Dr., at Arenas Rd., tel. 760/325–2794.*

Red Bird Diner. Host Gayla Morris serves '50s-style food at her diner, which is decorated with life-size murals of the decade's icons: James Dean, Ed Sullivan, and a bright-red T-Bird. Lamb is the Red Bird's specialty, but the chef also cooks country-fried steak, liver and onions, and chicken and dumplings.*35-955 Date Palm Dr., tel. 760/324–7707.*

UNDER $15 • Blue Coyote Grill. Diners sit under blue umbrellas and munch on burritos, tacos, fajitas, or more unusual items such as Yucatán lamb or orange chicken at this casual restaurant. Dinner entrées start at $8 and go up to $20. Two busy cantinas serve up tasty margaritas to a youngish crowd. *445. N. Palm Canyon Dr., Palm Springs, tel.760/327–1196.*

WORTH SEEING

On Thursday evening (6–10 PM), check out the **Palm Springs VillageFest** (tel. 760/320–3781), a sprawling street fair covering Palm Canyon Drive between Baristo and Amado roads. Bands play live music while merchants sell everything from velvet jester's hats to Guatemalan jewelry and decorative dried gourds. Look for the professional massage booth ($1 a minute) and plenty of barbecued eats. *Closed Aug.*

INDIAN CANYONS

The Agua Caliente Indians thrived in the inhospitable desert because they settled in cool, palm-shaded canyon oases. Today the tribe manages this preserve as a day-use area for hikers and horseback riders. The **Andreas Canyon** oasis has dozens of pools and shallow falls. To escape its occasional crowds, follow the easy 1½-mi trail southwest from the Andreas Canyon parking lot to **Murray Canyon.** The creek

DINOSAUR JUNCTION

Immortalized in the 1985 movie "Pee Wee's Big Adventure," Wheel-In truck stop is creepily avant-garde. Gigantic, proto–Jurassic Park models of a brontosaurus and a Tyrannosaurus rex loom over the parking lot—a great opportunity to take photos of your friend being eaten alive by a creature that bit the dust 65 million years ago. I–10 in Cabazon (between Palm Springs and Los Angeles).

here flows only after a season's rainfall, but stands of fan palms always provide a pleasant picnic spot. The large **Palm Canyon** oasis, also accessible by car, stretches 15 mi and contains over 3,000 palm trees. From the Trading Post parking lot, follow the steep West Fork Trail south 3 mi; at its juncture with West Fork Trail North, you'll see pre-Columbian petroglyphs and, if you're lucky, wild horses and desert bighorn sheep. *Tel. 760/325–5673. Follow signs from S. Palm Canyon Dr. Admission: $5. Open daily 8–5 (until 6 during spring).*

LIVING DESERT

To see some of the desert's nocturnal residents, check out this 1,200-acre wildlife park, located 15 mi east of Palm Springs. Eagle Canyon houses golden eagles, mountain lions, and Mexican wolves in landscaped natural settings. The park also has an assortment of exotics from around the world, including zebras, gazelles, and Arabian oryx. Abundant nature trails offer many views of the park and its inhabitants, and interpretive shows are scheduled throughout the day. Those who don't want to walk can take a tram through the park for an additional $4. Scheduled for completion in 1998 is the African Savanna Village, a replica of a typical village plus domestic and wild animals; plans call for interactive exhibits, a marketplace featuring African crafts, and storytelling. *47900 Portola Ave., Palm Desert, tel. 760/346–5694. From Hwy. 111, south 1½ mi on Portola Ave. Admission: $7.50. Open Oct.–June 15, daily 9–5; June 16–30, open daily 8 AM–noon. Closed Aug. Last admission to park ½ hr before closing.*

PALM SPRINGS AERIAL TRAMWAY

This Swiss-built tramway, 10 minutes' drive from downtown Palm Springs, makes a dizzying 1-mi ascent from the desert floor into the mountains of the **San Jacinto Wilderness**—a vast alpine park with over 500 mi of hiking trails (*see* Outdoor Activities, *below*). The mountaintop station house has postcard views, a moderately priced cafeteria-restaurant (full dinners $10), and a free 20-minute film on Francis Crocker, the man who planned the tram. Best of all, it's always 30°F cooler up here than in the city below. *Tel. 760/325–1391 or 760/325–4227 for recorded information on weather and visibility. From Hwy. 111, Tramway Rd. uphill 3½ mi. Admission: $18; $21 for ride and dinner combo. Operates weekdays 10–9:45, weekends 8 AM–9:45 PM. Trams depart every half hour; last tram at 8 PM (1 hr later during daylight savings time). Closed Aug.*

CHEAP THRILLS

You can get a sweeping (and free) **view** of the Coachella Valley from part way up Hwy. 74 out of Palm Desert. Stop at the **Santa Rosa Mountains National Scenic Area Visitor Center** (tel. 760/862–9984, 51-500 Hwy. 74, Palm Desert, open weekends) for insight into the natural history of the desert. The **Moorten Botanical Gardens** (1701 S. Palm Canyon Dr., Palm Springs, tel. 760/327–6555), an outdoor museum ($2), has short nature trails that feature more than 3,000 varieties of cacti, trees, birds, succulents, flowers, and a nursery. Open daily 9–4:30 (Sun. 10–4). You can also beat the heat at **Palm Springs Desert Museum** (101 Museum Dr., just west of the Desert Fashion Plaza, tel. 760/325–0189). The museum holds first class collections of works by Giacometti, Moore, and Frankenthaler; displays also include personal collections of celebrities. Not to be missed are the regional Native American artifacts and artworks and the sculpture gardens. It's open Tuesday–Sunday 10 AM–5 PM (Fri. until 8 PM), and admission is $5. You can see more art free at the luxurious **Westin Mission Hills Resort** (Dinah Shore and Bob Hope Dr., Rancho Mirage, tel. 760/328–5955), which has an ever-changing display of large outdoor sculptures by prominent local artists. If you're interested in local history, stop by the museums in the **Village Green Heritage Center** (221 and 223 S. Palm Canyon Dr., Palm Springs, tel. 760/323-8297, admission 50¢); the best venue here is the Agua Caliente Cultural Museum, which houses displays on Native American life and history.

AFTER DARK

Nightlife in the desert is eclectic—there's something for just about everyone. A popular gay club, **C. C. Construction Co.** (Smoke Tree Shopping Center, Sunrise Way at E. Palm Canyon Dr., Palm Springs, tel. 760/778–1234) has a huge disco that is open Friday through Sunday nights and a smaller dance floor that's open nightly. For other gay venues, consult the free biweekly publication *The Bottom Line* (*see* Visitor Information, *above*).

Zelda's Nightclub and Beach Club (169 N. Indian Canyon Dr., Palm Springs, tel. 760/325–2375, open nightly 8–2) attracts a young, mostly straight crowd with dancing; there are two rooms, one with a beachy atmosphere featuring techno jazz and another featuring Top-40 music. **Harley's Coffee and Beers Café** (168 N. Palm Canyon Dr., tel. 760/778–5750) serves, uh, coffee and beers. The 25 international and microbrewed ales cost $3–$5. Reggae, jazz, blues, and acoustic-guitar players drop in to jam on weekend evenings beginning at around 8. The retro poetry readings and live jazz at **Peabody's Jazz Studio and Coffee Bar** (134 S. Palm Canyon Dr., Palm Springs, tel. 760/322–1877) are the hottest tickets in town.

NEAR PALM SPRINGS

SAN JACINTO WILDERNESS

Head for the hills when you tire of the heat and glitter of Palm Springs. The cool, rugged, 8,000-ft peaks at the top of the Aerial Tramway (*see* Worth Seeing, *above*) are part of the sprawling San Jacinto Wilderness, and from their heights you'll have surreal views of the desert below. The highest peak in the San Jacinto Range is towering Mount San Jacinto, which stands 10,804 ft above sea level; the rest of the wilderness area is a paradise of subalpine forests and fern-shrouded glens. San Jacinto Wilderness is just a two-hour drive from Los Angeles or San Diego (*see* Coming and Going, *below*). The resort town of **Idyllwild,** with its clapboard cabins and quaint country shops, lies amid all this grandeur and provides an ideal base for forays into the forest.

VISITOR INFORMATION • If you're arriving from the aerial tramway, stop by the **Long Valley Ranger Station** (tel. 760/327–0222 for recorded weather and trail information), just below the tram's mountaintop station, for maps and hiking permits. If your starting point is Idyllwild, the **San Jacinto Ranger District** (54270 Pinecrest, off Rte. 243, tel. 909/659–2117), open daily 8–4:30, sells hiking maps ($1.25–$4) and distributes free mandatory wilderness permits for day hiking and overnight backpacking. You can request permits in advance by writing to: Box 518, Idyllwild 92549. A small portion of the wilderness area is designated a state park; the **Mount San Jacinto State Park Office** (Box 308, Idyllwild 92549, tel. 909/659–2607), in Idyllwild just around the corner from the ranger station, furnishes information and permits for that area. It's open weekdays 8–5 and weekends 8 AM–10 PM (shorter hours in winter).

Backpackers must obtain a wilderness permit before setting out: Call or write the ranger station closest to your destination. You can try to get a permit the day of your trip, but don't count on it—summer is usually booked full. Day-use permits can be obtained on the day of your trip by visiting any of the above ranger stations. Camping permits can also be obtained the same day of your trip by visiting the appropriate ranger station.

There are several developed campgrounds in the San Jacinto District of the San Bernadino National Forest; check with the ranger stations for more information. **Boulder Basin Campground,** 15 mi north of Idyllwild and 14 mi off Hwy. 243 on Black Mountain Road, has 34 sites ($9), half of which are available on a first-come, first-served basis. At an elevation of 7,800 ft, this site is too difficult for trailers to maneuver—all the better for tent campers. **Hike-in camping** is also available; stop by the ranger station for the required free permits and camping suggestions.

COMING AND GOING • The San Jacinto section of the San Bernadino National Forest can be accessed on Hwy. 243 from Banning, Hwy. 74 from Palm Desert, Hwy. 74 from Hemet, and Hwy. 371 from Aguanga. Much of this driving is on winding roads and is slow-going. In winter be sure to carry chains. Snow usually covers the wilderness from December–April.

HIKING • Miles and miles of trails wind through the San Jacinto Wilderness, including plenty to satisfy both the novice and the advanced hiker. Many hikers make the 12-mi ascent to **San Jacinto Peak,** a strenuous, six-hour round-trip beginning at the foot of theLong Valley ranger station. Your reward: to stand astride the summit, queasily admiring the near-vertical drop of the mountain's north face. Acrophobes may feel more at ease on the moderate 5-mi loop to **Long Valley Camp**; the hike begins at the Long Valley ranger station and affords good views of the backcountry. For a shorter trek with breathtaking panoramas, try the **Desert View Trail,** a 1½-mi loop.

CROSS-COUNTRY SKIING • The **Palm Springs Nordic Ski Center** (tel. 760/327–6002), at the top of the Aerial Tramway, is generally open from December to early April. Here you can rent equipment ($7 an hour, $16 a day) to tour adjacent Long Valley, which offers 1 mi of beginners' trails and 80 acres of excellent cross-country terrain. Lessons start at $10 for one hour. Experienced cross-country skiers will want to leave Long Valley to blaze their own trails in the San Jacinto Wilderness. To do this, obtain a free permit at the ranger station next to the tramway.

ANZA-BORREGO DESERT STATE PARK

About 90 mi east of San Diego and 70 mi southwest from Palm Springs lie the 660,000 acres of desert that make up the largest state park in the United States. At first glance, the terrain could be mistaken for a barren moonscape with scraggly, pasted-on brush—until you catch sight of a nimble-footed bighorn grazing on a mountain slope, a jackrabbit nibbling scrub at the foot of your tent, or a hummingbird going about its business in the shade of a palm oasis. The dozens of plant species seem almost indistinguishable until wildflower season in spring (usually from March to mid-April), when multicolored blooms literally carpet the desert floor. Viewing the spring blossoms is one of the most popular activities in the park. For information on the peak blooming period, call or send a stamped, self-addressed postcard to **Wildflowers** (Box 229, Borrego Springs 92005, tel. 760/767–4684). High temperatures (100°F plus) make it tough to enjoy the park in summer, but during the rest of the year this is a popular destination for hikers, fearless four-wheel-drive explorers of the unpaved roads, and, to a lesser degree, mountain bikers.

BASICS

VISITOR INFORMATION

Obtain detailed maps, self-guided trail brochures, and a schedule of park activities at the **Anza-Borrego Visitor Center** (200 Palm Canyon Dr., Borrego Springs 92004, tel. 760/767–4205 or 760/767–5311), 2 mi west of Borrego Springs at the end of Palm Canyon Drive. Rangers post updates on the condition of unpaved roads here daily. The center is open October to May, daily 9–5; summer, weekends only 9–5.

FEES

The day-use fee for Anza-Borrego State Park is $5 per vehicle. New in 1997, a **backcountry camping permit** is required for overnight stays, at a rate of $5 per day per vehicle. During the off-season (May–Oct.) fees are collected on a self-registration basis when you register at one of the developed campgrounds where all facilities, including potable water, are located.

COMING AND GOING

The town of **Borrego Springs** lies at the center of Anza-Borrego on Hwy. S22, which bisects the park. Borrego Springs and Hwy. S22 are accessible from Palm Springs via Hwy. 86, which skirts the brown, malodorous Salton Sea. From San Diego, take Hwy. S22 east from Hwy. 79 or catch a ride on the **Northeast Rural Bus System** (tel. 760/765–0145). Fare is $3.25 each way; service is infrequent and some stops require prior reservation, so be sure to call at least 24 hours in advance. You need a healthy car (four-wheel drive very strongly advised), since most attractions require some travel on graded dirt roads. Throughout the year, the state of the park's unpaved roads varies widely due to washouts and erosion, and during the bighorn sheep's summer mating season some unpaved roads are closed altogether; check road conditions at the visitor center (*see* Basics, *above*).

WHERE TO SLEEP

You'll find a few reasonably priced inns in Borrego Springs; most are booked several weeks in advance during the spring. At the **Oasis Motel** (366 Palm Canyon Dr., Borrego Springs, tel. 760/767–5409, closed July and Aug.), clean rooms with ceiling fans and photos of wildflowers on the wall start at $55 during peak season and $40 during summer. The motel has a swimming pool and Jacuzzi. **Palm Canyon Resort** (221 Palm Canyon Dr., Borrego Springs 92004, tel. 760/767–5341 or 800/242–0044), one of the largest properties around (60 rooms), offers you several options, including RV sites with hookups and TV. Room rates start at $55 in summer and $75 in winter and include use of two pools and an outdoor spa.

CAMPING

The best way to explore this vast park is by camping, either in open terrain or at one of the handful of primitive sites. If you prefer to set up camp at an established campground, head for **Borrego Palm Canyon,** 1 mi north of the visitor center, or **Tamarisk Grove,** near the intersection of Hwys. 78 and S3. These campgrounds have flush toilets, showers, water, and fire rings. Rates for both are $15–$22 during peak season, $10 during summer. Tamarisk has 25 tent/RV sites set among shady trees, while Borrego Palm Canyon offers 65 tent sites and 52 RV hook-ups in open desert. You can also set up camp in the splendid isolation of the backcountry; a permit is required (*see* Fees, *above*).

Before you go, check weather conditions and backcountry regulations with a ranger. The **Mountain Palm Springs** area, in the south part of the park off Hwy. S2, makes an excellent overnight destination: It's a pleasant, uncrowded oasis with dozens of primitive campsites. In the sweltering summer months, check out the half-dozen primitive campsites in **Culp Valley,** west of Borrego Springs on S22; the 3,400-ft elevation may offer some respite from the sun.

FOOD

Eating in Borrego Springs will not be your fondest memory of the desert, but you can at least find a passable and cheap meal here. In the shopping mall west of Christmas Circle on Hwy. S22, **Kendall's Café** (528 The Mall, at Palm Canyon Dr., tel. 760/767–3491) serves hearty Mexican and American fare for less than $10. The local favorite is the tasty, low-fat buffalo burger ($4.95)—made from ground-up bison buttocks. **Chefs for You** (551 The Mall, tel. 760/767–3522) is a delicatessen that has pizzas (vegetarian $11), hot and cold sandwiches ($3–$5), and an assortment of breakfast sandwiches ($2–$3). The **Coffee and Book Store** (590 The Mall, tel. 760/767–5080), open for breakfast and lunch, has a wide variety of sandwiches made to order ($3–$5) and assorted pastries. It also sells a good map of the Anza-Borrego Desert Region ($5) designed by a couple of knowledgeable locals.

EXPLORING ANZA-BORREGO

You'll see rare 10-ft elephant trees with swollen branches on the **Elephant Tree Discovery Trail,** south of Hwy. 78 on Split Mountain Road. The 1-mi loop provides a short and easy hike. To glimpse a palm oasis and, if you're lucky, some bighorn sheep, take the 3-mi round-trip **Borrego Palm Canyon Nature Trail,** which begins at the Borrego Palm campground. More experienced backpackers will enjoy the miles of trail-less canyons and ridges at **Bow Willow Creek** and **Mountain Palm Springs,** both located in the southern sector of the park off Hwy. S2. Off-trail exploration offers the possibility of discovering unmapped Native American petroglyphs and completely isolated oases; rangers at the visitor center can help you plan your trip.

Many mountain-biking enthusiasts count Anza-Borrego's routes among the best in Southern California. Bicyclists are allowed on all of the park's paved and unpaved roads (a total of 500 mi) but not on hiking trails or open ground. Though many unpaved roads are too sandy for cyclists, mountain bikers might try exploring **Indian Gorge,** which branches west of Hwy. S2 about 25 mi south of its intersection with Hwy. 78. The canyon road extends for several miles, but the curious should look for a side canyon 2 mi in and to the north, where a group of elephant trees was discovered in 1987. Blair Valley is a good bet for neophytes as the roads are less sandy and roads lead to excellent trailheads. Pick up the pamphlet "Bicycle Routes: A guide to bicycle riding at Anza-Borrego," available at the visitor's center, for a description of popular trails and their mileage. You can rent mountain bikes in Borrego Springs at **Carrizo Bikes** (648 Palm Canyon Dr., tel. 760/767–3872) or arrange a guided tour. Rental rates are $7 for the first hour, $5 each additional hour, or $29 for a full day.

Anza-Borrego Desert explorers should be aware that this area has been infiltrated by Africanized honey bees. These new immigrants, also called "killer bees," are identical to European honey bees but twice as ornery and less predictable. Rangers will caution you to listen for buzzing, but as any visitor to the desert knows, a half-million things buzz at any given moment. Use common sense and don't camp where you see bees swarming, and don't antagonize them by swatting furiously.

SCENIC DRIVES AND VIEWS

If you have a four-wheel drive and want to catch some breathtaking views of the Borrego Valley and the Borrego Badlands, stop at **Font's Point,** just east of Borrego Springs on a 4-mi dirt road south of Hwy. S22. Nearby is a self-guided auto tour known as **Erosion Road,** which offers views of the corroded landscape along an active fault that runs from 240 ft below sea level to the 8,700-ft Toro Peak. In **Blair Valley,** you can see prehistoric Native American pictographs in red and yellow hues at the end of a 4-mi dirt road off Hwy. S2 (south of Hwy. 78).

LAS VEGAS AND THE GRAND CANYON

13

UPDATED BY DEKE CASTLEMAN AND EDIE JAROLIM

Almost everyone reacts the same way at the first sight of Las Vegas. Shimmering in the distance—even during the day—the city grows brighter as you approach, eventually turning into street after street of flashing electric lights and frantic commotion. You may think it's kitschy, you may think it's corrupt—but suddenly you feel *lucky.* Standing at a roulette wheel in one of the more than 70 casinos, you may find yourself between a fresh-faced bride whose dress still sports a 7-ft train, and an obnoxious drunk in a pin-striped suit jacket and gym shorts. The booze is flowing, and if you feel a bit bewildered and outta control, the casinos have done their job. If you lose all your money, you can always throw yourself into the Grand Canyon, 300 mi to the east. Most of the national park's annual 5 million visitors, though, prefer just looking at its stunning views, countless buttes and pillars, and seemingly bottomless chasms. Both Las Vegas and the Grand Canyon are well within reach of southern California, and a four- or five-day jaunt that takes in the two destinations provides a surreal trip that scales the heights and plumbs the depths. Once you foray into the Southwest, however, it can be hard to turn back to California, since you'll have placed yourself close to a host of enticing destinations, including Bryce Canyon and Zion national parks, Flagstaff, and Lake Mead and Hoover Dam.

LAS VEGAS

Whether they call themselves gamblers, honeymooners, cultural critics, or plain old tourists, more than 30 million people visit Nevada's biggest city each year, making Las Vegas one of the top tourist attractions in the world. Apparently not content with having 9 of the 10 largest hotels on the planet, Las Vegas continues to develop at a dizzying pace: the skyline changes almost daily and a new casino can celebrate its grand opening out front while construction continues in the back. The family-oriented entertainment trend has reached its height—Vegas now has about as many roller coasters, theme parks, and magic shows as it has craps tables—and developers' newest angle is adult-theme casinos for grown-ups who want more glitz and a less day-camp ambience in their vacation. No matter the spin and no matter the facade, Vegas's raison d'être is to get *someone* in the family to empty his or her wallet into a slot machine. Gambling so permeates Nevada culture that you can play slot machines almost anywhere, including the airport, most bars, and even supermarkets. Gambling pays for everything, from the neon signs along Las Vegas Boulevard to

LAS VEGAS

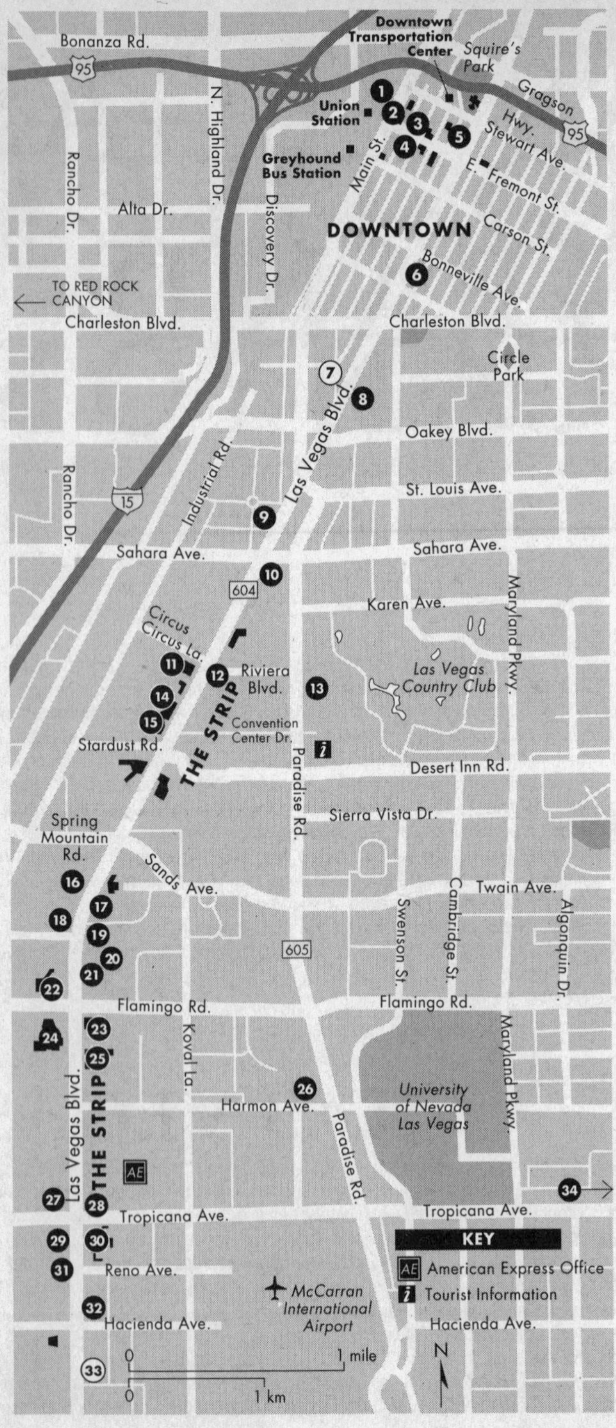

Sights ●

Graceland Wedding Chapel, **6**

Liberace Museum, **34**

Little White Chapel, **8**

Lodging ○

Las Vegas Independent Hostel, **7**

Laughing Jackalope, **33**

Hotel-Casinos ●

Aladdin Hotel, **25**

Bally's, **23**

Bellagio, **24**

Binion's Horseshoe, **3**

Caesars Palace, **22**

Circus Circus, **11**

Excalibur, **29**

Flamingo Hilton, **21**

Golden Nugget, **4**

Gold Spike, **5**

Hard Rock Hotel, **26**

Harrah's, **17**

Imperial Palace, **19**

Klondike, **32**

Las Vegas Club, **2**

Las Vegas Hilton, **13**

Luxor, **31**

MGM Grand, **28**

Mirage, **18**

New York, New York, **27**

O'Shea's, **20**

The Plaza, **1**

Riviera, **12**

Sahara, **10**

Slots A Fun, **14**

Stardust, **15**

Stratosphere Hotel and Casino, **9**

Treasure Island, **16**

Tropicana, **30**

the bicycle-mounted police that patrol it; the astronomical profits ensure some of the lowest state taxes in the country: no personal, corporate, or business income taxes and nominal property taxes.

You need not be discouraged, though, by the statistic that casinos keep about 25¢ of every dollar wagered in a machine and about 15¢ of every dollar risked at the tables. Though it's not a foregone conclusion that you will lose, if you're *willing* to lose all the money you convert into chips, you can have a great time here. You can even make your trip relatively inexpensive by taking advantage of cheap rooms, free drinks while you play, and all-you-can-eat buffets offered by casinos eager to attract your gaming dollars.

Beyond the vagaries of the gaming tables, Las Vegas remains an unparalleled cultural spectacle. This town, where marriages and divorces are a snap, liquor flows all night long, legal bordellos are nearby, and "anything goes," is also the paragon of control and surveillance—security cameras abound in every casino, and both gamblers and dealers are monitored night and day. Once dominated by mobsters and still associated with the shady side of American life, Vegas nonetheless hosts countless trade conventions and national gatherings of Elks and Rotarians. If you tear yourself away from the Strip and downtown, you'll notice a sprawling metropolitan area of more than 1 million people. For many, this is a city characterized by shopping malls and about 300 days of sunny skies every year. Las Vegas is also home to the University of Nevada at Las Vegas, whose high-profile basketball team, the Runnin' Rebels, usually plays to capacity crowds. Yet over in the casinos, their games hardly count: State law prohibits wagering on Nevada teams. Venture even further from the Strip and the spectacles continue: the refreshing natural beauty of Red Rock Canyon is only 25 minutes away, and the man-made wonders of Lake Mead and Hoover Dam are not much further. En route to any of these nearby spots you'll surely pass more than one casino—just in case the bug bites.

Vegas breeds strange attitudes toward money. Minutes after you add $5 to your blackjack wager because you "feel good," you'll pass up a $5 buffet because it's too expensive.

BASICS

VISITOR INFORMATION

"Official tourist centers" offering hotel reservations, bus tours, and show tickets pepper the Strip. These offices are really travel agencies in disguise, making their money off commissions from casinos and motels. Still, their services don't cost you anything, and you can pick up maps, information, and funbooks (full of discount coupons). A reliable source of information is the **Las Vegas Convention/Visitors Authority** (3150 Paradise Rd., in the Convention Center, tel. 702/892–7576), open daily 8–5 (weekdays until 6). There's an **American Express** inside Caesars Palace (3570 Las Vegas Blvd. S, Las Vegas 89109, tel. 702/731–7705) that accepts client mail and cashes cardholders' personal checks; the office is open daily 8–6.

The "Las Vegas Advisor," a monthly newsletter ($5), lists the best deals on everything from seafood buffets to slot tournaments to airport transportation. If you're trying to get by in Las Vegas on a small bankroll, this is your Bible. Copies of the "Advisor" can be purchased by phone weekdays 9–5 (tel. 702/252–0655) or picked up at the **Gambler's Book Shop** (630 S 11th St., tel. 702/382–7555) downtown. Detailed and up-to-date information on shows, buffets, and the casino scene, as well as coupons galore, can be found in weekly magazines like *What's On in Las Vegas* and *Today in Las Vegas,* available free in hotels, gift shops, tourist centers, and newspaper machines.

WHEN TO GO

Though the casinos never close, and there's really no slow season, you may want to time your visit with care. Las Vegas was built in the middle of the desert, and temperatures soar well over the 100°F mark during summer and rarely drop below 50°F even during the coldest days of winter. Summer heat can force you into the climate-controlled casinos more than you can afford, and hotel prices double on weekends and holidays. If you're here for the bargains, don't pull into town on Friday or Saturday.

COMING AND GOING

BY BUS

Buses to destinations throughout the United States leave from the **Greyhound Bus Station** (200 S. Main St., at the Plaza, tel. 702/384–9561 or 800/231–2222 for reservations). Small lockers are available for

$2 per 6 hours. Buses run to and from Los Angeles (7½ hrs, $58 round-trip) and San Francisco (16 hrs, $75 round-trip) several times daily.

BY CAR

Las Vegas sits along **I–15** in southern Nevada. There's a steady flow of traffic on the interstate and on the two other highways that serve the city, **U.S. 93** and **U.S. 95,** which merge near downtown. From Los Angeles (293 mi), take I–10 east and pick up I–15 north near Ontario. From San Francisco (570 mi), take I–580 east to I–5 south, pick up Hwy. 58 at Buttonwillow, and follow it east through Bakersfield and over to Barstow and I–15.

BY PLANE

Slot machines are spread throughout **McCarran International Airport** (5757 Wayne Newton Blvd., at Paradise Rd., tel. 702/261–5743), which is served by all major U.S. carriers. Luggage lockers ($2–$5 per 48 hrs) are available in each terminal. McCarran serves as a hub for **America West** (tel. 800/235–9292), which offers vacation packages that include discounted hotel stays; regular round-trip fares from L.A. are $97 and San Francisco about $131.

The cheapest way to get to the casinos from the airport is on a **Citizens Area Transit (CAT)** bus (*see* Getting Around, *below*). Bus 109 runs to downtown every 15 minutes, and Bus 108 runs every 30 minutes along Paradise Road, which parallels the Strip 1 block east. Fare is $1. Private shuttles cost $3.50–$5. A cab costs $10 to the south Strip and upwards of $20 to downtown. The south end of the Strip is just 1 mi from the airport; head north on Paradise Road and turn left on Tropicana Avenue.

BY TRAIN

Amtrak (tel. 800/872–7245) serves **Union Station** downtown (1 Main St., inside Jackie Gaughan's Plaza, tel. 702/386–6896); the station is open 6:30 AM–7:30 PM. Passengers can check luggage at the station for $1.50 per 24 hours. Trains head west to Los Angeles (6–7 hours) every morning, and trains from Los Angeles to Salt Lake City, Denver, and Chicago pass through Las Vegas in the early evening. When making reservations, ask about "casino fares," which can get you from L.A. to Vegas for as a little as $46 round-trip. Otherwise, round-trip fares from L.A. start at $70 (advance purchase). There is no direct service to Las Vegas from San Francisco, but with a connecting bus in Bakersfield, you can get there for $124 round-trip (15 hrs each way).

GETTING AROUND

Most of the action is concentrated in two parts of town: **the Strip** (a 3-mi stretch of Las Vegas Boulevard South) and **downtown** (centering on Fremont Street, near the bus and train stations). Downtown is easily navigated on foot; it's served by U.S. 95/93 (take the Casino Center exit). Distances between casinos can be considerable on the congested Strip, which is accessible from four well-marked exits off I–15. If you're headed more than a few blocks north–south, try one of the parallel thoroughfares, such as Paradise Road (east of the Strip), Industrial Road, or the interstate (west of the Strip). The major east–west streets are named for the big hotels they pass when they hit the Strip. Parking at nearly all casinos is plentiful and free (though you should tip valets $1–$2 if you use them). As you move about the city, be extra vigilant at night—especially around Fremont Street and the less populated blocks of the Strip, where even the bus stop signs warn of pickpockets.

BY BUS

CAT (tel. 702/228–7433) runs buses from 5:30 AM to 1:30 AM, with 24-hour service between downtown and the Strip. Normal fares are $1, but you pay $1.50 to travel along the Strip (transfers are free). All buses are wheelchair accessible and have bike racks. Most routes originate within walking distance of the major downtown casinos at the **Downtown Transportation Center** (300 N. Casino Center Blvd., at Stewart Ave.), where a customer service center provides maps, schedules, and trip-planning assistance weekdays 6 AM–11 PM and weekends 6–6. Bus 301 (every 10 min) serves the Strip from the downtown station.

BY CAR

While most of the action in Vegas is foot- and bus-accessible, outlying attractions are nearly impossible to get to without a car. What's more, low airfares and car rental rates make Vegas a plausible launch pad for trips to both the north and south rims of the Grand Canyon, each only six hours away by car. **Airport Rent-A-Car** (4990 Paradise Rd., tel. 702/795–0800) rents compacts with unlimited mileage for $27 daily and has free airport pick-up.

WHERE TO SLEEP

During the week, budget rooms are easy to find in small hotels just off the Strip, some of the fancy hotels, chain motels, and at the hostel. Plan ahead if you're arriving on a weekend, or you may face high prices and a round of neon NO VACANCY signs. If you're in a bind, call **Room Reservations** (tel. 800/332–5333), which provides last-minute availability information for hotels around town. The price categories below refer to weekday rates; on weekends, you'll generally pay double. All rooms come with private bath. Rates are lowest in mid-December and early August. Because room rates are so fluid, it's a good idea to ask about special promotions or discounts when making a reservation. Vegas adds an 8% tax on rooms (10% on Fremont Street).

You'll find some good deals at the giant hotel-casinos, where rates are kept low to attract vacationing gamblers. These places have comfortable rooms and sometimes offer special promotions, contingent upon a specific number of hours spent at the tables or on the slots; do the math first, though, since you can sometimes end up staking more cash than you save on the hotel room. Bright-blue **Bally's** (3645 Las Vegas Blvd. S, tel. 702/739–4111 or 800/634–3434) almost always has a decent package deal.

UNDER $35 • Klondike. It's not much to look at, but who's complaining with rooms that start at $29 on weekdays? Among the few "bonuses" at this comfortably run-down hotel-casino are the Olympic-size swimming pool and the low table minimums in the small casino. *5191 Las Vegas Blvd. S, tel. 702/739–9351. 150 rooms.*

Elvis married Priscilla at the Aladdin Hotel (3667 Las Vegas Blvd. S, tel. 800/782–5267) in 1967. Now you can be married by his look-alike mere blocks away.

The Plaza. The rooms are slightly older and less fancy than the imposing edifice might suggest, but spacious singles and doubles run $30 on weekdays most of the year, there's a pool, and the location is great. The hotel is next door to the bus and train stations and is only a couple of blocks from all the downtown casinos. Reserve ahead, and prepare for crowds and lines. *1 Main St., tel. 702/386–2110 or 800/634–6575, fax 702/386–2378. 1,037 rooms.*

UNDER $45 • Binion's Horseshoe. This Western-style hotel-casino was built in 1931 and was bought by Texan Benny Binion in 1947. Doubles in the east wing run $30–$35; newer rooms in the west wing start at $45 on weekdays. The adjoining Binion's Horseshoe Coffee Shop (*see* Food, *below*) offers a cheap Late-Night Steak Dinner. *128 E. Fremont St., between 1st St. and Casino Center Blvd., tel. 702/382–1600 or 800/622–6468, fax 702/384–1574. 80 Eastside rooms, 290 Westside rooms.*

UNDER $50 • Circus Circus. In *Fear and Loathing in Las Vegas,* Hunter S. Thompson took massive doses of psychedelics to help him get through his stay at Circus Circus. With acrobats swinging on trapezes high above hordes of weekend visitors, you might also feel as if you're hallucinating. Everything about the place is immense, including the number of rooms—nearly 4,000. Room rates sink as low as $29 per night (single or double) for a week or two during December but are generally in the $30–$40 range on weekdays and as much as $90 on weekends. *2880 Las Vegas Blvd. S, tel. 702/734–0410 or 800/634–3450, fax 702/734–5897. 3,741 rooms.*

Laughing Jackalope. For a break from the mega-hotels, try this family-run place next to the airport; rates vary wildly, but the lowest are real bargains: Recently remodeled rooms start at $35 ($65 on weekends). There's an English-style pub next door, with 15 draft beers and food available 24 hours daily. *3969 Las Vegas Blvd. S, tel. 702/739–1915, fax 702/736–7852. 34 rooms. Cable TV, key deposit ($2), pool.*

UNDER $65 • Excalibur. This enormous 4,032-room Arthurian castle is the supreme middle-class family resort. The medieval motif is hammered home endlessly, from lavish dinner shows to a Canterbury wedding chapel and regularly scheduled jousting tournaments. The rooms are more polished and modern than those at Circus Circus, and the rates are higher ($39–$59 for a double on weekdays, $74–$84 on weekends). The two hotels, along with **Imperial Palace** (3535 Las Vegas Blvd. S, tel. 702/731–3311 or 800/635–6441), tend to be the lowest priced on the Strip. *3850 Las Vegas Blvd. S, tel. 702/597–7777 or 800/937–7777, fax 702/597–7040. 4,032 rooms.*

HOSTEL

Las Vegas Independent Hostel. This well-managed hostel draws a refreshingly international crowd of backpackers and young travelers. Travelers with any type of hostel membership card save $2 off bed or room prices. Beds go for $14, and a private room for two is $28; this includes free lemonade, coffee, tea, and the use of the pool at the motel next door. *1208 Las Vegas Blvd. S, tel. 702/385–9955. 60 beds. No curfew, no lockout. Reception open 7 AM–11 PM, checkout 10 AM. Kitchen, laundry.*

CAMPING

The only place to pitch a tent within a dice roll of the Strip is at KOA's **Las Vegas Resort** (4315 Boulder Hwy., near Desert Inn Rd., tel. 702/451–5527), which provides a cement pad, two pools, a hot tub, laundry, and a free casino shuttle for $23 nightly. If you prefer starlight to the refracted neon glow of the Strip, drive about 40 minutes to the **Toiyabe National Forest,** where you can camp for free anywhere that's more than 100 ft from an improved road. There are designated campsites with fire pits and tables, but they cost $10. Drop by the ranger station (Hwy. 157, tel. 702/872–5486; open May–Sept.) for information on good free sites and fire regulations. Contact the Las Vegas office of the Toiyabe National Forest (2881 S. Valley View Blvd., Suite 16, tel. 702/873–8800) for conditions during the winter months and for general camping and hiking information. Winter brings snow and cold temperatures; drive-in campsites close, and walk-in camping is not recommended. To reach the forest, take U.S. 95 about 18 mi north and pick up Hwy. 157 west toward Mt. Charleston and Kyle Canyon. After 17 mi, you'll see the ranger station.

FOOD

For most, Vegas dining is synonymous with the all-you-can-eat buffet, an ironic combination of thrift and conspicuous consumption. Most buffets offer a mind-boggling range of items, and the quality may surprise you. You can also find great savings in the casinos' cocktail lounges, snack bars, and regular restaurants (the ones that actually dare to restrict your portions). Check local magazines (*see* Publications, *above*) carefully for coupons, which can save you even more money.

CASINO BUFFETS AND DINNER SPECIALS

Most major casinos offer some sort of buffet, for which you may have to wait. **Circus Circus** (*see* Where to Sleep, *above*) draws lines that resemble those at Disneyland with its $3–$5 buffets. The lines are shorter and the prices slightly lower ($2.50–$5.50) at the **Sahara** buffet (2535 Las Vegas Blvd. S, tel. 702/737–2111).

UNDER $5 • Binion's Horseshoe Coffee Shop—Late-Night Steak Dinner. This is *the* big bargain in a town of big bargains. Hostelers and baccarat players alike head downtown nightly for the $4 meal, which features a tasty 10-ounce steak, salad, a large baked potato, and rolls. Beverages are extra. *128 E. Fremont St., tel. 702/382–1600.*

UNDER $10 • Main Street Station. This is the best all-around buffet downtown. The room is huge and beautifully appointed and the many serving islands dish up everything from Southwestern and Italian food to barbecue and pizza. It'll be hard, but try to save a little room for the luscious desserts. Prices run $5–$9. *100 N. Main St., downtown, tel. 702/387–1896.*

Rio. When it opened in 1993, the Carnival World Buffet elevated the Las Vegas buffet experience to new heights. It introduced the "serving island" concept and set a new standard for a festive and colorful atmosphere. And the buffet's been expanded since! Check out the choices: American, Italian, Chinese, Mexican, Mongolian (grill), steaks, seafood, sushi, teppan, burgers and fries, salads, and Las Vegas's largest selection of sugar-free desserts. To avoid the long lines, go late for breakfast and early for lunch and dinner. Prices run $5–$9. *3700 W. Flamingo Rd., tel. 702/252–7777.*

Texas Station. Vegas's best buffet is at Texas Station in the northwestern suburbs. Here you'll find a Texas chili bar, Chinese food wokked on the spot, fajitas cooked to order, and a root beer float bar, along with steam-table Italian, Mexican, seafood, American, salads, and desserts. But the real stand-outs here are the high-quality ingredients and preparation. Prices are comparable to most other buffets: $5–$9. *2001 El Rancho Blvd., tel. 702/631–1000.*

RESTAURANTS

Though nowhere near as cheap as the buffets, non-casino eateries are a good way to avoid the gaming tables for a while. Vegetarians can take cover at either of two **Wild Oats Community Markets** (6720 W. Sahara, tel. 702/253–7050 or 3455 E. Flamingo, tel. 702/434–8115), health-food superstores with cafés attached that serve sandwiches, salads, smoothies, and hot dishes in the $3–$6 range. For a sit-down meal that's on the Strip (in locale) but off the Strip (in ambience), visit **Battista's Hole in the Wall** (4041 Audrie La., behind the Flamingo Hilton, tel. 702/732–1424), where Italian dinners (from $14) come with all the house wine you can drink.

CAFES

A couple good cafés offer some tranquillity. Only a short walk from the hostel, **Enigma Coffeehouse** (918½ S. 4th St., 1 block north of Charleston Blvd., tel. 702/386–0999) is a neighborly place that showcases local artists and hosts live music on a cool, leafy patio; it also serves nourishing eats in the $3–$5 range. **Cafe Michelle** (1350 E. Flamingo, tel. 702/735–8686), situated in a small strip mall, sports red-and-white-checkered tablecloths and the traditional Cinzano umbrellas above the tables in the plaza outdoors. Omelets, crepes, seafood, and salads are the fare; the Caesar salad is renowned far and wide.

WORTH SEEING

CASINOS

The walls are mirrored, bright lights shine from the ceilings, coins clang everywhere, time and direction are confused, and the exits are hard to locate. Part of the intended effect is to sap your will to gawk and stroll and encourage you to make yourself comfortable at a table or machine. Vegas hotel-casinos, which get more elaborate and extravagant each year, remain the focus of tourist interest even among non-gamblers, and you inevitably have to walk across the casino floor to get to any of the indoor attractions.

The cheapest food on the Strip is served at Holiday Inn Boardwalk (3740 Las Vegas Blvd. S, tel. 702/739–8481): all-you-can-eat spaghetti for $1, 24 hours daily.

THE STRIP • The newest, most dramatic addition to the Vegas skyline is, well, another skyline. At the south end of the Strip **New York, New York** (3790 Las Vegas Blvd. S, tel. 702/740–6969 or 800/693–6763) is a hotel-casino that recreates the Manhattan skyline—including Miss Liberty, the Brooklyn Bridge, and the Empire State—and throws in the Coney Island roller coaster for good measure. Another landmark is the needle-shape observation tower of the **Stratosphere Hotel and Casino** (2000 Las Vegas Blvd. S, tel. 702/380–7777), rising 112 stories above the north end of the Strip. Daring souls can ride the Space Shot ($5), launching themselves up the tower at dizzying speed, or race around the outside of the tower on an elevated roller coaster 100 stories above the ground ($5). The **Flamingo Hilton** (3555 Las Vegas Blvd. S, tel. 702/733–3111 or 800/732–2111) is the house that Bugsy built and has managed to stay open more than 50 years, a rare achievement in Las Vegas. Since the Flamingo was acquired by Hilton in 1970, it's undergone a half dozen expansions and nothing of the original creation remains. When completed in mid-1998, the **Bellagio** (3600 Las Vegas Blvd. S, tel. 702/791–7161) will be the most expensive and luxurious hotel ever built—and room rates will reflect this. The south end of the Strip is dominated by the upper-class **Luxor** (3900 Las Vegas Blvd. S, tel. 702/262–4000), a 30-story bronze pyramid fronted by a 10-story replica of the Sphinx. The emerald green **MGM Grand** (3799 Las Vegas Blvd. S, tel. 702/891–1111), the largest resort hotel-casino in the world, boasts 5,005 rooms and encompasses 112 acres, including its own 33-acre amusement park.

Another newcomer is the **Hard Rock Hotel** (4455 Paradise Rd., tel. 702/693–5000), luring a younger crowd with loud music, Sex Pistols slot machines, and music memorabilia. Check out the chandelier in the entryway—complete with 32 gold saxophones. A portion of the proceeds from some of the slots go to help preserve the rain forests.

You can beam aboard *Star Trek: The Experience* at the **Las Vegas Hilton** (3000 Paradise Rd., tel. 702/732–5111); the attraction features interactive voyages with the Starfleet, virtual reality games, and a Cardassian restaurant and lounge.

"Cultural mainstays" may be the wrong phrase, but the more established casinos on the Strip include **Caesars Palace** (3570 Las Vegas Blvd. S, tel. 702/731–7110), Las Vegas's preeminent theme casino replete with Greco-Roman statuary, centurion doormen, fountains, and the upscale Forum Shops. The opulent **Mirage** (3400 Las Vegas Blvd. S, tel. 702/791–7111) features a 100-ft-high domed rain-forest atrium, habitually sleepy white tigers, and an outdoor volcano that erupts every 15 minutes after dark.

DOWNTOWN • In an effort to compete with the spectacles of the Strip, the major downtown casinos in 1995 unveiled the **Fremont Street Experience,** a multisensory light-and-sound show projected from a 100-ft-high space frame that stretches over Fremont Street from Main Street to Fourth Street. In keeping with the traditional aesthetics of Glitter Gulch, this "experience" consists of 2 million lights and 100 concert-quality speakers. Stray a mere block or two, however, and you'll find that downtown has a sadder, more Western ambience. The fanciest hotel downtown is the **Golden Nugget** (129 E. Fremont St., tel. 702/385–7111), where you'll see a lot of the frenetic big-money gambling portrayed in the movies.

When you've cashed out, you can admire the world's largest gold nugget (a 63-pound chunk found in Australia), stored in a glass case near the hotel lobby.

IMPERIAL PALACE AUTO COLLECTION

On display are more than 200 rare and exotic cars, including Elvis's '76 Cadillac, an experimental car with a Naugahyde exterior, and cars dating back to the 1880s. Look for free-admission coupons in tourist magazines and at the casino entrance. *Imperial Palace, 3535 Las Vegas Blvd. S, tel. 702/731-3311. Admission: $7. Open daily 9:30 AM–11:30 PM.*

LIBERACE MUSEUM

Until his death in 1987, Liberace entertained legions of Las Vegas audiences with some of the purest camp ever concocted. The museum preserves the extravagance, flamboyance, and uninhibited tastelessness that marked the great performer's life. In the main building are his outrageous costumes. The library building houses his family photos and gold albums, and the gallery contains antique pianos and flashy cars from his extensive collection. *1775 E. Tropicana Ave., at Spencer St., tel. 702/798–5595. From downtown, Bus 109 south to Tropicana Ave., then Bus 201 east to Spencer St. Admission: $6.50. Open Mon.–Sat. 10–5, Sun. 1–5.*

WEDDING CHAPELS

In Las Vegas, marriage is more than an institution—it's an industry. Under Nevada law, if you're at least 18 years old and have identification, you can obtain a license at the **Clark County Marriage License Bureau** (200 S. 3rd St., downtown, tel. 702/455–4415) for $35 (cash only). The bureau is open weekdays 8 AM–midnight, weekends 24 hours (i.e., they open 8 AM Friday morning and don't close again until midnight on Sunday). Be aware that on special occasions—like Valentine's Day and New Year's Eve—lines can stretch around the block. Once you've got the license, you're ready for that special ceremony that only happens every once in a while in a person's life. Most chapels are open every day; nearly every casino has one, and there's always "Wedding Chapel Row," on Las Vegas Boulevard South between the Strip and downtown. If you're not ready for a lifelong commitment, there's no harm in merely sitting through a ceremony or two—just ask. The price of a wedding depends on its extravagance ($50 and up). At the **Graceland Wedding Chapel** (619 Las Vegas Blvd. S, near Charleston Ave., tel. 702/474–6655 or 800/824–5732), an Elvis impersonator will perform the ceremony for an extra $120. Michael Jordan and Joan Collins were married (not to each other) at the **Little White Chapel** (1301 Las Vegas Blvd. S, tel. 702/382–5943 or 800/545–8111), where you can also get married in your car at the drive-up wedding window.

GAMBLING

You can have a lot of fun trying to squeeze a few bucks out of the house in Vegas if you adopt the attitude that you're buying entertainment and a chance at an unexpected windfall. In picking a casino, look for low table minimums that will enable you to get cheap entertainment and free alcohol for your money. You get free drinks if you're gambling; just tell the cocktail waitresses what you want when they come by to take your order. A tip of 50¢ to $1 is customary.

Downtown, the cheap casinos cluster within a couple of blocks of one another and the lower minimums attract a younger crowd. At the low-key and low-rent **Gold Spike** (400 E. Ogden Ave., tel. 702/384–8444), penny slots and $2 blackjack tables are the norm, and you won't find yourself intimidated by impatient dealers or high-stakes players. **Jackie Gaughan's Plaza** (1 S. Main St., tel. 702/386–2110) is lively, with lots of low minimums, including penny slots, $2 blackjack, and 25¢ craps, which makes it easy to learn this game without risking the rent money. The most liberal blackjack rules can be found at the **Las Vegas Club** (18 E. Fremont St., tel. 702/385–1664). Feel confident in your gambling abilities before heading to one of the bigger casinos, where you won't find a blackjack table with a minimum lower than $5.

On the Strip, the budget choices are few and far between, although the entertainment value—with people-watching and casino gimmicks—is high. It gets zilch for atmosphere, but **Slots A Fun** (2880 Las Vegas Blvd. S, next to Circus Circus, tel. 702/734–0410) wins the lowest minimums prize. You might also head for **Silver City** (across the street), **O'Shea's** (next to the Flamingo Hilton) or the **Holiday Inn Boardwalk,** three comfortable low-roller joints situated in the middle of the Strip's action. One block east of the Strip, the **Las Vegas Hilton** has the sports book of choice. For nonsmokers, one consideration in selecting a casino is finding an environment you can breathe in. Most casinos have nonsmoking areas, but the **Stardust** (3000 Las Vegas Blvd. S, tel. 702/732–6111 or 800/634–6757), **Harrah's** (3475 Las

Vegas Blvd. S, tel. 702/369–5000 or 800/634–6765) and **Luxor** (*see* Casinos, *above*) seem to be contain the freshest air.

For many visitors, the casino matters less than the game. Some games offer slim shots at major payoffs (slots, roulette, big-six), while others give you better odds but no chance to win much more than you wager (blackjack, baccarat, pai gow). Some games are festive and group-oriented (craps and roulette) while others are more private (video poker). And then there's keno, which has terrible odds but is such a slow-moving game that you can play it while noshing at the buffet. Sports betting is a great value, since the games last a long time and the house edge is minimal. Blackjack (see box, above) remains the game of choice for most people visiting Vegas.

You might find a sympathetic dealer who will discreetly offer tips during the slower hours. Otherwise, most major casinos offer free instruction in all the games through hands-on classes in the casinos or on your TV set. Ask at any casino desk for more information.

CHEAP THRILLS

The best free entertainment on the Strip is the live-action cannon battle between a pirate ship and a British frigate at **Treasure Island** (3300 Las Vegas Blvd. S., tel. 702/894–7111). The show, which always results in the same victor, takes place daily every 90 minutes 4 PM–10 PM, until 11:30 on Fridays and Saturdays. "Funbooks"—available at the casino welcome centers—feature food and drink coupons, discounts on shows, and a couple of bucks of free gaming action. The funbooks at the **Lady Luck** (206 N. 3rd, tel. 702/477–3000) and the **Riviera** (2901 Las Vegas Blvd. S., tel. 702/734–5110) get the highest marks from the local cognoscenti.

The world-famous lights of Las Vegas can be seen from as far away as Death Valley, California. From any distance, the spectacle of nightfall in Vegas—when the sparkle of countless lights follows quickly on the heels of ocher-red sunsets—inspires awe for some, disgust for others, and dollar signs for electric companies. To take in the show, head west on Charleston Boulevard (Hwy. 159) for about 8 mi and pull over somewhere appropriate.

AFTER DARK

Las Vegas is renowned for its elaborate and gaudy stage shows. Ticket prices for headline acts range from $45 to $120, but the small revues (burlesque, celebrity impersonators, dirty dancin') can be seen for as little as $20. Away from the Strip, a hot bar and club scene attracts young people of various cultural predilections.

Drink. The innovative design of this restaurant and club has established it as the hottest nightspot in town. The interior courtyard is enclosed by two stories of adjoining rooms ranging in style from psychedelic to swank, with many incorporating a look of faux dilapidation. At any of the eight bars, your drink comes in your choice of container: jar, bucket, or bottle. The hip, escaped-from-L.A. crowd may even line up outside to gain access to the sounds of a DJ and occasional live acts. Thursday–Saturday arrive before 9 PM to avoid the $5 cover. *200 E. Harmon Ave., at Koval La., tel. 702/796–5519. Closed Mon.*

Gipsy. Of the city's various gay bars, this is the most unpretentious and lively dance spot—drawing a mix of men and women. Doors open at 10 PM, seven nights a week. There's no cover before midnight, $4 thereafter. Right next door, **Angles & Lace** (4633 Paradise Rd., tel. 702/791–0100), is a good spot to pick up a dancing partner for Gipsy. *4605 Paradise Rd., near Naples St., tel. 702/731–1919.*

NEAR LAS VEGAS

RED ROCK CANYON

The natural splendor of Red Rock Canyon, 18 mi west of Las Vegas, might help you forget about your gambling losses for a while. Created by a thrust fault, the striking red sandstone formations afford scenic views and can be explored on any one of several short hikes originating along the 13-mi Loop Drive or from the visitor center. One of the nicer short trails, the Calico Hills Trail follows its namesake—a range of checkerboard-patterned, bright-colored rock formations—for up to 4 mi; the trail parallels the road, so you can hike for as long or as short as you like. Along any trail or road in the area, keep your eyes peeled for wild burros, common to the area. Camping is available for $10 nightly at Oak Creek, which has drinking water and pit toilets but scant shade.

BLACKJACK TIPS

The game favors the dealer; if both you and the dealer bust (i.e., exceed 21), you lose. Still, many people do win money at blackjack, and self-proclaimed experts on the subject are everywhere. If you want to prolong your ride at the table, the following elementary rules may prove useful:

(1) In picking a table, consider rule variations that help the player, like the option of doubling down on any two cards, or the requirement that the dealer stand on "soft" 17 (a hand that includes an ace, which counts as 1 or 11). Even if you don't completely understand them, these rule variations can work to your advantage.

(2) Start with the basics: Since the dealer has to hit (take a card) on any hand 16 or lower, you'll never win with less than 17 unless the dealer busts. Take a hit on any hand below 17 when the dealer shows Ace, K, Q, J, 10, 9, or 8, all of which are unlikely to make the dealer bust. Stand on 12 or higher when the dealer shows a 4, 5, or 6, cards that will cause the dealer to bust more than 40% of the time.

(3) When you "double down," you double your bet and get one additional card. This is the player's chief advantage, so don't ignore this option. Double with 10 against a 9 or lower and with any hand of 11. Rules permitting, double with 9, or with "soft" hands totaling 13–17, against a 4, 5, or 6.

(4) If you are dealt two cards of the same value, you may "split" them, doubling your bet and playing two hands. Never split 5s, 10s, or face cards. Always split 8s or 7s against a dealer's card of equal or lower value. Always split 2s or 3s against a 4, 5, or 6. Always split aces.

(5) Tip (or "toke") the dealers, as they are not unionized, work for lousy wages, and depend upon your generosity. Unless you're winning serious stakes, a dollar chip every 20 or so hands is generally appropriate. If you want to make sure the dealer has your best interests at heart, place the tip right in front of your wagering circle, essentially turning it into a side bet on your hand. If you win, the dealer's tip doubles.

To get to Red Rock Canyon, take Charleston Boulevard (Hwy. 159) west and follow signs. The **visitor center** (tel. 702/363–1921 or 702/363–1922), is open daily and is loaded with hiking tips. Unfortunately, public transit is nonexistent; Bus 206 travels west out Charleston Boulevard from the intersection with Las Vegas Boulevard South but stops about 10 mi short of the park; a popular option in the cooler months is to travel the rest of the distance via bicycle, taking advantage of CAT's free bike racks.

LAKE MEAD AND HOOVER DAM

Fittingly for Las Vegas, a completely man-made environment in the middle of the desert, the nearest water-sport paradise is also artificial—110-mi-long Lake Mead, created by the construction of the Hoover Dam (U.S. 93, 7 mi east of Boulder City, tel. 702/293–8391). This Depression-era public works project is considered to be one of the great artificial wonders of the world. At its tallest, Hoover Dam is 70 stories high; at its widest, it equals the length of two football fields. Spanning the mouth of Black Canyon, the 1,244-ft-long dam successfully regulates the flow of the Colorado River in its intermittent periods of flooding and drought. Admission to the dam is $5 (includes parking), and there are tours Memorial Day–Labor Day, daily 8:30–6:30; off-season, daily 9–5.

You may want to begin your visit to the lake at the **Lake Mead National Recreation Area Visitor Center** (U.S. 93, at Hwy. 166 4 mi east of Boulder City, tel. 702/293–8906), which has maps, brochures, and information on boating and camping. The center is open daily 8:30–5 in summer, 8:30–4:30 in winter. All developed Lake Mead campsites cost $10 a night; primitive camping is plentiful and free—ask at the visitor center for tips on good spots. Campers seeking solitude might want to ignore large, developed **Boulder Beach,** 2 mi from the visitor center, and head to **Echo Bay,** with good camping and the best beach on the Nevada side of the lake. To get there, go straight on Hwy. 166, which becomes Lake Shore Scenic Drive, make a right on Northshore Road, and follow signs for 45 mi. **BC Water Sports** (1108 Nevada Hwy., just west of Buchanan Blvd. stoplight in Boulder City, tel. 702/293–5201 or 702/293–7526) will rent you a canoe or kayak for serious lake exploration for $25 daily. You'll have no problem finding a quiet, sandy beach for camping and swimming (in summer, the water gets close to 80°F). Several rough access roads lead to the water off Northshore Road (Hwy. 167). **Crawdad Cove** and **Ridge Road** are the nearest (unofficial) gay, lesbian, and nude beaches.

The lake is less than an hour's drive south of Vegas on U.S. 93. There is no public transit to the dam or lake from Las Vegas, but **Cactus Jack's Wild West Tours** (2217 Paradise Rd., tel. 702/731–9400) has $12, five-hour tours of Hoover Dam that originate in Vegas. **Lake Mead Cruises** (707 Wells Rd., Boulder City, tel. 702/293–6180) ferries you right up to the foot of Hoover Dam. The 90-minute cruise ($14.50) lets you see up close the amazing contrast between the lake and the surrounding desert terrain. Tours leave four times daily (twice daily in winter); reservations are advised.

GRAND CANYON

Native Americans inhabiting the Grand Canyon and the surrounding Kaibab Plateau have likened this breathtaking chasm to a "mountain lying upside down." It's a striking comparison. The enormous park covers 1,900 square mi, and the "big crack" itself averages 1 mi deep and 10 mi wide. A considerable chunk of the vast, largely unexplored canyon is inaccessible to travelers, while the tourist centers on the North and South rims are connected only by a circuitous 210-mi road. The canyon is especially grand in the morning and at dusk, when the sun's rays create a dazzling display of changing colors and patterns on the rock.

The canyon itself is 5 million years old, and the Colorado River's ongoing fantastic erosions have exposed rock dating back billions of years. The oldest human artifacts found within the canyon are animal-shape figurines and arrowheads about 4,000 years old, but little is known about the people who made them. The ancestral Pueblo people, who populated the region 1,500 years ago, are the earliest known group to dwell in the area around the canyon; only a few of their artifacts and cliff drawings remain in the canyon today. However, the Hopi, Havasupai, Navajo, Hualapai, and the southern Paiute continue to inhabit much of the canyon and its surroundings.

The first Europeans came this way in the 16th century, when Spanish explorer Francisco Vázquez de Coronado forged north in search of the fabled Seven Cities of Cíbola. After a stubborn four-day attempt to find a crossing, the expedition gave up, finally admitting "it must be as wide as the Indians had said." Few visited the canyon again for some 300 years, until Major John Wesley Powell boated 1,000 mi down the dangerous Colorado in 1869. The true tourism boom began in 1901, when the Santa Fe Railroad link to the South Rim from Williams, Arizona, shortened the trip from 11 hours by horse to 3 hours.

You can take the train from Williams, but most people today arrive by car or plane. Once you've arrived, you can hike into the canyon on several trails, maintained or rough, and camp on the canyon floor or

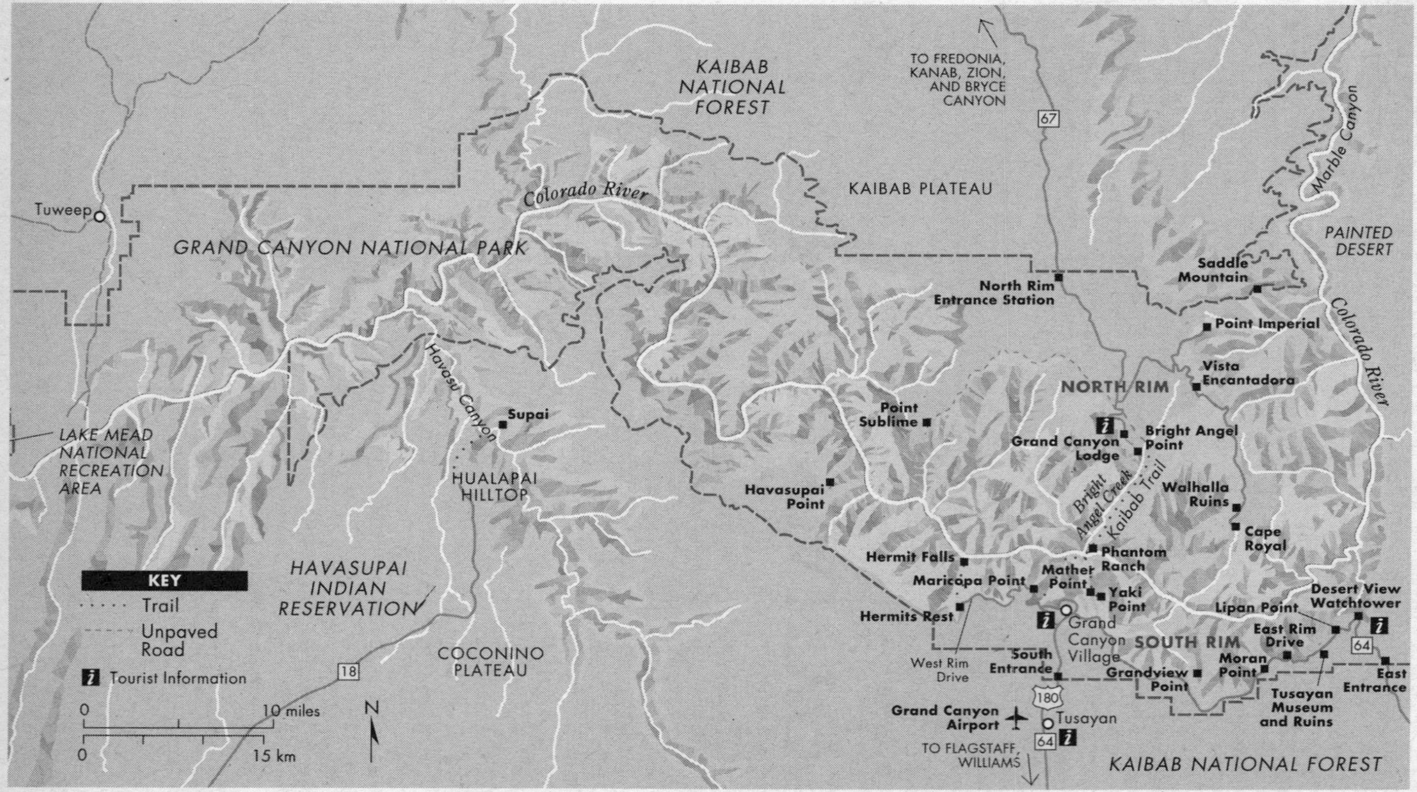

GRAND CANYON NATIONAL PARK

KAIBAB NATIONAL FOREST
TO FREDONIA, KANAB, ZION, AND BRYCE CANYON
67
KAIBAB PLATEAU
Colorado River
Tuweep
GRAND CANYON NATIONAL PARK
PAINTED DESERT
Marble Canyon
Saddle Mountain
North Rim Entrance Station
Point Imperial
Vista Encantadora
NORTH RIM
Point Sublime
Supai
Havasu Canyon
LAKE MEAD NATIONAL RECREATION AREA
HUALAPAI HILLTOP
Grand Canyon Lodge
Bright Angel Point
Bright Angel Creek
Kaibab Trail
Havasupai Point
Walhalla Ruins
Cape Royal
Hermit Falls
Phantom Ranch
Maricopa Point
Mather Point
Yaki Point
Hermits Rest
Desert View Watchtower
Lipan Point
Grand Canyon Village
SOUTH RIM
East Rim Drive
HAVASUPAI INDIAN RESERVATION
COCONINO PLATEAU
West Rim Drive
South Entrance
Grandview Point
Moran Point
Tusayan Museum and Ruins
East Entrance
64
180
18
Grand Canyon Airport
Tusayan
TO FLAGSTAFF, WILLIAMS
KAIBAB NATIONAL FOREST

KEY
Trail
Unpaved Road
Tourist Information

0 10 miles
0 15 km
N

along the rim. For the best perspectives from above and below, there are scenic air tours and Colorado River rafting trips, most of which originate in nearby towns and require a moderate to frightening outlay of cash. Finally, there's the possibility of riding a pack animal into the canyon—for about $100.

BASICS

Arizona is in the Mountain Standard Time Zone but does not observe Daylight Savings Time. This means that Grand Canyon National Park is on the same time as California in April through October but an hour ahead during winter. However, Utah and the Navajo Indian Reservation do recognize Daylight Savings Time, so these areas are always an hour ahead of California time.

VISITOR INFORMATION

For general information, maps, brochures, and trip planning guides, contact **Grand Canyon National Park Visitor Services** (Box 129, Grand Canyon, AZ 86023, tel. 520/638–7888 for recorded information). The **visitor center** (tel. 520/638–7771) in Grand Canyon Village, 6 mi north of the South Entrance Station, is open daily November–February, 8–5; March–October, 8–6. The **Desert View Information Center** (tel. 520/638–7893), near Desert View Watchtower at the East Entrance, offers similar services from March to October 9–5 (closed the rest of the year). Tips on North Rim services and activities are available at the **visitor center** adjacent to the Grand Canyon Lodge (tel. 520/638–7864); it's staffed daily from mid-May through mid-October, 8–5.

The average visitor to Grand Canyon spends only 17 minutes actually looking at the chasm. The rest of the time is spent eating and shopping.

For more detailed information on South Rim lodging, restaurants, rafting trips, and scenic flights, try the **Grand Canyon Chamber of Commerce** (Hwy. 64, in IMAX Theater, Tusayan, tel. 520/638–2901). The office, 2 mi south of the South Entrance Station, is open daily March–October, 9–5; November–February, 9–7. For similar information about the North Rim, contact the **Kane County Travel Council** (78 S. 100 E, Kanab, UT 84741, tel. 800/733–5263), open summer, daily 8–6, and winter, daily 8–5.

FEES

There's a $20 entrance fee for each car, good for seven days (bus passengers, hikers, and bikers pay only $10). The Grand Canyon Pass ($40) allows you to come and go as you please all year long. Travelers with disabilities can pick up a free Golden Access Passport at the South Rim visitor center.

WHEN AND WHERE TO GO

All but 400,000 of the 5 million annual visitors head for the South Rim, which turns into a giant RV park during the hot, dusty summers. During these months you'll have a better chance at solitude and serenity at either the East or North Rim, both of which are less accessible and have fewer, though comparable, tourist services. The geology and vistas of the East Rim closely resemble what you'll see from the South Rim, and the entrance is accessible from both the South Rim and Flagstaff. The North Rim, by contrast, lies a thousand feet higher than the South Rim and has a more alpine climate, with twice as much annual precipitation. Due to severe winters all North Rim facilities close between October 15 and May 15; that side of the park itself stays open for day use from October 15 through December 1, if heavy snows don't close the roads before then.

The South Rim's rainiest months are July–September. Spring and fall, when the weather is mild and the crowds aren't so heavy, are the best times to visit the South Rim. Even though this part of the canyon is at a lower elevation, it still suffers wet, cold winters. Don't let snow on the rim stop you from hiking down to the canyon floor, though; even when there's a blizzard up top, it may be just drizzling below.

PUBLICATIONS

Grand Canyon Guide is published in two editions, one for the North Rim and the other for the South. The guides tell you all you need to know about park activities, regulations, facilities, and ranger programs. Pick up free copies at any visitor center or at the information desk of any north or south rim lodge. Disabled visitors should request the free, slightly outdated, **Accessibility Guide** available at the same locations. For the "all-you-ever-needed-to-know" angle, rangers recommend *The Official Guide to Hiking the Grand Canyon,* by Scott Thybony. For a free catalog of all maps, trail guides, and other publications, contact the **Grand Canyon Association** (Box 399, Grand Canyon, AZ 86023, tel. 520/638–2481 or 800/858–2808, fax 520/638–2484).

GENERAL STORES

Babbitt's General Store (tel. 520/638–2262), in the Mather Business Center at Grand Canyon Village, has groceries, camping supplies, and equipment rentals. The in-store deli sells hot and cold sandwiches (about $3) and other picnic edibles. Other locations are in Tusayan (Hwy. 64, tel. 520/638–2854) and Desert View (near the East Entrance, tel. 520/638–2393); neither has rentals. You'll get a wider selection and more competitive prices in Flagstaff (*see* Near the Grand Canyon, *below*).

On the North Rim, the **Camper Store** (North Rim Campground, tel. 520/638–2611, ext. 270) has groceries, camping supplies, and a small snack bar serving pizza and sandwiches (under $5). It's open from mid-May to October. Five mi north of the park boundary, the **Country Store and Gas Station** (across Hwy. 67 from Kaibab Lodge, tel. 520/638–2383) carries groceries, automotive supplies, and camping and backpacking equipment when the North Rim is open.

COMING AND GOING

The routes to the North, East, and South rims are very different thanks to one small obstacle—namely, the Grand Canyon. South or East Rim visitors may want to use Flagstaff or Williams as a base camp; the nearest large city to the North Rim is Las Vegas, and smaller towns include St. George and Kanab, in Utah, and Fredonia, Arizona. There are more options for getting to the South Rim and more people using them. In contrast, the North Rim is only easily accessible by car, unless you care for an almost five-hour shuttle ride from the South Rim (*see below*) or an even longer shuttle from the hostel in Las Vegas.

BY BUS

There is no direct public transit into the park and no public transit to speak of to the East Rim. **Nava-Hopi Tours, Inc.** (114 W. U.S. 66, at Beaver St., Flagstaff, tel. 520/774–5003 or 800/892–8687) provides round-trip service between Flagstaff and the South Rim for $25 and to Williams for $14 round-trip (Apr.–Oct. only). Call to arrange morning pick-ups from the bus or train station or from motels in Flagstaff. The **Downtowner** hostel (*see* Where to Sleep, *below*) offers a shuttle to the South Rim in high season; the **Du Beau** (*see* Where to Sleep, *below*) also transports guests and nonguests to the grand Canyon. **Greyhound** (tel. 800/231–2222 for reservations) can get you to Flagstaff (*see* Near the Grand Canyon, *below*) from L.A. for about $100.

When the North Rim is open, **Trans Canyon Shuttle** (tel. 520/638–2820) links it to the South Rim (4½ hrs, $60 one-way, $100 round-trip). There's one round-trip daily that leaves the North Rim's Grand Canyon Lodge at 7 AM and the South Rim's Bright Angel Lodge at 1 PM. Reservations by phone or in person at either lodges' transportation desk are required. This service is used mainly by hikers making the 24-mi rim-to-river-to-rim trek. The **Las Vegas Independent Hostel** (*see* Where to Sleep *in* Las Vegas, *above*) also leads three-day bus tours of the Grand Canyon as well as Bryce and Zion national parks.

BY CAR

The **South Rim** is almost exactly 500 mi from Los Angeles. From either Southern or Northern California, take I–40 east from Barstow to Williams, Arizona (322 mi). From Williams, head north 60 mi on Hwy. 64. If you're arriving from the east, take I–40 to Flagstaff, Arizona, and then head north on Hwy. 180. To access the park via the **East Rim** Entrance, take Hwy. 89 from I–40 at Flagstaff, and hang a left in Cameron on Hwy. 64, which leads past the Little Colorado River Gorge to the East Rim.

To reach the **North Rim** from either Southern or Northern California, take I–15 east through Barstow and Las Vegas to southern Utah (about 350 mi from L.A.). Fifteen mi north of St. George, Utah, leave the interstate for scenic Hwy. 9, which runs east through the spectacular Zion National Park. About 50 mi later, Hwy. 9 intersects Hwy. ALT89, which you follow south 54 mi through Kanab, Utah, and Fredonia, Arizona, to Jacob Lake, Arizona. From there, Hwy. 67 (closed in winter) takes you directly to the North Rim.

BY PLANE

The **Grand Canyon National Park Airport** (near Tusayan, 4 mi south of park entrance, tel. 520/638–2446) is served from Las Vegas only by small commuter airlines, some of which also offer air tours of the canyon (*see* Park Activities, *below*). **Eagle Canyon** (tel. 800/446–4584) occasionally has round-trip fares as low as $140, though they more often go for around $200. On **Air Nevada** (tel. 702/736–8900 or 800/634–6377), one-ways run $59 and $109, depending on the flight; it's $159 round-trip on any combination of flights if you book ahead and stay overnight. **Scenic Airlines** (tel. 800/535–4448) charges $115 round-trip if you stay overnight, $202 if you want to come back the same day. **Air Vegas** (tel. 702/736–3599) flights cost only $29 each way if you're willing to go standby; it'll be $85 each way if you're the book-ahead type.

From the Grand Canyon airport, you can catch the **Grand Canyon–Tusayan Shuttle** (tel. 520/638–0821), which departs every hour and a quarter from 9 AM–5:45 PM for stops in Tusayan and Grand Canyon Village. All-day fare is $7. Nava-Hopi tours (*see above*) will also pick you up at the airport. Those who prefer to drive can rent economy cars from **Budget** (tel. 520/638–9360), located at the airport, for about $41 a day.

BY TRAIN

Amtrak (1 E. Rte. 66, at Leroux Ave., tel. 520/774–8679 or 800/872–7245 for reservations) makes daily stops in Flagstaff (*see* Near the Grand Canyon, *below*) where you can catch a bus to Williams or the South Rim (*see above*). The touristy **Grand Canyon Railway** (233 N. Grand Canyon Blvd., tel. 800/843–8723) winds its way across the mostly flat Colorado Plateau to the historic log depot in Grand Canyon Village. Passengers ride in an early-20th-century restored train, just as most travelers did before the automobile took over. Round-trip departure and arrival schedules allow little time to enjoy the sights at the canyon if you don't stay overnight; fares include park entrance fee and are $60 round-trip and $49 one-way. Reservations are advised.

GETTING AROUND

The **East Rim** has hassle-free driving and parking, but on the **South Rim,** village roads are crowded and parking spots are in short supply. Take advantage of the numerous free or low-cost shuttles that tool around the area April through October. The free **Village Loop** shuttle operates daily 6:30 AM–9:45 PM, stopping at the visitor center and other village facilities at 15-minute intervals—look for the blue signs designating shuttle stops. The **West Rim Loop** shuttle, also free, begins service at the West Rim interchange and continues to Hermits Rest (*see* Scenic Drives, *below*). Brown signs designate shuttle stops. A **hiker's shuttle** (round-trip $3) connects several points on the South Rim (Bright Angel Lodge, Maswik Lodge, the Backcountry Office) with the South Kaibab trailhead near the Yaki Barn. There are several daily; times depend on the season. Look for schedule information at pickup points or in the *Grand Canyon Guide*. On the **North Rim,** a **hiker's shuttle** travels between Grand Canyon Lodge and the North Kaibab trailhead daily between 6 AM and 8 PM. Purchase tickets ($5; $2 for each additional person) at the lodge's front desk.

WHERE TO SLEEP

Hotels are expensive and are usually booked months in advance. Contact **Amfac Parks and Resorts** (14001 E. Iliff, Aurora, CO, 80014, tel. 303/297–2757) about reservations for all park accommodations. It's possible to pick up a room because of a canceled reservation, but don't count on it. For short-term or same-day reservations at any North or South Rim lodge, either call the lodge directly—the park's main switchboard can connect you—or go to the lodge and inquire at the front desk. A word to the wise regarding park campgrounds: Arrive at your site before noon if you have not reserved in advance. To find truly budget lodging outside the park, bypass Tusayan and Valle and head for Flagstaff (*see* Near the Grand Canyon, *below*) or Williams, 56 mi south of the park, at the junction of I-40 and Hwy. 64. The friendly **Downtowner** (201 E. Bill Williams Ave., tel. 520/635–4041) consistently keeps its rates a few dollars below those of its neighbors and offers all kinds of discounts; dark but clean doubles go for $30–$45 in summer and plummet in price in winter.

SOUTH AND EAST RIMS

The most reasonably priced options within the park's South Rim are **Maswik Lodge** and the rustic **Bright Angel Lodge,** situated right on the rim. At Maswik, cabins are $59 and rooms start at $72. At Bright Angel, rooms with shared bath start at $38, and the knotty-pine cabins ($62) can sleep two or more; extra people pay $7–$9 each.

Phantom Ranch (tel. 303/297–2757) at Bright Angel Creek, accessible by mule or on foot (*see* Longer Hikes *and* Park Activities, *below*), has the only non-camping accommodations below the rim. Cozy cabins for two ($56) are usually filled up by mule riders; if they're available they can actually sleep 4–10; extra guests pay $11 each per night. Another option is single-sex dorm beds ($21). You can either haul your cookstove and supplies down the trail or reserve a meal in the canteen (breakfast $12, dinners $17–$28, box lunch $5.80). The food may be pricey, but it's good all-you-can-eat grub. Reservations are required and rooms are often booked almost a year in advance; the Bright Angel Lodge transportation desk (tel. 520/638–2383) resells Phantom Ranch cancellations (usually for the next two to four nights).

HOSTELS • Grey Hills Inn and Hostel. This spot lies between the South and North rims, on the Navajo reservation 60 mi east of the Grand Canyon—in a high school. Spotless, motel-style doubles with shared bath cost $24 per person for HI members. Nonmembers pay $47.50 and up for a double. The only drawback: you may have a tough time finding this place at night. *Box 160, Tuba City, AZ 86045, tel. 520/283–6271, ext.141. From U.S. 89, U.S. 160 east 10 mi to Tuba City, left on Warrior Dr. 62 beds. Reception open 24 hrs. Laundry.*

Red Lake Hostel. Only 43 mi south of the South Rim Entrance Station, this is the closest hostel to the Grand Canyon. Bare-bones dorm beds go for $11 in summer and $8 winters; a private double is $33. Showers are coin-operated, since the whole community has to have its water hauled in from a distance. *Hwy. 64, 8 mi north of Williams, tel. 520/635–9122 or 800/581–4753 for reservations only, fax 520/635–5321. 35 beds. Reception open 5:30 AM–10 PM; shorter hours winter. Laundry.*

CAMPING ABOVE THE RIM • At **Mather Campground,** conveniently located in Grand Canyon Village just south of the visitor center, towering pine trees disguise the fact that this 320-site tent city is within spitting distance of the business center's tourist mega-throngs. It's also an easy walk to the rim of the canyon. Sites ($12 Sept.–May, $15 June–Aug.) have toilets and drinking water. From March to November, you must reserve through Destinet (tel. 800/365–2267) up to five months in advance; in winter it's first-come, first-served. Near the East Entrance Station, the first-come, first-served **Desert View Campground** (tel. 520/638–7893) operates from mid-May to mid-October and has drinking water and toilets. The 50 sites seem shoehorned in, but if you take a short hike past the community campfire, you'll be rewarded with an incredible view of the canyon. Sites go for $10; no RVs over 40 ft are allowed.

The U.S. Forest Service maintains the **Ten-X Campground** in the enchantingly secluded Kaibab National Forest, 3 mi south of Tusayan off Hwy. 180. Yet to be discovered by the mobs, the 70 first-come, first-served sites ($10) fill up quickly in summer; the sites (open May–Sept.) have picnic tables, water, and toilets. Dispersed camping is available in the forest (*see* Camping *in* Chapter 1)—there's no fee and no permit is required. The basic rule is that you can pitch a tent or toss down a sleeping bag anywhere at least ¼ mi from a paved road. With a little help from a ranger at **Tusayan Ranger District** (Hwy. 64, about 3 mi north of Tusayan, tel. 520/638–2443), you can probably camp for free within 10 mi of the South Rim and 5 mi of the East Rim.

CAMPING BELOW THE RIM • To protect the inner canyon from overuse, backcountry camping is restricted. Anyone wishing to stay overnight at developed or primitive campsites below the rim must first get a $20 permit from the **Backcountry Office** (Box 129, Grand Canyon, AZ 86023), ¼ mi south of the visitor center near Mather Campground, and then pay a $4 per night impact fee. If you're planning to come often, consider the $50 frequent-hiker membership. Permit requests are taken no more than five months in advance, by mail or in person only. Rangers are available to field questions by telephone (tel. 520/638–7575) weekdays 1–5. Request the free ***Backcountry Trip Planner,*** an invaluable introduction to the permit procedure and the trails, with tips on pre-trip preparations. Though competition for reservations is fierce, it's still possible to obtain one of the few permits set aside for those without reservations by putting your name on the in-person waiting list. The first-come, first-served permits are issued every morning at 8 am. In summer it usually takes two or more days to reach the top of the list. Persistence is key.

Once you get the permit, you can camp inside the rim at **Bright Angel, Indian Gardens,** or **Cottonwood,** which have drinking water, chemical toilets, and emergency telephones. Indian Gardens (the closest developed campground but still a 4½-mi hike) and Cottonwood both have about 15 sites in canyon oases that stay green year-round. Bright Angel's 31 sites, next to Phantom Ranch along the Colorado River, offer few trees, but you can splash around in Bright Angel Creek. Reserve ahead (tel. 303/297–2757) and you can dine at nearby Phantom Ranch (*see* Where to Sleep, *above*). A number of more primitive, less crowded sites are located along unmaintained trails. **Horseshoe Mesa,** at the end of Grandview Trail, has great views but only pit toilets and no water. **Hermit Creek** and **Hermit Rapids** are designated camping areas along Hermit Trail. They offer pit toilets, water at year-round creeks (remember to purify), and shade in the form of cottonwood trees. For directions to these sites, *see* Longer Hikes, *below.*

NORTH RIM

The only North Rim hotel accommodations within the park are at the **Grand Canyon Lodge** (tel. 520/638–2611), which has 125 rim-side cabins and 38 motel units. Cabins that sleep two start at $59;

unexciting motel-style units start at $72. The lodge is open mid-May through mid-October and tends to book up three to four months in advance. For same-day reservations, ask at the registration desk at random times throughout the day in the hope that someone has canceled.

Travelers on a tight budget have to trek 74 mi from the North Rim to the Fredonia–Kanab area, two nearly identical towns straddling the Arizona–Utah border. The cheapest of the lodging lot is the **Blue Sage Motel** (330 S. Main St., on Hwy. ALT89, Fredonia, tel. 520/643–7125): standard doubles go for $30–$35 in summer, $5 less in winter. The cheapest kitchenette rooms in the area are to be found at **Sun-N-Sand Motel** (Jct. Hwys. 89 and ALT89, Kanab, tel. 520/644–5050 or 800/654–1868): $44 for one double bed, stove, and fridge.

HOSTELS • The **Grey Hills Inn and Hostel** lies between the South and North rims, on the Navajo reservation 60 mi east of the Grand Canyon's East Rim (*see* Where to Sleep *in* the South Rim, *above*). Otherwise, the **Canyonlands International Hostel** is the closest and cheapest place to stay. It has an extensive travel center and free buffet breakfast, coffee, tea, and lemonade; unfortunately there are no locks on the doors. The hostel costs $9 per night and has 36 beds; reservations are advised. *143 E. 100 S, Kanab, tel. 801/644–5554. 2 blocks north of stoplight. Reception open 7 AM–midnight. Kitchen, laundry.*

CAMPING ABOVE THE RIM • The sites at **North Rim Campground** are interspersed between stands of tall pine trees. The ground is adorned with pine cones, and layers of pine needles make your bed soft and altogether pleasant. Showers, a laundromat, and a general store are nearby. The 83 sites ($12) are open mid-May to mid-October. Since this is the only North Rim campground inside the park, it fills up fast; be sure to make reservations at least two weeks in advance through Destinet (tel. 800/365–2267). Your only alternative is to join the near-futile waiting list; sign up before 10 AM at the camp's registration kiosk.

Unlike on the South Rim, backcountry camping is allowed—with permit—along the piney trails above the rim on the north side, including the Widforss and Uncle Jim Point trails. Even better, a limited number of primitive campsites are available free of charge at the very edge of the canyon, near **Tuweep Ranger Station.** The route to this remote region of the national park is circuitous, to say the least, and involves a bouncy 55-mi dirt road trek from Fredonia; ask backcountry rangers for details about the location and quality of the road. Once you navigate the route, however, it's just you and a tent teetering on the edge of the grandest of canyons.

The U.S. Forest Service maintains two campgrounds in the **Kaibab National Forest,** which stretches for miles on either side of Hwy. 67, between Hwy. ALT89 and the North Rim Entrance Station. Stop by the **visitor center** (junction Hwys. ALT89 and 67, 30 mi north of entrance station, tel. 520/643–7298) in Jacob Lake for tips on forest activities and camping. The area closes from mid-October to mid-May due to snow. At **Jacob Lake Campground** (open mid-May to the end of October), near the visitor center, be prepared for the occasional roar of the adjacent highway, visible from many of the 56 first-come, first-served sites ($10). Gas, food, firewood ($5), and groceries are available. Closer to the park entrance on a rutted dirt road, **DeMotte Park Campground** is near a lush green meadow, 5 mi north of the North Rim Entrance Station off Hwy. 67. The 23 tent sites, with drinking water and pit toilets, go for $10 per night on a first-come, first-served basis. Pick up supplies at the nearby Country Store and Gas Station (*see* General Stores, *above*).

Dispersed camping is available in the forest free of charge from May through mid-October. Stop by the information center (*see above*) for current information and a look at the list of regulations. Then pull off on one of the dozens of dirt fire trails that branch off the highway and pitch your tent. There's no registration and no facilities. Some basic rules: Camp at least ¼ mi away from any paved road or water source and use existing fire rings whenever possible. There are a number of primitive camp sites scattered throughout the forest as well; ask at the visitor center about the location of secluded and panoramic **East Rim View.**

CAMPING BELOW THE RIM • Hikers spending the night below the rim must first obtain a $20 permit from the **North Rim Backcountry Reservations Office** at the North Rim Ranger Station ½-mi north of Grand Canyon Lodge; after that, there's a $4 person nightly impact fee. The same restrictions apply as for the South Rim (*see above*). The North Rim BRO is open daily 8 AM–noon and 1–5. The major backcountry campgrounds—**Bright Angel, Indian Gardens,** and **Cottonwood**—are accessible via both the North and South rims (for directions, see Longer Hikes, *below*); the closest one to the North Rim is Cottonwood, 7 mi down along the North Kaibab Trail.

ENVIRONMENTAL ALERT

In the last 30 years, the Grand Canyon has become less grand and more grimy. A nearby generating station belches 10 tons of sulfur dioxide into the air hourly, some 80,000 annual "flightseeing" tours add noise and air pollution, and Glen Canyon Dam's control of river flow has washed out beaches and turned the once ice-green river a murky brown color. The number of flights has finally been limited; there's talk of installing a light-rail system and prohibiting cars at the South Rim altogether; and 1996's artificial flood restored many beaches and cleared out accumulated debris, creating new breeding grounds for the river's endangered fish species. But it may be too little too late. The canyon needs more than an annual "spring cleaning" if it will be attractive and available to hikers of the 21st century. In the words of Theodore Roosevelt, "Leave (the canyon) as it is. You cannot improve upon it. The ages have been at work on it and man can only mar it."

FOOD

The Canyon's best cheap eats will cost you blood, sweat, and tears—they lie at the end of the long hike to Phantom Ranch (*see* Where to Sleep, *above*) and must be reserved ahead. Anywhere else, expect an all-American menu of hamburgers, soups, sandwiches, and salads, served with a dollop of grease and a grin.

SOUTH RIM

You wouldn't expect hunting lodge food—like that served at **El Tovar (Hotel) Dining Room**—to compete with canyon views, but this would be a really good restaurant regardless of its location. Dinners are pricey (entrées run as high as $24.75), but pastas at $14.75 are worth a splurge. Stop at the **Bright Angel Fountain,** open in summer in the Bright Angel Lodge, for ice cream and sandwiches (about $3). You can eat your Canyon Crunch ice cream while sitting on the terraced patio overlooking the canyon. The **Maswik Cafeteria,** in the Maswik Lodge (at the Village's west end), **Hermits Rest Snack Bar,** and the **Yavapai Cafeteria,** in the Yavapai Lodge across the road from the visitor center, offer the same cafeteria-style food at the same prices ($3–$7). The central switchboard can connect you to all these eateries—tel. 520/638–3631.

NORTH RIM

Maybe it's the higher altitude, but food at the North Rim just tastes better. The **Grand Canyon Lodge Dining Room** (tel. 520/638–2611, ext. 160) serves such delicacies as fillet of Utah red trout ($13), but you could eat tuna straight from the can and still be happy in this impressive room with rock walls, cathedral ceilings, and sweeping views. Lunch at the lodge ranges from the expected (burger; $5) to the unusual (smoked-trout salad; $5). Even the snack bar isn't bad, serving surprisingly good pizza slices ($3). They make (or, more likely, thaw) the same pizza at a counter in the **General Store** by the North Rim campground (*see* General Stores, *above*). In Kanab, **Nedra's Too** (Hwy. ALT89, at Hwy. 89, tel. 801/644–2030) serves decent Mexican food, with breakfast, lunch, and dinner for under $10. The eatery is open later and more often than anyplace else in Kanab. The original **Nedra's** in Fredonia (Hwy. ALT89, tel. 520/643–7591) may be closer to where you are staying.

EXPLORING THE GRAND CANYON

ORIENTATION PROGRAMS

In addition to its walk-through exhibits, the South Rim's **visitor center** (tel. 520/638–7771 or 520/638–7888 for recorded information) in Grand Canyon Village runs free 15-minute slide shows daily on the canyon's geology, discovery, and development. If groups don't bother you, join one of the free ranger-led talks or hikes at the canyon's rim. North Rim park rangers hold a variety of informative talks daily (mid-May to mid-October) at Point Imperial, the Campground Amphitheater, and the east patio of the Grand Canyon Lodge. They also lead short hikes throughout the park. Check the North or South Rim version of the *Grand Canyon Guide* (*see* Publications, *above*) for schedules, or check the posted schedule at any lodge. For information on raft, air, and mule tours of the canyon, *see* Park Activities, *below.*

GUIDED TOURS

SOUTH RIM • Fred Harvey Transportation Co. (tel. 303/297–2757) has several narrated bus tours to various locations west and east of Grand Canyon Village, including one at sunset. The tours ($7.50–$20) last anywhere from 90 minutes to a full day. Tickets can be purchased in advance or at the transportation desks at the Yavapai, Maswik, and Bright Angel lodges. **Nava-Hopi Tours** (*see* Coming and Going by Bus, *above*) has bus tours of the Grand Canyon and other northern Arizona attractions, including Monument Valley, the Petrified Forest, and the prehistoric dwellings at Montezuma Castle National Monument. Tours cost about $38–$75 and originate in downtown Flagstaff. **Hopi Polewyma Travel and Tours** (Box 210, Polacca, AZ 86042, tel. 520/737–2534) has an interesting approach to touring the canyon: You get to drive the guide around on a tour that costs $15 an hour and originates in Flagstaff. The Hopi owned-and-operated tour can also include villages, cultural centers, and artisans' workplaces within the Hopi reservation.

In summer, rangers rescue four or five canyon hikers daily who are injured, dehydrated, have heat stroke, or have a condition quietly referred to as Code W, for wimp.

NORTH RIM • Amfac has a three-hour van tour of Cape Royale, Angel's Window, and other scenic viewpoints for $20. Reservations and information are available at the registration desk of the Grand Canyon Lodge (tel. 520/638–2611).

SHORT HIKES

SOUTH RIM • The level, paved, and wheelchair-accessible **South Rim Trail** runs 1½ mi from the Yavapai Observation Station to the historic district of Grand Canyon Village. All along the trail, you'll see spectacular views of the inner gorge—but there'll be other people in the way. The less-trafficked, moderately challenging **West Rim Trail** begins where the South Rim trail ends. The path sometimes veers close to the edge of the canyon; in some parts it rises and falls several feet as it follows the rim 8 mi west, past Maricopa Point (where the pavement ends) and the Abyss Overlook to Hermits Rest; consider hiking one way and catching the free shuttle back (*see* Getting Around, *above*).

NORTH RIM • The paved **Bright Angel Point Trail** ascends a steep ¼-mi to a toe-curling view of the inner gorge. Far below, you can hear **Roaring Springs,** which supplies water and hydroelectric power to both rims. The trail begins at the log structure alongside the Grand Canyon Lodge parking lot and doubles back to end at the lodge's east patio. Pamphlets describing the ½-mi loop are available at the trailhead for a 25¢ donation. The **Cape Royal Trail,** an easy ⅔-mi paved path, begins at the Cape Royal parking area, 25 mi southeast of the lodge (follow signs). In addition to impressive views of the canyon, the Colorado River, and high-desert plateaus, look for **Angel's Window,** a huge trapezoidal hole in a rock wall. It's a product of erosion, not—as you might think—of tour operators' sledgehammers.

LONGER HIKES

You may want to start off with a shorter hike before tackling a below-the-rim trail, in order to acclimate yourself both to the high elevation and the specific hazards associated with canyon hiking. Cut your teeth on the corridor trails—**Bright Angel, North Kaibab,** and **South Kaibab.** These well-maintained, ranger-patrolled paths have water available year-round, but they're hardly easy trails. At the top, the trails are crowded with day hikers, but tourists thin out 1 or 2 mi below the rim. The rest of the way, you'll share the trails (and views) only with other dedicated backpackers. Call or visit the Backcountry Office (*see* Backcountry Camping, *above*) or ask at any information desk for trip-planning assistance, maps, and information on these and other trails.

HIKING IN THE GRAND CANYON

Unless you've used the Stairmaster in the sauna at level 9 for, oh, four or more hours, read on. The most important thing to do when hiking in the canyon is bring a gallon of water per person per day. Eating is also important, to prevent water intoxication. Raisins and banana chips are ideal because they're high in carbohydrates and natural sugars.

Keep your shoes on in the backcountry campsites, as scorpions are regular below-the-rim residents; their sting is extremely painful. Avoid hiking during summer's hottest hours (10 AM–3 PM) by rising early and finding a shaded midday picnic spot. The rule of thumb is that it takes twice as long to go up as it does to descend. Tote a flashlight, so that after-dark hiking is viable. You may be tempted to trek to the river and back again in one day, but anyone who's lived to tell about trying will strongly discourage you.

SOUTH RIM • Bright Angel Trail, which begins just west of Kolb Studio near Bright Angel Lodge, is the most heavily traveled route into the inner gorge. Shade is plentiful and water is available year-round at Indian Garden Campground (4½ mi down and a rewarding day hike destination) and from May to September at the two rest houses (1½ and 3 mi down). It makes for an exhausting day but continuing on 1½ mi beyond Indian Gardens to **Plateau Point** (3,120 ft below the rim) rewards you with a view of the Colorado River another 3,000 ft below. The return is strenuous: Allow 8–12 hours round-trip. Farther down, the 9½-mi trail terminates at Bright Angel Campground and Phantom Ranch after crossing the Colorado via suspension bridge.

The **South Kaibab Trail,** beginning near Yaki Point on East Rim Drive, is a steeper and shorter (6.5 mi one-way) route to the Colorado River, but there's no water and little shade along the way. Your reward? Unobstructed, spectacular views, as the trail follows exposed ridgelines rather than descending canyon walls. Iron-calved day hikers will enjoy the 3-mi round-trip journey part way down the trail to **Cedar Ridge,** requiring 2½–4 hours total—bring flashlights and warm clothing and experience an inner canyon sunset. Overnight hikers heading to Bright Angel Campground and Phantom Ranch will want to take South Kaibab down and return on the easier Bright Angel Trail. Overnight parking is possible at Yaki Point, but cars may be left in Grand Canyon Village where the hiker's shuttle will take you to and from (*see* Getting Around, *above*) the trailhead.

Steeper and more solitary still is the unmaintained **Grandview Trail** (3 mi one-way), beginning on the canyon side of the retaining wall at Grandview Point on East Rim Drive. The rocky and sometimes narrow trail descends 2,600 ft past funky wind-shaped rock formations through coniferous forest into a hot and stark desert landscape at the campgrounds at **Horseshoe Mesa,** where ruins of old Hopi mining works are visible—set aside 6–11 hours for the round-trip, depending upon your physical condition. There is no water and little shade along Grandview Trail. Day hikers should follow signs for the 6-mi round-trip hike to **Dripping Springs** (6–9 hours round-trip), where canteens can be refilled from the natural spring that drips from a rock overhang into a natural rock pool. Overnight hikers can continue 4 mi to the Hermit Creek and Hermit Rapids camps; the Colorado River is another 1½ mi away along Hermit Creek. Springs along this trail mean that water is available year-round—just remember to purify before drinking.

NORTH RIM • North Kaibab Trail, the only corridor trail from the North Rim into the inner canyon, is best after autumn frosts have turned the leaves of the cottonwoods that line the trail. The 14-mi trail begins on the mountain entrance road 2 mi north of the Grand Canyon Lodge (for information on shuttle service, *see* Getting Around, *above*) and ends at Bright Angel Campground and Phantom Ranch on the Colorado River after a 6,000-ft descent. Day hikers in excellent physical condition will enjoy the 4.7-mi descent on this trail to **Roaring Springs,** source of all the park's electric power and water—allow 6–8 hours total for the round-trip from the trailhead. The last 5 mi follow **Bright Angel Creek.** Overnight campers at Cottonwood (7 mi down) can trek the 3-mi round-trip to the small waterfall and emerald pools at **Ribbon Falls**; look for the **Spur Trail** 1 mi below camp.

A pleasant and less strenuous contrast to the sometimes crowded trails below the rim, the **Widforss** and **Uncle Jim Point trails** offer the tranquillity of cool, piney glens and ridge-top canyon views. The Uncle Jim Point trail (5 mi round-trip) picks up from the Ken Patrick trail ½-mi from the trailhead (east side of Kaibab Trail parking lot) and climbs through fir and aspen forest, teasing with quick canyon peeks, and then emerges at the point, where you can gaze till your eyes are full. The Widforss Trail (10 mi round-trip) follows the canyon rim for a short distance, then retreats into the cool, deer-spotted forest before emerging at stunning **Widforss Point,** overlooking Haunted Canyon. The trailhead lies at the end of a signposted dirt road 2¾ mi north of Grand Canyon Lodge, opposite the paved road to Cape Royal.

SCENIC DRIVES AND VIEWS

SOUTH RIM • The **West Rim Drive** runs 8 mi west from Grand Canyon Village to Hermits Rest. Along this tree-lined, two-lane drive are several scenic overlooks with panoramic views of the inner canyon—all of which are popular sunset destinations. The road is closed to automobile traffic from April through October, but you can catch the free shuttle bus at the West Rim Interchange near Bright Angel Lodge every 15 minutes (7:30 AM–6:45 PM). The shuttle stops at all eight scenic viewpoints on the way out to Hermits Rest (stops only at Mojave Point on the return), making a complete round-trip every 90 minutes.

To hike rim-to-river-to-rim, rangers recommend descending on North Kaibab and climbing out on Bright Angel; the total trip is 24 mi and takes at least 3 days.

The relatively uncluttered **East Rim Drive** also affords some beautiful views of the canyon and the raging river. The 23-mi, 45-minute (one-way) drive takes you past **Lipan Point,** the widest and perhaps most spectacular part of the canyon, where the rapids of the wild Colorado are clearly visible, as are its wide S curves and the delta where the ancestral Pueblo peoples farmed. The road continues to where you'll see partially intact ancient rock dwellings. About 30 of these ancestors of the modern Hopi and other Pueblo cultures farmed along the North Rim and the canyon floor until the 12th century, when they moved east (possibly because of a drought). The free **Tusayan Ruin and Museum** (3 mi west of Desert View on East Rim Drive, tel. 520/638–2305) has educational exhibits about various Native American tribes who have inhabited the region in the past 2,000 years. The museum is usually open daily 9–5 but may be closed during ruin tours. The drive ends at the East Rim Entrance Station and the 70-ft **Desert View Watchtower,** which clings precariously to the lip of the chasm. Built in 1932 to resemble southwestern Native American architecture, the watchtower is the highest point on the South Rim; not surprisingly, the views are spectacular (open daily summer 8–7:30, winter 9–4:30, admission: 25¢). A stairway inside leads to viewing windows and replicas of petroglyphs, Native American paintings, and a unique Hopi altar.

NORTH RIM • The scenic road to **Point Imperial** and **Cape Royal** intersects Hwy. 67 about 3 mi north of Grand Canyon Lodge and winds 8 mi through stands of quaking aspen combed neatly into a forest of unkempt conifers; it's most impressive after fall's first frosts, when the aspen leaves turn golden. When the road forks continue 3 mi north to Point Imperial—the views of the eastern canyon and Painted Desert are spectacular at sunrise. Or head south 15 mi to Cape Royal for the North Rim's only views of the Colorado River (*see* Shorter Hikes, *above*). On this leg of the drive, the road occasionally strays—no guardrails—to within inches of sharp canyon drop-offs.

PARK ACTIVITIES

MULE RIDES

Mules provide efficient and exhilarating (if expensive) transportation down steep canyon trails. Several mule trains depart daily from the South Rim's Bright Angel Lodge for day trips to Plateau Point ($100), overnight trips to Phantom Ranch at the canyon bottom ($250 per night), or two-night trips mid-November–March ($350). Trips book months in advance, but spontaneous sorts can place their names on a waiting list at the Bright Angel transportation desk; for the best chance, come at 6 AM on the day before the day you want to go. For the mule's safety, there's a 200-pound weight limit. Contact the **Amfac** (*see*

Where to Sleep, *above*; tel. 520/638–2631 for information, 303/297–2757 for reservations) for details. Mule trains on the North Rim don't descend to the canyon bottom, but they do spend a full day traveling into the canyon to Roaring Springs ($85); half-day trips are $35. A one-hour trip along the rim is mere mule feed at $15. Reservations are advised; write Box 128, Tropic, Utah 84776, or call **Canyon Trail Rides** (tel. 801/679–8665).

HORSEBACK RIDES

Though horseback rides are cheaper than rides on more stubborn creatures, the disadvantage is that they just go along the rim and not into the canyon. **Apache Stables** (Box 158, Grand Canyon, AZ 86023, tel. 520/638–2891 or 638–2424) offers short and affordable horseback rides through the Kaibab National Forest and along the canyon rim in high season. Rates start at $25 for one hour; rides originate at Moqui Lodge just south of the South Rim entrance station on Hwy. 64. **Allen's** (584 E. 300 South, Kanab, Utah 84741, tel. 801/644–8150) offers guided horseback rides through the North Kaibab Forest and along the North Rim for $15 per hour, $45 per half-day, or $75 per day. Rides originate at Jacob's Lake, near the forest service visitor center (*see* Camping Above the Rim, *above*).

RAFTING

The Colorado River's course through the Grand Canyon incorporates both rushing rapids and slow-moving stretches of crystal-clear water perfect for swimming. Guided rafting tours range from day trips to extensive (and expensive) two-week outings and are available from over 20 companies in both motorized (smooth water) and oar-propelled (white-water) boats, though smooth-water trips don't venture into the Grand Canyon itself. Trips originate in Flagstaff, Page, or Las Vegas, and the price usually includes transportation to the river. Trips of less than one week generally explore only half of the Colorado River's course through the canyon, starting or ending at Phantom Ranch; be prepared to hike one leg of the journey. You must reserve well in advance; for a list of all rafting companies, consult the *Grand Canyon Guide*. **Canyoneers, Inc.** (Box 2997, Flagstaff, AZ 86003, tel. 520/526–0924, 800/525–0924 outside AZ) offers a three-day trip into the canyon with all meals, transportation from Flagstaff, and river and sleeping gear included for $575 per person. **Hualapai River Runners** (Box 246, Peach Springs, AZ 86434, tel. 520/769–2219 or 800/622–4409) runs trips that begin at Diamond Creek and end at Pierce Ferry in Lake Mead; transportation is provided from Peach Springs, about 2½ hours west of Flagstaff on Rte. 66. A one-day trip with no accommodations but including food costs $221 per person; the same trip with food and one-night camp out on the river is $321.

SCENIC FLIGHTS

If you're considering "flightseeing," check your conscience first. Many environmentalists would like to see air tours—and the attendant pollution and noise—completely banned from the Grand Canyon (*see* Environmental Alert *box, above*). Helicopter and airplane tours of the canyon leave from the Grand Canyon Airport just south of Tusayan. Rates start at around $80 for 50-minute plane rides, $95 for 30-minute helicopter rides. The visitor center (*see* Basics, *above*) can supply you with the names and phone numbers of various companies.

NEAR THE GRAND CANYON

FLAGSTAFF

Tucked into a dense pine forest at the foot of 12,633-ft Mt. Humphreys, Flagstaff makes an appealing and sensible budget base camp and public transit hub for Grand Canyon exploration (*see* Coming and Going, *above*). Located 80 mi south of the national park at the junction of I–40 and I–17, "Flag" makes up for its relative distance with well-stocked camping supply stores, bountiful hostels and cheap motels, and a rambunctious population of locals and travelers, all of whom live for the outdoors during the day and for the hopping independent rock scene at night. Thursday–Saturday nights, **Monsoon's** (22 E. Rte. 66, near N. San Francisco St., tel. 520/774–7929) is the venue of choice for live music. After 8 on Friday and Saturday, the cover charge is sometimes as much as $20, but it's usually more like $3–$5; there are sometimes free shows Sunday through Wednesday. Lodging, dining, nightlife, and public transportation are all conveniently located in Flag's historic downtown district, with the train station as the hub of downtown.

Flagstaff Visitor Center (1 E. Rte. 66, at Leroux Ave. in the Amtrak Station, tel. 520/774–9541 or 800/842–7293) has a free map and tips on local activities.

COMING AND GOING • America West (tel. 800/235–9292) is currently the only commercial airline serving **Flagstaff Pullium Airport** (on I–17, 3 mi south of town, tel. 520/556–1234); the low-end round-trip fares to L.A. hover around $180. **Greyhound** (399 S. Malpais La., at Milton Rd., tel. 520/774–4573 or 800/231–2222 for reservations) provides service to L.A. (12 hrs one-way, $99 round-trip) and Vegas (6–7 hrs one-way, $99 round-trip). **Amtrak** (1 E. Rte. 66, at Leroux Ave., tel. 520/774–8679 or 800/872–7245 for reservations) stops daily in Flagstaff. You'll pay $96 for the 10-hour trip from L.A. to Flagstaff; round-trip prices run $104–$192, depending on how far in advance you book. **National** (Holiday Inn, 2320 E. Lucky La., tel. 520/779–1975) rents economy cars and will pick you up and drop you off anywhere within Flagstaff.

WHERE TO SLEEP • All budget lodging in Flagstaff—hotels and hostels—is nearly on top of the train tracks. About 80 trains roar through town daily, so pack earplugs. Most hotels are along Old Rte. 66, and while there is really no "strip" of cheap motels, a general rule of thumb is that prices go down as you head east out of town. Two more tips: hotel managers have been known to match a competitor's lower prices when challenged; and when you see a minimum price advertised in front of a hotel, ask specifically for that price instead of asking how much a room is. The **Western Hill Hotel** (1580 E. Rte. 66, at Enterprise Rd., tel. 520/774–6633) has a pool and a Thai restaurant open Monday–Saturday 11–10 and Sunday 4–10. Rooms start at $35.

Hotel Monte Vista. Michael J. Fox, Jon Bon Jovi, Carol Lombard, and more than 40 other stars have stayed at this historic, worn-around-the-edges hotel. Room rates can shoot as high as $85 a night, but a handful of rooms with shared bath go for $25–$50; reservations are strongly advised. The Monte V also has two live music venues (one a converted post office) that attract locals and travelers alike. *100 N. San Francisco St., at Aspen Ave., tel. 520/779–6971 or 800/545–3068, fax 520/779–2904. 47 rooms, most with bath. Laundry, luggage storage.*

The **Grand Canyon International Hostel** in downtown Flagstaff is also known as the **Downtowner** because of the five-story high sign out front, left over from the building's previous life as a motel. This meticulously decorated, too-nice-to-be-a-hostel hostel can sleep 60 people—options include a dorm ($12) or a private double ($30), breakfast included. The hostel provides free pickup from the bus station or airport and is two blocks from Amtrak. It also offers a shuttle to the South Rim and one to Page, near Lake Powell, where they run the **Lake Powell International Hostel** (141 8th Ave., Page, tel. 520/645–3898), a good place to look for rides to the North Rim or Monument Valley. *19 S. San Francisco St., at Phoenix Ave., tel. 520/779–9421. Reception open 7 AM–1AM. Kitchen, laundry. Cash only.*

The **Motel Du Beau International Hostel** in Flagstaff attracts a rowdy new bohemian crowd. It offers both dorm-style ($12) and private ($25) rooms, or you can pitch a tent for $6; breakfast is included. In high season, local chefs occasionally cook tasty dinners ($3–$4). The hostel picks you up for free from the airport or bus station (Amtrak is right around the corner) and regularly shuttles guests ($25) and nonguests ($35) to and from the Grand Canyon. *19 W. Phoenix Ave., at Beaver St., tel. 520/774–6731 or 800/398–7112, fax 520/774–4060. 70 beds. Reception open 6 AM–midnight. Kitchen, laundry.*

A faded beauty—it was established in 1897—the **Weatherford Hotel** is an AYH lodging that has 20 dorm-style beds that run $14 for members, $17 for nonmembers, as well as a few hotel rooms that range from $38 with private bath to $32 without. The hostel is directly above Charly's Pub and Restaurant, a drinking spot beloved by locals—only rooms facing Aspen Avenue get much noise. Guests of the hostel get dollar-off coupons for the restaurant and no cover and happy hour prices on beer and wine in the bar. *23 North Leroux St., at Aspen Ave., tel. 520/774–2731. Reception open 7 AM–10 AM and 5 PM–11 PM, curfew 1 AM, lockout 9:30–5 (dorm rooms) or 11:30–5 (private rooms).*

FOOD • For all its nightlife, it can be hard to get a decent meal in Flagstaff after about 9 PM. Go to the **Black Bean** (12 E. Rte. 66, tel. 520/779–9905) for great do-it-yourself burritos, as healthy or as guacamole-smothered as you like. **Macy's** (14 S. Beaver St., 1 block south of Rte. 66, tel. 520/774–2243) has mean coffee drinks, acoustic or spoken-word entertainment, hearty breakfasts, Dagwood-size sandwiches, and friendly company. Sooner or later you're likely to find yourself at **Café Espress** (16 N. San Francisco St., tel. 520/774–0541), which has the best stir-fries, veggie burgers, and healthy desserts in town. Check out the local art scene while you're here.

HAVASUPAI INDIAN RESERVATION

As an alternative to crowded Grand Canyon National Park, explore the **Havasupai Indian Reservation,** four hours west of the South Rim's Grand Canyon Village. The views from the 8-mi riverbed trail leading to the remote village of **Supai** at times rival those in the park. Life for the agrarian Havasupai hasn't changed much; this is the only town in the United States that still receives mail by mule train. The tribe maintains a campground for hikers (with pit toilets and water) 2 mi north of Supai, near a series of spectacular waterfalls that fill the narrow, red-walled canyon with a surprising abundance of greenery. There's a $15-per-person one-time entrance fee, plus a campsite fee of $10 per person per night. Reservations are required, and it's best to schedule several weeks in advance. Contact **Havasupai Tourist Enterprises** (Supai, AZ 86435, tel. 520/448–2141). To reach the trailhead, follow Hwy. 18 65 mi north from historic **Old Route 66** (parallel to I–40 between Kingman and Seligman). Parking is on Hualapai Hilltop at the end of Hwy. 18.

CAMERON AND THE PAINTED DESERT

Since 1916, Native Americans have been bringing their crafts to the **Historic Cameron Trading Post** at the intersection of Hwys. 64 and 89, 54 mi north of Flagstaff and 30 mi east of the Grand Canyon's east entrance. These days, though prices are occasionally inflated, it's still an ideal place to find finely crafted turquoise jewelry, kachina dolls, woven rugs, and pottery. On the premises are also a motel, art gallery, cafeteria-style restaurant, and dining room (try the $5.50 Navajo tacos). For information on any of the above facilities, contact the Cameron Trading Post (Box 339, Cameron, AZ 86020, tel. 800/338–7385).

Stretching for 70 mi north of Cameron, on either side of Hwy. 89, is the Technicolor sandstone of the **Painted Desert.** The lavender, red, saffron, and pink hues of the rocks, exposed by millions of years of erosion, are most spectacular at sunset. This is also the best place to shop for Native American jewelry—Navajo artists sell their crafts from roadside stands to passing motorists, but you'll have to haggle to get the best price. This portion of the desert is on the Navajo Reservation and off-road travel is prohibited. If you want to camp or hike, you'll have to travel 100 mi east to the **Petrified Forest National Park.**

BRYCE CANYON AND ZION NATIONAL PARKS

There seems to be no end to the bizarre contortions and colors that nature has wrought from solid rock. At **Zion National Park** (119 mi northwest of the North Rim), red- and pink-hued canyon walls of fragile sandstone are fissured, creating checkerboard patterns and striations reminiscent of a giant esophagus. Those passing through should pause long enough to climb the 2-mi round-trip trail to Canyon Overlook, beginning just east of the first of two park tunnels. To get to Zion from the Grand Canyon, take U.S. 89 north, which intersects Hwy. 9 at Fredonia. Hwy. 9 crosses the park before joining I–15. For more information on camping and other park activities, contact the Zion National Park (Springdale, UT 84767, tel. 801/772–3256). The visitor center, open daily 8–8 in summer, is located ½ mi inside the south park entrance. Admission ($10 per vehicle, $5 per person) gives you access to the park for one week.

Bryce Canyon National Park, 155 mi north of the North Rim, is a land of rock minarets. The spires that rise from the canyon floor are impressive year-round but become outrageously photogenic when capped with snow. If you only have a day to sample the park's unique vistas, hike the strenuous 8-mi Fairyland Loop from Sunrise Point, near the visitor center. To reach Bryce from the Grand Canyon, take U.S. 89 north to Hwy. 12. For more information contact Bryce Canyon National Park (Box 170001, Bryce Canyon, UT 84717, tel. 801/834–5322). Admission (good for one week) is $10 per vehicle, $5 for those on bus, bicycle, or foot.

INDEX

A

B

C

N

O

P

NOTES

NOTES

NOTES